Arnold Swanberg
December 26, 1987
————————— // —————————→

THE
NAVAL WAR
IN THE
MEDITERRANEAN
1914 – 1918

THE
NAVAL WAR
IN THE
MEDITERRANEAN
1914 – 1918

by
Paul G. Halpern

Naval Institute Press

Published and distributed in the United States of America by the Naval Institute Press, Annapolis, Maryland 21402

First published in 1987

Library of Congress Catalog Card No. 86–62238

ISBN 0–87021–448–9

Set in 10 on 11 point Bembo by Oxford Print Associates Ltd, Oxford and printed in Great Britain by Oxford University Press

To the memory of

Captain Stephen W. Roskill, CBE, DSC, Litt.D, FBA, RN,
who set such a high standard and helped so many in the field.

Contents

List of Maps and Charts

xi

List of Tables

Glossary of Abbreviations

ACS	Archivio Centrale dello Stato, Rome
Adm	Admiralty Archives, Public Record Office, Kew
Admiralstab	German Naval Staff
ANC	Allied Naval Council
AOK	Armeeoberkommando (Austrian High Command)
Auswärtiges Amt	German Foreign Office
BA-MA	Bundesarchiv-Militärarchiv, Freiburg im Breisgau
BdU	Befehlshaber der Unterseeboote im Mittelmeer (Commander of German submarines in the Mediterranean, Aug.–Nov. 1918)
BMK	Befehlshaber der deutschen Marinekommandos in ehemals russischen Schwarzmeergebiet (German naval commander in former Russian territory, Black Sea, 1918)
Cab	Cabinet Papers, Public Record Office, Kew
C.-in-C.	Commander-in-Chief
DGGSM	Direction générale de la guerre sous-marine
DNI	Director of Naval Intelligence, Admiralty
DOD	Director of Operations Division, Admiralty
DTD	Director of Trade Division, Admiralty
EMG	Etat-Major général (French Naval Staff)
FdU	Führer der Unterseeboote im Mittelmeer (Commander of German submarines in the Mediterranean, June 1917–Aug. 1918)
FO	Foreign Office Records, Public Record Office, Kew
HE	Homeward East (Through Mediterranean convoy)
k.u.k.	Kaiserlich und Königlich (Imperial and Royal, the designation applied to the Austro-Hungarian navy and those institutions common to both halves of the Dual Monarchy)
MAE	Archives diplomatiques, Ministère des affaires étrangères, Paris
MKSM	Militärkanzlei des Kaisers und Königs, Kriegsarchiv, Vienna
NARS	National Archives and Records Service, Washington
NATEKO	Nautisch-Technische Kommission für Schwarze Meere. (Inter-Allied Commission of the Central Powers to supervise Armistice with Russia in the Black Sea)

OE	Outward East (Through Mediterranean convoy)
OHL	Oberste Heeresleitung (German Army High Command)
OK/MS	Operationskanzlei/Marinesektion, Kriegsarchiv, Vienna
PRO	Public Record Office, Kew
RG	Record Group (designation used at NARS [q.v])
RMA	Reichsmarineamt (Imperial Navy Office)
SHM	Service historique de la marine, Vincennes
Stato Maggiore della Marina	Italian Naval Staff
SNO	Senior Naval Officer
USM	Ufficio Storico della Marina Militare, Rome

Preface

The novelist Nicholas Monsarrat, renowned for his evocative works with naval backgrounds, included a passage in *The Kappillan of Malta* in which the Kappillan recalls arriving at Malta in 1917 in A. B. Cunningham's destroyer *Scorpion* and glimpsing the Mediterranean Fleet. There was supposedly line on line of warships with five battleships, attendant cruisers, and at least twenty destroyers. The general impression is of a southern version of the Grand Fleet at Scapa Flow. Unfortunately, the author who had such a marvellous grasp of the Royal Navy in the Second World War has gone astray, for Malta in 1917 would probably have reminded him more of his experiences in the Second World War. Most warships in port would have been small anti-submarine craft, generally sloops bearing the same names of flowers as the corvettes Monsarrat immortalized. Any battleships at Malta would probably have been there in the earlier part of the war and until the spring of 1916 they would have been just as likely to have been French. The mistake is perhaps symbolic for outside of the *Goeben* episode and the Dardanelles campaign of 1915, the 1914–18 naval war in the Mediterranean is not very familiar and has been pushed even further into the background by the dramatic events of the Second World War. I hope this study may at least reintroduce those interested in naval history to the very complex situation which existed in the theatre during the First World War. There was no single Mediterranean campaign, but rather a number of different campaigns. The term 'Mediterranean mosaic' might be used to describe how the bits come together to form the picture. The diversity of the subject and the economic constraints of publication have caused me to cut an overly long manuscript and neglect certain factors such as the Italians in Libya – who felt even more neglected at the time – and the role of neutral Spain. I hope to treat the latter in another study. This work must therefore sacrifice some depth to obtain breadth and remain in one volume. With the general opening of archives in the past generation, the navies of France, Italy and Austria-Hungary certainly deserve studies of their own to supplement the official and semi-official accounts which appeared in the interwar period.

The question of geographical names, which have often changed, has been troublesome and I have tried to use those familiar to contemporaries. On the vexing problem of the names of Turkish and Russian warships, which appear in a bewildering variety of forms, I have tried for consistency to use whenever possible the style found in British documents, particularly those presented to the Allied Naval Council. This may not be pleasing to modern linguistic purists, but it avoids the absurdity of rendering them in a form contemporaries probably would not have recognized, and whatever its faults seems a reasonable compromise.

In the years I have been working on this project I owe a great debt to many people. The late Captain Stephen Roskill, to whom this book is dedicated, was a constant source of generous assistance and advice. I would particularly like to thank: Dr Nicholas Rodger and the staff of the Public Record Office, Kew; Mr Roderick W. A. Suddaby, Keeper, Department of Documents, and the staff of the Imperial War Museum, London; Miss Marion M. Stewart, Archivist, Churchill College, Cambridge; Dr R. J. B. Knight, Dr R. A. Morris, Mr Alan W. H. Pearsall and Mrs G. Vaz and the staff of the National Maritime Museum, Greenwich; Mr David Brown and staff, Naval Library, Ministry of Defence, London; Mrs K. V. Wheeler, House of Lords Record Office, London; Contre-amiral Duval, Chef du service historique, and the late Joël Audouy, former Chef du services des archives, and Jean-Pierre Busson, Chef du services des archives et des bibliothèques de la marine, Monsieur G. Labar and the staff of the Service historique de la marine, Vincennes; P. Enjalran, Conservateur en chef des archives and the staff, Archives diplomatiques, Ministère des affaires étrangères, Paris; Contrammiraglio Vittorio Dati, Capo and Capitano di fregata Eugenio Cochi, Sotto-Capo, Ufficio Storico della Marina Militare, Rome; Professor Enrico Serra, former Caposervizio, Ufficio Storico e Documentazione, Ministro degli Affari Esteri, Rome; Dr Mario Missori, Archivio Centrale dello Stato, Rome; Dr Walter Wagner, Director, Dr Peter Broucek, Mr Franz Bilzer and the staff of the Österreichisches Staatsarchiv-Kriegsarchiv, Vienna; Dr Fleischer, Dr Borgert and the staff of the Bundsarchiv-Militärarchiv, Freiburg im Breisgau; Mr Stuart L. Butler, Naval and Old Army Branch and Messrs Robert Wolfe, William H. Cunliffe and Harry E. Rilley, Modern Military Branch, National Archives and Records Service, Washington; Mr Joseph Evans, Micromaterials Division, Miss Marianne Donnell, Documents/Map Division and Miss Phyllis Holzenberg, Inter-Library Loan Office, Strozier Library, Florida State University.

Valuable assistance and advice came from: Dr Wilhelm Deist and Dr Gerhard Schreiber, Militärgeschichtliches Forschungsamt, Freiburg im Breisgau; Mr Erwin F. Sieche of the Arbeitsgemeinschaft für österreichische Marinegeschichte, Vienna; Professor Richard Georg Plaschka; Dr Horst Haselsteiner; the late Professor Arthur Marder; Professor Jan Karl Tanenbaum; Professor Philip V. Cannistraro; Professor Renzo De Felice; Professor Holger Herwig; Professor John D. Treadway; Professor Joel Blatt; and Dr Dean C. Allard. Ing. Erich P. Heyssler generously allowed me to see his father's unpublished memoirs and Mrs Nicholas Baker kindly provided me with a copy.

For permission to use or quote from unpublished material I would like to thank: the Trustees of the National Maritime Museum (Papers of Admirals Limpus, William Howard Kelly and Herbert Richmond); Captain Peter

G. C. Dickens (Papers of Admiral Sir Gerald Dickens); the 2nd Baron Keyes (Papers of 1st Baron Keyes); Mrs E. Drage (Papers of Commander C. H. Drage); Mr M. Wilkinson (Papers of Captain R. W. Wilkinson); Mrs M. Godfrey (Papers of Admiral J. H. Godfrey); Baron de Robeck and Mrs Jocelyn Proby (Papers of Admiral John M. de Robeck); 2nd Baron Hankey (Papers of 1st Baron Hankey); Mr T. Dumas (Papers of Admiral Philip Dumas); and Frau Clara Däubler (Papers of Admiral Wilhelm Souchon). Crown copyright material appears by permission of The Controller, Her Majesty's Stationery Office. I should also like to apologize to any holders of copyright I have been unable to trace.

I would like to thank Collins Publishers for permission to publish excerpts from Stephen Roskill, *Hankey: Man of Secrets*, Vol. I: *1877–1918*.

I also thank the American Philosophical Society and the President's Club of Florida State University for financial assistance while working on this study.

PAUL G. HALPERN

Tallahassee, Florida
January, 1986

[1]

The Mediterranean Naval Balance

The outbreak of the First World War was at first something of an anti-climax in the Mediterranean. Naval competition had been intense, rivalled only by that of the British and Germans in the North Sea and when the war began everyone assumed a naval battle would occur within a few days. This did not happen largely due to the decision of the Italian government to remain neutral which resulted in, at least on paper, a lopsided advantage for the Triple Entente. The fact that the Italian decision weighed so heavily was due less to Italy's inherent strength and more to changing strategic circumstances, notably the preoccupation of Great Britain with the rise of German naval power in the North Sea, coupled with a steady reduction of the British Mediterranean Fleet. At the same time Italy and Austria-Hungary imitated the other powers in the construction of the most powerful class of warships, dreadnoughts, while the development of the French fleet was slowed by political difficulties. Italy and Austria were traditional enemies, but also allies in the Triple Alliance. Their naval building was to a large extent directed against each other but the decline of British power eventually raised the possibility that an Austro-Italian combination might be able to gain control of the sea from the French and whatever British forces remained in the Mediterranean.[1] There was always something rather artificial about this as with similar paper calculations, but a closer look at the balance of power in the Mediterranean on the eve of the war explains how it could occur.

It is somewhat surprising to learn that the world's leading naval power was in July 1914 far from the leading Mediterranean naval power. The Mediterranean had traditionally occupied considerable attention in the Royal Navy and here the largest fleet and most modern ships were assembled, although in the late nineteenth century the most likely enemy had been Russia and France instead of Germany. British seapower probably peaked in the Mediterranean during the years 1902–5 with fourteen battleships in 1902, a record year. It was during this period, however, that the Anglo-French Entente became a reality, while Anglo-German rivalry intensified, and Admiral Sir John Fisher, when First Sea Lord, recognized

1

these changing strategic circumstances and reduced the Mediterranean Fleet from twelve to eight battleships in his 1904 reorganization of the Royal Navy. The Home Fleet became the Channel Fleet and the former Channel Fleet became the Atlantic Fleet, able to reinforce, at least in theory, either the Channel or the Mediterranean Fleet. In 1906 a further two battleships were taken from the Mediterranean for northern waters, and from 1907 to 1912 the Mediterranean Fleet based on Malta numbered six battleships, with another six in the Atlantic Fleet based on Gibraltar.[2] Winston Churchill, who became First Lord in October 1911, carried these trends caused by changing diplomatic and naval considerations to their logical conclusion when he proposed a drastic reorganization of the Royal Navy in March 1912. Churchill wanted to shift the former Atlantic Fleet (to be renamed 3rd Battle Squadron) from Gibraltar to home waters and the Mediterranean Fleet (now the 4th Battle Squadron) from Malta to Gibraltar. In theory its battleships could operate in either the Mediterranean or northern waters, but in practice it was obvious it would be called home in the event of war with Germany, leaving only a cruiser squadron at Malta. The proposed reorganization aroused considerable controversy, both in and out of the government, with much parliamentary and press debate. The Foreign Office was particularly opposed for diplomatic reasons to the Mediterranean reductions. The Admiralty backed down following a meeting at Malta between the vacationing Prime Minister Asquith, Churchill and Lord Kitchener, then Consul General in Egypt, and agreed to maintain permanently in the Mediterranean two to three battle cruisers, an armoured cruiser squadron, at least two of which were to be Devonshires (10,850 tons), a destroyer and submarine flotilla at Malta and a flotilla of long-range submarines at Alexandria.[3] The idea was to leave a force large enough when added to the French fleet to maintain a clear superiority over a combined Austrian and Italian fleet. In the subsequent debates in the Cabinet and Committee of Imperial Defence, Churchill and the Admiralty gained their major point: a reasonable margin of superior strength in home waters was the first requirement; but they conceded the facesaving device that subject to this, a Mediterranean force should be maintained equal to a 'one-Power standard excluding France'. Unfortunately, there were not sufficient dreadnoughts available after northern requirements and a true one-Power standard was not obtained. Two or three battle cruisers were obviously not the equal of the Italian or Austrian fleet. Churchill proposed four battle cruisers for the Mediterranean until a battle squadron of eight dreadnoughts – a real one-Power standard – would be available in 1915. Battle cruisers were used because in these innocent days before the Battle of Jutland exposed their fatal flaw in protection, they were considered powerful enough with their big guns to fight or fast enough to run when necessary. The Mediterranean was therefore devoid of British battleships – the accepted standard of naval strength – although a squadron of pre-dreadnoughts was temporarily deployed in the eastern Mediterranean during the Balkan Wars.

Only three of the four battle cruisers were actually on station when war began. The Mediterranean Fleet under Admiral Sir A. Berkeley Milne consisted of: the 2nd Battle Cruiser Squadron (*Inflexible, Indomitable* and *Indefatigable*); the 1st Cruiser Squadron, under Rear-Admiral Ernest C. T. Troubridge (armoured cruisers *Defence, Black Prince, Duke of Edinburgh* and *Warrior*); the four light cruisers *Chatham, Dublin, Gloucester* and *Weymouth*; and sixteen destroyers of the 5th Destroyer Flotilla.[4]

A British concentration in home waters left the French fleet as the major naval force in the Mediterranean. It was more than a match for the Italian or Austrian fleets when they were separated, but the major question was whether or not it would still prevail should they combine. The French navy had gone through a stormy period under the Third Republic with the strategic and tactical disputes of the 1880s centring around the theories of the Jeune ecole, which advocated torpedo boats or cruiser warfare directed against commerce as opposed to traditional battle fleets. A somewhat lax and confused building policy resulted in a heterogeneous 'fleet of samples', and in the early twentieth century there was an attempt to 'democratize' the navy and stress torpedo boat and submarine construction during the ministry of Camille Pelletan in the Radical Cabinet of Emile Combes. By 1905 the Germans overtook the French as the world's second naval power and the French fleet fell steadily behind. There was also a nightmarish problem with unstable powder which led to major catastrophes including the loss of battleships in 1907 and 1911 and which continued through 1912. Nevertheless by the end of 1912 the French navy appeared to have turned the corner. A pair of unusually effective Ministers of Marine, Vice-Admiral Augustin Boué de Lapeyrère and Théophile Delcassé gave new impetus and direction to naval affairs, and in 1912 a naval law provided for a regular programme of construction with the avowed aim of supremacy in the Mediterranean. According to the Naval Law of 1912 the French fleet by 1920 was to consist of 28 first-class battleships, 10 scout cruisers, 52 destroyers, 10 ships for overseas stations and 94 submarines. The first class of French dreadnoughts had been laid down in 1910 and 1911, somewhat belatedly compared to other powers. They were the four Courbets (23,470 tons, 21.5 knots, twelve 12-in. [305-mm] guns), and were followed by the three Bretagnes (23,600 tons, 20.5 knots, ten 13.4-in. [340-mm] guns) laid down in 1912. In 1913 the French programme was accelerated and the four Normandie class (25,230 tons, 21 knots, twelve 13.4-in. guns) were laid down followed by a fifth (*Béarn*) in 1914. Four of the even larger and more powerful Lyon class (27,600 tons, 21 knots, sixteen 13.4-in. guns) were to be laid down in 1915. Only the first portion of this programme was ever completed. When war began only *Courbet* and *Jean Bart* were in service while *Paris* and *France* were still completing their trials. The *Bretagne*, *Provence* and *Lorraine* had been launched in 1913 but would not enter service until the first quarter of 1916. The four Normandies, launched in 1914–15 to clear the slips, were never completed, while the fifth, *Béarn*, was finally converted to an aircraft carrier long after the war. The Lyon class were never laid down. However, once Italy was safely in the Allied camp these dreadnoughts were not needed. The ten scouts in the programme were, but they were not scheduled to be laid down until 1917 and the absence of fast light cruisers turned out to be a severe handicap for the French fleet.[5]

3

In August 1914 the French would have had only two dreadnoughts to face an Austro-Italian combination, with another pair to follow within a few weeks. The backbone of the French battle squadrons were the six Danton class (18,400 tons, 19.25 knots) which, with their mixed armament of four 12-in. and twelve 9.4-in. guns, are generally considered as semi-dreadnoughts, equivalent to the British Lord Nelsons or the Austrian Radetzkys. They are rather a controversial class, the first large ships in the French navy with turbine engines which experienced considerable teething troubles and had a reputation for excessive coal consumption. Supplementing them were five older and smaller Patries (14,865 tons, 18 knots, four 12-in. guns), the *Suffren* (12,450 tons, 18 knots, four 12-in. guns) and three Charlemagnes (11,200 tons, 18 knots, four 12-in. guns). The French had five to six older battleships but their value in a fleet action was questionable, however useful they might have been for secondary operations. One of the problems in assessing the strength of the respective navies and trying to determine the balance of power is the question of how many of the older battleships each possessed might be used in a fleet action. The fleets the Mediterranean powers might employ were far more heterogeneous than those the British and Germans were likely to use in the North Sea where, for example, at the Battle of Jutland only one of the German and none of the British battle squadrons included pre-dreadnoughts.

The French did have a relatively large number of armoured cruisers which were a dubious asset, and were one of the reasons why laying down of the scout cruisers in the programme had been deferred until 1917. They were big and to the uninitiated imposing looking, but employed correspondingly large crews. Unfortunately their maximum speed was only 23 knots at best, and their primary armament only 7.6-in. guns. They were therefore too slow to compete with new light cruisers, lacked the gun power or heavy armour protection to face battleships or battle cruisers, and were too slow to run away from the latter. The grevious losses suffered by similar British vessels at Jutland demonstrated their vulnerability in a major encounter. The French had nineteen armoured cruisers and nine older protected cruisers, of which six plus the *Jurien de la Gravière*, a protected cruiser used as a repeating ship, were allotted to the 1ère Armée navale, the French fleet in the Mediterranean.[6]

The French had, at least on paper, a sizeable number of flotilla craft. There were approximately 81 to 84 destroyers, 17 high seas torpedo-boats, 170 small torpedo-boats (*torpilleurs de défence mobile*) and 67 to 75 submarines and submersibles. Many of these were of little value, suitable only for local defence and only about half of them were in the Mediterranean. On the whole French flotilla craft were less robust than their British and German contemporaries. There were approximately thirty-seven destroyers in the Mediterranean, about twenty-four of which were attached to the 1ère Armée navale. Only twelve were 750 to 800 tons, the remainder 350 to 550 tons. Shortly after the outbreak of war the French Commander-in-Chief complained that many of his destroyers were not serious instruments of war.[7]

The French submarine service, both in numbers in service and boats under construction, was one of the largest in the world and Camille Pelletan and the Radicals had made much of this new and revolutionary weapon which was relatively cheap and ideal for the defensive. But despite their numbers, French submarines were a very mixed lot. Many were small and of little value and their torpedoes were inferior to foreign contemporaries. The experience of war would expose these defects, and despite the undoubted courage of the crews the results of French submarine operations were often frustrated by their technical limitations.[8]

The bulk of French naval forces were concentrated in the Mediterranean in 1914. This was widely assumed after the visible naval displacements of 1912 to reflect the Entente Cordiale, with an agreement for the British to look after northern waters and the French the Mediterranean. This was of course the underlying assumption, but the French had actually assembled their forces in the Mediterranean without prior agreement with the British for a very practical reason. They could no longer face the German fleet alone and any forces in the north were liable to be cut off and destroyed or shut up by superior forces. Moreover, the French had an immense distrust of the Italians and the growth of Italian and Austrian naval power threatened French control of the Mediterranean. Secure communications with North Africa were vital in the event of mobilization so that troops could be transported to metropolitan France for the decisive battles everyone assumed would take place along the frontiers.[9]

The British and French military and naval staffs had indeed been engaged in secret talks which, though non-binding, certainly gave a new dimension to the Entente Cordiale. These talks began around the time of the First Moroccan Crisis although the Royal Navy, probably due to the influence of Fisher, had been much slower to participate than the soldiers. Nevertheless in the spring of 1913 an agreement, F.010 – Joint Action in the Mediterranean, was one of a number of agreements concluded between the two admiralties.[10] The agreement was rather vague on details but the British hoped to maintain a force equal to dealing with the Austrians with a reasonable chance of success should they come out of the Adriatic. However, if North Sea requirements necessitated withdrawing so many ships that those remaining in the Mediterranean could not operate independently against the Austrian fleet, they would join the French and act under the French C.-in-C.'s orders, though they would be subject to recall if circumstances required it. The agreement was provisional, what *might* be done in an emergency. There was still no binding treaty. The bases of each country would be at the disposal of the other, although the fleets themselves would not form a single line of battle and would operate separately, but in mutual support.[11] The agreement simply confirmed the obvious, the North Sea was the decisive area for the British and the French were left largely to their own devices in the Mediterranean. This posed no problem to the French if all they had to deal with was the Italian fleet alone, but an Austro-Italian combination would have caused significant difficulties.

The Regia Marina would have been the major opponent for the French in the Mediterranean because of Italy's membership in the Triple Alliance. The Italians themselves had a high opinion of the training and ability of the

French and a healthy respect for the French fleet in general in the summer of 1914. A study by the Stato Maggiore della Marina, the Italian Naval Staff, in July 1914 concluded that the conditions in which Vice-Admiral Lapeyrère, the French C.-in-C., found himself were perhaps better than those of Admiral Togo on the outbreak of the Russo-Japanese War with many elements of victory in his hands.[12]

On the eve of the war the Italians were in the midst of a major building programme. The Naval Law of 27 June 1909 provided for 4 dreadnoughts, 3 scout cruisers, 12 destroyers, 34 torpedo-boats and 12 submarines. The first of the dreadnought type, the *Dante Alighieri* (19,500 tons, 23 knots, twelve 12-in. guns) had been laid down in June 1909, a year before any French or Austrian ship of that type. The *Dante* was considered rather lightly protected for a dreadnought, reflecting the traditional Italian practice of sacrificing protection for firepower and speed. It was followed in 1910 by three of the improved Cavour class (23,088 tons, 21.5 knots, thirteen 12-in. guns). In 1912 the Italians laid down the 2 Duilio class (22,964 tons) which were essentially Cavours with better secondary armament. Vice-Admiral Paolo Thaon di Revel, Capo di Stato Maggiore, proposed in July 1913 that the Italians aim at a minimum standard for their fleet of 60 per cent of the French and a 4:3 margin of superiority over their ally and rival Austria-Hungary. Revel also favoured expanding the number of destroyers to sixty-four and a large increase in the number of submarines. On the other hand, he favoured reducing somewhat the grandiose plans of Italian naval designers for the construction of large super-dreadnoughts. He was not completely successful in this for during the period of Italian neutrality four Caracciolos (34,000 tons, 28 knots, eight 15-in. guns) were laid down. These monster ships were never completed.[13]

Virtually all naval staffs overestimated their potential rivals in what is colloquially called 'the counting of beans'. It is an easy mistake to make – and one may be generous and call it a mistake – when requesting funds from reluctant parliaments. The real difficulty and most likely cause of alarmist reports was ascertaining when a ship would be completed. This was particularly true in the case of Italy where the programme fell far behind owing to the inability of Italian industry to provide prompt deliveries of armour plate, turrets and heavy cannon.[14] Therefore, of their original programme of six dreadnoughts, the Italians in July of 1914 had only the *Dante, Leonardo da Vinci* and *Guilio Cesare*, the latter two only recently commissioned and probably not yet worked up to full efficiency. The *Conte di Cavour* was not ready until April 1915 and the final pair, *Caio Duilio* and *Andrea Doria*, were not finished until May 1915 and March 1916 respectively. In pre-dreadnoughts, the Italians had the 4 Regina Elena class (12,600–13,000 tons, 21–22 knots) which were relatively lightly protected and armed with only two 12-in. guns, and therefore not classified as true battleships by some authorities; 2 older Brins (13,427 tons, 20 knots, four 12-in. guns) and the two small and older St Bons (9,800 tons, 18 knots, four 10-in. guns) which were not really in the same class as the more modern ships. The Italians also had: 7 armoured cruisers (four 10,000-ton Pisas and three 7,350-ton Garibaldis), which had the same disadvantages as their larger French counterparts; 3 recently commissioned and very useful light cruisers; 11 older protected cruisers of varying degrees of utility; 33 destroyers; 71 to 85 torpedo-boats (ranging from seagoing to coastal); and 20 to 22 submarines.[15] The Italians were well aware of their naval inferiority *vis-à-vis* France and quite conscious of how vulnerable their long coastline and exposed cities were to maritime pressure by the British and French if they were left unsupported in a general war resulting from their membership in the Triple Alliance. Paradoxically it was the activities of their traditional enemy and present ally Austria-Hungary which opened new perspectives.

The Kaiserlich und Königlich (k.u.k.) Kriegsmarine was in many respects the most revolutionary factor in the Mediterranean on the eve of the war. Until the turn of the century it had been primarily a coast defence force preoccupied with the Adriatic, with an anti-Italian tradition and a proud history, notably the naval victory of Lissa in 1866. The latter was an event which naturally the Italians always sought to avenge. During the period when Vice-Admiral Rudolph Graf Montecuccoli was Marine-kommandant (1904–13) the k.u.k. Kriegsmarine, with the enthusiastic support of the heir to the throne Archduke Franz Ferdinand, who had considerably more interest in the sea than his uncle the emperor, broke with past tradition and built the three semi-dreadnought Radetzky class (14,226 tons, 20.5 knots, four 12-in. guns) and followed them with four true dreadnoughts of the Viribus Unitis class (20,000 tons, 20.5 knots, nine 12-in. guns). The first pair, *Viribus Unitis* and *Tegetthoff* were laid down in the summer of 1910 as a speculation by the yards in advance of formal budgetary appropriations, while the second pair, *Prinz Eugen* and *Szent István*, were laid down in 1912. In the spring of 1914 the Austro-Hungarian Delegations approved construction of a second group of four dreadnoughts to replace the small, old Monarch class coast-defence ships. The first of the Ersatz Monarch class (24,500 tons, ten 14-in. guns) was scheduled to be laid down in the autumn of 1914.[16] When war broke out the *Viribus Unitis* and *Tegetthoff* were in service, *Prinz Eugen* had just commissioned, while the *Szent István* building at the Hungarian yards in Fiume was not completed until November 1915. In addition to the Viribus Unitis and Radetzky class the Austrians also had: the 3 Erzherzog class (10,600 tons, 20.5 knots, four 9.4-in. guns), 3 Habsburgs (8,300 tons, 20 knots, three 9.4-in. guns) and the 3 very old and small Monarchs (5,600 tons, 17 knots, four 9.4-in. guns). The Habsburgs and especially the Monarchs were far outclassed by this time and likely to be of limited use in any purely naval engagement. The Austrians also had: 2 old armoured cruisers; 2 good, fast light cruisers (Spauns), with 2 more under construction; 3 older protected cruisers (Asperns); 18 destroyers (six 870-ton Tátras and twelve 400-ton Huszárs); 44–51 sea-going and 40 coastal torpedo-boats; and 5 submarines.[17]

The Austrian building programme exerted pressure before the first large ships were completed. It was one of the factors in the British reorganization of 1912, for the new Austrian dreadnoughts would clearly have outclassed the older pre-dreadnoughts of the Mediterranean Fleet based on Malta. But by itself the k.u.k. Kriegsmarine was no match for the French. The situation changed if it combined with the Italians. When the initial dreadnought programmes were completed in 1915–16 there would be the 4 Viribus Unitis class, *Dante*, 3 Cavours and 2 Duilios, a total of 10 dreadnoughts against the 7 dreadnoughts (4 Courbets and 3 Bretagnes) of the French, which were to be reinforced by 4 British battle cruisers. Counting semi-dreadnoughts and pre-dreadnoughts there would be the 3 Radetzkys, 4 Regina Elenas and 2 Brins against the 6 Dantons, 5 Patries and *Suffren* making a total of 19 Austro-Italian ships against 19 French. A British battle squadron of eight had been promised for the Mediterranean some time in 1915 and pending its arrival it is easy to see the importance of the four battle cruisers as an interim reinforcement.

The Triple Alliance also had the prospect of German support, for in the crisis caused by the Balkan Wars of 1912–13 the new battle cruiser *Goeben* and fast light cruiser *Breslau* were sent out to the Mediterranean. The ships stayed on after the wars as the Mittelmeerdivision, a permanent and for the British and French most disturbing German presence in the Mediterranean, of great potential importance for diplomatic as well as military reasons given the close naval balance.

Of course, the difficulty in any calculation of this sort was how far down the list to go. Should you include, for example, the older Italian St Bons or French Charlemagnes or Austrian Habsburgs? Moreover, listing ships, or in common fashion of the day the weight of their broadsides, is a paper exercise. It is much more difficult to evaluate the effect of training or the cohesion of a fleet of mixed nationality with widely different classes of ships. Many observers would have argued, no matter how close the actual tally of ships, that this gave a clear advantage to the French, even without direct British support. Nevertheless, an exercise of this sort can demonstrate that the outlook for the Austrians and Italians, however unpromising it might have been for them individually, was significantly changed if they combined their forces. The logic of this was not lost on the Austrians and Italians and in the summer of 1913 they concluded the secret Triple Alliance Naval Convention.[18] The initiative came from the Italians who obviously felt more exposed in the event of war and whose military and naval authorities had apparently not been fully informed by the diplomats of the strictly defensive nature of the Triple Alliance. To tempt the Austrians to risk their precious fleet outside the Adriatic, the Italians offered the Austrian Marinekommandant, Anton Haus, command of the combined force which would assemble at the port of Augusta in Sicily. The Germans were, of course, delighted by all this and it was assumed that their Mediterranean force would join the combination. Naval supremacy offered them the prospect of cutting off French reinforcements from North Africa from the decisive land battles, and the possibility of an eventual Italian landing on the coast of Provence and advance up the Rhône valley to take the French armies in the rear. It was all very heady stuff although the war was apt to be over before such a landing and advance could take place. Thaon di Revel and Haus even travelled incognito to meet at a hotel in Zurich to talk matters over, and a combined signal book, the Triple Codex, was prepared for the use of the fleets. It was all slightly unreal. The realities of the Austro-Italian antagonism remained and both navies realized that they were just as likely to be at war with each other instead of allies and planned accordingly. The bubble burst on 2 August 1914 with the declaration of Italian neutrality. Revel certainly had few illusions on the chances of success. The day before the declaration of neutrality he painted a stark picture indeed for Prime Minister Salandra. The British and French had a 14 per cent advantage over the Triple Alliance in naval forces rising to 26 per cent when the pair of new French dreadnoughts entered service in the next few months. The situation might grow even worse since the Russian Black Sea Fleet and the Greeks might support the Triple Entente. The forces might be in balance if they only had to fight against the French, but if Britain intervened there was scant possibility of victory. Revel admitted that the Italian navy would not be able to protect the exposed and vulnerable Italian coastal cities and could not keep open communications with the Italian colonies. Revel's message to the Prime Minister was clear. Under present conditions chances for success were slight and it was desirable to avoid conflict.[19] From a naval point of view, Salandra could have had little temptation to go to war on the side of Germany and Austria-Hungary.

There were other naval factors in the Mediterranean which provoked a good deal of attention in 1913 and 1914, but with the outbreak of war and Italian neutrality they became unimportant. Spain, which had one dreadnought in service and two under construction and a relatively weak navy remained neutral. The Greeks and Turks had seemed on the verge of war in the spring of 1914 with a hot little naval race of their own as two powerful dreadnoughts under construction for the Turkish government in Britain neared completion. To meet this potential threat the Greeks scrambled for dreadnoughts under construction for other navies, failed to obtain any, and wound up with two old American battleships with a dreadnought on order in France and a battle cruiser on order in Germany. The Greek navy also included an Italian-built armoured cruiser, a light cruiser, 3 ancient coast defence ships, 14 destroyers, 17 torpedo-boats and 2 submarines. The Turkish navy included 2 ex-German battleships, an ancient coast defence ship, 2 cruisers, 8 destroyers and 9 torpedo-boats.[20] When war broke out the Admiralty took over the two Turkish dreadnoughts and Turkey ceased to be a serious naval factor, at least in the Mediterranean. The ex-American battleships reached Greek waters but ironically the major Allied interest in Greece from the naval point of view turned out to be control of the light craft once the submarine war became a serious threat.[21]

The Russians also had a sizeable naval programme before the war with extensive construction under way in both the Baltic and Black Sea. There were four dreadnoughts under construction in the Black Sea, but the first was not due to enter service until 1915. The Russian Black Sea Fleet included 3 pre-dreadnoughts, 2 old battleships, 1 cruiser, 26 destroyers, 10 torpedo-boats and 11 submarines. The Russian Black Sea Fleet obviously was preoccupied with naval supremacy over Turkey. However, the Russians were cut off from the Mediterranean by geography and their Black

Sea Fleet would have little direct influence until 1918, when the fear it would be taken over by the Germans following the Russian collapse caused considerable concern to the Allies.

This survey has tended to concentrate on battleships at the expense of other classes of warships. This has been deliberate for they were the accepted standard of naval strength at the time, took far longer to construct and are correspondingly easier to count. Moreover, most naval leaders expected a major naval encounter between battle fleets early in the war. This never occurred, largely because the defection of Italy from the Triple Alliance altered the naval balance of power irretrievably towards the British and French. As the war progressed it turned out to be the light craft, the cruisers, submarines, destroyers, sloops and drifters which became all-important, while the powerful dreadnoughts played a subsidiary, though always potentially important, role as fleets-in-being. By the latter stages of the war there would be a correspondingly different definition of naval power – one based on these light craft. There is something essentially artificial in speaking of French predominance in the Mediterranean and treating Britain as a minor factor. Ships are, after all, by their very nature mobile and it was always possible for the Royal Navy to reinforce the Mediterranean and alter the relative balance, provided they accepted the risk in subtracting forces from other areas. Moreover, as the definition of naval power changed the British played an increasingly important role. The size of the British merchant marine and fishing fleet which was the source of the anti-submarine drifters and trawlers, and the capacity of British yards to turn out scores of escort craft as well as the ability of British industry to produce large quantities of anti-submarine nets and materials resulted in a steady increase in Britain's relative strength in the Mediterranean. The British would never have the strength in capital ships that the French had, but through the swarm of light craft they would gradually recover much of the influence they had been willing to relinquish in 1912.

Notes: Chapter 1

1 The prewar period is examined in detail in Paul G. Halpern, *The Mediterranean Naval Situation, 1908–1914* (Cambridge, Mass., 1971).

2 ibid., pp. 2–3; Arthur J. Marder, *From the Dreadnought to Scapa Flow: The Royal Navy in the Fisher Era, 1904–1919* (5 vols, London, 1961–70), Vol. 1, pp. 40–3, 71–2; Peter K. Kemp (ed.), *The Papers of Admiral Sir John Fisher*, Vol. 1, Publications of the Navy Records Society, Vol. 102 (London, 1960), pp. 189–96.

3 Halpern, *Mediterranean Naval Situation*, pp. 17–18, 28–9; Marder, *Dreadnought to Scapa Flow*, Vol. 1, p. 287 ff.

4 Naval Staff, Training and Staff Duties Division, *Naval Staff Monographs (Historical)*, no. 21: *The Mediterranean, 1914–1915* (1923), p. 2, copy in Public Record Office, Kew (hereafter cited as PRO), Adm 186/618.

5 Halpern, *Mediterranean Naval Situation*, pp. 47–60, 121–3; Henri Le Masson, 'La politique navale française de 1870 à 1914', 'Les cuirassés du type "Normandie"' and 'Les cuirassés qu'auraient pu être', in *Propos maritimes* (Paris, 1970); Robert Dumas and Jean Guiglini, *Les Cuirassés français de 23,500 tonnes* (Grenoble, 1980), Vol. 1, pp. 11–13, 17, 83.

6 Le Masson, *Propos maritimes*, p. 230.

7 See below Chapter 2.

8 Le Masson, *Propos maritimes*, p. 222; idem, *De Nautilus (1800) au Redoutable* (Paris, 1969), pp. 222, 241–4.

9 Halpern, *Mediterranean Naval Situation*, pp. 71–5, 84–5.

10 The subject is examined exhaustively in Samuel R. Williamson, *The Politics of Grand Strategy: Britain and France Prepare for War* (Cambridge, Mass., 1969). See also, Halpern, *Mediterranean Naval Situation*, ch. 4.

11 Halpern, *Mediterranean Naval Situation*, pp. 107–9.

12 Ufficio del Capo di Stato Maggiore della Marina, IV Reparto, 'Memoria sull' efficienza delle forze navali francesi in Mediterraneo', n.d. [July 1914]. On the 15th the Chief of Staff forwarded a copy to Prime Minister Salandra. Archivio Centrale dello Stato, Rome (hereafter referred to as ACS), Carte Salandra 2/16.

13 Halpern, *Mediterranean Naval Situation*, pp. 190–3, 202–8; Giorgio Giorgerini and Augusto Nani, *Le navi di linea italiane* (Rome, 1962), pp. 183–8, 193–8, 205–8, 213–18.

14 Halpern, *Mediterranean Naval Situation*, pp. 191–3.

15 The various authorities do not agree, largely due to ships under refit, on detached service, or too old to be effective. These figures are from Ufficio Storico della R. Marina, *La marina italiana nella grande guerra* (8 vols, Florence, 1935–42) (hereafter cited as *Marina italiana*), Vol. 1, pp. 443–52; Fred T. Jane (ed.), *Fighting Ships, 1914* (hereafter cited as *Jane's 1914*) (London, 1914; reprint, Newton Abbot, 1968).

16 Halpern, *Mediterranean Naval Situation*, pp. 158–63. Details of the dreadnoughts are in: Arbeitsgemeinschaft für österreichische Marinegeschichte, *Die Tegetthoff Klasse: Österreich-Ungarns grosste Schlachtschiffe* (Vienna, 1979). For a general survey see: Hans Hugo Sokol, *Des Kaisers Seemacht: Österreichs Kriegsmarine 1848–1914* (Vienna, 1980).

17 Varying estimates from *Jane's 1914*; Hans Hugo Sokol, *Österreich-Ungarns Seekrieg* (2 vols, Vienna, 1933), Vol. 2, Beilage 5; René Greger, *Austro-Hungarian Warships of World War I* (London, 1976).

18 A full account is in Halpern, *Mediterranean Naval Situation*, chs 8–9. An exhaustive study with texts of documents including the earlier 1900 treaty is Mariano Gabriele, *Le convenzioni navali della Triplice* (Rome, 1969).

19 Revel to Salandra, 1 Aug. 1914, ACS, Carte Salandra 2/16.

20 Figures from *Jane's 1914*. For the Balkan naval race see, Halpern, *Mediterranean Naval Situation*, ch. 11.

21 See below, pp. 297–8.

[2]

The Beginning of the War in the Mediterranean and Adriatic

The Escape of the Goeben *and* Breslau

The naval war began in the Mediterranean in a far different manner than most had anticipated and the events of the first few days revealed how little the prewar plans and expectations of the Mediterranean naval powers corresponded with reality. Instead of a major naval battle between closely balanced fleets, there were the glancing blows associated with the pursuit of the *Goeben* and *Breslau* to the Dardanelles. The events might have been dramatic but they were hardly the titanic encounter everyone had anticipated and when they were over virtually everyone, except the Germans, was somewhat let down and left with feelings of disappointment, while quarrelling to varying degrees among themselves as to what had gone wrong.

The Mittelmeerdivision consisting of the battle cruiser *Goeben* and light cruiser *Breslau* had been commanded since October 1913 by Rear-Admiral Wilhelm Souchon. The *Goeben*, sent out immediately after her trials in 1912, suffered from boiler tube defects and was due to be replaced by *Moltke* in October 1914. Instead, after the Sarajevo assassinations she went into dry dock at Pola while specialists from Germany came south to help in the frantic work of changing boiler tubes. The Kaiser had warned the armed forces on 5 and 6 July to be prepared for all eventualities.[1] Souchon fretted in the hot, and for a North German, uncomfortable port while he marvelled at the Austrian *joie de vivre* and nonchalance which was so different from his own experience. As late as 25 July he did not believe, however, it would come to a major war.[2] When war did break out, *Goeben* could steam far faster than she did before docking, but nothing like the speed reached on her trials. The British and French, of course, did not know this and the French were conscious that they had nothing able to stand up to the *Goeben* that could come anywhere near her speed. Souchon, irrespective of any possible Triple Alliance combination, was determined to exploit that speed and firepower and disturb the transport of French troops from Algeria to metropolitan France. This potential weakening of French forces in the decisive encounter battles on land was a logical step for the Germans and

12

they had always shown considerable enthusiasm for it. The French, in turn, anticipated that this would be the primary German objective. Souchon displayed commendable energy in getting to sea although he was still convinced on 1 August they would not be drawn into a war. His ships were at Messina on 2 August, where he learned of Italian neutrality and experienced difficulties in obtaining coal.[3] Anticipating the outbreak of war with France, he sailed on the night of 2–3 August, received word of the formal declaration of war by wireless on the evening of the 3rd, and was off the coast of Algeria the following morning. At 6.08 a.m. *Goeben* bombarded Philippeville for ten minutes, while to the east *Breslau* fired on Bône at daybreak. French shore guns returned the fire. These were the opening shots of the war in the Mediterranean.[4] That afternoon Souchon received another wireless message from Berlin informing him of the conclusion of the alliance with Turkey and ordering him to break through to Constantinople. For this he needed coal and he headed for Messina. He met the battle cruisers *Indefatigable* and *Indomitable en route*, but Britain and Germany were not yet at war. No salutes were exchanged and the British turned to follow but could not keep up. Souchon made heroic efforts to increase *Goeben*'s speed to 24 knots for a brief interval so as to preserve her reputation for speed, an effective tactic since the British, like the French, would consistently overestimate it.[5] Souchon arrived back in Messina on the morning of the 5th and received unpleasant news. Not only had the Italian government declared neutrality, the port authorities now limited his stay to twenty-four hours. He did not believe this would allow sufficient time to fill his bunkers. He was correct and the Germans frantically arranged for a collier to meet them in the Aegean. Souchon also learned that the Austrian fleet was *not* coming to his assistance. So much for the grand designs of the Triple Alliance. Perhaps equally disturbing, Souchon received new information from Berlin that it might not yet be politically possible to call at Constantinople. With Austrian help not forthcoming, Souchon elected to gamble that the Turkish situation would improve and left Messina late in the afternoon on the 6th in an attempt to break through to the east. He had no desire to be bottled up with the Austrian fleet.[6]

Souchon's forces feinted towards the Adriatic before turning eastwards, shadowed by Captain Howard Kelly in the light cruiser *Gloucester*, whose actions were perhaps the one bright spot in the otherwise dismal British performance. *Gloucester* skirmished with *Breslau*, but finally had to break off the pursuit when her bunkers were nearly empty on the afternoon of the 7th. Rear-Admiral E. C. T. Troubridge and the 1st Cruiser Squadron (armoured cruisers *Defence, Black Prince, Duke of Edinburgh* and *Warrior*) was patrolling south of Corfu off Cephalonia near the entrance to the Adriatic. Troubridge could have intercepted *Goeben*, started to, and then, influenced by his Flag Captain, Fawcet Wray, decided it would be a violation of his orders not to engage a superior force and turned away. He was convinced that *Goeben* had the speed to destroy his ships with her 11-in. guns before his 9.2-in. and 7.5-in. guns would be in range. Souchon was therefore able to reach the Aegean unmolested, coaled at the island of Denusa near Naxos, and was finally allowed to enter the Dardanelles on the evening of the 10th.

The pursuit of the *Goeben* and *Breslau* has been examined in great detail and on the British side the conduct of Milne and Troubridge has been severely criticized. The criticism extends to the Admiralty and the Foreign Office, the latter for failing to draw attention to the likelihood of a Turkish-German treaty which would have had a bearing on Souchon's probable destination.[7] The Admiralty orders to Milne on 30 July had been ambiguous in telling him that his first task was to aid the French in transporting their African army by covering, and if possible bringing to action, individual fast German ships such as the *Goeben*, but to avoid being brought to action against superior forces except in combination with the French as part of a general battle.[8] He was also ordered not to be engaged seriously with Austrian forces before Italy's attitude was clarified. This happened on 2 August when it declared its neutrality, but this also complicated Milne's task for on 4 August the Admiralty ordered him to rigidly respect that neutrality, and not to allow any of his ships to come within six miles of the Italian coast, thereby effectively preventing him from sending warships into the two-mile-wide Straits of Messina.[9] Admiralty orders had the effect of turning Milne's attention towards the protection of the French transports, while the concept of avoiding action with superior forces, which implied the Austrian fleet, was interpreted by Troubridge as meaning the *Goeben*. An erroneous signal on 8 August to commence hostilities with Austria wasted twenty-four hours when Milne, pursuing with three battle cruisers, turned northwards to combine with Troubridge at the entrance to the Adriatic. Milne's conduct was approved by the Admiralty, at least on the surface, but he was never employed again. A Court of Inquiry decided to court martial Troubridge for failing to engage the *Goeben*. However, the court 'fully and honourably' acquitted him although he was not employed at sea again during the war.[10]

While the actions of the British and Germans have been examined in minute detail, the role of their respective allies, the French and Austrians, was equally interesting. The Austrians, in particular, deserve a closer look for at the very beginning of the war there was the appearance of discord in the Austro-German Alliance while the Triple Alliance Naval Convention was revealed as a mirage. The Italian navy had actually taken quiet preparatory measures to facilitate prompt and efficient mobilization, and on 29 July sealed orders were sent to various naval and maritime authorities for the event of mobilization. These orders, with one exception, were returned unopened after the declaration of neutrality.[11] But the Germans and especially the Austrians had, deep in their hearts, never really counted on the Italians. The Austro-German relationship was different.

Admiral Anton Haus, Marinekommandant and Chief of the Marinesektion of the Ministry of War since February 1913, and C.-in-C. designate of the Triple Alliance naval forces was in a critical position at the outbreak of war. The 63-year-old Haus was generally considered the outstanding man in the k.u.k. Kriegsmarine and enjoyed a high reputation. His photographs show him with a short, pointed white beard and mustache and alert intelligent eyes, and he was something of an intellectual, the author of a text on

14

oceanography and marine meteorology and an Austrian delegate to the Hague Peace Conference in 1907.[12] He was fond of music and multilingual, although fluency in languages was common, if not a necessity, in the multinational k.u.k. Kriegsmarine. Nevertheless, his private letters are peppered with French, Italian, Latin and English phrases. In the summer of 1913 he had undergone a serious operation for the removal of part of his large intestine and a stomach tumour which proved benign. Souchon described him at a dinner revelling in lively reminiscences of his time under sail, a narrative talent he apparently shared with other Austrian admirals who, the commander of the Mittelmeerdivision remarked, could talk about a toothpick for half an hour.[13] Haus had a sharp eye for human folly and an even sharper tongue. His sarcasm was well known in the officer corps and made him difficult to get along with, although there are indications from a prewar diary that he was ailing, often in pain, and had to resort to pain-killing medicines which may have affected his behaviour and how he was perceived by others. He sometimes had strong prejudices against an officer, frequently correct but occasionally unjustified, and he was also occasionally mistaken in his praise.[14] On the whole he does not seem to have been an individual who suffered fools gladly.

Haus experienced what must have been a disconcerting series of ups and downs as the Dual Monarchy moved from a limited war against Serbia to a general war against the Triple Entente. During this period he was to command the combined Austrian, Italian and German forces in the Mediterranean by convention and then, after the Italian declaration of neutrality, to go back to a rather reduced role as commander of a fleet forced to remain on the defensive. Initially he was concerned about 'our dumb' Albanian policy which had kept warships off the Albanian coast and deprived the fleet of cruisers and torpedo-boats badly needed for the defence of the southern Dalmatian coast or an eventual blockade of Montenegro, Serbia's likely ally.[15] On 22 July he ordered the II Division (three Radetzkys) to sail that evening for the Gulf of Cattaro – generally referred to as 'the Bocche' – to be followed by a gunboat, minesweepers, three Huszár-class destroyers and five high-seas torpedo-boats. The commander of the division, Rear-Admiral Anton Willenik, was specifically cautioned in any bombardment to ensure that his force saved sufficient munitions for action against an enemy fleet, and that situations which seriously threatened the combat readiness of his ships were to be avoided and landing detachments were not to be sent ashore.[16] This was an obvious precaution in case it did not remain a local war, but even in a limited war the southernmost portion of the Dalmatian coast was dangerously exposed, and subsequently evacuated. Haus was very anxious to get the II Division to Cattaro in case Montenegro attacked suddenly, as he wanted to avoid the disgrace of the navy being blamed for any disasters caused by the weak defences.[17] Haus also advised the Austrian Foreign Office that in case of war it would not be possible to keep warships off the Albanian coast. Here politics conflicted with sound strategy for the Austrians were supporting the Prince of Wied as uncertain ruler of Albania, and the Austrian Foreign

Office was afraid that withdrawal of the warships would signal disinterest and a free road to the Italians. In the absence of a final decision by the Kaiser, the Common Ministers ordered that all visible preparations by the navy be avoided until the evening of the 23rd, which meant until after the delivery in Belgrade of the Austrian ultimatum to Serbia.[18] The representative of the Marinekommandant at the Marinesektion in Vienna was Rear-Admiral Karl Kailer von Kaltenfels who felt that he was in a crossfire between Haus's irritation at not getting the ships south in time and the Foreign Office's desire for secrecy. Haus admitted to Kailer that he had not realized that the latter's opposition to sending the II Division south, ostensibly to avoid provoking Montenegro, reflected authoritative opinion, including that of Conrad von Hötzendorf, the Chief of the Austrian General Staff. Had it been just the opinion of the Ballhausplatz, it could be disregarded. But the Bocche was dangerously exposed and Haus reproached his deputy for being 'more military than he was' in presenting too little opposition to folly in high places.[19]

On 26 July Conrad informed the navy of the Kaiser's decision to order mobilization for Kriegsfall 'B' (Balkans) with action to begin against Serbia immediately on the opening of hostilities. Montenegro, whose artillery on Mount Lovčen dominated Cattaro, might still remain neutral, and therefore no action against the Montenegrins was to take place.[20] The melancholy series of events marking the beginning of the First World War are well known. Austria declared war on Serbia on 28 July, Russian intervention quickly followed and on 31 July Kriegsfall 'R' (Russia) was ordered with 4 August as the first day of mobilization.[21] Russian intervention was of little real meaning for the navy, but the possible intervention of Russia's ally, France, with its much more powerful fleet was of great importance and made the action of Italy crucial. As late as the 29th the Austrian naval attaché in Rome was optimistic. Korvettenkapitän Johannes Prince von und zu Liechtenstein was cordially received that day by Thaon di Revel, who mentioned that the Italian dreadnoughts *en route* to Taranto were ready for war and, as planned, coal supplies for the combined fleets were ready at Augusta along with colliers and lighters.[22] The mood changed swiftly and on 31 July the Marinesektion cabled Haus the sobering statement by the Italian Minister of Foreign Affairs that war against Serbia was an aggressive action which did not obligate Italy under the essentially defensive Triple Alliance.[23] Archduke Friedrich, titular commander of the Austro-Hungarian forces, in his formal orders to Haus concerning the conduct of the war authorized him to act according to the Triple Alliance Naval Convention, but explicitly stated that should Italy shirk its alliance obligations the fleet would be restricted to a defence of the Adriatic and cutting off contraband to Serbia.[24] Throughout 1 August, Liechtenstein forwarded a series of increasingly pessimistic reports on the imminence of Italian neutrality, which in fact came on the 2nd, and the Austrian naval attaché consoled himself with the observation that in the Italian officer corps one seemed ashamed of oneself. But, as he cynically observed little more than a week later, the epoch of feeling ashamed lasted at least two days before it began to change to open hostility towards their former ally.[25] Haus had been cheated of his chance to be a supreme allied naval commander with a decisive role, one way or another, in naval history.

The war had no sooner begun, however, than the question of a more active role for the Austrian fleet came up. This took two forms: first, a sortie to the rescue of the hunted *Goeben* and *Breslau*; and second, a move by the bulk of the fleet to the Dardanelles for operations in the Black Sea. On the afternoon of 4 August, Rear-Admiral Raisp, naval representative at the Austrian High Command (Armeeoberkommando or AOK), proposed to Conrad that after the Italians 'had done a bunk' the Austrian fleet was in danger of being destroyed by the overwhelmingly superior Anglo-French naval forces in the Adriatic, where the protection it could afford to the coast was only fictitious. On the other hand, the fleet might be used to good account for operations against the Russians in the Black Sea. Conrad, while sceptical about the remarks concerning the Adriatic, thought a move to the Black Sea would be useful for prodding Turkey and Bulgaria. He took Raisp to the Foreign Minister, Count Berchtold, who agreed to try and obtain permission from the Grand Vizier for the Austrian fleet to pass through the Dardanelles, and spoke of the desirability of delaying any declaration of war against France for at least three days in order to give the fleet time to reach the Straits. A premature declaration of war could attract French warships to the Adriatic.[26]

At 3 a.m. on the morning of the 5th Haus received the first concrete news of Souchon in several days. It was a somewhat garbled cable from Messina requesting the Austrians to come at once, reporting British but not French ships off Messina, and asking when the Austrians would arrive. It was an awkward request for Haus who, as C.-in-C. designate under the Triple Alliance Naval Convention, had known and approved of Souchon's proposed sortie against the French transports in the western Mediterranean. He was now, as he apologetically wrote to Admiral von Pohl, Chief of the German Admiralty Staff, in the bitter position of seeming to have left his ally in the lurch at a critical moment. However, general mobilization had begun only the day before Souchon's request. He therefore had ready for battle only the three dreadnoughts, three Radetzkys, two cruisers and around a dozen destroyers. This force would have a good chance of success against the British, particularly as their force was likely to be divided north and south of the Straits of Messina. The real problem was the superior French fleet which must have been aware of the *Goeben*'s location by then, and might have been hastening to ensure that this most dangerous opponent did not escape. Haus knew the French fleet had sailed from Toulon early on the morning of the 4th, and from various sources of information concluded on the morning of the 5th that all British ships were concentrating on blockading *Goeben* at Messina, with the French from Toulon and probably Bizerte on their way. He estimated that the ships from Toulon could arrive off Messina twenty to twenty-four hours earlier than the Austrians, and the ships from Bizerte might arrive even sooner. The Austrians could therefore run into overwhelmingly superior forces and risked the destruction of their two strongest battleship divisions without really helping Souchon. Haus assumed that the French C.-in-C. must realize that the real security of the

French transports lay in blockading *Goeben* at Messina rather than deploying capital ships to the western Mediterranean.[27] He was in this case perhaps more logical than his opponent.[28]

There was a further complication. The Austrian Ministry of Foreign Affairs was anxious to avoid war with Britain and Sir Edward Grey, British Foreign Secretary, had told the Austrian ambassador in London that even though Britain had declared war on Germany it would for the moment not act against the Dual Monarchy. AOK therefore ordered the k.u.k. Kriegsmarine to avoid acting against British ships and support *Goeben* and *Breslau* only when they were actually under the protection of the Austrian fleet or in Austrian territorial waters.[29] But it was likely to be difficult to combine these considerations with Austria's alliance obligations. The Admiralstab in Berlin forwarded a request to AOK for the k.u.k. Kriegsmarine to send all available strength to the southern Adriatic to facilitate the entrance of Souchon's force, now threatened by the British Malta Squadron, into the Adriatic. This was of course a naval question and the final decision belonged to Haus. In a hot pursuit under these circumstances it is difficult to see how hostilities between the British and Austrians could have been avoided.

The German naval and military attachés in Vienna both supported the request. When Conrad asked Korvettenkapitän von Freyberg why the *Goeben* had not come to Pola after Italy had declared neutrality, the German naval attaché answered cuttingly that it was impossible in war for a German ship to lie idle in harbour, that she went where she believed she could inflict the greatest damage on the enemy, and if her allies would not come with her she went alone.[30] Freyberg also passed on another wireless dispatch from the *Goeben* repeating that British warships were blocking the *Goeben*'s exit from Messina and it was urgent that Austrian warships should arrive there, and that French ships were still in the western Mediterranean.[31] This implied that in the absence of the French, Haus would have been assured of superiority over the British, but had he acted he might have violated the Austrian government's desire to avoid hostilities with Britain. Haus got out of the dilemma by citing technical difficulties. If *Goeben* were chased by British ships she could escape with her superior speed, while the much slower Austrian fleet 580 miles away could not help her. The French ships at Bizerte were 300 miles closer than the Austrians and to act on Souchon's request might mean the sacrifice of the two strongest divisions of the k.u.k. Kriegsmarine. Conrad was also concerned with the destructive potential of the French fleet and on both the 5th and 6th urged Berchtold to delay any declaration of war against the French for as long as possible, despite the fact that Austria's German ally was already at war with France. On 6 August there was another request from Berlin for assistance and AOK added that such action was politically desirable if militarily possible. Again it is difficult to see how AOK thought the fleet could act and yet avoid hostilities. Haus once again replied that the move was not opportune.[32]

Souchon broke out of Messina on the evening of the 6th and was reported heading for the Adriatic with the British in pursuit. The Admiralstab requested the Austrian fleet to come at least as far south as the parallel of

Brindisi. This put the situation in a different light and Haus sailed on the morning of the 7th with the I and II Divisions (6 battleships), Cruiser Flotilla (2 armoured cruisers), 6 destroyers and 13 torpedo-boats with the objective of protecting the *Goeben* in Austrian territorial waters.[33] For the Austrian officers the fleet made an imposing appearance, morale was excellent and the move to rescue the *Goeben* solemn but stimulating. The more thoughtful among them, however, realized the great responsibility that Haus had taken upon himself since the position of the superior French fleet was not known.[34]

The tension in the Austrian fleet had been unnecessary for the *Goeben*'s move towards the Adriatic had been only a feint, and on the afternoon of the 7th the Admiralstab transmitted its 'comradely thanks' to the Austrians, but informed them that the *Goeben* was on her way to the Dardanelles and had passed Cape Matapan at 1 p.m. The Germans added that it would be politically and militarily of the greatest value if the Austrian fleet also went to the Dardanelles for action against the Russian Black Sea Fleet. Haus, who received the news that evening when his fleet was off Cape Planka, turned about, cabled his best wishes to the Germans and was back in Pola by the following evening.[35]

The proposal to send the fleet to Constantinople, first raised by Raisp, had for a few days taken a back seat to the more pressing problem of the *Goeben*. Haus had, not surprisingly, turned down Raisp's proposal on the 5th, pointing out that it was not technically feasible without a secure base with coal stocks, and they must be certain that the fleet, whose speed would be slowed by the supply ships of the fleet train accompanying it, would not be attacked by superior forces on the way. Moreover, the state of mobilization at that time would not permit such a move. Berchtold was disappointed by the answer for he thought that the Austrian fleet in the Black Sea would be decisive for the actions of Romania and Bulgaria, who feared Russian warships off their coast. Berchtold enthusiastically remarked than when Odessa could be shelled, Bessarabia would be free and that the governments in Sofia and Bucharest were somewhat hesitant and needed a military spectacle. He complained of Haus's clumsy handling of the matter.[36] It was, considering the situation, a remarkably flippant approach.

Graf Hoyos, chief of Berchtold's Cabinet at the Foreign Office and his most trusted adviser, approached Conrad on the 8th about moving the fleet to Constantinople, and reiterated its importance on the attitude of Bulgaria and Romania. Conrad could only reply that Haus was not ready. But it was more than a question of being ready. Haus termed the German request 'impracticable' from a maritime-technical standpoint and 'ruinous' from a maritime-political standpoint. The Marinekommandant elaborated his reasons in a dispatch to AOK on the 8th. A move of the operational area of the k.u.k. Kriegsmarine outside of the Adriatic to the Black Sea was, given their means and in existing circumstances, an insoluble problem. A base secure from torpedo boat and submarine attack was the *conditio sine qua non* for the fleet and there were no bases on the Turkish, Bulgarian, or Romanian coasts. Constantinople was too far (300 miles) from the projected theatre of operations, and there were not sufficient stocks of coal and fuel on hand. Any temporary improvised base, while adequate in good weather, would require an immense apparatus whose procurement would last longer than the base itself. The difficulties would be insurmountable even if the way from the Adriatic to Constantinople was free. But that route was commanded by an overwhelming opponent who could easily cut sea communications. An expedition by the fleet and its fleet train outside of the Adriatic to Constantinople while the French fleet had no other serious opponent in the Mediterranean would be a frivolous gamble (*va Banque Spiel*) and the return home of the fleet would only be possible after the conclusion of peace. Moreover, the entire coast would be left defenceless and exposed to the greediness of Italy. Haus asked if it was conceivable that the Italians would resist such a temptation.[37]

The technical aspects of the problem certainly support Haus's position. As of the 8th the loading of two of the three colliers at Pola had not yet begun, while the third had 1,300 tons of coal on board and needed an additional five days to be filled. Another collier with 3,500 tons of Cardiff coal and 1,000 tons of anthracite was still at Fiume. Five steamers which were being fitted out for the fleet train would only be ready between the 18th and 25th, and another at Trieste required ten days' work.[38] Very few of the fleet's regular train were in service, most would not be ready until the 11th to the 20th. The technical factors alone would have prevented the fleet's departure until the last week of the month, but the question of the superior French fleet was even more critical and, most important of all, there was an understandable aversion towards leaving the Austrian coast to the mercy of the Italians. The Germans displayed a surprising insensitivity towards this aspect of the problem. On 12 August Korvettenkapitän von Arnim, on his way through Vienna to Romania to secure provisions for the *Goeben*, told the Marinesektion that the Admiralstab placed the highest value on the Austrians sending at least their II Division to co-operate with the *Goeben* in the Black Sea. Conrad, traditionally suspicious of Italy, used the Italian argument when Raisp brought this German officer to see him, but was also inclined to take the view that, while the fleet was already weak for the purpose of defending their own coasts, detaching a few ships would suffice to paralyse the Russian Black Sea Fleet.[39] Freyberg had the impression that Conrad, who deferred on naval matters to Haus, was rather unpleasantly affected by this new proposal and that von Arnim would not have any more success than he had. Raisp did manage to arrange for an automobile to be placed at Freyberg's disposal on the 14th for a trip to Pola, and the news that Britain had declared war on Austria-Hungary on the 13th led the German naval attaché to hope that perhaps they might yet accomplish something in the Adriatic. However his interview with Haus aboard the admiral's yacht, *Lacroma*, on the afternoon of the 15th confirmed his suspicions that there was nothing to be expected from the k.u.k. Kriegsmarine. They would shut themselves up in Pola in case of an Italian move, forsaking even a systematic reconnaissance of the lower Adriatic, and relying instead on the reports of signal stations and incoming steamers. The Austrians considered the thought of sending the fleet to the Black Sea very noble, but not feasible on account of supply and replenishment. But,

Freyberg complained, they did not seem to have oriented themselves on what coal was actually there or the possibility of coal supplies from the mines of Heraklea or via Romania. They were also convinced that the Italians would fall on their coast the moment the Austrian fleet left the Adriatic. Freyberg suggested sending only part of the fleet, even only two ships, to the Dardanelles, but this was termed not even under discussion once Britain had declared war. He suggested that the two ships might be escorted by the entire fleet as far as Corfu, or if necessary up to Cape Matapan and then detached, but this was termed impracticable and the sole thing he succeeded in obtaining from the Austrians was a few marine handbooks and maps of the Black Sea.[40]

The *Goeben* affair and subsequent refusal by the Austrians to rush either to Messina or send their fleet to Constantinople left at least a slight chill on Austro-German naval relations. Admiral von Pohl, Chief of the Admiralstab, tried to put a good face on the matter in his reply to Haus's letter of explanation, declaring that not for a moment had he or Souchon thought their brothers-in-arms had left them in the lurch in such a critical position. He knew 4 August was the first day of general mobilization for the Austrians and that the fleet was not ready for action against an overwhelming foe. The appeal for help was a cry to a friend who one assumed would follow up when he was in condition to do so. Those initiated in such matters had not the slightest reproach against a friend who could not do anything else, and the fact that the Austrian fleet eventually did sail, still under unfavourable conditions, would not be forgotten in the German navy.[41] Souchon also expressed his thanks for the attempt to relieve the *Goeben*, and added that he would gladly have fought shoulder to shoulder with the Austrians but had received the all-highest command to go to Constantinople. He hinted, however, that he regretted nothing had come of the plan to send Austrian ships to the Black Sea, as with them his chances for accomplishing something out there would be much greater.[42] The real reaction in the German navy was probably much closer to the exasperated comments of the naval attaché Freyberg, and as the war progressed the comments would become more barbed, even though the declarations of war by Britain and France ended practical hopes of sending out the entire fleet and possibly even individual warships.

The failure to come to the aid of the *Goeben* was a sensitive issue in the Austrian navy and the accusation of leaving their ally in the lurch was undoubtedly a painful one for those raised in the military ethic. Austrian officers writing after the war were anxious to justify and explain Haus's position.[43] Rear-Admiral Erich Heyssler, who was then Chief of Staff of the Cruiser Flotilla, described how Haus had assembled his admirals and their chiefs of staff aboard his yacht to discuss how far it was possible to assist the Germans. Heyssler termed a sortie by the fleet, which was still not totally prepared, to Messina to face a possibly overwhelming opponent as 'madness', and resented those German writers who with their 'usual arrogance' referred to this as slackness.[44] The technical arguments certainly support Haus. Even if he had wanted to send a few cruisers, the Austrians had available only the *Admiral Spaun*. The three Novaras, which would give such excellent service during the war, were not yet complete and the old armoured cruisers were too slow. The three Asperns, which would have been the most probable choice, were also slow and weak (as the fate of the *Zenta* would shortly demonstrate) and would not really have contributed much to any possible action in the Black Sea by the far faster *Goeben* and *Breslau*. On the larger strategical question, notably the future attitude of Italy, Haus's forebodings were also correct. He was, however, mistaken on one point. He regarded the French fleet as likely to appear in overwhelming strength at any moment. It did not, in fact, come anywhere near Messina while the *Goeben* was there and did not enter the Adriatic until 16 August.

Had the Italians honoured their Triple Alliance commitments, Haus's probable opponent would have been Vice-Admiral Augustin Boué de Lapeyrère. Lapeyrère was a Gascon who had made a great name for himself under Admiral Courbet in the operations against the Chinese fleet in 1884. Courbet had supposedly dubbed him the bravest of his captains. The 62-year-old Lapeyrère had been Minister of Marine from 1909 to 1911, and C.-in-C. of the 1ère Armée navale since 1911. His energetic command of France's major naval force in the Mediterranean had brought it to a high state of training and reflected a considerable improvement over the situation a few years before. This achievement had been noted by foreign observers, including his potential Italian foes.[45] Captain Howard Kelly, former British naval attaché, described him as a 'fine figure of a man with a ferocious expression . . . a kind heart, and . . . a very fine seaman'.[46] His future enemy, Souchon, who met him before the war dismissed him as a boor (*knoten*) who did not speak English or German, but acknowledged that he seemed more youthful and energetic than other French admirals.[47] He had the reputation of having a bit of the spirit of a *frondeur* in regard to the naval administration and as a former Minister of Marine was apt to treat the orders of the naval staff, and occasionally even the minister, in a rather cavalier fashion. While popular with the crews, he was also authoritarian and known for keeping his subordinates on their toes, never hesitating to correct a subordinate, perhaps too loudly, and often with the phrase 'vous manoeuvrez comme un pied' to the delight of the sailors. The Italian naval attaché summed him up as an energetic enemy to be feared, full of initiative, more apt to be bold than to stay on the defensive, not enjoying fame as a genius, criticized for a lack of perseverance and follow through, but not lacking in the confidence of his subordinates and faith in himself.[48]

Lapeyrère was thoroughly imbued with the spirit of the offensive, relished the thought of coming to grips with the enemy in a classic squadron encounter and trained his fleet for this purpose. He naturally assumed the enemy would be the Italians, possibly combined with the Austrians. But Lapeyrère was also charged with the duty of effecting the transport of the XIXème Corps from North Africa to metropolitan France. This transport was part of the mobilization plan and everyone assumed that the troops would be badly needed in the encounter battles which would follow the outbreak of war. The operation had been a matter of discussion and controversy between the Ministries of War and Marine for over forty years.[49] Lapeyrère opposed the idea of diverting the fleet from its offensive

22

mission to the role of convoy escort with the departure of the transports tied to the fixed schedule of the army's mobilization plans. The Ministry of War was willing to forgo convoys and allow transports to sail independently but insisted on the timetable, while Lapeyrère argued that only the naval commander could determine when it was safe to sail. The argument that the arrival of troops in time for the crucial land battles was the higher priority proved decisive, and in May 1913 the Conseil supérieur de la défense nationale decided that the transports would sail independently according to fixed schedule. They would be covered indirectly by the anticipated offensive of the French fleet at the beginning of hostilities, and somewhat more closely by a special division under the command of the Rear-Admiral commanding the Mediterranean Instruction Division which would consist of the old battleship *Jauréguiberry* and seven equally old armoured or protected cruisers. The division would concentrate south-east of the Balearics and east of the line Algiers–Toulon, roughly halfway between the French and Algerian coasts, with the mission of supplementing security by advising transports of the best route to follow, stopping suspicious ships and fighting any enemy trying to reach the transports.

Rear-Admiral Gabriel Darrieus, who was designated to command this special division, realized the illusory nature of the protection, especially when faced by a potential enemy such as the *Goeben*, and proposed minimizing risks by forming two convoys to be protected by his division, strengthened by the addition of two old battleships (*Charlemagne* and *Gaulois*) taken from the Division de complément.[50] Lapeyrère took up this proposal and on 28 July, the day Austria declared war on Serbia, proposed adding the entire Division de complément, when mobilized, to the Special Division to make a force of six battleships which would escort two successive convoys sailing from two, instead of the planned three, ports of embarkation (Oran and Algiers), while the major portion of the fleet energetically pursued the enemy. He concluded that any other way of proceeding was 'an adventure with which he did not desire to associate himself'. The exasperated ministry replied in a peremptory tone that the plan had already been decided and could not be changed on the eve of its execution. The transports would sail on fixed dates at full speed for Cette, while the fleet would provide distant cover by an offensive aimed at securing mastery of the sea in the western Mediterranean.[51]

By 1 August the situation had clarified itself and to some extent improved, for Lapeyrère now knew that the Italians would probably remain neutral and that the British would be allies, although he complained to one of his staff that the ministry had only informed him of Italy's official declaration of neutrality four days after one of his staff officers had learned of it by accident on the train to Paris.[52] But the *Goeben* and *Breslau* with their high speed and the former's big guns were his major worry, and Lapeyrère took advantage of a sentence in his orders authorizing the formation of convoys provided that no appreciable delay resulted. The main body of the French fleet sailed from Toulon at 4 a.m. on the morning of 3 August and divided into three groups steaming towards the coast of Algeria. The ministry's message announcing the opening of hostilities with

Germany reached the fleet at 1.15 on the morning of the 4th. The same message abrogated the clauses of Lapeyrère's instructions permitting the formation of convoys. In the next few days there were a flurry of messages between the fleet and the ministry which have been closely studied and could form the subject of a monograph by themselves. The French fleet never made contact with Souchon; one of the three groups might have, but was diverted by an erroneous report that Souchon was heading west. Perhaps the key to Lapeyrère's behaviour was his preoccupation with the 'transport spéciale', that is escorting the convoys which he had formed despite the orders from the ministry. He was reinforced in his beliefs by scattered information which filtered through the usual fog of war including reports that German liners were fitting out as auxiliary cruisers at Genoa, and that a German collier was at Palma and others might enter the Mediterranean through the Straits of Gibraltar. The evidence led him to believe that it was the *western* and not the eastern or central Mediterranean that would be crucial. There was indeed a general impression in the fleet that the Germans had colliers in the Balearics which would be used as a base for attacking French convoys.[53] Even after the presence of the *Goeben* at Messina was confirmed on the afternoon of the 6th, Lapeyrère, some of whose forces now needed to coal, believed that Souchon's ultimate objective would be the Austrian fleet at Pola or a breakthrough to the Atlantic. Moreover, the British, with whom Lapeyrère had no effective communication, were known to be present in force off Messina, and should have been able to handle the Germans, while no state of war yet existed between France and Austria.[54] French forces were consequently far from the decisive point when Souchon broke out of Messina and unexpectedly headed east. Moreover, it was unlikely any of the big gunned French ships would have been able to steam fast enough to damage the *Goeben*, especially as respect for Italian neutrality would have prevented a close blockade.

The escape of the *Goeben* and *Breslau* caused as much, if not more, controversy in France as it did in Britain, although this has understandably not always been reflected in English-language literature. Vice-Admiral Salaun, a distinguished officer, later wrote that a prompt concentration of the best French forces between the south of Sardinia and the Algerian coast should have been attempted and might have surprised and forced the *Goeben* to fight superior French forces, while there ought to have been more co-operation with the British in the prewar period for this purpose. This sentiment, though, ignores the fact that the British were determined to avoid that close co-operation before the war since the entente was not a binding alliance.[55] Capitaine de vaisseau Laurens, Chef du service historique after the war, is more severe in his implications and wrote of Lapeyrère's preconceived ideas influencing his interpretation of ministerial telegrams and constantly attracting his attention towards the west.[56] But these officers were writing calmly long after the events and are a pale reflection of the controversy which took place during the war. The attack on Lapeyrère, who relinquished his command in October 1915, was led by a retired naval officer, Vice-Admiral Bienaimé, nationalist deputy from the Department of the Seine, who began his inquiries in the summer of 1916. His attacks on

Lapeyrère became increasingly vitriolic and extended to the conduct of the war beyond the *Goeben* and *Breslau* episode. They eventually led to extensive testimony before the Chamber of Deputies Commission de la marine de guerre by Victor Augagneur, Minister of Marine from August 1914 to October 1915, Lapeyrère, and Vice-Admiral Pivet, Chief of the Naval Staff at the outbreak of the war. The testimony of Augagneur was particularly revealing with his description of the navy grouped into rival clans resembling cones with a vice-admiral at the point of each, and rear-admirals, captains and junior officers arranged appropriately below.[57] Personal animosities do appear to have played a role in the controversies in high naval circles, although the French navy was hardly unique in this. The fact that Augagneur was clearly a man of the left in politics while Bienaimé was of the far right may also have added a special note of bitterness. Augagneur claimed that Lapeyrère had remained independent of the rival clans, and as a result earned the hostility of the Naval Staff. The former minister added to the controversy by describing how he had been forced to remove Pivet as Chief of Naval Staff for lack of capacity. On the whole, Augagneur strongly and loyally defended his former Commander-in-Chief, Lapeyrère.[58]

The president of the Commission de la marine de guerre, Charles Chaumet, became Minister of Marine in August 1917 and conducted his own inquiry into the events of 3–8 August 1914, presumably through the officers of the minister's Cabinet. Their report concluded that: Lapeyrère had wanted to convoy transports despite orders; had not taken at the very beginning the necessary offensive measures according to intelligence received to execute his orders on the subject of the capture of the *Goeben*; had only partially done so afterwards; was not wrong in seeking the enemy in a false direction, in this case the western Mediterranean and Balearics, since everyone can be fooled in war; it could not be said that such offensive measures would have led to the certain destruction of the *Goeben*; and nothing could be asserted on the subject of whether or not the arrival of the *Goeben* at Constantinople had been the principal cause of Turkey's entry into the war.[59]

Lapeyrère testified before the Chamber of Deputies Commission de la marine de guerre in March 1918 and the latter presented its report in May. Their conclusions were similar to those of the minister. The commission agreed that Lapeyrère had used the fleet to convoy the transports, although he had received orders not to and to use his forces instead to destroy the enemy cruisers. However, from 4–8 August the C.-in-C.'s telegrams relative to protection of the convoys had been received without observation by the minister who declared he covered and fully approved the dispositions taken. The commission concluded:

> Vice-Admiral de Lapeyrère declared that, if he had not executed the orders given it is because these orders had not been conceived in view of the situation created by the presence of the *Goeben* and *Breslau*, superior in speed and in artillery to all the units of the French Fleet, which this case of *force majeure* obliged to take new dispositions.

25

By reason of the difference in speed and artillery existing between the ships making up the French Fleet and the *Goeben* and *Breslau* it is impossible to affirm that if offensive measures had been taken from the first day of operations the enemy cruisers would have been captured or destroyed.[60]

Vice-Admiral Bienaimé was not satisfied with this partial exoneration of Lapeyrère, but reserved further action for the duration of the war. He then published his own account which was highly critical of Lapeyrère and the two admirals continued their polemic in the press in the summer of 1921.[61]

Both the British and French had therefore started the war in the Mediterranean in a bumbling manner. Perhaps this was only to be expected after the long period of peace and the lack of effective plans for co-operation which spelt out all the crucial details so necessary for naval and military operations. The conflicting demands of diplomacy and military necessity complicated the situation, where the dates of the respective declarations of war differed. This also affected the Germans and Austrians and the much more elaborate German, Austrian and Italian plans for co-operation proved in the crisis to be no more effective than the vague Anglo-French designs. Possibly Souchon escaped because he was the one person who had a clear idea of what he wanted to accomplish in the confusion. But even Souchon had received conflicting advice from his superiors about permission to pass through the Dardanelles and had to waste precious time in the Aegean waiting for clearance. Perhaps too much has really been made of the *Goeben* episode. At first the Admiralty had indeed been inclined to minimize the escape and only later, particularly after Turkey entered the war on the side of Germany, did the enormity of the event sink in. It was certainly an affront to British and French pride, and the diplomatic dividends for the Germans were enormous. As a historian writing on the Turkish-German alliance put it, the *Goeben* greatly facilitated, but did not necessarily cause, Turkey's entry into the war.[62] The *Goeben* and *Breslau* subsequently played active, important but highly precarious roles against the Russians in the Black Sea. The Germans paid a price for this. *Goeben* and *Breslau* ceased to be important Mediterranean factors for the rest of the war and would come out into the Aegean just once in early 1918 with disastrous results for the Allies and themselves. In 1914 Souchon ended up far removed from any co-operation with the Austrian fleet, while the transport of French troops from North Africa was not seriously disturbed and for several months the free use of the Mediterranean by the British and French was not threatened.

The French and the Adriatic

Lapeyrère had little time to brood over the escape of the *Goeben*. On 6 August a convention was signed in London by Prince Louis of Battenberg, First Sea Lord of the Admiralty, and Capitaine de vaisseau Schwerer, Sub-Chief of the French Naval Staff, giving France the general direction of naval operations in the Mediterranean.[63] Until *Goeben* and *Breslau* were destroyed British naval forces in the Mediterranean would co-operate with the French fleet towards that end, but once this was accomplished the three battle cruisers and two or three armoured cruisers would regain their liberty of action, unless Italy broke neutrality. The remaining British forces in the Mediterranean, namely one to two armoured cruisers, four light cruisers, sixteen destroyers and the mobile defences of Malta and Gibraltar would be placed under the orders of the C.-in-C. of the French fleet and both Malta and Gibraltar would serve as bases for the French. The French navy would assure the protection of British and French commerce throughout the Mediterranean, and if war were declared between Austria and France would act against Austrian naval forces and, in any case, assure a rigorous surveillance of the entrance to the Adriatic. The French would also watch the exits of the Suez Canal as well as the Straits of Gibraltar and prevent enemy cruisers or auxiliary cruisers from entering the Mediterranean. The Anglo-French Naval Convention of 6 August was the high-water mark of French predominance in the Mediterranean.

The French, curiously enough, were as reluctant to declare war on the Austrians as the Austrians were to declare war on them. Pivet, acting on an erroneous report that Britain had just declared war on Austria, wrote to Lapeyrère on 7 August that France had an interest in delaying war against Austria despite its great desire to act in concert with Britain. The Chef d'état-major général's motive, possibly reflecting the minister's opinion, was to avoid pushing Italy into joining the Austrians as a result of past treaties. He stressed the importance of the French fleet showing no hostility whatever towards Italy, while also preparing for an approaching state of war with Austria. Pivet reported that according to reliable intelligence the Austrian fleet had left Pola and the Russians, upon whom the Austrians had already declared war, were afraid it might go to the Dardanelles; while the British at the mouth of the Adriatic might request Lapeyrère's assistance. The French should prepare for these eventualities, but for higher reasons of diplomacy it was essential for the fleet to wait at Toulon for further orders.[64]

When Pivet wrote the letter Lapeyrère was engaged in protecting the transports, but within a few days the situation began to clear, particularly in regard to Austrian and German intentions. Lapeyrère left the protection of transports to the Division de complément and older warships, and the core of the Armée navale had concentrated at Malta by the morning of the 13th.[65] The same morning the minister informed Lapeyrère that war had been declared on Austria-Hungary, and in order to influence the Italians asked for immediate action against the Austrians. He ordered Lapeyrère to sail as soon as possible with all available French and British ships, pass ostentatiously in view of the Italian coast while preserving amicable relations with the Italians, and undertake whatever operation he thought best against an Austrian port.[66]

The ministerial dispatch amplifying the bare telegram pointed out that the operation was a necessary demonstration from the point of view of grand policy, and might lead to the sortie of the Austrian fleet for a decisive battle and also cause the Austrians to lift their blockade of Montenegro. The government left Lapeyrère full liberty in the choice of his objective. The

Naval Staff considered a brusque attack by the fleet on Pola as absolutely impossible, involving losses out of proportion to the results likely to be obtained. Penetration into the Gulf of Cattaro seemed equally difficult. But support for the Montenegrins on the heights of Mount Lovčen might harm Austrian ships in the Gulf of Cattaro and facilitate subsequent operations. Lapeyrère was ordered to avoid any action which might give umbrage to the Italians, such as stationing a ship close to Valona, and any coastal bombardment should avoid as far as possible hitting private property. Many of the coastal areas were inhabited by Slavs who should be spared since their support might easily be gained by the French.[67]

Lapeyrère decided on a sweep into the Adriatic to surprise the Austrian vessels enforcing a blockade of Montenegro. The French fleet, joined by Troubridge's cruisers and destroyers, succeeded in cutting off and sinking the small cruiser *Zenta* off Antivari on 16 August. The *Zenta*, overwhelmed by a cascade of heavy gun fire, went down with her colours flying, while her consort, the destroyer *Ulan*, escaped to the north. The fire of the French fleet was not well co-ordinated and Lapeyrère's intervention in the normal gunnery procedures of the flagship caused considerable confusion and accounts for the excessive amount of firepower employed in sinking the small cruiser.[68] The Austrians, for their part, regarded the *Zenta* and her commander, Fregattenkapitän Paul Pachner, as heroes fighting to the end against overwhelming odds.[69] Despite French hopes the Austrian fleet did not come out, for Haus would have been foolish to oblige the French by steaming into the face of overwhelming force. This, in turn, presented Lapeyrère with a considerable problem. He did not have a base in the Adriatic and was consuming large quantities of coal daily. He informed the minister that if the fleet did not establish a base in the area it would be compelled to return to Malta. Operations might be fruitful only when they had a solid base at the entrance to the Adriatic and, in default of Corfu which belonged to neutral Greece, Lapeyrère suggested Valona. He warned that through lack of a base they would wear out personnel and material and risked being surprised in a defective situation.[70]

The hard and constant steaming which a blockade of the Adriatic required soon revealed defects in the material of the French navy, notably in the vital destroyers and torpedo-boats. Lapeyrère complained that the new 850-ton destroyers were perhaps suitable vessels for parades, but certainly not as warships. After accidents in the *Mangini* and *Renaudin*, Lapeyrère observed that a number of destroyers lived under constant threats of fire in their engine and boiler rooms, and that this series of ships could not be counted upon in an absolute fashion. The fragility of the torpedo-boats rendered them inapt for hard service and they had to be frequently supplied with fuel, water and food. Only ten of the thirty-five destroyers attached to the Armée navale were suitable for a projected sweep into the Adriatic by the cruiser division.[71]

The real problem for the French, however, was the lack of a base, complicated by the necessity of respecting the neutrality of Italian and Greek waters. All ships, whether large or small, coaled and took on water or fuel oil while at rest in the open sea. These improvised methods worked well in good weather, but would be very difficult when the weather turned in the autumn. The French also did not have all the vessels for the fleet train they might have desired. A staff officer complained that there had been no provision for colliers or oilers and that the authorities seemed to think that a naval battle would take place off the piers of Toulon in the first days of a war.[72] The quantities of fuel involved were also considerable. The daily consumption by the fleet was around 5,000 tons of coal and 1,000 tons of fuel oil. Ships also needed the opportunity to accomplish necessary technical chores, such as cleaning boilers and inspecting evaporating machinery. Consequently, Lapeyrère was forced after a few weeks to institute a system of rotation so that some ships could rest and tend to their needs. *Courbet* and 1ère Escadre de ligne and three flotillas (*escadrilles*) of torpedo-boats, for example, went back to Malta in the latter part of September and by early October the C.-in-C. reported the establishment of a continuous rotation between base and cruise so that a sufficient force was always ready for combat.[73]

Lapeyrère was also conscious that he was the Allied, as well as French, C.-in-C. in the Mediterranean and believed that according to the ministry's instructions his first objective was to protect shipping, making use of British cruisers. Unfortunately, the necessity of watching the Dardanelles, the Red Sea and other areas deprived him of British warships, and Lapeyrère found himself reduced to his own resources to assure protection of commerce. The Chef d'état-major général was irked by Lapeyrère's assertion that the ministry's instructions gave priority to the protection of commerce and Pivet noted in the margin of the dispatch: 'That has never been said.' His reply to the C.-in-C., prepared for the minister's signature, stated that the object which still seemed to hold Lapeyrère's attention deviated from that of the government. Protection of commerce would result naturally from closing the entrances to the Mediterranean at Gibraltar, Port Said and the Dardanelles. Pivet drew Lapeyrère's attention to his orders of 13 August about operations against the Austrian fleet and ports, and did not doubt that Lapeyrère would recognize the misunderstanding involved in his preoccupation with the commercial fleet and henceforth would employ the Armée navale to satisfy those orders. This implied, of course, a concentration on offensive operations against the Austrians. The dispatch reflected the Naval Staff's annoyance over the escape of the *Goeben* and Lapeyrère's preoccupation with the troop transports. What is interesting, however, is the minister's reaction. Augagneur noted that he could not sign the letter which was written in a comminatory and tart tone which was not employed in correspondence with the C.-in-C. of the fleet.[74] The incident demonstrated the friction between Lapeyrère and Pivet, as well as Augagneur's support of his naval commander against the staff.

Victor Augagneur, originally a physician, former Mayor of Lyon, and one-time Governor-General of Madagascar (1905–10) was associated with the group of republican socialists in the Chamber and became Minister of Marine on 3 August when his predecessor, Armand Gauthier, proved unequal to the strain of war. Gauthier had been minister for only a few months and was not very knowledgeable about the navy. He alarmed the

Cabinet by his nervousness and erratic actions which included a proposal to attack the *Goeben* before the outbreak of war. Raymond Poincaré, President of the Republic, described Augagneur as someone not accustomed to mincing his words, energetic, patriotic, a little trenchant in the expression of his ideas, but with a lively intelligence.[75] Augagneur had strong ideas and severely limited the Naval Staff's role in the conduct of operations, and the latter was also greatly weakened on the outbreak of war when fourteen of its seventeen junior officers left for other posts. Augagneur was not afraid to make decisions and assume responsibility himself, and subsequently replaced Pivet with an officer more to his liking.[76]

The sinking of the *Zenta* was a blow to the small, tightly knit Austrian naval officer corps and a sharp demonstration of the potentially overwhelming power of the French and British. Haus was critical of Rear-Admiral Richard Ritter von Barry, commanding the V Naval Division in the Gulf of Cattaro, for not having more extensive patrols which might have prevented the *Zenta* from being surprised and cut off. This opinion was not shared by everyone, but it might have been a major factor in Barry's replacement in this potentially important command by Rear-Admiral Alexander Hansa in October.[77] The loss of the *Zenta* must have confirmed Haus in his basically defensive strategy, with one eye always on his former ally. He wrote to Kailer:

> So long as the possibility exists that Italy will declare against us and attack us I consider it my first duty to keep our fleet intact as much as possible for the decisive struggle against this our most dangerous foe. Against the French and English I can therefore risk the least possible part of the operative fleet.

Haus added that even if it were possible to destroy these enemies in the Adriatic and in doing so suffer the loss of only half their fleet, such a 'glorious victory' would, under existing circumstances, be much more harmful than useful. From the caution that the French had displayed so far, he considered an attack on Pola or Sebenico to be out of the question, nor did he think that the French were likely to support the Montenegrins against Cattaro with any undertaking involving serious risk. He did not for the present fear loss of the Bocche, and considered everything there to be completely secure, while the battle readiness of the fleet was satisfactory and would be raised still further.[78] Kailer showed this letter to General Bolfras, the head of the Kaiser's Militärkanzlei, who had repeatedly asked about the navy. Bolfras, in turn, took it to Schönbrunn where Franz Joseph found Haus's opinions 'completely correct' and agreed to his policy.[79]

The two opposing commanders, Haus and Lapeyrère, therefore judged the essentials of each other's likely actions correctly. Neither a major fleet action nor a major landing would take place. But this did not prevent relatively minor actions on both sides which entailed limited risks. For the Austrians, it took the form of operations against the Montenegrin coast which was relatively limited in length. The French, for their part, made periodic sweeps into the Adriatic, often to cover ships carrying supplies to the Montenegrin port of Antivari only thirty-five miles from Cattaro, while observation posts equipped with wireless were established on Mount Lovčen. French submarines were posted off Cattaro and on 1 September battleships bombarded the forts at the entrance to the gulf. The logistical problems of the French persisted, however, and the use of various bays in the Ionian Islands by destroyers and torpedo-boats brought occasional protests from the Greek government, apparently instigated by the diplomatic agents of the Central Powers. The French assumed that the Austrians had a well-organized intelligence service to report on their movements in these ostensibly neutral waters. Eleutherios Venizelos, the pro-Allied Greek Prime Minister, was tolerant to the point of complicity in these technical violations of Greek neutrality, informing the Austrian minister that the use by the French of certain bays in the southern part of Corfu was a simple 'mistake' which would not happen again. He asked the French not to use the same bases any longer, but accepted their going to the other side of Corfu or some other Greek island adding, with what must have been a wink to the French minister, that if need be they could begin again the 'sham of explanation' (comédie de l'explication) with the Austrians.[80] The French navy also conducted what might be described as pin-prick operations which included cutting cables and destroying signal stations and lights on outlying islands such as Lissa. Their difficulties increased as the weather deteriorated in the autumn and the Bora, the nasty wind peculiar to the Adriatic, arrived. It was a frustrating war for the French and not likely to change given the basic strategy of the Austrians.

In the autumn of 1914 the Austrian naval base at Cattaro offered a tempting objective for an expedition. Located in the southernmost portion of the Dual Monarchy and relatively isolated, it could be dominated by Montenegrin guns on Mount Lovčen. The Bocche formed a complex series of bays and inlets and was slightly reminiscent of Norwegian fiords. The very complexity of the geographical layout meant that to secure it and the surrounding heights an army might have to employ a considerable number of troops. King Nicholas of Montenegro was enthusiastic about such a project and offered to take Cattaro with his army if the French provided support. The French government toyed with a project involving 4,500 men of the French-officered Italian Foreign Legion (including the grand-sons of Garibaldi) and 10,000 volunteers from Italy who, they hoped, would be joined by volunteers from Dalmatia. Augagneur was in contact with Reformist Socialist politicians in Italy and stated that they had promised 10,000 volunteers for whom the Minister of Marine was able to obtain rifles. Millerand, the Minister of War, also agreed to put the few thousand men of the Italian Foreign Legion at their disposal. Augagneur claimed that the project was squelched by Poincaré and Delcassé on the grounds that using Italians to conquer Cattaro would be too explosive in an area of growing Italian-Slav rivalry, and risked alienating Serbia. A further complication was undoubtedly the pro-republican, potentially anti-monarchical sentiments of many of the Garibaldini and the reluctance of the French to offend the Italian government, a neutral monarchy whom they were ardently courting.[81] Augagneur thought that they had missed a great opportunity, but Cattaro under the circumstances of 1914 was a far different proposition than Sicily in 1860 and the *Garibaldini* would have required substantial French backing, particularly in artillery, to have had any real chance of success. Moreover, the Italian government was unlikely to allow such a large-scale violation of its neutrality.

Lapeyrère, citing insufficient information about the defences of Cattaro, wanted more competent and precise intelligence. A French detachment under Capitaine de frégate Grellier was ordered to Montenegro, and Lapeyrère wanted Grellier's report on the conditions under which a methodical attack might be made.[82] The Grellier Mission, consisting of approximately 140 sailors and soldiers with four 155-mm and four 120-mm cannon landed at Antivari on 18 September but, due to difficulties in transportation and establishing itself at Kuk on Mount Lovčen, was not ready to actually commence firing until 19 October. Lapeyrère was not optimistic. He believed that there were six large forts at Cattaro (three of reinforced concrete), 150-mm cannon and an Austrian garrison of 10,000; while the poorly equipped Montenegrin forces numbered only 3,000–4,000. Capture of Cattaro would require a sizeable force with effective siege equipment, and this force did not exist. Lapeyrère did not believe that it was possible to take the Bocche without the assistance of the Serbian army. Moreover, considerable misery existed in Montenegro, with basic commodities such as flour, benzine and coal completely lacking. He feared that the King of Montenegro had illusions about the power of his army compared with the Austrians. Capture of Cattaro would require a long siege, and to hold the port an army would have to make all the heights which dominated two-thirds of its perimeter secure. French movements were already signalled from those heights by the enemy, and this made surprise difficult once their ships appeared on the horizon. Undoubtedly, Cattaro would be a precious naval base once it was taken but Lapeyrère thought the best and perhaps only thing they could do to acquire it would be to destroy the Austrian fleet, and to save their ships and munitions for this objective unless, of course, the Serbians would undertake the siege.[83]

Any expedition to Cattaro would be closely bound to the subject of assistance to Montenegro. Augagneur informed Lapeyrère that there was both political and military interest in a continuous surveillance of the Montenegrin coast, especially Antivari, and passed on the remarks of the Italian naval attaché in London that the reason Italy did not join the Entente was that Austria was being 'spared' by the inactivity of the Allied fleet in the Adriatic. King Nicholas told Delaroche-Vernet, French Minister in Cetinje, of the unfavourable impression on both public opinion and the representatives of neutral powers caused by the lack of effective French maritime action on the Dalmatian and Montenegrin coasts. The king complained that Antivari was practically blockaded by the Austrians and that the railway station at Gravosa, which could easily be bombarded from the sea, remained intact and was facilitating the transport of Austrian troops. Delaroche-Vernet added that he personally shared the impressions of the king.[84]

Lapeyrère was clearly annoyed over the accusation by this '*fonctionnaire*' of inactivity by the fleet and its leader. He pointed out that Antivari was an open port in a bay without defences of any sort, exposed to bad weather, absolutely inhospitable even for small ships, and situated only thirty-five miles from the enemy base at Cattaro where there were three battleships, two cruisers, and fourteen torpedo-boats sheltered behind forts and mine fields.[85] The French had only one moderately fast light cruiser, the *Jurien de la Gravière*, and a base of operations at Malta 480 miles from Antivari. They were ordered to blockade the entrance to the Adriatic and therefore forced to shelter and provision themselves in the Ionian Islands where Corfu, the principal island, had recently been forbidden to them because of the presence of numerous foreign diplomatic agents. Even these improvised bases were 190 miles from Antivari. In addition to these problems, there was also the necessity of rotating ships to Malta for the inspection of boilers and machinery. It was therefore impossible to keep ships permanently off Antivari or Cattaro. Lapeyrère also challenged the assertion that the Austrian blockade of Antivari was always effective, for that would require Austrian ships to be permanently off the port and this was far from the case. Austrian appearances were as intermittent as those of the French, despite the proximity of their base. Lapeyrère could only make brief appearances off Antivari and although he would multiply them the best he could, his present means did not permit him to conduct an effective blockade of Cattaro simultaneously with one of the Straits of Otranto. He needed at least six additional cruisers for that. Lapeyrère denied letting Montenegro starve, and pointed out that frequent reconnaisances and the destruction of cables and lighthouses rebutted any charges of inactivity. He reminded the minister that his orders had instructed him to spare the Slavic population and he had therefore refrained from destroying undefended places and, barring formal orders, would not commit depredations similar to those perpetrated by the Germans. As for Gravosa, the fleet had been off nearby Ragusa the day before yesterday and torpedo-boats had entered Gravosa harbour, but had found only two locomotives departing hastily and a calm population leaving religious services. They had not destroyed the railway station but this was only a small one at the end of the line and the vital line itself was sheltered from naval gunfire. Lapeyrère concluded that he could not forget that his principal obligation was to assure freedom of the Mediterranean, and he believed this could be achieved by a permanent blockade of the Straits of Otranto. He would do all in his power to assure communications with Antivari, even in the coming bad season, but he hoped that his efforts were appreciated more favourably and that the Ministry of Foreign Affairs was acquainted with the situation. Delaroche-Vernet's reproaches about inactivity had obviously touched a raw nerve and provoked the C.-in-C. into a long, revealing exposé of the situation.

Lapeyrère had other suggestions for action, for example a demonstration off Trieste with the objective of provoking the Austrian fleet to come out. He had studied such an operation but concluded:

> It is certain that if the presence of our ships before Trieste would have as a consequence the sortie of the enemy squadron the demonstration would impose itself on us even at the price of heavy sacrifices, but if this was not so one would have the right to ask oneself if the effect produced would really be in return to the risks run by our large ships.

If the Austrian fleet did come out the encounter would require all their resources, especially destroyers, which were vital for sweeping mines known to be scattered in profusion in the upper Adriatic. But their closest base, the precarious shelter of the Ionian Islands, was 550 miles from Trieste making a round trip of 1,100 miles, while the practical radius of action of their destroyers was limited for the most part to 700–800 miles, assuming an absence of breakdowns which were unfortunately so frequent with that type. Therefore the demonstration would be impossible without an intermediate refuelling in the open sea which would require exceptional weather, particularly in that season. Since the beginning of October bad weather had complicated their task, and re-supply, especially coaling, was very slow and uncertain. This was particularly true for the French cruisers because of their long lines of patrol. Since the British had given them responsibility for traffic in the Mediterranean, Lapeyrère asked for additional ships from the north. For an effective blockade of the Straits of Otranto he needed five cruisers on permanent patrol, with one specially placed at the northern exit of the Corfu Channel. There were three shifts, one at Malta, one on patrol and one coaling. He therefore required fifteen cruisers, but had only ten.[86]

The problems caused by geography, the sea and supply, as well as the technical limitations of some of his ships revealed in Lapeyrère's dispatches, demonstrate why the large paper superiority of the French over the Austrians did not result in more tangible results. There still remained, however, the question of Cattaro and Rear-Admiral de Bon, now Sub-Chief of the Naval Staff, was sent to Montenegro at the end of September to prepare a detailed report. De Bon was in Montenegro for approximately a fortnight and conferred with Lapeyrère on arrival and departure. The two were in basic agreement. De Bon concluded that, given the fortifications of Cattaro, its capture would require a considerable effort and that it was necessary to proceed as quickly as possible because of the approach of bad weather. He was, for example, told that by the end of November snow might render the positions of the batteries on Mount Lovčen at Kuk, and perhaps Krstac, untenable. The fortress should be attacked from the north by means of an expeditionary corps of 12,000 men who would be landed at Ragusa Vecchia, while 1,000 to 1,500 men would be landed at Budva to reinforce the Montenegrin army to the south. The troops to be used should be solid or elite forces, not scarcely trained volunteers, and should be accompanied by 12 field artillery batteries (10 for the north, 2 for the south), 4 batteries of mountain artillery and 10 batteries of machine guns. The artillery on Mount Lovčen should be reinforced by six 24-cm or 27-cm mortars and four 14-cm naval guns, and at least four of the latter were also needed for north of the bay to destroy vessels at anchor. The participation of the French navy was indispensable for landing the troops, reducing the coastal fortifications of Cattaro and destroying the warships sheltered in the bay. De Bon observed that, while it was not up to him to report on the consequences all of this might have for the fleet, he did call attention to the heavy consumption of munitions that would be required to reduce some of the well-protected fortifications such as Lustic and Radovic. They would also be subject to the attack of submarines which could easily come down from Pola behind the shelter of the Dalmatian Islands. De Bon believed that a venture against Cattaro would be successful, but they risked having to pay dearly for it, especially the fleet. It was up to the government to decide if the sacrifices were in accord with the benefits.[87]

Lapeyrère realized that the location of Cattaro was ideal for French operations. He agreed with de Bon that it was preferable to land at Ragusa and attack from the north instead of from the south, and saw no difficulty in landing troops at daybreak, provided the date of the landing could be kept secret.[88] The reduction of the coastal defences presented more difficulties, however, since the bombardment would be long and would require sweeping minefields, while they could expect submarine attacks by day and torpedo-boat attacks by night. Once the coastal forts were silenced and submarines and torpedo-boats destroyed, French submarines could penetrate into the gulf and it was reasonable to hope that the remaining enemy warships would be put out of action or destroyed, provided French troops occupied the surrounding heights and forts. Lapeyrère doubted that under these circumstances the Austrian fleet would remain immobile at Pola and the siege of Cattaro would therefore give them the much-desired opportunity to fight it under favourable conditions. If, on the other hand, the Austrians stayed in Pola the French would face the danger of emptying their magazines against land fortifications and then being surprised by fresh Austrian forces, with full magazines, coming down from the north. To avoid this, he proposed attacking Cattaro with the old battleships only, as well as submarines and part of the destroyer force, while the newer battleships and armoured cruisers would stand off ready to meet any enemy sortie from the north. Lapeyrère thought that 20,000 men would be required for the expedition, a higher estimate than that of de Bon.[89]

The actual French effort against Cattaro, the Grellier Mission on Mount Lovčen, did not fare very well. The French 15-cm cannon opened fire on 19 October against Fort Vermać, damaged the concrete emplacements, but could not completely reduce them.[90] The three Monarch-class battleships of the V Division in the gulf returned the fire and, while these small, old coast defence battleships were of little value in a battle at sea, their 24-cm cannon outranged the French. Moreover, the Montenegrins took little interest in defending the port of Antivari through which the French received their supplies, and ships could not use it unless covered by naval escorts which were then exposed to submarine and torpedo attack from Cattaro. Lapeyrère was forced to recommend conserving ammunition and taking advantage of the bad weather which had now arrived as an excuse to evacuate the positions on Mount Lovčen without appearing to have given in to Austrian counter-battery fire. The C.-in-C. was concerned that submarines, mines and Austrian aircraft were making their activities close to Antivari and the Adriatic coast more perilous every day. He thought it unexpected good fortune that they had avoided a serious incident so far, and recommended reducing the trips to a minimum.[91] Lapeyrère also complained of Montenegrin indifference and apathy, which led to their doing nothing to protect the port, and cited their laziness and sloth about moving valuable commodities, such as wheat, to a secure place after it had been disembarked.

The Grellier Mission received a further setback when Admiral Haus ordered the semi-dreadnought *Radetzky* to proceed to Cattaro on 21 October, escorted by torpedo-boats. The *Radetzky* remained an integral part of the battle fleet and was placed under the command of the V Division only for this operation. Her Captain was specifically ordered to economize on munitions and fire against targets on land no more than twenty shots per 30.5-cm gun or forty shots per 24-cm gun so as to guarantee the readiness of the ship for a real naval action.[92] *Radetzky*'s intervention was decisive and after two French guns were dismounted and twenty-four men killed or wounded, Grellier had to evacuate his initial positions for a less-exposed site. On 25 November the Minister of Marine ordered Grellier to return to France and turn over his remaining cannon to the Montenegrin government.[93] Lapeyrère had a long conversation with him after he was picked up and concluded that the evacuation ordered by the government was not only opportune but obligatory, and that the capture of Cattaro was clearly one of the biggest operations they could conceive.[94]

The expedition to Cattaro never occurred. The Montenegrin army was weak and ill-equipped for siege warfare while the scheme of recruiting Dalmatian and Italian volunteers was impracticable, if only because of the fierce Italian-Slav rivalry over the region. The intervention of the Serbian army could have been decisive, but the Serbs were locked in a deadly struggle against the Austrians far to the north, while the French government was loath to detach troops from the crucial battles at home.[95] General Joffre, Chief of the Army General Staff, was dead set against any project aimed at sending an army to operate against the Austrians, whether it was co-operation with the Serbs by way of Salonika or landing on the Adriatic coast. Early in the new year he ordered the Operations Bureau of the General Staff to draft a note to 'kill the project in the egg'. Any corps operating against Austria could only come from the western front where there were barely sufficient forces to cover its 600-km length. To weaken these forces would deprive them of any possibility of an offensive in the future and would, moreover, expose them to being attacked at a weak point and driven back. Joffre maintained that the objective was to defeat the enemy in the principal theatre of operations, and it was necessary to defeat the Germans, not the Austrians.[96] Given the attitude of Joffre and Lapeyrère's and de Bon's warning that the Cattaro expedition would be a very serious affair it is hardly surprising that the project came to nothing. After the beginning of 1915 the Dardanelles campaign and the possibility of Italian intervention on the side of the Allies transformed the situation. The reluctance to undertake any major expedition against Cattaro in the autumn of 1914 was probably logical when one takes the attitude of the major naval and military authorities into account. The next group to advance serious proposals towards attacking the base would be the Americans in 1918. If the French government could have foreseen the future use of Cattaro by the Germans in the deadly submarine war which followed within two years, the historian might legitimately ask if they would then have considered the potential cost of capturing it in late 1914 as excessive. The answer may still have been yes, for Cattaro was only one of two submarine bases. The major one was Pola.

On the Austrian side, Haus's defensive attitude was not appreciated by some of his own government or his German allies. Count Berchtold, in particular, annoyed Kailer with persistent questions about why the fleet did nothing to disturb repeated French excursions into the Adriatic.[97] Kailer replied that the fleet was indeed active with submarine and aircraft attacks against the French during their last incursion, while the reconnaissance of the I Torpedo Flotilla down to the parallel of Bari might have inflicted loss on the French if the latter had not withdrawn so quickly. They were undertaking raids and bombardments of Antivari, but any movement of the bulk of the fleet to oppose the French in the southern Adriatic was unjustified, and Kailer pointedly added that this attitude was fully approved by the Kaiser. Berchtold explained that his questions were prompted by conversations between the Duke of Avarna, the Italian ambassador, and Count von Tschirschky, the German ambassador, about the continuation of Italian neutrality and Avarna's alleged fears that the repeated and not seriously opposed French attacks on the Gulf of Cattaro were likely to become more serious with the installation of Montenegrin artillery on Mount Lovčen. This, in turn, would cause the Italians to seize the gulf themselves since they would never allow this important Adriatic harbour to fall into the hands of 'a Serbian power'. Berchtold feared that once the Italians had got a firm footing in the Bocche it would be impossible to get them out.

The multilingual Haus read the Italian papers every day and knew of their exaggerated reports about the entire Anglo-French fleet being continually off Cattaro with uninterrupted bombardments. He was therefore not surprised that Avarna, Salandra (the Italian Prime Minister), Tschirschky and Berchtold had a false notion of the situation.[98] In reality, the French made only temporary appearances off Cattaro, generally to cover transports to Antivari. After their first appearance he had sent the III Torpedo Division to Sebenico to attack them the following night, but the French had withdrawn before the end of the first day at sundown. When they repeated this on their second incursion, he had given up running after them. The French bombardments, despite exaggerations in the Italian press, did little serious damage. Haus concluded that the French would content themselves with blockading the Straits of Otranto, would not attack the Austrians and had no desire to risk anything to pull someone else's chestnuts out of the fire. There was nothing for them to win from the Austrians and in a major battle they might be weakened, leaving the Italians superior at sea. On these grounds, the Italians would enjoy nothing more than a decisive Austro-French naval battle which would leave the Italians masters of the Adriatic and the Mediterranean.

The Marinekommandant complained that their German ally was, strange to say, completely blind to their situation, and cited as an example the request to send the fleet on the second day of mobilization to join the *Goeben* and *Breslau* at Messina, followed by the 'incredible, quite absurd' request to move the fleet to the Black Sea, and later German requests to send at least the II or III Division. Haus said that he received, not long afterwards, a telegram from Souchon asking him to send a submarine to attack the British off Tenedos, about 1,000 miles away, which should then go on to attack the Russians in the Black Sea. With his usual sarcasm, Haus remarked that when such nonsense could flower out of the fresh wood of German naval professionals one need not wonder what grew out of the dead wood of the diplomats. As for the Italians, Haus doubted that Salandra was as naïve as his ambassador in believing that the French would risk a large part of their fleet for Cattaro, or that it would be easy for the Italians to obtain the Bocche without risking a very large portion of their fleet. Salandra knew that the French fleet would only be unleashed against Austria when the Italians had been seriously committed on land against Germany and Austria. The stronger the Austrians remained at sea, the higher the price to the Italians for any gain in the Adriatic and the stronger their disinclination to do anything. The entire navy joined with Salandra, Avarna, Tschirschky and Berchtold in the wish to inflict losses on the French and give them a lesson, but how difficult this was without weakening their own forces could be seen in the North Sea where, apart from the splendid successes of German submarines, all other German actions led only to considerable losses in small cruisers and destroyers. The Austrians did not have so many to lose and Germany's situation in the North Sea was incomparably more advantageous than Austria's in the southern Adriatic. Attacking the French with the bulk of their fleet would be an even more irresponsible mistake than if the German fleet attacked the British. They could not hope to defeat the French with a fleet half their strength, and the decision could not be final since the British Mediterranean Fleet would remain, and even a costly victory would leave Italy master of the Adriatic. In this long letter of 22 October to his representative in Vienna, Haus once again showed his fundamental mistrust of his former Italian allies and his exasperation at his present German ally, as well as Berchtold, for their lack of understanding of Austria's position in the maritime war.

The k.u.k. Kriegsmarine was clearly on the defensive with its military colleagues and German allies over its role in the war. The army may have suffered defeats against the Russians and Serbians, but at least it was fighting. Rear-Admiral Raisp, the naval representative at AOK, found most staff officers, particularly the prominent and younger more energetic ones, critical that the navy had exhibited little thirst for action and up to now had not accomplished anything.[99] These opinions were shared by the German delegates at headquarters, notably Lieutenant-General Freytag, and also by Lieutenant-Colonel Graf Kageneck, German military attaché. Raisp and Freytag had, at one point, exchanged heated words over the subject. The incident apparently ended on a satisfactory note for the Austrians, as Freytag, whom Raisp described as 'a very decent man', later apologized after he had been to a high-level meeting in Breslau where he found that Kaiser Wilhelm II and the Chief of his Naval Cabinet, Admiral von Müller, approved of the Austrians' attitude and described an offensive by the bulk of the fleet against the French as 'madness'. Kaiser Franz Joseph, when told of the incident, repeated his full support for the navy's strategy.[100]

The ever-sarcastic Haus remarked that he was not surprised the leading German authorities had finally recognized that their attitude was correct as they themselves had followed it since the beginning of the war. Unlike the Germans who had only to worry about the enemy fleet, the Austrians had to take their neutral neighbour into their calculations.[101] He continued to read the Italian press and noted the speculation about how Italy, through a clever policy, might acquire the Trentino, Trieste and Dalmatia on Austria's collapse without any sacrifice beyond mobilization. On the subject of the lack of appreciation of Austria's maritime position, Haus found as much to complain about his own army as he did about the Germans. The Austrian General Staff seemed very naïve on the question of sea strategy and the heir to the throne, Archduke Karl, unfortunately seemed to be under the influence of the General Staff.[102] Haus railed against the General Staff's failure to realize that they were not competent to judge naval questions and that they could not simply apply general principles. Naval war was more like a game of chess or bridge, mere knowledge of the rules was not sufficient if one could not actually play. Defeat at sea usually meant destruction, and lost ships could not be replaced as readily as regiments or divisions shattered through dumb leadership on land. Haus did not think the General Staff was conscious of the fact that without the navy the weakly held Gulf of Cattaro would have long since been lost. Without the Monarchs, the Montenegrin artillery would have dominated the Austrian forts Vermac and Gorazda, and without the *Radetzky* the forts would surely have been destroyed. He belittled what the French, despite overwhelming strength, had been able to accomplish in the Adriatic, and criticized the poor judgement and lack of comprehension of the military commander at Cattaro who had ordered the *Radetzky* to shell Cetinje, and when told it was impossible used his aircraft to bomb it when there were far more important military targets close to the Bocche.

While Haus may have strongly defended the Kriegsmarine from outside, and what he considered unfair, criticism, he was quite aware and highly critical of its internal shortcomings. He regarded the attack on Antivari on the night of 17–18 August as miserably executed by Korvettenkapitän Nowotny of the destroyer force.[103] He also lamented the fact that he did not find the restless spirit to risk everything among Austrian submarine commanders, whom he compared unfavourably with naval aviators. He praised the latter and termed them the first elite corps of the navy. Haus marvelled at the spirit shown by everyone once they could fly, and noted with approval that a call for aerial observers for reconnaissance flights had resulted in all Fregattenleutnants in the fleet at Pola, without exception, volunteering.[104]

Submarines were a weapon with great potential for the Austrians but there were only seven in service in the autumn of 1914. The two oldest (U1 and U2), based on the Lake design, were useful only for local defence, which left only the two Germania type (U3 and U4) built in Kiel, and the three Austrian-built Holland types (U5, U6, U12). One of the latter had been a speculative venture by the yard and was only commissioned by the Kriegsmarine in late August. There were six larger, Germania-type boats under construction at Kiel for the Austrians when the war began but in November 1914, in the belief that they could not be delivered during the war, they were taken over by the German navy.[105] Haus's role in submarine affairs is controversial. He has been criticized for a lack of interest in submarines, although this may have been more a case of personal dislike for the commander of the Austrian submarine service, Korvettenkapitän Franz Ritter von Thierry.[106] Haus had, in fact, experienced a dive and simulated attack in a submarine in 1913. Thierry complained of the ignorance of naval headquarters concerning submarines, and cited the example of a flag lieutenant specially sent to the submarine station on the second day of mobilization to inquire if you could also see aft through a periscope. According to Thierry, Haus had rejected a proposal on 17 August to send the five usable submarines to Cattaro on the grounds that he had intelligence that the British and French were planning to attack Pola.[107] Thierry complained that Haus had also frustrated a proposal to build additional submarines on either German or Whitehead's plans. The Marinekommandant asked Thierry how long construction would take, and when told ten months, provided the army released the necessary number of workers, replied that they would come too late for the war would end in four months' time.[108] Haus, for his part, found the more he conferred with Thierry, the more he found him more confused than convinced (*più confuso che persuaso*) and, when presented with Rear-Admiral Haus's plan to send two submarines down to the Straits of Otranto, became pale with horror, saying they might go, deliver an attack, but would then be lost. He could only give confused reasons why.[109] Haus criticized the performance of the submarine commanders as overcautious after a few unsuccessful attacks on French warships. He cited the example of the commander of U5 who had missed the cruiser *Victor Hugo* on 5 November largely because, Haus believed, he lacked the courage to wait five seconds to observe the torpedo track and fire a second shot. He remarked, 'and this trembling heart is according to Thierry number one!' Haus did note, though, that Hansa also considered the officer an able and determined commander who would hunt in the Straits of Otranto, a manœuvre which Thierry had characterized as madness. Whatever the differences between Haus and Thierry, they never reached breaking point and Thierry remained in command of Austria's submarines for the duration of the war. But it was never a warm relationship and, at the end of 1915, Thierry, although promoted to Fregattenkapitän, could still note that Kailer was the sole friend of submarines and someone who also understood them.[110]

French submarines were also active. In late November the *Cugnot* managed to penetrate part of the way into the Gulf of Cattaro. Haus gave a backhanded tribute to the French by remarking that, according to what Austrian submarine commanders had cited as dangers, the feat was pure madness.[111] On 8 December the *Curie* was caught and sunk in a gallant attempt to penetrate the defences of Pola. Most of her crew survived and in these still chivalrous early days of the war the Austrians treated her commander, Lieutenant de vaisseau O'Byrne, as something of a hero, even allowing his wife to come via Switzerland to care for the ailing officer. But the Austrians, after a number of near misses, finally had luck. On the tenth French sweep into the Adriatic, covering the movement of supplies to Montenegro, Lapeyrère's flagship *Jean Bart* was torpedoed on the morning of 21 December by U12. Fortunately, the torpedo hit the bow and the ship's water-tight compartmentation held allowing her to limp back to Malta.[112]

Lapeyrère concluded that not only could no secure use be made of Montenegrin ports, but that escorting a convoy into the Adriatic could not take place without excessive risk. Operations similar to the landing of the French artillery in September were now impossible, given the reinforcement of the enemy at Cattaro and the entry into action of Austrian submarines and aircraft. The presence of the *Radetzky* and three Monarchs at Cattaro necessitated the introduction of French battleships to protect the cruisers, transports and torpedo-boats, and the presence of submarines in the restricted waters made this too dangerous.[113] The French blockade in the Adriatic therefore became more and more of a distant blockade of the Straits of Otranto. It is ironic that both Lapeyrère and Haus faced criticism for their alleged inactivity. However, the seeming lack of activity had sound technical reasons behind it and both men were wise enough to realize that conditions of warfare had changed. Large warships could no longer steam where they wanted to with impunity, but must now be preserved as capital assets for use under special circumstances. By the end of the year a stalemate existed in the Adriatic similar to the one on the western front. The Austrians could not get out of the Adriatic, but the French could not operate big ships very far into it or too close to the shore without great risk.

Any discussion of the first few months of the war must also take into account the less-exciting aspects of maritime power. This involved the large movements of troops through the Mediterranean. Regular British troops from India, Malta, Egypt, Gibraltar and the Far East were brought back to Britain; Indian troops were brought to Egypt and France; and Territorial troops went out from Britain to the empire to relieve the regular garrisons.[114] The entrance to the Dardanelles was blockaded by British, later joined by French, warships, while diplomatic activity ensured that German liners in neutral Mediterranean ports which might have been converted into auxiliary cruisers were interned. The Mediterranean until the arrival of German submarines in the spring of 1915 was an Anglo-French lake, and in addition to the massive troop convoys the merchant shipping of Britain and France was free to exploit the resources of their empires and the Far East, with the Mediterranean an open highway. The entry of Turkey into the war on the side of Germany and Austria at the end of October brought with it the problem of defending the Suez Canal, but it did not challenge Anglo-French control of the sea. The *Goeben* was bottled up at the far-eastern end of the area and from this point of view much less of a threat, given her speed and firepower, than she might have been operating from an Austrian port through the sixty-mile-wide Straits of Otranto, instead of the narrow, easily blockaded entrance of the Dardanelles. She had ceased to be a significant factor in the Mediterranean and this must offset at least some of the enormous political advantage that the Germans gained from Souchon's escape. With the Adriatic stalemate, however, Germany's new ally, Turkey, would be the focus of British and French attention for much of 1915.

Notes: Chapter 2

1 Hermann Lorey, *Der Krieg in den türkischen Gewässern* (2 vols, Berlin, Vol. 1: 1928; Vol. 2: 1938), Vol. 1, pp. 2–3; V. R. Berghahn, *Germany and the Approach of War in 1914* (New York, 1973), pp. 188–9.

2 Souchon to his wife, 11, 17, 22 and 25 July 1914, Bundesarchiv-Militärarchiv, Freiburg im Breisgau (hereafter cited as BA-MA), Nachlass Souchon, N156/10.

3 Souchon to his wife, 1 and 2 Aug. 1914, ibid.

4 The first shots fired by naval guns in the war were those fired on 28 July by Austro-Hungarian monitors on the Danube against Serbian positions near Belgrade.

5 Lorey, *Krieg in den türkischen Gewässern*, Vol. 1, pp. 6–7.

6 Ulrich Trumpener, 'The escape of the *Goeben* and *Breslau*: a reassessment', *Canadian Journal of History*, vol. 6 (1971), pp. 175–6.

7 ibid., pp. 186–7; Julian S. Corbett and Henry Newbolt, *Naval Operations* (5 vols in 9, London, 1920–31), Vol. 1, pp. 67–8; Marder, *From the Dreadnought to Scapa Flow*, Vol. 2, pp. 31–41; Winston S. Churchill, *The World Crisis* (5 vols in 6, New York, 1923–31), Vol. 1, pp. 269–75; S. W. Roskill, *The Strategy of Sea Power* (London, 1962), p. 113.

8 E. W. R. Lumby (ed.), *Policy and Operations in the Mediterranean, 1912–1914*, Publications of the Navy Records Society, Vol. 115 (London, 1970), Doc. 62, p. 146.

9 ibid., Doc. 119, p. 157. In an unpublished note written after the war Churchill attacked Milne for failure to query the Admiralty on this point. Martin Gilbert, *Winston S. Churchill*, Vol. 3: *The Challenge of War, 1914–1916* (Boston, Mass., 1971), p. 42.

10 The full Court Martial is reproduced in Lumby (ed.), *Mediterranean, 1912–1914*, pt 3. For a short account see Marder, *Dreadnought to Scapa Flow*, Vol. 2, pp. 33–6. Troubridge spent an adventurous and taxing period as head of the British Naval Mission with the Serbian army and was later on the staff of Prince Alexander of Serbia at Salonika.

11 Halpern, *Mediterranean Naval Situation*, pp. 275–6.

12 Heinrich Bayer von Bayersburg, *Unter der k.u.k. Kriegsflagge, 1914–1918* (Vienna, 1959), pp. 7 ff; Sokol, *Des Kaisers Seemacht*, pp. 239–41.

13 Souchon to his wife, 11 and 13 July 1914, BA-MA, Nachlass Souchon, N156/10.

14 Wladimir Aichelburg, *Die Unterseeboote Österreich-Ungarns* (2 vols, Graz, 1981), Vol. 1, p. 65; Kontreadmiral Erich Heyssler, 'Erinnerungen' (1936), typescript in private possession, p. 388.

15 Haus to Kailer, 20 July 1914, Kriegsarchiv, Vienna, Nachlass Kailer.

16 Haus to Willenik, 22 July 1914, Kriegsarchiv, Vienna, Operationskanzlei/ Marinesektion (hereafter referred to as OK/MS) OK/MS IX-9/2 ex 1914, No. 3150.

17 Haus to Kailer, 22 July 1914, Kriegsarchiv, Vienna, Nachlass Kailer; Sokol, *Österreich-Ungarns Seekrieg*, Vol. 1, pp. 76–7.

18 Memorandum by Fregattenkapitän Konek on Haus to Marinesektion, 21 July 1914, OK/MS IX-9/2 ex 1914 No. 3115. For the ultimatium see Luigi Albertini, *The Origins of the War of 1914* (3 vols, London, 1952–7), Vol. 2, pp. 284–9.

19 Kailer to Haus, 24 July 1914, Kriegsarchiv, Vienna, Nachlass Haus; Haus to Kailer, 25 July 1914, ibid., Nachlass Kailer.

20 Conrad to Marinesektion, 26 July 1914, OK/MS IX-9/2 ex 1914, No. 3233.

21 Krobatin to Haus, 31 July 1914, OK/MS VIII-1/1 ex 1914, No. 3455.

22 Marineattaché, Rome to Marinesektion, 29 July 1914, ibid., No. 3404.

23 Marinesektion to Haus, 31 July 1914, ibid., No. 3454; Marineattaché, Rome to Marinesektion, 31 July, ibid., No. 3488.

24 Archduke Friedrich to Haus, 1 Aug. and Supplement, 2 Aug. 1914, ibid., No. 3848.

25 Marineattaché, Rome to Marinesektion, 1 and 3 Aug. 1914, ibid., Nos 3523, 3703; Marinesektion to Haus, 2 Aug., ibid.; Liechtenstein to Cicoli [?], 9 Aug., ibid., No. 4008.

26 Feldmarschall Conrad, *Aus Meiner Dienstzeit, 1906–1918* (5 vols, Vienna, Leipzig and Munich, 1921–5), Vol. 4, pp. 174–5.

27 Haus to von Pohl, 6 Aug. 1914, OK/MS VIII-1/1 ex 1914, No. 3912. Most of the letter is printed in Sokol, *Österreich-Ungarns Seekrieg*, pp. 70–2. Admiral Khuepach, writing after the war, said it was not possible to discover in the Austrian archives the text of Haus's first reply to Souchon, but that the version given by Souchon is apparently garbled. Admiral Khuepach, 'Warum hat Admiral Haus der deutschen Mittelmeerdivision seine Hilfe versagt?', Kriegsarchiv, Vienna, Nachlass Khuepach, B/200 Fasc. VI, No. 11.

28 See below, pp. 23–4.

29 AOK to Marinesektion, 5 Aug. 1914, OK/MS VIII-1/1 ex 1914, No. 3686; circular telegram from Marinesektion, 5 Aug., ibid., No. 3680; Marinesektion to Haus, 5 Aug., ibid., No. 3685.

30 'Aufzeichnungen des Marineattachés in Wien in der Zeit vom 5–16 August 1914 [17 Oct. 1914]', Reichsmarine Amt Archives, microfilm copy in National Archives and Records Service, Washington (hereafter cited as NARS), T-1022, Roll 537, PG 69132. In another report Freyberg used the more provocative phrase 'Austria and Italy had left Germany in the lurch' although it is not certain he actually said this to Conrad. 'Niederschrift über einen mündlichen Bericht des Korvettenkapitän Freiherr von Freyberg vom 14 Oktober, 1914', ibid.

31 Marinesektion to Haus, 5 Aug. 1914, OK/MS VIII-1/1 ex 1914, No. 3685; Fleischmann to Conrad, 5 Aug., ibid., No. 3686; Marinesektion to Haus (telephone), 5 Aug., ibid., No. 3733, Conrad, *Dienstzeit*, Vol. 4, pp. 179–80.

32 Haus to Kailer, 5 Aug., OK/MS VIII-1/1 ex 1914, No. 3686; Conrad, *Dienstzeit*, Vol. 4, pp. 178, 181, 184.

33 Marinesektion to Haus, 7 Aug., OK/MS VIII-1/1 ex 1914, No. 3804; Haus to Marinesektion, 7 Aug., ibid., No. 3806.

34 Heyssler, 'Erinnerungen', cit. at n. 14, p. 381.

35 Marinesektion to Haus, 7 Aug. (17.40), OK/MS VIII-1/1 ex 1914, Nos 3818, 3849; Haus to Marinesektion, 8 Aug., ibid., Nos 3822, 3867.

36 Haus to Marinesektion, 5 Aug., ibid., No. 3674; Conrad, *Dienstzeit*, Vol. 4, pp. 178–9.

37 ibid., p. 189; Flottenkommando to AOK (telephone), 9 Aug., OK/MS VIII-

1/1 ex 1914, No. 3881; Haus to AOK, 8 Aug. 1914, ibid., No. 3992; Sokol, *Österreich-Ungarns Seekrieg*, pp. 73–4.

38 Hafenadmiralat to Marinesektion (telephone), 8 Aug. 1914, OK/MS VIII-1/1 ex 1914, No. 3838.

39 Marinesektion to Haus, 12 Aug., ibid., No. 4022; Conrad, *Dienstzeit*, Vol. 4, pp. 205–6.

40 'Berichte des Marineattachés in Wien', 14 Oct. 1914; 'Aufzeichnungen des Marineattachés in Wien', 17 Oct. 1914, NARS, T-1022, Roll 537, PG 69132.

41 Von Pohl to Haus, 14 Aug. 1914, OK/MS VIII-1/1 ex 1914, No. 4400; substantially reproduced in Sokol, *Österreich-Ungarns Seekrieg*, pp. 72–3.

42 Souchon to Haus, 24 Sept., OK/MS VIII-1/1 ex 1914, No. 5551; Sokol, *Österreich-Ungarns Seekrieg*, p. 73.

43 Khuepach emphasizes the political and diplomatic aspect, notably the order to avoid war with Britain. 'Warum hat Admiral Haus der deutschen Mittelmeer-division seine Hilfe versagt?', pp. 6–9, loc. cit. at n. 27, Nachlass Khuepach, B/200, Fasc. VI, No. 11; see also Sokol, *Österreich-Ungarns Seekrieg*, pp. 67, 74.

44 Heyssler, 'Erinnerungen', cit. at n. 14, p. 381.

45 Etienne Taillemite, *Dictionnaire des marins français* (Paris, 1982), pp. 41–2; R. de Belot and André Reussner, *La Puissance navale dans l'histoire*, Vol. 3: *De 1914 à 1959* (Paris, 1960), p. 26; a rather critical description is in: Philippe Masson, 'Delcassé Ministre de la Marine', thèse, University of Paris, 1951, pp. 187–8.

46 Admiral Sir William Howard Kelly, 'Journal as Naval Attaché', National Maritime Museum, Greenwich, Kelly MSS.

47 Souchon to his wife, 5 Nov. 1913, BA-MA, Nachlass Souchon, N156/9.

48 Rota to Revel, 5 June 1914, Rome, Ufficio Storico della Marina Militare (hereafter cited as USM), Cartella 319/2.

49 Summarized in Halpern, *Mediterranean Naval Situation*, pp. 135 ff.

50 ibid., pp. 144–6.

51 Lapeyrère to minister, 28 July 1914. Vincennes, Service Historique de la Marine (hereafter cited as SHM), Carton A-89; Gauthier to Lapeyrère, 30 July 1914, ibid., Carton Eb-120.

52 Amiral Jules Docteur, *Carnet de bord, 1914–1919* (Paris, 1932), p. 18.

53 Vice-Amiral Dartige du Fournet, *Souvenirs de guerre d'un amiral, 1914–1916* (Paris, 1920), p. 4.

54 Good general accounts from the French point of view are: A. Thomazi, *La Guerre navale dans l'Adriatique* (Paris, 1925), pp. 21–31; Vice-Amiral Salaun, *La Marine française* (Paris, 1934), pp. 144–9; Adolphe Laurens, *Le Commandement naval en Méditerranée, 1914–1918* (Paris, 1931), pp. 31–45.

55 Salaun, *Marine française*, pp. 147, 149. On the British desire to limit prewar communications in the Mediterranean see Halpern, *Mediterranean Naval Situation*, pp. 128–30.

56 Laurens, *Commandement naval*, p. 40.

57 Audition de M. Augagneur, Commission de la Marine de Guerre, 18 July 1917, pp. 18–19, SHM, Carton Ed-76bis.

58 ibid., pp. 19–20.

59 Cabinet du Ministre, 'Les operations navales en Méditerranée du 3 au 8 août, 1914', enquête fait par M. Chaumet (Sept. 1917), ibid., Carton Ed-76.

60 Commission de la Marine de Guerre (Députés), *Rapport sur l'affaire du Goeben et du Breslau présenté par M. Abel, Député*, 14 May 1918, p. 35, ibid.

61 Vice-Amiral Bienaimé, *La Guerre navale, 1914–1915: fautes et responsabilités* (Paris, 1920); Lapeyrère, 'Qui a laissé echapper?', *L'Eclair*, 2 July 1921;

Bienaimé, 'Encore la fuite du *Goeben* et du *Breslau*', *La Libre Parole*, 6 July 1921; Lapeyrère to minister, 11 July 1921, copies SHM, Carton Ed-76bis.

62 Trumpener, 'Escape of the *Goeben*', loc. cit., p. 171. For the initial sanguine judgements and subsequent change in opinion see: Marder, *Dreadnought to Scapa Flow*, Vol. 2, pp. 31–2, 41; Churchill, *The World Crisis*, Vol. 1, pp. 273–4.

63 'Protocole de convention passés entre l'Amirauté Britannique et l'Etat-Major Général de la Marine Française', 6 Aug. 1914, SHM, Carton Es-11.

64 Pivet to Lapeyrère, 7 Aug. 1914, SHM, Carton A-135.

65 The movements of the French fleet can be followed in detail in Thomazi, *Guerre navale dans l'Adriatique*, pp. 36–7.

66 Marine to Armée Navale, 13 Aug. 1914, SHM, Carton A-31. The French actually had no plan for war against Austria alone, see Thomazi, *Guerre navale dans l'Adriatique*, p. 38.

67 Augagneur [or possibly Pivet] to Lapeyrère, 13 Aug. 1914, SHM, Carton Ed-80.

68 J. Le Comte, 'L'affaire de la *Zenta*', *Revue Maritime*, no. 204 (Nov. 1963), pp. 1254–9; Thomazi, *Guerre navale dans l'Adriatique*, pp. 39–40.

69 Sokol, *Österreich-Ungarns Seekrieg*, pp. 80–4. On 8 August *Zenta* and her sister cruiser *Szigetvár* had opened the naval war in the Adriatic by shelling the Montenegrin port of Antivari, ibid., pp. 77–8.

70 Lapeyrère to minister, 17 Aug. 1914, SHM, Carton Ed-83.

71 Lapeyrère to minister, 21 and 23 Aug., 3 Sept. 1914, ibid. On 800-ton French destroyers see Jean Labayle-Couhat, *French Warships of World War I* (London, 1974) pp. 101, 111.

72 Amiral Docteur, *Carnet de bord*, p. 15.

73 Lapeyrère to minister, 3 and 25 Sept., 6 Oct. 1914, SHM, Carton Ed-83; Thomazi, *Guerre navale dans l'Adriatique*, p. 41.

74 Lapeyrère to minister, 25 Aug. 1914, SHM, Carton Ed-83; EMG [Pivet] to Lapeyrère and note by Augagneur, 10 Sept. 1914, ibid., Carton Ed-76.

75 Raymond Poincaré, *Au service de la France* (10 vols, Paris, 1926–33), Vol. 4, pp. 509–10; Vol. 5, p. 179; Vol. 6, p. 11.

76 Laurens, *Commandement naval*, pp. 21–2.

77 Heyssler, 'Erinnerungen', cit. at n. 14, p. 383. There is no mention of this in the generally laudatory sketches of Barry and Hansa in: Heinrich Bayer von Bayersburg, *Österreichs Admirale* (Vienna, 1962), pp. 16, 74.

78 Haus to Kailer, 6 Sept. 1914, Kriegsarchiv, Vienna, Nachlass Kailer.

79 Kailer to Haus, 10 Sept. 1914, ibid., Nachlass Haus.

80 Deville to Minister of Foreign Affairs, 23 Sept. 1914; Minister of Marine to Lapeyrère, 24 Sept. 1914, SHM, Carton Ed-104.

81 Thomazi, *Guerre navale dans l'Adriatique*, p. 52; Commission de la Marine de Guerre, Audition de M. Augagneur, 18 July 1917, pp. 34–7, SHM, Carton Ed-76bis; Brunello Vigezzi, *L'Italia di fronte alla prima guerra mondiale*, Vol. 1: *L'Italia neutrale* (Milan and Naples, 1966), pp. 837 ff.

82 Lapeyrère to Augagneur, 8 Sept. 1914, SHM, Carton Ed-83. Lapeyrère's British liaison officer, Captain Huntingford, Royal Marines, supposedly knew the organization of the Cattaro defences and advised against attack from the seaward side where they would risk losses without obtaining any definite results. Lapeyrère to Augagneur, 25 Aug. 1914, ibid. See also Thomazi, *Guerre navale dans l'Adriatique*, pp. 52–3.

83 Lapeyrère to minister, 25 Sept. 1914, SHM, Carton Ed-83.

84 Augagneur to Lapeyrère, 21 Sept. 1914, ibid., Carton Ed-91.

85 Lapeyrère to Augagneur, 6 Oct. 1914, ibid., Carton Ed-92.

86 Lapeyrère to Augagneur, 13 Oct. 1914, ibid., Carton Ed-83.
87 'Extraits du rapport du Monsieur le Contre-Amiral de Bon sur sa mission au Montenegro', 27 Oct. 1914, pp. 8–9, 43–4, ibid., Carton Es-18.
88 Lapeyrère to Augagneur, 18 Oct. 1914, ibid., Carton Ed-83.
89 ibid., De Bon also differed by believing that the limited number of big guns in the old battleships would not be sufficient to do the job and, inevitably, the newer battleships would be required. De Bon, 'Extraits du rapport', pp. 8–9, ibid., Carton Es-18.
90 Lapeyrère to Augagneur, 25 Oct. 1914, ibid., Carton Ed-83.
91 Lapeyrère to Augagneur, 4 Nov. 1914, ibid.
92 Haus to Captain, S. M. S. *Radetzky*, 20 Oct. 1914, OK/MS VIII-1/1 ex 1914, No. 5978.
93 Sokol, *Österreich-Ungarns Seekrieg*, pp. 91–6; Thomazi, *Guerre navale dans l'Adriatique*, pp. 53–6. Thomazi, along with many French sources, incorrectly identifies *Radetzky* as *Zryni*.
94 Lapeyrère to Augagneur, 9 Dec. 1914, SHM, Carton Ed-83.
95 Thomazi, *Guerre navale dans l'Adriatique*, pp. 54–7; Laurens, *Commandement naval*, pp. 54–6.
96 J. J. C. Joffre, *Mémoires du Maréchal Joffre* (2 vols, Paris, 1932), Vol. 1, pp. 484–6.
97 Kailer to Haus, 20 Oct. 1914, Kriegsarchiv, Vienna, Nachlass Haus.
98 Haus to Kailer, 22 Oct. 1914, ibid., Nachlass Kailer.
99 Kailer to Haus, 12 Dec. 1914, ibid., Nachlass Haus.
100 Kailer to Haus, 15 Dec. 1914, ibid.
101 Haus to Kailer, 14 Dec. 1914, ibid., Nachlass Kailer.
102 ibid. Kailer had been anxious for a long time to have a naval officer attached to the suite of the archduke and had finally received the emperor's approval in October, Kailer to Haus, 27 Oct. 1914, ibid., Nachlass Haus.
103 Haus to Kailer, 29 Oct. 1914, ibid., Nachlass Kailer.
104 Haus to Kailer, 14 Dec. 1914, ibid.
105 Greger, *Austro-Hungarian Warships*, pp. 68–72; Aichelburg, *Unterseeboote Österreich-Ungarns*, Vol. 1, p. 69.
106 Aichelburg, *Unterseeboote Österreich-Ungarns*, Vol. 1, pp. 63–5.
107 Thierry Diary, pp. 6–7, 11, Kriegsarchiv, Vienna, Nachlass Thierry, B/755, No. 22.
108 ibid., p. 42.
109 Haus to Kailer, 14 Dec. 1914, loc. cit. at n. 78, Nachlass Kailer.
110 Thierry Diary, 3 Dec. 1915, pp. 32–3, loc. cit. at n. 107, Nachlass Thierry, B/755, No. 23.
111 Thomazi, *Guerre navale dans l'Adriatique*, pp. 64–5; Haus to Kailer, 14 Dec. 1914, loc. cit. at n. 78, Nachlass Kailer.
112 Thomazi, *Guerre navale dans l'Adriatique*, pp. 67–9; Sokol, *Österreich-Ungarns Seekrieg*, pp. 118–20, 135–9, 139–42; Aichelburg, *Unterseeboote Österreich-Ungarns*, Vol. 1, pp. 70–6.
113 Lapeyrère to Augagneur, 24 Dec. 1914, SHM, Carton Ed-83.
114 This aspect of naval operations is covered in: Naval Staff, *The Mediterranean, 1914–1915*, chs iv–v.

[3]

The Dardanelles Campaign

When Rear-Admiral Souchon and the Mittelmeerdivision were last mentioned in the preceding chapter they had just been allowed to pass through the Dardanelles to the safety of Turkish waters. The poor condition of *Goeben*'s boilers caused excessive coal and water consumption and affected her speed, and Souchon was glad to have nothing more to do with the superior British fleet. On the other hand, he was anxious to get at the Russians whom he considered proportionately weaker in the Black Sea.[1] *Goeben* and *Breslau* were joined by the liners *General* of the German East Africa Line, and *Corcovado* of the Hamburg–America Line which would serve as depot ships. Souchon's desire for action, however, would be frustrated for the next two and a half months. The inevitable protests by the diplomats of the Entente powers over the presence of the German warships in supposedly neutral Turkish waters led to a clever solution which initially satisfied the needs of both the German and Turkish governments. The Ottoman navy had been on the verge of taking over two super-dreadnoughts, *Sultan Osman I* and *Reshadieh*, which were building in Britain when the war began. The ships threatened to upset the naval balance in the Aegean and in the spring of 1914 the Greeks had spoken of either a preventative war or attacking the ships on their way out. Despite the fact that Turkish crews had already arrived in Britain, Churchill ordered their seizure once the war began. The *Sultan Osman* and *Reshadieh* became *Agincourt* and *Erin*, respectively, in British service. Turkish public opinion was, however, incensed, as the ships had been the object of considerable propaganda and public subscription had been used to raise some of the money for their acquisition, and Churchill was criticized for alienating the Turks.[2] The Admiralty offered the Ottoman government a fixed payment per day for their use for the duration of the war, but the Turkish government and public were not satisfied and felt cheated of the magnificent ships they thought rightfully theirs. Churchill's action had been farsighted, however, for a Turkish–German Treaty of Alliance had been signed on 2 August and the Ottoman government had promptly offered to send *Sultan Osman* to a German port as soon as she left Britain. Not surprisingly, the Kaiser and Admiral Alfred von Tirpitz, State Secretary of the Reichsmarineamt (the Imperial Navy Office responsible for administrative control of the navy), quickly informed the German Foreign Office that the *Sultan Osman* would be most welcome

47

in Germany. The Ottoman government, however, was able to use these circumstances to at least partially forestall retaliation by the British and French for allowing the *Goeben* and *Breslau* to pass through the Dardanelles. It announced that it had purchased the two German ships as substitutes for the two dreadnoughts confiscated by the British and in a formal ceremony on 16 August both ships hoisted the Turkish flag.[3] The *Goeben* was renamed *Jawus Sultan Selim* and *Breslau* became *Midilli*. Souchon subsequently became Chief of the Turkish Fleet (Befehlshaber der schwimmenden Türkischen Streitkräfte).[4] The sale was only a fiction and, at least initially, few Turkish naval personnel actually joined the ships. There are photographs of ruddy-faced Germans looking rather sheepish in Turkish fezzes, but Souchon confided to his wife that the fez and Turkish uniform were for ceremonial purposes only and worn as little as possible.[5] Back in Germany, Admiral Hugo von Pohl, Chief of the Admiralstab, protested against German sailors actually having to fight under the Turkish flag, but Kaiser Wilhelm ordered the fiction to be maintained so long as it was politically required, even in the event of military action. Souchon noted that he felt the bitterness associated with the change even more than his subordinates, but gulped it down and after awhile scarcely felt it. He consoled himself with the thought that in war personal feelings had to be suppressed.[6] The Germans never used the Turkish names of the ships outside of official reports and documents, but they quickly became trapped in their own fiction. Officials such as Baron von Wangenheim, the German ambassador in Constantinople and Lieutenant-Colonel von Feldmann, Chief of Staff to Liman von Sanders, warned that any attempt to take back the ships would instantly deprive Germany of Turkish sympathy.[7] Neither ship would ever fly the German naval ensign again.

The fictitious sale actually worked against German naval interests for the next two and a half months, and Souchon complained that he was sitting in the *Corcovado* like a 'chained lion', frustrated in his desire to get at the Russians. Had he wanted to do nothing, he would have joined the Austrians in the Adriatic. Ideally he would have liked to operate in the Black Sea with a benevolently neutral Turkey to fall back on. Taking over the leadership of the Ottoman fleet was, on the other hand, a very uncertain and thorny problem.[8] Souchon obviously suffered from his dual position, and indeed his formal appointment had been motivated by a Turkish desire to control him more closely so as to preserve Ottoman neutrality and, if necessary, disavow his actions as those of an insubordinate troublemaker.[9] Souchon was in the habit of writing long, rather introspective letters to his wife and has been described as cool, calm and inspiring trust, but rather unassertive when compared with some of his more boisterous colleagues in the military. An American diplomat pictured him as a 'droop-jawed determined little man in a long ill-fitting frock-coat looking more like a parson than an admiral'.[10] He does not appear to have had any great liking for the Turks nor any great feeling or understanding of the Ottoman Empire. This was in direct contrast with the commander of the German base (*Etappenkommando*), Korvetten-kapitän Hans Humann, who had formerly commanded the German stationnaire *Loreley* at Constantinople. Humann, the son of a noted archaeologist, was born in Smyrna, fluent in the language, and a friend of the Turkish Minister of War, Enver Pasha. On the other hand, Souchon had rather more leeway in handling the fleet than German officers working with the Turkish army. This was due to the fact that the Ottoman Minister of Marine, Djemal Pasha, was also commander of the IV Turkish Army and Military Governor of Syria from November 1914 until the end of 1917 and usually absent from the capital. Nevertheless, all really important decisions required the agreement of Enver Pasha and the Turkish High Command.[11] Relations among the various German authorities in Turkey were not completely smooth either. Souchon found Liman von Sanders a good field soldier, but beyond that childlike, silly and impeding co-operation.[12] In the future, the Germans in the Ottoman Empire would prove themselves the equals of their Entente enemies when it came to friction and personal rivalries.

The Ottoman fleet was not very promising in appearance. The major units were the old battleships *Heireddin Barbarossa* and *Torgud Reis*, launched in 1891, and purchased from Germany in 1910. Both were under repair in dockyards at the beginning of the war. There was also the ancient battleship *Messudiyeh*, launched in 1874, and ostensibly modernized in 1903. However, her big guns had been placed on shore and she was of little value. There were two protected cruisers, *Hamidieh* and *Medjidieh*, launched in 1903, which were potentially more useful but still relatively slow for working with the *Goeben* and *Breslau*. There were eight high-seas torpedo-boats, launched 1908–9. Four were German-built Schichau boats, and four were French-built. There were also at least three smaller and older Italian-built torpedo-boats. German officers and men, initially from the Mittelmeer-division, but later from Germany, were seconded to the Turkish ships. The larger ships had both a German and Turkish commander, the latter responsible for internal administration and command in harbour, the former to command in battle at sea. The torpedo-boat flotilla was directly under a German officer as commodore, and here the Germans found their best opportunity. Kapitänleutnant Rudolph Firle, one of the young German officers sent out from home who had passed through neutral Romania as a 'dockyard worker', found the Schichau boats of the I Half Flotilla still in relatively good condition, but conditions on board, especially the bugs, were a brutal shock, and increased the importance of the liner *General* which could at least provide the Germans with clean beds and good food.[13] It was, however, the material condition of the ships, their boilers, and watertight compartmentation as well as the state of Turkish training that really shocked the Germans. The Germans were indignant over the British Naval Mission under Admiral Sir Arthur H. Limpus which had supposedly been responsible for training the Turkish fleet. The Limpus Mission, awkwardly enough, remained in Constantinople after the outbreak of war and was not expelled until mid-September. The British officers had, however, been removed from the fleet itself and ordered to work on shore at the ministry. Souchon and his officers were convinced that the British Mission had systematically worked to sabotage the development of the Turkish fleet and had for years kept its battleworthiness at the lowest possible grade.[14] The charge is a serious one and Souchon could list a number of areas of apparent neglect. However, the British Mission had been in Turkey during a highly disturbed period of coup and counter-coup, as well as the Italo-Turkish War of 1911–12 and the Balkan Wars of 1912–13 during which its activities were greatly restricted. The Germans in August and September 1914 were fresh, more likely to be shocked by the contrast between the Ottoman navy and their own immaculate fleet, and were present in far greater numbers than the British Mission and would enjoy proportionately more authority. They might have become more tolerant of their British predecessors after they themselves had worked a long time under the conditions of the Ottoman Empire.

The first of the British cruisers pursuing Souchon, HMS *Weymouth*, reached the Dardanelles less than twenty-four hours after the Germans had passed through the straits and was warned off by blank Turkish shots. The British subsequently established a close watch on the Dardanelles with the battle cruisers *Indomitable* and *Indefatigable*, and light cruiser *Gloucester*, under the command of the senior officer, Captain Francis W. Kennedy of the *Indomitable*. On 15 August the Admiralty, after they had learnt that the German crews would remain aboard *Goeben* and *Breslau* despite their alleged sale to Turkey, ordered the armoured cruiser *Defence*, and all available British destroyers plus the destroyer tender *Blenheim* to the Dardanelles. After the former Mediterranean C.-in-C., Admiral Milne, had left for home, the British Mediterranean forces were divided in two. Rear-Admiral Carden, the senior British naval officer in the Mediterranean, was in charge of the naval establishments at Malta and the local defence craft, while Rear-Admiral Troubridge commanded vessels at sea. Both were in theory under the French C.-in-C., Vice-Admiral Lapeyrère, who was by now preoccupied with the Adriatic.[15]

Souchon recognized that at best he could only attempt a torpedo-boat attack on the British off the Dardanelles. The 'miserable Turkish fleet' simply could not compete with them, and his primary goal therefore remained striking at the presumably easier Russians in the Black Sea. The German officers worked with their customary energy to whip their Turkish charges and their ships into shape, and by 20 September Souchon believed that the Turkish ships were in good-enough condition to put to sea and use their engines with a certain amount of security, but they still could not shoot.[16] The more junior German officers were less confident. Firle, in command of the I Half Flotilla, thought that the Turkish officers with years of sea experience in independent positions treated their boats as merchant steamers, and had no idea of their military and tactical employment. Even an undertaking in the Black Sea was impossible until they became accustomed through steady practice to working together at sea.[17]

The defence of the Dardanelles and the Bosphorus was a much more pressing problem for the Germans. Souchon was convinced that the Germans should take over the work themselves and, apparently on his own initiative, cabled home for experts on 15 August. The result was the arrival by early September of approximately 400 naval artillerymen and specialists in mine warfare who constituted the Sonderkommando under Admiral

Guido von Usedom. The latter subsequently received the title of Inspector-General of Coastal Fortifications and Minefields.[18] The crucial command at the Dardanelles was given to Vice-Admiral Merten. The arrival of the Sonderkommando, whose numbers would grow, was a great relief for Souchon, who felt that within a short while his rear, the Dardanelles, would be secure and he could turn his attention to the Russians in the Black Sea. By 20 September, Souchon considered the Straits to be secure.[19]

The British government had remained intensely suspicious of the presence of German officers and men aboard the *Goeben* and *Breslau* and in other ships of the Ottoman fleet, and on 2 September the Cabinet decided to sink any Turkish warships which tried to come out of the Dardanelles. The Admiralty had anticipated the Cabinet decision in regard to *Goeben* and *Breslau* and on 27 August had ordered Troubridge to attack the pair whatever flag they flew. The order was repeated on 8 September.[20] Churchill, even before Limpus's formal expulsion by the Turks, considered his position to be untenable and wanted to use his unrivalled knowledge of Turkish conditions by giving him command in the eastern Mediterranean. These proposals were vetoed by the Foreign Office, acting on the advice of Sir Louis Mallet, British ambassador at Constantinople, who still believed it was possible to preserve Turkish neutrality. Battenberg also wanted Limpus for command off the Dardanelles, but after the government's intervention Limpus, when he finally left Constantinople, simply changed places with Carden and became Admiral Superintendent at Malta while Carden moved to the eastern Mediterranean.[21] It seems a great waste of his special knowledge out of a misguided sense of chivalry and a desire not to offend the Turks. On the other hand, Limpus was a prolific writer of memoranda and kept the British commanders off the Dardanelles well supplied with comments on the Turkish defences. It is, of course, impossible to say whether it would have meant any difference had he been in command of the forces off the Dardanelles, although in the autumn of 1915 he fully supported de Robeck's decision not to attempt another naval attack.

The Admiralty repeated its orders to Carden to sink the *Goeben* and *Breslau* no matter what flag they flew, but he was to use his discretion with minor Turkish warships which might seek to come out of the Dardanelles. They did not want to pick a quarrel with Turkey until its hostile intentions were clear. Because of the two old German battleships in the Turkish fleet, the British also asked the French C.-in-C. to send two Patri-class battleships to join Carden.[22] The blockade was tightened still further when the British informed the Turkish government on 25 September 'that knowing German methods' any Turkish warships coming out of the Dardanelles under present conditions were to be regarded as having the intention of attacking some British interest, and on the night of the 26th the British turned back a Turkish destroyer which had tried to enter the Aegean after discovering Germans on board. The Turks and Germans replied by closing the last narrow channel through the Dardanelles minefields, thereby completely cutting off all maritime communications with Russia via the Black Sea by the 29th.[23] Souchon was delighted that nothing could now go in or out of the Dardanelles and that British, French and Russian commerce was stopped, although he was somewhat disappointed that the Entente did not follow this violation of past treaties concerning the Straits with a declaration of war.[24]

The details of how Turkey was manœuvred into war during October by the pro-German, pro-war factions of the ruling Young Turk government are beyond the scope of this book.[25] On the morning of 9 October Souchon held a meeting of senior staff officers and the flotilla chiefs to discuss possible actions against Russia. The younger German officers in the flotilla were anxious to attack the Anglo-French ships off the Dardanelles near Tenedos, and thought that they had a good chance of success in a night attack with the three small (120-ton) Italian-built torpedo-boats. The proposal was apparently killed by Korvettenkapitän Busse, Souchon's Chief Admiralty Staff Officer (commonly known as Asto) who remarked that the boats were actually a danger to their own ships. The flotilla officers resented this, and felt Busse was unfairly applying German standards to their training.[26]

A few days later Souchon chose Odessa as the most promising objective for some of the Turkish torpedo-boats. Enver agreed to Souchon initiating hostilities with the fleet and on 22 October gave him sealed orders to win command of the Black Sea and attack the Russian fleet wherever it was found. Souchon deviated from the plan by deciding to attack the Russian coast in advance of any encounter at sea, which was rather an embarrassment for Enver and his supporters.[27] Souchon intended to use all Turkish warships fit for sea, but decided to leave the slow, old battleships *Barbarossa* and *Torgud Reis* behind. The *Goeben*, two torpedo-boats and a minelayer would attack Sebastopol, *Breslau* and a Turkish cruiser would attack the straits at Kertsch and then Novorossisk; *Hamidieh* would attack Feodosia; and two torpedo-boats and minelayers would attack Odessa. The scanty number of torpedo-boats available – only four – is striking. The Ottoman fleet left the Bosphorus on the evening of the 27th, supposedly for exercises, and initially steamed eastwards to deceive the Russian postal steamer stationed off the straits. The Turkish–German attack took place early on the morning of the 29th.[28] Although his flagship did not actually fire the very first shots against the Russians, Souchon has the somewhat dubious distinction of being the officer who initiated hostilities in two separate seas – the Mediterranean and Black Sea. The major result of the Turco-German raid was the sinking of the Russian gunboat *Donec* at Odessa and the old minelayer *Pruth* off Sebastopol. A few Russian warships were damaged and approximately six merchant ships were sunk by gunfire and mines or captured. The bulk of the Russian fleet was unscathed and so, too, were the Turks and the Germans.[29] Souchon realized that his undertaking had been extraordinarily favoured by luck and good weather and that, given the miserable state of Turkish personnel and material, bad weather or more efficient countermeasures by the enemy might have led to very different results. He did not believe that any extensive reforms or improvements could be achieved in the Ottoman fleet during the war, for the rot was too deep.[30] As an attempt to weaken the Russian fleet and tip the naval balance in the Black Sea with a surprise attack Souchon's sortie was a failure. But from the diplomatic point of view it was a brilliant success. Souchon proudly wrote to his wife that 'I have thrown the Turks into the powder-keg and kindled war between Russia and Turkey'.[31]

The Allied reaction was swift. Brushing aside the lame Turkish excuse that it was the Russians who had attacked first, the Russian government promptly declared war, while the British and French took naval action to back up their ultimatum. On 1 November the British destroyers *Wolverine* and *Scorpion* were ordered to cut out a large armed yacht in the Gulf of Smyrna. The yacht, supposedly laying mines, was set afire by her own crew and blew up. On a much larger scale, the Admiralty ordered Carden: 'Without risking the ships a demonstration is to be made by bombardment . . . against the Forts at the entrance to the Dardanelles.' Carden was ordered to retire before the return fire became effective. Early on the morning of 3 November Carden carried out the bombardment with the battle cruisers *Indefatigable* and *Indomitable*, allowing eight rounds per turret. The French battleships *Suffren* and *Vérité* under Rear-Admiral Guépratte joined in the attack. Turkish counter-fire was ineffective and considerable damage was done to the Seddul Bahr fort where a magazine exploded.[32] The formal British declaration of war followed on 5 November. There would subsequently be considerable discussion over this bombardment which many considered to be a serious mistake. As a military operation it was but a pin prick which served only to put the Turks on the alert. This argument is refuted by others, including the recent biographer of Churchill, Martin Gilbert, who points out that the Dardanelles were an obvious point for an attack and that the Germans and Turks had already been working feverishly to make them secure.[33] The German documents would seem to bear out this contention.

The German officers with the Turkish torpedo flotilla were anxious to retaliate with a torpedo attack on the British and French ships off the Dardanelles. The Germans realized, as one of them expressed it pithily, that 'lousy' Turkish personnel and material hampered their prospects of success but thought something might be achieved with the four Schichau boats, and were able to convince the somewhat reluctant Souchon to let them study the project. However, when they met with the commander of the Dardanelles fortifications, Vice-Admiral Merten, and his delegate at the Turkish high command, Korvettenkapitän Wossidlo, they found that the actual situation was different to what they had thought, and that the mining of the Straits made the undertaking impossible.[34] Souchon reported to the Kaiser that his forces could not accomplish anything off the Dardanelles as there was nothing to prevent the Turkish forts from firing on their own ships. Moreover, British torpedo-boats and submarines were so thick off the entrance that an unnoticed exit by one of their own torpedo-boats could not succeed, while British battleships and cruisers nearly always kept far from the coast.[35]

Contrary to Souchon's expectations, the Russian Black Sea Fleet under the command of Vice-Admiral Eberhardt turned out to be relatively more active than their countrymen in the Baltic. The Russians bombarded

Turkish ports, particularly the important coal port of Zonguldak, which was the outlet for the coal mines of the Heraklea district, and also frequently laid mines. The Ottoman fleet retaliated and *Goeben* and *Breslau* ran into the Russian fleet on 17 November approximately twenty miles off the Crimean coast. The Russians were returning to coal and numbered five pre-dreadnoughts, two cruisers and three squadrons of destroyers and torpedo-boats. Souchon, who had left the Turkish ships behind as unready or unsuitable, was outnumbered and received a nasty surprise when the Russians on their very first salve hit the *Goeben* in the starboard 15-cm casement killing twelve. It was their only hit, although Souchon told the Kaiser they shot well – he told his wife they shot badly. *Goeben*, in turn, concentrated her fire on the leading Russian ship, the flagship *Evstafi*, and damaged her with four hits. The encounter in misty weather lasted only ten to fourteen minutes and *Goeben*'s speed was decisive,[36] Souchon had kept the lightly protected *Breslau* out of effective range and *Goeben* was really on her own against superior strength. He confided to his wife that had the two old Turkish battleships been with him their fate would have been sealed. They were 24 years old, not fast enough to escape, less well protected than the Russians, and did not have all their artillery. The Russian navy was clearly superior to the Turks in the Black Sea and he could do nothing against their fleet and must limit himself to destroying Russian property.[37]

The Germans at sea had virtually all of their eggs in one basket – the *Goeben*. The precariousness of this situation was demonstrated on 26 December when *Goeben* ran into two mines off the Bosphorus. Because of the lack of proper docking facilities in the Ottoman Empire, the Germans realized that she would be out of action for around four months.[38] Time was not on the side of the Turks and Germans in the Black Sea for they also realized that the first of the Russian dreadnoughts was moving steadily towards completion.

The Germans at the beginning of the war had been extremely worried that the Allies would attempt to force the Dardanelles before their experts could strengthen the defences. The British and French, however, had far too many other concerns to consider this seriously and the means were not at hand. The British initially considered using the Greek army to seize the Gallipoli Peninsula, and at the beginning of September staff officers from the Admiralty and War Office had examined the problem while Churchill ordered Admiral Mark Kerr, head of the British Naval Mission in Greece, to approach the Greek government. The scheme finally foundered on Greek mistrust of Bulgaria. It was little more than a year after the Second Balkan War when the Bulgarians and Greeks had fought each other and the Greeks refused to move unless the Bulgarians simultaneously attacked the Turks with all their forces. Churchill, however, still considered the Dardanelles as the point where decisive pressure might be exerted on Turkey and an attack on the Gallipoli Peninsula as the ideal means of defending Egypt. He argued this point at a meeting of the War Council on 25 November.[39]

The origins of the Dardanelles campaign have been the object of intense scrutiny which began even before the war had ended with the Dardanelles Commission. The literature is therefore vast and a detailed account is beyond the scope of this book. The campaign was initiated due to the drive and persuasive powers of the First Lord of the Admiralty in a situation where some leaders sought a way to exert maritime pressure and avoid the bloody indecisiveness of the struggle on the western front. These men, later termed 'easterners', were opposed by those who considered the western front in France to be the decisive point of the war, and were unwilling to squander troops, of which they felt they had none to spare, on secondary theatres. The 'westerners' or 'continentalists' included Joffre, whose forces still far outnumbered the British on the western front. We have already seen Joffre's opposition to plans for an expedition to Salonika or Cattaro. The situation at the beginning of the year 1915 also contained elements of a crisis, notably the desperate struggle of the Serbs against the Austrians along the Danube and the apparent inability of the British and French to assist them. An attack on the Dardanelles might also have a beneficial effect on the uncertain attitude of the neutral Balkan states, Romania and Bulgaria. The Russian armies on the eastern front had also suffered enormous losses in the early months of the war, partially offset, perhaps, by the considerable losses the Russians had inflicted on Germany's ally Austria-Hungary. Early in January Grand Duke Nicholas, C.-in-C. of the Russian armies, had appealed for a diversion to offset the pressure of a Turkish offensive in the Caucasus mountains. Offensive action by the British and French would also be a means to forestall an expected Turkish attack on the Suez Canal. Churchill managed to secure agreement by the War Council for a naval attack on the Dardanelles, although it is apparent that the agreement of the British naval and military experts was far more qualified than he realized at the time and rested on the assumption that a naval attack, once begun, could easily be broken off if the prospects for success proved unappealing. The support of Admiral Sir John Fisher, First Sea Lord and Churchill's senior naval adviser, was certainly not wholehearted and the seeds of the discord which would eventually lead to Fisher's resignation were present from the very beginning.

Whatever the strategic merits of the Dardanelles campaign, it rested on certain, false tactical assumptions. This was particularly true in regard to overestimating the effects of flat trajectory naval gunfire against targets on land, and underestimating the difficulties of spotting and fire control as well as the inherent disadvantages more vulnerable ships suffered when engaging shore batteries. Turkish powers of resistance were also underestimated, although this might in part have been due to the easy successes enjoyed by Captain Frank Larken and the cruiser *Doris* in their operations off the Syrian coast in December 1914. There is also at least some doubt if even a successful naval attack destroying the Turkish forts at the Dardanelles would really have led to a Turkish surrender once an Allied fleet appeared off Constantinople.[40] Admiral Carden, who would have to carry out the operation, did not believe that the Straits could be rushed, but did think they might be forced after extended operations because of the superiority of his fleet's gunpower compared to that of the forts. A few days later he submitted a more detailed plan for successive phases of an attack in which first the entrance forts, then the inner forts, and finally the narrows defences would be reduced and the minefields cleared. The War Council concluded provisionally on 13 January that the Admiralty should prepare for a naval expedition in February to bombard and take the Gallipoli Peninsula with Constantinople as its objective. During the discussions Sir Edward Grey, the Foreign Secretary, had also suggested an attack on Cattaro, as he was anxious to do something to force Italy's hand, while David Lloyd George, Chancellor of the Exchequer, was in favour of a major attack on Austria, possibly via Salonika. Churchill turned aside the Adriatic suggestions by pointing out that the French fleet was already there in force.[41]

The French almost inevitably had to be consulted about the Dardanelles venture since the convention of 6 August had given them, at least in theory, command in the Mediterranean. On 26 December the Admiralty suggested in a memorandum given to the French naval attaché in London that the French give up naval operations in the Adriatic in favour of operations against Turkey, merely blockading the Straits of Otranto tightly enough to ensure that Austrian ships would not interfere in the Mediterranean. The French Naval Staff replied in a memorandum dated 28 December. They agreed with the British contention that mines and submarines made it too dangerous for large warships to operate in the Adriatic, unless the Austrian fleet gave them an opportunity by coming out of its bases. Military operations against these bases would require forces which could not be detached from the principal theatre of the war. The major role of the French fleet was therefore to totally blockade the Straits of Otranto so as to prevent any Austrian attempt to sortie. Because of the distance of Malta, their principal base, from the entrance to the Adriatic, and the necessities of being constantly at sea and rotating ships for refits, Lapeyrère believed that he must have a superiority over the Austrians by at least one-third. This would require the 1ère and 2ème Escadres (sixteen battleships) and five of the six destroyer *escadrilles*. The patrols which were necessary to prevent supplies for Germany and Austria passing through neutral Italian harbours required a minimum of nine cruisers or auxiliary cruisers. Under these circumstances, the only ships that could be detached from the Armée navale for operations against the Turks would be six old battleships and a few cruisers. Until the *Goeben* was sunk the French thought that the Dardanelles forces should include 1 battle cruiser, 4 battleships, 1 fast light cruiser (Dublin class), 12 destroyers, 6 submarines and 1 Blenheim-type depot ship. Augagneur believed that the naval forces destined to operate off the Dardanelles and on the coast of Asia Minor and Syria as far south as Jaffa should be under the orders of a French vice-admiral, assisted, if the Admiralty desired, by a British rear-admiral. Anglo-French forces in the Red Sea and on the coast of Egypt would be placed under the orders of a British vice-admiral, assisted if the Admiralty desired by a French rear-admiral. The French vice-admiral commanding the forces off Asia Minor and Syria would be under the authority of Lapeyrère. The British vice-admiral in Egypt would be independent. French control of operations off the Dardanelles was not at all what Churchill had in mind by this time and on 30 December he minuted that they could not give up the command and the matter was allowed to drop.[42]

Augagneur was alarmed by the operations of the British naval C.-in-C. in Egypt off Syria since the latter was a traditional focal point for French ambitions. He became increasingly impatient and annoyed when no reply was received from the British and asked the Foreign Minister to intervene to insure that the Allied forces destined to operate off the Dardanelles were placed under a French admiral. To signify his disapproval, he also rejected a British request for trawlers, aircraft and one or two light cruisers for the eastern Mediterranean, declaring that he could give nothing without knowing in advance the purpose for which they were intended.[43] The formal British reply to the French note of December finally came a few weeks later. Churchill sketched the plan for the Dardanelles expedition, stressed its importance, and argued that since Admiral Carden had so carefully studied the project and was well acquainted with the area and dispositions of the enemy the Admiralty did not believe a change of command in the Aegean would be opportune. After the operation was concluded and the German–Turkish fleet destroyed, nothing would prevent command in that part of the Mediterranean being exercised by a French admiral. They hoped that the French would participate in the operation with their forces currently off the Dardanelles under the French rear-admiral.[44] Churchill also mentioned the War Office's intention of occupying Alexandretta to cut the strategic Turkish railway lines which ran nearby.

On 8 January, Capitaine de vaisseau Le Gouz de Saint-Seine, French naval attaché, forwarded a study by the Admiralty War Staff on the subject of operations in the Gulf of Smyrna. The paper included a remark that to prevent reinforcements from Asia Minor reaching Egypt or the Persian Gulf the occupation of Adana or Alexandretta would be much more effective than that of Smyrna, and the occupation of Beirut or Jaffa also merited attention if troops or ships were available. This study might almost have been guaranteed to trigger a strong response from the French. The Dardanelles were one matter, but Syria and the Lebanon were quite another for the French had traditional and strong interests in this area. Saint-Seine had immediately pointed this out to the Admiralty, noting that French interests in Smyrna were at least equivalent to British interests, that they were certainly more important in Syria and especially at Beirut, and that no operation in Asia Minor should be undertaken without agreement between the two governments as to its scope. The Chief of Naval Staff quickly assured Saint-Seine that the British would undertake nothing without French agreement.[45]

Both Paul Cambon, French ambassador in London, and Saint-Seine were satisfied with Churchill's reply of 18 January which calmed the apprehensions aroused by the actions of a few British cruisers in the Levant, and Saint-Seine in a private letter to the Chief of the EMG said he was convinced that the British government was speaking in good faith when it declared military conquests, such as Alexandretta, made during the war were only provisional and subject to revision at the end of hostilities. Cambon warned, however, that only the ministers of marine, war and foreign affairs should know of the impending Dardanelles operations.[46] Saint-Seine was perhaps overly sanguine about British assurances, for the old adage about possession being nine-tenths of the law could easily hold true in the case of wartime conquests. Cambon thought that in view of potential misunderstandings it was essential that either Saint-Seine should go to Paris with full explanations or, preferably, that Augagneur should come to London. Augagneur elected to go to London and the Foreign Minister, Delcassé, in announcing the trip reiterated France's interest in Alexandretta and Syria, and that any action in this area should take place only after prior agreement with the French.[47]

Contrary to Cambon's warnings about secrecy, Augagneur was careful to get the French Cabinet's approval for his meeting with Churchill which took place on 26 January. This meeting later became highly controversial in French political and naval circles since the Minister of Marine agreed to French participation in the Dardanelles expedition.[48] Vice-Admiral Bienaimé, that impassioned critic of French naval policy, later criticized Augagneur for not taking Vice-Admiral Aubert, Chief of the EMG, with him to furnish a technical critique of British plans, and implies rather darkly that the minister had destroyed a critical memorandum on British naval plans subsequently written by Aubert.[49] There is also the suggestion that Augagneur, lacking both experience in naval affairs and technical advisers, was dazzled by Churchill and succumbed to pressure. This is rather unfair to Augagneur who by then had been in office for almost six months of war and from all accounts was a strong-minded individual who knew exactly what he wanted. Moreover, Augagneur did have Capitaine de vaisseau Henri Salaun, his Chef de Cabinet, with him. Salaun was an extremely capable officer who would soon rise to flag rank and later head the Directorate of Anti-Submarine Operations. The details of the talks are not known, but even Churchill would have lost a large amount of his famous oratorical power if he had had to speak in French or work through an interpreter.

The day after the meeting Churchill sent, after consultation with Grey and Kitchener, a letter summing up their agreement. Owing to renewed Turkish pressure in Egypt the capture of Alexandretta was not contemplated in the immediate future, and if it became necessary at a later date the British agreed to consult with the French beforehand on the political as well as military aspects of the expedition, and had no objection in principle to a joint enterprise both by land and sea. The British wished to retain the command at the Dardanelles and did not ask for any assistance except in regard to certain small craft suitable for minesweeping, but would welcome cordially the co-operation of the French squadron now at the Dardanelles in the general work of the bombardment. The British also agreed to a French vice-admiral being appointed to command on the Syrian coast and any British ships employed in the Levant would come under his command while naval operations in Egypt would remain in British hands. Churchill concluded by saying that they were relying on the French navy, especially during the Dardanelles operations, 'to maintain its effective control of the Austrian fleet and we are vy much impressed with the great advantages to the general political situation in the S.E. of Europe wh wd undoubtedly follow if a more pronounced offensive was found possible in the Adriatic'.[50]

Augagneur replied on the 31st that after consultation with the Premier, René Viviani, and Foreign Minister Delcassé, he adhered entirely to the propositions contained in Churchill's letter. Operations at Alexandretta or any point along the coast of Asia Minor would take place only after an agreement between the two governments. The French agreed to British command at the Dardanelles and would co-operate with the forces currently under the French rear-admiral there, notably four battleships, destroyers, submarines, minesweepers and the seaplane carrier *Foudre*. Augagneur was careful to note, however, that the Dardanelles operations were a special enterprise and distinct from those of the remainder of the Mediterranean which depended on Lapeyrère, the Allied C.-in-C. Regarding the Austrian fleet, Augagneur assured Churchill that they would not let any ship exit from the Adriatic and as soon as the possibility presented itself would take the most energetic offensive against that enemy fleet, convinced of the importance of that offensive on the general policy.[51]

Augagneur claimed that he found Churchill's plan acceptable since it permitted them to break off the attack as if it had been a simple demonstration if success seemed impossible, and thereby avoid the morale consequences of a reverse. Augagneur even claimed later on that the rash attack on the Straits was executed in opposition to the reserves he had formulated in his conversation with Churchill. Perhaps the real motives behind Augagneur's and the French actions were revealed in his testimony to the Commission de la marine de guerre in 1917. 'Not to take part in the operation', he declared,

> would be to see, should it succeed, the British fleet present itself alone before Constantinople. For we French, who have known stakes in the Near East, it would have been a very painful renunciation, perilous for our interests. We therefore decided that we would send 4 old battleships to be part of the game, without, however, engaging ourselves.[52]

Augagneur on this point really does not deserve the reproaches critics such as Vice-Admiral Bienaimé have directed at him. He had reaffirmed and won renewed British recognition of French command in the Mediterranean and special interests on the coast of Syria in return for a relatively minor commitment of old ships, which were expendable and for the most part already on the scene, and he had assured France of a say and position in an expedition which promised to pay big dividends if successful. The question of command off the Dardanelles which Augagneur gave up to the British ultimately came down to a case of *force majeure*. The British were ready to contribute a large force, while the French maintained the bulk of their fleet blockading the Austrians in the Adriatic. This was not a responsibility to be depreciated since the Austrians had the only sizeable modern enemy fleet afloat in the Mediterranean, and Churchill himself acknowledged this when he rejected Grey's suggestion of an attack on Cattaro by pointing out that the French were already there. Had the French really wanted command off the Dardanelles they would have had to transfer the bulk of their fleet there. But they did not have the strength to blockade both the Adriatic and force the Dardanelles. The seizure of Alexandretta would also remain a strictly academic question until either party had the actual intention and force available to take it.

Augagneur after his return to France met with Poincaré, and described the planned expedition as very uncertain. He did not have great illusions as to the success of the enterprise, but did not want to dissuade the British from it since they were taking nearly all the risks.[53] This statement has been interpreted as a clever political act on the part of Augagneur to dissociate himself from the venture and blame it on the British should the attack fail. He has also been criticized for committing himself to the British plans without consulting the experts of the EMG, who would probably have disapproved. His own C.-in-C. in the Mediterranean, Admiral Lapeyrère, apparently first learned of the project through British sources, despite the fact that his subordinate, Rear-Admiral Guépratte, was involved.[54] Vice-Admiral Aubert, Chief of the EMG, was indeed rather dubious. He remarked in a note to the minister on 7 February, 'One thing strikes the reader of the different English memoranda . . . in that expedition in which the English have taken the initiative and will have the direction one sees the beginning very well, but one does not see the ending'. This was largely due to the lack of provision for landing troops to seize places reduced by the fleet, and Churchill appeared to count solely on the effect on morale after the reduction of the forts of Chanak and Kilid Bahr. Aubert asked what would happen in the most favourable circumstances with the Allied fleet arriving off Constantinople and the Turkish government fleeing? What would they do without troops for a landing? Aubert's objections were very similar to those already raised by Admiral Sir Henry Jackson of the Admiralty War Staff in January, although he did admit that from the technical point of view the general method of the British attack appeared to be good.[55]

Augagneur consolidated French claims to command off the Syrian coast in new orders defining the limits of his authority to Vice-Admiral Dartige du Fournet, commanding the 3ᵉᵐᵉ Escadre. At that time the 3ᵉᵐᵉ Escadre consisted of the old battleships *Saint Louis, Jauréguiberry,* the coast defence ship *Henri IV,* and the cruiser *d'Entrecasteaux.* The French were to undertake landing operations only in the case of absolute urgency, such as the necessity to assist their protégés or destroy railways and bridges. Bombardments were to be directed only against troops or war material, and were to be carried out as far as possible by French ships. If it were ever necessary to use British ships, a French ship would always be associated with them. Augagneur specifically ordered that at least one French warship was always to be off Alexandretta so that any British ships there would always be assured of French support. French surveillance was to be exercised mainly in the region from Alexandretta to Beirut, especially at Alexandretta.[56]

The French rear-admiral who had been operating with Carden's British squadron off the Dardanelles since autumn 1914 was one of the most colourful characters in the French navy. Emile-Paul Guépratte, then 58, would become one of the legendary figures of the war, renowned for his courage and audacity. A member of an old naval family, he had served in

Indo-China and in the operations against Siam in 1893, as well as the more traditional commands in the Mediterranean. He began the war commanding the Division de complément escorting convoys between North Africa and France. Ironically, the ships under his command usually consisted of obsolete vessels, old crocks which 'sank like stones' as one British officer described them. Guépratte got on well with his British allies, something that was not always true in inter-Allied relations. Guépratte did more than merely get on with the British, however, he won the genuine respect and admiration of a wide variety of British officers and was, perhaps, the Royal Navy's favourite French admiral. Commodore Keyes, Chief of Staff during the Dardanelles expedition, described him as a 'gallant old knight who only lives for honour and glory', while Admiral John M. de Robeck referred to him as 'dear old soul, he is the most loyal friend one could have'.[57] Others compared him to the Chevalier Bayard, *sans peur et sans reproche*. He had his detractors, of course, and some considered him pompous and his statements vainglorious and later in the war, in the post of préfet maritime at Bizerte which involved administrative duties, he was termed hopeless.[58] The experiences of the campaign deepened the esteem in which he was held by the British even though by May he was no longer the senior French admiral on the scene. When he left the Dardanelles in October he was given a grand sendoff by the British squadron with crews manning ship and bands playing 'La Marseillaise'. The sincerity of the farewell went far beyond the bounds of perfunctory naval courtesy and some French politicians as well as Admiral Lacaze, then Minister of Marine, were not insensitive to these tributes.[59] Guépratte also appreciated the British attempts to dilute his bitterness with courtesies when he was relieved from command and he was, in turn, fiercely loyal to de Robeck and his reputation. Long after the war he indignantly took up his pen to reply to an article by Churchill implying that de Robeck had phrased his proposal for a renewal of the naval attack in May 1915 in terms that invited a refusal. He learned from Keyes, however, that the charge was true.[60]

A fire-eater like Guépratte was apparently not to the taste of everyone in the French navy either, and he evidently had enemies. Shortly after naval operations began at the Dardanelles in February, Augagneur cabled Lapeyrère that he had received disturbing information that Guépratte's demeanour and attitude aroused fears for his mental equilibrium and was likely to create a poor impression on the British. The minister asked if Guépratte appeared to be in a suitable state to continue his command and, if not, who would Lapeyrère suggest? Lapeyrère replied with the obvious, namely that Guépratte's relations with the British were excellent, and after suitable investigations the C.-in-C. reported that his health was also excellent and that he had given the officers and men of his division a remarkable élan which reflected honourably on the French navy, and in every respect there was no one more worthy of command.[61] Augagneur shifted his ground with the customary skill of a politician and cabled that his query had only been to confirm from the C.-in-C. his own good opinion of Guépratte, and that he was glad to know the campaign of denigration whose echoes had reached him was unjustified.[62] The minister had not, however, lost all his doubts concerning Guépratte and, as we shall see in the following chapter, he would act on them later during the campaign.

On 28 January the War Council approved the Admiralty undertaking a naval attack on the Dardanelles. Churchill had, at best, the lukewarm support of his naval experts who, as Professor Marder has put it, 'went along thinking that a naval operation could not lead to disaster because it could be broken off at any time' while 'he had dazzled – hypnotized almost – the politicians with his picture of the great political and military results which would follow a successful naval attempt to force the Dardanelles'.[63] The British force would consist of: the new super-dreadnought *Queen Elizabeth*, sent on account of her long-range 15-in. guns; the battle cruiser *Inflexible*; 10 pre-dreadnought battleships;[64] 4 cruisers; 2 destroyer depot ships; the seaplane carrier *Ark Royal*; 16 destroyers (8 Beagle and 8 River class); 21 minesweeping trawlers and 6 submarines. After the Turkish defences at the entrance had been put out of action, the Naval Staff expected the operations would develop into a slow, methodical progress of perhaps a mile a day, silencing the fire of concealed guns and keeping down fire from trenches or machine guns 'which will inconvenience the minesweepers'. The Admiralty emphasized the cautious approach: 'It is not expected or desired that the operations should be hurried to the extent of taking large risks and courting heavy losses. The slow relentless creeping forward of the attacking force mile by mile will tend to shake the morale of the garrisons of the forts at Kephez Point, Chanak and Kilid Bahr, and will have an effect on Constantinople.' Two battalions of Royal Marines would be sent out for temporary landing operations along with a squadron of merchant vessels with dummy upper-works altered to resemble 'dreadnoughts' and 'cruisers' to deceive the enemy. The Admiralty did not believe that any submarines had yet been assembled at Constantinople, but when operations began they expected Germany would try to either send submarines to the Mediterranean or induce the Austrians to send their own out of the Adriatic. They therefore intended to send submarine indicator nets as a preventative measure. Churchill endorsed the plan on 5 February as 'excellent'.[65] A few days later Fisher suggested adding the semi-dreadnoughts *Lord Nelson* and *Agamemnon* to Carden's forces. The two were sent and would, in fact, remain in the eastern Aegean until the end of the war.

While the naval forces gathered in the eastern Mediterranean, considerable doubt remained as to whether the naval attack alone would force the Straits. The influential Colonel Hankey, Secretary to the War Council, wrote to Balfour on 10 February: 'From Lord Fisher downwards, every naval officer in the Admiralty who is in the secret believes that the Navy cannot take the Dardanelles position without troops. The First Lord still professes to believe that they can do it with ships, but I have warned the Prime Minister that we cannot trust to this.'[66] Hankey's and other objections, including those from Admiral Jackson and Captain Herbert Richmond, Assistant Director of Operations, had their effect and on 16 February a partial War Council agreed to send the regular 29th Division, which had just been offered to the Greek government and rejected, to Lemnos – a Greek island forty to fifty miles off the Dardanelles. The 29th Division would be joined by Australian and New Zealand troops from Egypt. The move of the 29th Division was, however, blocked at a full meeting of the War Council on the 19th by Lord Kitchener, who argued that the Australian and New Zealand troops from Egypt, which had just been redeemed from the threat of Turkish invasion, would suffice. The War Council did not reach any firm decision.[67]

As soon as they learned that the British intended to send a division to the Dardanelles the French Cabinet resolved on 18 February to send a division of their own. The decision was taken quickly before Joffre was consulted, and for the same reason as Augagneur had engaged the navy – a fundamental disinclination to see the British establish themselves alone in the Levant. Preparations for the transport of the French force – grandly designated the Corps expéditionnaire d'orient and scraped together from depots throughout France – began on the 22nd. Delcassé suggested that naval operations should be postponed until the arrival of the troops. Churchill, however, had not been anxious for French military assistance and replied, with Kitchener's approval, 'The naval operations having begun cannot be interrupted but must proceed continuously to their conclusion, every day adding to the danger of the arrival of German or Austrian submarines & any lull in the attack prejudicing the moral effect on the Turkish capital'.[68]

Admiral Carden began the bombardment of the Turkish forts at the entrance to the Dardanelles on 19 February. Bad weather delayed further operations until the 25th and by 1 March the Allies considered the forts at the entrance sufficiently dominated so that the next phase of the operations, the destruction of the intermediate defences and the clearing of the minefields below Kephez Point, could begin. The outer Turkish defences were outranged by the guns of the fleet and had been relatively easy to silence. The real problem came when the ships began to operate in the more restricted waters of the Straits against the intermediate defences, where minefields kept the battleships at a distance, and mobile Turkish batteries including howitzers kept the battleships on the move reducing the accuracy of their fire against the forts and hampering sweeping. Admiral Jackson commented that Carden's report for this period clearly brought out the difficulty of spotting at long range, the necessity for ships to be anchored for accurate and deliberate long-range fire and the difficulty of doing this when within range of concealed guns and howitzers.[69] High-flying aircraft were necessary for reconnaissance work, but despite some useful work by the seaplanes with the fleet they 'were not equal to what was required of them'. Commodore Keyes had also noted of the seaplanes, 'They are gallant fellows, but they are not much use as their machines can only get up in a flat calm and take ages to get to a safe height, if they can get there at all'.[70] Carden reported that it was impossible to locate and silence concealed guns and howitzers solely by ship's fire. Sweeping with the slow trawlers manned by volunteer fishermen rather than regular naval personnel was also much more difficult than anticipated. Jackson, writing after the setback of 18 March, concluded on a sober note:

The comparative ease with which the outer forts were silenced and demolished solely by naval forces has, I think, led one to imagine the inner forts would succumb to the same forces with but little more difficulty. Were mines the only additional danger to be encountered this might be the case, but the military mobile artillery, concealed guns and howitzers, and the strengthening of Nos. 7 and 8 Forts, which, though not unexpected, were all unknown quantities, have now assumed such large proportions as to very seriously impede all operations in the Straits and have led several to remark in their reports that military assistance will be essential for the success of the further phases of the operation.[71]

As the British and French squadrons off the Dardanelles continued pounding away Keyes wrote to his wife: 'We are going to get through – but it is a much bigger thing than the Admiralty or anyone out here realized, and I am insisting as much as I can on the absolute necessity of telling the Admiralty by wire the exact position and what it all means.'[72] The arrangements for the troops slowly assembling at Mudros on the Island of Lemnos also caused concern. Rear-Admiral Rosslyn Wemyss, Senior Naval Officer at Mudros, complained: 'The General has been up here from Alexandria and he seems as much in the dark as everybody else – doesn't know where he is to disembark his army, or what the objective is when they are disembarked.' Wemyss added, 'The fact of the matter is that I am afraid they are trying to rush matters at home without giving the people who are to carry the job sufficient time or opportunity to organise the matter properly.'[73] Rear-Admiral Hugh Miller, who had been Wemyss's assistant on Mudros, recalled, 'In those early days the whole campaign seemed to me to have been very sketchily thought out' and 'the naval command was most unfortunate in its appreciation of the situation and . . . the strength of the Dardanelles defences was underestimated long after their strength was being made obvious to the most inexperienced layman'.[74] Kitchener did not finally agree to send the regular 29th Division out to the Dardanelles until 10 March, and there was no possibility of its being available for the impending naval attack. Moreover, the loading of the stores and equipment of the troops destined for Mudros was chaotic and the facilities on Lemnos were inadequate for rectifying the mistakes. General Sir Ian Hamilton, who received command of the Mediterranean Expeditionary Force, had to send some transports back to Alexandria and reroute others in a situation which can only be described as a logistic mess which required nearly a month to straighten out.[75]

The possibility of using Greek troops had frequently been discussed by the Allies. The Russians, however, had their own designs on Constantinople, subsequently recognized by their Allies, and had no desire to see a Greek army establish itself there. They therefore firmly and finally vetoed Greek participation. At almost the same moment Venizelos, the pro-Allied Prime Minister of Greece, was forced to resign, while King Constantine of Greece was determined to remain neutral. Constantine was married to the sister of Kaiser Wilhelm and was generally considered to be pro-German.[76] Direct or indirect Russian assistance for the Allies off the Dardanelles was also highly problematical. On 19 January, Churchill had written to Grand Duke Nicholas asking that the Russians co-operate at the proper moment by naval action at the mouth of the Bosphorus and by having troops ready to seize any advantage. The Russian reply was not encouraging. The Russians claimed that they did not have the means of directly assisting in carrying out a plan of action against Turkey. Russian dreadnoughts were not finished, there were no submarines of a modern type, and only an insufficient number of swift destroyers. The Russians thought that their Black Sea Fleet was 'not more than the equal of the Turkish Fleet and that only when all the ships were together'. Their ships carried only four days' coal and coaling at sea was impossible in bad weather, while their nearest base was over twenty-four hours from the entrance to the Bosphorus whose defensive batteries compared with the guns of the Russian ships 'were such as to give little hope of a successful attack by the latter'. Matters would improve once the dreadnought *Imperatriza Maria* was finished, but this reinforcement as well as more modern submarines and destroyers would not be available before May. The Russians were also unable to withdraw from the principal theatre of war the minimum two army corps considered necessary for any operation, although they fully supported the Allied plans for an attack on the Dardanelles.[77] The Russians, to put it bluntly, would cheer the British and French on but were not likely to do anything to help them.

Russian naval action since the beginning of hostilities seemed to be concentrated in the eastern half of the Black Sea where co-operation with the right wing of the Russian army undoubtedly had a high priority. However, Vice-Admiral Eberhard, C.-in-C. of the Black Sea Fleet, had already undertaken a potentially important operation at the end of December aimed at bottling up the coal port of Zonguldak with four blockships, and co-ordinated with the laying of a line of mines off the Bosphorus. The attempt to block Zonguldak failed, partially through bad weather, partially through faulty organization, but the line of mines laid off the Bosphorus eventually damaged the *Goeben*, a notable success. On 7 March the Russian squadron shelled the coaling facilities at Eregli and Zonguldak, sinking seven steamers and a sailing vessel, while from 5–8 March the new Russian submarine *Nerpa* operated off the Bosphorus for the first time.[78] On 28 February, after Carden's operations had begun, Grand Duke Nicholas did promise the Allies that the Black Sea Fleet would attack Constantinople and an army of 47,000 men would be employed, but only after the Allied fleets had entered the Marmara and appeared off the Princess Islands. The Russians considered the forcing of the Bosphorus without the assistance of the Allied fleets from the other side 'to be impossible', and Russian operations while the Allies were still off the Dardanelles would be limited to purely naval demonstrations. The Russian High Command subsequently designated the V Caucasian Corps (37,000 men) for the landing with the troops to be embarked at Batum.[79] Any serious Russian action therefore involved a big if – that the Allies would succeed at the Dardanelles. The Russian navy, however important and successful its struggle for command of the Black Sea, would have, at best, only indirect effects on the Mediterranean.

The Dardanelles were not the only Allied concern in the Mediterranean. The Suez Canal was an obvious objective for the Turkish army once Turkey entered the war and its capture would have had enormous consequences for the Allies. The long-anticipated Turkish offensive came at the end of January. The defence of the canal was largely in the hands of Indian troops assisted by a handful of British and French warships under Vice-Admiral Peirse. Fortunately for the Allies the Turkish attack, made with inadequate forces and preparation, was never close to success. After a few days' fighting in early February the Turkish forces were in full retreat and by the 11th the canal had been reopened for night traffic.[80]

There were various British plans for naval operations against the seaward flank of the Turkish army but these ran into obstacles that were as much political as military. The French ambassador in London objected to one Admiralty proposal to land 5,000 men at Jaffa to seize leading Turkish authorities and German representatives as hostages on the obvious grounds that, in addition to being of little military value, it would expose the numerous French nationals and protégés in Syria to reprisals.[81] Captain Richmond was another frequent advocate of harrying the Syrian coast to keep Turkish garrisons employed and favoured a landing in Syria together with the attack on the Dardanelles. He wrote to Hankey after the Turks had retreated from the canal and 'implored him to try & get someone to seize the psychological moment & sling the Egyptian troops into Alexandretta as well as feints and raids at other ports from Aleppo to Acre'. Richmond complained, 'It is damnable to see everyone sitting doing nothing'.[82] Fisher also favoured the capture of Alexandretta because of its value as an outlet for the Mesopotamian oil fields.[83]

The potentially strongest advocate for Alexandretta was Lord Kitchener who said in the War Council of 13 January that its capture should be kept in mind, but admitted that the troops in Egypt were not yet sufficiently trained to carry it out.[84] Churchill wanted an operation against Alexandretta to be so timed as to be practically simultaneous with an attack on the Dardanelles. If they were checked at the Dardanelles, they could claim it was a mere demonstration to cover the seizure of Alexandretta.[85] After the Turkish defeat before the Suez Canal, and with Carden actually bombarding the forts at the Dardanelles, Kitchener was even more emphatic at a War Council on 10 March. Lloyd George had expressed his misgivings over Alexandretta, saying he would prefer Palestine. Kitchener answered that Palestine was of no value while Alexandretta was an important communications centre, connected by a branch line to the Baghdad railway which was within easy striking distance, and was also a useful outlet for oil supplies from Mesopotamia. According to Kitchener, its location was also advantageous because it was beyond the French sphere of influence in Syria. Kitchener argued that its acquisition would compensate for recognizing Russia's control over Constantinople, and that they should not count on holding Egypt if Alexandretta was in the hands of some other power. If they did not take Alexandretta, it would be better not to take Mesopotamia.[86] The Admiralty also prepared a paper supporting the capture of Alexandretta largely because of the access it provided to Mesopotamian oil.[87]

Smyrna, the largest Turkish port on the Mediterranean, was another potential objective. The British planned naval rather than military action. They had received persistent reports that German or Austrian submarines were on their way to the eastern Mediterranean, and Smyrna was an obvious potential base since it was located within easy striking distance of the Dardanelles and the lines of communication in the Mediterranean. Two battleships, the *Triumph* and *Swiftsure*, were detached from the Dardanelles force to operate off the Gulf of Smyrna and on 2 March, Vice-Admiral Peirse, C.-in-C. of the Egypt and East Indies station, was ordered to proceed to Smyrna with the cruiser *Euryalus*, accompanied by minesweepers and a seaplane carrier, joined later by the Russian cruiser *Askold*. His orders were to destroy the forts protecting the harbour to facilitate a blockade and leave the port itself open to attack. Peirse began his attack on 5 March but the naval operations were accompanied by a curious attempt to negotiate with the Vali of Smyrna, alleged to be pro-Allied, to in effect neutralize the port and surrounding vilayet by surrendering to the British his small craft and permitting them to sweep a path through the Turkish minefields. This plan presupposed the destruction of the Turkish forts, whose military commanders might be assumed to have had other ideas. The naval operations paralleled those at the Dardanelles but on a much smaller scale. The ships could not close to decisively finish off the forts until the minefields were swept and the concealed mobile guns prevented the sweeping.[88] A young lieutenant wrote in his war diary, 'The press telegrams have got our little stunt in at last & talk glibly about "progress being made", batteries silenced & minefields cleared. Little do they know what a minute amount we have accomplished.'[89]

The negotiations with the Vali opened on a promising note but ultimately came to nothing, and on 15 March Peirse was ordered to return *Triumph* and *Swiftsure* for the impending attack at the Dardanelles. In the course of the operations a small German-commanded, Turkish torpedo-boat, *Demir Hissar*, which had sneaked out of the Dardanelles, managed to disable the seaplane carrier *Anne Rickmers*. The Turks as a defensive measure sank five steamers in the channels, blocking the port and making it unusable as a submarine base. The British objective was, rather ironically, at least partially achieved by the Turks themselves and Peirse was ordered back to Egypt on 15 March. Jackson later remarked on the detailed reports of the operations that, 'The results hardly seem commensurate with the losses & expenditure of ammunition'.[90]

Vice-Admiral Peirse's operations against Smyrna once again aroused French suspicions, although the port was far from the Syrian coast. This did not stop Augagneur from objecting that they were against the convention giving command of the Syrian coast to a French admiral, were unnecessary since the arrival of submarines was improbable and, even if they were necessary, should be executed by the French admiral. Peirse, according to the convention, commanded in Egypt and not in the Mediterranean.[91] Paul Cambon, the French ambassador in London, immediately wrote privately to Delcassé in an attempt to smooth over the matter. He pointed out that Smyrna was not on the coast of Syria and was in the Dardanelles sphere of operations, while the area of command recognized for the French admiral stretched from the Egyptian frontier to Mersina. He added that the Admiralty had intelligence that Austrian submarines, probably from Cattaro, had been seen off Saseno Island, Albania, and that six Austro-German submarines accompanied by several torpedo-boats had left Pola for the Dardanelles to attack transports and the bombarding squadrons. Cambon hoped that Delcassé could 'rectify certain errors of appreciation'. Despite Cambon's efforts to enhance Augagneur's geographical knowledge, the French Foreign Office, probably reflecting the very deep and real suspicions of British designs in the Levant, ordered him to deliver a protest similar to that of Augagneur.[92]

While Carden's fleet continued to hammer away at the Dardanelles defences, there was another British attempt at secret negotiations with the Turks which was even more bizarre than the effort to 'bluff' the Vali of Smyrna out of the war. Rear-Admiral William R. Hall – the legendary 'Blinker' Hall – now Director of Naval Intelligence, initiated secret negotiations with a member of the Turkish government at Dedeagatch, which was then Bulgaria's port on the Aegean. The plan was for Turkey to withdraw from the war, open the Dardanelles and surrender the *Goeben* in exchange for a large sum of money – £4 million was the sum mentioned. The British negotiators were Griffin Eady, a civil engineer, and Edwin Whittall, a businessman, who had both resided in Turkey for a long time. Fisher was taken aback when he learned that Hall had pledged £4 million on his own initiative without informing his superiors, the Foreign Office, or the Cabinet. Fisher, acting on intelligence that the Turks were short of ammunition, ordered the negotiations to be broken off. The British emissaries left Dedeagatch on 17 March, just a day before the ill-fated naval attack. The agreement was probably doomed to failure since Constantinople had already been promised to the Russians and it is questionable that the Turkish negotiators really had the power to deliver the goods, that is circumvent Enver Pasha or his German advisers and take Turkey out of the war. The affair remains mysterious and much of the detail will probably never be known. Not surprisingly the leading authorities give versions which differ in detail.[93]

As the British and French forces prepared for their climactic assault on the Dardanelles troubled only slightly, if at all, by the naval activities of their enemies, it would be well to stop and examine what the Austrian and German naval forces in the Mediterranean had been doing since the beginning of the year. The Turks and Germans had a warning that the defences of the Dardanelles were not completely secure on 13 December when Lieutenant Norman Holbrook brought the old submarine B11, especially fitted with mineguards, through the tricky currents of the Dardanelles and under five lines of mines to torpedo and sink the ancient Turkish battleship *Messudiyeh* which was being used as a guard ship. The *Messudiyeh* was very old, lacking her primary armament, and went down in shoal water so that much of her secondary armament was salved. Nevertheless, the feat was a notable one and Holbrook was awarded the Victoria Cross.[94] Souchon thought that the gap in the minefield had been disclosed to the British by spies, but noted that Usedom was working to close it so as to prevent similar exploits. He later believed that the fault had been Usedom's for anchoring the ship too far outside the inner defences where it was protected by only two lines of Turkish mines laid before the arrival of the Germans. Usedom put down additional mines, but Souchon deplored the poor state of Turkish security and the fact that it was not always possible to keep spectators away. He assumed that the British and French were well informed of their defensive measures.[95] By 6 January, Souchon was satisfied that the various passages had been blocked with mines and there were enough soldiers and guns on both shores of the Straits to force any attacker to undertake a considerable effort, with corresponding losses. Once in the Marmara, the attacker could not really accomplish anything without the assistance of strong landing detachments. At the most, his ships could fire off their munitions against the Turkish fleet or the mass of houses in Constantinople, risking further losses to himself, and achieving nothing except damage caused by fires. If the Turkish fleet did not oblige by giving battle and retired into the Bosphorus, the Allied fleet would have to withdraw back through the Dardanelles when they ran short of coal.[96] Souchon's opinions were remarkably similar to those of Admiral Jackson.

The major weakness of the Turkish position really lay in their stock of munitions. There were sufficient munitions to stop one Allied attempt, but should the Allies try a number of times and accept their losses they would probably break through, for mines alone could not stop the ships. In late 1914 the neutral Romanians had stopped permitting arms and munitions for Turkey to pass through their territory, and as long as the alternate route through Serbia was still not open the Turks and Germans were forced to be very economical.[97] The Germans had been pressing their Austrian allies on this question, but the latter had not been able to clear the Serbs from Belgrade or open the Danube. Nevertheless, in January 1915 there was a possibility that the Austrian navy might have been able to play a role and that crucial supplies could reach Turkey by sea. The Germans thought of using two Italian steamers sailing from Trieste with munitions stowed under a cargo of lumber but the Austrians doubted that secrecy could be maintained.[98] Haus in early January suggested that if the munitions transport was really a vital question for the common war effort it could be performed by the *Novara*, a fast light cruiser which was just entering service. Haus thought that breaking through the Straits of Otranto in the late evening and slipping into Smyrna the following evening between 4 p.m. and 6 p.m. was not too great a risk. *Novara* would not actually enter Smyrna but would anchor in the Gulf of Smyrna at Kalessi where lighters would be waiting for the munitions and also provide about 500 tons of coal for *Novara*. Haus had already discussed the plan with *Novara*'s commander, Linienschiffskapitän Nikolaus Horthy de Nagybánya, and *Novara* would be ready to sail in ten to fourteen days when the moon would be good – presumably Haus meant dark or moonless nights. It remained only to ascertain if the urgency of the munitions transport justified the risk of the *Novara*, and if she could receive the necessary 500 tons of coal at Smyrna for her return. Haus did not think that the risks were excessive and on his return Horthy might surprise the British off the Dardanelles or cruise along the line Port Said–Malta for one or two days and throw the entire Mediterranean into an uproar.[99]

Horthy had a reputation in the k.u.k. Kriegsmarine, which he would command in 1918, as a bold and decisive officer. The son of a Hungarian country squire, he was far from the best pupil at the Naval Academy, but had evolved from a somewhat frivolous young officer into a leader with a good understanding of human nature, a fine sportsman and an excellent ship handler. He had been an aide-de-camp to Kaiser Franz Joseph from November 1911 until May 1914, and began the war as captain of the *Habsburg*, flagship of the IV Division. The command of an obsolete battleship not likely to see much action was hardly to his taste and he applied for the *Novara* which was nearing completion. Haus had the good sense to realize that he would be an excellent choice for this type of command. A fellow officer and friend remembered him as the type who was always anxious for offensive action against the enemy, and after any mission was bubbling over with new ideas and proposals; in direct contrast to many others who might perform their duty faultlessly, but then quietly and passively merely wait for new orders.[100]

The plan proved to be impractical for a number of reasons. *Novara* could only stow 200 tons of munitions and the Austrians lacked essential intelligence on the Allied blockade of Smyrna.[101] Souchon could provide some of this information but had to advise abandonment of the scheme. There was no wireless station at Smyrna to advise the cruiser, the inner gulf was completely blocked by mines to the east of Vourlah and there were no signal stations on the coast to report enemy movements save for a few gendarmerie posts. Perhaps most important of all, it was impossible to provide suitable coal for naval boilers on the coast of Asia Minor.[102]

By the time Souchon's more detailed reply was written on 20 February, the possibility of operations by Horthy and the *Novara* on the coast of Asia Minor was probably out of the question. Haus had conceived the plan in early January well before the Allied attack on the Dardanelles, which by early March had been expanded to include Smyrna as well. The sizeable numbers of British and French ships which were now in the eastern Mediterranean greatly reduced the outlook for success by multiplying the chances *Novara* would be spotted and the alarm given. The plan is interesting, however, as one of the few really serious proposals originating from an Austrian source for operations outside the Adriatic. However, even with official approval – the Kaiser and Haus – and an able and willing commander such as Horthy, the Austrians lacked the matériel. The range of *Novara* was indeed limited, particularly if she had to use her greatest asset which was speed, but which carried the penalty of high coal consumption. She was not really suited because of this for a raid nor, for that matter, the transport of large quantities of cargo. Given the great value of this ship in the Adriatic – the four light cruisers of the k.u.k. Kriegsmarine really carried the brunt of the major operations – it was questionable whether the small quantity of munitions she might transport justified the risk.

The Ottoman fleet could only play a passive role as the Dardanelles bombardments began. When bad weather postponed operations after the first day of the Anglo-French bombardment, Souchon thought that the whole thing was a bluff, and also wondered why the Russians did not attack the Bosphorous at the same time as the British and French did at the Dardanelles. Souchon had the frustrated feeling of not being able to do anything and his best ships, *Goeben* and *Breslau*, were still in dock. The old battleships *Torgud Reis* and *Barbarossa* joined the available destroyers in the Marmara ready to fall on any damaged enemy ships in case of a break-through. Souchon hoped that their old short-range cannon might still be of use in the narrow channels. He did not, however, think that the Allies were ready to break through for they would have to employ the greatest part of their ships and he did not think that they would take the risk. Moreover, they could not accomplish anything without landing troops and they did not have them.[103] If the Allies succeeded in breaking through he expected them to demand the surrender of the Turkish fleet. He hoped that the Turkish government would not yield and that he might yet find a glorious end in the Black Sea. If the Turks did not give in, he planned to withdraw all available ships to the Bosphorus and defend it with mines and torpedoes. In the meantime, they were working night and day to repair the *Goeben*.[104]

The Germans received various reports of troop movements in the Mediterranean during February, including one about nine transports entering Corfu, and connected this with an attempt to break through the Dardanelles. The Admiralstab accordingly asked the Austrians to take countermeasures and try for at least a diversion with their submarines and torpedo-boat flotillas. Souchon thought that submarine operations off the Dardanelles might be very promising, but in view of Haus's past refusals to send submarines recommended exerting further pressure on the Austrians. He suggested offering to buy two of the Austrian boats, manning them with German crews and promised to be able to supply them on the coast of Asia Minor. Small, dismantled submarines sent by rail to Pola might be given to the Austrians as a replacement.[105] Kailer, however, told the German naval attaché that the transports reported at Corfu were in his opinion intended for an operation on the Austrian coast rather than the Dardanelles. The Germans, however, were worried about the Allied operations actually underway and not about a hypothetical attack on the Austrian coast.[106] Tirpitz warned the Austrian naval attaché in Berlin of the dangers of the situation at the Dardanelles and the unforeseeable consequences of a Turkish collapse. He asked the Austrians to send at least one of their submarines to the Dardanelles and offered to provide them with a small submarine as a replacement by the end of March. The German naval attaché in Vienna increased the offer to two disassembled submarines and assured the Austrians that Souchon could provide the necessary fuel oil on the coast of Asia Minor. If need be, German naval officers and engineers could be on hand to assist with material such as batteries. German aerial reconnaissance revealed that the British and French at the Dardanelles anchored every evening near Tenedos at the same place giving a submarine an excellent opportunity for an attack.[107]

In view of the consequences of an Allied breakthrough at the Dardanelles and Bosphorus, Enver Pasha was also extremely anxious for submarines to attack the British and French fleet, and even suggested that the Turkish government should purchase three boats from the Austrians at Pola. They could then be manned by the Germans and sent to the Dardanelles. The Turkish ambassador in Vienna in passing on the request pointed out that Romania and Bulgaria might attack Austria after an Anglo-French success at the Dardanelles, and submarines were the only effective way of guaranteeing the defence of the Straits.[108] In Constantinople the German ambassador, Baron von Wangenheim, suggested to the Austrian military plenipotentiary that the two submarines might be escorted or towed to the Dardanelles by a ship already outside the Straits and flying the Italian flag which belonged to an Austrian businessman residing in Constantinople. The shipowner would vouch for the reliability of the captain.[109]

This was a moment when the intervention of the k.u.k. Kriegsmarine could have produced dramatic results. The possibility that submarines would appear off the Dardanelles was certainly a factor in British discussions and a source of concern. Once again, however, technical considerations prevented the Austrians from acting. Haus claimed that only two of their submarines were fully ready for action, and one of these (U4) had a battery at only half capacity, while the second (U12) had a radius of action which in theory only just reached from the Straits of Otranto to the Dardanelles. Even this was possible only under the most favourable circumstances. There would have to be completely calm weather and they would have to avoid meeting enemy warships so that the entire trip could be made on the surface. Unfortunately, the Adriatic was blockaded by the French fleet and an undetected passage by the submarine through the Straits of Otranto without having to submerge was out of the question. The submarines used gasoline as fuel and a supply of this had to be guaranteed, while they could only carry four torpedoes, and after these were expended the boats were useless. Moreover, a new assault on Cattaro was always possible and the two submarines were required here, for the attitude of Italy was very doubtful. The remaining five submarines of the Austrian navy had either too small a radius of action, or due to docking, changing of engines, or replacement of batteries would not be available for several weeks. The dispatch of Austrian submarines to the Dardanelles was therefore out of the question. The Austrian naval attaché in Berlin received instructions to express Haus's regrets and to point out that the Flottenkommandant had seriously tried to do what was possible for the common cause and had already proposed sending the cruiser with munitions; but he was not in a position to initiate technically impossible operations, and he did not believe that the Reichsmarineamt would have made these proposals if they had known the actual condition of the Austrian submarines.[110]

The major question remains: could the Austrians really have done something with their submarines in March 1915 to affect the Dardanelles campaign? At first glance, given the small number of Austrian submarines (seven), and the even smaller number which had even a chance of executing the mission, it would have been highly unlikely that the Austrians would have deprived themselves of these potent weapons which had already imposed such caution on the superior French fleet in the Adriatic. Moreover, and this probably decided the matter, the attitude of Italy was more than 'uncertain'. The Italians were already in the process of the diplomatic bargaining that would bring them into the war within two months. The technical problems were also very real and difficult to overcome. Haus most probably would have liked to assist the Germans and when he discussed the question with the head of the Austrian submarine service he seemed very irritated with the technical problems that Korvetten-kapitän Thierry kept raising. The outspoken Thierry was anything but a 'yes' man, which he suspected Haus and his staff may have wanted, and in the end the Flottenkommandant accepted his advice which once again put him in an awkward position with his German allies.[111] Haus sent a long letter to Souchon on 5 March explaining the situation in regard to submarines and repeating his conditions for sending the *Novara* – a minimum quantity of 500 tons of good coal, and unloading and loading in a quiet place secured against enemy interruption. He also mentioned the obvious. This mission meant that Austria would give up a valuable ship for the common cause and the loss was not in proportion to the advantage to be gained – the transport of, at most, 300 tons of munitions. Haus also pointed out that, since Christmas, Austrian sorties into the Straits of Otranto up to the parallel of Corfu had been without success, largely because after the *Jean Bart* had been torpedoed the French had pulled their base further south to the waters of Corfu and Cephalonia, and had maintained the blockade of the Straits of Otranto primarily with destroyers.[112] After Haus's letter, Souchon could have had few illusions about the possibilities of Austrian help at the Dardanelles.

Korvettenkapitän Colloredo-Mannsfeld, Austrian naval attaché in Berlin for much of the war, believed that the German naval authorities appreciated Haus's standpoint and understood the impossibility of sending Austrian submarines. The Admiralstab explained to him that they had made the request when an Allied attack on the Dardanelles, irrespective of losses, seemed imminent but it now appeared that the Allies were not willing to run the risk and the main defensive positions were so strong that their reduction would require weeks, if not months, of effort. Nevertheless, the Germans did not want to loose sight of the likelihood of sending one or two submarines when the Austrians were in a position to do so. Their appearance among the hitherto secure British and French ships would be of great importance and might eventually decide the entire Dardanelles campaign. The Germans made the offer that when the *Curie* – the French submarine captured in December and now in dock at Pola – or another Austrian submarine with sufficient range, such as the Germania boats, set off for the Dardanelles, they would immediately send two small boats to Pola. The Germans emphasized that they would be offering two boats for one and that the pair would be sent via rail in three parts on special wagons and could be assembled and ready for action within a few days. The initial destination of the submarines might be Smyrna, or possibly some remote island in the Aegean archipelago or elsewhere on the coast of Asia Minor where fuel might be carried by a coastal sailing vessel or steamer flying the Greek or Italian flag. The Germans thought that their two small boats with a radius of action of 900 nautical miles were a valid substitution – especially on a two for one basis – for the submarine the Austrians would send to the Dardanelles. Colloredo-Mannsfeld was conscious of the widespread feeling in Germany that the Austrians were not pulling their weight in the war, and he warned that if they should decline the German offer it would be taken very badly and the Germans would not fail to put the blame on them should Constantinople fall.[113]

Haus was ready to accept the German offer as soon as a suitable Austrian boat was ready, but he did not think the political situation permitted him to denude the coast of the few available submarines and so made the departure of the Austrian boat conditional on the German substitutes actually being in hand. So long as the political situation was not clarified, he also could not promise to send a second boat. His two Germania submarines would be the ones most suitable for the mission, but they needed new batteries which would not be delivered until mid-April and the boats would be ready four weeks later. The Austrians in this matter appear to have had a complaint – its legitimacy was disputed by the Germans – against German bureaucratic procedures which were delaying the export of suitable batteries from Germany. Should the Reichsmarineamt be able to expedite their delivery, the boats might be ready a month sooner. If this were too late, the Austrians could send one of their Holland-type boats at the beginning of April, but this had the disadvantage of a small radius of action and used gasoline as fuel, and supply of the latter was likely to be difficult in Asia Minor. Haus seems to have overcome his technical reservations about the range of his boats and was ready to try. Haus favoured a German plan for a rendezvous with a Greek steamer carrying supplies. This steamer might eventually tow the submarine to an island in the Aegean archipelago, while other supplies could be deposited at some point on the coast of Asia Minor. The German naval attaché in Vienna, however, was not convinced of the truth of all his assertions, particularly concerning reasons for delay of the batteries which Freyberg claimed had been ordered through the Austrian branch of the German company. He had proposed that Germany should purchase the Austrian Germania boats U3 and U4 and put them in order themselves, presumably with German technicians sent to Pola. This would be the way to get something done much more quickly and circumvent what he termed the Austrian *'schlamperei'*.[114] The slow procedures of the Austrian yards would, perhaps more than any other action of their ally, plague the Germans for the remainder of the war.

Colloredo-Mannsfeld's fears over the German reaction were correct. While the reply in Berlin at the Reichsmarineamt or the Admiralstab was polite and understanding of the technical difficulties facing the Austrians, the reaction of the German officers on the scene in Turkey was far different when they learned of Haus's initial refusal to send submarines. Souchon exclaimed, 'These Alliance brothers! Shameless!' and sneered that Haus's letter had offered a thousand grounds but the sole true one was a lack of pluck.[115] Firle, representing sentiments undoubtedly widespread among the more junior officers, remarked that the Austrian allies were 'only big in beer table fraternization and enthusiasm' and referred sarcastically to 'these heroes', although he actually received a garbled version of the story. 'God knows', he remarked, 'two submarines would keep this society [the British] at a respectful distance.'[116]

By 10 March the Admiralstab considered the Dardanelles situation would be extremely serious if no further ammunition supplies arrived, and since Austrian military success against Serbia did not seem likely, suggested obtaining the Kaiser's decision on whether or not the sharpest diplomatic pressure, including the threat of military action, might be used against the Romanians to force passage of munitions. At the same time, in full agreement with the Reichsmarineamt the Admiralstab advised the Chief of the High Seas Fleet of the pressing necessity for at least one U-boat for the defence of the Dardanelles, and asked whether, in his opinion, it were possible for a specially selected boat of the U29 class to make the long sea voyage directly to Constantinople.[117]

Tirpitz, State Secretary of the Reichsmarineamt, was another German naval leader anxious to get Austrian boats out to the Dardanelles since his experts had told him that the Germania-type U3 and U4 had good prospects of success, especially if accompanied part of the way by a steamer, although their fuel would have to be replenished on the coast of Asia Minor. There would also be too long a delay before the Austrians had the captured *Curie* ready for service. Tirpitz accordingly offered the small UB7 and UB8 as a substitute for the Austrian boats. The two would be ready at the Germania yards for transport by rail in a disassembled condition on 15 March. In case rail transport through Romania became possible, the Germans were ready to send an additional two disassembled UB boats directly to Constantinople. Unfortunately, there appeared to be little likelihood of this taking place, so the participation of the Austrian boats in the defence of the Dardanelles was essential.[118]

Colloredo-Mannsfeld informed the Germans of the poor state of readiness of the Austrian submarines on 13 March. The news was sobering for the Germans. Allied pressure at the Dardanelles was increasing but it would be six to eight weeks before any of the Austrian boats would be ready to leave. Since the use of the Austrian boats was highly problematical, Rear-Admiral Behncke of the Admiralstab agreed with Tirpitz's proposal to send the disassembled UB7 and UB8 to Pola. This might exert pressure on the Austrians and should the Austrian boats still not be forthcoming they could be manned by German personnel and employed in the Mediterranean. A meeting of experts discussed the problem at the Reichsmarineamt on 15 March and agreed that UB7 and UB8 should be sent, while UB16 and UB17, originally meant for Constantinople, would be held in reserve for Pola. The conference also agreed to send a large submarine carrying 20 tons of extra fuel oil in her diving tanks directly to the Mediterranean. The Germans informed the Austrians that German engineers and workers would accompany the transport and asked for Austrian assistance in assembling the boats at the arsenal in Pola.[119] The Germans had taken the first significant step towards establishing themselves in the Mediterranean.

Meanwhile matters at the Dardanelles were moving towards their climax. On 11 March, based largely on intelligence concerning Turkish ammunition shortages, Churchill and the Admiralty ordered Carden to shift from his methodical bombardment and advance and press for a decision. The results to be gained were 'great enough to justify loss of ships and men if success cannot be obtained without'.[120] Efforts to sweep the Kephez minefields at night with trawler minesweepers continued to be unsuccessful when the warships were unable to knock out the searchlights which exposed the fragile trawlers to the deadly fire of the batteries protecting the minefields. Carden and his staff concluded that the only method to succeed would be a daylight attack to silence the forts at the Narrows as well as the batteries protecting the Kephez minefields. The trawlers could then clear a channel at night and permit the fleet to destroy the Narrows forts at short range the following day. This, in turn, would permit the trawlers to sweep the Narrows minefields and open the way into the Marmara. Shortly before the attack, Carden's health gave way and he was forced to relinquish his command on the 16th. Rear-Admiral Wemyss, SNO at Lemnos, was the senior admiral on the scene and should have taken over, but deferred to Rear-Admiral de Robeck, Carden's second-in-command who had been in on the planning from the beginning.[121]

The preliminaries, conduct and aftermath of the attack on 18 March have all been studied in great detail and there is no need for a detailed account here. The intermediate batteries were silenced and later the Narrows forts as well, but the Turkish mobile and hidden artillery still kept the trawlers from sweeping the Kephez minefields. Furthermore, an undetected row of twenty mines, moored parallel to the shore on 8 March in Eren Keui Bay by the minelayer *Nousret*, proved deadly. The battleships *Irresistible, Ocean* and *Bouvet* were sunk, while the battle cruiser *Inflexible* was badly damaged. The French battleships *Gaulois* and *Suffren* were also badly damaged by gunfire and the former had to be beached on Rabbit Island. The decisive element in the Turkish defence was the minefield rather than the artillery, and this had not been touched.[122] De Robeck, pushed along by his confident Chief of Staff, Commodore Keyes, was ready to renew the attack. Keyes set to work furiously reorganizing the sweeper force, fitting destroyers with sweeping gear. Had this been done before the attack of 18 March the results might have been different. The Admiralty sent the battleships *London* and *Prince of Wales* to follow *Queen* and *Implacable*, already *en route* to the Dardanelles, while the French sent the coast defence ship *Henri IV*. On 22 March, de Robeck changed his mind and decided he could not get through without troops and at a conference of naval and military leaders in the *Queen Elizabeth* decided to defer further naval attacks until a joint operation could take place in April. This had been the advice of Wemyss but Keyes was dismayed for he was, and would always remain, convinced that another attack after 4 April, when reorganization of the sweepers had been completed, would have resulted in the Allies forcing the Narrows, entering the Marmara, destroying the Turkish fleet and cutting the communications of the Turkish army on the peninsula. De Robeck, however, having made his decision, was firm and not even the eloquent arguments of Churchill could move him.[123] The success or failure of the Dardanelles campaign would henceforth become primarily a military question. The reasons for the failure of 18 March have been the subject of voluminous testimony which began during the war with a special commission to examine the entire campaign. The question of whether or not another naval attack would have succeeded after 18 March is one that can, of course, never be answered. Souchon was confident the Turkish forts would hold, but the Turkish ammunition situation was a source of grave concern to the Germans. Another naval attack probably would have succeeded, at some cost. But then what? Would the appearance of the Allied fleet off Constantinople have caused the Turks to give in? Could the British have maintained that fleet in the Marmara without control of both sides of the Straits? These questions are even more difficult to answer.[124]

Almost as a footnote to the Dardanelles attack, the Russian Black Sea Squadron appeared off the Bosphorus on 28 March. The force comprising five battleships, two cruisers and ten destroyers bombarded the forts at the entrance without significant result, and a renewal of the attack the next day was frustrated by thick fog. The following day portions of the Russian fleet shelled different ports in the coal district, again without significant results.[125]

At the same time as the Dardanelles operations were taking place, serious talks were also under way to bring Italy into the war on the side of the Entente. While the naval results of this would eventually prove to be disappointing, it would end once and for all any possibility of action by the Austrian navy outside the Adriatic, save for an occasional submarine. The Dardanelles operations also had another and most undesired result for the Allies. The Germans decided to send submarines to the Mediterranean. They would have had little effect on the Dardanelles campaign had the Allied attack on 18 March been successful, and would not have arrived in time to influence the situation had a renewed attack taken place by early April. They would eventually, however, cause the most serious threat to British and French control of the Mediterranean during the war. Both the Italian entry into the war and the arrival of German submarines will be the subject of the next chapter.

Notes: Chapter 3

1 Souchon to his wife, 11 and 12 Aug. 1914, BA-MA, Nachlass Souchon, N156/10.
2 Halpern, *Mediterranean Naval Situation*, ch. 11.
3 Tirpitz to Staatssekretär des Auswärtiges Amts, 2 Aug. 1914; Wangenheim to Auswärtiges Amt, 11 Aug. 1914, NARS, T-1022, Roll 587, PG 68126. See also: Ulrich Trumpener, *Germany and the Ottoman Empire, 1914–1918* (Princeton, NJ, 1968), pp. 30–2.
4 Lorey, *Krieg in den türkischen Gewässern*, Vol. 1, p. 31. Until late September, Souchon's title was only a pretence and he did not have actual command of the Turkish fleet. On 23 September the Turkish government formally offered him the appointment of vice-admiral in the Ottoman navy with actual command of

the Turkish fleet and general supervision of a naval reform programme to be undertaken by a German naval mission. He remained a rear-admiral on active service in the German navy. See Trumpener, *Germany and the Ottoman Empire*, pp. 40–3.

5 Souchon to his wife, 27 Sept. 1914, BA-MA, Nachlass Souchon, N156/11.

6 Müller to Souchon, 7 Sept. 1914, NARS, T-1022, Roll 785, PG 75208; von Pohl to Tirpitz [?], 11 Sept. 1914, ibid., Roll 587, PG 68126; Souchon to his wife, 7 Oct. 1914, BA-MA, Nachlass Souchon, N156/11.

7 'Aeusserungen des Oberstleutnant v. Feldmann über die Lage in der Türkei', 22 Sept. 1914, NARS, T-1022, Roll 687, PG 75214. See also Trumpener, *Germany and the Ottoman Empire*, p. 31.

8 Souchon to his wife, 12 and 15 Aug. 1914, BA-MA, Nachlass Souchon, N156/10.

9 Trumpener, *Germany and the Ottoman Empire*, pp. 42–3.

10 Lewis Einstein, *Inside Constantinople: A Diplomatist's Diary during the Dardanelles Expedition, April–September 1915* (New York, 1918), p. 255; 'Kriegstagebuch von Kapitänleutnant Rudoph Firle, 1914–1918', 8 Jan. and 1 July, 1915, BA-MA, Nachlass Firle, N155/21.

11 Trumpener, *Germany and the Ottoman Empire*, p. 70. On Humann see: ibid., p. 40; Einstein, *Inside Constantinople*, pp. 92–3; Ernest Jackh, *The Rising Crescent* (New York, 1944), pp. 118–20; Matti E. Mäkelä, *Auf den Spuren der Goeben* (Munich, 1979), pp. 22–5.

12 Souchon to his wife, 23 Aug. 1914, BA-MA, Nachlass Souchon, N156/10.

13 Souchon to his wife, 22 and 23 Aug. 1914, ibid.; Lorey, *Krieg in den türkischen Gewässern*, Vol. 1, pp. 32–4, 40–1; Firle, Kriegstagebuch, 31 Aug., 3 and 10 Sept. 1914, BA-MA, Nachlass Firle, N155/21.

14 Souchon to Tirpitz [?], 27 Aug. 1914, NARS, T-1022, Roll 1261, PG 60055; Firle, Kriegstagebuch, 16 Sept., 3 Oct. 1914, BA-MA, Nachlass Firle, N155/21; Souchon to his wife, 27 Sept. 1914, ibid., Nachlass Souchon, N156/11. On the condition of the Turkish fleet see also: Lorey, *Krieg in den türkischen Gewässern*, Vol. 1, pp. 36–8.

15 Naval Staff, *The Mediterranean, 1914–1915*, pp. 49–50, 54; Corbett and Newbolt, *Naval Operations*, Vol. 1, pp. 86–8.

16 Souchon to his wife, 20 Sept, 1914, BA-MA, Nachlass Souchon, N156/11.

17 Firle, Kriegstagebuch, 1 and 26 Sept. 1914, ibid., Nachlass Firle, N155/21.

18 Lorey, *Krieg in den türkischen Gewässern*, Vol. 1, p. 36, Vol. 2, pp. 4–10; Trumpener, *Germany and the Ottoman Empire*, pp. 35–6.

19 Souchon to his wife, 22 Aug., 9 and 20 Sept. 1914, BA-MA, Nachlass Souchon, N156/10, N156/11.

20 Gilbert, *Churchill*, Vol. 3: *The Challenge of War, 1914–1916*, p. 204; Churchill to Grey, 17 Aug. 1914, reproduced in Lumby (ed.), *Mediterranean, 1912–1914*, Doc. 415, pp. 441–2; Admiralty to Rear-Admiral *Indefatigable*, 27 Aug. 1914, ibid., Doc. 426, p. 448; Admiralty to SNO, Dardanelles, 8 Sept. 1914, ibid., Doc. 429, pp. 448–9.

21 Gilbert, *Churchill*, Vol. 3, pp. 207–9; Prince Louis of Battenberg to Limpus, 19 Nov. 1914, National Maritime Museum, Greenwich, Limpus MSS.

22 Admiralty to Carden, 20 and 21 Sept. 1914, Admiralty to Marine Bordeaux, 20 Sept. 1914, reproduced in Lumby (ed.), *Mediterranean, 1912–1914*, Docs 432–4, pp. 454–5.

23 Admiralty to SNO *Indefatigable*, 25 Sept. 1914, ibid., Doc. 435, p. 455; Gilbert, *Churchill*, Vol. 3, pp. 209, 212–13.

24 Souchon to his wife, 3 Oct. 1914, BA-MA, Nachlass Souchon, N156/11.

25 On Turkey's entry into the war see especially: Trumpener, *Germany and the Ottoman Empire*, pp. 54–62; Frank G. Weber, *Eagles on the Crescent: Germany, Austria and the Diplomacy of the Turkish Alliance, 1914–1918* (Ithaca, NY, 1970), pp. 72–86.

26 Firle, Kriegstagebuch, 9 Oct. 1914, BA-MA, Nachlass Firle, N155/21.

27 Souchon to Kaiser Wilhelm, 3 Nov. 1914, ibid., Nachlass Souchon, N156/3; Lorey, *Krieg in den türkischen Gewässern*, Vol. 1, p. 45; Trumpener, *Germany and the Ottoman Empire*, p. 55.

28 Lorey, *Krieg in den türkischen Gewässern*, Vol. 1, pp. 47–50.

29 The actions are described in great detail, ibid. A convenient summary is in René Greger, *Die Russische Flotte im Ersten Weltkrieg, 1914–1917* (Munich, 1970), p. 45.

30 Souchon to Kaiser Wilhelm, 3 Nov. 1914, BA-MA, Nachlass Souchon, N156/3.

31 Souchon to his wife, 29 Oct. 1914, ibid., Nachlass Souchon, N156/11.

32 Corbett and Newbolt, *Naval Operations*, Vol. 1, pp. 359–64; Gilbert, *Churchill*, Vol. 3, pp. 216–17; Admiralty to Admiral Superintendent, Malta, 1 Nov. 1914, Carden to Admiralty, 14 and 22 Nov. 1914, Lumby (ed.), *Mediterranean, 1912–1914*, Docs 438, 439, 443, pp. 456–9, 460–1.

33 Marder, *Dreadnought to Scapa Flow*, Vol. 2, p. 201; Gilbert, *Churchill*, Vol. 3, p. 218.

34 Firle, Kriegstagebuch, 3, 8, and 15 Nov. 1914, BA-MA, Nachlass Firle, N155/21.

35 Souchon to Kaiser Wilhelm, 25 Nov. 1914, ibid., Nachlass Souchon, N156/3.

36 Souchon to Kaiser Wilhelm, 25 Nov. 1914, ibid., Nachlass Souchon, N156/3; Lorey, *Krieg in den türkischen Gewässern*, Vol. 1, pp. 64–5; Greger, *Russische Flotte im Weltkrieg*, p. 46; N. Monasterev, *La marina russa nella guerra mondiale, 1914–1917* (Florence, 1934), pp. 247–55.

37 Souchon to his wife, 18 Nov., 16 Dec. 1914, BA-MA, Nachlass Souchon, N156/1, N156/12.

38 Greger, *Russische Flotte im Weltkrieg*, p. 47; Lorey, *Krieg in den türkischen Gewässern*, Vol. 1, pp. 72–3.

39 Gilbert, *Churchill*, Vol. 3, pp. 202–4; 209, 220–1.

40 For succinct recent accounts of the origins of the Dardanelles campaign based on voluminous published and unpublished records see: Marder, *Dreadnought to Scapa Flow*, Vol. 2, ch. 9; Gilbert, *Churchill*, Vol. 3, chs 6 and 8–10; and George H. Cassar, *The French and the Dardanelles* (London, 1971), ch. 3. For *Doris*'s operations on the Syrian coast see Corbett and Newbolt, *Naval Operations*, Vol. 2, pp. 74–6.

41 Secretary's Notes of a Meeting of the War Council, 13 Jan. 1915, PRO, Cab 22/1. See also Marder, *Dreadnought to Scapa Flow*, Vol. 2, pp. 205–7; Gilbert, *Churchill*, Vol. 3, pp. 248–53. Churchill spoke of using the code name 'Pola' for the Mediterranean project but appears to have done so only once in a memorandum on 13 January, ibid., p. 253.

42 Memorandum by Etat-Major général (hereafter cited as EMG), 28 Dec. 1914. Copy in Archives Diplomatiques, Ministère des Affaires Etrangères, Paris (hereafter cited as MAE), Série Y Internationale, Vol. 78, ff. 2–5; Historical Section Summary, 'Anglo-French Naval Co-operation', 26–30 Dec. 1914, PRO, Adm 137/1091.

43 Augagneur to Delcassé, 10 Jan. 1915, MAE, Série Y Internationale, Vol. 78; Commission de la Marine de Guerre, Audition de M. Augagneur, 18 July 1917, p. 44, SHM, Carton Ed-76bis; Laurens, *Commandement naval*, pp. 75–6.

44 Saint-Seine to Augagneur, 19 Jan. 1915, MAE, Série Guerre 1914–1918, Vol. 1060, ff. 9–13, 16; see also another version in Winston S. Churchill, *The World Crisis*, Vol. 2 (New York, 1923), pp. 112–13.
45 Saint-Seine to Augagneur, 8 Jan. 1915, SHM, Carton Ed-109.
46 Saint-Seine to Aubert, 18 Jan. 1915, MAE, Série Guerre 1914–1918, Vol. 1060, ff. 7–9.
47 Cambon to Delcassé [for Augagneur], 22 Jan. 1915, ibid., Vol. 1052, f. 67; Delcassé to Cambon, 24 Jan. 1915, ibid., f. 71.
48 The best account is Cassar, *The French and the Dardanelles*, pp. 56–60.
49 ibid., p. 58; Bienaimé, *La Guerre navale*, pp. 181–2.
50 Churchill to Augagneur, 27 Jan. 1915, PRO, Adm 137/1091.
51 Augagneur to Churchill, 31 Jan. 1915, MAE, Série Guerre 1914–1918, Vol. 1060.
52 Augagneur to Minister of Marine [Lacaze], 26 Feb. 1917, SHM, Carton Es-11; 'Audition de M. Augagneur', Commission de la Marine de Guerre, 18 July 1917, p. 46, ibid., Carton Ed-76bis.
53 Raymond Poincaré, *Au service de la France*, Vol. 6: *Les Tranchées 1915* (Paris, 1930), p. 34.
54 Cassar, *The French and the Dardanelles*, pp. 62–6; Laurens, *Commandement naval*, pp. 80–2.
55 Aubert, 'Note pour le Ministre sur l'action aux Dardanelles', 7 Feb. 1915, SHM, Carton Ed-109. Jackson's memorandum is: 'Note on forcing the passages of the Dardanelles and Bosphorus . . .', 5 Jan. 1915, PRO, Adm 137/1089.
56 Augagneur to Dartige du Fournet, 5 Feb. 1915, SHM, Carton A-132.
57 Keyes to his wife, 2 July 1915, reproduced in Paul G. Halpern (ed.), *The Keyes Papers*, Vol. 1: *1914–1918*, Publications of the Navy Records Society, Vol. 117 (London 1975, reprint 1979), Doc. 88, p. 156; de Robeck to Limpus, 16 May 1915, loc. cit. at n. 21, Limpus MSS.
58 Cassar, *The French and the Dardanelles*, pp. 127–8; Marder, *Dreadnought to Scapa Flow*, Vol. 2, p. 232.
59 Keyes to Jackson, 11 Nov. 1915, Halpern (ed.), *The Keyes Papers*, Vol. 1, Doc. 115, p. 242; Statement by M. Chaumet, President, Commission de la Marine de Guerre, 18 July 1917, SHM, Carton Ed-76bis; see also the tribute in Corbett and Newbolt, *Naval Operations*, Vol. 3, p. 171.
60 Vice-Amiral P.-E. Guépratte, *L'Expédition des Dardanelles, 1914–1915* (Paris, 1935), pp. 239–40, 251–2; Guépratte to Keyes, 16 Sept. and 23 Oct. 1930, Keyes to Guépratte, 1 Oct. 1930, reproduced in: Halpern (ed.), *The Keyes Papers*, Vol. 2: *1919–1938*, Publications of the Navy Records Society, Vol. 121 (London, 1980), Docs 226–228, pp. 279–82.
61 Augagneur to Lapeyrère, 10 Mar. 1915; Lapeyrère to Augagneur, 11 and 15 Mar. 1915, SHM, Carton A-29.
62 Augagneur to Lapeyrère, 16 Mar. 1915, ibid.
63 Marder, *Dreadnought to Scapa Flow*, Vol. 2, pp. 224, 228; for a full account of the War Council meeting and the equivocal position of Fisher see: Gilbert, *Churchill*, Vol. 3, pp. 270–5; Churchill, *The World Crisis*, Vol. 2, pp. 160–4.
64 *Swiftsure, Triumph, Cornwallis, Irresistible, Ocean, Albion, Canopus, Vengeance, Majestic, Prince George.*
65 Minute by Chief of Staff, Dardanelles Operation Orders, n.d. [5 Feb. 1915], PRO, Adm 137/1089. Also printed in Churchill, *The World Crisis*, Vol. 2, pp. 547–50.
66 Hankey to Balfour, 10 Feb. 1915, British Library, London, Balfour MSS, Add. MSS 49703, f. 165.

67 Minute by Jackson, 15 Feb. 1915, PRO, Adm 137/1089; Richmond, 'Remarks on Present Strategy', 14 Feb. 1915, reproduced in Arthur J. Marder, *Portrait of an Admiral: The Life and Papers of Sir Herbert Richmond* (London, 1952), pp. 142–5; Gilbert, *Churchill*, Vol. 3, pp. 288, 292–6.

68 Gilbert, *Churchill*, Vol. 3, pp. 296–7; Cassar, *The French and the Dardanelles*, pp. 73–5; A. Thomazi, *La Guerre navale aux Dardanelles* (Paris, 1926), p. 64.

69 Minute by Jackson, 7 Apr. 1915, PRO, Adm 137/38.

70 Keyes to his wife, 8 Mar. 1915, Halpern (ed.), *The Keyes Papers*, Vol. 1, Doc. 64, pp. 103–4.

71 Minute by Jackson, 7 Apr. 1915. On the minesweeping problem see Marder, *Dreadnought to Scapa Flow*, Vol. 2, pp. 263–5.

72 Keyes to his wife, 8 Mar. 1915, cit. at n. 70.

73 Wemyss to Limpus, 4 Mar. 1915, loc. cit. at n. 21, Limpus MSS.

74 Rear-Admiral Hugh Miller, unpublished autobiography, p. 136. Microfilm copy at Imperial War Museum, London, PP/MCR/16.

75 Gilbert, *Churchill*, Vol. 3, p. 332; Marder, *Dreadnought to Scapa Flow*, Vol. 2, pp. 236–9.

76 Paléologue to Delcassé, 5 Mar. 1915, MAE, Série Guerre 1914–1918, Vol. 1060; Gilbert, *Churchill*, Vol. 3, pp. 328–9.

77 Churchill to Grand Duke Nicholas, 19 Jan. 1915, Buchanan to Grey, 25 Jan. 1915, reproduced in Churchill, *The World Crisis*, Vol. 2, pp. 113–14, 155–6.

78 Monasterev, *La marina russa nella la guerra mondiale*, pp. 257–65; Greger, *Russische Flotte im Weltkrieg*, pp. 46–8.

79 Gilbert, *Churchill*, Vol. 3, pp. 315, 344; Greger, *Russische Flotte im Weltkrieg*, p. 48.

80 For a detailed account of the naval support see: Corbett and Newbolt, *Naval Operations*, Vol. 2, ch. 7; A. Thomazi, *La Guerre navale dans la Méditerranée* (Paris, 1929), pp. 77–81.

81 Cambon to Delcassé, 1 Mar. 1915, MAE, Série Guerre 1914–1918, Vol. 1060.

82 Richmond Diary, 16 Jan., 9 and 14 Feb. 1915, Marder, *Portrait of an Admiral*, pp. 135–6, 140–1.

83 Fisher to Churchill, 3 Jan. 1915, cited in Gilbert, *Churchill*, Vol. 3, pp. 234–5, 245.

84 Secretary's Notes of a Meeting of a War Council, 13 Jan. 1915, PRO, Cab 22/1.

85 Churchill to Kitchener, 20 Jan. 1915, reproduced in Gilbert, *Churchill*, Vol. 3, pp. 267–8.

86 Secretary's Notes of a Meeting of a War Council, 10 and 19 Mar. 1915, PRO, Cab 22/1. Kitchener's arguments were summarized and printed as: CID Paper G-12, 'Alexandretta and Mesopotamia: Memorandum by Lord Kitchener', [16 Mar. 1915], PRO, Cab 24/1.

87 CID Paper G-13, 'Alexandretta and Mesopotamia: Memorandum by the Admiralty', 17 Mar. 1915; Jackson, 'Remarks on the importance of Alexandretta as a Future Base', 15 Mar. 1915, PRO, Adm 137/1091, ff. 316–19. Subsequently printed as CID Paper G-15 [18 Mar.], copy in PRO, Cab 24/1.

88 Corbett and Newbolt, *Naval Operations*, Vol. 2, pp. 195–200; more details are in: Naval Staff, *The Mediterranean, 1914–1915*, pp. 118–23.

89 J. H. Godfrey, War Diary, 10 March 1915, Naval Library, Ministry of Defence, London, Godfrey MSS.

90 Corbett and Newbolt, *Naval Operations*, Vol. 2, pp. 209–10; Naval Staff, *The Mediterranean, 1914–1915*, pp. 123–4; Minute by Jackson, 2 [?] Apr. 1915, PRO, Adm 137/1091.

91　Augagneur to Saint-Seine, 3 Mar. 1915, MAE, Série Y Internationale, 1918–1940, Vol. 78, f. 21.

92　Cambon to Delcassé, 3 Mar. 1915, MAE, Papiers Delcassé, Vol. 3, ff. 343–5, Laurens, *Commandement naval*, p. 108.

93　Captain G. R. G. Allen, 'A ghost from Gallipoli', *The Royal United Service Institution Journal*, vol. 108, no. 630 (May 1963), pp. 137–8; letter by Admiral Sir William James, 7 Sept. 1963, ibid., vol. 108, no. 632 (Nov. 1963), pp. 374–5; see also his *The Eyes of the Navy: A Biographical Study of Admiral Sir Reginald Hall* (London, 1955), pp. 60–4; Gilbert, *Churchill*, Vol. 3, pp. 358–60; Patrick Beesly, *Room 40: British Naval Intelligence, 1914–18* (London, 1982), pp. 80–2. The French apparently picked up traces of the talks, Cassar, *The French and the Dardanelles*, pp. 167–9.

94　Corbett and Newbolt, *Naval Operations*, Vol. 2, pp. 72–3; Holbrook to Keyes, 17 Jan. 1915 reproduced in Halpern (ed.), *The Keyes Papers*, Vol. 1, Doc. 49, pp. 72–3.

95　Souchon to his wife, 16, 18 and 30 Dec. 1914, BA-MA, Nachlass Souchon, N156/12. A French attempt to penentrate the Dardanelles was unsuccessful when the submarine *Saphir* ran aground and was sunk on 15 Jan. See Thomazi, *Guerre navale aux Dardanelles*, pp. 38–40.

96　Souchon to his wife, 6 Jan. 1915, BA-MA, Nachlass Souchon, N156/12.

97　ibid.; Fernspruch des Admiralstabes, 30 Dec. 1914, NARS, T-1022, Roll 788, PG 75240.

98　Kailer to Haus, 15 Dec. 1914, Kriegsarchiv, Vienna, Nachlass Haus; Sokol, *Österreich-Ungarns Seekrieg*, pp. 175–6.

99　Haus to Kailer, 4 Jan. 1915, Kriegsarchiv, Vienna, Nachlass Kailer.

100　Heyssler, 'Erinnerungen' (1936) typescript in private possession, p. 392; further biographical details are in Bayer von Bayersburg, *Unter der k.u.k. Kriegsflagge*, pp. 27–35.

101　Kailer to Haus, 8 and 9 Jan. 1915, loc. cit. at n. 98, Nachlass Haus; Haus to Souchon, 11 Jan. 1915, OK/MS VIII-1/8 ex 1915, No. 1545.

102　Souchon to Haus, 22 Jan. and 20 Feb. 1915, Report by Lieut. Missuweit, 16 Feb. 1915, ibid. Copies are also in NARS, T-1022, Roll 421.

103　Souchon to his wife, 22 and 25 Feb. 1915, BA-MA, Nachlass Souchon, N156/12.

104　Souchon to his wife, 26 and 28 Feb. 1915, ibid.

105　Souchon to Admiralstab, 1 Mar. 1915; Admiralstab to Marineattaché, Vienna, 28 Feb. and 2 Mar. 1915, NARS, T-1022, Roll 726, PG 75258.

106　Kailer to Haus, 1 Mar. 1915, OK/MS VIII-1/8 ex 1915, No. 1376.

107　Marineattaché, Berlin to Marinesektion, 1 Mar. 1915, ibid., No. 1380.

108　Wangenheim to Auswärtiges Amt, 1 Mar. 1915, NARS, T-1022, Roll 726, PG 75258; Kailer to Haus, 3 Mar. 1915, OK/MS VIII-1/8 ex 1915, Nos 1414, 1415; Hilmi Pasha to Burián, 4 Mar. 1915, ibid., No. 1783.

109　Militärbevollmachtigter in Pera to AOK, 4 Mar. 1915, ibid., No. 1462; Wangenheim to Auswärtiges Amt, 2 Mar. 1915, NARS, T-1022, Roll 726, PG 75258.

110　Marinesektion to Marineattaché, Berlin, 3 and 4 Mar. 1915, OK/MS VIII-1/8 ex 1915, Nos 1416, 1445.

111　'Die Entsendung eines k.u.k. U-bootes nach den Dardenellen', Kriegsarchiv, Vienna, Nachlass Thierry, B/755, No. 23, ff. 8–10.

112　Haus to Souchon, 5 Mar. 1915, NARS, T-1022, Roll 421.

113　Colloredo-Mannsfeld to Marinesektion, 6 Mar. 1915, OK/MS VIII-1/8 ex 1915, No. 1549.

114 Haus to Marinesektion, 10 Mar. 1915, Marinesektion to AOK, 12 Mar. 1915, ibid., No. 1623; Freyberg to Tirpitz, 4 Mar. 1915, NARS, T-1022, Roll 726, PG 75258.
115 Souchon to his wife, 8 and 12 Mar. 1915, BA-MA, Nachlass Souchon, N156/13.
116 Firle, Kriegstagebuch, 18 Oct. 1914 and 5 Mar. 1915, BA-MA, Nachlass · Firle, N155/21.
117 Admiralstab, Fernspruch an Chef im GrHQ, 10 Mar. 1915, NARS, T-1022, Roll 726, PG 75258.
118 Capelle to Freyberg, 13 Mar. 1915, ibid.
119 Colloredo-Mannsfeld to v. Rheinbaben, 13 Mar. 1915, ibid., Roll 421; Behncke to Bachmann, 14 Mar. 1915, Protocol of meeting at Reichsmarineamt, 15 Mar. 1915, ibid., Roll 726, PG 75258; Colloredo-Mannsfeld to Marinesektion, 16 Mar. 1915, OK/MS VIII-1/8 ex 1915, No. 1736.
120 Churchill to Carden, 11 Mar. 1915, reproduced in Gilbert, *Churchill*, Vol. 3, p. 337.
121 Marder, *Dreadnought to Scapa Flow*, Vol. 2, pp. 242–5; Roger Keyes, *The Naval Memoirs* (2 vols, London, 1934–5), Vol. 1, ch. 12; Keyes to his wife, 15 and 17 Mar. 1915, Halpern (ed.), *The Keyes Papers*, Vol. 1, Docs 66, 68, pp. 108–10.
122 Marder, *Dreadnought to Scapa Flow*, Vol. 2, pp. 245–50; Corbett and Newbolt, *Naval Operations*, Vol. 2, ch. 13, pp. 213–23; Keyes to his wife, 21 Mar. 1915, Halpern (ed.), *The Keyes Papers*, Vol. 1, Doc. 69, pp. 110–15; Keyes, *Naval Memoirs*, Vol. 1, ch. 13; Eric Bush, *Gallipoli* (London, 1975), pp. 51–64.
123 Marder, *Dreadnought to Scapa Flow*, Vol. 2, pp. 251–7; Keyes to his wife, 27 Mar. 1915, Halpern (ed.), *The Keyes Papers*, Vol. 1, Doc. 72, pp. 116–22; Keyes, *Naval Memoirs*, Vol. 1, chs 14–15; Gilbert, *Churchill*, Vol. 3, pp. 356–8.
124 Keyes, *Naval Memoirs*, Vol. 1, pp. 185–6; Churchill, *The World Crisis*, Vol. 2, ch. 13; Marder, *Dreadnought to Scapa Flow*, Vol. 2, pp. 259–65; idem, 'The Dardanelles revisited: further thoughts on the naval prelude', in *From the Dardanelles to Oran* (London, 1974), pp. 1–32. On the Turkish ammunition situation, see below, p. 106.
125 Greger, *Russische Flotte im Weltkrieg*, p. 48.

[4]

German Submarines Arrive and Italy Enters the War

Italian War Plans

As we have seen in the preceding chapters, the Italian navy by its very presence weighed heavily in the minds of Austrian naval leaders such as Haus, and to a large degree influenced – the Germans might say paralysed – their action. The Austrian leaders were correct for, once free of the possibility or nightmare of having to fight as Austria's ally, the Chief of the Italian Naval Staff returned to the traditional problem of preparing for war in the Adriatic. Paolo Count Thaon di Revel was Capo di Stato Maggiore for most of the war except for the period from October 1915 to February 1917 when he was C.-in-C. at Venice. He would emerge from the war as the dominant figure in the Regia Marina. Authoritarian in temperament, he seemed the terror of his subordinates and displayed a ferocious energy not always found among the senior officers of that service. He would also be a thorn in the side of the Allies for his stubborn and singleminded determination to uphold what he considered to be Italy's vital interests in what critics have described as a naval form of *sacro egoismo*. Revel was a member of a noble Piedmontese family with a long tradition of service to the state. Admiral Sims, commander of US forces in European waters, described him with tongue in cheek as 'a source of continual delight' and went on to say:

> . . . Someone remarked that he was in reality an Irishman who had escaped into Italy; and this facetious characterization was not really inapt. His shock of red hair, his reddish beard, and his short stocky figure almost persuaded one that County Cork was his native soil. He delivered his opinions with an insistence which indicated that he entertained little doubt about their soundness; he was not particularly patient if they were called in question; yet he was so courteous, so energetic, and so entertaining that he was a general favourite.

Sims presumably added the final clause for diplomatic reasons. Admiral Howard Kelly, who had commanded the British forces in the Adriatic was more blunt. Although always kind to him, he found Revel, 'a real tough nut', and 'it was positively annoying to see the state of absolute subjugation to which he had reduced all his admirals. They trembled at the very thought of him . . .'[1]

In September 1914 Revel prepared a lengthy study on possible operations in the Adriatic.[2] He began with the traditional argument of how the geographical configuration of the Adriatic favoured the Austrians who had excellent bases in the north at Pola and in the south at Cattaro, good anchorages between the two, and numerous islands with navigable channels between them which would serve as a screen behind which the enemy fleet could move, ready to attack with overwhelming force at the opportune moment. The Italian side of the Adriatic, on the other hand, was open to attack with few secure anchorages except for Venice and Brindisi. The Austrian fleet could keep itself securely and in full efficiency, while the Italian fleet would have to keep to the seas exposed to torpedo attack, particularly at night. The most probable strategy for the Austrians would be the 'fleet-in-being', maintaining their strength in the security of their bases and waiting for the opportune moment to attack, while the Italians were whittled away by the attrition of mines and torpedoes. The major problem for the Italians would be how to provoke the Austrians to sortie and give battle under favourable conditions. Revel discussed various courses of action. These included: the blockade of the Straits of Otranto; the bombardment of the dockyards and factories at Fiume, difficult to reach up in the Quarnero and therefore best entrusted to ships of scant military value; and the bombardment of Trieste, which presented political difficulties because of the large Italian population, and where the enemy fleet would be close to its base and the bombarding ships exposed to torpedo attack at night. The Italians might also provoke enemy action by the temporary occupation of certain islands such as Lagosta, Curzola, Lesina and Meleda. Revel, in consideration of Italy's probable allies, also suggested that they threaten a landing near Antivari on the Montenegrin coast. Antivari in Italian hands would be particularly useful for strengthening Serbian and Montenegrin resistance through arms, munitions and supplies sent from Italy. Revel also talked about destroying Austrian semaphore and signal stations in the Dalmatian Islands, as well as mining important channels between those islands to make Austrian navigation hazardous. He wanted to concentrate a special division of old cruisers at Venice to oppose the advance of the enemy army or support that of their own. Although Revel devoted some space to submarines and aircraft, his study is very similar to a number of older plans prepared by Admiral Bettolo, Chief of Naval Staff, 1907–11, and very much in line with traditional Italian thinking about war in the Adriatic.[3]

Revel revised his remarks in a second study written in January 1915. By now the experiences of the war in the North Sea had demonstrated the effectiveness of mines and submarines. There still remained, however, the major problem of what diversionary action would induce the Austrians to sortie from their well-defended base of Pola. The Austrians might attack in the upper Adriatic, probably even initiating hostilities with an attack on

Venice. Venice would have to provide for its own maritime security by coastal batteries, minefields and aggressive action by submarines and torpedo-boats. A naval guerrilla war with these small craft was likely to unfold between Pola and Venice. Cattaro was the southern head of the Austrian maritime defensive system which ended in the north at Pola and Rovigno. An attack on Cattaro might therefore provoke an intervention by the enemy fleet. However, since the Italians lacked the means for such an attack, Revel recommended maintaining a group of warships notably superior to the Austrian forces at Cattaro and ready to attack and cut them off whenever they came out. This Italian force would require a base and Brindisi might fulfil the function, at least initially. The support the opposing armies expected from their navies also tied the actions of the fleet to the aims of the army. An army attacked from the sea between Monfalcone and Trieste would clearly experience difficulties and its stay in Trieste would become untenable. Conversely, the advance and capture of Trieste would be facilitated by the support of concentrated warships. The Italians must not expose themselves to losses from mines or torpedoes which would not be compensated for by equivalent damage to the enemy, and they had the duty to profit from their slight superiority in torpedo-boats and submarines to strike some blow which would assure their superiority in battleships over the enemy force which might come out of Pola. In pursuing their higher objectives, however, Revel insisted that they should never run the risk of putting their battleships in danger of mines or torpedoes, nor should the conduct of their forces be subordinated to opposing fleeting enemy attacks on undefended portions of the Italian coast. Revel concluded that the Gospel for operations by their fleet should always be to cause major damage to the enemy while receiving the minimum, and this was to be achieved by aggressive action on the part of light craft and torpedo-boats, while preserving major ships for combat against their peers.[4]

These general criteria for the use of the Italian fleet are worthy of note because of later misunderstandings of Italian policy. The Italians did indeed desire an engagement between the battle fleets. It was the most favourable hypothesis for them as they anticipated superiority over the Austrians. However, the experiences of the war convinced them that battleships must be preserved from mines and torpedoes and that much of the real fighting would be done by light craft with battleships maintained solely for use against their enemy counterparts. The relatively restricted waters of the Adriatic reinforced these considerations and they would form the basis for the conduct of the Italian battle fleet for the duration of the war. Allied charges that the Italians were afraid to risk their battle fleet are unfair and not true. The Italians would be ready and anxious to use it, but *only* against the Austrian battle fleet.

The memoranda and directives produced by Revel and his staff were, for the most part, rather general except for detailed instructions for the defence of Venice. How would the Italians employ the fleet itself? The powerful dreadnoughts, battleships and armoured cruisers which had caused so much comment before the war were under the command of His Royal Highness,

Vice-Admiral the Duke of the Abruzzi. Luigi Amadeo di Savoia was the third son of Amadeo di Savoia, Duke of Aosta, King of Spain, 1871–3, and was in fact born in Madrid two weeks before his father's abdication. His elder brother, Emanuele Filiberto, Duke of Aosta, commanded the Third Italian Army. Abruzzi, a cousin of King Victor Emmanuel III, was one of the best-known Italians of his time. Before the war he led a series of well-publicized expeditions to the North Pole, the Himalayas and the Ruwenzori mountains of Central Africa. He also commanded the Italian naval force sent to the USA in 1907 for the festivities marking the 300th anniversary of the founding of Jamestown. The duke became familiar to Americans as a result of his romance with Katherine Elkins, daughter of the prominent senator from West Virginia, and reports of their engagement tantalized the American press in the years 1908–10. The affair ended sadly when the engagement was broken off, allegedly over the Italian court's opposition to his marriage to a commoner. Abruzzi never married. His name was frequently in the press with a wide range of activities from mountain climbing expeditions to winning a Tango contest, and he projected the image of a dashing leader of whom much was expected. His manners and charm were supposedly perfect, as befitted a *grand seigneur*, and in 1913 even the old Emperor Franz Joseph spoke approvingly of him as a capable chief who after the conclusion of the Triple Alliance Naval Convention might one day lead a combined Austro-Italian fleet.[5]

Revel had some more specific proposals for Abruzzi at the beginning of March. He wanted to create a secure anchorage among the islands off the Dalmatian coast. Capitano di fregato Conz, Assistant Chief of Staff to Abruzzi and formerly one of Revel's most trusted officers on the Naval Staff in Rome, had prepared detailed studies on Sabbioncello. Conz, a clever officer fluent in French, English and German, had already played a leading role in the preliminaries leading up to the abortive Triple Alliance Naval Convention of 1913, and had allegedly visited Dalmatian ports before the war disguised as a mendicant friar or fisherman. His study established that a secure anchorage at Sabbioncello, or more correctly in the Sabbioncello Channel between the peninsula of that name and the island of Curzola, had certain advantages for conducting the war in the southern Adriatic. It was close enough to Cattaro (72 miles) for the Italians to establish patrols and attack any destroyer force coming out from the Austrian base, but it was far enough from Pola (195 miles) so that the Italians would not be surprised by the Austrian fleet. Revel was convinced that the Italian fleet had to be kept in readiness to frustrate any major enemy movement against their coast, which might include a landing to take the Italian army in the rear and hinder its mobilization. The Italian fleet would only intervene in the upper Adriatic after the Italian army had pushed victoriously beyond the Isonzo River. They would then proceed to the north of Pola or into the Gulf of Trieste to assist the army in the capture of Trieste and the Istrian Peninsula. Revel thought that maritime operations would fall into two principal phases. During the first phase the Italian fleet would be based in the lower Adriatic, and operations would take place in the lower and central Adriatic. The Italian objectives would be: indirect cover of Brindisi; surveillance of Cattaro and attack of any forces which might be forced out by the Italian air or land offensive (provided the army would co-operate); and provoking the Austrian fleet at Pola by means of attacks against the minor torpedo-boat bases at Ragusa, Spalato, Sebenico, and possibly Lussin and Zara, although in the case of the latter political reasons might preclude an attack on this port because of its large Italian population. The second phase of operations would be in the upper Adriatic. The Italian fleet would put to sea after (and not before) the army had succeeded in pushing the enemy out of Monfalcone back towards Trieste. The fleet would then help to speed the occupation of Trieste and the Istrian Peninsula, and cut Austrian lines of communication along the coast.[6]

Abruzzi, who had been asked to prepare detailed studies within this strategical framework, approved in principle the idea of occupying Sabbioncello as a base for the fleet in the first phase of a war, and submitted a list of personnel and equipment it would be necessary to have on hand in advance at Taranto to man a lookout station. The navy would need some military support, including, if possible, gunners for the 76-mm landing guns and mules and drivers. Abruzzi was also studying possible action against Cattaro by means of howitzers emplaced on Mount Lovčen, and believed that this was the most likely of the actions contemplated in the southern Adriatic to induce the enemy fleet to steam south. This action would, of course, involve considerable military participation, and since many of the detailed arrangements could not be improvised at the last moment Abruzzi asked Revel to obtain a decision from the army.[7]

General Luigi Cadorna, the Chief of the Army General Staff, was far from generous in his response. While promising to do everything possible to meet the navy's request for troops to occupy the territory adjacent to the proposed base at Sabbioncello, he pointed out that the unit designated for the role, the 149th Regiment of Mobile Militia (*milizia mobile*) from Palermo, had not yet received its allotment of machine guns and was not likely to get them for a few months. The 149th Regiment were second-line troops of the Reserve, hardly what one would have employed for a dangerous exposed position on enemy soil. Cadorna added that it was absolutely impossible for him to detach any mountain artillery or mule-carried batteries from the frontier district, nor could he spare any artillery officers, since the existing cadre was insufficient for the needs of the army. The best he could offer seemed to be 100–200 men of the fortress artillery. Revel admitted to Abruzzi that this was an inadequate response but nevertheless, in order to be ready for unforeseen eventualities, he asked Cadorna to deploy the 149th Regiment and 150 fortress artillerymen to the Puglia region, ready for embarkation at either Taranto or Brindisi.[8]

Revel was apparently having second thoughts about the Sabbioncello base, or 'Base Rossa'. The occupation and maintenance of Sabbioncello would be easy when the enemy fleet had been defeated, but might be difficult while the enemy was still at full strength. Sabbioncello could become a considerable burden, given the necessity of maintaining 3,000–4,000 men over a none-too-secure line of communication, and might tie down naval forces which could be more efficiently employed elsewhere.[9]

Moreover, Cadorna placed great importance on the support the navy might provide for the army's advance on Trieste. This might provoke the Austrian fleet to sortie from Pola and result in precisely the sort of battle the Italians desired. If the enemy sought battle at once, a base at Sabbioncello would not be an immediate necessity and if the enemy avoided battle Revel was certain that between the fifteenth and twentieth day after the declaration of war the bulk of the Italian fleet would be compelled to advance to the north whatever the risks and difficulties. The pressure from the Italian army for naval protection on the flank of its advance along the Gulf of Trieste would be hard to resist, and he did not see how the Sardegna division of old battleships at Venice could fulfil the mission without the bulk of the Italian fleet to cover it from an attack in force from Pola. Sabbioncello would be of little use if a major battle occurred at once, and if such a battle did not occur the base would be abandoned after a few days when the fleet left the lower and central Adriatic for the north.[10]

The various studies and exchanges of opinion which had been going on since the beginning of the European war finally resulted in a general plan for operations in the Adriatic which was approved by the Italian government, sanctioned by the king and subsequently transmitted by the Minister of Marine to the naval C.-in-C. on 18 April. The plan did not contain any specific instructions as to how its objectives were to be achieved as the government did not wish to bind Abruzzi to details, and left him full liberty for choosing the time and method for achieving the objectives.[11] The Italian plans should be no surprise after following the line of argument already outlined in this chapter. They began with something of a disclaimer, that the rational conduct of the maritime war and the attainment of its objectives should in no way be subordinated to the protection of undefended cities and the national coast in general. It would be a grave error which might lead to a disaster if the fleet compromised its efficiency by stretching itself thin and wearing itself out rushing to the defence of every threatened locality. Nevertheless, the fleet would provide such defence whenever it could do so effectively in relation to its deployment at the time, and provided it would not run the risk of suffering greater damage than it might presumably inflict on the enemy. The Italian army would employ all available forces for the advance beyond the frontier and was not able to divert any forces, even in a very limited measure, for the obtainment of other objectives such as the occupation of islands or places on the enemy coast. An attack on Cattaro was also out of the question, at least for the moment. The requisite artillery for attacking the land front was not available, and the land defences of the Austrian base had been strengthened so that an attack would now require substantial military forces.

The Italian plans contain the usual statement about objectives – primarily the destruction of enemy forces. Italian commanders were to push attacks to the limit without excessive preoccupation with losses so long as the enemy was destroyed or put out of action. A secondary objective would be the destruction of undefended or lightly defended facilities like signal or lookout stations that could be useful for torpedo-boats. In order to avoid excessive risk, forces employed on these operations were to be adequately supported by major ships close at hand. The Italians would also mine those channels likely to be used by enemy warships, and the latter would be closely watched by scouts and aerial reconnaissance, although such reconnaissance should not be pushed too far from the bulk of the fleet. Special measures would have to be taken to cover Brindisi, whose defences were still relatively weak, from an enemy attack and forces would have to be deployed to promptly meet such an attack, or at least give battle before the enemy force could return to its base. The Italian navy would assure the relative dominance of the upper Adriatic, particularly the Gulf of Trieste, with timely deployment of forces at least equivalent to the enemy at Pola, and when naval conditions permitted would support the advance of the army into the heart of enemy territory. If army operations went according to plan, this would probably be around the fifteenth day after the beginning of hostilities.

At the opening of hostilities the fleet would probably be deployed in the lower or mid-Adriatic, based either on Brindisi or Taranto. The advantage of using Taranto would increase if ships of other navies were attached to the Italian fleet because of the limited capacity of the anchorage at Brindisi. If the bulk of the enemy fleet came down from Pola to give battle, the outcome of the latter would be decisive for the further unfolding of the war. Should the enemy fleet remain in Pola most of the Italian fleet would pursue operations in the lower and mid-Adriatic until called north to support the advance of the Italian army. This would probably induce the enemy to sortie for a battle, exactly what the Italians desired, and it was essential that the bulk of the fleet be preserved in at least equivalent strength to the enemy. The secondary operations and those intended to support the army were always to be subordinated to this objective.[12]

The Italian war plans, general as they might have been, clearly reflect Revel's influence in their depreciatory and hesitating attitude towards temporary bases on the enemy coast. The Italians were seeking battle and desired nothing more than an encounter with the enemy fleet but, and this is important to remember in judging future Italian conduct, they considered it essential to preserve the battle fleet in the best possible condition for such an encounter. Operations against a tempting target such as Cattaro were also excluded, primarily because of a lack of support from the Italian army. Presumably, Cadorna jealously guarded all his strength for what he hoped would be the decisive push north-eastwards over the Italian frontier towards Trieste and refused to disperse men and material on what were to him secondary objectives. In this situation the Italian and French navies had similar experiences. Cattaro would be spared for the entire war, less because of its inherent strength, than because there always seemed more important or more profitable areas to employ the Allied armies, to which might be added political reasons – Italian jealousy towards others operating in the Adriatic.

In these early plans it is also clear that Revel and the Italian Naval Staff expected most of their fleet to eventually move to the upper Adriatic to support the advance of the Italian army. This, after the experience of several months of the world war, is probably the most questionable feature of the

Italian plans. After the *Jean Bart* had been torpedoed, the French were very chary of venturing into the relatively restricted waters of the Adriatic in the presence of submarines, however limited in number. The Italian plan had also made only a passing reference to possible Allies, followed by the automatic assumption that Allied ships would come under Italian command in the Adriatic. This subject, along with the Italian intention to move the fleet into the upper Adriatic, would cause considerable discussion and controversy when the Italians entered into the hard bargaining which accompanied their entrance into the war.

The assistance which the Italian army was ready to provide the navy for any possible base on enemy territory was very limited. It consisted of 65 officers and 1,080 men of the 149th Infantry of Mobile Militia and 150 artillerymen who would man four 76-mm landing guns to be furnished by the navy. Revel reported to Abruzzi on 20 April that the guns were at Venice and that the navy was in the process of acquiring mules to transport them. He suggested that the material be sent to Brindisi and authorized Abruzzi to use the force as he saw fit for the defence of future bases, notably Sabbioncello.[13] The seizure of 'Base Rossa' was, however, becoming more and more hypothetical. Abruzzi would have had to be firmly committed to the project, which he does not appear to have been, to continue in the face of the very discouraging remarks he received from Revel and the Naval Staff, and the scant support from the army.

Cattaro and operations on Mount Lovčen were another and more serious matter and the navy did not give up on its proposals. In March, Abruzzi had proposed sending 305-mm howitzers to Mount Lovčen, but in anticipation that these would not be ready in time he suggested using 280-mm howitzers with smokeless powder drawn from the fortifications on the island of Maddalena in the Tyrrhenian. With France an ally instead of enemy, these were hardly likely to be needed. Revel wrote to Cadorna on 25 April that the attack on Cattaro had been omitted in the naval war plans largely because the heavy artillery that would be necessary would not be available, but as the present period of waiting before they actually entered the war might be rather prolonged it was possible that this situation would change. He suggested to Cadorna that they ought to undertake a serious detailed study of such an operation and determine whether or not the army could detach the necessary troops without harm to its other operations. The investment of Cattaro would not be a decisive action for resolving the war, but it might induce the Austrian fleet to come south and provide the Regia Marina with the excellent opportunity for a decisive battle in waters favourable to themselves. If the Austrian fleet continued to avoid battle, their inaction would cause a serious loss of morale. Cattaro might also be a suitable objective in a second phase of operations, after the first phase had gone well for the Italians. The capture of Cattaro by a predominantly Italian force would also have the political advantage of sustaining the Italian point of view in peace negotiations on the future of the eastern shores of the Adriatic.[14]

Cadorna was almost totally lacking in sympathy. The Italian navy and army already had an agreement to initially send four 280-mm howitzers to

Montenegro to bombard the coastal forts of Radišević and Traste, which would permit Italian ships to close the coast and destroy enemy ships sheltering in the Bay of Teodo (part of the Gulf of Cattaro). In this case, the support of the army would be limited solely to providing the personnel to man the guns and their protection would have to be assured by the Montenegrin army, as the latter had already done for the French batteries on Mount Lovčen a few months before. Revel was, however, now speaking about an investment of the entire base of Cattaro, and Cadorna did not need any detailed studies to affirm *a priori* that this operation would require troops and material to such a degree as to constitute a grave and damaging dispersion of forces. Given the difficult task of the army along the extensive land front, the detachment from the principal theatre of operations of a force this size for a secondary objective such as Cattaro would constitute an error. A regular siege of Cattaro could not be undertaken unless the military situation was radically different from what it was at the present, and the army's support must therefore be limited to the men necessary to serve the four howitzers. Cadorna was ready to provide this small force whenever Revel wanted.[15] Revel naturally had no option but to accept Cadorna's judgement that action on the land front of Cattaro must be restricted to the four 280-mm howitzers. His more extensive measures would have been more effective, and he still hoped that they might be obtainable in the second phase of operations when the military and naval situation was sufficiently clarified.[16] The best, however, that Cadorna would offer would be to study the operation at a suitable time in the future based on their own and the enemy's strength. In the meantime the four 280-mm howitzers would be sent to Brindisi with the artillerymen to arrive on the tenth day of mobilization. The howitzers were eventually used on the island of Pedagne for the defence of Brindisi.[17]

After the abandonment of any prospect of an immediate investment of Cattaro, Abruzzi considered the occupation of Sabbioncello superfluous and preferred to establish the fleet's base at Brindisi where the watch over the Straits of Otranto could be more easily assured, and from which the fleet could eventually advance to the north without any restrictive obligation to support an exposed base. During the first phase of operations in the lower Adriatic the fleet, based on Brindisi, would undertake all operations that circumstances allowed to induce the Austrian fleet to leave its shelter and come southwards to give battle. The second phase of operations, involving the advance of the fleet to the north, was a difficult operation and implied the probable loss of some units which would perhaps leave them in a position of inferiority in regard to the enemy. The Naval Staff had apparently mentioned the Bay of Pirano on the Istrian Peninsula as a possible base. Abruzzi considered it too dangerous because of the difficulties inherent in establishing and maintaining it without command of the surrounding heights. Venice would have to be ready to receive the fleet if it was ever compelled to move north.[18]

The Anglo-French-Italian Naval Convention of 1915

The discussions of Italian actions in the event of war with Austria were, by this time, no longer a merely hypothetical question. On 26 April after long and difficult bargaining, particularly over Italian claims in the Adriatic, the Treaty of London was signed providing for Italy's entrance into the war. The Germans had made a considerable effort to keep Italy neutral and had prodded their Austrian ally into offering concessions, but the Entente had the inherent advantage of offering enemy rather than allied territory and could always outbid their enemies.[19]

In Article III of the Treaty of London the Allies had agreed: 'The Fleets of France and Great Britain will give their active and permanent assistance to Italy until the destruction of the Austro-Hungarian Fleet or until the conclusion of peace.'[20] The details of this co-operation were settled by a naval convention drafted in Paris where the first plenary session of naval and military delegates took place on the morning of 2 May.[21] Italian requirements were likely to be high. Almost a month before the Treaty of London had been signed, Revel told Prime Minister Antonio Salandra what Italy's minimum terms ought to be. Owing to the relative strength of the Austrian and Italian fleets and the advantages that the Austrians derived from the geographical configuration of the eastern shore of the Adriatic, Allied assistance to Italy would have to be at least twenty-four modern destroyers and six battleships armed with 30.5-cm (12-in.) cannon, and a speed of not less than 17 knots.[22] These figures were also given in the directives Revel sent to Capitano di vascello Mario Grassi, the Italian naval delegate in Paris for the forthcoming discussions. They were, however, the maximum for the opening of discussions; the minimum which Revel felt they could not compromise was underlined in red. Revel had hoped for six battleships, some of which might possibly be of the dreadnought type. His minimum, however, was four, two of which were to be dreadnoughts and two Dantons or Lord Nelsons. He preferred the twenty-four destroyers to be coal-burning with a speed of not less than 30 knots, and at least some of the destroyers to be armed with cannon superior to 76 mm. He would settle if twelve of the twenty-four did not have the desired characteristics. If the Italians could not get all the twenty-four destroyers at once, he would settle for twelve, and instead of the remaining twelve he would ask for three scouts or light cruisers, of necessity British since the French did not have any of this class. The Italians insisted that the Allies should keep up these numbers by replacing ships which were lost, or provide substitutes for units which would be under repair for more than ten days. Revel was willing to make concessions here, notably along the line that replacements should be compatible with the successful prosecution of the Dardanelles campaign. Revel claimed that operations in the upper Ionian and all of the Adriatic would be directed by the C.-in-C. of the Italian fleet.[23]

The Adriatic was a major headache for Lapeyrère now that the threat of submarines made the French blockade a rather distant one, enforced by armoured cruisers patrolling a line along the parallel of Paxo (north of

Corfu), accompanied by destroyers whenever the winter weather permitted. French submarines, based on Navarino and towed up to Fano before they were cast loose, struggled against the weather and managed only two days of blockade off Cattaro for every six days they were absent. The results were meagre and in the first four months of 1915 the French submarines appeared in the Adriatic an average of only one day out of four.[24]

The necessity of supplying Montenegro was also a heavy burden which exposed Lapeyrère's fleet to serious risk of loss, or so he assumed, when cruisers were used to convoy supply ships to Antivari. Lapeyrère actually wanted to use neutral shipping for the job, loading the ships in the Ionian Islands and sailing to the Albanian port of San Giovanni di Medua. The cargoes would then be transferred overland to shallow draught vessels on the Bojana River, and carried up stream to lighters for the trip across Lake Scutari to Montenegro. He entered into negotiations with an Italian entrepreneur named Di Chiara to effect the transport, but there were numerous difficulties caused by the hostility of the Albanians and the abominable state of roads on the Albanian–Montenegrin frontier. Peter Plamenatz, the Montenegrin Minister of Foreign Affairs, feared that Di Chiara would not be able to furnish more than 1,500 tons of grain per month while Montenegro required 3,000 tons. Lapeyrère was exasperated with the Montenegrins for he felt that they had done nearly nothing up until then to assist the French and he regarded it as increasingly imprudent to risk warships to guarantee a supply that could be assured by another route than Antivari.[25] The Russian and Serbian governments supported the Montenegrin demands and some shipments continued to go via Antivari. Di Chiara experienced financial difficulties purchasing a ship, which subsequently sank on its first voyage, while the French Ministry of Foreign Affairs refused to pay for any of the expenses. Shipments to Montenegro continued through various routes and on the evening of 24 February the destroyer *Dague* was mined and sunk off Antivari, the first French warship to be lost in the Adriatic. The Austrian navy raided Antivari on 1 March, while Austrian aircraft periodically bombed the port making it dangerous for shipping. By the end of March, Di Chiara's small Italian steamers were in service carrying supplies to San Giovanni di Medua, while other supplies were carried to Salonika and transported by rail to Ipek in Serbia, and then overland to Montenegro.[26]

Lapeyrère was really worried by the potential of Austrian submarine activity. He had already been forced to move the line of patrol from Fano–Santa Maria di Leuca further south to the parallel of Paxo in order to put his large armoured cruisers out of range of submarines. French surveillance therefore became less effective, although Lapeyrère still did not consider the cruisers secure and anticipated moving the blockade line even further to the south. He could not use his own torpedo craft to patrol the Straits of Otranto, for seven months of war had only corroborated his opinion that they were incapable of sustained service. To keep some of them in good condition he had refrained from employing them on a continuous blockade, which would have ended by putting them all out of service. He therefore asked for a certain number of passenger liners or auxiliary cruisers, which he could use with his own cruisers on a line moved further to the south where they would be out of reach of submarines.[27]

The continued reports concerning Austrian submarines, particularly information that German officers were taking over the direction of their operations in the Adriatic and Mediterranean – an exaggeration, of course, but indicative of growing German involvement – alarmed Lapeyrère, who was worried over the vulnerability of his large cruisers in the approaches to Navarino Bay where they coaled and took on supplies. He assumed these activities were well known to Austrian intelligence. Lapeyrère therefore moved their base of supply temporarily to Malta, but realized that this more distant base meant that he could not keep more than three large cruisers on the patrol line. Given the distance to be covered, this number was insufficient. He therefore repeated his request for more cruisers or auxiliary cruisers and warned that without them the blockade of the Adriatic by the French fleet was a net with an excessively large mesh and could not provide security against Austrian ships slipping into the Ionian unobserved.[28]

Lapeyrère's worst fears in regard to submarines came true on the night of 26–27 April when the armoured cruiser *Léon Gambetta* was torpedoed and sunk approximately fifteen miles south of Cape Santa Maria di Leuca by the Austrian submarine U5, commanded by Linienschiffsleutnant Ritter von Trapp, who would become the leading Austrian submarine ace of the war. Out of 821 officers and men aboard, 684 were lost including Rear-Admiral Sénès, commander of the 2ème Division légère. Lapeyrère had ordered a special watch on that area in anticipation of Austrian activity as a result of the negotiations with Italy, and the French patrol had been moved back to the north.[29] He was convinced that a series of clear, calm nights had induced the enemy submarines to operate outside their usual waters in the Adriatic, but immediately changed his dispositions. French cruisers would be kept south of the parallel of Géroghambo (Cephalonia), except for indispensable raids at high speed up to the entrance of, or even into, the Adriatic. He did not consider the base that the French submarines were using at Navarino to be secure any longer and, lacking ships to protect it, he moved the submarines back to Malta. The French torpedo-boats would also receive a new base, and when good weather permitted refuelling them at sea from battleships, the latter were to avoid showing themselves off the Peloponnesian coast or in the Ionian Islands.[30]

When Lapeyrère learned that German submarines had apparently entered the Mediterranean he again changed his dispositions. Malta was very busy with transports going to and from the Dardanelles and the large French cruisers wound up having to coal at Bizerte. The big cruisers would leave Bizerte separated by an interval of two days and would meet an *escadrille* of destroyers coming from Malta at a different rendezvous each time. The group would patrol for two days at a speed of at least 14 knots up to the vicinity of Navarino, where a collier and tanker had been left to ·resupply the destroyers. The group would then retrace its route with the destroyers peeling off for Malta and the cruisers returning to Bizerte.[31] This can hardly be considered an effective blockade of the Straits of Otranto and, under these circumstances, Italian intervention should have provided welcome relief to the French, if only for the secure bases closer to the action that it ought to provide.

By the time the Treaty of London had been signed and the naval representatives had met in Paris, the British and French armies had landed at the Dardanelles. The landing took place on 25 April and resulted in the Allies establishing at great cost a beach-head on the Gallipoli Peninsula.[32] While Turkish counterattacks and attempts to throw them into the sea failed, the British and French for their part did not succeed in breaking through to the commanding height of Achi Baba, and within a few weeks the situation on the Gallipoli Peninsula had turned into a stalemate similar to that on the western front. If it was not the disaster that some had feared might adversely affect Italy's decision to enter the war, it was also not the smashing success its supporters had predicted. The Dardanelles campaign also saddled the Royal Navy (and to a much smaller degree the French) with the major responsibility of supplying a sizeable army over open beaches. Moreover, by early May there was always in the background the shadow of an impending arrival of German or Austrian submarines in the eastern Mediterranean.

The negotiations in Paris for a naval convention to complement the Treaty of London proved to be unexpectedly difficult and seemed to foreshadow, if they did not actually set, the tone for Italy's naval relations with its allies for the remainder of the war.[33] The British and French objected to Italian plans to operate with large ships in the northern Adriatic which would expose them to submarine attacks from Pola in relatively restricted waters. The question of command was, not surprisingly, the most difficult. The Italians refused to consider any operations in the Adriatic which were not commanded by an Italian admiral, while the French would not consider placing the French fleet, superior in strength to the Italians, under an Italian admiral. Captain Grassi, the Italian delegate, may have been willing to bend slightly before the pressure of the Allied proposals and their sharp critique of Italian plans, but at home the redoubtable Thaon di Revel intervened with Baron Sonnino, Minister of Foreign Affairs, with the warning that Italy faced the danger of being left to bear the brunt of battle in the northern Adriatic without Allied assistance, and that it would be better not to conclude any convention. Sonnino was sufficiently alarmed to cable his representative in Paris that unless the French changed their line the entire Treaty of London might be invalidated.[34] Revel also warned the Duke of the Abruzzi about the difficulties they were encountering in Paris and stated that the proposal, if the Italian fleet went north, to form a second Allied fleet in the lower Adriatic under the French C.-in-C., ready to reply to the appeal of the Italian C.-in-C., was ambiguous and contrary to the unity of command so necessary for the successful prosecution of maritime operations. So far, it did not appear likely that the Italian battle fleet would be reinforced; consequently, even given the most favourable hypothesis that the Italians would annihilate the Austrian fleet, they would suffer grave losses and remain practically without a fleet while their interests in the Mediterranean would be severely compromised for some years. The French would be the first to profit from this state of affairs.[35]

Churchill arrived in Paris on 5 May and lobbied for some of his pet proposals at the session on the 6th. These included a strong argument for the capture of Sabbioncello, but he aroused little enthusiasm on the part of the French or other delegates, and the First Lord left Paris with the discussions at an apparent impasse over the subject of command. The Italians also met privately with the British who could afford to be somewhat more accommodating on the subject since they had no claim to command themselves. The Italians proposed that the British battleship contribution, originally to be under Lapeyrère's command, be placed instead directly under the Italian C.-in-C. The British were willing, once the Dardanelles operations were terminated, but since this qualification also posed problems because of its uncertainty, they suggested as a compromise that the designated British warships at the Dardanelles would leave for the Adriatic as soon as they had been replaced by an equal number of French warships. The impasse was broken and the naval convention was concluded with the final signature, that of Italy, on 10 May.[36]

The Anglo-French-Italian Naval Convention of 10 May 1915 consisted of seven articles and a codicil of eight points providing specific details of its execution.[37] It was essentially a compromise and there was a certain ambiguity to it which would haunt the Allies later in the war. The most important features included (Article II) the establishment under the command of the C.-in-C. of the Italian fleet of a First Allied Fleet. This would consist of: most of the Italian fleet and twelve French destroyers, to be joined by as many torpedo-boats, submarines and minesweepers as the French C.-in-C. could detach; if possible, a squadron of aircraft and a French seaplane carrier; four British light cruisers, to arrive as soon as they were replaced by four French cruisers at the Dardanelles; and a division of four British battleships. The C.-in-C. of the Italian fleet (Article III) would have the initiative and complete direction of operations executed in the Adriatic by this First Allied Fleet. If the First Allied Fleet had to move to the north of the Adriatic (Article IV) for any important operation which would appear to necessitate the intervention of the whole of the Allied forces, a Second Allied Fleet would be formed of French battleships and cruisers, and those Italian or British ships not already allotted to the Italian C.-in-C. This Second Allied Fleet, accompanied by its flotilla craft and placed under the command of the C.-in-C. of the French fleet, would be ready to reply to the appeal of the C.-in-C. of the Italian fleet. All bases on the Italian coast would be at the disposition of the Allies (Article V), but while the First Allied Fleet had Brindisi as a base, the Second Allied Fleet would use, preferably, Taranto, Malta and Bizerte. If the First Allied Fleet went north and took Venice as its base, Brindisi as well as Taranto would be at the disposition of the Second Allied Fleet. As long as enemy naval forces were in the Adriatic (Article VI), the Allies bound themselves to assure their support to the Italian fleet so as to maintain, as much as possible, Allied naval power clearly superior to the enemy.

The specific details in the codicil included: provision for six of the twelve French destroyers to be oil-burning and six coal-burning, and that the former should, as far as possible, have a displacement greater than 600 tons; the number of French submarines at the disposal of the Italian C.-in-C. would be at least six; the number of French cruisers at the Dardanelles would be brought to four as quickly as possible, and each French arrival would release a British cruiser for the Italian fleet; the number of French battleships at the Dardanelles would be brought as quickly as possible to six, and four British battleships with 12-in. cannon would leave the Dardanelles for Italy as soon as they had been replaced by the French. The major and deliberately unanswered question was who would command should the Second Allied Fleet, really the French battle squadrons, have to operate inside the Adriatic, for it was inconceivable to the French that their C.-in-C., who was after all Mediterranean C.-in-C. as well, would fall under Italian orders. This point would come back to plague the Allies whenever there was any prospect that the French would actually have to help the Italians.

Revel was not really satisfied with the convention and very annoyed at the Italian ambassador in Paris, Tommaso Tittoni, for authorizing its signature before his final approval. He was particularly alarmed over the provision that the British battleships and light cruisers that had been promised would not leave until they had been replaced at the Dardanelles by equivalent French units. He feared that this meant they would not arrive until after the outbreak of hostilities.[38] He was equally concerned, however, about a report from Tittoni that a large French squadron was ready to proceed to Taranto, for this would lead to excessive overcrowding and he preferred the situation outlined in the convention – the Allied squadron would arrive in Taranto only after the Italian fleet went north. Revel had more in mind than merely quibbling over details. In fact he admitted that while the terms of the convention and the criteria of the Italian government did not correspond exactly, the differences involved secondary questions which would not have a notable influence on the course of the campaign. It would suffice for the Italians to adopt a prudent temporizing conduct and give up any action beyond the parallel of Gargano until they were properly reinforced.[39] What really bothered Revel was his suspicion that the efficiency of the British and French fleets was actually less than one might expect. This seemed to have been demonstrated by the fact that the British could only send four battleships from the Dardanelles after they had been replaced by the French, and the British and French delegates in Paris had allegedly remarked to Captain Grassi that they were giving the Italians all they could. The Dardanelles campaign was far from over and other, and perhaps considerable, Allied losses might be expected before they succeeded in forcing the Straits. Revel did not see in what way France and Britain would be able to satisfy their obligation under Article III of the political convention to provide active and permanent support up to the destruction of the Austrian fleet or the conclusion of peace. He suggested that British and French losses had been even higher than officially announced, especially in the all-important light craft and torpedo-boats, and ten months of hard wartime activity had certainly notably diminished the efficiency of machinery and boilers. Revel concluded a memorandum to Sonnino with what amounted to a plea for continued neutrality. He admitted that he did not know if the political convention (that is, the Treaty of London) with the Allies specifically obligated Italy to take up arms. If it did, his arguments had no value; but if it did not, before deciding to do so it would be well to consider the possible consequences of the state of things he had just described.[40] Revel also wrote to Sonnino's secretary that if the Allies could not offer the very little that Italy was asking it would be proof that they were reduced to a bad way at sea and have 'more need of us than we of them'.[41] Thaon di Revel, one of the few naval leaders to play as large a role at the end of the war as he did at the beginning, evidently had serious reservations about his Allies even before Italy came into the war. He would not lose these reservations during the next few years.

The Italian government was, however, moving towards fulfilment of its obligation under the Treaty of London, and on May 14 Revel warned Abruzzi that the decision on war with Austria was close and would be taken at the latest by the 20th when Parliament met. As the Austrians might take the initiative, it was necessary that the fleet should complete its initial deployment by the 19th.[42] Abruzzi had already suggested that if the intervention of the fleet was indispensable in the northern Adriatic it would be preferable to complete the deployment to Venice *before* the opening of hostilities, leaving an adequate force at Brindisi. Revel replied that the move to the north was not indispensable, the government fully recognized its risks, and no specific obligation to do so existed between the navy and the Chief of the Army General Staff.[43]

Revel left the final choice of where to deploy the battle fleet to Abruzzi. It could be Brindisi or Taranto, but the Capo di Stato Maggiore warned that an Austrian submarine had been spotted a little more than ten miles southeast of Cape Santa Maria di Leuca, and a large German submarine was probably in the Mediterranean too. On the declaration of war, they could therefore anticipate that enemy submarines would be on the likely route between Taranto and Brindisi. Revel therefore considered it indispensable that in the days immediately following the opening of hostilities, the large Italian warships should not move out of their bases for any motive whatsoever, and Italian action at sea should be limited exclusively to torpedo-boats and light craft.[44]

Given Revel's line of thought, the general criteria he gave to the Italian C.-in-C. provide few surprises. Granted the absolute necessity of avoiding exposure to Austrian and German submarines whose threat was steadily increasing, and the desirability of waiting for Allied assistance to arrive, an essentially defensive character would be imposed on Italian operations in the Adriatic until the situation was clarified, especially with regard to the efficiency of enemy submarines and their mode of use.[45] In Revel's opinion, during the first phase of operations the essential objective was to defend Brindisi and from this base scour the sea with patrols, reconnaissances and undertake small surprise actions on the enemy coast. The Italian navy should, at the same time, destroy whenever the opportunity presented itself, and even at the cost of equivalent or even greater losses, enemy light craft, torpedo-boats and, above all, submarines. The best of the large warships, the Division of the *Dante*, Elenas, Pisas and Brins, should be saved and held ready for battle with the Austrian fleet if, and whenever, the opportunity came for it, and it was essential that they were not exposed in secondary operations. Revel also disagreed with Abruzzi's decision to initially deploy the best ships at Taranto. Although he realized that the government had left the decision up to Abruzzi, his personal opinion was that they should be at Brindisi where underwater defences were now sufficient, and where the bulk of the enemy fleet might come down from Pola and attack in force before the Italian fleet could arrive from Taranto. Austrian feints down the Dalmatian coast would also force repeated deployment of the Italian fleet to Brindisi and, if co-ordinated with submarine activity, would expose the Italian fleet to attack off Cape Santa Maria di Leuca.

Revel was obviously defensively minded, but it is important to note that this applied only to large ships. For light craft – destroyers and torpedo-boats – the Chief of Naval Staff was aggressive and showed a willingness to take risks and accept losses. He was also determined not to be caught napping and informed the Minister of Marine that in international law the declaration of war was a pure formality, and added a list of recent examples where hostilities proceeded any formal declaration.[46] Revel was also worried by press reports that German and Austrian merchant ships in Italian ports were getting ready for sea. There were many among them which might be turned into good auxiliary cruisers and their departure had to be prevented. He proposed an immediate embargo on the ships as a simple police measure, with special precautions to secure the vessels before their crews could scuttle them. Revel even suggested that they might avoid possible conflict through the ruse of having Italian port authorities invite the captains or part of the crews ashore on the pretext that they desired to speak with them and then seize the ships. Revel, in addition to using normal channels with the Minister of Marine, apparently tried to appeal directly to the Prime Minister. He was firmly rebuffed. Salandra told him that this was a matter for the Minister of Marine and that he himself had no part in the commencement of operations and could not meddle in them. The opportune agreements should be made verbally between the two Chiefs of Staff or their representatives. Salandra cautioned, however, that no operation could be undertaken without the Minister of Foreign Affairs certifying that war had been declared and the observance of this condition was to be absolute.[47]

The Italian navy may have been anxious to obtain assistance from the French and British, but Revel saw no need to conclude any war plans in advance with them. He justified this attitude by Article III of the Naval Convention, which left the full direction of operations of the First Allied Fleet and Allied units attached to it to the C.-in-C. of the Italian fleet. The preparation of a common plan of war with the Allies, or more precisely with the French C.-in-C., appeared to be necessary only when the Second Allied Fleet had to act in accord with the First Allied Fleet under the Duke of the Abruzzi. This would occur only when the First Fleet moved to the northern Adriatic, but this was likely to be far in the future when different and unforeseen circumstances would require radical modifications to any plan that was drawn up now.[48] Once again the Italians were sidestepping the tricky question of command. Abruzzi naturally agreed and his war plans covered only the first phase of operations in the south with the objective of obtaining mastery of the Adriatic up to the parallel of Spalato.[49]

Abruzzi envisaged three successive and distinct phases for his operations aimed at gaining command of the Adriatic in the first period of hostilities. The first phase would be the relentless sweep of the lower and mid-Adriatic by all torpedo-boats and light craft which would have no other duties except to seek and destroy enemy submarines and torpedo-boats. Once the lower Adriatic was relatively clear, the Italians would proceed to the second phase, the destruction of bases for enemy light craft. This would deprive the enemy of his bases of support and little by little confine him to a fixed locality. The Italians would proceed from this to gradual conquest of mastery of the sea. In this second phase it would be possible to use some cruisers of the Pisani or Garibaldi class as well as auxiliary cruisers. These larger ships would have been too exposed to submarines in the first phase. The chief objectives in the second phase should be: the destruction of torpedo-boat bases at Ragusa, Gravosa and possibly Spalato; the dismantling of lookout stations in the lower Dalmatian archipelago; cutting submarine cables; and the occupation of some small islands to establish advanced observation posts. Should it be desirable for reasons of a political nature to obtain some tangible result, however transitory, Abruzzi intended to proceed to a third phase of operations which aimed, above all, at provoking the enemy fleet and attracting it to the south. They would therefore occupy some island in the lower Dalmatian archipelago, such as Lagosta or Lissa, which would also be of value from the point of view of morale in counterbalancing possible enemy actions on their own coast. The Italians might then proceed to the occupation of some major islands, such as Curzola or Meleda, to once again tempt the enemy fleet to rush to the rescue and accept battle. Such occupations would have an essentially 'flying' or transitory character, and if they were not opposed by the enemy would raise morale in Italy and put the Italians in contact with the population of Dalmatia, whom they would try to incite to rebel in Italy's favour. The enemy could only oppose these actions by sending ships southwards which would give the Italians the opportunity to destroy them. The method and detail of the second period of the war – the advance to the north – would depend on the outcome of the first three phases and also the speed with which operations on land developed.[50]

These, then, were the plans with which the Italians entered the First World War. They would not proceed very far towards their objectives, if only because the realities of war belied the assumptions about 'cleaning' the seas. Submarines were, after all, a form of 'dirt' which could appear and disappear at will and easily evade the broom. The Austrians also failed to oblige by sending their precious battle fleet into southern waters where the situation was favourable to the Italians.

The k.u.k. Kriegsmarine and the Dardanelles

While the Italians moved steadily towards war in April and May of 1915, the k.u.k. Kriegsmarine came under renewed German pressure to play a more active role. Graf Tschirschky, the German ambassador in Vienna, appeared to be the instigator and told the former Austrian Minister-President Baron von Beck that 'the inactivity of the k.u.k. Fleet would weigh heavily in the final settlement of accounts', and in Germany they could not understand why, with so many French units tied to the Dardanelles, the Austrians did not use the opportunity to attack the French at the entrance to the Adriatic, or at least strongly harass them.[51] Beck considered it his duty to bring these remarks to Haus's attention and he repeated them to Rear-Admiral Kailer, the Marinekommandant's representative at the Marinesektion in Vienna, on the afternoon of 24 March. It was against Kailer's taste to burden Haus with remarks of this sort, but Beck had assumed that the German ambassador must have had the authorization of his government to make them. There is the possibility that Tschirschky was expressing not only the opinion prevalent in German headquarters but even that of the Kaiser himself.[52] There were also high-ranking Austrian officials, such as Graf Burián the Foreign Minister, who desperately wanted some success to offset in the eyes of the Italians the recent loss to the Russians of Premsyl in Galicia. Burián sent a secret letter to the Foreign Office representative at AOK asking him to try and interest Archduke Friedrich and Conrad in pushing the navy towards a more active policy, and also to take advantage of the recent Allied setback at the Dardanelles. Burián argued that an Austrian defeat of the French would certainly affect Italy and it was no use saving the fleet for a war against the latter. The Italians would not attack alone but in company with the French, and once the Dardanelles campaign ended, whether in success or failure, a large portion of the British and French forces in the Mediterranean would be freed to turn against the Austrians.[53]

These charges apparently provoked Haus into writing a long defence and explanation of his policy to Baron Beck. Reprinted in full in the semi-official Austrian naval history, it is the best known and classic explanation of Austrian naval strategy for much of the war.[54] Haus repeated his earlier arguments about the limited achievements of the French in the Adriatic and how their blockade line had been forced still further southwards since last Christmas to a point where Austrian torpedo-boats and submarines could not reach them in their bases. The French contented themselves with fulfilling their major task, preventing the Austrians from breaking out of the Adriatic, while Austrian shipping within the Adriatic was almost entirely undisturbed.

Since neither the one nor the other fleet had a goal achievable with their strength and important enough to gamble their existence on, or in other words a battle between them would *decide* no vital question for their states, that strategy of patient waiting is the sole rational one. In return though, the reproach of inactivity must fall on them both. The Dardanelles operation had not altered the situation since Lapeyrère had nothing to do with it, the landings were British and the few French ships participating played a secondary role. None of the French ships reported at the Dardanelles came from the Adriatic and it was unlikely any would be detached from the Adriatic to strengthen the Dardanelles. Austrian submarines, of which they had only two then ready for action, had made raids as far as they could into waters where enemy ships were suspected without finding any (this was written before the sinking of the *Léon Gambetta*) and the same was true for the torpedo-boat flotillas. Moreover, the torpedo-boats could not sail from Cattaro by day without being reported by the French observation post on Mount Lovčen, and if they sailed by night they had no hope of reaching the at least 180-mile distant foe, assuming they knew where he was, during darkness. A flotilla sailing unobserved from Sebenico with full bunkers had over 300 miles to steam, and they had few torpedo-boats whose radius of action and speed under very favourable conditions made an attack at this distance appear reasonable, especially when it remained a matter of luck to find the enemy. Moreover, the British and French admirals at the Dardanelles were in no way influenced if Lapeyrère was disturbed in the Ionian by submarines by day, or torpedo-boats at night. Even if the Austrian fleet succeeded in destroying all the French battleships in the Adriatic, the situation at the Dardanelles would not be altered. Should the Austrian fleet come out of such a battle entirely undamaged, they still could not think of attacking approximately 1,000 miles from their base a British and French fleet at the Dardanelles that was twice as strong.

Lapeyrère's fleet, even with the *Jean Bart* still in dock, was superior to the Austrians in tonnage and heavy calibre guns, and it would still be superior if two Courbets or five Dantons, or one Danton and five Patries were removed from it. Lapeyrère was four times stronger in armoured cruisers, twice as strong in torpedo-boat flotillas, and had an enormous superiority in submarines which could only come into action on the side of the French if the Austrians attacked more than 400–500 miles from their base. Haus wrote:

> To attack a superior fleet under these circumstances, when one does not know where to find it and how large their superiority is, is an unreasonable demand which I can only account for through the confusion war has brought to minds, to whom, as Bismarck said, the measure of things is completely missing.

Haus complained: 'It is difficult to make clear to many men that in many cases not to do anything is the only correct thing.' No one admired the spunk of the German fleet more than he did, explained Haus, but the much smaller k.u.k. fleet could not completely follow their example and had not as much to lose and could not risk as much. His impression of the activity of the German fleet after eight months of war was that all cruisers at large and active in three oceans at the beginning of the war had been destroyed. They had caused enormous losses to the British, but these German successes were for Britain only a 'pinprick' without any meaning for the outcome of the war. The German sorties into the North Sea had led to considerable losses in armoured and light cruisers as well as torpedo-boats, without any special success to set against it. All major actions during the war – Coronel, Falkland Islands, Heligoland – had, without exception, resulted in the defeat of the materially weaker squadron, and defeat was equivalent to destruction each time that squadron was far from its base. On the other hand, the German submarines had succeeded beyond all expectations. Within the radius of their action they had become the masters of the sea with one blow, and had given an entirely new stamp to naval strategy. The conspicuous inactivity of all battle fleets in waters where submarines are met leads directly back to these 'pests'. Haus concluded that if one can draw lessons from this, it is certainly not that the k.u.k. fleet, which is much weaker, should increase the activity of its battleships and cruisers. Haus repeatedly referred to an 'eminent German' diplomat in his rebuttal, although he obviously knew it was Tschirschky who had instigated Beck and must have suspected that there were other highly placed Germans, perhaps even the 'all highest' himself, behind him.

Haus and the Marinesektion not surprisingly considered the letter important enough for copies to be sent to General Bolfras, head of the Kaiser's Military Chancellery, Foreign Minister Burián, Rear-Admiral Raisp, the navy's representative at AOK, and the Austrian naval attaché in Berlin.[55] Haus's letter was timely, for along with the copy sent to Bolfras there was a copy of another of those prodding messages from the Germans. This time it was from Admiral Bachmann, Chief of the Admiralstab. Reconnaissance revealed that the British and French were apparently concentrating more ships for an attempt at forcing the Straits. Falkenhayn, the Chief of the German Army General Staff, therefore intended to direct a proposal to AOK that the k.u.k. fleet should undertake a sortie at least up to the southern boundary of the Adriatic for the relief of the Dardanelles. Bachmann supported the proposal since he thought this disturbance of the enemy promised to be successful in diverting enemy ships from their goal.[56] Haus's long letter to Beck was effective in offsetting this German pressure. General Bolfras reported that after reading it, Kaiser Franz Joseph had expressed the fullest confidence in Haus's energetic leadership of the fleet.[57] This was perhaps only to be expected, for the old emperor had never had much feeling for the navy and indeed had once admitted that he had little more competence in naval affairs than sailing boats in the pond with his grandson. His experiences during his long reign would hardly have inclined him towards a reckless gamble with the fleet.

Haus also had the full support of Archduke Friedrich, titular head of AOK. The Archduke agreed with Haus's arguments and expressed satisfaction with the firmness with which he had refuted the unreasonable demands of the German diplomat. However, he objected strongly to Haus having discussed possible courses of action for the fleet with Baron Beck, 'a private person and a layman', who had no right to discuss operative questions with the Flottenkommandant who was under AOK. The 'eminent German diplomat' should also have taken the 'loyal way' and gone to the Minister of Foreign Affairs, who would then turn to AOK for proper orientation. Archduke Friedrich ordered Haus to flatly refuse similar requests in the future.[58]

Korvettenkapitän Colloredo-Mannsfeld, the Austrian naval attaché in Berlin, for his part, reported that the 'opinions of the eminent German diplomat' were unknown to him and that in German naval circles there now appeared to be a fair understanding of Austria's situation and standpoint, especially after German experiences and expectations for the sea war had been very considerably scaled down, as was evident, for example, in the great hopes once expressed for the *Goeben*. He was, however, conscious of a tendency in Germany to blame Austria for the slow progress of the war and the recent requests by Falkenhayn and Bachmann for an Austrian sortie were further proof that leading German circles in certain matters lacked any understanding of Austria's position or interests, were indifferent to Austria's sacrifices and losses when they thought they could profit from them, and were, in this respect, 'thoroughly unscrupulous'.[59]

Baron Beck, the recipient of the original of Haus's letter, thanked the Flottenkommandant not only for the information but for putting him in a position to correct unjustified critics of whom there were always enough in Vienna. The former Minister-President recognized that Haus's self-denying and reserved strategy was not likely to gain the praise that a 'hurrah' action would. The German ambassador's remark had been made in a private conversation and Beck did not find in it any trace of a reproach or threat.[60]

Freyberg, the German naval attaché, had a full report from the ambassador and thought that the most interesting and striking point was that the word 'Italian' did not once appear, but knowing the views of local naval circles one could read between the lines of the conclusion. The general tone of Haus's letter seemed only to confirm the defensive-mindedness and lack of any offensive spirit in leading Austrian circles. Freyberg specifically criticized the Austrians over the fact that the k.u.k. Kriegsmarine knew very well that the French were making themselves at home in bays of the Ionian Islands but were satisfied to leave them in peace, fearing to 'provoke the lion'. He concluded that while this attitude was unfortunately prevalent in leading circles, there were some opponents and k.u.k. admirals who would have been willing to go to the rescue of the *Goeben* and *Breslau* the preceding August with all ships mobilized at the time, and in mid-August would have proceeded to the Dardanelles with, if not the entire fleet, at least the Erzherzog division. These critics would also carry out a keener reconnaissance in the Adriatic and Ionian, and not let the U-boats decay to the point that when they were most necessary only one was ready.[61] The German naval attaché had neither forgotten nor forgiven the events of the preceding summer, but what is most interesting is that he seems to be hinting that he had been talking to critics within the navy. Unfortunately, he was too discreet to name them.

The entire affair of the German ambassador, Baron Beck, and the Haus Memorandum may be nothing more than the proverbial tempest in a teapot, except that from a historian's point of view it provoked a valuable exposition of the Flottenkommandant's strategy, and also revealed the underlying friction in Austro-German relations and the strong German feeling that the Austrians, the weaker partners, were not pulling their weight in the war.

The question of munitions transport to the Turks also remained critical. Souchon was confident right after the Allied attack of 18 March that the forts would hold out and actually hoped that the Allies would come again to suffer similar losses. If they really wanted to succeed they would have to attack immediately and before the damage to telephone communications and earthworks was repaired.[62] Souchon sent the old battleships *Torgud Reis* and *Barbarossa* up to the inside part of the Dardanelles boom so that they could keep the inner portion of the Straits under fire without themselves being seen. They formed a substantial addition to the inner defences and should the enemy press forward, the *Goeben*, out of dock again, could also be sent. They would then have a total of twenty-two 28-cm naval cannon available for the defence. Souchon became so confident, in fact, that by 7 April he could write that the sole chance of conquering the position the Allies had would be to land an army of 200,000 men, and he considered this to be out of the question.[63] All of this confidence, however, presupposed sufficient ammunition. On 28 March the major batteries of the Dardanelles defences reported: 46 shells (8 modern, 38 old) for each of the five 35.5-cm cannon; 62 shells (12 modern, 50 old) for each of the three 24-cm cannon; 120 high-explosive shells for each of the thirty-two 15-cm howitzers; 230 shells (30 armour piercing, 200 practice) for each of the 3 British 15-cm cannon; and 140 shells for each of the five 15-cm Krupp cannon.[64]

Kapitän zur See Rösing, representing the Reichsmarineamt, appeared at the Marinesektion in Vienna along with Freyberg on 23 March and discussed a project by which munitions could be sent to Asia Minor via a Greek steamer whose captain they were trying to win over in Venice. The steamer could be loaded openly with non-contraband merchandise and the ammunition could be taken on later in a Dalmatian bay. The munitions might include ammunition for field guns as well as 15-cm, 24-cm and possibly 35.5-cm shells. However improbable the possibilities of success, it appeared as if the Germans would attempt the transport.[65] Rösing also knew about the proposal to send the Austrian cruiser *Novara*, but thought it best for Souchon to send a German officer directly to Haus. The officer might then accompany *Novara* on her mission, but even Rösing admitted that in present circumstances he did not see where *Novara* might arrive and discharge her munitions.[66] This did not, however, stop Falkenhayn from once again raising the question of using an Austrian cruiser, although his Austrian counterpart, Conrad von Hötzendorf, did not think that such an attempt was promising anymore.[67] Haus had little trouble fending off the request, for Souchon himself had stated that offloading of munitions and taking on coal in Smyrna was impossible, and he did not know of any other harbour on the coast of Asia Minor where this could be accomplished. Furthermore, the chances of success worsened as the nights became longer.[68]

German Submarines Arrive in the Mediterranean

The most promising, and certainly potentially the most important, activity on the part of the Germans was their plan to send submarines to the Mediterranean, either in sections by rail to Pola (UB7 and UB8) or directly by sea. Admiral Bachmann was anxious to get the U-boats in service and on 7 March asked if it might not be faster to take over the Austrian boats (U3 and U4) as soon as possible and make them ready with German experts and man them with German crews. After examination of the question, the Admiralstab and Reichsmarineamt did not agree. The assembly of UB7 and UB8, then *en route* to Pola by rail, would probably begin around 29 March and under favourable circumstances end around 10 April; running-in would take at least a week; the boats would leave Pola around the 20th and arrive in Asia Minor around the 27th or 28th. The Austrian boats U3 and U4 would take longer to make ready and would be less efficient than the German UB boats. Furthermore, the Germans did not have the crews to man them nor the personnel to make them ready. Admiral Behncke of the Admiralstab therefore recommended that the Germans should renounce their use and leave them to the Austrian navy.[69]

The dispatch of a submarine directly by sea to the eastern Mediterranean was, given the distance, a much more difficult task and another conference was held on the subject on 17 March, presided over by Behncke, representing the Chief of the Admiralstab. Kapitänleutnant Hersing, an experienced submarine officer, was also present since his boat U21 appeared the best choice for the mission. The meeting discussed a wide range of technical problems including a possible call at a northern Spanish harbour for refuelling or repair if necessary. Korvettenkapitän Ackermann, another Admiralstab officer, suggested chartering a small steamer in Barcelona which could meet and resupply the submarine in the Balearics. The German naval agent in Madrid had already been ordered to secure fuel and provisions and had left for Barcelona. A Greek harbour would be less favourable as a staging post because of difficult communications and the danger of betrayal. It would be possible to use the coast of Asia Minor, but mail and telegraphic communications in this area were not favourable. Fuel supplies would, however, have to be assembled on the coast of Asia Minor for the return to Pola. The staff decided that if the submarine commander should decide he had insufficient fuel for the entire trip, and if he missed his rendezvous with the auxiliary steamer, he could go to an Italian port, if Italy were still neutral, or failing that, a Spanish harbour, or possibly Cattaro. After surveying available U-boats, the conference decided on U21 and ordered that preparations for the trip should begin immediately.[70]

The Kaiser approved sending U21 to the Mediterranean on 30 March. U21 would go to Bodrum after refuelling in northern Spain. The supply of torpedoes would be a problem in the eastern Mediterranean for those already out there in *Goeben* and *Breslau* were not suitable for U21, although they could be used by the small UB boats. The Admiralstab thought of sending torpedoes to Asia Minor by means of a small steamer flying a

neutral flag and carrying a false cargo. If this were not possible, U21 coul
go to Pola once her torpedoes were expended.[71] The Germans did not full
trust their Turkish allies and Souchon warned the Admiralstab not t
inform them of the movements of the submarine in advance. He claime
from experience that their security was lax, and if the British and Frenc
were forewarned they could hamper operations by hindering the export o
fuel oil from Romania, instituting a tight watch on the coast of Asia Mino
with the assistance of the Greek population, and a special watch at th
Dardanelles and Smyrna.[72]

The Germans intended to acquire two auxiliary steamers to assist U21
voyage. The first would be obtained by the German naval agent in Spain
Korvettenkapitän von Krohn, and would carry as supercargo to th
rendezvous in the Balearics a German naval reserve officer drawn from on
of the interned German steamers. The second steamer would be Greek an
would also carry a reserve officer. The Germans decided that U21 woul
have to fuel in a Spanish harbour, and after careful consideration the
decided on the Gulf of Corcubion near Cape Finisterre. Von Krohn, wh
not very successfully tried to disguise himself as 'Juan Corona' in cable
chartered a small steamer in northern Spain. She was the *Marcella*, with
cargo capacity of 175 tons and would proceed to Vivero with a fake carg
and then appear at a prearranged series of meeting points.[73]

In the meantime Kapitänleutnant Adam, the officer detached to supervis
the assembly of the UB boats at Pola, reported on 1 April that the proje
was causing no difficulties and that the Austrian yard had taken the greate
trouble to expedite work and support the Germans. The German crews fo
the boats could therefore leave from home on the 6th. However, Adam als
reported the Austrians' passion for secrecy. They intended to designate th
UB boats as the Austrian U7 and U8 and had spread the rumour tha
German officers and men were only 'running-in' the boats before the
would be turned over to the Austrian navy. To make the rumour plausibl
they had even designated two Austrian officers as commanders. Th
Austrians went so far as to request that the Germans should travel to Pola i
Austrian uniforms. In Pola they would live in an accommodation hulk an
have either very restricted liberty or none at all. Adam pointed out that
was apparently well known in Austria that German boats were bein
assembled at Pola, but the Flottenkommando appeared to place the greate
value on the disguise and the Reichsmarineamt ordered the crews to trav
to Vienna in civilian clothing.[74] The Reichsmarineamt and Admiralstab als
decided to complete UB16 and UB17, originally meant for Turkey,
home. They considered it best not to send further UB boats to th
Mediterranean until they had proved themselves.[75]

The Germans suffered a setback when a leak damaged UB7 and delaye
her entry into service for approximately four weeks. The Admiralsta
decided to send UB8 out alone and since they expected the boat to
resupplied off the south-west coast of Crete by a Greek steamer, they d
not think it absolutely necessary for the submarine to be towed through th
Straits of Otranto unless circumstances were especially favourable and n
enemy counteraction was expected.[76] The tow turned out to be necessar

for the Greek steamer that the Germans had acquired had to be held ready for U21 and could not wait for UB8. Korvettenkapitän Ackermann of the Admiralstab, who had come down to Pola for the trials of the UB boats, was pleased with the torpedo-firing exercises of UB8 and the trials at towing by the cruiser *Novara*, which managed to achieve a speed of 10 knots. UB8 would make her landfall and meet a pilot boat on the coast of Asia Minor to the east of Bodrum between Orak Island and the mainland. Ackermann was also encouraged and favourably impressed with the captain of the *Novara*, who he thought would do his best to support the submarine.[77] He was correct in his judgement for the commander was Horthy whose reputation was well known.[78] Horthy was ordered to tow UB8 if possible up to the island of Sapienza off the south-west tip of the Peloponnese, and to support the submarine in its mission as far as it coincided with the safety of his own ship. If possible, he would pass through the southern part of the Straits of Otranto on a dark, moonless night and would keep the submarine out of sight of foreign warships or merchantmen. He was authorized to fly a foreign flag if necessary. The role of Italy would be crucial and the radio signal *Zwokvacuum* meant war with Italy had been declared and barring further orders the mission would be broken off, while *Zwokstorch* meant war with Italy was possible or imminent.[79]

Horthy began his mission on 2 May, refuelled at Curzola and safely passed through the Straits of Otranto, having rigged a false funnel of cloth and wire to simulate a transport. On 6 May he was finally intercepted by French warships about eight miles west of Cephalonia and forced to cast off the submarine, which was not observed. Horthy made a successful escape. The fact that he was able to get so far south of the Straits of Otranto without detection indicates how ineffective the French blockade had become because of the submarine threat. Shortly afterwards, on the night of 15–16 May the destroyer *Triglav* successfully towed UB7 through the Straits of Otranto.[80] Within three weeks of the Allied landing on the Gallipoli Peninsula, two small German submarines were actually *en route* to the area.

The presence of Ackermann in Pola provided Admiral Haus with the opportunity for some plain speaking to the Admiralstab officer aboard his flagship about the 'so-called inactivity of the Fleet which is yet more valuable than suicide in battle with the French fleet or travelling to the Dardanelles'. This, plus the solid example of co-operation with even a bit of dash which Horthy provided, must have had at least some effect. Bachmann, in thanking Haus for the support given in assembling and towing the submarines, assured him that he would not fail to oppose the utterances of those who, in their ignorance of military affairs and of the special situation in the Mediterranean, did not sufficiently appreciate the Austrians' work. Bachmann's letter was undoubtedly a source of satisfaction to Haus who had copies sent to the Kaiser's Military Chancellery and AOK, and the Flottenkommandant replied that he and the entire k.u.k. Kriegsmarine considered the cause of the Imperial German Navy as their own and in true brotherhood of arms were always ready and determined to do everything in their power towards reaching the common war aims.[81] Tirpitz's sarcastic remarks made in the preceding March probably reflected the real German view of the Austrians and their Flottenkommandant: 'Their Admiral Haus is reserving his fleet for Italy. He thinks he may bring off another Lissa, but whether another Tegetthoff comes on the scene is open to question. He conversed with our Naval Attaché chiefly on exotic water-plants, which is his hobby.'[82]

Hersing sailed with U21 on 25 April and made his rendezvous with the supply ship in the Gulf of Corcubion on the night of 2 May, apparently unnoticed by the Spanish. After taking on oil, he was out of sight of the Spanish coast by dawn. Hersing arranged another rendezvous with the steamer for the following night in nearby Arosa Bay, but during the day he made the alarming discovery that the fuel oil he had received was unsuitable for his diesel engines. He therefore had to dismiss the steamer without taking on further oil. Another part of the German plan went awry when Spanish authorities hindered the departure of a second steamer carrying fuel that von Krohn had chartered in Barcelona, allegedly because of a prohibition on the export of oil. Nevertheless, the Admiralstab ordered Krohn to get the steamer to sea to serve as a scout for the U-boat and possibly tow it for some distance to conserve fuel. Hersing, however, once he had discovered his fuel problem, coolly calculated his chances and elected to waive his stop in the Balearics and make directly for Cattaro which he reached by careful economy on 13 May with a mere 1.8 tons of his original 56.5 tons of fuel remaining. He was, however, spotted and attacked by British or French warships on at least three occasions, so the Allies were well aware that a German submarine was coming.[83]

Back in Spain, in view of the recent prohibition on the export of oil, Krohn thought it expedient that if further submarines were to be sent to the Mediterranean an agent should be sought in the south of Spain to whom cargoes could be forwarded. His agent in Barcelona seemed to be so highly suspect that he could no longer be used for equipping steamers. The Admiralstab replied on 8 May that the sending of further U-boats directly to the Mediterranean was, for the moment, not intended, but agreed that Krohn should prepare oil supplies in case they were needed and seek a confidential agent in the south of Spain.[84] Krohn's activities were at least partially uncovered, however, and there was considerable and sensational comment about them in the Spanish press, fuelled no doubt by British consuls and agents.[85] Krohn thought that some of the difficulties stemmed from his agents carelessly linking his name to activities when it was not necessary. There may be another explanation, but here the historian enters a murky world where information, if it still exists, is not to be found in normal files. The secret code-breaking organization at the Admiralty, the famous Room 40, may have been intercepting the German naval agent's messages to and from the Admiralstab. It is not clear how closely they followed his activities in the spring of 1915, or whether they had the manpower to decrypt at this stage everything they intercepted. They were certainly on to Krohn and followed him closely in 1917, and they would also intercept and read messages to U21 at Cattaro.[86] 'Blinker' Hall, the Director of Intelligence who had just tried to buy the Turks out of the war, was fond of what today would be known as 'dirty tricks', and the sensation in the Spanish press may not have been accidental or bad luck.

The attempt by the German navy to provide a U-boat supply ship disguised as an innocent Greek steamer in the eastern Mediterranean proved to be frustrating, expensive and ineffective. The German naval authorities entered into a formal contract with Michel Kouremetis, a Greek salesman in Hamburg, to proceed to Greece and purchase a steamer in his own name. The ship would then be placed at the disposal of the German navy for special purposes, that is, the resupply of submarines. To maintain secrecy, the Germans authorized him to carry on a regular trade to the extent that it was compatible with his duties. The navy ordered Kouremetis to maintain strict secrecy about his activities, even with his own family, but promised him a bonus of 25,000 marks if he was successful. They defined success as the undisturbed supply of a submarine during its activity on the coast of Asia Minor. Kouremetis would retain any profit or sustain any loss on his camouflage trade.[87] By 7 April, Kouremetis had purchased a 1,000-ton steamer, the *Proton*.[88] A complicated maritime shell game followed with fuel oil or lubricating oil either carried to various points in the Aegean by *Proton* or shipped there by other means to be picked up by Kouremetis later on.[89] The Germans became as mystified by the movements of *Proton* as the Allies were supposed to have been, and at one point even suspected that Kouremetis had defrauded them.[90] Kouremetis was hampered by Greek controls on the export of fuel oil which had been instituted through Allied pressure and *Proton* was eventually captured by a British warship on 18 May and taken in to Alexandria.[91] The British were apparently on the verge of releasing the steamer when, at the last minute, Kouremetis's name was linked to suspect oil seized by the Italians at Kalymnos in the Dodecanese. The steamer stayed although Kouremetis was allowed to return to Piraeus.[92] Kouremetis and the Germans had hopes of obtaining *Proton*'s release by legal means and as late as November the German naval attaché in Athens was still forwarding funds for *Proton*'s upkeep and the wages of her crew.[93] One might question his judgement in throwing good money after bad. The *Proton* was hopelessly compromised and, by this time, Italy was also in the war, a fact which undoubtedly contributed to the discovery of the incriminating oil on Kalymnos. There were simply too many British, French and Italian ships in the Aegean and eastern Mediterranean and Greek ships were the object of intense suspicion, some might almost say paranoia, on the part of Allied naval officers. The resupply of submarines from neutral flag ships by May 1915 – let alone November – was simply not a viable proposition, if it ever was. The affair of the *Proton* ended badly for the Germans, but they discovered that their submarines were able to operate quite effectively in the Mediterranean without the assistance of surface ships.

While the Germans withheld their decision on sending further larger submarines directly by sea to the Mediterranean, they did intend to increase the number of small boats assembled at Pola. A third UB boat (UB3) left via rail for Pola on 15 April. The Austrians also requested compensation for the submarines building in Germany on their account and taken over by the

German navy after the beginning of the war. Tirpitz considered sending another two UB boats to be taken over by the Austrians, but decided to wait until the boats were nearly finished and made his decision dependent on the war situation. The news from the Dardanelles after the Allied landing certainly tended to emphasize the potential importance of submarines Usedom described how the British and French fleet had repulsed Turkish attacks and said that the outlook for holding the Dardanelles was 'slight' (*gering*) if they did not succeed in paralyzing or compelling the enemy fleet to withdraw. Ambassador Wangenheim in Constantinople also pleaded for Tirpitz to send more U-boats.[94] A few days later, on 10 May, Tirpitz informed the Admiralstab that UB1 and UB15 would be sent to Pola and turned over to the Austrian navy; their crews would return to Germany as soon as the Austrians were sufficiently trained. Tirpitz also decided to send two minelaying submarines (UC14 and UC15) to Pola, but they would retain their German crews and would be used according to the situation in the Adriatic against either Malta or in Turkish waters, or possibly even to transport torpedoes to Turkish bases. The final decision as to their employment would follow as soon as the situation, especially the Italian question, was clarified.[95] The Admiralstab also tried to apply a bit of psychological pressure against Italy by asking the German Legation in Berne to spread the news, especially for the benefit of the Italian press, that at least eight submarines were *en route* for the Austrian navy.[96]

After U21 arrived at Cattaro on 13 May, the Admiralstab decided that Hersing should sail directly for the Dardanelles as soon as the submarine was ready and omit the contemplated call at some base on the coast of Asia Minor. They asked Souchon for information on the deployment of enemy ships. The German submariners were particularly anxious to learn the exact positions from which the Allied ships were shelling the Gallipoli Peninsula, as this was where Hersing would make his first attack. The information was duly sent by the Admiralstab and also intercepted and read by Room 40 who passed on the warning to Admiral de Robeck.[97] Enver Pasha, Turkish Minister of War, again appealed to Tirpitz for further submarines on 23 May. This time Tirpitz was able to reply that, at the moment, there were eight U-boats allocated to the Mediterranean and probably one large and three small U-boats were already in Turkish waters.[98] They would shortly make their presence known.

At the Dardanelles the Royal Navy shouldered a heavy burden supporting and supplying the army struggling on shore, well aware that German submarines were on their way. The fact that the army was unable to make further progress led Admiral de Robeck to cable the Admiralty on 10 May about the possibility of a renewed naval attack to force the Dardanelles and cut off supplies, which were largely water-borne, to the Turkish army on the Gallipoli Peninsula. De Robeck's proposals were, at best, lukewarm for he did not believe that the presence of an Allied fleet in the Marmara would be decisive, and much of the pressure for the cable probably came from his Chief of Staff, Commodore Keyes. Years later Keyes would describe how de Robeck recognized that a successful attack would be of vital importance to the army, but feared for the latter's fate if it failed, and declined to take responsibility for running the risk of failure. Keyes told him to place the responsibility on the government, but to make it clear that if ordered he would be prepared to attempt to force the Straits. De Robeck rejected the first draft of the telegram as too confident and it therefore had to be modified.[99] The French naval commander at the Dardanelles, the fiery Guépratte, although not at the conference with de Robeck, was delighted at the prospect of a renewed attack.[100] Churchill had just returned from the Paris Conference and negotiations for the naval convention with Italy, and was conscious of the need to provide ships for the Italians as well as the impending arrival of German submarines. He was ready for a 'limited operation', to try and sweep the Kephez minefield under cover of the fleet, compelling the forts to exhaust their ammunition, but even this was too much for Fisher who was dead against any attempt to rush the Narrows before the army had occupied the adjacent shores. In the end, as a compromise measure, Churchill sent a very weak telegram to de Robeck on the 13th telling him to let them know before taking any decisive step and to obtain Admiralty approval beforehand. Fisher, with the support of the other Sea Lords, was then able to get an additional telegram sent which flatly declared that the Admiralty thought the moment for an independent naval attempt had passed and would not arise again, and that de Robeck's role was to support the army.[101] The disappointed Keyes later summed it up:

> So the great opportunities which had been open to the Fleet since 4th April [when destroyer minesweepers were ready] were allowed to slip away, and the Allied Army, having suffered 26,000 casualties in its effort to secure the Gallipoli shore, was to continue the struggle, in order that the Fleet might steam by without any undue loss.[102]

British submarines did overcome the tricky currents and successfully penetrated the Dardanelles. The first attempt by E15 on 17 April ended in failure when the submarine ran aground and was captured, although the hull was later destroyed by a daring raid in small boats before the Turks could salvage it.[103] The Australian AE2 succeeded in passing the Straits on 25 April and torpedoed a gunboat off Chanak, but was subsequently sunk in the Marmara on the 30th by the torpedo-boat *Sultan Hissar*. The French *Joule* was unsuccessful and was lost with all hands on 1 May after hitting a mine. The most successful British submarine to date was E14 under Lieutenant-Commander E. C. Boyle who went through the Straits on 27 April, sank four ships including a large transport, thoroughly disturbed but did not stop Turkish reinforcements for Gallipoli, was hunted constantly, and returned in triumph to the cheers of the fleet on the evening of the 18th to learn he had been awarded the Victoria Cross.[104]

If the Allies succeeded in forcing the Dardanelles, the Germans planned to hold the Bosphorus in order to maintain the cross traffic between the Asian and European shores which was vital to the Turkish army. They would still be able to deny the British and French one of their main objectives, that is, access to Russia and the Black Sea.[105] Souchon was dissatisfied because the Dardanelles defence tied him down and prevented him from doing anything

113

on the Russian coast. He had to avoid 'useless' sorties into the Black Sea because of the necessity to economize on fuel, but thought he would be able to do something again as soon as the route through Serbia was free. Moreover, once German troops had opened the way for supplies to Turkey through Serbia and Bulgaria the British would feel threatened in Egypt, and that perhaps would have more effect on them than if the German army occupied more territory in Belgium and France.[106] In the overall view of the Dardanelles campaign, the importance of the strategic route from Germany and Austria through the Balkans is sometimes overlooked, and on a more local level, so too is the problem of coal for the Turks and Germans. On 9 May, while congratulating Enver Pasha on his recently awarded Iron Cross, 1st Class, Souchon reported to him on the coal difficulty. The Russians could easily cut off traffic through the Black Sea and it was incredible to Souchon that, with the help of their submarines, they had not done so long ago. The fleet might run out of coal in six weeks' time and, in the worst case, the Turks might be forced to conclude peace in three months. He did not think it was quite so serious, but the struggle against Turkish negligence was wearing.[107]

The Turks and Germans struck back at sea when they could. On 16 April the German-officered torpedo-boat *Demir Hissar*, which had come out from Smyrna the night before, attacked a British transport, failed to sink it, and hotly pursued by British destroyers was trapped and ran herself ashore on the Greek island of Chios where the crew was interned.[108] The Germans had a spectacular success on the night of 12–13 May when Kapitänleutnant Firle commanding the destroyer *Muvanet* succeeded in torpedoing and sinking the old battleship *Goliath* anchored in Morto Bay. The *Goliath* was in an exposed position where her close support of the army had made her obnoxious to the Germans and Turks. Firle in a sense stalked his quarry, surveying the entire panorama two days before the attack from an artillery observation post on the opposite shore.[109] The loss of life was heavy, including the captain. De Robeck thought it 'was a good ship thrown away' and reflected 'one ought not to have risked a ship there, but it was at the repeated & earnest request of the French general'. He later thought it the fault of *Goliath*'s captain who had 'no sort of arrangement made to meet a torpedo attack' and considered old ships like the *Goliath* 'badly officered' with the Officer of the Watch 'quite unfit for the work at hand'.[110] While a daring and skilfully executed surface attack might pick off an exposed ship, Souchon's main yearning was for the three U-boats which were just entering Turkish waters. If these were successful, the situation would be at once greatly altered.[111]

The most immediate effect of the loss of the *Goliath* was a renewed and much more vigorous insistence by Fisher on the recall of the new super-dreadnought *Queen Elizabeth* from the Dardanelles. The imminent arrival of German submarines also exerted a powerful influence on the First Sea Lord and he had been very nervous about the ship well before news of *Goliath* arrived. Fisher and Churchill agreed to replace *Queen Elizabeth* with the old battleships, *Exmouth* and *Venerable* and two 14-in. gun monitors. Lord Kitchener, however, protested on the effect that *Queen Elizabeth*'s departure would have on the army's morale. In the next few days Churchill's apparent intention to provide further reinforcements for the Dardanelles brought the long simmering dispute between himself and Fisher into the open. Fisher resigned and resisted all pressure from friends, the Prime Minister and Churchill to return to his post.[112] The resignation of the famous admiral coupled with a recent scandal about the shortage of artillery shells in France, threatened to overturn the government, and Prime Minister Asquith agreed to form a Coalition government with the Conservative opposition. The Conservatives insisted that Churchill should leave the Admiralty and he was finally relegated to the sinecure Duchy of Lancaster. The former Prime Minister, Arthur J. Balfour, became First Lord of the Admiralty and Admiral Sir Henry Jackson was appointed First Sea Lord.[113] The Dardanelles campaign had therefore lost its firmest and most eloquent supporter in the government.

The Russian navy also displayed considerable activity in the Black Sea striking exactly where Souchon feared at the coal traffic on the coast of Anatolia. On 15 April three large Russian destroyers destroyed four Turkish steamers and on 25 April – the day the Allies landed at Gallipoli – the Russian fleet bombarded the forts at the entrance to the Bosphorus. They repeated the performance on 2 and 3 May while cruisers and destroyers attacked Turkish shipping on the Anatolian coast. These activities continued and on 10 May the *Goeben* engaged the Russian Battle Squadron and was hit twice, but not seriously damaged. By the end of May the Russians had established a systematic blockade of the Bosphorus and groups of two to four destroyers made periodic sweeps along the Anatolian coast to cut off the coal traffic. Russian destroyers rather than submarines were the problem. The Russians had only two suitable submarines to employ on these activities at the time, and the boats did not achieve anything. The engagement of 10 May also provided a nasty shock for the Germans when they discovered that the 30.5-cm guns of the old Russian battleships outranged the 28-cm guns of the *Goeben* by about 2 kms, probably because they could be trained at a higher elevation.[114]

Souchon on 16 May also moaned about the frightful distress coal was causing him now that the Russians were diligently destroying all steamers along the open coast of the coal district. He was powerless against them and Turkish Headquarters did not fully recognize the seriousness of the situation. They had not restricted the use of coal by private firms and held the naïve opinion that the fleet could protect the colliers. Souchon estimated that the *Goeben* would burn as much coal protecting the slowly loading colliers on the open coast as they themselves would load. Once they could get coal from Germany freely through Serbia they would be able to renew the campaign against Egypt, and Souchon thought that a separate peace between the Turks and Russia would be desirable. He repeated his frequent lament, that the struggle against the Turks was more wearing than the struggle against the enemy. Souchon's one bit of real satisfaction from recent events was that *Goeben* could again make 28 knots, a considerable achievement for her leading engineer considering the poor coal available and the fact that her bottom had not been cleaned in twenty-one months.[115]

But what of the German submarines? Keyes noted that their impending arrival 'worries the Admiral horribly', but Keyes himself put the best face on the matter and told Churchill's brother Jack, then on Ian Hamilton's staff, that the submarines 'only added piquancy to the situation'.[116] Once one of his major concerns, the valuable *Queen Elizabeth*, had departed, de Robeck planned to meet the problem as best he could. All transports would go to the main base at Port Mudros and no further, with troops ferried to the Gallipoli Peninsula each night by fleet sweepers. Supply ships would go, if necessary, to Cape Helles, or Kephalo which would be made into an advance base with net defences and booms. Vital ammunition ships, however, would discharge at Mudros and their cargoes would be forwarded to the peninsula by means of fleet sweepers and trawlers. Ships required by the army as 'covering ships' were the only ones at sea, and they would cruise at night if possible, and anchor in their positions at daylight with their nets, if they had them, out at once. Ships had to anchor while firing, otherwise they would throw away ammunition. De Robeck concluded, 'Now my *most important* requirement are nets & lighters on which to hang the nets & place them round these ships'.[117]

The net defences proved to be inadequate. On 25 May U21 sank the battleship *Triumph* and on 27 May sank the battleship *Majestic*. Hersing eventually passed through the Dardanelles and reached Constantinople safely on 5 June.[118] Of the small UB boats, UB8 had arrived at Smyrna on 17 May and, off Mudros, on 30 May torpedoed and sank the British steamer *Merion*, part of the Special Service Squadron, which had been altered and camouflaged with dummy superstructure to resemble the battle cruiser *Tiger*. UB8 subsequently reached Constantinople on 4 June. UB7 arrived off Bodrum on 20 May and entered Smyrna on the 30th, where she had to be overhauled by engineers sent from Constantinople. UB7 later unsuccessfully attacked a transport *en route* to the Dardanelles and eventually arrived at Constantinople on 21 June. The third UB boat, UB3, left Pola on 23 May, was towed by the Austrians up to the Straits of Otranto and was never seen again.[119] The mystery of her fate has never been solved.

The British could also claim their own submarine successes. Lieutenant-Commander Nasmith took E11 through the Dardanelles on the night of 18 May immediately after conferring with Boyle on his experiences in E14. Nasmith had an adventurous and successful cruise and claimed a gunboat, 2 ammunition ships, 2 troopships and 2 steamers, while a third transport beached herself after he attacked. One of Nasmith's victims had actually been anchored alongside the Arsenal in the Golden Horn and Nasmith, too, was subsequently awarded the Victoria Cross.[120] However, Souchon could gloat that '*Triumph* and *Majestic* count more than old transports' which the British might sink in the Marmara, and that the success of the German submarines had far exceeded his expectations. For the first time no British or French warships, except for destroyers, could be observed off the coast. The battleships lay in a gulf on the island of Lemnos behind nets and booms. Souchon's confidence was tempered somewhat after UB8 and U21 arrived in Constantinople. The boats would require a thorough overhaul which would stop the German U-boat assault for the moment, and the UB boats were very fragile. Their machinery had been strained to the utmost and they were likely to cause him many troubles.[121]

The arrival of German submarines off the Dardanelles threatened the expedition but they did not, and would not, end it. De Robeck wrote: 'These submarines are the devil & are cramping one's style very much & until we can sink them there will be no peace', while his Chief of Staff, Keyes, told his wife 'I must say it is a problem which makes one think and requires all our courage and fortitude'.[122] The answers lay in more small craft, nets, booms, shallow draught monitors for artillery support and wiser tactics. Moreover, the actual number of German submarines off the Dardanelles was small, the capacity of the UB boats slight (they only carried two torpedoes), and the days they were on station were few, given the poverty of German resources in Turkey. On the other hand, the establishment of German bases and support facilities in Austrian harbours and the demonstration by Hersing that it was possible for submarines to go directly from German ports to Cattaro would be of tremendous importance for the future war in the Mediterranean. Ironically, those Germans did not come out of any desire to help their Austrian ally or to deliberately make war on Allied commerce. They came rather as a direct response to the British and French attack on the Dardanelles.

In the meantime Italy moved steadily towards fulfilment of her obligations under the Treaty of London to enter the war, despite the fact that this may have been against the wishes of a majority of the population. The Entente powers experienced a momentary scare when former Prime Minister Giolitti, who favoured continued neutrality, returned to Rome and seemed to enjoy widespread parliamentary support. The Salandra government resigned for a brief period, but Italy was too deeply committed to war, and in the end the forces favouring intervention won out.[123] The Austrians received a steady stream of reports from their naval and military attachés in Rome who saw their position change from ally to almost certain enemy and remarked how old colleagues and friends fell away and began to avoid them.[124] AOK noted the uncertain political attitude of Italy and its apparent arming and on 27 April, just one day after the signature of the Treaty of London, Archduke Friedrich advised Haus that a sudden opening of hostilities against the monarchy, possibly without a declaration of war, was not out of the question. Diverse intelligence, moreover, led to the suspicion that these hostilities would be accompanied by surprise attacks by land and sea.[125] The tension increased and on 9 May the Marinesektion cabled Haus: 'Unpublicized general mobilization in Italy as well as deployment to the north-east alleged to be already in progress. Soonest possible opening of hostilities probable.'[126] The German naval attaché, Freyberg, was not satisfied with the Austrians merely remaining on guard against a surprise attack. In the now-familiar pattern of the aggressive Germans prodding the quiescent Austrians into action, he informed the Marinesektion on 18 May that his sources had intelligence that the Italians would seek a cheap success, and it was of the utmost importance that Austria should deal the first blow with torpedo-boats or submarines as soon as war seemed unavoidable either without, or at the very moment of, a declaration of war. The Marinesektion replied that an attack against Italy was impossible without the authorization of the Kaiser and that the Foreign Minister had to give the sign for such a step and would scarcely take the responsibility himself. Freyberg argued that even if the Italians lost only two or three ships, it would be decisive for the entire war by lowering morale in Italy. Freyberg suggested to the Admiralstab that Falkenhayn should also apply pressure on Conrad.[127]

Haus really did not need German prodding to act aggressively against the Italians. In one sense, he had been waiting to do so ever since the Italian declaration of neutrality in August 1914. Early in May he sought approval to take action before any declaration of war against a possible Italian troop transport to Antivari, or attempt at landing on the Montenegrin coast. The Austrian Foreign Ministry eventually took the position that, since Antivari was blockaded, a possible move by Italian troops to Montenegro would constitute support of a state with whom Austria was at war and the transport could therefore be attacked before any declaration of war. However, this interpretation still needed the Kaiser's approbation, which was finally given on the 20th.[128] Haus was determined to strike the first blow for its effect on morale as soon as possible after the outbreak of war. He planned an action by the entire fleet against military targets on the eastern coast of Italy. From 19 May onwards Austrian light cruisers and destroyers guarded the line Gargano–Pelagosa–Lagosta to prevent surprise, aircraft conducted reconnaissance missions off the Italian coast, and to prevent raids and landing attempts two submarines were stationed in the Gulf of Trieste, one submarine in the waters of Lissa and another off the Montenegrin coast.[129] Haus had the fleet ready on the 23rd waiting for the declaration of war and prepared to sail as soon as it was dark. The news of the Italian declaration of war reached Pola around 4 p.m., greeted with spontaneous and spirited cheering by the crews, and around 8 p.m. the fleet sailed. Haus divided his forces to strike at Ancona with the bulk of the heavy ships while other Austrian forces attacked Corsini harbour (near Ravenna), Rimini, Senigallia, and the mouth of the Potenza. There would also be air raids against Venice and the airship hangers at Chiaravalle. The Austrian bombardments took place early on the morning of the 24th and almost all of the k.u.k. fleet was safely back in harbour before noon. Apart from damage inflicted on targets on land, the Italian destroyer *Turbine* was sunk by *Helgoland* and two destroyers in the south off Pelagosa.[130] The Austrian forces had never been near the bulk of the Italian fleet and the French fleet was, of course, even further away. The action in terms of numbers of ships employed would be their largest operation of the entire war.

By the beginning of June 1915 the naval war in the Mediterranean had entered a new phase. Although the Dardanelles campaign appeared to be stalemated, the British and French had gained the great prize among the European neutrals – Italy. The Italian fleet was a substantial one and the Germans, Austrians and Turks now had little hope for any lasting success by surface warships outside the Adriatic, while in the Black Sea the Russians had turned out to be a far tougher proposition than the Germans might have anticipated. On the other hand, the Dardanelles campaign had also brought German submarines to the Mediterranean and the German presence was destined to grow. Furthermore, due to the peculiar circumstances of the Adriatic, the Italian entry into the war would turn out to be less decisive than originally hoped.

Notes: Chapter 4

1 Rear-Admiral William Sowden Sims, *The Victory at Sea* (Garden City, NY, 1921), p. 261; Kelly, War Diary, National Maritime Museum, Greenwich, Kelly MSS, KEL/15. Kelly actually crossed out this unflattering paragraph in the diary, presumably with a view to possible publication. There is a biography of Revel by his former ADC, Guido Po, *Il Grande Ammiraglio Paolo Thaon di Revel* (Turin, 1936). See also my entry on Revel in Philip V. Cannistraro (ed.), *Historical Dictionary of Fascist Italy* (Westport, Conn., 1982), pp. 532–5.

2 'Promemoria No. 1. Esame di operazioni di guerra nell'Adriatico', Sept. 1914, USM, Cartella 354/3. Excerpts are printed in: Ufficio Storico, *Marina italiana*, Vol. 1, pp. 312–23.

3 For older plans see Halpern, *Mediterranean Naval Situation*, pp. 208–11.

4 'Nuovo esame di operazioni di guerra nell'Adriatico', 5 Jan. 1915, ACS, Carte Brusati/ 11 (VIII-2-46). Printed with slight changes in Ufficio Storico, *Marina italiana*, Vol. 1, pp. 325–8.

5 A serviceable biography is Giotto Dainelli, *Il Duca degli Abruzzi: le imprese dell'ultimo grande esploratore italiano* (Turin, 1967). On Franz Joseph's remark see Halpern, *Mediterranean Naval Situation*, p. 250; and the entry on Abruzzi in Cannistraro (ed.), *Dictionary of Fascist Italy*, pp. 489–90.

6 Revel to Abruzzi, 3 Mar. 1915, USM, Cartella 354/3. On Conz see Richmond to Rodd, 24 June 1915, National Maritime Museum, Greenwich, Richmond MSS, RIC/13/5.

7 Abruzzi to Revel, 5 Mar. 1915, Revel to Abruzzi, 8 Mar. 1915, USM, Cartella 354/4; Abruzzi to Revel, 26 Mar. 1915, ibid., Cartella 361/5.

8 Cadorna to Revel, 5 Apr. 1915, Revel to Abruzzi, 7 Apr. 1915, ibid.

9 Revel, 'Considerazioni sul Promemoria No. 1', 5 Apr. 1915, ibid., Cartella 354/3.

10 Revel to Abruzzi, 14 Apr. 1915, ibid. The obsolescent cruisers *Carlo Alberto, Piemonte, Etna* and *Etruria*, with medium artillery, were also designated to co-operate with the army.

11 Viale to Abruzzi, 18 Apr. 1915, ibid.

12 Viale, 'Piano generale delle operazioni in Adriatico', 18 Apr. 1915, ibid. The document is also printed virtually unchanged in Ufficio Storico, *Marina italiana*, Vol. 1, pp. 331–41.

13 Cadorna to Revel, 17 Apr. 1915, Revel to Abruzzi, 20 Apr. 1915, USM, Cartella 361/5.

14 Revel to Cadorna, 25 Apr. 1915, ibid.

15 Cadorna to Revel, 28 Apr. 1915, ibid.

16 Revel to Cadorna, 30 Apr. 1915, ibid.

17 Cadorna to Revel, 3 May 1915, Revel to Cadorna, 5 May 1915, Diaz to Revel, 10 May 1915, ibid.

18 Abruzzi to Revel, 29 Apr. 1915, ibid., Cartella 354/3.

19 On the Treaty of London see: Mario Toscano, *Il Patto di Londra. Storia diplomatica dell'intervento italiano, 1914–1915* (Bologna, 1934); idem, 'Rivelazioni e nuovi documenti sul negoziato di Londra per l'ingresso dell'Italia nella prima guerra mondiale', *Nuova antologia*, vol. 494–495, fasc. 1976–9 (Aug.–Nov. 1965); W. W. Gottlieb, *Studies in Secret Diplomacy during the First World War* (London, 1957); Albert Pingaud, *Histoire diplomatique de la France pendant la grande guerre* (3 vols, Paris, 1935–45); Antonio Salandra, *Italy and the Great War* (London, 1932); Sidney Sonnino, *Diario*, Vol. 2: *1914–1916*, ed. by Benjamin F. Brown and Pietro Pastorelli (Bari, 1972); a succinct account is in: Z. A. B. Zeman, *The Gentlemen Negotiators: A Diplomatic History of the First World War* (New York, 1971), ch. 1.

20 'Agreement between the Three Powers and Italy', 26 Apr. 1915, PRO, Cab 37/128.

21 A detailed account is in: Halpern, 'The Anglo-French-Italian Naval Convention of 1915', *Historical Journal*, vol. 13, no. 1 (1970), pp. 106–29; see also Mariano Gabriele, 'Le convenzione navale italo-franco-britannica del 10 maggio 1915', *Nuova antologia*, vol. 492–494, fasc. 1972–3 (Apr.–May 1965).

22 Revel to Salandra, 31 Mar. 1915, ACS, Carte Salandra 2/20.

23 'Promemoria per svolgimento della trattative circa concorso delle Marine Franchesa ed Inglese del operazioni militari in Adriatico', n.d., enclosed in Revel to Sonnino, 6 May 1915, USM, Cartella 356/1.

24 Thomazi, *Guerre navale dans l'Adriatique*, pp. 70–2.

25 Lapeyrère to Minister of Marine, 7, 15 and 24 Jan. 1915, SHM, Carton Ed-83.

26 Lapeyrère to Minister of Marine, 27 Feb. 1915, ibid.; Thomazi, *Guerre navale dans l'Adriatique*, pp. 74–7; Sokol, *Österreich-Ungarns Seekrieg*, pp. 100–5, 143–6.

27 Lapeyrère to minister, 11 Mar. 1915, SHM, Carton Ed-83.

28 Lapeyrère to minister, 10 Apr. 1915, ibid.

29 Thomazi, *Guerre navale dans l'Adriatique*, pp. 77–9; Sokol, *Österreich-Ungarns Seekrieg*, pp. 147–51.

30 Lapeyrère to minister, 4 May 1915, SHM, Carton A-75.

31 Lapeyrère to minister, 12 May 1915, ibid., Carton Ed-83.

32 Standard accounts of the landings are: Robert Rhodes James, *Gallipoli* (New York, 1965); Alan Moorehead, *Gallipoli* (New York, 1956); Cecil F. Aspinall-Oglander, *History of the Great War. Military Operations: Gallipoli* (2 vols in 4, London, 1929–32); Keyes, *Naval Memoirs*, Vol. 1, ch. 17; Bush, *Gallipoli*.

33 For a detailed account see: Halpern, 'Anglo-French-Italian Naval Convention', pp. 116–24.

34 ibid., pp. 121–2.

35 Revel to Abruzzi, 8 May 1915, USM, Cartella 356/1.

36 Halpern, 'Anglo-French-Italian Naval Convention', loc. cit. at n. 21, pp. 123–4; Churchill, *The World Crisis*, Vol. 2, pp. 344–5.

37 Text in Thomazi, *Guerre navale dans l'Adriatique*, pp. 82–5; Ufficio Storico, *Marina italiana*, Vol. 1, pp. 435–9.

38 Revel to Sonnino, 'Promemoria circa schema di convenzione militare navale', 9 May 1915, Revel to Viale, 15 May 1915, USM, Cartella 356/1.

39 Revel to Sonnino, 'Promemoria per S.E. il Ministro degli Esteri circa "Convenzione Navale con la Francia e l'Inghilterra"', 11 May 1915. Copy in ACS, Carte Salandra 2/16.

40 ibid. Revel apparently did not know the exact text of the Treaty of London on the 15th when he asked the Minister of Marine for the terms. Revel to Viale, 15 May 1915, USM, Cartella 356/1. The Italians had an unfortunate tradition of keeping their service chiefs in the dark about the exact nature of their

diplomatic obligations. In December 1912, when the Chief of the Army General Staff inquired about the exact text of the Triple Alliance he was advised that there were no military clauses he needed to know and would be advised by the Foreign Ministry in good time if there were danger of war. See Halpern, *Mediterranean Naval Situation*, pp. 223–4.

41 L. Aldovandi Marescotti, *Nuovi ricordi e frammenti di diario* (Milan, 1938), p. 222.

42 Revel to Abruzzi, 14 May 1915, USM, Cartella 354/3.

43 Ufficio del Capo di Stato Maggiore della Marina, 'Relazione generale sull' opera svolte dal 1 Aprile 1913 al 1 Ottobre 1915', pp. 151–2. Copy in ACS, 1° Aiutante di Campo Generale di S.M. il Re, Sezione Speciale, Filza 24.

44 Revel to Abruzzi, 14 May 1915, USM, Cartella 354/3.

45 Revel to Abruzzi, 16 May 1915, ibid., Cartella 444/2.

46 Revel to Viale, 18 May 1915, ibid., Cartella 354/3.

47 Revel to Viale (with memoranda), 20 May 1915, Salandra to Revel, 22 May 1915, ibid.

48 Revel to Abruzzi, 19 May 1915, ibid.

49 Abruzzi to Revel, 21 May 1915, ibid.

50 Abruzzi, 'Schema generale del piano di guerra in Adriatico', enclosed in Abruzzi to Revel, 21 May 1915, Abruzzi to Vice-Admiral Presbitero [C.-in-C. II Squadra], 20 May 1915, ibid.

51 Kailer to Haus, 25 Mar. 1915, Kriegsarchiv, Vienna, Nachlass Haus.

52 Erwin Sieche, 'Die diplomatischen Aktivitäten rund um das Haus-Memorandum vom März 1915', *Marine–Gestern, Heute*, vol. 9, no. 3 (Sept. 1982), pp. 102–3.

53 Burián to Graf Thurn, 23 Mar. 1915, reproduced ibid., pp. 100–1.

54 Haus to Beck, 31 Mar. 1915, OK/MS II-1/8 ex 1915, No. 2165. Printed in full in Sokol, *Österreich-Ungarns Seekrieg*, pp. 164–9; Sieche, 'Die diplomatischen Aktivitäten rund das Haus-Memorandum', loc. cit. at n. 52, pp. 93–7; also printed in translation with a few omissions in Laurens, *Commandement naval*, pp. 61–4; excerpts are in Ufficio Storico, *Marina italiana*, Vol. 1, pp. 300–3.

55 Letters of transmittal, 4 Apr. 1915, OK/MS II-1/8 ex 1915, No. 2165.

56 Freyberg to Kailer, 2 Apr. 1915, OK/MS II-1/8 ex 1915, No. 2163.

57 Bolfras to Haus, 7 Apr. 1915, Kriegsarchiv, Vienna, Militärkanzlei des Kaisers und Königs (hereafter referred to as MKSM), 69-6/12-1 ex 1915.

58 Erzherzog Friedrich to Haus, 8 Apr. 1915, OK/MS II-1/8 ex 1915, No. 2489. The Archduke sent a similar letter to Burián. Both are reproduced in Sieche, 'Die diplomatischen Aktivitäten rund das Haus-Memorandum', loc. cit. at n. 52, pp. 97–8.

59 Colloredo-Mannsfeld to Marinesektion, 11 Apr. 1915, OK/MS II-1/8 ex 1915, No. 2482.

60 Beck to Haus, 7 Apr. 1915, loc. cit. at n. 51, Nachlass Haus, B/241.

61 Freyberg to Staatssekretär des Reichsmarineamt [Tirpitz], 8 Apr. 1915, NARS, T-1022, Roll 537, PG 69132.

62 Souchon to his wife, 19 Mar. 1915, BA-MA, Nachlass Souchon, N156/13.

63 Souchon to his wife, 22 Mar. and 7 Apr. 1915, ibid.

64 Bachmann to Kaiser Wilhelm, 31 Mar. 1915, NARS, T-1022, Roll 587, PG 68126.

65 Marinesektion [Kailer] to Haus, 24 Mar. 1915, OK/MS VIII-1/8 ex 1915, No. 1934.

66 Excerpt of letter from Capt. Rösing [16 Mar.] in Humann to Generalinspektion [Usedom], 23 Mar. 1915, NARS, T-1022, Roll 1377, PG 6006.

67 Conrad to Haus, 12 Apr. 1915, OK/MS VIII-1/8 ex 1915, No. 2490.

68 Haus to Conrad, 12 Apr. 1915, ibid. Haus also sent Conrad copies of his

correspondence with Souchon, Haus to Conrad, 13 Apr. 1915, ibid., No. 2463.

69   Bachmann to Admiralstab, 17 Mar. 1915, Behncke to Bachmann, 23 Mar. 1915, NARS, T-1022, Roll 726, PG 75258.
70   Protocol, session of 17 Mar. 1915, Fernspruch from GHQ to Admiralstab, 20 Mar. 1915, ibid.
71   Bachmann to Admiralstab, 30 Mar. 1915, telephone query from Bachmann, 30 Mar. 1915, Operationsbefehl für U21, 6 Apr. 1915, ibid.
72. Souchon to Admiralstab, 27 Mar. 1915, ibid.
73   Ackermann [?] to Hersing, 31 Mar. 1915, Behncke to Bachmann, 3 Apr. 1915, Memorandum by Commander, III U-Boat Half Flotilla, 5 Apr. 1915, Krohn to Admiralstab, 15 and 16 Apr. 1915, ibid.
74   Adam to Reichsmarineamt (Werftsdepartment), 1 Apr. 1915, Reichsmarineamt to Admiralstab, 6 Apr. 1915, ibid.
75   Behncke to Bachmann, 8 Apr. 1915, ibid. Apparently U-boat personnel themselves 'were very sceptical of their possibilities', Eberhard Rössler, *The U-Boat: The Evolution and Technical History of German Submarines* (Eng. trans., London and Melbourne, 1981), p. 44.
76   Adam to Admiralstab, 9 Apr. 1915, Grasshoff to Adam, 15 Apr. 1915, Admiralstab to Adam, 20 Apr. 1915, NARS, T-1022, Roll 726, PG 75258.
77   Ackermann to Admiralstab, 28 Apr. 1915, ibid., PG 75259.
78   See above, Chapter 3.
79   Fiedler [Vice-admiral commanding the Austrian Cruiser Flotilla] to Horthy, 30 Apr. 1915, OK/MS I-5/4 ex 1915, No. 2930.
80   Sokol, *Österreich-Ungarns Seekrieg*, pp. 172–5.
81   Bachmann to Haus, 11 May 1915, Haus to Kailer [?], 15 May 1915, Haus to Bachmann, 15 May 1915, OK/MS II-1/8 ex 1915, No. 3448; the original of Haus's letter is in NARS, T-1022, Roll 727, PG 75259.
82   Grand Admiral von Tirpitz, *My Memoirs* (2 vols, New York, 1919), Vol. 2, p. 299.
83   Krohn to Admiralstab, 3 and 5 May 1915, Admiralstab to Krohn, 5 May 1915, NARS, T-1022, Roll 726, PG 75259; Lorey, *Krieg in den türkischen Gewässern*, Vol. 1, pp. 149–51; Otto Hersing, *U.21 rettet die Dardanellen* (Zurich, Leipzig and Vienna, 1932), pp. 43–7.
84   Krohn to Admiralstab, 5 May 1915, Admiralstab to Krohn, 8 May 1915, NARS, T-1022, Roll 727, PG 75260.
85   Report by Krohn with newspaper cuttings, 20 May 1915, ibid.
86   Beesly, *Room 40*, pp. 189–92. Beesly writes that the wireless traffic between Berlin and Madrid was increasingly at the mercy of Room 40 from mid-1915 onwards.
87   Contract between Kouremetis and the navy, 24 April 1915, NARS, T-1022, Roll 726, PG 75258. The navy also promised regular monthly payments to the Kouremetis family in Hamburg and a lump sum to his wife and children in the event of his death.
88   Kloebe to Admiralstab, 3, 7 and 9 Apr. 1915, ibid. These cables generally went out under the signature of Count Mirbach through the Auswärtiges Amt. Again, there is the question: were they read by Room 40?
89   Kloebe to Admiralstab, 10, 13 and 15 Apr. 1915, Admiralstab to Kloebe, 11 Apr. 1915, Mirbach to Auswärtiges Amt, 14 Apr. 1915, ibid.; Kloebe to Admiralstab, 20 Apr. 1915, ibid., PG 75259.
90   Kloebe to Admiralstab, 6, 7, 8, 9, 11 and 15 May 1915, Admiralstab to German Legation, Athens, 13 May 1915, ibid.

91 Humann to Admiralstab, 17 May 1915, Souchon to Admiralstab, 18 May 1915, Mirbach to Admiralstab, 18 May 1915, ibid., Roll 727, PG 75259.

92 Kloebe to Admiralstab, 14 June and 9 July 1915, Mirbach to Admiralstab, 26 June 1915, Humann to Admiralstab, 3 July 1915, ibid., PG 75260.

93 Grancy to Admiralstab, 28 Oct. and 5 Nov. 1915, ibid., Roll 791, PG 75262.

94 Usedom to Admiralstab, 4 May 1915, Wangenheim to von Treutler [the Chancellor's representative at GHQ], 5 May 1915, ibid., Roll 789, PG 75242.

95 Memorandum by Reichsmarineamt, 5 May 1915, Tirpitz to Admiralstab, 10 May 1915, ibid., Roll 727, PG 75259; Arno Spindler, *Der Handelskrieg mit U-Booten* (5 vols, Berlin, 1932–66), Vol. 2, p. 195. The UC1 class were essentially UB boats fitted with mines instead of torpedoes. The mine chutes could also be used to carry cargo.

96 Admiralstab to German Legation, Berne, 11 May 1915, NARS, T-1022, Roll 726, PG 75259.

97 Admiralstab to German Base, Constantinople, 13 May 1915, Adam to Admiralstab, 16 May 1915, ibid., Roll 727, PG 75259; Beesly, *Room 40*, pp. 82–3.

98 Humann to Admiralstab, 23 May 1915, Admiralstab to German Base, Constantinople, 25 May 1915, NARS, T-1022, Roll 727, PG 75259.

99 Keyes to Guépratte, 1 Oct. 1930, reproduced in Halpern (ed.), *The Keyes Papers*, Vol. 2, Doc. 227, pp. 280–1; the telegram itself is reproduced in Keyes, *Naval Memoirs*, Vol. 1, pp. 335–6; Churchill, *The World Crisis*, Vol. 2, pp. 350–1; see also Gilbert, *Churchill*, Vol. 3, pp. 117–18.

100 Keyes, *Naval Memoirs*, Vol. 1, pp. 336–7; Guépratte, *L'Expédition des Dardanelles, 1914–1915*, p. 147.

101 Keyes, *Naval Memoirs*, Vol. 1, p. 338; Marder, *Dreadnought to Scapa Flow*, Vol. 2, pp. 275–6; Gilbert, *Churchill*, Vol. 3, pp. 419–21, 428–9.

102 Keyes, *Naval Memoirs*, Vol. 1, p. 338.

103 ibid., pp. 288–9; Corbett and Newbolt, *Naval Operations*, Vol. 2, pp. 302–4; C. G. Brodie, *Forlorn Hope 1915* (London, 1956).

104 Corbett and Newbolt, *Naval Operations*, Vol. 2, pp. 374–5; Keyes to his wife, 19 May 1915, in Halpern (ed.), *The Keyes Papers*, Vol. 1, Doc. 81, pp. 138–9; Keyes, *Naval Memoirs*, pp. 347–50.

105 Unsigned memorandum [probably Usedom], 'Fortsetzung des Kampfes um die Meerengen, fall es den Gegner gelingt eine oder beide desselben fuer Kriegsschiffe zu oeffnen', 4 Apr. 1915, NARS, T-1022, Roll 1410, PG 60139.

106 Souchon to his wife, 10 and 16 Apr. 1915, BA-MA, Nachlass Souchon, N156/13.

107 Souchon to his wife, 9 May 1915, ibid., Nachlass Souchon, N156/14.

108 Covered in great detail by Lorey, *Krieg in den türkischen Gewässern*, Vol. 1, pp. 107–11; Corbett and Newbolt, *Naval Operations*, Vol. 2, pp. 300–1.

109 Firle, Kriegstagebuch, 10–12 May 1915, BA-MA, Nachlass Firle, N155/21; See also Lorey, *Krieg in den türkischen Gewässern*, Vol. 1, pp. 138–44; Corbett and Newbolt, *Naval Operations*, Vol. 2, pp. 406–8.

110 De Robeck to Limpus, 16 and 22 May 1915, National Maritime Museum, Greenwich, Limpus MSS.

111 Souchon to his wife, 10 May 1915, BA-MA, Nachlass Souchon, N156/14.

112 A succinct account is in Marder, *Dreadnought to Scapa Flow*, Vol. 2, pp. 276–86; Gilbert, *Churchill*, Vol. 3, pp. 422–9, 433–45; Churchill, *The World Crisis*, Vol. 2, pp. 360–80; Lord Hankey, *The Supreme Command, 1914–18* (2 vols, London, 1961), Vol. 1, pp. 314–18; Stephen W. Roskill, *Hankey: Man of Secrets* (3 vols, London, 1970–4), Vol. 1, pp. 173–6.

113 Marder, *Dreadnought to Scapa Flow*, Vol. 2, pp. 286–91; naturally covered in great detail in Churchill, *The World Crisis*, Vol. 2, pp. 380 ff.; Gilbert, *Churchill*, Vol. 3, ch. 14.

114 Greger, *Russische Flotte im Weltkrieg*, p. 49; Lorey, *Krieg in den türkischen Gewässern*, Vol. 1, pp. 128–33.

115 Souchon to his wife, 16 May 1915, BA-MA, Nachlass Souchon, N156/14.

116 Keyes to his wife, 10 and 11 May 1915, in Halpern (ed.), *The Keyes Papers*, Vol. 1, Doc. 78, pp. 135–7.

117 De Robeck to Limpus, 16 May 1915, loc. cit. at n. 110, Limpus MSS.

118 Lorey, *Krieg in den türkischen Gewässern*, Vol. 1, pp. 151–5; Corbett and Newbolt, *Naval Operations*, Vol. 3, pp. 28–31.

119 Spindler, *Handelskrieg*, Vol. 2, pp. 196; Lorey, *Krieg in den türkischen Gewässern*, Vol. 1, pp. 147–9, 156–60.

120 Corbett and Newbolt, *Naval Operations*, Vol. 3, pp. 32–5.

121 Souchon to his wife, 27 and 28 May, 1 and 5 June 1915, BA-MA, Nachlass Souchon N156/14.

122 De Robeck to Limpus, 3 June 1915, loc. cit. at n. 110, Limpus MSS; Keyes to his wife, 1 June 1915, in Halpern (ed.), *The Keyes Papers*, Vol. 1, Doc. 83, p. 143.

123 On the crisis see: Christopher Seton-Watson, *Italy from Liberalism to Fascism, 1870–1925* (London, 1967), pp. 443–7.

124 Report by Military Attaché, Rome, 10 Feb. 1915, OK/MS XI-1/6 ex 1915, No. 1220, Liechtenstein to Marinesektion, 22 Apr. and 5 May 1915, ibid., Nos 2768, 3143. See also the short memoir by the outspoken Prince Liechtenstein, 'Marineattaché in Rom, 1912 auf 1915', n.d. [1947], pp. 16–22, Kriegsarchiv, Vienna, Nachlass Liechtenstein, B718, No. 4.

125 Erzherzog Friedrich to Haus, 27 Apr. 1915, OK/MS II-1/1 ex 1915, No. 2894.

126 Kailer to Haus, 9 May 1915, OK/MS VIII-1/8 ex 1915, No. 3191.

127 Freyberg to Bachmann, 18 May 1915, NARS, T-1022, Roll 537, PG 69132.

128 Marinesektion to Haus and AOK, 20 May 1915 (with supporting memoranda), OK/MS VIII-1/17 ex 1915, No. 3558.

129 Haus to Marinesektion, 22 May 1915, OK/MS VIII-1/17 ex 1915; Haus's report of action of 24 May, 26 May 1915, ibid., No. 3948.

130 Widely differing interpretations of the action are in: Sokol, *Österreich-Ungarns Seekrieg*, ch. 7, pp. 193–218; Ufficio Storico, *Marina italiana*, Vol. 2, chs 1–2, pp. 1–70. A succinct account is in: Admiral Vittorio Prato, 'La nostra entrata in guerra nel 1915 e le prime operazioni in Adriatico', *Rivista marittima*, vol. 98, no. 5 (May 1965), pp. 42–7.

[5]

Stalemate in the Adriatic and the Germans Build Up Their Submarine Strength

The Adriatic

Shortly before Italy's formal entry into the war Admiral Sir Douglas Gamble, who had signed the convention of 10 May for Britain, proceeded to Rome, conferred with the Minister of Marine and Thaon di Revel, and continued on to Taranto to meet the Duke of the Abruzzi aboard his flagship *Conte di Cavour* on the morning of 23 May to discuss the details of naval co-operation. Gamble was favourably impressed with the charts of the anti-submarine defences of Taranto and Brindisi 'which appeared on paper, to be very well thought out'. Gamble politely advised the duke to exercise the greatest caution against submarines and emphasized how dangerous it would be to send battleships into the Adriatic before 'it was fairly cleared of these pests'. The duke took the suggestion 'in the most friendly way' and he and Gamble agreed that British ships using Taranto would coal directly from British colliers, while those at Brindisi would be supplied from Italian stocks. This would spare British colliers the dangers of passing through the Straits of Otranto, where submarines were suspected. Stores for ships at Brindisi would also be sent from Taranto via rail.[1]

Gamble arrived in Malta the morning of the 24th in an Italian destroyer, one of two bringing pilots for the French and British ships destined to join the Italian fleet. The British role in the Adriatic would be very limited. The big problem in relations with the Italians was apt to be the French as Gamble and Limpus, Admiral Superintendent at Malta, discovered when they, accompanied by Rear-Admiral Cecil Thursby who was commanding the battleship squadron attached to the Italian fleet, conferred with Lapeyrère aboard his flagship *Courbet*. They all agreed that the French and Italian commanders-in-chief should meet to exchange views, but Lapeyrère 'did not wish to meet the Italian C.-in-C. unless an English Admiral was present, and he would not propose it'. If Gamble suggested the meeting and arranged a date, he would come to Taranto in one of his ships. The British had to act as the go-betweens in the relationship and the meeting between Gamble, Thursby, Lapeyrère and Abruzzi took place in Taranto on the 27th. Abruzzi read the principal paragraphs of his instructions and Gamble considered that the encounter was apparently a success with good feeling being established between the French and Italians, although he 'was not at all sure, before the meeting took place, that this desirable result would be attained'.[2] Lapeyrère designated the twelve 'best units' of his destroyer flotillas to join the Italians at Brindisi along with six submarines, but warned the British that he could not guarantee absolute security of the extensive lines of communication in the Mediterranean with his restricted means, and recommended certain itineraries for maritime transport. The Italians would also have to take charge of escorting shipments of supplies to Montenegro which now lay within their zone in the Adriatic.[3]

While Lapeyrère may have sent his 'best' destroyers to the Italians, the British contribution could never have been described in these terms and the ships had been continually under fire and needed refitting. Revel, when warned of this by Gamble, was most concerned that the cruisers be efficient, and did not appear to consider the battleships. All four, *Queen*, *London*, *Implacable* and *Prince of Wales*, were pre-dreadnoughts, and *London* and *Implacable* had particularly severe defects. Three of the four all-important cruisers were even worse. *Dartmouth* had two boilers out of action and her speed reduced to 21 knots – it later fell to 16 – while the older *Amethyst* and *Sapphire* could not make more than 20 knots. Only *Dublin* was in reasonably good condition and she would be torpedoed in one of the early Italian operations. Acting Vice-Admiral Sir Henry Oliver, Chief of Staff, admitted that the position as to refits was not satisfactory, but no spare battleships were available and those at the Dardanelles were just as bad. Balfour, the new First Lord, commented that Thursby's report showed 'a serious state of things. The only ship that is praised without qualification is the one which has been torpedoed! We cut a very poor figure with our Allies in the Adriatic.' Admiral Jackson agreed, 'We are hardly keeping to our obligation owing to the drain in our resources elsewhere'. Midshipman Charles Drage in the *London* confided to his diary with the outspokenness of youth that the Italians must have been expecting *Lord Nelson*, *Agamemnon* or at least four King Edwards, but 'what their feelings must have been when this antediluvian quartette was fobbed off on them can well be imagined'.[4] The Italian suspicions about the real state of the Allied navies which had been so forcefully expressed by Thaon di Revel in the haggling over the Naval Convention appeared to be only too true.

The appearance of the submarine threat really called for small craft. At the Paris Conference, Churchill had offered fifty trawlers to the Italians as well as fifty miles of submarine indicator nets for the Straits of Otranto. The Italians would arm and man the little ships. The Italians tentatively accepted the offer but they were not enthusiastic. Revel doubted that the Duke of the Abruzzi really wanted them and thought that their draught was too great for effective use as minesweepers in the tideless Adriatic. Moreover, the Italians would have great difficulty in finding the necessary armament and crews.[5] The first British drifters ordered to the Mediterranean at the end of

May therefore did not go to the Adriatic, but joined de Robeck's forces in the Aegean where they proved extremely useful.[6]

Lapeyrère, on the other hand, welcomed the Minister of Marine's decision to send him ten armed trawlers which would permit him to rotate patrol duties to keep his precious destroyers and torpedo-boats in good condition.[7] He found his responsibilities as Mediterranean C.-in-C. to protect the long transport routes very difficult to fulfil. Shortly before Italy joined the war, he informed the minister that the means the Allies possessed to assure an active and intense pursuit of submarines were insufficient and, such as they were, would be concentrated at points where the presence of submarines was most probable, but their resources would not permit a continuous and systematic search for supply ships and bases. Like other naval leaders, he was obsessed with the idea that submarines needed secret bases and supply ships. Lapeyrère estimated that, counting patrols and the immediate protection of the battle fleet, he needed a minimum of fifty-six destroyers and torpedo-boats, but had only forty-seven, and five of these had been detached for service at the Dardanelles leaving a deficit of fifteen units. The ten armed trawlers to be sent to the Mediterranean would slightly ameliorate the situation, but it would remain precarious since the twelve destroyers he counted on for the immediate protection of the fleet were notoriously unreliable and he would really need at least twenty to be sure of always having ten ready to sail at any moment. Lapeyrère was also at his extreme limit in regard to cruisers, and he concluded that it was absolutely essential for the 5ème Escadrille of destroyers detached to the Dardanelles to be returned to his control until he could receive reinforcements and until the British could come to the assistance of the French in the general surveillance of the Mediterranean.[8] There was one measure, however, that the French did not intend to take. Augagneur informed the Minister of War that convoys, which reduced the speed of ships to that of the slowest, were only advantageous when enemy cruisers were feared, but in the presence of submarines drew attention from far off and might be more dangerous than useful. The dispatch of ships sailing alone at high speed on variable routes offered more security, but naturally an accident was always possible.[9] The French, like their British allies, would pay dearly for this attitude before the introduction of the convoy system in 1917.

Lapeyrère's problems were considerable, particularly since he thought exclusively in terms of hunting and pursuing submarines. He suggested that the French trawlers might be organized for continuous surveillance between Sicily and Tunisia with the objective of discovering enemy submarines and probably their supply ships. One wonders how much time and precious fuel the Allies wasted looking for those non-existent supply ships. Lapeyrère complained of the considerable disproportion between the responsibilities of the French navy in the Mediterranean and the means at its disposal to meet those responsibilities. The line of communications between Port Said and Gibraltar extended some 1,900 miles and Lapeyrère asked Augagneur to inform the Admiralty that he would hunt submarines as much as possible with the means at his disposal and recommend routes for shipping to avoid areas which appeared dangerous according to the latest intelligence, but he could not guarantee accidents would not occur on those routes.[10] The irony of the situation was that while the French had unchallenged superiority in terms of big ships, they did not have sufficient numbers of small craft and would be forced to make increasing calls in the future on the Royal Navy for assistance. Inevitably this would diminish the authority of the French C.-in-C.

Once Italy had entered the war, the actual Anglo-French operations with the Italians began with high hopes. The British and French sent liaison officers to the Italian fleet at Taranto. Happily for historians, they were Captain Herbert Richmond and Capitaine de vaisseau René Daveluy, both intelligent, articulate and outspoken officers who were also prolific writers. Their initial impressions of the Duke of the Abruzzi were highly favourable. Richmond found him 'young and vigorous', his Chief of Staff 'able', and Italian plans compared favourably with those of the Admiralty since 'thought has been given both to the general & the particular' and 'a coherent plan runs through the whole'.[11] Daveluy found the duke exercising a very exacting personal action, but with 'style', and the Italian C.-in-C. was very up-to-date in matériel matters and several times raised technical questions that Daveluy could not answer. He had navigated sufficiently in all the waters of the world to have as much experience of the sea as any Italian admiral and was a true and effective chief who inspired confidence in his subordinates, with a marked predilection for evolutions at high speed.[12]

The handling of the Allied fleet in a hypothetical action posed many problems since the ships were very diverse, ranging from dreadnoughts to pre-dreadnoughts and cruisers of different types and vintages. The Austrian fleet would have been equally diverse. An intellectual officer like Richmond obviously relished the problems which involved questions such as which part of the line the armoured cruisers of the Pisa class would be placed in, or which Italian and British ships would engage the Viribus Unitis class, and which ships the Radetzkys or the older Austrian classes? The questions had a certain abstract ring to them, rather like a war game at a staff college, and it was questionable that the Austrians would ever seek such a classic encounter. One thing was certain, real practice in joint manœuvring was necessary. The Cavours, Regina Elenas and Queens went out in the Gulf of Taranto on 5 June for steam tactics. Richmond confessed that the Cavours were not well handled with crash use of the helm and great variations in speed and failures to follow the ships ahead. Young Midshipman Drage was even more explicit. He confessed that, on the British side, their 'own manoeuvring was not remarkably good', but that of the Italians 'was abominable'. The 'amount of smoke they make is appalling. The heavens are literally darkened and it is difficult enough to keep station astern of them, apart from fighting our guns, in the kind of black fog they create. God help us if we have to tackle the Austrian battle fleet.' Thursby also commented on the excessive smoke made by the Italians and attributed it to their burning American coal.[13] The British and Italians went out again on 11 June for combined steam tactics, despite the fact that *Dublin* had been torpedoed by a submarine the day before. Richmond noted, 'Expect we shall be torpedoed if we go on playing the fool doing steam tactics off Taranto, especially as the whole fleet knows when we are going to sea'. Richmond failed to convince Thursby of his objections for the admiral's 'mind is still taken up with accurate station keeping & such like; he doesn't seem to see that you can't teach these things at 5 minutes' notice & that at this stage of the war it is too late to begin that part of nautical instruction when in the process of teaching we are likely to lose some of our pupils'. Thursby, after Richmond pointed out the danger, was so convinced of the importance of manoeuvres that he even suggested they ought to go to Malta and do the exercises there, far from the scene of possible operations in the Adriatic.[14] Thursby was perhaps more conscious of the submarine danger than Richmond admitted. He wrote privately to the First Lord that the fleet went out on these occasions without any proper screen of cruisers and destroyers. Each division had two torpedo-boats attached to it, but they were usually far astern and would not be much use.[15]

The Duke of the Abruzzi and Rear-Admiral Thursby were, as so often happened in the Mediterranean during the war, preparing for a contingency that would never take place. The real action involved cruisers, destroyers, torpedo-boats and submarines, and the British and French followed Italian plans by joining their allies in a series of raids and bombardments of Austrian coastal installations in the lower and mid-Adriatic on 1, 5 and 9 June, while they drew up other plans for a more serious bombardment of Spalato.[16] Naturally, the Allies did not catch any of the Austrian light craft at sea. Richmond recognized that these actions were 'pin-pricks' and Rear-Admiral Thursby wanted to send landing parties of a few thousand men to the Dalmatian coast and islands. The Italians had examined this before and the British soon learned that the Italian navy could not furnish the men and the Italian army would not. Richmond was inclined to favour purely naval action for the time being. But, as Daveluy wryly remarked, they would quickly exhaust the list of possible targets and wind up bombarding the same lighthouse, semaphore or viaduct ten times. Moreover, Abruzzi had congratulated himself that high speed had enabled his ships to escape Austrian submarine torpedoes. This good luck ended on 9 June when *Dublin* – ironically the British cruiser in the best condition – was torpedoed by the Austrian submarine U4, despite the fact that she was steaming at high speed with a strong destroyer escort.[17] *Dublin* was able to get back to Brindisi, even working up to 17 knots, but would be out of action for some time. Shortly afterwards the Austrians resumed their raids against points on the Italian coast. This, in turn, was partially responsible for one of the more disastrous decisions of the Italian Naval Staff. In order to have fast but powerful warships to back up the old Sardegna division at Venice, they decided to send the IV Division of four large Pisa-class armoured cruisers under Rear-Admiral Umberto Cagni to Venice, accompanied by a *squadriglia* of Indomito-class destroyers. Revel later justified the decision by claiming that the Pisas were fast enough to avoid an unequal encounter with battleships, and that their presence at Venice would limit the activity of Austrian light craft or force the Austrians to expose larger warships to support their flotillas. Revel apparently dreamed of a Pisa catching an Austrian

Novara-class light cruiser or one of the slower and weaker Austrian cruisers and, after the arrival of the Pisas at Venice, claimed Austrian naval activity in the upper Adriatic was, with the exception of submarines, reduced to virtually nothing. Richmond remarked that Abruzzi was 'furious' about the move which was also to partially satisfy army demands for naval support on their seaward flank, and Richmond, Thursby and Daveluy all considered it to have been a big mistake. As Richmond put it, the Pisas did not have the cruising speed to catch the Austrian Novaras, were a big target and unnecessarily large to fight the Novaras, and would now be cut off from the rest of the Italian fleet.[18]

The Italian war plans had included considerable discussion about the seizure of enemy islands or territory and the establishment of a temporary naval base. Abruzzi was anxious to undertake something bigger than pin-prick raids which did not seem to yield any tangible results. On 8 June he announced his intention of occupying the island of Lagosta by surprise in order to establish a line of lookout stations that would run eastwards from Monte Gargano on the Italian mainland. Lagosta would also provide a base for submarines to oppose enemy navigation in the lower Dalmatian archipelago and serve as a centre to gather intelligence for a further advance to Sabbioncello. He thought that Lagosta could be taken by around two hundred volunteers. Revel and the Naval Staff had no objections about the surprise capture of Lagosta but had some reservations about the further advance to Sabbioncello. While Lagosta was sufficiently distant from the mainland and other Dalmatian islands to be held without employing powerful forces, the same could not be said for Sabbioncello. The Italian army had explicitly excluded formation of a volunteer corps, but Revel pointed out that the 149th Regiment of Mobile Militia at Brindisi, originally destined to occupy the temporary naval base (Base Rossa), might be suitable for the operation against Lagosta. Revel also invited Abruzzi to consider, before undertaking the operation against Lagosta, permanently occupying and installing a signal station on the little island of Pelagosa.[19]

Abruzzi did not think that the occupation of Pelagosa by itself would compensate for the risks involved, and Pelagosa would only acquire value as the necessary compliment for Lagosta. Pelagosa might then represent the optical connection for signal stations between Lagosta and the Italian mainland since Abruzzi wanted to reduce wireless transmissions to cases of urgent necessity or when atmospheric conditions precluded visual signals. On 5 July he forwarded to Vice-Admiral Presbitero, commanding the Italian forces at Brindisi, a general scheme for the occupation of Pelagosa which must have a 'flying' character and be limited to the minimum force and supplies necessary to set up the signal station.[20] On 6 July he cabled Revel that the operation would take place within a few days and that he was also preparing for the occupation of Lagosta.

Revel was ready to accept the occupation of Pelagosa, but asked Abruzzi to consider recent developments before proceeding to Lagosta. The Italian army's operations in the north had not developed with the anticipated speed, the enemy enjoyed the advantage of terrain, and the breakthrough into enemy territory had not yet occurred. The Austrians instead of having to use all their forces to stop the Italian army might therefore be able to detach troops without excessive risk for a reoccupation of Lagosta. The 'ambiguous' policy of Montenegro and the present inaction of the Serbian army also eased the pressure on the Austrians, while relations between Italy and Greece were strained and the Greeks might fall into the orbit of the Central Powers. Furthermore, the offensive capacity of enemy submarines was growing and ships participating in the occupation of an island as close to the Dalmatian coast as Lagosta would be exposed to considerable risk. Revel advised waiting for the situation to clarify itself before taking a definite decision.[21]

Meanwhile Vice-Admiral Presbitero had prepared his study on how the occupation of Lagosta might take place. Because of the steep and nearly inaccessible nature of the coast, landings were only possible at the two points of Porto Largo Grande and Porto Largo Piccolo, and Presbitero estimated that the Italians would need approximately 620 men.[22] The question of Lagosta and Pelagosa revealed considerable indecision among Italian naval leaders and one can follow the frustrations in the various entries in Richmond's diary. On 12 June he noted that Rome had approved the plans for Lagosta: the duke was for it but the admirals and Naval Staff were against it. On 18 June he noted that Lagosta was held up and the admirals disagreed among themselves and the duke was undecided. By 23 June, Richmond heard from the duke's Deputy Chief of Staff, Captain Conz, that the Naval Staff in Rome was in favour of Lagosta and, on 9 July, Conz told him that they had decided to take Lagosta and Pelagosa. Richmond wondered 'why it has taken 4 weeks or so to make up their minds'.[23]

The Italians moved the four Regina Elenas from Taranto to Brindisi so the fast light battleships could take the place of the four Pisas sent to Venice. This had the effect of dividing the Italian fleet into three parts: the dreadnoughts, two pre-dreadnoughts and four old British battleships at Taranto; four Regina Elenas, Italian and British cruisers, and French and Italian destroyers at Brindisi; and the old Sardegna-class battleships, four Pisas, destroyers, torpedo-boats and submarines at Venice. It was not difficult to see, as Richmond pointed out, that the present dispositions were a temptation to the enemy to attack Ancona, Bari, or Brindisi, with the opportunity of defeating the separated Italian squadrons should they come out to give battle.[24] Abruzzi had intelligence from various sources that the Austrians were planning such an attack with their entire fleet timed to coincide with the anniversary of Lissa (20 July). There were also reports of submarines in the lower Adriatic and supply bases for submarines in the Corfu zone, and he suspected that this might be linked with an effort to draw out the Italian battle fleet from Taranto by bombarding Brindisi and Bari so as to lead the Italians into submarine-infested waters around Cape Santa Maria di Leuca. As soon as he had news that the bulk of the enemy fleet had left Pola, Abruzzi planned to meet such an attack by increasing the number of submarines waiting in ambush before Brindisi, keeping all the others ready to sortie, and also sending some to Bari for the defence of that port. If the bulk of the Austrian fleet did attack Brindisi, the Italian warships there should not exit but would co-operate with their artillery in the defence. As soon as the enemy retired, all destroyers and large torpedo-boats would exit to hunt enemy submarines, which would surely be posted off Brindisi. Italian submarines in the area should dive as soon as they saw the enemy retreating and get away from the waters around Brindisi so as not to encumber the hunt.[25]

An attack or feint by the Austrians against Taranto appeared improbable since they would, at the latest, be spotted by the blockade line in the Straits of Otranto which would give more or less five hours' warning of their approach. In this unlikely event, the Italian 1° Squadra (dreadnoughts) would sail at once, while the scout cruisers and destroyers would sortie from Brindisi to establish contact with the enemy and transmit information about his strength, course and speed. The large torpedo-boats at Brindisi would also patrol the waters around the port and clear them of submarines in preparation for the exit of the larger warships, notably the Regina Elenas, which would proceed at once towards the line of Otranto if contact between the enemy fleet and the 1° Squadra from Taranto took place. The Regina Elenas should be ready to attack the enemy when he retreated from combat with the 1° Squadra since the latter would not pursue the Austrians to avoid falling into a submarine ambush. If contact between the enemy fleet and the 1° Squadra did not take place because the enemy preferred to avoid combat, the warships at Brindisi would not come out since the enemy would still be in superior force. In this case, all submarines at Brindisi would be sent towards the Straits of Otranto to attack the enemy on his retreat.

What is most striking about Abruzzi's plans is the fact that even under the most favourable and unlikely circumstances in which the Austrians came south of the Straits of Otranto to do battle with the Italian fleet, he was disinclined to risk his own dreadnoughts in the Adriatic. Admiral Haus, although greatly inferior to the Allied forces, could really have steamed down the Adriatic and thoroughly pounded Brindisi, with the Italian warships there immobilized and firing back the best they could from the shelter of the port. The Italian dreadnoughts would never have come near him. But then Haus would have faced the risk of submarines himself and the same question as Abruzzi, that is, were the possible results commensurate with the risks? Haus obviously thought not. Submarines had, to a large extent, checkmated both sides in the Adriatic.

On 30 June the Minister of Marine placed all naval forces at Venice under the sole command of Rear-Admiral Cagni. Revel thought that Cagni's safe passage to Venice with the Pisa division completely eluding the enemy was a 'fine operation'. Cagni was ordered to facilitate and support the Italian army's operations and protect their seaward flank from enemy naval operations, and also to attack and destroy enemy naval forces in the upper Adriatic when he could do so with losses that would be compensated for by at least equivalent losses to the enemy. His torpedo-boats would hunt and destroy enemy submarines or torpedo-boats and might also attack the secondary Austrian bases on the Istrian Peninsula.[26] The event that Italy's allies feared in the upper Adriatic came on the morning of 7 July when the large cruiser *Amalfi*, escorted by only two torpedo-boats, came out to support a sweep by Italian destroyers and was herself torpedoed and sunk by UB14.[27] UB14 was commanded by Oberleutnant zur See von Heimburg, a German as were the other officers and men, although an Austrian officer was on board as pilot. The small submarine had only just been assembled at Pola and within a week would leave for Aegean waters. Italy and Germany were not yet officially at war and the submarine had the Austrian designation, U26. The identification of German and Austrian submarines in the Mediterranean can be confusing, as no doubt the Germans and Austrians intended, for German U-boats in the Mediterranean had Austrian numbers as well as their own. The k.u.k. Kriegsmarine did not follow the German practice of designating submarines by type – U, UB, or UC – but used the simple designation U for all. Early in the war, the Austrians used Roman numerals for submarines but gave up the practice for the more common Arabic numerals. German submarine officers paid little attention to the technicality that they were not at war with the Italians. UB14's commander, von Heimburg, for example, had recently been in command of UB15 (Austrian U11) with a German crew (but an Austrian officer as second-in-command) when he surprised and sank the Italian submarine *Medusa* on 1 June.[28] UB15 was then on trials before being turned over to the k.u.k. Kriegsmarine but, although under the Austrian flag at the time of the attack on the *Medusa*, she was not officially taken into Austrian service until the 18th and reports concealed her identity. The nationality point was confusing but obviously academic as long as a submarine attacked while submerged. It would cause complications later in the year when German submarines flying the Austrian flag destroyed Italian merchant ships while surfaced.

The loss of the *Amalfi* was the first major naval disaster for the Italians in the war. After receiving the preliminary reports, Revel was furious with Cagni for having risked the ship on a reconnaissance for which destroyers, acting *en masse*, would have sufficed, with the sailing of the *Amalfi* dependent on what they reported. Revel considered *Amalfi*'s escort to be woefully inadequate for six instead of two torpedo-boats should have been employed, and if Cagni did not have that number available he should not have let the cruiser sail. Her mission fulfilled none of the objectives cited in Cagni's orders of 30 June. Cagni received a preliminary letter of reprimand and his independence was curtailed by being placed, along with the three surviving ships of his division, under the orders of Vice-Admiral Cutinelli, commander of the base at Venice.[29] The question of further punishment would await the results of a full inquiry.

Revel was still convinced, despite Cagni's mistakes, that his own decision to send the large Pisas to Venice was a correct one. He argued in a letter to Abruzzi that the conflict with Austria would be resolved on land and the task of both the Italian and Austrian navies was primarily to assist either directly or indirectly their respective armies. Before the advent of the submarine the situation would have led either to a battle or blockade, but today the war was one of attrition and cunning in which more than ever one sought to arrive at one's aims with a minimum of risk. If Venice were destitute of powerful warships, the Austrians might risk their older ships of scant value to disturb the Italian position on land. As long as the Italians had naval units at Venice which could advantageously face the less important classes of the Austrian fleet, in order to act in the upper Adriatic the latter would be forced to employ more powerful warships and would therefore be forced to run graver risks. Abruzzi's forces in the south had been compensated for the four Pisas by the four British battleships. Revel repeated his contention that the Pisas were faster than the most powerful Austrian ships and stronger than the fastest Austrian ships. He had also not lost faith in Cagni who had certainly made mistakes and had learned a painful lesson, but also had the qualities to benefit from this lesson in the future.[30]

The Italians occupied Pelagosa without opposition on 11 July, establishing a garrison of ninety men who the following morning found a few Austrian lighthouse keepers hiding in a grotto. The barren little island was barely more than a kilometre in length and 330 metres wide, with a lighthouse as its principal feature. The same day, French destroyers carried out an aggressive and close reconnaissance of Lagosta which included sending a party ashore.[31] Richmond and Thursby had advocated taking Lagosta at the same time as Pelagosa but the Italians were undecided. Richmond complained, 'Why the deuce don't the Admiral go on & take Lagosta? If he waits, he will find they've defended it, & instead of walking in he'll have to fight his way. It is sheer madness to delay.' Daveluy had similar sentiments although he had doubts about its value: 'The most certain benefit one would draw from its possession would be the preoccupation with keeping it.'[32] The Italian liaison officer who had accompanied the French reconnaissance also had some discouraging news about Lagosta. The island had numerous points suitable for a landing and it would therefore require many troops to hold it securely.[33]

Abruzzi re-examined actions he might take in the south to draw the Austrian fleet out, since nothing could apparently be accomplished in the north until the military situation was delineated more clearly. The C.-in-C. considered operations against Lagosta (vetoed by the Minister of Marine and Chief of Staff), Ragusa and Spalato. Operations against the latter could only be an offensive demonstration since too many troops would be required to actually occupy the town. Abruzzi complained that he was not informed about the Italian army's operations in the north and learned about them only through the Stefani news agency press releases, and he was also not up-to-date on the operations of the naval units detached to the upper Adriatic which were directly dependent on the ministry. If he were better informed he might be able to co-ordinate his actions with the other forces and obtain better results.[34]

One of Abruzzi's objectives in an attack on Ragusa would be to cut the railway between Ragusa and Cattaro which had been shelled on 5 June and put out of action for approximately a month. The line apparently had been restored. The new operation against the railway led directly to the Italian navy's second major loss of the war, for on the morning of 18 July the armoured cruiser *Garibaldi* was torpedoed and sunk by the Austrian submarine U4 off the Dalmatian coast.[35] Revel was inclined to blame Rear-Admiral Trifari, commanding the V Division (Garibaldis) for not informing the C.-in-C. that his force had been spotted by an aeroplane shortly after leaving Brindisi the evening before. This would have given the C.-in-C. the opportunity to cancel the operation if he saw fit since the essential factor of surprise would be lacking.[36]

Ironically Haus was not satisfied with the extent of the Austrian success either. Haus criticized U4's commander, Linienschiffsleutnant Singule, for sinking only the *Garibaldi* when he had the whole Italian cruiser division spread out before him, and repeated this criticism before all the Austrian submarine officers on the 25th. Thierry, leader of the submarine service, tried to defend his subordinate by pointing out that U4 had been hunted for hours. The Flottenkommandant took his remarks very ungraciously and a few days later a staff officer arrived to warn him that he should not perpetually contradict the admiral. The outspoken Thierry replied that he would always maintain his point of view.[37] This was perhaps another example of that friction between Haus and the head of the Austrian submarine service. Surprisingly, Haus kept Thierry on.

The loss of the *Garibaldi* immediately affected the plans for Lagosta. On 17 July, Revel informed Abruzzi that he would reserve judgement until after he had conferred with the Army High Command and the government, but in the meantime preparations for the operation should continue. A detachment of 50 *carabinieri* and 36 *guardia di finanza* and two companies of 100 sailors each, equipped for landing operations, assembled at Brindisi, but the army was unable to provide artillery officers to direct the guns they were willing to send, and the officers would have to be furnished by the fleet.[38] The final decision of the government on 27 July was negative. Revel admitted that the plans for the operation were well conceived and employed ships which were well chosen – battleworthy but not too large. However, to implement the operation at the present moment would be inopportune, although it would not be excluded at some time in the future when the impression in the country caused by the nearly successive loss of two warships was somewhat dissipated. In the meantime, Revel authorized Abruzzi to prepare the small expeditionary corps, avoiding excessive expenditure.[39]

The Austrian reaction to the occupation of Pelagosa came slowly. A seaplane reconnoitred the island on the afternoon of 13 July and returned with the destroyer *Tátra* which shelled the Italian wireless station and moved off when the seaplane reported the presence of the French submarine *Fresnel*. The Italians had decided to station submarines in rotation for the defence of the island. *Fresnel* tried unsuccessfully to get in position for a shot at the *Tátra* and was, in turn, bombed by the seaplane. With the Italian presence on the island of Pelagosa confirmed, the Austrians extended their boom defence of the harbour of Largo Grande on Lagosta and prepared mines for the harbour of San Giorgio on Lissa, thereby justifying Richmond's warning that the once defenceless Lagosta should have been taken simultaneously with Pelagosa before the Austrians had been put on their guard.[40] The small Italian garrison on Pelagosa had two 75-mm cannon, and later four 76-mm landing guns, a 76-mm anti-aircraft gun and a pair of machine guns. Revel thought that they ought to have two or four

120-mm cannon instead of the 76-mm guns to hold off the Austrian Novara-class light cruisers which were armed with 100-mm guns. Abruzzi believed that the 76-mm guns on hand plus the trench and barbed wire defences prepared by the Italians, as well as the presence of the submarine, were sufficient to prevent a surprise enemy landing, but he promised to study the question of establishing a heavier battery of 120-mm guns.[41]

Austrian cruisers, destroyers and torpedo-boats raided the Italian coast from Grottamare to Termoli and the Tremiti Islands on 23 July, and joined by aircraft repeated the attacks between Ancona and Fano on the 28th. On the same day Austrian forces sailing from Sebenico and consisting of two light cruisers, six destroyers and a number of torpedo-boats, with UB14 scouting in advance, attacked Pelagosa. After a heavy bombardment, the Austrians landed 4 officers and 104 men, but met strong resistance and were eventually recalled. Before landing the Austrians had underestimated the garrison, thinking it to be only around 30; after their repulse they overestimated it at 200–400. The French submarine *Ampère* fired at, but missed, an Austrian destroyer and was, in turn, hunted. The Italians reported two wounded, the Austrian losses were two dead and ten wounded. The British cruiser *Topaze* and three destroyers from Brindisi arrived after the Austrians had departed.[42] It was a small affair but the Italians had defended the island and could claim a victory. The Austrians struck back on the morning of 5 August when Linienschiffsleutnant von Trapp in U5 succeeded in torpedoing the Italian submarine *Nereide* posted for defence of the island. Trapp might not have seen the submarine but for the fact that the Italian crew raised the flag after daybreak and he actually spotted the naval ensign under the cliffs of the island before he saw the submarine.[43]

Abruzzi was not content to let the decision on Lagosta rest and wanted to reopen the question. He now argued that the island would have been very useful as a submarine base, for the Italians with their relatively fragile submarines had difficulty in maintaining permanent patrols in the promising hunting grounds off the Zuri Channel near Sebenico. In conjunction with Pelagosa and the Gargano headlands the occupation of Lagosta would establish a barrage in the central Adriatic completely isolating Cattaro and shutting out the enemy from the lower Adriatic. The occupation force considered necessary had grown to approximately 870, of whom about 200 were the naval landing party and 300 were artillerymen to serve the guns.[44]

On 7 August, Abruzzi warned that it would take not less than thirty days from the moment the government decided to go ahead with the occupation to gather the landing parties, complete their training and assemble material. Moreover, the approach of autumn would increase the difficulties in preparing and executing the operation, while every passing day gave the enemy more time to reinforce his defences, create obstacles and lay mines where they had been nearly non-existent. From the strategic point of view, Lagosta constituted the natural and indispensable support of Pelagosa and completed the occupation of the latter, which in no case could be considered an end in itself and had been effected only as a first step towards the subsequent occupation of Lagosta. As winter approached aerial reconnaissance from Venice would become less frequent and consequently information on the enemy deployment would become more scarce, while reconnaissance by light craft would also become more difficult and the fleet would have serious trouble obtaining exact intelligence on the moves of the enemy. The occupation of Lagosta would therefore be of great assistance to the fleet since, along with Pelagosa, it would constitute a line of observation posts from the Gargano towards the Curzola Islands. Abruzzi placed a high value on this and considered it would compensate for the losses which might occur in occupying and maintaining the island. Moreover, there was an absolute lack of good ports to support submarines on the coast of Puglia and the frequent bad weather in the Adriatic during the winter would undoubtedly make it difficult and almost impossible for Allied submarines to maintain themselves near Pelagosa. This implied the danger of losing either the submarine deployed or the island itself since Abruzzi considered the submarine constituted the most valid and effective defence. Abruzzi argued that if the government intended to occupy Lagosta they should do so at once or definitely give up the idea. In case of the latter, it would be expedient to consider the eventuality of being obliged to also withdraw from Pelagosa.[45]

Revel refuted the arguments on the value of Lagosta, demonstrating the fundamental disagreement between the C.-in-C. of the fleet and the Naval Staff and helping to explain why the Italians seemed to have such great difficulty in making up their minds on the operation. The Capo di Stato Maggiore argued that the military situation on land continued to be such as to advise, at least for some time, against the occupation of Lagosta. The advance of the Italian army beyond the Isonzo River was proceeding with slowness and difficulty and the campaign was assuming the characteristics of trench warfare. The occupation of Pelagosa and Lagosta were not strictly tied to one another and the latter was not a necessary consequence of the former. Lagosta and Pelagosa would not really be of great utility for getting more prompt and secure intelligence on the enemy's movements during the winter season for the enemy had the ability to cross by night and arrive at dawn at whatever coastal point in the central and lower Adriatic which might be his objective. When bad weather prevented Italian submarines from maintaining themselves near Pelagosa, the occupation of Lagosta would in no way change the situation. Submarines might stay at Barletta, seventy miles from Pelagosa, while waiting for better weather, and with northerly winds could also stay at Manfredonia, sixty miles from Pelagosa. If they could stay at Lagosta the sole advantage would be that Pelagosa was twenty-three or thirty-three miles closer. The distance from the west coast of Lagosta to Pelagosa was thirty-seven miles and, if a submarine left Lagosta as soon as it received information that Pelagosa was under attack, most of the time it would still arrive at its post after the action was over. Moreover, in bad weather Pelagosa was secure from landing attempts and within certain limits also from bombardment by light vessels. The supply of Lagosta would be much more difficult and dangerous than that of Pelagosa. The latter was equally distant from the Austrian and Italian coasts, while Lagosta was much closer to the Austrian coast and would require more supplies and larger transports. There were also no spare officers available for the landing forces and they would have to be furnished from the fleet.[46]

In presenting their arguments, neither Abruzzi nor Revel had mentioned one of Captain Richmond's main ideas for the use of Pelagosa which was to use it as bait for enemy forces who could then be crushed with superior strength. This was not likely to occur, however, for Abruzzi had mentioned that the Pisas would not come out of Venice and he had also ruled out sending any of his own battleships into the Adriatic. By the beginning of August, Richmond was becoming thoroughly disenchanted with the Italians. 'These folk deserve to lose, for by heaven they do nothing towards trying to win', he complained, and later wrote, 'What the deuce is the use of a superior Fleet if you don't use it.' Thursby became concerned that Richmond's latest reports were so full of criticism of the Italians that he did not think it right to send them as an appendix to his own report of proceedings, although there was no difference of opinion between them.[47]

The Italian garrison which was working hard to fortify Pelagosa suffered acute discomfort from the heat on the barren island where fresh water had to be brought in by tank ships. On 9 August a small convoy landed more supplies, four 76-mm cannon, a pair of machine guns and another thirty sailors. On the 16th, Revel continued to advocate 120-mm guns to hold off the Austrian Spauns, but Abruzzi thought that the 76-mm guns were sufficient to prevent a landing and hold off attacks by destroyers. The 120-mm guns could not be in place during the current month and, with their crews, would add to the difficulties of supply, particularly in regard to water. Abruzzi wanted to keep the garrison of Pelagosa to a minimum.[48] The very next day, 17 August, the Austrians returned in force. Sailing from Sebenico to avoid observation from Mount Lovčen at Cattaro, the I Torpedo Flotilla and XII Torpedo Division deployed around Pelagosa where the light cruiser *Helgoland*, two destroyers and a torpedo-boat closed to shell the Italian positions. They were later joined by another pair of destroyers and the cruiser *Saida* as well as seaplanes. The Austrians thoroughly worked over the island, destroying installations including the fresh-water cistern. Later that day, Revel ordered immediate evacuation, all material which could not be quickly embarked was to be destroyed. Revel and the Naval Staff account of the affair stressed the lack of resources on the island where steep slopes made it difficult to enlarge the Italian emplacements. In short, inhospitable Pelagosa would be more trouble to hold than it was worth. The actual evacuation took place without incident on the 18th, covered by strong cruiser and destroyer forces from Brindisi.[49] Richmond's entry in his private diary that day was scathing:

> They have by this admitted that the Austrians have command of the sea in the Adriatic in spite of inferior naval force & without fighting an action! They have surrendered to them. They had better sell their Fleet & take up their organs & monkeys again, for, by Heaven, that seems more their profession than sea-fighting.[50]

Thursby, on the other hand, thought that it was useless to hold Pelagosa since the Italians had not taken advantage of its possession to attack the Austrian forces sent against it and had, at present, abandoned the idea of occupying any of the Dalmatian Islands. He acknowledged, however, that 'the practical abandonment of the control of the Adriatic may have very serious results' allowing the Austrians to blockade with submarines and mines and bombard undefended towns and attack the Otranto patrol. Thursby's solution was some action against Corfu which he asserted, incorrectly, 'is now to be used as a base for enemy submarines'.[51] Daveluy shared the sentiments about the Italians failing to use Pelagosa to draw the Austrians into an encounter because, as he suspected, the Italians did not really want one, and 'destruction of the enemy afloat did not constitute the objective of our Allies'. He did not share the suspicions of Thursby, Richmond, or many Italians about Corfu as a submarine base. Daveluy pointed out the obvious. It would be extraordinary for submarines to go and supply themselves in a clandestine fashion in a neutral harbour where they could not stay when they had the base at Cattaro at their disposal. He concluded: 'It is never necessary to suppose the enemy did things contrary to good sense.'[52]

The Austrians did not have it all their own way during the week before the evacuation of Pelagosa and suffered their first submarine losses. U12 struck a mine off Venice on the 12th (some sources give the 11th) and was lost with all hands, while U3 was sunk north-east of Brindisi by the French destroyer *Bisson* on the 13th. The Austrian torpedo-boat T51 also had its bows blown off by a torpedo from the French submarine *Papin* during a reconnaissance of Pelagosa on 9 September, but was towed to safety.[53]

The question of action against the Austrian base at Cattaro also came up again during the summer of 1915. The French Army General Staff suggested the possibility of a combined action by the Italian fleet and Montenegrin troops along the Adriatic coast, perhaps in conjunction with action by the Serbian army. The French asked the Italian military attaché in Paris if the Italian army had prepared any studies on the subject. The Italian army obviously had not and turned to the navy.[54] King Nicholas of Montenegro also appealed to King Victor Emmanuel III, who was his son-in-law, for eight long-range guns and some heavy howitzers. The guns would be established on Mount Lovčen and would make the stay of the Austrian fleet in the Gulf of Cattaro impossible. Montenegrin troops were ready to leave for the north and awaiting the signal for common action with the Serbs in Bosnia, but King Nicholas was unwilling to leave Cattaro and Ragusa untouched on their left flank when the two places, he claimed, might be taken without great difficulty or sacrifice by a combined action. He asserted that the Austrian forts at Cattaro, once they were under fire from Italian artillery on Mount Lovčen and the Italian fleet from the seaward side, would capitulate without difficulty. With Cattaro in their hands they could move on Ragusa which was nearly an open city, but important for its location as a terminus for the Bosnia railway.[55]

The navy's reply to these suggestions was delayed by Revel's absence from Rome but, in the interim, Vice-Admiral Viale, Minister of Marine, made it quite clear that it was likely to be negative. Viale seemed to see the project in the worst possible light. The transport by sea and landing of the artillery, considerable accessory material and munitions in a locality that was close to Cattaro would be a 'fairly perilous undertaking' because of submarines, and despite all precautions there might still be grave losses. The heavy artillery and munitions, let alone the men necessary to serve the guns, would have to be provided by the Italian army as the navy did not have cannon adapted for siege operations. The maritime transport necessary to supply the expeditionary force, especially in munitions, and to satisfy the probable requests for matériel from Serbian and Montenegrin troops once they had reached the coast near Cattaro, would be a serious burden for the Regia Marina and despite all precautions the transports in question would always be exposed to considerable risks.[56]

Revel, on his return to Rome, not only agreed with the minister, but went even further. The artillery requested by the King of Montenegro, namely eight long-range guns and some heavy howitzers, would be sufficient to prevent enemy ships from remaining securely in Cattaro, but would not be sufficient for a real siege aimed at forcing a surrender. The attainment of that objective, the only one which would result in considerable utility for the development of their campaign in the Adriatic, would require a more powerful rank of siege artillery. Consequently, the difficulty and risk of its transport and subsequent supply in munitions would grow. These risks were much graver because of enemy submarines whose numbers, aggressive spirit and ability of commanders in manoeuvre were manifestly superior to what could rationally have been foreseen before the opening of hostilities. The transport overland of the artillery from the point of landing to positions on Mount Lovčen might also be opposed and even prevented, with consequent loss of matériel to relatively more numerous enemy troops, and the operation therefore required the assistance of a strong military escort to guarantee security.[57]

With the evacuation of Pelagosa, the naval war in the Adriatic seemed to be winding down somewhat. Even before, Revel had sent a dispatch to Abruzzi on conserving matériel with specific orders to show it to the admirals under his command. Revel reiterated previous statements on the necessity of keeping the activities and services of the light craft and torpedo-boats, as well as submarines, within proper limits so as to avoid excessively frequent repairs and long periods out of service of these relatively (at least for the Italians) fragile craft. He also ordered Italian commanders to take into account the limited nautical capacities of these craft and avoid risking them in bad weather if it were not absolutely necessary, reducing and even suppressing their permanent patrols when needed. The war was likely to last for a long time, he cautioned, and the necessity for energetic naval action might only present itself after many months. Revel repeated these warnings after the evacuation of Pelagosa which had freed the light craft from the obligation of protecting the supply convoys to the island. The services of light craft were once again to be limited to avoid the necessity for frequent repairs. Rear-Admiral Millo, commanding the Scouting Division, an aggressive officer to whom the warnings may have been particularly directed, endorsed Revel's dispatch with the notation that use of light craft had been reduced to a minimum and cruises on the coast of Puglia were now seldom executed, generally only one day out of four.[58] This heavy emphasis on defensiveness and conservation of material went against the grain for Millo and he would shortly clash with the Chief of Naval Staff.

While conserving their own matériel, the Italians made every effort to gain more assistance from their own allies. The Stato Maggiore were well aware that fast light cruisers were of great importance in the Adriatic and would be even more important if they ever occupied some point or islands on the Dalmatian coast. However, this type of vessel was subject to frequent breakdowns requiring long periods of repair, for example *Dartmouth* had spent four months in dockyard hands and *Marsala*, five. The Italians also did not want to rely overly much on the assistance of their allies, either from a certain sense of independence or for the bad impression this made at home on public opinion. The only country with relatively large numbers of light cruisers under construction was Britain and on 26 August, Count Villarey, the Italian naval attaché in London, approached the Admiralty about the possibility of the Regia Marina purchasing two to four light cruisers of the Arethusa or Calliope class.[59] The Admiralty, although conscious of the disadvantage in speed suffered by the British cruisers in the Adriatic in comparison with the Austrians, not surprisingly declined to part with the latest light cruisers under construction which were all earmarked and whose arrival was eagerly awaited in the fleet.[60]

The fumbling performance of the Italian navy in the first few months of the war of which outside observers were so critical could not fail to have political consequences in Italy. The naval war was taking place right on the country's doorstep and a large part of the coastline was directly exposed to enemy attack. The citizens of towns subject to Austrian raids had their deputies, and politicians could hardly be deaf to their appeals. Revel, as Capo di Stato Maggiore, seemed to be in the centre of the storm, his position complicated by the fact that the Minister of Marine was also a retired admiral and the C.-in-C. of the Fleet, a duke and cousin of the king. All navies had some degree of internal friction, but the Italian situation was probably aggravated by a relative lack of success. Revel was also aggressive, unafraid of responsibility and did not hesitate to appeal to other ministers as he had done with Salandra and Sonnino before the war. He also corresponded with General Ugo Brusati, the king's first aide-de-camp with suggestions that certain subjects be brought to the sovereign's attention. He had been in office since April 1913 and wrote, after Italian participation in the war was barely a month old, how disgusted he was with the struggle to conquer slackness and apathy, and complained of the 'byzantine bureaucracy' and how the road was often blocked by jealousy and envy.[61] Revel also found himself blamed by Salandra for naval disasters such as the loss of the *Amalfi* caused by Cagni's rashness, and realizing the problems inherent in his position began to think that an eventual solution would be to combine the functions of minister and chief of staff in the same person.[62] The Italians would, in fact, try this experiment later in the year. As for the *Amalfi*, Revel continued to defend his decision to move the Pisa division to Venice; he simply had not foreseen the reckless and unjustified actions of Cagni.[63]

141

After the losses of the *Amalfi* and *Garibaldi*, and the repeated bombardments of towns on the Italian coast, Salandra had understandable doubts as to what the navy was doing. He wrote to his Minister of Marine on 24 July for details as to whether or not underwater defences and aerial defences were prepared, or could be prepared, to prevent without risking the fleet the all-too-frequent incursions of the enemy against cities from Rimini to Bari. He was also anxious to learn the results of the inquiry into the loss of the *Amalfi* and the submarine *Medusa*, especially as in the latter case the commander of an Italian torpedo-boat was alleged to have fled without attempting to rescue the survivors of the sinking submarine. Salandra also wanted to know whether the indispensable and complete agreement existed between the Capo di Stato Maggiore and the C.-in-C. of the Fleet on the future conduct of the war and the prevention of similar unfortunate incidents. He also warned that proceedings to determine responsibility and solutions to problems should be much more rapid and clear in time of war than they ordinarily were in time of peace. Salandra concluded by declaring it indispensable in time of war that the most complete unity of criteria should govern the supreme powers directing the fleet, and if it were lacking it should be restored at whatever cost so there would be no uncertainty on the responsibility for future events.[64] Salandra authorized Admiral Viale to show the letter to Revel who was immediately ready to resign. The Capo di Stato Maggiore thought that the Prime Minister, and perhaps all the Cabinet, felt the navy might do better, and unfortunately Admiral Viale was not a man capable of solving the difficulties of their maritime war. It would be better if Salandra had another Chief of Naval Staff in whom he could believe without reservation, and Revel did not think it just to share responsibility for Viale's slowness of decision, inertia and lack of energy.[65]

Viale replied to Salandra with a lengthy – twelve pages of typescript – lecture on 28 July giving the navy's explanation for what had or had not happened. The Minister of Marine answered the question of the preparation of underwater and aerial defences to prevent enemy raids with a full explanation of the geographical realities of the Adriatic.[66] He pointed out that mines were in use, and 6,000 were on order, but that frequent gales in the Adriatic tore them loose and the natural drift of the current made them a great peril to their own ships. Submarines could be effective and less dangerous for the defence of the Italian coast, but given the length of the coast, the limited radius of action of Italian submarines and the need for frequent resupply, they would need five times the number they had. Far too many anti-aircraft guns would also be necessary to cover the principal points on the coast between Rimini and Bari, and the army would have to provide them as well as aircraft. The Italians were not alone in their problems. Viale cited the example of the far more powerful Royal Navy in the North Sea which was unable to prevent raids on a stretch of coast roughly the same distance as Rimini to Bari. The German bases were 240 to 300 miles away while the average distance between the two shores of the Adriatic was only 60 to 80 miles. The Italian navy could not assume a precise obligation to defend the open coast from enemy incursions, but would arrange by means of mines, submarines, torpedo-boats and aircraft a defensive system to convince the Austrians that raids against the Italian coast were subject to risks not justified by the importance of the undertaking. This system had been, or was in the process of being, established and other projects such as the use of armoured trains carrying artillery which could be deployed rapidly along the coastal railway line were under study. The minister also quoted the relevant passages of the Italian War Plan of April about the futility of rushing to every point which might be attacked.

Viale then turned to the subject of the *Amalfi*. The results of the formal inquiry into the loss of the *Amalfi* had only just arrived and revealed that Admiral Cagni had not shown the necessary deliberation and sagacity. His independence from the C.-in-C. at Venice had already been revoked and, as additional punishment, he might now be relieved of his command. However, Cagni had a good record and with a character generally recognized as fearless enjoyed esteem in the navy and in the country at large. A severe penalty against him might cause it to be interpreted in the country as a lack of confidence in those fulfilling the difficult task of command at sea. These considerations were of a morale and political character of which Salandra was the better judge, and Admiral Viale would fully consent to Salandra's decision to put Cagni ashore, and if the Prime Minister did not want to go that far he would inflict a severe reprimand on him. Viale had performed here the neat trick of shifting the responsibility for Cagni's fate on to the shoulders of the politician Salandra.

Viale concluded his lengthy apologia with a discussion of the relations between the leading naval authorities, and here he deftly undercut Revel or, more accurately, hinted at a solution that Revel himself had advocated of combining the functions of the chief of staff and minister in the same person. This, of course, implied the departure of Revel. In Viale's opinion the work of the Capo di Stato Maggiore was generally good on technical, military matters, but he did not seem to always have an exact conception of the attributes belonging to his office. He was diligent and shrewd in the preparation of means, but this work all too frequently encroached beyond the boundaries of his logical role, especially in relations with the C.-in-C. of the Fleet. This was clearly demonstrated in his ordering the deployment of the Cagni division (the Pisas) from Brindisi to Venice despite the contrary opinion of the C.-in-C. The Chief of Naval Staff was in a different position from that of the Chief of the Army General Staff. The presence of the king at headquarters conferred on the orders of the Chief of the Army General Staff an authority which those of the Chief of Naval Staff could not have since they came from Rome rather than the field of action. Viale proposed modifying the present April 1913 decree concerning the functions of the Capo di Stato Maggiore and returning to the decree of February 1907, which would have had the effect of drastically reducing the powers of the office. Viale concluded by declaring that he firmly believed everyone in the navy was convinced that, for the moment, their war at sea should be limited to intense action with submarines and aircraft, keeping ships sheltered and well protected in their bases, while preparing the matériel and training personnel for submarines and aircraft.

Salandra took the course expected of an astute politician on the question of Admiral Cagni and sought to avoid overt controversy or, as he put it, he agreed with Viale that the navy should not be deprived of an intelligent and bold officer at the moment. He insisted, though, that a letter of reprimand should be sent at once and asked to see a copy.[67]

In September of 1915 the Italian navy suffered another case of severe dissension in the higher ranks when the Minister of Marine, on the advice of Revel, removed Rear-Admiral Enrico Millo from command of the Scouting Division in the lower Adriatic. Millo first gained fame during the Libyan war when he led a group of torpedo-boats in a daring night raid through the Dardanelles in an unsuccessful attempt to get at the Turkish fleet sheltering further up the Straits. He was promoted to Rear-Admiral, one of the youngest, and subsequently became Minister of Marine from July 1913 to August 1914. His rapid promotion had aroused considerable jealousy and there were many who claimed he had 'arrived in one night' and made a play on his name by calling him 'mille e una notte' after the legendary tales of the *Arabian Nights*. Like Cagni, he had the reputation of being a daring and aggressive officer and was certainly one of the best-known men in the navy.[68]

Millo got into trouble with Revel concerning his remarks on the evacuation of Pelagosa. He had covered the evacuation with his light cruisers and in his report to Abruzzi stated that, without entering into the merits or the motives which had determined the evacuation, the garrison had taken shelter during the bombardment by twenty-two enemy warships for two hours at close range and had suffered only 6 per cent casualties; and that with supplies, reinforcements and the support of submarines the occupation could have been prolonged indefinitely. In his opinion, the order to evacuate did not take due account of the importance of the island in the reconnaissance operations of the fleet. Millo's report, after Abruzzi had forwarded it to Rome, aroused the wrath of the staff and after the conclusion there is a pencilled remark in an unknown hand, 'What communication of sightings had Pelagosa given from 11 July to 17 August?', while elsewhere on the report someone had scribbled that Millo's remarks were 'inopportune'.[69] Revel subsequently visited Brindisi, had at least a brief conversation with Millo, and shortly after his return to Rome the letter of dismissal bearing Viale's signature was sent on the 11th. Millo was removed from his command of the Scouting Division and given command of the Naval Academy. The Chief of Staff charged that Millo's energetic nature and desire for action had caused him frequently to act inopportunely and, in the employment of his light craft, contrary to the Naval Staff's directives concerning excessive and unnecessary use of delicate material. Revel repeated these charges even more forceably after his return from Brindisi where he found that Millo had not hesitated to express in writing to the C.-in-C. opinions which were not in accord with directly given orders. Millo, who was also a Senator of the Kingdom of Italy, submitted a letter of complaint protesting at his treatment and pointing out that his position as commander of the Scouting Division was not directly dependent on the Chief of Naval Staff, but was under the C.-in-C. of the 2° Squadra at

Brindisi and the C.-in-C. of the Fleet at Taranto, and he had received the praise and approval of both of them. In forwarding the complaint Abruzzi gave Millo his full support. He praised the admiral and saw nothing in his remarks concerning the evacuation of Pelagosa that was harmful to discipline. Abruzzi personally regretted that he was suddenly deprived of the support of an admiral who, on every occasion, demonstrated that he was fully equal to the complex and difficult command entrusted to him.[70] Salandra's papers contain copies of the correspondence, so the Prime Minister was obviously well aware of the controversy.

Revel was also under increasing pressure and his own days in office were numbered. He was ready to resign again after government censors allowed an article bearing the signature of Deputy Enrico Arlotta to appear in the *Giornale d'Italia* on 10 September, a paper with which Salandra and Sonnino were closely associated. Arlotta made what Revel considered to be unjustified insinuations on the preparations for war, and asked if there was all the 'desirable mental agility' in the direction of the navy. The fact that the tight government control over the press had permitted this to be published led Revel to ask Viale to relieve him of his post if he no longer had the support of the government.[71] The only support Revel claimed that he received after he had complained to the Minister of Marine and the Minister of the Interior was a 'small and timid' communiqué inserted in page 3 of the newspaper the following day, while Arlotta's attack had been prominently featured on the first page. He had also written to the Prefect of Rome about preventing similar attacks in the future but feared that he was labouring in vain. Revel poured out his troubles in a long letter to General Brusati for the attention of the king. He pointed out that the war was going to be long and that the Austrian fleet was well commanded by a 'calm and balanced person who knew how to obtain good results with small means and who did not consider war as an "action of glory"'.[72] Perhaps next March, if their administration and military industry did not fail them, the Italian navy would have sufficient underwater and aerial offensive means to undertake a provocative action, but until then the war would be one of waiting. Revel did not think that the navy could continue with two heads and there needed to be unity in its direction. At the moment he could not move, punish, or correct an officer without long discussion and waiting for authorization, which when it came had lost its value and opportuneness because it was so late. Revel claimed that he had no further personal ambitions. After the recent death of his daughter, 'the vanities of the world no longer had any influence on me'. He concluded that things were not going well in the navy and if Admiral Viale believed it harmful to his prestige as minister to renounce some of his attributions during the war it would be preferable to also transfer to him the office of chief of staff with its relevant responsibilities.

There was still more criticism of the navy from influential people. Vice-Admiral Pasquale Leonardi-Cattolica, a senator of the realm and former Minister of Marine (April 1910–July 1913) was asked by Viale in mid-August to conduct an inquiry into the loss of the *Garibaldi*. Cattolica used his discussions with officers and men of the fleet to draft a report on the prewar preparations of the navy and its conduct of the first three months of war. Cattolica claimed that during the ten months of Italian neutrality the navy had not sufficiently taken into account the importance of submarines, and all the efforts of the dockyards had gone into finishing or laying down dreadnoughts, while the Naval High Command were dedicated to training the fleet for a classical but improbable naval battle. Only after war had broken out had submarines, seaplanes and fast light craft been ordered. Cattolica criticized the frequent changes in the organization of the fleet and alterations in Abruzzi's chiefs of staff which created an impression of instability and divergences of views. He also found much to criticize in the operations in the lower Adriatic in which the *Turbine* and *Garibaldi* had been lost and the *Dublin* torpedoed. Morale in the navy was not as high after three months of war as it had been at the beginning. Security was also a problem and operations at Brindisi were generally known on land some days before those on board the ships who were actually to perform them were informed. They would only lend themselves to Austrian tactics if they continued the war with the methods adopted up to now. Enemy incursions along the coast were also harming civilian morale and bringing the navy into disrepute. It could not defend the entire coast but it was possible to defend the zone close to Brindisi, which was fortunately a well-populated area. Cattolica's study was subsequently given to Salandra who forwarded it to the king with the remark that one could exclude a pessimistic predisposition on the part of the writer, but the criticism was widespread among the public and in the navy itself.[73] By this time, however, Admiral Viale himself had left office.

Viale resigned on 24 September, ostensibly for reasons of health having recently undergone minor surgery. The next morning his Cabinet chief, Capitano di vascello Galleani told Lieutenant d'Huart, the French naval attaché, that things could not go on that way, and that the navy needed one head, not two or three. The minister had learned of things only after they had been done and it was not sufficient for the minister merely to be the most senior of the admirals. D'Huart recalled that Galleani had also been Cabinet chief and a personal friend of Millo who had just been given the sack. In the interim between Viale's resignation and the nomination of a new minister, during which Salandra held the portfolio, the Italian navy suffered another major disaster. On the morning of 27 September the battleship *Benedetto Brin* blew up in Brindisi harbour with heavy loss of life including Rear-Admiral Rubin de Cervin, commanding the III Division. The mysterious explosion was later discovered to be the result of sabotage. A few days later, on 30 September, Vice-Admiral Camillo Corsi became the new minister. Corsi had commanded the dreadnought squadron at Taranto and was for a time Abruzzi's Chief of Staff. He was described by Richmond thus: 'Old Corsi . . . seems unable to do anything except shake his head & say the war is a very difficult one.' Thursby called him 'a politician, clever but cautious, and I do not think likely to do anything startling'.[74]

The latent conflict between the minister, the various directorates at the ministry and the Chief of Naval Staff remained. D'Huart reported the umours that Revel had offered to resign but, possessing the confidence of he king, had been asked to stay. The question was finally resolved on 1 October when Revel left to become C.-in-C. at Venice and was not eplaced. Instead Rear-Admiral Pino Pini, former Director of Armaments t the ministry, became Sub-Chief of the Naval Staff. Corsi had evidently hosen the solution of combining the functions of chief of staff with the ninister's office, although the decree of November 1913 which had stablished Revel's power was not immediately revoked. A series of hanges in personnel followed; among them Rear-Admiral Millo received a ommand afloat again, this time a division of the dreadnought squadron. The situation of the Chief of Staff was finally regularized by the decree of February 1916 marking the evolution of the Naval Staff from its origin as centre for technical studies to the directing organ of the navy under Revel, nd now back to the military Cabinet of the minister.[75] In the long run it vould be Thaon di Revel who would emerge triumphant and return to his old position with enhanced powers, but that would not be before February 917.

The war in the Adriatic by the end of the summer of 1915 was clearly a talemate with discontent in the Italian navy and disillusionment among taly's allies. Richmond left the Italian fleet on 12 September having asked o be relieved. He considered his stay in Taranto to have been a waste of noney since there was no need for a liaison officer. Richmond had also ubmitted a lengthy letter calling for a revision of the Naval Convention of May 1915, recall of British ships to home waters, and joint action by the French and Italians. The Admiralty filed it away without further action, Admiral Gamble remarking that he saw no need for a new convention, that he French and Italians would not approve, and Richmond's essay was well hought out, 'but like all his epistles too long'.[76]

Richmond's French counterpart, Capitaine de vaisseau Daveluy, stayed until December but by the end of August made this judgement on the naval var in the Adriatic:

> From these facts one can draw the following conclusion: submarines prohibit large warships from keeping to the sea, each party scratched their heads to 'do something' but one has not found any other thing to do except small operations which have no real significance [*portée*] and are, above all, intended to give the illusion one is acting. But, as one cannot fire indefinitely on the same bridge, the same station, the same railways, the same lighthouses and the same semaphores, it seems clear that now the Italians and Austrians are at the end of their resources; after having wanted to do 'something', one no longer knows 'what to do'.
>
> During this time commercial navigation remains forbidden to both parties, in a way that none of them can claim mastery of the sea; the latter belongs to submarines of all nationalities.[77]

German U-boats at Pola

At the conclusion of our discussion of Austrian and German submarine activities in the preceding chapter German submarines had just arrived in late May in the Aegean with spectacular results. The numbers involved, however, were small but growing. The Admiralstab report on U-boats in the Mediterranean as of 10 June 1915 listed U21 and UB8 at Constantinople, UB7 at Smyrna and UB3 probably lost. UB1 and UB15 were completing at Pola and destined for the Austrian navy, while UB14 was expected to arrive in Pola that day and be ready for departure to Turkish waters around the end of the month. The minelaying submarines, UC14 and UC15, were ready to leave Germany for Pola and with their longer range might be converted to transports, while UC12 would be ready to leave Germany around mid-June. At this date the k.u.k. Kriegsmarine had eight submarines of their own, not all of them serviceable and the early pair (U1 and U2) suitable only for training and local defence.[78] The Admiralstab felt some concern that the Italian entry into the war would threaten the rail line to Pola over which the disassembled UB14 was being sent, but the commander of the Austrian south-east front assured them that the line was secure, although they would have to ask about future movements.[79] This was, however, a threat which never really materialized since the Italian army failed to break through and conditions resembling the stalemate on the western front resulted.

The UB and UC boats in the Mediterranean were very small in size and this restricted their operations. This was quite clear from a report by Marine-Baumeister Weichardt on his experience in assembling the submarines at Pola. Larger versions of the boats, about 200–300 tons, would have a military advantage for the eastern Mediterranean but would still have to come by rail since Weichardt did not believe that they would have the necessary range to come via Gibraltar. The small UB and UC boats were unsuitable for long-range action since they had only one screw for surface or submerged travel, and this gave them an insufficient reserve of power. The boats needed two screws and engines powerful-enough to master the Dardanelles currents. The new type that Weichardt recommended would be a larger boat, but because of the restrictions of the special railway carriages which brought the boats to Pola these would have to be broken down into more than three sections. Weichardt thought that it would be technically possible to assemble such boats in Pola but emphasized that the pressure hull should as far as possible be riveted in Germany since skilled personnel were needed for this operation. Kapitänleutnant Hans Adam, the officer in charge of the German navy's Sonderkommando at Pola, agreed with the proposals. If the transport via rail to Pola of such boats was perhaps no longer possible during the war, it would still be of great importance for Germany to strengthen and expand its naval strength in the Mediterranean every time it was in a position to do so. The way for future building at Pola had already been paved and a few months after the conclusion of peace Germany would have a respectable U-boat formation in the Mediterranean.

If the German Empire did not intend to maintain a naval base in the Mediterranean, the submarines could be given to Austria or Turkey. Adam reported that the Austrians were building four boats in their own yards, but with their wretched organization and deficient experience in submarine building one could not count on these boats being either a useful type or ready in the foreseeable future. Adam thought that the Germans ought to undertake the building of Mediterranean U-boats in order to be in the position of exerting permanent strong pressure on the British with relatively little expense.[80]

UC14 was the first of the minelaying submarines to near completion and Adam proposed sending her against Malta, with a stop at Cattaro to refuel before setting out. This would have the effect of increasing the radius of action to 1,200–1,300 miles. He wanted to send UC15, when ready, against Taranto and the third UC boat (UC12) would be converted into a transport. Adam recommended caution about using the UC boat as a transport since the little craft had only one engine and a breakdown would mean the loss of a vital cargo. To reduce the danger, the submarine would top up at Cattaro, and then be escorted by Austrian torpedo-boats up to the Straits of Otranto. The submarine would have to travel alone about 400 miles, but to reduce the danger zone after that Adam suggested that Admiral Souchon should send U21 out from Constantinople to rendezvous with the transport submarine on the west coast of Crete and escort it to Aegean waters. He did not think it advisable to use the UC boats for minelaying in the Aegean; it was too far from their base and they would probably have more success against Malta and Taranto. Adam proposed using only larger U-boats in the Aegean and keeping the UC boats in the Ionian. The question of which was more important, using the UC boats in their original role as minelayers, or as transports for small quantities of vitally needed materials to Turkey, was obviously far too important for a relatively junior officer to decide. The Admiralstab judged that the critical situation in Turkey had priority and ordered UC14 and UC15 to be converted into transports. Souchon also decided that he could not do without U21, which had to be held ready for an Allied attempt to force the Dardanelles, and he arranged for a rendezvous on the coast of Asia Minor near Bodrum for the UC boats which would now have to make the long trip on their own.[81] The submarines had two pressure-proof containers fitted in each of their mine chutes and each also carried four torpedoes as cargo along with other vitally needed materials. The submarines could carry around 8 tons of cargo apiece, and to help them on their way they were towed to approximately fifty miles south of Cattaro by Austrian destroyers.

U21 was still the only German submarine in the Mediterranean in July 1915 with a long radius of action, while the small capacity of the UB boats tended to restrict their use. Souchon was well aware of the problem this posed for his Mittelmeerdivision. In the Black Sea the Russian naval base of Sebastopol where the Germans could inflict the most damage was about 275 miles from the submarine base at Constantinople. The submarines could be towed through the strong currents of the Bosphorus and the prevailing good visibility in the Black Sea aided submarine operations. On the other hand, the usually smooth sea made attacks more difficult. The Aegean was a different question. Souchon planned to establish a base at Chanak where submarines going to the Aegean could top up with fuel and receive the latest intelligence. The establishment of additional bases on the Mediterranean coast of Asia Minor was hampered by the difficulty of getting supplies to them and the readiness of the anti-Turkish and unreliable Greek population to provide information to the Entente forces, as well as the ruthless action of the latter in bombarding open places they suspected of being submarine depots. Apart from the beaches on the Gallipoli Peninsula, the Gulf of Kephalo (Imbros) and Mudros (Lemnos) offered promising opportunities for attack, as did the approach routes of transports heading for the Dardanelles. The old vessels employed by the British and French on blockade duties off the coast of Asia Minor would also be tempting targets. However, while the passage out of the Dardanelles would be aided by the current, the return against the current would pose difficulties for the weak UB boats, especially since the first ten miles would be under enemy fire and watched by destroyers, and there was also the danger that Turkish batteries would fire on them by mistake. In the Aegean the strong currents, clarity of the water, great depths which prevented a submarine resting on the bottom, and numerous islands with potential enemy observation posts all worked against the employment of the single-screw UB boats which Souchon claimed were not practicable for missions lasting longer than ten days for numerous technical reasons. He therefore intended to reserve the Aegean for the larger U-boats and to keep the UB boats for the Black Sea. To maintain a continuous disturbance of enemy activities, the permanent presence of a large U-boat in the Aegean and a small UB boat in the Black Sea was necessary, and Souchon also had his eyes on future missions in the eastern Mediterranean from Malta to Port Said. To accomplish this he would need a U-boat flotilla at Constantinople of three large and four small boats. He would determine the method of using the minelaying UC boats after their arrival and according to experience.[82]

Souchon's proposals raised the question of sending further large boats to the Mediterranean and the matter became pressing by the second week in July. Hersing took U21 through the Dardanelles for his second mission on 3 July and managed to sink the French steamer *Carthage* (5,275 tons) off the south-western tip of Gallipoli on the 4th. Keyes, de Robeck's Chief of Staff, thought that the transport had been risked unnecessarily:

> I watched a large French transport off Helles for days – he was of course torpedoed in the end, it could only be a question of time as I said to our French officer the day before . . . the silly transport . . . got exactly what the French deserved as they have any number of small craft and there was no excuse for using a big one.[83]

Obviously it was folly to offer a chance to a daring and skilled submarine commander such as Hersing. He saw an opening and exploited it, but he did not have any further success due to strong countermeasures by Allied destroyers and small craft, as well as the clarity of the water, and the mission had to be broken off after an underwater explosion, probably a mine, damaged the submarine's hull. U21 limped safely back to Constantinople and was docked on the 16th, but the only large German submarine in Mediterranean waters would be out of action for at least six weeks. This was enough for the Admiralstab to decide to send another two large U-boats to the Mediterranean. In a letter to the Chief of the High Seas Fleet asking him to choose two suitable boats, Bachmann noted that there would be no submarine off the Dardanelles for the next six weeks and that this was probably known to the British and French through their espionage system since British cruisers and battleships had just resumed shelling Turkish positions.[84]

The Admiralstab justified their request with a paper pointing out that the onset of bad weather and sea conditions in the autumn would reduce the U-boat campaign against Britain in the Atlantic and the approaches to the Irish Sea by increasing fuel consumption and sea damage to U-boats, lowering visibility and hindering accuracy when torpedoes were fired. The weather and sea conditions were better in the Mediterranean and when they were bad enough to hinder submarine operations those conditions did not last as long as they did in the north. The Admiralstab produced the expected statistics to point out the importance of the route through the Suez Canal to British imports. The following percentages of British imports passed through the Mediterranean: jute, 99 per cent; tea, 99 per cent; rice, 75 per cent; hemp, 73 per cent; wool, 70 per cent; gasoline, 65 per cent; manganese, 52 per cent; and rubber, 51 per cent. The average steamer encountered in the Mediterranean was also larger. The Admiralstab estimated that there was a daily traffic of eight to nine ships of 4,000 tons each. The Admiralstab also pointed out the importance of the Mediterranean trade to France and Italy, especially since the latter was dependent on Britain for coal, and its present harvest was also reduced thereby necessitating increased imports of grain. The Germans considered it nearly impossible for the British to divert their Mediterranean traffic around the Cape of Good Hope. This diversion on a voyage from Bombay to London would mean a 45 per cent increase in distance and time, and the limitations of the carrying capacity of a steamer's bunkers would mean coal stocks would have to be built up in South Africa. The Germans did not think that the British would be able to easily accomplish this. The possibilities for submarines in the Mediterranean were also promising since all traffic had to pass through four relatively narrow areas – the Suez Canal, Crete, Malta and Gibraltar. Success in the Mediterranean would add to the effect on morale of the submarine campaign and there would be fewer problems with neutrals. The Admiralstab took care to point out that they were not likely to meet American ships and not many United States citizens travelled through the Mediterranean, while Spanish traffic was mostly confined to the western part and Greek shipping was mostly coastal traffic in the Aegean. The Dutch had a sizeable trade but it should be possible to distinguish their boats through special markings and appointed times for passing through the narrow points. Submarine activity could also have an impact on the course of the campaign at the Dardanelles or, in case of a renewed Turkish attack, on Egypt. Pola and Cattaro would be suitable bases while intelligence of ships passing through the Straits of Gibraltar could be provided by observers at Algeciras in neutral Spain, and the newly arrived German naval attaché in Athens would expand this intelligence activity in the eastern Mediterranean. The newer U-boats could also improve on U21's performance in reaching Cattaro without refuelling. The Admiralstab recommended that at least two additional large U-boats were needed for carrying on economic war, or *Handelskrieg*, in the Mediterranean. With one usually under repair, this would allow at least one or, counting U21, two boats to be available on the steamship routes. The small UB boats could not be used for serious economic war in the Mediterranean; the distances to the waiting positions on the steamship routes were too great for them and they were also needed by Souchon for either the defence of the Dardanelles or to guard against Russian attack at the Bosphorus. The Admiralstab recommended sending the two large boats to the Mediterranean as soon as possible, for with the onset of bad weather in the Atlantic in September the risks of carrying out the trip would be considerably increased and the entire operation might become questionable.[85] The Admiralstab's arguments were compressed into an *Immediatvortrag* for the Kaiser on 20 July and promptly approved; two U-boats were to be withdrawn from the Baltic as soon as they had finished their current missions.[86]

Admiral von Pohl, the Chief of the High Seas Fleet, designated U34 (Kapitänleutnant Rücker) and U35 (Kapitänleutnant Kophamel) for the Mediterranean. Moreover, as of 1 July, the Sonderkommando in Pola was expanded to the 'German U-boat Half-Flotilla, Pola'.[87] The Germans had intelligence of large movements of troops from Britain and Egypt to the Dardanelles and were therefore anxious that the submarines should leave as quickly as possible with the greatest precautions for secrecy since they hoped that the British, knowing of the damage to U21 and the small radius of action of the UB boats, were not counting on serious attacks along the transport routes.[88]

The Admiralstab decided that U34 and U35 would go directly to Cattaro and that their great endurance rendered a call in a Spanish harbour unnecessary except in the case of an emergency. They also decided that it would be expedient to make use of Austrian bases for Aegean operations and to avoid the dangerous trip through the Dardanelles to Constantinople, as the British watch at the Straits seemed to have been strengthened. Furthermore, Austrian harbours obviously offered better repair facilities and a more secure supply of torpedoes.[89] The Admiralstab also added a supplement to the submarines' operational orders before they sailed. Souchon's proposed orders included the statement that neither Turkey nor Germany was then at war with Italy and therefore no hostile action should be taken against Italian ships. The Admiralstab wanted to emphasize that this prohibition applied only to the eastern Mediterranean where the Italians would normally expect that hostile action could only come from German submarines. In the western Mediterranean, up to the line of Cape Matapan, the standing orders for submarines remained valid. Italian warships would be considered hostile and in conducting cruiser warfare (that is, acting on the surface) against neutral and Italian merchant ships, the submarines were to appear as Austrian. These orders were modified slightly after 20 August when Italy declared war on Turkey. German submarines acting east of Cape Matapan could now represent themselves as Turkish but, although diplomatic relations had been broken off, there was still no state of war between Italy and Germany.[90]

Souchon was not happy with these developments, for it meant that U34 and U35 working from Austrian bases would not be under his command. His sense of isolation must have increased and he asked the Admiralstab to reconsider. He now tried to minimize the dangers of submarines passing through the Dardanelles. They were most dangerous for submarines with less-powerful engines, not the more powerful U-boats, and the recent extension of Turkish batteries on the Asiatic shore reduced the distance that enemy destroyers could pursue the submarines, while the Turkish gunners were now more accustomed to the passage of German submarines and less likely to make mistakes. U21 had been able to make the passage in a damaged condition with much less difficulty than anticipated. The British would probably strengthen their vigilance off the Dardanelles but were also not likely to seal off completely the entrance with obstructions as long as they intended to operate their own submarines in the Marmara. Souchon argued that sending submarines destined to operate in the Aegean to Austrian harbours would inevitably result in loss of time and their full capacity would therefore not be used. Moreover, it was now urgent to have a U-boat permanently on patrol in the Black Sea to counter difficulties experienced with the coal traffic from Zonguldak. The appearance of a large German submarine off the Crimea, with perhaps a lucky success, would not eliminate their shortage of coal, but undoubtedly would improve the situation and have a favourable effect on the attitude of Bulgaria and Romania.[91]

Rear-Admiral Behncke, who prepared the Admiralstab's reply, was not impressed with Souchon's arguments. The passage through the Dardanelles might have been easier for large submarines than it was for small ones, but it was still dangerous enough under present circumstances and even the large boats had to use up a large part of their battery reserve before getting into action. The British could establish mine and net barriers and still leave a passage open for their submarines that would be unknown to the Germans, and the British apparently had a large number of small craft on patrol between the Dardanelles and neighbouring islands. The Germans had learned in home waters these forces were apt to be well trained. Although approximately three days would be required for submarines to proceed from the Adriatic to their operational areas in the Aegean this was not lost time because of the opportunities for attack which might occur. Souchon had not really made a convincing case against the argument that repair and maintenance of submarines and supply of fuel, torpedoes and spare parts would be much easier in Austrian harbours than at Constantinople. Submarines based in the Adriatic could also operate in different parts of the Mediterranean and have a much greater effect on the enemy than those restricted to coming in and out of the Dardanelles, especially as their exact number and time of departure would probably be quickly signalled by the British and French espionage service which the Germans were convinced was well organized in the Marmara. The Black Sea was only a secondary theatre of war for the Admiralstab; the main theatre outside the Atlantic and North Sea was the Mediterranean, and success there would also have an effect on Romania and Bulgaria. Behncke suspected that there were more personal motives involved in Souchon's arguments rather than a purely objective reflection aimed at clarifying the question. The order establishing the Mittelmeerdivision in November 1912 had given its chief unbridled freedom of movement, but this was no longer the case and the Chief of the Mittelmeerdivision was now confined to the furthest corner of the Mediterranean and his direct influence on naval forces in the Mediterranean ceased as soon as they were a few miles from the coast of Asia Minor.[92]

German submarine successes in the Aegean in July and August certainly did not live up to their early promise. Oberleutnant zur See von Heimburg and UB14, fresh from the success in sinking the *Amalfi*, departed for the Dardanelles on 16 July, towed by an Austrian destroyer to about seventy miles south of Cattaro. Heimburg reached the little island of Orak near Bodrum on the 24th, and then operated on the transport route from Alexandria to the Dardanelles giving the Germans their major success that summer when, on 13 August, he sank the transport *Royal Edward* (11,117 tons) with a loss of over 900 lives and torpedoed, but did not sink, the transport *Southland* (11,899 tons) on 2 September before reaching Constantinople on the 4th. Heimburg found that the large number of small craft coupled with the weak battery capacity of his UB boat had hampered his efforts. A third UC boat, UC13, reached Pola on 19 July and was assembled with a special transport forecastle which permitted it to carry a cargo of 30 tons. Another transport submarine, UC15, discovered that it could only partially discharge its cargo at the rendezvous on the coast of Asia Minor. Souchon realized that unloading in these unsheltered areas was dangerous and the onward transport of the cargo over land was slow and difficult because of the lack of roads. He decided, since the Dardanelles seemed to be less closely watched at that moment, that unloading cargo in Constantinople would be the quickest and safest solution.[93]

At the beginning of August the Germans also took stock of their experiences with assembling the small UB and UC boats at Pola and the results were encouraging. Kapitänleutnant Adam reported that they appeared to be splendidly suited for the Adriatic and northern Ionian thanks to the short distances from the enemy coast, favourable weather and the simple navigation involved. The assembly had gone smoothly, the Austrians had provided a floating crane to unload them from the special railway carriages and carry them to the dock, and the assembly itself required, on average, three to four days for UB boats and five to six days for the UC boats, owing to more extensive riveting. The conversion of UC boats to transports with special containers took six to seven days. After launching, one to one and a half weeks were needed for engine trials, water tightness and pressure checks and the preparation of the crews. There were sufficient Austrian personnel on hand in Pola for unimportant work, but for riveting and caulking the pressure hull they could not have managed without German personnel. The sea trials and underwater firing of torpedoes took place in the twenty to thirty metre depths of the Fasana Channel east of Brioni and required eight days. Adam found that a comparatively long period of training was necessary for the Austrian crews who were far below the German level, and in his opinion lacked thorough and strict training and education. The situation of Austrian submarine commanders was therefore much more difficult and they also lacked the support of a leading engineer. Adam did not expect any submarine offensive from the Austrian navy. The small number of submarines available, their short radius of action and poor habitability made it impossible for the Austrian commanders to use them outside the Adriatic, and the Germans should not expect any change in this unfortunate situation. The answer to the problem was obvious; they needed more German submarines and larger ones at that. It had been a triumph for German submarine building and submarine personnel that they had been able to accomplish what they already had, but only larger boats had real prospects of success in the Aegean, and further operations in the eastern Mediterranean against, for example, the Suez Canal were prohibited by the small number of submarines available. For this expanded submarine war in the Mediterranean, Adam proposed that the German navy should order at once twelve submarines of an improved UB type which would be assembled at Pola and ready for service in the early months of the new year. The twelve boats would permit three to four submarines to operate at the same time in the central Mediterranean area around 500–600 miles from Cattaro.[94]

The eagerly awaited large U-boats, U34 and U35, sailed from Heligoland on 4 August, lost sight of one another, but eventually arrived safely at Cattaro within a few hours of each other on the 23rd. While U34 and U35 were on the way to Cattaro another cry for help came from Liman von Sanders. The British had landed at Suvla to the north of the original beachheads on 6–7 August and while they frittered away their initial surprise and chance for success the close naval support once again so evident off Gallipoli obviously annoyed the Germans and Turks. Liman von Sanders complained to the German embassy in Constantinople that the excellent shooting of the ships, directed by spotters in balloons, had already caused the Turks to lose 4,000 men, and they had no weapon to use against the ships. If it was considered necessary to hold the Dardanelles, then they could not be left without any assistance. Colonel von Lossow, the German military attaché, appealed again on the 14th for ten submarines at Constantinople so at least two to three were always ready for action. He also requested an additional three fighter aircraft to those already promised, with facilities for aerial reconnaissance including an observer and camera, large Gotha bombers, and three seaplanes to hunt British submarines in the Marmara. These appeals had their effect on the Kaiser and Admiral von Müller, Chief of the Kaiser's Naval Cabinet, asked Bachmann if the navy could send more submarines to the Mediterranean. The decisive point in the world war appeared more and more to be shifting to this area and the Kaiser was now pressing for the earliest possible decision.[95] The Admiralstab replied that another pair of submarines would leave for the Mediterranean within ten to fourteen days. They could not leave before this time as the boats chosen were at sea and on their return would require an overhaul before setting out on the long trip. This was not good enough for the Kaiser who asked if their departure could not be hastened and demanded a report as soon as possible.[96] State Secretary Tirpitz reported on 21 August that U39 and U33 would be ready at the yards on the 23rd and could leave on the 27th and 29th respectively. Because of necessary repairs and overhauls at the end of August, there would be a considerable decline in the number of submarines available, and new arrivals would not cause this number to rise again until the end of September at the earliest. Tirpitz, despite this weakening of strength in home waters, was in favour of sending the two additional submarines to the Mediterranean because of the dangerous situation at the Dardanelles and also, from the political standpoint, the impression that increased German submarine activity in the eastern Mediterranean would have on the fluctuating Balkan states.[97] U39 (Kapitänleutnant Forstmann) and U33 (Kapitänleutnant Gansser) sailed for the Mediterranean on the 27th and 28th.

The Admiralstab was reinforced in its decision to raise the number of large submarines in the Mediterranean by another lengthy report from the German naval attaché in The Hague, quoting extensively from the *Statesman's Year Book, 1915* on the importance of Mediterranean trade. There were also various intelligence reports of large troop movements to the eastern Mediterranean, as well as the possibility that the Italians would attempt a landing somewhere in Asia Minor after Italy's declaration of war on Turkey. Bachmann summarized all these events in another letter to Falkenhayn, linking the troop movements and arrival of additional British monitors at the Dardanelles with a new attempt to force the Straits or exert pressure on the Balkan states. Bachmann mentioned that the navy was sending the three seaplanes requested by Constantinople and emphasized the sacrifice involved in recently sending the two submarines from home waters. These sacrifices could, at best, only ease the pressure on Turkey, not remove it. The latter could only be expected when secure communications were opened between Germany and Constantinople. Falkenhayn replied that he shared in this view in its entirety and would take it into account as soon and as far as possible.[98]

At the beginning of September the Germans discussed the possibility of declaring the Mediterranean a 'war zone'. This was linked to the number of submarines to be sent there. The Kaiser was anxious to do so, and ordered Bachmann to consider once more whether the conduct of the war in the North Sea and Baltic would allow sending more submarines to the Mediterranean. This time Bachmann and the Admiralstab replied with a firm no. They had already sent five large submarines and eight small submarines (one of which had been lost), and transferred another two submarines to the Austrians. There were at the moment only eighteen submarines available for the war in home waters (fourteen for the North Sea and four for the Baltic) and Bachmann did not consider sending more U-boats to the Mediterranean to be possible. Furthermore, the effectiveness of submarines in the Mediterranean was also restricted because, on political grounds, the Foreign Office did not believe it was possible to declare it a war zone (*Kriegsgebiet*). Admiral Henning von Holtzendorff, Bachmann's successor as Chief of the Admiralstab, took the same view. The number of U-boats which had now been sent to the Mediterranean would suffice as long as the greater part of the Mediterranean was not declared a war zone and, when present and anticipated submarine losses were taken into account, to send more submarines would weaken them too much in the North Sea. Holtzendorff concluded most emphatically that the sending of further U-boats to the Mediterranean was neither necessary nor expedient.[99]

Admiral von Müller, possibly at the Kaiser's prompting, took up the idea of declaring the Mediterranean a war zone and asked what use it might have. Admiral von Holtzendorff replied that it would not have any. There were already sufficient military targets, warships or troop transports, on the approaches to the Dardanelles in the eastern Mediterranean and Aegean, and operations by submarines in the western part of the Mediterranean were out of the question for the moment because of the restricted number of U-boats available. If the British gave up the Dardanelles campaign and withdrew their naval forces from the Aegean, the Germans would then have to re-examine the question of declaring a war zone so that they could free the U-boats for a real attack on the sizeable British traffic through the Suez Canal. Until then, however, declaration of the Mediterranean as a war zone was of no use.[100]

The new German submarines in the Mediterranean were making their presence felt in September. Souchon was aggressive and wanted their operational orders to include the statement that submarines in the Aegean must carry on a ruthless economic war against all supplies for the enemy and destroy coastal ships which were necessary for the substantial needs of the British army. Relief would only arrive when submarines were noticed and Souchon asked for telegraphic reports of the successes of U34 so that he could have them published in the Turkish press. The Admiralstab did cable new instructions on 21 September, but they were still somewhat cautious. Large merchant ships in the Aegean could be attacked while submerged on suspicion that they were troop transports or auxiliary cruisers, but small merchant ships were to be sunk without warning only if it were apparent that they were supply ships, and that would be assumed if they were in the vicinity of and on courses to and from enemy bases. All supplies to the Dardanelles, even when carried on small ships, were to be cut off but mistakes (*verwechslung*) with Greek ships were undesirable.[101] As for the actual results of the first missions by U34 and U35 in early September, Kapitänleutnant Kophamel in U35 sank three ships for a total of 10,596 tons and U34 sank one steamer and a small French auxiliary warship for a total of 4,907 tons. U39 and U33 arrived at Cattaro in mid-September, the former having sunk three ships for a total of 6,776 tons after passing through the Straits of Gibraltar, while the latter had no successes in the Mediterranean but a number in the Atlantic. Allied shipping losses in the Mediterranean were now going to grow, especially as Kophamel had observed that Allied security and countermeasures were apparently very weak around the Dardanelles away from the swarm of light craft.[102]

As the Germans suspected, the k.u.k. Kriegsmarine was not likely to play a significant role in the submarine campaign outside the Adriatic for a long time. Haus, after realizing that it was going to be a long war, authorized the construction of additional submarines in March 1915, but that was far easier to propose than actually accomplish. The Austrians decided to order the so-called Havmanden class, named after a group of three submarines which the Whitehead yard at Fiume had built for the Danish government before the war. Haus was unenthusiastic about these relatively small boats and reduced the proposed order from ten to four. Their proponents thought that they were a proven design since the Danes had built an additional three themselves and the Austrians could therefore begin series production right away; but, of course, submarines in the service of neutral Denmark had never undergone the test of war. Furthermore, the submarines were of a modified Holland type originally built under licence from the Electric Boat Company of New York with many spare parts also protected by patent. Consequently, there was the additional complication of American neutrality preventing deliveries to a belligerent power. In an attempt to circumvent these difficulties, Whitehead established a new and ostensibly independent company, Ungarische Unterseebootsbau AG – commonly known as UBAG – with headquarters at Fiume and a branch at Linz. There were even more complications caused by the nature of the Austro-Hungarian monarchy itself. In a move reminiscent of the controversy over the prewar dreadnought building programme, the Hungarian government demanded a significant share of production for Hungarian firms. The question is too involved to recount in detail, but at the end of June a compromise decision was reached by which the four submarines were to be partially built in Linz and Pola and the final assembly was to take place at either Pola or Fiume. The contract was signed on 9 July but the first boat was not laid down until 29 September and construction went very slowly with sabotage a problem. Around two-thirds of the subcontracting came from Hungarian firms, approximately one-third from Austrian. The Havmanden submarines finally entered service between August and November 1917 but they were most unsuccessful. The design was decidedly obsolete by this time, they were unhandy and also had trouble with their engines.[103]

The new German-designed, enlarged UB type offered a better solution. These improved versions of the UB submarines were designated 'enlarged B types' by the Austrians and 'BII' by the Germans. Adam was very pleased to learn that in mid-August the Austrian naval attaché in Berlin had asked the Reichsmarineamt if it would be possible to order them at a German yard. Adam noted that, sad as the loss of two Austrian U-boats in August had been, it nevertheless had its positive side since the Austrians realized that it was high time they ordered new and sensible submarines and hasten their completion as soon as possible.[104] Adam, a relatively junior officer on the scene at Pola, may have been enthusiastic but the Reichsmarineamt and the German yards were somewhat hesitant. Understandably, the German naval authorities were reluctant to actually part with finished submarines or use the building capacity of their yards on Austria's account. Some Austrian firms were also negotiating with the German yards about purchasing plans for the BII boats and then building them in Austrian or Hungarian yards. The Austrians had other projects under consideration at the time, but Haus opted for the German design in what was probably a wise decision. The Germans not surprisingly turned down the request of the Austrians to take over two submarines in mid-August, but on 25 August the Weser yards agreed to sell plans to the Austrians for the construction of up to six BII submarines. There then followed the usual difficulties and complications about allocating production between Austrian and Hungarian firms. In the long run, and not without much argument, they settled on the Austrian firm, Cantiere Navale, building two and the Hungarian firm, Danubius, building four. The boats were not actually laid down until the winter and spring of 1916 and the delivery dates were not met, largely because of the unreliability of subcontractors who suffered from a lack of workers and materials. The six BII boats, numbered by the Austrians U27–U32, did not actually enter service until the first half of 1917. During 1916 the Austrians also laid down another pair of BII submarines, one (U40) a gift of the Österreichischen Flottenverein, the other (U41) a replacement for U6 which had been lost.[105] Given these circumstances, it is not surprising that the submarine war outside the Adriatic was essentially a German concern in 1915 and 1916, and even after the Austrian BII submarines began to enter service they were limited in numbers and still not the equal of the larger German U-boats which undertook most of the far-ranging missions in the western and eastern Mediterranean.

The arrival of German submarines in the Mediterranean had certainly complicated the role of the British and French navies at the Dardanelles, but even expert submariners had testified to the effectiveness of the counter-measures in the immediate vicinity of the Straits. UB14 might have uncovered a gap in the defences and sank the *Carthage* but, as we have seen, the typical British comment was similar to that of an officer in one of the destroyers, 'Well, she [*Carthage*] was asking for it'.[106] The real danger to the expedition would come along the supply routes rather than in the immediate vicinity of the Straits.

The entry of Italy into the war also brought changes in the French command. Augagneur decided to create a temporary squadron called Escadre des Dardanelles and gave the command to Vice-Admiral Nicol, with Guépratte remaining under his orders. Augagneur warned Nicol that in the 'adventurous' Dardanelles campaign de Robeck had given proof of an enterprising spirit which sometimes bordered on temerity. While recognizing de Robeck's authority and giving him dedicated support, Nicol's rank and the importance of the forces at his disposal would certainly give great weight to his opinions in de Robeck's decisions.[107] The description of de Robeck was hardly accurate and would have brought a wry smile from Keyes, his Chief of Staff, who had tried, and would continue to try, and prod the admiral into taking responsibility for another naval attempt on the Straits. De Robeck, for his part, regretted that 'dear old Guépratte, who is the most loyal of men', was no longer in charge of the French force and found Nicol 'a little man of the most unprepossessing appearance' who did not 'look a gentleman & don't think his name would be in the "Stud Book"'.[108]

Anglo-French friction in naval affairs at the Dardanelles seems to have been prevented by literally avoiding it. Nicol, a week after his arrival, reported that his personal relations with de Robeck were good. He saw him frequently when they were in the same anchorage and it was easy to come to an agreement with him, but de Robeck had just transferred his flag to the yacht *Triad* for mobility and Nicol had the impression that he would use the yacht to meet with him as little as possible, the separation permitting him to take actions, supposedly urgent, without having discussed them with the French except in the vaguest manner. The situation did not change and a month later Nicol could write that while the admiral showed the most perfect courtesy only insignificant results came from their conversation and that 'the English while accepting our collaboration in certain points did not appear to want it in others'.[109] De Robeck had, of course, really chosen *Triad* because of the better accommodation it afforded his staff and the mobility it gave him to shuttle between the scattered British bases and the beaches, but not having to practice diplomacy on an ally whom he found far less sympathetic than his predecessor Guépratte was probably something he appreciated and one less worry among the multitude he had.

The destroyer question was probably the one most likely to cause a dispute between the British and French at the Dardanelles. On 16 May, de Robeck claimed that Lapeyrère had taken four French destroyers away leaving them one 'which is hardly playing the game'. The German submarine threat and the French obligation to provide a dozen destroyers for the Adriatic complicated the matter. Lapeyrère claimed that it was materially impossible for him to replace the 5ème Escadrille at the Dardanelles and that on 23 May he had only twelve destroyers available to protect his fleet and patrol the vicinity of Cape Matapan and the approaches to Malta. Augagneur, after an urgent request by the Admiralty motivated by the submarine danger, considered it a duty to leave the British the 5ème Escadrille which de Robeck promised to maintain from the depot ship *Blenheim*. The minister therefore asked Lapeyrère to leave the destroyers at the Dardanelles, while he would try to make good, if possible, the gaps created in Lapeyrère's fleet.[110] This competition for precious destroyers between different commands would be one of the constants of naval war in the Mediterranean.

The real decision in the Dardanelles campaign had ceased to be a naval one and belonged to the military. De Robeck's responsibilities remained large, however, supplying the army over open beaches from island bases sixty miles away and providing the essential support by naval gunfire while guarding against the new menace of submarines. Wemyss claimed that at Mudros harbour there were always between 150 and 170 ships, not counting innumerable small craft.[111] The British made another effort on 6 and 7 August when fresh forces were landed at Suvla to the north of the original beachheads. The naval part of the landing went well but the military commanders failed to exploit the initial surprise by pushing on to seize the high ground dominating the bay when they might have done so, and within a short time the same stalemate prevailed. The army could not advance.[112] The French also had plans to break the deadlock. In August, General Sarrail, an able but controversial figure with strong ties to the political left in France, had been given command of a force grandly designated L'Armée d'orient. Sarrail had actually been removed from his command on the western front by Joffre, but his powerful political friends had been able to get him this new command. Sarrail planned to land on the Asiatic shore at Yukyeri opening what would have been, in effect, a second front at the Dardanelles.[113] Guépratte and successive commanders of the French army at Gallipoli had all complained of the deadly harassing fire from the Turkish batteries on the Asiatic shore. A conference between Sarrail and representatives of the Ministries of War and Marine decided on 2 September that Sarrail's force would consist of four divisions sent from France (and torn from a reluctant Joffre) and the two French divisions withdrawn from Cape Helles.[114] Whether or not the landing at Yukyeri would have been successful in breaking the deadlock and opening the Straits is another one of those questions that can never be answered. Keyes, that ardent believer in the Dardanelles campaign, told Sarrail a few months later in Salonika that he might have been 'Sarrail de Constantinople'.[115] However, later in September, Bulgaria mobilized and subsequently entered the war on the side of the Central Powers and Sarrail and his army, joined by British forces, were diverted to Salonika in a futile attempt to save Serbia which ended by opening yet another front.

Throughout the summer of 1915 the Royal Navy continued to make a major offensive contribution to the Dardanelles campaign through the continued operations of British submarines in the Marmara. On 10 June, Lieutenant-Commander Boyle went through the Straits in E14 for a second successful cruise sinking a brigantine, torpedoing a steamer in the harbour of Panderma and sinking a number of dhows. The majority of Turkish shipping appeared to be smaller ferry boats or sailing craft with the larger steamers kept prudently out of reach. In late June E12 (Lieutenant-Commander K. M. Bruce) achieved some success although plagued by engine trouble, and in July E7 (Lieutenant-Commander A. D. Cochrane) not only sank a number of ships but also shelled the Zeitunlik power works in the suburbs of Constantinople and attacked the railway line to Constantinople in the Gulf of Ismid. The Allies suffered a setback on 25 July when the French submarine Mariotte was caught trying to pass the Narrows and had to be abandoned. In early August, in conjunction with the landings at Suvla, both Boyle in E14 and Nasmith in E11 made a deliberate effort to cut the road to Gallipoli where it was exposed to the sea, shelling troops attempting to pass, while E11 torpedoed the gunboat Berc-i-Satvet and on 8 August achieved a major success by torpedoing and sinking the battleship Barbarossa which had come down to support the Turkish defences. E14, for her part, torpedoed a 5,000-ton supply ship which beached herself and a few days later the ship was hit by a torpedo dropped from an aircraft piloted by Flight-Commander C. H. K. Edmonds, a first in naval warfare. E2 (Lieutenant-Commander D. de B. Stocks) came into the Marmara on 14 August and also enjoyed a successful cruise but the British suffered another loss when E7 (Lieutenant-Commander Cochrane) was caught in the Nagara net on 4 September. The Turkish obstructions built under German supervision were making passage in and out of the Dardanelles increasingly hazardous and E14, E11 and E2 all had difficulties and close escapes with the Nagara net.[116] The exploits of these submarines were probably the brightest part of the British naval effort at the Dardanelles but by themselves they could not alter the course of the campaign.

The Germans placed great hopes on the Nagara net. In May, Tirpitz had suggested to Admiral von Usedom that he should consider laying a net similar to the ones the British had established in the Straits of Dover as well as deep minefields in the Dardanelles or Marmara aimed specifically against submarines. The Admiralstab co-operated by sending all the information they had on different types of net construction and reporting their own experiences with British anti-submarine measures.[117] Souchon appears to have been critical of what he considered to be Usedom's laxity in guarding against submarines, implying this had led to the loss of the *Messudiyeh* the preceding December, and privately wrote to his wife that he had let the net appear to be Usedom's invention so that he would not hinder it.[118]

In mid-July, Souchon described the Nagara net, which he emphasized Usedom had not finished in ten months of war, as making good progress and on the 17th he reported that the net was half finished. As soon as it was finished, he intended to net the Bosphorus as well and then, hopefully, U-boat visits in the Marmara would cease. The destruction of E7 at the beginning of September was the first success of the Nagara net and Usedom proudly reported it to the Kaiser, emphasizing that it was the sixth enemy submarine to be destroyed by the defences of the Straits, and claiming that two others had been destroyed in the Marmara, which was not true. He added that the net would be strengthened mechanically and by mooring mines at a greater depth. Souchon hoped they would get the other two British submarines which he knew were in the Marmara, but after a while was disappointed to realize that British submarines were still able to penetrate and operate there. Furthermore, through their own obstructions, the British had also made it impossible for the German U-boats to get out of the Dardanelles, and Souchon realized that the submarine war in the Aegean would have to be carried on from outside, while German U-boats at Constantinople would operate in the Black Sea.[119] British submarines, on the other hand, continued to work in the Marmara almost until the final evacuation of the peninsula.

After learning of the presence of U21 and UB8, the Russians temporarily halted operations by their large warships along the Anatolian coast, but the raids by fast Russian destroyers continued. On 11 June two destroyers on such a raid clashed with *Breslau* and one, *Gnyevni*, was disabled, but *Breslau* missed the opportunity for the kill and returned to the Bosphorus enabling *Derski* to tow her crippled consort to safety. The Russian raids continued, while on 18 July *Breslau* was mined on one of the early Russian fields and put out of action for a number of months. The Russian submarines were now more active and one, *Tyulen*, torpedoed and sank a steamer in a convoy escorted by *Goeben*, *Hamidieh* and three torpedo-boats, although the following day the submarine could not get off a shot at the biggest prize of them all, the *Goeben* herself. On 5 September two Russian destroyers, *Buistri* and *Pronziteini*, attacked a convoy of three steamers sailing from Zonguldak to the Bosphorus, escorted by the cruiser *Hamidieh* and the torpedo-boats *Noumoune* and *Muvanet*. The Russian gunfire was superior, the main armament of the *Hamidieh* ceased to function and the cruiser was forced to drop out of action, while the three steamers eventually were run aground.[120] Firle, in command of *Muvanet* acknowledged that: 'These Russian destroyers with their artillery and speed are the real masters of the sea and need fear no one'.[121] After the fiasco the chagrined German officers were ready to concede that the cruiser *Hamidieh* had no battle value and that it would be better for the remaining Turkish steamers, of which there were only eight or nine left, to sail without escort and be picked up by the torpedo-boats, again without *Hamidieh*, off the Bosphorus. Souchon tried to buoy up his officers by telling them of the conclusion of the Turkish-Bulgarian Treaty and the momentous events it was likely to have in the Balkans if they could hold out for the next few months. Souchon also elected to take the risk of sending out the *Goeben* to escort the vital coal transports from Zonguldak and on the 21st the battle cruiser opened fire on three Russian destroyers. The use of the German's major and irreplaceable asset to convoy slow colliers was commented on critically by Firle and cited as another example of the effect of the Russian destroyers. The activities of those destroyers on the Anatolian coast were, however, somewhat diminished in the second half of September as a number of them were employed hunting submarines after UB7 torpedoed and sank the British transport *Patagonia* (6,011 tons) off Odessa. On 1 October, however, the Russians returned in force with three battleships, two cruisers and seven destroyers, covered for the first time by the dreadnought *Imperatriza Maria* and five destroyers. The Russians shelled Kozlu, Zonguldak and Eregli on the Anatolian coast without inflicting great damage, but it was a clear affirmation of Russian supremacy at sea which would not be seriously threatened by the small UB7 or UB8.[122]

In September 1915 yet another factor in the naval war in the Mediterranean arrived on the scene. At the time Italy entered the war the British had offered to provide drifters and trawlers with anti-submarine nets for the Straits of Otranto, but the Italians had been unenthusiastic and the Duke of the Abruzzi declined them.[123] After the experience of two months of war the Italians apparently changed their minds and on 16 August their naval attaché in Paris asked for sixteen French trawlers to be sent to Taranto. The trawlers which had initially been requisitioned for the Italian government had been turned to other purposes after the Italian refusal, and the French had nothing to send except for four shallow-draught trawlers which Lapeyrère had been able to scrape together.[124] The Admiralty stepped into the breach, especially after it became apparent that German submarines were readily passing through the Straits of Otranto, and on 30 August ordered preparations to be made for a first group of trawlers to leave for the Adriatic. Eventually sixty drifters arrived at Taranto between 22 September and the end of the month. Rear-Admiral Thursby was delighted when he got the news for 'now we shall be able to do some submarine hunting. I think myself that they use Pola & Cattaro as bases & Corfu as a supply station so we may be able to catch them with some luck.' The actual arrival of the drifters was less than orderly however, and Thursby changed his tune: 'You can imagine my surprise when suddenly 60 Drifters were dumped on me with no organisation, provisions, stores or anything else.' Nevertheless Thursby allocated them, so many to each battleship, and as soon as possible sent two divisions out to lay nets in the Straits of Otranto with an Italian merchant ship to act as host ship at Brindisi. Thursby aimed at a pattern of two divisions out, one division in port, and hoped to keep thirty-five to forty of the drifters out at a time.[125] The British would subsequently place great hopes on this drifter line in the Straits of Otranto and until the very end of the war considerable efforts would be expended in their direction with questionable success.

The summer of 1915 had therefore witnessed the disappointment of the high hopes which accompanied Italy's entry into the war. A stalemate existed in the Adriatic with the Italians slipping into an increasingly defensive state of mind, a major preoccupation being the preservation of matériel for a long war. There seemed to be a progression on the part of the Italian Naval High Command from a sensible refusal to do foolish things with large ships to the habit of saying 'no' to almost any action which carried the least degree of risk. The stalemate at the Dardanelles also continued despite the unsuccessful British effort to break it at Suvla. The Germans and the Austrians were also building up their submarine strength in the Mediterranean. At first this was merely aimed at relieving pressure on the Dardanelles but it was about to expand into economic warfare against Allied shipping. While the Austrians had done relatively well with their handful of submarines in the Adriatic, it was the Germans who were about to begin the submarine war in earnest with major attacks on Allied shipping. This will form the subject of the next chapter along with the end of one Anglo-French expedition, the Dardanelles campaign and the beginning of a new and major commitment, the Macedonian campaign.

Notes: Chapter 5

1 Gamble to Admiralty, Letter of Proceedings, June 1915, PRO, Adm 137/1088.
2 ibid., also enclosures B and C.
3 Lapeyrère to Augagneur, 26 May 1915, SHM, Carton Ed–83.
4 Gamble, Letter of Proceedings, June 1915, and enclosure D, Minute by Oliver, 6 June 1915, PRO, Adm 137/1088; Thursby to Admiralty, Report of Proceedings, 4 June 1915, and minutes by Balfour, 20 July and Jackson, 21 July, ibid., Adm 137/780; Drage Diary, 26 July 1915, Imperial War Museum, London, Drage MSS, PP/MCR/99.

5 Minute by Churchill, 10 May 1915, Minute by Jackson, 10 May 1915, Gamble, Letter of Proceedings, June 1915, PRO, Adm 137/1088.
6 Naval Staff, *The Mediterranean, 1914–1915*, p. 204. A detailed account of the drifters is in E. Keble Chatterton, *Seas of Adventures* (London, 1936), ch. 6.
7 Lapeyrère to Augagneur, Nos 1550, 1557, 5 June 1915, SHM, Carton Ed-83.
8 Lapeyrère to Augagneur, 19 May 1915, ibid., Carton A-75.
9 Augagneur to Minister of War, 13 May 1915, ibid., Carton Gp–67.
10 Lapeyrère to Augagneur, 10 June 1915, ibid, Carton Ed-83.
11 Richmond Diary, 23 May 1915 reproduced in Marder, *Portrait of an Admiral*, p. 158. The complete diary is in National Maritime Museum, Greenwich, Richmond MSS, RIC/1/13.
12 Daveluy to Jonquières [?], 9 June 1915, SHM, Carton Ea-136.
13 Richmond Diary, 27 May, 5 and 9 June 1915, loc. cit. at n. 11, Richmond MSS, RIC/1/13; Drage Diary, 5 June 1915, loc. cit. at n. 4, Drage MSS, PP/MCR/99; Thursby to Limpus, 12 June 1915, National Maritime Museum, Greenwich, Limpus MSS.
14 Richmond Diary, 10–13 June 1915, loc. cit. at n. 11, Richmond MSS; Marder, *Portrait of an Admiral*, pp. 169–70.
15 Thursby to Jackson, 30 June 1915, Naval Historical Library, London, Jackson MSS. The Italians after spotting submarines on 13 and 14 August and sweeping submarine-laid mines finally stopped the fleet from going to sea for exercises. Thursby to Admiralty, Report of Proceedings, 25 Aug. 1915, PRO, Adm 137/780.
16 Richmond Diary, 1 June 1915, loc. cit. at n. 11, Richmond MSS; Ufficio Storico, *Marina italiana*, Vol. 2, pp. 83–9.
17 Richmond Diary, 4 June 1915, loc. cit. at n. 11, Richmond MSS; Daveluy to Jonquières, 9 June 1915, SHM, Carton Ea-136; Ufficio Storico, *Marina italiana*, Vol. 2, pp. 89-90; Sokol, *Österreich-Ungarns Seekrieg*, pp. 228–30.
18 Ufficio del Capo di Stato Maggiore della Marina, 'Relazione generale sull'opera svolta dal 1 Aprile al 1 Ottobre 1915', pp. 158–9, copy in ACS, 1° Aiutante di Campo Generale di S.M. il Re, Sezione Speciale, Filza 24; Ufficio Storico, *Marina italiana*, Vol. 2, pp. 116–18; Daveluy to Lapeyrère, 21 June and 5 July 1915, SHM, Carton Ed-91; Thursby to Limpus, 5 July 1915, loc. cit. at n. 13, Limpus MSS; Richmond Diary, 26 June 1915, in Marder, *Portrait of an Admiral*, p. 178.
19 Abruzzi to Revel, 8 June 1915, Revel to Abruzzi, 9 June 1915, USM, Cartella 363/1.
20 Abruzzi to Presbitero, 5 July 1915 (with enclosures of plan for occupation of Lagosta and Pelagosa), ibid., Cartella 474/1.
21 Revel to Abruzzi, 7 July 1915, ibid., Cartella 363/1. The Greeks had recently detained for a few days the auxiliary Italian steamer *Ganicolo* which had been sent to reconnoitre Corfu and look for submarine bases. Berthelot to Lapeyrère, 12 July 1915, SHM, Carton Ed-91.
22 Presbitero to Abruzzi, 7 July 1915, USM, Cartella 363/1.
23 Richmond Diary, 12, 18 and 23 June, 9 July 1915, in Marder, *Portrait of an Admiral*, pp. 169, 173, 175, 181.
24 Richmond Diary, 3 July 1915, loc. cit. at n. 11, Richmond MSS, RIC/1/13.
25 Abruzzi to Presbitero, 5 July 1915, USM, Cartella 361/3.
26 Revel to Brusati, 2 July 1915, ACS, Carte Brusati/12 (VIII-17-61); Viale to Cagni, 30 June 1915, ibid.
27 Ufficio Storico, *Marina italiana*, Vol. 2, pp. 120–8; Spindler, *Handelskrieg*, Vol. 2, pp. 196–7.

28 Aichelburg, *Unterseeboote Österreich-Ungarns*, Vol. 1, pp. 121, 133–4, Vol. 2, pp. 318–19, 337; Ufficio Storico, *Marina italiana*, Vol. 2, pp. 109–10.

29 Revel to Cagni, 10 July 1915, ACS, Carte Brusati/23 (VIII-17-61); Ufficio dell Capo di Stato Maggiore, 'Relazione generale sull'opera svolta dal 1 Aprile 1913 al 1 Ottobre 1915', loc. cit. at n. 18, pp. 159–60.

30 Revel to Abruzzi, 16 July 1915, ACS, Carte Brusati/12 (VIII-17-61).

31 Ufficio Storico, *Marina italiana*, Vol. 2, pp. 171–5.

32 Richmond Diary, 13 July 1915, in Marder, *Portrait of an Admiral*, p. 183; Daveluy to Lapeyrère, 26 July 1915, SHM, Carton Ed-91.

33 Capitano di fregata Petrelluzzi to Millo, 12 July 1915, USM, Cartella 363/1.

34 Abruzzi to Revel, 10 July 1915, ibid.

35 Ufficio Storico, *Marina italiana*, Vol. 2, pp. 178–85; Sokol, *Österreich-Ungarns Seekrieg*, pp. 233–5.

36 Revel to Abruzzi, 27 [?] July 1915, ACS, Carte Brusati/12 (VIII-17-61).

37 Thierry, *Tagebuch*, 20, 24, and 25 July 1915, Kriegsarchiv, Vienna, Nachlass Thierry, B/755, No. 23, pp. 23–4.

38 Revel to Abruzzi, 17 July 1915, USM, Cartella 363/1.

39 Revel to Abruzzi, 27 July 1915, ibid.

40 Ufficio Storico, *Marina italiana*, Vol. 2, pp. 175–8; Sokol, *Österreich-Ungarns Seekrieg*, pp. 232–3; Fiedler to Haus (and enclosures), 16 July 1915, OK/MS VIII-1/1 ex 1915, No. 5346.

41 Revel to Abruzzi, 23 July 1915, Abruzzi to Revel, 24 July 1915, USM, Cartella 363/1.

42 Ufficio Storico, *Marina italiana*, Vol. 2, pp. 191–7; Sokol, *Österreich-Ungarns Seekrieg*, pp. 236–8; Seitz to Haus (and enclosures), 25 July 1915, OK/MS VIII-1/1 ex 1915, No. 5741; Fiedler to Haus (and enclosures), 2 Aug. 1915, ibid., No. 5743.

43 Sokol, *Österreich-Ungarns Seekrieg*, pp. 238–9; Aichelburg, *Unterseeboote Österreich-Ungarns*, Vol. 2, pp. 288–91; Ufficio Storico, *Marina italiana*, Vol. 2, pp. 199–202.

44 Abruzzi to Revel, 28 July 1915, USM, Cartella 474/1; Commando-in-Capo dell' Armata Navale e del Basso Adriatico, 'Piano per l'occupazione di Lagosta', n.d., ibid.

45 Abruzzi to Revel, 7 Aug. 1915, ibid., Cartella 361/2.

46 Revel to Abruzzi, 12 Aug. 1915, ibid., Cartella 363/1.

47 Richmond Diary, 29 July and 1 August 1915, in Marder, *Portrait of an Admiral*, pp. 184–5; Thursby to Jackson, 30 July 1915, loc. cit. at n. 15, Jackson MSS.

48 Ufficio Storico, *Marina italiana*, Vol. 2, pp. 202–5; exchange of telegrams between Revel and Abruzzi, 16 Aug. 1915 reproduced in: Ufficio Storico, *Occupazione dell' Isola di Pelagosa* ('Chronistoria Documentata della Guerra Marittima Italo-Austriaca, 1915–1918. Collezione: L'impiego delle Forze Navali-Operazioni, Fascicolo VIII', [Rome, June, 1922]), p. 58.

49 Sokol, *Österreich-Ungarns Seekrieg*, pp. 239–40; Ufficio Storico, *Marina italiana*, Vol. 2, pp. 206–12; Ufficio Storico, *Occupazione dell' Isola di Pelagosa*, pp. 66–7; Ufficio del Capo di Stato Maggiore, 'Relazione generale sull' opera svolta dal 1 Aprile 1913 al 1 Ottobre 1915', loc. cit. at n. 18, p. 163.

50 Richmond Diary, 18 Aug. 1915, in Marder, *Portrait of an Admiral*, p. 192; more temperate remarks are in Richmond to Rodd, 21 Aug. 1915, loc. cit. at n. 11, Richmond MSS, RIC/13/5.

51 Thursby to Admiralty, Report of Proceedings, 25 Aug. 1915, PRO, Adm 137/780.

52 Daveluy to Lapeyrère, 23 Aug. 1915, SHM, Carton Ed-91.

53 Aichelburg, *Unterseeboote Österreich-Ungarns*, Vol. 2, pp. 258–9, 328–32;

Ufficio Storico, *Marina italiana*, Vol. 2, pp. 247–52; Haus to Marinesektion, 28 Sept. 1915, OK/MS VIII-1/1 ex 1915, No. 6943.

54 Bregarte to Diaz, 17 July 1915, Diaz to Marzolo, 3 Aug. 1915, USM, Cartella 361/5.

55 King Victor Emmanuel to Sonnino, 5 Aug. 1915, Sonnino to Viale, 5 Aug. 1915, ibid.

56 Viale to Sonnino, 7 Aug. 1915, Marzolo to Porro, 7 Aug. 1915, ibid.

57 Viale to Sonnino, 13 Aug. 1915, Revel to Commando Supremo, R. Esercito, 14 Aug. 1915, ibid.

58 Revel to Abruzzi, 30 July 1915, ibid., Cartella 356/3; Revel to Abruzzi, 27 Aug. 1915 with endorsement of Admiral Millo, 29 Aug., ibid.

59 Note by Stato Maggiore [initials illegible], 'Opportunità di aumentare il numero di nostri esploratori', n.d., ibid., Cartella 361/6; Villarey to Admiralty, 26 Aug. 1915 and minutes by Oliver and Wilson, PRO, Adm 137/1140.

60 Gamble to Oliver, 28 Aug. 1915, Memorandum by Gamble, 'Comparative Strengths of Austrian & Allied Fast Cruisers in Adriatic', 28 Aug. 1915, Oliver to Jackson, 28 Aug. 1915, minutes by H. B. Jackson, 29 Aug. and 2 Sept. 1915, Balfour to Jackson, 30 Aug. 1915, Memorandum by Oliver, 1 Sept. 1915, ibid.

61 Revel to Brusati, 2 July 1915, ACS, Carte Brusati/12 (VIII-17-61).

62 Revel to Brusati, 13 July 1915, ibid.

63 Revel to Brusati, 28 July 1915, ibid.

64 Salandra to Viale, 24 July 1915, ibid.

65 Revel to Brusati, 28 July 1915 (enclosing what is apparently a draft letter of resignation addressed to the Prime Minister), ibid.

66 Viale to Salandra, 28 July 1915, ACS, Carte Salandra, 2/16.

67 Salandra to Viale, 30 July 1915, ibid.

68 Report of US Naval Attaché, No. T-90, 26 Mar. 1914, NARS, Record Group (hereafter referred to as RG) 38, E-7-a, File No. 327. For further details of the Millo ministry see: Halpern, *Mediterranean Naval Situation*, pp. 197–8.

69 Abruzzi to Revel, 22 Aug. 1915, enclosing Millo to Abruzzi, 20 Aug., USM, Cartella 474/2.

70 Viale to Millo, 11 Sept. 1915, Millo to Viale, 14 Sept. 1915, Abruzzi to Viale, 14 Sept. 1915, ACS, Carte Salandra, 2/16.

71 Revel to Viale, 11 Sept. 1915, Carte Brusati/12 (VIII-17-61).

72 Revel to Brusati, 12 Sept. 1915, ibid. Revel had met Haus in Zurich before the war when they were allies in the Triple Alliance and had discussed, in secret, possible joint action in the event of war. See Halpern, *Mediterranean Naval Situation*, pp. 256–8.

73 Leonardi-Cattolica to Viale, n.d. [Sept. 1915]; Salandra to King Victor Emmanuel, 2 Oct. 1915, ACS, Carte Salandra, 2/16. Revel would hotly dispute the charge that he had neglected destroyers, torpedo-boats and submarines. See Ufficio del Capo di Stato Maggiore, 'Relazione sintetica sull'opera svolta dal 1 Aprile 1913 al 1 Ottobre 1915', pp. 3–8, copy in USM, Cartella 1451/740.

74 Reports of US Naval Attaché, T-303, 27 Sept. 1915, T-307, 1 Oct. 1915 and cuttings from *Rivista nautica*, Oct. 1915, p. 145, NARS, RG 38, E-7-b, No. 3041 and E-7-a, No. 327; D'Huart to Minister of Marine, 30 Sept. 1915, SHM, Carton Ea-136; Richmond Diary, 3 July 1915, in Marder, *Portrait of an Admiral*, p. 180; Thursby to Jackson, 19 Oct. 1915, loc. cit. at n. 15, Jackson MSS. On the loss of the *Benedetto Brin* see: Ufficio Storico, *Marina italiana*, Vol. 2, pp. 309–14; Sokol, *Österreich-Ungarns Seekrieg*, p. 244.

75 D'Huart to Minister of Marine, 6 and 14 Oct. 1915 and 23 Feb. 1916, SHM, Carton Ea-136.
76 Richmond Diary, 6 and 13 Aug. 1915, in Marder, *Portrait of an Admiral*, pp. 189–91; Richmond to Rodd, 6 Aug. 1915, and remarks by Admiral Gamble, 20 Aug., PRO, Adm 137/1088; paper by Richmond, 'Italian Naval Operations', ibid.
77 Daveluy to Lapeyrère, 30 Aug. 1915, SHM, Carton Ed-91.
78 Memorandum by Admiralstab, 'U-Boote im Mittelmeer', 10 June 1915, NARS, T-1022, Roll 727, PG 75260.
79 Colloredo-Mannsfeld to Admiralstab, 29 May 1915, ibid., PG 75259.
80 Marine Baumeister Weichardt, 'Bau von Unterseebooten für das Mittelmeer', 15 June 1915, Adam to Chef des Admiralstabes, 17 June 1915, ibid., PG 75260.
81 Adam to Chef des Admiralstabes, 14 June 1915, Souchon to Admiralstab, 16, 19 and 25 June 1915, Admiralstab to Adam, 26 June 1915, ibid.; Spindler, *Handelskrieg*, Vol. 2, p. 197; Adam to Admiralstab, 'Bericht über die Tätigkeit des deutsches-Marine-Spezial-Kommandos bezw. der Unterseeboots-halbflotille Pola', 3 Aug. 1915, NARS, T-1022, Roll 727, PG 75261.
82 Souchon to Chef des Admiralstabes, 29 June 1915, ibid., PG 75260.
83 Keyes to his wife, 5 July 1915, British Library, London, Keyes MSS 2/13.
84 Spindler, *Handelskrieg*, Vol. 2, pp. 197–8; Bachmann to Chef Hochseeflotte, 16 July 1915, Admiralstab to Hochseechef, 18 July 1915, NARS, T-1022, Roll 727, PG 75260.
85 Admiralstab, 'U-Bootskrieg im Mittelmeer', 9 July 1915, ibid. The Admiralstab also produced a paper on the importance of keeping the Dardanelles closed to the export of Russian grain. The neutral states such as the United States had not made up the deficit caused by the closure. Admiralstab, 'Die russische Getreidsausfuhr und die Dardanellen', 17 July 1915, ibid.
86 Bachmann to Kaiser Wilhelm, 20 July 1915, Bachmann to Admiralstab, 20 July 1915, ibid.
87 von Pohl to Admiralstab, 21 July 1915, Adam to Admiralstab, 1 July 1915, ibid.
88 Admiralstab to von Pohl, 21 July 1915, Bachmann to Admiralstab, 23 July 1915, ibid.
89 Admiralstab to Chef Hochseeflotte and Souchon, 29 July 1915, ibid.
90 Admiralstab to U-boat Half Flotilla, Helgoland, 3 Aug. 1915, 'Operationsbefehl für U34 und U35' (and supplement), n.d. [July 1915], ibid.
91 Souchon to Chef des Admiralstabes, 15 Aug. 1915, ibid., PG 75261.
92 Behncke to Bachmann, 27 Aug. 1915, Bachmann to Souchon, 3 Sept. 1915, ibid., Roll 728, PG 75261.
93 Souchon to Admiralstab, 4 Aug. 1915, ibid., Roll 227, PG 75261; Spindler, *Handelskrieg*, Vol. 2, pp. 196–202.
94 Adam to Chef des Admiralstabes, 3 Aug. 1915, NARS, T-1022, Roll 727, PG 75261.
95 Hohenlohe to Auswärtiges Amt, 12 Aug. 1915, Zenker to Admiralstab, 13 and 15 Aug. 1915, ibid.
96 Bachmann to Admiralstab, 17 Aug. 1915, ibid.
97 Tirpitz to Kaiser Wilhelm, 21 Aug. 1915, ibid., Roll 587, PG 68126; Spindler, *Handelskrieg*, Vol. 2, pp. 203–5.
98 Bachmann to Falkenhayn, 24 Aug. 1915, Bachmann to Admiralstab, 25 Aug. 1915, ibid., Roll 662, PG 75243; Erich Müller [naval attaché, The Hague] to Tirpitz, 16 Aug. 1915, ibid., Roll 727, PG 75261.

99 Bachmann to Kaiser Wilhelm (excerpt), 3 Sept. 1915, Holtzendorff to Kaiser Wilhelm (excerpt), 8 Sept. 1915, ibid., Roll 728, PG 75261.

100 Holtzendorff to Chef des Marinekabinetts, 13 Sept. 1915, ibid., Roll 587, PG 68126.

101 Souchon to Admiralstab, 19 Sept. 1915, ibid., Roll 728, PG 75261; Spindler, *Handelskrieg*, Vol. 2, pp. 205–6.

102 Spindler, *Handelskrieg*, Vol. 2, pp. 202–5.

103 Aichelburg, *Unterseeboote Österreich-Ungarns*, Vol. 1, pp. 92–100; Greger, *Austro-Hungarian Warships*, p. 76; on the Hungarian complication in the prewar dreadnought programme see: Halpern, *Mediterranean Naval Situation*, pp. 160–4, 171–9.

104 Adam to Korvettenkapitän [unnamed but probably a member of the Admiralstab], 16 Aug. 1915, NARS, T-1022, Roll 727, PG 75261.

105 Aichelburg, *Unterseeboote Österreich-Ungarns*, Vol. 1, pp. 110–17.

106 Dickens Diary, 7 July 1915, Imperial War Museum, London, Dickens MSS, PP/MCR/93.

107 Augagneur to Lapeyrère, 13 May 1915, SHM, Carton A-29; Augagneur to Nicol, 14 May 1915, ibid., Carton Ed-108. The French contingent at this date was five battleships, a coast defence ship, and four cruisers.

108 De Robeck to Limpus, 22 May 1915, loc. cit. at n. 13, Limpus MSS; de Robeck to Jackson, 15 June 1915, loc. cit. at n. 15, Jackson MSS.

109 Nicol to Augagneur, 27 May and 23 June 1915, SHM, Carton Ed-109.

110 De Robeck to Limpus, 16 May 1915, loc. cit. at n. 13, Limpus MSS; Lapeyrère to Augagneur, 23 May 1915, Augagneur to Lapeyrère, 29 May 1915, SHM, Carton A-29.

11 Wemyss to Limpus, 6 Sept. 1915, loc. cit. at n. 13, Limpus MSS.

12 There is a large literature on the Suvla landings. See: Corbett and Newbolt, *Naval Operations*, Vol. 3, pp. 68–70, and ch. 5; Aspinall-Oglander, *Military Operations: Gallipoli*, Vol. 2; Keyes, *Naval Memoirs*, Vol. 1, ch. 22; James, *Gallipoli*, chs 10–11; Bush, *Gallipoli*, ch. 22.

13 On the Sarrail affair see: Jan Karl Tanenbaum, *General Maurice Sarrail, 1856–1929* (Chapel Hill, NC, 1974), pp. 56–65; Jere Clemens King, *Generals and Politicians* (Berkeley and Los Angeles, Calif., 1951), ch. 4; Cassar, *The French and the Dardanelles*, ch. 8. A significant number of documents on the French plans are printed in: Ministère de la Guerre, Etat-Major de l'Armée – Service Historique, *Les Armées Françaises dans la Grande Guerre*, Tome VIII–ler Volume, Annexes–ler Volume (Paris, 1924).

14 Jonquières to Augagneur, 2 Sept. 1915, studies by French Naval Staff, 30 Aug. and 2 Sept. 1915, SHM, Carton Ed-108; Memorandum by Admiralty on French Plans, 21 Sept. 1915, ibid., Carton Ed-109.

15 Keyes to his wife, 1 Apr. 1916, in the Halpern (ed.), *The Keyes Papers*, Vol. 1, Doc. 154, pp. 347–9; Keyes, *Naval Memoirs*, Vol. 1, pp. 521–2.

16 Corbett and Newbolt, *Naval Operations*, Vol. 3, pp. 75–9, 100–2, 114–19.

17 Communication from AIV to B, BIII and BI [Admiralstab], 27 May 1915, NARS, T-1022, Roll 727, PG 75259.

18 Souchon to his wife, 18 June, 15 and 17 July, and 6 Aug. 1915, BA-MA, Nachlass Souchon, N156/14, N156/15.

19 Usedom to Kaiser Wilhelm, 8 Sept, 1915, NARS, T-1022, Roll 791, PG 75262; Souchon to his wife, 5 Sept. 1915, BA-MA, Nachlass Souchon, N156/15; idem, 15 and 16 Sept. 1915, ibid., N156/16. Lorey, *Krieg in den türkischen Gewässern*, Vol. 1, p. 193; Vol. 2, pp. 146–9.

20 Covered in great detail, ibid., Vol. 1, pp. 166, 175–6, 185–7; a succinct account is in Greger, *Russische Flotte im Weltkrieg*, pp. 49–51.

121 Firle, Kriegstagebuch, 5 and 9 Sept. 1915, and excerpts from Kriegstagebuch, I Halbflotille, 4–5 Sept. 1915, BA-MA, Nachlass Firle, N155/21.

122 Firle, Kriegstagebuch, 27 Sept. 1915, ibid.; Lorey, *Krieg in den türkischen Gewässern*, Vol. 1, pp. 193–5; Greger, *Russische Flotte im Weltkrieg*, p. 51.

123 Remarks by Admiral Gamble on Richmond to Jackson, 21 June 1915, loc. cit. at n. 15, Jackson MSS.

124 Jonquières to Italian Naval Attaché, 19 Aug. 1915, SHM, Carton Gp-67.

125 Naval Staff, *Mediterranean, 1914–1915*, pp. 204–6; Thursby to Limpus, 1 and 28 Sept. 1915, loc. cit. at n. 13, Limpus MSS.

[6]

Macedonia, the End of the Dardanelles Campaign and the Submarine War Intensifies

The Expedition to Salonika

While the Dardanelles campaign remained at a stalemate in September 1915 and the Germans built up their submarine strength in the Mediterranean, the entire Balkan situation was about to be radically changed by the entry of Bulgaria into the war on the side of Germany and Austria. This also had its effect on the naval war in the Mediterranean for it resulted in a major new commitment for the British and French in the form of the Salonika expedition, provided new opportunities for the Austrians in the Adriatic, opened up direct rail communications between Germany and Constantinople and, finally, and perhaps inevitably, generated strong pressures for the liquidation of the Dardanelles campaign. The Germans and Austrians were eventually successful in the long diplomatic duel to win over Bulgaria and on 6 September concluded an alliance and military convention which included provisions for a combined German and Austrian military campaign to begin against Serbia within thirty days, which the Bulgarians were to join five days later. The Bulgarian army began its mobilization on 21 September and the Serbian government appealed to Greece, with whom it was bound by the treaty of May 1913 for assistance. This assistance was contingent, however, on the Serbians supplying 150,000 troops to any campaign, a requirement the outnumbered and hard-pressed Serbs could not now meet. The pro-Allied Prime Minister of Greece, Eleutherios Venizelos, suggested that the British and French supply this force and secured the consent of King Constantine for an Allied landing at Salonika with the objective of marching up the Vardar Valley to support the Serbs. The Greek political situation was extremely complicated and King Constantine was strongly opposed to actually joining the war. The Greeks publicly refused the Allied request to land at Salonika, despite the private assurances of Venizelos. Nevertheless, a British division and a French division began to land at Salonika on 3 October. Venizelos resigned on the

171

5th over King Constantine's refusal to join the war and the succeeding cabinets of Alexandros Zaimis (6 October–5 November) and the more anti Allied Stephanos Skouloudis held fast to the policy of neutrality. Th German Eleventh Army and the Austrian Third Army under Field Marsha August von Mackensen began their offensive on 6 October and Belgrad fell on the 9th, while on the 11th two Bulgarian armies began their invasion The British and French declared war on Bulgaria on the 15th and 16th an on the 21st the Allied naval forces bombarded Dedeagach and other point on Bulgaria's Aegean coastline. The Allied forces at Salonika were place under the command of General Sarrail and were reinforced by two Frenc divisions with more British troops to follow. The original British an French plan to march up the Vardar Valley to support the Serbs did no appear very promising given the forces arrayed against them, and the nov uncertain attitude of the Greek government with Venizelos removed fron power added yet another element of great danger. There was a very real fea that the Allied troops might be attacked in their rear by the pro-Germa elements in the Greek army, sensing victory once it appeared likely tha Serbia would be overrun.[1]

As the Balkan crisis deepened during the month of October, there wer two major changes in the French naval command. Admiral Boué d Lapeyrère, theoretically the Allied naval commander in the Mediterranean had actually been in command of the 1ère Armée navale since 1911 and thi period before the war was one in which a significant number of new ship had entered service and the French fleet had undergone intensive training a it attempted to surmount the technical and political difficulties of the earlie years of the century. Lapeyrère had his enemies and not everyone in th navy admired his methods or thought highly of his technical competenc After the outbreak of the war he had been denied the naval battle he s ardently desired, and after over a year of frustrating war he found that h responsibilities were sharply increasing with the initiation of the Macedonia campaign and the large troop movements this involved. These troo movements were an obvious target for the growing number of Germa submarines in the Mediterranean. Lapeyrère was not sure he had the mear to fulfil those responsibilities, especially when he compared his resources t those of other sectors. On 4 October he pointed out that French forces i the English Channel had, in addition to port and harbour defences, no fewe than 2 *escadrilles* of destroyers and 80 trawlers, while at the Dardanelles th Anglo-French forces under de Robeck included 72 light cruisers, destroye and torpedo-boats, plus 134 sweepers, small steamers and trawler Lapeyrère's Armée navale had, in contrast, only 27 light cruisers an destroyers and 28 auxiliary gunboats and trawlers to cover the remainder the Mediterranean outside the Adriatic. With this material, which was ofte under repair, he had to guard a surface of more than a million squa kilometres, including a line of communications extending over a length 1,900 miles, as well as the Greek archipelago presently 'swarming' wit enemy submarines. Once these submarines appeared on the Syrian coast would also have to withdraw the large ships of the 3ème Escadre and repla them with small ships, already in short supply. The situation caused hi serious concern by imposing on him large responsibilities with few means to face them. He was now forced to ask the Italian C.-in-C. to return the 2ème and 6ème Escadrilles of destroyers from Brindisi so that he could cover the troop movements.[2]

Lapeyrère also ordered reinforcements to the western approaches to Crete and the passages around Cerigo and Cerigotto where heavy losses to submarines were now taking place. The action of enemy submarines also led Lapeyrère to recommend that *all* ships, not just troop transports, should be armed if they sailed in waters where they were likely to meet submarines, while all troop transport or shipment of critical material should only be by ships able to maintain a good rate of speed. On 8 October Lapeyrère was faced with the problem of protecting a sizeable movement of troops from Alexandria to the Greek archipelago. The British did not provide this protection, and Lapeyrère complained to the minister that he did not have the means to do so. On the 9th Augagneur ordered Lapeyrère to take the dispositions necessary to assure security in the transport of troops from Alexandria through dangerous regions and, in what seemed like a rebuke, stated that destroyers hunting enemy submarines without any indication where they actually were would be better employed in giving direct protection to the transports. Lapeyrère was ordered to fix the itineraries of the transports and assure their protection both coming and going. At this critical moment Lapeyrère cabled the minister on 10 October: 'My state of health does not permit me to assure the responsibilities which fall on me in present circumstances.' He asked the minister to relieve him of his command. Augagneur thanked him in the name of the government for the 'eminent' services he had rendered to the country as leader of their principal naval force for four years and named Vice-Admiral Louis-René Dartige du Fournet as his replacement. Lapeyrère requested that there be no ceremony when he received Dartige aboard his flagship *Courbet* at Malta and, again without ceremony, lowered his flag at sunset on the 15th.[3] The first of the major Allied commanders in the Mediterranean then departed quietly from the scene.

There is something vaguely unsatisfactory about the suddenness with which Lapeyrère relinquished his command. To the President of the Republic, Poincaré, Augagneur's order of 9 October concerning convoys seemed a rebuke and he did not think that Lapeyrère had attempted to justify himself in his reply and had probably used his health as a pretext. Poincaré added that according to Augagneur his authority in the fleet was so weakened that most of its officers would easily reconcile themselves to his departure.[4] There were some in the fleet who indeed spoke of his star as a great chief having waned and that he had not lived up to his early promise.[5] His enemies, such as Vice-Admiral Bienaimé, later charged that Lapeyrère's correspondence revealed that he had felt himself absolutely run over by events which he had not foreseen in time to master. Furthermore, he had never found the support he needed at the ministry, where defence against submarines was misunderstood, and finally 'saw deliverance from his worries only in the abandonment of his post'.[6] But Bienaimé's attacks on Lapeyrère and Augagneur were part of the ferocious nature of French politics, and the fire-eating nationalist deputy's role in the Commission de la marine de guerre was well known. In British naval circles some thought that Lapeyrère had been relieved on account of the French failure to deal with submarines, especially in the Cerigo Channel.[7] This was definitely not so. Lapeyrère retained the confidence of Augagneur, or so Augagneur claimed despite his remarks to Poincaré, to the very end, and the former minister made this quite clear in his testimony before the Commission de la marine de guerre in July 1917 when he added that the men who had succeeded Lapeyrère had not done better from any point of view.[8] Of course, in defending Lapeyrère, Augagneur was also to a large extent defending his own administration.

Vice-Admiral Dartige du Fournet, then 59, had started the war as Préfet Maritime at Bizerte and later commanded the 3ème Escadre on the coast of Syria. He subsequently relieved Nicol as commander of the Escadre des Dardanelles but was in the Aegean barely a month before Lapeyrère departed. Before the war he had also acquired a certain reputation for handling with great tact and ability the numerous problems of protocol which came up when he was SNO in the International Fleet which had assembled at Constantinople during the Balkan Wars in 1913. Captain Howard Kelly, former British naval attaché in France, described him as 'small and dapper (it would be an impertinence to say perky) and does not immediately convey to the unobservant the impression of a great naval chief'. Nevertheless, Kelly added, 'The friends of Admiral de Lapeyrère say that everybody is agreed that his successor has the necessary qualities, whilst those who were not admirers of the late chief were prepared to accept anybody in exchange, so that everybody is apparently satisfied.' This was close to Limpus's reaction: 'I think the new man should do', although a few days before he had written 'Admiral de Lapeyrère I regard as a real loss. I confess that it took time to convince him of the urgent need of energetic action. But he was convinced, and he was acting.' Keyes was somewhat more blunt, and referred to Dartige as a 'nice 2nd rate little man'.[9]

In one respect Dartige was to cause some embarrassment to his British hosts at Malta. During the winter of 1916 a French lady, 'young and quite alone', arrived in Malta and was described by Dartige as a relation. Limpus and others had suspicions about the nature of the relationship, but as it was a private matter they took no official notice of it. The less-gallant censors confirmed from opened letters that the young lady was indeed the C.-in-C.'s mistress. This again need have caused no official attention since Dartige was not the first sailor to have a mistress and the British had only to look at their own naval heroes, such as Nelson, or for that matter Beatty. However, the affair took on another dimension when the censors discovered that the young lady was corresponding with persons on the suspected list and mentioned naval movements she had learned from the C.-in-C. Shortly afterwards the French fleet left for Argostoli and the young lady departed. The following autumn the British were dismayed to learn that she intended to return to meet Dartige when he planned to visit in November. However, the Governor of Malta was adamant that she would not be allowed to return and Rear-Admiral Ballard, now Admiral

Superintendent, had the delicate task of informing Dartige by means of Capitaine de vaisseau Mornet, the French naval delegate at Malta. Mornet apparently knew quite well about the relationship and admitted to Ballard that he was relieved the matter had come to a head without a widespread scandal. Dartige was, after all, married. The potential for scandal, however, was still there if he insisted on her return and the British believed he was so indiscreet in the information he gave the young lady who was 'associated with some very doubtful characters' that they would have to watch his correspondence while he was in Malta 'using every precaution to avoid offence'. They recognized, however, that Dartige had means of transmitting letters privately via French ships. To the great relief of Ballard and Mornet, Dartige privately wrote to the latter that he had told the young lady in question not to come to Malta, and expressed surprise that she had written to suspected individuals but doubted she was intentionally guilty of doing harm. The threat of a potentially awkward situation therefore evaporated and Dartige seems to have taken the matter well, perhaps mollified by the recent receipt of a British decoration.[10]

On 29 October the Viviani government resigned and a new Cabinet was formed under Aristide Briand. Rear-Admiral Lucien Lacaze replaced Augagneur as Minister of Marine. There was a particularly lively scene at the last meeting of the Viviani Cabinet when Augagneur attacked Viviani for calling Lacaze to Paris without his knowledge to offer him his portfolio. Augagneur was particularly angry since he claimed that he had inflicted a punishment of thirty days' confinement on Lacaze when the latter was relieved of his command at Lapeyrère's request in the winter of 1915.[11] Lacaze had indeed been relieved of command of the 2ème Division of the 1ère Escadre de ligne at Lapeyrère's request on 9 March 1915 but the reasons are not clear. Augagneur gave his version of the affair before the Commission de la marine de guerre in July 1917. He claimed that Lacaze allegedly had second thoughts about his vote after a council of admirals was held by Lapeyrère to discuss the conduct of the Adriatic campaign. Lacaze supposedly refused to commit himself, while complaining that Lapeyrère did not keep his subordinates *au courant* of intelligence which ought to be communicated to them regularly. Lapeyrère had then demanded his relief stating that his 'double dealing' attitude made him think that Lacaze had ulterior motives.[12]

Lacaze himself was not new to politics. He had been Chef de Cabinet to Théophile Delcassé when the latter was Minister of Marine from March 1911 to January 1913 and was familiar with the intricacies and patronage that went with that politically sensitive position. Lacaze was of the Germinet' school, that was closely associated during his past career with Vice-Admiral Paul-Louis Germinet, and had been his Chief of Staff in the Mediterranean fleet. Germinet was an exceptionally able and popular officer who had been relieved of his command in 1908 when he publicly complained about the unpreparedness of the fleet due to lack of munitions. Lacaze had also served as naval attaché in Rome in 1906. Kelly described him as 'small, slight and delicate, and belongs to the not uncommon type of Frenchman who always appears to be on the point of death, but lingers on in a manner worthy of the most robust'.[13] It was, on the whole, a shrewd judgement for Lacaze lived until 1955 when he was in his 94th year.

The new French naval leaders immediately had to face the deteriorating situation in the Balkans. By 23 October the Bulgarian Second Army had captured Veles, cutting off Sarrail's forces moving up the Vardar Valley from reaching the Serbian army. The Anglo-French intervention in Macedonia had been a classic case of too little and too late. The British contingent had only advanced to the Greek–Bulgarian border and Sarrail's forces, hopelessly outnumbered, would obviously have to retreat back into Greece with large Greek forces of uncertain attitude between them and their base at Salonika. General Dousmanis, Chief of the Greek General Staff, and Colonel Metaxas, his Assistant Chief of Staff, certainly discussed action against the Allies and on 31 October and 1 November posed a series of questions to Captain von Falkenhausen, the German military attaché in Athens. King Constantine approved their action, although the wily monarch asked von Falkenhausen to represent the questions as emanating from himself rather than the Greeks. Colonel Metaxas described how the difficult position of Greece was well known, and that the Greek fleet had no proper and secure base and thus had to avoid a naval war against Britain. The events in the Balkan theatre could, however, compel Greece to come out openly against the Entente. This might mean enforcing the obligation to disarm Entente troops when they retreated over the Greek frontier from Serbia. The Greeks had therefore to prepare for this and a probable declaration of war by the Entente, and they would need support from the Central Powers. Colonel Metaxas wanted to know how many German U-boats could be available in Greek waters on the outbreak of hostilities, and by what means could Greece support these submarines? Could the U-boats together with the Greek fleet protect at least the sea route from Salonika to the straits of northern Euboea and the route from Salonika to Chalkis, as well as the Saronic Gulf and with it Athens and Piraeus? The latter question was important because of the need for food supplies from old Greece, that is Greek territory before the conquests of the Balkan Wars. Only a quarter of Greek requirements could be transported to northern Greece over the land route. Metaxas also asked about the protection of the Aegean Islands and the Ionian Sea. The Aegean Islands might best be protected by blocking the passages on both sides of Crete and turning the Aegean into a *mare clausum*. Metaxas asked if this would be possible with German submarines working together with the Greek and Turkish fleets? Greece could do little to protect the Ionian Islands itself, but Metaxas asked how much assistance the Austrian fleet could provide if the islands were placed at its disposal. They could probably not avoid partial occupation of the Ionian Islands by the Entente, but if Germany struck at Britain in Egypt the Entente Powers would be compelled to give them up in future peace negotiations. Metaxas also asked about artillery support from the Central Powers, both in the form of munitions and heavy batteries for coastal defence. In the case where the Greeks disarmed the Entente troops, Metaxas argued that it would be desirable on political grounds for the French to be interned in a country other than Greece. Metaxas emphasized, however, that the Greeks were anxious to avoid war with the Entente and this would be achieved if the Entente could be brought to evacuate Salonika. German submarine activity on the approach routes to Salonika would assist the attainment of this goal since Greece could not delivery any foodstuffs to the British and French and they would have to import them by sea.

Colonel Metaxas, a future dictator of Greece (1936–41), displayed, at best, a rather hazy and unrealistic appreciation of seapower and the potential naval support that the Greeks could receive from the Central Powers. Von Falkenhausen was intelligent enough to realize that while Metaxas's remarks might reflect the views of the king and the General Staff, it was doubtful whether the responsible ministers would make them their own. Moreover, he thought it desirable for Greek neutrality to be preserved for the moment, since Greece as an ally would make considerable claims for war material and foodstuffs and would require strong support at sea. For Greece to maintain its neutrality it would suffice for Bulgarian troops to refrain from following the retreating British and French over the Greek frontier. Von Falkenhausen did agree with Metaxas's argument that increased activity by German submarines in the eastern Mediterranean would be strong support for King Constantine's policy of neutrality, and he recommended raising the numbers of submarines in the Mediterranean, although he doubted, correctly as it turned out, that the Greek government would succeed in getting Entente troops off Greek soil.[14] Certain of the Greek claims, such as making the Aegean a *mare clausum*, have an air of unreality about them and possibly revealed a considerable ignorance about the realities of seapower on the part of King Constantine and the Greek General Staff. This is a bit surprising, since the Greek navy had performed well in the Balkan Wars of 1912–13 and the Naval Staff at least must have been conscious of the large British and French forces already in the Aegean. Perhaps the questions were just talk, or an unspoken justification for continued neutrality by posing requirements that the Germans could obviously not fulfil.

Admiral Holtzendorff stressed submarine warfare in his reply. It was, realistically, all the German navy could do. German submarines were already permanently operating in Greek waters and as many as could be detached from home waters would be sent, although the exact number available on any outbreak of hostilities between Greece and the Entente could not be established in advance. It would not be necessary for the Greeks to furnish material support to the German submarines. The bases available in the Adriatic would suffice since the latest U-boats had a large radius of action and could maintain themselves for weeks at sea. The Greeks might best support submarines by the transmission of intelligence and by providing wireless facilities, as well as granting them unlimited stay in remote gulfs and harbours. However, the Admiralstab did not recommend permanently stationing U-boats in Greek harbours as a defensive measure. The submarines would be lost for operations while they were idle and real protection would be best achieved by their activity at sea inflicting harm on the enemy at various points. Holtzendorff also pointed out that due to the strengthening of enemy anti-submarine measures they could not restrict the activities of their submarines to narrow waters or certain well-defined areas as the Greeks wanted in regard to protection of their coastal routes. If U-boats could not give absolute protection to Greek harbours and coastal trade, they could nevertheless hinder long and undisturbed operations by the British and French in the vicinity of the Greek coast. The attack on enemy traffic on the approach routes to the Aegean south of Crete would considerably shake the enemy's position in Salonika. Holtzendorff quickly dismissed the Turkish fleet as a source of assistance. It was confined to the Marmara for the moment because of the danger of a Russian landing on the Black Sea coast – he might also have mentioned the obvious, that the Dardanelles expedition closed off its exit to the Aegean. The Admiralstab would send an officer to Pola to discuss possible Austrian support, although it is doubtful whether the Admiralstab could have had any realistic expectation of this.

Kapitän zur See Zenker, the Admiralstab representative with the Army High Command, did discuss the problem with Falkenhayn. The naval position was, after all, only common sense. Zenker noted that, at the moment, they had in the Mediterranean only four large U-boats available, a fifth would not be available until the end of November and a sixth in the middle of December. The closure of the Aegean Sea by submarine activity around Crete and the protection of the Salonika–Euboea coastal route or the port of Piraeus by submarines was not possible and the prospect of a combined Turkish–Greek fleet closing the Aegean was hopeless because o the great superiority of the British and French. It was also hopeless to expec the Austrians to protect the Greek islands in the Ionian, especially as the Entente had an ideal base in Taranto and the Austrians were restricted by the fear of an Italian landing on their coast. Falkenhayn agreed with the navy's argument. They could scarcely guarantee much security to the Greeks with the means at their disposal. He added that, from the military point of view, they could make only limited deliveries of munitions since a the moment they had to supply Turkey and Bulgaria. They could establish heavy coastal batteries if they were clearly necessary.[15] It is hard to avoid reading between the lines the conclusion that Greece was also more valuable as a neutral than an ally for the German army. The Admiralstab put the best face on it by ordering their naval attaché in Athens to assure King Constantine that the success of German U-boats in the Mediterranean would be, in the future as it had been in the past, a strong support for his policy of neutrality.[16] This argument had received strong reinforcement on 23 October when the British transport *Marquette* (7,057 tons) carrying troops from Egypt to Salonika was torpedoed and sunk in the Gulf o Salonika by U35, although most on board were rescued.[17] All in all, the German proposals and means to render maritime support to the Greek were not likely to tempt King Constantine out of his policy of neutrality.

None of this was known, however, to the senior Allied naval officer a Salonika, Vice-Admiral Dominique-Marie Gauchet, a 58-year-old Norman who had assumed command of the French Dardanelles squadron afte Dartige succeeded Lapeyrère as Mediterranean C.-in-C. Gauchet, flying hi flag in the battleship *Patrie*, was a prickly individual with a reputation in the

French navy for being 'difficult'. He was jealous of his prerogatives and the terror of his subordinates, quick with reprimands for any presumed slight. Not surprisingly, he did not get on well with the British of whom he was intensely suspicious. The situation was not helped by the divergence of views between the British and French governments over the Salonika campaign. There were a bewildering series of inter-Allied conferences as the two governments grappled with the changing situation and the apparent about-face of the Greeks, while the British were consistently far less enthusiastic over Salonika than their French allies. The British government in this and in the parallel Dardanelles campaign gave the impression of vacillation and uncertainty over the proper course to follow. This uncertainty was widely denounced by the sailors on the scene.[18]

Gauchet was worried about the Greeks and their intentions until enough Allied troops had arrived to secure the port, city and surrounding roads from the large concentration of Greek troops in the vicinity. In case of difficulty, he was particularly anxious to destroy the forts at Point Kara which commanded the entrance to the Gulf of Salonika and the anti-submarine net established by the Allies on their arrival, but recognized that they would have to proceed cautiously until they were solidly ashore.[19] Gauchet was suspicious of the British and brusquely rejected an Admiralty proposal for an international commission to direct movements at the port. He accused the British authorities at Salonika of being nervous and fidgety as well as unnecessarily blunt with the Greeks, while it was the French who were doing most of the fighting and the British who were ready to evacuate. Gauchet concluded that there were two operations in the Aegean which should be clearly separated. One was the Dardanelles, a dead weight which the Allies could only think of getting rid of and which was a British affair. The other was Macedonia, and here the responsibility of France was clearly engaged and it could not place the direction of the operation into any other hands than its own. Briand and Lacaze agreed.[20] Gauchet was also worried about Dartige's proposal to use Suda, Milo and Corfu as bases if it came to armed conflict with the Greeks. He maintained that the Escadre des Dardanelles must cling to Salonika to the last ship while they had a single soldier in Macedonia.[21] Gauchet also reported to Dartige that the resistance of the Serbian army in the region of Monastir was weakening and that the position of their troops would rapidly become difficult with the possibility of a Greek attempt to disarm them as they retreated back into Greece. He alleged that German officers were working openly with the Greek General Staff. The best chance of remaining master of the situation would be to transport with extreme urgency another 50,000 men to Salonika. The operation could be accomplished in a dozen days and, until then, they should avoid furnishing the Greek General Staff with any pretext for action. The British appeared to have around 40,000 men available at Mudros but, according to Gauchet, their ally floated in indecision and was guided by considerations which were not identical to their own.[22]

There was considerable substance to Gauchet's charges about British indecision and lack of enthusiasm concerning the Salonika expedition, but the French admiral's personality undoubtedly exacerbated the situation.

The British also had the Dardanelles campaign in which they had by far the dominant role to worry about. They suspected that Gauchet was scheming to make himself independent of de Robeck in an area of the Mediterranean that had been assigned to the British. They were convinced that Gauchet resented their presence at Salonika and in the next few weeks there were a whole series of petty slights, assumed affronts and similar incidents indicating a far higher degree of friction than normal. Personality, even in a mass war such as 1914–18, could still be important in certain situations, particularly when inter-Allied co-operation was necessary. Until now Anglo-French friction in naval affairs in the Mediterranean had been kept to a minimum if only because both sides consciously worked at reducing it. Lapeyrère had been very diffident about even visiting de Robeck's sphere of operations lest he be accused of butting in, but when the long-expected visit did occur in September 1915 it went off well.[23] De Robeck could be a charmer and was, by all accounts, a great gentleman; but he and Gauchet simply did not like each other and were, to quote de Robeck's Chief of Staff Keyes, 'like a couple of dogs with their hackles up whenever they met'. Lacaze later admitted to Keyes that Gauchet was 'un peu difficile' and undoubtedly his own navy must have found him almost as difficult to handle as the British.[24] Anglo-French friction in naval affairs probably reached its peak in late 1915 and early 1916 when Gauchet commanded French forces in the Aegean. Ironically, it seemed to diminish after Gauchet became Mediterranean C.-in-C. at the end of 1916, presumably because his close contact with foreigners diminished, and probably also because his authority was now recognized and he was no longer in competition with others of similar rank. Perhaps he also mellowed a bit, for in 1918 American officers sent to establish a base on Corfu for the submarine-chasers that were going to operate at the entrance to the Adriatic found him extremely helpful, almost fatherly, and reported that he could not do enough for them.[25] But then again, they were relatively junior in rank and represented no challenge to his authority.

The British and French both made plans to exert naval pressure on the Greeks when the moment of truth arrived and Allied troops retreated over the Greek frontier.[26] The diplomatic and naval manœuvring is far too detailed to discuss here. Certainly the Allies felt themselves in a vulnerable position, although when Kitchener passed through Athens in November King Constantine reassured him that Greece would never attack Allied forces.[27]

While King Constantine was making reassuring noises to the British and French, his Chief of Naval Staff was inquiring about possible German naval assistance in the event of threats to the Greek coast by the naval forces of the Entente. He asked the German naval attaché in Athens if mines and U-boats could be placed at their disposal. Holtzendorff replied, with Tirpitz's approval, on 22 November that the German navy was ready to make mines available to the Greek navy at once. They could be brought to Greece by submarines and most expediently unloaded at a suitable harbour in the western Peloponnese. Direct transport to Athens was not advisable because of the distance involved, and submarines obviously could not pass unseen through the Corinth Canal. The Greek government would also have to ensure that the British Naval Mission, still in Greece, did not learn the details of the mines' construction. The Germans also promised to send experts along with the first shipment. Coast-defence materials for Salonika, however, could only go by the land route as soon as the railway was clear of Entente troops. Several U-boats would also be held ready to attack the Allied blockade line. Simultaneously, the Admiralstab ordered the minelaying submarine in the German Flotilla at Pola, UC14, to be ready to undertake the transport to Greece of the mines, while U39 was to be ready to attack the Allied blockade line and also to tow UC14 up to the Straits of Otranto if the Austrian navy could not provide a torpedo-boat for this purpose. King Constantine and his Chief of Naval Staff thanked the Germans for the offer of mines and U-boats and promised to keep the details of the mines' construction secret. The Greek Chief of Naval Staff also promised to make detailed proposals within the next few days for implementation of the transport, but he did not think at the moment it would come to a blockade. Nevertheless, it was best to be prepared and until the final departure of Entente troops from Macedonia they had to be ready for surprises from the British and French. On the other hand, he assured the Germans that, for the present, it was not necessary to take Greece into consideration when deploying U-boats in the Mediterranean.[28]

One is left with the question how serious was all this? The promised German support would have been very scanty indeed, for the carrying capacity of UC14, which seems to have been all the Germans intended to use initially, was limited to about a dozen mines. The use of U39 would have been a definite threat to the Allies, but it was hardly anything more than the Germans were already doing to their supply lines, and since any blockade was likely to be enforced by light vessels rather that large warships, U39's employment against them would have been far less profitable for the Germans than operations against merchantmen in the economic war. What the Germans were proposing, or could provide, in the way of naval support was therefore not very much and the Greeks must have realized it.

A combined Allied squadron under Vice-Admiral Le Bris anchored in Milo harbour on 25 November. The French contingent included the battleships *Vérité*, *Justice* and *Démocratie*. The British contribution included the old battleships *Hibernia*, *Zealandia* and *Russell* under Rear-Admiral Sydney Fremantle. Le Bris had around thirty British and French light craft as well as the token participation of the Italian armoured cruiser *Ferruccio* and the Russian cruiser *Askold*. The handful of mines that the Germans could have provided would have made little impression on this force. The U-boats would have been a more serious threat, but only one or possibly two would have been available, and once their presence was known it can be safely assumed that the big ships would have been kept behind nets in harbour and the actual blockade left to the light craft. The Greek fleet itself was composed of: 2 battleships recently acquired from the United States; 3 ancient coast-defence battleships of relatively little value; 1 very good armoured cruiser (*Averoff*); 1 light cruiser; 14 destroyers; 13 coast-defence torpedo-boats; and 2 submarines. The *Averoff* and the fourteen destroyers four of which were large and modern, were potentially the most valuabl and troublesome portion of the fleet.

The British and French ministers had this threat of force behind then when they began negotiating in Athens for the necessary Greek guarantee for security at Salonika. These guarantees included the neutralization o those batteries which bothered Gauchet so much. The French governmen informed Sarrail that they intended to stay and ordered him to plac Salonika in a state of defence for the troops retiring from Serbia. Sarrail als intended to make the surrender of the Greek batteries at Kara Point a gaug of Greek good will.

The actual situation finally showed signs of easing, however. Th stoppage of Greek ships, as well as all cargoes destined for Greece in French British and Italian ports, produced strong emotion in Athens and, accordin; to the French minister, the Greek government apparently recognized th necessity of yielding. On 11 December they ordered the Greek army t evacuate Salonika, leaving only a division whose presence was accepted b Sarrail.[29] Fremantle's squadron departed for the Dardanelles on the 12t while the French light craft resumed their anti-submarine patrols and escor duties. The French soon had second thoughts about dispersing the Mil squadron when new difficulties occurred in the negotiations with th Greeks and the Naval Staff wanted to reconstitute it.[30] The French navy and indeed the entire French government, were by this time receivin; consistent advice towards an aggressive policy from the French nav attaché in Athens, Capitaine de frégate de Roquefeuil, who had bee appointed in mid-November. Roquefeuil was another of 'l'équipe Germine and had been with Lacaze on Germinet's staff in the Mediterranean fleet. H had also taught the course on foreign navies at the Ecole de Guerre Naval before the war, and in Athens made no secret of the fact that his diplomati position as naval attaché was a cover for the establishment of an intelligenc service. He was a zealous, if controversial, individual who apparently ha few hesitations about meddling in Greek politics and his actions alarme many, including the French C.-in-C., Dartige. On the other hand, h definitely had the ear, and probably the great confidence, of his minister.[3]

The crisis passed at Salonika when the Allied troops retreated from Serbi in good order over the Greek frontier. The much-feared disaster did no occur, the Greeks remained quiescent and the allies were able to fortify th position securely, while they received additional troop reinforcements fror France or Gallipoli. Perhaps most important of all, the German an Bulgarian forces refrained from an all-out assault on Salonika. While th German navy might have been able to provide little assistance to th Greeks, the German army was quite another story. The German Hig Command regarded the Balkans as a secondary theatre and were no inclined or, at least initially, in a position to push south into Greece. Th Allies were therefore reasonably secure in what the Germans supposedl referred to with a sneer as their largest internment camp.[32] Relation between the Greeks and the Allies remained difficult, at least unt Constantine was deposed in June 1917, and in the course of 1916 the Frenc

C.-in-C., Dartige, would find more and more of his attention taken up by the Greek problem which would ultimately be the cause of his dismissal at the end of the year. The supply of the Salonika forces would also be a continuing and substantial naval commitment.

The End of the Dardanelles Campaign

By the end of September 1915 the Dardanelles campaign was also entering its final stage. The stalemate on the peninsula and the deflection of Sarrail's forces to Salonika ended hopes of the French opening up a second front on the Asiatic shore, and the British were faced with the prospect of preparing for a winter campaign. Given the stalemate at Cape Helles, Anzac and Suvla, de Robeck had regarded the French landing as 'the true solution'. As for the military operations themselves, de Robeck on 8 October described the British troops on the peninsula as 'marking time' and secure in their positions, incapable of making much headway against the Turks, suffering from a high rate of sickness, largely dysentery, but not likely to be easily turned out unless an overwhelming force of artillery could be brought against them.[33] The impending collapse of Serbia and the opening of direct rail communications between Germany and the Ottoman Empire made this a distinct possibility.

On 16 October the commander of the Mediterranean Expeditionary Force, General Sir Ian Hamilton, and his Chief of Staff, Major-General Walter P. Braithwaite, finally paid the penalty for the army's lack of success and were replaced. The new commander was General Sir Charles Monro who had been in command of the Third Army in France and had served on the western front since the beginning of the war. Monro would turn out to have very different ideas on the Dardanelles campaign and shortly after his arrival recommended evacuation. There was another alternative. Ever since the check at Suvla in August, de Robeck's Chief of Staff, Keyes, had been trying without success to persuade him to propose another naval attack. Keyes believed that the navy would succeed where they had failed on 18 March because they now had long-range monitors, an efficient air service for spotting and, perhaps most important of all, an efficient minesweeping flotilla. De Robeck did not agree, noting that in his opinion they had never tackled the real minefield last March and he did not think that their sweepers were capable of clearing it under fire.[34] Captain William W. Godfrey, a Royal Marine officer on de Robeck's staff, was Keyes's ally and prepared a plan for forcing the Straits which Keyes submitted with a warm letter of support on 23 September. De Robeck was not moved. Keyes wrote to his wife on 28 September, 'I can think of nothing but the project', but de Robeck told him 'Well Commodore, you and I will never agree on this subject – but there is no reason why we should not remain good friends'.[35] Keyes kept nagging the remarkably tolerant de Robeck and prepared another plan, dated 18 October, which he hoped would meet some of de Robeck's chief objections.[36] Finally de Robeck, always the great gentleman, sent Keyes home to plead his case, insisting it was not a dismissal and that he expected Keyes to return as Chief of Staff, and Keyes was only doing his duty, as he was himself, in giving his opinion against the attack. De Robeck gave Keyes private letters to Balfour and Jackson stating his own case. The Turks would not lay down their arms if four or five ships got into the Marmara (which he doubted) and bombarded Constantinople, for they had several months' supply on the peninsula. The British could not carry on an effective campaign in the Marmara until they could pass soft-skinned colliers and supply ships through the Dardanelles, and to do this they had to take and destroy all the Turkish forts in the Straits. That could only be done in a combined operation with the army. If the attack failed, the loss of personnel and ships would be great and it would have a heavy effect on the morale of the army while encouraging the enemy. The position of the army would then become critical.[37]

The government in London was in a state of great indecision over the eastern Mediterranean where the critical position in Macedonia complicated the situation. Keyes, with the handicap of de Robeck's negative opinion, did not have as much influence as he hoped or later thought, although perhaps more than some of the Sea Lords gave him credit for. Jackson wrote to de Robeck, 'Keyes has not made much impression except perhaps on K. [Kitchener]' but admitted 'things here change daily thanks to the indecision of our rulers. They don't know how to save their face so talk, talk, talk & let things slide.' Balfour was intrigued with Keyes's scheme, perhaps because it offered a way out of an evacuation with its assumed horrors. He told Keyes on 30 October that it was not often when one considered a hazardous scheme that the more one examined it the more one liked it. The Admiralty were inclined to favour a renewal of the attack but combined with a major military movement. However, Monro reported in favour of evacuation and the army, dominated by western front generals, was never very enthusiastic about major overseas ventures.[38] Their French allies were becoming heavily involved in Macedonia, although the Minister of War in the Viviani Cabinet, Alexandre Millerand, and in the succeeding Briand Cabinet, General Gallieni, were opposed to a complete evacuation of the peninsula.[39]

Kitchener, Secretary of State for War, initially did not accept Monro's report in favour of evacuation and resolved to make a personal tour of inspection before reaching a final decision. On his way back to the Dardanelles, Keyes called on Lacaze, the new French Minister of Marine, in Paris. The two were old friends since they had been naval attachés together in Rome before the war. Lacaze was ready to support a renewed naval attack and ask his government to provide six French battleships as he feared an evacuation would result in the loss of large quantities of men and material.[40] De Robeck was horrified at the degree of success Keyes had achieved. He wrote to Limpus on 7 November:

> The Admiralty, probably on the advice of Roger Keyes, are evidently anxious that we should again attack the Dardanelles with the Fleet. I am perfectly determined to do nothing of the sort, as it would probably lead

to a colossal disaster & then Roumania & Greece would come in against us & we should lose our army on the Peninsula & Salonika. Unless we can clear the mines away & destroy the torpedo tubes it is madness, fancy bringing these old battleships into the Narrows to be torpedoed. It is like sending an unfortunate horse into the bull ring blindfolded![41]

Limpus, former Head of the Naval Mission with the Turkish fleet, backed de Robeck to the hilt and replied:

You are absolutely right. It wants an independent and strong man to tell the Admiralty so. I am horrified to hear that they even contemplated such an operation. It is true that some armoured ships might get through – and we have always known that. It is equally true that they could do nothing real if they *did* get into the Marmara, unless collier transport supply ships and other soft vessels got in too . . . I believe that an attempt by the Fleet to rush the Dardanelles would provide us with the biggest disaster of the whole war. Imagine my thankfulness – this time – we have a man who is strong enough to say *no*.

But Limpus also feared that evacuation 'would be a costly business in men & stores & almost as bad as a visible failure of the Fleet to force a passage'.[42] The fate of a renewed attack on the Dardanelles will always be a subject of speculation. Would it have exposed the Turkish artillery positions to enfilading fire, shaken the grip of the Turkish army on the peninsula, cut off their supplies, permitted the army to push forward in a combined attack and, with Constantinople under the guns of a British fleet, perhaps have knocked Turkey out of the war? Or, as de Robeck and Limpus feared, would the result have been a major disaster? The answer will never be known.

The final decision to terminate the Dardanelles campaign has been examined in great detail elsewhere.[43] Kitchener, always mercurial, once he had actually seen the peninsula and no doubt heavily influenced by Monro, recommended evacuation. De Robeck estimated that it would take at least six weeks and that they would 'lose at least 30 per cent in men & material unless we have the most wonderful luck'.[44] Kitchener added yet a new complication. He coupled his decision to evacuate with a new proposal to employ two of the divisions withdrawn from Gallipoli, combined with two divisions taken from Egypt, in a new landing at Ayas Bay in the Gulf of Alexandretta. The objective would be to move inland sufficiently far to cut Turkish communications with Syria, thereby forestalling a new attack on the Suez Canal and offsetting the political effects in the Muslim world of the evacuation of Gallipoli. Kitchener had toyed with the idea of a landing at Alexandretta earlier in the year, but his new scheme ran into what seemed like universal objections. The proposal would end up requiring large numbers of troops for they would have to hold a sizeable perimeter. The Admiralty were opposed to the idea of trying to keep an army supplied over an open beach or through a port which was being shelled by the enemy from surrounding heights or was open to submarine attack. The General Staff thought that the minimum 60,000 men required would have to push inland about twenty-five miles and would have to hold a perimeter of around fifty miles. The General Staff, not surprisingly, thought that the troops would be better employed if concentrated for a great offensive in a decisive theatre of the war, and efforts outside the main theatre of operations should be limited to holding in check dangerous political and military developments which might threaten the security of British or French possessions or interests. The Admiralty also pointed out that small craft and lighters required for the evacuation at Gallipoli would not be available for use at Ayas Bay, and the expedition would require guarding a new transport route of approximately 400 miles in addition to existing routes, which were already imperfectly protected. The Admiralty could undertake the Ayas Bay expedition if it were not for the large drain on resources caused by the Dardanelles and Salonika expeditions, the protection of Egypt and transport routes in the Mediterranean, as well as the protection of the sea communications with the army in France, the United States and the detachments sent to the Adriatic and Archangel. The French objection was equally strong. Admiral de Jonquières, Chief of Naval Staff, noted on the margin of a translation of the note by the British General Staff that he associated himself in the most formal fashion with their considerations, and the army's Section d'études de la défense nationale – the permanent secretariat of the Conseil supérieur de la guerre – in their report on the subject recommended that the best defence of Egypt was on the banks of the Suez Canal itself. They also raised the obvious political consideration. French interests in Syria required French participation in any expedition of this sort and this would probably consist of a French division withdrawn from Gallipoli.[45]

The Ayas Bay scheme was rejected by the British government and at an Anglo-French Conference at the Ministry of Foreign Affairs in Paris on 17 November, Prime Minister Asquith himself declared that they would set the idea aside for the moment.[46] Even de Robeck and Keyes could agree on this subject. De Robeck thought that the scheme was a great mistake and that the defence of Egypt on the Suez Canal where they had mobility and seapower was preferable, while Keyes remarked about the scheme: 'As if Gallipoli wasn't the place to fight for Egypt in – the maddest thing.'[47] The Ayas Bay scheme was so roundly condemned that one historian has argued that it was actually concocted by a member of Monro's staff as a diversion to gain time for the principle of evacuation to be accepted and was never meant as a serious proposition.[48] Kitchener actually had a potential supporter for his Ayas Bay scheme in the French C.-in-C. in the Mediterranean. Dartige du Fournet was also predisposed towards an expedition to Cilicia or Asia Minor with, of course, full French participation and, preferably, control. He apparently argued in favour of the subject with de Robeck when the latter passed through Malta on 18 December. Dartige probably kept his other motives to himself on that occasion – the fear that the British would supplant the French in Syria. Lacaze called him sharply to order. The French government had decided for numerous and serious reasons to concentrate their efforts in the east at Salonika and Lacaze ordered

Dartige to say nothing in his conversations with Allied admirals, even personal conversations, which might appear contrary to that view.[49]

Kitchener made his final recommendation for the evacuation of Suvla and Anzac but the temporary retention of Cape Helles on 22 November and two days later left for Britain. The War Committee accepted the recommendation but added that Cape Helles must also be evacuated. The news to people like Keyes, who learned of it on the 24th, was devastating, but he was determined to

> turn what promises to be the most appalling disaster in history into a
> great and glorious victory . . . We can't win if we always wait to see
> what will turn up and risk nothing. The worst that can happen is that a
> few old ships will be sunk. The Army can be evacuated afterwards if they
> must be, but they must be in a position to take advantage of our success if
> we have one.[50]

The opportunity for a reversal of the decision on the renewal of a naval attack was ironically provided by de Robeck himself. The admiral's health was breaking down from the strain of months of command and he suffered particularly from insomnia. He was obviously in need of at least a brief period of rest and, once the crucial decisions had been made, he departed for a short leave in Britain leaving Wemyss in command. He wrote: 'I hate running away even for a day but Rosie Wemyss is such a good fellow, he will not be induced into any foolish action by R. Keyes.'[51] De Robeck was wrong, for Wemyss and Keyes launched a furious campaign to change the decision. Wemyss tried to explain to de Robeck:

> It required no urging on the part of the Commodore to make me see that
> . . . something must be done, or at least proposed, as an alternative. You
> know that I have not, at any rate lately, been against the actual deed of
> forcing the Straits. My difficulty has been that my vision afterwards has
> been somewhat clouded. But now something must be done to stop them
> leaving the Peninsula and that seems the only something left.

He told the First Sea Lord:

> I believe attack is the only Policy left to us – beaten in Servia,
> outmanœuvred by Greece, evacuation of the Peninsula would be
> disastrous politically and when I contemplate the operation and think of
> what it means I positively shudder. The principal difficulties are almost
> prohibitive even with good luck – with a little bad luck our losses would
> be prodigious and horrible. I really don't think the soldiers realise the
> situation.[52]

The efforts of Wemyss and Keyes did not succeed. The Cabinet finally decided on 7 December to order the evacuation of Anzac and Suvla. While he was in London, de Robeck had been called to a War Council meeting on 2 December and made a strong impression with his opposition to a renewed naval attempt, and in France an Anglo-French military conference at French headquarters unanimously concluded in a request for immediate and complete evacuation. By this stage, the British decision to evacuate was probably more political than military.[53] Once evacuation had been ordered, Wemyss and Keyes took the line that Helles by itself could not be held during the winter months with supply ships and supporting squadrons exposed to storms, submarines and the expected large-scale infusion of German heavy artillery and munitions. It was now a question of 'get on' (with a renewed attack) or 'get out'. Keyes and Wemyss naturally hoped that the government would 'get on', but after the successful evacuation of Suvla and Anzac the Cabinet opted to 'get out'.[54]

The actual evacuation of Suvla and Anzac was successfully completed the night of 19–20 December. By careful organization, and of course with a good bit of luck, the much-feared disaster and heavy losses did not occur.[55] De Robeck arrived back just after the first evacuation and was magnanimous and remarkably tolerant:

> They pulled off a great performance here & every credit is due to those who did it & Wemyss & Keyes especially. They certainly were very foolish & sent many telegrams that showed they had no true appreciation of their responsibilities, however all's well that ends well. R. W. [Wemyss] is off as C.-in-C. Egypt & I have had a heart to heart talk with R. Keyes & told him that he must in future be C.O.S. & not "leader of the opposition"! I had not the heart to send him away.[56]

The Cabinet on 27 December decided to evacuate Cape Helles and again after careful organization and remarkably good luck the evacuation was successfully completed on the night of 8–9 January.[57] The Dardanelles campaign was over.

The British submarines continued their operations in the Marmara until the very end of the campaign, although these were not without loss. In September and October Lieutenant-Commander Bruce in E12 and Lieutenant W. B. Pirie in the small H1 operated successfully, despite the Nagara net which damaged E12 on her way out on 25 October and resulted in an experience for Bruce which de Robeck termed 'the like of which few officers have had to undergo'. E20 (Lieutenant-Commander C. H. Warren) and the French *Turquoise* (Lieutenant de vaisseau Ravenel) also successfully entered the Marmara in late October. *Turquoise* was actually the first French submarine to succeed in penetrating into the Marmara but the outcome was doubly unfortunate. The submarine suffered from numerous technical faults and her commander tried to return, ran aground on 30 October and the boat was captured intact. Unfortunately, the Germans discovered confidential papers which gave the rendezvous with E20. This enabled Heimburg with UB14 to set a trap and torpedo E20 on 5 November.[58] When the Germans turned the captured *Turquoise* over to the Turks Souchon inspected the submarine and found it wretchedly arranged and remarked, 'How the French commander could come into the Marmara in the defective boat is incomprehensible'. From his point of view he probably obtained greater satisfaction at being able to extract 15 tons of badly needed oil from the submarine's tanks than in capturing the boat itself.[59] The Turks never used the *Turquoise* operationally.

Nasmith in E11 returned to the Marmara on 6 November and added to his brilliant record, sinking among other ships the destroyer *Yar Hissar* on 3 December, and returned safely on the 23rd. Lieutenant-Commander Stocks with E2 entered the Dardanelles on 9 December and was the last submarine to operate in the Marmara during the campaign. After the decision to evacuate had been taken Keyes saw 'no object in running such great risks' and de Robeck ordered Stocks to return at his own convenience, which he successfully accomplished on 3 January.[60] The submarine campaign in the Marmara was costly for the British and French. Eight submarines, four of them French, were lost in the Marmara or trying to pass through the Dardanelles. The German official history grudgingly credits them with 25 steamers (c. 26,000 tons) totally destroyed and 10 steamers (c. 27,000 tons) badly damaged and out of action for the Dardanelles campaign, as well as the destruction of around 3,000 tons worth of small craft for a total bag of 56,000 tons. The British claims were 1 battleship, 1 old coast defence ship, 1 destroyer, 5 gunboats, 11 transports, 44 steamers and 148 other vessels.[61] Part of the discrepancy between British and German claims may come from the fact that some of the torpedoed Turkish ships were beached and later salvaged.

The evacuation of the Dardanelles was a welcome relief to the Mittelmeerdivision, although somewhat to their chagrin the Germans were in no position to play a role in hindering it. In the closing days at Cape Helles, Liman von Sanders once more begged for U-boat assistance against the bombarding Allied ships which were helping to keep the Turks at bay. Souchon once again had to confess he could send none. Help from outside the Dardanelles was not readily available either. The Admiralstab informed Souchon that for submarines to appear off the Dardanelles to attack the bombarding ships they would have to be notified, if possible, four to six weeks in advance. As the year ended, the earliest that the Admiralstab could promise a U-boat was around the middle of January.[62] The German submarines at Constantinople were used in the Black Sea and after Bulgaria entered the war some were stationed at Euxinograd, which served as an auxiliary base near Varna. They achieved some successes, but not against warships, and UC13 was lost when it ran aground. The Russians also kept up the pressure against the Turkish coal districts and, in the course of covering the now-precious colliers, *Goeben* had two torpedoes launched against her by a Russian submarine off the Bosphorus on 14 November. Once again the Germans stopped using the battle cruiser for this purpose. Ominously, the second Russian dreadnought, *Imperatriza Ekaterina II* took part in an operation for the first time on 24–26 December. The Russian activities against the coal coast compelled Souchon to employ the *Goeben* again in an effort to secure the colliers, for by the end of the year they had only five left. The result, on 8 January 1916, was an encounter between *Goeben* and *Imperatriza Ekaterina II* and a group of destroyers. *Goeben* was too late to save one of the colliers, fought an artillery duel at long range and once again escaped thanks to her superior speed. Despite the German submarines, the Russians had the upper hand in the Black Sea and their own submarines posed a threat to the major asset of the Germans, the *Goeben*.[63]

With the evacuation of the Dardanelles though, the naval war in the Black Sea faded from the concern of those in the Mediterranean. It was really a totally separate struggle, almost in another world, out of sight and out of mind until 1918 when the collapse of Russia brought about fears that the Germans would get their hands on the Black Sea Fleet and employ the surviving portions of it in the Mediterranean.

The Submarine War Intensifies

The German submarine campaign against Allied shipping in the Mediterranean began in earnest in October 1915. At the beginning of the month the Germans had five large U-boats and two small UC (minelayers) in the Mediterranean. But it is important to remember that the number of boats actually at sea in any given moment was only a fraction of the total number of boats on station. On 15 October, for example, only U35 was at sea and the famous U21 (which had left the Dardanelles before Allied obstructions made the passage too dangerous) was under long refit and would not be back in service until early December. UC13 was about to leave for Asia Minor as a transport while UC14 had just been converted back to minelaying after serving in the transport role.[64] After Bulgaria began to mobilize, there was the possibility of an Allied naval demonstration off Dedeagach and Souchon asked for German submarines to operate in the northern Aegean to at least show the flag, as he put it, although one wonders if that traditional phrase was really apt for submarines. The Admiralstab ordered U33 and U39 to the Aegean to work on the shipping lanes to Salonika and Kavalla and, as the occasion offered, off Dedeagach. They sank thirteen steamers (35,000 tons) and eight steamers (27,000 tons) respectively. The Kaiser was particularly anxious for submarines to work off Salonika and the Admiralstab were able to advise him on 4 October that a third submarine, U35, would sail within a few days.[65]

The improved UB boats (UBII class) which the Austrians were anxious to build themselves were considered a promising type for the Mediterranean. At the beginning of October the Admiralstab wanted six of the class (UB42–47) under construction at the Weser yards for use in the Mediterranean. However, their radius of action was too small to permit them to proceed from Wilhelmshaven to Cattaro by sea and, unlike the earlier UBI boats, they were too large to be sent to Pola by rail in a half-finished condition. The solution to the problem would be to send the materials for the six U-boats to Pola where they would be assembled by German workers. Tirpitz pointed out, however, that this meant that they would not be able to use the boats in the coming winter and their transport and assembly in the less-well-equipped yard at Pola would delay completion for at least two months. The first boat would not be finished until around 1 April and because of trials and training would not be ready for action until mid-May at the earliest. The other boats would follow at intervals of two to three weeks. The detachment of German workers to Pola would also mean a delay in the completion of U-boats for home waters. Under these circumstances, Tirpitz asked the Admiralstab if they really wanted the materials to be sent? The Admiralstab did, and as soon as possible. They asked for the Kaiser's approval which was forthcoming on 7 October. The Kaiser optimistically scribbled in the margin next to the statement that the boats would not be ready before next April or May that hopefully they would no longer be necessary by then. The Admiralstab also added to their proposal to assemble the UB boats at Pola a request to send a sixth large submarine to the Mediterranean. This would permit them to keep at least two permanently at sea. The Chief of the High Seas Fleet had already approved and U38 under the famous (or infamous depending on your point of view) Kapitänleutnant Max Valentiner was chosen. This proposal was also approved and U38 sailed on what would be a controversial cruise in mid-October.[66]

The steady growth in numbers of German submarines in the Mediterranean also necessitated a change in organization. The new large submarines could not really be placed under the German U-Boat Half Flotilla which was joined to the German Naval Special Command in Pola since most of the U-boat commanders were actually senior to the current Half Flotilla leader, Kapitänleutnant Adam. The submarines were therefore formed into an independent U-boat flotilla with its headquarters at Cattaro under the command of the senior U-boat commander in the Mediterranean, Kapitänleutnant (shortly to be promoted to Korvettenkapitän) Kophamel of U35. Kophamel would assume his duties as soon as a substitute commander for the submarine could be obtained, and would receive his orders directly from the Admiralstab. Adam would remain in command of the Marine-Spezial-Kommando at Pola in charge of repair, assembly of new boats and maintaining close contact with the Austrian authorities.[67]

While the deliberations were in progress Kophamel sailed on his first and highly successful cruise on 12 October. U35 sank twelve ships (48,813 tons) including the transport *Marquette* in the Gulf of Salonika. The new organization did not take effect until 18 November after Kophamel's return. His successor in command of U35 was Kapitänleutnant von Arnauld de la Perière, who would become perhaps Germany's most successful U-boat commander during the war.[68]

The major strategic objectives of the Germans were the shipping lanes and approaches to the Aegean, but a secondary objective quickly appeared along the North African coast. The Senussi, the religious sect in Cyrenaica, had been successful in winning control of substantial portions of Libya from the Italians who were forced back to a few coastal cities. Senussi forces in Cyrenaica were, according to the German Army General Staff, well armed with captured weapons and in a position to threaten the western frontier of Egypt, and the Germans naturally had every reason to support them. At the beginning of October, Enver Pasha asked for a German submarine to carry munitions, valuable gifts and an autograph letter from the caliph to a suitable bay west of Sollum where the coast was entirely in the hands of Senussi forces. Souchon suggested that the mission should be entrusted to a large submarine which after finishing its cruise in the Aegean could call at a designated point on the coast of Asia Minor, embark the material and proceed to Cyrenaica before returning to Cattaro. The most suitable choice for the Admiralstab was Kophamel and U35 which was on the point of sailing.[69] After U35's successful cruise in the Aegean, Kophamel called at the signal station established by the Germans on the Gulf of Xeros side of the Gallipoli Peninsula and named 'Hersingstand' in honour of the commander of U21 who had pioneered the route. Hersingstand was the usual point where submarines could receive the latest intelligence. U35 then proceeded to Orak Island near Bodrum and embarked ten Turkish officers, as well as munitions, and sailed for Cyrenaica, towing during periods of calm two Turkish schooners laden with 120 soldiers and munitions. After a difficult voyage in the overcrowded submarine Kophamel discharged his cargo at Bardia and on 5 November torpedoed and sank the British armed boarding steamer *Tara* in the Gulf of Sollum, subsequently towing the lifeboats crammed with survivors to Bardia as prisoners for the Senussi. Kophamel then destroyed one and damaged another Egyptian gunboat at anchor in the harbour of Sollum.[70] The sudden and unexpected appearance of a U-boat in these waters, combined with U35's successful cruise, represented a spectacular success.

Falkenhayn was intrigued by the potential ability of the Senussi to make trouble for the British in Egypt and was anxious to repeat U35's performance and send machine guns. The Germans had the little minelaying submarine UC12 converted to transport duties, but until the end of October the transport of cargoes to Turkey had a higher priority. However, once the Danube was cleared through von Mackensen's offensive there was no need to send cargoes to Turkey via submarine and UC12 was available for the North African missions.[71] Enver Pasha was also anxious for German submarines to again tow schooners from Turkish ports in Asia Minor to Cyrenaica. The Germans denied this request on technical and political grounds. The transport from southern Asia Minor to Cyrenaica could only be accomplished by large submarines and in the latter part of November these were urgently needed for attacks on the transport routes to Salonika, or for political reasons in Greek waters. Furthermore, the experiences of U35 demonstrated that it was extremely difficult to tow sailing craft, and both U-boat and schooners were threatened with destruction if enemy forces were encountered. Holtzendorff therefore preferred all transport to the Senussi to be accomplished via submarine and directed the Turks to dispatch whatever men and material they wished to send to an Austrian base.[72]

U38 sailed from Cattaro on 9 December towing the small transport UC12. Allied patrols in the Straits of Otranto forced U38 to abandon the tow and in the following days the two submarines failed to make contact with each other. In the end U38 proceeded to Bardia on her own to discharge her cargo. UC12 was picked up by another large submarine, U39, on the 13th and the latter interrupted her operations against merchant shipping to tow the transport to the vicinity of Bardia. After discharging her cargo, UC12 had to make the over 700-mile return trip alone on her own power. In the meantime on 20 December the Admiralstab had ordered another large submarine, U34, to load as many munitions as possible (about

1.5 tons) for the Senussi without delaying either her departure or hindering her freedom of movement, and to try and make contact with U38 and UC12 in case it was necessary to tow UC12 home. U34 met UC12 in the Ionian, but towing was not possible in this closely guarded area and both submarines continued on opposite paths alone.[73] The experience of UC12 was complicated and the attempt to carry what was, after all, a relatively small quantity of supplies wound up involving a substantial portion of German submarine strength in the Mediterranean. These operations, which really pushed the smaller submarines beyond their capacities, were forced on the somewhat reluctant navy by Falkenhayn and the Army General Staff, anxious to honour the wishes of their ally, Enver Pasha. The Admiralstab tended to regard them as a costly diversion.

The use of submarines for transport purposes to foster mischief against the Allies by rebellious tribesmen was indeed a diversion from their major strategic purpose, that is, economic warfare – *Handelskrieg* – against the Entente, and here the Mediterranean offered a rich and promising field, especially after protests by the United States government following the sinking of the *Lusitania* in May and other incidents had resulted in the German government ordering submarine commanders not to sink large passenger liners on sight. There were further American protests after the *Arabic* was sunk off Ireland in August with the loss of a number of American lives, and by the second half of September unrestricted submarine warfare had virtually ended in northern waters. There was considerable disagreement within the German government about how to handle the situation and sharp cleavages between Chancellor Bethmann Hollweg and Admiral Müller, Chief of the Kaiser's Naval Cabinet, on one side, and advocates of unrestricted submarine warfare, such as Tirpitz, on the other. The tension between the two groups was rising. Tirpitz, whose position was deteriorating, had already threatened to resign and Admiral Bachmann, Chief of the Admiralstab, did resign in August.[74] The Mediterranean offered an attractive escape from the difficulties in the north with the added advantage that American interests were not as pronounced here and there were fewer chances of diplomatic complications with the United States government. The Germans would achieve spectacular success in the Mediterranean in the autumn of 1915 but that success was not quite as free of diplomatic complications as they had hoped. Fortunately for them, they had Austria-Hungary to take the blame.

The results of operations by U-boats in the Mediterranean in autumn of 1915 against Allied shipping and excluding successes against warships are shown in Table 6.1.[75] It is particularly striking to note how large a proportion of the total sinkings the Mediterranean represented at this period, with November being a particularly fertile month. The majority of the sinkings occurred in the waters north and south of Crete and along a line running roughly from Malta to Cape Matapan.

Kapitänleutnant Max Valentiner in U38 also left a trail of destruction (14 ships, 47,460 tons) along the coast of North Africa on his voyage from Heligoland to Cattaro in November. The sinking of the French transport *Calvados* (c. 6,000 tons) off the coast of Algeria on 4 November made a

Table 6.1   *Shipping Losses due to Submarines, October–December 1915*

	Sunk by Mediterranean U-Boat Flotilla		Sunk by Submarine-laid Mines		Total All Theatres
	Ships	Tonnage	Ships	Tonnage	Tonnage
Oct. 1915	18	63,848	—	—	83,714
Nov. 1915	44	152,882	—	—	167,043
Dec. 1915	17	73,741	1	2,952	107,735

particularly strong impression on the French authorities since, although unarmed and without wireless, she was carrying a battalion of Senegalese troops from Marseilles to Oran. The loss of life was extremely heavy and led to the suspension of traffic between metropolitan France and Algeria for thirty-six hours. Valentiner claimed that panic had broken out among the coloured troops and his attempt to fish a white officer out of the sea for intelligence purposes after the sinking failed because the European crew had fled towards the coast in two lifeboats leaving the troops to their fate.[76]

Valentiner left a trail of diplomatic complications as well as sunken ships. On 7 November off Bizerte he attacked the Italian passenger liner *Ancona* (8,210 tons) *en route* from Messina to New York. While surfaced, Valentiner naturally flew the Austrian flag since Germany was not at war with Italy. The *Ancona* initially attempted to escape but could not outrun the submarine which shelled her until she stopped, and as the passengers and crew were abandoning ship Valentiner fired a torpedo. The loss of life was very heavy, more than 200 of whom around 20 were alleged to be American citizens. Robert Lansing the American Secretary of State called the action 'more atrocious than any of the submarine attacks which had previously taken place. For cold-blooded inhumanity the conduct of the submarine commander scarcely found an equal in the annals of modern war.' The question of atrocities in wartime, particularly in regard to submarines, is sometimes a matter of perspective. Valentiner's version was that he had taken the *Ancona* for a troopship at first and that during the chase some boats with crews were thrown into the water and overturned, while there had been great panic on board. He had given the *Ancona* forty-five minutes to abandon ship and had fired a torpedo because smoke revealed another ship, possibly summoned by the *Ancona*, approaching. The *Ancona* had sunk slowly, lasting another forty-five minutes, and the heavy loss of life was due to the Italian crew who had taken to the boats without regard to rescuing passengers, although there were many unused lifeboats on hand so all passengers could have been saved. Two days later on the 9th, U38 sank the Italian steamer *Firenze* (3,960 tons), again after a short chase and loss of life, and again while flying the Austrian flag.[77]

Regardless of who was to blame for the heavy civilian casualties, and whether they were due to the panic and irresponsibility of the Italian captain and crew or the cold-blooded action of the German submarine commander, the diplomatic controversy could not be escaped. The Admiralstab were desperately anxious as soon as news of the sinking of the *Ancona* arrived to learn the details to refute the 'enormous lies' spread by their enemies. They were reassured by one of the staff temporarily in Pola, Kapitän zur See Grasshoff, that Admiral Haus was ready to assume responsibility for the act and that the Austrian High Command was ready to publish an official communiqué refuting 'the hair-raising stories of their enemies', while in the case of the *Firenze* the Austrians would take the line that guilt for loss of life rested with the Italian captain who while travelling at full speed had launched lifeboats which capsized, and they had recovered Italian documents ordering Italian merchant captains not to obey submarine commands to stop, but to attempt to flee or ram the submarine.[78]

Haus may have been inclined to back the Germans but on 11 November the Austrian Foreign Office asked what agreement existed with the Germans about flying the Austrian flag. Haus replied that on his part no agreement existed, but as far as he knew the Germans intended to fly the Turkish flag in actions against Italy in the Aegean and the Austrian flag in the western Mediterranean. Haus at first favoured issuing a declaration justifying the sinking of the *Ancona* but without the express declaration that one of their own (Austrian) submarines was responsible. On 13 November AOK approved publication of the German-Austrian communiqué but the logic of the situation, not to mention the Americans, was pressing the Austrians into taking full responsibility. The Italians asked the Germans in a direct manner if the submarine which sank the *Ancona* really was Austrian and the State Secretary of the German Foreign Office, put on the spot in this fashion, announced with the agreement of Graf Burián, the Austrian Foreign Minister, that the submarine was indeed Austrian, and on 21 October U38 was entered into the k.u.k. List of Warships along with its crew.[79] This was a wise precaution, for on 16 November Lansing asked the American ambassador in Vienna to examine the Austro-Hungarian list of submarines and report whether the vessel attacking the *Ancona* appeared on the list.[80] The Austrians apparently never identified the submarine, but had the issue actually gone to arbitration they probably would have been forced to do so.

The Germans and Austrians naturally faced the problem of co-ordinating their stories once the Austrians had agreed to take responsibility for acts committed by the Germans under their flag. The most pressing problem was the *Ancona* affair where the United States government had demanded an explanation of the circumstances of the sinking. The two allies obviously had to concoct this story, but there also remained the problem of how to announce successes in the Mediterranean. The Germans wanted to go beyond the Entente practice of merely announcing sinkings and publish the location and cargo carried of the ship they had sunk. The propaganda advantage to be derived from this in justifying *Handelskrieg* was obvious. However, they also had to maintain the fiction that Austrian submarines were active outside the Adriatic, which at the moment they were not. To maintain that fiction they obviously could not publish the list of successes in Berlin alone. The Germans therefore proposed to Haus that the Austrians issue the list simultaneously with the Germans as a semi-official publication.[81] Haus objected that the proposed list did not contain the names of any Italian ships and appeared 'too German'. Freyberg suggested that this might have been due to the heading of the list which announced ships sunk 'since the beginning of the Salonika expedition', and at this stage the Italians had not yet sent any troops to Salonika. The solution was simple. Freyberg proposed that they add a section headed: 'Moreover, the following Italian ships have been sunk by Austro-Hungarian submarines'. This proposal was accepted by both parties and the list of sinkings appeared with an explanatory statement as to how they had slowed down the flow of troops to Salonika.[82]

The Austrians, while willing to cover for their allies, wanted to be as conciliatory as possible towards the United States government whose initial *note verbale* delivered by the American ambassador, Frederic C. Penfield, included a request for details and if possible the report of the submarine commander. The Generalauditor of the Marinesektion discussed the situation with representatives of the Foreign Office, and Haus personally prepared a proposal for the specific points to emphasize. This was submitted to the Germans for approval on 1 December. The Austrians had a final question. Did the Germans actually approve of Austria taking full responsibility?[83] Tirpitz agreed, but insisted that if the Austrians wanted to provide the Americans with excerpts from the submarine's log these would have to be carefully edited first so that the professional terms used did not betray the least trace of Imperial German origin.[84]

The United States government was not easily mollified. Lansing personally agreed with the Italian experts who considered the submarine which sank the *Ancona* to have been German for 'the act was that of a Prussian and not an Austrian'. The American Secretary of State readily fell into the common stereotype of the 'soft' Austrian as opposed to the 'harsh' Prussian and appears to have had considerable sympathy for the Austrian chargé d'affaires Baron Zwiedinek who had claimed that 'no Austrian officer is capable of an inhumane act' only to be undercut by his own government when it assumed full responsibility for the sinking. On 6 December the United States government delivered what President Wilson termed a 'peremptory note' demanding that the Austro-Hungarian government denounce the sinking of the *Ancona*, punish the officer responsible and pay an indemnity as reparations for the American victims. Lansing found the Austrian reply, presumably worked out in conjunction with the Admiralstab, 'a quibble over the facts and the reliability of the witnesses' which was 'almost an insult to one's intelligence'. The American answer on the 19th was, in effect, an 'ultimatum' and two days later Lansing bluntly told the Austrian chargé d'affaires that the Austrian government should either punish the officer concerned or assume responsibility and the guilt themselves.[85] The Austrians were getting more than they had bargained for and it would have been ironic indeed if the United States government had broken off relations or even gone to war with the Dual Monarchy over submarine warfare *before* Germany, when at that moment the Austrians had virtually no capacity to actually conduct submarine warfare outside the Adriatic. They were, to Haus's disgust, having little luck with their own submarine arm that autumn. The submarine on which they had placed great hopes because of its large radius of action, the captured French *Curie*, raised and rebaptized U14, was giving endless trouble and Haus dubbed it a 'child of sorrow [*schmerzenskind*] as far as it was warm'.[86]

The Austrians asked the Germans to send an expert to Vienna with full powers to help them settle the issue and, perhaps to alleviate the situation and avoid further friction with the Americans, the Admiralstab ordered the U-Boat Flotilla in the Mediterranean to sink American ships only when more than half their cargo consisted of absolute contraband. But the Austrians were preparing to climb down. The Austrian ambassador in Berlin asked the Germans to refrain in the future from attacking both enemy and neutral passenger liners when their submarine commanders were obligated to fly the Austrian flag.[87]

The Austrians caved in to the United States government in their note of 29 December. While they maintained that the commander of the submarine (neither the name of the commander or number of the submarine was mentioned) had given sufficient time to abandon ship and that there would have been no loss of life if the crew of the *Ancona* had not 'left the passengers in the lurch', they also:

> . . . came to the conclusion that he had failed to take into sufficient consideration the panic which occurred amongst the passengers rendering the embarkation more difficult and the spirit of the regulation that Imperial and Royal naval officers should not refuse help to anyone in distress, not even to the enemy. Hence the officer has been punished in accordance with the rules in force in this matter for exceeding his instructions.

The Austrians also agreed to pay an indemnity. The exact nature of this punishment was never stated, as Lansing himself noted, although on 21 October the submarine had been taken into the k.u.k. Naval List along with the crew so that they would be able to appear in a Prize Court in Austrian uniform. The German government had, in fact, been very anxious for the Austrians to give in and on 23 December an official of the German Foreign Office, Dr Klüge, was sent to Vienna to advise the Austrian Foreign Office that any American declaration of war against Austria-Hungary would soon extend to Germany and would have serious effects on German ships interned in American ports which would be seized and German capital sequestered. The American action would also affect the attitude of Romania and Greece.[88]

Haus actually wanted to take a much tougher line with the Americans in a reversal of the 'tough Prussian' and 'soft Austrian' stereotype. In a reply to a request from the Austrian Foreign Office for the naval point of view, written on 10 December and subsequently quoted by the German naval attaché, Haus termed the conduct of the U-boat commander 'utterly irreproachable' and that from the humanitarian standpoint he had done even more than his duty in allowing an unusually long time to abandon ship. The U-boat commander would have violated his duty if he had not torpedoed the *Ancona* or had let her go free. The *Ancona* on her return voyage could have brought back reservists, that is future soldiers, from the United States and also have been used as a transport or munitions ship. The commander of a warship had humanitarian obligations not only to those on board a captured prize but also *and above all* to his own countrymen. The submarine commander had tried to resolve these conflicting obligations by not letting the steamer fall back into enemy hands, but also doing everything possible to rescue passengers with measures which would have sufficed if others, that is, the Italian crew, had also done their duty. Moreover, Haus argued, the steamer approaching when *Ancona* was torpedoed had probably been summoned by *Ancona* and that constituted an act of resistance. The torpedoing of an enemy merchant ship which used its wireless was necessary and justified. When the Austrian Foreign Office declined to follow this line in its response to the United States government, Haus wanted to oblige the United States only so far as promising that any passenger liner to be sunk would be challenged first as long as this could be done without danger to the submarine, although he added that if the ship had a wireless set available this already meant danger to the submarine under certain circumstances. If the steamer halted on call, it would not be sunk before its crew and passengers could abandon ship *as long as there was no resistance*, and if the crew did not use this interval to rescue themselves this would be treated as resistance. Haus's line was so hard that the German naval attaché was reluctant to send this report through the usual channels, that is by means of the German ambassador for transmittal to the Chancellor. The Admiralstab agreed, for after the Austrian reply to the Americans there was nothing further to be gained with the German civilian authorities, and if they learned of the Flottenkommandant's attitude it might cause friction which could harm the good relations between the two navies.[89]

Chancellor Bethmann Hollweg and the German Foreign Office were nervous about the masquerade under Austrian colours in the Mediterranean for the deception could easily be unmasked. Submariners by the nature of their profession were a scruffy lot at sea and victims of the U-boats were hardly likely to get close enough to note the insignia on an officer's cap, even if they knew the difference between the Austrian and German cap badge. The flag was something else, and there had been occasional reports that flags were switched from German to Austrian in the midst of an attack. This had already led to Italian protests over the sinking of the Italian steamer *Cirene* (3,236 tons) on 30 September in which sworn testimony by survivors indicated that the submarine had flown German colours at the beginning of the attack on the steamer, which initially showed no colours itself, and then substituted the Austrian flag after learning that the ship was Italian.[90] Holtzendorff assured the Chancellor on 23 November that action against Italian or neutral ships carrying contraband to Italy was permissible only under the Austrian flag and if, in the course of an inspection begun by a submarine flying the German flag, a ship turned out to be Italian or carrying contraband to Italy the submarine commander was obliged to release the ship. Holtzendorff quoted a telegram to Kophamel specifically ordering him to give oral instructions to U-boat commanders that under no circumstances should a flag be changed once an action had commenced.[91]

Holtzendorff also justified German use of the Austrian flag to the German Foreign Office on the grounds that if they restricted themselves to use of the German flag in surface actions and were thereby obligated to treat Italian ships as neutral, their enemies would quickly learn of it and misuse the 'neutral' flag in the Mediterranean to protect their own shipping as they had done in the north. This would lead to incidents similar to the *Baralong* affair, endangering German submarines and leading to the virtual suspension of submarine warfare in the Mediterranean.[92] However, submarine activities had considerably slowed and rendered more difficult the Allied expedition to Salonika. Holtzendorff argued that sinking Italian ships was a very real German contribution to the Austrian war effort and was greatly appreciated by them. Holtzendorff offered some concessions to the Foreign Office to avoid giving nourishment to the British press campaign which was stirring up hatred of Germany. For the time being, he was ready to order German U-boat commanders to allow Italian ships to pass unmolested and later from time to time, say every four to six weeks, while flying the Austrian flag to sink an Italian freighter – not passenger liner – in order to prevent the enemy from thinking that the Italian flag gave immunity. The measure was to be kept a strict secret, even from the Austrian authorities.[93]

The Admiralstab shared the Chancellor's and Foreign Office's concern, however, that an indiscretion could lead to the true identity of a submarine being discovered and a possible Italian declaration of war. Therefore, what should have been a stroke of luck from the point of view of intelligence turned into a source of considerable alarm. On 4 December U33 under Kapitänleutnant Gansser stopped the Greek steamer *Spetse* and, while releasing the ship, took off two British officers as prisoners. One was Lieutenant-Colonel H. D. Napier, former British military attaché in Bulgaria and currently military attaché in Athens, and the other was the King's Messenger, Captain Seymour Wilson, who was also a Member of Parliament. The couriers had thrown their dispatch cases overboard, but these, or some of them, were fished up by the Germans. They turned out to be an intelligence coup for in addition to service correspondence from the legation in Athens there were numerous private letters written by members of the British Legation or Naval Mission who had taken advantage of the uncensored Foreign Office bag to send very frank comments about the Salonika expedition and the Greek government and its policies. The Germans eventually passed copies of this correspondence to the Austrians and naturally both exploited the unflattering comments about the Greeks by making sure that those Greek officials they were courting learned of them. The tactic was effective. The Chief of the Greek Naval Staff, for example, a known enemy of the British Naval Mission, was very anxious to learn the names of those who had written the passages, although the exact or full names were not always readily apparent from the excerpts.[94]

That was the positive side of the Napier Affair. The negative side was that the submarine had flown the Austrian flag and the two British prisoners knew this. The Admiralstab ordered that they were not to be sent to Germany but turned over to an Austrian prison and their mail strictly censored. Napier, in his memoirs written after the war, referred to the submarine commander as 'Captain Ganzer' and told him that he recognized the officers and crew as North Germans by their accent. According to Napier, the submarine commander had detailed his first lieutenant and some bluejackets to escort them to Berlin by rail, but they were taken off the train at Vienna and put into an Austrian prison. Ironically, Napier and Wilson had actually applied to be treated as Austrian prisoners since they were captured under the Austrian flag.[95] They got their wish but their inconvenient knowledge probably caused them to spend a much longer period in captivity than would normally have been the case. In February 1916 the Prussian Ministry of War asked the Austrians about the possibility of exchanging Napier for a German officer captured on a trip from the United States and threatened by legal proceedings. Freyberg quickly pointed out that this would mean that German use of the Austrian flag would become public. Freyberg recommended that if any exchange took place it ought to be the 'harmless' Wilson instead of the military professional Napier. Gansser, when queried on the subject, was dead set against any exchange. Napier was an able military and diplomatic personality who would find special employment in the Balkans, and since he spoke very good German he had seen and heard more than was desirable in his two-and-a-half-day stay in the submarine as well as at the submarine base. Napier and Wilson, whom Gansser referred to as 'sly' rather than harmless, had also been in contact with French prisoners from the recently sunk submarine *Fresnel*. All in all, the pair knew too much to be released and the German navy accordingly declined the Prussian Ministry of War's request for an exchange. Napier remained a prisoner of war until 1917.[96]

The flag question continued to cause trouble, however, and Freyberg had to play detective following up reports of a German doctor, unfit for military service and reportedly director of a factory in Sebenico, who had talked about German submarines under the Austrian flag and had photographs alleged to have been taken from U38 of the sinking of the *Ancona*. Valentiner, on leave in Germany, thought that the photos were of an earlier sinking, not the *Ancona*. The Germans and Austrians also had to co-operate over a joint communiqué about the sinking of the Italian steamer *Porto Said* (5,301 tons) by U39 (Kapitänleutnant Forstmann) on 10 December, but compared to the furore over the *Ancona* this appears to have caused few difficulties.[97]

The year 1915 ended with another incident in the Mediterranean. On 30 December the P & O liner *Persia* (7,974 tons) was torpedoed by Valentiner in U38 approximately seventy miles south of Crete. The ship's boilers exploded and she sank very quickly with a loss of 334 lives including 2 Americans. Valentiner had attacked without warning and while submerged so that there would be no problem about the flag. The United States government could only ask the German, Austro-Hungarian and even Turkish governments if their submarines had been involved, and had no means to challenge their inevitable denials, which led the French ambassador in Washington to remark that they were being asked to believe that the *Persia* had sunk of her own accord committing a kind of suicide.[98] The renewed negotiations with the United States government, this time over the *Persia*, caused the Admiralstab to cable new instructions to the U-Boat Flotilla at Cattaro. Once again passenger steamers were to be left unharmed, even when they were armed, with the exception of enemy liners either in the Aegean or under escort on the approaches to the Aegean. The *Persia* had been armed with a 4.7-in.gun on her stern and Valentiner could claim he had taken her for an armed transport.[99]

The arming of merchantmen raised a host of diplomatic and legal problems, for while submarines often outgunned them they were also more vulnerable to a lucky shot and were therefore forced to attack while submerged and without warning. This eliminated problems about use of the flag and blurred responsibility, but it also reduced the time a submarine could cruise since the number of torpedoes they could carry were limited. Submarine commanders obviously preferred to sink enemy ships, preferably unarmed enemy ships, with explosives or gunfire. The American Secretary of State recognized the changed conditions of warfare and, on 18 January, Lansing made his *modus vivendi* proposal to the Entente powers. Submarines would have to obey international law in stopping and searching vessels and assuring the safety of passengers and crew before sinking them but, in turn, merchant vessels could not be armed. If they were armed, they might be treated as armed merchant cruisers or auxiliary cruisers. This was an argument which the British in particular rejected, but again there is no space here to enter into a lengthy discussion of an intricate subject.[100]

In the Mediterranean the rules seemed to be always changing for the submarine commanders. This reflected the continuing tug of war within the German government between those who were partisans of unrestricted submarine war and those who desired to be more accommodating towards the United States government. Holtzendorff pointed out to Bethmann Hollweg in mid-January that British and French anti-submarine measures in the Mediterranean, such as escorting important ships with destroyers and submarines, arming nearly all ships and employing numerous patrol craft, were producing a situation similar to that in northern waters. Submarines would have to attack while submerged if they did not want to experience heavy losses. However, errors with neutral ships had not taken place and were not likely. On German instigation, the Greeks had adopted markings which were visible from a great distance, and after the Dutch had given up passage through the Suez Canal Holtzendorff claimed that they were unlikely to meet neutrals. He was also anxious to release his U-boats against Italian shipping, for the supply of Italy by the Allies would always be difficult due to the shortage of shipping space, and the destruction of a considerable amount of shipping could lead to a catastrophe for the Italians. The major goal of the U-boats in the Mediterranean would remain as it was before, that is, the interruption of the supply lines to the British and French armies in Salonika and Egypt and, at the same time, the destruction of traffic passing through the Suez Canal, and a general reduction of British and French shipping capacity. With the U-boats then available and up until the beginning of the summer, they were able to permanently occupy two stations in the Mediterranean, one east of longitude 18°E, extending to the Syrian coast, and the other to the west of this line extending to Gibraltar. In the latter, they could also attack French traffic from Gibraltar to Marseilles and from France to North Africa. When the six UBII boats under construction at Pola entered service in the summer, they would be able to occupy an additional two stations and the operations of the large U-boats in the western Mediterranean could be extended under certain circumstances into the Atlantic against the shipping lanes from South America and South Africa to Britain.[101]

Kophamel argued that his Mediterranean U-Boat Flotilla had some very real problems with the recent order to permit certain steamers to pass. Now that German successes had caused their opponents to arm nearly all steamers, U-boat successes were down and the new restrictions would make it impossible to bring Britain to its knees through economic warfare. Losses for the British would be disagreeable pin-pricks and could never be decisive. Kophamel maintained that they could achieve success with a ruthless attack in which everything going to and from Britain would be treated as an enemy and destroyed. He asked if it would be possible for neutrals to be notified that all armed steamers would be treated as warships and sunk on sight. Kophamel pointed out that a steamer armed by its government was really a warship and some now even had military gun crews on board. There were no armed 'merchant ships' unless they were pirates. Kophamel also asked, somewhat sarcastically, if the neutrals, meaning the United States, could tell them how they would be able to distinguish an auxiliary cruiser from an armed passenger liner since all large steamers appeared to be passenger liners outwardly, and his commanders now had to let everything worthwhile pass. Flags, as the *Baralong* case proved, were no means of distinguishing armed patrol vessels or yachts in naval service from ordinary merchant vessels carrying guns. He also asked if they could treat the crew of an armed steamer which fired on a U-boat as pirates, and wondered about Turkey's relations with the United States and if they might act more freely flying the Turkish flag.[102]

The Germans decided to attack armed steamers. On 3 February, Holtzendorff advised Kophamel of substitute orders for U38 which was about to sail for the western Mediterranean after landing, weather permitting, Turkish officers and supplies for the Senussi on the coast of North Africa. As of 20 February armed French and British ships could be attacked while submerged and without warning. The Kaiser's order permitting the attack on armed steamers was dated 11 February and authorized the commanders to attack only after they had actually recognized the armament. The order would take effect on 29 February after warning to neutrals. The Austrians issued similar orders. Holtzendorff, in a supplement to these orders, also ordered submarines which had attacked while submerged not to surface after firing the torpedo but to depart while still under water. Furthermore, merchant ships which were listed by the Admiralstab as armed could be treated as warships even if their armament was not discernible as long as there was no doubt about their identity.[103] Diplomatic considerations forced the Admiralstab to revise these orders on 24 February before they could go into effect. Passenger liners, whether armed or not, were not to be attacked. This provision had a crippling effect

1 the Mediterranean, given the problem of distinguishing large troop
ransports and auxiliary cruisers from ordinary passenger liners. On the
•ther hand, the effect of the new orders would have been to initiate virtually
nrestricted submarine warfare on the west coast of Britain. The diplomatic
•ressures against this remained strong, however, and the government
vobbled. At Charleville on 4 March a Crown Council of German leaders
ed to the Kaiser reaching a somewhat ambiguous decision that after 1 April
nrestricted submarine warfare against Britain was unavoidable, but until
hen the Chancellor was to try and make the United States understand the
ituation with the object of giving Germany a free hand. Meanwhile the U-
•oat war would be carried on as effectively as possible under orders issued
•n 1 March, which meant 'sharpened' rather than 'unrestricted' submarine
varfare. Within the German government the disagreement between Tirpitz
nd Bethmann Hollweg reached its climax and on 10 March the Kaiser
nally accepted Tirpitz's resignation. Moreover, there was soon another
risis with the Americans. On 24 March the French channel steamer *Sussex*,
upposedly mistaken as a troop transport, was torpedoed and more
merican lives were lost. This provoked a United States ultimatum on
) April and the unrestricted submarine campaign in the north was called
ff. On 4 May Bethmann Hollweg promised that submarines would not
nk ships without warning and without saving lives as long as they did not
ttempt to escape or offer resistance.[104] The partisans of unrestricted
ibmarine warfare had suffered a definite setback.

The Austrian role in this was obviously only a secondary one. However,
1e Austrian naval attaché in Berlin reported that he had been questioned
bout it at the Admiralstab. Bethmann Hollweg had supposedly claimed
1at Austria-Hungary was opposed to the extension of submarine warfare
1d the Admiralstab wanted to know if this was true. Colloredo-Mannsfeld
aturally knew nothing about it. Haus, when asked his opinion about the
•ntroversy surrounding Tirpitz's resignation, replied that he did not know
1e number of German submarines available and could not, therefore, judge
1e chances of success for Tirpitz's plans, and even less the significance for
•ermany of war with the United States. Haus was personally inclined to
•eat war with the United States as a minor evil since the latter could not
inder militarily the action of German U-boats when they were strong
1ough to paralyse traffic to Britain for months. The season for this was
•w becoming more advantageous. Supposing Germany, in the life-and-
•ath war against Britain, refrained from ruthless use of its resources out of
•spect for the United States and then, later on, war with the United States
•uld not be avoided. Such a situation was not foreseen but easily possible
1d Germany would then be in a very unpleasant situation for having let
ip so much irretrievable time for weakening the British. Haus thought it
•vious that their own diplomats knew nothing of Tirpitz's plan. The
•1arinesektion subsequently pointed out to the Austrian Foreign Minister
1at Burián had never asked the Marinesektion nor the Flottenkommandant
•r their opinions on the question of the German submarine war. Burián
sured the navy that the report that Austria-Hungary had spoken out
;ainst the 'sharpened Submarine war' did not correspond to the facts in

that form. They had restricted themselves to suggesting that, on th question of sinking passenger liners, the Germans should not go beyond th scope of the German Memorandum exempting them from attack in orde to avoid the danger for both Central Powers of a break with the Unite States.[105] There was nothing of the 'soft' Austrian about Haus on th question of the submarine war and, if he could have known his opinions Tirpitz would have found nothing to complain of. Haus lacked, howevei the material means. Had the Austrian submarine service been a potent forc or had Austria-Hungary the industrial capacity for its rapid expansion Haus might have played the same role in his own government that Tirpit played in the German government. It was an ironic position for a man wh had doubts about his own submarine service.[106]

German successes in the Mediterranean declined markedly in the firs quarter of 1916 (see Table 6.2).[107]

Table 6.2 *Shipping Losses due to Submarines, January–March 1916*

| | Sunk by Mediterranean U-Boat Flotilla | | Sunk by Submarine-laid Mines | | Total All Theatres |
	Ships	*Tonnage*	*Ships*	*Tonnage*	*Tonnage*
Jan. 1916	5	27,979	4	4,459	49,610
Feb. 1916	12	44,410	4	2,969	95,090
Mar. 1916	4	20,245	3	430	155,186

The Admiralstab attributed the comparative lack of success to the change conditions in the Aegean where strong Allied countermeasures in the forr of patrols and extensive intelligence facilities made chances for succes proportionately small. U39, for example, sank only one transport on he January cruise off the Dardanelles and approaches to Salonika and the ship *Norseman* (9,542 tons), was able to beach herself in the Gulf of Salonika However, the Admiralstab still considered it desirable for a submarine to le itself be noticed in the Aegean so as to disrupt transport and force the Britis and French to spread their patrols. Outside the Aegean, the Admiralsta attributed the lack of success to the new orders which impeded submarin activity. Indeed, in this first quarter of 1916, German successes tended to b along the line Malta–Crete, in the Gulf of Lyon, along the North Africa coast and in the Adriatic. The Admiralstab also found fault with the recer cruises of their crack commanders Valentiner and Hersing, for U38 an U21 had been diverted from *Handelskrieg* to operate against warships. Thi was the cruise on which Valentiner had sunk the *Persia* with such heavy los of life, but he had actually spent only five days out of a thirty-three da cruise on economic warfare. Hersing in U21 sank the old French cruise *Amiral Charner* off the Syrian coast but his engines gave him trouble and h claimed only one merchant steamer. Holtzendorff wanted all submarin commanders to be reminded that the reduction of shipping space was th most important means of pressure against their main enemy, Britain, an consequently a much more effective means of pressure than sinkin warships.[108]

The flag question continued to be a source of potential embarrassment in the first quarter of 1916 as reports continued to appear in the British and French press about German misuse of the Austrian flag. One incident concerned the British steamer *Commodore* (5,858 tons) which had been sunk by Gansser and U33 at dawn on 2 December, shortly before he captured Napier and Wilson. The captain of the steamer charged that, in coming alongside the submarine to hand over the ship's papers, he had noticed two flags, one German, the other Austrian, ready to be raised according to the nationality of the steamer. In this case, the Germans claimed that the German naval ensign had been flown throughout the action but when the *Commodore*'s captain came alongside there had been little wind and the flag was not waving. They suggested that the captain might have seen two signal flags which were ready for use, notably for the signal 'AB' which meant 'Abandon ship as quickly as possible'. Moreover, the Germans ingeniously suggested, the captain of the *Commodore* was in an unwashed, half-dressed condition, obviously fresh from his bunk, and an erroneous judgement on his part was perhaps understandable. The other incident concerned reports in *Le Temps* that the French troopship *Amiral Hamelin* (5,051 tons) had been sunk on 7 October by a German submarine flying the Austrian flag. The submarine involved turned out to be U33 again and the Austrians were ready to issue a reply covering for the Germans, but unfortunately the excerpt from Gansser's log which they had been provided with did not give any details about the flag. Freyberg suggested that if the order had not already been issued, all submarine commanders in the future should be told to always specify under what flag they conducted an action.[109]

The Evacuation of the Serbian Army

The other major naval event at the close of 1915 and the beginning of 1916 has so far only been mentioned in passing. This was the attempt, after Bulgaria entered the war, to supply Serbia by means of the Adriatic coast and, after Serbia was overrun, the evacuation of what remained of the Serbian army. These operations presented serious problems for the Allies, exacerbated at one point relations between Italy and the French, and also provided the Austrian navy with opportunities for a more active role.

The Adriatic had been relatively quiet after the summer actions and the sixty British drifters which arrived at the end of September began that long and ultimately unsuccessful effort to bottle up the Straits of Otranto. The commander of the British Adriatic Force, Thursby, quickly realized in regard to the drifters that 'I haven't half enough' for 'it is a big place to watch & we want more depth to our screen'. He wired home for twenty additional drifters and was promised the eighteen which had been sent to the Dardanelles when de Robeck was finished with them, but somewhat cynically doubted that they would ever materialize. Thursby knew that the winter weather in the Adriatic was bad and in a rough sea nets were lost and boats frequently had to take shelter. He considered that they needed at least forty boats out at a time and with the necessary docking and repairs this meant that they needed around eighty drifters on the station.[110] By 8 November, Thursby had been able to arm virtually all of the drifters, although the very steep seas now often obliged them to take shelter. Thursby wanted them to stay out on patrol even if it was too rough to work their nets, but after a tour of inspection in a destroyer 'fully realized what a very small chance one has of catching a submarine with so few'. The Admiralty finally decided in mid-November to send an additional forty drifters which began to arrive on 7 December.[111]

The other British contributions to the naval war in the Adriatic also suffered from material deficiencies. The hard-worked British light cruisers operating with the Italians at Brindisi suffered frequent mechanical problems and Thursby complained that they 'are always breaking down'. When *Dublin* departed in December, Thursby remarked that it was the fourth cruiser of that class which had had to be sent away for boiler trouble. The six 'B'-class submarines sent to Venice under Commander Wilfred Tomkinson were also old boats and found the short steep seas in the northern Adriatic very trying and frequently came in damaged. Tomkinson was also worried about their battery capacity and annoyed that the boats had been sent from Malta without a proper six months' overhaul. He also could not see why the Admiralty had not sent better submarines, such as the more modern and capable 'E' class which had done so well at the Dardanelles, 'for it is criminal to be sending them out to make attacks on torpedo craft if a better class of boat is available'. Obsolete as the 'B' boats might have been, they were far more robust than the Italian submarines which Tomkinson noted were flimsy, required frequent repair after little running, and some 'could not stand any weather on the surface with their planes out', while the Italian submarine commanders seemed to seek any excuse for not going out. The Italian submarines had, according to Tomkinson, one very good feature however. Their battery capacity was 'miles ahead of ours'.[112]

The British battleships at Taranto were virtually inactive and had not left the outer harbour since August when submarines had been reported. One of their British officers thought this was an advantage in a way since in the *Duncan* he had a 'kindergarten of boys and old seamen' who were still undergoing rudimentary training and knew nothing when they joined. The French contribution in the Adriatic was now largely confined to submarines, as the 2ème Escadrille of destroyers had been withdrawn on 1 October and the 6ème Escadrille on 5 October to cover the troop movements to Salonika. The shortage of destroyers was aggravated, according to Thursby, because the Italian destroyers were slightly built and would not stand much rough work and too large a proportion of them were constantly under repair.[113]

The Italians were most unhappy over the departure of the twelve French destroyers from Brindisi. The Duke of the Abruzzi had immediately pointed out to the Minister of Marine what this meant to his forces in the southern Adriatic and asked for reinforcements from the Italian naval force at Venice. Corsi sent, or intended to send, five destroyers which he admitted was inadequate, but argued that at the moment it was not possible to diminish by too much the naval forces at Venice without lowering and perhaps rendering null the protection they could give to the right wing of the Italian army. The entry of Bulgaria into the war which caused the withdrawal of the French destroyers had not been foreseen when the naval convention between Italy and the Allies had been concluded the preceding May, but Corsi ordered the Italian naval attaché in Paris to tactfully ask the French that the absence of the destroyers from Brindisi last as little time as possible, while he warned the Italian Foreign Minister, Sydney Sonnino, that the uncertain attitude of Greece might prolong the absence of those destroyers beyond the time needed to transport troops to Salonika with prejudicial results for the Italians. The French tried to reassure the Italians that the move was only temporary and that the destroyers would return to Brindisi once their presence on the lines of communication ceased to be a necessity.[114]

This was the situation in the Adriatic when the Serbian question became acute once the Bulgarian armies had cut off the Allied supply route to Serbia via Salonika. Supplies could henceforth reach the hard-pressed Serbs only via Adriatic ports in a zone which was now an area of Italian responsibility. The flow of supplies to Montenegro had also been going through San Giovanni di Medua in northern Albania and then overland to the Bojana River. Montenegro's own port of Antivari was an open harbour, now partially blocked by sunken ships, and too close to Cattaro. The Montenegrins had been receiving relatively small quantities of material. Serbian needs would be much greater, but the prospects for getting that material to them were not very bright. The French Minister of War thought that the only way to supply Serbia would be through San Giovanni di Medua or Antivari whatever the risks. The French naval C.-in-C., based on past experience, absolutely rejected those ports and claimed that the supply could only take place through Valona and Santi Quaranta in southern Albania. However, Dartige quickly learned that Valona had no communications with the interior, so of necessity Santi Quaranta would have to suffice, with material sent to establish a protected base.[115] Albania, under Ottoman rule until just before the war, was one of the most backward regions of Europe and roads and facilities in general were few. Dartige also discovered that there were political complications involved in the use of Santi Quaranta. It was in the southern portion of Albania where the Greeks had claims and had in fact been occupied by Greek forces whose attitude was always uncertain. Furthermore, the communications from Santi Quaranta ran inland to Monastir rather than to the north. There were also certain political and diplomatic complications involved with the use of Valona which had been occupied by the Italians. The latter, taking advantage of the semi-anarchical situation which prevailed in Albania after the outbreak of the world war and the collapse of the government of the Prince of Wied, had occupied the island of Saseno in September 1914 and the town of Valona itself in December. In November 1915 they were preparing an expeditionary corps to fortify Valona and the surrounding area. The diplomatic and political situation, the miserable state of communications in Albania and the location of the Serbian army itself, all caused the Allies to reconsider using the northern Albanian ports. The French accordingly asked the Italians what naval support they could give the supply route through San Giovanni. Neither the Duke of the Abruzzi nor Corsi would provide very much. Abruzzi did not think it would be possible for Allied steamers to go directly to San Giovanni and the sole solution in his eyes would be to send the ships to Brindisi where the cargo could be transferred to small sailing craft which could get up the Bojana River or be towed to Scutari. These coasters would be protected in the approximately 100-mile journey from Brindisi to the mouth of the Bojana by a submarine patrol between Cattaro and the Bojana. Capitaine de vaisseau Daveluy, the French liaison officer with the Italian fleet, remarked with a heavy dose of sarcasm: 'The support of the Italian Navy would limit itself, therefore, in the eventuality envisaged to sending a *French* submarine south of Cattaro.' Daveluy warned that it would be dangerous to count on the Italian navy to support their action and even if they acquired that support in principle, which would be surprising since up until then the Italians had need of the French, it would not be effective. The Italians were offering their support in good faith but they were not capable of a sustained effort. Dartige shared these sentiments. Moreover, the solution proposed by Abruzzi would not be effective. The small sailing craft would be subject to variable crossings because of wind. They could not carry the estimated 500 tons per day which would be required, the protection offered by the Italians would be illusory and they had a good chance of being captured by the fast Austrian ships.[116]

The Allies after considerable negotiation reached an agreement on 13 November by which the British would provide the supplies sent to Brindisi, the expenses would be shared by Britain, France and Russia, and the Italian navy would provide protection, supported by the Allies, for the transit across the Adriatic. An inter-Allied commission, known as the Serbian Relief Committee was formed and met for the first time in Rome on 24 November. The committee was presided over by Rear-Admiral Pino Pini, Sub-Chief of the Italian Naval Staff, and consisted of the Allied naval and military attachés and selected Italian authorities. This body concluded that due to difficulties in the lines of communication, whatever the dangers the bulk of the supplies to the Serbs would have to go through the northern ports of San Giovanni or Durazzo, or in small ships up the Bojana to Scutari. Unfortunately, by the time the committee met the measures for protection of the supply route had already been revealed as totally inadequate.[117]

At the end of October, Conrad advised Haus that Serbia had been cut off from Salonika and could only be supplied through northern Albanian or Montenegrin ports, and pointed out the importance of an attack on that supply route.[118] Haus took three weeks to react. On the night of 22–23 November, Linienschiffskapitän Heinrich Seitz, commanding the light cruiser *Helgoland*, led the similar *Saida* and the I Torpedo Division of modern Tátra class destroyers on a sortie to the Straits of Otranto and reconnaissance along the Albanian coast. The Austrians ran into the Italian motor schooner *Gallinara* and small steamer *Palatino* which were carrying supplies of flour for Serbia and sank them both. It was a sharp reminder of how vulnerable the supply route across the Adriatic to northern Albania was, but Vice-Admiral Fiedler, commanding the Austrian Cruiser Flotilla, was actually dissatisfied with the results since in his opinion the two sinkings had been somewhat hasty and used an excessive amount of ammunition, while the time lost, approximately an hour, meant that they had to give up the reconnaissance of the Albanian coast. This failure to finish the reconnaissance was very disappointing to Kophamel since one of his submarines, U34, had just had an encounter with a net carried by one of the drifters. The Austrians at first did not plan any further reconnaissance into the straits. They considered it too dangerous since they assumed that they were strongly watched, but then on 26 November they changed their minds and warned the Germans that in the future they intended other sorties by the Spauns and Tátras into the southern Adriatic and the German submarines should therefore only attack ships that they clearly recognized as the enemy. AOK, once they had reports of Italian troop transport to Albania, directly ordered Haus on the 29th to institute a permanent patrol of the Albanian coast and to disrupt enemy troop transport according to his own judgement. Haus, in turn, ordered *Helgoland*, *Novara*, 6 Tátra destroyers and around 6 T-74 class torpedo-boats, as well as the oiler *Vesta*, to be stationed at Cattaro.[119] These were the newest and fastest of the Austrian light forces.

There were other attacks by Austrian aircraft and Austrian or German submarines against the supply route across the Adriatic, and on 4 December the transport *Re Umberto* (2,952 tons) and Italian destroyer *Intrepido* were lost to mines laid by UC14 in the vicinity of Valona. The Austrian light forces struck again at dawn on 5 December when *Novara*, four destroyers and three torpedo-boats raided the coast from the Bojana to San Giovanni, which they bombarded, sinking three steamers and a number of small sailing craft. On their return the destroyer *Warasdiner* caught the French submarine *Fresnel* aground on a sand bank off the mouth of the Bojana and destroyed the submarine and captured the crew. On 6 December *Helgoland* led six destroyers on a raid to Durazzo, where two destroyers entered the port and sank two large and three small schooners. *Novara* and the I Torpedo Group were also out on the night of 18 December after intelligence that King Peter of Serbia was to travel on an Italian destroyer from Durazzo to Brindisi. The Austrians, with bad weather hampering the torpedo craft, found nothing and later learned that the destroyer in question had not sailed.[120]

The heavy losses incurred by the first group of ships attempting to supply Serbia by means of the northern Albanian ports apparently shook the Italian Minister of Marine. Corsi told the French naval attaché that under these conditions, at least while the French destroyers were not in the Adriatic in support, it appeared impossible to continue this way and it would be necessary for the supply ships to fall back on Valona and Santi Quaranta. Lacaze noted on the margin of the dispatch that this was equally his impression – until they were free of submarines they had to operate in a harbour closed against attack and only Valona and Santi Quaranta fulfilled these desiderata. Thursby, who was actually on the scene, thought that 'i only Valona could be used it would solve all our difficulties' for the Italian had established a properly fortified harbour, while Durazzo and Sar Giovanni were open harbours with no facilities for unloading and in easy reach of Cattaro. There was no protection in the ports for the smal steamers after the Allies had escorted them there, and no force available to remain permanently cruising in the vicinity which 'would be asking fo trouble' because of the submarine menace. Unfortunately for the Allies, Sar Giovanni was the only place with a reasonable road to Scutari.[121]

The necessity of protecting the supply route to Serbia gave the Italian another lever for insisting on the return of the twelve French destroyers Those twelve destroyers seem almost to have become for the Italians a symbolic test of how sincere the British and French were in their alliance and how much they really intended to support them. The Regia Marina moreover, was preoccupied with the transport of their own troops to Valona. Sonnino asked Tommaso Tittoni, the Italian ambassador in Paris to raise the question with Briand, while Capitano di vascello Grassi, th Italian delegate to a naval conference which met in Paris at the end o November to co-ordinate anti-submarine measures, also planned to bring up the subject as well as a request for more assistance. Grassi soon realize that it was impossible to ask for anything more than the restoration of th twelve destroyers, for the French were hard pressed to maintain the suppl line to Salonika, and he suggested that they turn to the British. He wa wrong, the Admiralty turned down an Italian request for eight Britis destroyers in the Adriatic with the reply that they had none to spare Briand, who was acting as his own Foreign Minister at the time, wa responsive to Tittoni's claim that the Italians were not really asking for ai increase in assistance but merely for fulfilment of the engagement made t them in the naval convention. Briand was aware that the Serbia government had asked for all supplies formerly sent via Salonika to go vi Brindisi to Albanian ports and told Lacaze that the situation merite examination without delay and proposals for a solution. This was clearly crisis in Franco-Italian naval relations. As of 1 December the Italian claimed to have only thirteen destroyers available and the French nav attaché in Rome warned of the consequences of a French refusal to restor the destroyers, namely, Corsi would take personal offence, there would b general rancour directed especially at the French and the supply of Serb would be more or less intentionally badly performed.[122]

Lacaze tried to reassure the Italians. He had never thought of making th slightest modification in the Naval Convention and the destroyers had onl been withdrawn to protect commerce because of the new situation create by the appearance of German submarines in the Mediterranean. He wa presently taking measures which would permit him to free a certain numbe of destroyers from escort service, and they would be returned to the Italiar as they became available. He would also willingly put at the disposal of th Italians more French submarines armed with cannon. Lacaze intended t release destroyers by reorganizing the supply services of Sarrail's Armé d'orient. He would transport troops in auxiliary cruisers and material i armed freighters leaving in groups of two. These measures would do away with convoys to Salonika and free destroyers within a short time. On 2 December Lacaze ordered Dartige to send six to Brindisi as soon as they became available.[123]

By the end of November the situation on land was becoming increasingly critical as the Austrian–German–Bulgarian advance continued and the first groups of Serbian refugees, both civil and military, as well as thousands of Austrian prisoners taken in earlier fighting, streamed into the northern Albanian ports suffering from cold, hunger and disease. The Italians, however, stopped the supply of the Serbian army and declared that they would only resume it when at least one of the two *escadrilles* of French destroyers was returned to them. Sonnino bluntly told the French ambassador in Rome, Camille Barrère, that it was not Italian good will that was lacking but rather the means, and that they had to envisage facts as they were. The Austrian fleet, thanks to its submarines, torpedoes and bases, had the upper hand in the Adriatic to the point of exposing the transport of Italian troops to Valona to serious danger. Sonnino claimed that destroyers or submarines could not be created by royal decree, and with what they had the defence of transports supplying San Giovanni di Medua appeared to be impossible. The Italians wanted the Serbs to force their way overland southwards to Valona. With the number of Serbs in Albania growing, the supply of flour at San Giovanni and Durazzo was altogether insufficient and the situation threatened to become very grave. The Italian pressure worked. Lacaze ordered Dartige to send destroyers as quickly as possible and on 10 December the C.-in-C. detached five destroyers and two submarines from his command to join the one French destroyer and one French submarine which had just reached Brindisi. This brought the number of French destroyers in the Adriatic up to six, an *escadrille*, and Lacaze accordingly asked the Italians to resume the supply of the Serbian army.[124]

Dartige was finally able to get away to meet Abruzzi at Taranto on the 13th and the French C.-in-C. emphasized French concern over the danger of thousands of Serbian refugees dying of hunger in Albania. Abruzzi, pleased that he was getting at least half the French destroyers back, promised that supplies would immediately go via Valona where unloading was easier. They would try to resume landing food and material at Durazzo and San Giovanni but those two points, close to Cattaro, were a very uncertain operation with unprotected harbours lacking facilities for unloading, and now partially blocked by sunken ships. Dartige concluded privately that the good will of the Italians was certain, what was lacking was ardour and confidence in themselves. He decided that the only places they could supply the Serbian army and, if necessary evacuate it, were Durazzo and Valona, and they ought to try and concentrate the debris of the Serbian army at these points. Montenegro could only be supplied by means of the Bojana if the munitions requirements were not large, but the convoys would have to be escorted and not left to themselves as the Italians had done. The idea of protecting them by submarine patrols meant protection was illusory by day and non-existent at night.[125]

By the middle of December it was no longer a question of supplying the

Serbian army. The conditions in Albania were so chaotic that evacuation seemed to be the only feasible solution. This evacuation was extremely difficult at San Giovanni where troops had to be ferried out to the ships and the Allies were anxious to get as many of the Serbians as possible southwards to Durazzo or Valona. The commission in Rome approved evacuation from Valona in principle on 10 December. The Italians had attempted to secure Durazzo by ordering a brigade of troops to move northwards from Valona to the port on the 5th, but the troops did not arrive until the 19th because of poor to non-existent roads turned into quagmires by the winter rains. The Italians also landed their expeditionary corps at Valona and had over 28,000 men ashore by the 12th. The story of the evacuation of the Serbian army along with refugees and substantial numbers of Austrian prisoners is a complicated one with confusion, suffering, disease, harassment of the retreating Serbs by Albanian bands, and bickering among the British, French, Italian, Serbian and Montenegrin authorities. The Austrian advance, slowed as much by logistical problems as anything else, was for a long time a relatively minor threat.[126] The French sent the armoured cruisers *Jules Michelet* and *Victor Hugo* to bolster the Italians in covering the evacuation, although Dartige now bitterly complained of their haggling, while Thursby and Abruzzi tried to get the Italian Minister of Marine to shift the three surviving Pisa-class armoured cruisers from Venice to Brindisi where they might deal with the Austrian armoured cruisers, the *Sankt Georg* or *Kaiser Karl VI* reported at Cattaro.[127]

Towards the end of the year, another Austrian raid on Durazzo resulted in the most significant cruiser action so far in the Adriatic. On the evening of 28 December, Haus cabled the commander of the V Division at Cattaro that aerial reconnaissance and other intelligence had revealed that two Italian destroyers had brought approximately 300 troops to Durazzo. If the weather was not too stormy, Haus ordered the Austrian Cruiser Flotilla to attack them. Vice-Admiral Fiedler gave oral instructions to Linienschiffskapitän Seitz of the *Helgoland* to sail with the I Flotilla and search the stretch of water between Durazzo and Brindisi for the two destroyers. If he did not encounter them, he was to proceed to examine Durazzo at dawn and sink the destroyers or any cargo ships which might be there. The Austrian force consisting of *Helgoland* and the destroyers *Balaton*, *Csepel*, *Tátra*, *Lika* and *Triglav*, had a stroke of luck on their way southwards. They surprised the French submarine *Monge* which was sunk by the destroyer *Balaton*. The Austrians did not encounter the Italian destroyers at sea and at daybreak reached Durazzo. The Italian destroyers were not there either but four Austrian destroyers entered the harbour and sank a Greek steamer (with Italian crew), one large and one small schooner. As they were leaving, the destroyers came under fire from shore batteries and turned sharply to port supposedly to avoid masking *Helgoland*'s line of fire. This was a fatal error for they ran into a minefield and *Lika* was sunk and *Triglav* badly damaged. *Csepel* attempted to tow *Triglav*, but the tow fouled her screw thus greatly reducing her speed. *Tátra* subsequently succeeded in getting *Triglav* under tow, but picking up survivors of *Lika* and arranging the tow had taken around one and three quarter hours and the alarm was out, while the

Austrian Cruiser Flotilla could not make more than 6 knots because of the necessity of towing *Triglav*. Once the alarm had been given at Brindisi shortly after 7 a.m., Admiral Cutinelli ordered Captain Addison and the British light cruiser *Dartmouth* to sail along with the Italian light cruiser *Quarto*, to be followed by the French destroyers *Casque, Bisson, Renaudin, Commandant Bory* and *Commandant Lucas* as soon as they had steam up. The other British light cruiser, *Weymouth* under Captain Crampton, was ordered to raise steam but not sail until Cutinelli had further intelligence of the Austrians. Cutinelli did not in fact order *Weymouth* to sail until after 9 a.m. when she left in company with the Italian light cruiser *Nino Bixio* and the Italian destroyers *Abba, Nievo, Mosto* and *Pilo*. Rear-Admiral Belleni, commander of the Scouting Division, flew his flag in the *Bixio* and was senior Allied officer afloat during the action. By mid-morning there were four British and Italian cruisers (armed with 6-in. and 4.9-in. guns) and nine French and Italian destroyers racing to cut off *Helgoland* (armed with 3.9-in. guns) and the three destroyers (one with damaged screw) towing the crippled *Triglav*. Seitz was in a dangerous position and radioed for assistance. Fiedler ordered the armoured cruiser *Kaiser Karl VI* (two 9.4-in. guns, 20 knots), which was under steam at Cattaro, out in support along with the torpedo-boats T70, T71, T81 and T80. The small old battleship *Budapest*, cruiser *Aspern* and light cruiser *Novara* raised steam and sailed later in the day but were never near the scene of action. *Kaiser Karl VI* with her 9.4-in. guns was more powerful than any individual ship in Belleni's squadron, but could easily have been outmatched by the three Regina Elena-class battleships (two 12-in. guns, 20 knots) at Brindisi if Cutinelli had ordered them to sea. He did not, but although close enough to observe the enemy's smoke, *Kaiser Karl VI* did not come into action either. The Allied ships were actually between Cattaro and Seitz's force and he had to abandon *Triglav*, attempting to scuttle the destroyer. The submarine U15 was patrolling nearby and the Austrians hoped that it would be in position for an attack on any of the Allied ships which arrived. That hope was not fulfilled when the *Casque* group of destroyers arrived and finished off the wreck of the *Triglav*. However, the French destroyers could not catch up with the cruisers and did not get into action again during the day. The real action throughout the afternoon was a high-speed chase with most of the gunnery exchanges at extreme range and *Helgoland* frequently outranged. With the Allies between him and safety, Seitz's only salvation was speed and he steamed westwards and south-westwards almost up to the Italian coast while he tried to work around his pursuers, until nightfall permitted him to escape.[128]

The action of 29 December left the Allies with a feeling of dissatisfaction for their strength at sea had been three times that of the Austrians and their potential strength was even larger since the battleship division and another *escadrille* of destroyers at Brindisi had never been ordered to sea. They had for a time even been between the enemy and his bases yet the Austrians had still managed to escape. Thursby explained to Limpus: 'You can imagine how furious I am over losing the "Novara" and 3 "Tátras" on the 29th. ½ an hour more day light would have done it and if Belleni had only done the right thing we might have done it as it was, but what can you expect from an old admiral who has been 8 years ashore.' Captain Crampton of the *Weymouth* described how on the morning of the 29th 'I finally said to Cutinelli *"For God's sake let me go out"* & then he consented'. Crampton subsequently greeted the news that Belleni would be superseded with the remarks 'victory for me' and 'it is quite right & he is not fit to be in command of light cruisers'. Admiral Sir Francis Pridham, who was then a young officer in the *Weymouth*, wrote: 'The more one hears of the affair . . . the more disgusted one becomes. The Italians themselves are very sick. The Duke of the Abruzzi . . . has been over here and has straffed Bellini and Cutinelli severely.' The distant French C.-in-C., Dartige, when he read reports of the action, also commented on the glaring lack of co-ordination and unity of command of the larger Allied forces, but did not spare the French commander of the *Casque* group of destroyers from criticism especially for having wasted so much time on the wreck of the *Triglav*.[129]

The Austrians, however, had their own dissatifactions. Seitz was praised even by his opponents for his cool handling of his flotilla and his escape from a difficult position. He arrived back in port to the cheers of other Austrian warships. He must therefore have been shocked by the reception he received from Haus who apparently blamed him for getting into the difficult position in the first place. Haus had harsh words for Seitz instead of the praise the latter must have expected. He growled: 'Herr Captain, you thus ran away, you ran away very ably.' The Flottenkommandant termed the failure of *Lika* and *Triglav* to follow in the wake of their leader in waters suspected of mines an inexcusable error which resulted in the loss of the two destroyers and later brought the entire flotilla into the greatest danger. He referred to the fouling of *Csepel*'s screw in the attempt to tow *Triglav* as 'ineptitude' and 'carelessness' and criticized the apparent slowness in sending wireless reports to Cattaro which delayed the dispatch of the relief force, and the neglect in sending important reports to Cattaro left the supporting forces in ignorance of the whereabouts of the destroyers. Haus had no criticism with the conduct of the flotilla during the long pursuit, but criticized Seitz for not planning or executing a torpedo attack on the two closest pursuing cruisers with his three surviving destroyers after dark. Seitz was relieved of his command, and there were many Austrian naval officers who believed that this was an injustice.[130] Haus's ire is understandable however, for he had lost two of the six best destroyers his fleet had in return for a French submarine, a Greek steamer and two schooners, and the remainder of the flotilla, again his most modern fast light forces, had been in the gravest peril and only narrowly escaped. Haus must have realized that the Austrians had been extremely lucky and the action of 29 December undoubtedly served to strengthen that reluctance to risk his few precious assets against potentially overwhelming forces. They could not count on the errors of their enemies all the time.

The Austrian offensive against Montenegro at the beginning of 1916 brought one notable advantage to the k.u.k. Kriegsmarine. From 8–10 January the old ships of the V Division, notably *Budapest*, *Kaiser Karl VI*, *Aspern*, *Panther* and the ancient *Kaiser Franz Joseph I*, provided substantial and effective artillery support to the operations of the XIX Austrian Army Corps in the capture of Mount Lovčen. The elimination of the observation posts on Mount Lovčen which could report all Austrian ship movements during daylight hours enabled Haus to transfer the Austrian Cruiser Flotilla from Sebenico to Cattaro.[131]

The Montenegrins requested an armistice on 12 January. With Montenegro out of the war, the evacuation of refugees and soldiers from San Giovanni di Medua ended by 22 January. The centre of the evacuation now shifted southwards to Durazzo where the evacuation of Serbian forces was completed by 9 February. The remaining evacuations took place through Valona, and the majority of the Serbian army was reassembled on the island of Corfu. Durazzo still had its Italian garrison, which was now threatened by the Austrian advance, but the Italians delayed the evacuation perhaps longer than they should have if they did not mean to hold the port and it took place on the nights of 25–27 February under fire, with difficulty, and with over 800 casualties.[132]

The subject of the evacuation of the Serbian army merits a monograph of its own. Relations between the Italians and the French were strained, despite the cordiality between Abruzzi and Dartige when they met. The Italians and Serbians were also potential rivals in this area, especially in Albania, and this is reflected in the tone of the relevant volume of the Italian official history published in 1936. Dartige was certainly dissatisfied with the performance of the Italians. He complained on 5 January that the return of the French destroyers to Brindisi had not been for the Italians a motive for doubling their activity but rather an excuse for remaining at rest. Although the Italians claimed that they had no destroyers to escort supply convoys to Serbia and Montenegro and let them sail without protection, they had found enough destroyers when it was a question of escorting their own troops to Valona. The Italian troop transports sailed at night and with a luxury of protection that the French troop movements to Salonika had never known. The French also complained of an almost interminable series of disagreements with the Italians over the method of evacuation.[133] Undoubtedly, *sacro egoismo* was evident, and the Italians were inclined to give priority to their own interests in Albania. Nevertheless, when all is said and done the evacuation was accomplished successfully and Italian ships played the largest role, although the British drifters also had an important part in protecting the evacuation between Valona and Corfu. The British official history acknowledges that one-half to two-thirds of the transports used in the evacuation were Italian flag. The Italian official history provides detailed statistics which, since they included the supply and transport of the Italian expeditionary corps to Albania and run up to 5 April 1916, naturally magnify the role of the Italians (see Table 6.3).[134] Six Italian and two French steamers were lost during the evacuation. Statistics are, of course, open to interpretation and totals may vary. Undoubtedly, as the rise in numbers of the Italian expeditionary corps to Albania by spring 1916, indicate much of the Italian activity was connected with furthering purely Italian interests. On the other hand, we are still left with the fact that the Italian contribution to the evacuation was a very considerable one. Unfortunately, the hard

Table 6.3   *Evacuation of the Serbian Army*

Number of Passages by Steamers

	Italian	French	British	Total
Foodstuffs to Serbia	51	20	3	74
Transport of Serbian army	151	81	16	248
Transport of Italian expeditionary corps to Albania (to 5 April 1916)	208	—	—	208
Evacuation of Italian garrison at Durazzo	30	—	—	30
Total	440	101	19	560

Men, Animals, Pieces of Artillery and Material Transported

	Men	Animals	Artillery	Tons of material
Supplies to Serbian Army	Allied missions (unknown total)	—	—	28,299
Evacuation of Serbian army, refugees and Austrian prisoners	260,895	10,153	68	unknown
Transport of Italian expeditionary corps to Albania	73,355	16,215	254	39,500
Evacuation of Italian garrison at Durazzo	8,500	—	16	unknown

feeling between the French and Italians which had been evident to varying degrees since the beginning of the war was going to continue. Thursby, who by this time could have had few illusions about the Italian navy, paid tribute to the role of the Duke of the Abruzzi when he wrote in a private letter to the First Sea Lord on 20 February:

> We have moved altogether in the last two months over 200,000 people including Servians [sic], Austrian prisoners & Italian troops with hardly a casualty. I do not think that with the scratch pack we have had to deal with, ships & material being supplied by 3 different nations, anyone but the Duke could have done it. In addition to being able & energetic, his position enables him to do more than any ordinary Admiral could do.[135]

The evacuation should have provided the k.u.k. Kriegsmarine with an excellent opportunity to affect the war, and while the Austrians did attack with light craft, submarines and aircraft they never seriously interfered with the operation. The day after the action of 29 December and in order to efface the impression created by the loss of the two destroyers, *Helgoland* and five torpedo-boats swept to a point fifteen miles north-east of Brindisi, turned towards the Gulf of Drin at midnight and then returned to base at dawn without encountering any hostile craft. On 27 January the V Division commander, after learning through aerial reconnaissance of the presence at

Durazzo of eight steamers and five destroyers, ordered Captain Horthy in *Novara* to raid the port along with the destroyers *Orjen* and *Csepel*, but *en route* the two destroyers were damaged in a collision with each other and had to return to Cattaro. *Novara* continued alone but encountered the old Italian cruiser *Puglia* and French destroyer *Bouclier* and, with surprise gone, *Novara* broke off action and returned home. On 6 February, Seitz's successor Linienschiffskapitän Benno von Millenkovich led *Helgoland* and six torpedo-boats in a raid on the transport route between Durazzo and Brindisi. They ran into *Weymouth* and *Bouclier* and in the ensuing action two torpedo-boats collided with one another, and one, T74, had to drop out. Millenkovich assumed his opponents had made wireless contact with their base and again, with surprise gone, broke off action and returned home. On the same day *Liverpool* and the Italian destroyer *Bronzetti* chased the destroyer *Wildfang*, which had been out on reconnaissance, back to Cattaro. On 23 February bad weather frustrated an attempt by three Austrian destroyers to attack a cruiser reported off Cape Rodoni. The following day Fiedler sent *Helgoland*, four destroyers, and five torpedo-boats against Durazzo to support the advance of the XIX Austrian Army Corps, but the flotilla action, as well as efforts by German and Austrian submarines, were frustrated by bad weather until the 26th when *Helgoland* and six destroyers failed to find any enemy craft off Durazzo in the sector Cape Pali–Cape Rodoni.[136]

The activity of the k.u.k. Kriegsmarine during the period of the evacuation of the Serbian army was therefore relatively ineffective. The operations of the light flotilla craft were either frustrated by bad weather or clashes with Allied screening forces which destroyed the possibility of surprise and exposed the Austrians to the danger of being cut off and destroyed by potentially superior forces if they pressed on. Linienschiffskapitän Heyssler, Chief of Staff in the Austrian Cruiser Flotilla, had the impression that the I Torpedo Flotilla was not led with the necessary energy by Millenkovich and his own admiral, Fiedler, had not intervened sufficiently. Heyssler himself did not want to intrigue behind the back of a comrade so near to him in rank, an attitude he admitted was perhaps a weakness.[137] This was a local matter. The big question is would the Austrians have had more success and been able to inflict considerable losses if they had employed their heavier units? The naval representative at AOK reported that there were some grumblers who had expressed surprise that the navy had not helped more at Durazzo, but that this had no significance since those in authority understood that on the Austrian side it could only be a question of submarines taking part. Haus had reportedly denied an AOK suggestion about helping at Durazzo by pointing out that there were over forty heavy units of the Entente in Ionian waters. Haus has been criticized for this relative lack of activity in which some claim that the k.u.k. Kriegsmarine missed a great opportunity. Hans Sokol, a former naval officer who prepared the official history was rather reticent, but admitted that the reasons for not employing the heavy ships to back up the clearly outnumbered Austrian light craft, which were also frustrated by the weather, cannot be established from the archives and are probably no longer accessible. Sokol suggests that the extent of the Serbian evacuation may not have been precisely known while it was taking place, and there was consequently no apparent necessity for employing a larger number of heavy units. Another former naval officer who wrote extensively on maritime subjects, Bayer von Bayersburg, suggested in somewhat contradictory fashion to Sokol that Haus may have been anxious to spare the Austrian prisoners of war whom he knew were being evacuated by sea. Sokol's younger brother, Anthony, writing close to forty years after publication of the Austrian official history was much more critical. So, too, is a recent article by Lothar Baumgarten. Both argue that the inactivity of the fleet was a mistake and point out the future significance of the more than 130,000 Serbian troops who were rescued, reorganized, rearmed and later used in the Macedonian campaign. The Austrian advance in Albania also stopped short of Valona, another mistake, but one in which AOK instead of the navy must assume most of the blame for, with Valona in Austrian hands, the blockade of the Straits of Otranto might have been broken or forced much further to the south.[138]

This argument, like all 'what might have beens' in history is one that can never really be settled. However, if we remember Haus's line of thinking in March 1915 it is not hard to understand what motivated him. He had just lost two precious modern destroyers and, given the larger forces of all classes available to his enemies which he thought might be used against him if he was so foolish as to put his head in the noose, Haus was understandably reluctant to risk his most precious and irreplaceable assets to stop the evacuation of the Serbian army or assist the advance of the Austrian army on land. He could not count on Italian mistakes all the time to escape disaster. The 'fleet in being' was all-important to him and he was willing to pass up the opportunity for success if it meant excessive, in his mind, risk. There were also, one should remember, sizeable numbers of Allied submarines in the Adriatic. They had achieved relatively little success so far, largely through a lack of suitable targets and opportunities. What ardent French submarine officer off the Dalmatian coast would not have loved to get an Austrian battleship in his periscope? The Austrians knew that the submarines were there, for on 28 December the French *Archimède* torpedoed and sank the transport *Kupa* off Cape Planka. Haus may have lacked that killer instinct in regard to the Serbian army, although from his writings on the *Ancona* case and on the unrestricted submarine war one could never accuse him of soft-heartedness. Having said 'no' so often in the past, he perhaps got into the habit of saying 'no' even when the case for employing offensive action was much stronger. This was a fault he perhaps shared with some of his Italian opponents. Haus may indeed have missed an opportunity to accomplish great things, although it is sobering to remember that when the daring Horthy came to lead the k.u.k. Kriegsmarine in 1918 and undertook a major offensive action the results, as we shall see, were not happy for the Austrians. However, that argument could also be answered by pointing out that at the beginning of 1916 the Italians did not have the means that were available to them in 1918.[139]

With the evacuation of the Dardanelles and Serbian army by early 1916, he naval war in the Mediterranean became to a large extent simplified. The ubmarine war would now become the dominant theme with the Adriatic a ideshow, although the Austrian 'fleet in being' was a potential threat to the talians, and French and Italian friction over the question of command ontinued. In the following chapter we shall examine the Allied response to he submarine danger.

Notes: Chapter 6

1   There is an extensive literature on the tangled Greek situation. See: George B. Leon, *Greece and the Great Powers, 1914–1917* (Thessaloniki, 1974); Christos Theodoulou, *Greece and the Entente: August 1, 1914–September 25, 1916* (Thessaloniki, 1971); Alexander S. Mitrakos, *France in Greece during World War I* (Boulder, Colo., 1982); and Tanenbaum, *Sarrail*. The maritime aspects are succinctly covered in: Thomazi, *Guerre navale dans la Méditerranée*, pp. 127–31; Corbett and Newbolt, *Naval Operations*, Vol. 3, pp. 155–66, 172–6, 179–80.
2   Lapeyrère to Augagneur, 4 Oct. 1915, SHM, Carton Ed-83.
3   Lapeyrère to Augagneur, 10 Oct. 1915, Augagneur to Lapeyrère, 10 Oct. 1915, Lapeyrère to Amiral, *St. Louis* [Dartige], 14 Oct. 1915, ibid., Carton A-29.
4   Poincaré, *Au service de la France*, Vol. 7, pp. 170–1.
5   Hector de Béarn, *Souvenirs d'un marin* (Geneva and Paris, 1960), p. 114. Béarn was not particularly impressed with Lapeyrère's successor. He characterized the change as putting a 'blind horse' (*cheval borgne*) in place of a 'lame horse' (*cheval boiteaux*), ibid., p. 133.
6   Bienaimé, *La Guerre navale*, pp. 238, 241; Briand's biographer wrote sarcastically that for some time Lapeyrère was depressed and confided the guard of his ships to the Holy Virgin. Georges Suarez, *Briand: sa vie – son œuvre avec son journal et de nombreux documents inédits* (6 vols, Paris, 1938–41), Vol. 3, p. 164.
7   Keyes to his wife, 5 Jan. 1916, in Halpern (ed.), *The Keyes Papers*, Vol. 1, Doc. 137, p. 304.
8   Audition de M. Augagneur, Commission de la Marine de Guerre, 18 July 1917, p. 64, SHM, Carton Ed-76bis.
9   Kelly to Rear-Admiral cmdg 3rd Lt Cruiser Sqdn, 30 Oct. 1915, PRO, Adm 137/1136; Limpus to de Robeck, 24 Oct. 1915, Churchill College, Cambridge, de Robeck MSS, DRBK 4/36; Limpus to Jackson, 18 Oct. 1915, Naval Library, London, Jackson MSS; Keyes to his wife, 5 Jan. 1916, in Halpern (ed.), *The Keyes Papers*, Vol. 1, Doc. 137, p. 304.
10   Ballard to Jackson, 4 and 24 Oct. 1916, loc. cit. at. n.11, Jackson MSS. Ballard had thought it expedient to write privately to the First Sea Lord for guidance.
11   Abel Ferry, *Les Carnets secrets (1914–1918)* (Paris, 1957), p. 119; Alexandre Ribot, *Lettres à un ami: souvenirs de ma vie politique* (Paris, 1924), p. 141.
12   Augagneur to Lapeyrère, 9 Mar. 1915, Lapeyrère to Amiral *Gambetta*, 10 Mar. 1915, SHM, Carton A-29; Audition de M. Augagneur, Commission de la Marine de Guerre, 18 July 1917, pp. 22–3, ibid., Carton Ed-76bis.
13   Kelly to Rear-Admiral cmdg 3rd Lt Cruiser Sqdn, 30 Oct. 1915, PRO, Adm 137/1136.
14   Falkenhausen to Falkenhayn, 3 Nov. 1915, NARS, T-1022, Roll 791, PG 75262.

15   Holtzendorff to Zenker, 5 Nov. 1915, Zenker to Admiralstab, 7 Nov. 1915, Falkenhayn to Military Attaché, Athens, 7 Nov. 1915, ibid.

16   Holtzendorff to Marineattaché, Athens, 8 Nov. 1915, ibid.

17   Corbett and Newbolt, *Naval Operations*, Vol. 3, pp. 175–6.

18   The records of the inter-Allied conferences are in PRO, Cabinet Papers, I.C. (Allied Conferences) Series, Cab 28. Particularly useful for the early stages of the Salonika expedition are the summary paper I.C.-0 and papers I.C.-1 to I.C.-6, Cab 28/1.

19   Gauchet to Lacaze, 27 Oct., 3, 4 and 12 Nov. 1915, SHM, Carton Ed-112.

20   Lacaze to Gauchet, 9 Nov. 1915, Gauchet to Lacaze and Dartige, 9 and 13 Nov. 1915, ibid.

21   Dartige to Gauchet, 14 Nov. 1915, Gauchet to Lacaze, 15 Nov. 1915, ibid.

22   Gauchet to Dartige, 15 Nov. 1915, ibid.

23   Keyes to his wife, 9 Sept. 1915, in Halpern (ed.), *The Keyes Papers*, Vol. 1, Doc. 99, pp.192–3; de Robeck to Jackson, 16 Sept. 1915, loc. cit. at n.11, de Robeck MSS, DRBK 4/70.

24   Keyes to his wife, 5 and 16 Jan. 1916, 30 Mar. 1916, in Halpern (ed.), *The Keyes Papers*, Vol. 1, Docs 137, 143, 153, pp. 304–5, 330–1, 346.

25   Captain R. H. Leigh to Admiral Sims, 30 July 1918, NARS, RG 45, TD File, Box 552.

26   Asquith to Joint Staff, 27 Oct. 1915, Memorandum by Admiralty War Staff, 'Naval Measures Suggested against Greece', 29 Oct. 1915, H. B. Jackson and A. J. Murray, 'The Question of Coercive Action against Greece', 1 Nov. 1915, PRO, Adm 137/1142; Lacaze to Dartige, 14 and 17 Nov. 1915, Dartige to Lacaze, 14 Nov. 1915, SHM, Carton A-29.

27   Gauchet to Lacaze, 21 Nov. 1915, Guillemin to Gauchet, 22 Nov. 1915, ibid., SHM, Carton Ed-112.

28   Holtzendorff to Marineattaché, Athens, 22 Nov. 1915, Holtzendorff to Falkenhayn and Auswärtiges Amt, 23 Nov. 1915, Holtzendorff to U-Flotilla, Pola, 22 Nov. 1915, Marineattaché, Athens to Admiralstab, 24 Nov. 1915, NARS, T-1022, Roll 791, PG 75263.

29   Guillemin to Gauchet, 9 and 11 Dec. 1915, SHM, Carton Ed-112.

30   Thomazi, *Guerre navale dans la méditerranée*, pp. 130–1; Laurens, *Commandement naval*, p. 216; E.M.G.-4ᵉ Section [Capitaine de vaisseau Grasset, Sous-Chef], 'Note relative à l'action des Flottes Alliées contre la Grèce', 25 Dec. 1915, SHM, Carton Ed-103.

31   There is a lively and admittedly partisan account by one of his fellow officers in Athens in Béarn, *Souvenirs d'un marin*, and favourable treatment by his successor in Commandant Emmanuel Clergeau, *Le Commandant de Roquefeuil en Grèce* (Paris, 1934). Understandably a very different view is taken in Vice-Amiral Dartige du Fournet, *Souvenirs de guerre d'un amiral*.

32   An account of German motives is in General von Falkenhayn, *General Headquarters and its Critical Decisions* (London, 1919), ch. 7.

33   De Robeck to Jackson, 16 Sept. and 8 Oct. 1915, loc. cit. at n. 11, de Robeck MSS, DRBK 4/70.

34   Proposal by Keyes for a renewal of the naval attack on the Dardanelles and de Robeck's comments, 17 Aug. 1915, in Halpern (ed.), *The Keyes Papers*, Vol. 1, Doc. 98, pp. 188–92; Memorandum by Captain Godfrey, 13 Sept. 1915, Keyes to de Robeck, 23 Sept. 1915, ibid., Docs 100(b), 100(c), pp. 194–204.

35   Keyes to his wife, 27 Sept. 1915, ibid., Doc. 102, p. 206.

36   Keyes to his wife, 12 and 17 Oct. 1915, ibid., Docs 105, 107, pp. 210–11, 213–14. The memorandum of 18 Oct. is printed in Keyes, *Naval Memoirs*, Vol. 1, pp. 440–3.

37 Keyes, Diary of 17 Oct.–10 Nov. 1915, in Halpern (ed.), *The Keyes Papers*, Vol. 1, Doc. 109, p. 216; de Robeck to Jackson, 20 Oct. 1915, ibid., Doc. 110, pp. 232–3; de Robeck to Balfour, 20 Oct. 1915, loc. cit. at n. 11, de Robeck MSS, DRBK 4/69.

38 Jackson to de Robeck, 7 Nov. 1915, loc. cit. at n. 11, de Robeck MSS, DRBK 4/31; Balfour to Keyes, 1 Nov. 1915, in Halpern (ed.), *The Keyes Papers*, Vol. 1, Doc. 112, pp. 234–5; see also Keyes's Diary, ibid., pp. 220–1, 226–7.

39 Millerand to Minister of Foreign Affairs, 9 Oct. 1915, MAE, Série Guerre 1914–1918, Vol. 1067, f. 38; for the French aspect see especially Cassar, *The French and the Dardanelles*, pp. 212–16.

40 Keyes to Jackson, 11 Nov. 1915, in Halpern (ed.), *The Keyes Papers*, Vol. 1, Doc. 115, pp. 241–2; Memorandum by Keyes, n.d., ibid., Doc. 113, pp. 235–6.

41 De Robeck to Limpus, 9 Nov. 1915, loc. cit. at n. 3, Limpus MSS.

42 Limpus to de Robeck, 12 Nov. 1915, loc. cit. at n. 11, de Robeck MSS, DRBK 4/36.

43 On the decision to evacuate see: James, *Gallipoli*, pp. 321–32; Marder, *Dreadnought to Scapa Flow*, Vol. 2, pp. 309–29; Aspinall-Oglander, *Military Operations: Gallipoli*, Vol. 2, chs 28–30.

44 De Robeck to Limpus, 26 Nov. 1915, loc. cit. at n. 3, Limpus MSS.

45 Admiralty War Staff, 'Operations in Syria', 18 Oct. 1915, PRO, Adm 137/1147; Imperial General Staff and Admiralty War Staff, 'A Statement of Military Considerations as to the Advisability of Undertaking an Expedition, as Proposed by Earl Kitchener, for the Purpose of Severing and Keeping Severed, the Turkish Communications from Asia Minor via Adana to Baghdad and via Aleppo to Syria and Egypt', n.d. [16 Nov. 1915], SHM, Carton Es-11. The document included statements concerning the naval considerations and the opinions of the French Naval and Military Staffs; Section d'études de la Défense Nationale, 'Rapport sur un projet soumis par Lord Kitchener à son gouvernement', 13 Nov. 1915, ibid., Carton Es-23.

46 Conférence tenue au Ministère des Affaires Etrangères à Paris, 17 Nov. 1915 [I.C.-3], PRO, Cab 28/1.

47 Keyes Diary, 18 Nov. 1915, in Halpern (ed.), *The Keyes Papers*, Vol. 1, Doc. 116, p. 245.

48 James, *Gallipoli*, pp. 329–31. This argument is not accepted by Sir Llewellyn Woodward, *Great Britain and the War of 1914–1918* (London, 1967), pp. 92 n. 1, 95–6.

49 Dartige to Lacaze, 17 Dec. 1915, SHM, Carton Ed-84; Dartige to Lacaze, 19 Dec. 1915, Lacaze to Dartige, 20 Dec. 1915, ibid., Carton A-29.

50 Keyes Diary, 29 Nov. 1915, in Halpern (ed.), *The Keyes Papers*, Vol. 1, Doc. 116, p. 254.

51 De Robeck to Limpus, 26 Nov. 1915, loc. cit. at n. 3, Limpus MSS.

52 Wemyss to de Robeck, n.d. [probably 29 Nov. 1915], in Halpern (ed.), *The Keyes Papers*, Vol. 1, Doc. 120, pp. 257–8; Wemyss to Jackson, n.d. [late Nov., early Dec. 1915], ibid., Doc. 124, pp. 268–9; Keyes, *Naval Memoirs*, Vol. 1, pp. 473–5.

53 James, *Gallipoli*, pp. 337–8; Roskill, *Hankey*, Vol. 1, pp. 236–7; Cassar, *The French and the Dardanelles*, pp. 233–4; Military Conference of the Allies held at the French Headquarters, December 6–8, 1915, [I.C.-5], PRO, Cab 28/1.

54 Keyes to his wife, 14–17 Dec. 1915, in Halpern (ed.), *The Keyes Papers*, Vol. 1, Doc. 129, pp. 278–82; Wemyss to Jackson, 15 Dec. 1915, ibid., Doc. 131, pp. 283–4.

55 James, *Gallipoli*, pp. 339–42; Keyes to his wife, 18–24 Dec. 1915, in Halpern

(ed.), *The Keyes Papers*, Vol. 1, Doc. 132, pp. 286–93; Keyes, *Naval Memoirs*, Vol. 1, ch. 26; Bush, *Gallipoli*, pp. 300–5. The very detailed account is Aspinall-Oglander, *Military Operations: Gallipoli*, Vol. 2, ch. 21.

56 De Robeck to Limpus, 20 Dec. 1915, loc. cit. at n. 3, Limpus MSS; de Robeck to Jackson, 24 Dec. 1915, in Halpern (ed.), *The Keyes Papers*, Vol. 1, Doc. 134, p. 295.

57 James, *Gallipoli*, pp. 344–7; Keyes to his wife, 12 Jan. 1916, in Halpern (ed.), *The Keyes Papers*, Vol. 1, Doc. 141, pp. 315–21; Bush, *Gallipoli*, pp. 305–6; Aspinall-Oglander, *Military Operations: Gallipoli*, Vol. 2, ch. 32.

58 Details in Corbett and Newbolt, *Naval Operations*, Vol. 3, pp. 167–8, 177–9, 205–6, 217; Bush, *Gallipoli*, pp. 219–25; Lorey, *Krieg in den türkischen Gewässern*, Vol. 1, pp. 198–201, 207–8; Thomazi, *Guerre navale aux Dardanelles*, pp. 207–8.

59 Souchon to his wife, 5 and 7 Nov. 1915, BA-MA, Nachlass Souchon, N156/16.

60 Keyes to his wife, 1 Jan. 1916, in Halpern (ed.), *The Keyes Papers*, Vol. 1, Doc. 136, p. 302; Keyes, *Naval Memoirs*, Vol. 1, p. 510.

61 Lorey, *Krieg in den türkischen Gewässern*, Vol. 2, pp. 149–50; Bush, *Gallipoli*, p. 225; Marder credits the submarines with: 2 battleships, 1 destroyer, 5 gunboats, 9 transports, over 30 steamers, 7 ammunition and storeships, and 188 sailing vessels, Marder, *Dreadnought to Scapa Flow*, Vol. 2, p. 313. See also Kenneth Edwards, *We Dive at Dawn* (London, 1939), p. 182.

62 Souchon to his wife, 30 Dec. 1915, BA-MA, Nachlass Souchon, N156/17; Admiralstab to Souchon, 18 Dec. 1915, Souchon to Admiralstab, 30 Dec. 1915, Bronsart to Admiralstab, 31 Dec. 1915, Admiralstab to Bronsart, 1 Jan. 1916, NARS, T-1022, Roll 792, PG 75263.

63 Greger, *Russische Flotte im Weltkrieg*, pp. 51–2; Souchon to his wife, 8 Jan. 1916, BA-MA, Nachlass Souchon, N156/17.

64 Admiralstab to Kaiser Wilhelm, 15 Oct. 1915, NARS, T-1022, Roll 791, PG 75262. On 15 October two UB boats and two UC boats (one a transport) were at Constantinople and another UB boat at Varna.

65 Souchon to Admiralstab, 23 Sept. 1915, Admiralstab to U-Flotilla, Pola, 24 Sept. 1915, Müller to Admiralstab, 4 Oct. 1915, Admiralstab to Müller, 4 Oct. 1915, ibid.

66 Tirpitz to Holtzendorff, 2 Oct. 1915, Holtzendorff to Tirpitz, 6 Oct. 1915, Holtzendorff to Kaiser Wilhelm, 6 Oct. 1915, Holtzendorff to Chief, High Seas Fleet, 9 Oct. 1915, ibid.

67 Holtzendorff to Tirpitz, 2 Oct. 1915, Tirpitz to Holtzendorff, 18 Oct. 1915, ibid., Roll 607, PG 68231.

68 Spindler, *Handelskrieg*, Vol. 3, pp. 10, 24–6, 37.

69 Souchon to Admiralstab, 6 Oct. 1915, Admiralstab to Adam (for U35), 9 and 10 Oct. 1915, Nadolny to Admiralstab, 11 Oct. 1915, NARS, T-1022, Roll 791, PG 75262.

70 Spindler, *Handelskrieg*, Vol. 3, p. 25; R. H. Gibson and Maurice Prendergast, *The German Submarine War, 1914–1918* (London, 1931), p. 76.

71 Holtzendorff to Souchon, 29 Oct. 1915, Holtzendorff to Reichsmarineamt, 29 Oct. 1915, NARS, T-1022, Roll 791, PG 75262.

72 Souchon to Admiralstab, 20 Nov. 1915, Admiralstab to Souchon, 24 Nov. 1915, ibid., PG 75263; Holtzendorff to Souchon, 21 Dec. 1915, ibid., Roll 792, PG 75263.

73 Spindler, *Handelskrieg*, Vol. 3, pp. 32–4, 46–7; Admiralstab to U-Flotilla, Pola and Cattaro, 20 Dec. 1915, NARS, T-1022, Roll 792, PG 75263. This was UC12's last mission as a transport. She was converted back to minelaying and

subsequently lost with all hands off Taranto on 16 March 1916, probably as the result of the detonation of one of her own mines.

74 A concise summary is in Holger Herwig, *'Luxury' Fleet: The Imperial German Navy, 1888–1918* (London, 1980), pp. 164–6.

75 Figures from Spindler, *Handelskrieg*, Vol. 3, pp. 388, 390.

76 Thomazi, *Guerre navale dans la Méditerranée*, p. 163; Spindler, *Handelskrieg*, Vol. 3, pp. 26–8; Holtzendorff to Kaiser Wilhelm, 19 Nov. 1915, NARS, T-1022, Roll 791, PG 75262. The troopship *Mercian* (6,305 tons) successfully beat off an attack by U38 with a loss of life of 23, plus 31 lost among those who had taken to lifeboats which capsized: Gibson and Prendergast, *German Submarine War*, p. 77.

77 Robert Lansing, *War Memoirs of Robert Lansing* (Indianapolis, Ind., 1935), pp. 87–8; Grasshoff to Admiralstab, 12 Nov. 1915, Holtzendorff to Kaiser Wilhelm, 19 Nov. 1915, NARS, T-1022, Roll 791, PG 75262. There is a good discussion of the American reaction in Arthur S. Link, *Wilson: Confusions and Crises, 1915–1916* (Princeton, NJ, 1964), pp. 62–3, 66–72.

78 Admiralstab to U-Flotilla, Cattaro and Pola, 10 and 13 Nov. 1915, Grasshoff to Admiralstab, 12 Nov. 1915, Zenker [Admiralstab representative at Supreme Command] to Admiralstab, 13 Nov. 1915, Holtzendorff to Kaiser Wilhelm, 19 Nov. 1915, NARS, T-1022, Roll 791, PG 75262; V Divisionskommando to Marinesektion, 12 Nov. 1915, OK/MS VIII-1/19 ex 1915, No. 7926.

79 Marinesektion to Haus, 11 Nov. 1915, Haus to Marinesektion, 12 Nov. 1915, Marinesektion to Ministerium des Äussern, 14 Nov. 1915, OK/MS VIII-1/19 ex 1915, No. 7895; Haus to Marinesektion, 13 Nov. 1915, Marinesektion to AOK, 13 Nov. 1915, AOK to Marinesektion, 13 Nov. 1915, ibid., No. 7919; Aichelburg, *Unterseeboote Österreich-Ungarns*, Vol. 1, pp. 130–1.

80 Wilson to Edith Bolling Galt, 17 Nov. 1915, enclosure II, in Arthur S. Link (ed.), *The Papers of Woodrow Wilson*, Vol. 35: *October 1, 1915–January 27, 1916* (Princeton, NJ, 1980), pp. 208–9.

81 Admiralstab to Austrian Naval Attaché, Berlin, 27 Nov. 1915, Admiralstab to U-Flotilla, Pola, 27 Nov. 1915, Admiralstab to Freyberg, 27 Nov. 1915, NARS, T-1022, Roll 791, PG 75263.

82 Kophamel to Admiralstab, 3 Dec. 1915, Freyberg to Admiralstab, 7 Dec. 1915, Admiralstab to U-Flotilla, Pola, 8 Dec. 1915, Holtzendorff to Freyberg, 9 Dec. 1915, ibid.

83 Penfield to Burián, 19 Nov. 1915, Memorandum by Generalauditor Leopold Feigl with annotations by Haus, 24 Nov. 1915, Marinesektion to Reichsmarineamt, 1 Dec. 1915, OK/MS VIII-1/19 ex 1915, No. 8144.

84 Tirpitz to Holtzendorff, 7 Dec. 1915, Holtzendorff to Marinesektion, 8 Dec. 1915, NARS, T-1022, Roll 791, PG 75263.

85 Lansing, *War Memoirs*, pp. 88–92; Lansing to Wilson, 3 Dec. 1915, in Link (ed.), *Papers of Woodrow Wilson*, Vol. 35, p. 282; Wilson to Lansing, 5 Dec. 1915, ibid., pp. 286–9; Lansing to Wilson, 17 Dec. 1915, ibid., pp. 364–6; Wilson to Lansing, 18 Dec. 1915, ibid., pp. 368–70; Lansing to Wilson, 21 Dec. 1915, ibid., pp. 378–80; for a general view of the American reaction see also: Ernest R. May, *The World War and American Isolation, 1914–1917* (Cambridge, Mass., 1959; paperback edn Chicago, 1966), pp. 163, 165–6.

86 Haus to Kailer, 30 Oct. 1915, Nachlass Kailer. On problems with U14 see Aichelburg, *Unterseeboote Österreich-Ungarns*, Vol. 2, pp. 333–4.

87 Freyberg to Admiralstab, 12 Dec. 1915, Admiralstab to U-Flotilla, Pola, 11 Dec. 1915, NARS, T-1022, Roll 791, PG 75263; Austro-Hungarian embassy, Berlin to Admiralstab, 28 Dec. 1915, ibid., Roll 792, PG 75263.

88 Burián to Penfield, 29 Dec. 1915, United States, Department of State, *Papers Relating to the Foreign Relations of the United States 1915, Supplement: The World War* (Washington, DC, 1928), pp. 655–8; Spindler, *Handelskrieg*, Vol. 3, pp.28–30; Aichelburg, *Unterseeboote Österreich-Ungarns*, Vol. 1, pp. 129–32; Lansing, *War Memoirs*, p. 94.

89 Freyberg to Holtzendorff, 5 Jan. 1916, Admiralstab to Holtzendorff, 7 Jan. 1916, Admiralstab to Freyberg, 8 Jan. 1916, NARS, T-1022, Roll 792, PG 75263.

90 Auswärtiges Amt to Admiralstab, 4 Nov. 1915, ibid., PG 75262. *Cirene* had been sunk by U39 (Kapitänleutnant Forstmann).

91 Holtzendorff to Bethmann Hollweg, 23 Nov. 1915, Holtzendorff to Kophamel, 22 Nov. 1915, ibid., PG 75263.

92 The *Baralong* was a British 'Q' ship under the command of Lieutenant-Commander Godfrey Herbert which on 19 August had used the United States flag while approaching the German submarine U27, surprised while attacking the British steamer *Nicosian* off the Scilly Islands. U27 was sunk and, in a controversial sequel, Marines from the *Baralong* killed four of the German submariners who had climbed back aboard the *Nicosian*, believing that they might scuttle the ship or had been responsible for the recent sinking of the liner *Arabic*. The Germans denounced Herbert as a war criminal and demanded that he and his crew be tried for murder. See Gibson and Prendergast, *German Submarine War*, pp. 52–3; Corbett and Newbolt, *Naval Operations*, Vol. 3, pp. 131–4.

93 Holtzendorff to Zimmerman, 7 Dec. 1915, NARS, T-1022, Roll 791, PG 75263.

94 Holtzendorff to Tirpitz, Falkenhayn, Zimmerman and Müller, 16 Dec. 1915, ibid., Roll 587, PG 68126; Marineattaché, Athens to Marinesektion, 11 Feb. 1916, Marinesektion to Foreign Office, 21 Feb. 1916, OK/MS VIII-1/14 ex 1916, No. 1042. Keyes for a time was very worried that the bags might have contained a letter with highly sensitive material on the Dardanelles campaign which he had written to Admiral Oliver. The bag with his letter, however, was apparently concealed by one of the passengers, Keyes to his wife, 8 Dec. 1915, in Halpern (ed.), *The Keyes Papers*, Doc. 128, p. 276.

95 Kophamel to Admiralstab, 7 Dec. 1915, Admiralstab to Kophamel, 7 Dec. 1915, Admiralstab to Freyberg, 9 Dec. 1915, NARS, T-1022, Roll 791, PG 75263. Napier describes the incident in H. D. Napier, *The Experiences of a Military Attaché in the Balkans* (London, n.d.), pp. 234–7.

96 Freyberg to Holtzendorff, 16 Feb. 1916, Prussian Ministry of War to Austro-Hungarian Ministry of War, 9 Feb. 1916, Memorandum by Kapitänleutnant Gansser, 20 Feb. 1916, Note by Kophamel, 21 Feb. 1916, NARS, T-1022, Roll 792, PG 75264; Napier, *Experiences of a Military Attaché*, pp. 240–1. Wilson was exchanged four months before Napier.

97 Freyberg to Holtzendorff, 10 Jan. 1916, Valentiner to Admiralstab, 20 Jan. 1916, Freyberg to Holtzendorff, 4 and 18 Feb. 1916, NARS, T-1022, Roll 729, PG 75293; Marinesektion to AOK, 29 Dec. 1915 and 6 Jan. 1916, OK/MS VIII-1/19 ex 1915, No. 8906.

98 Cited by May, *World War and American Isolation*, p. 164; Lansing, *War Memoirs*, pp. 94–5.

99 Admiralstab to U-Flotilla, Pola, 3 Jan. 1916, NARS, T-1022, Roll 792, PG 75263; Spindler, *Handelskreig*, Vol. 3, pp. 35–6; Gibson and Prendergast, *German Submarine War*, p. 78.

100 Short accounts are in: Gibson and Prendergast, *German Submarine War*, pp. 82–3; May, *World War and American Isolation*, pp. 185–6; Corbett and Newbolt,

Naval Operations, Vol. 3, pp. 282–3. The subject is discussed at length in Lansing, *War Memoirs*, pp. 99–108; and Link, *Wilson: Confusions and Crises*, chs 5–6.

101 Holtzendorff, 'Führung des U-Bootskrieges im Mittelmeer', 12 Jan. 1916, NARS, T-1022, Roll 792, PG 75263.

102 Kophamel, 'Der U-Bootskrieg im Mittelmeer', 15 Jan. 1916, ibid., PG 75264.

103 Holtzendorff to Kophamel, 3 Feb. 1916, Holtzendorff, 'Befehl für des Vorgehen gegen Armierte feindliche Handelsschiff' [print], 11 Feb. 1916, Haus, 'Reservat befehl', 20 Feb. 1916, Holtzendorff to Kophamel, 19 Feb. 1916, ibid.

104 Short account in Herwig, *'Luxury' Fleet*, p. 165; great detail in Spindler, *Handelskrieg*, Vol. 3, pp. 87–104; and May, *World War and American Isolation*, ch. 11.

105 Haus to Marinesektion, 24 Mar. 1916, Marinesektion to Burián, 28 Mar. 1916, OK/MS VIII-1/14 ex 1916, No. 1726; Burián to Kailer, 3 Apr. 1916, ibid., No. 2105. See also Sokol, *Österreich-Ungarns Seekrieg*, pp. 338–40.

106 At the beginning of 1917 Haus was a strong supporter of the fatal decision for unrestricted submarine warfare and again depreciated the danger of war with the United States. See Count Ottokar Czernin, *In the World War* (London, 1919), p. 124.

107 Figures from Spindler, *Handelskrieg*, Vol. 3, pp. 388, 390.

108 Zenker to Müller, 29 Jan. 1916, NARS, T-1022, Roll 587, PG 68127; Spindler, *Handelskrieg*, Vol. 3, pp. 34–6; Holtzendorff to U-Flotilla, Pola, 14 Mar. 1916, ibid., Roll 792, PG 75264.

109 Holtzendorff to Reichsmarineamt, 11 Feb. 1916, Freyberg to Holtzendorff, 27 Mar. 1916, ibid.

110 Thursby to Limpus, 17 Oct. 1915, loc. cit. at n. 3, Limpus MSS; Thursby to Jackson, 19 Oct. 1915, loc. cit. at n. 11, Jackson MSS.

111 ibid.; Thursby to Limpus, 8 Nov. and 1 Dec. 1915, loc. cit. at n. 3, Limpus MSS; Naval Staff, *The Mediterranean, 1914–1915*, pp. 203–7.

112 Thursby to Limpus, 22 Dec. 1915, loc. cit. at n. 3, Limpus MSS; Tomkinson Diary, 18, 22 and 25 Oct., 2, 4 and 17 Nov. 1915, 31 Jan. and 13 Mar. 1916, Churchill College, Cambridge, Tomkinson MSS, 170/2. The Admiralty did send in December the redoubtable E21 to Brindisi to work off Cape Planka and Ragusa, but the submarine broke down soon after arrival, Naval Staff, *The Mediterranean, 1914–1915*, pp. 212–13.

113 Hugh Heard to De Chair, 19 Dec. 1915, Imperial War Museum, London, De Chair MSS, DEC/4/2(c); Thursby to Jackson, 10 Nov. 1915, loc. cit. at n.11, Jackson MSS; Jonquières to Naval Attaché, Rome, 1 Oct. 1915, Roque to Naval Attaché, Rome, 5 Oct. 1915, SHM, Carton Es-9.

14 Corsi to Abruzzi, 7 Oct. 1915, Corsi to Sonnino, 8 Oct. 1915, USM, Cartella 361/6; Corsi to Leone [French translation], 14 Oct. 1915, Augagneur to Leone, 20 Oct. 1915, SHM, Carton Ed-105.

15 Marine Paris to Dartige, 29 Oct. and 1 Nov. 1915, Dartige to Marine Paris, 29 and 30 Oct. 1915, SHM, Carton A-29; Ufficio Storico, *Marina italiana*, Vol. 2, pp. 338–9.

16 Daveluy to Dartige, 8 Nov. 1915, SHM, Carton Ed-91; Dartige to Lacaze, 20 Nov. 1915, ibid., Carton Ed-84.

17 Thomazi, *Guerre navale dans l'Adriatique*, p. 108; Ufficio Storico, *Marina italiana*, Vol. 2, pp. 344–7; Corbett and Newbolt, *Naval Operations*, Vol. 4, pp. 101–2; Naval Staff, *The Mediterranean, 1914–1915*, pp. 210–11.

18 Conrad to Haus, 29 Oct. 1915, OK/MS VIII-1/1 ex 1915, No. 7648.

19 Sokol, *Österreich-Ungarns Seekrieg*, pp. 242–3; Ufficio Storico, *Marina italiana*,

Vol. 2, pp. 353–4; Fiedler to Haus, 29 Nov. 1915, OK/MS VIII-1/1 ex 1915, No. 8347; AOK to Flottenkommando, 29 Nov. 1915, Flottenkommando to V Divisionskommando, 30 Nov. 1915, OK/MS VIII-1/9, ex 1915, No. 8312.

120 Ufficio Storico, *Marina italiana*, Vol. 2, pp. 365, 367–71, 386–9; Thomazi, *Guerre navale dans l'Adriatique*, p. 109; Sokol, *Österreich-Ungarns Seekrieg*, pp. 246–9.

121 D'Huart to Lacaze, 25 Nov. 1915, SHM, Carton Ed-92; Thursby to Jackson, 1 Dec. 1915, loc. cit. at n. 11, Jackson MSS; Thursby to Limpus, 2 Dec. 1915, loc. cit. at n. 3, Limpus MSS.

122 Grassi to Corsi, 29 Nov. 1915, USM, Cartella 361/6; P. de Margerie to Lacaze, 29 Nov. 1915, D'Huart to Lacaze, 1 Dec. 1915, Attaché naval, London to Lacaze, 2 Dec. 1915, SHM, Carton Ed-105. A very interesting detailed exposé of the situation (30 Nov.) by Cutinelli Rendina, Italian C.-in-C. at Brindisi, is printed in: Ufficio Storico, *Marina italiana*, Vol. 2, pp. 348–51.

123 Lacaze to D'Huart, 1 Dec. 1915, Lacaze to Dartige, 2 Dec. 1915, SHM, Carton Ed-105.

124 Camille Barrère to Briand, 8 Dec. 1915, ibid.; Lacaze to Dartige, 10 Dec. 1915, Dartige to Lacaze, 10 Dec. 1915, Lacaze to D'Huart, 11 Dec. 1915, ibid., Carton Es-9.

125 Dartige to Lacaze, 17 Dec. 1915, ibid., Carton Ed-84.

126 For details see, Ufficio Storico, *Marina italiana*, Vol. 2, ch. 14; Corbett and Newbolt, *Naval Operations*, Vol. 4, pp. 102–5.

127 Dartige to Lacaze, 5 Jan. 1916, SHM, Carton Ed-84; Thursby to Admiralty, Report of Proceedings, 21 Dec. 1915, PRO, Adm 137/780; Thursby to Limpus, 22 Dec. 1915, loc. cit. at n. 3, Limpus MSS; Thursby to Jackson, 24 Dec. 1915, loc. cit. at n. 11, Jackson MSS.

128 Detailed studies of the action are in: Corbett and Newbolt, *Naval Operations*, Vol. 4, pp. 106–17; Ufficio Storico, *Marina italiana*, Vol. 2, ch. 15; Thomazi, *Guerre navale dans l'Adriatique*, pp. 110–14; Sokol, *Österreich-Ungarns Seekrieg*, pp. 250–63; Naval Staff, *The Mediterranean, 1914–1915*, pp. 216–25.

129 Thursby to Limpus, 5 Jan. 1916, loc. cit. at n. 3, Limpus MSS; Captain D. B. Crampton, Diary, 29 Dec. 1915 and 9 Jan. 1916, Imperial War Museum, London, Crampton MSS, 71/29/1; Admiral Sir Francis Pridham, War Diary, 1914–1918, Vol. 2, 31 Dec. 1915, Churchill College, Cambridge, Pridham MSS; Dartige to Lacaze, 22 Jan. 1916, SHM, Carton Ed-84.

130 Haus, 'Besprechung über die Aktion . . . am 29 Dezember, 1915', 6 Jan. 1916, OK/MS VIII-1/1 ex 1916, No. 238; Heyssler, 'Erinnerungen' (1936), typescript in private possession, p. 394. Some Austrian officers could not understand the delay in bringing the units at Cattaro into action since the *Kaiser Karl VI* was more powerful than all their opponents and could have altered the situation. Khuepach, Tagebuch 1915, 29 Dec. 1915, Kriegsarchiv, Vienna, Nachlass Khuepach, B/200, No. V/1.

131 Sokol, *Österreich-Ungarns Seekrieg*, pp. 264–70; Haus to Commander, Kreuzer-flottille, 26 Jan. 1916, OK/MS II-1/1 ex 1916, No. 619.

132 Detailed treatment from the Italian point of view in Ufficio Storico, *Marina italiana*, Vol. 2, chs 17–18. See also Corbett and Newbolt, *Naval Operations*, Vol. 4, pp. 118–25.

133 Dartige to Lacaze, 5 and 22 Jan. and 8 Feb. 1916, SHM, Carton Ed-84; Annex to Note by 4[e] Section, EMG concerning objectives proposed for Italian naval activity, 8 Feb. 1916, ibid., Carton Ed-91.

134 Corbett and Newbolt, *Naval Operations*, Vol. 4, p. 121; Ufficio Storico, *Marina italiana*, Vol. 2, pp. 514, 515, 615–16. Sokol provides statistics for the actual ports used: S. Giovanni di Medua, 8,338 men; Durazzo, 88,153 men

Valona, 157,965 men (and all animals). The transport fleet itself numbered: 45 Italian or Italian chartered (130,000 tons); 25 French or French chartered (43,000 tons); and 11 British or British chartered (50,000 tons). There were also 5 Italian and 1 French hospital ships. Sokol, *Österreich-Ungarns Seekrieg*, pp. 271–2.

135   Thursby to Jackson, 20 Feb. 1916, loc. cit. at n. 11, Jackson MSS.

136   Horthy, Operations Journal, 28 Jan. 1916, OK/MS VIII-1/1 ex 1916, No. 1090; Millenkovitch, Gefechtsbericht (with comments by Fiedler), 7 Feb. 1916, ibid., No. 1058; Fiedler to Flottenkommando, 24 Feb. 1916, ibid., No. 1243; idem, 28 Feb. 1916, ibid., No. 1456; Sokol, *Österreich-Ungarns Seekrieg*, pp. 273–8, 285; Ufficio Storico, *Marina italiana*, Vol. 2, pp. 520–7; Thomazi, *Guerre navale dans l'Adriatique*, p. 117; Corbett and Newbolt, *Naval Operations*, Vol. 4, pp. 121–3.

137   Heyssler, 'Erinnerungen', loc. cit. at n. 132, pp. 399–400.

138   Winterhalder to Kailer, 1 Mar. 1916, Kriegsarchiv, Vienna, Nachlass Kailer, B/242; Sokol, *Österreich-Ungarns Seekrieg*, pp. 286–7; Heinrich Bayer von Bayersburg, *Die Marinewaffen im Einsatz, 1914–1918* (Vienna, 1968), p. 29; Anthony E. Sokol, *The Imperial and Royal Austro-Hungarian Navy* (Annapolis, Md, 1968), pp. 116–18; Lothar Baumgartner, 'Österreich-Ungarns Dünkirchen? Ein Gegenüberstellung von Berichten zum Abtransport der serbischen Armee aus Albanien im Winter 1915/16', *Marine – Gestern, Heute*, vol. 6, no. 2 (June 1982), pp. 46–53.

139   The historian of these events is hampered by the fact that many Austrian naval records have apparently not survived in Vienna. The papers of the Flottenkommandt at Pola probably fell into the hands of the Italians in 1918 and other records may have been destroyed. This seems to have included much internal memoranda and correspondence of the fleet in which records are extant only if a copy was sent to the Marinesektion in Vienna. Unfortunately, some Austrian historians believe much business was discussed at the Marinekasino – the officers' club at Pola – and no written record exists. The answer to some of these historical puzzles may lie in the large number of cartons of relatively uncatalogued 'documents in German language' listed in the registers at the Ufficio Storico della Marina Militare in Rome. Haus also kept a diary in shorthand, but the volume covering the war years is missing.

[7]

The Allied Failure to Meet the Submarine Challenge in 1916

The Malta Conference

The French C.-in-C. was in theory responsible for all of the Mediterranean beyond the immediate vicinity of the Straits of Gibraltar, the Italian area in the Adriatic, the British zone in the Aegean and, of course, the territorial waters of British and Italian possessions. The French C.-in-C. was also the individual who arranged the routes for transport through the Mediterranean and changed them according to circumstances, promulgating his arrangements to the British admirals in the eastern Mediterranean, Egypt, Malta and Gibraltar. The British authorities, in turn, implemented them and also brought their local arrangements regarding patrols for the protection of transports and trade in conformity with the French C.-in-C.'s measures on the subject.[1] The submarine war was therefore his problem and the enormity of the task may have had something to do with Lapeyrère's decision to retire. The number of light forces suitable for anti-submarine warfare was continually changing and growing. The Naval War Staff's estimate of these, as of 15 November 1915, excluding the Adriatic, is shown in Table 7.1.

Table 7.1 *British and French Anti-Submarine Forces, 15 November 1915*

Type of Vessel	British	French	Total
Scouts, sloops and gunboats	13	3	16
Destroyers	32	53	85
Torpedo-boats	19	44	63
Armed boarding steamers and armed yachts	24	1	25
Armed trawlers	66	42	108
Net drifters	48	—	48
Minesweeping trawlers and steamers	60	5	65

On this date there were also an additional forty-two net drifters in the Straits of Otranto and more were on the way. Many of the small craft listed, however, were actually tied up by the Dardanelles campaign in the Aegean.[2]

The theoretical position of the C.-in-C. did not correspond to reality. Dartige recognized his situation clearly. In his very first report to Lacaze he declared that while his title of Commander-in-Chief implied that he was responsible for everything, in reality the present circumstances of the war relegated him to Malta and Bizerte, far from all theatres of operations, and kept him in a sort of impotence. The most active operations were in the Italian or British zones. De Robeck had been willing to send flotilla craft and even submarines to the area around Cerigo when submarine activity there became dangerous, but there had been dangerous misunderstandings because there was no unity of command. Instead, there was discordant effort together with the relative impotence of the C.-in-C. Dartige recognized that commanders such as the Duke of the Abruzzi and de Robeck and the French forces directly under them should be able to develop their actions freely, but a co-ordinated effort was indispensable and liaison between the different theatres was necessary for limits had to be assigned to each, reinforcements given to one, and unnecessary ships taken from the other. Dartige recognized that he could always have recourse to the Minister of Marine's authority by asking him to intervene with foreign governments, and while awaiting the results of that intervention Dartige could try to use persuasion. But persuasion was better in time of peace than in time of war. Unfortunately everyone recognized that the French fleet in the Mediterranean formed a sort of reserve, devoted to supporting external actions, whose genesis and development escaped it until the day it would have to palliate errors for which it was not responsible but would have to bear the weight.[3] The submarine war with its potential for action throughout the entire length of the Mediterranean rather than in restricted areas was perhaps where lack of unity would be felt the most. The quest for that co-ordination and unity would be another constant throughout the war.

The immediate problem in the submarine war was the protection of troop transports. The British in home waters escorted them with small fast vessels on the scale of two destroyers for an ocean transport and one for a fast packet steamer of the Cross-Channel type. In mid-November 1915 the British claimed virtual immunity from loss with this protection. Unfortunately, the Admiralty regarded the method as feasible only where distances were comparatively short since they did not consider destroyers capable of continuous, long-distance steaming because of their light machinery and limited fuel capacity. The distances in the Mediterranean were long, with over 3,000 miles of routes to guard from Gibraltar to Mudros, with deviations to Egypt or Salonika. They had approximately twenty-two transports at sea each day which, on a northern scale of protection, would have required forty-four destroyers to escort them and an equal number as reliefs, given the length of certain passages and necessities of refuelling and boiler cleaning. Those resources simply were not available. The result was a compromise: transports were escorted through dangerous points where patrols were also provided and the routes were frequently varied. The

Admiralty also were in the process of arming all transports and vessels carrying supplies for the army and navy, but sufficient guns were not yet available.[4] The problem was complicated because few 12-pdr guns were available and the 3-pdr and 2½-pdr guns many steamers had been given were frequently outranged by the 3.4-in. guns of a submarine but, as Limpus put it, 'any gun is better than no gun' and preferably concealed, since an obviously gunned ship was more likely to attract a topedo.[5] The objective was, of course, to arm all vessels, not just transports.

The Mediterranean required more resources and with submarine activity apparently shifting from north to south the local British commanders thought that they had a good and justifiable argument. Vice-Admiral Peirse, C.-in-C. Egypt and East Indies, declared: 'Now that it is an obvious fact that their centre of activity has been shifted to the Mediterranean, it is high time we were provided with the necessary destroyers & other small craft such as have achieved success in home waters, to rid us of this pest.' Furthermore, running transports unarmed would 'be an unjustifiable risk for some time to come' as neither the French C.-in-C. nor de Robeck could provide escorts. Vice-Admiral Currey, SNO at Gibraltar, argued that seventy-two destroyers for all the Mediterranean routes were 'none too much', while Limpus in discussion with Dartige spoke of eighty to eighty-four British destroyers joined to fifty-seven French. This would not make the routes absolutely safe but could be used so as to make them 'reasonably safe' and was the number to aim at.[6] The First Sea Lord confided to Jellicoe that 'the demands on our resources are beyond our capabilities' and owing to the demands of the Salonika expedition and Dardanelles the Mediterranean transports would be employed to the end of the year carrying one quarter of a million troops 'almost unescorted'. In the latter part of November he complained: 'Everyone is screaming for destroyers, especially the French & I have to harden my heart to all such requests but they are very annoying.'[7] Jellicoe's answer to all of this was predictable: 'I confess to being quite unable to recognize the necessity for sending further ships to the Mediterranean. The whole French battle fleet is there and it seems extraordinary to me that we can't persuade the French to do their part. It was always recognized as their sphere of action', and somewhat later, regarding minesweeping sloops, 'I would, however, suggest that charity begins at home, and that we should not run, what in my opinion, is a serious risk of so weakening the Grand Fleet as to make it possible for us to lose the command of the sea in home waters for the sake of satisfying our Allies.'[8]

Dartige realized that the British had their hands full and could provide little assistance to the major French preoccupation, the protection of their troop transports on the way to Salonika. This involved some 1,600 miles of steaming from French ports and had already forced the French to reclaim the destroyers they had sent to work with the Italian fleet in the Adriatic. The incessant escort service caused considerable fatigue to the French personnel as well as material, but Dartige considered it necessary, as much for reasons of reassuring public opinion and the troops themselves as for the actual protection it afforded the transports. The French were particularly sensitive to losses after disasters such as the *Calvados*. The presence of a destroyer could at least exclude an attack on a transport by gunfire and force the submarine to act while submerged and use torpedoes which Dartige, perhaps wrongly, thought less accurate, and more correctly, harder to replace. The hard work performed since the beginning of the war had already forced many of the small number of destroyers and torpedo-boats available into the yards for repair and refit. Consequently, Dartige could not always give each vessel leaving France an escort and he complained that many of the transports left as soon as they were ready, often incompletely or poorly loaded, instead of being grouped for mutual protection. The voyage from France to Salonika took nearly a week and the French escorts were divided into three stages, with reliefs at Malta and the Doro Channel. In default of escorts the French, like the British, tried to provide indirect protection by patrolling the routes and operating against the submarines and their alleged supply bases. As a result of the pattern of sinkings, the French were particularly concerned with the channels between Crete and Greece. Dartige complained that because they had to concentrate so much of their effort on the direct protection of convoys they had to limit their offensive action against submarines and their supply bases, and also had to curtail their surveillance of the transport routes. As a result, some routes such as Gibraltar to Malta were not patrolled. Dartige warned: 'In scattering our efforts, we would risk being feeble everywhere.' He attempted to remedy the problem by sending transports on routes which were patrolled and away from dangerous areas, a measure which often added to the duration of the voyage.[9]

The loss of the *Calvados* had made a particularly strong impression on both the European and native population of Algeria. Lacaze assured the Minister of War that a new flotilla of torpedo-boats and trawlers was being sent from the north, and that henceforth all troop transports would be armed and escorted. He did point out, however, that the *Calvados* was an ordinary steamer not specially assigned to the transport of troops and the latter had been embarked without his knowledge. He asked the Ministry of War to inform him in the future of actions of this sort so that special measures could be taken.[10] The local naval commanders in Algeria, in view of the great emotion caused by the sinking, clamoured to Paris for the creation at Algiers and Oran of a flotilla centre which might be made up of worn-out destroyers and some trawlers. Lacaze replied that this would really be up to Dartige who was responsible for the direction of the patrol service in the Mediterranean, but he urged the C.-in-C. to provide some of his smaller trawlers. Dartige quickly answered that while he understood and shared the emotion produced in Algeria by recent sinkings, he could not strip one service to fill another.[11]

The obligation to provide destroyers to escort those troop transports which were insufficiently armed or not equipped with wireless required more destroyers than the French had, and threatened to wear out prematurely the relatively fragile craft the French employed, especially as bad weather arrived with the winter season. On 19 November, according to Lacaze, thirteen of the fifty-two destroyers of the 1ère Armée navale were already immobilized through breakdowns, although intensive convoying had only been in effect a relatively short time. Moreover, as Lacaze explained to the Minister of War, it was also necessary to reduce the number of ships taken from commercial service for military purposes since the supply of France's civilian needs was suffering. He did not mention that by this date Italian demands for the return of the destroyers to the Adriatic had also become pressing. Lacaze was forced into proposing a new organization for the supply of Sarrail's army which would provide sufficient security yet avoid convoys and diminish as much as possible the number of ships used. The transport of men would be completely separated from that of matériel and animals and would be accomplished by large passenger liners such as *La Provence* and *La Lorraine* which were armed as auxiliary cruisers, commanded by naval officers, provided with naval gun crews, had a minimum speed of 15 knots and were equipped with powerful wireless. They would sail alone and without escort and the six liners available would permit two departures per week carrying a total of 3,000–4,000 men. Material and animals would be carried by fifteen steamers, all armed and equipped with wireless, sailing in groups of two for mutual support. They would not be convoyed unless there was a particularly valuable cargo or military necessities would require using an unarmed ship. The measures were forced by the lack of steamers for carrying freight and the need to conserve destroyers.[12] The problem of excessive wear on destroyers was growing and Dartige reported that at the end of November, of sixty-one destroyers (including two minelayers) of the Armée navale, twenty-eight were broken down or under refit. This was a wastage of 46 per cent and was likely to increase with the intensive service imposed on them and the now frequent bad weather.[13] Dartige was so distracted that he even proposed imitating German ruthlessness by placing hostages taken from prisoner-of-war camps on French passenger liners. He claimed that 'well-fed, well-housed and well-treated, the hostages would have no reason to complain', but the French would have to take care that the number of hostages on each ship was too large to be embarked in a submarine after destruction of the liner.[14]

The submarine problem in the Mediterranean really called for co-operation between the Allies and Lacaze recognized this. On 12 November he ordered Dartige to reach an agreement with de Robeck about a general plan for patrols.[15] The result was Dartige's memorandum of 20 November which established the total of 140 British and French destroyers as necessary for patrolling the Mediterranean. Dartige had arrived at this figure by aiming at one destroyer for every 140 miles of transport routes, except for one every 40 miles in certain narrow channels such as those leading to the Aegean, and making allowance for detachments to the Adriatic and refits and breakdowns. In addition to destroyers Dartige wanted a total of 280 trawlers and small craft, allocated at 128 for British and 152 for French areas. They would work in groups of two to four searching for submarines and their supply bases in the narrow passages of the Mediterranean, the Aegean islands and along the coast of Asia Minor. Dartige admitted that the area the French had to look after was beyond their resources and that, at best, they could only man 78 trawlers or drifters leaving 202 to be provided y the British. Dartige's proposal came while de Robeck was on leave and Wemyss replied, not surprisingly, that the number of destroyers or similar raft required appeared 'prohibitive' in view of their present resources. There was little hope that the Admiralty could provide the additional seventy-five destroyers needed for the scheme when at present they had some difficulty meeting their own requirements in the Aegean. Wemyss proposed an alternative scheme which might be carried out with fewer raft. To use flotillas to their fullest advantage, an 'Admiral of Patrols' would control all patrol and search flotillas in the Mediterranean from one centre. Furthermore, since night attacks by submarines were then rare, ships would travel as much as possible by night while a system of 'safe' anchorages (that is, protected by nets) would be prepared where ships could be during daylight hours when submarine activity made this desirable. Wemyss, in forwarding his own proposal to the Admiralty, remarked that the system of convoy in his opinion was 'a very expensive method' of employing their craft and did not render their ships immune from submarine attack by torpedo although it certainly increased the difficulties of attack. He cited the example of the *Dublin* recently torpedoed in the Adriatic although escorted by six destroyers.[16] The system of 'safe' anchorages would, in fact, be adopted in desperation some time later, but by the time Wemyss's report reached London the Allies had already taken a first bumbling step towards dividing the Mediterranean coasts into zones at a conference in Paris.

The purpose of the conference which began on 29 November was to seek means of collaborating in the hunt for submarines. Captain H. W. Grant, the British delegate, did not arrive until the afternoon of 2 December and found that the French and Italians had already drawn up a chart of their respective zones of surveillance to submit to their governments. Grant had the impression that the patrols and zones envisaged by the French and Italians were entirely coastal with the sole objective of trying to find submarine bases and possibly intercepting submarines when they returned to resupply. The agreement concluded on 3 December divided the Mediterranean coast into eighteen patrol zones of which four were British, four were Italian, and ten were French. The divisions were fairly obvious. The Italian zones were adjacent to their own coasts and islands or Libyan colony; the British zones were also adjacent to their possessions – Gibraltar, Malta and Egypt, plus the Dardanelles – and the remainder of the Mediterranean coastal zones, including the Ionian Islands, were French. The limits were not to be too strictly adhered to and in the unassigned areas outside the patrol zones each nation should allot the requisitioned vessels it could provide for control, the French to the west of Malta and the British to the east.[17]

The other important result of the conference was an agreement on abbreviated wireless signals concerning submarines. These included the sign 'SOS–SOS–SOS–SSSS' repeated three times, followed by co-ordinates and the name of the ship. This indicated that the latter had been attacked by submarine and had stopped and requested help. There were variations of the basic signal to indicate that the ship was being chased by a submarine and requested help. The other signal, and one that would become widespread, was the 'ALLO' signal followed by co-ordinates which indicated that a submarine had been seen.[18] Every twelve hours the major wireless stations in the Mediterranean would transmit bulletins summarizing the information received. These would, at least in theory, warn merchant ships away from the areas where submarines were reported to be operating.

The December 1915 Mediterranean agreement caused dissatisfaction and revealed grave flaws even before it went into effect. Keyes complained 'They made a ridiculous convention in France . . . it is simply futile and impractical.' Keyes and his ally on de Robeck's staff, Captain Godfrey, drafted a telegram 'pointing out how rotten the scheme is and suggesting an alteration' which de Robeck, perhaps wisely, toned down. The core of the complaint was that 'experience gained in working with the French showed that the zones should be considerably larger and allotted as far as possible to facilitate rapid wireless communication'. The proposed division of the zones in the Aegean would have had the opposite effect, and unfortunately wireless communication between the British and French 'has always been unreliable'. If zones were larger it would be easier to quickly reinforce the patrol in any area temporarily threatened by enemy submarines. De Robeck even suggested that if the small craft were available the British should assume responsibility for the whole of the Aegean, thereby giving them unbroken control from Salonika to Egypt. The Admiralty quickly squelched this proposal for it would necessitate very large modifications in other parts of the Mediterranean and lead to much discussion and long delay. They could ask the French and Italians for modifications 'if after sufficient trial it proves a failure'. A disgusted Keyes commented, 'I wonder how many lost ships, transports, etc. equal experience! We always must pay for our experience.'[19]

Dartige also had problems with the agreement. He worried about the British enclave at Malta creating a duality of command. Moreover, since he was obliged to remain at Malta in order to be as close as possible to both the Adriatic and the Aegean, he found himself surrounded by a zone where the command did not belong to him. Dartige complained that his authority as C.-in-C. was only a word which did not respond to any serious reality. The role allotted to Italy also troubled him for the zones attributed to the Italians were vast given the relative poverty of Italian resources. The Italians with a fleet far superior to the Austrians had not been able to effectively watch the Adriatic and were constantly asking for assistance from their Allies. How then could they fulfil their obligations in the other zones allotted to them? Dartige wondered if, once again, the Italians would need the assistance of their Allies. If so, the latter ought to have command.[20]

It was perhaps fortunate that Limpus and Dartige, as they both acknowledged, had a good working arrangement and that Limpus, perhaps benefiting from experience with the diplomatic necessities of his prior service with the Ottoman navy, apparently had the knack for avoiding potentially awkward situations. Limpus found that with Dartige 'a little judicious "suggesting" beforehand paves the way for Dartige to agree the more easily to what one wants. In fact he sometimes comes to regard thing

his own ideas – and that is better still!'[21] Limpus probably needed all his
plomatic finesse, for Dartige was inclined to be suspicious of the British,
ith good reason. In reading the Admiralty orders to Limpus he was struck
y the absence of the words 'Commander-in-Chief of Allied Fleets in the
lediterranean' and the sole prerogative left to him was to fix the
commended routes for transports, without having the means to control
e effectiveness of the surveillance in the Italian or British zones or in the
n-delimited zone to the east of Malta. Moreover, even his only
erogative was reduced by the latitude left to the respective Allied
mmanders to change the prescribed itineraries within their zones after
tifying the C.-in-C. De Robeck's proposal to expand the proposed
itish zone in the Aegean only confirmed Dartige's suspicions and he
fused.[22]

Dartige really doubted that effective collaboration between two different
vies was possible in the same zone. On 8 February he wrote that
perience had shown that it was essential to have not only unity of views
t also unity of methods of action. No matter how loyal the support he
d de Robeck gave to each other, the differences between the nature
ractère) of the British and French officers and men were too deep for the
me work to be fruitfully followed in parallel in the same region. If he did
t have sufficient strength to effectively patrol the zones given to him,
artige would prefer to turn them over entirely to their allies rather than to
ntinue to operate simultaneously but separately at the same points.[23]
artige was not, of course, totally wrong in his suspicions about the British
d at this stage of the war it was difficult for the British and French to
erate together, although commanders on both sides had a tendency to
come exasperated with their respective ally and his methods with perhaps
cessive speed. Given these perceptions, however, it is easy to see why
lied co-operation in the Mediterranean during the 1914–18 war was never
ry easy.

Dartige had a number of other questions concerning the Paris agreement
nging from wireless transmission procedures to a proposal to declare the
tire Mediterranean a War Zone and strictly control the movements of
utral vessels. The latter proposal was at least partially motivated by
artige's almost pathological suspicion of the Dutch and the assistance he
ought that they might be providing to German submarines.[24] Limpus,
o, had his problems working with a plan 'made with very scant or no
ference to the Admirals on the spot', but was pragmatic in his approach
d concluded: 'However, there it is and the only thing to do is to take it
d try and work it as well as we can, and introduce some very necessary
odifications as we go along.' Limpus did not intend to stress the
odifications in correspondence with the Admiralty; he would 'simply
range to do them with the other Admirals as they became possible'.[25]
caze preferred a different approach and took the initiative for a formal
nference to meet at Malta under Dartige's direction with the objective of
hieving unity of effort for the common purpose. The agenda for the
nference expanded after the suggestions of the other admirals to include
bjects beyond the question of the zones. These included the establishment

of a plan of action in case of certain contingencies, such as action by th
Austrian or German fleet, and the organization of an intelligence network.[2]

The British were not enthusiastic about the prospect of yet anothe
conference and anti-French sentiment, stimulated by annoyance over th
Salonika expedition, seemed to be running high at the Admiralty. Jackso
wrote de Robeck:

> I'm sorry to drag you to a joint conference at Malta. It is due to th
> French Minister of Marine Admiral Lacaze, a man full of words, who see
> they have taken on a great deal more than they can do efficiently, but wh
> wants all the 'commands' he can get hold of. The bottom of it all is tha
> he wants us to put our light craft under the French C.-in-C. & we are jus
> as determined not to do it. Of course this does not appear on the surface
> The French are a great trial at present. Their politicians have th
> whiphand of ours, & the naval & military heads would like to do the sam
> but we don't let them. They are thoughtless & excitable & don't seem t
> possess more brains than our people, & won't stick at a thing like w
> generally do however well they may fight their ships. I see you find you
> opposite number at Salonika rather a trial too.[27]

Limpus was also brutally frank in telling the First Sea Lord of his ow
aims and strategy for the forthcoming conference at Malta:

> . . . I am convinced also that gallant, spirited and charming as ou
> French Allies are, they are 25 years behind us in hard, practical, dogge
> sea patrol work. They will never learn in a year how to do it. We mus
> therefore do the business part, that is Malta to Egypt and Egypt t
> Salonika, *ourselves*, while all the time humouring their susceptibilitie
> making our own patrol schemes and work them ourselves, carefull
> 'suggesting' what we are doing to the Commander-in-Chief so that he
> under the impression that . . . in accordance with the original conventio
> the British exercise command in the North, the French provide th
> general command in the Mediterranean and delegate this little sidesho
> here to us 'uns, and there to the Italians, and so forth. But all the tim
> with smoothness and with constant deference.
>
> The blunt point is that we have the *men* (officers) who can do patre
> work, and though we may be, and are, pressed to find a real sufficiency
> small fast sea keeping craft, yet we *can* manage the areas allotted to us an
> they can *not* for want of both the craft and the alert, sea bitten men t
> handle them.
>
> But it is very important while we do it, to say smooth, nice things t
> them, to keep them in good humour with themselves and with us, in fa
> to play the extremely difficult game of working efficiently and loyal
> and with full friendliness nominally under the people who have not y
> acquired the capacity to do it themselves.[28]

Limpus somewhat later added the remark: 'As to the Italians, they a
children at the game of the sea compared to the French.' Given the
sentiments, or perhaps because of Limpus's tactic of blatant flattery, it
remarkable that the Malta Conference would come off as well as it did. It

also important to see certain things in their proper perspective. Limpus may have been critical of the French but his own ideas about anti-submarine warfare would not stand the test of time either. Limpus wanted to make the transport routes as simple, close together and direct as possible, thickly patrolled with 'packs of hounds', with a pack of six to work west of Malta, another pack of six to work between Malta and Crete, and a pack of six to work between Crete and Egypt. With the three 'packs of hounds' added to the ordinary patrols, Limpus thought that submarines 'ought to have very little chance of doing any harm on the transport route'. Oliver criticized Limpus's ideas about denying the littoral to enemy submarines as subscribing to the 'fallacy' that submarines needed secret bases; but his major worry was that Limpus's talk of 'packs of hounds' would give a false impression that larger numbers of small craft would be sent to the Mediterranean than those already provided, for they were 'down to bed rock at home'.[29]

At the same time as the Malta Conference was taking shape the British were wrestling with another problem concerning the Mediterranean. This involved the diversion of traffic from the Mediterranean route around the Cape of Good Hope. The Admiralty had proceeded very cautiously on the subject. On 11 December Captain Richard Webb, Director of Trade Division, replied to a query from Sir Aubrey Brocklebank of the Anchor–Brocklebank line concerning the advisability of diverting Calcutta-bound liners to the Cape route. Without giving any definite reply, Webb pointed out that if a large number of vessels were diverted to the Cape route a very considerable increase in tonnage would be required to carry the same quantity of cargo which would, in turn, have a serious effect on freight generally and raise the additional question of the supply of bunker coal on the Cape route. Webb did not think it would be desirable at present to divert 'a large number' of vessels to the Cape route, but 'would be in the general interest' if vessels with specially valuable cargoes from Australia, the Far East and east coast of India went via the Cape.[30] The Board of Trade also became interested in the question and Mr Hipwood of their marine department began regular discussions with Commander Fisher of the Admiralty Trade Division. Both soon found that the question was more complex than they had at first supposed. They tended to be against a general diversion but in favour of diverting the Australian and Far Eastern trade. The issue reached crisis proportions with the sinking of the P & O liner *Persia* at the end of the year. The Orient Company wanted to divert their own ships around the Cape and gave the reasonable argument that the increased time involved was inconsiderable while the loss of a valuable ship would be irreparable.[31] The issue was discussed at a conference at the Admiralty on 18 January with representatives from shipping companies, the War Office, the Commonwealth of Australia and the India Office.[32] Given the mass of complications which accompanied the decision, Captain Webb must have smiled wryly if he had but half a sense of humour at the letter from one of the British shipping companies which asked plaintively, 'Cannot the Navy make the Mediterranean rather more safe—:—this would be much the best solution'.[33] The final outcome of all these discussions, however, was the notice issued by the Admiralty through the Liverpool and London War Risks Insurance Association that on or after 15 March 1916 vessels proceeding to or from Atlantic ports and ports in the Far East or Australia would take the Cape route while those proceeding to or from ports in India would continue to use the Suez Canal.[34] The measure only applied to vessels using the Mediterranean as a highway to the Suez Canal and on long voyages where diversion to the Cape involved proportionately less of an increase in time. Nevertheless, it was a first significant step which would be expanded at the end of the year and in a sense represented a notable success for the German submarine campaign.

The Malta Conference which opened on 2 March was the largest conference to take place in the Mediterranean up to that time. Limpus and de Robeck were the senior British officers present, for Wemyss had been detained in Egypt because of the operations around Sollum against the Senussi, and since only a few questions on the agenda concerned Egypt and the East Indies station he contented himself with sending his Flag Commander.[35] The distant Senior Naval Officer, Gibraltar, was not represented at all. Dartige presided with Gauchet, commanding the 4ème Escadre in the Aegean, and Moreau, commanding the 3ème Escadre on the Syrian coast, representing the major French commands in the Mediterranean. Rear-Admiral Pini, Sub-Chief of Naval Staff, represented Italy. By the time the conference opened even de Robeck, who was assumed to have been reluctantly dragged away from his command, was anxious for it to begin. He wrote to Limpus: 'I wish this conference would come off & clear the air, the French or rather Gauchet is becoming very impossible . . . the French W/T [wireless] is now a positive danger & they don't appear to be taking any steps to improve it.' On the question of patrol zones, de Robeck argued: 'Our friends issue wonderful orders which if carried out would be excellent, but they have not the craft & also what craft they have got, spend far too long in harbour.' De Robeck blamed the French for the loss of the transport *Royal Edward* the past summer when they failed to patrol a route they had promised to, and concluded: 'We shall have to speak very plainly to the French, it is no good being all smiles. Their present government want to take charge everywhere & in order to entitle them to do so at sea, they must do far more work!'[36] Limpus agreed: 'We must persuade the French C.-in-C. that *he* wants to reduce this [?] W/T roar to a minimum', while on the question of patrols he added, 'I hope we shall get him to want a British line of patrols right through to mine on the one side & to Wemyss' on the other'.[37]

During the conference the Allied admirals, with Dartige presiding, agreed with little difficulty to a revision of the Mediterranean zones substantially along the lines de Robeck had suggested. The zones were enlarged and reduced in number from eighteen to eleven. The large unassigned area in the eastern basin disappeared, most of it going to the British, except for an extension of the French area in the Ionian. The British also assumed control of most of the Aegean including Crete, with the French adding the coast of Greece south of the Doro Channel and the islands west of Syria. The Italian area was left unchanged, especially since

Pini, the Italian delegate, had admitted that at the moment the Italians could not effectively patrol their four zones since they needed seventy-six patrol craft for the job and only had fifty.[38]

There were also two methods for protecting the routes, escorting and patrolling. The admirals claimed that experience had condemned the former for it had resulted in rapidly breaking down the light craft used for the purpose and could only be effective as long as the convoying ship had only two vessels to look after. Limpus pointed out that the number of Allied vessels circulating each day in the Mediterranean was 'infinitely greater' than the number of small ships which could be detailed to escort them. For example, on the average day there were more than 100 British ships at sea on government charter and as many as 50 had sailed from Malta in one day. Therefore they could ordinarily protect vessels only by patrolling routes, with the use of escorts reserved for special cases. The admirals considered that Allied forces in the Mediterranean were not sufficient to ensure the desired security and should be increased. A large proportion of that increase should be used for strengthening the barrages at Gibraltar and Otranto, and the remainder for increasing the density of patrols on the routes.[39]

On the question of the routes themselves, the admirals agreed that they should be altered when necessary, but to avoid delays and complications recommended having a certain number of routes prepared in advance for each journey and lettered 'A', 'B', 'C', etc. The C.-in-C. could then simply order a ship to follow, for example, route 'B' from point to point. When possible the different routes should be at least thirty miles apart. On de Robeck's recommendation, the conference agreed on a single route both coming and going, with ships to move out five miles to starboard at night or in thick weather. The admirals agreed that 'a Naval Authority who would understand the importance of these recommendations should be appointed in all the Allied Ports for the duty of informing ships what route they should follow' and captains of Allied ships for their own safety would be advised to follow the prescribed routes which were the only ones patrolled and guarded, and those routes were to be kept as secret as possible.[40]

The Malta Conference also devoted a considerable amount of time to the contingency of German and Austrian surface action. The disagreement between Gauchet and his colleagues was most evident on this question, especially over the subject of what force was to be left to guard Salonika. Pini could not give absolute assurances that the Austrian fleet would not be able to get through the Straits of Otranto before they were intercepted by the Italians. The conference accordingly recommended that the French fleet shift its base from Malta to Argostoli where it would be in a better position to intercept them. This was indeed a hypothetical question and in the long run far less important than the submarine problem, but the conference gave much time to this and other purely theoretical questions involving possible surface action by the Germans and Austrians.[41] The discussion of actions to take if the German fleet came down to the Mediterranean is of interest from the point of view of a naval war game. It had little basis in reality. The admirals also discussed a wide range of technical subjects, such as wireless

traffic, but the decisions concerning patrolled routes and zones were th
most important.[42]

The Malta Conference set the ground rules for the conduct of the Allie
naval war in the Mediterranean for the next year. Dartige thought that th
conference had been fruitful. He did not know what the results of th
recommendations by the Allied admirals would be and was realistic enough t
note that nearly all involved obtaining reinforcements for the Mediterranean
Nevertheless, the Allied admirals had at least got to know one another an
many exchanges of views had had an immediate result, they were able t
settle many questions on the spot, and many misunderstandings wer
dispelled.[43] Limpus was also convinced that the conference had been o
considerable value, and not merely for the formal conclusions an
recommendations. In a classic evaluation of what an international meetin
of this sort could accomplish he wrote:

> Not only did the Admirals meet and talk informally and get to knov
> one another, but their staffs, especially their Intelligence and W/T
> officers, saw a good deal of one another; and though it would be to
> much to say that 'especial national aspirations' were entirely subordinatec
> or, to use a rougher term, that international jealousies and mistrusts wer
> entirely cleared away, it is a fortunate fact that a good many rough angle
> and sharp corners were adjusted.[44]

The role of the Italians at the conference had been relatively limited
Limpus thought that Admiral Pini was 'rather inclined to hold up his hand
when any suggestion was made involving either action on a large scale o
the provision of any fresh aid by the Italian Government', while de Robecl
interpreted his role as 'only anxious for the conference to realise that it wa
impossible for the Italians to do anything'.[45] The British ambassador i
Rome, Sir James Rennell Rodd, had been even more blunt in his language
Rodd declared: 'the trouble is that Italy *thinks* she is a great power but i
nothing of the sort' and they must 'not count on her for great things, bu
she is really trying to do the little that she can'.[46]

Pini and Dartige had tried to use the conference to meet privately in orde
to smooth over some of those 'rough angles' that Limpus had spoken of
The problems included the status of Capitaine de vaisseau de Cacqueray
commander of the French destroyers at Brindisi, who had complained of hi
treatment by the local Italian commander. De Cacqueray had difficult
getting permission to take out his destroyers for exercises and was kept ir
the dark and not consulted on plans for Adriatic operations. Pini had th
impression that de Cacqueray was well thought of in the French navy an
resembled a racehorse who needed special treatment in order to yield all h
was capable of. The private talk was effective, for even before he ha
learned of Dartige's intervention with Pini, de Cacqueray reported that hi
situation had improved significantly.[47] The improvement, unfortunately
was only temporary.

The Admiralty approved the new zones on 20 March. When Limpus me
Lacaze on his way home he found him anxious for British assistance
notably small fast craft. The British could do little more than promise tha

hey were sending new sloops to the Mediterranean as fast as the vessels
became available from their builders. Lacaze had also been 'most nervous'
about the Austrians slipping into the Black Sea. The Russians had
repeatedly issued warnings about a move by the Austrian fleet since the
beginning of the war and Lacaze was anxious to follow the suggestion of the
conference to move the French fleet's base to a position where it would be
better placed to intercept the Austrians. Lacaze even proposed yet another
conference, which some of the British including Limpus considered a waste
of time. De Robeck wrote that once the French battle fleet was established at
Argostoli 'there should be little anxiety as regards movements of the
Austrian fleet'.[48]

De Robeck's Eastern Mediterranean Squadron was in the process of being
steadily reduced after the Dardanelles campaign. The First Sea Lord put it
very plainly in a private letter:

> We are very much worried indeed with mines & submarines round our
> coast & want all the small craft we can get & shall have to commandeer
> your 2 'L' [class] T.B.D.s The Army people here say they don't want
> help at Salonika & we are not in a position at home to offer to do anything
> for anybody else abroad, so you must really work on that basis and
> anything not really essential for holding the islands, hunting submarines
> & holding the exit of the Dardanelles should be returned to us at home
> where we can use everything that floats or can move.[49]

As a result of the recommendations of the conference Dartige was faced
with the prospect of changing his base. He had inclined towards Corfu but
on the recommendations of his allies finally opted for a base further to the
south and better situated for intercepting the Austrian fleet. His choice lay
between Argostoli on the island of Cephalonia or Navarino on the mainland
of Greece. Dartige, like de Robeck, favoured Argostoli since it was
probably healthier than Navarino and at Navarino their cable communications would be in the hands of the Greeks. Oliver also presented a
memorandum to the French giving strong British support to the recommendation of the conference for Argostoli. The preparation of the base,
notably the accumulation of the extensive but necessary nets, took time.
Dartige intended to reduce French patrols in the Aegean and shift more of
the French effort to the Ionian to establish a barrage to link up with the
British drifters to the north of Otranto, and also patrol the Greek coast and
islands up to Cerigo. He still thought that they would have to net Corfu in
the future for the fleet would be immobilized at Argostoli and needed the
large harbour of Corfu for ships to exercise and continue their training.[50]
Dartige knew that he had to leave Malta and not merely because of the
threat of the Austrian fleet. The British, despite what he described as their
habitual courtesy, did not hide the fact that they considered the harbour
much too crowded, especially with dreadnoughts for which there were only
limited number of moorings. Moreover, at Malta the French could not
conduct any training exercises and Dartige feared that the officers and men
would grow stale.[51]

The major portion of the French fleet moved to Argostoli during April

1916, and by the end of the month Dartige reported that the base was completely installed and protected, at least as well as the means at their disposal permitted. Dartige was pleasantly surprised by the extent of the harbour and he concluded that they could perform more exercises than at Malta, if not as many as they would have been able to do at Corfu. The Corfu Channel, however, once barrages had been established between the mainland and the northern and southern extremities of the island, was used for training by the French battleship squadrons starting in the month of July. The redeployment of the French fleet coincided with a major maritime operation, the transfer of the reformed and re-equipped Serbian army from Corfu to Salonika, a voyage of approximately 550 miles around the Peloponnese. The movement began on 12 April and was largely undertaken by the French, assisted by the British, and after the usual haggling, the Italians. The troops moved in closely escorted convoys and when the operation ended on 30 May over 125,000 men had been safely transported.[52]

There was one recommendation by the admirals at Malta that was not implemented. This concerned an Allied declaration of the Mediterranean a a 'war zone' together with taking control of postal and telegraphic communications at Salonika, Mudros, Mytilene and Corfu. Lacaze strongly supported the measure but Briand and the French Foreign Office had doubts about such a general declaration, based on the reaction by neutrals to similar declarations by the British and Germans concerning the North Sea earlier in the war which conflicted with the principle of freedom of the seas Briand suggested that more specific police measures as a control over neutrals might be more opportune.[53] The Italians also turned out to be against it. Italy, unlike Britain and France, was totally dependent on the Mediterranean for its maritime communications, and the proposed measure almost certainly would provoke protests from neutrals like the United States as well as Spain and Greece. Furthermore, by creating difficulties for navigation, the measure would diminish the number of ships visiting the Mediterranean and thereby raise the cost of freight to the detriment of Italy The Italians suggested other measures, such as placing an Allied supercargo aboard the neutral ships at Suez or Gibraltar and issuing special passes Sonnino told the French ambassador that the moment was badly chosen to arouse the susceptibilities of the Americans now that a break in German-American relations was possible in the aftermath of the *Sussex* incident. But according to Barrère, Sonnino did not hide the fact that his real concern was over causing difficulties to neutral shipping, for the Italian problem of inadequate freight and shipping space was far from solved. Sonnino also claimed that he was experiencing difficulty obtaining support from Britain and that the coal situation was extremely precarious. In the light of the Italian reaction, the British Foreign Office saw serious objections to the proposal and asked the French Government to reconsider the suggestion of the Allied admirals and French C.-in-C.[54] The proposal to declare the Mediterranean a 'war zone' was dead for the moment.

Just a few days before the Malta Conference opened the French had experienced one of their worst disasters of the war. On 26 February Kapitänleutnant von Arnauld de la Perière, in command of U35, torpedoed and sank south of Cape Matapan the auxiliary cruiser *Provence II* (13,753 tons) which was carrying more than 2,000 troops to Salonika. The *Provence*, one of the Cie Générale Transatlantique's fast liners, was travelling without escort and, well armed, had been one of the ships that Lacaze had chosen to transport troops to Salonika. The *Provence* after being hit took on an immediate and severe list and many of the lifeboats could not be used. The resulting loss of life was heavy, close to 1,000.[55] Lacaze answered the inevitable question from the Ministry of War, namely, from a military point of view the loss of the *Provence* still did not appear to justify modifying the measures adopted for transporting troops to Salonika. He could not assure the army that danger to navigation in the Mediterranean was only momentary for it was a consequence of the length of their lines of communication. The Naval Staff had always told the army at conferences that if auxiliary cruisers used as transports had nothing to fear from attack by cannon, they were exposed like all ships no matter how fast or powerful to a lucky torpedo from a well-placed submarine. Destroyers were ineffective in protecting fast armed liners since the slightest bad weather obliged them to abandon their attempt to keep up. Lacaze therefore saw augmenting the patrols as the only military remedy for the present state of things. He offered, given the small number of men left to transport and the need to avoid the effects on morale that an accident involving a large number of human lives would cause, to embark only 1,000 men per voyage in the auxiliary cruisers. The best solution would be transport by rail from France to southern Italy and from Patras to Salonika, limiting the journey by sea to the stretch from southern Italy to Patras.[56] But horrible as the loss of the *Provence* was, it actually came at a moment when German submarine activities in the Mediterranean and the losses they caused were far lower than they had been in the last quarter of 1915. The respite was caused by a lack of submarines at sea due to the large number under refit, poor weather, and the restrictive orders against sinking passenger liners. This relief was destined not to last beyond the first quarter of 1916 and Arnauld in the U35 would be a particular scourge to Allied shipping. The self-satisfied pronouncements of Dartige and Limpus over the Malta Conference concealed the fact that in their actual discussions the Allied admirals were on the wrong track when it came to facing the submarine problem. They were talking of thickening patrols on the recommended routes and strengthening barrages. With, of course, the benefit of hindsight, we know that these were not the measures to reduce the submarine menace.

The Successful 1916 U-Boat Campaign in the Mediterranean

Korvettenkapitän Kophamel, commander of the German U-boat flotilla in the Mediterranean, attributed the general lack of success by German submarines in the month of March 1916 to the fact that the single large submarine available for operations at the beginning of the month, U33, had been detached by the Admiralstab to the Black Sea.[57] It was only towards the end of the month on the 20th that Arnauld was able to sail with U35 once again and on the 23rd sank the British transport *Minneapolis* (13,543 tons) in the central Mediterranean. It was, however, his only success. This relative lack of activity may have caused a certain optimism on the part of the Allies during and just after the Malta Conference, but in April the total of sinkings rose sharply once again. Furthermore, the German submarine force in the Mediterranean was reinforced by the large minelayer U73 (Kapitänleutnant Siess) which laid a row of mines off Malta on its way to Cattaro that claimed the battleship *Russell* and sloop *Nasturtium* on 27 April and the armed yacht *Aegusa* on the 28th. To offset these gains, the Germans lost the minelayer UC12 which blew up on her own mines off Taranto. The first of the improved UBII boats under construction at Pola also began to enter service, UB42 on 23 March, UB43 on 24 April and UB44 on 11 May, but initially they had little success.[58] The weight of the submarine campaign was carried on by the handful of large submarines under crack commanders, U35 (Arnauld), U39 (Forstmann), U34 (Rücker) and U21 (Hersing). The vast majority of sinkings were in the western portion of the Mediterranean, and mostly, but not exclusively, in zones which were French or Italian responsibility. The measures for the protection of those large areas, full of rich targets for submarines, were therefore revealed very quickly after the Malta Conference to be inadequate.

The blockade of the Straits of Otranto was not a serious barrier to submarines either. An Austrian officer, Linienschiffsleutnant Gaston Vio, reported on his experiences during a cruise with Forstmann in U39 in May and June. The submarine had passed through the Straits of Otranto in good weather on a clear moonlit night. They had indeed spotted ten trawlers either standing still or moving very slowly, but Forstmann elected to break through at high speed on the surface between the two central groups of trawlers. The latter had apparently spotted the submarine and from the heavy smoke they began making probably tried to follow, but thanks to the submarine's high speed they were soon left far behind. U39's return after the cruise was a bit more difficult. This time the submarine was obliged to submerge and raise her periscope every hour. Each time during the day they saw a group of three trawlers and a destroyer. The submarine got through on the surface at night, but at one point had to submerge when a destroyer approached. Vio surmised that the British and Italians had recognized that the attempt to block the straits through a line of nets was not effective, and had attempted to patrol the surface so as to force a submarine to remain under water and exhaust its battery. He thought that the British and Italians could achieve this by expanding the surface area they patrolled. Forstmann noted in his log that he had been compelled to remain under water for twelve hours and he did not think it out of the question that the patrols would eventually be expanded further to the north and south causing serious difficulties for a submarine. The cruise itself, from 16 May to 6 June had been one of the most successful of the war and Forstmann claimed 21 ships (9 British, 10 Italian, 1 Norwegian and 1 Spanish) representing 52,812 tons. U39 had expended only five torpedoes and five explosive charges, but fired 365 rounds of 8.8-cm ammunition. The particularly high consumption of shells was undoubtedly due to an eighteen-minute bombardment o 'ortoferraio (Elba), but Vio reported that Forstmann had generally elected o destroy ships by shell fire while surfaced during daylight hours, but >referred to use explosive charges at night so that the flash of gunfire and :xplosions would not attract patrols.[59]

The picture in regard to the Otranto blockade was not clear, however. Dn 13 July, Kophamel related that recently returned boats reported a very :trong watch in the Straits of Otranto which had endangered them, and that 1e repeatedly asked the Austrian staff if Austrian warships could raid it. Nevertheless, an Austrian officer, Linienschiffsleutnant Dürrigl, who had iccompanied UB46 on its cruise from 19 July to 12 August, reported >assing through the Straits of Otranto on the surface both coming and ;oing without any disturbance by enemy patrols.[60] Obviously, it was a /ery uneven situation. The actual results for the second quarter of 1916 are hown in Table 7.2.[61]

Table 7.2   *Shipping Losses due to Submarines, April–June 1916*

	Sunk by Mediterranean U-Boat Flotilla		Sunk by Submarine-laid Mines		Total (All Theatres)
	Ships	Tonnage	Ships	Tonnage	Tonnage
Apr. 1916	18	51,186	2	4,822	187,307
May 1916	37	72,092	—	—	119,381
June 1916	43	67,125	—	—	87,293

Although by the summer of 1916 sinkings in the Mediterranean once gain represented a major proportion of all ships sunk by submarines, the ;erman conduct of a sustained *Handelskrieg* against Allied shipping in the Mediterranean was constantly threatened by demands for a diversion of ubmarines to other purposes, notably operations in the Black Sea and ssistance to the Senussi in North Africa. The Senussi invasion of Egypt vas defeated by the British and by the end of March the Senussi had been orced back from Sollum. Enver Pasha, backed by the German Army ;eneral Staff, was anxious for the Germans to transport men, matériel and oodstuffs to Libya. Kophamel, backed by the Admiralstab, was reluctant or both strategic and technical reasons.[62]

Freyberg also received urgent pleas from Hilmi Pasha, the Turkish mbassador in Vienna. Freyberg had his own suggestion about helping the 'enussi and this involved playing the Austrian card. He wondered if it vould be possible to obtain a small Adriatic steamer, or perhaps a schooner, o attempt the trip to North Africa. The Admiralstab had considered the ossibility of sending a steamer out of the Adriatic but did not think that here was any prospect of success as long as Valona was not in their hands, owever they had no objection to Freyberg raising the subject with the Austrians.[63] Freyberg promptly approached Rear-Admiral von Keil, flag fficer appointed to the Marinesektion. Keil spoke of the steamer *Graf Wurmbrand* (952 tons) belonging to Tripcovich & Company which was urrently at Sebenico. This steamer was especially suitable because of its comparatively low profile which might permit it to slip through the Allied patrols unnoticed. A few days later the plan collapsed when Admiral Keil learned more about the *Graf Wurmbrand*. The steamer could carry around 300 tons of supplies but its normal speed was only 11 knots, its maximum 15. Unfortunately, at 11 knots its endurance was around 70 hours or 770 miles. As the distance to North Africa from the Adriatic was approximately 750 miles, the *Graf Wurmbrand* would not have had much margin for error, or even sufficient fuel if she had to steam at a less economical speed in order to escape Allied patrols. Moreover, it could only be a one-way voyage since there would be no way to provide the ship with coal for the return voyage. The *Graf Wurmbrand* was therefore out of the question and the Austrians claimed that they did not have any other steamer that was suitable for the mission.[64] Once again a plan to use Austrian ships outside the Adriatic was frustrated through the lack of technical means.

The actual mission was finally undertaken by Hersing with U21, which sailed from Pola on 10 April carrying Oberleutnant Freiherr von Todenwarth, four Turkish officers and NCOs, arms and munitions, and a wireless set. Hersing had orders to operate against shipping after landing the mission. U21 failed in the first attempts to land the party at several places because of heavy surf and a lack of understanding with local leaders, and Hersing returned to operations along the shipping lanes, but without success. He eventually returned to the coast and futilely tried to establish communications with the shore. Hersing returned again to operations against shipping, but when he returned to Cattaro with the Todenwarth party still aboard on 4 May he had only bagged one ship and the Admiralstab had an understandable reluctance towards missions of this sort in the future.[65]

Once again the Sektion Politik of the Army General Staff played the major role in prodding the navy with various schemes, generally impractical, but this time the German Foreign Office added its weight to the requests.[66] The mission was eventually carried out by U39 before proceeding to her operational area in the western Mediterranean. U39 sailed on 5 July with von Todenwarth and a seven-man mission as well as war material. This time they landed successfully. Kophamel had the impression that the missions sent by the Turks were pointless if they did not establish a permanent regular communication, and since this was not possible he asked the Admiralstab to deny all further requests for transport by submarine to North Africa. He personally did not believe that von Todenwarth would ever return and his mission appeared hopeless, but naturally he was obliged to ask for a submarine to be ready to pick him up from the beginning to the middle of October.[67]

Enver Pasha had other requests of the German navy. On 9 May he appealed for assistance against the Russian advance and threat of new Russian landings on the Turkish Black Sea coast. Turkish artillery could no match the heavy guns of the Russian fleet and the Turkish Minister of War once again appealed for the Austrian fleet to try and break through to the Dardanelles. This old project, which the Russians feared, therefore came up again. Souchon, from his vantage point in Constantinople, considered the breakthrough of an Austrian naval force expedient only if it included at least three large battleships and a flotilla of light craft for protection against submarines. Souchon was experienced enough by now to realize that any move of the sort was out of the question, and the use of such a force if it even reached Constantinople – and it was a big if – was problematical because of the lack of coal. From the surviving records, the Germans this time do not appear to have even mentioned the scheme to the Austrians. Submarines were therefore the only possible naval assistance that the Germans could provide, but the sole large German submarine at Constantinople, U33, was under repair at the time. Souchon claimed that the last cruise of U33 had shown submarine successes in the Black Sea were possible only by chance, and the four small UB boats at Constantinople were not suited for operations in the distant eastern portion of the Black Sea. He proposed directing some of the new BII boats to Constantinople when they were ready and, if feasible, sending a large submarine as a temporary reinforcement. Falkenhayn added his weight to the request for more U-boats in the Black Sea and the Admiralstab finally agreed to send U38 under the redoubtable Valentiner. They ordered him to make his presence known in the eastern Mediterranean, presumably to draw Allied patrols from the western and central portions, before proceeding to Hersingstand to pick up a pilot for the tricky passage through the Dardanelles minefields. His stay in the Black Sea would only be temporary, for the Admiralstab intended U38 to return to Pola once the new UB42 had worked up and was able to reach Constantinople.[68] They also intended UB43, the second of the UBII class, to follow as soon as its work-up period was over, while the large U33 would return to Pola from Constantinople when its repairs were completed. If the situation in the Black Sea required it, the Admiralstab were ready to send out yet a third UBII boat (UB44).[69]

U38's stay in the Black Sea turned out to be far longer than expected. By the time Valentiner's relief reached the Aegean renewed Allied mining activity had made the Dardanelles too dangerous for a submarine to pass. UB42 had to return to Pola after topping up with fuel at Hersingstand. UB42 had achieved no successes on the fruitless cruise to and from the Dardanelles, while Valentiner during U38's period of operations in the Black Sea sank only four ships (c. 4,968 tons) and U33 sank only one ship (5,350 tons). Compared with the rich possibilities in the Mediterranean, operations in the Black Sea were clearly a loss as far as *Handelskrieg* was concerned, especially as losses inflicted on the Russians would have less effect than those on the principal enemy, Britain, in the overall strategic picture. U38 was not able to leave Constantinople for Pola until 11 August, and U33, under long repair, did not leave Constantinople until 15 November and had no successes on its cruise to Pola. UB42 finally reached Constantinople on 16 August while UB44 sailed from Cattaro on 4 August but never reached Hersingstand. Its fate is unknown. A second UBII boat, UB45, arrived at Constantinople on 12 August and a third, UB46, on 7 October. Their accomplishments in the Black Sea were relatively meagre. On the other hand, the Black Sea turned out to be a comparatively unhealthy place for submarines and four were lost in 1916: UB7 sailed from Varna on 27 September and was never heard from again; UB45 was mined off Varna on 6 November; UC15 sailed from Constantinople on 13 November and disappeared; and UB46 was mined thirty miles off the Bosphorus on 7 December.[70]

It is probably not accidental that the Admiralstab preferred to substitute UBII boats for large submarines in the Black Sea. The new class had proved to be something of a disappointment in service. Kophamel analysed the problem on 7 June. The UBII boats were not well suited for *Handelskrieg* on the surface since their surface speed was relatively slow. Unfortunately for the Germans, slow steamers were gradually disappearing and more and more steamers in the Mediterranean were being armed. It was now an exception to encounter an unarmed steamer in the central and eastern Mediterranean. However, the more distant western portions of the Mediterranean were reserved for the long-range large submarines. Consequently, they could only employ the UBII boats in submerged attacks, but existing restrictions prohibited underwater attack on anything but warships. Kophamel on 7 June requested an exception to this rule for the entire Aegean where, with the exception of Greek trade, they were not likely to encounter neutrals and every steamer they met was probably serving the enemy.[71] Kophamel gained his point. Once more and for technical reasons – the need to employ the UBII class – the Admiralstab changed the rules. Armed cargo ships could be attacked under water as long as their armament was clearly recognized, but passenger liners whether armed or unarmed were to pass freely *with the exception* of the Aegean north of Crete, where large passenger liners could be attacked underwater without regard to visible armament when they could safely be assumed to be troop transports. Kophamel in his orders to submarine commanders warned them to be very cautious in executing the new provisions and to absolutely avoid errors since they could lead to new restrictions on the conduct of submarine warfare.[72]

The Germans had particular reason to resent restrictions on submarine warfare in the Mediterranean for, as a result of the vital coastal route down the Dalmatian coast, their Austrian allies were exposed to attacks from Allied submarines. The German naval attaché in Vienna was especially bitter after the Austrian Lloyd steamer *Albanien* (1,122 tons) had been sunk without warning on 4 June by the Italian submarine *Atropo*. Freyberg claimed that their own UB42 had recently lost several opportunities for attacking armed steamers on the Malta-Cerigo route because of the existing restrictions. Freyberg pointed out that the *Albanien* was the fourth case of a steamer being attacked without warning off the Dalmatian coast, and one attack had even involved a hospital ship, the *Elektra* (3,199 tons). The Austrians and Germans wondered why President Wilson of the United States had not taken the slightest exception to this.[73] The torpedoing of the *Elektra* on 18 March had apparently been a mistake on the part of the French submarine *Ampère* and the ship was beached with only a few casualties, but the situation was ironic since the Austrians did make extensive use of coastal steamers for military purposes. The Allies, too, had the problem of distinguishing between ships used for military purposes and those carrying innocent civilians in an area where the proximity of the enemy coast also forced the submarine to attack while submerged. It was a curious reversal of roles in the war and an example of the shoe being on the other foot.

The logic of the war in the Mediterranean led towards a further lifting of restrictions by the German government. Arnauld had another highly successful cruise in U35 from 6 June to 3 July, sinking forty ships representing 56,818 tons. This led the Kaiser to ask on 5 July about sending additional submarines to the Mediterranean and the Admiralstab agreed that U72, another large minelayer, would leave as soon as possible which turned out to be 20 August.[74] Despite a successful cruise like the one of U35, the German submariners felt that they could do much more with a relaxation of restrictions, and the presence of an Admiralstab officer in U35 on that four-week cruise gave Holtzendorff an eyewitness and considerable ammunition for his arguments. It was, according to German experience in the Mediterranean, almost impossible to determine if a steamer was armed or not since guns were hidden from view. This was, of course, perfectly true and Limpus and Captain Webb of the Admiralty Trade Division had corresponded over how to conceal those guns at the end of 1915, and in March 1916 Webb reported that the Admiralty had changed its initial policy of advertising armament to one of concealment after the Germans announced that they would sink armed steamers on sight.[75] Holtzendorff also argued that there were other signs besides guns to indicate a freighter was employed on military purposes. These included designating numbers painted on the hull, wireless outfits and escorting warships. They would not mistakenly attack neutral ships since the latter bore clear neutrality markings in addition to their flag and were not normally found on the transport routes. Holtzendorff therefore requested permission for U-boat commanders in the Mediterranean to attack, from a submerged position, freighters along the transport routes between Malta and the Aegean which were clearly military transports even though their armament was not visible.[76] Chancellor Bethmann Hollweg met with Holtzendorff on 12 July and gave what was probably his reluctant consent. However, commanders who mistakenly attacked a ship which turned out not to have been a transport would be held responsible and the Chancellor wanted this point to be clearly emphasized in operational orders. These new orders altered German assurances to the United States and, consequently, in their execution conflict with the United States was to be avoided in all cases.[77] The Kaiser agreed, subject to the Chancellor's reservations, and the new orders were issued to the Mediterranean U-Boat Flotilla on 15 July. Henceforth all ships recognized as transports, whether carrying visible armament or not, could be attacked while submerged throughout the Aegean and on the transport route between Malta and Cerigo.[78] There was the general assumption on the part of everyone that they were unlikely to meet American ships in those waters.

The Germans missed an opportunity to provide submarine assistance to land operations against the Suez Canal in July. Colonel von Kress informed the navy on 4 July that on the 15th he would launch an offensive from El Arish in the direction of Kantara and requested submarines to hinder British naval operations on his seaward flank. The Admiralstab intended to send three UB boats and a large minelayer, but had incorrect information about when the boats would be ready to sail. There were also garbled or unreceived wireless messages and eventually only one submarine belatedly cruised off the desired position, but found nothing in sight and returned to *Handelskrieg* on the way back to the Adriatic.[79] Thanks to this series of blunders the concentration of U-boats to assist the Turkish offensive against the Suez Canal never materialized.

Enver Pasha was not easily discouraged in his requests for regular submarine traffic to North Africa where he had great plans for exploiting the success of the tribesmen who controlled most of the Libyan coast. Unfortunately, he could not reach them and the Admiralstab at the beginning of September once again had to pour cold water on his plans. Given the small number of U-boats available for military purposes, the establishment of regular submarine communications with North Africa was unfortunately not possible. Moreover, during the winter season heavy surf and difficult navigational conditions made it rarely possible to unload cargo. There were no protected harbours on hand and the Admiralstab intended only one more trip in October in order to pick up the Todenwarth party.[80]

Communication with the Senussi in North Africa and co-operation with the Turkish army were not the major objective of German submarines in the Mediterranean. The assault on Allied and especially British shipping – the *Handelskrieg* – was and the activities that Enver Pasha and the German General Staff were so fond of were time-wasting diversions. Nevertheless, in the summer of 1916 the Germans were able to achieve a new level of success in the *Handelskrieg*. Their task was eased somewhat by the fact that in late July through intercepted wireless messages, they had learned of the prescribed transport routes which were patrolled. Moreover, by log books, maps and other documents recovered from merchant ships before they were sunk, as well as a copy of sailing directions for British steamships on the route between Mudros and Algiers supposedly obtained from an Indian seaman aboard a British steamship in New York, the Germans thought they had a pretty good idea of what certain of those prescribed routes were. They also knew of the directive to move out five miles right or left of the prescribed route at nightfall or in heavy fog.[81] The prescribed routes favoured by the Malta Conference were not a very effective defence against German submarines and the figures for sinking in the third quarter of 1916 demonstrated this (see Table 7.3).

Table 7.3 *Shipping Losses due to Submarines, July–September 1916*

| | Sunk by Mediterranean U-Boat Flotilla | | Sunk by Submarine-laid Mines | | Total (All Theatres) |
	Ships	Tonnage	Ships	Tonnage	Tonnage
July 1916	33	86,432	—	—	107,103
Aug. 1916	77	129,368	—	—	156,918
Sept. 1916	39	101,430	6	4,312	229,163

This quarter included Kapitänleutnant von Arnauld de la Perière's record cruise in U35 from 26 July to 20 August during which he sank in the western Mediterranean 54 steamers and sailing craft (11 British, 32 Italian, 2 French, 1 Japanese, 8 neutrals – none American) representing over 90,150 tons. This was the most successful cruise of any submarine commander during the war and Holtzendorff boasted to the Kaiser that U35 had sunk close to 50,000 tons of coal, causing a further increase in the already high price of coal in Italy, and thereby increasing pressure on the Italian economy.[82]

The outstanding record of the Mediterranean U-Boat Flotilla helped to eventually assure a favourable response to Kophamel's request on 22 August for another three large submarines. Kophamel pointed out that the spectacular Mediterranean successes had been achieved despite the small number of boats available for operations and, in fact, counting boats under long overhaul or detached for service in the Black Sea, they had only been able to average one large submarine at sea at any one time. The additional three submarines would permit them to keep at least one more submarine at sea all the time.[83] Over a month later, when a decision had still not been taken, Kophamel expanded his request to five additional large submarines which, joined to their existing submarines, would enable them to average at least three boats at sea all the time. Kophamel justified his request by arguing that the impending bad weather in autumn and winter would restrict submarine activities in northern waters, while the political situation in the Balkans was one in which Greece might become an open enemy. There was consequently an excellent opportunity to inflict serious damage on Greek shipping before the Greeks could arrange with the British for the protection of their commerce. By the time Kophamel's request reached Berlin, the Admiralstab had already received the Kaiser's approval to send U32, U63, U64 and U65 to the Mediterranean as quickly as possible.[84] Kophamel had therefore got more than he originally asked for, but not quite as much as his latest request. Kophamel also had another cause for satisfaction. The August report of submarine activity in the Mediterranean revealed that the total tonnage sunk by Mediterranean submarines during the war had exceeded 1 million tons, and after Holtzendorff's prompting of the Chief of the Kaiser's Naval Cabinet the Kaiser sent Kophamel a special telegram of congratulations.[85]

On 28 August the Italian government finally declared war on Germany. This should have ended the necessity for German submarines to fly the Austrian flag and the occasional complication it caused. These complications had continued right up to the Italian declaration of war and one may doubt if anyone really took the fiction seriously. For example, at the beginning of August, the Auswärtiges Amt transmitted an Italian *note verbale* delivered through the Swiss Embassy concerning the sinking of an Italian schooner off Minorca by a submarine which, after some delay, had hoisted the Austrian flag. However, the very same day in nearly the same waters a French schooner had been sunk by a submarine flying the German flag. The Italians wanted to know if a German submarine had also sunk the Italian ship, and if so asked if the German goverment would acknowledge its mistake and pay damages. The Admiralstab simply lied and told the Auswärtiges Amt that it was not a German submarine.[86] Did anyone really believe two submarines, one Austrian and the other German, would be operating in virtually the same waters far from the Adriatic on the same day? The deed was in fact done by U35 shortly before the submarine called for propaganda purposes at Carthagena. The Italian declaration of war eliminated the need for this type of deception in the future, but the Germans still had to cover their past actions. The German and Austrian governments were actually discussing this question even before the Italian declaration of war. As a result of various incidents and the possibility of international arbitration the Austrian Foreign Office asked if it would not be desirable to take all German submarines and their crews which had used the Austrian flag formally into the k.u.k. Kriegsmarine with a date *preceding* the Italian declaration of war against Austria-Hungary. Holtzendorff agreed. Furthermore, submarines sent later on would be taken into the Austrian naval list on the date they passed through the Straits of Gibraltar. Although Italy had declared war on Germany by the time Holtzendorff replied to the Austrian proposal, he still considered it expedient for German submarines to fly the Austrian flag at least some of the time. Otherwise the Austrian flag would completely disappear from the Mediterranean. This was likely to cause undesirable comment in the enemy or neutral press and possibly create difficulties in prize courts. Holtzendorff also pointed out that it would help to conceal the actual number of German submarines operating in the Mediterranean.[87] Freyberg found Kailer a bit reluctant for German submarines to continue using the Austrian flag after there was no longer any necessity to do so since he did not like to 'deck himself out in borrowed plumes', but the argument about camouflaging the actual number of Mediterranean submarines apparently convinced him. Kophamel and Haus reached an agreement at Pola on 10 September. The six large submarines which had conducted operations against Italy were formally and retroactively taken into the k.u.k. Kriegsmarine as of the moment they had passed Gibraltar, without altering their actual subordination to the Admiralstab or the latter's responsibility for issuing orders. Subsequently, three of the submarines (U33, U34 and U21) would pass out of the k.u.k. list at the end of September. Haus had proposed that the simplest solution for preventing the Austrian flag from suddenly disappearing from the Mediterranean would be for half the boats to continue to operate under the Austrian flag. In this case, U35, U38 and U39 would continue to use the Austrian flag and the Austrians agreed to represent them in any subsequent prize court or negotiations. The other German submarines in the Mediterranean which had not passed as Austrian, notably UC14, U72, U73, UB43, UB46 and UB47, would not be taken into the Austrian naval list.[88] Kaiser Franz Joseph gave his formal consent to the arrangement on 1 October.[89]

Despite the deterioration in weather, the sinkings in the Mediterranean remained high during the last quarter of the year (see Table 7.4).[90] The unusually high tonnage for the few ships sunk by submarine-laid mines in November was due to the line of twelve mines laid by U73 (Kapitänleutnant

Table 7.4   *Shipping Losses due to Submarines, October–December 1916*

	Sunk by Mediterranean U-Boat Flotilla		Sunk by Submarine-laid Mines		Total (All Theatres)
	Ships	Tonnage	Ships	Tonnage	Tonnage
Oct. 1916	44	125,152	—	—	337,358
Nov. 1916	36	91,547	4	74,583	325,218
Dec. 1916	43	132,319	2	4,398	307,847

Siess) in the Zea Channel on 28 October. The minefield claimed the French liner *Burdigala* (12,009 tons) on 14 November and the huge hospital ship *Britannic* (48,158 tons) on the 21st. The *Britannic* was the largest ship sunk during the war, although fortunately empty of wounded at the time she struck the mine and the loss of life was relatively small. UB47 (Oberleutnant zur see Steinbauer) also demonstrated that the UBII class, despite their relative lack of speed, could achieve spectacular results. On 4 October he torpedoed and sank the empty troopship *Franconia* (18,150 tons), a former Cunard liner, 195 miles south-east of Malta.[91]

The Austrians also proposed a special mission for one of the German submarines but the Admiralstab declined. In early November Haus spoke with Kophamel about a plan to rescue ten Austrian officers from an Italian prison on Sardinia. The officers would be picked up by submarine at night in the latter part of December. Kophamel, because of the great co-operation Haus had extended to the U-Boat Flotilla and Spezialkommando in Pola, was anxious to agree and ready to use one of the boats that would be available at the time, probably U39 or UB47. The Admiralstab, however, rejected the proposal. UB47 was not in a position to carry out the plan which would curtail military operations and in the Admiralstab's judgement the usefulness of the project was not in proportion to the danger to be expected.[92] A cynic might wonder if the verdict would have been different if German instead of Austrian officers were to have been rescued.

The German forces in the Mediterranean were growing. On 25 October, Holtzendorff reported to the Kaiser that there were 10 large U-boats (including 1 in the Black Sea and 4 *en route*); 2 large minelayers; 5 UBII boats (including 3 in the Black Sea); 1 small UBI boat; and 8 UC boats (including 1 in the Black Sea, 1 *en route* and 4 preparing to leave Germany).[93] Kophamel was conscious of the larger number of U-boats he would soon have at his disposition and during the winter months thought that it would be especially desirable to use them to disturb supplies on the way to Italy with the objective of provoking an internal crisis. The conduct of the submarine war was made up of many bits and pieces and it is difficult to discern any particular strategy within the overall concept of *Handelskrieg* against the major enemy, Britain. Kophamel would propose the operational area for each submarine; the Admiralstab would accept it or order variations for reasons that are not always clear. The Admiralstab always had its eye on reports of movements to or from Salonika and would adjust its dispositions accordingly. There were also the occasional special missions, such as one to

Madeira or the reluctantly conceded diversions to the Senussi or the Black Sea. On the whole, however, it is difficult to distinguish any particular pattern to the German deployment. Kophamel, perhaps reflecting the Austrian environment at Pola, was somewhat more inclined to think of a strategic concentration against Italy, the weak link of the Allies. But Kophamel was a relatively junior officer and the Admiralstab apparently preferred to look at the bigger picture, *Handelskrieg* against the *Hauptfeind* – Britain. The Germans seemed to scatter their submarines in different portions of the Mediterranean with the long-range boats operating in the western basin and the smaller UB boats in the centre. Kophamel also tried to take weather conditions in the different portions of the Mediterranean at various times of the year into account when making his plans. The weather around Malta, for example, was bad in December and it was not expedient to send UB boats to the area at that time.[94]

By late 1916 the pressure for unrestricted submarine warfare regardless of the diplomatic consequences was building up and the crucial decision would soon be taken. On 2 December the Admiralstab issued new orders for the Mediterranean. As a result of the recent *Marina* and *Arabia* incidents,[95] the Kaiser ordered that for the near future all complications with the United States must be avoided. However, the General Orders for the Mediterranean contained no new restrictions and merely systematically summarized existing ones. The Germans would conduct the *Handelskrieg* in the Mediterranean under prize rules with a long list of exceptions, notably freighters which were clearly armed could be attacked while submerged along with freighters whose armament was not visible but which were clearly used for transport purposes on the route Malta-Cerigo and in Cretan waters. Passenger liners and hospital ships were to be unharmed, except that in the Black Sea, in the Aegean north of latitude 36°20′N, in the Adriatic and in the Ionian north of the line Cape Colonna–Cerigo all enemy ships could be attacked under water except hospital ships. Spanish ships which had a pass from the German embassy in Madrid or a German consul in Spain stating that their cargo was merely produce were to be allowed to go and American ships would only be sunk when half their cargo was war material, as defined in Article 22 of the Declaration of London (26 February 1909), or aircraft and automobiles. After attacking underwater submarines would not surface but, if at all possible, leave the area while still submerged. Mistakes as to the nature of a ship attacked could have serious consequences for German interests. Therefore, in doubtful cases submarine commanders should abstain from attacking.[96] Even before the introduction of unrestricted warfare, these orders gave fairly wide latitude to submarine commanders in the Mediterranean, especially the eastern portion. Moreover, as a practical matter they obviously preferred to sink ships by gunfire while surfaced in order to preserve precious torpedoes of which they could carry only a limited quantity. On the other hand, there were undoubtedly cases when the restrictions prevented submarine commanders from firing at a particularly attractive target. The major advantage that unrestricted submarine warfare would have in the Mediterranean would be the freedom to make submerged attacks on freighters throughout the sea and liberty to attack passenger liners.

The Austrian contribution to the submarine campaign during 1916 was minimal, largely because Austrian submarines did not usually operate outside or very far outside the Adriatic (although U4 did work in the Gulf of Taranto and off Cape Spartivento) and none of the four Havmanden or Type UBII submarines under construction for the k.u.k. Kriegsmarine entered service that year. These were the only new submarines that the Austrians would commission during the war, although in July 1917 the Germans transferred to them the UBII boats, UB43 and UB47. The Austrians had, or would lay down, other submarines, notably six 850-ton high-seas types and ten of a modified UBIII type, but none of these were commissioned or completed before the end of the war. There were other Austrian projects, including six large high-seas 900-ton submarines which were ordered at the end of 1917 but never laid down. Austrian submarine officers were always conscious of the fact that in regard to material they were very much poor relations when compared to the Germans.[97] Once the submarines under construction during 1916 began to enter service in 1917 the Austrians could participate in the *Handelskrieg* outside the Adriatic. In 1916 Austrian submarines sank sixteen ships, most of them small coastal steamers or sailing craft, but including the French destroyers *Renaudin* and *Fourche*, the Italian destroyers *Impetuoso* and *Nembo*, and the Italian auxiliary cruisers *Principe Umberto* (7,929 tons) and *Città di Messina* (3,495 tons). The Austrians lost two submarines: U6 was caught in the nets in the Straits of Otranto on 13 May and scuttled by its crew before they were captured; while U16 was rammed and sunk off Albania on 17 October by the Italian steamer *Bermida* just after the submarine had torpedoed the *Nembo*.[98] However limited their activities outside the Adriatic might have been, the handful of Austrian submarines continued to have an immense influence in inhibiting Allied, and especially Italian, movements in the Adriatic.

This account of the submarine campaign in the Mediterranean during 1916 should indicate that from the Allied point of view the hopes arising out of the Malta Conference, namely that following the division of the Mediterranean into zones and the assignment of shipping to patrolled routes the depredations of German submarines could be controlled, proved to be false. Some had doubts from the very beginning. Captain Webb of the Admiralty Trade Division disliked the idea of a definite transport route which a ship had to follow. Unless the route could be closely patrolled by small craft at intervals of not less than five miles it was easy for a submarine to sit on the route and torpedo without warning. Webb preferred dispersal unless a route could be patrolled very carefully. However, Limpus disagreed and added the marginal comment: 'If dispersed – no ship can be patrolled', and if they dispersed 100 ships a day a submarine could always find one, and if sunk the crew would stand a poor chance as they would not learn of the loss. On a patrolled route, they always learned of the attack, the crew was picked up, and the patrols had a fair chance of keeping the submarine down.[99]

During the first half of 1916 the British had a dispute among themselves over the routes given to shipping. The Admiralty Trade Division, the War Office and the Board of Trade carried on a long acrimonious correspondence over sending frozen meat ships through the Mediterranean. The Admiralty argued that it was too dangerous to risk these valuable ships and that they should go around the Cape, while the Board of Trade claimed that the requirements of providing adequate supplies to the army precluded the loss of time that a journey round the Cape would involve.[100] Oliver, thoroughly exasperated, wrote on one of the lengthy minutes: 'Better that the soldiers in Egypt should eat tinned beef for a week than that ships & lives should be stupidly risked.'[101] Even the War Committee could not resolve the problem. Private owners and masters usually followed Admiralty advice as to trade routes, but government departments controlling movements of merchant ships did not alway do so, preferring to save time by using routes that the Admiralty pronounced as dangerous. The War Committee could not prescribe any rule or principle which could apply in all cases and simply recommended what was in effect better liaison. When circumstances required the Board of Trade or another department to disregard Admiralty advice, the Admiralty Director of Trade Division should be informed at once. The decision, as Webb noted, provided convenient machinery for keeping other departments in touch with the Admiralty War Staff but did not touch on the question of ultimate responsibility.[102] The controversy continued.

If the British had such difficulty among themselves, it was small wonder that the three Allied navies had trouble co-operating in the Mediterranean. Wemyss, now C.-in-C. Egypt and East Indies, was convinced that the Italians and, to a minor degree, the French were 'quite incapable of safeguarding their areas properly' and that P. & O. captains commonly said that they never saw any patrolling vessels except in the British zones. The French had complained of not having enough small craft but Wemyss, judging by their patrol of the Syrian coast in his area, termed the proportion of French craft in harbour to those at sea 'perfectly ridiculous'.[103] During July the losses in British merchant ships within 50 to 100 miles of Algiers were so serious that the Shipping Control Committee asked the Foreign Office to make representations to the French government for a more effective system of defence. The Admiralty reacted strongly against this, for in their eyes the Allied authorities in the Mediterranean were working in close touch with each other and the French Ministry of Marine was fully aware of the situation and doing all that was possible. Representations through diplomatic channels would give the impression that the British and French admirals were not acting in harmony and to the utmost, and would undo much of the good results of the recent conference.[104]

By September 1916 submarines had made the Mediterranean route so dangerous that the Admiralty was forced to propose modifications to the War Office in regard to troop transport. Henceforth troops going to or returning from Salonika and Egypt should be sent overland via Marseilles. Troops going to or returning from India would go via the Cape as would Australian and New Zealand forces *en route* to Britain.[105] The War Office eventually agreed, as did the British C.-in-C. in France and the French government, that Le Havre should be the port of arrival and the number of troops should be limited to not more than 3,600 per week. The service, which had the effect of cutting the long haul through the Bay of Biscay, Straits of Gibraltar and western Mediterranean, would begin around 20 October, although as a temporary measure at the end of October the War Office asked for drafts from Britain to proceed directly by sea to Salonika.[106] The French also decided to hasten talks, already begun, with the Italians and Greeks about establishing a supplementary line of communications designed to speed transport of troops to Salonika and reduce the risks of the journey at sea.[107]

By the second half of November, the Director of the Trade Division of the Admiralty was also considering the diversion of more ships from the Mediterranean route to the Cape route. This involved a careful balancing of the disadvantages from the loss in carrying capacity that the longer route would entail with the advantage of diminished risk, and also meant building up stocks of coal in South African ports. The latter would be facilitated by persuading certain neutral shipping companies to divert their ships from Cape to the Suez Canal. Presumably the ships would be protected in the Mediterranean by their status as neutrals. The Admiralty decided that the most convenient means of giving effect to the decision would be to prohibit issuing insurance for vessels entering the Mediterranean unless they were provided with a special licence from the Ship Licensing Committee appointed by the Board of Trade. This procedure, rather than a rigid rule, permitted them to make exceptions in special cases. Normally, they expected to issue licences to ships carrying cargo to Mediterranean ports or using the Mediterranean as a highway to and from ports in India west of Colombo.[108] In practical terms, as compared with the restrictions of the preceding March which had applied to ships trading to ports east of 100° East Longitude (that is, Singapore and beyond), the new restrictions shifted shipping from ports such as Rangoon, Calcutta and Madras to the Cape route. The new measures went into effect on 11 December.

Although the majority of the tonnage sunk by U-boats was British, the French were also suffering severely from the submarine attack. Unfortunately, they too kept coming up with the same old answers. The ministry, either Lacaze or De Bon, rebuked the Préfet Maritime at Bizerte in June for concluding from the reports of captains whose ships had been sunk by submarines that the system of patrols was bad and it would be advantageous to replace them with convoys. The authorities in Paris accused the Préfet of forming his opinion from too limited a number of facts. Convoys were a method which had been definitely abandoned after past experience. They did not give absolute security since ships convoyed by destroyers had been sunk, and the speed of patrol vessels, even destroyers, in a rough sea was often very inferior to that of the ships in the convoy. Convoys therefore imposed a reduction in speed and increased the time at sea, thereby increasing the exposure to danger. They also reduced speed to that of the slowest ship. Moreover, the French navy had reached the limit of auxiliary vessels that they could purchase for patrol and the number available was far inferior to that required for convoying the multitude of transports presently in service. The sole effective measure was the one presently ordered by the C.-in-C. which consisted of hunting without respite submarines wherever they were signalled, to prevent them from doing further harm. Once this method was perfected they could hope to keep contact with submarines and destroy them.[109] The method was not working, however, for submarines were hardly likely to remain obligingly on the surface to await destruction at the hands of French patrols dashing to the scene. In the month of July the increased activity by patrols of French torpedo boats, auxiliary craft and aircraft along the French North African coast did force U39 to move its operations further to the east.[110] This was a tactical decision by a submarine commander and merely shifted sinkings to another locality. Unless there were sufficient forces to literally saturate every point on a route, it did not really reduce the amount of tonnage lost.

The French did make considerable efforts to increase the numbers of small craft available for patrols. They ordered a series of twelve destroyers from Japanese yards, possibly the first example of a European power having recourse to Japanese industry on a large scale. The French also purchased sizeable numbers – eventually over 250 – of trawlers from their Allies and neutrals. The sources were diverse, notably: Belgium, Brazil, Britain, Greece, Iceland, Japan, the Netherlands, Norway, Sweden, Spain and the United States.[111] They also took great pains to reorganize their patrol system. Rear-Admiral Fatou, Admiral of Patrols, with headquarters at Bône, and eventually Malta, was directly under the C.-in-C. Fatou's subordinates, Capitaine de vaisseau Violette, with headquarters in the yacht *Hélène*, commanded the patrols in the eastern basin of the Mediterranean from Argostoli or Milo, and Capitaine de vaisseau Fossey worked the patrols in the western basin from Bône.[112] Nevertheless, the sinkings continued and August represented an increase over July. Lacaze naturally had to face criticism, especially from deputies like Bergeon who represented Marseilles. The minister gave careful and sometimes detailed explanations to questions concerning subjects such as providing armaments for merchant ships, introducing convoys, or the reasons for a lack of adequate patrols. The general tenor of these replies was that the navy was doing all that it could.[113] That often did not seem to be enough, particularly after more of those spectacular disasters which aroused considerable emotion. On 2 October U35 torpedoed and sank the sloop *Rigel* off Algiers and on 4 October torpedoed and sank off Cape Matapan the troopship *Gallia* (14,900 tons). The *Gallia* had been full of troops and over 600 lives – perhaps many more – were lost. The reaction in France was strong enough to cause Lacaze to prescribe special measures in the future for movements of large numbers of troops by sea. The C.-in-C. would deploy destroyers and patrol craft along the route, especially in the most dangerous areas, so that without being directly escorted, the transport would only remain out of sight of a patrol vessel for a short time.[114] At the close of the year, however, in reporting his patrol dispositions Admiral Fatou was still explaining why he preferred the system of patrols to that of direct escorts.[115]

Neither the French nor the British had really found an answer to the submarine challenge in the Mediterranean at the end of 1916. Small wonder that commanders such as Arnauld and Forstmann had made such record cruises during the year. The British, French and Italians were all moving towards another series of conferences in 1917 to thrash out the problem and the supreme challenge of unrestricted submarine warfare was about to come. However, before turning to this we shall examine the Adriatic and Aegean in the next chapter and particularly the difficulties between the French and Italians over command. Unfortunately, the good will created by the Malta Conference did not last very long. Moreover, the French C.-in-C. became increasingly preoccupied with the Greek muddle which would eventually cost him his job.

Notes: Chapter 7

1 Naval War Staff, 'The Submarine Situation in the Mediterranean', 15 Nov. 1915 [Print], PRO, Adm 137/1136.
2 ibid.
3 Dartige to Lacaze, 2 Nov. 1915, SHM, Carton Ed-84.
4 Naval War Staff, 'The Submarine Situation in the Mediterranean', 15 Nov. 1915 [Print], p. 7, PRO, Adm 137/1136.
5 Capt. Richard Webb [Director of Trade Division] to Limpus, 18 Nov. 1915, Limpus to Webb, 17 Dec. 1915, National Maritime Museum, Greenwich, Limpus MSS.
6 Peirse to Limpus, 19 Nov. 1915, Currey to Limpus, 23 Nov. 1915, ibid.; Peirse to Jackson, 4 Dec. 1915, Naval Library, London, Jackson MSS; Limpus to Admiralty, 7 Dec. 1915, PRO, Adm 137/1136.
7 Jackson to Jellicoe, 1 and 21 Nov. 1915, British Library, London, Jellicoe MSS, Add. MSS 49009.
8 Jellicoe to Jackson, 8 Nov. 1915, reproduced in A. Temple Patterson (ed.), *The Jellicoe papers* Vol. 1: *1893–1916* Publications of the Navy Records Society, Vol. 108 (London, 1966), Doc. 169, p. 186, Jellicoe to Balfour, 23 Feb. 1916, ibid., Doc. 189, p. 202.
9 Dartige to Lacaze, 4 Nov. 1915, SHM, Carton Ed-84.
10 Lacaze to Minister of War, 12 Nov. 1915, ibid., Carton Gp-67.
11 Lacaze to Dartige, 14 Nov. 1915, Dartige to Lacaze, 15 Nov. 1915, ibid., Carton A-29.
12 Lacaze to Minister of War, 26 Nov. 1915, ibid., Carton Gp-67.
13 Dartige to Lacaze, 6 Dec. 1915, ibid., Carton Ed-84.
14 ibid. Lacaze had copies of the proposals sent to Poincaré and Briand, but the subject seems to have quickly died.
15 Lacaze to Dartige, 12 Nov. 1915, SHM, Carton A-29.
16 Dartige to de Robeck, 20 Nov. 1915 (and enclosure), Wemyss to Dartige, 1 Dec. 1915, Wemyss to Admiralty, 2 Dec. 1915, PRO, Adm 137/499.
17 Report by Captain H. W. Grant, n.d. [c. 7 Dec. 1915], and Agreement of 3 Dec. 1915, ibid.
18 An example of an 'Allo' signal: 'ALLO (5 times) – 3725 – 0520 – E – 0218 – Sydney' which meant 'Sub seen Long. 37°25′ North, 5°20′ East at 2:18 by *Sydney*', ibid.
19 Keyes to his wife, 30 Dec. 1915, in Halpern (ed.), *The Keyes Papers*, Vol. 1, Doc. 135, p. 299; de Robeck to Admiralty, 29 Dec. 1915, Admiralty to de Robeck, 29 Dec. 1915, PRO, Adm 137/499.
20 Dartige to Lacaze, 17 Dec. 1915, SHM, Carton Ed-89.
21 Limpus to de Robeck, 16 Feb. 1916, Churchill College, Cambridge, de Robeck MSS, DRBK 4/36.

22 Dartige to Lacaze, 5 Jan. 1916, SHM, Carton Ed-84.
23 Dartige to Lacaze, 8 Feb. 1916, ibid.
24 Dartige to Lacaze, 5 Jan. 1916, ibid.
25 Limpus to Thursby, 30 Jan. 1916, PRO, Adm 137/2123.
26 Lacaze to Saint Seine, 25 Jan. 1916, Admiralty to Limpus, de Robeck and Wemyss, 25 Jan. 1916, ibid., Adm 137/499; Lacaze to Dartige, 24 Jan. 1916, SHM, Carton Es-15.
27 Jackson to de Robeck, 28 Jan. 1916, loc. cit. at n. 21, de Robeck MSS, DRBK 4/31.
28 Limpus to Jackson, 2 Feb. 1916, loc. cit. at n. 6, Jackson MSS.
29 Limpus to Thursby, 30 Jan. 1916, PRO, Adm 137/2123; Memorandum by Limpus (for Dartige, de Robeck and Wemyss), 1 Feb. 1916, Minute by Oliver, 27 Feb. 1916, Admiralty to Limpus, 25 Feb. 1916, ibid., Adm 137/499.
30 Webb to Brocklebank, 1 Dec. 1915, ibid., Adm 137/2894.
31 Memoranda by Webb, 23 Dec. 1915 and 5 Jan. 1916, Minute by Webb, 9 Jan. 1916, ibid.
32 Report of Mr Hipwood and Cmdr Fisher, 12 Jan. 1916, Notes on a Conference, 18 Jan. 1916, ibid.
33 Richard Holt (Alfred Holt & Co.) to Webb, 11 Feb. 1916, ibid.
34 Circular No. 511, Liverpool and London War Risks Insurance Association, 9 Mar. 1916, ibid.
35 Wemyss to de Robeck, 24 Feb. 1916, loc. cit. at n. 21, de Robeck MSS, DRBK 4/32.
36 De Robeck to Limpus, 16 Feb. 1916, loc. cit. at n. 5, Limpus MSS.
37 Limpus to de Robeck, 23 Feb. 1916, loc. cit. at n. 21, de Robeck MSS, DRBK 4/36.
38 Procès Verbaux, 1st and 2nd Session, Malta Conference, 2 and 3 Mar. 1916, and General Report, 9 Mar. 1916, PRO, Adm 137/499.
39 General Report, 9 Mar. 1916, pp. 6–7, ibid.
40 ibid., pp. 7–10.
41 Procès verbaux, 3rd Sitting, 4 Mar., 4th Sitting, 5 Mar. 1916, General Report, 9 Mar. 1916, pp. 12–16, ibid.
42 Procès verbaux, 4th, 5th and 6th Sitting, 5–7 Mar. 1916, General Report, 9 Mar. 1916, pp. 16–28, ibid.
43 Dartige to Lacaze, 20 Mar. 1916, SHM, Carton Ed-84.
44 Limpus to Admiralty, 9 Mar. 1916, PRO, Adm 137/499.
45 Limpus to Admiralty, 9 Mar. 1916, ibid.; de Robeck to Balfour, 17 Mar. 1916, loc. cit. at n. 21, de Robeck MSS, DRBK 4/69.
46 Notes by Vice-Admiral Limpus, 15 Mar. 1916, PRO, Adm 137/499.
47 Pini to Corsi, 11 Mar. 1916, USM, Cartella 533/2; Dartige to Lacaze, 20 Mar. 1916, SHM, Carton Ed-84.
48 Note by Vice-Admiral Limpus, 17 Mar. 1916, Minute by Oliver, 29 Mar. 1916, Jackson to Lacaze, 20 Mar. 1916, PRO, Adm 137/499; de Robeck to Balfour, 17 Mar. 1916, loc. cit. at n. 21, de Robeck MSS, DRBK 4/69.
49 Jackson to de Robeck, 10 Mar. 1916, loc. cit. at n. 21, de Robeck MSS, DRBK 4/31.
50 Dartige to Lacaze, 19 Mar. 1916, SHM, Carton Ed-83; Memorandum by Oliver, 16 Mar. 1916, ibid., Carton Es-11.
51 Dartige to Lacaze, 10 Apr. 1916, ibid., Carton Ed-84.
52 Dartige to Lacaze, 15 May 1916, ibid. Thomazi, *Guerre navale dans la Méditerranée*, pp. 41–43.
53 Lacaze to Naval Attaché, London, 7 Apr. 1916, PRO, Adm 137/499; Lacaze to

Briand, 7 Apr. 1916, Briand to Lacaze, 22 Apr. 1916, MAE, Série guerre 1914–1918, Vol. 1055.

54 Rodd to Foreign Office, 23 Apr. 1916, Italian Note Verbale (trans.), 24 Apr. 1916, PRO, Adm 137/499; Sonnino to Barrère, 24 Apr. 1916, Barrère to Briand, 26 Apr. 1916, MAE, Série Guerre 1914–1918, Vol. 1055; Note from British Embassy (Paris) to Minister of Foreign Affairs, 24 Apr. 1916, ibid.

55 Thomazi, *Guerre navale dans la Méditerranée*, pp. 169–70. Thomazi claims that over a thousand lives were lost. On the 23rd Arnauld had just missed getting a shot at the huge British liner *Olympic* (46,439 tons).

56 Lacaze to Minister of War, 7 Mar. 1916, SHM, Carton Gp-67.

57 Kophamel to Admiralstab, 'Tätigkeit der deutschen U-Flotille im März 1916', 12 Apr. 1916, NARS, T-1022, Roll 792, PG 75265; Spindler, *Handelskrieg*, Vol. 3, pp. 41, 46–7.

58 Spindler, *Handelskrieg*, Vol 3, p. 169.

59 Gaston Vio, 'Bericht über Mission mit U39', 4 July, 1916, OK/MS VIII-1/14 ex 1916, No. 4219; Kriegstagebuch, U39, ibid.

60 Kophamel to Admiralstab, 13 July 1916, Endorsement by Kophamel to Kriegstagebuch UB42, 8–30 June 1916, NARS, T-1022, Roll 12, PG 61801; Report of Linienschiffsleutnant Dürrigl and copy of Kriegstagebuch UB46, 23 July 1916, OK/MS VIII-1/14 ex 1916, No. 5052.

61 Spindler, *Handelskrieg*, Vol. 3, pp. 388, 390.

62 Humann to Admiralstab, 16 Mar. 1916, Admiralstab to Holtzendorff, 17 Mar. 1916, Kophamel to Admiralstab, 21 Mar. 1916, Lossow to General Staff, 25 Mar. 1916, NARS, T-1022, Roll 792, PG 75264; Nadolny to Admiralstab, 23 Mar. 1916, ibid., PG 75265.

63 Freyberg to Holtzendorff, 31 Mar. 1916, Admiralstab to Freyberg, 4 Apr. 1916, ibid.

64 Freyberg to Holtzendorff, 7 and 12 Apr. 1916, ibid., Roll 505, PG 69081.

65 Spindler, *Handelskrieg*, Vol. 3, pp. 43–4.

66 Nadolny to Admiralstab, 3 May 1916, Admiralstab to Sektion Politik, Generalstab, 3 May 1916, NARS, T-1022, Roll 792, PG 75265.

67 Jagow to Holtzendorff, 23 May 1916, Holtzendorff to Jagow, 31 May 1916, Kophamel to Admiralstab, 2 and 9 May and 1 June 1916, Kophamel to Holtzendorff, 13 July 1916, Roll 793, PG 75265; Spindler, *Handelskrieg*, Vol. 3, p. 159.

68 Souchon to Admiralstab, 9 May 1916, Buelow to Admiralstab, 9 May 1916, Holtzendorff to Buelow, 11 May 1916, Holtzendorff to Souchon, 11 May 1916, NARS, T-1022, Roll 793, PG 75265.

69 Admiralstab to Reichsmarineamt, 19 May 1916, ibid.

70 Admiralstab to Kophamel, 24 June 1916, Souchon to Admiralstab, 17 and 20 June 1916, ibid., Spindler, *Handelskrieg*, Vol. 3, pp. 164, 169–71, 177–8, 335.

71 Kophamel to Holtzendorff, 7 June 1916, NARS, T-1022, Roll 793, PG 75265.

72 Admiralstab to Kophamel, 15 June 1916, Admiralstab to Souchon, 18 June 1916, Kophamel, 'Operationsbefehl für S.M. Unterseeboot UB44 & UB43,' 20 June 1916, ibid.

73 Freyberg to Capelle, 20 June 1916, ibid., Roll 505, PG 69081.

74 Müller to Admiralstab, 5 July 1916, Admiralstab to Müller, 6 July 1916, ibid., Roll 793, PG 75265; Spindler, *Handelskrieg*, Vol. 3, pp. 155–6.

75 Webb to Limpus, 14 Mar. 1916, loc. cit. at n. 5, Limpus MSS.

76 Holtzendorff to Kaiser Wilhelm (with copy for Bethmann Hollweg), 12 July 1916, NARS, T-1022, Roll 793, PG 75265.

77 Bethmann Hollweg to Holtzendorff, 12 July 1916, Holtzendorff to Müller, 13 July 1916, ibid.

78 Müller to Admiralstab, 14 July 1916, Admiralstab to Kophamel, 15 July 1916, ibid.; Spindler, *Handelskrieg*, Vol. 3, pp. 160–1.

79 Souchon to Admiralstab, 4 July 1916, Admiralstab to U-Flotilla, Pola, 17 July 1916, Holtzendorff to U-Flotilla, Pola, 13 July 1916, NARS, T-1022, Roll 793, PG 75265; Spindler, *Handelskrieg*, Vol. 3, pp. 170–1.

80 von Hülsen to Admiralstab, 16 Aug. 1916, Lossow to Politische Abteilung, Generalstabes, 12 Aug. 1916, Admiralstab to Sektion Politik des Generalstabes, 2 Sept. 1916, NARS, T-1022, Roll 803, PG 75266. Von Todenwarth and party were eventually picked up by U39 on 13 Oct. as part of an operational cruise in the western Mediterranean.

81 Auswärtiges Amt to Admiralstab, 19 July 1916, Holtzendorff, Immediatvortrag, 28 July 1916, NARS, T-1022, Roll 793, PG 75265.

82 Spindler, *Handelskrieg,* Vol. 3, pp. 161–3; Holtzendorff to Kaiser Wilhelm, 28 Aug. 1916, NARS, T-1022, Roll 803, PG 75266.

83 Kophamel to Holtzendorff, 22 Aug. 1916, NARS, T-1022, Roll 803, PG 75266.

84 Kophamel to Holtzendorff, 9 Oct. 1916, Holtzendorff to Hochseekommando, 6 Oct. 1916, ibid.

85 Holtzendorff to Müller, 26 Sept. 1916, Kaiser Wilhelm to Kophamel, 1 Oct. 1916, ibid.

86 Auswärtiges Amt to Admiralstab, 7 Aug. 1916, Admiralstab to Auswärtiges Amt, 22 Aug. 1916, ibid.

87 Note from Austro-Hungarian Embassy, Berlin, 12 Aug. 1916, Holtzendorff to Auswärtiges Amt, 1 Sept. 1916, ibid.

88 Freyberg to Holtzendorff, 8 Sept. 1916, Haus to Kophamel, 10 Sept. 1916, Kophamel to Holtzendorff, 10 Sept. 1916, ibid.

89 Kailer to Kaiser Franz Joseph, 30 Sept. 1916, MKSM 66–5/12 ex 1916.

90 Spindler, *Handelskrieg*, Vol. 3, pp. 388, 390.

91 ibid., pp. 172, 343.

92 Kophamel to Holtzendorff, 3 Nov. 1916 and Notation by BIII Section, 24 Nov. [?] 1916, NARS, T-1022, Roll 803, PG 75267.

93 Holtzendorff, Immediatvortrag, 25 Oct. 1916, ibid., PG 75266.

94 Kophamel to Holtzendorff, 10 Nov. 1916 (with annotations by Admiralstab), ibid., PG 75267.

95 Only the *Arabia* concerned the Mediterranean. The *Marina* (5,204 tons) of the Donaldson line was sunk off Fastnet on 28 October with the loss of eighteen lives including six Americans. The armed P & O liner *Arabia* (7,933 tons) was torpedoed off Cape Matapan by UB43 (Kapitänleutnant von Mellenthin) on 6 November. The passengers were saved but eleven crewmen were lost.

96 Holtzendorff to U-Flotilla, Pola, 2 Dec. 1916, NARS, T-1022, Roll 803, PG 75267.

97 Details, not always in agreement, on the subject are in: Aichelburg, *Unterseeboote Österreich-Ungarns*, Vol. 1, pp. 172–85; Greger, *Austro-Hungarian Warships*, pp. 79–81. On Austrian feelings of inferiority see: Georg von Trapp, *Bis zum letzten Flaggenschuss: Erinnerungen eines österreichischen U-Boots-Kommandanten* (Salzburg and Leipzig, 1935), pp. 58–9.

98 Aichelburg, *Unterseeboote Österreich-Ungarns*, Vol. 2, pp. 90–1, 302–3, 356–8.

99 Webb to Limpus and marginal comment by Limpus, 14 Mar. 1916, loc. cit. at n. 5, Limpus MSS.

100 War Office to Admiralty, 29 Jan. and 12 Feb. 1916, Admiralty to War Office, 31 Jan. and 21 Feb. 1916, Admiralty to Board of Trade, 21 Apr., 3 and 5 May 1916, Board of Trade to Admiralty, 26 Apr. and 13 May 1916, PRO, Adm 137/1193.

101 Minute by Oliver, 25 May, 1916, ibid.
102 War Committee, Extract from Proceedings of Meeting, 6 June 1916, Minute by Webb, 10 June 1916, ibid.
103 Wemyss to Jackson, 23 Aug. 1916, copy in Rear-Admiral Hugh Miller MSS, Imperial War Museum, London, 73/11/12.
104 Shipping Control Committee to Foreign Office, 23 Aug. 1916, Admiralty to Foreign Office, 7 Sept. 1916, PRO, Adm 137/1221.
105 Admiralty to War Office, 15 Sept. 1916, Admiralty to the Commonwealth of Australia Shipping Representative, 15 Sept. 1916, ibid.
106 War Office to Admiralty, 2, 10 and 25 Oct. 1916, ibid.
107 Joffre to Lacaze, 26 Oct. 1916, SHM, Carton Es-12. This decision was taken by the Conseil supérieur de la défense nationale.
108 Memorandum by Webb, 18 Nov. 1916, Webb to Secretary, Liverpool and London War Risks Association, 5 Dec. 1916, PRO, Adm 137/2894.
109 Lacaze or De Bon to Vice-Amiral, C.-in-C., Préfet Maritime à Bizerte, 16 June 1916, SHM, Carton Gp-67.
110 Spindler, *Handelskrieg*, Vol. 3, p. 160.
111 Labayle-Couhat, *French Warships of World War I*, pp. 121, 221–6.
112 Report by Captain Kelly, 19 Aug. 1916, PRO, Adm 116/1429.
113 Lacaze to Bergeon, 7 Sept. and 30 Nov. 1916, EMG – 4ᵉ Section, Note pour le Cabinet du Ministre [concerning replies to Bergeon], 30 Oct. 1916, SHM, Carton Es-8.
114 Lacaze to Dartige, 16 Oct. 1916, ibid., Carton A-29.
115 Fatou to Dartige, 22 Dec. 1916, ibid., Carton Gp-67.

[8]

The Adriatic, the Aegean and the Eastern Mediterranean in 1916

The Adriatic

While the spectacular cruises of the crack German submarine commanders attracted most of the attention in the Mediterranean in 1916, the only place where the surface forces of the Entente and the Central Powers were actually in contact remained the Adriatic. Here, as they were fond of pointing out, the Italian navy bore the brunt of the struggle, assisted somewhat grudgingly by the French and the British, while at the entrance to the Adriatic the Allies – primarily the British – attempted the controversial experiment of trying to hinder the passage of enemy submarines through a blockade of the Straits of Otranto. The Italians invariably wanted aid, but should that assistance go beyond a certain scope it inevitably raised the touchy question of command. This would form the subject of considerable, and ultimately sterile, discussion in the course of the year.

The situation in the Adriatic had altered to the disadvantage of the Italians after the Austrians captured Mount Lovčen and Montenegro dropped out of the war. They lost those valuable observation posts overlooking Cattaro which had provided information on the movements of the Austrian fleet, and Admiral Corsi, Minister of Marine, became worried that Valona and Brindisi could be exposed to sudden attack without sufficient warning while the bulk of the Italian fleet at Taranto would be too far away to render effective assistance. Abruzzi did not think that the loss of Mount Lovčen had really changed the actual situation very much, for thanks to the channels between the Dalmatian Islands the Austrians had previously been able to undertake surprise operations against the Italian coast by sailing from Sebenico or Spalato. The Austrians could now use Cattaro as a point of departure, but since the Italians did not have sufficient forces for a permanent patrol off Cattaro or the Dalmatian channels, whether the Austrians came out of Cattaro or through the channels they could still be off

Brindisi at dawn after only six hours steaming and, barring unusual circumstances, before Italian forces at anchor in the port would have time to sortie. The same would be true for Valona. Abruzzi therefore thought it best to retain their present dispositions, that is, the Italian dreadnoughts and British Queens at Taranto; the Regina Elenas, scouting division and flotillas at Brindisi; and the *Regina Margherita*, older battleships and cruisers at Valona. Abruzzi favoured intensifying work towards making Valona secure against underwater attack. Once this was accomplished they could consider moving forces from Taranto to Valona but this, in turn, would necessitate making provisions far in advance for their logistical requirements and acquiring additional steamers for a fleet train.[1]

A month later the impending fall of Durazzo to the Austrians led Corsi to anticipate the possibility that the latter would displace the centre of their naval activity to the lower Adriatic. This would require, as a preventative measure, a corresponding move by the Italians. The anchorage at Valona would therefore have to be made absolutely secure against submarine attack, and sufficient supplies assembled here in advance so as to avoid logistical worries. Abruzzi used the opportunity to request some of Thaon di Revel's forces at Venice, notably the armoured cruisers of the Cagni division, which had been relatively inactive at Venice since the loss of the *Amalfi*. The armoured cruisers were moved to Valona in early April, and in May changed places with the Regina Elenas at Brindisi.[2] Corsi, however, still urged Abruzzi to move the main portion of the fleet to Valona. The Italians could not maintain a continuous or thick patrol across the Adriatic and the Austrians might be able to get out unobserved. In that case it would be up to the British and French in the eastern basin of the Mediterranean to stop them. Corsi was afraid, however, that on the way the Austrians might arrive at dawn off Brindisi and Valona and conduct a destructive bombardment before continuing on out of the Adriatic. The bulk of the Italian fleet at Taranto would be unable to prevent this.[3]

The prospect did not really worry Abruzzi. That type of action would jeopardize the Austrian escape from the Adriatic by exposing them to submarine attack, and also warn the Allies who could then concentrate along the route that they had to follow. Such action by the Austrians would also be foolhardy, as the loss of the *Garibaldi* had demonstrated to the Italians. The Italians had never exposed their capital ships off Pola or Cattaro for the purpose of a mere bombardment; the Austrians were not likely to do so off Brindisi. Abruzzi was also opposed to using capital ships to oppose Austrian raids. The big ships could not be kept under steam at all times – that would waste too much precious coal – and they would be exposed to submarine or mine ambush if they came out. Consequently, he did not see any advantage in deploying to Valona where the Italian fleet would be closely observed by Austrian aircraft operating from Durazzo. Valona was also less secure than Taranto and would become a magnet for submarines.[4]

The plan to occupy one or more of the islands off the Dalmatian coast, notably Lagosta, had been one of the Italian preoccupations the preceding summer.[5] In January 1916 Corsi apparently decided to re-examine the project. Abruzzi was not enthusiastic about Lagosta. It might be a good base for submarines and torpedo craft, but it would require support from Brindisi which was 140 miles distant, while Cattaro and Sebenico were scarcely 70 miles and the Sabbioncello Channel barely 20 miles away. To properly protect Lagosta they would need another anchorage able to contain light cruisers and torpedo craft in numbers superior to the maximum force of similar vessels that the enemy might use against them. Abruzzi did not think that Lagosta could be the primary objective of Italian action. Its capture would be the consequence of a larger and more significant action, notably the establishment of a naval base on the island of Curzola and a portion of the nearby Sabbioncello Peninsula. Corsi agreed with the C.-in-C., but pointed out that the Italian navy itself did not have sufficient men to occupy Curzola and could not rely on the Italian army for support. Nevertheless, he ordered that the project should be re-examined in case circumstances changed.[6]

On 14 March Abruzzi submitted his study on the occupation of Curzola and the possible formation of a naval base for light torpedo craft and submarines on the Sabbioncello Peninsula. The plan included seizure of the most important inhabited places on the peninsula and adjacent island of Curzola, and establishment of a battery of mountain guns on the commanding height of the peninsula, Monte Vipere. The area between the southern shore of Sabbioncello and the northern coast of Curzola would form the base whose protection would require a new deployment of the Italian fleet to meet an Austrian counteroffensive. The C.-in-C. of the 2ª Squadra with the Regina Elena division, three French armoured cruisers temporarily attached to Brindisi, Pisani class (protected cruisers), light cruisers, large destroyers, and submarines, along with sweepers and supporting ships, would be at Sabbioncello; the C.-in-C. of the Fleet and dreadnoughts *Doria* and *Duilio*, the British Queen division, smaller French destroyers and defensive submarines would move to Brindisi; while the C.-in-C. of the 1° Squadra (Cavour-class dreadnoughts) and the battleship *Regina Margherita*, along with the Nembo-class destroyers, auxiliary cruisers and defensive submarines, would move to Valona. The net effect would be to abandon the now distant Taranto as a major base since ships from here would arrive too late to counter any Austrian action. The enemy naval force at Cattaro would be enclosed by a 'strategic triangle' Sabbioncello–Brindisi–Valona. Abruzzi concluded that the operation would not present any great difficulty from the maritime point of view but the big question would be whether the Italian army could provide sufficient forces to hold the Sabbioncello Peninsula from the expected Austrian counterattack from the mainland.[7]

The occupation of the western portion of the Sabbioncello Peninsula would, in a second phase of operations, be extended to other islands and along the peninsula to a line some twenty kilometres east of Monte Vipere approximately between the little harbours of Giuliana and Bratkovica. These operations would require substantial military support well beyond the three companies of Alpini, battalion of infantry, and battery of mountain artillery to be used in the initial landing. Corsi eventually approached General Cadorna, Chief of the Army General Staff, in May, pointing out that, in addition to their military value, Curzola and the Sabbioncello Peninsula would constitute useful bargaining chips in any subsequent peace negotiations aimed at improving Italy's current unfavourable strategic situation in the Adriatic. The operation itself could not take place before the end of July.[8] Cadorna, however, would have none of it. He judged that the force which the navy intended to use for the initial landings was sufficient, but to hold the three-kilometre front between Giuliana and Bratkovica six battalions with the requisite quota of artillery, engineers and service troops would be required. These might also have to be reinforced if the Austrians made serious efforts to regain lost territory. Under the present circumstances, Cadorna did not anticipate that the army could provide the desired support at the end of July, although should the situation change the army might reconsider the proposal.[9] This had not been the best moment to ask Cadorna for troops because, on 15 May, Conrad von Hötzendorf had launched his *Strafe* or 'punishment' offensive in the Trentino directed towards the rail centre of Padua. The Italians were caught off balance and the Austrians captured Asiago, but difficult terrain and Italian reinforcements from the Isonzo front slowed down the Austrian advance, while Italian counterattacks coupled with a major offensive by the Russian army in Galicia ended the Austrian advance by 17 June. The Austrians eventually withdrew to a line substantially close to their original position. Conrad's *Strafe* offensive did not yield the desired results, but it was easy to understand why Cadorna was likely to pay little attention to naval requests for the diversion of troops from the main front.

The military situation improved for the Italians during the summer with Cadorna devoting his attention to a series of offensives along the Isonzo River which resulted in the capture of Gorizia in August. It was probably the most notable Italian success on land so far during the war, but certainly not a major breakthrough in the direction of Trieste. In September, Corsi again approached Cadorna about an amphibious operation. This time it concerned landing troops on the Istrian Peninsula between Salvore and Cittanova in order to draw Austrian troops from the main front and take the entrenched camp of Trieste from the rear, possibly isolating Pola. Once again, however, Cadorna preferred to use all of his forces on the main front.[10]

Corsi also wondered about his French ally. Later in September he noted that the French press was agitating in favour of an Italian counteroffensive and landing along the coast of Montenegro and Albania, or in the Dalmatian Islands. Durazzo, San Giovanni di Medua, Antivari and Curzola were the names most frequently mentioned. Corsi assumed that such articles in the normally censored press must have been inspired by the French government. He expected the French to bring the subject up in any future discussions and resolved to echo Cadorna – for the present and foreseeable future they could not withdraw troops from the major front. In the unlikely event that the Allies should make an offer of Allied troops, he would also decline it for obvious political reasons. In Corsi's personal opinion it would not be a great evil if operations of this sort were put off until a more propitious moment since the risks involved were not in proportion to the benefits of a success. Not surprisingly, Cadorna fully agreed. The troops employed in winning bridgeheads at the locations mentioned would be squandered since they would not be aimed at any vital points of the enemy. To establish bridgeheads here and there as an end in themselves might be useful for political purposes, but would certainly be harmful for their military interests. Cadorna warned that their adventure at Durazzo the preceding winter ought to serve as both an example and warning. The occupation of Curzola and Sabbioncello would require fewer troops than objectives on the mainland, but this number would still be substantial and, at the moment, the army could not provide the requisite artillery to block the nearby channels and protect the stronghold.[11] Once again, Cadorna had rejected the prospect of amphibious operations on the Dalmatian coast. The next people to seriously push the idea would be the Americans in 1918.

The Italians had conflicting emotions about French assistance. They were none too sure of their own superiority over the Austrians, given the necessity to disperse their forces in more than one base. On the other hand they were jealous whenever French forces approached the Adriatic or appeared to be operating off the Albanian coast since they had their own aspirations in Albania. In March the Italians found the impending move of the French fleet from Malta to Argostoli, and perhaps Corfu, equally disturbing. Capitano di vascello Mario Grassi, then liaison officer with the French fleet, was quick to signal the danger. If the French fleet moved to support the Italians, Dartige might try to assume direction of the operation in the Adriatic by virtue of his title of 'Commander-in-Chief in the Mediterranean'. The Italians always insisted that this title excluded the Adriatic. Grassi thought that they could avoid potential interference in the Adriatic if any French squadron in Ionian waters was under another French vice-admiral who did not have the title 'Commander-in-Chief'. Dartige would then remain at Malta or in the Aegean ready to intervene in a second phase of operations should the Austrians overcome the first obstacle represented by the Italian fleet and any French squadron previously attached to it. In other words, the Italians wanted the C.-in-C. Mediterranean to stay well clear of the Adriatic. Grassi warned of Dartige's inclination to interfere and that the French C.-in-C. would seek the first opportunity to modify the situation in which the French had so far played only a secondary role in the maritime war.[12]

Abruzzi readily admitted that with the means for reconnaissance that the Italians had at hand, particularly in the winter months when it was difficult for aircraft from Venice to watch Pola, he was not able to guarantee that the Austrian fleet could not escape from the Adriatic. He regarded such an event as improbable but not impossible. Even if he moved the Italian fleet to Valona, there was still no guarantee that the Austrians would not get out since his big ships could not remain under steam all the time. Abruzzi therefore planned to concentrate all his forces south of the Straits of Otranto if the Austrians should ever break out. The Italian fleet would then prevent them from *returning* to the Adriatic, while it would be up to the other Allied navies to actually pursue them. The best preventative measure would be to concentrate the large French ships at Argostoli. Abruzzi, however, was adamant on the question of command. He did not believe that the French C.-in-C. at Argostoli or Corfu could impose his influence on operations in the Adriatic unless the respective governments modified the Naval Convention of May 1915. He was certain that the French C.-in-C. would have absolute command of operations in a French zone – which included the Ionian south of the Straits of Otranto – and Abruzzi would not hesitate to put himself under his orders if the Italian fleet ever had to co-operate with the French here. On the other hand, Abruzzi claimed the full direction of operations in the Adriatic and French co-operation here ought to take place through a French vice-admiral under Abruzzi's orders.[13]

However adamant Abruzzi might have been about command in the Adriatic, he nevertheless felt that he needed French assistance in any classic encounter with the capital ships of the Austrian fleet. This at first glance might have been somewhat surprising, but the Italian C.-in-C. feared that in terms of dreadnoughts or semi-dreadnoughts the Austrians might, by a clever tactical manœuvre, neutralize the slight Italian superiority. Abruzzi assumed that the Austrians would use only their best ships, the four Viribus Unitis-class dreadnoughts and the three semi-dreadnought Radetzkys in any serious encounter, and discounted the assistance of the British Queen division of old battleships which were too slow to match the Radetzkys and whose 305mm/40 calibre guns he considered inferior to the Austrian's 305mm/45 calibre. The four Regina Elenas had an advantage in speed but this was nullified by their excessive inferiority in armament, each had only two 305-mm guns. Abruzzi would therefore have to face the seven Austrian capital ships with six Italian dreadnoughts (*Dante*, three Cavours, two Dorias). The broadside of the Italians was superior but in certain tactical formations, notably with both fleets in line abreast, the Italians, even in pursuit, would only be able to employ twenty-eight against thirty 305-mm guns.[14] The diagrams in naval annuals confirm the duke's contention that in certain circumstances the Italians might have been fighting at a slight disadvantage, although one wonders if a real encounter would have developed in such a neat fashion so as to give the Austrians this theoretical advantage. Was it also realistic to assume that the four Regina Elenas would have played absolutely no part in the battle and would not have used their superior speed to take up a position where they could contribute some firepower and perhaps divert the Austrian fire? Abruzzi did not mention that the Italians also had, at least in theory, an advantage in speed. There was a real Italian disadvantage, but the duke did not speak of it or perhaps was not fully aware of it. British observers were almost uniformly critical of the unrealistic nature of Italian gunnery exercises and primitive fire-control procedures. There is some doubt whether the big guns of the Italian fleet at long range and high speed really would have been able to hit anything.[15] The inevitable question would then be how good was Austrian gunnery in comparison? The issue was never put to the test.

Abruzzi's solution to his assumed dilemma was simple. He needed a group of ships from an Allied navy whose artillery was more modern and speed greater than the British Queens. He was realistic enough not to expect the British to send ships of this sort from the North Sea and therefore turned to the French for a division of three semi-dreadnought Dantons. Abruzzi wanted the Dantons to be sent to the Ionian (that is, Corfu) and be ready to co-operate with him in any action.[16] Abruzzi approached the French through Capitano di vascello Grassi, his liaison officer with Dartige, and provided the French with a copy of his General Orders to the Italian fleet dealing with the contingency of an Austrian sortie. These directives included the suggestion that on receipt of intelligence that the Austrian fleet was out, the French fleet would sail from Argostoli towards a position approximately fifty miles south of Cape Santa Maria di Leuca and Fano, ready to intercept should the Austrians attempt to proceed through the straits. Under certain conditions, such as an Austrian move towards Brindisi or Valona, a division of Dantons would join the Italian fleet in its attempt to intercept. In case of a general Italian offensive in the Adriatic, Abruzzi desired a French division to join the British division to add to his superiority and share in the victory. He offered, in turn, to place himself or a portion of his fleet at the disposition of the Allied forces if circumstances carried the struggle *outside* the Adriatic. Dartige expressed disappointment at the 'defensive' nature of the Italian plans, given their superiority in numbers and Grassi had to give the, what should have been familiar, explanation that under present circumstances there was little 'offensive' action that could be undertaken that would justify the risks. Dartige offered to send the division of Dantons when they were required, but not at the moment for he did not want to weaken his fleet or disturb gunnery exercises. Dartige considered his own forces to be decisively superior to the Austrians should they try to escape from the Adriatic. But, whatever his superiority in capital ships, Dartige thought that the French were really in a bad way through their lack of destroyers. He had at the moment only six, all the others were assigned tasks which had nothing to do with his fleet. On this subject the discussion quickly took an alarming turn for the Italians. Dartige's talk about badly needed destroyers which had been assigned to Italy by the Naval Convention gave Grassi the impression that the French wanted to get them back by offering submarines as substitutes.[17]

Dartige replied to Abruzzi in a *note verbale* which he was careful to emphasize had no official character. He vaguely agreed with the duke's plans for the destruction of the Austrians should they sortie and promised his support within the limits of the convention of May 1915, but anything that was not contained in this convention could only be granted by the French government. If the French and the Italian fleets ever joined for battle with the Austrians, Dartige thought it desirable for the French fleet to attack the head of the enemy line while the Italians attacked the tail. He had no personal objection towards a division of three Dantons reinforcing the Italian fleet at Taranto if the French fleet left the area, nor did he object to the division proceeding to Taranto when the situation required in order to familiarize itself with Italian methods. However, while the French fleet was at Bizerte, Malta, Corfu, or Argostoli, Dartige preferred to keep it grouped together under its own C.-in-C., ready to act in accordance with the convention of May 1915. He reported that the French fleet on 25 May was deployed as follows: 6 armoured cruisers (less 1 under refit) at Corfu; the C.-in-C., 6 dreadnoughts and 6 Dantons (less 1 dreadnought and 1 Danton under refit) at Argostoli; and 5 Patries and *Suffren* (less 1 under refit) at Salonika and Mudros.[18]

Grassi summed up Dartige's reply as clinging to the Naval Convention and claiming that any variation from it was beyond his competence and could only be decided by the government. Even the concession to send a division of Dantons whenever the French fleet was absent from Argostoli, Corfu, Malta, or Bizerte was weakened by the inclusion of the latter two. Grassi could not imagine where the French fleet might go if it was not at one of the four ports, and hoped that they might reduce the French reservation to Argostoli and Corfu. He thought that the subject might be a topic of discussion in a forthcoming meeting between Abruzzi and Dartige and could then form the basis of discussions between the respective ministries.[19] The French Naval Staff, for its part, was also inclined to think that the best thing would be a conference between the two commanders about the different contingencies which might occur, followed by the drafting of a *memorandum de combat* for their flag officers.[20]

Abruzzi paid a brief visit to the French C.-in-C. at Argostoli on 31 May. The duke's visit was announced only the evening before and he arrived in the scout *Nino Bixio*, escorted by a single destroyer. On the surface all was charm and the duke presented a silver vase to the French flagship *Provence*. He insisted that his visit had a purely 'personal' character. The two commanders discussed their action in liaison should the two fleets ever have to meet the Austrians, and from that point of view Dartige thought that the interview had not been useless. But the question of the deployment of the Danton division was left to their respective governments and the Italians noted that all of Dartige's concessions were also on a purely 'personal' basis. Dartige had less charitable thoughts about his allies. He thought that the Italians had little confidence in their squadrons and even their latest dreadnoughts were not up to the mark. They had abdicated all thought of an offensive and had seeded their coasts with numerous minefields which hampered their own movements as much as those of the enemy.[21] Abruzzi, for his part, was alarmed at Dartige's claim that he could recall the French destroyers at Brindisi to work with the French fleet when necessary, since this would probably occur at the very moment that the Italian fleet was going into action. Abruzzi also wanted the promise of the three Dantons to be something more than a mere personal pledge. He preferred a firm agreement between the two governments which would be valid whenever the French fleet was away at Malta or Bizerte.[22]

The prospect of eventual Franco-Italian co-operation was not improved by the continuing problem of the relations between Capitaine de vaisseau de Cacqueray, commanding the French Adriatic Flotilla, and the Italian authorities at Brindisi. The optimistic view that the private talks between Dartige and Pini at the Malta Conference in March would improve the situation had proved to be false. The tangled subject of command relationships in the multi-national force at Brindisi is too lengthy to recount in detail, but de Cacqueray reported directly to the Minister of Marine rather than to Dartige, and the desperate need of the latter for destroyers which the French were convinced that the Italians were misusing added a particular edge to the controversy.[23]

The French were concerned enough to query the British about the situation of British ships attached to the Italian fleet. Thursby explained in a private letter to the First Sea Lord that there was no preferential treatment between any of the allies and that the French commander at Brindisi attended all Flag Officers' meetings along with the British SNO. However, Thursby thought that the real cause of de Cacqueray's discontent was the fact that all operations in the southern Adriatic were initiated and directed by the Italian C.-in-C. at Taranto (that is, Abruzzi) with the necessary orders given to the ships concerned by the Italian admiral at Brindisi. Thursby met with Abruzzi daily and the latter asked for concurrence before issuing orders for British ships, who subsequently received those orders from the Italian admirals under whom they were serving. Thursby held the British SNO responsible for seeing that the ships were fit for service, that he understood the orders and that he considered them reasonable and safe. If he did not, he was not to execute them without further reference to Thursby. As for Abruzzi, Thursby declared that he 'runs his own show' and thought it was better that he should do so instead of it being run by a committee of foreign officers. Thursby's only qualification was that if Abruzzi should go he did 'not think there is anyone they could put in his place'. Thursby's account seemed to indicate that the British really did have a more favourable situation in that they had a flag officer in proximity to the Italian C.-in-C. at Taranto. The French did not enjoy this advantage and if Thursby's explanation is correct, de Cacqueray by definition could play only a minor role in the initiation of operations. The Admiralty passed on Thursby's comments to the French, but rather tactfully omitted certain remarks about de Cacqueray. The French commodore was 'very anti-Italian & Pro-British. He dislikes the Italians & they don't like him. Our people are friendly with both, but prefer working with the French, who are gallant & good seamen but cannot stick it at sea for long. The Italians lack initiative, avoid responsibility, and are not accustomed to Fleet work.'[24] Thursby had expressed rather succinctly the British outlook after their experience in the Adriatic and was also reflecting opinions which, justly or unjustly, were widely held in the Royal Navy.

The assumed inviolability of the respective national zones in the Mediterranean was also another problem, but fortunately this one proved relatively easy to solve. Lacaze protested to the French naval attaché in Rome that on 4 and 5 June a hunting group of French flotilla craft had been in pursuit of two German submarines believed to be returning to Cattaro from the western Mediterranean. The Italian authorities were notified and sent two destroyers from Brindisi to take up the hunt at the Otranto barrage. When the Italian destroyers arrived, the French group suspended its chase 'considering that they were not authorized to cross the limits of the Adriatic zone'. Lacaze argued that the boundaries of the zones ought not to be 'impassable barriers' and that an action begun against a common enemy in one zone should not be abandoned at the boundary of that zone. On the contrary, the Allies should send all available forces to reinforce the action already begun, and if the Italian Minister of Marine agreed with this proposition he ought to direct Abruzzi to come to an understanding towards the realization of these goals. The French had replaced their naval attaché in Rome, Lieutenant d'Huart, with Rear-Admiral Pigeon de Saint Pair on 1 May. Saint Pair had held the position a few years before the war and the French had obviously and somewhat belatedly recognized that a flag officer would carry more weight at the Italian Ministry of Marine than a lieutenant. Saint Pair reported that Corsi readily agreed with Lacaze's argument, as indeed any reasonable man would have. Corsi also asked a basic question. Had the French broken off the hunt as a result of any initiative on the part of the Italian authorities? Saint Pair admitted that he had no knowledge of such an act, but assumed from Lacaze's letter that the French commander 'by discretion' and from a strict observation of the Naval Convention had stopped at the boundary of the Straits of Otranto and invited the Italian commander to continue the operation. Corsi immediately agreed that the demarcation line should not apply to operations of this sort and that Dartige had every latitude to pursue in the Adriatic operations which began outside those waters. Corsi then made a startling admission. If, in the course of operations of a large scope, Dartige was led to enter the Adriatic in person, Abruzzi would immediately come under the orders of the Allied C.-in-C. Saint Pair concluded that Corsi did not seem to have consulted the duke on this subject and had the impression that in questions of a general nature the Ministry of Marine did not seem very concerned with his opinions. He therefore suggested that in questions of this sort Dartige would do well to deal directly with the ministry in Rome.[25] Abruzzi had often told Thursby that he would gladly place himself under the French C.-in-C.'s orders if it would shorten the war,[26] but Corsi's statement that this would occur in the Adriatic – assuming that the French naval attaché had reported it correctly – was surprising. Or perhaps it was less than it seemed, for it was difficult to imagine the circumstances that might cause the French fleet to enter the Adriatic. They were positioned to prevent the Austrian fleet from *breaking out*, but who was likely to *break in*, unless it would be a highly improbable German attempt to reach Pola with ships from the North Sea or perhaps the *Goeben* from Constantinople? The Italians did, somewhat later, give the French a list of regulations concerning prior notice to Italian naval authorities about French forces in hot pursuit of submarines in order to avoid 'incidents' with their patrols along the line of British drifters in the Straits of Otranto.[27] The question of the Danton division could not be disposed of so easily.

Throughout the summer and autumn of 1916 the Italians and French exchanged notes and memoranda, with the Italian ambassador in Paris, Tittoni, also ready to intervene. The two navies simply could not agree on when and under what circumstances the Dantons would join the Italian fleet. The French were reluctant to break up their homogeneous squadron and even more reluctant to place their ships under Italian command while weakening their own C.-in-C. The Italians were reluctant, as ever, to see the French commander intervene in their Adriatic. The arguments produced by the Stato Maggiore, the Etat-Major Général, Abruzzi and Dartige were all cogent and appealing from their own point of view. There is no space to go into them in detail. They produced a small mountain of paper but no agreement and a certain amount of ill will. They were also slightly unreal since they rested on the increasingly unlikely hypothesis that the Austrian fleet would attempt to break out of the Adriatic. Unfortunately, in the long run this lack of agreement meant that it would take two battle fleets rather than one to check the Austrians, and this represented a substantial waste of Allied resources.[28]

The Regia Marina suffered a major catastrophe on 2 August when the dreadnought *Leonardo da Vinci* caught fire, blew up and capsized in Taranto harbour with heavy loss of life. The Italian government, while notifying families of the victims, did not initially make any official announcement of the loss, a procedure which was probably a mistake since it contributed to the spread of wild rumours. The Italians had lost the battleship *Benedetto Brin* under similar circumstances the year before and the implications of this latest disaster were serious. Either Italian procedures on board ship were defective and had caused the catastrophe, or the Italians suffered from the nightmare of unstable powder which had plagued the French navy in the years before the war. On the other hand, if the loss was due to enemy action, notably sabotage, the Italian authorities could be accused of criminal negligence in regard to counterespionage and the surveillance of Germans, Swiss-Germans and even Austrians still resident on Italian soil. The only mitigating factors, according to the French ambassador, were the recent successes of the Italian army along the Isonzo River which would lessen the effect on morale.[29] The Italians inevitably appointed a commission to conduct a detailed inquiry into the catastrophe, and eventually Italian espionage activities, notably a break-in and ransacking of a safe at the Austrian consulate in Zurich in 1917, confirmed that the loss of the *Leonardo* was indeed due to Austrian sabotage.[30] The Italians were certainly not the only ones to lose warships to explosions in harbour during the war. The British lost the dreadnought *Vanguard*, battleship *Bulwark* and armoured cruiser *Natal*; the Russians lost the dreadnought *Imperatriza Maria* and the Japanese lost the dreadnought *Kawachi*. But the catastrophe had a particularly heavy effect in Italy given the sensitivity over its national performance so far during the war. The French very quickly drew the immediate and obvious conclusion. The Italians had just lost one of their best units and this would inevitably accentuate their obsession with numerical inferiority, and they could expect renewed demands for French battleships to be sent to Taranto.[31]

The French were right, but Corsi also took advantage of the loss of the *Leonardo da Vinci* to ask for additional British assistance, notably either more battleships or the substitution of superior ships for the obsolete Queen division. Jackson could not diminish Jellicoe's fleet at the moment, but promised to substitute dreadnoughts for the old battleships in the British Adriatic squadron as soon as the situation in the North Sea permitted.[32]

The Italians also asked for British monitors in the northern Adriatic. Corsi would have liked four, with at least two armed with 12-in. guns. The

Admiralty eventually sent one, the *Earl of Peterborough*, armed with two 12-in. guns, which did not arrive at Venice until December.[33] The Italians had more success in October with an appeal for additional destroyers or trawlers of recent construction with adequate speed for submarine hunting on the Otranto barrage. They even offered to man the trawlers themselves, and the reinforcements might free some Italian torpedo-boats to operate elsewhere in the Mediterranean to the benefit of Allied traffic. Corsi appealed to the Italian Foreign Minister for diplomatic support, arguing that the Italian fleet had not received the adequate naval support it had been promised on entering the war. The appeal on these terms evidently had some effect. After the Taranto Conference at the end of October the Admiralty agreed to send four H-class destroyers and a second monitor.[34]

The question of the supreme command in the Adriatic which so divided the French and Italians involved a contingency that was not likely to take place – sustained offensive action by the Austrian fleet. Ironically, the Italian C.-in-C. himself doubted such action would ever materialize. The Duke of the Abruzzi did not believe, for example, that the Austrians would ever attempt a landing on the Italian coast or permit a major encounter with the Allied squadrons. The Austrians might use their fleet to oppose the right wing of the Italian army in any advance by the latter, but would quickly understand the difficulty of operating in an area thick with mines and threatened by the submarines from Venice. Abruzzi believed that it was more probable that the Austrians would use some of their large warships in operations similar in concept to those followed by Austrian light craft, that is raids against the Italian coast and bombardments of coastal towns and cities. Abruzzi recommended that the Italians counter this by improving their underwater defences at all ports important enough to justify the enemy risking his big ships. This would mean laying minefields at a great enough distance from shore to exclude the possibility of long-range bombardment.[35]

By October 1916 Lacaze was anxious for a meeting between the respective commanders-in-chief. He managed to manufacture a propitious occasion by inducing the President of the Republic to confer the Grand Cross of the Legion of Honour on the Duke of the Abruzzi. Dartige would proceed to Taranto to make the award in person and naturally use the opportunity to discuss a number of outstanding questions. These would include potential operations against the Dalmatian coast. Lacaze apparently wanted to act on a suggestion made by the French naval attaché in Rome that they use General Joffre to intervene with Cadorna to provide the necessary troops. Lacaze also wanted to revise the conditions of the Otranto barrage which was not yet effective, but which he considered to be the best means of hindering submarine action. He suggested organizing a small conference over the barrage to which they might invite the local British commander.[36] The Italians were equally anxious for a conference by the beginning of October. They were alarmed by the sinking of their merchant shipping off the Spanish coast or the Balearics, where they suspected submarine bases, and were not pleased by the French view that it was better to concentrate light craft on the Otranto barrage rather than reinforce the patrols in the western Mediterranean.[37]

The French were able to turn Italian concern over sinkings on the western Mediterranean routes into what turned out to be primarily a conference on the Otranto barrage scheduled to open at Taranto on 27 October. Rear-Admiral Fatou, the French Admiral of Patrols, would have to represent Dartige who was now completely tied down by the Greek situation. Fatou and de Cacqueray prepared a plan for stiffening the Otranto barrage, but Fatou was always conscious of the need to constantly protect over 2,500 miles of routes in the French zones of the Mediterranean and did not intend to modify any of the arrangements for patrolling currently in force. Therefore, when he took into account French needs for escort and normal patrols in the Ionian he only had sufficient forces for a much less elaborate Otranto barrage then he had originally intended.[38] It was also apparent that if it should prove desirable to place direction of the Otranto barrage under a single individual, Lacaze intended to propose de Cacqueray.[39] That proposal was likely to cause difficulty.

The Italians had certain fundamental criteria which governed their attitude to the Otranto barrage. They could not exclude the possibility that the Austrian fleet might some day change its defensive attitude and always had to hold their fleet ready to meet the Austrians alone, since Allied assistance might not arrive in time. This meant that they had to provide an adequate number of destroyers to work with their fleet in the lower Adriatic. The Italians also had to maintain a sufficient number of destroyers and torpedo-boats at Venice to serve as a threat and restrain the Austrian potential to damage operations on land. These needs were of primary importance to the Italians and came before any contribution to the Otranto barrage whose efficiency, Corsi maintained, was only relative. Up to now only the British had been able to increase their support of the barrage. The Italians could not do so without damage to their other interests. On the other hand, even though the Straits of Otranto were in the Italian zone, their effective blockade contributed to the security of all Allied shipping throughout the Mediterranean. Corsi went back to the old Italian complaint about inadequate support in terms of light craft compared to what had been promised in the Naval Convention and pointed out that if the British had been unable to bar the passage of submarines through the much narrower Straits of Gibraltar, it was unreasonable to suggest that the Italian navy by itself could bar the Straits of Otranto.[40]

The Otranto Barrage

In retrospect the Otranto barrage at the entrance to the Adriatic was, because of its implications for the submarine war, the most important Allied operation in this area during 1916. This is not to imply that there were no other operations or actions in the Adriatic, for there were many but they were relatively small in scope and would be too numerous to include in a book of this kind. On a careful reading of the record, the Italians were also more active than their detractors realized or were perhaps willing to admit. The same might also be said for their Austrian enemies. But their options given the geographical setting and the changed nature of the war, were relatively limited. In the course of 1916 the Italian submarine *Pullino* was lost on the Galiola reef off the island of Unie in the Quarnero on 31 July during an attempt to reach Fiume. The incident provided the Italians with one of their martyrs, Nazario Sauro, an Istrian (and still an Austrian subject) who had been serving as pilot and was captured and subsequently executed by the Austrians. The following day the submarine *Salpa*, sent to bombard the wreck of the *Pullino*, blew the stern off the torpedo-gunboat *Magnet*.[41] Corsi acknowledged the explanation of the C.-in-C. at Venice, Thaon di Revel, that the *Pullino*'s mission had been a useful contribution to their operations against Fiume, but cautioned him that in the present situation offensive activity in the upper Adriatic, while undoubtedly useful, would not be a contribution of primary importance to the supreme ends of the war and should be kept within just limits.[42]

The Allies had other submarine successes and losses in the Adriatic. The new Italian submarine *Balilla* was lost off Cape Planka on 19 July after action with the Austrian torpedo-boats Tb65 and Tb66, and the British submarine H3 were mined off Cattaro on 15 July. The French submarine *Bernouilli* managed to blow the stern off the Austrian destroyer *Csepel* near the entrance to Cattaro on 4 May, but on 15 September the French submarine *Foucault* was destroyed ten miles off Cattaro by Austrian aircraft, assisted no doubt by the extreme clarity of Adriatic waters which worked to the disadvantage of Allied submarines. The action also demonstrated the potential effectiveness of aircraft in the struggle against submarines. In a surface action on 2 August Capitaine de frégate Frochot, leading the French destroyers *Commandant Bory*, *Bisson* and the Italian destroyers *Ardito* and *Impavido* returning from escorting a raid by Italian motor torpedo-boats on Durazzo, chased the Austrian destroyers *Wildfang* and *Warasdiner*, which had bombarded Molfetta at dawn, while forces from Brindisi and Valona came out in pursuit. *Commandant Bory* and *Abba* fired at long range after the fleeing Austrians but broke off pursuit about 15 miles off Cattaro when the cruiser *Aspern* and two torpedo-boats came out in support. The French and Italians were in turn attacked, unsuccessfully, by the submarine U4 while returning to Brindisi.[43] This inconclusive action was fairly typical of the war of ambush and counter-ambush in the Adriatic. Aircraft played an increasing role but one that is difficult to recount in a work of this scope since, by its nature, it involved many small actions. On the whole the Italians, with some assistance from the French, gradually reduced the initial Austrian advantage and brought about a more balanced situation.[44]

The Italians shifted their commanders once again in May 1916 and, after the armoured cruisers came back from Venice, Cagni became C.-in-C. at Brindisi, Millo, C.-in-C. at Valona, and in September Rear-Admiral Acton replaced Pini as commander of the Scouting Division. Cagni and Millo enjoyed the reputation of being among the more aggressive of the Italian admirals and Cagni gave his full support towards the deployment of the one weapon which the Italians developed that was well suited to Adriatic conditions. In April of 1915 the Italians had ordered the first group of what subsequently became known as the Mas (*motobarca armata silurante*). These were fast (22–25 knots) motor torpedo-boats which could be fitted with two torpedoes and had a crew of eight.[45] The Mas scored a notable success on the night of 7 June when Mas5 (Tenente di vascello Pagano di Melito) and Mas7 (Tenente di vascello Berardinelli), towed by two torpedo-boats to the Albanian coast and escorted by an *escadrille* of French destroyers, succeeded in torpedoing the steamer *Locrum* (924 tons) in Durazzo harbour. After aerial reconnaissance confirmed the presence of two steamers they repeated the raid on the night of the 25th–26th, escorted by the scout *Marsala* and Italian destroyers, and sank the steamer *Sarajevo* (1,100 tons), which was, however, later salved.[46] The Mas were clearly a weapon with a future and one that the Italians adapted to readily. It is important to remember, however, that not all Mas operations were successful, they were relatively fragile and limited in range, and the Austrians would improve the net and boom defences of their harbours. Nevertheless, they would achieve a spectacular success in 1918 when they sank an Austrian dreadnought.

From the strategic point of view the Adriatic skirmishes were far less important than the Otranto barrage and one of the major reasons why they have been relegated to the multi-volume official or semi-official histories of the naval war. The barrage was different. Thursby had applied for an extra forty to fifty drifters in April. By then the British net drifters based on Brindisi had been continuously at work since September 1915, patrolling the Straits of Otranto and assisting in the evacuation of the Serbian army. Their patrol area extended to a distance of eighty miles from Brindisi and was forty miles wide at its narrowest point, and the strain on the personnel to achieve maximum efficiency with the numbers available was beginning to tell. Thursby also asked for forty or more motor launches to assist the drifters and thought that the approaching summer weather would provide ideal conditions for them to work. He expected the Italians to deepen their patrol to the north while the French would do so to the south. He also thought that the number of additional vessels he asked for was 'the minimum with which it is possible to maintain an efficient patrol line across the Straits of Otranto'.[47] The docket of Thursby's report grew thick with comments and minutes as the Admiralty attempted to scrape together additional drifters. There were no more available in Britain and the Admiralty tried to obtain some from the Orkneys area or the Grand Fleet.[48] At first, Jellicoe was willing to 'eventually' release from the Orkneys area some twelve to fifteen drifters, a concession Oliver branded as 'not much use', and added 'it does not seem to be realized in the Grand Fleet that these drifters are required for active service against enemy submarines for the preservation of our merchant shipping & the lives of the crews'. Oliver wanted all drifters not required or used for protecting bases against submarines. In the end, and for very good reasons, the Admiralty could not obtain more than ten drifters from the C.-in-C. of the Home Fleets.[49]

Thursby had few illusions about the effectiveness of the Otranto patrol. On 6 May he wrote that after having to detach twenty-four drifters to Corfu to help the French admiral during the transfer of the Serbian army to Salonika, his Otranto patrol was 'practically useless at present', and less than a week later, with the Italian destroyers busy covering a movement of

Italian troops, Thursby conceded that the Otranto patrol was 'practically non existent'.[50] He had reluctantly parted with the drifters on Jackson's orders and was inclined to 'blame the French C.-in-C. who has done nothing to assist it & much to hamper it. I am afraid it is not spectacular enough to appeal to them. They are very gallant & brave & full of dash so long as it does not involve hard & continuous work.'[51]

This was an old lament on the part of Thursby but his connection with the drifters ended at the end of May when he succeeded de Robeck in command of the Eastern Mediterranean Squadron. Rear-Admiral Mark Kerr, formerly head of the Naval Mission in Greece, took over command of the British Adriatic Squadron. Kerr was an air-minded officer, the first British flag officer to qualify as a pilot in 1914, and almost immediately spoke enthusiastically to the Duke of the Abruzzi about an air raid on the torpedo factory at Fiume by seaplanes carried to within sixty miles of their objective by cruisers and other vessels. The aircraft would then make for Ancona while a submarine ambush would be established off Cape Promontore in case the Austrians came out in pursuit. The plan stalled, however, when they could not obtain more than fifteen seaplanes. Kerr wanted forty or fifty and they were also short of destroyers and effective sea-going submarines.[52] He was quickly brought down to earth by more mundane matters. The Otranto patrol, weakened as it was, had its first success when the Austrian U6 was caught in the nets of the drifters and subsequently destroyed on 13 May. But retribution came quickly and on the night of 31 May–1 June the destroyers *Balaton* and *Orjen* along with three torpedo-boats, backed up by the cruiser *Helgoland*, raided the drifter line and sank the *Beneficient*.[53]

The situation improved somewhat on 3 June when six French destroyers and twenty-four drifters which had been covering the transport of the Serbian army to Salonika returned to the Adriatic. Kerr was now alive to the danger and feared a major raid on the vulnerable drifters, but also felt handicapped in having to rely on foreign aid in the matter of destroyers, submarines and light cruisers. He thought that the situation might be improved if the British had a permanent senior officer at Brindisi, a commodore who would balance de Cacqueray. The latter was a junior captain, allegedly not so easy to deal with, but 'as always with foreigners, his broad pendant [commodore's flag] carries a lot of guns'. By this time Kerr was cognizant of the potential importance of the Straits of Otranto since Italian wireless intercepts seemed to confirm a constant stream of submarines passing through, with the big ones diving under the net area. He learned that the French C.-in-C. was anxious to put a line of drifters southwards of the British with destroyers in between, and asked the First Sea Lord for some E-class submarines armed with 4-in. guns to deploy ready to attack enemy destroyers when they came for the drifters. He also wanted four British destroyers to serve as a good example for the Italians and French who 'buck up when our fellows are in competition'.[54]

Kerr became even more committed to the Otranto barrage as time went on. He regarded the Mediterranean as a trade artery which had been cut and would bleed them to death if not tied up. His ultimate goal was now to obtain 150 drifters, 4 fast destroyers and 2 or more E-class submarines to help protect the drifters, and 30 to 40 seaplanes with 1 or 2 seaplane carriers so that they could raid Fiume, Cattaro, and afterwards Pola. Kerr feared that the drifters, which had practically no protection, would be raided and 'wiped out' the next time they bagged a submarine.[55] Kerr's schemes for a carrier-launched raid on Fiume were apparently stifled by the Admiralty, while Abruzzi proved unable to get more destroyers from his government: in fact they removed two from his command. Kerr doubted that he would get seaplanes from the French and complained 'in the meantime, whether it is their business or ours, we pay the bill in losses from submarines'.[56]

The protection given to the drifters was steadily reduced as a result of losses. On 23 June the Austrian submarine U15 torpedoed and sank the Italian auxiliary cruiser *Città di Messina* twenty miles east of Otranto. The French destroyer *Fourche*, which accompanied her, depth-charged the submarine and, seeing an oil slick mistakenly assuming it was sunk, began to rescue survivors. The *Fourche* was then cut in two and sunk by a torpedo. The Italians gave up, probably wisely, protecting the drifter line with a cruiser during daylight hours. The protection of the drifters was reduced to a section of destroyers, but on 10 July the Italian *Impetuoso* was torpedoed and sunk by the Austrian U17. The drifters also suffered another loss on 9 July when Captain Horthy in *Novara* raided the line, sank two drifters and damaged two others, took nine British sailors prisoner, and got away before the arrival of Allied reinforcements. The Italians then decided that they could no longer protect the drifters and the line was brought south to a somewhat less vulnerable position between Cape Santa Maria di Leuca and Fano. Here the drifters had the advantage of being more secure, on the whole as effective, but suffered the disadvantage of being further from their base.[57] The vulnerability of the drifters to raids had now been demonstrated but the really large-scale massacre that Kerr feared would not come until the following year.

The term 'barrage' or even 'line' of drifters is a bit misleading for it conjures up a picture of a continuous line of small craft with nets out forming a serious barrier to submarines. The reality was far different. Capitaine de vaisseau Lejay, French liaison officer with the Italian fleet, provided an interesting sketch made by a destroyer specifically sent to inspect the line of drifters between Cape Santa Maria de Leuca and Fano on the morning of 13 July (see Map 8). Only thirty-seven of what should have been a daily average of fifty were out, and only ten actually had their nets in the sea, while the unpredictable Adriatic currents had caused the groups to drift far apart. The barrage was completely illusory and the number of drifters quite insufficient to obtain serious results. They needed a minimum of seventy-five constantly on the barrage but Kerr had reported that the British could not supply them.[58]

Kerr in fact had only ninety-six drifters as of 10 September – one had recently been sunk by an air raid on 26 August. A dozen motor launches did arrive on station and were based on Gallipoli, with a sub-base at Tricase, but the launches were only good in fine weather. The base of the drifters themselves was moved from Brindisi to Taranto, where they would work under Kerr's direction, and the drifter line was established between a point five miles north of Santa Maria di Leuca and Fano Island, turning down to Samothraki, with a few left over to form a small second barrier which would shift from time to time. Unfortunately, the drifters still had no real protection from attacks from the sea or air and, according to Kerr, had enjoyed immunity in the past only because the enemy knew that it was desirable to leave them alone since they were doing no harm. As soon as they got a submarine, they were raided. Kerr complained of the constant refusals by the Admiralty of his requests and remarked that the latter must have misread the bible and interpreted the passage in Matthew: 'Ask and ye shall be refused, seek and ye shall be "straffed"; knock and we will jolly well lock the door.'[59] In October, Kerr claimed that convoying transports to Salonika, Valona and Santi Quaranta took every destroyer and torpedo-boat that Abruzzi had and left none for the drifter line.[60] The British contribution to the Adriatic also changed. The *Topaze* and *Sapphire* at Brindisi were far too slow compared to the Austrian cruisers, locked up valuable officers and men, and required destroyer escorts when they were at sea. After consultation with the Italians, Kerr suggested their recall, and they were eventually replaced with the faster *Bristol* and *Gloucester*. The major Italian concern was that the number of British light cruisers remain at four, as stipulated in the Naval Convention. Moreover, the four surviving antiquated B-class submarines were recalled from Venice in October after the arrival of four W-class submarines sold to Italy.[61]

The long-delayed conference concerning the Otranto barrage took place aboard the Duke of the Abruzzi's headquarters ship the *Trinacria* (the former Royal yacht) at Taranto on 30 October. Rear-Admiral Fatou, the French Admiral of Patrols, brought a number of proposals, but even before he arrived at least one of them provoked a note of warning. Lacaze, in order to assure unity of direction, wanted command of the Otranto barrage to be entrusted to de Cacqueray, whom he considered highly competent and well acquainted with the situation. Corsi, when approached by the French naval attaché, was unenthusiastic and full of excuses.[62] Kerr reported the problem more straightforwardly. The choice of de Cacqueray would be very unpopular, he warned before the conference, for he had quarrelled with the Italians continually ever since he was there, had no tact, hated the Italians and was very rude to them.[63]

At the opening of the conference Fatou proposed shifting the drifters northwards to operate with the line San Cataldo–Saseno as their northern limit.[64] This was unacceptable to Kerr and Abruzzi. The drifters had been moved southwards to the Fano–Leuca line to protect them from raids by Austrian destroyers, and they considered that French and Italian destroyers from Brindisi would have time to cut off the Austrians if they came as far south as Fano, but the Austrians would hardly be threatened on the northern line since they did not have to go any further from Cattaro or Durazzo than the French and Italians had to come from Brindisi. The drifters could also take up the southern line easily from their base at Taranto, but it would take them too much time to proceed up to the proposed French line. Kerr also argued that the drifters had no better chance of catching a submarine in the north than they did in the south. De Cacqueray apparently argued strongly for the French proposal and, in the end, Abruzzi suggested a compromise. The drifters would be put on a line from Otranto to Asproruga (south of Cape Linguetta) and Abruzzi promised to lay a minefield running east from Otranto for ten miles, and to try and have two destroyers out on patrol as long as other obligations for escorts permitted. Kerr consented, for this kept the most dangerous part of the drifter line some way south of Valona. The French were somewhat pleasantly surprised that the Italians were willing to transfer twenty-two of the fifty-two trawlers currently in the Tyrrhenian to the Duke, but were disappointed when he absolutely refused to risk any more costly destroyers (of which three had been torpedoed) in protecting them. The Italians also promised to add eighteen small 300-ton coastal torpedo-boats to the barrage and send an additional twenty-two aircraft to Brindisi and sixteen to Valona. They would be in addition to the thirty that the French planned to provide for Corfu. Abruzzi promised to keep one light cruiser always under steam at Brindisi and ready to sail at half an hour's notice, and politely declined the two antiquated Bruix-class cruisers that the French offered him. The Italian offers were better than Fatou had hoped for.[65]

The one area where there was sharp disagreement was, of course, over the question of command. Fatou seemed nervous in putting forward the name of de Cacqueray and emphasized that the suggestion came from Lacaze rather than Dartige. He was stopped short by Abruzzi, whom Kerr reported as saying 'he could not entertain for a moment the idea of placing the control of the Straits of Otranto under a foreign officer'. Fatou even quoted Abruzzi as saying that he would ask to be relieved of his functions rather than sanction the proposition, and noted that Abruzzi had added he would similarly oppose the candidacy of a British captain, while 'Admiral Kerr had the discretion not to formulate any opinion'. Fatou realized that the Italian support for the barrage was much larger than anticipated and consequently diminished the relative importance of what help the French were bringing. He therefore let the matter drop.[66]

When Abruzzi returned Fatou's official visit, the two had a long heart-to-heart talk about the situation aboard the French Admiral of Patrol's flagship, the yacht *Atmah*. It soon became apparent that beyond reasons of national *amour propre*, there was a special problem with de Cacqueray's candidacy, namely his lack of tact. Fatou, while agreeing that many of de Cacqueray's complaints against the Italians at Brindisi were legitimate, was forced to admit in private to Lacaze that Abruzzi's charges were well founded.[67] It was, as Fatou later confirmed with the French ambassador and naval attaché in Rome, a case of de Cacqueray expressing opinions of the Italian navy a little too freely and loudly in a country where the walls had ears.[68]

Fatou's stay in Rome from 3–4 November was primarily to discuss the question of protecting trade in the western Mediterranean, a subject beyond Abruzzi's authority. Nevertheless, according to Kerr it threatened to upset the decision of the Taranto Conference, for Abruzzi made it quite clear that if the decisions regarding command of the Straits of Otranto were reversed at the ministry he would be forced to resign, and he had already recommended that the Italian government should ask that de Cacqueray be replaced at Brindisi by another officer. Kerr may have been trying to steer clear of this Franco-Italian imbroglio, but his own views were predictable:

The problem of closing the Adriatic would not be efficiently dealt with until the British Government could spare sufficient destroyers and small craft capable of keeping the sea to be under the command of the Senior British officer controlling the drifter line and with enough drifters to have at least a double line across the Straits at all times allowing for boats resting and repairing. This would not interfere with the French and Italian patrols northward and southward of the barrage.[69]

It said something about the relationship between the French and the Italians that at one point during Fatou's stay in Rome the French naval attaché cautioned him against giving the Italians the *verbatim* text of a message Lacaze had just cabled for the Italian Minister of Marine lest this enable the Italian cryptographers to discover the French codes.[70] In assessing the results of the negotiations Fatou rather shrewdly guessed the one fundamental factor which explained, at least in Fatou's mind, the line of argument taken by Abruzzi. Unlike Dartige, he was not C.-in-C. in all the Italian zones and was not charged with the protection of commercial navigation. His major concern, therefore, was still the possibility of having to meet the Austrian fleet, and for this he would need all of his destroyers. He did not intend to see them absorbed in the Otranto barrage while their numbers were whittled down in what for him was only a secondary operation, especially as his own fleet was relatively safe from submarines in hermetically sealed bases.[71]

Capitaine de vaisseau de Cacqueray, the object of so much controversy, had his own judgement of the Taranto Conference. It had been one of pure form, without clear result, especially hindered by the British admiral, and the Italians had agreed to it only as a formality to evade inconvenient questions; but the Italian authorities wanted to keep their habit of acting in complete independence.[72] However, de Cacqueray's days were numbered despite Lacaze's strong and continued support. Lieutenant Mario Arlotta, the Italian naval attaché in Athens, was in Paris in early November on what was ostensibly an unofficial visit, but which included a long private meeting with the Minister of Marine. The affair was arranged by de Roquefeuil, his redoutable colleague in Athens, who was also in Paris at the same time and apparently prepared the ground in advance on the de Cacqueray question. The subject of Otranto was only part of the long interview and Lacaze stressed the need for a 'commandement unique et special' for the barrage. De Cacqueray had demonstrated a special competence for this position, but Lacaze saw no drawback in the command going to an Italian officer, and according to Arlotta, two or three times let escape nearly unconsciously the words, 'Yes, certainly by an Italian officer, better than an Englishman, better than by an Englishman'.[73]

Arlotta's experience in Paris also tipped off the Italians that the French were reading their codes, although it is not clear whether they attempted to correct the problem. If they did, they were not successful for the French continued to do so in 1918. De Roquefeuil had complained to the Italians that he had received a scolding from his minister for a private conversation about Greece that he had had with Capitano di fregata Leone, the Italian naval attaché, on the train from Rome to Paris. Leone had reported the conversation to the Italian Minister of Marine, but since he had personally encoded the message with the aid of his petty-officer secretary and burned his notes, he was puzzled by what method the French had found out. Rear-Admiral Marzolo, to whom Arlotta gave an account of the talks, noted sarcastically on the margin of the letter: 'Poor Leone had not guessed one! The French had our cypher.'[74]

Lacaze finally shifted de Cacqueray to command of the Naval Division of Morocco and on 15 November named Capitaine de frégate Frochot to succeed him as commander of the French flotillas in the Adriatic. Frochot, who had led the destroyers in the action of 2 August, was initially cool to his allies. A fortnight after assuming command he reported that out of a spirit of solidarity with his profoundly esteemed former chief he was led to cease or limit camaraderie with the Italians and was only resuming, little by little, the habit of seeing nearly every evening the Italian vice-admiral or persons in his entourage.[75]

Kerr was anxious to get a British officer in charge of the barrage, but he found a reflection of Lacaze's anti-British sentiments among the Italian authorities, for he suspected that having just refused a French officer the Italian Minister could hardly put a British officer in the post. But Kerr was convinced that regardless of who was in command they needed a far greater number of drifters to make the barrage work. The strength of the Adriatic currents and their unpredictability was such that even when the drifter line had been accurately placed in the evening there was hardly a day in which the groups had not drifted ten miles apart during the night. Kerr thought that they needed drifters deployed in two or three lines, with intervals between them of ten to fifteen miles. The ninety-six drifters that he now had worked ten days at sea and spent three and a half days in harbour, and using this standard it would require 300 drifters to make a really effective barrage.[76]

On the night of 11 December the Italians suffered another disaster. The battleship *Regina Margherita* while leaving Valona for docking in Taranto was mined and went down with heavy loss of life.[77] Captain Grassi conducted the inquiry which placed the blame squarely on the battleship's captain, who had gone down with his ship, for failing to follow instructions for leaving the mined harbour and taking a route dangerously close to a minefield. In order to maintain secrecy regarding the defences of Valona, Abruzzi suggested that for the duration of the war the loss should simply be attributed to an 'act of war'.[78]

The British added around twenty additional drifters to the barrage after the Taranto Conference but it remained relatively ineffective at the close of the year, and the four H-class destroyers promised by the Admiralty were held up at Malta and used for the protection of trade. The Italians provided approximately twenty trawlers taken from their west coast to patrol north of the drifter line, but the Italian and French gunboats mentioned at the conference did not materialize either. They, too, were diverted for escort duties or the protection of bases. The Italians had established a base at Santi Quaranta at the beginning of October and with the expansion of the area they occupied in Albania the protection of the base and the traffic to it became a major concern.[79]

The drifters narrowly escaped loss on the night of 22 December when the Austrian destroyers *Scharfschütze*, *Velebit*, *Reka* and *Dinara* (all of the older 600-ton Huszár class), led by Korvettenkapitän Nowotny in *Scharfschütze*, attacked the drifter patrol line. Fortunately six French destroyers (*Casque*, *Protet*, *Commandant Rivière*, *Commandant Bory*, *Dehorter* and *Boutefeu*), *en route* from Brindisi to Taranto to escort transports, were in the vicinity, and constituted a force superior in numbers and armament to the Austrians. The drifters replied to the Austrian attack as best they could and gave the alarm signal, and Capitaine de frégate de Boisanger in *Casque*, commanding the French group, steered for the sound of the guns. A confused night action followed. *Protet*, the next in line, did not see the signal to turn and only *Commandant Rivière* followed *Casque* into action, but the former was momentarily put out of action by a hit in the boiler room. *Casque* kept up pursuit alone until a hit reduced her speed to 23 knots. In the meantime, reinforcements had sailed from Brindisi, notably a *squadriglia* of Italian destroyers made up of *Abba* (Tenente di vascello Civalleri) leading *Nievo*, and *Pilo*. This *squadriglia* was soon followed by the British light cruiser *Gloucester* escorted by the Italian destroyers *Impavido*, and *Irrequieto*, all steering to intercept the Austrians presumed to be heading towards Cattaro. The French and Italian groups ran into each other and in the darkness and confusion *Abba* rammed *Casque* and shortly afterwards *Boutefeu* rammed *Abba*. The damaged destroyers were towed back to Brindisi the following morning. The French and Italians had missed the opportunity to cut off and destroy an inferior Austrian force, but this first night action at high speed in the Adriatic graphically illustrated the difficulties of command and control.[80] The only happy circumstance on the side of the Allies was the fact that only one of the drifters was slightly damaged and this was, perhaps, not much to show for the grave risks the Austrians had run. They might not be so lucky in future escapes. On the whole, however, the action of 22 December was not an auspicious ending to the year for the Allies and the fundamental difficulties of command of the barrage and the question of French battleship reinforcements for the Italian fleet remained unresolved.

The k.u.k. Kriegsmarine in 1916

The capital ships of the k.u.k. Kriegsmarine, the object of so much concern and hypothetical planning on the part of the Italians, remained quiescent during 1916 fulfilling the essential lines of Haus's strategy of maintaining a 'fleet-in-being'. Haus did not budge from this fundamental strategy although it caused a sharp exchange between himself and AOK. On 22 February AOK issued directives to Haus bearing the signature of Archduke Friedrich, titular head of the armed forces, but obviously inspired by

Conrad, Chief of the General Staff. AOK announced its intention to begin a major offensive at the end of March against the Italians in the Tyrol. This was Conrad's celebrated *Strafe* (or punishment) offensive which, in fact, did not start until mid-May.[81] AOK expected the Kriegsmarine to undertake in the second half of March a 'major action aimed at inflicting serious damage on the enemy'. On the more immediate and concrete side, AOK directed all available naval aircraft to participate in a general air raid on railway bridges over the Piave planned by the commander of the south-west front for 10 March.[82] Haus's reply was negative. A study made by a naval staff officer in July 1915 had revealed that there was no effective way that the big guns of the Austrian battleships could assist the southern flank of the army and there was no prospect of seriously harming the Italians through naval artillery between the front and south of the mouth of the Po River, with the exception of the coastal fortifications around Venice. Haus rather acidly remarked that had there been a serious opportunity to damage the enemy the fleet would not have remained inactive for nine months. An attack on the coastal fortifications of Venice could be justified if it would have a decisive effect on the Tyrol offensive but, according to Haus, the destruction of coastal works would not have the least effect on the battle in the Tyrol or near any of the other frontiers. The navy would provide fifteen seaplanes for the 10 March air raid, but even here Haus warned that the chances of simultaneous action by naval aircraft with army aircraft operating from the Tyrol were not good because of the weather. Enemy warships were only to be seen in the southern Adriatic where nearly all the Austrian cruisers and the I (modern) Torpedo Flotilla were at Cattaro, while the older II Torpedo Flotilla was, after detachment of ships to Sebenico for the escorts of transports, so reduced that the units remaining in Pola sufficed only for local purposes.[83]

Conrad replied that AOK did not expect direct co-operation with the army, but rather a 'ruthless undertaking' similar to the one that the fleet had effected on the Italian east coast at the beginning of the war.[84] Haus answered with a long lesson on the strategy and tactics of the naval war. He wanted a clarification of three important points in AOK's request: (1) its strategic purpose; (2) what was meant by 'serious damage to the enemy', that is, destruction of military objectives or destruction of cities and towns?; and (3) the meaning of the term 'ruthless undertaking', that is, without regard to the stake or their own losses or without regard to the enemy civilian population? The Flottenkommandant described how the situation had altered since 24 May 1915. The Italians were now on the alert with strong coastal defences, minefields, armoured trains and Italian and Allied submarines. The k.u.k. Kriegsmarine was correspondingly weaker in terms of destroyers and torpedo-boats. All had been available at the beginning of the war, but at the moment only two of the six modern Tátra-class destroyers were ready for action – two had been sunk and the remaining two were under repair – while four of the Huszár class, one older destroyer and eighteen torpedo-boats were also in dockyard hands. Haus attributed the decline in available torpedo craft to the excessive demands for service by the army, ranging from escorting transports between Fiume and Durazzo to clearing and securing the newly won harbours on the Montenegrin and Albanian coast. There would have to be a complete redeployment of those units now in the south for any fleet action. Haus also described how Austria's favourable situation and apparent immunity at sea rested not so much on their own strength as on the astonishing passivity and lassitude of their materially superior enemies. This situation could alter through a change in leadership on the Italian side or after a serious Austrian naval reverse. Haus claimed that the offensive spirit in the Italian fleet had vanished as a result of the loss of the *Garibaldi* but could be restored as a result of a similar loss on the Austrian side. He argued that it would be folly to employ their battleships at sea against the only Allied vessels at sea in the upper Adriatic, namely submarines, and the more battleships they employed the better the chances for an enemy submarine. He cited the examples of the failure of the Allied fleets at the Dardanelles, the torpedoing of the *Jean Bart* in the Adriatic, and the relative lack of activity of the battleships of the High Seas Fleet in the North Sea. Haus claimed that Austrian torpedo-boats, destroyers and small cruisers had had twenty-five more or less narrow escapes from torpedo attacks, and despite the sharpest lookout, without in most cases having spotted the submarine's periscope before the attack. Haus made a convincing case for not risking battleships in any action which could have no real military effect on the enemy. If the sole operational. purpose was damaging the enemy, they could do so with incomparably less risk and cost through air raids.[85] Haus was therefore as checked in the movement of his major assets, dreadnoughts, as the Duke of the Abruzzi, and both were far more constrained by the smaller area of the Adriatic than their British and German counterparts in the much larger North Sea. AOK could only agree to refrain from ordering the 'ruthless undertaking'[86] although there may have been some disgruntled army staff officers who wondered what the value had been of all the money spent on battleships before the war.

The Austrian fleet therefore remained firmly in its defensive posture, with the big ships most of the time secure in harbour. But while there was no major fleet action, there was considerable activity by the smaller craft in terms of escorts, sorties against the Italian transport routes and minor raids on the Italian coast. The same has been said for the Italians but a full account is beyond the scope of this book and the interested reader is directed to the detailed work of Sokol. Haus certainly did not suffer by his clash with AOK. In May 1916 he was honoured by being raised to the rank of Grossadmiral, the first and only one the k.u.k. Kriegsmarine would ever have. Haus, sarcastic as ever, remarked that he was taking the congratulations which flooded in as calmly as he had taken the many anonymous letters and satirical poems in the first half year of the war which criticized him for his defensive conduct, but the latter at least had the advantage of not requiring a reply.[87]

The avoidance of risks to large ships also had another justification. Aside from submarines and small torpedo-boats, the k.u.k. Kriegsmarine was able to accomplish little new building during the war. Haus, as well as his Chief of Staff, Linienschiffskapitän Rodler, would have liked to put their primary emphasis on improved versions of the Tátra-class destroyers. Large ships and even battle cruisers were mentioned, but the Austrian leaders realized that they were not likely to get beyond the planning stage during the war.[88] The k.u.k. Kriegsmarine took over a small destroyer, the *Warasdiner*, under construction for the Chinese government, but completed only four new Tátras during the war, two of them replacements for the pair lost on 29 December 1915.[89] The fact that the important yards at Monfalcone were virtually in the front lines and subsequently lost was a major disadvantage.

The air war over the Adriatic and Italy might have intensified, perhaps significantly, in the late summer of 1916 when some German authorities raised the question of sending Zeppelins to the area. The Italian declaration of war on Germany in August would have ended any necessity for them to masquerade under Austrian colours. The matter seems to have begun when Freyberg had a long conversation with the Austrian naval aviator Linienschiffsleutnant Gottfried Freiherr von Banfield, who was in Vienna to be recognized by the Kaiser for his successes.[90] Banfield expressed the opinion that the effects of air raids were satisfactory, but that Zeppelin raids would have even greater success on the easily excitable Italians, and he did not think that they could endure a series of air attacks similar to the ones the Germans had launched against Britain. These sentiments coincided with Freyberg's own ideas on the value of dirigibles in the war against Italy and their usefulness for reconnaissance up and down the long 'tube' of the Adriatic. He took every opportunity to argue these points with Austrian authorities who usually agreed with him, but Freyberg complained that not a single individual had the energy to take up the matter and at least attempt to turn the wish into reality. This was a familiar complaint of the naval attaché as well as many Germans about their Austrian allies. Two days after his conversation with Banfield, Freyberg obtained powerful support when he visited AOK at Teschen on business and managed to interest Conrad in the matter. Conrad was anxious to know if the Germans would put Zeppelins at Austria's disposal.[91] The German government was actually far less enthusiastic about this than Freyberg assumed. Chancellor Bethmann Hollweg and the Kaiser had serious reservations about air raids on Italian cities and wanted attacks limited to strictly military targets.[92] The Admiralstab was more forthcoming and ready to turn over at least two airships if the Austrians would build hangars for them at Agram.[93] Haus, however, considered seaplanes sufficient for the Kriegsmarine's needs under Adriatic circumstances and lacked the personnel to man the airships. The Austrian army also needed all its aviators for aircraft.[94] The Marinesektion reversed itself on 5 October, largely because the airships would have the range to reach Italian industrial centres hitherto immune from air attack, and agreed to build the hangars wherever the Germans wanted them. They could not, however, provide any personnel beyond a naval officer to accompany them on missions. The Germans would have to provide both flight and ground crews.[95] The Germans, with the Kaiser opposed to the project, decided that as a result of losses and accidents they needed all their airships themselves and quietly let the matter drop.[96] German and Austrian airship operations in the Adriatic and Italian theatre never materialized and a number of Italian cities were spared from aerial attack, at least for this war.

The Eastern Mediterranean and the Aegean in 1916

With the close of the Dardanelles campaign the Aegean became a backwater in the naval war. The British and French retained sizeable numbers of older warships to support their forces at Salonika and the burden of protecting this long vulnerable supply route grew increasingly onerous as the German submarine campaign developed. But the major portion of submarine operations against the route tended to be outside the Aegean and in other parts of the Mediterranean, for example along the stretch from Malta to Cerigotto. The Salonika expedition also involved the navies in the complex Greek political situation and the periodic steps of coercion directed against the widely mistrusted government of King Constantine. This was especially true of the French and events in Athens in December would result in the removal of the French (and Allied) C.-in-C. However, Dartige came to grief over what were essentially political, diplomatic and military factors rather than naval questions.

The British in this area maintained the watch over the Dardanelles and were especially anxious to prevent the *Goeben* from breaking out. It was, unfortunately for them, debatable whether the slower semi-dreadnoughts *Lord Nelson* and *Agamemnon*, assisted occasionally by older and slow French battleships, would really have been able to catch the battle cruiser. The British also continued a threat against Smyrna through operations in the Gulf of Smyrna and the occupation of Long Island at the entrance to the gulf. These operations were not without loss, and the monitor M30 was sunk by Turkish gunfire on 13 May and Long Island was evacuated on 27 May. Starting in the spring of 1916 de Robeck also launched a series of raids by Greek irregulars based on islands off the Anatolian coast and supported by a heterogeneous collection of warships and auxiliary craft. Further to the south and west British naval forces, assisted by the French, continued to protect the Suez Canal and support the seaward flank of the Egyptian Expeditionary Force in its eventual advance towards Palestine, while French warships operated off the coast of Syria where the French, of course, had political ambitions. It would require a multi-volume work to provide an adequate account of these many and varied operations which were usually conducted with obsolete warships and were, on the whole, outside the major thrust of the naval war. They were, in effect, taking place in a backwater of the Mediterranean which tended itself, except in time of crisis, to be considered a secondary theatre of the British naval war.[97]

The raids on the Anatolian coast are perhaps among the more interesting of these minor operations and involved the Royal Navy in the rather unusual role of cattle rustling. Captain Frank Larken, commanding the 6th Detached Squadron off the coast of Anatolia, authorized Lieutenant-

Commander B. G. Drake, RNR, commanding the fleet sweeper *Whitby Abbey*, to undertake a raid on the Anatolian coast to seize cattle which the British were convinced the Ottoman government was commandeering for dispatch to Germany. Larken also gave permission for refugees from Anatolia on the island of Samos to take part in the raid and be given half the spoils. Commander Drake conducted the raid on 22 March in the Bay of Lebedos, north of the Gulf of Skala Nuova, towing six caiques with approximately thirty-six Greek irregulars. The irregulars clashed with a small Turkish patrol, killing some and capturing six, and made off with over 600 livestock of various types, mostly sheep. Drake reported: 'In the particular work of this occasion, no better men could have been found than the Irregulars, they acted with promptitude and pluck, obeying the orders given them', and he recommended that the British make more extensive use of them.[98]

De Robeck was, of course, conscious of the minor role to which he and his command was relegated after the Dardanelles campaign and was anxious for action. He wanted to carry out raids on the coast of Asia Minor between Samos Straits and the latitude of Rhodes 'with the object of destroying any submarine bases or stores and to otherwise harass the enemy'. De Robeck, however, wanted to use troops of the Royal Naval Division then garrisoning the islands of Lemnos, Imbros and Tenedos.[99] As he explained to Balfour, the raids with small forces would 'make the Turks put more troops in those parts' and also capture cattle and sheep at present being exported to Germany, and 'as these were largely the property of the Greeks who have been driven from their homes they cannot well accuse us of robbery'.[100] De Robeck promised to obtain the approval of the Admiralty before any specific operation and the latter approved, subject to the raids being on a small scale and not requiring the retention of any transports specially for the purpose.[101] The Malta Conference in March had discussed the prospect of using Greek or Armenian volunteers for raids, and the Army Council also wanted to keep the Turks under threat of landings along the coast of Syria and Asia Minor to prevent troops garrisoned here being sent elsewhere. The War Office, however, thought that it would be extremely difficult to provide the munitions to equip the 30,000–40,000 men that the members of the conference had so glibly mentioned, but agreed to instruct the general officer commanding in Egypt to assist any raids with such troops as could be made available.[102] However, the Army Council decided to take over the Royal Naval Division – the troops de Robeck actually wanted to use – and transfer it to France, and consequently did not want it to get mixed up in any expedition.[103]

De Robeck appears to have wanted the raids to be undertaken by regular troops. He wrote to the First Lord on 21 April: 'The importance of starting raids on the Asiatic coast cannot be too strongly impressed on the War Office' and they would be of little value unless carried out within the next few weeks. He favoured a raid at Bodrum to draw troops far from a railway to an area where communications were difficult.[104] However, when the navy applied to the general commanding in Egypt for two battalions for a minor operation in the Bodrum area it was told that no troops could be spared for the purpose. De Robeck was therefore forced to conduct these operations with irregular bands, recruited as far as possible from Anatolian refugees.[105]

A projected cattle raid – and the naval officers in 1916 used the term 'cattle' in the older sense to denote all types of livestock – in the Gulf of Skala Nuova, had to be called off in early April because the Turks were keeping too good a look out but, on the night of 30 April–1 May, Lieutenant-Commander Gerald Hodson led a raid nine miles east of Gaidaro Island with the sweepers *Aster* and *Whitby Abbey* towing fourteen caiques with 150 irregulars. There was some opposition, *Aster* was attacked by an aircraft, two of the Samians were killed and, 1,870 head of cattle captured. The British had high praise for the Samian leader Asfalia, known as 'Longshanks'.[106] The raids, however, had diplomatic complications. The Greek minister in London, Gennadius, protested that these acts of 'pillage' against the Turkish population had led to reprisals by the Turks on Greek subjects in neighbouring districts and begged the British not to encourage such descents on the mainland. The Admiralty had in fact few details when the Foreign Office first forwarded the protest on 30 April and were not sure exactly what incidents the Greeks were referring to, but once they had obtained more information W. Nicholson, of M Branch (Secretarial) advised that the Foreign Office might be told the outline of the proceedings, but that 'the details might perhaps lead to controversy & would be better suppressed'. Jackson was inclined to be unsympathetic to the Greek protests. The Greek government, after all, was not held in particularly high repute at that moment. He advised that they would have to supply more definite information in such cases with dates and places, but that the British really could not have their strategy dictated by the Greeks. The Admiralty also stressed, in their formal reply to the Foreign Office, that the seizure of cattle 'was a military object as they were being commandeered by the Ottoman government for dispatch to Germany' and that the naval authorities would use part of the booty to relieve distress among Anatolian refugees in Mytilene or elsewhere.[107]

Sir Francis Elliot, the British ambassador in Athens, also complained of the proceedings to de Robeck in what the admiral termed 'a devil of a letter' which 'might have been written by the Greek Foreign Minister', and de Robeck sent a 'corker' in reply. Since, he claimed, all cattle were now commandeered by the Turkish government and sent to Germany, and were stolen from Christians in the first place, de Robeck objected to being 'classed as a brigand by Elliot or anybody else'.[108]

On 12 May, Lieutenant-Commander England in the destroyer *Chelmer* along with *Whitby Abbey*, three ketches and a motor lighter led a cattle raid at a point north of Makaronia. The raid was successful, some 236 head of cattle were taken without loss, and Captain Larken's report gave the colourful detail:

> The *Whitby Abbey* embarked the majority of the cattle her officers and men working with most remarkable dexterity, slinging on board Camels, Horses, Water buffaloes, Bulls, etc., till the ship was crowded

from stem to stern. Some of the Bulls were very fierce and one went mad after being embarked. It was a novel sight.[109]

The scope of the raids expanded in June when Captain Dent, commanding the 1st Detached Squadron, authorized Lieutenant-Commander Myres, RNVR, to conduct a raid on Karada on 3–5 June with twenty-five irregulars from Samos, Kalymnos and Kos. The irregulars attacked a Turkish patrol, killed eight and captured seven, although the spoils were disappointing. Myres, a professor of classics in civilian life, was the type of academic who apparently had a flair for this type of unorthodox warfare and subsequently obtained a reputation as the 'Blackbeard of the Aegean'. The British were also not the only ones to make raids. Dent complained that 'indiscriminate raiding' had been going on for some months past from the Italian islands in the Dodecanese and was likely to interfere with the organized raiding, and he intended to approach the Governor of Rhodes to bring the raids under control.[110]

De Robeck turned over the Eastern Mediterranean Squadron to Vice-Admiral Sir Cecil F. Thursby on 20 June and left to assume command of the 3rd Battle Squadron in home waters. Thursby initially elected to continue the raids, although he too complained about the Italians permitting independent raids from the island of Symi which, in ignorance of each other's intentions, could lead to 'regrettable incidents'.[111] Some degree of co-operation was apparently obtained, for Captain Clifton Brown, later commanding the 1st Detached Squadron, reported a successful raid by the Symi men led by Lieutenant Charnaud in Pedala Bay (latitude 36°46' N, longitude 28°7' E) on 19 July while, on 20 July, Myres led eighty Samians in a raid on Karakisi Bay.[112] Further to the north near Smyrna and Mytilene, the 4th Detached Squadron conducted a raid near the mouth of the Tuzla River with 172 irregulars armed with British rifles on 24 July. The irregulars, supported by the destroyer *Renard*, monitor M33, a sweeper and other auxiliaries, made off with 3,200 head of cattle, mostly sheep, and at one point were bombed by an enemy seaplane.[113]

There is no space here to cover all of these raids in detail. They continued over the summer and on into the autumn of 1916. Thursby thought that the raids 'keep the Turks busy, but would do much more good if we could use service troops instead of the ruffianly crew we now employ'.[114] The operations were not without cost, although on the whole the British were lucky. Commander H. T. England, commanding the destroyer *Harpy* supporting Myres's irregulars in the Gulf of Mendelyah, was severely wounded by rifle fire from a Turkish village on 28 September.[115] Operations of this sort could easily have involved the Royal Navy in unjustified attacks on civilians. Thursby tried to ward off the danger by ordering that a town or village was liable for bombardment if fortified, but that an enemy minefield off the town would not classify it as a fortified position. Whenever the Eastern Mediterranean Squadron bombarded enemy positions in close proximity to towns and villages, the ships would fly a red flag at the masthead in addition to their colours. The Ottoman authorities were informed that when they saw a ship flying a red flag all inhabitants must immediately leave the vicinity and, when circumstances permitted, the inhabitants should be given sufficient time to reach a place of safety. Thursby carefully specified that rifle shots alone fired from a village did not entitle a ship to consider the entire village a fortified position and subject to a general bombardment, although the specific house or locality from which the shots had been fired could and should be bombarded.[116]

Whatever restrictions the British tried to place on the activities of warships along the coast, they could not alter the unpleasant fact that the use of irregular troops in an area where blood feuds and hatreds went back decades, if not centuries, could easily lead to difficulties. The Ottoman government did in fact protest to the United States in a *note verbale* delivered on 30 July about certain raids in the Gulf of Kos the preceding June, claiming that the use of irregular bands instead of regular armed forces was contrary to the principles of international law as universally admitted. The Admiralty, when the protest eventually reached them in October, continued to maintain that the raids were 'legitimate and desirable operations of war'.[117] Nevertheless, the period of raiding by irregulars was drawing to a close as the necessity for collecting small craft to serve a squadron sent to Salamis in a new coercive measure against the Greek government in September forced Thursby to cut down his patrols and raids on the Anatolian coast.[118] In the latter part of October and with the approval of the Allied C.-in-C., Dartige du Fournet, Thursby ordered the cattle raids to cease, although raids against gun positions, lookout posts and other objectives of a military nature would continue. Thursby explained that the cattle raids 'have now served their purpose; and their utility is more than counterbalanced by the difficulties they add to the maintenance of the blockade, the number of craft employed on them, and the impossibility of controlling the irregular volunteers taking part'. The operations against military objectives, on the other hand, took place in close proximity to the coast where the irregulars were more easily controlled and 'opportunities for looting, etc., do not exist'.[119] One wonders what multitude of sins were included under 'etc.' and it is not difficult to read between the lines that Thursby was rather dubious about some of the activities of the irregulars. Within a month their role was virtually over. Thursby reported on 24 November that all Anatolian refugees were required for Venizelos's new anti-royalist forces in formation at Salonika or for their own labour corps. Operations with irregulars were therefore no longer desirable and he discontinued the use of Port Laki on Leros as a base, merely using it as a harbour of refuge for patrols blockading the southern coast of Anatolia.[120] One of the odder roles played by the Royal Navy, that of cattle rustler, therefore came to an end.

Both the British and French navies found a considerable amount of their attention taken up by Greece in 1916. But this was a problem that was more diplomatic than naval and involved many and complex factors. General Sarrail, Allied commander at Salonika and a highly political general supported at home by the Left against the military establishment, was worried over the safety of the Allied expedition in the face of the still equivocal attitude of the Greek government where King Constantine was widely suspected of acting secretly on Germany's behalf. The British were still relatively reluctant partners in this Macedonian campaign, and the Allies were far from united in their approach. De Robeck was always intensely suspicious of, and hostile to, King Constantine, although the King had his British defenders, notably King George V and Admiral Mark Kerr, former head of the British Naval Mission in Greece.[121] The general opening of the archives in the past generation has produced a number of studies of this complicated question.[122] From the naval point of view Capitaine de frégate de Roquefeuil, the French naval attaché in Athens, played a role out of all proportion to his rank. An energetic and controversial officer, he played an active part in politics and one recent historical monograph devoted an entire chapter to him, while another former associate, Hector de Béarn, linked him with Joffre and Foch as one of the three men who won the war, and another associate wrote a book in his defence after the war.[123] Roquefeuil undoubtedly had the ear of his minister; both he and Lacaze had been members of 'l'équipe Germinet' in the Mediterranean fleet before the war and even his younger Italian colleague, Lieutenant Arlotta, could confirm to his interested superiors after a brief visit to Paris that Roquefeuil did indeed have real influence despite the bombastic style which made so many suspicious of him.[124] British authorities, such as de Robeck, tended to be unimpressed with many of Roquefeuil's claims, especially his propensity to see secret submarine depots everywhere which de Robeck complained was causing much wasted effort in futile searches.[125] Dartige also came to regard Roquefeuil as alarmist and thought the money spent by the French intelligence service in Athens ill used, since much of the information received proved to be incorrect. Lacaze did not agree, but felt the more information they received the better, since he believed intelligence gathering to be like many business affairs at their beginning. Many apparently unprofitable expenditures had to be made before arriving at a result which might occur suddenly and recoup in a single stroke all their past efforts.[126] This was typical of the protection Roquefeuil enjoyed.

The Greek affair, while unimportant from the point of view of the main thrust of the naval war, did lock up sizeable numbers of warships above and beyond those necessary to assist the army at Salonika where the right flank of the British force conveniently rested on Stavros and the Gulf of Orphani. It is true that the old battleships and obsolete cruisers that the British and French employed in the diplomatic muscle-flexing might not have found any other useful employment in the war, but the smaller craft which were now so essential for the indispensable netting of anchorages and the performance of auxiliary services could most certainly have found far more useful work in the anti-submarine campaign. Moreover, there was always potential danger should the Greeks resist. The final outcome would naturally never have been in doubt but there was always the possibility of losses to mines and torpedoes. Furthermore, German submarines were likely to be present to take advantage of an opportunity, and towards the close of the year, on 27 December, the old battleship *Gaulois*, a survivor of the Dardanelles campaign, was torpedoed and sunk by UB47 (Oberleutnan zur See Steinbauer) thirty miles east of Cerigo while *en route* from Corfu to Salonika, and despite the escort of a destroyer and two trawlers. [127]

The naval events in Greek waters in 1916 are associated with a succession of crises which, in outline, were in three major stages. The first came in June with the assembly of an Allied squadron at Milo ready for another naval demonstration at Phalerum, which would accompany a landing by approximately 7,000–8,000 troops. The second came in September with another naval demonstration at Keratsini on the Bay of Salamis and culminated with the seizure or neutralization of the Greek fleet in October. The final and major event took place on 1 December with a landing at Piraeus and march into Athens by French and British forces in support of renewed Allied demands. This led to fierce fighting when the Greeks attacked the landing parties, loss of life and the replacement of Dartige du Fournet. [128]

The first crisis was provoked by a Bulgarian advance down the Struma Valley and the surrender by the Greek army of Fort Rupel with little resistance to this violation of Greek territory. This, in turn, alarmed General Sarrail about the security of the Allied army and the French suspected collusion between the Greek government and the Central Powers. On 3 June, Sarrail declared a state of siege at Salonika and took over control of public services such as the police and railways. Sarrail's actions caused strong resentment in Athens, anti-Allied demonstrations, and the Allied ministers asked for a naval demonstration to be linked with demands to insure the benevolent neutrality of Greece. These included the demobilization of the army, the replacement of the ministry, dissolution of the Chamber of Deputies, the calling of new elections and the expulsion of Baron Schenck, the director of German propaganda in Greece. On 8 June the French government ordered all Greek merchant ships to be held in port or stopped at sea, while the naval demonstration was prepared by Dartige who, conveniently, had been in Greek waters on a tour of inspection. The Allied battle squadron was placed under the command of Vice-Admiral Moreau, the French admiral at Salonika, and consisted of five French and one British battleships, and two old French armoured cruisers, while the Escadre légère, some fifty ships of all classes at Milo, was placed under the command of Rear-Admiral Fremantle, who had also commanded the British contingent in the proposed demonstration the preceding autumn. The Allied naval forces were to arrive in the Gulf of Athens on 22 June and eventually anchor in Salamis Strait to back up the demands of the Allied ministers. Dartige had originally planned only a naval demonstration but, at the request of the French minister in Athens, this was expanded to include the landing of 7,000–8,000 troops transported from Salonika. The operation was called off at the last moment, with some of the troop transports already at sea, when the Greek government agreed to the Allied demands. [129]

The Allies were perhaps lucky that the operation did not come off. Thursby 'was not at all struck with their plan of operation, especially the military part of it – which would have led to endless trouble'. [130] Fremantle also thought that the occupation of Athens would have been resisted by the

Greek army and would not have achieved their purpose, a benevolently neutral Greece. He later recommended that if new coercive measures were necessary against Greece, they should be limited to naval action without warning to the Greek government, and when their immediate demands had been met the Battle Squadron should remain in Salamis Strait. That suggestion did not find favour with the Chief of Staff at the Admiralty, for the squadron at Salamis would require a large increase in small craft and other auxiliary vessels which could only come from Mudros, Salonika, or off the transport routes. Oliver argued that they could not give up Mudros or Salonika to establish Salamis.[131]

The Anglo-French force dispersed after the crisis passed, but the naval authorities expected further trouble and agreed to establish a force, dubbed Escadre A, for future demonstrations. The ships for this force were designated in advance and would assemble at a specified location when necessary. The new crisis came in August when a German–Bulgarian offensive against the Allied army captured Florina before it was stopped by counterattacks, while to the east the Bulgarians captured Demir Hissar, east of the Struma, and steadily advanced towards Kavalla on the Aegean which they occupied on 11 September. The Bulgarians had, in effect, overrun eastern Macedonia with little or no Greek resistance. The French Minister of Marine ordered Dartige to assemble Escadre A at Milo and, although the French C.-in-C. would have preferred to delegate the command to one of his admirals, Lacaze ordered him to take charge of operations in person. The French component consisted of Dartige's flagship the dreadnought *Provence*, the battleships *Vérité*, *Démocratie*, *Justice* and *Patrie*, the armoured cruisers *Waldeck-Rousseau* and *Ernest Renan*, the protected cruiser *Jurien de la Gravière*, the seaplane carrier *Campinas*, the minelayer *Pluton*, 12 destroyers and torpedo-boats, 2 gunboats and 6 trawlers; while the British contingent, now commanded by Rear-Admiral Hayes-Sadler in the battleship *Exmouth*, included the light cruisers *Sentinel* and *Forward*, the seaplane carrier *Empress*, the minelayer *Perdita*, 3 monitors, 4 destroyers, 2 small torpedo-boats, 2 sweepers, 1 sloop, 2 netlayers (a vital contribution without which Dartige really could not have moved) and 20 trawlers. Although superfluous to Allied needs, the Italian cruiser *Libia* and the old Russian battleship *Chesma* (captured by the Japanese in 1905 and returned to the Russians during the world war) subsequently joined the squadron to add to its representative character.

The Allied squadron on 1 September anchored off Keratsini near the eastern entrance to the Bay of Salamis and in proximity to the Greek fleet, with orders to back up a new set of demands by the Allied ministers. These included Allied control of Greek posts and telegraphs, the expulsion of enemy agents and punishment of their Greek accomplices, and the surrender of German and Austrian steamers which had taken refuge in Greek ports at the beginning of the war.[132] The Allies promptly seized thirteen Austrian and German steamers including the Austrian Lloyd liner *Marienbad* (8,000 tons), and on 3 September the Greek government yielded to the demands of the Allied memorandum. However, the situation grew yet more complicated. A portion of the Greek garrison in Salonika rebelled against the government in Athens and formed a Committee of National Defence which advocated intervention in the war on the side of the Entente. Venizelos eventually took charge of what was in effect a provisional government in Salonika, while Greek liberals in Athens, where royalist sentiment was strong, feared for their safety and began to take refuge in Allied warships. In turn, reservist leagues were formed in Athens and elsewhere as a pro-royalist, pro-neutralist, anti-Venizelist, anti-Allied force. The Allies themselves disagreed on the course of action to follow, with the British generally inclined to be softer on the Greeks than the French. However, the French also disagreed among themselves, notably Dartige and Roquefeuil. Dartige complained of the 'impassioned levity' of the information he received from the French intelligence service in Athens and was appalled at their apparent ignorance of the Greek fleet and inability to deliver the concrete information he needed for planning to neutralize it. He did not know what information they were sending to Paris unknown to him, and demanded to be informed immediately.[133] The situation was both complex and potentially explosive.

The Greek fleet itself became a focus of attention when the ancient coast defence ship *Hydra* and two small torpedo-boats went over to the Allies. Admiral Condouriotis, a hero of the Balkan Wars who was pro-Venizelist, had hoped to win over more of the fleet but there was no unanimity in any of the ships and further desertions appeared unlikely.[134] The Greek royal government, not surprisingly, began a purge of officers and men. Without entering into the details, the net result was Dartige's decision to seize or neutralize the Greek fleet. On 10 October, under the threat of the big guns of the Allied squadron, Dartige delivered an ultimatum demanding sequestration of the light vessels, disarmament of the big ones, and Allied occupation of certain coastal batteries. The Greeks yielded again under protest to *force majeure*, and on 1 October breech blocks, munitions and torpedoes were landed from the battleships *Lemnos*, *Kilkis* and the armoured cruiser *Averoff*, and their crews reduced to one-third normal size, while Allied destroyers, torpedo-boats and trawlers towed the light cruiser *Helle*, fourteen destroyers and torpedo-boats, five small torpedo-boats, two submarines and a dozen auxiliary vessels to Keratsini. Allied landing parties occupied the batteries on the island of Lipso which commanded the entrance to Keratsini. The Allied ships had cleared for action during the operation, but the Greeks made no resistance.[135]

Dartige intended to put the sequestered Greek ships to work and his first priority was fitting out the five small 150-ton torpedo-boats to patrol the Gulf of Athens, while his second priority would be fitting out the eight 350–400-ton destroyers which he intended to use to free French destroyers at Salonika for work in the western Mediterranean. It would also demonstrate to the Greeks, according to Dartige, that a good portion of their fleet was being used to guarantee their own interests as well as those of the Allies. Dartige relegated the fitting out of the four large Aetos-class (980 tons) and two Keravnos-class (562 tons) destroyers to third priority, for potential use against their Austrian counterparts in the Adriatic.[136] The Italians were also interested in the fate of those Greek destroyers but were politely put off by the French.[137] On the other hand, Thursby turned down a request by Admiral Condouriotis that the two small torpedo-boats of the *de facto* Venizelist regime at Salonika be permitted to patrol the coast. Thursby refused to countenance these boats acting independently in the war zone and, if needed, they would have to work under British or French patrols. The Foreign Office backed his decision.[138] The British were in one sense rather embarrassed, for Admiral Palmer was still in Athens as head of the British Naval Mission with obviously little to do after the Greek fleet was sequestered. When the French took control of the Arsenal at Salamis and formally raised the tricolour over the Greek light craft on 7 November Admiral Palmer himself proposed the withdrawal of the mission. The Admiralty were at first reluctant to withdraw the mission completely, less other powers supplant British influence, but finally agreed at the end of the year and the Naval Mission departed on 6 January.[139] The Greek employees at the Arsenal of Salamis continued to work under the supervision of Allied engineers.

When the Greek situation remained uncertain beyond mid-November Admiral Thursby sorely missed some of his forces now locked up at Salamis. But this did not include Hayes-Sadler and his battleship. Thursby wrote: 'I can spare *them*, but not the 2 destroyers & 4 trawlers who are wanted for escort & patrol work in our own areas.'[140] The relations between the Greek government and the Allies continued to fluctuate against the background of Romania's entry into the war on the side of the Allies only to be overrun by the Central Powers. The next crisis came with the Allied demand for cession of war materials, including cannon, rifles and munitions, as compensation for the material surrendered by the Greeks to the Bulgarians at Fort Rupel and Kavalla. Sarrail wanted to use the material to arm pro-Allied Greek volunteers, while to ensure the safety of the Allied army at Salonika the Greek army would be reduced to peacetime strength and redeployed back to the Peloponnese. Dartige initially demanded 16 field batteries, 16 mountain batteries, 40,000 Mannlicher rifles and 140 machine guns. King Constantine, while apparently ready to yield once again to *force majeure* on most points, wanted assurances that the arms would not be used by the insurgents against the regular Greek army, and that coercive measures would be relaxed as soon as he began executing Allied demands. The negotiations continued throughout November with the spectre of civil war present after a Venizelist detachment clashed with royalist forces at Ekaterini near Mount Olympus on 2 November. The negotiations are too complicated to follow in detail but on 22 November Dartige, with the approval of Lacaze, delivered an ultimatum for the delivery of a first instalment of matériel – ten batteries of mountain artillery – on 1 December with the remainder to follow on the 15th. After talks with King Constantine, Dartige placed perhaps too much reliance on the king's good will and assurances that order would be maintained, and probably paid too little attention to the alarmist reports of Roquefeuil whom he found had exaggerated so often in the past. Dartige assumed that the Greeks would yield to pressure in the form of a peaceful demonstration, that is, a landing by Allied sailors and marines at Athens on 1 December. The assumption turned out to be wrong.

The Allied landing parties were approximately three battalions strong, mostly French, but included three companies of Royal Marines and a small detachment of Italians. While the initial landings were unopposed, later in the day the Allies were suddenly attacked by Greek troops in what French texts invariably refer to as the *guet-apens* or 'ambush' of Athens. There was heavy fighting and for a time Dartige himself was cut off and surrounded with the detachment at the Zappeion theatre and, on at least one occasion, the battleship *Mirabeau* opened fire with her big guns on the Greek positions. *Mirabeau* fired only four rounds, but one of them landed near the Royal Palace with good effect; the Greek royal family, according to some accounts, hastening to take shelter in the cellar. The Allied ministers eventually managed to arrange a cease-fire, the landing parties withdrew to Piraeus, and the Greek government promised to deliver six batteries of mountain artillery immediately. The accounts of the affair differ about the number of casualties, Hayes-Sadler reported 44 French and 8 British dead, and total casualties for the French and British as 191 and 21, respectively. At least 40 Greek soldiers were killed. The withdrawal of the Allied landing parties to Piraeus was followed in Athens with attacks by soldiers and armed reservists on Venizelists and a general roundup and widespread arrests of the latter followed.[141]

Dartige was now prepared to bombard Athens if the Greeks did not deliver the six batteries, allowing a time-limit for the evacuation of the Allied colony, and promising to spare ancient monuments, but on December the Greek government confirmed the promise that it would deliver the batteries. Unfortunately for Dartige, the first reports in France of the action appear to have come from Roquefeuil to Sarrail via wireless telegram and were highly alarmist. The king and his government had 'rolled' (*roulé*) the negotiators, the events were a profound humiliation and they had had to negotiate the re-embarkation of their troops, while they remained at Athens, veritable hostages in the hands of the Greeks. Roquefeuil claimed that they could only get out of the grave situation by quick vengeance, such as a bombardment of Athens. Dartige protested against the misinformation in this telegram and commented tartly that Roquefeuil had assured him the night before the landing that there would be no resistance and the arms would be brought to them by the Greeks 'on a platter' at the end of two days. He had not seen Roquefeuil at the Zappeion on 1 December, the naval attaché was ostensibly sick in his room, and this was probably the reason for his errors.[142] Roquefeuil's general line in subsequent reports was, naturally, that disaster had occurred because the recommendations of his intelligence service had not been followed.[143]

The government in Paris gave the direction of operations to General Sarrail who ordered arrangements to be made for the evacuation of Allied nationals from Athens along with preparations for a bombardment of Greek wireless posts and the Royal Palace, and cutting the bridges to the Peloponnese over the Corinth Canal. On 6 December, the French

government declared a blockade of Greece and on 11 December Vice
Admiral de Bon, Chief of the EMG, arrived at Salamis to assess th
situation. Dartige, rightly or wrongly, quickly paid the penalty. On 1
December, Lacaze relieved him of his command and two days later hi
successor, Vice-Admiral Gauchet, arrived to take over. Dartige coul
hardly conceal his emotion at his final meeting with the Allied officers o
the 14th with, according to the Italian commander of the *Libia*, particularl
warm thanks to Hayes-Sadler.[144] The French naval attaché in London als
reported that the Admiralty, while deploring the sad events, were no
inclined to throw stones at Dartige nor recriminate against the decision
taken by him in such tragic circumstances. In general, the Admiralty ha
preferred blockade to any sort of a landing as a means of pressure on th
Greeks.[145] On the whole, Dartige also received sympathetic treatment i
the British official history, as well as in its French equivalent written b
Captain Thomazi, perhaps reflecting the influence of his memoirs which h
was quick to get into print immediately after the war.[146] He is a sad exampl
of an officer placed in a difficult position, in which the divergence of view
and interests among the Allies added to his troubles, and he was finall
undone by political events rather than mistakes associated with his ow
profession.

The Greeks, under strong Allied pressure, were forced to submit to
public ceremony in which the Greek army marched past and dipped it
colours in salute to the flags of the Allies on 29 January.[147] Moreover, th
Greeks did agree to withdraw their army to the Peloponnese where it woul
have to communicate with the rest of the country by the bridges over th
Corinth Canal which could easily be destroyed by the Allied fleet. The rea
of Sarrail's army was in theory safe, but the Greek situation remained
complicated and unsatisfactory muddle until the Allies finally forced th
abdication of King Constantine in June 1917. By then, however, the Frenc
and British admirals had far more important things to worry about, for th
German submarine campaign would call into question the very existence c
the Salonika expedition itself. The unrestricted submarine campaign of 191
with its effects in the Mediterranean will be the subject of the next chapte

Notes: Chapter 8

1 Corsi to Abruzzi, 20 Jan. 1916, Abruzzi to Corsi, 25 Jan. 1916, USM, Cartell
   519.
2 Corsi to Abruzzi, 23 Feb. 1916, Abruzzi to Corsi, 13 Mar. 1916, USM
   Cartella 533/1; Ufficio Storico, *Marina italiana*, Vol. 3, pp. 69–70, 224.
3 Corsi to Abruzzi, 24 Mar. 1916, USM, Cartella 533/1.
4 Abruzzi to Corsi, 27 Mar. 1916, ibid.
5 See above, Chapter 5.
6 Corsi to Abruzzi, 24 Jan. and 10 Feb. 1916, USM, Cartella 363/1; Abruzzi t
   Corsi, 6 Feb. 1916, USM, Cartella 518/2.
7 Abruzzi to Corsi, 'Occupazione delle isole Curzolari – formazione di una ba
   eventuale', 14 Mar. 1916, ibid., Cartella 518/4.

8 Corsi to Cadorna, 21 May 1916, ibid., Cartella 519.

9 Porro [Deputy Chief of the General Staff] to Corsi, 1 June 1916, ibid.

10 Ufficio del Capo di Stato Maggiore della Marina, 1° Reparto, 'Relazione sui servizi di competenza del I Reparto dal 1 Ottobre 1915 al 1 Ottobre 1916', pp. 40–2; ibid., Cartella 507/7.

11 Corsi to Cadorna, 19 Sept. 1916, Cardona to Corsi, 23 Sept. 1916, ibid., Cartella 519.

12 Grassi to Abruzzi, 20 Mar. 1916, ibid., Cartella 533/1.

13 Abruzzi to Grassi, 26 Mar. 1916, ibid., Cartella 519.

14 Abruzzi to Corsi, 8 Apr. 1916, ibid., Cartella 533/1.

15 Comments on Italian gunnery are in: Lejay to Lacaze, 25 Apr. and 13 Aug. 1916, SHM, Carton Ed-93; Caulfield to Thursby, 22 Apr. 1916, PRO, Adm 137/2124; Kerr to Admiralty, 14 July and 12 Aug. 1916, ibid., Adm 137/781.

16 Abruzzi to Corsi, 8 Apr. 1916, USM, Cartella 533/1.

17 Grassi to Abruzzi, 16 May 1916, ibid.; French translation of Grassi's Promemoria (Dartige's copy dated 9 July 1916) is in SHM, Carton Ed-93.

18 Dartige, 'Note Verbale', 25 May 1916, ibid., Carton Ed-105.

19 Grassi to Abruzzi, 28 May 1916, USM, Cartella 533/1.

20 Marginal comment [probably by De Bon] to a copy of Dartige's Note Verbale of 25 May, SHM, Carton Ed-105.

21 Grassi to Corsi, 4 June 1916, USM, Cartella 533/1; Dartige to Lacaze, 2 June 1916, SHM, Carton A-75.

22 Abruzzi to Corsi, 13 June 1916, Abruzzi to Grassi, 14 June 1916, USM, Cartella 533/1.

23 The lengthy correspondence is to be found in SHM, Carton Ed-105. The question is, curiously, glossed over in Laurens, *Commandement naval*, pp. 184–6.

24 Thursby to Jackson, 12 May 1916, Naval Library, London, Jackson MSS. Extracts from Thursby's letter are in Lostende to Lacaze, 18 May 1916, SHM, Carton Ed-105.

25 Lacaze to Saint Pair, 16 June 1916, Saint Pair to Lacaze, 23 June 1916, ibid. The submarines were probably U34 (Rücker) and U39 (Forstmann), the latter reporting that as a result of extensive patrols he was compelled to make a twelve-hour submerged passage through the Straits of Otranto, Spindler, *Handelskrieg*, Vol. 3, pp. 154–6.

26 Thursby to Jackson, 12 May 1916, loc. cit. at n. 24, Jackson MSS.

27 Saint Pair to Lacaze, 13 July 1916, Dartige to Abruzzi, 8 Aug. 1916, SHM, Carton Ed-105.

28 The extensive correspondence and memoranda are located in SHM, Carton Ed-105 and USM, Cartella 533/1. Copies of Italian cables intercepted and decoded by the French are in SHM, Carton Ed-93.

29 Barrère to Briand, 9 Aug. 1916, MAE, Série Guerre 1914–1918, Vol. 1057.

30 Ufficio Storico, *Marina italiana*, Vol. 3, pp. 215–20.

31 Dartige to Lacaze, 8 Aug. 1916, SHM, Carton Ed-105; Saint Pair to Lacaze, 8 Aug. 1916, ibid., Carton Ea-139.

32 Corsi to Italian Naval Attaché, London, 24 Aug. 1916, Italian Naval Attaché, London, to Corsi, 26 Aug. 1916, USM, Cartella 533/1.

33 Corsi to Villarey, 21 Sept. 1916, Villarey to Corsi, 5 Oct. 1916, ibid.; Ufficio Storico, *Marina italiana*, Vol. 3, pp. 88–9.

34 Corsi to Villarey, 19 Oct. 1916, Corsi to Sonnino, 19 Oct. and 23 Nov. 1916, Corsi to Abruzzi, 24 Nov. 1916, USM, Cartella 533/1.

35 Abruzzi to Corsi, 23 Aug. 1916, ibid., Cartella 519.

36   Lacaze to Dartige, 8 Oct. 1916, SHM, Carton Es-9. On Dalmatian operations see: Saint Pair to Lacaze, 20 Sept. 1916 and marginal comments by Lacaze, ibid., Carton Ea-136.
37   Leone to Lacaze, 7 Oct. 1916, Ruspoli to Briand, 12 Oct. 1916, ibid.
38   Lacaze to Italian Naval Attaché, 20 Oct. 1916, Lacaze to Fatou, 24 Oct. 1916, ibid.; Fatou to Lacaze, 29 Oct. 1916, ibid., Carton Ed-93; Lacaze to de Cacqueray, 24 Oct. 1916, ibid., Carton Es-15.
39   Lacaze to Fatou, 24 Oct. 1916, ibid., Carton Ea-136.
40   Corsi to Abruzzi, 18 Oct. 1916, USM, Cartella 519.
41   Thomazi, *Guerre navale dans l'Adriatique*, p. 122; Ufficio Storico, *Marina italiana*, Vol. 3, pp. 177–83; Sokol, *Österreich-Ungarns Seekrieg*, pp. 436–8.
42   Corsi to Revel, 9 Aug. 1916, USM, Cartella 519.
43   Thomazi, *Guerre navale dans l'Adriatique*, pp. 127–32; Ufficio Storico, *Marina italiana*, Vol. 3, pp 423–7, 435–41; Sokol, *Österreich-Ungarns Seekrieg*, pp. 402–6, 433–5, 438–9.
44   Sokol covers the subject of air operations in great detail, ibid., chs 10, 18 and 27. See also Thomazi, *Guerre navale dans l'Adriatique*, p. 122; Ufficio Storico, *Marina italiana*, Vol. 3, pp. 167–8.
45   Ufficio Storico, *Marina italiana*, Vol. 3, pp. 50–5. There are variations on the name. Originally *motobarca armata*, they became *motobarca anti-sommergibile* or *motoscafo anti-sommergibile* for those in the anti-submarine role and *motobarca armata silurante* for the torpedo attack role. Succinct details are in Aldo Fraccaroli, *Italian Warships of World War I* (London, 1970), pp. 129 ff. and extensive detail in Erminio Bagnasco, *I Mas e le motosiluranti italiane 1906–1966* (Rome, 1967).
46   Thomazi, *Guerre navale dans l'Adriatique*, pp. 126–7; Ufficio Storico, *Marina italiana*, Vol. 3, pp. 371–4, 394–7; Sokol, *Österreich-Ungarns Seekrieg*, pp 422–4.
47   Thursby to Admiralty, 19 Apr. 1916, PRO, Adm 137/1197.
48   Minutes by Flint, 9 May, Jackson, 9 May and Commander Yacht Patrols, 28 Apr. and 9 May 1916, Minute by Oliver, 30 Apr. 1916, ibid.
49   Halsey to Admiralty, 8 May 1916, Minute by Oliver, 13 May 1916, Admiralty to C.-in-C. Home Fleets, 1 June 1916, ibid.
50   Thursby to Limpus, 6 May 1916, National Maritime Museum, Greenwich, Limpus, MSS; Thursby to Jackson, 12 May 1916, loc. cit. at n. 24, Jackson MSS.
51   Thursby to Limpus, 20 May 1916, loc. cit. at n. 50, Limpus MSS.
52   Kerr to Jackson, 29 May 1916, loc. cit. at n. 24, Jackson MSS.
53   Ufficio Storico, *Marina italiana*, Vol. 3, pp. 300–3; Sokol, *Österreich-Ungarns Seekrieg*, p. 360. The incident is not reported in Corbett and Newbolt, *Naval Operations*.
54   Kerr to Jackson, 2 June 1916, loc. cit. at n. 24, Jackson MSS.
55   Kerr to Jackson, 8 June 1916, ibid.
56   Kerr to Jackson, 16 June 1916, ibid.
57   De Cacqueray to Lacaze, 16 July 1916, SHM, Carton Ed-83. The action is described in Ufficio Storico, *Marina italiana*, Vol. 3, pp. 301–2, 313–14, 388–92; Thomazi, *Guerre navale dans l'Adriatique*, pp. 127, 135; Sokol, *Österreich-Ungarns Seekrieg*, pp. 362–3, 427–8.
58   Lejay to Lacaze, 23 July 1916, SHM, Carton Ed-93.
59   Kerr to Limpus, 10 Sept. 1916, loc. cit. at n. 50, Limpus MSS.
60   Kerr to Jackson, 27 Oct. 1916, loc. cit. at n. 24, Jackson MSS.
61   Kerr to Admiralty, 24 Sept. 1916, PRO, Adm 137/2124; Admiralty to

Villarey, 11 Oct 1916, ibid., Adm 137/1227. One submarine, B10, was damaged beyond repair in August by an air raid while in dock at Venice.

52 Saint Pair to Lacaze, 28 Oct. 1916, SHM, Carton Ea-136.

53 Kerr to Jackson, 27 Oct. 1916, loc. cit. at n. 24, Jackson MSS. Kerr quoted the British SNO at Brindisi as claiming de Cacqueray was a cousin of Lacaze.

54 Fatou to Dartige, 9 Nov. 1916, SHM, Carton Es-15.

55 ibid., Kerr to Jackson, 4 Nov. 1916, loc. cit. at n. 24, Jackson MSS; Kerr to Admiralty, 9 Nov. 1916, copy in British Library, London, Jellicoe MSS, Add. MSS 49035; Abruzzi to Fatou, 1 Nov. 1916 [French translation], SHM, Carton Es-15.

56 Kerr to Jackson, 4 Nov. 1916, loc. cit. at n. 24, Jackson MSS; Kerr to Admiralty, 9 Nov. 1916, loc. cit. at n. 65, Jellicoe MSS, Add. MSS 49035; Fatou to Dartige, 9 Nov. 1916, SHM, Carton Es-15.

57 Fatou to Lacaze, 1 Nov. 1916, SHM, Carton A-29.

58 Fatou to Dartige, 9 Nov. 1916, ibid., Carton Es-15.

59 Kerr to Admiralty, 9 Nov. 1916, loc. cit. at n. 65, Jellicoe MSS, Add. MSS 49035.

70 Fatou to Dartige, 9 Nov. 1916, SHM, Carton Es-15. The French were reading Italian cables in Paris. See below, p. 284.

71 Fatou to Lacaze, 5 Nov. 1916, SHM, Carton A-29; amplified in Fatou to Dartige, 9 Nov. 1916, ibid., Carton Es-15.

72 De Cacqueray to Lacaze, 2 Nov. 1916, ibid., Carton Ed-93.

73 Arlotta to Marzolo, 8 Nov. 1916, USM, Cartella 533/1.

74 Marginal note by Marzolo, ibid.

75 Lacaze to Saint Pair, n. d. [end Nov. 1916] and marginal notation, SHM, Carton Ed-91; Frochot to Lacaze, 1 Dec. 1916, ibid., Carton Ed-83.

76 Kerr to Admiralty, 18 Nov. 1916, loc. cit. at n. 66, Jellicoe MSS, Add. MSS 49035. This is amplified in his memorandum, 'Situation in the Mediterranean', 30 Nov. 1916, ibid.

77 Ufficio Storico, *Marina italiana*, Vol. 3, pp. 514–18.

78 Abruzzi to Corsi, 28 Dec. 1916, ACS, Carte Boselli 1/14. Corsi and the Stato Maggiore were not satisfied with all aspects of the conduct of this inquiry, Corsi to Abruzzi, 4 Jan. 1917, ibid.

79 Lejay to Lacaze, 6 Jan. 1917, SHM, Carton Ed-94.

80 Thomazi, *Guerre navale dans l'Adriatique*, pp. 138–9; Ufficio Storico, *Marina italiana*, Vol. 3, pp. 520–33; Sokol, *Österreich-Ungarns Seekrieg*, pp. 367–75.

81 Brief accounts of the *Strafe* offensive in which the Austrians made sizeable initial gains but ended with the Austrians back near their original positions are in: Piero Pieri, 'Italian Front', in Vincent J. Esposito (ed.), *A Concise History of World War I* (New York, 1964), pp. 165–6; Cyril Falls, *The Great War, 1914–1918* (Paperback edn, New York, 1961), pp. 232–4.

82 Erzherzog Friedrich to Haus, 22 Feb. 1916, OK/MS VIII-1/1 ex 1917, No. 1118.

83 Haus to AOK, 28 Feb. 1916, ibid. Most of the correspondence is also printed in Sokol, *Österreich-Ungarns Seekrieg*, pp. 394–400.

84 Conrad to Haus, 3 Mar. 1916, OK/MS VIII-1/1 ex 1917, No. 1118.

85 Haus to AOK, 12 Mar. 1916, ibid.

86 Erzherzog Friedrich to Haus, 17 Mar. 1916, ibid.

87 Haus to Bolfras, 28 May 1916, Kriegsarchiv, Vienna, Nachlass Bolfras B75/21.

88 Rodler to Kailer, 4 Dec. 1915 and 21 Jan. 1916, ibid., Nachlass Kailer B/242.

89 Details of construction and projects are in Greger, *Austro-Hungarian Warships*,

passim. The projects for large warships are reviewed in: Erwin Sieche 'Grosskampfschiffs-Projekte des MTK aus der Zeit des Ersten Weltkrieges' *Marine – Gestern, Heute*, vol. 8, no. 4 (Dec. 1981), pp. 123–40.

90   At the beginning of 1984 Banfield was the last living Knight of the Militar Maria Theresa Order.

91   Freyberg to Capelle, 31 Aug. 1916, NARS, T-1022, Roll 538, PG 69132.

92   Bethmann Hollweg to Kaiser Wilhelm, 7 Sept. 1916, and marginal note by th Kaiser, n.d. [c. 21 Sept. 1916], ibid.

93   Freyberg to Conrad, 20 Sept. 1916, OK/MS XV-5/11 ex 1916, No. 5804.

94   Marinesektion to Flottenkommando, 7 Sept. 1916, Flottenkommando t Marinesektion, 8 Sept. 1916, ibid., No. 5346; Conrad to Flottenkommandc 23 Sept. 1916, ibid., No. 5804; Haus to AOK, 1 Oct. 1916, ibid.

95   Marinesektion to Flottenkommando, 5 Oct. 1916, ibid., No. 5853; Marine sektion to Marinereferent, AOK, 6 Oct. 1916, ibid., No. 5881; Marinesektio to Marineattaché, Berlin and Flottenkommando, 14 Oct, 1916, ibid., Nc 6033.

96   Captain [unnamed] to Freyberg, 16 Oct. 1916, NARS, T-1022, Roll 505, PC 69081; Marinesektion to Marinereferent, AOK, 13 Dec. 1916, OK/MS. XV 5/11 ex 1916, No. 7138; Kriegsministerium to Marinesektion, 18 Dec. 191€ ibid., No. 7233.

97   For example, the loss of the M30 and operations on Long Island in the Gulf c Smyrna in May 1916 are not even mentioned in Corbett and Newbolt's *Nav Operations*, which is perhaps understandable since they occurred shortly befor Jutland. The episode is covered in Chatterton, *Seas of Adventures*, pp. 209–1? and ch. 23. The French are better served in Thomazi, *Guerre navale dans I Méditerranée*. De Robeck provided a succinct summary when he turned ove his command. See de Robeck to Admiralty, 13 June 1916, PRO, Adr 137/365.

98   Drake to Larken, 25 Mar. 1916 and Minute by Larken, ibid., Adm 137/36^

99   De Robeck to Admiralty, 25 Mar. 1916, ibid., Adm 137/1199.

100   De Robeck to Balfour, 31 Mar. 1916, British Library, London, Balfour MSS Add. MSS 49715.

101   Admiralty to de Robeck, 6 Apr. 1916, de Robeck to Admiralty, 6 Apr. 191€ PRO, Adm 137/1199.

102   War Office to Admiralty, 11 Apr. 1916, ibid.

103   Minute by Hamilton [Second Sea Lord], 14 Apr. 1916, ibid.

104   De Robeck to Balfour, 21 Apr. 1916, loc. cit. at n. 100, Balfour MSS, Ad€ MSS 49715.

105   Thursby to Admiralty, 10 Aug. 1916, PRO, Adm 137/1229.

106   Hodson to Larken, 4 May 1916, Larken to de Robeck, 4 May 1916, ibid., Adr 137/365; De Robeck to Admiralty, 5 May 1916, ibid., Adm 137/1199.

107   Foreign Office to Admiralty, 30 Apr. 1916, minutes by Nicholson, 1 and May, H. B. Jackson, 3 and 4 May, and Gamble, 2 and 4 May 1916, Admiralt to Foreign Office, 5 May 1916, ibid.

108   De Robeck to Limpus, 12 May 1916, loc. cit. at n. 50, Limpus MSS.

109   Larken to de Robeck, 14 May 1916, PRO, Adm 137/365.

110   Dent to de Robeck, 13 June 1916, ibid. For a full account of Myres see: Taffra [Captain Taprell Dorling], *Endless Story* (London, 1931); and J. N. L. Myre: *Commander J. L. Myres, RNVR: The Blackbeard of the Aegean* (London, 1980^

111   Thursby to Admiralty, 3 July 1916, PRO, Adm 137/366.

112   Clifton Brown to Thursby, 25 July 1916, ibid.

113   Larken to Thursby, 30 July 1916, ibid.

14 Thursby to Jackson, 3 Aug. 1916, loc. cit. at n. 24, Jackson MSS.
15 SNO, Port Laki to SNO 1st Detached Squadron, 3 Oct. 1916, Myres to SNO, Port Laki, 30 Sept, 1916, PRO, Adm 137/545.
16 Eastern Mediterranean Squadron, Confidential Memoranda, No. 68, 8 Sept. 1916, ibid., Adm 137/698.
17 Ottoman Ministry of Foreign Affairs to United States Embassy, 30 July, 1916, US Chargé d'Affaires to Foreign Office, 5 Oct. 1916, Admiralty to Foreign Office, 15 Oct. 1916, ibid., Adm 137/1229.
18 Thursby to Jackson, 2 Sept. 1916, loc. cit. at n. 24, Jackson MSS.
19 Thursby to Admiralty, 26 Oct. 1916, PRO, Adm 137/367.
20 Thursby to Admiralty, 24 Nov. 1916, ibid.
21 De Robeck to Limpus, 8 and 15 June 1916, loc. cit. at n. 50, Limpus MSS. For King George V's views see: Memorandum by Lord Bertie of an Audience with the King, 10 Apr. 1916, PRO, FO 800/190; Admiral Mark Kerr, *Land, Sea and Air* (London, 1927), *passim*,
22 On the French role, *Sarrail* is indispensable. See also: Leon, *Greece and the Great Powers*; Mitrakos, *France in Greece during World War I*; Theodoulou, *Greece and the Entente*; and S. P. Cosmin [Phocas S. Cosmetatos], *Dossiers secrets de la triple entente: Grèce, 1914–1922* (Paris, 1969).
23 Mitrakos, *France in Greece during World War I*, ch. 5: 'Roquefeuil: coercion, controls and plots of revolution'; Béarn, *Souvenirs d'un marin*, p. 54; Clergeau, *Le Commandant de Roquefeuil en Grèce*. See also Compton Mackenzie, *Greek Memories* (London, 1939).
24 Arlotta to Marzolo, 8 Nov. 1916, USM, Cartella 533/1.
25 De Robeck to Admiralty, 8 June 1916, PRO, Adm 137/1199.
26 Lacaze to Dartige, 22 May 1916, SHM, Carton A-132. Dartige presents his story in detail in his *Souvenirs de guerre d'un amiral.*
27 Thomazi, *Guerre navale dans la Méditérranée*, p. 46; Spindler, *Handelskrieg*, Vol. 3, p. 342.
28 Fairly clear accounts of the Greek complications from the naval aspect are in: Thomazi, *Guerre navale dans la Méditérranée*, chs 9–10; Corbett and Newbolt, *Naval Operations*, Vol. 4, ch. 5.
29 Dartige to Lacaze, 26 June, 1916, SHM, Carton Ed-110; Memorandum by Fremantle, 8 Aug. 1916, PRO, Adm 137/1228.
30 Thursby to Limpus, 28 June 1916, loc. cit. at n. 50, Limpus MSS.
31 Fremantle to Admiralty, 8 Aug. and Minute by Oliver, 9 Aug. 1916, PRO, Adm 137/1228.
32 Lacaze to Dartige, 26 and 31 Aug. 1916, SHM, Carton A-29.
33 Dartige to Lacaze, 8 Sept. and 6 Oct. 1916, ibid.
34 Elliot to Hardinge, 1 Oct. 1916, copy in House of Lords Record Office, London, Lloyd George MSS, E/3/15/2.
35 Accounts of the seizure are in Thomazi, *Guerre navale dans la Méditérranée*, pp. 136–8; Corbett and Newbolt, *Naval Operations*, Vol. 4, pp. 151–3.
36 Dartige to Lacaze, 5 Oct. 1916 [probably misdated and should be Nov.], SHM, Carton A-29; Dartige to Lacaze, 11 Nov. 1916, ibid., Carton Ed-104.
37 Arlotta to Corsi, 8 Nov. 1916, USM, Cartella 533/1.
38 Thursby to Admiralty, 27 Oct. 1916, Admiralty to Foreign Office, 28 Oct. 1916, Foreign Office to Admiralty, 30 Oct. 1916, PRO, Adm 137/1228.
39 Historical Section Summary, 'Greece – Naval Mission', (17 Oct. 1916–21 Apr. 1917), ibid., Adm 137/1229.
40 Thursby to Jackson, 21 Nov. 1916, loc. cit. at n. 24, Jackson MSS.
41 Corbett and Newbolt, *Naval Operations*, Vol. 4, pp. 166–72; Thomazi, *Guerre*

navale dans la *Méditérranée*, pp. 143–9; Ufficio Storico, *Marina italiana*, Vol. 4, pp. 341–5. Dartige's report is in Dartige to Lacaze, 8 Dec. 1916, SHM, Carton Ed-105; Hayes-Sadler to Thursby, 6 and 7 Dec. 1916, PRO, Adm 137/546.

142 Dartige to Lacaze, 4 Dec. 1916, SHM, Carton Ed-104.

143 Roquefeuil to Lacaze, 11 Dec. 1916, ibid.

144 Colli di Felizzano to Corsi, 23 Dec. 1916, USM, Cartella 614/2.

145 Lostende to Lacaze, 3 Jan. 1917, SHM, Carton Ed-105.

146 Corbett and Newbolt, *Naval Operations*, Vol. 4, pp. 156–71; Thomazi, *Guerre navale dans la Méditérranée*, pp. 150–1; Dartige du Fournet, *Souvenirs de guerre d'un Amiral, passim*. Compton Mackenzie is far less kind in *Greek Memories, passim*.

147 Hayes-Sadler to Thursby, 1 Feb. 1917 (with enclosure giving programme), PRO, Adm 137/368.

The Submarine Crisis – 1917

The Germans Introduce Unrestricted Submarine Warfare

The year 1917 was undoubtedly the crisis of the naval war for the Entente powers as a result of the introduction of unrestricted submarine warfare. In December of 1916 Admiral von Holtzendorff circulated his memorandum of the 22nd incorporating portions of earlier studies and ending decisively his own somewhat wavering attitude. Holtzendorff recommended that unrestricted submarine warfare should be introduced no later than 1 February so as to reach a decision in the war by autumn. He estimated that German submarines, unfettered by concern about prize rules or safety of crew and passengers, would be able to sink 600,000 tons of British shipping per month and that Britain would be forced to make peace within five months, thereby making the possible threat of American intervention irrelevant.[1] The Germans reached the decision to resume unrestricted submarine warfare at the famous conference in Supreme Headquarters at Schloss Pless on 9 January.[2] Holtzendorff's memorandum had not specifically referred to the Mediterranean which was, naturally, but a part of the general struggle against Britain. The Admiralstab had actually been thinking of intensifying the submarine war in the Mediterranean before the Schloss Pless decision. On 4 January Abteilung B (Overseas Operations) proposed that as of 1 February all merchant ships, with the exception of hospital ships, encountered outside Greek territorial waters east of the line 20° 30′ East (that is, running due south of Cape Matapan) should be sunk without warning. However, Holtzendorff decided to defer the question momentarily so as not to complicate the major negotiations in progress over the general submarine war.[3] The Germans had, in fact, more extreme plans for the Mediterranean and in the operational orders opening unrestricted submarine warfare most of the Mediterranean was declared a prohibited area (Sperregebiet) where all ships, with the exception of hospital ships, could be attacked without warning. Neutral shipping was permitted in certain areas, notably west of a line running south-east from Point de l'Espiguette (near the mouth of the Rhône) and including the Balearics to sixty miles from the French North African coast. There was also a twenty-mile-wide corridor running through the Mediterranean to Cape Matapan and Greek territorial waters. In these neutral areas only armed steamers would be attacked without warning and prize rules for neutrals and hospital ships would be observed. However, in the corridor leading to Greek waters all enemy vessels encountered east of longitude 6° E would be considered armed.[4]

The Germans also planned to strengthen their Mediterranean U-Boat Flotilla. The successes of the first UC boats (minelayers) sent to the Mediterranean indicated that this type of craft was well suited for Mediterranean or Black Sea waters because of the proportionately short distances from their bases to well-known transport routes, favourable weather conditions and numerous possibilities for mining operations against enemy harbours. Holtzendorff claimed that without prejudice to the campaign in home waters they could send an additional nine UC boats to the Mediterranean as the new craft were completed in the next few months. One of them would be converted to a transport according to experience already gained with UC20 for conveyance of war material to North Africa. This was an operation on which the Army High Command continued to place great value. Holtzendorff also believed that there were similar favourable opportunities for the improved UB boats which would be completed during the summer of 1917, and he proposed sending another ten to the Mediterranean. They would, in addition to sinking ships, force the enemy to divide his anti-submarine forces thereby facilitating the activity of U-boats in British waters.[5] The great attraction of the Mediterranean for the smaller submarines was the relatively short distance from their bases in the Adriatic to the central Mediterranean shipping lanes, particularly the busy stretch between Malta and Cerigotto.

The Germans, once they had reached the decision for unrestricted submarine warfare, naturally turned to their Austrian allies for support. This was obviously more for diplomatic reasons and the need for the appearance of solidarity in the alliance than for the relatively slender resources that the Austrians would be able to contribute beyond the use of their bases in the Adriatic. The leading Austro-Hungarian authorities, including the new Emperor Karl, Foreign Minister Czernin and the Hungarian Prime Minister Tisza were decidedly unenthusiastic about or opposed to the German action. Haus, however, was strongly in favour of the German plans and was probably the most important advocate of unrestricted submarine warfare in the Habsburg monarchy. This was consistent with his past statements on the subject when, as in the *Ancona* case, he was apt to take a tough line and back the Germans to the hilt. He appears, however, something of the odd man out in leading circles of the Dual Monarchy, finding little support except from Conrad. Nevertheless the navy's courtship of Karl while he was still heir apparent had some effect. The new Kaiser seems to have had a high regard for the k.u.k Kriegsmarine and was certainly more interested in naval affairs than his predecessor.[6]

Haus was determined to do all he could to support the Germans and arranged for a conference to be held at the Marinesektion in Vienna on the measures to be taken to provide for an increased number of German ubmarines at Cattaro. These measures included fitting out workshops, fuel anks, additional mooring buoys and providing sufficient quarters for the personnel of eight to ten submarines.[7]

On 20 January, Holtzendorff arrived in Vienna along with the German Foreign Secretary, Zimmerman, to persuade the Austrians to support the policy of unrestricted submarine warfare. The Germans obviously thought that their allies needed some arm twisting for Czernin had recently sent Count Flotow, a Foreign Office official, to Berlin to support the Austrian ambassador in an unsuccessful attempt to dissuade the Germans from their action.[8] Holtzendorff in a meeting presided over by Kaiser Karl claimed, with some exaggeration, that the Germans had 120 submarines, of which 42 would be in the Mediterranean, and that they hoped to bring Britain to reason within four months. The counter-arguments of Czernin and Tisza had no effect on the Germans, and Haus, their major supporter among the Austrians, discounted the immediate effects of the United States joining the Entente powers. The Flottenkommandant also brought up one aspect of the question which was frequently overlooked. He claimed that the Entente was already practising 'unrestricted' submarine warfare against the Austrians and was able to cite examples of harmless transports or hospital ships which had been attacked without warning by submarines in the Adriatic. This argument was ultimately useful to Tisza when he later tried to justify the decision in the Hungarian Parliament. The Austrians and Hungarians could cite nine specific cases, including the hospital ship *Elektra* torpedoed in error by a French submarine in March 1916.[9] The Kaiser took no immediate decision, although in a private talk with Czernin after the meeting he claimed he had the same aversion to unrestricted submarine warfare and fears about its result as the Foreign Minister. Karl had given a private audience to Haus before the meeting with the Germans and the Flotten-kommandant had argued that unrestricted submarine warfare was the sole means to achieve the peace they longed for.[10] There were obviously still limits to the navy's influence, but in the end the Austrians went along with their ally. Holtzendorff is supposed to have argued that it was too late to change the decision for the U-boats were already on their way to their stations, and Czernin claimed after the war, with the benefit of hindsight, that the U-boat efforts would have been nullified if the Mediterranean were exempted. Moreover, once they allowed the Germans to use their bases they were involved in the campaign anyway, and if they refused to let Austrian submarines participate they 'would be attacking Germany in the rear' which would lead to a definite severance of the alliance. Czernin pleaded that it was 'one of those instances that prove that when a strong and weak nation concert in war, the weak one cannot desist unless it changes sides entirely and enters into war with its former ally. None who were in the Government would hear of that, and with a heavy heart we gave our consent.'[11] The Crown Council, meeting on 22 January with the Minister of War General von Krobatin and Conrad, but with neither Haus nor any representative of the navy being present, unanimously agreed to unrestricted submarine warfare. Conrad fully supported the German position. The general feeling of the more reluctant non-military members of the Council, such as the Austrian Minister-President Graf Clam-Martinic, was that there was nothing else left to do if the war continued.[12]

Once the difficult decision had been taken, Karl wrote to Kaiser Wilhelm, declaring his agreement, but requesting that no announcement be made until they had discussed the details in a forthcoming meeting at Schloss Pless on the 26th. Wilhelm readily agreed, but specifically requested that Karl's naval adviser should be present as well. Haus and his Chief of Staff, Rear-Admiral Rodler, therefore accompanied the Emperor to meet with Holtzendorff and Müller to concoct a note declaring the Mediterranean a prohibited zone. It was hurried, 'working in shirtsleeves' labour, according to Müller, since the Germans insisted on a 1 February date for the commencement of unrestricted submarine warfare. They agreed that U35, U38 and U39 would continue to fly the Austrian flag.[13] Holtzendorff inquired if the Austrians were in a position and willing to have so large a number of German submarines in their bases and to supply an abundant number of workers for fitting them out. Haus promised the Germans all possible support and told them that he had ordered the disarmament of the old armoured cruiser *Kaiserin und Königin Maria Theresia* and the torpedo cruiser *Panther* to obtain workers. He also intended to take other old ships out of service when the submarine question required it.[14] The Austrians, to the great joy of the Germans, announced that they would send their own submarines out of the Adriatic to operate against the transport route between Malta and Cerigo, and the Admiralstab promised to assist them in every possible way, including the provision of intelligence and the (already compromised) FVB code. They requested that the Austrians should co-ordinate their movements with the U-Boat Flotilla at Pola in regard to dates, times and operational areas.[15]

The Schloss Pless Conference literally proved fatal for Haus. He apparently caught pneumonia in the unheated railway coach during the journey and died aboard his flagship in Pola early on the morning of 8 February. The k.u.k. Kriegsmarine had lost a commanding presence. Kaiser Karl, Archduke Karl Stephen and Minister of War Krobatin all came to Pola for the funeral, while Kaiser Wilhelm sent a telegram of condolence to Karl expressing the hope that the seeds sown by Haus would bear rich fruit in the difficult struggle in which they were engaged and in which their naval forces were now called to special efforts.[16] Haus's successor as Flottenkommandant was Vice-Admiral (quickly promoted to Admiral) Maximilian Njegovan, a 58-year-old Croatian in command of the 1 Geschwader. Kailer, promoted to Vice-Admiral, became Chief of the Marinesektion in Vienna thereby returning to the old division of authority between Pola and Vienna. It did not last long for Kailer died suddenly on 28 April and on the 30th the Kaiser named Njegovan as Chief of the Marinesektion, thereby uniting once again the two offices in the same person. Njegovan had apparently been chosen because he was the senior flag officer, but he was an energetic officer who apparently clashed with the administration at the Marinesektion.[17] Njegovan's strategic thought was similar to that of his predecessor. Despite the recent changes in the Italian naval command – the replacement of the Duke of the Abruzzi – he did not regard increased activity by major Italian forces in the Adriatic as probable. Close support by capital ships for army operations in the Gulf of Trieste would be fatal for whatever side attempted it because of mines and submarines, while an enemy landing would be too risky or costly.[18] Njegovan was therefore compelled by circumstances to recognize the stalemate which existed as regards large surface ships in the Adriatic. He quickly realized what the decisive weapons now were and on 7 March urgently asked Kailer to hasten as much as possible the construction of Austrian submarines along with fast motor boats equipped with torpedoes, mines and nets.[19]

The Germans actually began unrestricted submarine warfare in the Mediterranean at something of a disadvantage for, as Holtzendorff explained to the Kaiser, the heavy demands on submarines during the past year meant that in January the larger part of the Mediterranean flotilla was at Pola or Cattaro undergoing necessary repairs and refits and it was therefore not possible at the beginning of February to undertake full U-boat activity in all areas of the Mediterranean. Holtzendorff claimed that this was not as harmful as it appeared at first glance, for the mere declaration of the prohibited zone had reduced ship traffic. Spanish crews had allegedly refused to enter the blockaded zone, at least for the present, and according to the reports of German agents Italian crews had also been deterred. They could, however, expect that higher wages and the pressure of the respective governments would bring crews back to travel in the forbidden zone and, once again, provide numerous chances for submarine attack, and with the arrival of better weather they could expect an increase in success. Holtzendorff was really explaining the relative lack of success in January when submarine sinkings had been fewer than in the preceding months.

On 10 February the Germans had ten U-boats at sea in the Mediterranean. They included five large U-boats, two small UB boats and three UC minelayers. The Austrian U11 was also working off Bari. Most of their activity was in the central or western Mediterranean and for a short time, except for a UC boat in the northern Aegean, the eastern Mediterranean would be completely unoccupied.[20]

As of 2 April – the beginning of a record month – the Admiralstab reported that the Mediterranean flotilla had fourteen German submarines at sea (one of them still in northern waters on the way to the Adriatic) and two Austrian boats were also operating in the Mediterranean. The flotilla during the month of May had a strength of twelve large U-boats (including two minelayers), two UB boats and fourteen UC boats. Significantly, this total of twenty-eight was far below the forty-two submarines that Holtzendorff had promised the Austrians. In the first half of June the Germans had eighteen submarines either on operations or about to put to sea. They were divided as follows: seven in the western Mediterranean, mostly the large U-boats; six in the central Mediterranean, all UB or UC boats; three UB or UC boats in the Aegean; and two UC boats in the eastern Mediterranean.

There were an additional two UC boats on their way to the Mediterranean from Kiel and three to four Austrian submarines were operating in the Ionian or on the Malta–Cerigo sector.[21]

The submarine successes in the first half of 1917 are spectacular, peaking in April – the best month for the Germans in the entire war – and falling off in May and June, possibly as a result of countermeasures ordered by the Corfu Conference. The figures cited below from the authoritative history of the submarine war by Admiral Spindler give only those sinkings credited to the U-Boat Flotilla at Pola. They do not include the success of the handful of submarines at Constantinople which operated in both the Black Sea and the Aegean. However, those totals were relatively small and do not affect the main picture. The Admiralstab, when faced with the problem of where credit was due, normally assigned the successes to the authority who had issued the operational orders. With these qualifications, the results were as shown in Table 9.1.[22]

The Kaiser noted the decline in sinkings in May, although the total was still higher than anything achieved in preceding months, and possibly spoiled by the spectacular successes of April and conscious of the great gamble the entire campaign represented, querulously demanded an explanation when UC35 returned from a twenty-five-day cruise in the Gulf of Genoa and reported that little tonnage had been destroyed. Holtzendorff attributed the poor results to frequently hazy weather and bad visibility, as well as an engine breakdown later in the cruise, but realizing the Kaiser's propensity to meddle he took the precautionary step of ordering submarine commanders when they first reported back from a cruise with relative lack of success to avoid the necessity for further explanation by including the reason – engine breakdown, strong countermeasures, little traffic, bad weather, and so on – in their initial report.[23]

The interference of the General Staff, notably Ludendorff, was probably much more disturbing to the Admiralstab and its execution of the

Table 9.1   *Shipping Losses due to Submarines, January–June 1917*

	Sunk by Mediterranean U-Boat Flotilla Tonnage	Sunk by Submarine-laid Mines Tonnage	Total Mediterranean Tonnage	Total (All Theatres) Tonnage
Jan. 1917	75,541	—	78,541	328,391
Feb. 1917	105,630	40	105,670	520,412
Mar. 1917	58,820	3,097	61,917	564,497
Apr. 1917	251,187	3,724	254,911	860,334
May 1917	165,834	4,792	170,626	616,316
June 1917	142,338	21,961	164,299	696,725

During this period Austrian submarines sank:

	Tonnage		Tonnage
Jan. 1917	—	Apr. 1917	23,037
Feb. 1917	—	May 1917	10,270
Mar. 1917	—	June 1917	6,174

unrestricted submarine war than the occasional quibbling of the Kaiser. This interference took the form of demands for secondary operations which had the effect of removing submarines from *Handelskrieg* to carry agents or supplies to Turkish supporters in Tripolitania or operate against the seaward flank of the British army advancing towards Palestine. With the return of better weather, the General Staff intended to resume shipments of war materials to North Africa on a larger scale than in the past. Unfortunately, the only boat available for transport purposes in the Mediterranean, UC20, would not suffice for the volume the army desired and Holtzendorff inquired about converting one of the additional UC boats scheduled to go to the Mediterranean. The choice was UC73 which was expected to sail around 20 March.[24]

UC20 and UC73 were employed successfully on these supply runs to North Africa which were not without incident, but unfortunately there is no space to recount them in detail. For a time during the summer of 1917 they did not even conduct the usual operations against shipping going to and from North Africa in order to speed deliveries of rifles and munitions. UC20 on her second mission in May also carried Expedition 'Mirr', which consisted of Rittmeister Freiherr Wolff von und zu Todenwarth and six men who intended to establish a wireless station in the vicinity of Misurata.[25] The real military value of the expedition in the long run was, at best, questionable.

The requests for assistance to military operations on the coast of Palestine were more difficult for the navy to evade since they rested on concrete military requirements rather than ill-defined and vague plans for influencing tribal politics in the interior of Tripolitania. In February, Colonel Kress von Kressenstein with the Turkish–German forces defending Gaza reported that he expected a British advance towards Gaza in March, and that the British would partially supply their army by sea and employ naval gunfire against the seaward flank of the Turkish positions. The presence of one or more German U-boats in the area between Port Said and Gaza would greatly help their defence of Palestine. The Admiralstab declined the request for both technical and strategic reasons. The British transport would probably be escorted by light craft and hug the coast where shallow water less than fifty metres deep extended ten to thirty miles out to sea. Furthermore, the employment of all available U-boats in *Handelskrieg* after the declaration of unrestricted submarine warfare precluded stationing a submarine on the Syrian coast for a long period of time.[26]

Enver Pasha complained to the German General Staff that he did not have the military strength to defend the entire Syrian coast behind the Sinai front against a landing with any chance of success. He therefore asked OHL's (*Oberste Heeresleitung*) intervention with the navy for U-boats to block the free movement of enemy ships which were conducting shore bombardments and launching seaplanes for air raids. Enver succeeded in getting Ludendorff's attention and the latter asked Holtzendorff on 27 February to what extent they could comply with the Turkish request. Holtzendorff yielded slightly. He explained that submarines in the eastern Mediterranean earlier in the year had met little traffic and therefore had correspondingly little success.

Nevertheless, he was ready to comply with Enver's request and send to the Syrian coast a large submarine, U63, which had been scheduled to go to the western Mediterranean, and a second submarine, UB42, would also come out from Constantinople. Holtzendorff warned, though, that a U-boat was not real protection against a landing because of the shallow water, and emphasized that every submarine sent to the eastern Mediterranean represented a diversion of their forces which had been primarily engaged in cutting off traffic to Italy in the western Mediterranean, and also encountered in those waters a large portion of the steamers going through to the eastern Mediterranean.[27] Souchon continued to advance his own and Turkish fears of possible landings on the coast of Palestine and Syria and the Admiralstab passed these reports by wireless to the few submarines that eventually reached this area. These submarine cruises were, as predicted, fruitless, and UB42 reported from Beirut, where she had stopped to refuel, that she had only encountered light craft under 1,000 tons and that attacks were not possible because of shallow waters or anti-submarine barriers.[28] On the whole, U-boats were not a really effective means of defence for the Palestine coast and in the spring of 1917 the Admiralstab had far more profitable uses for them. The Admiralstab attitude was perhaps best reflected by Holtzendorff's comments after another profitless mission early in the year to the Gulf of Orphani in the northern Aegean. This experience confirmed that attacks by a submarine through lines of trawlers, nets and warships protected against submarines by steamers lying alongside them in the narrow waters of the Aegean did not yield the results which observers on land or in the air might anticipate.[29] In other words, it was not always as easy as it looked to laymen.

In March, Ludendorff also attempted to interfere with the deployment of U-boats. Colonel von Bartenwerffer, head of the Political Section of the General Staff, began to quote intelligence reports about the deteriorating internal situation of Italy and the importance of cutting off traffic to Italian ports. Kapitän zur See von Bülow, the Admiralstab representative at Supreme Headquarters, found this a good opportunity to point out that the Admiralstab was quite cognizant of the importance of cutting off traffic to Italy but the proportionately small number of Mediterranean U-boats made the outlook for blockade runners rather more favourable than in the Atlantic. This was especially so as OHL always placed strong emphasis on the disruption of transport to Salonika and on operations in the eastern Mediterranean, where they had recently demanded U-boats for protection of the army's flank in Palestine. If they discontinued these secondary tasks they would be able to increase the pressure on Italy.[30] This was, of course, a polite way of telling Ludendorff and the General Staff that they could not have their cake and eat it, and that at sea as well as on land they would have to set priorities. Bartenwerffer quickly replied that Ludendorff regarded disturbance of the Salonika transport as less important, particularly once the use by the Entente of hospital ships for military purposes was really restricted, and that due to the present unrest in Italy the disruption of Italian traffic was more important. Ludendorff asked the navy to keep at least one U-boat in the eastern Mediterranean, assuming that it would also work against Port Said, and suggested a *concentration* of U-boats against a single, particularly important port. Holtzendorff may have welcomed another opportunity to demonstrate to Ludendorff the disadvantages of detaching U-boats to the Palestine front and also give him another lesson in naval strategy. He announced that, with the postponement of operations in the eastern Mediterranean, all available U-boats would be sent in the near future to the western Mediterranean to operate against traffic to Italy. However, Ludendorff's proposal for a concentration at a specific point was not expedient since this would inevitably result in augmented counter-measures at that point and the outlook for success would diminish. For the moment the Admiralstab compromised. At least one UC boat and, temporarily, a UB boat would remain in the eastern Mediterranean.[31]

The best-known and most important effect of the resumption of unrestricted submarine warfare was the direct intervention of the United States in the world war, with momentous consequences for its outcome. The United States broke off diplomatic relations with Germany on 3 February and declared war on 6 April. Relations between Austria-Hungary and the United States were broken off, but the United States did not declare war against Austria-Hungary until 7 December.[32] Turkey broke off diplomatic relations with the United States on 20 April but the latter never declared war on either Turkey or Bulgaria. Curiously enough, the Germans tried to maintain the fiction that they were not really at war with the Americans and it was not until 20 May that the Kaiser ordered the navy to regard American warships encountered in the blockaded zone as hostile. This message went out to the U-Boat Flotilla in the Mediterranean on the 21st. American cruisers had been engaged on humanitarian operations in the eastern portion of the Mediterranean earlier in the war, but there was now likely to be relatively little contact with American ships and one suspects that the American flag was sometimes used as a flag of convenience by certain Greek shipowners. Consequently, the immediate effect in the Mediterranean of one of the more critical events in the war was small.[33]

The question of how to treat the neutral Spanish was probably more important at first, and this was reflected in the exclusion of the western portion of the Mediterranean and the Balearics from the prohibited zone. The Germans did respect Spanish territorial waters and, after a Spanish complaint about the capture of a Norwegian steamer in what the Spanish claimed were their waters, all U-boat commanders were told that under no circumstances were they to conduct operations in Spanish waters. Later on, the Admiralstab even ordered submarine commanders to observe a four-mile limit on the Spanish coast to make certain that they did not violate the legal three-mile limit. They could, however, attack a particularly important target in that fourth mile if it was clearly established by terrestrial navigation that they were outside the three-mile limit.[34] The German operational orders for submarines usually contained the injunction that because of the uncertain political situation they were to enter Spanish harbours only when forced to for nautical reasons.[35]

While the Germans made some exceptions for Spanish ships carrying produce provided they had a pass from German consular or diplomatic authorities, the overall tendency was to crack down. Ludendorff on 25 March, after learning of intelligence reports stating that some Entente steamer captains claimed their ships followed the neutral corridor to Greece, wanted to know if they still had to leave it open. Holtzendorff answered that as long as Greece was not hostile they had to leave the lane open but that, up to now, U-boats had met little traffic in it. Nevertheless, submarine commanders were ordered to consider any enemy steamers encountered in that corridor as armed and therefore to be attacked on sight. Moreover, both inside and outside the prohibited zone all blacked-out ships not showing the usual navigational lights would be sunk without warning.[36] As the convoy system developed, the Admiralstab decreed that any neutral steamer in a British convoy would be considered hostile and liable to be attacked without warning, as in fact would any steamer regardless of the flag it flew since under these circumstances a neutral flag would be considered a *ruse de guerre*.[37]

By the late spring the Germans had close to thirty U-boats operating in the Mediterranean under the command of a relatively junior officer, Korvettenkapitän Kophamel. This in itself was not unusual in the submarine war which was generally recognized as one conducted by lieutenants, but it may have caused problems in Austrian bases, particularly at Pola where senior officers were common. The commander of the Mediterranean U-Boat Flotilla was therefore raised in status and, as of 9 June, Kapitän zur See (a full captain) Püllen became 'Führer der Unterseeboote im Mittelmeer' with the rank of commodore. Püllen, commonly referred to as the FdU in documents, remained directly under the Admiralstab for operational matters and directly under the Inspektion des Unterseebootswesens of the Reichsmarineamt for technical matters. The status of the Spezialkommando in Pola, directly under the Reichsmarineamt, remained unchanged.[38]

The Hospital Ship Question

Along with the sinking of passenger ships carrying women and children, the treatment of hospital ships, notably the threat to sink these vessels crammed with helpless sick and wounded, was probably one of the most emotionally charged issues of the entire war. It could be argued that it was difficult to distinguish a large passenger liner from a troopship or auxiliary cruiser in a war zone, but given reasonable conditions of visibility there should have been no question about the character of a hospital ship carrying the prescribed markings of white hull, distinctive green stripe, large red crosses and, of course, well-lit at night. The Germans, however, were no worried about recognizing hospital ships. They were convinced that the Entente was using them for military purposes and charged that a large number of ships were designated hospital ships during the Dardanelle campaign and it seemed that the British were adding and dropping ship from the list so frequently that there was insufficient time for submarines to be notified. The Germans claimed to have witnesses among prisoners they had taken who confirmed the misuse of hospital ships to carry healthy troops and munitions. The British in November 1915 had the large liner *Mauretania* inspected at Naples by consuls of the neutral powers to prove that it was being used for medical purposes only, but the Germans were not convinced. There is evidence that Allied hospital ships might have been guilty of sometimes signalling the presence of submarines, something which could be considered a belligerent act. Lacaze, for example, warned on 22 January that it had been drawn to his attention that hospital ships giving intelligence to maritime authorities had been mentioned in reports and this could lead to 'serious inconvenience'. Consequently, any hospital ship which might occasionally provide intelligence should never be mentioned by name.[39] This was certainly not the widespread misuse of hospital ships to carry troops and munitions that the Germans suspected and whether or not their harsh response – legally correct or not – was justified is debatable. The amount of tonnage involved compared with the total volume of Allied shipping and the multitude of other targets available to the Germans at this time was small. They might receive some dividend by forcing the Allies to divert precious escorts to protect hospital ships, but this could in no way compensate for the furious reaction which this new example of German brutality caused. The loss to the Germans in terms of propaganda was enormous and the failure to appreciate this is a clear example of that blindness to non-military factors for which Germany's wartime leadership has been condemned.

On 19 March, Holtzendorff was able to obtain the Kaiser's approval for an announcement that henceforth hospital ships would no longer be spared in the Mediterranean. Holtzendorff apparently wanted to include the neutral corridor to Greece in his restrictions but Foreign Secretary Zimmerman proposed to Hindenburg and Ludendorff that this route should be left open and the General Staff recommended that Holtzendorff should accept the suggestion. Holtzendorff did, but the navy added stringent conditions. Hospital ships would have to sail from Kalamata in the Peloponnese and follow a specified route at a predetermined speed, while arrivals and departures from Gibraltar and Kalamata had to be announced at least six weeks in advance, and a representative of a neutral government had to give for each voyage an express declaration that the ship carried only wounded and medical personnel and no other cargo.[40]

These provisions, at best, would have taken care of the wounded from the Salonika front. There was no provision for the wounded from the Palestine front or any hint of how they might get up to Kalamata to join the hospital ship for the voyage home. The restrictions on hospital ship movements in the Mediterranean had been preceded by restrictions on their movements in the area between Flamborough Head–Terschelling and Ushant–Land's End, that is the southern part of the North Sea and the English Channel. The British indignantly refuted the charges that they had misused hospital ships but quickly realized that the Germans meant business on 1 March when the *Glenart Castle* (6,807 tons) was torpedoed, but fortunately not sunk. On 20 March the well-lit *Asturias* (12,002 tons) was torpedoed and on the 31st it was the turn of the *Gloucester Castle* (7,999 tons). This was decidedly different from hospital ship incidents up to then which had usually involved the ship hitting a mine. There could be no doubt that it was now a deliberate policy on the part of the Germans to attack them and it is not hard to detect in contemporary British documents and literature dealing with the subject a tone of cold fury. In northern waters the British dropped the distinctive markings of hospital ships and used vessels designated as 'ambulance-transports' which carried no special markings and could enjoy no claim to immunity, but could carry a defensive armament.[41] They might suffice for the relatively short journeys across the Channel, but the long sea routes through the Mediterranean were obviously another problem. In the Mediterranean the Admiralty detached four destroyers which had been destined for work on the Otranto barrage to serve as escorts for hospital ships which were held in harbour until their arrival. From mid-April on, hospital ships were treated as troopships, zigzagging, showing no lights at night and escorted by two destroyers whenever they carried sick and wounded. They also received precedence over troopships in the provision of escorts. But, as the Allies had learned, the presence of an escort or escorts did not guarantee safety from a determined submarine commander who might be able to get into a favourable position. On 26 May the hospital ships *Dover Castle* and *Karapara*, escorted by two destroyers, were attacked by Oberleutnant zur See Karl Neumann in UC67 off the coast of Algeria. *Dover Castle* (8,271 tons) was torpedoed and sunk, although fortunately there was time to transfer the wounded to one of the destroyers and the loss of life was relatively small. *Dover Castle* was the only hospital ship to be torpedoed and sunk (as opposed to losses from mines) in the Mediterranean during the war, but this time there had been a witness in the form of a captured British master in UC67 who later reported how the submarine had stalked the well-marked hospital ships. In June 1921 Neumann was tried in Leipzig for war crimes but acquitted on the ground that he was obeying higher orders. Neumann, for his part, claimed the *Dover Castle* was zigzagging in company with another 'hospital ship' – he used quotation marks – and escorted by two destroyers, which was a violation of the Hague Convention. He spoke of his trial as a bitter moment that Germans could have humbled themselves so.[42]

The French government replied to the attacks on hospital ships by embarking German officer-prisoners on hospital ships after 15 April and informing the German government of the fact. The Germans soon learned that seventy German officers were in the French hospital ships *Sphinx*, *André Lebon*, *Samandria*, *Duguay-Trouin* and *Navarre* as protection against submarine attack during their regular voyages between Toulon and Salonika. The Germans replied by sending triple the number of French officer prisoners to sectors of the front exposed to Allied bombardment.[43] The vicious cycle of reprisals was on. The Germans may have believed quite sincerely, based on sometimes questionable intelligence, that the Allies were misusing hospital ships, but it is hard to escape the conclusion that the actions of certain commanders, such as Oberleutnant zur See Helmut Patzig of U86 against the hospital ship *Llandovery Castle* and its survivors in the

Atlantic in June 1918, are among the nastiest incidents of the war at sea and constituted a stain on the honour of the German navy. Up until the spring of 1917 there had frequently been time for crews to take to lifeboats and, certainly in the Mediterranean, it had been possible to regard the high-scoring submarine aces such as Arnauld in a very different light from the men who now deliberately attacked hospital ships.

The Austrians had strong reservations and the question of attacking hospital ships caused a distinct difference between the allies. On 31 March, Freyberg informed the Marinesektion that as a result of 'further proof' of the misuse of hospital ships the Germans were taking the prescribed measures. The 'further proof' cited by the Germans largely consisted of assertions by a French non-commissioned officer prisoner that the hospital ship *Lafayette* had left Bordeaux in mid-March with a cargo of munitions for Salonika, and that on 21 February the location of a German U-boat had been signalled to enemy forces by a hospital ship, an unqualified act of war. The Germans asked the Austrians to act in concert with them.[44] The Austrian naval authorities were, however, opposed to the measure largely on pragmatic rather than humanitarian grounds, or at least that is what they chose to emphasize. The configuration of the Adriatic coastline was such that Austrian hospital ships carrying sick and wounded from Albania were exposed to submarine attack and the commander of the Austrian Cruiser Flotilla cabled from Cattaro that sea transport was of great importance to the XIX Austrian Army Corps, and since August 1916 no fewer than 15,600 sick had been transported by sea from Albania. As the Italians were in approximately the same situation on the Valona–Brindisi route, the commander of the Cruiser Flotilla therefore suggested reaching a separate convention for the Adriatic with them, a suggestion also supported by the Flottenkommandant.[45]

The Germans took alarm and claimed that exemptions for the Adriatic were not possible and against their joint conduct of the war. Furthermore, the measures against hospital ships in the Mediterranean had been instituted after urgent demands by the OHL and had also been discussed by Holtzendorff and Haus and, the Germans claimed, suggested by the latter. The Admiralstab asked if transport of the sick of the XIX Corps could not at least partially be accomplished by land, and sea transport restricted to dark moonless nights with blacked-out ships which could make the proportionately short passage between Albanian harbours and Cattaro in a single night.[46] The Austrian Foreign Office, however, was attracted to the idea of a separate convention with Italy and ready to initiate negotiations towards it by means of neutral powers, but also thought that an agreement between the Marinesektion and German naval authorities ought to precede any action on their part. In addition, they wanted to know the more technical maritime details of such a convention, for example the southern boundary of the area in which it would be valid.[47]

General Baron Arz von Straussenburg, who had replaced Conrad as Chief of the General Staff in March 1917, was against the idea of any convention with Italy. The proposition was hopeless and more or less illusory in view of the possibility of meeting French and eventually British

forces at sea, and would also provide the Entente with the opportunity to
use hospital ships to carry material for the Salonika army from Brindisi and
Otranto to Valona and Santi Quaranta. Arz seemed to reflect the German
line very closely. Retaliation by the Entente against Austrian hospital ships
evacuating sick from Albania would cause a more difficult but probably not
impossible situation, and the local commanders would have to be advised in
good time to use land routes for evacuation of the sick and wounded, and
use sea transport only when absolutely necessary, and then under all
appropriate precautionary measures. Arz added that Austrian submarines
would have to have identical operational orders to those employed by the
German submarines, some of whom, he reminded the Austrian Foreign
Office, still flew the Austrian flag.[48]

The German ambassador in Vienna provided the Austrian Foreign Office
with the German memoranda of 29 January and 29 March justifying the
measures against hospital ships. Count Flotow of the Foreign Office was
still inclined to favour the convention with Italy, but in the face of AOK's
objections the Marinesektion dropped the project and the Flottenkommando
prepared a draft of an order to go out under Njegovan's signature which
would have been virtually identical to the German orders.[49] The new orders
were never issued for in this case the Austrians held back from imitating
German brutality. Kaiser Karl may have played the decisive role. On 21
April, Arz informed Hindenburg that Karl had decided Austrian submarines
would not attack hospital ships and, in addition, the Austrians requested
that German submarines which acted in this manner should not fly the
k.u.k. flag.[50] The Admiralstab promptly issued the relevant orders
although by this stage in the war the question of what flag a submarine
'flew' appeared rather quaint, especially since hospital ships were now
escorted and any attack would most probably have been made from a
submerged position.

On 2 May, Admiral Holtzendorff, accompanied by Kapitän zur See
Grasshoff, the head of Abteilung B, visited AOK in Baden in what was
intended to be a courtesy visit to pay respects to the new Chief of the
Austrian General Staff. However, General Cramon, the German plenipotentiary at AOK, succeeded in obtaining an audience for the visitors with
Kaiser Karl and an invitation for Holtzendorff and his entourage to breakfast
with the imperial couple. According to Rear-Admiral Winterhalder, the
Austrian naval representative at AOK, the real purpose of the interview was
to counter the influence of Count Czernin who still harboured doubts about
the ultimate success of the submarine campaign. The Austrians, in turn
used the opportunity to raise the question of delivery of oil supplies from
newly conquered Romania where there was apparently friction between
German and Austrian authorities over the subject. Winterhalder reported
that both Holtzendorff and Grasshoff were wildly optimistic about the U-
boat war – and after April 1917 this was understandable – and convinced
that Britain and the entire Entente would be compelled to give in within
another two or three months. They also hoped that when all reports were
in, the total of sinkings in April would reach or exceed 1 million tons
Holtzendorff seems to have had a tendency to exaggerate to his allies in this

just as he had about the number of U-boats that would have been available, for while the Germans did very well indeed they did not do that well and the total sinkings in April in all theatres were around 860,000 tons. The Germans also kept up that curious fiction that the United States had not yet declared war on Germany, apparently ignoring the vote of Congress and the fact that at 1 p.m. on 6 April President Wilson had signed the proclamation declaring a state of war with the Imperial German government and that Secretary of State Lansing immediately countersigned the document and affixed the great seal of the United States. Nevertheless, the Germans told the Austrians that they would give American warships 'the honour of the first shot' although American merchant ships would not be spared.[51] Holtzendorff and Grasshoff were probably reflecting the Kaiser's and Zimmerman's desire to avoid unnecessary provocation of the Americans, hoping to strengthen the neutralist or anti-war spirit in the American mid-west with its large population of German origin. This was another illusion for by this date the first flotilla of American destroyers were already steaming across the Atlantic and would arrive at Queenstown on 4 May.[52] Although Winterhalder thought that the interview between the Kaiser and Holtzendorff had been successful and that the imperial couple had been extremely gracious both during and after the breakfast, the reality was somewhat different. Count Arthur Polzer-Hoditz, head of the Emperor's private office, gives a very different picture with a glacial exchange between the Empress and Holtzendorff over submarine warfare.[53]

On the highest level, of course, Karl had during the winter of 1917 made an attempt to secure peace for Austria-Hungary through the intermediary of his wife's family, notably Prince Sixtus and Prince Francis Xavier of Bourbon-Parma. The attempt proved abortive and Austria-Hungary remained locked in that close – some would say stifling – embrace of her more powerful ally until the bitter end in 1918.[54] The navy most probably had no inkling of these secret talks at the highest level. For the k.u.k. Kriegsmarine it was war as usual with the Italians as the primary enemy. Nevertheless, the divergent approach to the hospital ship question was, at the least, a pale reflection of this different attitude to the war, even though the Austrian action might have been based as much on pragmatic as on humanitarian grounds.

The use by German submarines of the Austrian flag had long since served its purpose by the summer of 1917. Italy had been at war with Germany for almost a year and given the scope of German submarine activity the fear that the disappearance of the k.u.k. flag from the western Mediterranean would cause comment was an irrelevant issue if ever there was one. However, it could still create difficulties for the Dual Monarchy. On 18 July, Arz raised the inevitable question. He asked Njegovan if, given the numerous differences in operational orders between German and Austrian submarines, it was still advisable to continue the agreement with the Admiralstab whereby certain German submarines flew the k.u.k. flag and were nominally carried on the k.u.k. list. If the submarines in question acted only under the German flag, the freedom of action of their commander would be increased, while the long period of time which had

321

elapsed since the first German submarines arrived and numerous alterations in strength of Austrian and German submarines would suffice to camouflage the situation. Njegovan agreed, there were only three German U-boats involved and now that Austrian submarines were active in the central basin of the Mediterranean – as a proposal to announce the shelling of Derna by one of them would demonstrate – what had formerly been fiction would be fact and the apparent disappearance of k.u.k. U-boats from the western Mediterranean would not have any special significance.[55] Arz also wanted to include in any discussion with the Germans about a new flag agreement the subject of the corridor for neutral shipping to Greece now that the Greeks had come into the war on the side of the Entente.

The Austrians really did not expect any objections from the Germans since only U35, U38 and U39 were involved in the 1 October 1916 agreement with the Admiralstab. The Germans themselves, according to the Austrians, appeared to place little importance on the issue. Although the commanders of the three submarines were carried on the k.u.k. Naval List, the Germans had published their names in official German reports, and even photographs of them had appeared in the German press. They also happened to be Arnauld de la Perière, Forstmann and Valentiner, who were about the most successful U-boat commanders and everyone knew that they, and the submarines they commanded, were German.[56] The Admiralstab, as the Austrians anticipated, made no objection and in early September ordered the change. As for the neutral corridor to Greece, the Germans preferred to keep it open for the moment since the Greek government had broken relations with Germany but had not yet declared war, and closing it would merely play into the hands of Venizelos. Moreover, they conceded, there was little traffic in it and the corridor had no significance in practical terms.[57] In September 1917 the flag issue therefore ended quietly and with little notice. It had been extremely troublesome for the Austrians earlier in the war and earned them a good deal of odium when they had to cover German actions.

The Spanish government eventually provided the warring powers with an escape from the cycle of reprisal and counter-reprisal on the hospital ship question. The Germans had specified that hospital ships would have to be certified by the representative of a neutral power at Kalamata or Gibraltar as carrying only wounded and medical supplies. Prince Hohenlohe, Austrian ambassador in Berlin, reported on 22 April that the Spanish Cabinet had declared itself willing to provide that control through visitation of the hospital ships but the German government, while gladly accepting the proposal, insisted that the Spanish representatives must remain on board to prevent the ship being used for illegal purposes after the inspection had taken place.[58] The negotiations for an agreement seemed to take an excessive amount of time, possibly because the belligerents were not talking directly to each other but rather through the Spanish government, and the inevitable requests for clarification of the German terms by the British had to be passed via Madrid and were time-consuming. Nevertheless, on 29 July, de Bon informed the French C.-in-C. in the Mediterranean that the German terms had been accepted in principle and after the date they would take effect, which remained to be settled, French hospital ships would conform strictly to the provisions of the Hague Convention and navigate at night with lights burning and would no longer be escorted by warships or armed vessels, while instructions would be sent in sufficient time for landing the German officers who had been embarked as hostages. The Admiralstab, in turn, agreed on 15 August that as soon as the French government had made the necessary statement about disembarkation of the hostages the Germans would evacuate the reprisal camps. The Admiralstab also announced that from now on – as far as possible – submarines in the Mediterranean would be ordered not to attack hospital ships and that by 10 September all of them should be in possession of the order. The Admiralstab also announced that it had 'been secured' that the Austrians would act on the same principles, a statement that irritated the Austrians who had not been consulted but who, of course, had never agreed to attack hospital ships in the first place.[59]

The Admiralstab initially ordered submarines to permit hospital ships to pass even if they were escorted or in convoy.[60] This was merely for the transitional period. Once the agreement went into effect hospital ships escorted by warships or armed vessels would be regarded as belligerents. The Germans did agree to drop the demand that hospital ships follow specific routes and agreed to spare them in all parts of the Mediterranean, although they would and could give no guarantee against mines. The price for this German concession was that the neutral commissioners should remain permanently aboard the hospital ships, with these undertakings guaranteed by the King of Spain. The Germans were in fact adamant on this question of the Spanish commissioners remaining permanently on board and the absence of the man could in no cases be covered by a certificate. They therefore suggested that to get around the difficulty of one becoming ill there ought to be two commissioners for each ship. The Germans also warned of the dangers of incidents if a hospital ship allowed itself to be accompanied by a merchant vessel since they now assumed all British merchant ships were armed, and they reserved the right to stop and inspect vessels bearing hospital ship markings. More ominously, the Germans clearly specified that these provisions applied only to the Mediterranean and declined to give any assurances for hospital ships in other waters, including the English Channel. Under these circumstances, the Spanish government insisted that the Spanish delegates disembark before the ship passed through the Straits of Gibraltar into the Atlantic.[61]

The Spanish government named eight officers for British ships and thirteen for French. The French were startled to learn that the Spanish were sending naval officers. During the discussions they had understood that the commissioners would be members of the Spanish Red Cross and they asked if the British would accept them, for they thought the presence of Spanish naval officers on board their ships and in their bases might be undesirable. The Admiralty expert, C. R. Brigstock, minuted that it was obviously desirable to avoid neutral officers capable of making professional observations of defences entering defended ports but some trust must be placed in Spain if the arrangement was to work, while Jellicoe saw no objection.[62] The

Admiralty ordered all mercantile codes and other confidential material issued to hospital ships during the period they had been escorted to be landed, and stressed that no ship was to sail without a commissioner, even if the ship had to wait in port for a substitute. The Admiralty also ordered ships to take the greatest care to avoid all cause of complaint which might imperil the agreement itself or the possibilty that the latter might later be extended. They still hoped to get German agreement to extend it outside the Mediterranean and also asked the Foreign Office to approach the Spanish about naming additional commissioners as a reserve, a fairly obvious step since the eight commissioners assigned to the British would only have been able to handle four hospital ships at a time. The Spanish did extend their service to Italy and on 22 October a delegation of Spanish officers arrive in Rome for work aboard Italian hospital ships.[63]

The Germans evaded attempts to extend the agreement outside the Mediterranean and made threatening noises from time to time. For example, they announced that if one of the Allies did not observe all of the conditions, the agreement with all the others would cease. It would be nice to end this act of humanity during the war on a pleasant note, but it must also be reported that, human nature being what it is, AOK later passed on a report to the Marinesektion that their intelligence sources in Madrid claimed that the majority of the Spanish commissioners were the type who would try and improve their financial situation from their mission and were liable to allow a variety of misconduct, especially in regard to the conveyance of healthy troops from Salonika to Italy. There were even allegations that, on these grounds, a conscientious Spanish officer had requested to be relieved.[64] But, on the whole, the arrangements worked despite the quibbling and hospital ships were not *deliberately* attacked *in the Mediterranean* for the remainder of the war, although the *Goorkha* (6,335 tons) was damaged by a mine off Alexandria on 17 October. It was a different story outside the Mediterranean, and on 4 January 1918 the well-lit hospital ship *Rewa* (7,308 tons), which had carried Spanish commissioners as far as Gibraltar, was torpedoed and sunk by U55 in the approaches to the Bristol Channel, waters supposedly open to hospital ships. Fortunately, most of the wounded were taken off before the ship sank and the loss of life was small.[65]

Ineffectual Allied Countermeasures – Dispersion

Even before the Germans unleashed unrestricted submarine warfare the Admiralty were worried about the situation in the Mediterranean. These worries were largely centred on the heavy maritime commitments of the Salonika expedition where the British had never been as enthusiastic as the French. Jellicoe reported to an Anglo-French Conference in London at the end of December 1916 that from a naval point of view they were able with great difficulty to maintain their present forces at Salonika and Egypt as regards merchant shipping, had even greater difficulty providing escorts for transports and store ships, and it was practically impossible for them to add

:o their forces in Salonika or Egypt. Moreover, destroyers to escort transports or munitions ships to the Mediterranean would have to be withdrawn from 'offensive' work against enemy submarines which meant that the number of enemy submarines could increase rapidly and losses would rise.[66] Jellicoe was obviously still clinging to the concept of offensive' hunting of submarines. Prime Minister Lloyd George argued early in January in a memorandum for the delegates to an Allied Conference in Rome that after exhaustive examination the British had come to the conclusion that the grave shipping situation provided an overwhelming case against the dispatch of further British divisions to Salonika. The French proposed reducing the dangers of the movement by sea through the development of a route from Santi Quaranta to Monastir for the supply of Sarrail's army. This would have an additional advantage. The short passage from the Italian shore to the Albanian coast could be covered in a single night thereby reducing the amount of shipping needed. The French also wanted to develop rail communications to Salonika through Italy and Greece for troops, and eventually supplies and munitions, again with the objective of reducing the sea passage and exposure to submarines. The conference approved these proposals, although the Italian Minister of Transport pointed out that the question depended largely on the amount of rolling stock the Allies, notably the French, could put at the disposition of the Italian government. These were the primary decisions at Rome concerning the naval war. The remainder of the discussions concerned land operations, and a technical naval and shipping conference was scheduled for the earliest possible date in London.[67]

There was an urgent need for such a conference since at the beginning of 1917 there were notable differences between the Allies on a wide range of subjects, including how best to meet the submarine challenge, and the old problem between the French and Italians over supreme command in the Adriatic in case of joint action. The submarine losses remained painful. Although January was a relatively quiet month there were some spectacular casualties. On the very first day of the year Steinbauer in UB47, returning from the cruise in which he had already sunk the battleship *Gaulois* in the Aegean, torpedoed and sank the large troopship *Ivernia* (14,228 tons) off Cape Matapan with a loss of 125 men, while on 4 January the Russian battleship *Peresviet* (returned by Japan to Russia after the war began) was mined and sunk off Port Said, probably on a field laid by U73. On 9 January, Kapitänleutnant Hartwig in U32 torpedoed and sank the British battleship *Cornwallis* off Malta and on 25 January, while the Allies were meeting in London, Forstmann in U39 sank the French troopship *Amiral Magon* (5,566 tons) which was *en route* to Salonika.[68] A British officer on a destroyer in the Aegean commented on the *Cornwallis*: 'Do you realize we have lost 7 battleships out here since the show started – of course they were old – I'd give anything to push a submarine's face . . . ', and Mark Kerr added: 'The *Cornwallis* was sunk in the place where 2 submarines have been at work for a long time. I never send men of war on the transport routes, they are all marked by submarines & very unhealthy places.' Thursby, on the loss of the *Ivernia*, said: 'I am very strongly of opinion that the arrangements for the protection of transports and shipping will not be satisfactory until a single officer is appointed to control the routes and escort of all British ships in the Mediterranean.'[69] He would repeat this proposal to an Allied conference at Corfu at the end of April and this time the chastened Allies would agree.

Some British authorities had already expressed disillusionment with the arrangements well before the new year. In October, Rear-Admiral Ballard, Limpus's successor as SNO at Malta, argued that the system of patrolled routes had been in force long enough for a judgement as to its efficiency and in view of the increasing rate of loss, unless more patrol vessels were forthcoming, some other system should be given a trial. They would need at least four times the number of patrol vessels on the routes to ensure a submarine being brought to action whenever it appeared. The submarines had few difficulties discovering the Allied routes and Ballard proposed a system of convoys and accepting the delays to shipping which would be involved. If the system of patrols were abandoned in Zones I, V and X (British zones east of Gibraltar, around Malta in the central Mediterranean, and between Crete and Egypt in the eastern Mediterranean, respectively), sufficient patrol vessels would be released to provide escorts for one 12-knot and two 8½-knot convoys sailing from Port Said and Gibraltar every week, with enough left over to escort slow warships and transports. Merchant ships steaming faster than 12 knots usually required a destroyer for an escort and since there were not enough available these ships might be allowed to travel alone, trusting to their speed and zigzagging. Ballard asked for Admiralty approval before approaching the French C.-in-C. as he had been informed that the latter (it was still Dartige) was sensitive about suggestions from officers of junior rank.[70] Oliver was interested enough in Ballard's convoy proposals to order the Naval Staff to compile figures on the amount of British shipping under 12 knots along the main routes in the Mediterranean each week.[71] The results at the end of November were embodied by the Director of Trade Division in a diagram (see Figure 9.1). The Admiralty did not accept Ballard's proposal for convoys at this stage, but they were prepared to modify the system. In December, Captain H. W. Grant, the Assistant Director of Operations Division, suggested establishing throughout the western basin of the Mediterranean a number of 'Ports of Refuge', protected by guns and nets, to which ships could be directed during daylight hours when submarines were reported to be active in the

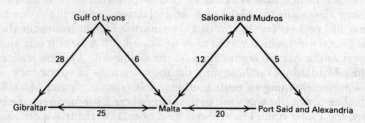

Figure 9.1 Average weekly volume of British traffic in the Mediterranean[72]

area. Ships would then proceed during the night to the next anchorage, if necessary, and keep as close to the coast as possible and make full use of Spanish territorial waters. In the eastern basin shipping in open waters would no longer follow a fixed route, the present procedure, but after passing Cape Bon would spread out on diverse routes to Malta, Alexandria, Port Said and the Aegean. Ships would enter the Aegean through either of the channels between Crete and Cape Malea and then proceed by fixed routes through the Aegean on the same principle as in the western basin, anchoring by day in protected ports and steaming by night. The proposal was supported by Captain Webb, Director of Trade Division, since he had also been advocating hugging the coast in the western basin and dispersal of ships in the eastern basin. Oliver also considered the scheme 'a great improvement' because the extensive coasting made it more difficult for submarines to attack and the system of dispersal in the open sea eliminated the ability of a submarine to lie on a track and wait for ships to come to it. Submarines would now have to cruise over wide areas to pick up single ships, thereby reducing their bag and consuming fuel which would shorten their cruise. The Admiralty approved the scheme, but sought French agreement before submitting it to the Italians.[73] Wemyss, too, was seeking a more effective system of protection for shipping and asked Ballard on 11 December if he thought that the French C.-in-C. would consider instituting in Zone X a system of convoys for slow merchantmen not fitted with wireless and therefore unable to benefit from the 'ALLO' signals warning of submarines. The convoys would follow a route different from the fixed transport routes. Ballard could only reply that he had already urged a system of convoys for slow traffic but that the French C.-in-C. did not agree 'and until he does I do not anticipate any material reduction in the present rate of loss'.[74]

Neither Wemyss's nor Ballard's suggestions about convoys found favour at the Admiralty. Rear-Admiral Thomas Jackson, Director of Operations Division, maintained that if vessels were taken from patrol duties on the transport routes in order to convoy slow merchant ships on different routes, the transport routes would become more unsafe than at present. Webb tried to counter by arguing that even if convoys were not possible, comparatively fast vessels should not be allowed to proceed along a definite fixed route easily located by the enemy. Rear-Admiral Duff, Director of the Anti-Submarine Division, was willing to see a trial of the convoy system in the Mediterranean, for they had 'no definite experience of its value', but was against Ballard's suggestion of a 12-knot fast convoy and thought fast ships should make the most of their speed and zigzag. Trawlers would be too slow to escort even an 8½-knot convoy and they would therefore have to use sloops, while the number of convoys possible every month would be very limited and, consequently, congestion at both ends of the journey would be great. Duff thought that in open waters such as those of the eastern basin of the Mediterranean the principle of dispersion would give the greatest safety, and once all British merchant ships in the Mediterranean were armed they ought to try and send them in pairs when their speed was the same.[75]

Despite hesitation over the introduction of convoys, the Admiralty was anxious to try the system of dispersal, at least for British ships and, in view of the delay likely to occur while the French Ministry of Marine referred the matter to the French C.-in-C. in the Mediterranean, it decided to implement the plan itself on 11 January. The system of dispersal would be used between Cape Bon and the Aegean, while coasting would be employed as far as possible elsewhere.[76] Ballard immediately inquired if his new orders authorized him to withdraw patrols from routes established by the French C.-in-C., and pointed out that the system of zones involved a British promise to protect all Allied vessels on routes passing through the British zone. He anticipated that the French C.-in-C. would expect him to continue the patrols as they were at present until he received orders to the contrary from Paris. This was indeed a delicate question for there were hardly likely to be enough ships to patrol the fixed routes properly and convoy ships on dispersed routes. The Admiralty reply was somewhat equivocal: 'Routes ordered by the French C.-in-C. should still be patrolled as far as practicable but you should so dispose the vessels that they will be more readily available to hunt submarines in any locality where they may be operating.'[77] There was also confusion at Alexandria where British authorities were sailing French as well as British steamers under the new orders, while the French continued to use the old routes when they controlled movements. Ballard concluded that the best way out of these difficulties – one is tempted to say mess – would be a conference of Allied naval officers to come to some arrangement, and until then the new routes ought to apply only to British steamers. The Admiralty agreed to the procedure but this unilateral introduction of the system of dispersed routes by the British understandably produced considerable friction with the new and prickly French C.-in-C., Gauchet.[78]

The French officer most concerned with anti-submarine warfare was Rear-Admiral Fatou, Admiral commanding (French) Mediterranean Patrols. Fatou held similar opinions to some of his British allies at the Admiralty, that is he was against the system of 'escorts' and staunchly in favour of 'patrols', despite the fact that in his very first report to the new C.-in-C. outlining the situation he acknowledged that of the total number of French forces available, deducting ships in harbour for repair or refit, they had only eighty-two vessels available for sea duty at any one time, and these eighty-two had to patrol 2,500 miles of French routes giving a density of one patrol for every 30 miles, provided the vessels could be distributed equally. This was also only a theoretical figure because of what Fatou termed the overly frequent detachment of destroyers, sloops and trawlers for escort duties. Fatou claimed naval opinion was nearly unanimous in recognizing the uselessness of escorts, at least for fast, well-armed vessels. Unfortunately this was exactly the type that public opinion in Britain as well as France insisted ought to be convoyed, a procedure which resulted in the squandering of resources. The smaller torpedo craft were, he alleged, useless in defending a large ship against the gunfire of submarines when the large ship was frequently better armed than the escort and a more stable gun platform. The so-called escort was impotent, as numerous cases had demonstrated, in defending against a torpedo attack, and in a rough sea the ship under escort had to reduce speed if it did not want to lose its escort which thereby increased its danger by lengthening the duration of the voyage.[79]

Fatou amplified his views in another paper written in early January. He dismissed the system of protection based on convoy and escort with frequently modified routes, or navigation along the coast with ports of refuge for daylight hours. The scarcity of transport and shipping would not permit such a lengthening of routes and the delays involved and as far as escorts were concerned, the French had a mere twenty-five craft which would really be suited for everyday service as escorts. An escort, in order to have any chance of thwarting an attack, ought to number at least three ships, one ahead and two on the flanks of the convoy. When the escort was reduced to a single ship it was useful only for its effect on morale, maintaining the discipline of the route, receiving wireless signals and saving victims of a disaster. Furthermore, Fatou argued, the principle of a continuous escort from Marseilles to Salonika was difficult to reconcile with the division of the Mediterranean into national zones, each patrolled by a different navy. If escorts systematically crossed an Allied zone to accompany vessels of their own nationality, they would be redundant. If they did not, the transference of protection of a convoy from zone to zone would involve complications which might be resolved for certain itineraries, but which would remain difficult to overcome and if the method was generalized could involve, at the very least, new delays. Fatou's own project involved a combination of systems: (1) permanently patrolled recommended routes for ordinary commercial navigation; (2) special secret routes for troop transports or important ships faster than 12 knots; and (3) detours signalled after information was received about the position or operational areas of submarines.[80]

Lacaze and the French Naval Staff were a bit more open to the Admiralty plan of dispersed routes, and in submitting it to Gauchet for study commented that it might have certain advantages once the majority of merchantmen were armed and equipped with wireless. Gauchet had, however, a number of his own complaints about the British, particularly their wireless procedures which he considered lax and frequently betraying routes to the enemy. He was absolutely convinced that any route used by the British would very quickly become known.[81] The French C.-in-C. now received predictably negative advice about the new Admiralty scheme from Fatou who maintained that the British system would put into question the principles of collaboration and unity of command which had been the rule up to then. Navigation along the Spanish coast offered certain guarantees only as long as the enemy respected Spanish neutrality, and there was relative protection along the Tunisian and Algerian coast, although Fatou admitted there were gaps here. There was, however, nearly no surveillance at all in Italian waters except for semaphore stations on shore. The Tyrrhenian patrols had never been more than feebly organized and had been diminished, admittedly at French request, in order to reinforce the Otranto barrage. Fatou claimed that the principle of dispersed routes in the central

Mediterranean was seductive a priori, and he had no doubt that initially it would produce satisfactory results when submarines became confused after no longer being able to find their prey on the same fixed routes. But once submarine commanders realized that the routes had been abandoned, they would logically proceed to hunt their targets at those points of convergence where the dispersed routes fanned out, that is in straits or on the approaches to ports. Moreover, on dispersed routes there would be little chance of rescuing the crew of a ship which had been sunk without being able to get out a wireless distress call for there would be no patrols passing at regular intervals. Fatou warned of the consequences that the British action would have for French shipping, for Ballard had already loyally informed him that he did not have the resources to meet all of the demands for escort of convoys and continue to patrol the old routes. Henceforth, the Allies would no longer patrol, they would only escort. To be fair, Fatou added, the British when informed of an important French ship crossing their zones had tried with good grace to assure its escort if their resources permitted after assuring the protection of their own ships. The French could no longer expect this benevolence in the future, however, because of the large number of British ships at sea, and the French certainly could not patrol their own zones and escort French transports themselves through the zones of their Allies. The Admiralty's decision annihilated the work of the Malta Conference and Fatou was delighted when ordered to London for the conference since he considered a new agreement to be absolutely necessary.[82]

The Mediterranean was only part of the agenda for the forthcoming London Conference but it was an important one. Jellicoe ordered the War Staff to include in the British agenda proposals for altered zones in the Mediterranean and for the French and Italians between them looking after the Austrian fleet and the Dardanelles without any help from the British. The latter, Jellicoe thought, should concentrate in home waters and outside the Mediterranean, although he conceded that they might have to leave patrol craft to assist. The British were particularly anxious to improve protection for the drifters on the Otranto barrage and pay off the old battleships at Taranto in order to provide crews for new ships at home.[83]

The Italians had their own agenda for the conference, linked partially to the long-running and still unsettled dispute over supreme command in the Adriatic and French reinforcement for the Italian fleet, the same problems which had occupied so much of 1916. The Stato Maggiore della Marina, despite the impending submarine threat, still seemed hypnotized by the Austrian fleet, although the Italians would have been quick to add that they were the only ally in the Mediterranean in actual and close contact with an enemy fleet. The activities of the Italian army in southern Albania and the use of Santi Quaranta as a port also led the Italian Naval Staff to comment how desirable it would be for the same power to control both sides of the Corfu Channel, which in one paper the Stato Maggiore referred to as the 'key to the Adriatic'. The Italians, in effect, now wanted to occupy the island of Corfu with its useful harbour and, to avoid the touchy question of command, wanted to adjust the boundary between the French and Italian zones so that the island fell within the Italian sphere. This implied Italian ommand. It was important, the Stato Maggiore maintained, that whoever ontrolled the Albanian mainland opposite Corfu also controlled the island self.[84]

The EMG clung to the principle that whenever the French C.-in-C. ntervened personally he would command. They also rejected the Italian esire to place Corfu in their zone. The French had used it as an important lace for training for close to a year, a French general served as governor of he island and, while only part of the French fleet was currently there and he French C.-in-C. had, to date, made only short visits, this was only a uestion of circumstances which could change from moment to moment. he line of demarcation would therefore remain as it was: Cape Santa Maria i Leuca–Fano. Lacaze assured Gauchet that in his formal response to the alians he would maintain the intangibility of the principle of a French C.-n-C. of all Allied forces in the Mediterranean.[85]

The Allied Naval Conference which met in London on 23–24 January as perhaps the most important to take place to date. Lacaze decided to ome along with de Bon and Fatou, while Corsi and Marzolo, Sub-Chief of he Stato Maggiore, represented Italy along with General Dall'Olio, Minister of Munitions. The conference was important enough for the Prime Minister himself to make the opening speech and Lloyd George, on the eve f unrestricted submarine warfare, set something of a crisis tone. The tuation was grave and was becoming increasingly so. The Germans had iscovered what a formidable weapon they had in the submarine and the mount of Allied tonnage sunk was alarmingly great and was going to be ncreased. The success of the Allies 'depends entirely on the arrangements vhich can be made for the protection of the mercantile marine during the ear' and the Prime Minister regarded the conference as one of 'the most erious and most important conferences which had been held since the war egan'. As for the Mediterranean, it was 'not as well managed as it ought to e', and 'unless something is done to get better co-operation and co-rdination among the Allied fleets . . . you will find the Mediterranean a losed sea for the Allies'. The Prime Minister claimed that the French and alian fleets ought to be enough for the Mediterranean, for the British vanted the crews from their battleships for arming merchantmen, and dvocated a really effective joint board at, perhaps Malta, with power to act r control of all fleets in the Mediterranean. Lloyd George concluded by nviting all those present to act as if they were really one country, as they all ad one cause and the failure of one meant the failure of all, and the success f one meant the success of all.[86] After the Prime Minister had left, Lacaze choed the call for unity. He added, however, that he did not see things in as ark a light and that, although tonnage destroyed was an inconvenience to nem, it was a negative success for the enemy since it would not feed him nd his populations were suffering. It was also essential to act with an ffensive spirit and not to be occupied mostly with measures to defend nemselves against the enemy's submarine campaign. They ought to onsider offensive actions, even if only small ones, and show the enemy that ney were not downhearted and could dare and act.[87] This rhetoric would ook odd in the light of what was about to happen.

In the discussions over specific issues the participants tended to repeat
each other face to face the arguments that they had already put on pap
over the past few months. The issue of bringing back the obsolete Quee
division from Taranto – a measure with overwhelming logic behind it give
the Franco-Italian superiority in battleship strength over the Austrians
proved surprisingly difficult. Corsi held out for compensations. The Sta
Maggiore in preparing its agenda had indeed stressed the point that they ha
not received everything promised to them in the Naval Convention
1915. They wanted dreadnoughts to replace the Queen division. In th
course of the arguments Jellicoe revealed that the British were pressing th
Japanese very strongly for a flotilla of destroyers for the Mediterranea
offering to pay for coal, for officers and men, or for anything if they wou
just send the destroyers. Count Villarey, the Italian naval attaché in Londc
and far from a favourite at the Admiralty, was fairly blunt in his requests fc
compensation, notably in the form of more destroyers, and readir
between the lines of the minutes it is fairly safe to assume that both Jellicc
and Sir Edward Carson, now First Lord, did not improve their opinion
their Italian ally during the meeting. At one point Corsi even asked, 'B
what will they say when I go back to Italy with empty hands?'[88]

In the end the conference agreed to the withdrawal of the Briti
battleships, but the Italians forced the inclusion of a long qualifyir
statement about the British withdrawal taking place only if a 'substantia
French force was permanently stationed at Corfu and the British mac
'every effort' to reinforce them by a 'convenient number of light craft whc
available'. The Italians finally agreed to the withdrawal on the Frenc
promise that a squadron of battleships 'would be constantly available
Corfu'. The Italians also agreed to the French C.-in-C. taking command
the 'greater part' of French naval forces in the Mediterranean ever took pa
in operations in the Adriatic. The British obtained approval for th
withdrawal of all their other battleships in the Mediterranean except for th
Lord Nelson and *Agamemnon* in the eastern Mediterranean. Henceforth tw
French Patries would join them in watching the Dardanelles.

The British and French had a lengthy discussion over their respectiv
schemes for protecting shipping, fixed or dispersed routes, and in the er
had to settle on a compromise. In the western basin of the Mediterranea
coastal routes would be used as much as possible and each country wou
decide if their ships would take the direct route from Marseilles to Algiers
arranged by the French navy. They would look into the question
protecting certain ports as refuges and if the British could spare the nets the
should advise the French and Italians where they wanted them placed. In th
eastern basin of the Mediterranean, the Allies agreed on what w
essentially a trial of the two systems. The French system of fixed route
frequently changed, would be used for traffic to and from Salonika and th
Aegean, and the British system of dispersal would be used for traff
between Cape Bon and Port Said by all British ships and any Allied vesse
which cared to join them. After a period of trial, the length was n
specified, there would be another conference to compare results and sett
on a permanent system. The British promised to maintain their patrols c

French routes in their zones and not divert any patrol craft for work on the dispersed routes.

In Adriatic questions the Allies admitted that the means presently employed on the Otranto barrage were not sufficient, but agreed to put the system directly under the command of a British naval officer with the status of commodore who would be under the Italian C.-in-C. and in those waters enjoy the use of all French and Italian craft not used elsewhere. The British commodore was also empowered to call on Allied forces in the vicinity for assistance when needed. The Allies agreed that no major naval operations in the Adriatic were possible at the moment but that minor operations 'should be carried out with vigour'. The Allies also recommended 'more frequent' conferences in the Mediterranean. On more general matters, the conference agreed to restrict the importation of non-essential articles, established a Standing International Shipping Committee to exchange information on the employment of merchant shipping, and recommended to the British and French governments a redistribution of available shipping according to needs. The latter was largely motivated by the unequivocal statements by General Dall'Olio that if Italy did not get the necessary tonnage for coal the production of ammunition would be stopped in March. The British promised to help meet French requirements for materials, steel and engines, and to assist the Italians, especially with coal, as much as possible.[89]

The conference had taken place just in time for there was apparently considerable confusion among the Allies in the Mediterranean. Gauchet protested on 26 January that, as a consequence of the new Admiralty orders, patrols had almost completely disappeared between Pantelleria and Cerigo and they were presented with a *de facto* rupture without preliminary notice of past agreements. Gauchet admitted that Ballard was doing what he could to escort French transports, but they were sometimes diverted in directions contrary to the instructions they had received from French authorities and which Gauchet occasionally considered dangerous. He thought the London Conference would bring order to what he termed 'this anarchy'. Thursby also reported from the eastern Mediterranean that 'considerable confusion and uncertainty' reigned as regards transport routes and escorts and various senior officers were trying to co-operate as far as British ships were concerned, but he had received no communication from the French C.-in-C. regarding his own wishes.[90]

Changes in the Italian High Command

The decision of the London Conference resulted in the immediate recall of the battleships *Duncan*, *Prince of Wales*, and *Africa* from Taranto. However, the Italians required the Italian depot ships used as a base by the drifters, and *Queen* therefore remained as a floating depot, reduced to a care and maintenance party. Kerr continued to fly his flag in *Queen* while Commodore Algernon Heneage took over the drifters.[91] The really big changes in this theatre would come in the high command of the Italian fleet. From the late autumn of 1916 on there appeared to be a growing campaign of criticism against the Duke of the Abruzzi in both political circles and the press, which was also coupled with dissatisfaction with the performance of the minister, Admiral Corsi, and with the overall record of the navy in general. The inquests into the various disasters, such as the *Leonardo da Vinci*, were in progress and there was a general sense of unease. According to the more specific charges against Abruzzi, he was authoritarian, intolerant and not disposed to welcome expert advice. His critics made much of the forced retirements under a decree setting age limits for active command of five admirals senior to him, and alleged that in the case of Leonardi Cattolica it was a reprisal for a courageous inquest that the latter had conducted into the sinking of the *Garibaldi* which revealed serious deficiencies in the navy and high command. The duke's frequent changes of his chief of staff were used against him as evidence that it was impossible to serve under him. The naval losses of 1915 were dragged up again along with the Pelagosa affair, and there were the usual more scurrilous charges about the duke's private life and pleasures.[92] By 12 January the French naval attaché could report that people with a reputation for being well informed were saying that the duke would soon leave his command, criticized not only for failing to accomplish anything but also for turning a deaf ear to all proposals for operations made to him. Saint Pair's sources claimed that the British were extremely discontented with him for the mediocre handling of their force on the Otranto barrage and that Admiral Cagni was his likely successor. These suggestions were false. There is no evidence that the British were strongly against Abruzzi, in fact just the opposite is true. There is also no real evidence that the duke had lost the confidence of the bulk of the officers and men of his own fleet at Taranto. Unlike the French C.-in-C., he had no responsibility for the defence of traffic and hence could escape blame for submarine losses. Nevertheless, even if the details were false or not known, it must have been fairly obvious to any observer that something was happening. The fiery ultra-nationalist paper *Idea Nazionale* also turned its guns on Corsi in a scathing attack, subsequently censored. There were similar attacks in *Secolo*, but also speculation that some of the fire was really directed at Abruzzi and the minister was the scapegoat to avoid direct attacks on a member of the royal family. The belated announcement, over a month after it happened, of the sinking of the *Regina Margherita* only added fuel to the fire.[93]

Corsi's experiment of combining the office of minister with that of Capo di Stato Maggiore also had not worked well in practice and on 18 January, while passing through Milan *en route* to the London Conference, Corsi had a meeting with Thaon di Revel, former Capo di Stato Maggiore and currently C.-in-C. at Venice. Corsi informed Revel of his intention to name him Capo di Stato Maggiore, C.-in-C. of the Fleet and commander of the 1° Squadra. Revel claimed to be surprised by the suddenness of the announcement and asked for time to reflect, observing immediately that it would be difficult to exercise the functions of Chief of the Naval Staff at the same time as he had the obligations of direct command of the fleet and one of its squadrons. Furthermore, he could not agree with other aspects of Corsi's plans, namely movements in personnel and the projected creation of a Committee of High Commissioners. Revel made it clear that he did not want to face the same conditions which had forced him to resign in 1915, notably insufficient authority for the exercise of his office, particularly on the question of executive action and the ability to order changes in personnel.[94] At first, Revel's conditions may not have been acceptable to the Minister of Marine and the former met with King Victor Emmanuel near Mestre a few days later, although there are apparently no records of what was said.[95] The sovereign's intervention may have been decisive for on the 28th Revel wrote to General Brusati, the King's first aide-de-camp, that Prime Minister Boselli had told him he would ask the Minister of Marine to renounce the creation of the Committee of High Commissioners and institute, instead, the office of Inspector General. Revel added that it would be necessary to see that the attributions of that office did not allow interference in the conduct of the war. Revel appears to have gained his point in regard to past decrees restricting the right of the Capo di Stato Maggiore to interfere in the employment of admirals. The decree naming Revel 'Chief of the Naval Staff and Commander of the Mobilized Naval Force' was signed on 3 February, and he congratulated himself on escaping the 'ambush' of a Committee of High Commissioners and the 'nonsense' of having direct command of a specific naval squadron.[96]

Revel's appointment and title meant that he would, in effect, replace Abruzzi, although the announcement on 3 February stated that the duke would relinquish his command for reasons of health. This was a bare pretext and the French ambassador termed it a disgrace, or as much as a prince of the blood could be disgraced. Two leading admirals linked to Abruzzi were transferred to sedentary posts, notably Cagni from C.-in-C. at Brindisi to Maritime Prefect at La Spezia, and Millo from command at Valona to C.-in-C. of the Maritime Department of Naples. Vice-Admiral Cutinelli-Rendina was named interim commander of the fleet at Taranto. Cagni and Millo were, of course, the men most identified with a more active and offensive policy. There was a general impression that Corsi, in an effort to save his own position, had jettisoned some ballast, but it was questionable how long he would or could remain.[97] There was also the problem of what to do now with Abruzzi. He was still popular with a substantial portion of the fleet and there was a large and spontaneous demonstration in which virtually every officer turned out to see him off at the station when he left Taranto. Mark Kerr, who did have a reputation of being excessively fond of royalty, reported that had the 'shelving' occurred in peacetime 'every officer would have resigned'. Kerr's attitude was that 'the politicians' had got rid of the three best admirals – Abruzzi, Cagni and Millo – and had 'done it in a hole & corner way'.[98]

Abruzzi's high social standing, a factor some people had a tendency to emphasize, may actually have worked against him in a certain sense. Revel's biographer, his former aide-de-camp Guido Po who was later chief of the navy's historical office, implies that the agreement at the London Conference for a French C.-in-C. to take command in the Adriatic if he ever arrived with the bulk of the French fleet meant that a 'prince of the blood' would have been placed under foreign command and this would have been unacceptable. Therefore the duke stepped down. However, another former officer, a partisan of Millo, hinted at a certain rivalry, even jealousy, between the King and his more glamorous cousin. There may have been something to this.[99] After the war, the King was far from reticent in talking of Abruzzi's alleged faults, but then the latter's own brother the Duke of Aosta, while in command of the Third Army during the war, also was quoted – admittedly secondhand – as saying, 'My brother still believes he can make war as in the time of Garibaldi', and then citing the same mistakes that the duke's enemies usually did.[100] Boselli was apparently ready at one point to appoint the duke to a newly created position as Inspector General of the Royal Navy. Indeed, there is a draft of the terms of reference for the office endorsed by the Prime Minister as having been modified in regard to the duke, but those terms made it clear that the office would not compete with the powers of the Chief of Naval Staff – something Revel had insisted on – and Abruzzi apparently preferred to decline a hollow position. He received no further employment during the war although the subject of the Inspectorate apparently came up again in 1918 when the Minister of Marine spoke to him about it in May, and there were also rumours that he was being considered for command of a Franco-Italian combined force at Corfu. After the duke had heard nothing further from the government about employment by August, he requested the King's permission to go abroad in order to escape from what he termed his position of idleness and uselessness, and in order not to create difficulties and accusations of meddling he intended to go to a locality where there were no military operations.[101] After the war Abruzzi became head of an agricultural society in Somalia where he spent the majority of his time until his death in 1933. Abruzzi's dismissal in February 1917 marked the disappearance of one of the more glamorous and colourful figures of the time but a leader who through his own faults, or more likely the force of circumstances, somehow never quite lived up to the expectations others had of him.

Saint Pair explained that the reshuffling of the Italian naval command marked a return to the old monarchical tradition which the Italian army had never ceased to follow. The King was considered to be Commander-in-Chief but delegated power to his Chief of the General Staff who exercised command, while the minister had no effect on the actual direction of military operations, with his role limited in principle to representation of the service before Parliament and the administration of the budget.[102] Corsi, contrary to some expectations, did not leave office until the following June, although immediately after the reshuffle he wrote to the Prime Minister offering to resign if he no longer enjoyed the confidence of Boselli and his colleagues in the Cabinet. Boselli's endorsement on the letter indicates that he did not reply.[103] There was, however, considerable speculation and political manœuvring over Corsi's successor. Cutinelli in practice remained in command of the fleet at Taranto as interim C.-in-C. while Revel spent most of his time in Rome with Marzolo (after 1 April Rear-Admiral Triangi) as Sub-Chief of Staff under his direct orders. The

Capo di Stato Maggiore was, however, theoretically empowered to take direct command of the fleet and all naval forces.[104]

Revel's priorities were essentially defensive, namely ensuring the supply of the country by facing the submarine menace and reducing losses to a minimum. He favoured reducing overseas military commitments, such as the Italian force at Salonika, because of the maritime transport they required, for he would have preferred using these ships for the supply of Italy. With this in mind he was also ready to renounce the Otranto barrage since he thought its practical efficiency had proven to be nil and it would be preferable to use part of the patrol craft from the barrage on the mercantile routes. He gave high priority to the arming of all merchantmen, although sea transport in general should be reduced to an absolute minimum. Revel also placed great emphasis on the construction of small craft, including the Mas, submarines and the use of aircraft. These were all points he and his followers liked to emphasize, particularly after the war.[105]

One of Revel's first acts was to establish an Ispettorato della Difesa Traffico, instituted by the decree of 27 February 1917, to co-ordinate the defence of merchant shipping. The first head of the Inspectorate, Rear-Admiral Mortola, took his orders directly from the Chief of Naval Staff and was specifically charged with: (1) the provision, distribution and utilization of offensive and defensive measures against submarines and the organization of harbours of refuge; (2) the arming of merchant ships and provision of suitable rewards to masters who sank submarines; (3) the conclusion of agreements with neutral states regarding the treatment of armed merchant vessels in their territorial waters; and (4) the control of navigation to ensure its safety.[106] The rules which the Inspectorate put into force for all merchant shipping proceeding to and from Italian ports, and strongly recommended to Allied or neutral vessels traversing Italian waters, were based on the idea that ships should navigate by night as much as possible at full speed in order to reduce the distance they would have to cover in daylight. When the distance between two ports was too great to travel in a single night, the vessel would hug the coast as closely as hydrographical conditions permitted during the day, and would do the same on clear nights, especially when there was a full moon. Those sections of a voyage which required daylight navigation would be escorted, with priority for escorts going to unarmed vessels. Armed vessels equipped with wireless could dispense with an escort. The Italians recognized that 70 per cent of their imports came via the Gibraltar–Genoa route and these ships were ordered to stay well within the three-mile limit of Spanish territorial waters during daylight hours, and to put into any Spanish port by day if they felt threatened. The voyage would be regulated so that ships would be south of the Franco-Spanish frontier at sunset and would leave Spanish waters well after sunset and proceed on the course they considered best across the Gulf of Lyon, with the final sector timed for night and entry into Genoa at dawn. Fast vessels would proceed towards Toulon or further east and then hug the coast until Genoa so as to arrive before sunset. Ships travelling from Sicily to Gibraltar would cross to Tunis by night and then hug the African coast.[107]

The Italian approach to the submarine question was therefore highly defensive in line with Revel's general policy. Revel was a realist and just as conscious of Italy's weakness as those German submarine commanders who concentrated on Italian shipping. There is also something markedly similar in his outlook and approach to that of his old Austrian enemy, Anton Haus. His was not a heroic policy, and he renounced any major risks. It was far better to score when one could with less expensive means, such as aircraft or the Mas. Although of a distinguished family, he was not the *grand seigneur* that Abruzzi had been and his Allies would find him far less conciliatory. Revel's staunch defence of what he considered to be Italian interests would make him a difficult ally and his single-minded realism would sometimes seem to the British, French, and later the Americans, a naval version of *sacro egoismo*.

The Corfu Conference

Shortly after the Admiralty introduced dispersed routes in the Mediterranean Wemyss reported that in his area, Egypt, the dispersal of traffic had proved highly successful 'but whether from the dispersion of traffic or whether from the absence of enemy submarines I, of course, am not in a position to judge'.[108] The Germans, who were concentrating on the central and western Mediterranean, soon made the answer painfully clear. Dispersal did not work any better than fixed routes and losses in the Mediterranean rose sharply in February, partially because the large number of submarines under refit the preceding month began to come back into service, fell off somewhat in March and soared to record levels in the month of April – the worst month of the entire war as far as submarine sinkings were concerned. There were some particularly cruel losses. On 15 February the Italian troopship *Minas* (2,854 tons) carrying over 1,000 men was sunk south of the Ionian by Forstmann in U39 with a loss of 870 lives. This was a tragic example of lack of co-ordination, for the ship had been left alone after the Italian escort turned back upon reaching the British zone, while Ballard had never been ordered to send an escort from Malta. On 17 February Kapitänleutnant von Fischel in U65 sank the French troopship *Athos* (12,644 tons) approximately 200 miles east of Malta with heavy loss of life. The French navy was particularly hard hit at this time. On the night of 2 February the minelayer *Cassini* was sunk off Bonifacio and there were stories, included in some of the more authoritative accounts after the war, that the submarine had fired on survivors. This is probably one atrocity story that was false, and *Cassini* was in all likelihood sunk by a mine in field laid by UC35 a few days before. The French lost the battleship *Danton* off Sardinia on 19 March, probably the most valuable unit in the French navy to be sunk during the war. The *Danton* was on her way back from refit and despite zigzagging and the presence of a destroyer, Kapitänleutnant Moraht in U64 was able to sink her with heavy loss of life. In the disastrous month of April the British liner *City of Paris* (9,239 tons) was sunk south of Nice by UC35 on the 4th with an eventual loss of 122 lives, and on the 15th he troopship *Arcadian* (8,929 tons) – Ian Hamilton's former headquarters during the Dardanelles campaign – was sunk by UC74 26 miles north-east of Milos with a loss of 279 lives, while on the same day Kapitänleutnant Siess in U33 sank the troopship *Cameronia* (10,963 tons) 150 miles east of Malta with a loss of 140 lives and despite an escort of two destroyers. On the following day Siess sank the French troopship *Sontay* (7,247 tons), even though the ship was part of a convoy of three escorted by a destroyer and armed yacht. Although the sea was rough, thanks to good discipline and the heroism of merchant Captain Mages, who went down with the ship, the loss of life was only forty-five. These were only the spectacular losses. The steady attrition of the smaller and less glamorous freighters with their vital cargoes was even more important for the German hope of forcing the Allies to their knees. Losses along the Algerian coast were so heavy that after 7 March the Admiralty abandoned the coastal route in favour of British vessels hugging the Spanish coast from Gibraltar to Cape San Antonio and then following dispersed routes eastwards to Malta. Naturally submarines began to appear on the points where those routes converged, for example off Alexandria.[109]

In the first quarter of the year the Allies could not really claim any success against German submarines in the Mediterranean, although on 31 March the Austrian U30 sailed from Cattaro and was never heard from again. It may have been sunk by a mine in the Straits of Otranto on 1 April, but its exact fate is uncertain. Unfortunately the Allies did sink one of their own. On 10 March the British sloop *Cyclamen* rammed and sank the Italian submarine *Guglielmotti* off the island of Capraia when the submarine crossed the north–south convoy route east of Corsica during the night and was mistaken for a German. The *Cyclamen*, whose charge included a troopship, had been warned of German submarines off the Tuscan coast and promptly made the signal which achieved a certain amount of notoriety in the Royal Navy: HAVE RAMMED AND SUNK ENEMY SUBMARINE. SURVIVORS APPEAR TO SPEAK ITALIAN. But the incident was tragic and fourteen Italian seamen were lost. To avoid similar accidents in the future the Italians insisted that they should be informed in sufficient time in advance of all convoys crossing the Tyrrhenian, and whenever these convoys passed along the Corsican coast the authorities of that island should also notify the Italian authorities at La Maddalena. The Italians did not feel any happier over the episode when they discovered the *Cyclamen*'s convoy had been at Porto Vecchio in Corsica just before sailing and the French had failed to notify La Maddalena, although the latter had informed the French about the departure of the *Guglielmotti* from La Spezia for Maddalena. Lacaze gave precise orders to the relevant authorities and all hoped that there would be no repetition of this embarrassing incident. The Allies were luckier in May when Lieutenant de Cambourg in *Circé* sank UC24 in the Adriatic on the 24th, one of only two German submarines sunk in the Mediterranean theatre in all of 1917. The Austrian U5 was also mined while on a practice cruise in the Fasana Channel off Pola on 16 May but was subsequently raised and rebuilt.[110]

The Italian Ministry of Marine decided at the end of February that ships *en route* to Italian ports must form a convoy at Gibraltar, even if it meant delay, but British ships continued to be sent independently via the coastal route.[111] The fact that the British and Italians were following different systems in the western Mediterranean was another example of the lack of unity. Gauchet, who was never really reconciled to the decisions of the London Naval Conference, summed up collaboration with the British, at least on the Malta–Cerigo route, as 'Everyman for himself'. The French C.-in-C. complained that while the French were maintaining more than eighty patrol craft of all kinds on patrolled routes in the western basin of the Mediterranean, the British were escorting with either two sloops or two destroyers all British troopships or important vessels and making use of routes entirely different from the French. This meant a disproportionate effort for the French to patrol the Algiers–Marseilles route, given the number of French ships profiting from it. Furthermore, after the British began using double escorts they had only trawlers left to patrol the routes through their zones, and according to Gauchet the latter were commanded by fishermen, grouped under a reserve officer. These trawlers frequently could not be counted on to relay wireless orders since many were not equipped with receivers, and it would therefore be an illusion to depend on them to detour ships from threatened routes. Even trawlers were not very numerous between Malta and Cerigo, where patrols were nearly non-existent, and the French were forced to escort all their important ships themselves. It was, on the whole, Gauchet claimed, a very poor utilization of their common resources.[112] There was a happy exception to this. Capitaine de vaisseau Violette, Chief of the French Division of Patrols of the Eastern Mediterranean at Milo, was quick to point out when he learned of Gauchet's complaints that there ought to be a distinction between the British authorities at Malta and those at Suda Bay, for the latter furnished escorts to the French nearly every day and Violette did not believe that there could be more complete collaboration, and without British support he would not know how to get by.[113]

Lacaze faced parliamentary criticism over the conduct of the naval war which is hardly surprising. There were somewhat over a dozen deputies, frequently representing port districts, who were traditionally concerned with maritime affairs and who could be anticipated to direct a stream of written questions to the ministry throughout the war. There had been a particularly long discussion of naval affairs lasting three days in December 1916 when the Chamber of Deputies voted to constitute itself a *comité secret,* that is a secret session in which the government could not retreat behind the device of censorship.

Emile Goude, Socialist deputy from Brest, was a particularly persistent critic of the navy from prewar days. He had actually served on the lower deck, and his arguments sometimes went back to the old Jeune École controversy or the rhetoric of the Radical minister, Camille Pelletan, in the early years of the century. He submitted a motion calling for the navy to establish a new directorate specifically charged with organizing and intensifying offensive and defensive measures against submarines. After a detailed study, the Commission de la marine de guerre unanimously approved the proposal on 13 March 1917 with the subordinate clause that the maritime arsenals should specialize in the construction of patrol craft, submarine hunters, submarines and merchant vessels, while warships which had lost their value through the evolution of naval warfare should be disarmed and their artillery used, when possible, at the front, for coastal defence, or for arming merchantmen, patrol-craft, or sub-hunters.[114] These conclusions represented parliamentary concern over the alleged disinterest by the Naval Staff in submarine warfare and this concern was naturally strengthened by the progress of the submarine war. At the end of May in another *comité secret*, Jules Cels compared the submarine war with a cancer patient who awaited the discovery of a serum before the cancer had done its work.[115] Lacaze preferred to reply this time in a public debate on 7 June which was followed on the 8th by a vote of confidence in the government, 286 to 125. Nevertheless, the Chamber passed a motion on the 12th adopting the conclusions of the Commission de la marine de guerre and a decree of 18 June formally established the Direction générale de la guerre sous-marine (DGGSM). Rear-Admiral Merveilleux du Vignaux became the first head with approximately twenty officers under him. Parliamentary criticism continued, notably with the charge that the DGGSM was not sufficiently independent of the supposedly hidebound Naval Staff, and later, after the resignation of Lacaze as minister during the summer, the DGGSM was made completely independent of the EMG by September 1917. The DGGSM was now directly responsible to a secretary of state and given a new head, Rear-Admiral Salaun.[116] The French in establishing the special direction for submarine warfare were, of course, acting in line with their Allies who had also set up special departments to handle this new problem. We have seen how Revel instituted the Ispettorato della Difesa Traffico in February, while the Anti-Submarine Division had been established by Jellicoe immediately after he became First Sea Lord of the Admiralty in December 1916.

The Italians, who tried and failed again in March to get British light cruisers for the Adriatic, now had another potential source for assistance, even if it was only indirect. They were neither blind nor unintelligent and quickly became aware of the resources of the United States. The enterprising Villarey reported in April that the American Admiral Sims was in London to establish a naval agreement with the British and this would lessen the burden on the Royal Navy and thereby permit the latter to give more help to the Italians, notably in terms of destroyers. Revel quickly approved an approach to the Admiralty on these lines, as well as direct negotiations with the Americans based on press reports the latter had already turned over light craft and submarine hunters to the British.[117] The Italian naval attaché in Paris also learned of the American mission – he referred wrongly to Admiral 'Simpson' – but Lacaze and de Bon probably deliberately played down the amount of naval assistance that the United States could immediately supply. They claimed that the uncertainty as to whether the Germans would use submarines on the American coast would

341

prevent the United States from making formal engagements and that the Americans, although possessing a superb fleet, did not have sufficient light craft to detach them for foreign needs.[118]

Villarey did not get anywhere with Jellicoe either. With the submarine crisis at its height, the First Sea Lord was hardly likely to be receptive. He claimed that the American destroyers only numbered six at present and all destroyers were currently fully employed protecting merchant shipping, with intensive service which prevented necessary dockyard work and threatened their efficiency. Jellicoe considered the situation in the Adriatic to be secure and doubted that the Austrian or German fleets would leave their bases seeking battle and, given Cadorna's communications on the coal shortage, from the Italian point of view destroyers would be better employed protecting merchant shipping than in the Adriatic where there was not an urgent necessity for them. Jellicoe pointed out that in the past week German submarines had sunk an average of nine ships per day and if they did not reduce losses it would also have effects on British supplies to their Allies. Someone at the Ministry of Marine, probably Revel, pencilled between the relevant lines of the telegram: 'Then why does he want to keep so many destroyers with the Grand Fleet?'[119] Revel would later display a certain personal animus towards Jellicoe. It may well have had its origins in Jellicoe's remarks about the Adriatic.

The Otranto barrage was obviously very closely linked with the question of submarine warfare in the Mediterranean. The French wanted to turn the barrage into something more than a loose term and in February proposed laying down, all the way across the Adriatic, a real obstacle in the form of a fixed net fitted with mines. They submitted a plan for the project, prepared by Lieutenants Fromaget and de Quillacq of the Mining Commission at the Ministry of Marine, to both the Italians and the British.[120] Captain Learmonth, Captain Supervising Submarine Defences at the Admiralty, considered the approximately forty-mile barrage, about three-quarters in depths varying from 200 to 500 fathoms, to be a very ambitious scheme and that the French had very much underestimated the time and floating plant required for its construction, while the maintenance work would be very heavy if the defence was to be effective. He advocated a practical trial before proceeding, that is the French ought to lay down a barrage of at least one mile in depths similar to those existing in the Straits of Otranto. Admiral Duff, the Director of the Anti-Submarine Division, believed the scheme to be 'impracticable' and, even if successfully laid, the work of maintenance 'would be enormous', while there would be little difficulty in avoiding the nets. However, for diplomatic reasons, that is since the French had obviously taken so much trouble with the scheme and to avoid charges of jealousy, Oliver suggested agreeing to a one-mile trial.[121]

The Italians had their own scheme for a barrage and submitted at the end of March a request to a rather dubious Admiralty for materials, particularly nets, with costs to be shared by the British and Italian governments. As Revel explained to Kerr, there would be a continuous net from Santa Maria di Leuca to Fano Island, approximately forty-seven miles, with the top of the net about 8 metres or 26 feet below the surface and the bottom of the net

200 feet below the surface, while drifters would be used ten miles north and ten miles south of it. Revel wanted the British to supply all of the material except for the mines to be placed in the nets. The Italians intended to ask the French for the mines and, since everyone would benefit, Revel suggested that the costs ought to be borne by Britain, France and Italy in equal parts. Although the Italians mentioned manufacturing some items such as buoys themselves, Kerr doubted that they would be ready in time and anticipated that everything except the mines would have to come from the British. Commodore Heneage was 'not at all sanguine' about the possibility of maintaining a net of that length. Revel, for his part, gave the impression that he had little faith in the British drifters by themselves – an impression confirmed in his other writings – and Kerr was unable to obtain from him a promise of more than a few Italian trawlers to work under Heneage. Kerr agreed that without small craft the drifters were practically useless, but the Capo di Stato Maggiore said submarine sinkings had forced him to send nearly all his small craft to the west coast of Italy. Moreover, Revel seemed to think that torpedo-boats and armed patrol trawlers would be at excessive risk on the drifter line.[122] The technical question of the continuous net fixed barrage was still up in the air when the Corfu Conference met, but virtually all concerned agreed that the Otranto barrage was in an unsatisfactory state.

At the same time, the Salonika expedition was very much on the minds of the Admiralty at this crisis in the submarine war. The Anglo-French Conference at Calais, 26–27 February, had agreed that the decisive defeat of the Bulgarian army was not a practical objective and the mission of the Allied forces at Salonika was to hold on their front the enemy forces now there and take advantage of striking the enemy if the opportunity offered. General Sir William Robertson, Chief of the Imperial General Staff, was dubious about the entire expedition which he regarded as a failure and quoted naval opinion that the strain on naval and shipping resources to maintain Salonika was 'becoming unendurable'. From a naval point of view, it would be less disadvantageous to have the enemy at Salonika than to be compelled to provide the naval force and shipping required to maintain their forces there. If they could not abandon the expedition completely, Robertson himself favoured confining their action to defending the town and harbour and using any troops not required for that purpose in Palestine, where he thought the results to be obtained were more likely to contribute to winning the war than anything they could achieve in the Balkans.[123]

The logic of Robertson, that the war would be more readily won in Palestine than the Balkans, is of course part of grand strategy, highly debatable and one suspects subject to at least some ulterior motives about future colonial gains. Jellicoe's position was more straightforward and understandable. The submarine losses were painful and Salonika meant so many more miles of steaming, so many more ships and so many more escorts, which were all badly needed elsewhere. On 6 April, Robertson approached Jellicoe about a definite statement to the Cabinet from the two of them concerning what reduction was necessary to enable Britain to continue the war in 1918, and whether the complete withdrawal or reduction of British forces at Salonika was necessary to achieve this. Jellicoe was only too happy to oblige for the Admiralty was 'no longer able to safeguard adequately the communications of the armies in Salonika and Egypt'. The opening of a land route from Cherbourg to Taranto, when accomplished, would shorten the sea route to Salonika by more than one-half, but this was counterbalanced by the German intention to attack hospital ships. Jellicoe recommended the immediate reduction or withdrawal of the British contingent at Salonika, although if the Cabinet expected the war to continue beyond 1917 he advocated a complete withdrawal. They would then be able to give better protection to their communications with the army in Egypt, gain a number of patrol craft for safeguarding commerce in home waters, and free a large amount of shipping to build up a reserve of food and to supply their Allies with coal and other necessities.[124] The Allies met with the Italians at St Jean de Maurienne on 19 April but there was no decision taken on Jellicoe's proposals. There were naturally many other considerations involved in a radical step of this nature, certain to be opposed by the French. Nevertheless, Lloyd George did use Jellicoe's statements as the basis for a warning about new commitments in Greece which were likely to arise from French support for Sarrail's plans for an advance on Larissa in Thessaly and further meddling in Greek politics.[125] The fate of the Salonika expedition was therefore unsettled when the Allies met at Corfu.

There was probably only one encouraging event for the Allies in the Mediterranean during that disastrous month of April. The naval ensign bearing the rising sun made its somewhat incongruous appearance. While American aid was only a very distant hope, the 10th and 11th Japanese Destroyer Flotillas arrived at Malta in mid-April under the command of Rear-Admiral Kozo Sato, flying his flag in the cruiser *Akashi*. The eight Japanese destroyers of the Kaba class (665 tons) were modern, well-handled and destined to work with the British out of Malta, particularly in the escort of troopships. Sato's force was nominally independent, but he carried out whatever orders the British C.-in-C. at Malta gave him. The Japanese quickly established a good reputation, especially when U63 torpedoed the troopship *Transylvania* (14,315 tons) off Genoa on 3 May. The *Matsu*, one of the two escorts, went alongside the stricken ship and, although nearly torpedoed herself, helped to rescue the majority of the almost 3,000 troops on board. The Mediterranean venture was not without cost to the Japanese either. On 11 June the *Sakaki* was torpedoed off Crete by the Austrian U27 blowing the bows off the destroyer and killing sixty-eight men who had been concentrated forward for their noonday meal. Although the ship was salved and later repaired, this represented a very high proportion of the crew. In August the armoured cruiser *Idzumo* arrived at Malta to relieve *Akashi* as headquarters ship and brought with her the 15th Flotilla, an additional four destroyers of the new Momo class (835 tons). The British also turned over to the Japanese the H-class destroyers (c. 760 tons) *Minstrel* and *Nemesis*, renamed *Sendan* and *Kanran* respectively, and manned by Japanese crews.[126] This made a total of fourteen Japanese destroyers to provide badly needed assistance at a critical point in the war. The French and Italians also made use of Japanese industrial capacity or maritime resources. The French ordered a series of twelve destroyers, the Arabe class (685 tons), virtually identical to the Kaba class. The ships, ordered in November 1916, were built in record time and completed between September and October 1917. In 1916 the Italians purchased from the Japanese the so-called G Group of Vedette boats, some forty-seven former fishing vessels, approximately 350–450 tons and of recent construction, which were all commissioned in the first quarter of 1917. The French also acquired thirty-four trawlers from Japan in 1916.[127]

After initial confusion as to whether it should take place at Malta or Corfu, the long-awaited conference finally opened aboard Gauchet's flagship *Provence* at Corfu on 28 April. Gauchet, probably delighted that his authority as Allied C.-in-C. was recognized by all, proved to be a surprisingly gracious president, and even Rear-Admiral Marzolo, the senior Italian officer present, acknowledged that he acted with much tact and impartiality. Thursby and Kerr were present, but distant Gibraltar was not represented and both Wemyss and Ballard contented themselves with sending their chiefs of staff. As far as Wemyss was concerned, 'We shall never get much forwarder in dealing with the submarine situation in the Mediterranean until we have the defence of the traffic organized under one head and that head an English Admiral'. He was certain that the French C.-in-C. should have nothing to do with it and defence of the lines of communication should be entirely separate from any other naval operation.[128]

Gauchet proceeded briskly through the agenda, welcoming the new arrival, Rear-Admiral Sato, who discreetly declined to express any opinions on the grounds that Japan had few interests to protect in the Mediterranean.[129] The assembled naval officers must have been in a chastened mood after the disastrous month of April and unanimously agreed not to return purely and simply to the system of patrolled fixed routes established by the Malta Conference in 1916. Someone at the Ministry of Marine in Paris wrote a large 'Hurrah!' on the telegram announcing this.[130] The conference then proceeded to unanimously recommend navigation by night only and along the coast whenever possible. These coastal routes would be patrolled, along with certain strategic straits. As for routes far from the coast, for example Malta–Suda Bay, Crete–Egypt, Malta–Egypt, or Marseilles–Algiers, the conference unanimously recommended protecting ships by means of convoys and escorts following dispersed routes, the latter meaning routes not fixed in advance but chosen according to the circumstances of the moment by the routing officer at the port of departure and assigned to the convoy at the last minute. These major principles were adopted with little disagreement. There was far more discussion on more specific details of how they were to be applied. For example, all the British delegates insisted that large troopships must *always* have an escort and ought not to be obligated to follow the coastal route. The conference decided it was desirable that convoys did not include more than three ships but, given the limited number of escorts available, the number of ships to be placed in a convoy and the organization of escorts were left entirely to the responsibility of the routing officer at the port of departure.

The net result of the Corfu decision was to establish what was in effect a hybrid system. Ships entering the Mediterranean had to stop at Gibraltar for instructions and formation into convoys for the voyage to Oran, although the authorities were left the option of allowing ships to navigate independently without escort if there was no submarine danger. Ships would follow the patrolled coastal route from Oran to Bizerte, although they would not necessarily be escorted in these waters. The ships would then be formed into convoys at Bizerte for the remainder of their journey eastwards with the obligation to cross the sector Sapienza–Cerigotto only by night. The number of *ports de garage* where ships could take refuge would be increased and provided with nets as soon as possible.[131] Traffic from Gibraltar to Marseilles or Genoa would continue to follow the Italian method of using Spanish territorial waters as long as circumstances allowed, but should they change and German submarines cease to respect Spanish neutrality, shipping would be diverted to the North African coastal route as far as Algiers, or possibly Bizerte, and then by convoy across the Mediterranean to Marseilles. The Allies also adopted *in toto* the Italian regulations for navigation along the coast of Italy.

The conference, with a view towards reducing the number of ships at risk to a minimum, recommended that all traffic from the Atlantic to ports east of Aden should proceed via the Cape of Good Hope, with the reservation inserted by the British that the necessities of the military expeditions, that is, Egypt and Mesopotamia, would always be satisfied by the most direct means. The Allied admirals also recommended the greatest possible use of Italian railways to carry men and material destined for Salonika and Egypt as far as Taranto, as well as use of the route inland from Santi Quaranta, and the Corinth Canal.[132] All of these measures would have the effect of reducing exposure at sea.

The question of the Otranto barrage caused what was probably the greatest amount of disagreement. Kerr claimed that, until now, the Allies had simultaneously employed three different systems in the Mediterranean against submarines: escorts, patrols and the inadequate barrage at Otranto. He thought that these were only half measures and no one system had really been pushed to the utmost, and therefore proposed experimenting with two of the systems for a month or two by giving them all available resources. Since the Otranto barrage was ineffective for lack of a sufficient number of ships, Kerr proposed pulling the 100 or so drifters immobilized for meagre results off the line and using them on patrols. If the results were not satisfactory, he proposed putting them back on the barrage and reinforcing them with enough units taken from patrols and escorts to make a really effective system. Heneage painted a bleak picture of the barrage. Approximately 70 of his 124 drifters were employed each day on the line, but as each drifter could only cover half a mile and the passage was forty-four miles wide there were open spaces through which submarines succeeded in passing freely. The barrage was therefore ineffective but could be rendered effective if given the necessary means, notably an increased number of ships, aircraft, a fixed net barrage and hydrophones. Heneage reluctantly supported Kerr's proposal to pull the drifters off the line for a trial period, provided there would be no interruption in the preparations for more aircraft, the fixed net and hydrophones. Fatou also favoured installing the fixed net and withdrawing the drifters. However, while agreeing on the importance of the barrage, Thursby did not believe it was possible to reduce patrols or escorts. The vote was 5 to 3 against Kerr who was supported only by Heneage and Fatou. Gauchet, Thursby, Marzolo and Captains Burmester and Veale (Wemyss's and Ballard's Chiefs of Staff respectively) all opposed Kerr's experiment. The members unanimously agreed, however, to hasten construction of the fixed net barrage. Furthermore, they also recommended fixed barrages at the Dardanelles, in the Gulf of Smyrna, Gibraltar and, when enough experience had been obtained, they would consider one between Cape Bon and the coast of Sicily.[133]

The arguments over the Otranto barrage were part of a general discussion involving the more effective use of flotillas and this led the Allies to recommend that, by virtue of the grave situation of maritime transport, it would be expedient to reduce as much as possible the number of patrol craft assigned to military or political operations, such as the blockades of the coast of Syria, Asia Minor, or Greece. Gauchet, on the grounds that they ought to consider offensive as well as merely defensive measures, successfully introduced a proposition in favour of the formation of submarine-hunting groups as soon as means permitted. Veale and Burmester were the only dissenting votes because of the poor results this procedure had achieved in the Channel and the North Sea.[134] The fallacy that a submarine could be successfully hunted by roving patrols died hard.

Gauchet was responsible for introducing the motion which led to one of the most important results of the Corfu Conference and which, ironically, in the long run reduced his own importance. The French C.-in-C. proposed establishing at Malta, the central point of the Mediterranean, a 'Direction Générale' composed of officers delegated by the different navies who would, under the control of the C.-in-C., be charged with direction of everything concerning transport routes and their protection. The discussion of this was deferred to permit further study and allow subcommittees at the conference enough time to prepare information on the resources which were available to the Allies. When the Allies returned to the subject on the final day of the conference, Thursby used the opportunity to introduce a new proposal. Without modifying the present arrangement of a French C.-in-C. for the whole Mediterranean, all British naval forces would be placed under a single commander. This would allow distributing British ships for the common interest and eliminate the need for the French C.-in-C. to deal separately with four or five different officers. The British C.-in-C. would have an officer of flag rank to deal with protecting transport routes who would be the British representative on the central authority which Gauchet proposed to establish at Malta. The conference unanimously approved, subject to the reservation introduced by Captain Burmester protecting the interests of his chief, Wemyss, that military operations in Egyptian and Palestinian waters would not be under the new central authority which would control only patrols and escorts.[135]

Gauchet readily accepted the proposal for he was seduced by the prospect of dealing with a single authority under a system which he assumed would be like that already employed by the French, that is a C.-in-C. and under him a flag officer commanding patrols and escorts. Gauchet was therefore satisfied with the results of the conference, although the details of the Direction Générale would have to be worked out after Admiralty approval was obtained. Gauchet was less happy about the situation at Otranto which, he admitted, remained a problem.[136] What Gauchet may not have fully realized at first, however, was that the balance of anti-submarine forces in the Mediterranean by this date was such that in any centralized control of protection the British were certain to play a predominant role. The division of British forces in the Mediterranean into separate commands – Gibraltar, Malta, the drifters, Egypt and the eastern Mediterranean – had tended to obscure this. The report of the subcommittee on Allied resources in the Mediterranean made it clear.[137] The strength of all patrol vessels in the Mediterranean is shown in Table 9.2.

After deductions for ships necessary for blockade, sweeping and the defence of bases, the Allies' resources for the protection of maritime traffic are shown in Table 9.3.

The report of the subcommittee also demonstrated the degree to which the Allies were unable to meet the needs of the system they had just proposed. Because of the need for re-supply and repair of patrol vessels, the Allies could only hope to have half the total at sea at the same time, except for the Italians who, because of the special nature of their service (that is, in their own coastal waters), could anticipate two-thirds of the total at sea. This meant 112 escorts and 89 patrol-craft at sea at any one time. However, for an effective patrol they needed a ship every ten miles. The length of

Table 9.2   *Allied Patrol Vessels in the Mediterranean, May 1917*

	British	Italian	Japanese	French
Destroyers	37	6	8	38
Sloops and gunboats	34	—	—	21
Large patrol boats	26	8	—	6
Large trawlers	176	33	—	102
Small trawlers and sweepers	59	30	—	84
Vedettes and small torpedo-boats	97	42	—	51
Total	429	119	8	302

Table 9.3   *Allied Resources for the Protection of Maritime Traffic, May 1917*

	British	Italian[a]	Japanese	French
Ships suitable for escort	127	23	8	59
Ships suitable for patrol	52	24	—	94
	179	47	8	153

[a]The Italian ships were considered suitable for either role.

coastline to be patrolled by decision of the conference was 2,030 miles, which therefore required 203 patrol-craft at sea at the same time, but the Allies would have only 89. There were, and the subcommittee lacked precise information, approximately 300 ships at sea to protect each day in all parts of the Mediterranean, but about 100 at any given moment were on coastal routes. This left 200 at large to be escorted and the subcommittee estimated that each convoy of 3 ships required at least 2 escorts. They therefore needed 140 escorts at sea each day and would have only 12.[138]

The conclusions of the Corfu Conference were only recommendations and needed Admiralty approval. This was for the most part readily given. By the time the voluminous minutes and appendices of the conference reached London for study, the Admiralty had taken the important step of moving towards the introduction of the convoy system in northern waters. There had been limited experience with 'controlled sailings' protecting the coal trade to France in February and 'protected sailings' to Scandinavia, and on 27 April the Admiralty took the plunge and ordered the first trial convoy from Gibraltar to Britain.[139] Jellicoe approved most of the conclusions of the Corfu Conference by the end of May, but the question of a British C.-in-C. and the central direction at Malta was deferred for special attention at a later date.[140] It would require some delicate negotiations with the French and, in the meantime, the Austrian navy gave a striking demonstration that it could not be disregarded and that the situation at Otranto was truly dangerous and unsatisfactory. Both subjects will be covered in the following chapter. On the whole, the Corfu Conference by eliminating the discredited system of fixed routes and dispersed ships sailing in isolation, opening the door to convoys, even on a limited basis, establishing the foundation for a central direction of the anti-submarine war and proposing the reintroduction of a British C.-in-C., was one of the most important conferences of the naval war.

Notes: Chapter 9

1 A succinct account is in Holger Herwig, *'Luxury' Fleet*, pp. 194–8; idem, *The Politics of Frustration: The United States in German Naval Planning, 1889–1941* (Boston, Mass., 1976), pp. 121–6. Much more detail is in Spindler, *Handelskrieg*, Vol. 3, ch. 15. The Germans provided their Austrian allies with the memorandum and supplementary studies on 17 January. Copies in OK/MS VIII-1/19 ex 1917, No. 473.

2 There is, given the fateful consequences of the decision, a large literature on the subject. Standard accounts are: Gerhard Ritter, *The Sword and the Scepter: The Problem of Militarism in Germany*, Vol. 3: *The Tragedy of Statesmanship: Bethmann Hollweg as War Chancellor* (English trans. Coral Gables, Fla, 1972), pp. 308–15; Konrad H. Jarausch, *The Enigmatic Chancellor: Bethmann Hollweg and the Hubris of Imperial Germany* (New Haven, Conn., 1973), pp. 298–302; Fritz Fischer, *Germany's Aims in the First World War* (English trans. New York, 1967), pp. 300–9; May, *World War and American Isolation*, pp. 412–15.

3 Memorandum by BIII [East Asia, East Africa and Mediterranean Section of Overseas Operations Dept.], 4 Jan. 1917, NARS, T-1022, Roll 804, PG 75268.

4 Holtzendorff, Allgemeiner Operationsbefehl für U-Boote im Mittelmeer, 27 Jan. 1917, ibid.
5 Holtzendorff, Beitrag zum Immediatvortrag, 'Entsendung weiterer Unterseeboote nach dem Mittelmeer', 7 Jan. 1917, ibid.
6 On the Kaiser and the navy see entry from Haus's private diary reproduced in Sokol, *Österreich-Ungarns Seekrieg*, pp. 340–1. On the *Ancona* affair see above Chapter 6.
7 Haus to Marinesektion, 10 Jan. 1917, Marinesektion, Sitzungsprotokoll, 17 Jan. 1917, OK/MS VI-1/14 ex 1917, No. 206.
8 Czernin, *In the World War*, pp. 116–20; Ritter, *The Sword and the Scepter*, Vol. 3, pp. 325–6.
9 Report reproduced in Czernin, *In the World War*, pp. 121–4. A slightly different version from Haus's diary is in Sokol, *Österreich-Ungarns Seekrieg*, pp. 340–1; another version critical of Czernin is in: Arthur Count Polzer-Hoditz, *The Emperor Karl* (London and New York, 1930), pp. 192–3. Details on the specific cases of attacks on Austrian ships are in: Freyberg to Holtzendorff, 6 Feb. 1917, NARS, T-1022, Roll 538, PG 69132.
10 Czernin, *In the World War*, p. 124; Sokol, *Österreich-Ungarns Seekrieg*, p. 340.
11 Czernin, *In the World War*, p. 125.
12 Protokoll, Ministerrates für gemeinsame Angelegenheiten, 22 Jan. 1917, Miklós Komjáthy (ed.), *Protokolle des Gemeinsamen Ministerrates des Österreichisch-Ungarischen Monarchie (1914–1918)* (Budapest, 1966), pp. 452–8.
13 Kaiser Karl to Kaiser Wilhelm, 23 Jan. 1917 and Kaiser Wilhelm to Kaiser Karl, n.d., MKSM 69-6/1-7 ex 1917; Note to Neutrals and Maritime-Technical Portion of the Agreement of Pless, 26 Jan. 1917, OK/MS VIII-1/19 ex 1917, No. 473; Memorandum by Rodler, 31 Jan. 1917, ibid., No. 662. Walter Görlitz (ed.), *Regierte der Kaiser?* (Göttingen, n.d. [1959]), pp. 252–3; copy of Haus's general orders to Austrian submarines reproduced in Aichelburg, *Unterseeboote Österreich-Ungarns*, Vol. 1, pp. 150–1.
14 Rodler to Njegovan, 13 Feb. 1917, OK/MS VIII-1/19 ex 1917, No. 892.
15 Admiralstab to U-Flotilla, Pola, 28 Jan. 1917, NARS, T-1022, Roll 804, PG 75268. On the compromised German codes see Beesly, *Room 40*, pp. 25–8.
16 Sokol, *Österreich-Ungarns Seekrieg*, p. 463; Kaiser Wilhelm to Kaiser Karl and Karl to Wilhelm, 9 Feb. 1917, MKSM, 36-4/2 ex 1917; details of funeral in Khuepach, Tagebuch, 8–10 Feb. 1917, Nachlass Khuepach B/200, No. V/1.
17 Biographical details of Njegovan in Heinrich Bayer von Bayersburg, *Unter der k.u.k. Kriegsflagge, 1914–1918* (Vienna, 1959), pp. 21–6; on appointments see Khuepach, Tagebuch, 17 Feb., 28 and 30 Apr. 1917, Kriegsarchiv, Vienna, Nachlass Khuepach B/200, No. V/1; Walter Wagner, *Die Obersten Behörden der k.u.k. Kriegsmarine, 1856–1918* (Vienna, 1961), pp. 99, 111–13.
18 Njegovan to Conrad, 24 Feb. 1917, OK/MS VIII-1/1 ex 1917, No. 1046.
19 Njegovan to Kailer, 7 Mar. 1917, Kriegsarchiv, Vienna, Nachlass Kailer B/242.
20 Holtzendorff to Kaiser Wilhelm, Immediatvortrag (and annex), 9 Feb. 1917, NARS, T-1022, Roll 804, PG 75268; Holtzendorff to U-Flotilla, Pola, 8 Feb. 1917, ibid., Roll 678, PG 75435.
21 Holtzendorff, Immediatvortrag, 3 Apr. 1917, ibid., Roll 804, PG 75269; Admiralstab to Vertreter des Admiralstabes im Grossen Hauptquartier, 8 June, 1917, ibid., Roll 664, PG 75270.
22 Spindler, *Handelskrieg*, Vol. 3, pp. 388, 390; ibid., Vol. 4, pp. 194–5, 376–7. The fifth and final volume of this series published after the Second World War contains a comparison of the totals given by the leading authorities. The

Admiralstab decision on crediting submarine successes is in Admiralstab to U-Flotilla, Pola, 3 May 1917, NARS, T-1022, Roll 730, PG 75295. Austrian figures from Aichelburg, *Unterseeboote Österreich-Ungarns*, Vol. 2, pp. 490–1.

23 Müller to Holtzendorff, 1 June 1917, Holtzendorff to Müller, 17 June 1917, Admiralstab to commanders of submarine flotillas, 9 June 1917, NARS, T-1022, Roll 664, PG 75270.

24 Holtzendorff to Reichsmarineamt, 12 Jan. 1917, ibid., Roll 804, PG 75268; Holtzendorff to Sektion Politik, Generalstabes, 5 Mar. 1917, ibid., Roll 731, PG 75297.

25 von Hülsen to Admiralstab, 4 Jan. 1917, 'Bestimmung für die Expedition "Mirr"', n.d.; U-Flotilla, Pola to Admiralstab, 9 June 1917, von Hülsen to Admiralstab, 18 June 1917, Todenwarth to U-Flotilla, Pola, 17 Aug. 1917, ibid.; Spindler, *Handelskrieg*, Vol. 4, p. 188.

26 Souchon to Admiralstab, 18 Feb. 1917, Admiralstab to Souchon, 25 Feb. 1917, NARS, T-1022, Roll 804, PG 75268.

27 Ludendorff to Holtzendorff, 27 Feb. 1917, Holtzendorff to Chef des Generalstabes, 9 Mar. 1917, Admiralstab to U-Flotilla, Pola, 7 and 8 Mar. 1917, ibid.

28 Souchon to Holtzendorff, 18 Mar. 1917, ibid., Roll 688, PG 75251; Souchon to Admiralstab, 17 and 19 Apr. 1917, ibid., Roll 804, PG 75269. UC74, ordered by wireless from the Aegean to the Syrian coast, fired under difficult conditions on 19 April at an old French battleship bombarding coastal positions north of Gaza but missed. Spindler, *Handelskrieg*, Vol. 4, pp. 185–6. For U63's and UB42's report of little traffic see ibid., pp. 169, 189–90.

29 Holtzendorff to Chef des Generalstabes, 6 Jan. 1917, NARS, T-1022, Roll 804, PG 75268.

30 Bartenwerffer to Bülow, 25 Mar. 1917, Bülow to Politische Abteilung, Generalstab, 26 Mar. 1917, ibid., PG 75269.

31 Bartenwerffer to Bülow, 27 Mar. 1917, Bülow to Holtzendorff, 27 Mar. 1917, Holtzendorff to Bülow, 30 Mar. 1917, ibid.

32 A succinct account is in May, *World War and American Isolation*, ch. 19.

33 Holtzendorff to Admiralstab, 21 May 1917, NARS, T-1022, Roll 731, PG 75298. On United States warships in the Mediterranean see: William N. Still, *American Seapower in the Old World: The United States Navy in European and Near Eastern Waters, 1865–1917* (Westport, Conn., 1980), ch. 11.

34 Holtzendorff to Admiralstab, 18 May 1917, Admiralstab to U-Flotilla, Pola, 29 May 1917, NARS, T-1022, Roll 731, PG 75298.

35 See, for example, 'O-Befehl für UC52', 19 May 1917, ibid., Roll 735, PG 75298; Holtzendorff to Staatssekretär des Auswärtiges Amts, 4 June 1917, ibid., Roll 664, PG 75270.

36 Bülow to Holtzendorff, 25 Mar. 1917, Holtzendorff to Bülow, 27 Mar. 1917, Holtzendorff to U-Flotilla, Pola, 27 Mar. 1917, Admiralstab to U-Flotilla, Pola, 28 Apr. 1917, ibid., Roll 804, PG 75269.

37 Admiralstab to U-Flotilla, Pola and Mittelmeerdivision, 30 June 1917, ibid.

38 Allerhöchste Kabinetts-Order, 9 June 1917, ibid., Roll 664, PG 75270.

39 De Bon to Gauchet and other naval authorities, 22 Jan. 1917, SHM, Carton A-133.

40 Note by Holtzendorff, 19 Mar. 1917, Holtzendorff to Zimmerman, 27 Mar. 1917, NARS, T-1022, Roll 804, PG 75269.

41 Gibson and Prendergast, *German Submarine War*, pp. 138–9, 163–6; the German note and allegations of 28 Jan. and the British reply are published in Archibald Hurd, *The Merchant Navy* (3 vols, London, 1921–9), Vol. 3,

pp. 308–14, other details in ch. 11, 'The sinking of hospital ships'; a short account is in: John H. Plumridge, *Hospital Ships and Ambulance Trains* (London, 1975), ch. 3.

42   Corbett and Newbolt, *Naval Operations*, Vol. 4, pp. 309–10; Gibson and Prendergast, *German Submarine War*, pp. 249–50; Spindler, *Handelskrieg*, Vol. 4, p. 184. Neumann's account is in: 'Avec l' UC.67 en Méditerranée', in Vice-Amiral E. von Mantey (ed.), *Les Marins allemands au combat* (Paris, 1930), pp. 271–3.

43   Thomazi, *Guerre navale dans la Méditerranée*, pp. 186–7; Gibson and Prendergast, *German Submarine War*, pp. 164–5.

44   Freyberg to ? [probably Kailer], 31 Mar. 1917, OK/MS VIII-1/19 ex 1917, No. 1705. The report about the *Lafayette* came from an unidentified German naval officer. The French prisoner-of-war had actually spoken about the *Le Canada* and *La France* at the Dardanelles. German Memorandum, 29 March 1917, ibid., No. 1824; Representative of Prussian Ministry of War at Austro-Hungarian Ministry of War to Marinesektion, 22 and 26 May 1917, ibid., No. 2706.

45   Marinesektion to Ministry of Foreign Affairs, AOK, and German Naval Attaché, 1 Apr. 1917, Flottenkommando to Marinesektion, 1 Apr. 1917, ibid., No. 1705.

46   Admiralstab to German Naval Attaché in Vienna, 3 Apr. 1917, ibid., No. 1820.

47   Flotow to Marinesektion, 4 Apr. 1917, ibid., No. 1788.

48   Arz to representative of Foreign Ministry at AOK, 6 Apr. 1917, ibid., No. 1853.

49   Flotow to Marinesektion, 6 Apr. 1917, Marinesektion to Flottenkommando, 9 Apr. 1917, Marinesektion to Foreign Ministry and AOK (with draft order), 15 Apr. 1917, German memoranda of 29 Jan. [also published by Hurd, *The Merchant Navy*, Vol. 3, pp. 308–11] and 29 Mar. 1917, Wedel to Foreign Ministry, 3 Apr. 1917, ibid., No. 1824.

50   Arz to Hindenburg, 21 Apr. 1917, Admiralstab to U-Flotillas, Pola and Constantinople, 22 Apr. 1917, Freyberg to Admiralstab, 22 Apr. 1917, NARS, T-1022, Roll 804, PG 75269; Marinesektion to Ministry of Foreign Affairs, Flottenkommando and German Naval Attaché, 21 Apr. 1917, Marinesektion to Flottenkommando, 20 Apr. 1917, OK/MS VIII-1/19 ex 1917, No. 2075.

51   Details on the American declaration of war are in Lansing, *War Memoirs*, p. 244; on German statements see Winterhalder to Njegovan, 2 May 1917, OK/MS VIII-1/19 ex 1917, No. 2328.

52   David F. Trask, *Captains and Cabinets: Anglo-American Naval Relations, 1917–1918* (Columbia, Mo., 1972), pp. 68–70; Herwig, *Politics of Frustration*, p. 128.

53   Polzer-Hoditz, *The Emperor Karl*, pp. 193–4.

54   On the Sixtus affair see Zeman, *The Gentlemen Negotiators*, pp. 131–40; Ritter, *The Sword and the Scepter*, Vol. 3, ch. 10.

55   Chief of General Staff to Marinesektion, 19 May 1917, OK/MS VIII-1/1 ex 1917, No. 2452; AOK to Flottenkommando, 13 July 1917, ibid., No. 3755; Njegovan to FdU, 16 July 1917, OK/MS VIII-1/19 ex 1917, No. 3888.

56   Arz to Njegovan, 21 July 1917, ibid., No. 3975; Extraktbogen für die Militärkanzlei S.M. des Kaisers und Königs, 5 Aug. 1917, MKSM 66-5/13 ex 1917.

57   Marinesektion to Militärkanzlei, 6 and 12 Sept.1917, MKSM 66-5/13-2 ex 1917.

58 Hohenlohe to Czernin, 22 Apr. 1917, Flotow to Marinesektion, 24 Apr. 1917, OK/MS VIII-1/19 ex 1917, No. 2159.
59 De Bon to Gauchet and Fatou, 29 July 1917, SHM, Carton A-133; Koch to Auswärtiges Amts, 15 Aug. 1917, Admiralstab to FdU Pola, 15 Aug. 1917, Winterhalder to Mirtl, n.d. [c. 29 Aug. 1917], OK/MS VIII-1/19 ex 1917, No. 4654.
60 FdU Pola to Admiralstab, 14 Aug. 1917, Admiralstab to U-Flotilla Pola, 14 Aug. 1917, NARS, T-1022, Roll 731, PG 75298.
61 Memorandum by Admiralstab [translation], 17 June 1917, Merry del Val to Balfour, 29 Aug. 1917, Admiralty to Foreign Office, 21 Aug. 1917, PRO, Adm 137/1412.
62 Marine Paris to Admiralty, 31 Aug. 1917, Minute by Brigstock and Jellicoe, 31 Aug. 1917, ibid.
63 Admiralty to British C.-in-C. Mediterranean and other Mediterranean authorities, 5 Sept. 1917, Admiralty to Foreign Office, 6 Sept. 1917, ibid.; Note from Spanish Ambassador in Vienna, 4 Nov. 1917, OK/MS VIII-1/19 ex 1917, No. 5939.
64 *Note Verbale* from Spanish Embassy, Berlin, 10 Sept. 1917, Admiralstab to Auswärtiges Amt, 30 Sept. 1917, NARS, T-1022, Roll 731, PG 75298; AOK Nachrichtenabteilung to Marinesektion, 29 Dec. 1917, OK/MS, X-12/1 ex 1918, No. 123.
65 On *Goorkha* and *Rewa* see Gibson and Prendergast, *German Submarine War*, pp. 260, 285–6.
66 Paper I.C.-13, Anglo-French Conference, London, 26–28 Dec. 1916, pp. 4–5, PRO, Cab 28/2.
67 Paper I.C.-15(a), Memorandum by the Prime Minister, n.d., Paper I.C.-15, Conclusion of a Conference of the Allies, Rome, 5–7 January 1917, ibid.
68 Gibson and Prendergast, *German Submarine War*, pp. 134–5; Spindler, *Handelskrieg*, Vol. 3, pp. 340–3.
69 Lieut.-Commander Ralph W. Wilkinson to his brother-in-law, 12 Jan. 1917, Imperial War Museum, London, Wilkinson MSS 76/230/1; Kerr to Jellicoe, 17 Jan. 1917, British Library, London, Jellicoe MSS, Add. MSS 49036; Thursby to Admiralty, 19 Jan. 1917, PRO, Adm 137/368.
70 Ballard to Admiralty, 14 Oct. 1916, ibid., Adm 137/1221.
71 Admiralty to Ballard, 18 Nov. 1916, minutes by Oliver, 14 Nov. and Webb [Director of Trade Division], 30 Nov., ibid.
72 ibid.
73 Memorandum by H. W. Grant, 23 Dec. 1916, minutes by Webb and Oliver, 24 Dec., Admiralty to Kelly [liaison officer in Paris], 25 Dec. 1916, ibid., Adm 137/1412.
74 Wemyss to SNO Malta, 11 Dec. 1916, SNO Malta to Wemyss, 12 Dec. 1916, Wemyss to Admiralty, 13 Dec. 1916, ibid., Adm 137/1230.
75 Minutes by T. Jackson, 27 Dec. 1916, R. Webb, 1 Jan., Duff, 3 Jan. and Oliver, 11 Jan. 1917, Admiralty to Wemyss, 21 Jan. 1917, ibid.
76 Minutes by Grant, 10 Jan., Oliver and Jellicoe, 11 Jan. 1917, Admiralty to Mediterranean authorities, 11 Jan. 1917, ibid., Adm 137/1412.
77 SNO Malta to Admiralty, 13 Jan. 1917, Admiralty to SNO Malta, 14 Jan. 1917, ibid.
78 SNO Malta to Admiralty, 16 Jan. 1917, Admiralty to SNO, Malta, 17 Jan. 1917, ibid.
79 Fatou to Gauchet, 22 Dec. 1916, SHM, Carton Gp-67.
80 Fatou, 'Projet d'organisation d'un service des Patrouilles . . .', n.d. [7 Jan. 1917], ibid., Carton Gp-70.

81   De Bon to Gauchet, 12 Jan. 1917, ibid., Carton A-133; Gauchet to Lacaze, 10 Jan. 1917, ibid., Carton A-29.
82   Fatou to Gauchet, 18 Jan. 1917, ibid., Carton Gp-70.
83   Minute by Jellicoe, 11 Jan. 1917, Foreign Office to Bertie [Paris], and Rodd [Rome], 13 Jan. 1917, PRO, Adm 137/1420; Lostende to Lacaze, 15 Jan. 1917, SHM, Carton Es-13.
84   Ufficio del Capo di Stato Maggiore, Promemoria, 20 and 26 Dec. 1916, and 9 Jan. 1916 [probably misdated and should be 1917], USM, Cartella 519.
85   Etat-Major Général, 1ère Section, Note Verbale, n.d. [c. 19 Jan. 1917], Lacaze to Gauchet, 16 Jan. 1917, SHM, Carton Ea-136.
86   Minutes of Allied Naval Conference, 23 Jan. 1917, PRO, Adm 137/1420, ff. 53–5.
87   ibid.
88   ibid., ff. 55–8, 61–3.
89   Agenda and Conclusion, Allied Naval Conference, London, 23–24 Jan. 1917, ibid.
90   Gauchet to Lacaze, 26 Jan. 1917, SHM, Carton A-29; Thursby to Admiralty, 26 Jan. 1917, PRO, Adm 137/368.
91   Admiralty to Villarey, 5 Feb. 1917, Admiralty to Kerr, 5 Feb. 1917, ibid., Adm 137/1420; Kerr to Jellicoe, 6 Feb. 1917, loc. cit. at n. 69, Jellicoe MSS, Add MSS 49036.
92   Nicolo Maura to Brusati, 2 Nov. 1916, ACS, Carte Brusati, 11bis, III-8-52, f. 199; unsigned typescript summarizing charges against Abruzzi in Prime Minister's papers, n.d., ACS, Carte Boselli 1/14.
93   Saint Pair to Lacaze, 12 Jan. 1917, SHM, Carton Ea-94; idem, 12 Jan. 1917, ibid., Carton Ea-139; Barrère to Briand, 20 Jan. 1917, MAE, Série Guerre 1914–1918, Vol. 574.
94   Revel to Brusati, 22 Jan. 1917, ACS, Carte Brusati/12 (VIII-17-61).
95   Oscar di Giamberardino, *L'Ammiraglio Millo* (Livorno, 1950), p. 107.
96   Revel to Brusati, 28 Jan. and 3 Feb. 1917, draft of a decree establishing a 'Comitato di guerra' consisting of the minister and 2 admirals (marked with the names of Abruzzi and Presbitero), n.d., ACS, Carte Brusati/12 (VIII-17-61).
97   Barrère to Briand, 3 Feb. 1917, SHM, Carton Ea-139; Barrère to Briand, 7 Feb. 1917, MAE, Série Guerre 1914–1918, Vol. 575; Rodd to Balfour, PRO, FO 371/2946; unsubstantiated accounts of a heated meeting between the duke and Prime Minister Boselli are in the 'Notizie Riservato', 14 Feb. 1917, ACS, Carte Brusati, 11 bis, VIII-9-53.
98   Giamberardino, *L'Ammiraglio Millo*, pp. 108–9; Kerr to Jellicoe, 6 Feb. 1917, loc. cit. at n. 69, Jellicoe MSS, Add. MSS 49036.
99   Po, *Il Grande Ammiraglio Paolo Thaon di Revel*, p. 113; Giamberardino, *L'Ammiraglio Millo*, p. 107. See also the discussion in Ufficio Storico, *Marina italiana*, Vol. 4, pp. 281–4.
100   For Victor Emmanuel's comments see: Enrico Caviglia, *Diario* (Rome, 1952), pp. 112–14; on Aosta's remarks about his brother see Saint Pair to Lacaze, 9 Mar. 1917, SHM, Carton Ea-136.
101   Draft of Decree for the Inspector General, n.d., ACS, Carte Boselli 1/14; Mattioli Pasqualini to Orlando, 8 Aug. 1918, Abruzzi to King Victor Emmanuel, 6 Aug. 1918 [copy], ACS, Carte Orlando, Busta 7. On the command of a combined squadron at Corfu see below, Chapter 11.
102   Saint Pair to Lacaze, 8 Feb. 1917, SHM, Carton Ea-136; Frochot to Lacaze, 5 Feb. 1917, ibid., Carton Ed-91.
103   Corsi to Boselli, 5 Feb. 1917, ACS, Carte Boselli, 1/14.
104   Saint Pair to Lacaze, 27 Feb. 1917, SHM, Carton Ea-139.

105 Revel's agenda, 'Compiti impellanti che debbono prevalere . . . ', n.d., Revel to Brusati, 20 Feb. 1917, ACS, Carte Brusati/12 (VIII-17-61); Revel, 'I primi cinque mesi dal ritorno alla carica di Capo di Stato Maggiore della Marina', n.d., USM, Cartella 738/2.

106 Ufficio Storico, *Marina italiana*, Vol. 4, pp. 76–9; Rodd to Balfour, 8 Mar. 1917, PRO, Adm 137/1414.

107 Commander Alfredo Baistrocchi, 'Rules for the Services of Defence of National Sea-Borne Trade', n.d. [English translation, 20 Apr. 1917], ibid.

108 Wemyss to Jellicoe, 7 Feb. 1917, loc. cit. at n. 69, Jellicoe MSS, Add. MSS 49036.

109 Gibson and Prendergast, *German Submarine War*, pp. 240–4; Corbett and Newbolt, *Naval Operations*, Vol. 4, pp. 276–86; Thomazi, *Guerre navale dans la Méditerranée*, pp. 58, 185–8; Ufficio Storico, *Marina italiana*, Vol. 4, pp. 181–4, 236–7; Spindler, *Handelskrieg*, Vol. 4, pp. 160, 170–2, 180, 185. Moraht's own account of the sinking of the *Danton* is in: Robert Moraht, *Werwolf der Meere: U64 jagt den Feind* (Berlin, 1933), pp. 56–62.

110 Ufficio Storico, *Marina italiana*, Vol. 4, pp. 181–4; *Cyclamen*'s signal reproduced in Jack Broome, *Make Another Signal* (London, 1973), p. 225; Saint Pair to Lacaze, 29 Mar. 1917, idem (with marginal comments by Lacaze), 5 Apr. 1917, SHM, Carton Gp-70; Spindler, *Handelskrieg*, Vol. 4, p. 177; Thomazi, *Guerre navale dans la Méditerranée*, p. 199; Le Masson, *Du 'Nautilus' au 'Redoutable'*, p. 231; Aichelburg, *Unterseeboote Österreich-Ungarns*, Vol. 2, pp. 295–6, 404–5.

111 Villarey to Admiralty, 3 Mar. 1917, Admiralty to Villarey, 4 Mar. 1917, PRO, Adm 137/1410. The first three experimental convoys, consisting of three ships each, escorted by a destroyer, left Gibraltar on 27 February. Unfortunately the official history provides no detail on the circumstances behind the decision. Ufficio Storico, *Marina italiana*, Vol. 4, pp. 156–7.

112 Gauchet to Lacaze, 10 Mar. 1917, Fatou to Gauchet, 27 Feb. 1917, SHM, Carton Ed-85.

113 Violette to Fatou, 6 Mar. 1917, ibid.

114 Chambre des Députés, *Rapport fait au nom de la Commission de la Marine de Guerre par M. Tissier* Annexe au procès-verbal de la séance du 13 février, 1917, pp. 40–42. Copy in SHM, Carton Ca-8.

115 Chambre des Députés, *Journal Officiel–Comités Secrets*, Comité Secret du 25 mai 1917, p. 317.

116 Georges Bonnefous, *Histoire politique de la troisième république*, Vol. 2: *La Grande Guerre (1914–1918)* (Paris, 1957), pp. 238–9; Laurens, *Commandement naval*, pp. 267–9; Thomazi, *Guerre navale dans la Méditerranée*, pp. 193–4; Vice-Amiral Salaun, *La Marine Française* (Paris, 1934), pp. 263–4.

117 Villarey to Corsi, 14 Apr. 1917, Revel to Villarey, 17 Apr. 1917, Revel to Corsi, 14 Apr. 1917, Corsi to Villarey, 19 Apr. 1917, USM, Cartella 740/1.

118 Leone to Revel, 19 Apr. 1917, ibid.

119 Villarey to Corsi, 25 Apr. 1917, ibid.

120 Lostende to Admiralty, 15 Feb. 1917, de Bon to Lostende, 12 Feb. 1917, PRO, Adm 137/1416.

121 Directions for 'De Quillacq-Fromaget's Sweep', 'Project for Deep Water Barrage' [Translation], minutes by Learmonth, 26 and 27 Feb. and 12 Mar. 1917, Duff, 3 Mar. 1917, and Oliver, 4 Apr. 1917, Admiralty to Lostende, 13 Mar. 1917, ibid.

122 Villarey to Admiralty, 27 Mar. 1917, minutes by Hope, 28 Mar. and Oliver, 1 Apr. 1917, ibid.; Kerr to Admiralty, 20 Apr. 1917, ibid., Adm 137/1414.

123 Conclusions, Anglo-French Conference held at Calais, 26 and 27 Feb. 1917,

p. 6, PRO, Cab 28/2; Robertson, 'Situation at Salonika', with Note by First Sea Lord, 2 Apr. 1917, ibid., Adm 137/1417.

124 Robertson to Jellicoe, 6 Apr. 1917, Jellicoe, 'Protection of Shipping in the Mediterranean', 17 Apr. 1917, ibid., Adm 137/1413; Paper G.T.-481A, Note by Robertson, 17 Apr. 1917, ibid., Cab 24/10.

125 Paper I.C.-20, 'Memorandum on the Anglo-French-Italian Conferences', April 19, 1917, p. 4, ibid., Cab 28/2.

126 Lacaze to Gauchet, 3 Mar. 1917, SHM, Carton A-135; a Japanese squadron also operated in the Indian Ocean, Corbett and Newbolt, *Naval Operations*, Vol. 4, pp. 295–6; O.N.I., 'Japanese Naval Operations during European War', n.d., NARS, RG 38, U-4-b, No. 11083; Train to Sims, 26 June 1917, Train to ONI, 21 Aug. 1917, ibid., RG 45, OT File, Box 335; Admiralty (Training and Staff Duties Division), *Mediterranean Staff Papers*, Jan. 1920, p. 21, London, Naval Library, Ministry of Defence.

127 Henri Le Masson, *Histoire du torpilleur en France* (Paris, n.d. [1966]), pp. 197–200; Labayle-Couhat, *French Warships of World War I*, pp. 118–21; Fraccaroli, *Italian Warships of World War I*, pp. 170 ff.

128 Marzolo to Revel, 2 May 1917, USM, Cartella 470/2; Wemyss to Jellicoe, 27 Apr. 1917, loc. cit. at n. 69, Jellicoe MSS, Add. MSS 49036.

129 Minutes of Corfu Conference, 28 Apr. 1917, PRO, Adm 137/1421.

130 Gauchet to Lacaze and marginal note, 2 May 1917, SHM, Carton Es-15.

131 Minutes of Corfu Conference, 28 Apr. 1917, PRO, Adm 137/1421.

132 Minutes of Corfu Conference, 29 Apr. 1917, ibid.

133 Minutes of Corfu Conference, 29 and 30 Apr. 1917, ibid.

134 Minutes of Corfu Conference, 29 and 30 Apr. 1917, ibid.

135 Minutes of Corfu Conference, 29 Apr. and 1 May 1917, ibid.

136 Gauchet to Lacaze (telegram and dispatch), 2 May 1917, SHM, Carton Es-15.

137 Report of Sub-Committee, Minutes of Corfu Conference, Annex I, PRO, Adm 137/1421.

138 ibid.

139 This controversial subject is covered in detail in Marder, *Dreadnought to Scapa Flow*, Vol. 4, ch. 6; see also: John Winton, *Convoy: The Defence of Sea Trade, 1890–1990* (London, 1983), ch. 5.

140 Minute by Jellicoe, 20 and 26 May 1917, PRO, Adm 137/1421.

[10]

The Otranto Action and the Introduction of Convoys

The Action of 15 May in the Straits of Otranto

The Allies recognized that the Otranto barrage was inefficient and up to May 1917 they could only be sure about destroying one submarine, the Austrian U6 caught in the nets in May 1916. Naturally, they thought they had accounted for more and perhaps some submarines which disappeared, like the German UB44 and the Austrian U30, may also have been claimed by the barrage, but one will never know. The Allies also liked to think that the Austrian raids on the drifters were invariably provoked or were a form of retaliation, which meant that the drifters, at the very least, were causing the enemy serious inconvenience. After the heavy losses of 15 May, Rear-Admiral Mark Kerr consoled himself with the thought that probably some of the submarines reported in the nets in the past month had been destroyed, despite unconvincing evidence. The Austrians had never raided the line except after losing a submarine and this time used a larger force and undertook a greater risk. Commodore Heneage also thought that only serious inconvenience caused by the drifters made the Austrians think it was worth risking three light cruisers against the powerful Allied forces at Brindisi.[1]

The real origins of the raid are more complex and while the annoyance and potential danger from the drifters naturally had a big role there was probably also a bit of that need to 'do something' that the more enterprising officers of both sides felt in the particularly frustrating circumstances of the Adriatic war. Unfortunately there are gaps in the Austrian archives caused by the circumstances of the Dual Monarchy's collapse in 1918 when the records at Pola were lost, and often only copies of material sent to the Marinesektion in Vienna have survived. It is very difficult to find traces of the internal correspondence of the fleet or discussions between the Flottenkommandant and his subordinates if, indeed, these ever existed on paper. Consequently, the historian is frustrated when he tries to learn *why* things happened as opposed to *what* happened. We know far more of the 15 May action itself than its origins. Captain Horthy, that enterprising officer who had made a name for himself, seems to have been the prime mover. In his own memoirs Horthy says that conversations with U-boat commanders at Cattaro revealed that they all agreed 'it was becoming more and more difficult if not impossible to break through' and Horthy made up his mind that 'it was time to make a clearance'.[2] Horthy's memoirs, however, were written in exile after the Second World War, apparently without access to official records, and are therefore unreliable on details. Horthy's statement tends to make the barrage a more formidable obstacle than it probably appeared at the time. According to Linienschiffskapitän Erich Heyssler, then Chief of Staff in the Austrian Cruiser Flotilla and soon to receive command of the *Helgoland*, Horthy arrived in the Bocche with *Novara* at the end of February having convinced the Flottenkommando to approve of a plan to mop up the drifters with a raid by the three best cruisers, *Novara, Helgoland* and *Saida*. Horthy had removed the mainmast of *Novara* and replaced it with a short steel mast so that its appearance from afar or at night resembled a large British destroyer. The turbines were also cleaned and overhauled and a 7-cm anti-aircraft cannon was installed. The appearance of the other cruisers was also altered. At first only a few knew of the plan and, again according to Heyssler, there was relatively little activity in M.. ·h beyond regular escorts and air raids so as to lull the Allies into a false sense of security.[3] It was not all that quiet in April, three destroyers thrust south to the transport routes to Albania on the nights of 22–23 April, 26 April and 5–6 May, without result.[4] *Helgoland* did not leave Pola where she had been in dock until 10 May. The operational orders were issued on 13 May under the signature of Rear-Admiral Alexander Hansa, the new commander of the Austrian Cruiser Flotilla, who determined the date of the operation. The plan was based on the assumption that the three cruisers, led by Horthy in *Novara*, would be taken as destroyers at first because of their shortened main mast and therefore gain time before overwhelming forces were called out. The Austrians would sail at nightfall and the three cruisers would separate during the night to attack different portions of the drifter line at dawn. They had orders to reassemble fifteen nautical miles west of Cape Linguetta by 7.15 a.m. at the latest for the dash home. There would be a parallel action led by Fregattenkapitän Prince von und zu Liechtenstein (former naval attaché in Rome) in the destroyer *Csepel* accompanied by the destroyer *Balaton*. The destroyers – originally there were to have been three, but *Tátra* was relegated to escort service because boiler trouble reduced her speed – would cruise off the Albanian coast seeking transports and would confuse enemy reporting on the movements of the Austrian forces. The Austrians also deployed three submarines, their own U4 off Valona and U27 off Brindisi, while the German UC25 would lay mines off Brindisi before dawn. Aircraft from Durazzo and Kumbor (in the Gulf of Cattaro) would support the action, while at Cattaro the armoured cruiser *Sankt Georg* and the destroyers *Warasdiner* and *Tátra* and a torpedo-boat escort would be ready to sortie in support if required, to be followed by the old coast-defence battleship *Budapest* and three torpedo-boats.[5]

The Allied force at sea that night consisted of the flotilla leader *Mirabello* (Capitano di Vascello Vicuna) and the French destroyers *Commandant*

Rivière, Bisson and *Cimeterre*. A fourth destroyer, the *Boutefeu*, had been compelled by condenser trouble to return to port. Captain Vicuna's force was well to the north of the drifter line, and was described by Kerr's Flag Commander Pipon as 'carrying out some sort of irregular patrol – what I haven't quite discovered'. The Italian admiral at Brindisi actually had intended the *Mirabello* force to be in a position to intercept any potential raiders returning from the drifter line. Furthermore, the Italian submarine F10 was south of Cattaro and the French submarine *Bernouilli* south of Durazzo.[6] The Italians also had a convoy of three ships escorted by the small destroyer *Borea en route* to Valona. At approximately 3.24 or 3.26 a.m. – Austrian and Italian reports vary – *Balaton* and *Csepel* attacked the convoy, sinking *Borea* and the munitions ship *Carroccio* (1,657 tons) and leaving the steamer *Verità* ablaze, although later salved.[7]

The Austrian cruisers passed through the line of drifters between Cape Santa Maria di Leuca and Fano without causing alarm, assumed in some cases if seen to be friendly. The attack on the drifters began around 3.30 a.m. and continued until after sunrise.[8] The drifters, manned by fishermen and armed at best with a six-pounder or 57-mm guns, stood little chance against the cruisers with their 3·9-inch guns. The Austrians appear to have acted with considerable chivalry, particularly *Helgoland*, dipping their ensign and blowing their sirens to give the drifter crews time to abandon ship before they opened fire. This act of humanity was appreciated by the British who recognized that it slowed the work of destruction and required considerable coolness since Brindisi, with its more powerful forces, was closer to Cattaro than the drifter line.[9] The cruisers also had to do some tricky manœuvring in places to avoid tangling their screws in the nets which some drifters had abandoned. Despite the heavy odds there were some drifter men who fought back and one, Skipper J. Watt of the *Gowan Lee*, which survived in battered condition, was subsequently awarded the Victoria Cross. Heyssler admired their courage and in his report described how one brave man manned his small gun and trained it on the cruiser, and when Heyssler was forced to fire he regretted that the life boat and the remainder of the crew on deck were in the line of fire.[10] The task was indeed, as Commodore Heneage surmised in his report, 'probably somewhat distasteful to him'. Heyssler's own wife was Australian and he had relations and friends in the Royal Navy. When the attack was over, fourteen of the forty-seven drifters on the line that night had been sunk and four damaged, three badly. The Austrians picked up seventy-two prisoners. Their damage done, the Austrians now had the problem of getting back safely with Brindisi forty miles closer to Cattaro than the drifter line.

Once the alarm had been raised there would be sizeable forces in pursuit. Rear-Admiral Alfredo Acton took command of the chase. At approximately 4.35 a.m. he ordered the *Mirabello* group southwards from their position north of Durazzo. Acton ordered the Brindisi light forces to sea as soon as they were ready and embarked with his staff in the British light cruiser *Dartmouth* from which he commanded the action, although Captain Addison of the *Dartmouth* noted that he did not fly his flag, and the staff tended to get in the way on the cruiser's bridge.[11] By approximately 6.45

the light cruisers *Dartmouth* and *Bristol*, the Italian destroyers *Mosto*, *Pilo*, *Schiaffino*, *Acerbi*, and the flotilla leader *Aquila* were steaming north-eastwards to head off the Austrians, while the scout cruiser *Marsala*, the flotilla leader *Racchia* and the destroyers *Insidioso*, *Indomito* and *Impavido* at Brindisi were either getting up steam or ready to sail. Acton did not actually send the wireless signal from *Dartmouth* for them to sail until 8.25, something Revel criticized him for since he believed the *Marsala* group could have sailed at least an hour before. The forces at Valona, particularly the potentially useful fast flotilla leader *Riboty*, also failed to intervene.[12]

The *Mirabello* group was the first to make contact with Horthy's cruisers around 7.00 and there was a brief artillery exchange in which the Italian commander, outgunned, did not close. Vicuna, instead, made a wide circle to avoid U4 and turned north to maintain contact with the three cruisers, but the three French destroyers could not sustain *Mirabello*'s speed and slowly fell behind. The *Dartmouth* group first made contact with the destroyers *Csepel* and *Balaton*, rather than the cruisers, at 7.45 according to Italian reports, and 7.35 according to Austrian reports. Acton apparently did not realize that the destroyers were present and it was twenty minutes before the faster *Aquila* and four destroyers closed the Austrians and an artillery duel at high speed resulted. At approximately 8.30 a lucky shot from *Csepel* cut a steam pipe and hit one of *Aquila*'s boilers thereby disabling the ship. *Csepel* and *Balaton* escaped behind the shelter of the Austrian coastal batteries at Durazzo. One British officer considered the disablement of the *Aquila* in retrospect to have been 'cruel bad luck', for in an action in which speed was at a premium the value of her 34–35 knots and pair of 6-in. guns would have been great.[13]

The Allies were still between Horthy's three cruisers, followed by the *Mirabello* group, and their base, and the main portion of the action was about to begin. Throughout the day, on which visibility was very good, aircraft from both sides intervened with reconnaissance, signalling by wireless or lamp, bombing and strafing. On balance the Austrians were probably more effective and one Italian seaplane was shot down. However, no ship was disabled or seriously damaged by bombs, although as Captain Addison of the *Dartmouth* put it, the attacks were 'most annoying'.[14] At approximately 9.00 *Bristol* reported smoke astern. It was Horthy and his cruisers and Acton turned to meet the Austrians. The battle now would be primarily between the three Austrian light cruisers armed with 100-mm (3·9-in.) guns and the two British cruisers, *Dartmouth* armed with 6-in. guns and *Bristol* armed with two 6-in. and the remainder 4-in. guns. The Austrians were outgunned but the Allied superiority in numbers rapidly fell away. Acton detached the destroyers *Schiaffino* and *Pilo* to guard the disabled *Aquila*. *Mirabello* was forced to stop for a time because of water in her fuel. She was back to her normal speed a little before 11.00 but at 11.45 *Commandant Rivière* broke down with condenser trouble. *Cimeterre* and *Bisson*, in turn, had to remain behind to protect the disabled ship from submarine attack. *Bristol* had been due to enter dock just before the action and her bottom was foul. She therefore could not keep up with *Dartmouth* and gradually fell behind, while her 4-in. guns were soon outranged. This eft *Dartmouth*, accompanied by the destroyers *Acerbi* and *Mosto*, to carry the brunt of the action.

Horthy also had his troubles, for *Saida* could not make more than 25 knots and thereby held back her consorts who were capable of 2–3 knots more speed. *Novara* was also outgunned by the 6-in. cannon of *Dartmouth* and a shell struck *Novara*'s forebridge killing the First Officer. Horthy used a smoke screen to try and close the range to where his 3·9 in. guns would be more effective. *Dartmouth* was straddled and, on occasion, well splashed and was also hit a few times. Addison admitted that they were lucky that one shell did not explode for it would have put the port propellor out of action.[15] At 10.10 Horthy was wounded by a shell splinter, tried to direct the action lying on the deck, but lost consciousness for a period and *Novara*'s Gunnery Officer, Lieutenant Witkowski, took command.

By now other forces were at sea. The Italian scout *Marsala*, the flotilla leader *Racchia* and destroyers *Indomito*, *Impavido* and *Insidioso* were racing to join the action while Gauchet at Corfu, on intercepting wireless reports of the action and without receiving any request for assistance, sent the destroyers *Casque*, *Faulx* and *Commandant Lucas*, northwards. The destroyers had been part of the French force normally based on Brindisi. On the Austrian side the armoured cruiser *Sankt Georg*, the destroyers *Warasdiner* and *Tátra* and the torpedo-boats Tb84, Tb88, Tb99 and Tb100 were teaming to support Horthy.

Dartmouth had been bearing the brunt of the action and at 11.00 Acton ordered her to open the range and ease to 20 knots to permit *Bristol* to catch up. This was fortunate for the Austrians as *Novara* had sustained damage to her main feed pumps and an auxiliary steam pipe to the starboard turbine and was losing speed. Acton apparently had turned away at 11.05 in an unsuccessful attempt to cut off the straggling *Saida* and then, sighting the smoke from the Austrian reinforcements from Cattaro on the horizon, he turned southwards to join the *Marsala* group from Brindisi, met them at 1.30, and turned back towards the *Novara*. This respite saved the Austrians, for *Novara* had been forced to stop and Captain von Purschka of *Saida* took the cruiser in tow, while Heyssler in *Helgoland* covered them from attack by Acton's reinforced group. This was indeed a critical moment for the Austrians and Purschka has been criticized for taking an excessive amount of time to complete the manœuvre. Acton, however, turned away with the approach of the *Sankt Georg*, whose pair of 240-mm guns (9·2-in.) outgunned anything in his force. By now *Budapest* with Tb86, Tb91 and Tb95 had also been ordered to sail. Acton apparently did not, at least initially, realize that *Novara* had been forced to stop, just as the Austrians earlier in the battle had not realized that *Aquila* was immobilized. Acton knew that the Austrian cruisers were likely to have the edge in speed and he did not want to run the risk of being drawn closer to Cattaro and having any damaged ships cut off by the presumably superior Austrian forces which he assumed were now out. The destroyer *Acerbi* misread the recall signal, obscured by smoke, for an attack signal and her enterprising commander, Vannutelli, manœuvred to deliver a torpedo attack but, unsupported, was driven off by the concentrated Austrian fire. *Racchia*,

Impavido, and later *Marsala*, also had approached the Austrians but were recalled by Acton. By the time Acton realized that *Novara* was disabled the *Sankt Georg* was approaching and at 12.05 he ordered a general retirement. At the time, Addison thought that Acton's recall was justified. He had been in the thick of the fighting and his trials that day were far from over. He wrote: 'By this time we were nearing Cattaro & 2 at least of the "St. Georges" were coming up fast & the Italian admiral decided to leave it at that & I think rightly.' The Austrians did not entirely understand the sudden breaking off of action on the appearance of the *Sankt Georg* for they thought that the enemy was at least five cruisers strong and had time to destroy at least *Novara*. Rear-Admiral Hansa speculated that the Allies might have been short of ammunition. Heyssler also commented on how, to their astonishment, the enemy turned away at the most critical moment, with *Sankt Georg* to their reckoning still twenty-five kilometres away.[16] Addison, when he corresponded with Heyssler after the war, admitted that he did not realize the Austrian cruisers were stopped and if he had 'I think I shall have disobeyed orders'. After studying the British reports, Kerr also came to the conclusion that Acton had discontinued the action 'a little too soon' for a few minutes at close range against the *Novara* would have probably finished her.[17] But all of this was hindsight. Kerr was not on the scene, Acton was, and the responsibility was his. Clearly though, he was not a Nelson.

The Austrians were lucky and escaped that day. The French submarine *Bernoulli* fired at *Balaton*, but missed, and *Balaton* and *Csepel* joined the *Sankt Georg* group with *Novara* in tow on their return to Cattaro, where they were met by *Budapest* and three torpedo-boats which had come out in support. The Allies had their own cripples to bring in. *Mirabello* took *Commandant Rivière* under tow with *Bisson* as escort and sent *Cimeterre* ahead to join the group around the crippled *Aquila*, under tow by *Schiaffino*, screened by *Pilo*. *Mirabello* was also reinforced for a time by the *Commandant Lucas*, one of the three French destroyers from Corfu which could not keep up with the other pair and arrived too late to join the action. *Commandant Lucas* was subsequently sent on to join the *Dartmouth* group. *Faulx* and *Casque* also joined the *Dartmouth* group around 13.00, too late to take any part in the action. The route home brought the Allies within range of UC25 (Kapitänleutnant Feldkirchner), which had already laid mines off Brindisi. At 13.30 Feldkirchner torpedoed *Dartmouth* approximately thirty-six miles from Brindisi. Depth-charge attacks by the French and Italian destroyers prevented the submarine from making any further attack, but the torpedo had struck the cruiser on the port bow and for a time the ship was abandoned. Addison later reported that the fore part of the ship was wrecked with the armoured deck holding the ship together, and they were lucky that the shell room had not blown up. When it became apparent that *Dartmouth* would not sink, Addison and sufficient officers and men to work the ship reboarded, partially righted the ship with counter-flooding, raised steam and, with the assistance of tugs sent out from Brindisi, got the cruiser stern first into port early in the morning. The Allied troubles were not over however. On receipt of the news that *Dartmouth* had been torpedoed

Boutefeu put to sea to assist, only to strike one of UC25's mines a few minutes after clearing the boom. The destroyer sank within a minute and a half. It was a dismal end of the day for the Allies. They had not used all their forces. The British light cruiser *Liverpool* was held at Brindisi, where she had been at six hours' notice when the action began, and the Italian admiral in charge in Acton's absence refused to let her sail. The Pisa division had also raised steam. Captain Vivian of the *Liverpool* was chagrined, for his natural instinct was to help and he thought that his ship might have been useful if heavy units came out of Cattaro, particularly if any of the Allied cruisers had been damaged in the running fight. Revel, who had arrived on a tour of inspection that morning, sent a wireless message to Acton inquiring if he wanted the Pisas. Acton's reply, with the action nearly over, was negative. Even Vivian considered this wise, for there were no destroyers left to escort them, enemy submarines obviously were outside and they would have arrived too late to be of any use. The fast battleship *Napoli* at Valona had also remained in port along with the flotilla leader *Riboty*. The inertness of the latter was also regrettable since her speed would have been useful, but the admiral at Valona had received neither direct information nor orders.[18]

The Allies thought – or rather hoped – that the damaged Austrian cruiser might have sunk. They were wrong. All Austrian ships returned to Cattaro safely to the enthusiastic cheers of the other vessels stationed there. The Austrian navy considered the action of 15 May, the largest encounter at sea would have during the war, to be a victory, the successful culmination of a successful raid, and this view has been cherished by the dwindling ranks of its veterans in later years. Certainly the k.u.k. Kriegsmarine had nothing to be ashamed of. The three cruisers and two destroyers had between them sunk a destroyer and a munitions ship, fourteen drifters, and badly damaged another three to four drifters, a transport and a flotilla leader, with the added bonus of the German UC25 sinking a destroyer and badly damaging a cruiser. *Novara*, the most heavily damaged Austrian ship, was ready for sea in eight days while *Dartmouth*, which was lucky to get back to port, would be out of service for months.[19] Nevertheless, rumours about the naval encounter assumed 'fantastic dimensions' in Vienna stock exchange circles and the Marinesektion recommended publication of an authorized communiqué as soon as possible.[20]

There was relatively little recrimination about the action and missed opportunities on the Allied side. Kerr's Flag Commander admitted, 'I can't help wishing we'd had some British destroyers, & some of our submarines off Cattaro, also a British admiral running the show'. Kerr and Vivian were inclined to put primary emphasis on the want of speed by British ships, and despite the fact that *Dartmouth* made more revolutions than she had ever done before she could not keep up with the Austrians who seemed to have the advantage of a knot or more. Moreover, *Bristol's* 4-in. guns were outranged and the British suspected, incorrectly, that the Austrians had regunned some of their cruisers with 6-in. guns. The signalling, always a problem in an inter-Allied force, also left much to be desired. The Italians did not provide the British with the call signals of their ships, thereby reducing the value of intercepted signals, while at one point *Mirabello* misled everyone by either coding her signals badly or using the squared chart incorrectly.[21] The commander of the French destroyers with the *Mirabello* also had difficulty. His own ship had not intercepted the wireless message ordering the group southwards after the attack on the drifters and he could not make out *Mirabello*'s semaphore signal executed in the Italian method and despite repeated demands for repetition could not understand it. All he knew was that 'something had happened' and that *Dartmouth* and *Bristol* had left Brindisi. This resulted in a painful surprise when the four-funnelled cruisers they encountered turned out to be Austrian. The French were, as usual, critical of Italian leadership, especially the 'dribbling way' that vessels were sent out from Brindisi. The Italians must have agreed, for Rear-Admiral Bollo, Admiral-in-Command at Brindisi in Acton's absence, was superseded.[22]

The question of the drifters caused more emotion. Commodore Heneage reported after the raid that the driftermen had expressed their disgust, not so much at being attacked with no protecting force to back them up, but because the Austrians had been able to get back unmolested. Heneage argued that, notwithstanding their fighting spirit, the driftermen could not be expected to fight warships unless backed up by something armed with more than 3-pdr guns. Kerr was sure that until they could attach some British destroyers to the barrage the drifters would be raided as before. The destroyers were not available and the Admiralty ordered the drifters to be withdrawn from the line at night, which naturally reduced its value. The drifters put in to Otranto, Port Palermo and Fano Island, laying nets between 5 and 10 a.m. and taking them up again at 3.00 p.m.[23] The Italians could not provide any protection until July and then only on an irregular basis. Protection of the drifters turned into another source of disagreement. The Italians, claiming they had not got enough destroyers to establish patrol to protect the drifters, delivered another petulant note about the British failure to live up to their promise at the London Conference to improve the quality (that is, *fast* light cruisers) and quantity (that is destroyers) of British forces in the Adriatic. The increase in the number of British cruisers from three to four through the impending arrival of the *Weymouth* meant little since she was the same class as the *Dartmouth* and therefore inferior to the Austrians in speed. The Italians wanted at least eight British destroyers and any additional reinforcements available from the United States or Japan. The British did not accept the argument. According to their own reports, the real problem was that Italian and French destroyers already at Brindisi spent too little time at sea compared with British destroyers. There were, according to the British, fourteen Allied destroyers, three Mirabello-class flotilla leaders and three large destroyers available for patrol of the barrage, yet out of these twenty the Italians could only provide three for a patrol on three nights out of six. It was 'farcical' for the Italians to say that they could not maintain a regular patrol without British assistance.[24] Moreover, the British claimed that the Italian arguments ignored the presence of the powerful French fleet at Corfu and the fact that the eighteen American destroyers, which the Italians asserted had reinforced the British fleet, were actually employed in the Atlantic escorting British and American trade rather than reinforcing the Grand Fleet. As for the Adriatic, the British claimed that the superiority of British and Italian light cruisers and flotilla leaders was 'infinitely greater' than that possessed by the light cruisers of the Grand Fleet over the High Seas Fleet in the North Sea, and it was therefore not possible to weaken the Grand Fleet in order to strengthen the Italian fleet. These arguments were deeply offensive to the Italians and Revel noted on his copy that he thought Jellicoe was trying to pull their leg and 'use their wood to make a fire'.[25]

The Admiralty finally prevailed on the Commonwealth Government of Australia to send three Australian destroyers, *Parramatta*, *Warrego* and *Yarra*, to the Mediterranean. The Australians agreed and went further. They also offered the destroyers *Swan*, *Torrens* and *Huon*, currently based on Singapore, if the Admiralty could provide an additional cruiser for the protection of Australian waters against a potential raider. Cruisers were obviously better for this type of work than a destroyer whose capacities for anti-submarine work were wasted in an area where the submarine danger was nil. The six Australian destroyers were supposedly earmarked for patrol of the Otranto barrage.[26] Before they arrived, however, they were diverted to escort duties and did not actually reinforce the Otranto barrage until October, after which the British were able to keep two of them permanently on patrol as protection for the drifters.[27]

On the whole, the action of 15 May 1917 was both a tactical and, to a lesser extent, strategic success for the Austrians. Not only had they inflicted heavier losses and escaped with little damage, but the line of drifters was rendered even less effective by restricting it to daylight operations. On the other hand, there is at least some similarity between the largest action in the Adriatic during the war and Jutland. It may sound odd to compare an encounter between a handful of cruisers and destroyers with the gigantic battle in the North Sea. The Otranto Straits action was, however, more of a battle in three dimensions with aircraft and submarines playing proportionately a far greater role than they had at Jutland. But the overall result was the same. As that American newspaper said of Jutland, 'The German Fleet has assaulted its jailor and is back in jail'. Nothing had really changed in the Adriatic either. The big dreadnoughts on both sides had never come near to going into action and the Austrians, at least as far as surface craft were concerned, were still shut off from the Mediterranean, while the lines of communication of the Allied armies in the Balkans and Near East were still threatened only by submarines. There is also the nagging question of whether the risk of using the most useful and irreplaceable units of the Austrian fleet, the 3 Novaras, had really been worth it? There had only been forty-seven drifters out the night of 14–15 May and, as Heneage pointed out, a drifter could effectively cover only half a mile. This meant that only twenty-three to twenty-four miles of the forty-mile-wide strait was covered. Horthy had therefore made a not very effective barrage temporarily even less effective. The Allies might not be able to protect the drifters but the Austrians might not always escape unscathed either. They had been very lucky that day; they might not be so lucky in the future.

The British undertook a raid of their own in the Adriatic on 24 May which was distinctly different from Horthy's high-speed dash. This one involved the plodding monitors and took place right in the Austrian's backyard, the Gulf of Trieste. Kerr managed to convince the Italians to risk the 12-in. gunned monitors *Earl of Peterborough*, in which he flew his flag, and *Sir Thomas Picton*, in a bombardment of the crossroads and airfield of Prosecco, only a few miles from Trieste. The monitors, protected by Italian torpedo-boats and motor-boats, were attacked by a number of aircraft, one of which was shot down by an Italian Nieuport. One bomb hit the *Earl of Peterborough* without causing serious damage, although Kerr later thought that splinters from it had inflamed his eye and he apparently revelled in his Nelsonic appearance. What the bombardment itself accomplished is questionable. Kerr hinted that the monitors were recalled prematurely because it appeared to the Italian commander at Grado that they were being smothered by bombs, although the reason the latter gave for the recall was that heavy ships were reported to be coming out from Pola. The submarines U1 and U2, ancient craft now normally used only for training, had in fact sailed from Trieste and perhaps the recall was not unjustified.[28] The affair is another example of the need 'to do something'.

The fixed net barrage was the other important component of the Otranto barrage, but so far it existed only on paper. The British, who would have been required to furnish most of the material for the project about which they were dubious, insisted on a preliminary trial. Lieutenant de Quillacq, one of the authors of the French scheme, had been at the Corfu Conference and had also inspected a trial barrage laid by the Italians off Taranto. The result was a revised Franco-Italian design which de Bon heartily recommended to the Admiralty. There would be a submerged barrage between Santa Maria di Leuca and Fano Island, some forty-seven miles. It would be supplemented by a French-designed mobile surface barrage consisting of a floated hawser in sections one and one-third miles in length, with mines at intervals. The surface barrage would be towed out after dark by patrol parallel to, and on either side of, the fixed barrage. The objective was to force submarines to either submerge and foul the moored underwater defence or navigate on the surface and strike the mined hawser. The French offered to supply 2,400 mines, the Italians the concrete sinkers and the British would have to furnish all the rest. Captain Learmonth, Captain supervising Submarine Defences, remained dubious. The Admiralty, after all, had had a long series of frustrating experiences with mine and net defences in the Dover Straits. The British realized, however, that it might not be politic to decline to participate and at the end of May recommended supplying material for a trial, laying a portion of the barrage eastwards from Cape Santa Maria di Leuca to around the 100-fathom line. If this approximately fifteen-mile trial was successful, they would try for greater depths. They also insisted on reviewing the trial at Taranto, but since deliveries of mooring buoys could not take place for some months owing to the pressure of work on qualified firms, they did not anticipate any real start on laying the barrage until the autumn.[29] Revel was not pleased and claimed further trials were unnecessary and that the British authorities at Taranto vere aware of the excellent results obtained. He objected most to the delay vhich would prevent them from working under favourable weather onditions in the summer. The Admiralty, who were going to have to foot nost of the bill which given the length and depth of the barrage was apt to be considerable, insisted on a repetition of the Taranto experiment in the deep waters of the Straits of Otranto and the French agreed.[30] It would herefore be a long time, if ever, before any mechanical obstacle appeared in he Straits of Otranto.

The Greek Imbroglio Is Settled

The tangled Greek situation in which King Constantine continued to rule a neutralist government in Athens while Venizelos led a provisional pro-Allied government in Crete and Salonika finally came to a climax in June of 917. The shipping problem by then had become more and more dominant n Allied arguments. An Anglo-French Conference attended by Lloyd George and Jellicoe thrashed out the Greek problem in Paris on 5 and 6 May. The British intended to withdraw one infantry division and two avalry brigades from the Salonika force starting 1 June. Jellicoe put it to the onference in harsh terms. Unless the Salonika force was evacuated before he end of the year it would starve there, and unless they began to reduce it t once it would be too late, for a little later there would be no ships to take he troops away. Lacaze supported Jellicoe on these points.[31] This naval essimism came, of course, after April 1917 which was the worst month of he war as far as submarine sinkings were concerned.

At the end of May the British and French met in London and finally greed to cut the Gordian knot. Realizing that they had often worked at ross purposes with one another in Greece, the Allies agreed on what could be termed a unified diplomatic command. A Frenchman, Charles Jonnart, vould be sent to Greece as High Commissioner to represent both Britain nd France and demand the abdication and withdrawal of King Constantine.[32] onnart's mission was backed by French naval forces including battleships nd armoured cruisers under Vice-Admiral de Gueydon. The French ecured the northern and southern entrances to the Corinth Canal cutting off the Peloponnese and a significant portion of Constantine's potential upport. With Athens and Piraeus under the threat of French naval cannon, Constantine yielded to Jonnart's demands and abdicated in favour of his son Alexander. The former king left for exile in Switzerland shortly afterwards. The French landed approximately 9,500 troops at Piraeus and unlike the preceding December there was no resistance. The Greeks had yielded to orce majeure. Neither the British warships nor the Italian cruiser at Piraeus vere invited to take part in the operation or notified beforehand.[33]

The Allied blockade of Greece was lifted on 16 June, freeing, incidentally, ome badly needed small craft for anti-submarine patrols. On 21 June, Venizelos arrived in Piraeus to form a new government which declared war n the Central Powers on 2 July. Now that Greece was officially an ally here was also the question of what to do about the Greek fleet. Earlier in the year the French had been extremely reluctant to tolerate the provisiona government using more than a handful of small torpedo-boats, and the were not anxious to see the bigger Greek ships such as the pair of battleship purchased in the United States back in service. The latter were certainly nc needed under present circumstances and their large crews were harder t control and a potential source of royalist agitation.[34]

With Greece actually in the war the French had little excuse to retain th Greek fleet and on 18 July de Gueydon gave the Greek Minister of Marin the welcome news that the Greek light cruiser *Helle* and the majority of th destroyers and torpedo-boats would be given back a few at a time. For th moment, the French would retain the four large destroyers of the Panthe class which were currently refitting in French yards. When the Greeks wer able to man enough ships, they would be given responsibility for patrollin and sweeping the Gulf of Athens under the command of the French vice admiral who was Senior Allied Naval Officer at Salamis. The Greeks woul obviously use the smaller torpedo-boats for this service. As they becam ready, the larger craft would be used for escort work farther afield in th Aegean or between Salamis and Corfu. The Greeks would not put th battleships *Kilkis* and *Lemnos* back in service, but would use the big ships a depots for the torpedo-boats or for training.[35] Gauchet was somewhat les than pleased at the whole procedure and did not share de Gueydon's fu confidence in the zeal and ardour of the Greek officers and crews wh would man the ships once they were returned. He, in fact, expecte considerable difficulties for the material was fragile and kept in service onl by well-trained and devoted personnel, and he could not forget th Germanophile spirit which he considered had been so evident in the Gree navy earlier in the war and could only have very limited confidence in it.[3]

De Bon would have liked to keep the Greek destroyers currently i French yards, the *Hierax*, *Leon*, *Panther* and *Aetos*. Under presen circumstances, these 980-ton, British-built vessels were potentially the mos useful portion of the Greek fleet, but Lacaze cut off his objections with th statement that the decision had been taken to return everything the Frencl had seized. The actual return of the ships went slowly, as Gauchet ha foreseen, because of the difficulty that the Greeks experienced in obtainin; reliable crews and, as of 13 August, they had only the *Helle*, two destroyer and two torpedo-boats, and these did not have full crews yet.[37]

Once the French began to return Greek warships, the British wer anxious to re-establish their Naval Mission. Admiral Condouriotis, Gree Minister of Marine, was at first inclined to want only a few liaison officer and technical advisers, but the Allied Conference in Paris in July agreed to British Naval Mission to balance the French Military Mission which wa now with the Greek army, and Venizelos accepted the idea of a full missio on 30 July. Captain Clifton Brown was given command with the rank o rear-admiral in the Hellenic navy. It was not an enviable position and he ha to expect a certain amount of friction with the French. Salamis and Athen were in a French zone and the French were reluctant to give up thei commanding position and use of the Salamis arsenal.[38] There was a lot o ink spilt over the issue at the time and not all of it very edifying. It wa

nother example of that dark underside of the Allies' relations to each other
with its finger pointing and elbowing for position. Nevertheless, what was
really important was getting the Greek navy back into the war where every
possible effort was needed to meet the challenge of the German submarines
nd this, happily, was eventually accomplished. In 1918 the armoured
cruiser *Georgios Averoff* and four Aetos-class destroyers joined the British
Aegean Squadron at Mudros, while the remainder of the Greek destroyers
nd torpedo-boats performed escort service, primarily in the Aegean. The
inal verdict of the staff of the British Mediterranean C.-in-C. was: 'The
ecord of these Greek ships was a most satisfactory one and they performed
;ood, and where the opportunity offered, gallant service.'[39]

The Appointment of a British Mediterranean C.-in-C.

The majority of the recommendations of the Corfu Conference had been
ccepted right away. One of the most important was the institution of
onvoys in the eastern portion of the Mediterranean. The British introduced
 Malta–Alexandria convoy on 22 May with four ships escorted by four
rawlers. The Malta–Alexandria convoy was considered a success, only two
hips were lost between 22 May and 16 July.[40] There were another two
ecommendations of the Corfu Conference that had been deferred – the
omination of a British C.-in-C. for the Mediterranean and the establish-
nent of a central direction for routing at Malta. Both issues were closely
nked with one another. Admiral de Bon was in London on 28 May and in
he course of discussions over the introduction of convoys in the
Mediterranean put forward a paper which may have surprised the British.
De Bon agreed that a central direction at Malta for the general control of
outes in the Mediterranean was the best means to concentrate all resources
f the Allies and ensure maximum efficiency, and conceded that the French
C.-in-C. could not himself act in that capacity since his other duties would
ot allow him the freedom to follow movements or minor operations
which required constant attention. This was only common sense, Malta
was obviously better placed for control of traffic through the Mediterranean
han the somewhat out-of-the-way Corfu. What de Bon proposed though,
was more controversial. Under the general control of the French and Allied
C.-in-C. there would be a Direction of Routes which would have free and
omplete direction of commercial traffic and its protection. De Bon
eclared – and this was the heart of his argument – that in order to facilitate
he liaison between the French C.-in-C. and the Direction of Routes it
eemed advisable to put a *French flag officer* at the head of the inter-Allied
ommittee exercising control.

The argument was not very convincing to the British and Jellicoe was
lunt in his reply. The head of the control at Malta should be a British flag
fficer because British interests in regard to shipping in the Mediterranean
ar exceed those of any other nation' and the British were providing more
atrol vessels than anyone else. The Admiralty did not think it essential for
he French C.-in-C. to have general control over the organization, although

it was necessary that he should be fully informed and that his arguments should receive the fullest consideration by the central authority.[41]

The French did not press the point very hard and one wonders if it was a serious proposition. The French Premier, Alexandre Ribot, was a pragmatist and had no objections to the British proposals 'based on the supremacy of their merchant marine', and Lacaze was content that the principle of a French commander of all Allied forces in the Mediterranean was established and admitted without dispute by the British. Gauchet, the man most concerned, also had no objection in principle provided that the essential condition was secured, that is, the Direction Générale functioned under the supervision (*contrôle*) of the C.-in-C. This was essential because it was impossible to provide his fleet with the destroyers and trawlers it required and it was therefore necessary that, at any moment, he could dispose of all or part of these units without having to negotiate with an authority equal to his own.[42]

This provisional acceptance, supported by Lacaze, had one potential difficulty. To what extent would Gauchet exercise that term beloved of French bureaucrats – *contrôle*? None the less, Jellicoe thought that the arrangements, while not wholly satisfactory, would 'be a distinct improvement upon that at present in force, and, presuming that the French Commander-in-Chief does not interfere except in cases where the operations of the Fleet are concerned, it may be expected to work well'. He thought that was as far as the French were willing to go at present and did not think it desirable to press for anything more at the moment. Jellicoe suggested that Wemyss should be appointed as British Mediterranean C.-in-C. for he considered him peculiarly suited for an appointment involving close co-operation with other nationalities. Wemyss, an urbane aristocrat noted for his characteristic monocle, had earned a good name for himself a commander of the British base at Mudros during the Dardanelles campaign. He might, indeed, have had the naval command of the expedition for he was senior to de Robeck when the original commander, Carden, went sick on the eve of the Allied attack in March 1915, but courteously stepped aside. He had been C.-in-C. Egypt and East Indies ever since the Dardanelles campaign. Wemyss was fluent in French and rather more knowledgeable about matters outside the navy than the average sailor. The appointment would not have been a sea-going one, however. Wemyss would fly his flag ashore at Malta and the boundaries of his old command would be rearranged with Egypt separated from the East Indies station and falling under the Mediterranean C.-in-C., while the northern limits of the East Indies command would be set at some point to be decided in the Red Sea. Rear-Admiral Thomas Jackson was named to replace Wemyss in Egypt.[4]

Wemyss and his staff had very definite ideas about what he was going to do. In addition to command of all patrols, he intended to take supreme control of the direction of all mercantile traffic in the Mediterranean, and exercise control through British, French and Italian Admirals of Patrols who would execute his orders and co-operate closely in regulating convoys and escorts. He asked for an increase in staff since good staff work was probably at the heart of his programme. Wemyss wanted an Intelligence Department to ascertain and predict movements of submarines based on the usual sources: espionage, interception of wireless communications, reports of sightings and close analysis of known methods and tactics. The objective would be to divert or regulate traffic before losses occurred. He also wanted statistics and diagrams of Allied trade in the Mediterranean so as to allocate protection according to the relative threat, for he recognized the Corfu Conference had been hampered by a lack of this information. Wemyss was understandably vague about the details of offensive and defensive operations, but apparently intended to make as much use as possible of aircraft and to examine possible operations against submarine bases, as well as the use of British submarine minelayers off those bases. He was, however, unenthusiastic about trying to use 'hunting squadrons' against submarines, the method favoured by those who liked 'offensive' tactics, and he discounted the potential advantages of hydrophones in the Mediterranean because of the great depth of the water. Wemyss was also a partisan of 'escorts' as opposed to 'patrolled routes', for if escorts were not an absolute safeguard they were certainly a deterrent. However, to keep the requirements for escorts within bounds, traffic would have to be formed into convoys with staff analysis of that traffic to show what the requirements were.[44]

Wemyss himself was fated never to take up the command but his staff was firmly established at Malta. The Mediterranean Staff was therefore destined to play a large role and by 1918 some disgruntled officers in other parts of the Mediterranean might even grumble that it was excessive. However, the nucleus Wemyss had about him undoubtedly included exceptionally able officers such as his Chief of Staff, Captain Rudolph Burmester, as well as Lieutenant-Commander John H. Godfrey who would later be the Director of Naval Intelligence at the beginning of the Second World War.[45] The ideas of the Malta Staff were not always new but the staff had the advantage that others such as Fatou and Limpus did not have, notably the authority to centralize information-gathering and to attempt to co-ordinate what had been separate and distinct commands.

Wemyss never returned to the Mediterranean to take up his command. There was a general shake up at the Admiralty and on 20 July, Sir Eric Geddes, a railway engineer who had been Director-General of Transportation on the staff of the C.-in-C. of the British armies in France and subsequently Controller of the Admiralty since May 1917, became First Lord, and as part of the reorganization appointed Wemyss Second Sea Lord on 7 August. Wemyss, who had always had the Mediterranean command as the height of his ambition, was disappointed and wrote to his friend Keyes, 'that you know, as well as I do, that personally my appointment is not a matter of congratulation'.[46] Nevertheless, it marked a rise in the fortunes of Wemyss who was raised to Deputy First Sea Lord in September and would replace Jellicoe as First Sea Lord in December. The Mediterranean went to Admiral Hon. Sir Somerset Gough-Calthorpe, second son of the seventh Baron Calthorpe, who had commanded the 2nd Cruiser Squadron earlier in the war and served as Second Sea Lord in 1916. Calthorpe seemed an odd choice for this key appointment. He is certainly not one of the names that spring to mind in any talk of naval leaders during the war and indeed to this day is relatively little known. This is hardly surprising since one officer described him, perhaps unfairly, as having 'not one ounce of magnetism'.[47] Godfrey provides one of the few extensive descriptions of him:

> Gough-Calthorpe, a most gentle, unassuming and modest man never, I am sure, sought greatness, but it was certainly thrust upon him, so much so that the British Government insisted that he should sign the armistice with Turkey, and later made him High Commissioner Constantinople and the Black Sea with Ambassadorial status. He was a man of profoundly good judgment, wise and level with a very alert twinkle in his eye.[48]

Calthorpe had some difficulty imposing his authority on the different British commands in the Mediterranean where people such as Thursby in the Aegean had got used to considerable independence, and where Ballard, SNO at Malta, found his status much diminished by the arrival of the new C.-in-C. Gibraltar, under Rear-Admiral Heathcote Grant, was a happy exception to this, but Godfrey thought that some of the subordinate rear-admirals needed to be told exactly 'where they got off'. Unfortunately Calthorpe:

> . . . was not sufficiently sure of himself – he temporised and waited. He knew what to do but was too considerate to do it. He has been described as ninety per cent wisdom and ten per cent initiative . . .
>
> Later, however, when he got his second wind and was appointed High Commissioner Turkey and the Black Sea, Admiral Gough-Calthorpe became tougher. He was a shrewd negotiator with the Turks and did not hesitate to order Maude and Allenby to halt their armies in Mesopotamia (as it was then called) and Syria.[49]

The Royal Navy was not the only one to have a change in its central leadership in the summer of 1917. There were also changes in the ministries in Italy and France. In Rome it was doubtful whether Corsi and Revel could have remained together indefinitely, especially after Revel had been able to thwart attempts to restrict the powers of the Capo di Stato Maggiore. Among other things, Revel had never forgiven Corsi for his concession in 1916 giving supreme command in the Adriatic to the French, should they ever enter with the bulk of their fleet, and sought to rescind it.[50] There had been rumours of Corsi's impending departure for a long time and the minister had indeed offered his resignation to Boselli in February. Finally, on 16 June during a Cabinet reshuffle he was replaced by Rear-Admiral Arturo Triangi, who had been Deputy Chief of Staff since March and, before that, Revel's Chief of Staff at Venice. Vice-Admiral Vittorio Cerri, C.-in-C. of the Military Maritime Department of Taranto, replaced Cutinelli-Rendina on 23 June as interim head of the fleet, subject of course to Revel's direct intervention. Triangi had actually been retired as a captain on reaching the age limit before the war, promoted to flag rank in the reserve, and then recalled on mobilization. He was obviously considered to be Revel's man but he did not last long. Unfortunately, according to various sources, the politically inexperienced Triangi put his foot in his mouth in the Chamber of Deputies when, in reply to a question from a Socialist deputy about the value of American support, he answered with astonishing frankness that such assistance appeared very problematical because of the difficulty of transport and apparently took a very gloomy view of the prospect of defeating the submarines. Triangi resigned after the subsequent outcry, ostensibly for reasons of health. He had, according to wits, 'torpedoed himself' (*auto-silurato*).[51] Boselli, with Parliament in recess, on 18 July nominated Vice-Admiral Alberto Del Bono to be minister, a nomination that was well received in the press. Del Bono had been Maritime Prefect of La Spezia at the beginning of the war and was currently Secretary-General at the Ministry of Marine. He would remain minister until the end of the war, but it was a purely representative position as the navy was really directed by Revel.[52]

Lacaze also left office in the summer of 1917. Captain Howard Kelly, the British naval liaison officer in Paris, reported that there was a growing war weariness in France following the failure of Nivelle's offensive on the western front in the spring and subsequent mutiny which affected large portions of the French army. By mid-July, Ribot, his own position eroding, allegedly wanted to jettison Lacaze whose presence in the Cabinet was offensive to the Socialist Party, and Kelly feared that he would be replaced by a Socialist and it was likely there would be more obstructionism to British proposals.[53] After more than a year and a half in office Lacaze was, perhaps inevitably, the target of considerable discontent over the submarine war. He had also quarrelled with the Commission de la Marine de Guerre, possibly because, as Ribot put it, he showed open disdain for his critics and disdain was what the Chamber of Deputies pardoned the least. On 2 August Lacaze submitted his resignation when Ribot accepted the demand by the commission for inquisitory powers.[54] He considered such an investigation to be harmful to discipline since it would involve subordinate officers testifying against their superiors in time of war, and pointed to events in Russia as an example of the fatal consequences which could follow.[55] Lacaze departed to become Préfet Maritime at Toulon. Ribot intended to replace him with Albert Thomas, a Socialist, but after the government had denied passports to Socialists who wanted to participate in the Stockholm Peace Conference the Socialists declined to enter the Cabinet and, probably to the relief of many, the more moderate Charles Chaumet, Deputy for the Gironde and a member of the Commission de la Marine de Guerre, became minister. Chaumet was described as a moderate Radical and allegedly the ministry 'had no decided objections' to him. He was only minister for a few months for, with the advent of the Clemenceau Cabinet, Georges Leygues succeeded him on 16 November. Leygues, Deputy for the Lot-et-Garonne, was going to have a long association with the navy and would be one of the most influential ministers of marine in modern French history, but his major accomplishments would not take place until after the war.[56]

Italy: The Recalcitrant Ally

In one way or another by the summer of 1917 Italy occupied, and would continue to occupy, a central role in naval affairs in the Mediterranean. There were two aspects to the problem. On the one hand, the Italians were difficult allies, particularly with Revel in full control of the navy, and co-operation and joint efforts could be troublesome given Italian aspirations in the Adriatic and in Albania. On the other hand, the Italians were the weak link in the Entente in regard to war materials, as the German naval leaders had ascertained, and there was a constant Italian demand for assistance. This, in turn, caused resentment on the part of the British and French at having to meet those persistent demands at a time when they themselves were hard pressed. The Italians undoubtedly resented their own role of always having to stand cap in hand asking for assistance, and felt that they were neither appreciated nor their needs understood. It was something of a vicious circle and it did not make Allied co-operation any easier. At the same time, the Italians were trying to play the role of a great power in the Balkans, notably in Albania, their coal situation was becoming a source of desperate anxiety. There were repeated calls to the British for aid and the Italians faced the dilemma of having to close factories or dip into naval reserves, with the knowledge that those reserves could not easily be replaced.[57]

These subjects were very much in mind in the naval portions of the inter-Allied conference held in Paris on 24–26 July. The more specific naval agreements included placing the Otranto barrage under the authority of the new British Mediterranean C.-in-C. with the area to the north of the Leuca–Fano–Corfu line under the command of the Italian C.-in-C., just as the remainder of the Mediterranean was under the command of the French C.-in-C. The Allies also agreed to draw up a list of their naval vessels in the Mediterranean to determine the number and quantity of ships which each nation would put at the disposal of the admiral commanding the Mediterranean patrols. The movable Otranto barrage, that is, the drifters, would be maintained, and the laying down of two types of fixed barrages would be continued as fast as possible. Both Jellicoe and Revel agreed on concentrating the largest possible number of aircraft at Otranto and the Allies agreed to form a base for operations against submarines at Gibraltar under Rear-Admiral Grant. They also agreed to study attacks by land and sea against enemy bases in the Adriatic and put all available means at Italy's disposal for the operation when required. The discussions with Revel, according to the Italian official history, had been harsh at times and undoubtedly contributed to the Capo di Stato Maggiore's distaste for some of his allies, notably Jellicoe. All of this would have its effect the following year when the Allies tried to establish an 'Admiralissimo' in the Mediterranean.[58]

There was another high-level, inter-Allied conference in London on 7 and 8 August which included Lloyd George, Ribot and Sonnino. The Allies accepted the British request to withdraw one division from Salonika for Palestine, although the British had to promise not to withdraw any further troops unless unexpected events occurred. The French also reserved the right to withdraw troops from Salonika, possibly for Palestine or Syria, and this, in turn, prompted the Italians to insist on the right to send troops to Palestine if the French did. If they were all implemented, those troop movements would involve substantial shipping resources. The Allies also agreed to study operations against the Austrians and to consider how they could provide more heavy guns for an Italian offensive.[59]

The British had their own internal conference devoted to the Mediterranean on 14 August. Calthorpe was present along with Rear-Admiral J. A. Fergusson, who would serve as British Admiral of Patrols, and Rear-Admiral Sydney Fremantle, who was replacing Thursby in command of the British squadron in the Aegean. There were other changes about to take place in the Mediterranean. Kerr was recalled, on Revel's suggestion, since the presence of a British rear-admiral was really superfluous with the withdrawal of the British battleships at the beginning of the year.[60] Commodore Heneage took over command of the British Adriatic Force while Captain Kelly went from the Ministry of Marine in Paris to Brindisi as commodore 2nd class commanding the British light cruisers. Finally, Ballard, SNO at Malta, reverted to the status of Admiral Superintendent of the Dockyard. The limits of the Mediterranean station were extended to include Gibraltar and as far west as the meridian of Cape Saint Vincent, and as far south as the Straits of Bab-el-Mandeb. This meant that the whole of the Red Sea was under Calthorpe's authority, with Rear-Admiral Thomas Jackson the new SNO Egypt and the Red Sea.

There was one glaring omission in Calthorpe's authority to direct anti-submarine operations. For the moment he could not direct the anti-submarine operations of the Italian naval forces.[61] This was particularly troublesome in view of the War Cabinet's decision that the conveyance of an additional 100,000 tons of coal per month to Italy was necessary at once, and that an increased tonnage of wheat would be required later on. Sir Joseph Maclay, the Shipping Controller, proposed obtaining the extra tonnage by diverting a considerable proportion of traffic going east via the Cape back to the Suez Canal route, which would economize on tonnage by greatly decreasing the time required for a round voyage to the east. Moreover, steamers heading east could also carry part cargoes of coal to Port Said which would thereby release colliers presently carrying coal to Port Said to carry coal directly to Italy. He expected that by the end of August the Admiralty would be able to supply the necessary protection, implying the formation of convoys. This was a big expectation, for most navigation in the Mediterranean to date was by coastal routes with convoys limited to the east where this was not possible, for example, on the Malta–Suda route. According to Jellicoe, an analysis of the present Mediterranean streamline traffic showed that approximately 372 convoy and escort vessels were required for protection of trade on the main routes, but there were only 212 available, leaving a deficiency of 160. Moreover, this did not take into account convoying the large number of troop transports and other special vessels requiring safe protection. Maclay's proposal would mean, including return journeys, an extra ten vessels always at sea on the Italian route and an extra fifty on the Port Said route. Jellicoe, under present conditions, could not give any undertaking that they could provide an escort with the resources available.

The Italians were a potential source of assistance since Jellicoe considered that their destroyer forces in the Adriatic were more than adequate for strategical requirements. Revel was likely to think otherwise and Jellicoe was realistic enough to admit it was improbable that the Italians would consent to release any destroyers for general convoy work since they had continually pressed the British for four additional destroyers for the Otranto barrage. Geddes now tended to see the Italians as the villains, and was annoyed enough to point out that since the additional convoy requirements were almost entirely due to the supply of coal to Italy, the latter was directly interested in giving additional assistance. The problem remained, however: where could the extra escort vessels come from since the shortage existed everywhere and the vessels could not be withdrawn from the Atlantic for the Mediterranean? Increasing the size of convoys was a potential solution but the Admiralty did not consider it practical and claimed, according to Italian experience, that there was a greater risk to large convoys in the Mediterranean than in the Atlantic. This taboo against convoys of more than a few ships took a long time to overcome. Moreover, the British also considered the entire Mediterranean to be a danger area, unlike the Atlantic where only about 350 miles required special protection to get convoys safely in.[62]

Calthorpe would not find Revel and the Italians easy to deal with on the question of contributing vessels to the common pool, but he had the means to exert pressure when he met with Revel in Rome on 22 August. He announced that the Admiralty desired a large destroyer escort to assure the protection of steamers going by convoy from Gibraltar to Genoa and had suspended the loading of steamers destined for Italy while they awaited the result of these talks. This pressure worked and the talks were satisfactory, up to a point. Revel agreed to detach four Italian destroyers to escort the first convoy of four or more steamers leaving Gibraltar for Italy, but he made it clear to Calthorpe that the necessities of the naval war in the Adriatic and the obligation to protect Italian national traffic abroad and in the Tyrrhenian, as well as ships proceeding from Italy to Albania, Salonika and Libya, prevented him from making any formal engagement to provide similar escorts for future convoys from Gibraltar. He asked for support from British and Japanese destroyers. Revel also asked Sonnino to make diplomatic approaches to the Japanese about providing direct assistance to the Italians just as they did for the British and, while conceding that Calthorpe had shown good will and was cognizant of Italian difficulties, the British government itself had to be made aware of those problems and not start out with a curt threat to suspend supplies to Italy if they did not get destroyers. Revel warned Calthorpe that if shipments of coal ceased he would be forced to suspend naval operations, and even now he was forced to limit operations to those strictly necessary to protect traffic.[63] These efforts by the British to link shipments of supplies to adequate defence in terms of Italian escorts were a polite form of blackmail and they had their effect. Riccardo Bianchi, Minister of Transport, after similar talks with a British representative from the Ministry of Shipping, begged the Prime Minister to intervene with the navy to satisfy the British requirements.[64]

The participation of the United States in the war was about to assume more concrete form in the Mediterranean area. On 18 August the scout cruiser *Birmingham*, flagship of the Patrol Force of the US Atlantic Fleet, arrived at Gibraltar flying the flag of Rear-Admiral Wilson. The US Navy Department had been strongly impressed with the necessity for adequate anti-submarine efforts at the entrance to Gibraltar and made the light cruisers *Birmingham*, *Chester*, *Salem* and seven older gunboats available. The cruisers would initially work on the Atlantic side of Gibraltar and the situation was a bit murky if US forces encountered an Austrian submarine since the United States was not yet at war with the Dual Monarchy. Nevertheless, this was the beginning of the American effort in the Mediterranean for those old gunboats would eventually work on the eastern side of Gibraltar. Furthermore, the Americans also had five old destroyers *en route* to Gibraltar from the Philippines via the Suez Canal.[65]

Admiral Mayo, C.-in-C. of the US Atlantic Fleet, was in London at the beginning of September and on the 4th and 5th another conference took place to discuss how the US Navy could most effectively participate in operations. The Italians had their own ideas on this. Revel and Del Bono, acting on press reports that the Americans were building a large air fleet, wanted part of it diverted to Italian use.[66] Revel was particularly attracted to aircraft and air raids on Austrian submarine bases as a means, and a relatively cheap one at that, to break the deadlock in the Adriatic. The Italian ambassador and naval attaché in the United States did manage to get a promise out of Admiral Benson, Chief of Naval Operations, that those five destroyers *en route* to Gibraltar from the Philippines might participate in escorting convoys from Gibraltar to Genoa or Naples. The Italian agenda for the forthcoming conference with Admiral Mayo was therefore simple. Revel sent his Sub-Chief of Staff, Vice-Admiral Cusani Visconti, with orders to ask for American support in the destruction of Austrian naval bases, and that the US government should expedite deliveries of motor-boats and other material ordered in the United States. To get around the argument that the United States was not at war with Austria-Hungary, Revel proposed that the United States give the percentage of light craft it would have assigned to Italy if it was at war with the Austrians to the British so that the latter could then transfer a corresponding number of destroyers to the Adriatic. It was an ingenious solution, but Revel also asked Sonnino for diplomatic efforts to end the awkward situation by having the United States declare war on Austria.[67]

The London Conference with the Americans opened on 4 September. Mediterranean affairs occupied only a small portion of the time but the question of introducing a Mediterranean convoy system was probably one of the more important issues discussed. Rear-Admiral Duff, now Assistant Chief of Naval Staff, pointed out that no organized convoy system yet existed in the Mediterranean as a whole and present convoy arrangements were disconnected and local. There was, for example, no direct convoy from Gibraltar to Alexandria. Duff proposed a number of regular convoy routes. Predictably, Cusani was adamant against changing the existing Italian coastal system where he maintained losses were relatively low. This argument was not really very relevant for the rest of the Mediterranean and the pressing need to get coal to Italian waters or economize on shipping by diverting it from the Cape route. A subcommittee, on which the United States did not wish to be represented, met with Admiral Duff on the issue and established a series of recommendations subsequently approved by the conference.

The conference recommended certain convoy routes in order of priority. They were: (1) Gibraltar–Genoa; (2) Gibraltar–Bizerte; (3) Bizerte–Port Said; (4) Marseilles–Bizerte; (5) Marseilles–Algiers; (6) Malta–Suda Bay; (7) Naples–Bizerte; (8) Malta–Taranto; and (9) Oran–Gibraltar. The order of precedence indicates that convoys to Genoa for the supply of coal to Italy had the highest priority followed by through convoys to Egypt via Bizerte, as well as convoys between France and its North African possessions; while convoys to southern Italian ports were given relatively less importance. On the other hand, the conference was careful to specify that these routes included mainline traffic only, and that coastal traffic could continue as at present. This was obviously a sop to the Italians. Captain Lovatelli, the Italian member of the subcommittee, had also pushed Revel's argument in favour of maintaining the Spanish coastal route since there were not enough escorts for both the coastal route and direct ocean convoy between Gibraltar and Genoa. Duff objected to the Spanish coastal route since it took twice as long (as much as thirteen days compared to four to six for a direct convoy) and might therefore prevent sufficient tonnage being sent to Italy. The Italians were firm on this point, however, because it was the safer route and the question was left to the Malta Commission. The subcommittee also ventured into tactical details, recommending that for convoys of twelve or more ships the escort should be at least six and preferably eight, and that for convoys of four to twelve ships the escort should be at least four and preferably six. These recommendations are interesting for they indicate that the Allies were finally moving away from the idea that a convoy could not number more than a handful of ships.[68]

The question of the Otranto barrage produced some heat when the British announced that they would shortly commence laying their portion of a trial fixed barrage and asked for a permanent destroyer patrol to protect the drifters so that they could be kept out constantly until a fixed barrage was established. Cusani insisted that regular patrols were too dangerous and pointed out that the Italians had already lost a destroyer on this service. Jellicoe depreciated the danger for it had not been the British experience, particularly at night. Geddes once again was indignant that the driftermen were being sent out as 'live bait' for the Austrians because the Italians would not risk warships. Cusani had no authority to promise destroyers and there was no agreement. There were also few operations that the Allies could realistically propose for the Adriatic.[69]

Cusani naturally brought up the subject of American assistance, mentioning the delays in obtaining material and motor-boats ordered in the

United States and asking Admiral Mayo's assistance in overcoming them. The main Italian requirements included around 15,000 tons of steel plate, 50 motor-boats for anti-submarine work and around 96 engines. Mayo could not himself comment beyond promising to pass on the request and suggest that the Italians approach the United States government through the usual channels, that is, their diplomatic representatives in Washington which, of course, they had already done. Cusani also brought up the more ticklish question of American destroyers and here Jellicoe did promise that if the situation permitted and if more American destroyers were sent to work in British waters or the Altantic one of the first things that the Admiralty would do would be to reinforce the Mediterranean.[70] This was an important point for the Italians but, of course, at this stage every promise was preceded by that very big little word 'if'. Nevertheless, when the London Conference ended the Allies had taken a long step towards implementation of a real convoy system in the Mediterranean. What remained to be seen, however, was how successful Calthorpe and the Malta Commission would be in turning these general recommendations into concrete facts and, above all, would they be able to get the necessary escorts?

Calthorpe had left a memorandum with Revel when he passed through Rome on the way to take up his command giving a broad survey of his views concerning the Mediterranean situation and stressing the need for 'pooling' Allied resources to make the proposed convoy system effective. The situation was rendered particularly acute by the necessity of supplying Italy with more coal and the British would be willing to risk larger and more valuable cargo vessels if reasonable protection could be given them. Calthorpe asked what additional assistance Italy could give to the common cause. He understood Revel's difficulties in transferring any torpedo craft from the Adriatic and suggested that Italy could assist Allied anti-submarine operations by intensifying its offensive measures with destroyers, submarines and aircraft in the lower Adriatic, strengthening the protection of the drifters in the Straits of Otranto so they could be more effective in stopping submarines, and assisting in the convoying of British ships from Gibraltar to Genoa with a few destroyers drawn from Italy's forces on its west coast.[71]

Revel replied formally in a memorandum of 3 September giving the Italian point of view. He made some good points and his argument is, in any case, something more than an example of naval *sacro egoismo*, although to what degree is a matter of opinion. Revel considered present methods of anti-submarine warfare were ineffective, for surface craft were not really a means for offensive action against submarines and merely served to warn them, and an enormous force was uselessly employed for this purpose which might be more profitably applied in other directions. Surface craft were essentially defensive measures, as with convoy escorts, but not an effective means of destroying submarines. Submarines really had to be fought under water, but not by Allied submarines for that would be a case of two blind men fighting. The only other underwater weapon would be fixed nets and mines established in areas where the submarine's freedom of movement was somewhat restricted, notably at the entrance to the Adriatic and in the Straits of Gibraltar. Revel put as much stress on the latter as the former for he claimed, incorrectly, that the newer, long-range German submarines worked in the Mediterranean from their bases in the North Sea. A truly effective barrage at the Straits of Otranto would free a large force of drifters and patrol craft for more useful work escorting convoys and the number that would have to remain to protect the fixed net barrage would then be doing effective service thereby justifying their protection by destroyers. Revel used a telling phrase in what was an apparent justification of the Italian refusal to provide a regular destroyer patrol to protect the drifter line. At present 'the destroyers only protect the drifter, i.e., a unit that has no value because the drifter defends a system which as a matter of fact does not yet exist'. Therefore employment of destroyers to protect drifters was not rational because potential losses were not compensated for by potential advantages since the drifters in the Straits of Otranto were, at the moment, absolutely incapable of preventing the free passage of enemy submarines. Revel also justified his reluctance to divert Italian escorts from the protection of coastal traffic to the Gibraltar convoys. Geography had a certain amount to do with it. Supplies for Italy arrived at relatively few ports such as Genoa, Leghorn and Naples where rapid unloading was possible. The Italians then had to distribute those supplies to the various points of the Italian peninsula which was difficult due to geography. The normal means of distribution would be accomplished relatively easily by rail, but owing to the shortage of coal three-fourths of the trains had been taken out of service and those still running burned partially wood and partially coal drawn from Italian naval reserves. Unfortunately, there were not enough trains left running to ensure the distribution of important supplies. Consequently, the Italians had to make use of ships and the coastal route to distribute foodstuffs to small secondary ports along the long Italian coastline for final distribution to the interior. Unfortunately, they could not use small steamers because of the lack of coal and therefore had to make extensive use of sail. However, as Revel put it, the wind does not blow when it should, and the uncertainty of the wind meant that sailing craft had to follow routes that were not always the safest, and these craft which were such a vital element in the distribution of food had to be protected just as much as larger steamers. Italy's problem of defending trade therefore did not end when a large ship reached Genoa, for it was even more difficult to defend traffic between the large and small Italian ports. Consequently, Revel found it impossible to diminish the means he had to defend this traffic in the Tyrrhenian. He complained, 'It is often believed that Italy has little inclination to support with all her forces the general interests of the Entente. In truth, however, one must needs say [*sic*] that the Italian problem and its grave difficulties, which have to be faced, have never been thoroughly studied by our Allies and hence they are completely ignored.' Revel also favoured gradual substitution of the drifters and small surface craft on patrol by aircraft, intensified air raids on enemy bases, the development of a system of hydrophones at the same time as the fixed net barrage was laid and, after the latter had been installed and submarines could not get out, the concentration of torpedo craft, motor-boats and other light forces now scattered all over the Mediterranean for an intensified search for, and destruction of, submarines in a limited zone.[72]

Revel had made a good case for the Italians for even if their methods and arguments were not always accepted it could also be said that their problems were not always appreciated. The reluctance to detach forces from the Tyrrhenian might have been justified, given the need to protect the vital coastal trade, but the Allies could make a counter-argument that the Italian destroyer forces in the Adriatic were excessive. Moreover, Revel made an erroneous assertion which the Naval Intelligence Division at the Admiralty were quick to point out. German submarines did not normally work in the Mediterranean from their bases in the north, and while a submarine based in the Adriatic might occasionally cruise in the Atlantic for a short period of time, the amount of German submarine traffic through the Straits of Gibraltar was very small compared with the traffic through the Straits of Otranto. Thus it certainly would not justify the enormous expense and effort that would have been necessary to master the formidable technical obstacles facing the establishment of a barrage.[73] Calthorpe diplomatically limited himself to acknowledging Revel's 'admirable' summary and agreeing with his desire to strengthen Adriatic anti-submarine defences, and promised to take up the question of similar measures at Gibraltar when the material was available. But Calthorpe defended using the drifters and in the interval between then and the time the fixed barrage was completed, he thought that they could be usefully employed in hampering submarines, and gaining sea experience and training in the use of hydrophones.[74]

Revel was sensitive to criticism at home about the defence of traffic and this must have contributed to his reluctance to detach forces from the Tyrrhenian. He reacted sharply when Bianchi, the Minister of Transport, brought to the Prime Minister both foreign and domestic criticism about the ineffective surveillance of the Italian coasts, particularly Liguria and eastern Sicily, where submarines seemed to be sinking ships carrying important cargoes with impunity after those same ships had already made long passages through waters supposedly infested with submarines. Revel termed the reports malicious and tendentious falsehoods and expressed surprise that a person as highly placed in the technical and political field as Bianchi had repeated them. He asked Del Bono, for the honour of the navy, to use an opportune moment to refute the rumours which were assuming the form of a real anti-patriotic and defamatory campaign. Revel then proceeded to cite statistics from the Ispettorato della Difesa Traffico which showed that in terms of ships which were either Italian, Allied, or neutrals acting on Italy's account, 36 ships representing 86,441 tons had been sunk in waters under Italian jurisdiction since the beginning of hostilities, while 173 ships representing 542,700 tons were sunk in waters outside Italian jurisdiction. Moreover, since the institution of the Ispettorato della Difesa Traffico they had convoyed 701 steamers to date on the Gibraltar–Genoa route and only 1 had been torpedoed and 1 sunk by a mine. Revel concluded that if one could judge the goodness of the method by the results, the Italian system of defending traffic was up until now the best among the Allies.[75] What Revel did not mention, however, was that these statistics might have been misleading since the Italian zones were relatively small compared with the others and essentially limited to the Tyrrhenian, Adriatic (where there was little traffic), Libyan coast and waters around Italy. The voyage from Gibraltar to Genoa took place mostly through waters which were either neutral Spanish or under French or British control.

The British thrashed out the problem of getting coal to Italy at a special conference held on 14 September under the presidency of Lord Milner and the Shipping Controller, and Admiralty representatives who were present concluded that if the Italians could provide eleven destroyers the British could provide approximately fifteen to twenty liners at Gibraltar approximately every fourteen days. These ships would be diverted from the Cape route and would have to be escorted to Genoa and then on to Malta, where the Admiralty would pick them up in the through convoy between Gibraltar and Port Said. The ships would then go on to the East to pick up commodities such as sugar for the return voyage. The British aimed at sending 700,000 tons of coal to Italy per month, including shipments from the United States of 60,000–70,000 tons, and had shipped 690,000 tons in August, but would only be able to send 460,000 tons in September.[76] The Italians would therefore be given the same choice which Calthorpe had recently posed – if coal deliveries were wanted, destroyers would have to be provided for the common pool.

Revel still opposed providing the eleven destroyers, for they would have to be larger ones and the new type could only be taken from Venice which would 'leave him at the mercy of Austria'. He also assumed that the Italian destroyers would be required for the Malta–Port Said route which would take them far from their bases. Both Revel and the admiral commanding the Ispettorato della Difesa Traffico reaffirmed their opinion that ships bound for Genoa should go unescorted, hugging the Spanish coast within territorial waters, for there had been no losses within the three-mile limit. The admiral commanding traffic defence privately suggested that since the British did not share these views it might be possible to come to some arrangement whereby all convoys were sent to Bizerte, where ships bound for Port Said could proceed as usual and those bound for Italy could be met by Italian destroyers and escorted to Naples and then follow the Italian coastal route to Genoa, or else proceed directly to Genoa from Bizerte.[77]

The 'eleven Italian destroyers' were the controversy of autumn 1917. Revel's basic argument against providing them, for which he again enlisted Sonnino's diplomatic support on 24 September, revolved around the fact that he had only forty destroyers, twenty-one of them antiquated and worn-out by long use, to fulfil the multiple obligations from the Tyrrhenian to the Adriatic, or the protection of communications to Libya and Albania. The 11 destroyers requested by the British therefore represented more than a quarter of their already insufficient strength, and the request came from the most powerful maritime nation in the world who had, Revel claimed, more than 375 destroyers, reinforced by American and Japanese craft. Moreover, the Italians had to be prudent and conserve their light craft because of the difficulty of making rapid repairs and the slowness of Italian yards caused by the lack of raw material. The repair of damaged vessels was therefore very uncertain, ships were wearing out from hard use and it appeared impossible in the future to fill gaps caused by losses through new construction. If they detached those eleven destroyers to distant waters they would not be able to meet their obligations in home waters. Revel shared the idea that the Italian flag ought to be represented, even in a reduced measure, in all operations by land, sea, or air so as to avoid the pretext of Italian absenteeism being used as an excuse to evade Italy's legitimate aspirations. However, it seemed to him that, in the naval field, the Italians had already contributed a great deal by facing the entire Austrian fleet alone while assuring imports which enabled Italy to continue the struggle which otherwise it would be forced to cease through exhaustion, thereby depriving the Entente of the Italian contribution which did not always seem to be appreciated. The British provided for their own interests in the north and they could also provide for their interests in the Mediterranean by detaching a small quantity of their light forces from home.[78]

There was another point on which Revel and the Italians felt badly used. The convoys between Gibraltar and Britain were initially only in a northbound direction. Ships carrying supplies to Britain were therefore protected. On the other hand, ships proceeding from Britain to Gibraltar, including those carrying vital supplies to Italy, were allowed to sail alone and without any protection. The Italians resented this and made a request through diplomatic channels for regular convoys between Britain and Italy. This implication that there was some sort of Machiavellian intent on the part of the British to neglect Italian interests was patently absurd since obviously any ship sunk on the outward journey would be unable to bring supplies back to Britain. But, right or wrong, it was indicative of the Italians' attitude and stiffened their resistance to what they considered to be unfair demands. That resistance, in turn, seemed like selfish egoism to their Allies. These attitudes would be deeply ingrained by the end of the war. This particular problem fortunately had been corrected by the time the Italian note reached London. Starting in mid-August all ships employed in the Italian coal trade had been convoyed from British ports clear of the immediate submarine danger zone, following which the convoy was dispersed and ships proceeded independently to Gibraltar. By early October, twenty-eight Italian ships had been included in these convoys and had received the same protection as British ships. Moreover, through convoys to Gibraltar had been approved and commenced by mid-October. These convoys would also be escorted through the danger zone west of Gibraltar and in the future no ships would sail independently.[79]

The British were equally unimpressed when they eventually got a translation of Revel's memorandum of 24 September justifying the refusal to provide the eleven destroyers. The Admiralty considered it to be a repetition of the arguments which they had already heard including the fallacy that the Italians faced the Austrian fleet alone. This completely ignored the presence of the French fleet at Corfu and French destroyers at

Brindisi, as well as the two British monitors in the Adriatic. The French had looked after the Adriatic without any British assistance before Italy had entered the war and British warships were protecting Italian shipping all over the world.[80]

The Japanese and Americans inadvertently provided Revel and the Italians with a way out of the impasse. On 4 September the Japanese naval attaché in Rome reported that Rear-Admiral Sato's force at Malta had just been reinforced and he would therefore be very happy to escort from time to time Italian warships or transports as he had been doing for the British and French. Revel immediately ordered the Italian naval delegate at Malta to ask Rear-Admiral Sato to assign a congruous number of Italian destroyers to the Italian C.-in-C. at Taranto for escort service. Sato politely refused, for this procedure would spoil the Japanese system of command and might cause trouble in the future if the French or British were to ask for a similar detachment. All Japanese forces in the Mediterranean had to be kept together under Rear-Admiral Sato's direct command, but if he were asked by the Italian authorities for a Japanese destroyer escort he would be pleased to detach them for such duty, assuming that he had some destroyers available and the convoy was a suitable one for destroyer escort.[81] While not quite what the Italians had in mind, it was nevertheless encouraging for, in reply to a request for Japanese co-operation in the Adriatic, the Japanese naval attaché in London had just been advised by his government that the most modern available units had already been sent to the Mediterranean and that the Japanese would find it difficult to send more since the US Navy had transferred the bulk of its naval forces to the Atlantic leaving the Japanese to provide for the Pacific. At the same time, Revel learned through the Italian chargé d'affaires in London that the Italians were mistaken in thinking that the British wanted those eleven destroyers for service between Gibraltar and Egypt. The British intended to use the destroyers in question to protect the grain and coal transports between Gibraltar and Genoa. Revel also learned from the British ambassador that the destroyers would only be used a few days for the convoys and only three times in two months. This put a different light on the picture for the Capo di Stato Maggiore, or as he put it, the British point of view had changed completely. Despite what he termed the grave inconveniences to the Italian organization, he would be able to assist the supply of Italy by temporarily assigning escorts for grain and coal convoys from Gibraltar to Genoa. He needed at least a fortnight's advance notice of the arrival of a convoy at Gibraltar so that he could get an adequate escort there in time. Moreover, to alleviate the Italian burden he asked Sonnino to approach the American and Japanese ambassadors about Sato's offer of Japanese destroyers and Benson's remarks that the five American destroyers from the Philippines might help escort convoys to Genoa.[82] In short, the Italians would now provide limited assistance to the British and expected Japanese and American assistance in return.

The Italian naval attaché in London wanted a reply to Revel's proposals as quickly as possible, but the Admiralty thought that the Italians were under some misapprehension about the American and Japanese destroyers. All available Japanese and American warships were already employed on escort work where Italian ships received the same protection as British merchantmen. Admiral Sato, although not formally under British orders, worked in consultation with the British C.-in-C. and any arrangement for the employment of Japanese destroyers would be made through Calthorpe. The five American destroyers from the Philippines which had just arrived were under the orders of the SNO, Gibraltar, and the Admiralty was not clear which American authority had promised anything to the Italians, but surmised it must have been only a vague statement.[83] The American authority was, of course, Admiral Benson, Chief of Naval Operations, who had made the statement to the Italian naval attaché in Washington just before the five destroyers reached Port Said. Benson left open the prospect of diverting them to the Italian coast and told Vice-Admiral Sims, 'Should action be taken by a break with Austria I think undoubtedly we would sent the five destroyers to the Adriatic'.[84]

All this intervention by diplomats and naval attachés was apt to cause trouble and Vice-Admiral Sims, commanding US Naval Forces in European waters, recommended referring all requests on the distribution of forces, however plausible they might be, through him. Sims, after discussion with the British and French, wanted the five American destroyers at Gibraltar to take part in the extension of the convoy system to the Mediterranean. They had to accept the risk that one of their ships would come into contact with an Austrian submarine, although everyone realized that 'we are actually, though not technically, at war with Austria', and Sims hoped that the situation would be cleared up soon so they would have greater liberty of action.[85] Sims could not have known it but the risk of meeting an Austrian submarine in the western Mediterranean was virtually nil and, by this time, they would not even encounter a German submarine masquerading under Austrian colours.

The Foreign Office thought that it was desirable for the Admiralty to accept the latest Italian offer although Jellicoe was adamant that they could not give up any Japanese or American destroyers in the Mediterranean. Wemyss conferred with Sims's Chief of Staff and the Japanese naval attaché and they confirmed the British viewpoint. All British, French, American and Japanese torpedo craft available in the Mediterranean were used for escorting convoys of Allied merchantmen of *all* Allied nations. Wemyss recommended, therefore, that in accepting the Italian offer as better than nothing they should make it clear to the Italians that the Gibraltar–Genoa convoys which Italian destroyers would escort must include other Allied merchantmen and not merely those carrying wheat and coal to Italy.[86]

In fairness to the Italians, it should be pointed out that the statements of Benson and Sato, probably meant as general civilities, caused a certain amount of misunderstanding and had both men been fully aware of the situation between Italy and its Allies they might have been a bit more reticent. Moreover, Rear-Admiral Wilson, commander of the US Patrol Force at Gibraltar, muddied the waters still more with some loose talk to Lieutenant Romanelli, head of the Italian naval office at Gibraltar, about the US Navy having gunboats which would be useful in escorting Gibraltar–Genoa convoys, and how he (Wilson) would not be adverse to sending the two Chester-class light cruisers to the Adriatic whenever the Italian Minister of Marine asked. Revel was interested, but admitted that he was quite aware Calthorpe was responsible for co-ordinating the use of Allied anti-submarine forces on the main traffic line. Nevertheless, the vital importance of the Gibraltar–Genoa route for Italy obliged them to consider its protection from a strictly national point of view. This, of course, meant the Capo di Stato Maggiore thought they would be justified in seeking to outflank the British and French in obtaining American aid. Sims was certainly wise to have recommended all requests for such assistance be funnelled through him. The Italians made the expected request in Washington only to be told to discuss the question with Benson who was on his way to Europe for an inter-Allied conference to take place in Paris.[87] At the very least, Rear-Admiral Wilson's remarks were unauthorized.

The official British reply to Revel's offer of limited assistance was delayed for a long time for it was overtaken by events. While the papers were circulating at the Admiralty, the Austro-German offensive and breakthrough at Caporetto took place and the British did not think it likely that the Italians would adhere to their offer. The Italians themselves eventually repeated the offer in late November when the front in Italy had been stabilized, and the British gave their conditional acceptance. The US Navy Department arranged for a convoy of twenty-three merchant ships bound for Italy to leave Hampton Roads on 5 December and to arrive at Gibraltar around the 23rd, with the Italian naval authorities providing a special escort of eight destroyers.[88]

The five American destroyers from the Philippines and now at Gibraltar which had been the subject of so much comment were not all that impressive. They were the oldest destroyers in the US Navy, the Bainbridge class, and were all 16 to 17 years old, only 420 tons and had no guns heavier than 13-pdrs (3-in.). They were in no way comparable to the modern destroyers that the United States sent to the British in the north. They and the gunboats at Gibraltar, the latter even more ancient, were not employed initially eastwards of Gibraltar. The light cruisers *Birmingham*, *Chester* and *Salem* were also not suitable for patrol work or escorting a slow convoy in the danger zone, and Rear-Admiral Grant, the SNO at Gibraltar, intended to use them for ocean escort work. Grant's most urgent plea, like that of everyone, was for at least four more destroyers for offensive patrols. He was told, however, that destroyers could not be sent until the large requirements for convoy escort had been met.[89]

The Mediterranean Convoy System

Calthorpe's printed instructions for patrol commanders and shipping control officers, dated 18 September, contained the statement: 'On all open sea routes Merchants Ships voyaging in the Mediterranean should be protected by being sailed in convoys, provided with suitable escort.' The scale of escorts was laid down at one escort for a convoy of two ships, two escorts for a convoy of three to four ships, three escorts for five to six ships and four escorts for convoys over eight ships, with a limit of twelve ships per convoy for the present. These were recommendations only, and officers had to use their discretion about sending convoys off if the requisite number of escorts was not available, but delays incurred in collecting ships to form convoys were of little importance compared with considerations of safe voyage. For purposes of the scale of escorts, two trawlers were considered to equal one 'escort'. Troop transports required special protection and when actually carrying troops never more than two sailed together and only then if of similar speed. Whenever possible, escorts for troop transports should be able to remove all troops if the transport was sunk. Oilers, munition ships, cable ships and important merchant ships, such as empty troop transports or P & O liners, would receive preferential treatment over ordinary mercantile traffic in regard to escorts and varying degrees of special protection.[90] This was, at least, the ideal.

The reality of the Mediterranean situation belied the broad promises or statements of the inter-Allied conferences or the Mediterranean Staff at Malta, and the convoy system did not spring into existence overnight. In September the British established shipping control officers in different Mediterranean ports with orders to provide Malta with information, collect ships for convoys and expedite discharge of cargo. The British vessels suitable for escort work were reallocated and redeployed in October between the Aegean, Malta, Egypt and Gibraltar, and the convoy systems began that month. The so-called streamline convoys under British control were Bizerte–Alexandria (every five days) and Bizerte–Malta–Milo (every five days), while the British and French ran the Milo–Alexandria convoy (every four days). The French escorted a Marseilles–Bizerte fast convoy (twice a week), Marseilles–Bizerte slow convoy (twice a week), Marseilles–Algiers fast convoy (twice a week) and Marseilles–Algiers slow convoy (three times a week), as well as a Bizerte–Corfu convoy to supply the fleet. Initially, there was no convoy along the Algerian coast. The British, later joined by the Americans, escorted small convoys from Gibraltar to Oran and ships then trusted to French surface and air patrols and ports of refuge until they reached Bizerte. The Allies also continued to use the Spanish coastal route between Gibraltar and French and Italian Mediterranean ports, but this route became controversial as the year drew to a close. The British later added streamline convoys between Gibraltar–Genoa and Alexandria–Port Said, while the Milo–Alexandria convoy was shifted to Milo–Port Said. Whenever a ship had to discharge at a port not on the convoy route, it would join a convoy to the port closest to its destination and then wait for an escort, if available, or make the final journey during the night, sheltering in a protected harbour during daylight hours.[91]

The introduction of through convoys between Port Said and Britain was a major improvement in the Mediterranean system. On 15 October the Admiralty asked Calthorpe if he was ready for the diversion of the Indian trade for Britain from the Cape route to the Suez Canal, with vessels detained at Port Said for a through convoy to Gibraltar and Britain. At the time, the Admiralty estimated that this would be about eight to ten vessels per week. The savings in tonnage by the elimination of the long voyage around the Cape was obvious. Calthorpe replied that he was ready and, for the economical working of escorts, sailings from Port Said would be governed by the dates of sailings from Gibraltar, and the number of convoys to east and west had to be identical with sailings from Britain and Port Said at intervals of sixteen days. These OE (Outward East) and HE (Homeward East) convoys were comparatively large, sixteen to twenty vessels, and the route was arranged so that the convoy would pass through the narrow waters between Cape Bon and Sicily at night. Careful co-ordination was also necessary to ensure that there would be escorts for the danger area which extended 200 miles west of Gibraltar. Moreover, virtually no escort craft could carry sufficient coal to steam from Gibraltar to Port Said without refuelling and a complete relief of escorts for each OE and HE convoy took place when they passed Malta. With convoys at sixteen-day intervals, the British had to have three escort groups of five fast ships exclusively detailed for the OE–HE service. Refits, breakdowns and the necessity for boiler-cleaning meant that the number of escorts had to be much larger than fifteen and the system of through convoys therefore absorbed a considerable portion of escort strength. All ships included in OE and HE convoys had to be capable of maintaining a speed of at least 10 knots and slow ships which were not capable of at least 7 knots could not join any convoy and had to sail unescorted or use coastal waters.[92]

The convoy system was later extended with a Gibraltar–Genoa (direct) route every four days, a Gibraltar–Bizerte convoy (every four days) co-ordinated with a Bizerte–Alexandria route (every four days), and an Alexandria–Port Said route (every four days). There was also a Bizerte–Malta–Milo convoy (every five days) co-ordinated with a Milo-Port Said convoy (every five days). These were streamline convoys. There were also a number of small local convoys which developed in the Mediterranean by the end of the year. The British ran a Port Said–Palestine route and Oran–Gibraltar route and, along with the French, ran a Port Said–Cyprus (Famagusta) convoy. The French had a Milo–Salonika route and eventually an Oran–Algiers convoy as well as an Oran–Cape Palos route for ships making for Marseilles and adjacent ports via Spanish territorial waters. The Italians, for their part, ran a convoy between Bizerte and Palermo.

Troop transports were an additional and heavy responsibility because of the potential for loss of life in the event of disaster. The normal method of transporting troops was a special convoy of four to five fast ships between Taranto and Port Said at fifteen-day intervals, or two large fast transports with an escort of two destroyers between Taranto and Itea (in the Gulf of Corinth) at weekly intervals. The Japanese were largely responsible for escorting troopships, in fact the postwar study by the Mediterranean Staff concluded that without the assistance of the Japanese forces 'the situation would have been impossible'. In the autumn of 1917 the threat of a Russian collapse freeing German and Turkish troops for an offensive in Mesopotamia or Macedonia raised the possibility that the British would have to move large numbers of troops from one theatre to another. This threatened to disrupt all escort arrangements. However, special emergency movements, as well as congestion on the Italian railways, sometimes necessitated transports running between Marseilles and Alexandria, which was an additional burden on the escort forces since many destroyers could not proceed from Marseilles to Alexandria without refuelling and had to be relieved at Malta.[93]

It took a great deal of effort to make this system work, particularly the not always successful attempt to co-ordinate sailings and to avoid excessive delay, one of the major objections to the convoy system. The problem was frequently complex and there were inevitable mistakes. Both the French and British archives contain numerous horror stories of ships taking an inordinate amount of time for a voyage due to having to wait for a convoy or to follow an indirect route. There was also the heartbreaking problem of a large fast ship being forced to travel with a much slower convoy, thereby increasing its exposure to danger and naturally wasting tonnage. There is no space in a study of this scope to go into these problems in detail and it can only be said that, as so often happens, it was far easier to say what should or should not be done than to actually do it.

Inter-Allied co-operation also seemed far more complete in those grand resolutions at the conferences than it actually was in practice. The Commission de Malte met regularly with Calthorpe presiding over Rear-Admiral Fergusson, the British Admiral of Patrols, and his French counterpart Rear-Admiral Fatou (replaced in November by Capitaine de vaisseau [later Rear-Admiral] Ratyé), the Italian delegate Capitano di vascello Como and Rear-Admiral Sato. They had useful discussions but the Italian delegate was little more than a liaison officer who always had to refer back to Rome when matters concerning Italy were mentioned. This did not prevent him from making a very useful suggestion regarding escorts, however. Since escorts could not prevent a submerged submarine from attacking a convoy, they ought to be deployed so as to enable them to make an immediate and concerted attack as soon as a submarine made its presence known. This suggestion interested the Admiralty and, of course, was recognition that the convoy was not a strictly 'defensive' measure but had 'offensive' attributes as well, in that it attracted submarines to where they could be attacked and destroyed.[94] The participation of Italian escorts in the general system remained, for the most part, limited or relatively irregular, as on the Gibraltar–Genoa route. The Italians were basically concerned with their coastal waters, although they participated in escorts on other routes or ran their own convoys from time to time. The 'pool' of resources that the delegates at the inter-Allied conferences had spoken of never really materialized. While there could be some mixing of escorts at times, particularly on the Gibraltar–Genoa run, the French and British tended to run their own separate convoys and, of course, had distinctly different interests. The French were concerned with communications with their North African possessions while the British were primarily concerned with communications to and from Egypt.

At the end of the year the authority of the French delegate at Malta was also considerably reduced when the Ministry of Marine transferred control of patrols in the western Mediterranean to the prefects of Provence, Algeria and Tunisia. The ministerial decree of 30 December was based on the recommendation of Rear-Admiral Salaun, head of the DGGSM, and was supposed to enhance unity of local command by ending the division of authority between control of the major routes out at sea and control over the extensive coastal routes of North Africa and Provence. It also followed in the wake of an earlier decree placing the patrol divisions of the Channel and Atlantic coasts under the local maritime prefects. Ratyé was now merely the French Delegate-General of the Mediterranean routes rather than an Admiral of Patrols, for authority over French patrols in the eastern Mediterranean went directly to Gauchet, the C.-in-C. Gauchet was surprised by the decree and interpreted the failure of the minister to consult him as a lack of confidence. Leygues and de Bon smoothed his ruffled feathers by pointing out that the whole organization was, in theory, under his authority and that his distance from Paris did not always permit full consultation. The adoption of the new organization was imposed more rapidly than anticipated by the influence of public opinion and France's Allies because of numerous sinkings along the Algerian and Tunisian coast, and its principal purpose was to establish a closer liaison between the different authorities responsible for the protection of transports. Leygues, in a cable apparently drafted by de Bon, asked Gauchet to designate an officer for frequent trips to Paris for closer liaison, and assured the C.-in-C. that he believed the interests of the fleet could not be in better hands. Gauchet was 'profoundly touched', but the exchange pointed out how far removed the French C.-in-C., preoccupied with the big guns of his flagship *Provence* and the other dreadnoughts waiting for the Austrian fleet to come out, was from what was now the real war in the Mediterranean, that is, the struggle against submarines.[95]

The decision might be considered a victory for Paris and the DGGSM and a blow to Allied unity. Just as Calthorpe's appointment almost inevitably diminished, in fact if not in theory, Gauchet's position as Allied C.-in-C. so, too, did the French action inevitably dilute the authority of the Malta Commission. It also reinforced the tendency for the French and British to go their own separate ways, each doing what they had to do. The British, with their preponderance of trade, concentrated on the system of convoys running the east–west route through the Mediterranean to Egypt and the supply of their overseas expeditions, while the French concentrated on communication with their North African possessions or army at Salonika. The British staff at Malta thought that these convoys between Provence and North Africa were run on an overly frequent schedule, given the amount of traffic, but the French answer to this charge was that the schedule was necessitated by public opinion which would not tolerate delays given the desperate need for tonnage.[96] Again, the French were doing what they had to do. There were definite limitations to Allied co-operation.

Calthorpe himself remained somewhat ambivalent about the convoy system. Convoys were by no means a guarantee of immunity. Moreover, the escorts themselves could often give only limited protection and their numbers were frequently minimal. Each streamline convoy had one sloop and three armed trawlers, even when the convoy contained up to thirty ships. The trawlers often could not maintain the speed of the convoy and if a ship were torpedoed would have to remain behind to protect the damaged ship. Once left behind, the trawler lacked the speed and reserve of power to catch up again.[97] Once again the reality was very different from the scale of escort so carefully set down by the Mediterranean Staff. All of this was hardly encouraging to Calthorpe, especially since losses to submarine attacks which had decreased in June and July increased again in August and September.[98] Although Calthorpe could report at the end of November that the system of convoys between principal ports in the Mediterranean was fully started, he could also add his own apprehension that submarine activity was on the increase and, in several cases, ships in convoys had been attacked and sunk. Consequently, he feared 'that this form of protection is not so efficacious as hitherto'. Calthorpe thought that convoys were a deterrent at best, not a reliable safeguard, and that protection was hampered by the restricted areas (that is, straits) through which ships had to pass.[99] Calthorpe regarded the anti-submarine *offensive* as the most important function of the navy in the Mediterranean and considered that maximum effort should be employed in the Straits of Otranto, with other areas depleted in order to form hydrophone-equipped hunting flotillas. He wanted to reduce the numbers of vessels employed in minesweeping, patrol, blockade and 'other less important duties' to concentrate on offensive tactics. These measures in their broad outline involved a shift in resources from the Aegean to Otranto and were, for the most part, approved by the Admiralty.[100]

Calthorpe wished to develop the hydrophone-equipped hunting flotillas to replace the netting drifters which he considered to be a failure, and also wanted to increase the number of aircraft to search for submarines or attack their bases. The Admiralty promised him twelve modern drifters equipped with Mark I hydrophones for the Otranto barrage and six more sloops, with another six to follow in the near future, for escort service. Unfortunately, the shortage of shipping hindered delivery of additional aircraft, while the lack of suitable hangers at Otranto had forced the Admiralty to transfer six Caproni bombers purchased on the recommendation of Commodore Sueter to the Royal Flying Corps on the Italian front in the north. On 13 December the Admiralty did order all available naval aircraft at Otranto to concentrate on improving the patrols in the straits since the resources available were not adequate for other projects.[101] The projects included those of Commodore Sueter, commanding No. 6 Wing, RNAS, which had commenced patrols from Otranto in June. Sueter had extensive plans for an air offensive against Pola and Fiume requiring thirty to fifty bombers and twenty-five fighters, as well as an additional sixty-five aircraft for work over the barrage in the south. On 2 September he had attempted an operation in which six Short seaplanes, loaded with torpedoes, were towed on skids by motor launches to a point fifty miles south of Traste Bay for a raid on Cattaro. The operation unfortunately had to be cancelled because of heavy seas and gale-force winds.[102]

Unfortunately for Calthorpe's hopes about 'hunting flotillas' the British hydrophones, as they existed in late 1917, left much to be desired. Captain

Henderson in the convoy section at the Admiralty wrote at the end of December that they did not yet have anything which defeated the submarine and although the submarine was harassed and chased for twelve to fourteen hours, at the end in 99 cases out of 100 the submarine still existed. Henderson did not advocate taking additional risks with convoy protection until more forces were available and the various anti-submarine devices and the personnel who manned them had improved.[103]

Some of Calthorpe's scepticism about convoys was probably due to the losses suffered by the first through convoys. OE1 (eleven vessels under the escort of two sloops) lost two ships, while HE1 lost three ships. Calthorpe's remarks were enough to renew the convoy debate at the Admiralty, at least in certain quarters. Rear-Admiral Hope, Director of Operations Division, now suggested that they might make better use of destroyers by reducing the numbers employed on escort duty and using those released to hunt submarines, working by divisions, and possibly employing hydrophones. They would still use destroyers to escort troop transports and those ships which were too fast for a sloop escort. Captain Whitehead, the Director of Mercantile Movements, refuted these notions for Calthorpe's inference about the ineffectiveness of convoys had not been borne out by the experience of convoys in danger zones outside the Mediterranean, and four subsequent OE convoys (thirty-five ships) had arrived at Port Said without loss. Rear-Admiral Duff also considered it too soon to judge the system as a whole, and to reduce escorts for submarine hunting would be 'a fatal policy to adopt', especially since this type of activity had not been generally successful. The through convoys in the Mediterranean in December were still in an experimental stage and, according to Duff, they could revert to the Cape route at any time if necessary.[104]

The idea that convoys were merely defensive and that offensive action was needed in order to win the war was deeply entrenched. Even as knowledgeable an officer on the Mediterranean Staff as Lieutenant-Commander Godfrey could still write in late November:

> Of course, one can only regard this system of convoys as a palliative. The only way to reduce our losses in the Mediterranean is to sink more submarines. I know this is a platitude, but nevertheless until we are provided with suitable craft, I do not expect that you will see any startling results. Organisation of existing forces will I hope accomplish a good deal, but unless the quality of the forces improves in proportion to the power of enemy submarines, losses will continue and very likely increase.[105]

Godfrey, of course, knew and accepted the value of the convoy system, but he was still longing for that magic key that would really defeat the submarine.

Godfrey had, however, put his finger on a major problem, that is, the lack of fast escorts which really meant that the convoys were not escorted on anything approaching the desired scale and, with OE and HE convoys and troop movements absorbing practically all available destroyers and sloops, an increase in those troop movements without a corresponding increase in fast escorting craft would probably mean the end of the OE and HE convoy system. They would then have to go back to sending ships by coastal routes or including them in slow convoys out of Bizerte. And that, needless to say, wasted tonnage. They also needed something better than trawlers as escorts. Rear-Admiral Grant at Gibraltar pleaded for at least ten destroyers or equivalent good sea-going vessels with a speed of not less than 18 knots and an armament of not less than 4-in. guns. Grant pointed out that on the night of 3–4 November there were eighteen merchant vessels over 800 tons each in the harbour. Calthorpe could only agree with him but the Admiralty, while realizing that the resources of Gibraltar were inadequate compared with the enormous volume of traffic, regretted that there were no destroyers available or likely to be available in the near future to send. The best they could offer, in addition to the twelve sloops already promised for the Mediterranean, would be the prospect of fifteen additional American yachts, of which barely one-third ever materialized.[106] It is hardly suprising that Jellicoe wrote in his celebrated memorandum for the War Cabinet of 18 November: 'It is not too much to say that the whole of our naval policy is necessarily governed by the adequacy of our destroyer forces.'[107] He was, of course, referring to operations by the Grand Fleet in the north, but the effects of those irreducible needs were felt in the Mediterranean. Thaon di Revel, on a much smaller scale, would have agreed with him in regard to the Italian battle fleet at Taranto, and Gauchet and the French fleet at Corfu were in an unenviable position, too, should the Austrian dreadnoughts ever come out. Gauchet's theoretical power to recall French destroyers from other services was apt to mean little in reality, for it might take a number of days before they were back and fuelled. Fortunately the contingency did not arise.

In the second half of 1917 the Allies were also able to put increased pressure on the activities of the U-boats by means of wireless direction finding, intercepts and code breaking. Rear-Admiral Hall, the DNI, had been out to the Mediterranean earlier in the year, and in the late spring of 1917 a team of British cryptographers had been sent from Room 40 at the Admiralty to Taranto and later to Rome to co-operate with Italian naval intelligence in working on Austrian codes, and by the end of 1917 the supply of intelligence had improved greatly. As usual, co-operation among the Allies was difficult, particularly in a sensitive area like this. The British appear to have limited their interchange of information with the Italians to Austrian codes and apparently were reluctant to share information about German U-boat traffic with either the French or the Italians. The French understandably resented Hall's attitude that it would be better to lose a ship (especially a French ship) than risk disclosing the extent of their crypto-analysis to the Germans.[108] A full discussion of the subject is beyond the scope of this book, but it is possible to say that the Allies developed an extensive network in the Mediterranean of direction finding centres and stations. The Naval Staff's *Mediterranean Staff Papers* lists 11 centres and 14 stations for the British, 20 stations for the Italians and 14 stations for the French.[109] It is possible to attribute the destruction of UB71 east of the Straits of Gibraltar in April 1918 at least indirectly to wireless intercepts.

French intercepts were also responsible for the damage inflicted by aircraft on U39 in May 1918 which forced the submarine to seek internment in Spain. The greatest contribution of wireless intelligence, however, was the ability to track U-boats and route convoys and shipping away from danger areas.[110]

Mediterranean arrangements were given a jolt by the Italian defeat at Caporetto at the end of October and the urgent need to reinforce Italy and the concomitant fear of an Italian collapse tended to be the prime problem in the latter part of 1917. Before examining that, however, we should really turn to how, if at all, the changes in Allied strategy and tactics during the summer and autumn of 1917 affected the operations of the Germans and Austrians.

The Austro-German Response

At the end of June, in addition to disturbing transport to Salonika, the Admiralstab set as the primary objective of the Mediterranean U-Boat Flotilla, the cutting off of communications to and from France and Italy. A concentration in the western and central Mediterranean was necessary to achieve this and U-boats operating in the western Mediterranean were also authorized to sortie into the Atlantic. As increased traffic from Salonika to Egypt had not been reported, the Admiralstab decided that no new U-boats need occupy the eastern Mediterranean. The Admiralstab did ask the FdU Pola to order some submarines, including the Austrians, working on the Malta–Cerigo route to thrust south of Crete towards the east. The Aegean would be occupied alternately by a UB and a UC boat. The majority of the minelaying UC boats in the Mediterranean would operate in the areas that the Naval Staff had designated for them, which meant scattered off important ports without any attempt at concentration, but the Admiralstab were particularly anxious to sow mines in the Gulf of Lyon in order to force coastal traffic further out into the open sea where, presumably, submarines were able to operate more readily.[111]

The German naval leaders faced renewed pressure in July to divert submarines from *Handelskrieg*, and British pressure in Palestine prevented the Admiralstab from completely neglecting the eastern Mediterranean. The British had suffered setbacks in attacks on Gaza in March and April but were obviously going to try again. Once again Ludendorff intervened. On 9 July he informed Holtzendorff that they would have to consider combined operations by the British against the rear of the Turkish army on the Palestine front. The Admiralstab had to confess that the Allies could land from boats along the greater portion of the open Syrian coast during good weather, and that U-boats could probably do little to prevent a sudden concentration and landing. Holtzendorff agreed to keep a U-boat permanently operating in the eastern Mediterranean to counter such a landing and, once the landing site was known, some of the submarines operating in the eastern Mediterranean and Aegean would be ordered by wireless to proceed to the area. As soon as a suitable minelayer was available around the beginning of

394

August, the navy also intended to mine the coastal route between Port Said and Gaza as well as the positions from which Allied ships were supporting the left flank of the British army. The options open to the Germans were relatively limited. Holtzendorff admitted that the establishment of a U-boat base in Asia Minor or in Syrian waters was not feasible. They had kept supplies and provisions at different points on the Turkish coast in the past but as a result of lively espionage these sites had been betrayed, particularly after they were actually used by a submarine, and very quickly visited by Allied patrols and henceforth kept under constant surveillance and occasionally shelled at random. Beirut had also been shelled after U-boats had called the preceding spring.[112] Holtzendorff was really admitting the relative impotence of the Mediterranean U-Boat Flotilla to influence events in Palestine and was, in effect, paying tribute to the little recognized efforts of British and French patrols on the coast of Asia Minor and Syria.

While General Allenby, the new British commander in Egypt, gathered his forces for a new offensive at the end of the summer, Ludendorff returned to the charge and asked the navy in September if they could employ more U-boats off the Palestine coast. The Admiralstab took the position that Ludendorff and the General Staff would have to decide which was more important: undiminished prosecution of the U-boat war *throughout* the Mediterranean or a more intense attack on traffic to the Sinai at only *one* place in the Mediterranean. From past experience a concentration of a large number of U-boats in the eastern Mediterranean off Alexandria, Port Said and on the Syrian coast would not threaten loaded transports *en route* east as much as the same number of U-boats deployed against the stream of ships throughout the Mediterranean, especially in the narrow waters around Gibraltar, the area between Sicily and Cape Bon, Malta and the Malta–Cerigo route. Moreover, the strong anti-submarine patrols in the vicinity of Port Said and Alexandria combined with the disadvantageous depth of water and the danger of mines, both their own and the enemy's, forced submarines to operate further out from the coast. There were also no straits which restricted the route of enemy steamers so that meeting a convoy or single ship in the eastern Mediterranean was more or less accidental. The Admiralstab argued that to have any chance of success they would have to employ at least five boats at the same time: two off Alexandria, two off Port Said, and one on the Syrian coast. This required fifteen U-boats, taking into account transit time, refuelling and refitting, and that number represented half the total number of U-boats on hand in the Mediterranean. A concentration such as this would also mean considerable neglect of *Handelskrieg*, particularly the pressure on Italy. The Admiralstab ordered for the moment at least three boats to be maintained in the eastern Mediterranean and Aegean including UC23, a minelayer from the U-Boat Half Flotilla at Constantinople.[113]

The actual successes by the submarines did show a falling off from the heady days of the spring.[114] Figures for sinkings by the Mediterranean U-Boat Flotilla at Pola are shown in Table 10.1.

These figures do not give comfort to those who confidently assumed a steady decline in sinkings as a result of the introduction of the convoy

Table 10.1   *Shipping Losses due to Submarines, July–December 1917*

	Sunk by Mediterranean U-Boat Flotilla Tonnage	Sunk by Submarine-laid Mines Tonnage	Total Mediterranean Tonnage	Total (All Theatres) Tonnage
July 1917	84,319	6,015	90,334	555,514
Aug. 1917	73,403	6,146	79,549	472,372
Sept. 1917	111,241	—	111,241	353,602
Oct. 1917	143,793	810	144,603	466,542
Nov. 1917	94,329	10,150	104,479	302,599
Dec. 1917	144,290	4,041	148,331	411,766

Austrian submarines claimed:

	Tonnage		Tonnage
July 1917	16,969	Oct. 1917	12,663
Aug. 1917	38,823	Nov. 1917	4,016
Sept. 1917	—	Dec. 1917	—

system. Ships may have been much safer in convoys, but they were no immune and not all traffic was in convoy or well protected. Consequently there was no steady decline in sinkings and there could still be alarming jumps in losses during certain months. The long-term trend was down, but no one could foresee that. Sinkings declined in July and August, but the rose in September and went even higher in October, the month that the convoy systems were established. The sinkings fell off in November, the first month that the convoy systems were really working, but then ros sharply in December to a level above that of June for tonnage sunk by submarines, although decidedly less in terms of losses due to mines. Mining remained responsible, however, for only a small portion of the losses. Th Austrian successes were more erratic, largely due to the small number o boats involved which exaggerated the effect of periods in dockyard hands

The fact that losses did rise sharply during certain months obscured th fact from the Allies that they were doing better than they thought. The could not know the figures for the German standard of success, tonnag sunk per U-boat day. When the Admiralstab made an analysis of this i September they made an alarming discovery. The sinkings per U-boat da in the first half of 1917 were as shown in Table 10.2.[115]

Table 10.2   *Sinkings per U-boat Day, January–June 1917*

	Tonnage sunk per U-boat day
January 1917	719
February 1917	673
March 1917	336
April 1917	802
May 1917	554
June 1917	543

These figures were even more disturbing because the conditions in May and June, with good weather, long days and bright nights were much more favourable for U-boat warfare than in January and February. Even the most spectacular month, April, would have been only 633 tons per day if the unusually successful cruise of U35 was excluded, and this too would have been below the winter months. The temporary assistants on the Admiralstab (*Hilfsarbeiters*) who compiled the statistics had no hesitation in attributing the decline in the rate of success to Allied counter-measures, although the Deputy Chief of the Admiralstab emphasized that this was their personal opinion not thoroughly shared by the Admiralstab. These figures did not improve for the remainder of 1917. The commander of the Mediterranean flotillas pointed out that the March 1918 total of 517 tons per U-boat day was above the average for the second half of 1917, and the February 1918 figure of 574 tons (later revised downwards) was the highest since May 1917.[116]

On the other hand, life was getting a lot harder for the Mediterranean U-Boat-Flotilla whose successes no longer represented as large a proportion of the total German successes as had been the case in the past. The Germans may have continued to exact their toll but they did not come anywhere near their record for April. They would have to work much harder for their victories now, but not all of the decline in sinkings was due to Allied tactics. There were material reasons as well. The Germans could have surmounted the decline in sinkings per U-boat day and increased total Allied losses if they could have increased the number of U-boats at sea. This was not the case. U35, the boat of the redoutable Arnauld de la Perière, was out of service for repairs for four months along with U47, in fact the mechanical difficulties of the latter were so great that the boat remained out of service for the rest of the war. To counterbalance this, the first of the UBIII class, UB48 and UB50, reached Cattaro by October along with UC52. On her way out the latter had been forced to put into Cadiz for a time because of engine difficulties. The Germans, in turn, handed over the last two UBII boats at Pola, UB43 and UB47, to the Austrians in July. By the end of the year the UBIII boats, UB49, UB51, UB52 and UB53, had reached Cattaro. UB49 had been forced to seek refuge in Cadiz after sustaining damage in an encounter with an escort in September, but in October her commander, Kapitänleutnant von Mellenthin, broke out of internment with the submarine and succeeded in reaching Cattaro. Nevertheless, the Pola flotilla was plagued by engine problems. The new UB52 and six other boats of the flotilla were out of service during most of the last quarter of the year and this undoubtedly contributed to the decline in sinkings.[117]

The troubles encountered by the Germans in maintaining their submarines far from home in Austrian bases were growing and, in October, a team of technical experts led by the Director of the Dockyard Department of the Reichsmarineamt investigated the problem. Moreover, there was a growing threat from another direction – the sky. On 16 October, Commodore Püllen warned that although enemy air raids on Pola and Cattaro had so far caused only minor military damage it was purely by chance, for neither the anti-aircraft defences nor air-raid shelters were sufficient. They could expect the attacks to increase with the end of the winter bad weater. Anti-aircraft guns at Pola were insufficient in number and lacked unified fire control with batteries firing pell mell. The situation was even worse at Cattaro. They also required generators to put up smoke screens and air-raid shelters. The strength of local fighter defences fluctuated according to the needs of the land front and they therefore needed fighter units to be assigned on a permanent basis. The objective of the proposals made by the German technical commission was to bring Pola up to the highest level of efficiency and to develop Cattaro for intermediate repairs and as a reserve for Pola, while the Danubius yard at Fiume would also be considered as a reserve. Unfortunately, this was something far easier said than done. Labour was a major problem and the technical experts did not expect to be able to satisfy a need for around 150 additional skilled workers from Germany. Njegovan promised the Reichsmarineamt delegation extensive support, but remained noncommittal about German suggestions concerning taking obsolete ships out of service in order to free their officers, men and artillery for other purposes. The Austrians, for their part, raised the question of deliveries of fuel oil, a problem which was also becoming more and more difficult.[118]

While the technical problems grew, the Mediterranean U-Boat Flotilla was once again called upon to contribute to the defence of Palestine. On 30 October the Turkish army reported a concentration of transports southwest of Gaza and that a British attack was imminent. They asked for the cooperation of submarines. Allenby's attack began on the 31st, and Falkenhayn, now commander of the Turkish-German forces, appealed for the intervention of U-boats since he thought that there were British preparations for a landing north of Gaza behind the Turkish front. This was not correct, for at this stage of the battle the thrust at Gaza and the ostensible preparations for a landing were merely a feint. Allenby's real thrust was directed inland at Beersheba. Nevertheless, the Admiralstab ordered by wireless that those submarines already at sea near Cerigo or Crete, UC34, UC37 and UC38, should proceed to the Syrian coast, while UB52 should sail as soon as possible. The latter, however, suffered from a faulty thrust-bearing in the port shaft and UB51 took her place, sailing on 10 November and expected to arrive on the scene around the 15th, long after the other submarines which were due between the 4th and 5th.[119] UC34 and UB51 found few opportunities for attacks on the Syrian coast and achieved no success, while UC37 apparently continued to work around Crete and in the Aegean and never arrived on the scene.[120] Oberleutnant zur See Wendlandt in UC38 had better luck. He skilfully eluded the protecting trawlers and nets and torpedoed and sank the monitor M15 and the destroyer *Staunch* off Gaza on 11 November. Falkenhayn later profusely thanked the navy for their rapid and successful intervention which he claimed had undoubtedly substantially relieved the threatened position of his army. Jackson had indeed withdrawn the remainder of the bombarding squadron to Port Said, and beyond protecting the army's line of supply with Egypt active naval participation in the campaign ceased, at least for the time being.[121] However, by this time it was irrelevant. Allenby captured Gaza on 7 November, took Jaffa on the 16th and would capture Jerusalem itself on 9

December. The German submarines, despite their limited success, had failed to alter the progress of the campaign and the diversion of the U-boats to generally profitless operations on the Syrian coast may be one of the reasons behind the decline in tonnage sunk during November.

Wendlandt was perhaps an excessively bold officer and UC38 did not return from her next cruise, one of a mere two German U-boats lost in the Mediterranean in the whole of 1917. On 14 December he torpedoed the large old French cruiser, *Chateaurenault* (carrying 985 troops for Salonika), between Saint Maure and Ithaca near the entrance to the Gulf of Corinth. UC38 tried for a second shot at the slowly sinking cruiser and was, in turn, depth charged, forced to surface, and sunk by the French destroyers *Mameluck* and *Lansquenet*. Wendlandt survived and thanks to good discipline so, too, did the great majority of the *Chateaurenault*'s passengers and crew.[122]

Kaiser Wilhelm honoured the Mediterranean U-Boat Flotilla with a visit on 12 November and spent six and a half hours in Pola inspecting German and Austrian facilities. There was a breakfast on the flagship *Viribus Unitis*, tea at the Marinekasino (the officers' club), and the Kaiser during a trip around the harbour with Njegovan apparently tried to convince his Austrian hosts to lay up their obsolete ships and use the crews for more important purposes.[123] The Mediterranean U-Boat Flotilla was going to be substantially reinforced at the end of the year or in early 1918. In the latter part of November UB68, UB69, UB70, UB71 and UB105 were all under orders to sail for the Mediterranean. They represented the second half of the ten UBIII class destined for the Mediterranean U-Boat Flotilla which, as of 1 January, was divided in two with the I Mediterranean U-Boat Flotilla at Pola and the II Mediterranean U-Boat Flotilla at Cattaro. Kapitänleutnant Otto Schultze assumed command of the First Flotilla at Pola and Korvettenkapitän Rudolf Ackermann, already head of the station at Cattaro, received command of the Second Flotilla.[124]

On 22 November the Germans and Austrians tidied up a probably meaningless exception to their prohibited zone in the Mediterranean. At the same time that they extended the blockade zone to the west of Britain and established a new prohibited zone around the Azores and Madeira, they also closed the twenty-mile wide corridor through the Mediterranean to Greece.[125] The Admiralstab also proposed to expand the blockade zone in the Gulf of Lyon to include the port of Cette, where cargo destined for neutral Switzerland was allowed to unload, but both the Army High Command and civil government had doubts and, for the time being, this small area in the western Mediterranean outside Spanish territorial waters remained open, at least in theory.[126]

The German submarines ended what, from their point of view, had been a highly satisfactory year with a striking success. On 30 December the troopship *Aragon* (9,588 tons) was torpedoed and sunk by UC34 off Alexandria and the destroyer *Attack*, engaged in rescuing survivors, was either torpedoed or ran on to one of the mines laid by the submarine and sank. The combined loss of life was 610. To make matters worse, the following day the fleet auxiliary *Osmanieh* (4,041 tons) struck one of the mines in the same field and sank with a loss of 198 lives.[127] All in all, it was a dismal end to a disastrous year for the Allies, although with the introduction of the convoy system they could at least hope that they had turned the corner. The fog of war obscured the fact that they had.

The Aftermath of Caporetto

On 24 October the Austrians, reinforced by seven German divisions, began the offensive along the Isonzo front which is generally known as the Battle of Caporetto. The Germans broke through the defences of the Second Italian Army and a general retreat followed. The Italians had hoped to hold the line of the Tagliamento River, but this proved untenable and on 4 November Cadorna ordered a withdrawal to the line of the Piave River where the front was finally stabilized on 10–12 November. The Caporetto disaster cost the Italians over 320,000 killed, wounded and missing, and the Austrian and German forces advanced over seventy miles into Italian territory capturing thousands of pieces of artillery. There was some question as to whether or not the Italians could hold Venice with the enemy only thirty miles away, and there were serious doubts on the Allied side that Italy would even remain in the war. These fears were typified by a memorandum written by 'Blinker' Hall, Director of the Intelligence Division, and circulated to the War Cabinet. Hall described how the Central Powers were counting on the collapse of the Allied cause through the situation in its weakest link – Italy.[128] The Italians showed surprising resilience and, in the emergency, underwent something of a national revival. Victor Emmanuel Orlando became Prime Minister and General (later Field Marshal) Armando Diaz replaced Cadorna as Chief of Staff, while five British and six French divisions were rushed from the western front.[129] The Italians held the line of the Piave, where those two British monitors, the *Sir Thomas Picton* and *Earl of Peterborough*, participated in the defence from positions in the lagoons north of Venice. The Italian resurgence could not be foreseen immediately and the fear of a complete disaster on the Italian front formed the background to naval events in the latter part of the year.

The Italian Minister of Marine was apprehensive that there would be a naval accompaniment to the offensive. Revel suspected a German-Austrian submarine concentration in the Adriatic which would account for an apparent lull in submarine activity in the Mediterranean. He also expected that Austrian light craft would undertake action aimed at cutting the railway communications of the Italian army which ran near the coast. This could have serious consequences in the situation which followed the retreat from Caporetto, but the Italians did not think that they could transfer any torpedo craft from the west coast of Italy to the Adriatic because of the pressure of the submarine war. They therefore asked the French, British and Japanese governments, through diplomatic channels, to contribute twenty destroyers between them as a temporary reinforcement for the Adriatic.[130] The history of the submarine war outlined so far indicates how little chance

here was that the Italians would receive, even temporarily, no fewer than
twenty precious destroyers at this stage of the war. The Italians could
hardly have been unaware of this and increased their efforts at obtaining
assistance from what might have been their best hope, the United States.
Just before the Caporetto disaster Washington had replied to the Allied
requests made at the London Conference with Admiral Mayo in early
September. The Americans agreed to give serious consideration to sending
a division of four coal-burning dreadnoughts to reinforce the Grand Fleet,
but unfortunately the US Navy did not consider an increase in the numbers
of destroyers overseas to be practical at that time, although they promised
to increase the number as rapidly as new destroyers became available. There
were also fifty submarine chasers – 110-foot wooden craft – assigned to
France, and four more squadrons (seventy-two boats) would be available in
the near future for service in foreign waters if found useful for such duty.
The British had already indicated to the Americans that they needed forty
submarine chasers for the Mediterranean. The Americans were also
arranging to commandeer additional yachts and tugs, fit them out and arm
them, and send them abroad as rapidly as possible. They promised little
specifically for the Italians, however, except to use the good offices of the
Navy Department towards preventing delay and expediting delivery of
matériel already on order or required in the future.[131]

The news that an American mission had arrived in London on 8
November to co-ordinate Allied actions and make the most efficient use of
their resources inspired Sonnino to alert the navy to join other Italian
authorities in presenting their requirements. The different departments at
the ministry and sections of the Naval Staff drew up their lists which could
be summed up as: ELCO (Electric Boat Company) motor launches; small
steamers (800–1,200 tons) for use as convoy escorts; minesweepers; material
for naval construction; and, of course, the assignment of American
destroyers and escort craft to work in the Mediterranean. The Minister of
Colonies, Gaspare Colosimo, and Governor of Libya, General Ameglio,
made their own special plea since the naval resources available to patrol the
long coastline of that neglected colony were totally inadequate.[132]

These were long-term goals, however. The most immediate problem
involved the threat in the Adriatic and concerned the twenty Allied
destroyers which the Italians wanted. The request received the expected
response. Jellicoe was very frank in his conversation with Count Villarey,
but that frankness must have caused considerable offence to Revel. The First
Sea Lord suggested that the Italians should concentrate as many submarines
as possible in the vicinity of Venice to counter any move by the Austrian
fleet against the city. He also expressed the somewhat surprising opinion –
assuming that Villarey reported his words correctly – that the French and
Italian fleets ought to make a combined demonstration in the upper
Adriatic, although they would have to return south because of the difficulty
of supply, and also asked how many battleships could be anchored at
Venice. Revel's marginal comment in characteristic red ink to the
suggestion about the demonstration was: 'To be torpedoed?' Jellicoe termed
the lines of communication of the Italian army in the Adriatic as solid as a

401

rock and they had nothing to fear. Moreover, any destroyer sent to the Adriatic had to be drawn from the protection of traffic with consequent increase in sinkings and damage to all the Allies. He also added that it was the unanimous opinion of all the British officers at present in Italy that Italian destroyers spent too much time in port compared with British destroyers which spent 70 per cent of their time at sea or with fires lit. The French response was equally negative. De Bon regretted that the French had no large destroyers to put at the disposal of the Italians beyond those already at Brindisi which Revel could use in the northern Adriatic if he saw fit. Revel's position was equally predictable. Naval operations in the northern Adriatic with the bulk of the French and Italian forces were not advisable since mines and submarines would expose them to considerable losses not compensated for by the insignificant results obtainable, and would only play the game of the enemy who presumably would have concentrated his submarines in anticipation of Allied moves. Revel termed the remarks of the British officers in Italy about the employment of Italian destroyers as 'irreverent and inopportune' and concluded that the Italian battle squadrons would intervene only in case the bulk of the Austrian fleet came out of the Straits of Otranto, and then their principal objective ought to be to prevent at any cost, the Austrians getting back into the Adriatic. Otherwise, Italian operations should be based on a wide use of mines, submarines and light craft.[133]

The Italian request for the twenty destroyers provoked a naval conference in Rome with Wemyss, de Bon, Calthorpe and Vice-Admiral Darrieus (commanding the 2ème Escadre) representing Gauchet. The Americans were not represented. Wemyss and de Bon travelled to Rome together and during the journey essentially agreed beforehand that there had not really been any change in the naval situation as a result of Caporetto. Revel, who actually had been spending most of his time near the front at Venice since Caporetto, presided over the conference and began with horror stories based on Italian intelligence. The Austrians might land between Rimini and Ravenna to take the Italian army in the rear should Venice fall, while eleven transports were at Buccari (near Fiume) and three at Trieste apparently preparing to embark troops reportedly destined for a landing at Bellaria near Rimini. There was also a major concentration of German and Austrian submarines in the Adriatic with small submarines sent by road from Germany, while large numbers of workers had recently arrived from Kiel to help assemble them. The British and French had little difficulty disposing of these suppositions, especially regarding submarines, since they were fantastic. Wemyss pointed out that the number of transports mentioned would not carry sufficient troops to make a landing effective, and the convoy would have to be protected by the Austrian battle fleet which could then be brought to action or exposed to submarines. The suggestion about large numbers of workers from Kiel was equally absurd. We have just seen how the Germans despaired of getting even 150 workers from home for Pola, although the Allied leaders could not have been expected to know this. De Bon offered to send French submarines from Brindisi to the upper Adriatic and to reinforce Brindisi with others. Wemyss offered the Italian

1,200 mines and minelayers. That was the most the Italians got for they gave up their request for twenty destroyers and made no mention of fast ships with long-range guns (meaning battle cruisers) to bombard Pola, an idea apparently floated by Revel through Villarey before the conference. The Italians also agreed to consider the idea of basing the Italian fleet at Corfu. De Bon had been anxious for joint gunnery exercises and manœuvres with the French fleet and Wemyss emphasized the disadvantages of Taranto, 120 miles further from their objective than Corfu with an easily blocked exit between the inner and outer harbour, and the possibility of a submarine ambush in the Gulf of Taranto. Revel maintained that this redeployment could only be accomplished after they had satisfactorily taken care of the problem of supply, but the difficulties, although numerous, did not appear insurmountable. An exchange of views, 'but no firm decision' was the way Vice-Admiral Darrieus summed up the subject. The French also impressed on the Italians the importance of holding Valona and the coast of Epirus opposite Corfu. Its loss would threaten the Otranto barrage and cause the French fleet to leave the island. The British, for their part, agreed to hasten the laying of their barrage near Otranto, although the results were not promising, and the Franco-Italian barrage would be started between Fano and Corfu.[134] Wemyss formed the opinion during the conference

> that the Italian naval authorities had somewhat lost their heads, probably owing to the representations of General Porro [Cadorna's Chief of Staff], and that their telegrams asking for assistance were directly due to this cause. By the time that the conference had assembled, however, they seemed to have regained their presence of mind, and took a less pessimistic view of the situation.[135]

The Italian situation had been regarded seriously enough in London to cause the Admiralty to ask Calthorpe in early November to report on the situation in the event that Italy was compelled to make a separate peace. Calthorpe, in his report dated 13 November, assumed that Italy would make peace before being compelled to withdraw from its positions in Albania. If this was not the case, however, and the Italians were forced out of Albania before making peace, a close blockade of the Adriatic would become impossible and the French fleet might be compelled to leave Corfu. Aside from the Adriatic, however, the main line of British strategy in the Mediterranean would not change, provided the neutrality of Italy was not grossly infringed on by the Central Powers. Calthorpe also did not consider it a reasonable possibility that the British could continue to use their current naval bases in southern Italy. The Allies would have to occupy any positions evacuated by the Italians on the Albanian coast in order to protect their position at Corfu. Valona also had to be occupied by naval forces and used as an advance base for their large monitors, submarines and light cruisers. This would give some protection to the barrage forces and cover the flank of the Allied army in Albania. If the Italians were required by the terms of the peace treaty to cede the Dodecanese Islands in the eastern Mediterranean to the Turks, the British would have to seize them or arrange for the Greeks to do so. The British cruiser and submarine forces, with the exception of two cruisers left at Valona, would shift to Corfu along with the drifters and motor launches of the barrage force and aircraft currently based in southern Italy. They would try to maintain the Otranto barrage in the same tactical position but would have to block the use of Italian territorial waters by submarines by placing, ostensibly on behalf of the Italians, around 1,000 mines between the shore and the three-mile limit.

The fate of the Italian fleet was a sensitive subject and, in many ways, the most interesting part of this contingency planning. Calthorpe placed his first priority on ships in the Adriatic and in preventing them from falling into enemy hands. The estimated thirty-five destroyers were the most important part of the Italian fleet from Calthorpe's point of view and the British and French would have to obtain as many of them as they could hope to man and get the rest away to the west coast of Italy before Italian neutrality became an accomplished fact. The ships would be acquired presumably by 'purchase or agreement, backed perhaps by a show of "Force majeure"'. If they had sufficient time, they might scrape together enough officers and men from ships on the Mediterranean station and crews of ships refitting at British bases to steam fifteen to twenty destroyers and flotilla leaders to adjacent British and French bases, and the French would doubtlessly be able to handle 'a fair number' too. Calthorpe did not think that it was practicable to remove any of the Italian cruisers but did not think it mattered if the Italians kept them, provided they were not left in the Adriatic. The British would have to take measures, such as the development of Piraeus and Salamis shipyards and increasing the resources of Malta, to compensate for the loss of Italian repair facilities, and naturally Allied codes and cyphers in Italian hands would be compromised.

There was one area, according to Calthorpe, where the Allies stood to gain by the Italians dropping out of the war. They could withdraw from Italian service some, if not all, of the large number of British ships employed in supplying Italy. On the other hand, they would have to add to British escorting craft if the present standard of escorts was to be maintained. The escort question was examined in detail by Rear-Admiral Fergusson, the British Admiral of Patrols. The increase in the number of escorts would be required by the fact that British and French troop movements to Egypt or Salonika would have to go via Marseilles instead of by the much shorter and less exposed route via Taranto. They might also have to replace the Italian troops on the Salonika front which meant that more ships would be required to maintain the British and French forces.[136]

Neither Calthorpe nor the Mediterranean Staff appear to have had any serious thought that the Italians would resist this Allied acquisition of a portion of their fleet the way, for example, the French would at Mers-el-Kébir in 1940. Nevertheless, in forwarding a copy to Heneage in the Adriatic, Calthorpe cautioned: 'It is, of course, of the utmost importance that the Italians should be unaware that the question is under consideration by us, and every precaution is to be taken by you to avoid the fact coming to their knowledge.'[137] After obtaining Admiralty approval for his plans, Calthorpe approached Gauchet on 10 December, pretending to be acting entirely on his own initiative. By this time, with the Piave line holding, the likelihood that Italy would be forced out of the war was diminishing, but the bureaucratic machine had been set in motion and the British continued to make their contingency plans. The different Mediterranean authorities were brought into the schemes. Ballard, Admiral Superintendent at Malta, reported that he could normally supply enough men to man fifteen destroyers and Rear-Admiral Fremantle in the Aegean, by accepting the risk of a raid by Turkish-German forces and temporarily demobilizing his two battleships, could provide navigating parties for twelve destroyers and flotilla leaders at short notice. Heneage, however, did not think that they could hold Valona with less than one army corps equipped with corps artillery.[138]

Gauchet had a rather interesting response. He was inclined to take a much broader view of the consequences of an Italian defection, stressing its implications for Albania, Epirus, Greece and the entire Balkans. He anticipated that the left wing of the Salonika army would be thrown back opening Thessaly and the road to Athens to German troops with the possibility of a restoration of King Constantine. They could not retain Valona and the enemy might then occupy the coast of Epirus, which would make Corfu untenable as a base for large French warships. The French fleet would then have to fall back to Argostoli holding, or trying to hold, Corfu with only light forces in order to support the Otranto barrage. Gauchet seemed more worried about the Greeks than the Italians. He maintained that they would have to seize the arsenal at Salamis and possibly the Greek fleet. He said nothing, though, about taking over Italian warships.[139] Gauchet reflected traditional French concerns about Greece and his own personal mistrust of the Greeks so evident from his reports. He had the support of his minister, Georges Leygues, and the naval staff in his ideas over Corfu and the necessity to evacuate the big French warships if the enemy was ever to take control of the mainland opposite the island. Nevertheless, the French would have to do all they could to prevent the enemy from capturing and making use of Corfu as an anchorage, and they regarded continuing to maintain the Otranto barrage as equally important. As for Salamis, if the French were compelled to abandon the arsenal they ought to put it out of action before leaving.[140]

By 22 January, Calthorpe concluded that he had in hand a sufficient outline of the organization required to take the necessary steps should the contingency arise. He was confident that by temporarily demobilizing the battleships in the Aegean and drawing on the crews of ships under repair at Malta he could man twenty to thirty Italian destroyers and flotilla leaders, and evacuate British naval forces from Italian ports within forty-eight hours, except for the old hulk *Queen* at Taranto which would require four to five days. By this time, Calthorpe did not propose to go into the subject very fully for the contingency 'appears, fortunately, less probable than hitherto', although he advised the other Mediterranean authorities to maintain a skeleton organization just in case.[141] Nevertheless the planning continued, though at a much slower pace. It was not until 11 April that Calthorpe replied to an Admiralty letter of 8 January about measures to be taken in regard to merchant shipping should Italy make a separate peace. Although approved by the Admiralty in June, by this time it was happily nothing more than a theoretical question.[142] Presumably the Italians never learned of the plans their ally had for a portion of their fleet.

The Italians would have another opportunity to make their case with the Americans at the naval conference to be held in Paris at the end of November when Admiral Benson, Chief of Naval Operations, would be present. As usual, the Italian ambassador in Washington was active, requesting allocations of fuel oil, mines and personnel to assemble them, submarine chasers to operate in Italian coastal waters, and the establishment of American air bases in Italy.[143] Orlando thought that the impending conference was imporant enough for Revel to be present but the latter refused to leave Venice because of the proximity of the enemy and the possibility of Austrian naval moves.[144]

The Paris Naval Conference actually preceded by a few days the first meeting of the Supreme War Council. This inter-Allied body had been formed for the better co-ordination of the war effort after an agreement by the Allies at Rapallo early that month. The decision was taken in the threatening atmosphere created by the disaster at Caporetto and the Bolshevik seizure of power in Russia. The principal topic discussed by the Allied naval leaders when they met concerned the formation of a similar body for the naval war. The French suspected that the British were pushing the idea as at least partial compensation for the Rapallo Conference which had seemingly given military pre-eminence to France. The French noted that British public opinion was not satisfied with naval affairs being handled within the inter-Allied General Staff and obviously the British would have pre-eminence in any separate naval organization.[145] The result of these discussions was the Allied Naval Council, created to 'ensure the closest touch and complete co-operation between the Allied Fleets' with the task of watching over 'the general conduct of the Naval war' and ensuring 'the co-ordination of effort at sea as well as the development of all scientific operations connected with the conduct of the war'. The Council had no executive authority, but would 'make all the necessary recommendations to enable the government to make decisions' and keep in touch with their execution with members of the Council sending to their respective governments all the reports which might be necessary. However, 'The individual responsibility of the Chiefs of Staffs, and of the Commander-in-Chief at sea, towards their Governments as regards operations in hand, as well as the strategical and tactical disposition of the forces placed under their command remains unchanged'.[146] The Mediterranean and particularly the Italian role would give this Council some of its livelier moments in the coming year.

Jellicoe's verdict was:

> The conference, as usual, has been a waste of time and mostly for purposes of eyewash, but it was as well not to leave the French and Italians to discuss matters along with the U.S. people. Benson is very helpful and as long as we are together all will be done that can be done by

the U.S. Navy to help the general cause. They are really heart and soul in the business and they are not influenced by the national jealousies which apparently must always exist between European nations.[147]

Benson must have been well courted, especially by the Italians.

Cusani presented a paper at the conference setting out Italy's need for an increase in tonnage at its disposal by new ships totalling at least 100,000 tons deadweight for the conveyance of coal to replenish Italian stocks which were 'suffering continuous and alarming depletion'. Furthermore, the Italians needed another tanker to carry naphthaline from Texas. Cusani also enumerated Italian requirements in terms of destroyers, escorts and minesweepers. De Bon countered with a request that Italian yards share in the repair of damaged Allied ships which, due to the shortage of tonnage, had to be returned to service as soon as possible. Cusani promised to examine the question but stipulated nothing could be done unless the Allies provided the necessary material.[148] He also had a private meeting with Benson on the morning of 1 December, and handed him a memorandum on Italian needs from the United States, mostly minesweepers, tugs, small armed ships to escort convoys, and some 5-in. guns for coast defence or arming merchant ships. Benson was 'well disposed' and promised that the United States would put at the disposal of the Italians five 5,000-ton merchantmen and two or three tankers.[149]

Orlando was able to obtain a promise in Paris of 150,000 tons of coal within a short time, but in the interim the most important Italian factories, such as the Ansaldo works, would have to suspend operation. Orlando therefore asked the navy to make another sacrifice, hopefully for only a brief period, and transfer 100,000 tons from its stocks. Orlando thought that the navy would still have sufficient coal for an adequate number of months.[150] The coal situation of the Regia Marina was indeed serious. The month before Revel had even tried to make the French themselves provide fuel for the French destroyers attached to the Italian fleet at Brindisi. The French found that request, which bordered on the brazen, to be completely unacceptable. Revel in December had to issue a printed memorandum to the Italian naval authorities stating that the navy could not rely on new supplies and would have to live on what was on hand. Italian coal stocks had been around 780,000 tons at the beginning of the year and had fallen to around 360,000 tons. The navy used around 50,000 tons per month which meant that the stocks would be completely exhausted within six or seven months' time. Revel therefore issued rules for the strictest economy.[151]

Given the Italian situation, Revel was thoroughly exasperated to receive on 9 December a request from Calthorpe for four to six Italian destroyers and twelve to eighteen Italian trawlers for escorting a convoy system between Syracuse and Egypt. The convoys would carry grain to Italy and the Minister of Marine, probably under heavy pressure from the Cabinet because of the alarming crisis in supply, asked Revel to make every sacrifice and to do what was possible to improve the situation. Revel, of course, refused and for the same reasons that he had denied the request for eleven destroyers a few months before. To Revel it seemed that this renewed insistence on Italy undertaking new obligations for escorting convoys, thereby thinning out even more its light craft facing the enemy in the Adriatic, showed little knowledge of Italy's condition and an incorrect appreciation of the real requirements of the Entente in the Mediterranean. It also demonstrated what little confidence Italy could put on the good will of its allies in prosecuting the war. Italy was the sole nation in the Mediterranean in direct contact with the enemy, resulting in the maximum wear on its material. The problem of supplying Italy was not only an Italian problem, it was an inter-Allied problem as well. He repeated the familiar numbers: of their forty-two destroyers, sixteen were in the Adriatic and twenty-six were in the Mediterranean, and not all of them were always available.[152] Revel's basic argument, for which he sought the assistance of Sonnino and Orlando, and passed on to Admiral Sims through the Italian naval attaché in London, ran: it was up to the United States, possibly joined by Japan, to send twenty-five armed yachts and twenty destroyers to the Mediterranean. The US Navy was, according to Revel, in the privileged position of having fresh and abundant matériel. Orlando promised to do what he could and these Italian requests would form an important topic at the new Allied Naval Council when it began to meet in 1918.[153]

Despite the shortages of coal, the British concluded the year on a relatively hopeful note as far as the naval aspects of the Italian situation were concerned, provided Venice did not fall. The greatest immediate disadvantage was denial of the use of Italian railways for troops going to Salonika and Egypt. Those railways were now fully absorbed with British and French troops going to reinforce the Italian front. However, those movements would soon end provided the situation remained the same. If Venice fell, however, the naval situation in the Adriatic would alter for the worse with no naval base between Venice and Brindisi and Austrian raids aimed at cutting the coastal railway would be exceedingly difficult to frustrate. The British had also recently honoured an Italian request for 2,000 mines which were being laid off Otranto as an anti-submarine measure.[154]

The mines off Otranto were badly needed, for the Otranto barrage itself had not improved significantly by the end of the year. In October the British laid an experimental fixed-net barrage about two and a half miles long. The barrage, based on a British design with surface buoys and connecting mines and nets, proved to be a dismal failure and did not survive more than seventeen days of continuous strong winds and rough seas. The British abandoned the project, whereupon the Italians promptly asked for material to lay the Franco-Italian designed fixed net. Captain Learmonth, the Captain Supervising Submarine Defences, termed the Franco-Italian submerged barrage 'a still more doubtful project', and the British still refused to provide the large quantity of material required until after the Italians had laid a trial section of the Franco-Italian barrage not over two miles in length in depths exceeding 100 fathoms. The Admiralty did agree to furnish material for this trial.[155] Commodore Heneage did not consider any system of fixed nets to be practical in the Adriatic because of the depth of the waters, and when the French expert, de Quillacq, presented a scheme for an improved fixed barrage Learmonth wrote that there was 'no prospect whatever of the success of the scheme which would in a very short time become a hopeless tangle'. He termed the scheme somewhat similar to one which had failed in its early stages in the Dover Straits. The Admiralty therefore politely thanked de Quillacq for his effort and informed him that they did not consider it practicable to give his scheme a trial. They would rely on surface, air and submarine patrols rather than a fixed obstruction to make the Otranto barrage as hazardous as possible for submarines.[156]

There were schemes for this three-dimensional attempt to seal the Straits of Otranto floating about the Admiralty in December of 1917 when the consensus was reached about the impracticability of a fixed barrage and the ineffectiveness of a single line of drifters. Calthorpe had strengthened the barrage somewhat during the autumn by shifting some trawlers, drifters and motor launches from the Aegean, but much more was needed to make it really effective. Captain Fisher, Director of the Anti-Submarine Division, had one plan involving trawlers, destroyers, CMBs (high-speed, coastal motor-boats), motor launches, aircraft, hydrophones and minefields out to the 100-fathom line. The idea was to create a zone around sixty-five miles deep which Fisher considered a greater distance than a submarine could travel in a single night. The only problem, as Fisher and others had recognized, was that the forces to put the scheme into operation were not yet in existence. Rear-Admiral Hope, Director of Operations Division, and already on record as being dubious about convoys, introduced a dangerous wrinkle and proved again that fixed ideas died hard. He proposed strengthening the barrage by taking destroyers from convoy escort duties which would be left to sloops. Hope argued that with the exception of escorting troop transports, destroyers 'would be far more usefully employed' at Otranto 'worked by Divisions under their proper commands'.[157]

The Admiralty cabled these considerations to Calthorpe on the 31st and asked how far north his authority over the patrol had to be extended, the total number of craft required, and how many he could provide himself or obtain from the French and Italians. In estimating destroyer strength, the Admiralty told Calthorpe to give consideration to withdrawing all destroyers from escort duties, except for troop transports and certain fast steamers not included in convoys. Calthorpe, who had been lukewarm about convoys himself, agreed with the general idea on 9 January and, as soon as improved weapons were available and personnel trained in their use, intended to carry out a much stronger patrol than before by employing all destroyers and torpedo-boats from the Aegean in addition to Adriatic vessels. This meant that the operation could only continue for a limited period of one month. To make the increased patrol permanent more destroyers and aircraft were essential. Calthorpe wanted a free hand from Italian authorities between approximately the parallels of latitudes 39° 30' and 41° 15' N. He did not expect operations to begin for about two months and, in the meantime, asked for the River-class destroyers to be relieved by more modern vessels, trawlers to replace wooden drifters whose hulls were affected by marine organisms, a hastening as much as possible of the supply of steam winches for kite balloons and more Fish hydrophones.[158] A major reinforcement of the Straits of Otranto was therefore on the agenda for

1918, although how far this would be accomplished at the expense of convoy escorts remained to be seen. It was a classic debate over strategy: would it be better to concentrate on stopping submarines from getting out to attack merchant shipping or concentrate on defending that shipping in convoys?

The disaster of Caporetto and its aftermath and the constant Italian appeals for assistance in one form or another have sometimes obscured the fact that, as far as the naval war in the Adriatic was concerned, things were not as bad as they seemed. The Austrians never attempted those extensive raids and landing schemes the Italians had been so worried about. Freyberg, the German naval attaché in Vienna, quoted a private letter from an unnamed Austrian flag officer who was critical of Austrian naval leadership. The flag officer criticized its lack of effort in hampering the Italian retreat or harassing the seaward flank of the Italian army, for example, trying to catch those slow monitors as they steamed southwards during the evacuation, or more energetically shelling coastal railway bridges. The naval leadership was also, according to Freyberg's source, lethargic in supporting waterborne supply of the advancing Austrian forces in areas where bridges had been destroyed. The navy had also failed to disturb Italian traffic to and from Valona in the south.[159]

The k.u.k. Kriegsmarine did not repeat its spectacular raid of 15 May. There were occasional sorties against the Brindisi–Valona transport route, such as *Helgoland* and the I Torpedo Division (plus two submarines) on the night of 18–19 October, but they met no hostile vessels. Moreover, the Austrian commanders were warned to avoid encounters with equal or stronger forces in the vicinity of enemy bases.[160] After Caporetto, *Novara* and three torpedo-boats repeated the attempt against the Valona–Brindisi route on the night of 12–13 November, but the torpedo-boats were forced back by bad weather and *Novara*, after approaching to within twenty-three miles of Brindisi, encountered nothing. A sortie by three torpedo-boats against the same route on 22 November had to be broken off because of bad weather. *Tátra*, *Balaton* and *Csepel* sortied against the Valona–Otranto line on the night of 13–14 December and encountered four destroyers. *Tátra* fired a torpedo, which missed, against one of the enemy group but, with orders to avoid combat with superior forces close to enemy bases, the Austrians returned home apparently unnoticed.[161] The Austrians, in sum, were unable to either disturb communications with Valona or attack the drifter line in its new and admittedly less effective position.

The k.u.k. Kriegsmarine had enjoyed considerable luck up to now and had the appearance of at least denying the Adriatic coast of the Dual Monarchy to far superior enemies. That luck was going to desert the Austro-Hungarian navy in the final year of its existence. There was also a warning sign that the navy also could not remain immune to the internal tensions of the Dual Monarchy. On 5 October part of the crew of the torpedo-boat Tb11, led by a Slovene and a Czech rating, locked the officers in their cabin and brought the boat from Sebenico to the Italian coast where they surrendered. Tb11, rebaptized *Francesco Rismondo* in Italian service, had little military value in itself and the incident may have been an isolated one, more connected with anarchist and anti-war sentiment than the nationality problems which would tear the monarchy apart.[162] Nevertheless the incident and the uncertainty it caused, since the Austrian authorities did not know exactly what had happened, was obviously disturbing to the Austrians and their German allies.[163] Was it a harbinger of events to come?

In the northern Adriatic the old coast-defence battleships *Wien* and *Budapest* had been shifted to Trieste in October to support the army. On 16 November, escorted by fourteen torpedo-boats, they bombarded the coastal batteries at Cortellazzo near the mouth of the Piave, while on the 28th Austrian destroyers and torpedo-boats bombarded the coastal railway near Senigallia. The old battleships at Trieste were a tempting target for the ambitious and energetic officers who served with the Mas boats and on the night of 10 December the commander of the torpedo flotilla at Venice, Capitano di vascello Pignatti, led a long-planned expedition against Trieste. The torpedo-boats 9PN and 11PN, towed Mas9 (Tenente di vascello Rizzo) and Mas11 (Capotimoniere Ferrarini) respectively, to the vicinity of Trieste. The two Mas boats managed to break through the obstructions of the port and Rizzo succeeded in torpedoing the *Wien*, which sank within a few minutes. The Italians escaped unharmed in what had been a daring and well-executed stroke that had significant results in raising Italian morale at a difficult moment.[164] This was the worst Austrian loss so far during the war and there was suspicion that treachery may have played a role in letting the Italians into the harbour. The old battleship *Arpád* reinforced Trieste and, on 19 December, Linienschiffskapitän Vuković led *Arpád*, *Budapest* and the light cruiser *Spaun*, escorted by six destroyers and a large number of torpedo-boats and minesweepers, to bombard the coastal batteries at Cortellazzo again, but on 20 December the battleships and *Spaun* were brought back to Pola. Furthermore, in order to obtain personnel for the submarine and air service Njegovan recommended taking the three old battleships of the Habsburg class (*Habsburg*, *Arpád*, *Babenberg*) out of service and the Kaiser authorized the decision at the end of the year.[165] By this time the German naval attaché was reporting considerable criticism of Njegovan and the High Command within the Austrian navy, undoubtedly stirred by the loss of the *Wien* and perhaps best expressed with the remark by an unnamed officer: 'Since Haus is dead the slovenliness [*schlamperei*] does not cease.'[166] For if the sinking of the *Wien* had important effects in raising morale in the Italian Navy, it had the opposite, although less pronounced, effect on the Austrians. Certainly, the old spell had been broken as the final year of the war began.

Notes: Chapter 10

1 Kerr to Admiralty, 21 May 1917, Heneage to Kerr, 3 June 1917, Appendix VII, p. 7, PRO, Adm 137/782. Kerr incorrectly states in his memoirs that a submarine was caught in the nets on the 13th and implies this brought about the raid on the 15th. Admiral Mark Kerr, *The Navy in My Time* (London, 1933), p. 195.

2   Horthy, *Memoirs*, p. 81.
3   Heyssler, 'Erinnerungen' (1936), typescript in private possession, pp. 412, 414.
4   Sokol, *Österreich-Ungarns Seekrieg*, p. 363. Sokol unfortunately says nothing on the origins of the action. According to French sources four Austrian destroyers were also out on the night of 1 March when *Gorgone* spotted them but could not attack. Thomazi, *Guerre navale dans l'Adriatique*, p. 147; Ufficio Storico, *Marina italiana*, Vol. 4, p. 459.
5   Hansa, 'Angriff auf die Überwachungslinie LEUCA-FANO', 13 May 1917, Hansa to Njegovan, 17 May 1917, OK/MS VIII-1/1 ex 1917, No. 2716.
6   Pipon to Mediterranean Intelligence Officers, 21 May 1917 enclosed in Pipon to Admiral F. Hamilton, n.d., National Maritime Museum, Greenwich, Hamilton MSS, HTN/118b. Italian dispositions are in Ufficio Storico, *Marina italiana*, Vol. 4, pp. 493–8; Corbett and Newbolt, *Naval Operations*, Vol. 4, p. 298.
7   Attack on the convoy in Ufficio Storico, *Marina italiana*, Vol. 4, pp. 498–507; Otto Rauscher, 'Auf S.M.S. "Csepel" im Otranto-Gefecht' [with excerpt from *Csepel*'s log], *Marine – Gestern, Heute*, vol. 7, no. 3 (Sept. 1980), pp. 89–92.
8   Standard and detailed accounts are in Corbett and Newbolt, *Naval Operations*, Vol. 4, pp. 297–306; Ufficio Storico, *Marina italiana*, Vol. 4, ch. 20; Sokol, *Österreich-Ungarns Seekrieg*, pp. 376–93; Thomazi, *Guerre navale dans l'Adriatique*, pp. 147–53.
9   Heneage to Kerr, 3 June 1917, PRO, Adm 137/782.
10 Heyssler to Hansa, 29 May 1917, OK/MS VIII-1/1 ex 1917, No. 3310. See also his 'Erinnerungen', loc. cit. at n. 3, pp. 418–20, and his short account 'Les croiseurs autrichiens dans le canal d'Otrante' in Mantey, *Les Marins allemands au combat*, pp. 293–304. It is not clear exactly what drifter Heyssler is referring to, although it may have been the *Admirable* whose crew abandoned ship after the boiler exploded and wheel house was shot away. The second hand (A. Gordon) was cited as killed after scrambling back on board and trying unsuccessfully to reach the gun. The details, of course, do not coincide. See Heneage's account in Heneage to Kerr, 3 June 1917, Appendix V, PRO, Adm 137/782.
11 Addison to Crampton, 28 May 1917, Imperial War Museum, London, Crampton MSS, 71/29/1; Addison to Heyssler, 19 Nov. 1921, Heyssler MSS, in private possession.
12 Ufficio Storico, *Marina italiana*, Vol. 4, pp. 521–2.
13 Pipon, Account for Intelligence Officers, 21 May 1917, loc. cit. at n. 6, Hamilton MSS, HTN 118b.
14 Addison to Crampton, 28 May 1917, loc. cit. at n. 11, Crampton MSS 71/29/1.
15 ibid.; Addison to Heyssler, 28 Oct. and 19 Nov. 1921, Heyssler MSS.
16 Addison to Crampton, 28 May 1917, loc. cit. at n. 11, Crampton MSS 71/29/1; Hansa to Njegovan, 17 May 1917, OK/MS VIII-1/1 ex 1917, No. 2716; Heyssler to Hansa, 29 May 1917, ibid., No. 3310.
17 Addison to Heyssler, 19 Nov. 1921, Heyssler MSS; Kerr to Admiralty, 21 May 1917, PRO, Adm 137/782.
18 Vivian to Kerr, 18 May 1917, ibid.; Admiral Casanova at Valona had no information. See Ufficio Storico, *Marina italiana*, Vol. 4, p. 517.
19 Franz Robert Oedl, '50 Jahre Otranto', *Österreichische Militärische Zeitschrift* (1967), pp. 244–8; Hansa to Njegovan, 17 May 1917, OK/MS VIII-1/1 ex 1917, No. 2716. Recent scholarship is more critical. See: Karl von Lukas, 'Das

Gefecht in der Otrantostrasse am 15 Mai 1917: Versuch einer kritischen Betrachtung', *Marine – Gestern, Heute*, vol. 4, no. 2 (June 1977), pp. 34–40.

20 Präsidialkanzlei, Marinesektion to Flottenstabschef, 16 May 1917, OK/MS VIII-1/1 ex 1917, No. 2610.

21 Pipon to Hamilton, n.d. [c. 21 May 1917], loc. cit. at n. 6, Hamilton MSS, HTN 118b; Vivian to Kerr, 18 May 1917, Kerr to Admiralty, 21 May 1917, PRO, Adm 137/782; Kerr to Jellicoe, 29 May 1917, British Library, London, Jellicoe MSS, Add. MSS 49036.

22 Report by Maj. Huntington [liaison officer with French fleet], 20 June 1917, PRO, Adm 137/782; Ufficio Storico, *Marina italiana*, Vol. 5, p. 150.

23 Heneage to Kerr, 3 June 1917, Appendix VII, p. 7, Kerr to Admiralty, 21 May 1917, minutes by Hope, 25 May, Oliver, 27 May and Jellicoe, 27 May 1917, Admiralty to Villarey, 30 May 1917, PRO, Adm 137/782.

24 Memorandum by Italian Embassy, London, 18 June 1917, ibid., Adm 137/1414; Kerr to Admiralty, 14 July 1917, minutes by Coode [for DOD], 15 and 21 July, Oliver, 17 July, and Jellicoe, 19 July 1917, ibid., Adm 137/496; Minute by Hope [DOD], 3 July 1917, ibid., Adm 137/1420.

25 Admiralty to Foreign Office, 6 July 1917, PRO, FO 371/2946; original with Revel's annotation in USM, Cartella 740/1.

26 Corbett and Newbolt, *Naval Operations*, Vol. 4, p. 306; Admiralty to Colonial Office, 6 and 18 May 1917, Governor General of Commonwealth of Australia to Secretary of State for Colonies, 12 May 1917, Admiralty to Vice-Admiral, Eastern Mediterranean Squadron, SNO Malta and Rear-Admiral, British Adriatic Squadron, 4 June 1917, PRO, Adm 137/1414.

27 Admiralty to Kerr, 16 July 1917, SNO Malta to Admiralty, 21 Aug. 1917, ibid.; Naval Staff (Training and Staff Duties Division), *Mediterranean Staff Papers*, p. 102; Calthorpe to Commodore, British Adriatic Force, 24 Sept. 1917, ibid., Adm 137/1415.

28 Somerville to Admiralty, 27 May 1917, ibid., Adm 137/782; Kerr to Jellicoe, 29 May 1917, loc. cit. at n. 21, Jellicoe MSS, Add. MSS 49036; Pipon to Hamilton, 30 May 1917, loc. cit. at n. 6, Hamilton MSS, HTN/118; Sokol, *Österreich-Ungarns Seekrieg*, pp. 473–4.

29 De Bon to French Naval Attaché, London, 12 May 1917, minutes by Learmonth [CSD], 23 May, Fisher (DASD), 26 May, Memorandum (including the preceding), n.d., Admiralty to Heneage, 25 May 1917, PRO, Adm 137/1416.

30 Villarey to Admiralty, 1 June 1917, Learmonth to Heneage, 2 June 1917, Lostende to Admiralty, 7 June 1917, ibid.

31 I.C.-21, Summary of the Proceedings of the Anglo-French Conference, Paris, 4–5 May 1917, PRO, Cab 28/2; G.T.-775, Memorandum by Jellicoe and Robertson, 18 May 1917, ibid., Cab 24/13.

32 I.C.-22, General Conclusions of an Anglo-French Conference, London, 28–29 May 1917; I.C.-23, Note of Anglo-French Conference, London, 28 May 1917; I.C.-23(a), Appendix II, Jellicoe, 'The Shipping Situation', p. 5, ibid., Cab 28/2.

33 Gauchet to de Gueydon, 31 May 1917, Gauchet to Rear-Admiral, 2ᵉ Division Légère, 6 June 1917, de Gueydon to Gauchet, 17 June 1917, SHM, Carton Ed-105; the British account is: Hayes-Sadler to Admiralty, 17 June 1917, PRO, Adm 137/398. Published accounts are in Thomazi, *Guerre navale dans la Méditerranée*, pp. 154–6; Corbett and Newbolt, *Naval Operations*, Vol. 4, pp. 313–14.

34 Lacaze to Gauchet, 25 June 1917, SHM, Carton A-133; de Gueydon to Gauchet, 2 July 1917, ibid., Carton Ed-105.

35   British Naval Attaché Athens to Admiralty, 20 July 1917, PRO, Adm 116/1574; Gauchet to de Gueydon, 26 July 1917, de Gueydon to Gauchet, 22 July 1917, Protocol between de Gueydon and Admiral Condouriotis [Greek Minister of Marine], n.d., SHM, Carton Ed-105.
36   Gauchet to Lacaze, 26 July 1917, ibid.
37   De Bon to Lacaze and marginal note by Lacaze, 27 July 1917, Gauchet to Minister of Marine, 12 Aug. 1917, ibid.
38   Foreign Office to Crackanthorpe, 27 July 1917, Crackanthorpe to Foreign Office, 30 July and 24 Sept. 1917, PRO, Adm 116/1574; Naval Staff (Intelligence Division), 'Greek Navy', 10 Sept. 1917, Minute by Coode, 17 Sept. 1917, Jellicoe to de Bon, 12 Oct. 1917, Historical Section Summary, Greece: British Naval Mission, ibid., Adm 137/1418.
39   Admiralty (Training and Staff Duties Division), *Mediterranean Staff Papers*, p. 21.
40   Gibson and Prendergast, *German Submarine War*, pp. 256, 258.
41   Translation of paper read by Admiral de Bon, 28 May 1917, minutes by Hope [2 DOD], 29 May and Jellicoe, 30 May 1917, PRO, Adm 137/1421; G.T.-789, Jellicoe, 'The Naval Position in the Mediterranean', 21 May 1917, PRO, Cab 24/13.
42   Lacaze to Gauchet, 4 June 1917, Gauchet to Lacaze, 5 June 1917, SHM, Carton A-29.
43   Minute by Jellicoe, 12 June 1917, PRO, Adm 137/1421. Attributes of Wemyss are described in Marder, *Dreadnought to Scapa Flow*, Vol. 5, pp. 4–5.
44   Wemyss to Jellicoe, 27 June 1917, Wemyss, 'Organisation of Mediterranean Command', n.d., PRO, Adm 137/1576.
45   On the Mediterranean Staff see Patrick Beesly, *Very Special Admiral: The Life of Admiral J. H. Godfrey, CB* (London, 1980), pp. 44–7; Godfrey has a more detailed account in his own memoirs [copy in Churchill College, Cambridge], J. H. Godfrey, *The Naval Memoirs of Admiral J. H. Godfrey* (7 vols in 10, Hailsham, Sussex, 1964–6), Vol. 2, pp. 85–90.
46   Wemyss to Keyes, 13 Aug. 1917, in Halpern (ed.), *The Keyes Papers*, Vol. 1, Doc. 192, p. 407. See also Lady Wester Wemyss, *The Life and Letters of Lord Wester Wemyss* (London, 1935), p. 357. On the Admiralty reorganization see: Marder, *Dreadnought to Scapa Flow*, Vol. 4, ch. 8; N. A. M. Rodger, *The Admiralty* (Lavenham, Suffolk, 1979), pp. 133–5.
47   Lambart to Keyes, 19 Nov. 1918, in Halpern (ed.), *The Keyes Papers*, Vol. 1, Doc. 254, p. 515. There is a scathing portrait of Calthorpe in Richmond's diary characterizing him as 'a fusser & a meddler' and a 'very stupid little man' likely to rise to command of a fleet through influence. In my opinion this is totally unjustified by his record as C.-in-C. In the complex and delicate situation in which Calthorpe performed on the whole successfully, the censorious Richmond, for all his brilliance, would most likely have been a disaster. Richmond Diary, 12 Nov. 1910 in Marder, *Portrait of an Admiral*, p. 72.
48   Godfrey, *The Naval Memoirs*, Vol. 2, p. 96.
49   ibid., pp. 99–100.
50   Ufficio del Capo di Stato Maggiore della Marina, 'Promemoria – Comando Navale Supremo in Adriatico', n.d. [29 Apr. 1917], USM, Cartella 741/4.
51   Rodd to Balfour, 17 June and 5 July 1917, PRO, FO 371/2945; Saint Pair to Lacaze, 19 June 1917 and 9 July 1917, SHM, Carton Ea-136; US Naval Attaché to ONI, Report No. T-122, 18 June 1917, NARS, RG 38, E-7-a, File No. 327. A detailed but, of course, undocumented account of intrigue involving a Giolittian deputy named Battaglieri, Assistant-Secretary of the Navy, is to be

found in the 'Notizie Riservato' of General Brusati, the King's aide-de-camp. See: 'Il caso Triangi . . .', n.d., ACS, Carte Brusati/Ilbis (VIII-10-54). Corsi received command of the dreadnought squadron at Taranto.

52 Saint Pair to Lacaze, 18 July 1917, SHM, Carton Ea-136; US Naval Attaché to ONI, Report No. T-144, 18 July 1917, NARS, RG 38, E-7-b, Box 786, File 5860; Rodd to Balfour, 18 July 1917, PRO, FO 371/2945.

53 Kelly to Carson, 13 July 1917, House of Lords Record Office, London, Lloyd George MSS, F/6/2/38.

54 Alexandre Ribot, *Letters à un ami: souvenirs de ma vie politique* (Paris, 1924), p. 342; Dr Al. Ribot (Pub.), *Journal d'Alexandre Ribot et correspondences inédites, 1914–1922* (Paris, 1936), p. 166. The most detailed account of Lacaze's resignation is in Poincaré, *Au service de la France*, Vol. 9, pp. 190, 195, 219, 221, 225–9.

55 Lacaze to Ribot, 2 Aug. 1917, MAE, Papiers d'Agents, Jules Cambon, Vol. 15, f. 61; Lacaze to Barrère, 5 Aug. 1917, ibid., Papiers Barrère, Vol 3, ff. 22–3.

56 George Grahame to Lord Bertie, 13 Aug. 1917, PRO, FO 800/191. On Thomas and the Socialists see Poincaré, *Au service de la France*, Vol. 9, pp. 234–5; on the careers of Chaumet and Leygues see entries in *Dictionnaire des parlementaires français*.

57 Coal for Italy forms the subject of Cabinet Papers G.T.-187, 22 June 1917, G.T.-1309, 5 July 1917, G.T.-1340, 9 July 1917, G.T.-1510, 28 July 1917, PRO, Cab 24/19.

58 Ministry of Marine, General Staff, 4th Section, Decisions at Paris Conference, 24–26 July 1917, Minute by Jellicoe, 28 July 1917, PRO, Adm 137/1420; Ufficio Storico, *Marina italiana*, Vol. 5, pp. 304–13.

59 I.C.-25(C) Decisions of Conference [London], 7–8 Aug. 1917, I.C.-25(D), Resolutions of Meeting [London], 8 Aug. 1917, PRO, Cab 28/2.

60 Larking to Rodd, 19 July 1917, minutes by Oliver, 31 July and 6 Aug. 1917, Jellicoe, 6 Aug. and Everett, 20 Aug. 1917, ibid., Adm 137/1415.

61 Admiralty to Calthorpe, 6 Aug. 1917, ibid., Adm 137/1421.

62 Record of Conference on Trade Protection in the Mediterranean, 14 Aug. 1917, Naval Staff (Operations Division), Memorandum on Situation in the Mediterranean, 15 Aug. 1917, National Maritime Museum, Greenwich, Fremantle MSS, FRE/301. There is also an annotated copy of the record of the conference in: Naval Library, Ministry of Defence, London, Godfrey MSS, Mediterranean Papers (II).

63 Revel to Sonnino, 23 Aug. 1917, USM, Cartella, 740/1.

64 Bianchi to Boselli, 24 Aug. 1917, USM, Cartella 915/1.

65 Navy Department to Sims, 5 July 1917, NARS, RG 45, TP File, Box 560; 'The American Effort in the Mediterranean', n.d. [postwar], ibid., OD File, Box 308; Grant to Admiralty, 20 Aug. 1917, Minute by Coode, 5 Sept. 1917, PRO, Adm 137/1411.

66 Revel to Boselli, 11 Aug. 1917, USM, Cartella, 361/6.

67 Vannutelli to Revel, 31 Aug. 1917, USM, Cartella 740/1; Cusani Visconti to Revel, 25 Aug. 1917, Revel to Sonnino, 25 Aug. 1917, ibid., Cartella 827.

68 Minutes of Proceedings, Naval Conference, London, 4 Sept. 1917, ff. 277, 284–5, 289, Reports and Conclusions, ff. 275–7, Appendix II, Report of Sub-Committee on Convoys, ff. 290–1, PRO, Adm 137/1420.

69 Minutes of Proceedings, London Conference, 5 Sept. 1917, ff. 286–8, Report and Conclusions, ff. 275–7, 288–9, ibid., Adm 137/1420; Villarey to Wemyss, 8 Sept. 1917, USM, Cartella 743/1.

70 Minutes of Proceedings, London Conference, 5 Sept. 1917, ff. 288–9, Conclusions, PRO, Adm 137/1420.

71 Memorandum by Calthorpe, 22 Aug. 1917, ibid., Adm 137/1415.

72 Revel, 'Traffic Defense and the Submarine Menace in the Mediterranean from the Italian Point of View', English translation either by the Admiralty or Italian naval attaché, 3 Sept. 1917, ibid.

73 Minutes by NID, 26 Sept. Fisher [DASD], 8 Oct., Learmonth [CSD], 13 Oct. 1917, ibid. The US naval attaché sent a copy of the Calthorpe–Revel exchange to ONI with his own comments, Train to ONI, Report No. T-199, 23 Sept. 1917, NARS, RG 45, WX-4 File, Box 749.

74 Calthorpe to British Naval Attaché, Rome, 19 Sept. 1917, PRO, Adm 137/1415.

75 Bianchi to Boselli, 24 Aug. 1917, Revel to Del Bono, 6 Sept. 1917, Del Bono to Boselli, 7 Sept. 1917, USM, Cartella 915/1.

76 G.T.-2059, 'Coal for Italy', 14 Sept. 1917, PRO, Cab 24/26; Foreign Office to Rodd, 19 Sept. 1917, ibid., Adm 137/1415.

77 Erskine (Rome), to Foreign Office, 21 and 27 Sept. 1917, ibid.

78 Revel to Sonnino, 24 Sept. 1917, USM, Cartella, 740/1.

79 Note by Italian Embassy, 27 Sept. 1917, minutes by Whitehead [DMM], 12 Oct. and Coode, 13 Oct., Admiralty to Foreign Office, 15 Oct. 1917, PRO, Adm 137/1415.

80 Translation of Revel's Memorandum, 26 Sept. 1917, minutes by Coode and Oliver, 17 Oct. and Jellicoe, 18 Oct. 1917, ibid.

81 Japanese Naval Attaché, Rome to Cusani, 4 Sept. 1917, Revel to Como, 6 Sept. 1917, Sakano to Como, 30 Sept. 1917, USM, Cartella 740/1.

82 Villarey to Revel, 20 Sept. 1917, Revel to Sonnino, 10 Oct. 1917, ibid.

83 Villarey to Admiralty, 15 Oct. 1917, Minute by Coode, 22 Oct. 1917, PRO, Adm 137/1415.

84 Benson to Sims, 24 Sept. 1917, NARS, RG 45, TD File, Box 552.

85 Sims to Benson, 28 Oct. 1917, ibid., TD File, Box 553.

86 Foreign Office to Admiralty, 17 Oct. 1917, Note by Italian Embassy, 12 Oct., minutes by Duff, 20 Oct., Oliver and Jellicoe, 22 Oct., and Wemyss, 26 Oct. 1917, PRO, Adm 137/1415.

87 Revel to Del Bono, 24 Oct. 1917, Sonnino to Del Bono, 4 and 23 Nov. 1917, Vannutelli to Del Bono, 7 Nov. 1917, Revel to Italian Naval Attaché, Paris, 11 Nov. 1917, USM, Cartella 740/1.

88 Minute by Everett, 9 Nov. 1917, Note from Italian Embassy, 23 Nov. 1917, Admiralty to C.-in-C. Mediterranean and SNO Gibraltar, 5 Dec. 1917, Admiralty to Foreign Office, 7 Dec. 1917, Admiralty to Calthorpe, 10 Dec. 1917, PRO, Adm 137/1415.

89 Grant to Admiralty, 21 Sept. 1917, minute by Coode, 1 Oct. 1917, Admiralty to Grant, 31 Oct. 1917, Sims to Admiralty, 13 Sept. 1917, Admiralty to Sims, 29 Sept. 1917, ibid., Adm 137/1411.

90 Mediterranean Naval Staff Offices, 'Instructions to Patrol Commanders and Shipping Control Officers', 18 Sept. 1917, ibid., Adm 137/2757.

91 Naval Staff, *Mediterranean Staff Papers*, pp. 59–61, 67; C. Ernest Fayle, *Seaborne Trade* (3 vols, London, 1920–24), Vol 3, pp. 184–5.

92 Admiralty to Calthorpe, 15 Oct. 1917, Calthorpe to Admiralty, 18 Oct. 1917, PRO, Adm 137/2757; Naval Staff, *Mediterranean Staff Papers*, pp. 60–1, 67.

93 Naval Staff, Mediterranean Staff Papers, pp. 61–5. On the threat of a Turco-German offensive see: Oliver, Notes on an Interview with the CIGS, 15 Sept. 1917, PRO, Adm 137/1413. For a discussion of what the contemplated troop transport would involve see: G.T.-2085, Jellicoe, 'Provision of additional sea

transport fof the movement of troops', 20 Sept. 1917, ibid., Cab 24/26; W.P.-54, Jellicoe, 'Question of Reinforcing the Army in Palestine', 11 Oct. 1917, Memorandum by the Ministry of Shipping, 13 Oct. 1917, W.P.-57, Jellicoe, 'Reinforcement of the Army in Palestine', 15 Oct. 1917, ibid., Adm 116/1349.

94 Report of Proceedings at Allied Conference, Mediterranean Naval Staff Offices Malta, 24 Dec. 1917, Minute by Coode DOD(F), 27 Jan. 1918, ibid., Adm 137/1413.

95 Naval Staff, *Mediterranean Staff Papers*, pp. 56–7, 60; Salaun, Rapport au Ministre, 30 Dec. 1917, SHM, Carton Gp-70; Leygues, 'Arrêté sur l'organisation du commandement des forces de patrouilles dans la Méditerranée', 30 Dec. 1917, ibid., Carton Gp-67; Gauchet to Leygues, 11 and 14 Jan. 1918, Leygues to Gauchet, 13 Jan. 1918, ibid., Carton A-29. Further discussion on the French action in Thomazi, *Guerre navale dans la Méditerranée*, pp. 201–3; Laurens, *Commandement naval*, pp. 280–4.

96 Godfrey to Henderson, 9 Dec. 1917, loc. cit. at n. 62, Godfrey MSS, Mediterranean Papers (I).

97 Naval Staff, *Mediterranean Staff Papers*, p. 69.

98 Calthorpe to Admiralty, 28 Oct. 1917, PRO, Adm 137/1413.

99 Calthorpe to Admiralty, 27 Nov. 1917, ibid.; idem, 28 Nov. 1917, ibid., Adm 137/2178. See also Corbett and Newbolt, *Naval Operations*, Vol. 5, pp. 81–2.

100 Calthorpe to Admiralty, 22 Oct. 1917, Admiralty to Calthorpe, 23 Oct. 1917, PRO, Adm 137/1413.

101 Calthorpe to Admiralty, 28 Oct. 1917, Admiralty to Calthorpe, 12 and 13 Dec. 1917, ibid.

102 H. A. Jones, *The War in the Air*, Vol. 5 (Oxford, 1935), pp. 392–3.

103 Henderson to Godfrey, 22 Dec. 1917, loc. cit. at n. 62, Godfrey MSS, Mediterranean Papers (I). For a discussion of hydrophones, see Vice-Admiral Sir Arthur Hezlet, *Electronics and Sea Power* (New York, 1975), pp. 148–53.

104 Minutes by Hope, 10 Dec., Whitehead, 15 Dec. and Duff, 18 Dec. 1917, PRO, Adm 137/1413.

105 Godfrey to Henderson, 25 Nov. 1917, loc. cit. at n. 62, Godfrey MSS, Mediterranean Papers (I).

106 Grant to Admiralty, 8 Nov., Calthorpe to Admiralty, 19 Nov., minutes by Hope and Duff, 23 Nov., Oliver, 24 Nov. and Jellicoe, 2 Dec., Admiralty to Calthorpe, 2 Dec. 1917, Grant to Admiralty, 8 Feb. 1918, Minute by Coode, 12 Feb. 1918, PRO, Adm 137/1411.

107 G.T.-2750, Jellicoe, 'The Influence of the Submarine upon Naval Policy and Operations', 18 Nov. 1917, ibid., Adm 116/1349.

108 Beesly, *Room 40*, pp. 178–80; David Kahn, *The Code Breakers: The Story of Secret Writing* (New York, 1967), p. 277.

109 Naval Staff, *Mediterranean Staff Papers*, p. 32. For a full discussion of communications in the Mediterranean, see ibid., pp. 110–20.

110 Hezlet, *Electronics and Seapower*, pp. 142–5; Robert M. Grant, *U-Boat Intelligence, 1914–1918* (London, 1969), pp. 134–42.

111 Holtzendorff to FdU Pola, 28 June 1917, NARS, T-1022, Roll 731, PG 75298.

112 Ludendorff to Holtzendorff, 9 July 1917, Holtzendorff to Ludendorff, 16 July 1917, ibid., Roll 664, PG 75270.

113 Retzmann to Admiralstab, 16 Sept. 1917, Memorandum by BIII Admiralstab, 17 Sept. 1917, Admiralstab to FdU Pola, 29 Sept. 1917, Admiralstab, 'Besetzung des östlichen Mittelmeer mit U-Booten', n.d., Roll 664, PG 75271.

114 Spindler, *Handelskrieg*, Vol. 4, pp. 376–7, 496–7; Austrian results from Aichelburg, *Unterseeboote Österreich-Ungarns*, Vol. 2, pp. 490–2.

115 Admiralstab, 'Statistisches über den U-bootskrieg im Mittelmeer während der ersten Hälfte des Jahres 1917', 28 Sept. 1917, NARS, T-1022, Roll 665, PG 75272.

116 FdU to Admiralstab, 29 Mar. and 13 May 1918, ibid., Roll 927, PG 76415.

117 Spindler, *Handelskrieg*, Vol. 4, pp. 341–2, 359–60, 466, 474–5.

118 Püllen to Holtzendorff, 16 Oct. 1917, Püllen, Report on Cattaro, n.d., NARS, T-1022, Roll 665, PG 75271; Püllen to Holtzendorff, 27 Oct. 1917, Roll 731, PG 75296; Report by Director of Dockyard Dept, RMA, Roll 665, PG 75272.

119 Souchon to Admiralstab, 30 Oct. 1917, ibid., Roll 731, PG 75298; Admiralstab to Wireless Station Nauen, 31 Oct. 1917, FdU Pola to Admiralstab, 1 Nov. 1917, Holtzendorff, Immediatvortrag, 4 Nov. 1917, Roll 688, PG 75252.

120 Spindler, *Handelskrieg*, Vol. 4, pp. 476–7, 479–81.

121 ibid., pp. 481–4; Falkenhayn to Admiralstab, 22 Nov. 1917, NARS, T-1022, Roll 688, PG 75252; Corbett and Newbolt, *Naval Operations*, Vol. 5, pp. 79–81.

122 Spindler, *Handelskrieg*, Vol. 4, p. 485; Thomazi, *Guerre navale dans la Méditerranée*, pp. 59–60, 199.

123 Khuepach, Tagebuch, 12 Nov. 1917, Kriegsarchiv, Vienna, Nachlass Khuepach B/200, No. V/1; Freyberg to Capelle and Holtzendorff, 23 Dec. 1917, idem (with marginal comments by Kaiser Wilhelm), 21 Jan. 1918, NARS, T-1022, Roll 538, PG 69132.

124 Admiralstab to U.K. Flotilla, Kiel, 17 Nov. 1917, Admiralstab to U-Flotilla Pola, 27 Dec. 1917, ibid., Roll 665, PG 75272.

125 Freyberg to Marinesektion, 17 Nov. 1917, OK/MS VIII-1/19 ex 1917, No. 6210; Winterhalder to Marinesektion, 25 Nov. 1917, ibid., No. 6357.

126 Admiralstab to Capelle, Representative of Admiralstab at Supreme Headquarters, naval attachés in Vienna, The Hague, Christiana and Stockholm, 9 Oct. 1917, NARS, T-1022, Roll 664, PG 75271.

127 Gibson and Prendergast, *German Submarine War*, p. 262; Spindler, *Handelskrieg*, Vol. 4, p. 480.

128 Hall, 'Italy, Germany's Hope', 25 Oct. 1917, PRO, Adm 116/1768.

129 Short accounts of Caporetto and its aftermath are: Pieri, 'Italian Front', in Esposito (ed.), *A Concise History of World War I*, pp. 169–72; Falls, *The Great War*, pp. 306–10; and in greater detail, idem, *Caporetto 1917* (London, 1966). On the general situation in Italy see Seton-Watson, *Italy from Liberalism to Fascism*, pp. 477 ff.

130 British Naval Attaché Rome to Admiralty, 8 Nov. 1917, PRO, Adm 137/1415; Saint Pair to Minister of Marine, 8 Nov. 1917, SHM, Carton Ea-136.

131 Sims to Admiralty, 23 Oct. 1917, Minute by Fisher [DASD], 1 Nov. 1917, PRO, Adm 137/1420.

132 Sonnino to Del Bono, 10 Nov. 1917; Mortola to Revel, 20 Nov. 1917, Bellavita to Sotto Capo di Stato Maggiore, 25 Nov. 1917, Ameglio to Colosimo, 2 Nov. 1917, Colosimo to Revel, 28 Nov. 1917, USM, Cartella 741/2.

133 Villarey to Revel (with marginal comment by Revel), 14 Nov. 1917, Villarey to Revel, 16 Nov. 1917, Grassi to Revel, 16 Nov. 1917, Revel to Villarey, 19 Nov. 1917, USM, Cartella 740/1.

134 As there was no formal procès-verbal of the conference the French and British minutes differ in emphasis and detail. They are: Minutes of Naval Conference at Rome, 21 Nov. 1917, Minute by Wemyss, 26 Nov. 1917, PRO, Adm

137/1420; Etat-Major Général, Sécretariat [de Bon], 'Note pour le Ministre', 27 Nov. 1917, SHM, Carton Gp–67; Darrieus to Gauchet, 29 Nov. 1917, ibid., Carton A–136.

135 Minute by Wemyss, 26 Nov. 1917, PRO, Adm 137/1420.

136 Calthorpe to Admiralty, 13 Nov. 1917, Memorandum by Fergusson, 6 Nov. 1917, ibid., Adm 137/2180.

137 Calthorpe to Commodore commanding British Adriatic Force, 14 Nov. 1917, ibid.

138 Admiralty to Calthorpe, 4 Dec. 1917, Calthorpe to Gauchet, 10 Dec. 1917, Ballard to Calthorpe, 13 Dec. 1917, Fremantle to Calthorpe, 19 Dec. 1917, Heneage to Calthorpe, 30 Dec. 1917, ibid.

139 Gauchet to Calthorpe, 24 Dec. 1917, ibid.

140 Leygues [or de Bon] to Gauchet, 9 Jan. 1918, SHM, Carton Ed-103.

141 Calthorpe to Admiralty, 22 Jan. 1918, Calthorpe to Gauchet, 22 Jan. 1918, Calthorpe to Commodore, British Adriatic Force and Rear Admiral, British Aegean Sqdn, 22 Jan. 1918, PRO, Adm 137/2180.

142 Admiralty to Calthorpe, 8 Jan. 1918, Memorandum by Fergusson, 7 Apr. 1918, Calthorpe to Admiralty, 11 Apr. 1918, Admiralty to Calthorpe, 2 June 1918, ibid.

143 Daniels [Secretary of the Navy] to Benson, 21 Nov. 1917, NARS, RG 45, TT File, Box 565.

144 Orlando to Del Bono, 28 Nov. 1917, Del Bono to Revel, 29 Nov. 1917, Revel to Del Bono, 30 Nov. 1917, USM, Cartella, 741/2.

145 Unsigned, Note pour le Ministre, 22 Nov. 1917, SHM, Carton Es-14. On Rapallo and the formation of the Supreme War Council see Hankey, *The Supreme Command*, Vol. 2, pp. 719–26; Roskill, *Hankey*, Vol. 1, pp. 451–7. On the Allied Naval Council see: Laurens, *Commandement naval*, p. 304; Trask, *Captains and Cabinets*, pp. 175–9.

146 Memorandum by Geddes, 'Naval Allied Council', 11 Dec. 1917, PRO, Adm 116/1769.

147 Jellicoe to Beatty, 30 Nov. 1917, reproduced in A. Temple Patterson (ed.), *The Jellicoe Papers*, Vol. 2, Publications of the Navy Records Society, Vol. 111 (London, 1968), Doc. 98, p. 229.

148 Paper produced by Admiral Cusani, 30 Nov. 1917, PRO, Adm 137/1415; Report by Cmdt Bellavita, 5 Dec. 1917, USM, Cartella 741/2.

149 Cusani to Benson, n.d. [2 Dec. 1917], Cusani to Revel, 3 Dec. 1917, Revel, Verbale della Seduta [conference at the ministry], 10 Dec. 1917, ibid.

150 Orlando to Del Bono, 2 Dec. 1917, ibid.

151 Saint Pair to Minister of Marine, 2 Nov. 1917, SHM, Carton Ed-94; Revel, 'Economia di combustibili', 17 Dec. 1917, USM, Cartella 1209/1.

152 Del Bono to Revel, 17 Dec. 1917, Revel to Del Bono (with copies to Orlando, Sonnino and the King's ADC), 18 Dec. 1917, Revel to Sonnino, 18 Dec. 1917, USM, Cartella 740/1.

153 Revel to Villarey, 19 Dec. 1917, Orlando to Revel, 22 Dec. 1917, Revel to Orlando, 27 Dec. 1917, Del Bono to Nitti, 29 Dec. 1917, Del Bono to Sonnino, 28 Dec. 1917, ibid.; Villarey to Sims, 30 Dec. 1917, NARS, RG 45, QC File, Box 464.

154 G.T.-3052, Jellicoe, 'Naval Aspects of the Italian Situation', 19 Dec. 1917, PRO, Cab 24/36.

155 Lieut. Bannatyne to Heneage, 1 Dec. 1917, Minute by Learmonth, 14 Dec. and Coode, 18 Dec. 1917, Heneage to Admiralty, 9 Dec. 1917, Admiralty to British Liaison Officer, Paris, 14 Dec. 1917, ibid., Adm 137/1416.

156 Heneage to Admiralty, 28 Dec. 1917, minutes by Learmonth, 17 Jan., and Coode, 18 Jan. 1918, Admiralty to Heneage, 22 Jan. 1918, ibid. For a defence of the de Quillacq system see: Thomazi, *Guerre navale dans l'Adriatique*, pp. 164–5.

157 Minutes by Fisher, 4 Dec., Duff, 5 Dec., Pound [for Director of Plans), 11 Dec., Hope, 18 Dec. and Oliver, 19 Dec. 1917, PRO, Adm 137/1420.

158 Admiralty to Calthorpe, 31 Dec. 1917, Calthorpe to Admiralty, 9 Jan. 1918, ibid.

159 Freyberg to Holtzendorff and Capelle, 7 Nov. 1917, NARS, T-1022, Roll 505, PG 69082. The detailed but semi-official Austrian account of naval activity during the Italian retreat is in Sokol, *Österreich-Ungarns Seekrieg*, pp. 480–4.

160 Hansa, 'Aktionen gegen feindliche Transporte nach Valona', 17 Oct. 1917, Report by Heyssler to Hansa, 20 Oct. 1917, OK/MS VIII-1/1 ex 1917, No. 5757.

161 Hansa to Marinesektion, 14 and 23 Nov. and 14 Dec. 1917, ibid., Nos 6128, 6319 and 6684. Printed account in Sokol, *Österreich-Ungarns Seekrieg*, pp. 548–50.

162 Full accounts in Ufficio Storico, *Marina italiana*, Vol. 6, pp. 177–80; Sokol, *Österreich-Ungarns Seekrieg*, pp. 651–2.

163 Freyberg to Capelle and Holtzendorff, 12 Oct. 1917, NARS, T-1022, Roll 505, PG 69082.

164 Ufficio Storico, *Marina italiana*, Vol. 6, pp. 431–5; Sokol, *Österreich-Ungarns Seekrieg*, pp. 621–3.

165 Njegovan to Kaiser Karl, 18 Dec. 1917, MKSM 66-5/16 ex 1917; Rodler to Marinesektion, 28 Dec. 1917, MKSM, 66-5/16-2 ex 1917.

166 Freyberg to Capelle and Holtzendorff, 23 Dec. 1917, NARS, T-1022, Roll 538, PG 69132.

[11]

The Final Year of the War: Part One

The Sortie of the Goeben *and* Breslau

The eastern Mediterranean and Aegean had, from a strictly naval point of view, enjoyed what might be termed benign neglect for much of the last half of 1917. The real action in the Mediterranean, especially as far as the submarine war was concerned, was elsewhere, notably in the central and western portions. The Allied naval forces off the Dardanelles, particularly the British Aegean Squadron, were steadily run down and consisted essentially of the semi-dreadnoughts *Lord Nelson* and *Agamemnon*, the Patrie-class French battleship *République*, the light cruiser *Lowestoft*, a few scouts and eight destroyers, as well as the usual flotilla of miscellaneous light craft. It was a shadow of the imposing force it had been under de Robeck at the time of the Dardanelles campaign. The French battleship was, in theory, to replace one of the British battleships at Mudros whenever it went off for refit, with the objective of always keeping two battleships off the Dardanelles. How any of them would have been able to catch the much-faster *Goeben* was a question no one could answer. The British commanders, Cecil Thursby until the end of August 1917 and then Sydney Fremantle, were also hard put to maintain the minimum number of destroyers on patrol. Calthorpe considered eight destroyers to be the minimum necessary to maintain the Dardanelles patrol. There were only four available in September 1917 and there had been no real improvement by December, with six available at the beginning of the month but only four around Christmas.[1] This was truly a backwater of the war, or so it seemed.

There were schemes for operations in the area. The fertile mind of Captain Richmond produced a plan in May for offensive operations along the Syrian coast by a detached force. Beatty liked the project enough to forward it to the War Staff, without naming Richmond, for further consideration. The operations against Turkish communications would range from Mersina to Gaza and would be conducted by monitors, seaplane carriers, destroyers, drifters with mines, self-propelled lighters and fast motor-boats, with a military force embarked for raids inland. Contrary to what Richmond might have thought, the Operations Division of the War Staff did give it careful and, on the whole, favourable consideration but the final Admiralty verdict was that minor operations such as these were apt to develop and tended towards a further dispersal of forces.[2] This attitude was understandable in view of the submarine war. Wemyss, whose past experience gave him a natural interest in the eastern Mediterranean, did not deviate from this attitude when the War Office approached him at the end of October about possible operations. Beyond direct naval assistance to Allenby's army, he did not think that any demonstration by the forces at their disposal would have an appreciable effect in drawing Turkish troops towards the threatened coastline, and would involve the use of ships currently assisting Allenby. Wemyss did not rule out such operations at a later date.[3]

Among the many plans circulating in the Admiralty was one for an attack on *Goeben* and *Breslau* at Constantinople. A large Handley Page bomber had, with great difficulty, been flown out to the Aegean in May 1917 by Squadron Commander K. S. Savory and a few raids were carried out from Mudros before the machine was lost at the end of September. The distance of Constantinople and the *Goeben* from the British air bases made large bombers the only really suitable craft to carry the heavier bombs that experienced airmen recommended using against the warship. The Naval Staff estimated that they would need thirty-six aircraft to keep up a sustained attack, but only twenty machines existed in France and there would be no increase in numbers until the following March. The aircraft were too large to ship and would have to be flown out in stages, no mean feat, and there was no certainty that their attacks on the *Goeben* after a seven-hour flight would end in destruction of the ship.[4] It was therefore obvious that it would be a long time before any of these plans would materialize.

Fremantle was ambitious. He was 'not proud of the part the Navy is playing here' and looked towards raids against Turkish lines of communications. He was less confident about anti-submarine operations in his area for the 'Commander-in-Chief has pinched me of no less than 55 units, and has put an end to my hopes of energetic anti-submarine action, but there are other fields of activity still open'.[5] At the end of December, Fremantle formally proposed resuming the policy of raiding the Anatolian coast during the next spring and summer. The forces employed would be 500 to 600 men, which meant that the operations would have been on a slightly larger scale than those conducted with irregular forces in 1916. The proposal, after extensive discussion, did not find favour at the Admiralty. The basic problem was that they could discern no really important objective or anticipate any significant results. Calthorpe shared the Admiralty view and was annoyed that Fremantle's proposal had not gone to him as British C.-in-C. in the first place, for 'It is impossible for me to dispose my forces satisfactorily if operations are planned and proposed direct to the Admiralty without my concurrence.'[6]

The relationship between the C.-in-C. and Rear-Admiral Aegean was not smooth. Captain Philip Dumas of the *Agamemnon* was somewhat acid in his diary concerning Fremantle 'who has every sense but common sense' and was 'full of half digested plans and evidently going off half cocked in many directions'.[7] Dumas, when coaling ship at Malta, found 'Sydney seems to have got everyone's back up' and was 'rabid with Calthorpe' while the latter was 'angry with the Admiralty, generally pessimistic & annoyed with Sydney' and asked Dumas to help smooth matters between them'.[8] Relations between the respective British authorities in the Mediterranean could be as touchy as those between the different Allies.[9]

The more immediate problem for the British commander in the Aegean was, of course, what action to take if the *Goeben* tried to break out of the Dardanelles. The battle cruiser was faster and her guns outranged those of the individual British ships, and she had an even greater superiority over the older French Patrie battleships that might have been present. The *Goeben* had already been the subject of memoranda by the respective commanders, de Robeck, Thursby and Fremantle, but they seemed more concerned with the protection of trade or German attempts to block the Suez Canal in a suicide raid. Dumas did not consider Fremantle's latest plan much of an improvement, for 'no one seems able to take the menace seriously' and Fremantle had left out the most likely possibility of the *Goeben* emerging for a momentary raid on Allied forces off the Straits.[10] This is, of course, exactly what happened but Fremantle was not present to pay the bill. He returned to London at the beginning of the year to succeed Oliver as Deputy Chief of Naval Staff leaving Rear-Admiral Hayes-Sadler in command. Hayes-Sadler could not have known when he assumed command that the Germans had been planning a sortie by the *Goeben* for a few months.

Souchon, the long time commander of the Mittelmeerdivision, had finally returned to Germany in September 1917 to take over the IV Battleship Squadron in the High Seas Fleet. His successor, Vice-Admiral Rebeur-Paschwitz, received a request from Falkenhayn in early November for naval support off the coast of Palestine. The Admiralstab ruled out sending any of the small Half Flotilla of submarines at Constantinople and preferred to use boats from the Adriatic. Rebeur-Paschwitz therefore decided that he could best help Falkenhayn by a sortie against Lemnos and Imbros with the objective of tying down strong forces off the Dardanelles and drawing them from the Syrian coast. He asked Usedom, who commanded the defences at the Straits, about securing a passage through their own minefields and nets and for aerial reconnaissance to determine the extent of the British minefields.[11] Rebeur-Paschwitz admitted that he could provide only indirect relief to the Turkish forces on the Syrian front but he was determined to make the attempt as soon as he had sufficient coal on hand. Unfortunately, over the past year and a half the relatively idle ships had fallen somewhat below full combat-readiness and on 4 December he asked for replacements from Germany to make up the gaps in the ships' complement caused by officers and men being drawn off for other duties.[12] Rebeur-Paschwitz also thought that a sortie would be good for purposes of morale to make up for the recent loss of Jerusalem and to strengthen Turkish naval spirit by demonstrating that ships were meant to be used.

Naturally he accepted the risk of the Allied minefields whose extent he thought he knew through aerial reconnaissance, and whose effectiveness in the absence of new minelaying he thought diminished over a period of time.[13] This confidence was misplaced.

With incredibly poor timing and even poorer judgement the new British commander, Hayes-Sadler, set off for Salonika in the *Lord Nelson* on 16 January. Dumas, now SNO at Lemnos, commented: 'Personally I think it is mad & if anything could make the *Goeben* come out this will & we with hopelessly divided forces.'[14] The French battleship was also away in dock. *Goeben* and *Breslau* did come out on the morning of 20 January, accompanied by Turkish destroyers which did not venture far beyond the entrance to the Dardanelles. Despite slight damage to the *Goeben* from a mine on her way out, the Germans achieved tactical surprise. The Germans sank the 14-in. gun monitor *Raglan* and 6-in. gun monitor M28 in Kusu Bay, Imbros. They paid a heavy price for this success. While proceeding to attack Mudros, followed by the destroyers *Tigress* and *Lizard*, they ran into a minefield and *Breslau* suffered fatal damage while *Goeben*, in an attempt to get into position to tow her sinking consort, was herself mined. The attack on Mudros was cancelled, but *Goeben* suffered further damage from mines getting back into the Straits and to make matters worse ran aground through a navigational error near Nagara Point. British aircraft attacked the motionless battle cruiser but unfortunately the weight of bombs that they could carry was too light to do serious damage.[15] Hayes-Sadler got back from Salonika on the 21st and, according to Dumas, was 'quite cheerful and actually looking for credit whereas in my opinion he is damned forever'. Calthorpe was also on his way in a light cruiser, but to Dumas's disgust the one British submarine on the scene, E12, was not employed because she had a fractured propellor shaft. It took a few days for her replacement E14 to arrive from Corfu. Dumas was frustrated: 'The whole idea seemed to be wait and see whereas both of us [*Lord Nelson* and *Agamemnon*] should be out bombarding & very long range ships telegraphed for at once. There is altogether a complete lack of energy or understanding, only a cynical disbelief in anything.'[16]

Calthorpe finally arrived on the 25th and Dumas proposed manufacturing a potentially more lethal bomb, the idea of one of his officers, from an 18-in. torpedo head. On the 27th Calthorpe sent Lieutenant-Commander G. S. White and E14 into the Straits against the *Goeben*. Calthorpe and others had the general feeling that they were sending him to his death – they were. The defences were more formidable than they had been in 1915 and the Germans and Turks had managed to tow *Goeben* off the sandbank the day before. E14 was lost and the two officers and nine men who survived were taken prisoner.[17] *Goeben*, on the other hand, was badly damaged and could not be entirely repaired at the Constantinople yards. She was immobilized for the time being with improvised bulkheads and cofferdams around her damaged hull.

The Mittelmeerdivision with the loss of the *Breslau* and the immobilization of the *Goeben* had ceased to exist as an effective fighting force, at least for the time being. Rebeur-Paschwitz tried to put the best face on the matter, inflating British losses and claiming that Turkish pride in the deeds accomplished under their flag outweighed sadness over the losses. Austrian intelligence sources reported a very different sentiment on the part of the Turks and Souchon when he finally saw a copy of his successor's report much later, was even less complimentary. He thought it carelessness to do without the services of torpedo-boats outside the Straits when they might have provided some protection against mines, particularly since no grounds for this omission were given. The failure to establish a mine-free outwards and inward course, the breakdown of the compass on the *Goeben*, the breaking off of operations to rescue the *Breslau*'s crew and, finally, running *Goeben* aground, could hardly have strengthened the reputation of the German navy.[18] Neither the British nor the Germans had cause for satisfaction over the sortie. Nevertheless, the complete collapse of Russia and the ability of the Germans and their allies to seize part of the Russian Black Sea Fleet and its bases and yards would soon give the *Goeben* and the Mittelmeerdivision a new lease on life. Over the next few months the British would certainly regret that they had not been able to finish off that ship while they had the chance.

While *Goeben* was still aground, Revel, prompted by the Italian naval attaché, offered at the meeting of the Allied Naval Council in London to contribute a pair of Italian Mas boats armed with torpedoes under the command of Tenente di vascello Berardinelli and an expert crew. The boats would be shipped by rail from Venice to Taranto and were due to be loaded on to a British steamer bound for Mudros, but the escape of the *Goeben* caused the plan to be cancelled.[19] It must have been gratifying to Revel to have been able to offer assistance and the Mas boats, which would later sink an Austrian dreadnought, might have been effective if there had been a way of getting them out to the Dardanelles in time.

Wemyss, now First Sea Lord, was disgusted at the whole affair. He wrote to Beatty: 'The *Goeben* getting away is perfectly damnable and has considerably upset me, since we at the Admiralty were under the happy delusion that there were sufficient brains and sufficient means out there to prevent it: of the latter there were; of the former, apparently not.'[20] Calthorpe, however, was not to be deflected from his primary concern. Despite the unusual political importance of the *Goeben*, submarines operating out of the Adriatic were the major problem in the Mediterranean. Whatever dispositions they made with the present forces now available, there was no guarantee that *Goeben*, once repaired, would be sunk or fail to do great damage if she took the risk and came out again. But if they depleted their anti-submarine forces to concentrate at the Dardanelles, they would suffer very heavy losses to their mercantile marine. Calthorpe discerned, correctly for the most part, that the sortie was intended to force the Allies to immobilize many of the craft that were now interfering with the freedom of German submarines. He therefore proposed to do nothing more than replace *Lord Nelson* and *Agamemnon* with two of the older dreadnoughts of the Grand Fleet, which would mean longer-range guns and a 4-knot increase in speed. He also wanted to strengthen the minefields off the Dardanelles, station a cruiser with the battleships at Mudros and looked for possible assistance from the Greek fleet in the future. But he still intended to keep only a small force of destroyers and submarines off the Dardanelles. The Admiralty approved, but informed him that two dreadnought battleships were not available for the Aegean. It was not possible to send strong reinforcements of any type to the Mediterranean and any light forces that could be spared should be used against submarines.[21]

Hayes-Sadler was perhaps the inevitable victim. When Geddes came out to the Mediterranean in February the First Lord and Calthorpe in conference at Malta criticized him for not leaving two battleships at Mudros, and proceeding to Salonika in *Lord Nelson* instead of the yacht *Triad* which would have been available in a few days. Hayes-Sadler admitted to Geddes when the First Lord visited Mudros that he had made an error in judgement in not keeping the two battleships together, although he claimed he did not know that there was any very definite understanding *Lord Nelson* and *Agamemnon* should be kept together, although this had been the practice in the six months he was there.[22] Calthorpe decided he should be replaced. No one seems to have asked what even two battleships might have accomplished against *Goeben* on 20 January, assuming that the Germans had not run into the minefield and reached Mudros. Dumas reported that when the British had long-range gunnery exercises on 8 February the firing was poor and slow, and 'it is heaven's kindliness that we didn't have to fight *Goeben*'.[23] Hayes-Sadler, according to Dumas, was very depressed by his relief and alarmed him by hinting at suicide. He was replaced by Rear-Admiral Cecil Lambert on 16 March.[24] The Aegean command returned to its status as a backwater of the war with Geddes determined to whittle it down ever more, but the danger that the Germans might get their hands on the Russian Black Sea Fleet would give it potential importance once again in the next few months. This time, however, it would seem as if the French were the ones who would come to the rescue.

Geddes's Mediterranean Tour

The first meeting of the Allied Naval Council took place in London on 22–23 January in the immediate aftermath of the *Goeben*'s sortie and Mediterranean affairs would be the subject of a considerable portion of that body's deliberations. This was understandable since four different navies operated in that sea, and the Council could have been a vehicle toward achieving a degree of unity which was difficult in the Mediterranean itself with its widely scattered commands. Wemyss was sanguine about its prospects and, after the first sitting wrote to Beatty: 'I think that no harm will come of it but that on the contrary some good may ensue. The representatives of our Allies appear quite tame and ready to follow our lead which is, of course, as it should be.' Duff, Assistant Chief of Naval Staff was less happy and referred to 'that most unsatisfactory body' where the cry of the Italians was 'give, give' and 'to obtain real disinterested co-operation appeared an ideal impossible of attainment'.[25] In the long run Duff's prognostication was probably more correct. The Allied Naval Council ame to be more the focus of Allied disunity than the opposite, a debating ground for conflicting strategies and concerns and where the necessity for unanimous agreement paralysed action.

Both de Bon and Revel travelled to London for this first meeting of the Allied Naval Council. Sims, whose headquarters were in London, was naturally present to reflect the increasing American role. The various staffs presented an almost bewildering variety of memoranda which were generally printed and circulated and help make 1918 the most heavily documented year of the war. The agenda, discussions and memoranda are far too extensive to quote in detail but the basic problems concerning the Mediterranean which appeared at the meeting would be themes for the remainder of the war. The subject of the Russian Black Sea Fleet came up the very first morning of the conference in the discussion over greater economy in use of the naval resources of the Allies. The fear that the Germans might use a substantial portion of this force put a brake on Allied plans to lay up older warships, particularly capital ships, in order to use their crews for light craft. The Allies were hampered by a lack of intelligence and, in the end, the conference decided to refer the matter to their respective staffs.[26] The use by enemy submarines of neutral territorial waters and what the Allied response should be was another subject which provoked disagreement. Ironically, the Germans profited from Norwegian territorial waters in the north while the Allies profited from Spanish waters in the south. Calthorpe thought that raids on Allied shipping in Spanish territorial waters were being made occasionally and might be increased in the future, while de Bon and Revel considered that, on the whole, they derived advantages from the use of Spanish waters. The conference decided to recommend that the respective Mediterranean Commanders-in-Chief confer and issue a joint statement on the exact degree of German violations and the numbers of ships actually sunk in Spanish waters, while the legal experts of each country were also asked to submit relevant memoranda. The issue was not considered to be particularly pressing and obviously the Italians and French were far more attached to those Spanish coastal routes than the British Mediterranean C.-in-C. whose staff were now pushing the direct Gibraltar–Genoa convoys.[27]

The question of Mediterranean convoys and escorts produced extensive discussion. Revel explained at length the Italian difficulties and how the threat of Austrian raids to destroy dykes and inundate the countryside forced the diversion of Italian destroyers to meet the threat. Revel did concede that the six to seven Italian ships used to shepherd Italian vessels on the Spanish coastal route and keep them within territorial waters would be placed at the disposal of the Allies for the Gibraltar–Genoa convoys, while he would make every effort to find another three for the Bizerte–Naples service. Geddes acknowledged that, 'At the present time the Mediterranean is not in a very healthy position', and with everyone clamouring for more destroyers admitted that he personally did not understand the Mediterranean and Adriatic situation and proposed making a personal tour of inspection before the next meeting of the Allied Naval Council. Again, in the absence of sufficient information or agreement, the Allies decided that a special commission would meet in Rome in a fortnight to discuss Mediterranean and Adriatic problems, as well as British proposals for the Otranto barrage.[28] In general, the really important questions concerning the Mediterranean were deferred for the future. Nevertheless, Wemyss judged the Council meeting 'on the whole a success', with Geddes 'a past master at the art of conducting a meeting and things went harmoniously'.[29] Revel' perspective was slightly different. He reported that no important decision had been reached with particular and often divergent interests always acting in the background of common interests, but the British mentality was somewhat reluctant to accept the proposals of others and decide problems which did not interest them directly.[30]

The Mediterranean was for a variety of reasons occupying an increasing portion of Geddes's and Wemyss's attention. Calthorpe submitted his extensive plans for a strengthened Otranto barrage on 16 January. To provide the forces to make the barrage effective he would be required to reduce the number of vessels employed on what he termed defensive duties such as escorts and patrols. Moreover, in the period just after the initiatio of the strengthened barrage when submarines would still be operating against shipping, he wanted to borrow a certain number of destroyers and sloops from outside the Mediterranean to replace those escorts withdraw for the barrage. He intended to withdraw all British destroyers and torpedo-boats from the Dardanelles patrol and detached squadrons in the Aegean, and reduce Mediterranean escorts by seven destroyers, eight sloops and twelve trawlers. The destroyers could come from the OE and H through convoys, their place being taken by sloops. The sloops could be provided from the station if promised reinforcements arrived, or by reducing the strength of escorts and accepting a slight delay in traffi eastbound from Malta. Calthorpe's general idea was to deploy the forces of the barrage to cover sufficient depth from north to south to force enemy submarines passing through the straits to surface within sight or hearing of surface craft or aircraft. There would be lines of hunting vessels equippe with hydrophones to make it difficult for the submarine while it was submerged and force it to continually change its course, thereby reducing the amount of distance it covered, exhausting its battery and eventuall making it necessary to surface. There would also be new minefields off the enemy coast north of Valona, submarines on patrol on the northern side of the barrage and kite balloon ships. Calthorpe argued that, for maximum efficiency, the barrage should be as far as possible composed of ships of on nationality. He meant, of course, Britain, and the entire barrage therefor would be under British direction. The major concession the British neede to obtain from their Allies would be for the British SNO of the barrage to command all vessels employed on the barrage south of latitude 41° 15′ N The twelve French destroyers attached to the Italian fleet at Brindisi wou also come under the orders of the British SNO of the barrage force, bu revert to Italian orders if the Allied light cruisers at Brindisi put to sea to meet the enemy. The destroyers forming the northern unit of the barrag and Allied submarines north of the barrage would also come under Itali orders.[31]

The Admiralty also faced pressure from the Ministry of Shipping over the state of affairs in the Mediterranean. The ministry in a memorandum of 10 January called attention to the rise in sinkings in December and the problem of delay of ships awaiting escort. They pointed out 'that delay to any vessel of whatever nationality not only affects the nation to which the ship is bound, but reacts upon all the countries of the Alliance', and that there were still some officers – naval, military and civilian – in Mediterranean ports who did not understand 'that the result of the war depends on cargo carrying merchant steamers' with shipping resources of the world strained to the utmost to keep the civilian populations from starving and to maintain supplies of munitions to the armies. Geddes replied by asking the ministry to send a representative to the forthcoming meeting in Rome.[32] It had been a long time since a First Lord had been forced to devote so much attention to the Mediterranean.

Revel naturally would preside over the meeting in Rome and prepared a memorandum, dated 8 February, summarizing quite clearly the Italian view of the situation and containing few surprises. An offensive by the Allied fleet in the Adriatic 'would be an unpardonable error' and the only means of destroying the Austrian fleet would be to make it the target for an incessant bombardment from the air. If it came out, even for only a brief period, the ships would fall victim to submarines and mines. Geographical conditions – the chain of islands on the Austrian side of the Adriatic – enabled the Austrians to easily concentrate destroyers and torpedo-boats at Pola, Cattaro, or Sebenico, and the Italians were forced to divide their destroyer strength between Venice and Brindisi with each group, of necessity, equal to the total enemy destroyer force. Any reduction of destroyers in the Adriatic would therefore be a great error. There were other aspects of the geographical conditions in the Adriatic which favoured the Austrians. At daybreak, when weather conditions were best for air activity, the defenders of the low-lying Italian coast had the sun in their eyes and were blinded, while the high Dalmatian coast was obscured in the shade. The waters on the Austrian side were crystal-clear making submarines easier to detect; the waters on the Italian side were dark and murky favouring Austrian submarine activity. Moreover, the Adriatic currents caused any enemy mines that broke their moorings to be carried to the Italian side. Revel also gave a full explanation of Italy's need to import coal, fuel oil, steel plate and foodstuffs, the chronic shortage of tonnage and the need to use coastal shipping to distribute essential commodities. He combined this with statistical evidence on the relative safety and effectiveness of the Spanish coastal route.[33]

Revel's exposition was, in many ways, an excellent review of the strategic situation in the Adriatic and Italian difficulties and, allowing for some understandable exaggeration, it was a remarkably frank confession of weakness. It was not appreciated. As Geddes described it to Lloyd George, 'A more plaintive wail was never I think issued from a Naval Commander-in-Chief and First Sea Lord. It is unimportant in substance, but I think it is useful as showing the spirit in which they view the war.' Wemyss when he saw Revel's paper exclaimed: 'Good Lord, what a screed from di Revel. It is not pleasant reading when one thinks that these are our allies.' Ratyé, who was also present in Rome, summarized it pithily: 'We can give nothing more than what we have given up to now; it is even necessary if the Allies wish us to continue this war in a good position that they assist us with more aid.'[34]

The meeting in Rome lasted only two days, 8 and 9 February. Rear-Admiral Hope, Deputy First Sea Lord, led the British delegation on the floor and Calthorpe came up from Malta. Geddes, although present, did not take part in the discussion. The major part of the time was taken up with the British plans for Otranto; the other subjects on the agenda, notably Italian participation in a general system of escorts, were left to the last minute and received scant attention. This was probably deliberate for, as Ratyé explained, Revel's preliminary memorandum followed the usual tactic of emphasizing Italian difficulties and asking for assistance in terms of destroyers and escort craft in order, if not actually to obtain them, to at least not be required to diminish their own resources. There was little likelihood of agreement and, perhaps naturally, the conference concentrated on a subject where something positive might be obtained – the Otranto barrage. The British were at odds with the French and Italians since the latter two placed great faith in the fixed barrage whereas, after the failure of their own design, the British wanted to abandon it. The British favoured what came to be termed the 'mobile barrage', that is, destroyers and drifters. The French Minister of Marine ordered Ratyé to insist on the simultaneous employment of the two systems. Because of his subordinate position to Calthorpe at Malta, Ratyé tried to avoid any open disagreement at the full session of the conference by reaching a preliminary accord the day before. This attempt failed, partially because Calthorpe himself claimed that he had not yet reached a definite agreement with the First Lord about the barrage. The French, who supported the other British proposals concerning the barrage, eventually got rather grudging conditional agreement from the British to continue construction of the fixed barrage with completion subject to favourable results. Whatever reservations the French might have had about the British proposals for the mobile barrage, including strong doubts about how effective hydrophones would really be, they recognized the value of the considerable effort the British barrage would involve and that it would be a formidable obstacle for submarines, even if it did not prove to be an impenetrable barrier. The French and Italians did unite on one point: escorts should not be weakened until the barrage had proved itself.[35]

The British gained their major point. The conference accepted the proposals for a mobile barrage with a British officer in command of the patrols. In turn, the British agreed that during the period of preparation for the barrage they would not diminish escorts except in case of absolute necessity, and would even augment them if possible. Revel managed to get a clause inserted into the conclusions calling attention to the necessity for adequate protection until the next harvest of ships carrying wheat to Italy and continuous protection for vessels carrying coal, and Ratyé secured approval for a resolution to be submitted to the next Allied Naval Council hat the new American submarine chaser squadrons expected in European waters should be allocated equally between the Mediterranean and western oceans, with the first squadron going to the Mediterranean to be put at the disposal of the Malta Commission and to be used in the best manner possible for the protection of coastal convoys.[36]

Geddes thought that the conference had gone 'tolerably well' since they had been able to get British control of the only means suggested by any naval authority of attacking the submarine in the Mediterranean or Adriatic, and hoped they would be in a position to initiate the scheme within a couple of months.[37] Revel mentioned barring other passages used by submarines, such as the Dardanelles and Straits of Gibraltar. He did this less for strategic reasons than for political opportunism, for he did not wish it to be taken for granted that all submarines entered the Mediterranean through waters controlled by the Italians. Revel was practical in outlook. The Italians were neither able to eliminate British influence on the barrage, given the size of the force they were employing, nor was it expedient to separate responsibility for the system from its principal supporters. Consequently, for Revel the agreement was all they could hope for, secured eventual advantages for them and safeguarded the authority of the Italian command. Revel had, of course, insisted that the Adriatic constituted a question quite apart from the general command in the Mediterranean.[38]

The meeting in Rome had another benefit for the Italians. Geddes was impressed with the crying need of coal for the Italian railways and navy after seeing the problem first hand. Sims, too, had noted the extensive cutting down of timber for firewood throughout his journey south to Rome. The Italians could expect a more sympathetic hearing on this subject.[39] The Italians may have been less satisfied with another of Geddes's concerns, an attempt to reorganize arrangements for the repair and salvage of merchant ships in French and Italian yards with representatives at major shipping centres to try and end haggling over raw materials and costs while the ships lay idle.[40]

Geddes continued his tour of inspection to Brindisi, Taranto, Corfu (to meet with Gauchet), and then on to Malta and eventually Mudros. He was not impressed with the command situation at Brindisi where Vice-Admiral Cerri 'merely keeps the place warm' for Revel, but unfortunately the latter was a whole night's journey away if any excitement did take place. If the British were going to sink any submarines they would have to do it themselves, and he hoped that the Admiralty would be able to provide the craft which Calthorpe wanted for the Otranto barrage. The idea that if you wanted to get anything done you would have to do it yourself was, of course, typical of the British attitude in the Mediterranean. Geddes also looked into the delays and problems associated with the convoy system and Captain Henderson, Duff's Naval Assistant and champion of the convoy system, and Lieutenant-Colonel Beharrell, the Director of Statistics, were with the First Lord at Malta to attack the thorny shipping problem. Beharrell would eventually require statistics in reports whose scope and detail were the bane of the Mediterranean Staff. Geddes's general conclusion was to send a shipping expert to the Mediterranean to handle the

431

commercial side of the naval arrangements for handling cargo ships. They needed men with commercial shipping experience to handle duties 'which naval officers before the war never dreamt they would have to undertake'.[4]

The question of shipping delays in the Mediterranean as distinct from losses was a significant one and there were serious charges against the British system. An unnamed correspondent of Lloyd George described the naval officers at Algiers, Oran and other ports as 'totally incompetent either from old age, drink, want of staff or general slackness' with prewar conditions existing everywhere and no one recognizing the great importance of tonnage. Lieutenant-Commander Kenworthy found the same situation on a trip to the Algerian coast in February. With virtually all shipping on time charter to the government there was not the same inducement to owners, masters, or agents to get ships turned around and off to sea as there was in peacetime.[42] Calthorpe, for his part, was 'impressing on everybody concerned the absolute necessity of "speeding up" the mercantile traffic' and also emphasized that no vessel which could steam should be employed as depot ship or hulk.[43] The French had similar problems with convoy causing delays, but since the volume of British trade was much greater so too, was the scope of the problem.

Sir Joseph Maclay, the Shipping Controller, eventually appointed Oswald Sanderson, managing-director of Ellerman's Wilson line, to go out to the Mediterranean with a small staff to study the problem.[44] There was a certain amount of skirmishing, too tedious to go into, between the Admiralty and Ministry of Shipping over their respective spheres of influence but, in the long run, Sanderson's mission was successful. Calthorpe and Sanderson agreed on an organization in which A. C. F. Henderson, managing-director of the Anchor Line, would be appointed to Calthorpe's staff with the title of Director of Commercial Transport and Mediterranean representative of the Shipping Controller. His position would be equivalent to that of Commodore Baird, Director of Shipping Movements, the new title adopted in April 1918 for the British Admiral of Patrols. Shipowners with the title 'Representative of the Ministry of Shipping' would be stationed at principal Mediterranean ports to work in close co-operation with naval authorities, the senior naval officers and naval transport officers. The new representatives of the Ministry of Shipping would exercise authority over local owners and agents, and work toward eliminating delays in loading, discharging, docking and bunkering, with full consideration for convoy timetables. Calthorpe emphasized the slogan 'Time is tonnage'.[45]

The new scheme for the Otranto barrage resulted in a reorganization of the British Adriatic Force. Howard Kelly, now a Commodore, was placed in detailed control of the barrage in command of all British seagoing and air forces in the Adriatic with headquarters at Brindisi. He also continued to command the 8th Light Cruiser Squadron under Italian orders, as well as the two monitors based on Venice. He was directly responsible to the British Mediterranean C.-in-C. for other matters, but would keep the Italian C.-in-C. constantly informed of operations he was about to undertake on the barrage so that the Italians could co-ordinate their action

f the British cruisers put to sea to engage the enemy, Kelly was authorized
o use the destroyers in the northern area of the barrage to co-operate with
he cruisers. Kelly and the destroyers would then come under the orders of
he Italian admiral until the operations were completed, when the
estroyers would revert to their duties on the barrage. Commodore
Ieneage, promoted to rear-admiral, was reappointed British SNO in Italy
vith his flag in the *Queen* at Taranto in charge of all general naval questions
ot connected with sea going, and administration of the drifter and motor-
aunch forces, Royal Naval Air Service, and transport services in southern
taly.[46]

The task of finding an adequate number of small craft for Calthorpe was
ot an easy one, but Geddes considered the submarine situation in the
Mediterranean to be serious enough to justify sending out more craft at the
xpense of home requirements. Calthorpe complained that the vessels in the
Mediterranean were suffering badly from wear and tear and that he needed
etter destroyers – replacing the older River and Beagle class – better
rawlers and more submarines. Calthorpe wanted a reinforcement of, at
east six modern destroyers and eighteen trawlers. Wemyss wrote to
Geddes that he was 'routing about to see what we can do' for Calthorpe and
o doubt should 'pick up something'.[47] This was easier said than done in
iew of the extensive requirements for trawlers in home waters and the
Northern Barrage Patrol. Captain Fuller, Director of Plans, proposed
urning to the Americans and sending a complete unit of thirty-six
ubmarine chasers in lieu of trawlers. While inferior to trawlers in sea-
eeping qualities, according to Fuller, they could do the work required in
ummer months and by mid-summer would be relieved by the larger
American Ford submarine chasers. It was probably natural for Plans
Division to think of the Americans for they worked in close co-operation
vith the US Planning Section, but the forecast of Ford chasers by mid-
ummer would prove to be over optimistic. These craft were not ready
ntil the end of the war. Fuller suggested that six American destroyers
hould work with the chasers, to be drawn from Queenstown, Gibraltar, or
he French coast, but Duff opposed any reduction in the Queenstown
estroyer force because of the large numbers of US troops expected to be
rossing the Atlantic that summer. Calthorpe, for his part, did not think the
ubmarine chasers had the sea-keeping qualities to replace trawlers on the
Otranto barrage, and it was also desirable that vessels employed on the
arrage were of the same nationality. Moreover, local petrol-storage
acilities were insufficient to maintain the chasers and he would need an oiler
o supply them. Calthorpe preferred to employ the chasers in Egypt where
he fuelling question was simpler and where they could relieve escorts on
he Palestine coast earmarked for Otranto.[48]

The decision to use the American submarine chasers in Egypt rather than
Otranto reckoned without the Allies and the Allied Naval Council.
Moreover, however much it made the Admiralty's own requirement to find
ubstitutes for craft drawn from the Palestine coast easier, it was a
amentable misuse of the submarine chaser's capacities since there was
elatively little submarine activity in those waters. The submarine chasers

were designed to work in groups of four using listening devices to locate submarines and most submarine traffic was at the Straits of Otranto, not the Palestine coast.

The desperate need to economize on escorts had already caused some British authorities to re-examine the whole concept of the OE–HE through convoys. On 16 January, Rear-Admiral Fergusson, British Admiral of Patrols, urged Calthorpe to abolish these through convoys which were so expensive in terms of escorts compared with the number of ships involved. Calthorpe, no doubt heavily influenced by his staff, eventually concurred and on 15 February submitted the proposal to the Admiralty, arguing that the institution of the Gibraltar–Bizerte convoy had altered the situation which should be reviewed again so that available escort craft could be used to the best advantage. Lieutenant-Commander Godfrey agreed with the example that Fergusson had cited, the absurdity of an OE convoy of eight to nine ships escorted by half a dozen fast sloops or destroyers passing in sight of a Gibraltar–Bizerte convoy of twenty-four ships accompanied by three or four yachts. Godfrey termed this 'ludicrous'.[49] Calthorpe and Fergusson were not arguing for the abolition of convoys in general, merely for a certain type which they did not consider justified the effort in terms of escorts. Nevertheless, there may have been at least some doubt in the C.-in-C.'s mind about the whole process which he tended to think of as a necessary evil until the barrage he put so much faith in had been fully instituted. Fleet Paymaster Manisty, Organizing Manager of Convoys at the Admiralty and another architect of the convoy system, successfully rebutted the arguments. The main advantage of running the through fast convoys was economy of tonnage and increased safety owing to the shorter time in the danger zone and use of the vessel's speed. The fact that these convoys got greater attention was no argument against them, for while their abolition would mean the release of twenty escorts which would constitute a small gain for the slow convoys, it would not compensate for the loss of the fast convoys. The OE–HE convoys remained.[50]

The American Project for an Offensive in the Adriatic

Vice-Admiral Sims in the course of the discussions at Rome over the Otranto barrage had stressed the idea that it was necessary to adopt a strategic offensive in the Adriatic to occupy, destroy, or blockade enemy submarine bases and, at the end of the session, disclosed an American plan to the senior delegates for operations in the Adriatic. Sims had been supported by the Japanese delegate in the discussion which put the Americans and Japanese on the opposite side of Revel who in his memorandum was on record as describing an offensive by the Allies in the Adriatic as inexcusable. To further muddy the waters, Ratyé claimed that the question of an offensive had not been submitted to the conference and really depended on the Allied C.-in-C., Gauchet, which caused Revel to assert that the Adriatic was a special sphere under Italian command.[51] The American proposal would not have been a complete surprise to Revel, for

Sims and Benson had spoken of its broad outline to the Italian naval attachés in London and Washington.[52]

The American scheme originated with the Planning Section of Sims's staff in London. Sims had very quickly formed the opinion at the first meeting of the Allied Naval Council in January that the United States and Britain were the only countries who had anything to give, notably foodstuffs and raw materials. They were regarded, as Wemyss expressed it to Sims 'rather as milk cows and the other chaps as calves'.[53] The United States therefore was in a position to take the lead and the Planning Section operated in this atmosphere. The Planning Section in which Captains F. H. Schofield, D. W. Knox and H. E. Yarnell played leading roles, was a source of pride to Sims who thought that American naval officers had much more thorough training in that type of staff work involving the establishment of general principles to guide the conduct of war and preparation of estimates of the situation.[54] This was true: staff work had been neglected in the prewar Royal Navy and this was the basis of so much of the criticism by people such as Richmond.

The specific problem for Problem No. 5 (Planning Section Memorandum No. 9) was to prevent the use of ports in the Adriatic as bases for enemy submarines operating in the Mediterranean. The general conclusion was to seize and secure a base between Curzola Island and the Sabbioncello Peninsula, and simultaneously with the seizure of the base to raid the railway leading to Cattaro on the mainland destroying bridges and tunnels, occupying a position astride the railroad as long as possible, and when compelled to retire, falling back on the Sabbioncello Peninsula which would be held permanently. There would be sufficient naval forces stationed at Curzola to completely interrupt all traffic by surface vessels between the northern Adriatic and Cattaro. At a later stage when troops and transports were available, the Allies would seize and hold Lissa, Brazza, Lesina, Lagosta, Meleda, Gazza and Pelagosa. The Planning Section also favoured laying a mine barrage from the Italian coast (Gargano Head) to Curzola Island. They also wanted to execute a surprise raid on Cattaro with the objective of sinking all enemy vessels in the gulf. They maintained that the approaches to Cattaro were not difficult from a navigational standpoint and the defences, while undoubtedly strong enough to resist a bombardment from the sea, were probably not strong enough to prevent running the batteries at night. The Planning Section wrote: 'The tactical problem involved is somewhat intricate and difficult, but the advantage of success would be so great that the risk of four or five battleships with the necessary sweepers and destroyers is more than counterbalanced by the probable results that they could achieve.' The patrols in the southern part of the Adriatic would be strengthened and equipped with listening devices and depth charges, while there would also be continuous air raids on Cattaro. The success of the operation required a single commander for the combined forces, and Sims naturally thought it should be an American. The Planning Section estimated that approximately 30,000 troops would be needed for the operation and US Marines could reinforce the Italian troops who would probably make up the landing party. Since the United States was not affected by any balance of naval power in the Mediterranean, the Americans should supply the battleships for the naval raid, listening devices for anti-submarine work, and also furnish the mines for the portion of the barrage assigned to the United States. Sims suggested 5 Virginia- or Connecticut-class pre-dreadnoughts for the raid on Cattaro and estimated that the United States would have to supply 25,000 mines, as many destroyers as could be spared from other areas, and thirty-six submarine chasers with a tender. Sims, in asking for the views of the US Navy Department, deemed it 'very important that radical steps be taken in the Adriatic'.[55]

Sims had not actually obtained the approval of the Navy Department when he presented the American plan in Rome to the senior Allied officers. He also had to admit that the American estimate of the situation in the Adriatic was based only on such detailed information as was available in London, but the Italians offered to supply their own more extensive and up-to-date intelligence, while the Americans agreed to restudy their plan with Plans Division at the Admiralty to see if it required any changes. The Italians, for their part, promised to study the plan thoroughly and that the question would be brought up at the next Allied Naval Council meeting. Sims had been warned by the American ambassador in Rome about Italian susceptibilities and 'refrained from expressing my opinion of their attitude as I should have been inclined to do'. Initially, he believed that the co-operation of all governments could be secured but the burden of active operations would fall on the United States and Britain, and it was necessary for the success of the plan that the troops for the landing operation should be American or British, particularly US Marines. He was less confident when he got back to London, and was not hopeful that the Italians would decide on the kind of offensive which the Americans would like to see carried out. Sims did not think that the Italians wanted anyone to attack Austrian bases except themselves, and did not intend to until they were practically sure they could do so with success and without much loss.[56]

Benson cabled Sims on 10 February that, in general, the broad plan was approved for study and consideration and the details affecting American co-operation could be taken up after the general plan was considered abroad.[57] Commander Train, the American naval attaché in Rome, had a talk with Revel about the plan on 15 February but Revel and the men around him were 'more or less reserved in their statements', and Revel wanted a more definite statement about the American contribution in ships and troops. Revel pointed out that the matter would have to be approved by the Italian army and eventually the Italian Cabinet. The Italians used the failure of the Dardanelles campaign as a justification for careful preparation, with much depending on the actual situation on the Italian front since it would be disastrous if troops had to be recalled from the islands for the main front once the operation had begun. The Italians also mentioned their own plans for Curzola and Sabbioncello earlier in the war, but Train thought that 'there is some ulterior motive' that will prevent them from accepting the American plan and thought they were 'afraid of it', since in case of failure a strong anti-war spirit might sweep aside the government with possible revolutionary results. Train was an industrious officer with unusually broad interests which went beyond purely naval affairs. He prepared daily summaries and analyses of the Italian press, war communiqués and parliamentary debates that are useful to this day for a student of wartime Italy, although one sometimes wonders how much attention was paid to it in Washington. He was, however, relatively junior in rank, certainly not an insider, and his opinions may occasionally seem a bit naïve. Nevertheless, after a few years in Rome he had a good grasp of the Italian situation, was allowed to see and hear much more after the United States entered the war, and could give a competent evaluation of events, at least as far as they could be deduced from the surface. Sims had a high regard for this officer who would later be a naval aide to President Herbert Hoover and there was a cordial and frank semi-official correspondence between them. Somewhat disarmingly, Train wrote that he had not argued with Revel over the objections the latter made to the American plan, 'Chiefly because arguing with an Italian in Italian is too much for me', but his report undoubtedly reaffirmed Sims's belief that 'the resistance behind the whole thing is more political than otherwise'.[58]

Plans Division at the Admiralty considered the American plan in detail and was on the whole favourable. The Admiralty had put forward their own proposal about occupying a base on Curzola in the summer of 1917 but the Italians were not interested. The British had some doubts that the occupation would cut off all supplies to Cattaro since the Austrians would probably develop alternate land routes, but the number of submarines able to operate from Cattaro would be considerably reduced. The American proposal would be a complement, not an alternative, to Calthorpe's Otranto barrage plan. Plans Division also favoured the American proposal for a mid-Adriatic minefield, provided it did not interfere with the extensive mining project for the North Sea. The raid on Cattaro would have to be treated as a separate operation whose feasibility could only be judged by the commander responsible for its execution. It would have considerable morale and material results if successful and, even if a failure, 'the moral effect would probably be great as evidence of a new fighting spirit amongst the Allies'. There was no reason to believe that the American pre-dreadnoughts which would be risked could be more profitably employed elsewhere and the short duration of the operation involved no additional drain on mercantile tonnage. In case of a joint French–American–Italian expedition, Plans Division suggested that command might be given to the American admiral. They were silent about British participation beyond the 8th Light Cruiser Squadron at Brindisi. Rear-Admiral Hope had the inevitable reservation. An operation involving land forces must affect the military position on the western front and therefore had to be considered by the Supreme War Council.[59] Sims realized this, too, and on 10 March gave Wemyss a short memorandum to more clearly define American objectives with the idea of reaching agreement before the Council.[60]

With British and American agreement on the essential features of the Adriatic plan, the issue would go forward to the next Allied Naval Council. However, because of the large number of people who had access to the minutes of the Council, the Planning Section considered it undesirable to submit detailed plans. The Council would agree only to the general features of the plan, that is, C.-in-C. and resources to be supplied by each nation. The detailed plans would be decided by the C.-in-C. appointed to carry out the operation. The Americans also assumed that the British would join them in providing troops, transports, cruisers and destroyers. This was not evident in the discussion by Plans Division at the Admiralty. The Planning Section thought that the troops employed should be seasoned forces, speaking the same language, and suggested US Marines, British troops from the Mediterranean area, or both. They concluded: 'Unless the Allies are able to inaugurate offensive operations in contra-distinction to purely defensive operations, the outlook as to our success in this war is extremely dubious.'[61] Sims admitted to Benson that there was agreement on essential features of the project between the Planning Section and Plans Division, 'but no definite undertaking' had been reached yet with the Admiralty. To provide for prompt action in case the plan was adopted, Sims suggested taking immediate steps to furnish a force of 20,000 Marines, including artillery, signal forces, aeroplanes and engineers, and since early and rapid action would be an essential element for success, recommended that mobilization begin immediately and without waiting for any definite adoption of the plan. Benson and the Navy Department demurred, however. Before taking any action they wanted to know if the plans had been presented to the Supreme War Council and British War Cabinet for opinion. The logistic demands of the western front were so great that no eccentric move, regardless of how attractive, could be contemplated without full discussion by all parties concerned. Shipping was now working to its full capacity to supply General Pershing and American forces on their way to the western front and Sims's plan now contemplated a landing force of 20,000 additional men with longer and new lines of communication. Benson ordered Sims not to commit the department to any plan until its full details were submitted and Washington's decision rendered.[62] Ironically, Sims was now experiencing the same tyranny of the western front that Churchill, Keyes and other partisans of the Dardanelles expedition had complained of three years before.

The inevitable question is: what about the reaction of those most concerned – the Italians? There is a copy of Planning Section Memorandum No. 9, Problem No. 5 in the Italian archives with marginal comments, sometimes sarcastic, by Revel and others, although unfortunately for a historian they are often merely question or exclamation marks – which may be eloquent in their own way. The statement that the weakened morale of Italy following recent reverses required the Allies to make extraordinary efforts to bring that morale again up to its former high standard prompted the remark 'Grazie!' and anything about the question of command brought the firm note 'Italiano'. The Stato Maggiore did prepare a reply to the American plan which is, however, endorsed as not having been communicated to anyone. It pointed out that the Italian plans had been abandoned in 1916 because the Italian army did not have the troops to spare for the occupation of Sabbioncello and surrounding islands, and the situation to date had not improved enough to regard the project as practical. The Italians would support the American project with all possible means but, in truth, the Italian navy's means were slender since the army had justly absorbed nearly all the resources of the country and nearly all imports from abroad. The Italian navy could not, and should not, risk too much without justification since losses could not be replaced. Moreover, the Italians argued, only one-third of all submarine losses occurred in the Mediterranean and in order to diminish that activity public opinion would not accept the Italians risking more than other and more powerful nations were willing to risk to combat the other two-thirds. The occupation of Sabbioncello would require supply ships escorted by destroyers exposed to enemy attack, and also coastal artillery on Curzola sufficiently powerful to repel at least the Austrian light cruisers and, on the Sabbioncello Peninsula, powerful enough to repel pre-dreadnoughts. The Italian navy could provide only modest support. As for Cattaro, the type and quantity of Austrian warships normally there did not seem to justify the great risks of an attack which would end up giving an easy triumph to the enemy. Mount Lovčen really dominated Cattaro and to take it and Cattaro would require around 200,000 men, and an investment by land had to take place simultaneously with an attack by sea. The Italian Naval Staff, however, had no objection to discussions with their Allies, and if judged useful would give orders to the Italian C.-in-C. in the Adriatic to execute the operation for which the Allies would provide adequate forces.[63] In short, this was a polite way of saying that the command must be Italian and it was perhaps well that the paper was never communicated for it would only have justified the least charitable thoughts of the Americans and British over the lack of offensive spirit in the Italian navy.

There was one portion of the American memorandum which Revel found totally unacceptable. This was the statement that 'Enemy operations in the Adriatic so far both of his surface vessels and his submarines, have resulted in making the Adriatic practically an Austrian lake in which no Allied Naval operations of importance are undertaken'. Plans Division at the Admiralty had not only agreed with the statement but cited their own examples. Revel, however, informed the President of the Allied Naval Council before the meeting that he could not accept discussion of the American Memorandum No. 49 (the printed version of the Planning Section paper) unless the 'contentious and unjustified phrase' was removed. The Council accepted Revel's demand and the offending phrase was cancelled in all copies distributed to various members of the Council and would be omitted in any new printing.[64] All in all, the omens for acceptance of the American plan were not promising.

The second meeting of the Allied Naval Council in London, 12–14 March, discussed a wide range of topics, many of them problems deferred for further information at the first meeting. The American proposal was given to a separate committee composed of Admirals de Bon, Wemyss, Revel, Funakoshi and Sims, which reported to the Council at its third session and was then discussed in a joint meeting with the military representatives of the Supreme War Council on the 14th. This smaller committee and the secret, rather than open, sessions of the Council were recommended by Geddes because of the secret nature of the material. The lines of argument were predictable, with Revel stressing the dangers and insisting that before they proceeded any further officers should be sent to Rome to examine the work that the Italians had already done in previous plans, and adding that any action in the Adriatic should be controlled by an Italian officer. De Bon, Wemyss and Funakoshi all supported the idea of some offensive in the Adriatic and Sims took issue with Revel that the Adriatic was essentially an Italian question, for no coastline which contained enemy bases could be the affair of any particular ally when the submarines operating from Cattaro affected all the Allies. Sims concluded that 'it was a matter of indifference to him who undertook the command so long as he was a fighter'.[65]

The committee of five admirals managed to settle their differences and submitted to the closed session of the council on the afternoon of 13 March a report in which they unanimously agreed that it was necessary to undertake operations as soon as possible with the object of cutting enemy connections between the bases in the north and south of the Adriatic. The committee considered these operations necessitated seizing certain islands in the Adriatic and thought that the naval personnel and material to carry them out could be made available, but the army's co-operation was necessary. The admirals therefore wanted to ascertain the opinion of the military representatives of the Supreme War Council as to whether or not troops and artillery would be available to carry out the operations and, if so, when and the strength the military believed necessary. The details of the admirals' committee deliberations are not reproduced and remained secret, but Geddes interpreted their decision as meaning all of the operations proposed by the Americans were not considered desirable or practicable, but some were recommended for execution. The first step, however, would be a joint meeting with the military representatives who, conveniently, were assembling in London for a meeting of the Supreme War Council the next day. The Allied Naval Council failed to reach any decision on the chief command and further discussion was deferred, although Revel continued to insist that, according to past conventions, it must be Italian and he could have no authority to renounce this without previously consulting his government.[66]

Wemyss, de Bon, Revel and Sims met with the military representatives at the Admiralty on the morning of 14 March. The meeting lasted less than an hour. The generals were Weygand, Rawlinson, Giardino and Bliss, representing France, Britain, Italy and the United States respectively. Their reaction was perhaps predictable. Rawlinson said that the whole question must be considered with care as to its effect on the whole Allied front from Salonika to Valona, as well as on Austria. After hearing more of the plan, General Giardino remarked that the limited scope suggested for military operations would, in practice, probably have to be considerably expanded once operations began, and it was impossible to foresee the number of troops that might be eventually required. While the United States had offered to send the initial troops, any reinforcements would have to be supplied by Italy and the Italians did not have the troops available. Giardino did not consider the general situation on the Allied fronts permitted them to disperse the forces this operation would involve, and he therefore did not consider the scheme practicable. Nevertheless, he and his military colleagues agreed to study it carefully.[67] With this dash of cold water, the American plan was deferred for further consideration, the Allied navies in varying degrees being favourable, the Allied military dubious.

It would be wrong to assume that the Italians were totally negative about the project or were evading it for ulterior motives. This was not the case, at least initially. Of course they insisted that the command should be Italian. They had, after all, studied a similar plan very closely themselves earlier in the war. What really mattered for Revel would be called in today's financial terms 'the bottom line'. Would the Allies, particularly the Americans, commit enough of their resources, especially manpower, to ensure success? Revel thought it would be useful to gain time while the military pondered their response and suggested, in thanking the United States for their offer, making a request to send the troops at once. Even if the military decided against the expedition, the men might be usefully employed in some other way in their war against Austria. It was necessary to urge the prompt dispatch of the forces offered by the United States, leaving to a later phase the examination of the questions involving their employment.[68] Revel's subsequent orders to the Italian naval attaché in Washington seemed to indicate that, at worst, the US Marines could be used alongside the Brigata Marina, the Italian naval force fighting in the marshes north of Venice.[69] This Italian desire to get the US Marines committed to fighting on the Italian front is not at all what Sims, Benson, or the Navy Department are likely to have had in mind.

Sims did not really have the firm commitment of the Navy Department that he had implied. When Benson learned from the Italian naval attaché that the Italian government was inclined to look with favour on the plan, he cabled Sims once again that before committing itself the Navy Department wanted to know the opinion of the Joint War Council and the details of a definite plan.[70] By this time, other events had occurred which indefinitely delayed any implementation of the Adriatic operations. On 21 March, Ludendorff began the long-expected German offensive on the western front, another consequence of the collapse of Russia. The Germans made gains on a scale not seen in four years of fighting in this great gamble to win the war before the American army arrived in force. Sims himself reported how it had taken thirteen hours to go from Paris to Boulogne because his train had been held up repeatedly to allow troop trains to pass. He realized the implications for his Adriatic plans and on 5 April reported to Benson that it was improbable the project 'will receive much consideration for the present, and may prove to be unnecessary or impracticable, depending on the outcome of the German offensive'. Sims wrote to another friend on 10 April: 'Only after the Huns are definitely checked on the western front can we hope that the proposition will be even considered again.'[71]

While the leading admirals debated the Adriatic project in private, the open sessions of the second meeting of the Allied Naval Council handled a number of issues of direct interest to the Mediterranean. They were for the most part a continuation of issues already raised, such as the use of neutral

Spanish waters and the Russian Black Sea Fleet. On the subject of Spain there was a joint report by the British, French and Italian commanders-in-chief that, under present conditions, it was desirable to maintain and respect the neutrality of Spanish waters, but as the Council had not yet received full reports or lists of ships allegedly sunk in territorial waters, the subject was deferred until the next meeting.[72] The Council did recommend gathering extensive evidence and proof since so far the Spanish government had been able to refute charges of violations of neutrality, which was hardly surprising since German submarine commanders had strict orders to respect it and most losses off the Spanish coast probably occurred when vessels strayed out of territorial waters.

The Russian Black Sea Fleet caused extensive discussions and lengthy memoranda. It would continue to do so until the end of the war. On the whole, the Allies considered that if the Germans wanted to they would be able to obtain possession of it without great difficulty and man the most modern units, which included two dreadnoughts, at least thirteen oil-burning destroyers and six submarines. The Germans would have difficulty finding crews, whether Russian, Turkish, or personnel transferred from Germany, and would require time to train them. Furthermore, the ships had not carried out any sea-going service for a long period of time and were not in good condition, and it would take two to six months after their acquisition to restore efficiency. The Allies were therefore confident that their intelligence would give them sufficient notice to make the necessary arrangements in the eastern Mediterranean if the Germans acquired the ships, and the minesweeping activities necessary before they could get out of the Dardanelles would provide further warning. They did not think that they had to consider the subject in detail at present since there were sufficient forces in the Mediterranean to meet the threat and the Allied C.-in-C. could make the necessary rearrangements in a few days. The Russian Black Sea Fleet, however, caused enough uncertainty to force the Allies to defer paying off any of their older capital ships in the Mediterranean in the interests of economy.[73]

This complacency was going to be shaken very soon. Moreover, while the Allies enjoyed a great superiority on paper, their forces were not united and any attempt to do so raised those delicate questions of command which had plagued Franco-Italian relations in particular since the beginning of the war. Gauchet, who in theory would direct Allied operations against the Russian–Turkish–German forces, gave a warning when first informed of the contingency in February. His position as Allied C.-in-C. left much to be desired. Italian forces escaped his control completely and enjoyed absolute independence. His authority did not even extend over the light craft and drifters operating in sight of Corfu. British forces recognized his authority, but only as a mark of gracious courtesy towards France and any attempt to exercise that authority, especially in the northern Aegean, aroused strong susceptibilities and was stoutly resisted. Franco-British relations could be characterized as official dependence under very courteous forms but complete independence in practice. Gauchet could really be sure only of having the French forces under his direct command to meet the new eventuality, and those forces he was only too aware were either wearing out or in the slow process of disorganization after three and a half years of war. The machinery and boilers of the French destroyers had suffered extreme wear thereby reducing their endurance, while the disorganization in the battleships and cruisers was the result of the ministry considering the officers and men as a reserve from which to draft the best elements to other services such as aviation, the bureaux and establishments on shore. Gauchet compared the situation with the case of an architect constructing an annexe to an important building by drawing on the foundations of the latter for the material necessary for his new construction, until the first strong wind brought everything down. After taking these general considerations into account, Gauchet planned to meet the specific problem of an Aegean sortie by using as many mines and mine nets as possible in the area between Mudros, Imbros and the coast of Asia Minor, uniting scouts, torpedo forces and submarines at Mudros, and concentrating battleships at the double base of Milo and the Egripo Channel (between Euboea and the mainland). The defence of Salonika would be assured by mines, two submarines and British monitors, and Gauchet also wanted to establish minefields and mine nets in the Doro, Steno and Mykonos channels, the major passages through the Cyclades. The EMG in Paris discussed and amended these proposals and the final French dispositions would have been for all French forces currently in the Adriatic, that is, the French destroyers at Brindisi, to return to the control of the French C.-in-C., while the French fleet at Corfu would be reinforced by Italian battleships, and a French force of three Justice-class and three Danton-class battleships, two cruisers with submarines and one of the destroyer flotillas currently in the Adriatic would be detached to the Milo–Euboea area to guard the Aegean.[74] This was all far easier to say than to do and when the possibility arose that the French might really have to make such a redeployment the Allied Naval Council and Supreme War Council would see some of their livelier moments.

The second meeting of the Allied Naval Council also confirmed the conclusions of the committee which had met in Rome regarding the British scheme for the Otranto barrage. The Council decided to recommend that the first two squadrons of American submarine chasers to reach European waters should be allocated to the Mediterranean, except for six to eight which were sent to northern waters for experimental work involving listening devices. Sims had made a particular point that they were designed to work in groups of four for submarine hunting and were not suitable for convoy escort or other duties.[75]

The Allies had been forced to seek naval support from unlikely sources as a result of the submarine campaign. We have already seen how Japanese destroyers provided invaluable assistance in 1917. The Allies approached the Japanese again about additional destroyers in 1918 but received a polite refusal. The Japanese authorities regretted that they had no more vessels available for European waters since their naval forces had already been sent to the Pacific, the Indian Ocean, Australian waters, the Mediterranean and recently to Vladivostok. The situation in Siberia, unsteady conditions in China and danger of a possible German raider in eastern waters prevented the Japanese navy from sparing any additional force.[76]

The Japanese refusal was offset by the prospect of naval assistance from another unlikely source – Brazil. The Brazilian government had declared war on Germany on 26 October 1917 and subsequently announced that it would send a naval force consisting of two scout cruisers, four destroyers and a tender to European waters. They left open the question of exactly where they might operate and some of the Admiralty staff thought of using them at Gibraltar to release British destroyers for the Otranto barrage, if the Brazilians could be relied on.[77] The Americans had other ideas and here the United States lost its attitude of the disinterested newcomer in European affairs unfettered by historic rivalries. The American ambassador in Brazil recommended inviting the Brazilian naval division to join the American naval squadron patrolling in the Mediterranean or between the Azores and Gibraltar, although he was not even sure there was one. Jellicoe, when approached by Benson, thought that Gibraltar would be the best place to send the Brazilians.[78] The Italians, never one to miss an opportunity, also tried to get the assistance of at least some of the Brazilian craft.[79] The Brazilian government agreed to send its naval force to Gibraltar, but the American ambassador in Brazil became alarmed that here it would probably co-operate with British rather than American forces since the British rear-admiral controlled forces operating from that historic British base. This was not acceptable to Benson, for however well meaning the British were, he feared that the American influence in the Brazilian navy would be impaired.[80] According to Benson the American attitude towards South American navies was definitely established with the objective of increasing friendly relations, and they had agreed to send several naval officers to instruct officers of the Brazilian navy. Benson cabled Sims:

> We are therefore anxious that no steps should be taken which tend to affect excellent relations now existing with any one of these countries. For this reason request was extended to British that their [Brazil's] force co-operate with us in European waters. It is believed that by continuing present policy of impressing upon these countries the inter-dependency of North and South friendly relations will be fostered and chances for their remaining permanent greatly increased.

If the US State Department was able to induce the Brazilian government to ask if it could co-operate with American naval forces, Benson authorized Sims to take up the question at the next Allied Naval Council, and suggested that the Brazilians operate first from the Azores and then move to the west coast of France.[81] Sims found the Admiralty agreeable to the Brazilians co-operating with American forces at Gibraltar and the Allied Naval Council at its first meeting in January also agreed that, for administrative purposes, the Brazilians would work with American naval forces.[82]

This extension of the Monroe Doctrine to European waters was not as simple as it seemed, probably because both the Americans and Brazilians would be operating under an SNO who happened to be British, and the US State Department feared a misunderstanding. Benson called the final result 'of vital importance' and the American chargé d'affaires in London saw Balfour twice over the subject, while the Foreign Office sent a special message to the British minister in Rio de Janeiro clearly stating that the Brazilian squadron operating at Gibraltar would be regarded as part of the American forces for administrative purposes. By this time the Brazilians themselves had thrown a monkey wrench into the situation by appointing Rear-Admiral Frontin to command the squadron destined for European waters and, on checking, Sims discovered that his date of rank preceded that of the American admiral at Gibraltar, thereby creating an embarrassing situation. Small wonder that Geddes, on hearing of the tangle while on his Italian trip, wrote to Wemyss, 'I expect you will have to handle the Americans with a little bit of care'.[83]

The Brazilian naval situation grew more tangled and the British submitted a memorandum for the second Allied Naval Council meeting asking for a clarification on the ruling that the Brazilians would operate for 'administrative purposes' under the admiral commanding United States naval forces operating in European waters. There was even more confusion over where the Brazilians would actually work. The Brazilian government apparently assumed that they would co-operate with American forces on the west coast of France, probably reflecting Benson's and the US State Department's views, while the French wanted them to assist in protecting Franco-American traffic. The Brazilians then asked the British for coal and supplies at Sierra Leone, and requested information about the British SNO at Gibraltar, apparently anticipating that their forces would be based there. The French proposed that the Brazilians should protect traffic between South America and Europe in the area between Dakar and Gibraltar. The Brazilian rear-admiral turned out to be senior to any of the American rear-admirals afloat, and Sims admitted to Wemyss that this ruled out operating under an American admiral, and the most they could do to carry out American wishes was to allocate the Brazilians so that their ships would always be operating 'in the same area' as American vessels.[84] Unfortunately this would not be the case if they followed French desires and worked off the African coast. One shudders to think of the complications if the US Navy decided to promote the American rear-admiral at Gibraltar to vice-admiral, which would have solved the problem as far as the Brazilians were concerned, but would have made him senior to the British SNO.

The Allied Naval Council decided that the Brazilians would be based on Gibraltar at first, and their exact employment should be left for discussion between the local senior officers and the Brazilian rear-admiral upon his arrival, with special consideration for the French proposals to operate off the African coast.[85] The Italian desires to get the Brazilians in the Mediterranean or Adriatic seem to have been tossed aside, if they were even brought up. There was still at least some possibility that the Brazilians might have operated in the western Mediterranean, but this was not to be. The Brazilian naval force – the scout cruisers *Bahia* and *Rio Grande do Sul*, four destroyers and a tender – did not leave for European waters until May and were then delayed for a long time at Freetown, Sierra Leone, by illness among the crews. The US State Department and Navy Department followed them with paternal interest. The Brazilians did not arrive at Gibraltar until the closing days of the war, just in time, however, to open fire on American submarine chasers during an anti-submarine operation on 10 November. The low superstructure of a submarine chaser could easily be mistaken for the conning tower of a submarine in a heavy swell and the mistake was understandable. Fortunately, there were no casualties.[86] The Brazilian squadron turned out to be another of those 'what might have beens' in the Mediterranean.

The American naval forces at Gibraltar were under the command of Rear-Admiral A. P. Niblack, a witty rather ironical individual who had formerly been naval attaché in Brazil and was known as 'Nibs' to his friends. The ships operated in both the Atlantic and Mediterranean. The idea that this force might have served as an inspiration to the Brazilians might have brought an ironic smile to the faces of most of its officers. There is a well-known painting in the US Naval Academy at Annapolis by Bernard Gribble entitled *The Return of the 'Mayflower'* which depicts fishermen watching a line of American four-stack destroyers arrive during the crucial days of the submarine war in 1917. There is a tradition among American destroyer-men that those forces at Queenstown surprised many by their arrival in good-enough condition to commence operations immediately. But if the Queenstown forces represented in many ways the elite of the US Navy, the Mediterranean forces were a heterogeneous collection of antiques – including gunboats from the time of the Spanish-American War – and converted yachts or, as Niblack put it, 'a lot of junk here that has to be continuously rebuilt to keep it going' and any immunity of ships in the area was largely due to an absence of submarines. The four old destroyers at Gibraltar about which the Italians had been so anxious were less than inspiring. Niblack reported: 'They were condemned in the Philippines as being unable to go out of sight of land, but since then have made over thirty thousand miles. Everytime they go out I feel a bit anxious until they get in again.'[87] In one, the *Barry*, someone carelessly lifted out a piece of cement and a part of the bottom came along with it. The ship had to go into dock to have some plates renewed. Niblack wrote: 'These four destroyers have to be handled very gingerly or they crack something. The Commanding Officers deserve great credit for keeping them going, and the prayers of the congregation are requested by all everytime they go out.' Niblack compared his operation with a horse race: 'I enter one of our ships to sail in a given escort and then I have to scratch her because she blows a tube. It is simply a game of checkers [draughts] and we constantly have ships' orders ready for them before they actually arrive from a previous one.'[88] Of course after three and a half years' hard steaming in war there were many British, French and Italian officers who might have had similar complaints about their ships, but somehow more must have been expected from the supposedly fresh forces of the New World.

Gibraltar was important, although rather neglected. Niblack claimed that 'More tonnage comes in or out of here now than any other port in the world, by long odds'. In December 1917, 751 merchant vessels arrived, 252 coaled, 47 discharged coal or cargo, 9 took on complete cargo, and 107 had repairs or other work at the dockyard. Unfortunately there were only around two-thirds the number of ships necessary to furnish escorts for the convoys. The operations were truly international. Niblack described the scene:

> If there should be a sudden lot of sinking around Gibraltar it would raise an interesting question as to who is responsible because every morning at 10 o'clock the British, American, Italian and French representatives gather around a table and plan for the day. It is the Allied Conference really working with all of the material available at the moment. Angels could do no more. Possibly devils could, but it is hard to be a devil with a back numbered type of ships we have here, most of which are on their last legs.[89]

The escorts could be very mixed. A British officer in the Flower-class sloop *Lychnis* remembered of 1918: 'My most fantastic convoy from Genoa to Gibraltar consisted of my sloop as a fast escort (14½ knots!), a United States yacht, an Italian armed merchantman, a French trawler and a Portuguese trawler.'[90] Despite the material difficulties, Gibraltar was improving, particularly in regard to inter-Allied cooperation, and Niblack thought that out of considerable chaos some simpler instructions and standard procedures were emerging. He was optimistic in May: 'This base is growing rapidly and will soon be ready for any thing that can come this way. For one thing, Rear-Admiral H. S. Grant, R.N. is the best thing I have seen yet in any Navy.'[91] The reader will have learned enough to realize that this was a refreshing spirit in the tangled Mediterranean world and perhaps symbolic of the fact that the Entente was growing stronger. Could the same be said of the Germans and Austrians in the first half of 1918?

Growing Problems for the k.u.k. Kriegsmarine and the Mediterranean U-Boat Flotilla

The year 1918 did not open on a happy note for the k.u.k. Kriegsmarine, with the repercussions of the loss of the *Wien* still reverberating. The German naval attaché in Vienna was perhaps inevitably the sounding board for discontented officers. Much of that discontent was directed at the naval leadership, particularly Njegovan, who was reputed to be interested solely in regular meals and rest, always refused anything proposed to him and seemed to have given up. The social and economic scene was darkening and there were signs of dissolution. The strike by German workers at the Pola arsenal was of particular importance for the naval war because it delayed the refits of submarines. The workers were alleged to be in the hands of the worst sort of agitators, and there were even reports that sailors had sympathized with the strikers. There were also reports of demonstrations in the fleet.[92] The commission investigating the loss of the *Wien* judged the Sea Defence Commander of Trieste, the SNO and captains of the *Budapest* and

447

Wien guilty of not taking all possible measures to secure the ships anchored at Trieste, or taking all possible measures to hinder the sinking of the *Wien*. Although the commission thought judicial proceedings were justified, Njegovan did not recommend them in view of the long service of the officers concerned who were replaced or retired. Njegovan also asked for the removal of Vice-Admiral Alfred Freiherr von Koudelka, the naval district commander (*Seebezirkskommandant*), who would have been the highest-ranking victim of the purge.[93] He was not successful. Koudelka did not retire until August.

The k.u.k. Kriegsmarine soon had graver things to worry about, notably a serious mutiny in some of the ships stationed at Cattaro. The revolt broke out on 1 February aboard Admiral Hansa's flagship, the armoured cruiser *Sankt Georg*, which became the centre of the revolt with the officers overpowered and one badly wounded. There were similar developments in the depot ship *Gäa* and the armoured cruiser *Kaiser Karl VI*. The revolt was strongest in the bigger ships. Heyssler and Liechtenstein, commanding the scout cruisers *Helgoland* and *Novara* respectively, managed to preserve their authority although the two cruisers and all destroyers and torpedo-boats were eventually compelled to raise the red flag.[94] The sailors' demands included peace without annexations, demobilization, complete independence from other powers, self-determination for all peoples, a loyal answer to President Wilson's peace proposals, democratization of the regime, as well as more specific issues related to the service such as better food, regular leave, improved conditions, equitable distribution of ship's food between officers and men, and a common kitchen for officers and men. The sailors would, however, resist any Italian attack on Cattaro. The author of one of the most detailed studies of the event has therefore argued that the events in Cattaro had their primary motivation in social and economic causes rather than the nationalism which motivated conspiracies in Pola that May and the events which would accompany the final collapse of the Dual Monarchy at the end of October.[95] The mutineers at Cattaro failed to win over the military garrison on land and on 2 February coastal batteries fired on the old guardship *Kronprinz Erzherzog Rudolph*, killing a mutineer, when it tried to shift position and move towards the centre of the rebellion in the middle gulf. *Novara* and *Helgoland* and nearly all the torpedo-boats and destroyers were able to break away from the immediate threat of the big guns of the armoured cruisers and enter the innermost gulf where they had the assistance of the German submarines, ready to torpedo any ships led by mutineers which might try to break in. The red flags were promptly lowered. The revolt collapsed on the 3rd with an ultimatum to the mutineers from the forces on land, while the III Division, three Erzherzog-class battleships, arrived from Pola. There was also a counter-movement led by Germans and Magyars, for the most part, on the armoured cruisers. One of the leaders of the revolt, Seefähnrich Sesan, a reserve ensign, fled to Italy with two petty officers in a seaplane. There was relatively swift justice, forty sailors were tried and four promptly executed. Approximately 800 men considered to be of questionable loyalty were removed from their ships. This is, of course, only a rough summary of a complex event which has, not surprisingly, generated a particularly large literature in Yugoslavia.[96]

The Kaiser sent Admiral Erzherzog Karl Stephan to Cattaro to make a full report on these events which precipitated significant changes in the k.u.k. Kriegsmarine. The idea most frequently heard was that a 'rejuvenation' of the Naval High Command was necessary and on 28 February the 59-year-old, but even more elderly looking, Njegovan hauled down his flag on the *Viribus Unitis* and turned over command temporarily to Vice-Admiral Seidensacher, commander of the III Battleship Squadron. Ten days later, and to the surprise of many, Kaiser Karl promoted Linienschiffskapitän Horthy, then only 49, to the rank of rear-admiral and named him Flottenkommandant. Vice-Admiral Franz Ritter von Keil became the Kaiser's naval adviser (*Admiral zur disposition des Allerhöchsten Oberbefehles*) and Rear-Admiral Franz Holub, Njegovan's former Chief of Staff, became Chief of the Marinesektion.[97] According to one officer, Horthy's nomination 'exploded like a bomb' in naval circles for he had been relatively junior and consequently jumped over the heads of many more senior officers. He had, however, a reputation for daring and initiative gained through his handling of the light cruisers in the southern Adriatic. Horthy, at least according to his memoirs, attempted to persuade the Kaiser to change his mind, arguing that his appointment would cause much controversy and was without precedent, and that he could not be expected to perform miracles in the fourth year of hostilities. The Kaiser, however, insisted that young blood was needed in the higher ranks of the navy and this, too, was the impression of others – Horthy would bring an innovative spirit.[98]

The Germans were pleased as well. Freyberg reported that the Austrians were energetically working at high pressure to make the fleet ready for action with gunnery exercises and manœuvres resumed, he claimed, for the first time in three and a half years. Keil had reported, however, that the fleet would not be battle-ready before two to three months. Kaiser Wilhelm's marginal comment to all of this was a characteristic: 'Now! Finally!' Coal, however, was a difficult problem for the Austrians. There were only 95,000 tons on hand in Pola and every hour the fleet steamed it consumed around 1,000 tons. Freyberg hoped that the Germans would do all they could to help, but transporting the coal was another difficulty since the southern railway was loaded to capacity and coal shipments had to go via Hungary to Fiume and then by collier to Pola. Keil had recently used the same route to raise the oil reserves at Pola from 300 to 2,000 tons. Freyberg reported that both Keil and Holub seemed different men; they had formerly been depressed, and performed their duty without finding the least support. The attaché used a nautical metaphor. They now had the difficult task of refloating the ship which had been stuck deeply in the mud, but their hands were no longer tied and Freyberg was convinced that Kaiser Karl had called the ablest men to the most important posts. There were other tangible signs of change as well. The fleet now consisted of only seven battleships, the four Viribus Unitis-class dreadnoughts and the three semi-dreadnought Radetzkys. The 'old ballast', that is, obsolete ships of questionable value, was taken out of service, while the three Erzherzogs were now kept at Cattaro for local defence. The armoured cruisers *Sankt Georg* and *Kaiser Karl VI* were disarmed, along with the coast-defence battleship *Budapest*.[99] The Austrians also took the coast-defence battleship *Monarch* and the cruisers *Aspern* and *Szigetvár* out of service to gain the crews for merchant ships to be employed in the Black Sea. All of these changes made for greater economy in manpower and an increase in genuine fighting efficiency. The three Erzherzogs could no longer really be counted as battleships, their primary armament was only four 24-cm (9.4-in.) cannon, but they could still perform useful service at Cattaro supporting the Austrian Cruiser Flotilla in place of the two armoured cruisers, centres of the recent mutiny, whose age and diminished speed made them of doubtful value.[100]

Some of these measures, such as the permanent deployment of the three Erzherzogs to Cattaro in place of the now-disarmed armoured cruisers, were at least partially motivated by the fear that the three mutineers who had fled to Italy would betray exact information about the defences of Cattaro. This could possibly lead to an attack with the objective of destroying warships and the U-boat base. Keil, as a defensive measure, recommended intensive reconnaissance of the southern Adriatic by air and sea. Horthy was ordered to take all appropriate measures at Cattaro to ensure all the operative modern ships got out of the gulf before it was closed, which meant intensive reconnaissance to avoid the surprise appearance off the gulf by an enemy fleet. Stocks of coal and fuel oil should not exceed a certain amount. The Germans were advised not to keep any U-boats at Cattaro that required long refit and could not be made ready to submerge in four to six hours. AOK intended to strengthen the Austrian artillery at Cattaro with heavy howitzers, and increase the troop strength in this portion of the Dual Monarchy to guard against operations directed at San Giovanni di Medua and Durazzo, the supply ports of the XIX Austrian Army Corps in Albania. The permanent deployment of the Erzherzogs to Cattaro was actually delayed because of the necessity for docking the ships, while the reduction in coal and fuel-oil supplies took care of itself. Because of a lack of transport the Austrians had been unable to maintain more than one month's supply at best. The Austrians also expected to have four submarines available for the defence of Cattaro by May.[101] The Austrians and Germans probably could not have known that the Americans had plans to raid Cattaro at this time, but the fact that a few U-boats might have been diverted, at least temporarily, from operations in the Mediterranean to defend Cattaro was an unexpected dividend for the Allies, although they were of course unaware of it. Most of the submarines that the Austrians kept at Cattaro were not really suitable for long-distance operations, but at least one, U29 (a UBII type) was. The Austrians and Germans did learn through press reports of Geddes's presence in the Aegean and the inevitable speculation that this might lead to some action in the Mediterranean, but Horthy, in view of the possible losses compared with possible gains, did not consider an offensive against Durazzo or Cattaro probable. He would, however, keep the submarines ready.[102]

Horthy was also able to fight off another attempt to detach some of his small submarine force. Kaiser Karl asked in April if it would be possible to send one of the Austrian submarines to operate in the Black Sea where the attitude of the Russian Black Sea Fleet was unreliable. Horthy replied that one of the UBII types, U28, could sail for Constantinople in ten to twelve days but, given their small number of submarines and their many tasks in the Adriatic and the Mediterranean, he could not recommend it. The Austrian flag was already represented in the Black Sea by the Danube Flotilla and the scant outlook for success and risks involved in the trip did not justify sending a submarine. The argument was well taken, for it was not terribly clear exactly what the single small submarine was expected to do except chase after the Black Sea Fleet in case it refused to submit meekly to German control or threatened the Ukraine, now occupied by the Central Powers. Karl dropped the idea.[103]

The naval guerrilla war continued in the Adriatic and the Italians had a useful weapon in the form of the Mas boats. They were also becoming more aggressive, something their Allies did not always acknowledge after listening to Revel's usual discourse about protecting his precious dreadnoughts at Taranto. On the night of 10–11 February, three Mas boats were towed to the vicinity of the Gulf of Buccari near Fiume to attack four laid-up steamers. The attack failed to sink any of the ships, partially because of faulty torpedoes which failed to explode, but it was immortalized by the author Gabriele D'Annunzio, who took part as the 'Beffa di Buccari' and, as a glance at the map will show, it was an audacious attack deep in Austrian waters. The Austrians countered with a raid on Ancona in an attempt to seize a Mas boat and blow up the submarines reported to be based there. On the night of 4–5 April Linienschiffsleutnant Joseph Veith, five cadets and fifty-five men landed to the north of Ancona, unfortunately in the wrong location due to a faulty compass. The attempt did not succeed and the entire party was eventually captured, while the Austrian Naval Command could only speculate on what had happened. The Italian authorities were equally shaken that the raiding party had got so close to its objective.[104]

The Italians also built four of the ingenious Grillo-class *barchini saltatori* (literally 'jumping boats'), which were a form of naval tank armed with two torpedoes and equipped with two lateral caterpillar chains to enable them to climb over the barrages protecting a harbour. The Italians made a few attempts against Pola. The first, on the night of 8–9 April, was frustrated by the arrival of dawn before they could get into the harbour, and similar delays ended the attempt on the night of 12–13 April when two of the craft, *Cavalletta* and *Pulce*, had to be scuttled on the approach of Austrian aircraft. Mechanical difficulties frustrated an attempt by the *Grillo* on the night of 6–7 May. Finally, on the night of 13–14 May, Lieutenant Mario Pellegrini managed to get past some of the barriers at Pola before the *Grillo* was discovered, sunk and the crew taken prisoner. The Austrians subsequently raised the *Grillo* and eventually began construction of two similar craft of their own which were, however, incomplete when the war ended. The Austrian versions of the motor torpedo-boats were also, for the most part, still incomplete at the end of the war.[105] There is no space to go into the details of all these operations, which could be fascinating, but they tended to provide the Italian navy with a tradition of daring and audacity of its own that was not fully appreciated by the Allies and would have some effect in stiffening the attitude of Italian leaders in negotiations.

Horthy was fully aware of the danger to the base at Pola and considered it a solemn obligation to preserve the irreplaceable battleships for combat or for Austria-Hungary's position as a great power. He, too, was not immune to the influence of 'the fleet-in-being'. On 15 April he ordered a series of special measures aimed at increasing the protection of the fleet against the sort of raid that *Grillo* attempted, and that heightened readiness may have led to the failure of the endeavour. Italian Mas boats also attempted to raid Trieste on the night of 14–15 May and failed. Horthy warned, however, that they could expect continuous activity by them.[106]

Austrian surface forces made another sortie against traffic in the Straits of Otranto on the night of 22–23 April when Fregattenkapitän Herkner in *Triglav* led *Uzsok*, *Dukla*, *Lika* and *Csepel* on a sweep southwards. Approximately fifteen miles west of Valona the Austrians encountered the British destroyers *Jackal* and *Hornet*, who were on patrol that night with *Alarm*, *Comet*, the Australian *Torrens* and the French *Cimeterre*. *Hornet* was badly damaged in the ensuing fight but the alarm went up and the Austrians turned for home, pursued by *Jackal* who had lost her main mast. The remaining Allied destroyers joined in the chase but the Austrians gradually pulled ahead and the Allied destroyers finally turned back west of Cape Pali. The Austrians suffered no damage or losses, but the British had seven dead and twenty-five wounded. Heyssler, now Commodore commanding the Austrian Cruiser Flotilla, commented on *Triglav*'s report that he thought Herkner could have sunk the damaged destroyer by energetically pushing the attack, but really could not be reproached since this was the first operation of his division and had been intended as a training mission. Moreover, they were in the vicinity of Valona with a bright moon and had to avoid being cut off by superior forces.[107] The action seemed to duplicate those of the past, a night encounter and high-speed chase, but also tended to demonstrate that the Allied defences were both stronger and more alert than they had been in the past. The massacre of the drifters which had occurred in May 1917 would not happen again.

There was another Austrian raid which was frustrated on the night of 8–9 May when the destroyers *Turul*, *Huszár*, *Reka* and *Pandur* attempted to land a raiding party to cut the coastal railway near Silvi to the north of Pescara. The attempt was discovered and the raid had to be broken off. What was perhaps more interesting and certainly ominous from the Austrian point of view, was that the destroyers *Turul* and *Reka* suffered different types of mechanical breakdowns on the return run which greatly reduced their speed. The destroyers were of an older class which had seen hard use but, when Keil saw the reports of the operation, he inquired about the nationality of the crewmen on duty in the engine rooms at the time, and asked about the possibility of sabotage. The men in question in the *Turul* were German, but the pair in the *Reka* were Czech and Hungarian. Nothing was ever proven but the very fact that these questions were now asked was indeed ominous and Keil added a note to the report recommending that machinists in the fleet be chosen with care.[108] The k.u.k. Kriegsmarine had been a multinational institution, certainly to a far greater extent than the army since each ship was mixed, whereas on land there might be whole regiments of the same nationality. In the aftermath of Cattaro, and with the example of the Russian revolution before them as well as the deteriorating condition of the Monarchy, many officers undoubtedly did have an eye over their shoulder, particularly towards the non-German members of the crews. Heyssler admitted as much to a British friend after the war, although in his opinion the socialist spirit did more mischief than nationalism. The submarine commander, von Trapp, remembered with apparent bitterness Czech workers in the arsenals always sitting together, speaking Czech and smiling at reverses, and remarked how the boat had to be carefully watched and all work personally checked.[109] One should not exaggerate all this. The fleet continued to function loyally until the very end of the war, but when all is said and done there was something in the atmosphere that had changed.

The situation was also changing for the worse as far as the German U-boat flotillas at Pola and Cattaro were concerned, and the convoy system was having its effect. In the eastern Mediterranean where once traffic proceeded along a few prescribed routes, the convoys apparently travelled dispersed courses and it was no longer advantageous for a submarine to wait in a single position. The submarine commanders noted that after a single success traffic was now energetically steered away from the submarine, compelling it to leave its position, and success could only be anticipated in the vicinity of harbours where steamer routes converged.[110] Anti-submarine defences had also improved and were intensified, and there were now losses. UB69, *en route* to Cattaro from Kiel, never arrived and was probably sunk on 9 January by an explosive sweep used by the sloop *Cyclamen* north-west of Cape Bon. UB66, *en route* to Cattaro from Constantinople, disappeared during operations in the eastern Mediterranean in the second half of January.[111] The Germans therefore lost as many U-boats in the first month of 1918 in the Mediterranean as they did in all of 1917. This was not a good omen for the future.

In January the Germans had an average seven to eight boats on operations at the same time, concentrated for the most part against traffic in the western Mediterranean, but one of their major problems continued to be the backlog of submarines awaiting repair and refit. This reached a high of seventeen on a single day in Pola and fourteen on one day in Cattaro. The operations in Pola were also badly affected from 22–27 January by a strike of the German workers at the technical department in common with the arsenal workers. Cattaro also suffered from a shortage of labour as well as a slow down in completion of refits by both inept and slow work of personnel in the depot ship *Gäa*. Minor refits which, as a rule, took three weeks now took four to five weeks. To improve communications between the flotillas at Cattaro and Pola, the Germans shipped the torpedo-boats A51 and A82 in sections by rail from Germany and assembled them in the

Adriatic. They also took over the laid-up Österreichischen Lloyd liner *Wien* (7,367 tons) as an accommodation ship at Pola, and in June even sent six seaplanes for a courier and postal service up and down the Adriatic.[112]

The situation in Pola improved a bit in February with the end of the strike and the dismissal of the bad elements among the workers and, in the interests of the whole, the Germans realized they had to put up with the reduction in manpower which resulted. However, the unrest in Cattaro, in which the greater part of the workers in the *Gäa* had participated and had to be removed, made refits almost exclusively dependent on the German crews themselves, assisted by some reserve personnel. The German commanders realized that they had to stand on their own feet at Cattaro as much as possible and, since labour posed the greatest difficulty, the solution would be to fit out a repair ship under German naval personnel.[113] That was likely to remain a dream.

The Germans had an average ten boats at sea at the same time during March and, according to Commodore Püllen, the FdU Mittelmeer, the standard of success, tonnage sunk 'per U-boat day', was higher on the average (517 tons, revised later to 539) than the second half of 1917 despite the handicap of bad weather. The success per U-boat day for the UBIII class was now greater (760 tons, revised later to 754) than that of the large U-boats (635 tons, revised later to 655), a reversal of the previous situation. Clearly the brunt of the war was being carried by the smaller types and the large boats which had enjoyed such spectacular success earlier in the war were not usually replaced if lost, worn out, or when they went home for long refits. The backlog of U-boats awaiting repair cleared a bit in March and April, with yards at Trieste and Fiume taking some of the pressure off Pola and Cattaro, but only in very small numbers. The submarine commanders reported an even greater increase in anti-submarine measures in the month of April and it was apparent to them that the British had taken over the direction of the anti-submarine war. There were also more losses, UB71 and UB70 never reached Cattaro on their voyages from Germany in April. UB71 may have been sunk by the Gibraltar forces off Ceuta on the 21st, but the circumstances of both losses are not clear. The number of tons sunk per U-boat day fell to 499.[114]

The Germans experienced their worst month of the war in the Mediterranean as far as U-boat losses were concerned during May. Of the twenty boats at sea during the month, three were lost and a fourth, U39, was forced by heavy damage to seek shelter in Carthagena on the 18th where it was interned for the duration of the war. U32 was probably sunk on 8 May by gunfire of the sloop *Wallflower* while attacking a convoy forty miles north-west of Malta, while UC35 was sunk by the gunfire of the French trawler *Ailly* west of Sardinia on the 16th. UB52 was sunk some forty miles south of Cattaro while returning from a cruise by the British submarine H4 on the 23rd. Although sinkings per U-boat day rose to 518 tons, the FdU Mittelmeer concluded that that month anti-submarine measures had been sharpened still more and unsecured steamers were no longer encountered. Convoys were protected with all types of weapons and the Germans found increased air reconnaissance and the kite balloon ships which accompanied some convoys particularly unpleasant. Püllen also considered the use of U-boat traps and Q ships on the rise and attributed, incorrectly, the loss of UC35 to one. The fact that certain classes of British sloops were deliberately designed with a merchant ship silhouette undoubtedly contributed to this German nervousness. Püllen complained that increasing numbers of air raids also threatened the base at Cattaro. Nevertheless, he did not attribute German losses to any new weapon, but rather to the assumption by the British of leadership in the anti-submarine effort and the intensive use of known weapons, as well as weather which had been favourable to anti-submarine forces. Püllen also warned that enemy submarines could now be encountered anywhere in the Mediterranean, but particularly in the Straits of Otranto and southern Adriatic. The Otranto barrage was now in British hands and they could encounter every conceivable anti-submarine weapon. The greatest danger came from aircraft by day and fast motor-boats by night, and passage of the Straits of Otranto had to be considered an undertaking in itself, and under no circumstances should the saving of time influence a submarine commander's conduct.[115]

The leader of the German U-boat station in the Gulf of Cattaro, Korvettenkapitän Ackermann, submitted a particularly gloomy report on the situation in the southern Adriatic on 11 June. The increase of British directed measures against U-boats at sea and against the secure entry and exit of U-boats from their bases, as well as against the bases themselves, threatened to paralyse the U-boat war unless the Germans took energetic countermeasures. Ackermann found the British air raids against Cattaro increasing with the good weather and very troubling. The British attacked in broad daylight, flew as low as 1,500 metres and were unharmed by the irregular fire of the ships or laughable number of anti-aircraft guns on land. Fighter aircraft were not available for the defence. The air raids were curtailing the U-boat war by delaying the repair and refit of submarines and exhausting the crews, while shelters were not available and torpedoes, munitions, material and rations were entirely unprotected. With frequent air raids, they could expect damage to personnel and material under present circumstances, and might even be compelled to give up the base. Moreover, the British might not be content with air raids only, as the recent attacks on Zeebrugge and Ostend demonstrated. They had to consider similar naval raids on the Dalmatian coast. The Entente could reckon on the support of the hostile population in the hinterland, and prisoners taken by the Austrians and Germans, probably airmen who were shot down, indicated that they were well informed about the weaknesses of the defence. Enemy naval forces might break into the gulf and destroy naval installations and ships, and a surprise attack could be expected at dawn when their own warships were not ready to sail. Ackermann considered Cattaro to be the only base from which the Austrian fleet could, under proper weather conditions, move on to attack the Otranto barrage. He recommended more and better defences, including motor torpedo-boats, motor-boat mine-sweepers, anti-aircraft guns, balloons, searchlights, harbour barriers and nets. Ackermann also recommended the immediate transfer of two

Jagdstaffeln of fighter aircraft to Cattaro. The Austrians had so far supplied a mere four Phoenix fighters, four weeks after the first air raids. Ackermann naturally wanted German fighters and, although Cattaro might appear a quiet post compared with the western front, it was a promising field for their activity. He argued that if it was possible to send German fighter aircraft to help the Turks in Palestine, it ought to be possible to send some to Cattaro in the interests of the U-boat war. To confirm these warnings, sinkings per U-boat day in June fell to 476.3 tons.[116] H. A. Jones in his official history *The War in the Air* expressed uncertainty about the effects of the British air raids on Cattaro.[117] The commander of the U-boat station could have given him his answer. The raids were indeed having a direct effect on the submarine war although the British did not realize it. By themselves they would not have ended the submarine war, and Cattaro was a relatively unprotected, somewhat geographically isolated and vulnerable place far to the south. The Germans would still have had Pola even if Cattaro was rendered untenable. But the air raids were slowing down the U-boat war and were therefore of at least some strategic importance.

The days when German submarines could expect to secure easy successes in the Mediterranean were gone and the war was much more dangerous for them. But whatever their difficulties they were still able to exact a heavy toll and this was obvious by the worries of Geddes, the Admiralty and the Ministry of Shipping. The Germans were below their record of 1917 but their substantial successes in the first half of 1918 are shown in Table 11.1.

Table 11.1 *Shipping Losses due to Submarines, January–June 1918*

	Sunk by Mediterranean U-Boat Flotillas		Sunk by Constantinople Half Flotilla		Total (All Theatres)	
	Ships	Tonnage	Ships	Tonnage	Ships	Tonnage
Jan. 1918	48	103,738	6	12,408	160	295,630
Feb. 1918	32	83,957	5	161	138	335,202
Mar. 1918	60	110,456	1	2,891	190	368,746
Apr. 1918	37	75,866	5	4,221	134	300,069
May 1918	43	112,693	1	97	139	296,558
June 1918	23	58,248	—	—	110	268,505

Austrian submarines in the first half of 1918 sank:

	Ships	Tonnage		Ships	Tonnage
Jan. 1918	7	26,020	Apr. 1918	1	40
Feb. 1918	—	—	May 1918	12	9,923·5
Mar. 1918	4	15,273	June 1918	—	—

The Austrian figures include the British destroyer *Phoenix* sunk by U27 in the Straits of Otranto on 14 May, the first British destroyer lost on the barrage. The Austrians, however, lost the U23, one of the unlucky Havmanden-type, to the Italian torpedo-boat *Airone* off Valona on 21 February. On the other hand, the French submarine *Bernouilli* was lost to unknown causes (probably mines) in the Adriatic around 13 February, while on 17 April another of those fatal accidents occurred when the Italian submarine H5 was torpedoed and sunk in error by the British H1. The figures show that the U-boats were still capable of inflicting serious losses and there was always the chance of a disaster, but after May 1918 sinkings in the Mediterranean would not exceed 100,000 tons per month for the remainder of the war.[118] In June the Germans suffered another loss on the 17th when the veteran Moraht in U64, who had sunk the battleship *Danton* in 1917, attacked a convoy between Sardinia and Sicily but was sunk by the sloop *Lychnis* and trawler *Partridge II*.[119] The German naval authorities in Berlin scoffed at Lloyd George's statement that the Allies were sinking submarines faster than the Germans could build them and building merchant ships faster than the Germans could sink them, and they were still telling the Austrian naval attaché in Berlin in June that Britain would soon be compelled to make peace.[120] Lloyd George's language may have been exaggerated but, as far as the Mediterranean was concerned, there was no substance for the German claim. The submarine menace, while far from eliminated, had been at least contained by the middle of the year.

The Threat of the Black Sea Fleet and Failure to Achieve Allied Unity

The subject of the Russian Black Sea Fleet had been discussed early in the year in purely theoretical terms and received a relatively low priority at the first two meetings of the Allied Naval Council. But just as the second meeting concluded in London, the subject became more urgent. The French naval attaché in Jassy (Romania) sent a cable on 21 March saying he had received intelligence that seven trains carrying German sailors had been reported in Kiev heading towards southern Russia. The implication was that they would man the Russian Black Sea Fleet at Sebastopol and many of the merchant vessels of all types immobilized in Russian ports. There was further intelligence that the Germans might man other vessels to be used as sweepers and, while this was understandable since the Black Sea was strewn with mines, no one forgot that those same sweepers might be used to clear the Dardanelles minefields for a sortie.

The French planned to concentrate a battleship force at Milo and lay new mine barrages between the Dardanelles and surrounding islands. This redeployment of French forces, in turn, raised the question of possible support by the Italian battle fleet. The British agreed that if the Italian battle squadron were at Corfu, a French battle squadron could be spared for Milo, where in conjunction with *Lord Nelson* and *Agamemnon* it would be well placed for preventing the exit from the Aegean of a combined Russian–German–Turkish force. Under these circumstances only light craft would be required at Mudros, but given the urgent requirements of the Otranto barrage there was no need to send more British destroyers to the Aegean until the threat from the Russian Black Sea Fleet became more definite. The most important point, the Admiralty thought, was to get the Italians to bring their battle fleet to Corfu under the direct orders of the Allied

C.-in-C. Once this was accomplished, the remainder of the redistribution to cope with the new danger would be easy.[121]

Calthorpe worked out his own solution for the problem in which the Allied Aegean Fleet would be based on Port Trebuki (Skyros), and for him the simplest answer would be for the American fleet to undertake the blockade of the Dardanelles, although this would have the undesirable result of straining the already overworked British dockyards and repair bases in the Mediterranean. It would also be even more of a waste of resources since, as far as capital ships were concerned, the Allied forces already in the Mediterranean should be sufficient to face the Austrian–Turkish–Russian fleet if they were properly distributed. Moreover, the United States was not at war with either Turkey or Bulgaria.[122]

The actual situation of the British Aegean Squadron at the beginning of April was not good, even if all they had to worry about was stopping another sortie by the *Goeben*. The commander, Rear-Admiral Cecil Lambert, former Fourth Sea Lord and commander of the 2nd Light Cruiser Squadron in the Grand Fleet, was by all accounts a brusque and fairly formidable character. Lambert had two battleships which could not catch the *Goeben*, lacked the mines necessary to renew the minefields off the Dardanelles, and had virtually all of his patrol vessels withdrawn for the Otranto barrage. Calthorpe, however, considered the submarine menace to be the most pressing danger and one to be met at the expense of forces in the Dardanelles area. Mines ought to be used to deter the enemy from breaking out, and he claimed that the Aegean had always been given priority in the supply of mines and the present shortage was merely due to the unforeseen loss of two mine carriers on their way out from Britain. He intended to keep eight destroyers off the Dardanelles – four British and four Greek. While the Greek destroyers were not yet up to the same standard of efficiency as the British, they were large and well-armed vessels which should be a match for any Turkish destroyers they were likely to encounter.[123]

Lambert was not happy with Calthorpe's proposed dispositions. He thought that an American squadron offered better prospects for victory than a mixed squadron, aside from the insuperable dockyard difficulties, and objected to French command of any mixed squadron to meet the Russian–Turkish–German fleet. He thundered: 'The conduct and proceedings of the French Fleet from the beginning of the War up to the present time suggest reasons for hesitating to acquiesce in such a proposal.'[124] Lambert complained in a private letter to Geddes that he had been 'bled white' by way of patrol vessels, submarines and light craft, and the Greek destroyers sent to him were quite undisciplined and 'not above suspicion as to their loyalty'. He could not use them on the Dardanelles Patrol and they were looking after Mytilene and protecting their own countrymen from the Turks. Geddes assured Lambert that mines were on their way, that the Greek destroyers had recently been refitted at Toulon and would be useful when trained, and since the United States was not at war with Turkey and Bulgaria, American battleships would be out of place in the Aegean. The

First Lord hoped to get three French dreadnoughts out to the Aegean shortly.[125]

Lambert and Calthorpe clashed over those Greek destroyers. At the end of April the British C.-in-C. noted that they were not employed on the Dardanelles Patrol as he had ordered and demanded to know when this would be done. Lambert answered that the disposition of ships within his command was a responsibility which belonged to the Rear-Admiral Aegean who would have to do the fighting when the enemy came out, and the Greek destroyers were disposed to meet a definite military necessity, notably the threat of a Turkish landing on the island of Goni, where they could also watch the southern route in case the *Goeben* broke out. Until the situation in the Gulf of Smyrna was clearer, the Greek destroyers would not be moved. The two exchanged sharply worded telegrams and there was the danger of another of those affairs which the navy could well avoid.[126] By mid-May the Greek destroyers were back on the Dardanelles Patrol and the storm blew over.[127] The episode certainly shows the difficulty that Calthorpe had in getting his authority accepted in some of those Mediterranean subcommands which were used to operating as independent fiefdoms.

In early April, Geddes instigated a letter from the Prime Minister to Clemenceau and Orlando concerning the Black Sea Fleet, Mediterranean, Aegean and Adriatic situations, and arguing that the whole naval question in the area ought to be considered by the Supreme War Council at its next meeting, with the Allied Naval Council in attendance so that naval matters could be discussed. Geddes also asked for a report on the relative efficiency of American battleships with the Grand Fleet compared with their own battleships so that they would be in a position to ask for similar information from the Italians and French to determine actual fighting efficiency as opposed to paper strength in the Mediterranean.[128] The motivation behind the First Lord's request was obvious. The basic British argument, and one that Sims fully agreed with, was that it took considerable practice before the American and British warships were really able to fight and work together as a team. The British would make the same argument in regard to the French and Italians.

The ability of the Allies to redeploy their forces to face any potential threat from the Black Sea Fleet depended to a certain extent on the willingness of the Italians to join the French fleet at Corfu. The arithmetic was simple. The Austrians had four dreadnoughts and three good semi-dreadnoughts. The Italians had only five surviving dreadnoughts, while the French had seven at Corfu, although at least one was always likely to be away in dock. The French dreadnoughts just balanced the Austrian battleships in numbers but were, of course, superior in firepower since not all the Austrians were dreadnoughts. The variables were the five surviving semi-dreadnought Dantons, some of which might be sent to the Aegean. If they could only combine, the French and Italians would have a crushing superiority over the Austrians. But that agreement had eluded them throughout the war.

The Italians went through another shake-up in their naval high command at the beginning of March. Revel was, of course, the instigator for he found the interim commander of the fleet, Vice-Admiral Cerri, too calm at times, excessively mild and in danger of excusing deficiences and errors in his subordinates, as well as prone to accept certain events as nearly inevitable when energetic and opportune action might easily have avoided them.[129] Revel was convinced that the fleet needed a more agile intellect and a firmer hand and, disregarding seniority, eventually chose Vice-Admiral Cusani, Chief of Naval Staff, as interim commander of the fleet in March. Cusani added the phrase 'C.-in-C. of the lower Adriatic' to his title and transferred his headquarters to Brindisi. The dreadnought squadron remained at Taranto. Rear-Admiral Triangi returned as Sub-Chief of Staff, the same position he had held before his brief and unhappy spell as minister in 1917. Vice-Admiral Solari replaced Corsi, who was retired, in command of the battle squadron at Taranto.

Rear-Admiral Pigeon de Saint Pair, the French naval attaché, judged the new men harshly. Cusani had never seemed destined for a post of that importance and was amiable but unobtrusive and not very active. Solari had not been up to his former job as Maritime Prefect of Taranto, had an agitated spirit, was restless, frightened of responsibility and did not seem made to lead the sole Italian battleship force under fire. Capitaine de frégate Isabey, French liaison officer with the Italian fleet at Taranto, had similar opinions on Cusani but was more positive about Solari who had been 'energetic and intelligent'.[130] The American naval attaché was much more optimistic; as a result of the recent changes 'a lot of dead wood had been put on the shelf', and sending Cusani to sea was a good move as 'he is young, active and able'.[131]

The opinions of these men who knew the Italians well are of more than passing interest now that the question of co-operation by the Italian fleet with the Allies had become so important again. The French were the most concerned and certainly the naval staff in Paris must have had serious doubts about the value of the Italian battle fleet. This did not diminish their desire to have those big ships join them at Corfu, but the union had to take place well before any action for the joint training they considered absolutely essential. The British and Americans, based on their experience in the Grand Fleet, strongly agreed. The Italians, notably Revel, were less sure and thought that there need only be a minimum of joint training, for any tactical co-operation with the French would be very loose. This different concept lay at the heart of much of their subsequent disagreement.

The French observers were inclined to be particularly critical. Capitaine de vaisseau Frochot, commanding the French destroyers at Brindisi, described the support of the Italian battle fleet as counting for nothing, with the Italian battleships at Brindisi partially disarmed and depleted of officers and men drawn off for the Brigata Marina fighting on land along the Piave. In fact, he reported, many Italian officers criticized Revel as being too 'grey-green' (the colour of the army uniform), while the dreadnoughts at Taranto were full of officers and men who never saw the sea or manœuvred in company and were imbued with the idea they would not fight. The smal cruisers and destroyers, on the contrary, were truly ready for combat.[132] Frochot, who was in a position to know, made a distinction between Italian light craft and heavy units which is often overlooked.

Geddes had also come away with negative impressions after his visit to Italy which were shared by the naval experts he brought with him. He told the Prime Minister that the only exercises or practice the Italian battleships obtained was occasionally when one ship at a time went into the outer harbour at Taranto for gunnery practice with sub-calibre ammunition, and under those conditions it was impossible for the fine ships – and no one denied the Italian dreadnoughts were imposing designs – to become truly efficient. Geddes thought that they would never be a source of strength to the Allies until they could be got away to another base and exercised as a fleet and put through a rigorous course of gunnery and torpedo practice. The base at Taranto was also unsuitable, if not dangerous, because of the narrow passage between the inner and outer harbour and the swing bridge which might be destroyed or damaged by sabotage at a critical moment, thereby bottling up the fleet.[133]

The problems of the Italian battle fleet are well known and have been frequently commented on. Perhaps less well known is the fact that the French were affected by similar troubles. Gauchet frequently complained about the erosion of his own battleship crews for other services, and in early March he reported that the fleet at Corfu had only been able the preceding month to resume exercises which had been interrupted for several months, and that the dreadnoughts of the 1ère Escadre had not been able to carry out any gunnery exercises since August 1917.[134] How efficient would the French have been? The problem was widespread in the Mediterranean. Captain Dumas has already been quoted about his unfavourable impression of the two British battleships at Mudros. And, finally, what of their potential Austrian opponents? Obviously they had similar problems for one of Horthy's avowed purposes was to restore the fleet to battleworthiness. Keeping the ships of a 'fleet-in-being' efficient was a major difficulty given the restrictions on movements caused by submarines and, especially in the Mediterranean, a lack of coal, not to mention the pressing demands of other naval services for manpower.

Revel was ready to co-operate with the French up to a point and promised that Gauchet would always be able to count on an Italian force of four dreadnoughts and two armoured cruisers of the San Giorgio class, but there were serious grounds for not sending the Italian battleships to Corfu in advance, notably the absence of docks and difficulties in supply and repair. Since the French did not have light craft or fast units available at Corfu, the Italians informed Gauchet what Italian light cruisers and destroyers were at Brindisi and exactly what was their normal state of readiness.[135] Under certain circumstances Italian forces would therefore join Gauchet, but it is important to note that this would be *outside* the Adriatic and they would *not* proceed to Corfu *in advance*.

The arrival of Horthy as commander of the Austrian fleet helped to strengthen rumours of some Austrian naval action and one of those reports had important consequences. In early April the Italians received intelligence from their own agents, supplemented by British intelligence from Malta, about an apparent concentration of submarines in the Adriatic. The Italians feared that when the Austrian offensive on land resumed there would also be a strong naval attack against Venice and Brindisi with heavy ships accompanied by submarines and minelayers, while light forces would attack Taranto. Older submarines would try to force the entrance of the ports, and there might also be a landing as a diversion. Neither Gauchet nor the EMG in Paris considered this probable, but it was enough to cause Revel to remove three of the four Regina Elena-class battleships from Brindisi. Only the *Napoli* was left behind, really to serve as what amounted to a floating battery. Revel supposedly had reports that the Viribus Unitis-class dreadnoughts had been moved to Cattaro and the Regina Elenas, with depleted crews and outgunned – they had only two 12-in. guns – were in danger of being seriously damaged without being able to effectively reply. If, on the other hand, the Regina Elenas were not at Brindisi, the Austrians might not consider the bombardment of the port worth the risk and the place would be spared. This was not the type of reasoning likely to appeal to the British or French. Frochot disliked the decision, for the battleships had provided the Allied light forces at Brindisi with, at least, moral support even though the coal shortage prevented them from keeping fires lit, which meant they were at only five hours' notice for sea.[136] Commodore Kelly had similar views and Calthorpe was disturbed that this might leave the barrage open to enemy raids in which the Allied light cruisers would be unsupported against Austrian heavy ships. Kelly thought that the best solution would be to base two or three Italian dreadnoughts at Brindisi, for the Regina Elenas or Pisa-class armoured cruisers which had been there were either too big or not big enough.[137] Revel used these British concerns as another opportunity to press for faster British light cruisers at Brindisi, although he hinted that if coal supplies there were improved the large armoured cruisers *San Giorgio* and *San Marco* might return. Once again he justified the removal of the battleships. He simply could not leave them exposed, unable to move because their fires were not lit through lack of coal.[138]

The transfer of the three battleships from Brindisi to Taranto produced a minor disaster. They were naturally screened by seven – some accounts give eight – Italian and French destroyers during the voyage. Around midnight the steering of the French destroyer *Mangini* broke down and she rammed the French destroyer *Faulx* which subsequently sank. Approximately an hour later, under similar circumstances, the Italian destroyer *Carini* rammed and sank her sister ship *Cairoli*.[139] This simple transfer wound up costing the Allies the services of four precious destroyers, two sunk and two out of action for a long time, *Carini* for the duration of the war.

The question of moving the Italian dreadnoughts to Corfu was only one of the many Mediterranean problems due to be thrashed out at the forthcoming Paris meeting of the Allied Naval Council at the end of April. The British, for example, were anxious for some agreement about pooling docking resources, for Rear-Admiral Ballard had been shocked on a recent trip to Taranto to find the Italian dockyard apparently underutilized while the facilities at Malta were overworked.[140] But the question of moving the Italian squadron was potentially the most important and probably the hardest on which to find agreement. The Italians seemed to evade giving the French a firm promise as to when their ships would come, and the French naval attaché suspected that it was over the question of command.[141] We have seen how Geddes considered the question important enough to instigate the letter from Lloyd George to Clemenceau and Orlando about bringing the whole Mediterranean situation before the Supreme War Council.[142] Agreement was likely to be difficult and the prospect of American operations in the Adriatic added yet another difficulty. Revel had already indicated how touchy he was about the Adriatic before the March meeting of the Allied Naval Council when he wrote privately to Geddes that as far as the American plan for Adriatic operations was concerned he could not accept any decision that was not in accordance with past conventions. Geddes did not enter Revel's note in the official minutes of the conference, and he told Revel that he hoped he would not prevent the American plan from being considered for the situation was now different. He went on to say that the United States hardly came within the limits of past conventions and they could, as Allies, surely settle the question of the commanding officer of an individual operation, having regard always to the supreme command in any particular area.[143]

While Geddes may have succeeded in keeping this disagreement off the floor of the Allied Naval Council in March, Revel was adamant once he got back to Rome. He wrote to Geddes on 2 April that considerations of a military order, internal Italian politics and existing conventions all required that direction and command of operations in the Adriatic should be Italian, just as those in the North Sea were British. The Italian navy in its duel with its traditional adversary had an essential debt of honour with itself and with the nation which would not tolerate an unjustified abdication of the responsibility it had assumed on this particular front of the naval war in the name of Italy and the Allies. They would welcome American forces just as they had French and British forces, and would give them the benefit of their practical knowledge and experience in this theatre, but the command-in-chief in the Adriatic was, by definition, Italian and this subject admitted no argument. Revel asked Geddes to consider the question as closed, avoiding further discussions in which to his regret he could not participate.[144] There was even some difficulty in getting Revel to attend the meeting in Paris; the British naval attaché visited him at his home with a personal plea and there was also diplomatic intervention. Revel finally agreed, but the meeting in Paris was delayed to accommodate his wishes and fit his schedule.[145]

The third meeting of the Allied Naval Council took place in Paris on 26 and 27 April. Revel did attend after all, but requested that future meetings be held in a central place like Paris since under present conditions of travel it took four to five days to go from Rome to London. The British delegation was somewhat less exalted this time and was led by Rear-Admiral Hope, Deputy First Sea Lord. The conference got the easier subjects out of the way, either deferring them for further study or following the time-honoured custom of referring them to a committee. This was the case with a British proposal for an Allied board to control existing establishments for the repair of warships in the Mediterranean. As for Spanish territorial waters, the evidence did not show any systematic violation of them and since the Allies benefited from their use they would maintain and respect the principle of their neutrality. Any Allied action taken as a result of enemy infringement of neutral waters should be confined to the particular territorial waters concerned.[146]

The project for operations in the Adriatic had been discussed by the military representatives of the Supreme War Council on 8 April. They decided, for the moment, that they would not divert any troops for the operation – hardly surprising in view of the German offensive on the western front – but that the project should be studied and detailed information furnished so that it might be eventually realized. Sims therefore pushed for further study since the situation could change rapidly and the Allies agreed to hold a conference in Rome on 15 May to study the plan and prepare a preliminary report.[147]

The question of the redistribution of Allied naval forces in the Mediterranean produced the expected disagreement. De Bon and Hope tried to meet Revel's objections concerning coal, stores and repair facilities at Corfu, and Sims chimed in with an account of how it had been necessary for the American battleships with the Grand Fleet to exercise with the British for several months before they were a real source of strength. Revel did not consider more than a month's joint training necessary since Gauchet had apparently told the Italians that because of the difference in speed and range of their guns he would probably use the Italian battleships as a separate division in any joint action. Revel also claimed the alleged disadvantages of Taranto had been exaggerated, for experiments showed that it took only twenty minutes to get a battleship from the inner to the outer harbour and, even assuming it took thirty minutes, the five Italian battleships would be clear in two and a half hours and the fleet with two cruisers in three and a half hours. That did not appear excessive to Revel.[148] He said nothing about the problem with the swing bridge.

The Allies failed to reach unanimous agreement despite an adjournment overnight and a private meeting between Revel, Leygues and de Bon. Revel read the French a memorandum which he had not given to the conference in which he promised, at the proper moment, to send all of the Italian battle fleet to Corfu when, and if, the Italian C.-in-C. deemed it necessary. The Italians would then act in liaison but not fuse with the French fleet, and for this a preventive accord between the two commanders-in-chief was all that was necessary.[149] Under these circumstances, full agreement was not possible. The Allied Naval Council, with the exception of Italy, agreed it was possible, and even probable, that the Germans would acquire at least the modern portion of the Russian Black Sea Fleet and they had to take countermeasures for the contingency that it might be used in the Mediterranean, including an attempt to join the Austrian forces. The Allies had sufficient forces to meet this and only a redistribution of those forces was necessary. The Aegean Squadron would be reinforced by six French battleships which would join *Lord Nelson* and *Agamemnon*. To enable the

French fleet at Corfu to meet the Austrians with decisive force in all eventualities after this detachment, four of the Italian dreadnoughts currently at Taranto should be permanently attached to, and incorporated in, the French fleet as soon as possible. In an obvious attempt to mollify Revel, the Allies agreed that the Italian battleships should not be transferred to Corfu until the Italian C.-in-C. was satisfied with arrangements for coal, fuel, stores and small repairs, while the ships would, one at a time, be docked at least once every six months. The Allies would make advance plans for sufficient destroyers, other than Italian which were needed in the Adriatic, to be allocated either for the Franco-Italian force at Corfu or the Anglo-French force in the Aegean, but no actual diversion would be made until the Allied C.-in-C. in the Mediterranean decided an emergency was imminent. The Allies would allocate sufficient submarines for the Aegean squadron and would plan additional minefields at the Dardanelles as well as anti-submarine nets in the approaches to the Dardanelles and various channels leading to the Aegean.

Revel did not agree and submitted a separate note incorporated into the conclusions. The union with the French would be desirable in principle but it should not be considered as a fusion of the Italian squadron with the French fleet since the former 'must keep intact the character of distinct grouping and be always ready to transfer themselves and intervene anywhere that it would appear desirable with regard to the Adriatic situation'. The Italians also did not accept the principle of subordinating the deployment of some French units from Corfu to the Aegean to the arrival of Italian dreadnoughts at Corfu. The advisability of such a movement was entirely dependent on events in the Adriatic which could not be foreseen and were distinct from the Aegean. There had been no change in the naval situation in the Adriatic to justify reducing Allied forces and if the Aegean required reinforcement those forces should be supplied by the other Allies, especially since, at present, there was not a single Allied ship with speed equal to, or greater than, the *Goeben*. This was, of course, an indirect request for British battle cruisers. Without unanimous agreement, the Allied Naval Council could not make any report to the Supreme War Council and the entire question was referred back to the respective governments.[150] De Bon told Gauchet that the question would be put before the chiefs of the governments when they met at the next Supreme War Council and the inevitable jockeying for position began.[151] Sims thought that it was apparent that Revel was instructed to agree in principle to the transfer of the battleships but to obstruct the plan by raising all possible objections to its practical execution. Revel had spoken at great length and with considerable heat at the conferences and in private meetings with the French. Sims realized that Revel would lose the most important part of his command by the transfer and his opposition might therefore have been motivated by personal motives. But Sims suspected that Italian policy was to see their ships were superior to Austria after the war. He reported the British impressino that Revel would have to be removed before any real work could be expected from the Italian navy.[152]

A few days after the meeting of the Allied Naval Council, Orlando went to France for the fifth meeting of the Supreme War Council at Abbeville Barrère suggested on 1 May that it might be opportune to profit by his presence and expose to him the situation created by Revel's refusal to co-operate in a vital task. Barrère thought that, in concert with the British they should very seriously contemplate the replacement of Revel. Revel had already anticipated much of this. The day before, 30 April, he cabled Rear-Admiral Grassi, now Italian naval attaché in Paris, that he was to inform Orlando at once on his arrival of the Allied Naval Council's discussions, the impossibility of accepting the Allied proposals, and the criticism of them expressed in Revel's memorandum. Grassi managed to catch Orlando that same day and the Prime Minister approved Revel's argument and promised to make use of it at the Supreme War Council. The next day Del Bono sent supplementary remarks, notably that the Italians only needed one battleship squadron, preferably the Dantons, at Corfu to be guaranteed superiority over the Austrians. The remainder of the French forces were superfluous and any reinforcements for the eastern Mediterranean should be drawn from them. This message arrived too late to catch Orlando but it had not been necessary.[153] When Clemenceau introduced a motion at the meeting at Abbeville on 2 May calling on the Italian government to give their consent to the proposals of the Allied Naval Council concerning transfer of the Italian dreadnoughts to Corfu to free French battleships for the Aegean Orlando quickly replied that he had not yet had the opportunity of talking with Revel about the subject but he understood that Revel had certain technical objections and there were also objections of a political character Orlando claimed he had to learn the views of the Italian War Committee before he and his government could accept the recommendation. The Supreme War Council adopted the resolution regarding the advisability of the transfer, subject to its acceptance by the Italian government.[154]

Orlando had even tried to prevent any discussion of the issue at all in the absence of a representative of the Italian navy, but Wemyss pressed the point with an alarmist telegram about the Black Sea situation allowing no delay. Wemyss believed the 'so called technical difficulties have been put up as an excuse for the Italians not doing something which I can quite understand is somewhat distasteful to them'. Wemyss was heartened by the information from the British naval attaché in Rome that the Italian Naval Staff, if not Revel, was in favour of the proposal and suggested a line of argument to Larking which he hoped would help them carry their point and obtain the enthusiastic support rather than the sullen acquiescence of the Italians. Wemyss's argument centred on the experience of the American battleships with the Grand Fleet and how well the British and American mingled together, while far from any friction arising the mingling had produced nothing but good results. Revel's idea that more ships should be sent to the Mediterranean was ridiculous. It would add to the difficulties of supply and, even with the Russian Black Sea Fleet, they had sufficient heavy forces out there 'to eat them up over and over again, if only they are properly disposed of'. Unfortunately, Wemyss warned, there was 'a chance of a very disagreeable debacle in the Eastern Mediterranean' as things stood and the Italians would be the first to feel the bad effects.[155]

The British by this time were genuinely concerned about the Russian ships, both in the Baltic and in the Black Sea. They were relatively confident that the Bolsheviks would destroy the Baltic ships if the Germans attempted to take Petrograd but the Black Sea was less secure. By now, the Germans and Austrians were moving deep into Russia, and Odessa was taken on 13 March and Nikolaiev fell on the 15th along with a number of ships under construction and the potentially valuable yards. The British knew the bulk of the Black Sea Fleet was probably at or near Sebastopol in the Crimea and the Germans now apparently intended to occupy the Crimea as well. The British were not confident that the Russian government had enough control over the chaotic situation to enable the fleet to escape capture by heading further eastwards to Novorossisk or elsewhere. The Germans might therefore get their hands on two useful and powerful dreadnoughts, two to three cruisers, thirteen oil-burning destroyers and some submarines. The British were not too concerned about the older battleships in the Black Sea which were likely to be worth little. But there were enough modern units to worry about. The best that Wemyss could recommend to the Cabinet was for the British authorities and ambassador in Russia to bring as much pressure to bear as possible on Trotsky and the Russian government to safeguard the ships. Trotsky had allegedly at one point asked for British officers to reorganize the Black Sea Fleet, but Geddes did not think the chances of him taking definite action were very great. The Cabinet supported his action but the options open to the British were not very great and the risk that the Germans would get the ships was now a large one. General Milne, commanding the British army at Salonika, was sufficiently alarmed by conversations with Lambert to make special representations about the dependence of his forces on naval co-operation in the Aegean.[156]

British, French and Italian diplomats and naval officers now entered a few weeks of intense negotiations on the subject with the Americans and their Adriatic project playing a role as well. The situation was also complicated by the fact that the French cryptographic services were reading with relatively few gaps the Italian diplomatic cables between Paris, London and Rome. The transcripts translated into French were discreetly given by the Quai d'Orsay, in at least one case with the calling card of Pierre de Margerie, Director of Political Affairs at the Foreign Ministry, to the Ministry of Marine under the label 'Informations Secrets'. The French consequently learned that on 7 May the Italian War Committee had met and decided to send the ships to Corfu but would not renounce the command as implied in the Supreme War Council resolution. If the bulk of the Italian battleship squadron were to go to Corfu it was necessary that it should preserve its tactical freedom, and the Italian commander would extend his control over the French units incorporated in it. Otherwise, as Orlando told Count Bonin, the Italian ambassador in Paris, by such a merger with the French, Italy would no longer have its own fleet and to renounce the duty of defending its own sea would create a bad impression in the navy and in the country and would give defeatism a new weapon. If one wanted to safeguard the principle that command belonged to the nation that had the largest number of warships, the majority of ships at Corfu would be Italian. This seemed to imply that Gauchet would have to take the bulk of his forces to the Aegean. Orlando dropped a bombshell in his message to Imperiali. If the majority of ships at Corfu were Italian, command would probably be given to the Duke of the Abruzzi who by his high rank and competence could well assume these functions without disturbing Allied susceptibilities.[157]

Barrère conferred with Orlando on the morning of the 8th and the Italian Prime Minister admitted that it was a difficult problem to resolve, for if they had five to six battleships and then incorporated four in the French squadron what would be left for them? Barrère tried to explain that all this was a matter of form, and asked if the Italians would consent to send four dreadnoughts to Corfu if they found a *modus vivendi* which would establish the autonomy of the Italian ships while assuring their co-operation. Orlando replied affirmatively.[158] This was, of course, in contradiction to his telegram to Imperiali the preceding day implying that the Italians would send enough ships to Corfu to justify claiming the command. The French could therefore be excused for concluding that the Italians were bargaining in bad faith although it is not always clear how quickly the cryptographers worked or the Ministry of Marine received transcripts of the Italian cables. They do bear a notation that three copies were made on 16 May and one given to the Minister on 5 June, but again it is not certain if this refers to the cryptographers or the Naval Staff. However, it is sufficient to say that the French knew their ally's hand at some point in the negotiations. They did not apparently pass on this knowledge to the British.

The Italian naval attaché in London – now Rear-Admiral De Lorenzi – discussed the question of transferring the dreadnoughts with Wemyss on the 9th and came away with the impression that the British considered displacement of the Italian fleet to the Ionian as only secondary to reinforcement of the Aegean with part of the French squadron at Corfu. Wemyss thought the question of command should be discussed directly between the French and Italians and indicated that the Admiralty would only intervene if, as probable, the French made reinforcement of the Aegean dependent on reinforcement of Corfu by the Italians. Imperiali, in another telegram read by the French, described this as the attitude of Pontius Pilate, but noted that Di Lorenzi's impression confirmed the one he had received in talks with Lord Milner, the Secretary of State for War. He thought that the Italians ought to change the British attitude and get them to make the French see reason. The question had enough political importance to counsel the Italian government to hold firm, and if the Allies wanted the transfer of ships they would have to do so on Italian terms. Revel, for his part, ordered the Italian naval attaché in London to refrain from opening discussions on the subject. If any one else initiated them, Di Lorenzi was to give his personal opinion that while it was relatively urgent to reinforce the eastern Mediterranean, the move of Italian forces to Corfu could take place when circumstances required it and command of forces destined to fight the Austrians must be Italian.[159]

On the morning of 10 May, ironically the third anniversary of the Naval Convention between the Allies and Italy, Clemenceau employed his usual forceful style to impress on Count Bonin the importance of removing all difficulties about sending the dreadnoughts to Corfu and how a refusal would have the most unfortunate effect in London. Bonin replied that the Italians were not refusing to send the ships but were claiming command. Clemenceau let the Italian ambassador clearly understand that he himself was indifferent to the question of command – a remark which produced some strong underlining and marginal marks perhaps signifying deep emotion when the Ministry of Marine obtained a copy of the intercepted Italian cable – but Bonin doubted that the French Naval Staff and Ministry of Marine could have the same sentiments and they had to expect Clemenceau to back the French navy's conclusions in the end. Orlando seemed impressed by the strong French reaction and hoped the problem could be overcome by an inter-Allied naval committee to handle the technical solutions. Geddes suggested a possible solution in a talk with Imperiali on the 10th. Both men had been careful to speak in terms of 'personal observations' rather than formal proposals. Imperiali found Geddes convinced that unified command of the Allied fleets in the Mediterranean and Adriatic was as important for the Allied navies as it had been for the Allied armies on land, and with their disaccord they were heading towards certain disaster despite the crushing superiority of the Allied fleets. The French would categorically refuse to put their fleet, superior in numbers, under Italian command. Geddes then flew his trial balloon. There might be an 'admiralissimo' to command all Allied squadrons in the Mediterranean and Adriatic and this supreme command, if all the Allies accepted, might be given to a British admiral, for example Jellicoe. Imperiali warned Sonnino that the conversation with Geddes had given him the impression that Italian claims to command would meet a serious obstacle in London. Orlando did not think these proposals by Geddes were as provisional as he made out since the British ambassador in Rome on the morning of the 12th had passed them off as his own ideas. Orlando had no objections since his sole purpose was to preserve the morale and political unity of their squadron. If the British did not want to take the initiative to avoid disobliging the French, it was even more difficult for the Italians to do so since it might be believed they had acted merely to thwart French command.[160]

The French knew the contents of these telegrams and that the British had proposed Jellicoe to the Italians. However, Clemenceau could not have yet had the information when he cabled Lloyd George after his interview with Bonin to warn him about the flagging of Orlando on the question of sending the dreadnoughts to Corfu. It seemed to him that a refusal of Italian military support pushed to that extreme would be absolutely intolerable, and he asked Lloyd George's intervention to avoid it.[161] Geddes had also prepared an *aide-mémoire* of the conversation between Imperiali, Lord Milner and himself for the War Cabinet, summarizing the arguments and advancing the proposal for an admiralissimo, to serve under the Allied Naval Council and be bound by the decisions of the latter as approved by the Supreme War Council. In this way the naval forces, whether Italian or Allied, allotted to the Adriatic by the Naval Council could remain under direct Italian command and forces elsewhere in the Mediterranean under other Allied command. Moreover, under this arrangement it might be strategically unnecesary for Italian battleships to leave Taranto since they would all be under one admiralissimo and the co-operation and co-ordination with the Corfu force would thus be secure. While the British did not ask for, or desire to press for, this command and were content to continue with general French command in the Mediterranean, they would be prepared if it eased matters and was acceptable to their allies to suggest a British admiral for approval by the Supreme War Council as admiralissimo. Geddes's proposal was approved by the War Cabinet on 11 May and promptly transmitted to Rome and Paris. Lloyd George in his personal reply to Clemenceau, drafted of course by Geddes and the Admiralty, suggested Jellicoe's name, adding that it was essential that the Mediterranean situation should be dealt with promptly.[162]

In Rome, Revel was fortifying his position with a memorandum dated 10 May on the transfer of the Italian battle squadron and command of the fleet destined to face the Austrian squadron. Revel went through the long unhappy controversy over the French fleet at Corfu and stressed that the Italian fleet could not be sure of defeating the Austrian fleet by itself without suffering excessive loss, but required only modest support. The French force at Corfu was excessive, possibly because the French fleet had nowhere else to go, and the French had used that preponderant force to claim command. The Italians needed only one French squadron in support and its speed was of more interest than tactical efficiency. Revel also refuted the argument that submarines could blockade the Gulf of Taranto. In the end Revel's arguments came down to what the Allies always suspected, *amour propre*. All the things said in the too numerous naval councils, as Revel put it, could not weaken the text or the spirit of the Naval Convention of May 1915 giving the Italians command in the Adriatic. It was not equitable that the Italians in order to obtain that relatively modest support necessary to secure victory renounce command of an eventual battle destined to cancel forever the memory of Lissa. If the government deemed it indispensable for the present and future prosperity of the country that they could be great only by becoming a significant maritime nation, then they should vigorously sustain his argument and make the Allies accept their legitimate point of view.[163] It all could be summed up by that simple elemental desire: Lissa must be avenged.

Orlando was buttressed by these arguments and used them when he met with the British ambassador, Sir James Rennell Rodd, on the 12th. He made it quite clear that, while overruling Revel's objections to sending the battleships to Corfu, he could not accept incorporating them in the French fleet for he could not be expected to merge the Italian flag with the French flag in their own sea. Orlando did indicate that a British admiral would remove every objection on his part and he would welcome the proposal for an admiralissimo. Rodd, who had been floating these proposals as his own opinion, concluded that there was something more than *amour propre* on the part of the minister over the issue, and that 'something' was Italian public opinion which they could not help considering, but conditions were evidently ripe for submission of the British proposal.[164] The same day in Paris the Italian ambassador met with Clemenceau and Leygues and the three went over the familiar terrain, the French promising that the four Italian dreadnoughts at Corfu would preserve their autonomy and that the Italian commander in the upper Adriatic would retain the facility of calling on them if he had to face superior forces. The French, however, would not concede command at Corfu to the smaller Italian force for this would also imply giving the Italians command in two distinct seas – the Adriatic and Ionian. Leygues finally suggested that they let seamen resolve the problem and since the next Allied Naval Council meeting was not until June offered the services of a French staff officer, Capitaine de vaisseau Lanxade, who was in Rome for the committee studying the American proposals for Adriatic operations. Bonin recommended that Orlando should accept this in order to gain time for the British to put forward their proposals. Orlando noted – in another cable read by the French – that the French proposal represented a modification of the Allied Naval Council resolution which had spoken of a fusion of units. Now Leygues was speaking of an Italian squadron going to Corfu under its own command. It remained to be seen how far this second idea could be reconciled technically with the situation. He had no objection to the conversations with Lanxade in Rome, but it went without saying if the British proposal came into discussion the conference in Rome would no longer have any reason for taking place. Geddes, in a talk with Imperiali on the 13th, also recognized that it was up to the British to take the lead in talking with Paris and, most embarrassingly since the French were decrypting the message, complained how difficult it was to deal with the French who were always so irritable. Imperiali, speaking privately and personally, replied that it was their own fault for encouraging French pretensions and the best means of protecting themselves from French irritability was to proceed in amiable accord with the Italians.[165]

Clemenceau did not receive the British proposal until the 14th, but did not seem to disapprove at first sight of the suggestion about a British admiralissimo. The following day he cabled French acceptance of examining the principle and asked for a British representative to come to Paris to help draw up the text for a common accord. Geddes also met with Jellicoe, unemployed since he had been relieved as First Sea Lord the preceding December, and Jellicoe indicated that he would be prepared to accept the command provided it was not essential he left Britain before 15 June, although he might leave earlier if Lady Jellicoe's health permitted. She was seriously ill at that moment. Jellicoe assumed the whole of the forces in the Mediterranean would be under his command and he would fly his flag in a suitable vessel to enable him to carry out the work.[166] This was a large assumption.

If the impending displacement of Italian dreadnoughts to Corfu in exchange for French battleships sent to the Aegean was displeasing to Revel, the displacements were almost as distasteful to Calthorpe. He cabled the Admiralty on 14 May that before the conclusions of the Allied Naval Council were put into execution he wished to draw the attention of the

Board to the fact that they were at variance with the principle that the Aegean command should be British and the Aegean squadron should therefore include an adequate force of British modern capital ships in order to justify British command in that area. The decision also violated the principle that no British destroyers or submarines should be withdrawn from present anti-submarine operations in the Mediterranean since the addition of the Black Sea menace had in no way eased the submarine situation elsewhere. He considered that the proposed combined fleet at Corfu should have Italian destroyers and, in an emergency, all French and British destroyers from the Otranto barrage, while the Aegean fleet should have the French destroyers at present allocated to the French battle fleet as well as the British and Greek destroyers and British scouts now in the Aegean. Calthorpe warned that it would be most difficult to recede subsequently from the strategic dispositions made now. The Admiralty quickly reminded him that Allied forces in the Mediterranean were sufficient to meet the situation and it was unnecessary to send reinforcements of British ships. Moreover, control of operations to meet the situation caused by the threat of the Black Sea Fleet remained in the hands of the French, and the sphere of the admiral commanding the British force in the Aegean was limited to minor operations in the Aegean or preventing the escape of the *Goeben* when she was the only large ship at Constantinople. Calthorpe and Lambert were both alarmed over British memoranda for the Allied Naval Council which spoke of withdrawing destroyers from the Otranto barrage for the Aegean, and both disliked the plan to base the reinforced Aegean Squadron at Milo for, according to Lambert, a worse base could not be found. It was a bad anchorage affording little or no shelter and a fleet based there could not cover Stavros or Mudros. Lambert was equally opposed to being placed in the hands of French naval authorities. The Admiralty did assure Calthorpe that the destroyers on the barrage would be withdrawn only when an emergency in the Aegean was imminent.[167]

This exchange should be seen in the context of the officers and men in the Mediterranean feeling left out and neglected. Captain G. O. Stephenson, the Captain commanding the mobile barrage force, asked the First Lord's Secretary, Steel: 'For God's sake get a move on and help us to win this war.' He complained that in late April they still had no Fish listening devices, no flares, star shells, delay-action fuses, or kite balloons. He asked: surely if the barrage was worthwhile doing at all it was worthwhile doing quickly? Stephenson, however, reflected that division over convoys in naval circles. He supposed that 'my friend Henderson [that champion of convoys] and his beastly escorts are grabbing everything' and that one heard of convoys at home 'with almost a sufficient force of escorts to block the Adriatic'.[168] It is, of course, superfluous to point out that in the judgement of history the convoys were far more important and accomplished infinitely more than the Otranto barrage, but the fixed ideas died hard. Commander Gerald Dickens, Calthorpe's Flag Commander, complained perhaps a bit unfairly on 9 May,

So few people at home seem to bother much about this part of the world. The problems that arise from time to time in the Mediterranean appear to be looked upon as being so many nuisances, having no connection with the home problems, and are brushed aside, or settled by the Allied Council, which means that, our representatives being more or less indifferent, the French and Italian opinions are those that govern the decisions.

Moreover, by not consulting Calthorpe before the last council meeting they were 'on the verge of chaos' concerning the possibility of pulling destroyers off the barrage for the Aegean.[169] Much of Dickens's complaint concerned the anti-submarine war where he had valid grievances that in terms of destroyers and other material the Mediterranean had not got its fair share. He was wrong, however, about the lack of concern for, whatever may have been the case in the past, by the time his letter probably reached Britain the Mediterranean was very much on the minds of the Admiralty.

Geddes set off to Paris along with Rear-Admiral Hope to meet with Clemenceau and Leygues over the admiralissimo question on 17 May. He was armed with a memorandum giving the tangled history of the Mediterranean command, something all staffs now had to prepare for their leaders, but he was blissfully unaware that some of his more indiscreet remarks about French irritability were known to his French hosts. Perhaps Geddes was the type of individual who would not have been very bothered about this. Clemenceau also had a reputation for plain speaking and, after reviewing the situation, stated that if the Italians definitely said they would not send their battleships to Corfu to serve under Gauchet's command, he was prepared to consider a naval arrangement on the lines of the one agreed to in regard to Foch and the Allied land armies. Clemenceau asserted that by naval custom the French were entitled to claim the command because of the preponderance of their forces in the Mediterranean, but Geddes was quickly able to counter that the British forces preponderated in the particular class of craft, namely, the more powerful destroyer for which there was a great need, and it would be useless and wasteful to send more battleships. Clemenceau did not press the point, for the French were only too aware of it. Moreover, Clemenceau had told the Italians that he was personally indifferent to who commanded as long as the job got done. Clemenceau did add that, in order to lead public opinion to the right point of view, he proposed that if the Italians had not agreed to the French proposals in three or four days he would agree to an undertaking that Jellicoe would be charged by the French and British governments with co-ordinating the action of the Allied fleets in the Mediterranean for the preparation and conduct of naval operations. It would be up to the British to obtain the assent of the Italians, Americans and Japanese. After the meeting with Clemenceau, Geddes, de Bon and Leygues agreed that the admiralissimo would be under the Allied Naval Council and not directly under the Supreme War Council. Clemenceau did not say so, but Geddes and Lord Derby, the British ambassador, thought he was not prepared to enter into any agreement with the British until he put himself in the position of being able to declare publicly or to his colleagues that the Italians had forced him into accepting a British admiralissimo because they refused to put their ships under a French commander in the Mediterranean.[170] The entire question had to be handled carefully for, as Geddes wrote to Wemyss privately, de Bon was afraid that the proposal to appoint Jellicoe would make his own position with the French navy impossible and was 'very much down on his luck & talked of resigning'. De Bon, according to Geddes, was anxious about the actual command of the forces in action. The French apparently did not like the idea of an admiralissimo 'in action' but found the idea of a 'First Sea Lord' to the Allied Naval Council acceptable, that is, an officer whose status was similar to that of Wemyss *vis-à-vis* Beatty. Geddes suggested a meeting between Wemyss and de Bon, for he did not want a change in Paris and de Bon was 'such a fine straight man that personally I'll go a long way to meet him'.[171] He also authorized Wemyss to let Sims see all the correspondence.

While the French and British were attempting to collaborate on a Mediterranean admiralissimo, the subcommittee of the Allied Naval Council met in Rome on the 15th to consider the American project for the Adriatic. The British representative was Captain Dewar of Plans Division and the Secretary of the Allied Naval Council suggested that the French might want to send an officer with the rank of rear-admiral – Saint Pair was absent from Rome – so as to have more weight alongside Revel. The Admiralty feared that if all the other delegates were captains or lower rank they would be effaced by the personality of Revel. Nevertheless, the French sent Capitaine de vaisseau Lanxade who was, however, Sub-Chief of Naval Staff and Lanxade was joined by Capitaine de vaisseau Frochot from Brindisi, a man thoroughly familiar with Adriatic conditions.[172]

Captain Harry E. Yarnell of the Planning Section led the American delegation accompanied by Lieutenant-Colonel R. H. Dunlap, a Marine officer, and Commander Train. Sims instructed Yarnell that the American project was originally conceived with the main object of paralysing enemy submarine activities in the Mediterranean and was essentially a naval offensive for which certain military operations on shore were necessary as a support. It was neither necessary nor desirable for the Supreme War Council to pass on the strictly naval features of the project and the purely naval aspects of the operations should not, at that stage, be made the subject of a detailed report for general circulation. The Planning Section did have a detailed study on the seizure of a base at Sabbioncello–Curzola, dated April 1918, but did not officially submit it.[173]

The meeting in Rome was accompanied by the now familiar, detailed memoranda, subsequently printed by the Allied Naval Council. The Stato Maggiore prepared a series of notes in advance which are heavily annotated by Revel who apparently did not agree with all the points made by his staff. There were a few which stand out, notably the statement that Italy would not oppose any navy that wanted to carry out a bombardment of Cattaro provided the light craft for the protection of the battleships were those normally employed on the Otranto barrage and the command would go to the nation sending the battleships. Revel, however, added: 'The command of the squadron certainly, but the superior direction of the operation should be Italian', and in the margin there were the words 'Remember the Dardanelles'. The Italian Naval Staff did not consider an actual raid on Cattaro to be worth the probable losses, and the Allies could not hold the place without Mount Lovčen. Air raids were cheaper and more effective. Revel agreed with this point, but not the staff's suggestion of an attack on Durazzo as an alternative.[174]

The major part of the meeting referred to the seizure of the Sabbioncello–Curzola base, not the raid on Cattaro. Colonel Ugo Cavallero, the head of the Operations Division of the Italian Supreme Command – and later Chief of Staff during the disastrous days of the Second World War – put in a brief appearance with a detailed memorandum on the number of troops the Italian army considered necessary to carry out the operation. They numbered over 44,500, well above the original American estimate of 30,000, and Yarnell and Dunlap proposed 20,000 American Marines, 10,000 of whom were already in France, as ideally suited for operations of this sort. This would still have left over half the force to be supplied by the Italians for there had not been any serious discussion in London about committing British troops, despite the assumptions and desires of the Planning Section. Cavallero was most explicit that the Italian Supreme Command, while welcoming the study, could not for the present or foreseeable future remove a single man from the Italian front for the operation. The Italians were still anticipating the equivalent of Ludendorff's offensive in France on their own front. Given this situation, the remaining discussions of the subcommittee in Rome have a highly theoretical ring to them. Moreover, the Allies disagreed among themselves whether or not the battle squadron and flotillas to be based in the waters between Curzola and the Sabbioncello Peninsula should be composed of the main Allied forces in those waters and strong enough to encounter the whole Austrian fleet. This, in turn, had a distinct bearing on the scale of land defences required to protect the base against attack from the sea and might also affect the military operations. The French favoured using only older pre-dreadnoughts, in other words, secondary forces. The British and Americans also argued that the operation should not be undertaken unless they also decided to lay the mine barrage Gargano–Pelagosa–Cassa–Curzola at the same time or shortly afterwards. The French wanted the question of the barrage to be considered independently of the main operation, and the Italians later insisted that this mid-Adriatic barrage should not be undertaken until the fixed barrage in the Straits of Otranto had been completed and tested because of the shortage of materials and the insufficient number of small craft to complete and patrol both effectively. There was little disagreement about the military objective on Sabbioncello which would be to hold the four-kilometre line on the Isthmus of Gradina between Vallone Vranik and Porto Trstenik. The Italian High Command was dubious about the other American plans to operate against the railway on the mainland. The naval support necessary was also considerable. In addition to the battle squadron at the proposed base, they would require several scouts, forty to fifty destroyers, about twenty submarines, not less than forty torpedo-boats, patrol-boats, trawlers and drifters, as well as the inevitable troop carriers and supply ships. The mine barrage across the Adriatic required 30,000 mines.[175]

The operation was not likely to take place for a long time, if ever. Revel naturally informed General Armando Diaz, Chief of the Army General Staff, of the proceedings and his own reflections. Diaz agreed with Revel that the command of any offensive by land or sea against Austrian territory had to be Italian, but it was absolutely impossible for him to detach enough troops from the front to enable the Italians to claim command, nor could he determine if he would be able to do so in the distant future. Consequently, he asked Revel to continue to use all his influence with the Allied naval representatives to ensure that the proposed operation had no sequel.[176] The Italian High Command was therefore apparently willing to forgo the possible benefits of the capture of Sabbioncello–Curzola if they could not command the operation themselves.

There were other Allied naval meetings taking place at the same time, one less glamorous, if not more important, and the other just as theoretical. Another subcommittee met in Rome from 10–14 May to wrestle with the question of joint control of repair facilities in the Mediterranean. There was no agreement.[177] On the same day that the subcommittee met in Rome, the Allied Naval Council held an emergency meeting in London which had been called at short notice. The American military representative at the Supreme War Council had posed the question whether, from a military point of view, it was desirable for the United States to declare war on the Ottoman Empire and Bulgaria. The military representatives of the Supreme War Council, not surprisingly, decided to recommend that the United States should immediately declare war on Turkey and, if Bulgaria could not be detached by diplomatic means from the Central Powers, on Bulgaria as well. The Supreme War Council made a specific point that under no circumstances must any American troops be diverted from the western front. The British members of the Allied Naval Council then brought up the matter for discussion from a strictly naval standpoint.[178] Sims was rather cautious at this venture into diplomacy. Moreover, the US Naval Planning Section had actually produced a memorandum on 4 March recommending that the Allies should make peace with Turkey, the terms to include free passage of the Dardanelles. The paper had been the subject of extensive, generally favourable and very interesting comment at the Admiralty, and the substance was incorporated in the American Memorandum No. 69 printed by the Allied Naval Council.[179] The memorandum, however, had not been circulated to the Supreme War Council or anyone outside the Allied Naval Council.

Sims anticipated that the subject of an American declaration of war on Turkey was going to come up because of the threat of the Russian Black Sea Fleet and the Italian refusal to transfer dreadnoughts to Corfu. All of this was perhaps bound to create pressure for American naval forces to move eastwards in the Mediterranean and Sims warned Benson on 13 May that the Navy Department should be prepared for a possible request to send a division of American dreadnoughts to the Mediterranean. Oil-burning vessels would be preferred since they could be supplied with fuel oil via the

Suez Canal much more readily than coal could be brought from Britain for coal burners. Benson apparently got the staff in Washington to investigate the subject based on the average consumption of four oil-burning dreadnoughts per month, taking into account the known output of the eastern refineries in Burma, Sumatra, Persia and Borneo. Captain William Pratt, the Assistant Chief of Naval Operations, determined the monthly consumption of fuel oil would be a little beyond the capacity of one tanker of the *Standard Arrow* type (7,794 tons), but the oil situation of the American dreadnoughts at Corfu could be met by the eastern supply of oil via the Suez Canal. Pratt considered it was wiser to accept supplies from the east rather than take the risk of one of their big tankers running through the Mediterranean at least once a month.[180] American dreadnoughts at Corfu might have fought the Austrians, not necessarily the Turks. However, as Wemyss pointed out at the Council, the closer the Americans got to the eastern Mediterranean, the greater the paradox. The fact that the United States was not at war with Turkey meant that if the *Goeben* came out flying the Turkish flag the American forces in the Mediterranean 'would have to be spectators while the Allied forces engaged'. Sims had no objection to a Council resolution from a purely naval standpoint and the Allied Naval Council accordingly unanimously adopted a resolution in general terms supporting the Supreme War Council on the desirability of the United States declaring war on the Ottoman Empire and, if necessary, Bulgaria.[181]

The drive towards getting those Italian dreadnoughts to Corfu and appointing an admiralissimo in the Mediterranean now moved towards its climax, but there was another and unexpected complication which appeared in mid-May. What about the Duke of the Abruzzi? Commander Train, the American naval attaché in Rome, reported that Del Bono was fairly open about wanting to appoint him to command the combined Franco-Italian squadron at Corfu. When he met with Clemenceau in Paris on the 17th, Geddes arranged for a special cable to Larking requesting him to ascertain the reason for the recent promotion of Abruzzi to full admiral. This request may have been instigated by the French who by now would have deciphered Orlando's telegram to Imperiali of 7 May suggesting the duke for the command. Naturally they were not likely to have told Geddes how they obtained the information, but the suggestion was enough. It might have seemed a marvellous Machiavellian plot to suddenly spring the duke as a distinguished officer with high social standing and rank, and then use him to ensure the command went to the Italians. Larking learned that the duke had actually been promoted two months before without any special command in mind and largely to keep him quiet. The Minister of Marine had supposedly been trying to find something for him to do and Larking understood that he would offer him the Corfu command if the Allies agreed on an Italian admiral.[182]

The Anglo-French negotiations over the admiralissimo stalled after Geddes's meeting with Clemenceau while the French awaited a final decision on whether or not the Italians would send their battleships to Corfu. Leygues ordered Lanxade to prolong his stay in Rome until he had received a definite reply from the Italian navy, and added that it was important the latter do so as soon as possible. Del Bono said he was personally favourable to the plan but deferred the decision until Revel returned to Rome.[183] Unfortunately, Revel was more uncompromising than ever in his encounter with Lanxade on the 19th. Revel did not consider that the question of principle had been resolved by the Abbeville Conference, nor did he see any necessity to send Italian dreadnoughts to Corfu since he was certain the Austrian fleet would not come out before seven or eight months. The proposed combination was in contradiction with the agreements of 1917 which called for only one French squadron at Corfu after the departure of the British Queen division from Taranto, and even after the detachment of the French forces for the Aegean those French forces remaining at Corfu would still be superior to what Revel judged necessary to reinforce the Italians. Revel also brought up the difficulties that Gauchet experienced obtaining coal at Corfu, and cited the loss of the *Danton* on her way to dock as a good reason for battleships not moving unless circumstances absolutely required them to. When Lanxade, in what must have been a stormy meeting, raised the subject of Revel's incurring a heavy responsibility in going against the unanimous agreement of the other Allies, the Capo di Stato Maggiore accepted full responsibility. Lanxade went over all the usual arguments, such as the need for joint manœuvring and gunnery exercises, but to no avail. Revel announced that he would see Orlando presently, but could give no date when the Italian government would announce its final decision. Barrère lost no time in meeting Orlando the very next day, apparently before the Italian Prime Minister had learned of the Lanxade– Revel interview. Barrère spoke of Revel 'going on strike' against an urgent naval enterprise of the Allies. Orlando recognized that despite Revel's opposition it was necessary to send the dreadnoughts to Corfu, and promised to bring up the subject at the Italian War Committee the next day. He claimed not to have heard from the Italian ambassador in Paris about the French offer whereby the four Italian dreadnoughts would preserve their national homogeneity. Orlando also complained that the British did not want to send any ships to Corfu. There had never been any question of this and it is difficult to guess what he was talking about, unless he meant a request for faster light cruisers in the Adriatic. Barrère concluded from the remark that, whatever it was, the Italians had not received what they expected from London. Barrère, for his part, protested that it was desirable the British did not leave them alone in the task of making the Italians agree to assist, without haggling, in work which touched British interests more than their own. In this case, as unfortunately in others in Italy, he complained, the support of their British ally was lacking.[184]

Revel was not the only naval leader to give his government trouble. De Bon, Chief of the EMG, was highly regarded by the British but despite the good face he had put on the matter he was not happy about relinquishing overall direction of the naval war in the Mediterranean to the British because, as he expressed it, Italy, the weakest of the naval powers, had pretensions to command. He wrote to Leygues on 21 May that the consequences of this renunciation were not limited solely to the question of the naval war, but involved French prestige in the Mediterranean where more than half the coastline in the western basin was French and where they had considerable present and future interests in the eastern basin. Their communications with Algeria and Morocco also depended on command of the sea, as did the supply of their fleet at Corfu and their army at Salonika. De Bon prepared a draft of a letter of protest for Leygues to submit to Clemenceau and it is likely that his arguments had some effect as the minister had been prominently associated with the group favouring the advance of French interests in Syria.[185] It is not clear, however, whether the letter was ever submitted or what effect, if any, it would have had on Clemenceau who dominated the Cabinet and took the lead in pushing the issue. He was willing and able to keep the military in check, as he would later on during the armistice negotiations at the end of the war. As Lord Derby, the British ambassador, put it: Clemenceau was the only man in the government and whether it was Pichon at the Foreign Ministry or Leygues at the Ministry of Marine or anyone else who spoke to you, 'it really is Clemenceau and Clemenceau alone who can give a definite answer on any subject'.[186] Moreover, in the long run the Italians might do the work of the French navy for them in frustrating the British admiralissimo. Clemenceau might control his admirals, the question was could Orlando control Revel, or did he really want to?

Revel submitted a hefty memorandum to Orlando on 21 May summarizing all his arguments and the past history of the agreements all the way back to the Naval Convention of May 1915. The gist of his argument was that the French concentration of the most important part of their fleet at Corfu did not respond to any diplomatic obligation or military requirement and was clearly intended to subvert all previous agreements regarding Italian command in the Adriatic. He submitted a table of warships and their total number of cannon to show that the Italians needed only a squadron of five Dantons, not dreadnoughts, to support them in the Adriatic. The French request, supported by the British, to send four Italian dreadnoughts to Corfu was aimed at abolishing the entity of the Italian fleet in the presence of the Austrian fleet and substituting the French flag for the Italian flag in the Adriatic and in the Ionian, with grave political and morale damage to Italy. Revel's solution for facing the new danger represented by German control of the Russian Black Sea Fleet was to give the task of facing and fighting the Austrian fleet to the First Allied Fleet created by the Naval Convention of 1915. This fleet would be under an Italian C.-in-C. and composed of the Italian Fleet, the division of five French Dantons and other Allied ships attached to the Italian fleet in the Adriatic. The task of fighting all other enemy forces which might appear in the Mediterranean would go to the remaining Allied ships in the Mediterranean under the command of the French C.-in-C., and deployed to whatever base he judged convenient. The Italian C.-in-C., with regard to the potential threat of the Austrian fleet, could choose the right moment to move to Corfu or, possibly and with less risk, bring the five Dantons to Taranto.[187] Revel's proposal was a reversion to the original Naval Convention of 1915 and would have had the effect of splitting the French fleet and perhaps even incorporating a portion of it in the Italian fleet at Taranto. It was not likely to be accepted.

Revel did succeed in convincing Orlando who informed Barrère that his Chief of Naval Staff had brought into relief elements which he had not understood perfectly. Barrère concluded that Orlando had gone back on his promise to send the four dreadnoughts to Corfu and that the French government could not accept these pretensions and would have to submit the issue once again to the Supreme War Council. He suggested that the action to adopt in the face of the dilatory Italian measures would be to ask for the immediate dispatch of four American dreadnoughts to Corfu to replace the ships which the Italians hestitated to provide.[188]

The British were growing impatient over the lack of progress in Rome and there were anxious cables from Geddes to Lord Derby. Derby saw Clemenceau and Leygues on the 22nd and Clemenceau said that he was most anxious to settle the matter forthwith. He asked, perhaps reflecting de Bon's and Leygues's concerns, if they might insert a paragraph in the Anglo-French agreement over the admiralissimo giving the French admiral leave to appeal to his government if the admiralissimo ordered him to do something he considered would endanger his fleet. Clemenceau was also true to his word. On the evening of the 22nd he cabled Barrère a characteristic message. It was absolutely impossible to let the matter drag on and while one quibbled events might be precipitated. He could not lend himself any longer to this system of inertia which might be dangerous. Clemenceau demanded a 'yes' or 'no' answer from Orlando.[189]

Clemenceau's cable actually crossed the one from Barrère informing him that the Italians would not send the dreadnoughts. Barrère did not feel he could make a communication in the form Clemenceau indicated – the refreshing request for a simple 'yes' or 'no' answer. 'We have forms to keep up if we do not want to fall out', he explained, and besides Orlando had already given his reply which was essentially negative. This could not have been a pleasant situation for Barrère who had been in Rome a long time and worked so hard at the process of Franco-Italian *rapprochement* during which Italy moved from membership in the rival Triple Alliance to neutrality and then an active alliance. Barrère was inclined to blame the British for encouraging Italian resistance and considered their attitude in the affair doubtful. For the higher interest of the war, for the future and for the power of the Alliance after the war, France and Britain should always present themselves as united. This was unfortunately not so in Italy and Barrère blamed the 'venomous diplomat' who represented Italy in London, that is Imperiali, for pushing the British to seek support in Rome against the French. The next day Barrère learned of the proposal to substitute Jellicoe for Gauchet as commander of the Allied fleets in the Mediterranean, and of the Italian plan to make Abruzzi commander of the Allied forces in the Adriatic and at Corfu. By this combination the French would be evicted from all direction of naval operations and their national and military prestige in the Mediterranean would suffer a severe blow. Barrère hoped that the French government would reject such a clandestine transaction.[190] He apparently did not realize how far Clemenceau had gone.

De Bon on the evening of the 24th ordered Lanxade to consider all conversations on the subject of the Italian dreadnoughts as terminated, and if the Italians brought up the subject again to say nothing without further instructions. The British naval attaché in Rome now believed that there was not the slightest hope of any satisfactory solution and that the proposal for a British admiralissimo should be put forward as soon as possible. On the 23rd the War Cabinet approved placing the subject of the admiralissimo on the agenda of the next Supreme War Council meeting if the issue had not been settled before that date.[191]

Clemenceau definitely turned to the British on the 23rd with a telegram to Lloyd George announcing that Orlando had gone back 'for reasons which he omits to mention' on the principle that he had accepted at Abbeville of moving the dreadnoughts. It is not clear that Orlando ever really accepted that principle, but Clemenceau thought he had and had then reneged. Clemenceau commented with typical sarcasm about Revel's contention that the Austrian fleet was not likely to attack for seven or eight months: 'Even if Austria had made a formal engagement to this effect, I should still have doubts.' Clemenceau accepted the principle of a British C.-in-C., 'but on the absolute condition that such command must apply to everyone, and that the Italians who have made a pretext of the danger of being torpedoed between Taranto and Corfu, shall consent to proceed to sea when the order is given them'. He also wanted to add that clause giving each commander the right of appeal if he thought Jellicoe's orders endangered his force. Clemenceau pointedly told Lord Derby that the appointment would be impossible if confined only to the British and French, and should only be operative when Italy assented. He, too, wanted to bring the matter up at the next Supreme War Council meeting and promised the British his active co-operation.[192] Rodd had made a similar point a few days before. He reported that not all of the Italian Naval Command apparently agreed with Revel, and the Minister of Marine's Chief of Staff privately suggested that should the scheme of admiralissimo be adopted it should be clearly laid down that the admiralissimo will take command in the whole of the Mediterranean including the Adriatic. If that was not done, the door would be open to further discussion and, while Revel would probably oppose this provision, he would be ruled out if the command was clearly defined.[193] Those unnamed Italian officers were perhaps over optimistic given Revel's influence.

The Admiralty could not accept the clause giving each Allied C.-in-C. the right of appeal for 'the rapidity with which a Naval battle situation develops makes the clause of different import to what obtains in land warfare'. This referred to the argument that Haig had the right to appeal against Foch's orders on land. Geddes, however, had no objection to the suggestion as far as 'the general disposition of forces' was concerned, that is, a right of appeal on long-term strategical issues rather than tactical problems requiring an immediate decision, but thought it best to discuss the question at the next Supreme War Council with their advisers.[194]

There was almost as much potential for Anglo-French discord over the matter as there was for friction with the Italians, as the attitude of Barrère demonstrated. French suspicions were of course fuelled by reading the Italian cables or, as Clemenceau expressed it to Barrère: 'From London, I learn from a reliable source [*source sûre*] that the proposition was the result of a preliminary accord between the English and the Italians.' The 'reliable source' was, of course, Imperiali's intercepted telegram to Orlando. Clemenceau's reference was part of a summary for Barrère in a caustic manner of the negotiations as seen from Paris. He wrote that one had to believe the Italians would not accept British command any more than they would French since Orlando had suddenly, baldly and flatly refused to run the risk of sending ships from Taranto to Corfu – ships which did absolutely nothing in the Mare Piccolo at Taranto, performing neither training exercises, nor preparation for combat or manœuvres. Clemenceau had immediately informed Lloyd George, whom he felt must be as embarrassed as he was since the British command, if it materialized, would presume that the Italians would at least risk the voyage to Corfu. Clemenceau ordered Barrère not to discuss the issue any further.[195]

Barrère seemed to think that Clemenceau had overreacted. Orlando had not refused baldly and flatly his support, for he had couched his reply in amicable expressions and sent a second letter claiming that Barrère had interpreted his thoughts in too absolute a fashion. Orlando had not refused to have his ships run the danger of a submarine blockade of Taranto, that observation was from Thaon di Revel, and the Italians, far from refusing British command, had provoked the proposition. Orlando had met with him that morning and spontaneously declared that the question could be easily settled by sending the four battleships to Corfu and deciding the question of command by seniority, and the French admiral being senior would command. Barrère had reservations about that assertion since command at Corfu belonged to France by treaty, but the conversation seemed to indicate that Orlando had evolved, and now supported sending the dreadnoughts to Corfu and would accept French command under another form.[196]

Clemenceau was not mollified, but then he probably knew that the Italians had the Duke of the Abruzzi waiting in the wings, suitably senior and therefore ready for command. For Clemenceau, all the amicable expressions in the world would not change the brutal facts and when Barrère distinguished between the reasoning of Orlando and Thaon di Revel and said it was only the admiral who feared meeting torpedoes, it was because Barrère had not heard the same arguments in Orlando's mouth at Abbeville. Clemenceau denied that he had said Orlando would not accept British command since it was Orlando who had asked for the British in order to avoid the French. Clemenceau had merely observed that the Italians, by refusing to send their fleet to Corfu, aspired to withdraw in advance that fleet from the same British command they were claiming for the French. Clemenceau added that he was personally wounded by the procedure which he had not merited because of the absolute loyalty of his declarations and acts in regard to the Italian government. He would undoubtedly forget this in the interests of France, but in the gravest crisis of the war the French government had not received from the Italian Cabinet the treatment it had a right to. Barrère believed that if he had not been ordered to suspend the talks something could have been accomplished in

Italian ships which went to Corfu had been guaranteed the maximum autonomy compatible with the necessities of combat. He denied that there was any unpleasant intention on the part of Orlando and the Italian Naval Staff towards France or Clemenceau. The Italians had merely tried to get their hands on a naval command which had a political importance for them.[197] If they failed to reach an agreement with the Italians, Barrère argued, they should turn to the Americans for assistance. Despite Barrère's attempts to smooth matters over, the outlook for the Supreme War Council was not good.

Some of the British were a bit more hopeful. Sonnino privately agreed with the British ambassador on the 24th that the whole of the Mediterranean sea command should be British instead of French, and Rodd thought that the Italian Minister of Marine and chief naval authorities would welcome this, whatever the views of Revel. Captain Larking, the British naval attaché, even rather naïvely believed that the Italians would let them run the whole Adriatic for them if they succeeded in ousting the French from the Mediterranean control.[198]

There was virtual agreement among the Allies, though, that Revel who was due to accompany Orlando to the Supreme War Council meeting was perhaps the major villain. Sims thought that 'the obstructing official should be relegated to the background in some position where he has not sufficient authority to ball the game', and a week later wrote, 'It is a great pity these people could not set aside their national pride and personal jealousies or whatever is the trouble and get along with the war'. Rodd referred to Revel as an 'arch-obstructionist' and Geddes termed him 'rather awkward when we want him to do things' and ridiculed his paper about battleships not going to sea lest they be sunk by submarines as a 'depressing document', not true for the Grand Fleet. Geddes doubted that the Italian battleships since the beginning of the war 'have steamed as many miles as the Grand Fleet battleships do each month'. Wemyss wrote: 'Our dear Allies the French and Italians are really almost more difficult to deal with than is the enemy – Several times have I flattered myself that I was actually at the point of success, but each time I have been disappointed.' Barrère also singled out Revel as the author of their difficulties and advised at the forthcoming meeting, while remaining within proprieties, that there was no need to humour him. Barrère claimed that the entire Italian navy – and that was to its honour – disapproved of the negative and egoistic policy of its Chief of Staff and would not regret if that policy received a striking check in the Council of the Allies.[199] Unfortunately, it seemed as if the Allies were almost spoiling for a fight at the forthcoming meeting, and they were not going to be disappointed. They would be disappointed, however, if they seriously thought that Orlando and the Italian government would not back Revel.

The sixth session of the Supreme War Council which met at the Trianon Palace at Versailles 1–3 June 1918 was possibly the low point of the war as far as relations among the Allies in the Mediterranean were concerned. Revel came armed with a memorandum that he had asked one of his staff officers to prepare on the advantages, or preferably disadvantages, facing the two enemy groups coming out of the Adriatic or Dardanelles and seeking to unite, taking account of their autonomy at high speed and the distance they would have to cover.[200] Revel used this fairly effectively in the presentations by naval experts in the first meeting of the council on 1 June. With more than 800 miles between Nagara in the Dardanelles and Cattaro, he asked what the Austrian fleet could hope to achieve if it came out. He repeated the argument that the Italians needed only the Danton division to reinforce them and that only urgent reasons would justify the risk of sending the Italian battleships to Corfu. De Bon gave the familiar British and French argument that it was a question of principle that the Allies could not accept Revel's contention that the Italian fleet was only for service in the Adriatic and not the Mediterranean as a whole. Units which were to fight together must be trained together and it would take three to six months before those combined units would achieve complete cohesion. The Italian division at Corfu could always be recalled by the Italian admiralty if a special operation required its intervention. There was little in any of the statements by the naval experts that had not been said many times before and the general meeting broke up to enable the heads of government to thrash out the problem in private.

The Americans played a distinctly minor role and at these high-level naval talks were represented only by Mr A. H. Frazier, the First Secretary of the American Embassy in Paris. Sims, incidentally, was not at the meeting. Lloyd George, Geddes, Clemenceau and Leygues essentially squared off against Orlando and Sonnino. The Italians argued that Revel had been totally misunderstood. It was not that he did not want to run any risks at all, but he had merely asked if the possible advantages were worth those risks. By this time all parties must have been well briefed on the naval questions and, possibly, all the less likely to accept each other's arguments as a result. The arguments were essentially the same and in the end Sonnino indicated that the Italians would accept unity of command, that is the British admiralissimo, but with a clause giving a C.-in-C. the right of appeal to his government if he thought the safety of his squadrons was being compromised. The conference then tried to hammer out the draft of a resolution appointing Jellicoe to co-ordinate the movements of the Allied naval forces in the Mediterranean with each national commander having the right of appeal. The details of Jellicoe's duties and powers would be laid down by the Allied Naval Council on the basis that it was the intention of the Supreme War Council that Jellicoe would have the general direction of Allied forces from the strategic point of view in the Mediterranean, Adriatic and Aegean.[201] The Allies were close to agreement. Geddes was most anxious that Jellicoe must have complete control over the grand fleets but recognized that the Italians wanted freedom to be able to carry out small defensive operations in the Adriatic against Austrian raids. Geddes, however, thought the two objectives could be reconciled with a little good will since he was really anxious that Jellicoe should not have the responsibility for defending the little towns along the Adriatic coast. He could not do it and the failure would have a bad political effect in Italy.[202] The Italians were not the only ones who could be Machiavellian.

Unfortunately the whole agreement unravelled the next day, probably after Revel had had a chance to get at Sonnino and Orlando. In the afternoon session of the 2nd the Italians challenged the decisions of the preceding day and, once again, the leaders of the Supreme War Council went into private session between the heads of government, only this time the naval experts were present. The Italians made a counter-proposal to the resolution appointing an admiralissimo. The conduct of all special operations of war in the Adriatic would be assigned to the Italian C.-in-C. and it would be understood that all naval units already assigned to the Italian fleet in preceding agreements would continue to remain at the disposal of the Italian C.-in-C. This was totally unacceptable to Clemenceau. Either there would be an Allied C.-in-C. or there would not be one, and the Italians apparently wished to retain complete independence. Orlando stressed the need for the Italians to control the local daily operations of war in the Adriatic. Geddes tried to find a compromise, distinguishing local tactical command from strategic command, but he could not agree to the proposal about units assigned to the Italian fleet by past agreement remaining at the disposal of the Italian C.-in-C., for that would have the effect of withdrawing the whole Italian fleet from the Allied C.-in-C., and the net result would be only the substitution of Jellicoe for Gauchet. Soon all participants were back to their old arguments. Revel must have endeared himself still more by interpreting the British and French proposals as a censure on both the direction of the war in the Adriatic and the Italian C.-in-C. He claimed that they had done nothing to warrant that, for nowhere had naval war been conducted more effectively. He argued that the Adriatic, with the enemy at the door, required special treatment and for the last six months no major Italian warships had left their harbours and that explained why there had been no losses. If the admiralissimo were to have ordered them out, losses might have been incurred and, in his opinion, there was no good reason for a change or running useless risks. The discussions grew heated and there were debates over various drafts and corrections of resolutions, particularly over the meaning of the term 'special operations' in the Adriatic. Finally, Lloyd George had had enough. He stated that no useful purpose would be served by passing resolutions that were not intended to be realized, 'that were mere shams', and he withdrew his resolution about the admiralissimo. If necessary, he said, special agreements could be entered into by the British and French.[203]

The formal minutes do not give a picture of the atmosphere. Hankey, Secretary to the War Cabinet, gives a vivid description in his diary:

> We had thought this [the admiralissimo question] to be settled the previous day, but Sonnino was extraordinarily obstinate and insisted that the Italians must retain command of the Adriatic . . . I am bound to say that Geddes was just as difficult and uncompromising as the Italians. On the one hand he would concede nothing to their *amour propre* and on the other he would insist on Jellicoe's dispositions being subject to the Allied Naval Council which the Italians would not accept. The reason for this was that he doesn't really trust Jellicoe sufficiently to place him in the

same position as Foch. The end of the *séance* was screaming farce. Orlando, Sonnino and the Italian Admiral di Revel were all shouting at the top of their voices at once, and gesticulating like monkeys. Sonnino's brick-red face looked like apoplexy, his eyes were bulging out of his head and flashing fire-real sparks, and his body was lolling about with his gesticulations. All this was provoked because Ll.G said the Italians wanted to make his proposal for an Admiralissimo a sham, that he would not insult Jellicoe by offering him the job on such terms, and that his proposal was withdrawn. Admiral di Revel was an altogether contemptible person. Yesterday he distinguished himself by saying that he could not join the Italian fleet at Taranto with the French fleet at Corfu, because the voyage between the two ports was too dangerous for ships going to and fro to dock. To-day he still further distinguished himself by boasting that the Italian fleet had not been to sea for 18 months and consequently, had not lost a ship! The meeting broke up in some confusion.[204]

That night Geddes cabled Wemyss, who had returned to London with the impression that the entire Mediterranean question had been settled entirely to their satisfaction, the disturbing news that the Italians 'have ratted completely'. Lloyd George had, in effect, broken off negotiations and prevented Geddes from seeing Sonnino again at the meeting. Hankey's point about the First Lord not trusting Jellicoe and insisting he should be under the Allied Naval Council is interesting. Geddes had, after all, relieved Jellicoe as First Sea Lord six months before. The major Italian objection to the Allied Naval Council was that it took too long to get from Rome to Paris. They would have preferred Jellicoe to deal directly with the admirals and governments concerned. But the issue was certainly not the one that wrecked the agreement. The question of command in the Adriatic which the Italians wanted to pre-empt for themselves was responsible for that. Before leaving Paris, Geddes did, however, send a note to Hankey impressing on the Secretary and the Prime Minister his strong view that it would be undesirable to place the admiralissimo directly under the Supreme War Council. He wrote: 'I am convinced that the Allied Naval Council is the proper body to supervise him, especially as the responsibility of the First Sea Lord, & myself in this matter is so great, as also is that of the French Minister of Marine.'[205]

Geddes also left a memorandum concerning command in the Mediterranean with Hankey on 3 June, for he did not think that the Supreme War Council should separate without dealing with the question. But the matter was dead for that session, which had also been a stormy one because of other problems dealing with the war on land. Things had been so rough that, when asked how the conference was getting on, General Tasker H. Bliss, permanent US military representative on the Supreme War Council, made the cruel remark: 'Well, they are all at sea, except the Italian Admiral and he won't go there.'[206] Geddes wrote to Jellicoe on the 5th about the failure at Versailles, asserting that he was the one to advise Lloyd George to break off negotiations when the Italians wanted to control the powers of the admiralissimo so drastically. However, Geddes claimed that the Prime

Minister anticipated the talks would resume 'before very long' on a more satisfactory basis. Geddes did not provide the justification for this and he or Lloyd George may have been over optimistic. Just before leaving Paris, Revel told de Bon that he was not disinclined to send his ships to Corfu to constitute a squadron to which two French battleships would be added. That squadron would be commanded by an Italian admiral under the French C.-in-C., Gauchet. The Italians would keep command of ordinary naval operations in the Adriatic while the ensemble of Allied forces in the Mediterranean would not be called into that sea.[207] This would, in effect, be a return to former agreements but without any place for Jellicoe.

This first effort at Allied unity had ended in failure, but the British would try again. It is hard not to place much of the blame on Revel and the Italians, particularly the egoistic refusal to send the ships to Corfu for badly needed joint training with the French, and the questionable technical difficulties they raised to justify this which reflected so badly on them. But Hankey was a shrewd-enough observer to note that Revel may have had the last laugh since the Russian Black Sea Fleet never materialized as a real threat, just as Revel had predicted all along, and the Italians, as we shall see, were about to sink an Austrian dreadnought and break up an Austrian attack on their own.[208] Moreover, no one really addressed the problem of why all those French ships were actually necessary at Corfu when the Italians only needed the support of the five older Dantons. Gauchet would have had perfect freedom to take the French dreadnoughts to the Aegean and that would have taken care of any potential threat from the Black Sea. We shall examine that threat more closely and how the Allies met it in the final chapter.

Notes: Chapter 11

1 Calthorpe to Admiralty, 18 Oct. 1917, minutes by Coode, 19 Oct. 1917, 5 and 23 Jan. 1918, PRO, Adm 137/400.

2 Beatty to Admiralty, 8 June 1917, Anon. [Richmond], 'Proposal for the Employment of a Detached Force on the Coast of Syria', n.d., Remarks by Operations Division, War Staff, 26 June 1917, Minute by Hope [DOD], 17 June 1917, ibid., Adm 137/1419. See also Marder, *Portrait of an Admiral*, pp. 250–1, 388.

3 W. Kirke, Note on Interview with Admiral Wemyss re Demonstrations on Syrian Coast, 31 Oct. 1917, Kirke to Wemyss, 1 Nov. 1917, PRO, Adm 137/2710.

4 Minutes by Plans Division, 19, 22 and 24 Nov. and 15 Dec. 1917, ibid. On the aerial operations see: Jones, *The War in the Air*, Vol. 5, pp. 406–10.

5 Fremantle to Hall, 13 Nov. 1917, National Maritime Museum, Greenwich, Fremantle MSS, FRE/301.

6 Fremantle to Admiralty, 30 Dec. 1917, minutes by Coode, 28 Jan. and 1 Feb., Fuller [D of P], 30 Jan., Hall, 11 Feb., and Wemyss, 19 Feb. 1918, Calthorpe to Admiralty, 21 Jan. 1918, PRO, Adm 137/1417.

7 Dumas Diary, 13 and 31 Aug., 1 Sept. 1917, Imperial War Museum, London, Dumas MSS, PP/MCR 96, Reel No. 4.

8 Dumas Diary, 16 Nov. and 5 Dec. 1917, ibid.

9   See above, Chapter 10.
10 Dumas Diary, 20 and 21 Dec. 1917, loc. cit. at n. 7, Dumas MSS, PP/MCR 96, Reel No. 4.
11 Rebeur-Paschwitz to Usedom [?] 4 Nov. 1917, Usedom to Rebeur-Paschwitz, 9 Nov. 1917, NARS, T-1022, Roll 1410, PG 60139.
12 Rebeur-Paschwitz to Holtzendorff, 4 Dec. 1917, ibid., Roll 663, PG 75247, Rebeur-Paschwitz to Marinestation Ostsee and Nordsee, 4 Dec. 1917, ibid., Roll 664, PG 75248.
13 Rebeur-Paschwitz to Kaiser Wilhelm II, 20 Jan. 1918, copy in BA-MA, Nachlass Souchon, N156/4.
14 Dumas Diary, 16 Jan. 1918, loc. cit. at n. 7, Dumas MSS, PP/MCR 96, Reel No. 4.
15 Corbett and Newbolt, *Naval Operations*, Vol. 5, pp. 83–92; Jones, *The War in the Air*, Vol. 5, pp. 409–14; Lorey, *Krieg in den türkischen Gewässern*, Vol. 1. chs 28–29; Marder, *Dreadnought to Scapa Flow*, Vol. 5, pp. 12–20.
16 Dumas Diary, 21 Jan. 1918, loc. cit. at n. 7. The censorious Dumas himself declined to take the risk of sending E12 up the Dardanelles because of her propellor shaft. Hayes-Sadler confirmed his decision. The Admiralty, however, considered the risk should have been taken because of the great value of the *Goeben*. See: Geddes, Memorandum of Consultation with C.-in-C. Malta, 15 Feb. 1918, PRO, Adm 116/1807.
17 Dumas Diary, 25, 27–30 Jan. 1918, loc. cit. at n. 7, Dumas MSS; Corbett and Newbolt, *Naval Operations*, Vol. 5, pp. 91–2.
18 Rebeur-Paschwitz to Kaiser Wilhelm II, 2 Feb. 1918 with remarks by Souchon, 31 Aug. 1918, BA-MA, Nachlass Souchon, N156/4; Einsichtsakt des Marineevidenz Büros über die politische Wirkung des Verlustes der *Breslau* in Konstantinopel', 17 Feb. 1918, OK/MS VIII-1/8 ex 1918, No. 760. See also report by the German naval attaché in Constantinople, Grancy to Capelle and Holtzendorff, 26 Jan. 1918 and Rebeur-Paschwitz to Holtzendorff, 29 Jan. 1918, NARS, T-1022, Roll 663, PG 75246. The Admiralstab backed Rebeur-Paschwitz, Remarks by Holtzendorff, 7 Feb. 1918, ibid.
19 Revel to Cusani, 23 Jan. 1918, Cusani to Cerri, 24 Jan. 1918, Gordon to Cerri, 28 Jan. 1918, Heneage to Cerri, 28 Jan. 1918, USM, Cartella 1137. See also: Ufficio Storico, *Marina italiana*, Vol. 7, pp. 53–4.
20 Wemyss to Beatty, 7 Feb. 1918, Wemyss MSS. Microfilm copy in the library of the University of California at Irvine.
21 Calthorpe, 'Remarks on the Situation in the Aegean', 7 Feb. 1918, PRO, Adm 116/1807; Admiralty to Calthorpe, 23 Feb. 1918, ibid., Adm 137/1575.
22 Memorandum of Consultation with the Commander-in-Chief, Malta, 15 Feb. 1918, Geddes to Calthorpe, 21 Feb. 1918, ibid., Adm 116/1807; Geddes to Wemyss, 17 Feb. 1918, ibid., Adm 116/1806.
23 Dumas Diary, 8 Feb. 1918, loc. cit. at n. 7, Dumas MSS.
24 ibid., 27 Feb., 6 and 16 Mar. 1918.
25 Wemyss to Beatty, 22 Jan. 1918, loc. cit. at n. 20, Wemyss MSS; Duff to Bethell, 28 Jan. 1918 quoted in Marder, *Dreadnought to Scapa Flow*, Vol. 5, p. 20.
26 Allied Naval Council [hereafter referred to as ANC], 1st Meetings, Report of Proceedings, 1st Session, 22 Jan. 1918, and Conclusions Nos VI and VIII, PRO, Adm 137/836, ff. 19, 31–4.
27 ANC, 1st Meetings, Report of Proceedings, 2nd Session, 22 Jan. 1918, and Conclusion No. IX, ibid., ff. 19, 34–6.
28 ANC, 1st Meetings, 3rd Session, Report of Proceedings, 23 Jan. 1918, Conclusion No. XXV, ibid., ff. 21–2.

29 Wemyss to Beatty, 28 Jan. 1918, loc. cit. at n. 20, Wemyss MSS.
30 Revel to Del Bono, 6 Feb. 1918, USM, Cartella 1209/2.
31 Calthorpe, 'The Otranto Barrage', 16 Jan. 1918, ANC, Report of Second Meetings, Appendix I, Enclosure II, PRO, Adm 137/836, ff. 156–61.
32 Maclay to Geddes, 22 Jan. 1918, Money to Geddes, 25 Jan. 1918, Ministry of Shipping, 'Memorandum on the Mediterranean Position', 10 Jan. 1918, Geddes to Maclay, 24 Jan. 1918, PRO, Adm 116/1806.
33 Revel, 'Preliminary Notes by Italy for the Commission in Rome', 8 Feb. 1918, ANC, Report of Second Meetings, Appendix I, Enclosure No. 1, PRO, Adm 137/836, ff. 149–55.
34 Geddes to Lloyd George, 9 Feb. 1918, PRO, Adm 116/1807; Wemyss to Geddes, 16 Feb. 1918, ibid., Adm 116/1806; Ratyé to Leygues, 15 Feb. 1918, SHM, Carton Es-16.
35 ibid.; Ratyé to Gauchet, 15 Feb. 1918, ibid., Carton A-136; Revel to Del Bono, 14 Feb. 1918, USM, Cartella 1138.
36 Conclusions of the Rome Commission, 8–9 Feb. 1918, in ANC, Report of Second Meetings, Appendix I, PRO, Adm 137/836, f. 147.
37 Geddes to Lloyd George, 9 Feb. 1918, ibid., Adm 116/1807.
38 Revel to Del Bono, 14 Feb. 1918, USM, Cartella 1138.
39 Rodd to Foreign Office, 10 Feb. 1918, PRO, FO 371/3229; Geddes to Lloyd George, 9 Feb. 1918, ibid., Adm 116/1807; Geddes, 'Coal for Italy', 8 Mar. 1918, ibid., Adm 116/1810; Sims to Admiral Sir Lewis Bayly, 15 Feb. 1918, NARS, RG 45, TD File, Box 553; Sims to Benson, 14 Mar. 1918, ibid., WA-4 File, Box 602.
40 Geddes to Lloyd George, 9 Feb. 1918; Memorandum of Meeting with Signor Bianchi, Minister of Transport, 11 Feb. 1918, PRO, Adm 116/1807.
41 Geddes to Wemyss, 14 and 17 Feb. 1918, Geddes to Wemyss, Duff and Fourth Sea Lord, 17 Feb. 1918, Geddes to Maclay, 17 Feb. 1918, ibid.
42 Stevenson to Steel, 14 Mar. 1918 (enclosing extract from Lloyd George's correspondent in Algiers), ibid.; Kenworthy to Richmond, 14 Mar. 1918, National Maritime Museum, Greenwich, Richmond MSS, RIC/7/4. It is, of course, possible that Kenworthy was Lloyd George's unnamed correspondent.
43 Calthorpe to Geddes, 20 Mar. 1918, PRO, Adm 116/1807.
44 Geddes to Maclay, 19 and 22 Mar. 1918, Maclay to Geddes, 21 Mar. 1918, Geddes to Calthorpe, 23 Mar. 1918, Geddes to Sanderson, 21 Mar. 1918, ibid., Adm 116/1605.
45 Maclay to Geddes, 3 Apr. 1918, Geddes to Maclay, 3 Apr. 1918, Admiralty to Calthorpe, 4 Apr. 1918, Sanderson to Geddes, 24 Apr. 1918, Calthorpe, Mediterranean Memorandum No. 4910, 30 Apr. 1918 [Print], ibid. See also Naval Staff, *Mediterranean Staff Papers*, pp. 4–46, 89–90.
46 Geddes and Revel, Approved Arrangements for Reorganization of British Adriatic Force, 11 Feb. 1918, PRO, Adm 137/1577.
47 Minute by Hope, 14 Feb. 1918, ibid., Adm 137/1420; Wemyss to Geddes, 16 Feb. 1918, ibid., Adm 116/1806.
48 Minutes by Fuller, 18 Feb., Duff, 19 Feb., and Hope, 25 Feb. 1918, Calthorpe to Admiralty, 22 Feb. 1918, ibid., Adm 137/1420. The Ford chasers (430 tons) derived their name from their builder, the Ford Motor Company. They were known in the US Navy as Eagle boats, Paul H. Silverstone, *U.S. Warships of World War I* (London, 1970), p. 184.
49 Fergusson to Calthorpe, 16 Jan. 1918, Calthorpe to Admiralty, 15 Feb. 1918, PRO, Adm 137/1575; Godfrey to Henderson, 9 Feb. 1918, Naval Library, Ministry of Defence, London, Godfrey MSS, Mediterranean Papers (I).

50 Minutes by Manisty, 4 Mar., and Duff, 5 Mar. 1918, Admiralty to Calthorpe, 5 Mar. 1918, PRO, Adm 137/1575.
51 Ratyé to Leygues, 23 Feb. 1918, SHM, Carton Es-16.
52 Villarey to Revel, n.d. [early Feb. 1918], USM, Cartella 1138; Vanuttelli to Del Bono, 12 Feb. 1918, ibid., Cartella 1210/2.
53 Sims to Admiral Sir Lewis Bayly, 24 Jan. 1918, NARS, RG 45, TD File, Box 553.
54 Sims to Benson, 7 Mar. 1918, ibid.
55 Planning Section, Memorandum No. 9, Problem No. 5, 30 Jan. 1918, ibid., TX File, Box 570; Sims to Benson, 2 Feb. 1918, ibid., Box 567.
56 Sims to Benson, 14 Feb. 1918, ibid., QC File, Box 464; Sims to Benson, 15 Feb. 1918, ibid., TD File, Box 553.
57 Benson to Sims, 10 Feb. 1918, ibid., QC File, Box 464.
58 Train to Sims, 15 Feb. 1918, Sims to Train, 23 Feb. 1918, ibid., TD File, Box 553. The Director of ONI, however, had not been satisfied with Train's reports in November 1917, believing him too closely tied to his office and not active enough in seeking out information. See: Jeffrey M. Dorwart, *The Office of Naval Intelligence* (Annapolis, Md, 1979), p. 127.
59 Plans Division, 'Remarks on U.S.N. Planning Section Problem No. 5 . . .', 2 Mar. 1918, minutes by Fuller, 7 Mar. and Hope, 8 Mar. 1918, PRO, Adm 137/2708.
60 Sims to Wemyss, 10 Mar. 1918, Memorandum by Sims, 10 Mar. 1918, NARS, RG 45, TD File, Box 553.
61 Planning Section, Memorandum No. 16, 7 Mar. 1918, ibid., TX File, Box 567.
62 Sims to Benson, 8 Mar. 1918, Benson to Sims, 11 Mar. 1918, ibid., QC File, Box 464.
63 Copy of Planning Section Memorandum No. 9, Problem No. 5 with marginal notes by Revel and Sechi, unsigned [Stato Maggiore], 'Risposta al Memorandum N. 9', 3 Mar. 1918, USM, Cartella 1210/2.
64 Revel to Villarey, 7 Mar. 1918, Villarey to Revel, 8 Mar. 1918, ibid., Cartella 1209/2. A revised version of the Planning Section Memorandum is printed as Allied Naval Council, Memorandum No. 49, 'The Situation in the Adriatic as Affecting the Mediterranean and the Decisions that Should Be Taken to Further Successful War', ANC, Second Meetings, Appendix II, PRO, Adm 137/836.
65 ANC, Second Meetings, 1st Session, 12 Mar. 1918 (morning), Committee report printed in ANC, Memorandum No. 81, 'Adriatic' [28 Mar. 1918], ibid., ff. 240–5.
66 ANC, Second Meetings, 3rd Session, 13 Mar. 1918 (afternoon), ibid., ff. 245–8.
67 Joint Meeting with Military Representatives, 14 Mar. 1918, ibid., ff. 249–50; Sims to Benson, 25 Mar. 1918, NARS, RG 45, TD File, Box 553.
68 Revel to Orlando, 24 Mar. 1918, Orlando to Revel, 24 Mar. 1918, USM, Cartella 1210/2.
69 Revel to Italian Naval Attaché, Washington, 30 Mar. 1918, ibid.
70 Benson to Sims, 2 Apr. 1918, NARS, RG 45, QC File, Box 464.
71 Sims to Benson, 5 April 1918, ibid.; Sims to Benson, 25 Mar. 1918, Sims to Rear-Admiral Ralph Earle [Chief of Bureau of Ordnance], 10 Apr. 1918, ibid., TD File, Box 553.
72 ANC, Report of the Second Meetings, Conclusion No. XLI; Appendix VI, Memorandum No. 46, PRO, Adm 137/836, ff. 116, 178.

73 ANC, Second Meetings, Conclusions Nos. XLIV(X), XLIV(A), Report of Proceedings, 1st Session, 12 Mar. 1918 (afternoon); Appendix VI, Memoranda Nos. 57, 58, 69 and 74, ibid., ff. 116–17, 131–3, 195–8, 200.

74 Leygues to Gauchet, 9 Feb. 1918, SHM, Carton Es-14; Gauchet to Leygues, 25 Feb. 1918, ibid., Carton Ed-83; ANC, Second Meetings, Appendix VI, Memorandum No. 74, 'Appreciation of the General Situation in the Mediterranean, the Black Sea, and the Adriatic–France', PRO, Adm 137/836, f. 206.

75 ANC, Second Meetings, Conclusions Nos. XXXVIII, XLVI, XLVII, XLVIII, Report of Proceedings, 1st and 2nd Session, 12 Mar. 1918, ibid., ff. 116–17, 124–8.

76 ANC, Second Meetings, Appendix VI, Memorandum No. 62, Reply from Japan [Iida to Crease] regarding the Dispatch of Additional Destroyers to European Waters, 7 Mar. 1918, ibid., f. 207.

77 Minute by Coode, 21 Jan. 1918, PRO, Adm 137/1420.

78 Benson to Sims, 3 Jan. 1918, NARS, RG 45, QC File, Box 465; Jellicoe to Benson, 10 Dec. 1917, ibid., OT File, Box 335.

79 Del Bono to Sonnino, 7 and 15 Jan. 1918, USM, Cartella 1191.

80 Benson to Sims, 11 Jan. 1918, Sims to Benson, 13 Jan. 1918, NARS, RG 45, QC File, Box 465.

81 Benson to Sims, 17 [or 18] Jan. 1918, ibid.

82 Sims to Benson, 20 Jan. 1918; ibid.; ANC, First Meetings, Report of Proceedings, 4th Session, 23 Jan. 1918, PRO, Adm 137/836, f. 54; Sims to Benson, 27 Jan. 1918, NARS, RG 45, QC File, Box 464.

83 Benson to Sims, 3 Feb. 1918, Laughlin to State Dept., 9 and 11 Feb. 1918, Sims to Benson, 10 Feb. 1918, ibid., OT File, Box 335; Geddes to Wemyss, 17 Feb. 1918, PRO, Adm 116/1806.

84 ANC, Second Meetings, Memoranda Nos. 55, 63 and 67, ibid., Adm 137/836, ff. 178–80; Sims to Wemyss, 10 Mar. 1918, NARS, RG 45, TD File, Box 553.

85 ANC, Second Meetings, Conclusion No. XLII, PRO, Adm 137/836, f. 116.

86 Benson to Sims, 26 June 1918, NARS, RG 45, TT File, Box 565; Daniels to Sims, 5 Sept. 1918, Sims to Benson, 26 Sept. 1918, Raguet to Sims, 27 Nov. 1918, ibid., OD File, Box 309.

87 A. P. Niblack to Sims, 28 Mar. 1918, ibid., TD File, Box 553.

88 Niblack to Sims, 29 Mar. 1918, ibid.

89 Niblack to Sims, 19 Jan. 1918, ibid.

90 'Yamew', 'Mediterranean Convoys, 1918', *Naval Review*, vol. 58, no. 3 (1965), p. 242. The author compares the Gibraltar staff very unfavourably with the Malta staff in regard to handling of escorts.

91 Niblack to Sims, 8 May 1918, NARS, RG 45, TD File, Box 553.

92 Freyberg to Holtzendorff and Capelle, 28 Jan. 1918, ibid., T-1022, Roll 505, PG 69082.

93 Njegovan to Kaiser Karl, 16 Jan. 1918, MKSM, 66-1/4 ex 1918. The captains of the *Wien* and *Budapest* were recalled to service in April due to a shortage of officers. Holub to Militärkanzlei, 8 Apr. 1918, ibid., 66-1/4-2 ex 1918.

94 Full accounts of the Cattaro mutiny are in Sokol, *Österreich-Ungarns Seekrieg*, ch. 30; and from an Italian perspective in Ufficio Storico, *Marina italiana*, Vol. 7, ch. 5; see also Anton Wagner, 'Die k.u.k. Kriegsmarine im letzten Jahr des Ersten Weltkrieges', *Österreichische Militärische Zeitschrift*, Heft 6 (1968), pp. 409–12. An extremely detailed study is Richard Georg Plaschka, *Cattaro– Prag: Revolte und Revolution* (Graz and Cologne, 1963). Unpublished sources

include: Johannes Prinz von und zu Liechtenstein, 'Die Matrosenmeuterei in der Bocche di Cattaro', Kriegsarchiv, Vienna, Nachlass Liechtenstein, B/718; Khuepach, Tagebuch, 1 Feb. 1918, ibid., Nachlass Khuepach, B/200, No. 5/1; and Heyssler, 'Erinnerungen' (1936), typescript in private possession, pp. 440–8.

95   Richard Georg Plaschka, 'Phänomene sozialer und nationaler Krisen in der k.u.k. Marine 1918', Militärgeschichtlichen Forschungsamt, Freiburg im Breisgau (ed.), *Vorträge zur Militärgeschichte*, Vol 2: *Menschenführung in der Marine* (Herford and Bonn, 1981), pp. 50–68.

96   Extensive bibliographies are in: Jorjo Tadić (ed.), *Ten Years of Yugoslav Historiography 1945–1955* (Belgrade, 1955), p. 383; idem, *Historiographie Yougoslave* (Belgrade, 1965), p. 389; and Dragoslav Janković (ed.), *The Historiography of Yugoslavia, 1965–1975* (Belgrade, 1975), pp. 284–5. I am indebted to Professor John D. Treadway for calling my attention to this reference.

97   Kaiser Karl to Chief of Marinesektion and Chief of General Staff, 27 Feb. 1918, MKSM, 66-1/7 ex 1918.

98   Linienschiffskapitän Remy-Berzenkovich von Szillás, Tagebuch, 28 Feb. 1918, Kriegsarchiv, Vienna, Nachlass Rémy, B1087/18; Horthy, *Memoirs*, pp. 88–9.

99   Freyberg to Capelle, Holtzendorff and Püllen, 9 Mar. 1918, NARS, T-1022, Roll 538, PG 69132; Freyberg to Capelle and Holtzendorff, 18 Mar. 1918, ibid., Roll 505, PG 69082. *Budapest* was actually taken out of service before the change in command, Rodler to Militärkanzlei, 15 Feb. 1918, MKSM, 66-5/5 ex 1918.

100 Rodler to Militärkanzlei, 20 Feb. 1918, ibid., 66-5/6 ex 1918; Holub, 'Alleruntertänigster Vortrag', 14 Mar. 1918, ibid., 66-5/7 ex 1918.

101 Keil to Horthy, 8 Mar. 1918, OK/MS VIII-1/1 ex 1918, No 1110; Horthy to Keil, 12 Mar. 1918, OK/MS VIII-1/9 ex 1918, No. 1264; Freyberg to Capelle, Holtzendorff and FdU Pola, 9 Mar. 1918, NARS, T-1022, Roll 538, PG 69132.

102 Arz to Marinesektion, 22 Mar. 1918, OK/MS VIII-1/9 ex 1918, No. 1422. The diary of Khuepach, for example, is full of reports about possible Allied landings. See Khuepach, Tagebuch 1918, loc. cit. at n. 94, Nachlass Khuepach, B/200, Nr. V/1.

103 Marinesektion to Horthy, 4 Apr. 1918, OK/MS I-5/1 ex 1918, No. 1643; Horthy to Marinesektion, 4 Apr. 1918, Keil to AOK, 5 Apr. 1918, ibid., No. 1665; Keil to Horthy, 9 Apr. 1918, ibid., No. 1763. See also Aichelburg, *Unterseeboote Österreich-Ungarns*, Vol. 1, p. 171.

104 Sokol, *Österreich-Ungarns Seekrieg*, pp. 624–7; Ufficio Storico, *Marina italiana*, Vol. 7, pp. 364–70 and ch. 7; Flottenkommando to Marinesektion, 5 Apr. 1918, OK/MS VIII-1/1 ex 1918, No. 1683.

105 Sokol, *Österreich-Ungarns Seekrieg*, pp. 627–30; Bagnasco, *I Mas e le motosiluranti italiane*, pp. 619–27; Ufficio Storico, *Marina italiana*, Vol. 7, ch. 20; Fraccaroli, *Italian Warships*, pp. 162–3; on Austrian measures see Greger, *Austro-Hungarian Warships*, pp. 65–7, and the authoritative Franz F. Bilzer, *Die Torpedoboote der k.u.k. Kriegsmarine von 1875–1918* (Graz, 1984), pp. 136 ff.

106 Horthy to Marinesektion, 15 Apr. 1918, OK/MS VIII-1/1 ex 1918, No. 1944; Horthy to naval base commanders, 16 May 1918, ibid., No. 2481.

107 Heyssler to Horthy, 24 Apr. 1918, Report by Herkner with comments by Heyssler, 25 Apr. 1918, OK/MS VIII-1/1 ex 1918, No. 2071; Sokol, *Österreich-Ungarns Seekrieg*, pp. 550–1; Corbett and Newbolt, *Naval Operations*, Vol. 5, pp. 287–8.

108 Braun to Heyssler, 9 May 1918, Keil to Heyssler, 28 May 1918, Heyssler to Marinesektion, 8 June 1918, and marginal note by Keil, 2 July 1918, OK/MS VIII-1/1 ex 1918, No. 2583. The printed account of the raid without the aftermath is in Sokol, *Österreich-Ungarns Seekrieg*, pp. 497–9.
109 Heyssler to Keyes, 1 Mar. 1921, in Halpern (ed.), *The Keyes Papers*, Vol. 2, Doc. 38, p. 52; Georg von Trapp, *Bis zum letzten Flaggenschuss: Erinnerungen eines Österreichischen U-Boots Kommandten* (Salzburg and Leipzig, 1935), p. 126.
110 Remarks on Kriegstagebuch UB53 (4 Dec. 1917–11 Jan. 1918), 11 Feb. 1918, NARS, T-1022, Roll 67, PG 61813.
111 Spindler, *Handelskrieg*, Vol. 5, pp. 166, 231–2.
112 Püllen to Admiralstab, 18 Feb. 1918, NARS, T-1022, Roll 927, PG 76415. On difficulties refitting and repairing submarines see also: Andreas Michelsen, *La Guerre sous-marine (1914–1918)* (Paris, 1928), pp. 70–1, 171–2.
113 Püllen to Admiralstab, 29 Mar. 1918, NARS, T-1022, Roll 927, PG 76415.
114 Püllen to Admiralstab, 13 and 31 May, 1918, ibid.; Spindler, *Handelskrieg*, Vol. 5, pp. 166–7. The UC II class, primarily minelayers but armed with 3 torpedo tubes and carrying 7 torpedoes, always brought down the average.
115 Spindler, *Handelskrieg*, Vol. 5, pp. 151, 157, 162–3, 185; Robert M. Grant, *U-Boat Intelligence, 1914–1918* (London, 1969), p. 188; Püllen to Admiralstab, 26 June 1918, NARS, T-1022, Roll 927, PG 76415; Püllen, Allgemeine Ausführungsbestimmungen für die Führung des U-Bootskrieges im Mittelmeer, 31 May 1918, ibid., Roll 980, PG 76400.
116 Ackermann to Püllen, 11 June 1918, ibid., Roll 928, PG 76417; Püllen to Admiralstab, 15 Aug. 1918, ibid., PG 76421.
117 Jones, *War in the Air*, Vol. 6, pp. 321–2. Between 11 May and the end of August there were twelve British air raids on Cattaro and seven on Durazzo.
118 Spindler, *Handelskrieg*, Vol. 5, pp. 364–5. Unfortunately, in this final volume Spindler does not differentiate losses from mines. Austrian figures are from Aichelburg, *Unterseeboote Österreich-Ungarns*, Vol. 2, pp. 492–3. See also: Gibson and Prendergast, *German Submarine War*, pp. 266–72; Thomazi, *Guerre navale dans l'Adriatique*, p. 193.
119 Gibson and Prendergast, *German Submarine War*, p. 272; for an account by an officer in the *Lychnis* see 'Yamew', 'Mediterranean Convoys, 1918', p. 243; Moraht survived to write an account of his experiences: Moraht, *Werwolf der Meere*, pp. 130–7.
120 Avray to Marinesektion, 10 June 1918, OK/MS VIII-1/15 ex 1918, No. 2984.
121 Leygues to Gauchet, 23 Mar. 1918, SHM, Carton A-29; de Bon to French Naval Attaché, London, 1 Apr. 1918, PRO, Adm 137/1580; Minute by Coode, 18 Apr. 1918, Admiralty to Lostende, 17 Apr. 1918, ibid., Adm 137/2180.
122 Memorandum by Calthorpe, 3 Apr. 1918, minutes by DNI, 18 Apr., Fuller [D. of P.], 24 Apr., Coode, 28 Apr. and Hope, 1 May 1918, ibid., Adm 137/1580.
123 Lambert to Calthorpe, 3 Apr. 1918, Calthorpe to Lambert, 10 Apr. 1918, minutes by Coode, 13 and 19 Apr. and Wemyss, 16 Apr. 1918, ibid. On Lambert see Marder, *Dreadnought to Scapa Flow*, Vol. 2, pp. 9, 306–7. Dumas described his brusque manners as causing comment but his bark was worse than his bite. Dumas Diary, 18 Mar. 1918, loc. cit. at n. 7, Dumas MSS, PP/MCR/96, Reel No. 4.
124 Lambert to Calthorpe, 14 Apr. 1918, PRO, Adm 137/2180.
125 Lambert to Geddes, 3 Apr. 1918, Minute by Coode, 11 Apr., Geddes to Lambert, 15 Apr. 1918, ibid., Adm 116/1807.

126 Calthorpe to Lambert, 26 and 28 Apr. 1918, Lambert to Calthorpe, 27 and 29 Apr. 1918, Calthorpe to Admiralty, 1 May 1918, ibid., Adm 137/1580.

127 Minutes by Coode, 10 May, and Hope, 15 May 1918, ibid. Lambert was relieved in the Aegean in August and brought back to conduct a survey by the Admiralty into the possibilities of effecting economies in the use of manpower at naval bases and shore establishments.

128 Geddes to Crease, 5 Apr. 1918, Geddes to Wemyss, 5 Apr. 1918, PRO, Adm 116/1605.

129 Revel to Del Bono, 31 Jan. 1918, USM, Cartella 738/1.

130 Lieutenant de la Chapelle [interim naval attaché] to Leygues, 10 Mar. 1918, Saint Pair to Leygues, 20 Mar. 1918, SHM, Carton Ea-136; Isabey to Leygues, 24 Apr. 1918, ibid., Carton Ea-139. On the changes see Ufficio Storico, *Marina italiana*, Vol. 7, pp. 240–1.

131 Train to Sims, 19 Mar. 1918, NARS, RG 45, TD File, Box 553.

132 Frochot to Leygues, 5 Apr. 1918, SHM, Carton Ed-91.

133 Geddes to Lloyd George, 6 Apr. 1918, House of Lords Record Office, London, Lloyd George MSS, F/18/1/11.

134 Gauchet to Leygues, 8 Mar. 1918, SHM, Carton Ed-86.

135 Revel to Cusani-Visconti, 24 Mar. 1918, Cusani-Visconti to Solari, 27 Mar. 1918, USM, Cartella 1191.

136 Gauchet to Leygues, 11 and 19 Apr. 1918, Leygues to Gauchet, 19 Apr. 1918, SHM, Carton A-29; Frochot to Leygues, 13 Apr. 1918, ibid., Carton Ed-95.

137 Kelly to Admiralty and Calthorpe, 9 Apr. 1918, Calthorpe to Kelly, 10 and 11 Apr. 1918, Kelly to Calthorpe, 12 Apr. 1918, PRO, Adm 137/1420.

138 Triangi to Larking, 15 Apr. 1918, USM, Cartella 1191; Admiralty to Calthorpe, 4 May 1918, PRO, Adm 137/1420.

139 Thomazi, *Guerre navale dans l'Adriatique*, p. 176; the incident is relegated to a footnote in Ufficio Storico, *Marina italiana*, Vol. 7, p. 408, n. 1.

140 Geddes to Bell, 4 Apr. 1918, Ballard to Calthorpe, 26 Mar. 1918, PRO, Adm 116/1807.

141 Saint Pair to Leygues, 11 Apr. 1918, SHM, Carton Es-14; Saint Pair to Leygues, 19 Apr. 1918, ibid., Carton Ed-95.

142 Geddes to Lloyd George, 6 Apr. 1918 (with draft for letter to Clemenceau and Orlando), loc. cit. at n. 133, Lloyd George MSS, F/18/1/11.

143 Revel to Geddes, 14 Mar. 1918, Geddes to Revel, 18 Mar. 1918, USM, Cartella 1192.

144 Revel to Geddes, 2 Apr. 1918, ibid. Revel sent copies to Orlando, Sonnino, Del Bono and the king's principal aide-de-camp.

145 Train to Sims, 16 Apr. 1918, NARS, RG 45, TD File, Box 553.

146 ANC, Third Meetings, 26–27 Apr. 1918, Conclusions Nos. LXII, LXIII, LXV, LXX, PRO, Adm 137/836, ff. 294–7. The detailed legal opinions on the subject of neutral waters make up Appendix III of the report of the meeting.

147 Naval Liaison Committee, Versailles to Secretary, Allied Naval Council, 9 Apr. 1918, SHM, Carton Es-12; ANC, Third Meetings, Proceedings, 2nd Session, 26 Apr. 1918 (afternoon); Conclusion No. LXVIII, PRO, Adm 137/836, ff. 295–6, 309–10.

148 ANC, Third Meetings, Proceedings 2nd Session, 26 Apr. 1918, ibid., ff. 311–14.

149 Revel, Promemoria [explaining his stand at Paris], 29 Apr. 1918, Memorandum read privately by Revel to Leygues and de Bon, n.d., USM, Cartella 1210/1.

150 ANC, Third Meetings, Conclusion No. LXIX, PRO, Adm 137/836, ff. 296–7. The Italian note is in SHM, Carton Es-18.

151 De Bon to Gauchet, 29 Apr. 1918, ibid.

152 Sims to Benson, 30 Apr. 1918, NARS, RG 45, QC File, Box 464.
153 Saint Pair to Leygues, 1 May 1918, SHM, Carton Es-14; Revel to Grassi, 30 Apr. 1918, Grassi to Revel, 30 Apr. 1918, Del Bono to Grassi, 1 May 1918, Grassi to Del Bono, 3 May 1918, USM, Cartella 1191.
154 Supreme War Council, Fifth Session, 2nd Sitting, 2 May 1918, Paper I.C.-60 (S.W.C.), Resolutions passed at the 5th Session . . ., Resolution No. 3, PRO, Cab 28/3. French text in SHM, Carton Es-12.
155 Wemyss to Larking, 3 May 1918, University of California, Irvine, Wemyss MSS. On the American battleships with the Grand Fleet see Marder, *Dreadnought to Scapa Flow*, Vol. 5, pp. 124–7.
156 Geddes, 'Future of the Russian Fleets', 25 Apr. 1918, Extract from Draft Minutes of War Cabinet Meeting, 26 Apr. 1918, PRO, Adm 116/1808; Milne to War Office, 28 Apr. 1918, Minute by Coode, 13 May 1918, ibid., Adm 137/1580.
157 Orlando to Bonin, 7 May 1918, Orlando to Imperiali, 7 May 1918, transcripts in SHM, Carton Es-14. Orlando by the end of the war was aware of the French activity and mentions it in his memoirs, Vittorio Emanuele Orlando, *Memorie (1915–1919)* (Milan, 1960), p. 556. For a discussion of the so-called *cabinet noir*, – the secret cipher office at the Quai d'Orsay – see Christopher Andrew, *Théophile Delcassé and the Making of the Entente Cordiale* (London, 1968), pp. 69–74.
158 Saint Pair to Leygues, 8 May 1918, SHM, Carton Es-14; Barrère to Pichon, 8 May 1918, MAE, Série Y Internationale, 1918–1940, Vol. 78.
159 Di Lorenzi to Ministry of Marine, 9 May 1918, Revel to Di Lorenzi, 10 May 1918, USM, Cartella 1191; French transcript of Imperiali to Orlando, 9 May 1918, SHM, Carton Es-14. There were other leaks of Italian documents. Friends of the American attaché in Rome, anxious to settle the situation, provided him with a copy of Di Lorenzi's cable of the 9th. Train to Sims, 11 May 1918, NARS, RG 45, TD File, Box 556.
160 Bonin to Orlando, 10 May 1918, Orlando to Bonin, 10 May 1918, Orlando to Imperiali, 10 and 12 May 1918, Imperiali to Sonnino, 10 May 1918, French transcripts in SHM, Carton Es-14.
161 Clemenceau to Lloyd George, 10 May 1918, loc. cit. at n. 133, Lloyd George MSS, F/50/2/33.
162 Note upon Naval Situation in the Mediterranean, 11 May 1918, Foreign Office to Derby [Paris] and Rodd [Rome], 11 May 1918, Lloyd George to Clemenceau, 13 May 1918, PRO, Adm 116/1649.
163 Revel, 'Dislocazione squadra da battàglia italiano – Commando in capo della flotta da battàglia destinata a fronteggiare la squadra austriaca', 10 May 1918, USM, Cartella 1192. Summarized in Ufficio Storico, *Marina italiana*, Vol. 7, pp. 424–5.
164 Rodd to Foreign Office, 13 May 1918, PRO, Adm 137/1576.
165 Bonin to Orlando, 13 May 1918, USM, Cartella 1192; Orlando to Bonin, 14 May 1918, Imperiali to Orlando, 13 May 1918, French transcripts in SHM, Carton Es-14.
166 Grahame (Paris) to Foreign Office, 14 May 1918, Clemenceau to Balfour, 15 May 1918, Geddes to Jellicoe, 15 May 1918, Jellicoe to Geddes, 16 May 1918, PRO, Adm 116/1649.
167 Admiralty to Calthorpe, 7 May 1918, Calthorpe to Admiralty, 9 and 14 May 1918, ibid., Adm 137/2180; Admiralty to Calthorpe, 15 May 1918, ibid., Adm 137/1576; Calthorpe to Admiralty, 6 May 1918, Lambert to Admiralty, 11 May 1918, ibid., Adm 137/1580.
168 Stephenson to Steel, 26 Apr. 1918, ibid., Adm 116/1807.

169 Dickens to Dewar, 9 May 1918, National Maritime Museum, Greenwich, Dewar MSS, DEW/2 (Pt 1).

170 Fremantle [?], Memorandum on Naval Command in Mediterranean, 15 May 1918, PRO, Adm 116/1649; Geddes to Lloyd George, 17 May 1918 (enclosing memorandum of meeting with Clemenceau), 17 May 1918, loc. cit. at n. 133, Lloyd George MSS, F/18/1/20 and 20(a); French records of the meeting are in SHM, Carton Es-14.

171 Geddes to Wemyss, n.d. [17 May 1918], Geddes to Wemyss, 17 May 1918, PRO, Adm 116/1649.

172 Rothiacob to Ministry of Marine (telephone dispatch), n.d., SHM, Carton Es-20; Revel to Del Bono, 4 May 1918, USM, Cartella 1210/1.

173 Sims to Yarnell, 8 May 1918, NARS, RG 45, QC File, Box 464; USN Planning Section, 'Seizure of a Base Sabbioncello–Curzola', Apr. 1918, ibid., TX File, Box 570.

174 Anonymous, Appunti per la Riunione del 15 (with annotations by Revel), n.d., USM, Cartella 1210/2.

175 ANC, Report of the Sub-Committee on Plans which Met in Rome on May 15th to May 21st 1918 [1 June 1918], Memoranda Nos. 140, 140A–140E, Memorandum No. 140F, 'Memorandum by Italy', 29 May 1918, Note by Secretary on Report of Sub-Committee on Adriatic Plans, 6 June 1918, PRO, Adm 137/836.

176 Revel to Diaz, 23 May 1918, Diaz to Revel, 30 May 1918, USM, Cartella 1192. Copies of this exchange went to Orlando, Sonnino, Del Bono and the Minister of War.

177 Procès-Verbaux de la Sous-Commission, 10–14 May 1918, Laubeuf, Rapport de Mission à Rome, 16 May 1918, SHM, Carton Es-18.

178 ANC, Emergency Meeting, 15 May 1918, PRO, Adm 137/836, ff. 484–5.

179 Plans Division, Remarks on USN Planning Section Memorandum No. 15, 11 Mar. 1918, minutes by DOD(F), 16 Mar. and 22 May, Fuller, 26 Apr. 1918, Hope, 23 May, and Wemyss, 24 May 1918, ibid., Adm 137/2708.

180 Sims to Benson, 13 May 1918, NARS, RG 45, QC File, Box 464; Pratt, Memorandum for CNO, n.d., ibid., OR-1 File, Box 334.

181 ANC, Emergency Meeting, 15 May 1918, PRO, Adm 137/836, ff. 386–7. For more on Sims's role see Trask, *Captains and Cabinets*, pp. 258–9.

182 Sims to Benson, 11 May 1918, NARS, QC File, Box 462; Liaison Officer Paris to Admiralty, 17 May 1918, Larking to Admiralty, 18 May 1918, PRO, Adm 116/1649.

183 Lanxade to Leygues, 16 May 1918, Leygues to Lanxade, 17 May 1918, SHM, Carton Es–14.

184 Lanxade to Leygues, 20 May 1918, SHM, Carton Es–19; Barrère to Pichon, 19 and 20 May 1918, MAE, Série Y Internationale, Vol. 78.

185 De Bon, Rapport au Ministre, 21 May 1918, Draft of letter to Clemenceau, 22 May 1918, SHM, Carton Es–14. On Leygues and the Syrian group see: Christopher M. Andrew and A. S. Kanya-Forstner, *The Climax of French Imperial Expansion, 1914–1924* (Stanford, Calif., 1981), *passim*.

186 Derby to Balfour, 24 May 1918, loc. cit. at n. 133, Lloyd George MSS, F/52/1/35.

187 Revel to Orlando, 21 May 1918, USM, Cartella 1187.

188 Barrère to Pichon, Nos. 1052, 1053, 1055, 22 and 23 May 1918, MAE, Série Y Internationale, Vol. 78; Lanxade to Leygues, 23 May 1918, SHM, Carton Es–19.

189 Geddes to Heaton Ellis (for Lord Derby), 21 May 1918, Derby to Geddes, 22

May 1918, PRO, Adm 116/1649; Clemenceau to Barrère, 22 May 1918, MAE, Série Y Internationale, Vol. 78.

190 Barrère to Pichon, Nos. 1058–1059, 23 May 1918, Barrère to Pichon, 24 May 1918, ibid.

191 De Bon to Lanxade, 24 May 1918, SHM, Carton Es-14; Naval Attaché Rome to Admiralty, 23 May 1918, Extract from Draft Minute of War Cabinet Meeting, 23 May 1918, PRO, Adm 116/1649.

192 Clemenceau to Lloyd George, 23 May 1918, loc. cit. at n. 133, Lloyd George MSS, F/18/1/21; Derby to Geddes, 24 May 1918, PRO, Adm 116/1649.

193 Rodd to Foreign Office, 20 May 1918, ibid., Adm 137/1576.

194 Geddes to Lloyd George (with suggested reply for Clemenceau), 24 May 1918, loc. cit. at n. 133, Lloyd George MSS, F/18/1/21.

195 Clemenceau to Barrère, 24 May 1918, MAE, Série Y Internationale, Vol. 78.

196 Barrère to Clemenceau, 26 May 1918, Barrère to Pichon, 27 May 1918 (enclosing translations of Orlando to Barrère, 21 and 23 May and Barrère to Orlando, 23 May), ibid.

197 Clemenceau to Barrère, 21 May 1918, Barrère to Clemenceau, 28 May 1918, ibid.

198 Rodd to Geddes, 28 May 1918, PRO, Adm 116/1649; Larking to [?], 25 May 1918, PRO, Adm 137/1576.

199 Sims to Train, 16 and 23 May 1918, NARS, RG 45, TD File, Box 553; Geddes to Rodd, 27 May 1918, PRO, Adm 116/1649; Wemyss to Beatty, 29 May 1918, loc. cit. at n. 155, Wemyss MSS; Barrère to Pichon, 29 May 1918, MAE, Série Y Internationale, Vol. 78.

200 Sechi to Bellavita, n.d., Chart by Capitano di fregata Bellavita showing autonomy of German–Austrian–Russian Ships, 25 May 1918, Bellavita, Promemoria, 30 May 1918, USM, Cartella 1192.

201 I.C.-64, Supreme War Council, 6th Session, Procès–verbaux, 1st Meeting, 1 June 1918 (p.m.), PRO, Cab 28/4, ff. 1–7. French records of the Council meeting are in SHM, Carton Es-12.

202 Secretary's Note of a Meeting of the Supreme War Council, 1 June 1918, (5.30 p.m.), Adm 116/1649, ff. 72–8; Hankey to Geddes, 1 June 1918, Notes by Wemyss and Geddes, ibid., ff. 74–5, 85; Anon., Note on Appointment of Interallied Admiralissimo and suggested powers, n.d., ibid., ff. 34–5.

203 Secretary's Note of a Meeting, 2 June 1918 (4 p.m.), ibid., ff. 93–106.

204 Hankey's Diary, 2 June 1918, partially reproduced in Roskill, Hankey, Vol. 1, pp. 558–9; see also Hankey, The Supreme Command, Vol. 2, pp. 811–12.

205 Wemyss to Beatty, 3 June 1918, loc. cit. at n. 155, Wemyss MSS; Geddes to Wemyss, 2 June 1918, Geddes to Hankey, 3 June 1918, PRO, Adm 116/1649. Italian notes of the conference are in USM, Cartella 1192; and a summary of the statements made by Revel in USM, Cartella 1187.

206 Geddes, Memorandum on Command in the Mediterranean, 3 June 1918, PRO, Adm 116/1649; Bliss's comment in Hankey Diary, 3 June 1918, Roskill, Hankey, Vol. 1, p. 559.

207 Geddes to Jellicoe, 5 June 1918, British Library, London, Jellicoe MSS, Add. MSS 49037; Pichon to Barrère, 6 June 1918, MAE, Série Y Internationale, Vol. 78.

208 Hankey, The Supreme Command, Vol. 2, p. 812.

[12]

The Climax of the War

New Allied Dispositions

The potential threat that the Germans would acquire the Russian Black Sea Fleet or a substantial part of it brought about a shift in the deployment of Allied forces in the Mediterranean in June. Gauchet, despite the lack of agreement with the Italians about sending Italian dreadnoughts to Corfu, decided to reinforce the Aegean with the 2ème Escadre under Vice-Admiral Darrieus comprising the 4 Danton-class semi-dreadnoughts *Diderot*, *Mirabeau*, *Vergniaud* and *Condorcet*, to be followed by the older *Justice* as soon as she got out of the Taranto dockyard. Gauchet ordered the battleships to sail for Mudros as soon as they had finished their gunnery exercises in early June and he was able to gather a sufficient number of destroyers to escort them. He appears to have acted because he believed that the Dardanelles minefield was in a poor state and the Germans and Turks might really be able to make a successful sortie and seize the base at Mudros. This, in turn, threatened communications with Salonika and supply of the Armée d'Orient. He also proposed sending as many submarines as possible – which turned out to be four – to the Aegean as soon as they had finished their training at Corfu, thereby bringing the total number of French submarines in the Aegean up to ten. Gauchet also repeated his request for British battle cruisers. Both the British and French took steps to strengthen the minefields off the Dardanelles, but the battle cruisers which alone seemed to have the speed and gunpower to match the *Goeben* were not likely to be forthcoming.[1] The British needed them in the North Sea where the Grand Fleet's margin of superiority in battle cruisers was not large.

The arrival of a French vice-admiral at Mudros brought up the old problem of command in the Aegean, for Darrieus would have been senior to Rear-Admiral Lambert, commanding the British Aegean Squadron. However, the northern Aegean had been a British zone since the Dardanelles campaign in 1915. The French and British admiralties finally agreed that Darrieus would command the combined squadron. The Admiralty justified this to a somewhat annoyed Calthorpe with the argument that dispositions to meet the menace of the Black Sea Fleet 'come under the head of major operations for which Allied C.-in-C. is responsible as always'. Lambert would remain responsible to Calthorpe for administration of the British zone, carry our minor operations and anti-submarine measures, assure efficiency of the minefields and conduct air operations. The Greek fleet would also continue to work in close co-operation with the British Aegean Squadron, which apparently was very comforting to the Greeks since there were reportedly very strong feelings in the Hellenic navy against the French commanding in the Aegean. Admiral Condouriotis, the Greek Minister of Marine, claimed to have no confidence in them and feared the slacker discipline in the French navy and the fact that it was less active compared with the British would have a bad effect on Greek discipline.[2] Obviously too much had happened in French and Greek relations since the beginning of the war for cordial collaboration.

Lambert was even less pleased with the new arrangement than Calthorpe and, as Captain Dumas of the *Agamemnon*, put it, 'his nose is rather out of joint'. Dumas mentioned that the French captain of the *Mirabeau* was astonished 'at our letting them get a footing in this place'. Dumas, however, found Darrieus an 'impressive little man with much personality' and indeed the French admiral enjoyed some reputation as a naval writer. Rear-Admiral Amet, the French second-in-command who was conveniently promoted to vice-admiral in June to succeed Darrieus, made less of an impression.[3]

The Allied admirals met in a series of conferences and had little difficulty in deciding their forces were not up to the situation in case the combined Russian–Turkish–German fleets came out. They all agreed to recommend to their respective admiralties both quantitative and qualitative reinforcement. Darrieus characteristically produced a detailed study and provided copies for the British authorities. Darrieus maintained that Allied forces in the Aegean had to be increased to 3 dreadnoughts, 4 pre-dreadnoughts (2 Dantons, 2 Justice), 2 battle cruisers, 3 cruisers, 5 scouts or light cruisers, and 25 destroyers. The battle cruisers would be stationed at Syra or Suda to counter a possible raid by the *Goeben* against Port Said.[4]

Lambert, hardly a model of tact himself, thought that the French had 'much sounder views on strategy than our Naval Authorities, but no ability to carry it into practical effect'. In a private letter to the First Lord he warned that 'the French are not battle winners at sea. They have never been so in the past, and there is nothing about their ships as we see them which inspires us with confidence in their ability to achieve success.' Lambert therefore recommended sending British ships whenever it was possible to spare them. He saw no use in leaving the *Lord Nelson* and *Agamemnon* out there for they could 'do no good, and lock up 2,000 men'. Lambert told Darrieus that their gunnery equipment was obsolete for they were not fitted for 'director firing' and 'could not live ten minutes in action against a modern ship', while their low speed reduced the speed of the rest of the squadron by at least one and a half knots. Lambert suggested to Geddes that they might even turn over that part of the line to the French altogether to 'save duplication of responsibility and anomaly of present arrangements'. It was obvious what really rankled Lambert. He complained: 'One Amet – a Frenchman of no great attainment, is put in direct authority over me' while Italian and Greek participation added another complication. On the mixing of nationalities, Lambert warned: 'In fact, the number of cooks endanger the fate of the Aegean broth. For it is in the Aegean that the next Naval fight will probably be, and on its decision will rest the command of the Mediterranean and all that that means.'[5]

Lambert was guilty of considerable exaggeration. Moreover, by the time Darrieus's study reached London one of the two Russian dreadnoughts in the Black Sea had been sunk, and the Admiralty also found that Darrieus had overestimated the number of Russian destroyers likely to be available to the Germans in the Black Sea. This obviously reduced Allied requirements for the Aegean, just as the recent loss by the Austrians of a dreadnought reduced requirements for the Adriatic. The Naval Staff in London doubted that the remote possibility of a raid by the *Goeben* on Port Said justified withdrawing two battle cruisers from the Grand Fleet and immobilizing them at Suda or Syra. Moreover, as Captain Coode, the Director of the Overseas Operations Division, pointed out correctly, anti-submarine warfare was still the most important duty for destroyers in the Mediterranean and they ought not to be withdrawn from the Otranto mobile barrage for the Aegean until the barrage was proven a failure or the situation at the Dardanelles became more urgent. In the latter case operations on the barrage could be suspended and eight to sixteen British destroyers sent at once to Mudros. The Admiralty, unfortunately, had no additional light cruisers or scouts to spare, and Rear-Admiral Hope admitted that their present force in the Aegean was not a satisfactory one to meet even the now diminished threat from the Black Sea. The Allies had a preponderant force of battleships and light cruisers at the entrance to the Adriatic and a weak one in the Aegean. Hope put his finger on the problem: 'If we had an Admiralissimo in the Mediterranean, he would, no doubt, redistribute his battleships so as to provide a suitable squadron in the Aegean, with the exception of battle cruisers, which can only be provided from home waters and cannot be spared.' But since there was no admiralissimo, they could only urge the French to reconsider their decision and send at least two dreadnoughts to the Aegean.[6]

All this talk of numbers and types tends to obscure the important problem of how they would have actually worked with one another – the same question that had been raised about the French and Italian fleets in the Adriatic. The account by Captain Dumas of the *Agamemnon* is not encouraging. Admittedly Dumas was critical of Lambert, and on 2 July reported a near collision with the *Lord Nelson* during manœuvres 'due to her carelessness' and 'Lambert's ignorance of first principle of tactics'. On 8 August he described exercises with the *Lord Nelson* and the Greek armoured cruiser *Averoff* as 'quaint & one [manœuvre] dangerously impossible & it is astonishing what a little grasp Lambert has of what he can or cannot do'. Joint exercises with the French and under French command only compounded the problem. On 29 July Dumas described the situation: 'Out with the French ships & *Lord Nelson* manoeuvring with the Aegean code & really rather an historic occasion as this is probably the first time British warships have been commanded & manoeuvred by a French Admiral. Their manoeuvring was miserable & we shone by comparison.' The scene was even more chaotic on 2 August:

Out with the squadron at 6.30 & being ordered to let go paravanes when steaming 15 knots not unnaturally lost one while the other went & remained under the bottom. Wild manoeuvring under Amet & it would be almost impossible to imagine anything worse than the French. In the midst came in the *Averoff* the Greek armoured cruiser & made angry by Amet's discourtesy in so manoeuvring as to drive her out of the swept channel & if I were the Greek Captain I should be furious. It is interesting to reflect that we had no signal to show her at a distance who we were & its shows very bad international staff work.[7]

Clearly the Allied force in the Aegean would need a lot of work before it would function effectively as one unit. Fortunately for the Allies, the prospect of a German-controlled Russian Black Sea Fleet turned out to be largely a mirage.

The redistribution of Allied naval forces in the Mediterranean, particularly the difficult question of how to provide adequate numbers of destroyers for the Aegean, was scheduled to be taken up at the Fourth Meeting of the Allied Naval Council in London on 11 and 12 June. This would have been the first Allied meeting since the stormy session of the Supreme War Council at Versailles and feelings were probably still strong. Revel, in fact, decided not to attend and sent his Sub-Chief of Staff, Rear-Admiral Triangi, to represent him. The Capo di Stato Maggiore doubted that the Black Sea forces would ever appear in the Mediterranean, and also asserted that it would be a long time until the Austrian fleet was ready for battle – an assertion which brought forth much sarcastic comment from Clemenceau. Revel was wrong about this, but on this occasion he and the Allies were going to be extremely lucky, although they might have had a narrow escape from suffering serious damage.

Horthy planned an attack on the Allied forces in the Straits of Otranto for dawn on 11 June. His motives were ostensibly to relieve the pressure on the passage of submarines exerted by the Allied mobile barrage and, probably even more important, to raise morale by giving the battle fleet something to do. Horthy planned for the light cruisers *Novara* and *Helgoland* with four Tátra-class destroyers to attack the line Fano–Santa Maria di Leuca, while the *Spaun* and *Saida* and four torpedo-boats would sweep the waters off Otranto and attack the seaplane station located there. The action would be, in some respects, a repeat of the 15 May 1917 raid with one major difference. This time the four dreadnoughts from Pola and three Erzherzog-class battleships from Cattaro would be out in seven separate support groups, each accompanied by destroyers and torpedo-boats. Austrian aircraft would, of course, co-operate and German and Austrian submarines were deployed off Brindisi and Valona. Horthy expected the Allies to repeat their reaction to previous raids and send light cruisers and perhaps even armoured cruisers out from Brindisi in an attempt to cut off the raiders. If they did, they were likely to encounter the big guns of the Austrian battleships. The dreadnoughts left Pola in two separate echelons. The first with Horthy in his flagship *Viribus Unitis* together with *Prinz Eugen* left Pola the evening of 8 June, arrived at Tajer the next morning and the following

501

night proceeded to Slano where it anchored on the morning of the 10th. The second echelon, the *Szent István* and *Tegetthoff*, sailed from Pola the evening of the 9th, escorted by the old destroyer *Velebit* and six torpedo-boats. Around 3.30 a.m. on the 10th, approximately nine nautical miles south-west of the island of Premuda, two Italian Mas boats encountered the Austrians. Capitano di corvetta Luigi Rizzo in Mas15 attacked *Szent István* and hit the dreadnought with two torpedoes, while the two torpedoes fired by Mas21 missed the *Tegetthoff*. The Mas boats escaped. The *Szent István*'s damage was fatal and shortly after 6 a.m. the dreadnought capsized and sank with a loss of four officers and eighty-five men. The sinking was filmed and was, and is, frequently included in documentaries, although the actual ship and incident are only rarely identified. Horthy called off the operation. He did not believe that the all-essential surprise was possible any more and there was now every chance that they might meet a superior force of dreadnoughts from Corfu or Taranto and submarines off Brindisi or the Albanian coast, while other submarines and Mas boats would converge on the approaches to Cattaro.

The Allies were, in fact, already alert to some Austrian move because of the increase in Austrian wireless traffic and air activity. The Austrian light cruisers and destroyers raiding the drifter line would have risked encountering ten British, Australian and French destroyers on patrol north of the drifter line. The drifters therefore would not have been as defenceless as they had been the preceding year and neither side is likely to have got off unscathed. What would have happened if Rizzo had not chanced on the *Szent István* group is, of course, impossible to say. However, the Austrians had now lost 25 per cent of their dreadnought force and while the episode demonstrated that the Allies could not afford to relax, it also demonstrated that the Austrians could not seriously alter the situation at the mouth of the Adriatic.[8] Rizzo's gallant deed also provided the psychological impetus to stiffen Revel and the Italian resistance to Allied demands about integrating their fleet. It also contributed to the persistent belief that the Otranto barrage must really have been effective if the Austrians had been willing to take such a big risk to attack it.

The news of Rizzo's success arrived after the meeting of the Allied Naval Council had begun in London on 11 June. The Italians mistakenly believed that they had sunk two dreadnoughts and there was the expected round of congratulations. It did not sweeten the atmosphere very much for Triangi frustrated agreement over improving arrangements for the repair of Allied warships in the Mediterranean. The British, French and Americans favoured a system of pooling resources and co-ordination, but the Italians argued that this should be confined to the eastern Mediterranean and no advantage could accrue to the Allies by introducing the system in the western basin. Triangi pointed out that Bizerte and Toulon were the only suitable ports for the proposed arrangement – Gibraltar was too far away – and they were so fully occupied that they could not be considered as available. Malta was also fully employed and a large portion of the burden would therefore fall on Italian ports which Triangi alleged were already quite full. The British certainly would not have agreed that Italian facilities were being used to the utmost, but in the absence of unanimity once again the Allied Naval Council could not reach any conclusion or make any recommendation.[9]

There was considerable disagreement with the Italians again about how to solve the problem of the lack of light cruisers and destroyers with the French fleet at Corfu and the Allied squadron at Mudros. On Geddes's suggestion the five naval members adjourned for a private discussion but the talks were difficult. Wemyss once again regretted that the most economical use of their forces could not be settled by an admiralissimo in the Mediterranean to move ships according to the circumstances at the required moment. Sims described the unsatisfactory situation:

> If the ships from the Black Sea and Dardanelles made a sortie in order to combine with the Austrian Fleet, the Austrian Fleet might come out of the Adriatic. We would then have the French Fleet at Corfu with no Light Cruisers or Destroyers attached, and the British Light forces on the Barrage unable to join them. These conditions were not only absurd, but it would be a disgrace to any Naval Officer concerned if when such an event happened he did not move his forces to join the Fleet at Corfu.

In the end, Triangi agreed that the Italians 'would be prepared to consider fresh arrangements' for the British destroyers on the Otranto barrage coming under the general direction of Gauchet, but only if they were convinced that the menace from the Russian Black Sea Fleet 'was serious and imminent' which they did not consider to be the case at the present time. They were not prepared to discuss any modifications of existing Allied naval conventions in regard to the British light cruisers in the Adriatic and regarded any serious depletion of barrage forces as 'highly dangerous' for the security of Allied naval and merchant fleets operating in the Mediterranean. Once again, in the absence of unanimity the Allied Naval Council failed to record any conclusion.[10]

Sims later reported that 'the position assumed by the Italian member was such a bar to amicable discussion' and if supported by his government would offer so serious an obstacle to efficient operations that the British, French and American members, including Geddes, held a special informal meeting to discuss the situation and action that might be taken. They agreed that each of the naval members should urge on his government the desirability of bringing pressure on Italy to induce it to co-operate.[11]

The major American effort in the Mediterranean was the allocation of thirty-six submarine chasers to the Straits of Otranto. The bulk of them under the command of Captain Charles P. ('Juggy') Nelson arrived at Corfu together with their tender *Leonidas* on 7 June. The submarine chasers had been long awaited – their very name aroused hopes of an answer to the submarine problem – and much was expected of them. They were actually 110-foot, wooden-hulled vessels, nicknamed the 'splinter fleet', of 75 tons displacement, with gasoline engines and able to make 17 knots. They had a complement of twenty-six and were armed with a 3-inch gun and depth charges, and equipped with listening devices. Their crews were reservists and amateurs, for the most part, with college graduates or undergraduates well represented. The crews of the submarine chasers were enthusiastic, morale was generally high and the ocean crossing itself in the small craft, which were refuelled at sea, a great adventure. The real basis for the hopes that the submarine chasers would live up to their name were the American listening devices. Captain R. H. Leigh, commander of submarine chasers on distant service (that is, European waters), considered them superior to British devices such as the Fish hydrophones. Leigh had been in Corfu in advance of the submarine chasers' arrival in order to establish a base at Govino Bay and stayed for the first few hunts.[12]

One of the men who served in them reported the tactical procedure of submarine hunting in units of three, generally 500–1,000 yards apart, with the leader in the centre ship. These intervals varied and appear to have been much greater at Otranto. The chasers would, on signal, stop all engines and machinery, down listening tubes and then hydrophone operators would listen while the leader plotted the bearings of his own sound contact and those of the other craft, with their intersection theoretically the source of the sound. If there really was a submarine present, the experienced U-boat commander might, in turn, stop his own engines when the submarine chasers stopped theirs and wait for larger ships to pass at a distance to cause enough interference to enable him to stay out of range. Submarine hunting therefore became frustrating and 'largely a matter of luck' if the chasers could get close enough for a depth-charge attack.[13] It also took a good deal of experience and, at the very least, the men at Otranto were at a distinct disadvantage during their first few weeks. The submarine chasers produced no miracles.

Benson and the Navy Department expected the submarine chasers 'to be used offensively and efficiently against hostile submarines', and Sims emphasized to the British that they were to be used exclusively for hunting submarines and not for other purposes, except in cases of emergency.[14] This precluded work as convoy escorts, for which they were not suited anyway. Sims acknowledged that the little craft were all right as long as the sea remained smooth but, in any sort of a blow, the chasers, while perfectly safe and seaworthy, could not make enough speed to keep up with even a slow convoy. The offensive power of the chasers was also limited. Calthorpe went out in one when they stopped at Malta *en route* to Corfu and watched her fire her depth charges and try her hydrophones. He found the chasers good sea boats, well fitted with hydrophone gear, but some were built of green wood and he doubted whether they would last long without a good deal of nursing. The keenness of officers and men impressed him but he thought the gun armament poor and the number of depth charges barely sufficient. Geddes passed some of these remarks on to Sims who issued instructions to increase the number of depth charges carried to twelve.[15]

The submarine chasers were really supposed to operate with a 'killing vessel' for each group. The little craft would find the submarine; a more heavily armed ship would finish it. Calthorpe did ask for additional destroyers or P boats – 613-ton patrol boats – to work with them. Not surprisingly, the Admiralty could not provide them and advised that the chasers would have to rely for their protection on the same covering force to the north of the barrage as the other vessels of the mobile barrage force. This evaded the question of a 'killing vessel', but Sims agreed to operate the chasers without support for the present. He actually intended to attach three American destroyers from Queenstown to work with the chasers but, as he explained to Niblack, the promises made by the Navy Department about destroyers coming to European waters 'had fallen down nearly completely'. This meant that the large American-building programme was behind schedule and the Americans had a shortage of destroyers too. The Navy Department was understandably most interested in protecting American troop transports and augmenting their escorts, even at the expense of other merchant shipping. Sims, consequently, did not feel justified in sending any destroyers to Corfu and no American destroyers ever operated on the Otranto barrage during the war.[16]

The first hunt took place 12–16 June on the latitude 40° 10′ N with nine chasers in three units at intervals of three miles between vessels of a unit and a five-mile interval between units. Leigh commanded the hunt in person and, writing after the war, Nelson thought that they might have destroyed a submarine. Leigh's primary impression was the untrained condition of the personnel and the necessity for an experienced submarine chaser officer to be present. While the submarine chaser officers were willing and enthusiastic, they knew practically nothing about submarine hunting on arrival. The sound-detection devices were effective but sound interference by other vessels on the barrage had to be reduced and the 'silent' period more carefully observed. By Hunt No. 4 (24–28 June) Leigh found that the listeners were beginning to get accustomed to the noise made by the destroyer patrol to the north and recognize it as such, as well as when destroyers made turns to go away from the line of patrol. A dozen chasers could cover the line on latitude 40° 10′ N very well and Leigh thought it was quite difficult for a submarine to pass without being heard. Experience counted. The first time the chasers were out on a hunt they had the impression that the straits were full of submarines. The 'submarines' turned out to be destroyers and the chasers were pursuing circulating pumps. On another occasion the target turned out to be a school of fish. There were also narrow escapes when the chasers were fired on by friendly forces.[17]

Leigh turned over command of the Corfu base (officially Base No. 25) to Nelson on 10 July and returned to Britain with praise for the assistance that Gauchet had given the Americans in establishing their base. The chasers continued their hunts with Nelson frequently complaining about a lack of experience by reserve officers which, on occasion, resulted in missed opportunities. The Italians to alleviate this provided the submarine *Nautilus* to give the chasers practice in underwater detection off the Italian coast near Gallipoli.[18]

The listening devices did not prove the panacea in anti-submarine warfare that everyone had hoped for. Sims himself was disappointed with their practical development and believed that enemy submarines were rapidly developing the ability to run silently, and that submarine crews were trained before going to sea in both balancing and operating at very low speeds with practically no noise. Experiments with a destroyer equipped with an MV listening device and a submarine revealed that, with the submarine making only 3 knots, it could not be heard consistently over 1,500 yards, even with the destroyer's engines and auxiliaries stopped.[19] The noise problem on the barrage was also very difficult to solve. Lieutenant-Commander Frank Lofton, commanding Hunt No. 22, reported on 9 September that there was entirely too much avoidable noise on the barrage caused by ships not stopping and starting promptly on time and running auxiliary machinery. By the beginning of October, Sims seemed to be losing patience. He attributed the trouble during the early hunts to lack of experience but now that they had considerable experience 'it is reasonable to expect an improvement'. He ordered Nelson to take up the matter with the barrage commander about strict adherence to the silent periods. Nelson replied that there had probably never been a meeting between himself and the commander of the mobile barrage when the problem had not been discussed, and no man could have made a greater effort to get all vessels passing through the area to observe listening periods. Nelson added the obvious: it was human nature that everyone considered the duty they were engaged on as paramount 'and it has been very difficult to induce people to believe that the safety of their vessels was enhanced by stopping them for set periods while in waters traversed by enemy submarines'.[20] Actually by mid-October the efforts by the mobile barrage commander began to pay off and the commander of Hunt No. 31 reported that the two convoys which had passed through the line observed listening periods, but it was unfortunate that this compliance had not been achieved before rough weather set in. The weather conditions by late October were very bad and the short steep seas seriously interfered with listening.[21] Consequently, there would not likely have been much of an improvement in the achievements of the chasers during the winter had the war not ended.

The submarine chaser line of patrol by late August was along the line of latitude 39° 15' N, from the southern end of Corfu to Cape Neto, Italy, a distance of about 125 miles, and this could not be effectively covered throughout its entire length with the number of submarine chasers available. Sims asked for an additional thirty-six for Otranto, if these could be spared from those already built, and he was careful to explain that this was not to be interpreted as a recommendation for constructing more vessels of that type. The Navy Department declined, however, to send any more submarine chasers abroad before the following spring, when they also planned to send thirty-six of the forthcoming Eagle (or Ford) boats. If an additional thirty-six submarine chasers ever arrived in Otranto, some might have been sent to the Straits of Messina to honour a request by the Italians, although Sims was careful to insist that the final recommendation would depend on the Allied Naval Council.[22]

By the time the war ended the submarine chasers had conducted thirty-seven hunts and Captain Nelson thought that they had made nineteen kills, although these were never officially allowed by Sims's headquarters in London. They were absolutely convinced that they had accounted for two submarines at the time of the Durazzo bombardment on 2 October. The sad fact is, however, that no submarines could be credited to the chasers. Sims and the Americans believed that, at the very least, the chasers had added to the difficulties of submarines in passing through the Straits of Otranto, which was true, but Sims badly overstated the case in his otherwise admirable memoirs when he claimed that, according to the tale told by former Austrian officers after the war, the chasers were responsible for a mutiny in the Austrian submarine force and two weeks after their arrival it was impossible to compel an Austrian crew to take a vessel through the straits, while attacks on German boats so lowered morale that in the last months of the war German officers were obliged to force their crews into submarines at pistol point. Heyssler later scoffed at this: 'We hardly knew the presence of Americans in the Adriatic Straits.' The story does Sims or his collaborator in writing, Burton J. Hendrick, little credit and may have had its origin in a long account that Nelson wrote for Sims after the war about the activities of the submarine chasers. Nelson recounted that after the Armistice they had met Yugoslavs at Cattaro or Pola who were supposedly former submarine commanders and who stated that Austrian crews had refused to go through the barrage for two months prior to the Armistice, though German boats had continued to pass through with their crews driven aboard at the point of the bayonet. The Yugoslavs alleged that during the time that the chasers were on the barrage, eight Austrian and five German submarines had left their bases and never returned, while the German and Austrian crews had an exaggerated idea of the submarine chaser's abilities which were thought to include all kinds of listening devices, 25 knots speed, 4-in. guns and thirty depth charges. Every U-boat that returned had been bombed severely and many were more or less crippled.[23] The Yugoslavs may have had reasons of their own for telling these tall tales to the victors and Nelson, proud of his enthusiastic men, was all too ready to believe them.

During the war Sims had been well aware of the limitations of the submarine chasers and admitted to Rear-Admiral Ratyé that they were using them 'because we have them' even though they were not very efficient for the purpose, having been designed before the difficulties of anti-submarine operations were realized. The Americans then tried to make the best of what they were stuck with. Sims told his friend Admiral Bayly: 'Having these boats, the Navy Department went with considerable enthusiasm into the question of developing their use in connection with listening devices of various kinds.' The Americans had not got very far in developing tactics for their use and the submarine chasers at Corfu and Plymouth were really in competition with one another to see who could first develop a system of successful tactics. The drawback so far, according to Sims, had been in the 'kill' rather than in detection of submarines by the listening devices. The Americans, realizing that the chasers were unsuitable for escort work, were determined to use them 'offensively', that is, tracking down submarines, and Sims told of having to counter considerable pressure from the French and Italians to use them for other purposes. The French wanted them for patrol and convoy work on the Algerian coast and the Italians wanted them for work on the west coast of Italy.[24]

Unfortunately, the whole concept of the submarine chaser might be questioned for the experience of two world wars has demonstrated that the real antidote to submarines was the well-armed and equipped escort guarding convoys, rather than futile attempts to 'catch' or 'hunt' submarines. This, in turn, put into question the whole concept of the Otranto barrage, whether fixed or mobile. The Americans would have done well in the long run to concentrate the very considerable resources they devoted to building the submarine chasers – over 400 were built – into a smaller number of larger but more lethal craft which were truly able to escort convoys and seriously attack any submarines that attacked those convoys.

The Americans were not the only ones who believed that they were on the verge of success in hunting submarines. Captain G. O. Stephenson, the Captain commanding the Otranto Mobile Barrage Force, reported in mid-August that the mobile barrage had 'proved itself to be sound in principle', and they were 'able to locate, hunt, and attack enemy submarines in the area through which they must pass', but they had 'just fallen short of achieving the desired object, which is to ensure the destruction of enemy submarines with a reasonable degree of certainty'. Stephenson, speaking primarily of the drifters, attributed this failure to kill to weaknesses in signalling and communications, deficiencies in training of personnel, the need for additional and more efficient detecting devices, and hunting craft with a greater margin of speed over a submerged submarine.[25] Success it seemed was always elusive.

Mediterranean Mining Projects

The United States was prepared in the summer of 1918 to make another major effort in the Mediterranean in the form of extensive mining projects. The Navy Department firmly believed that 'the Mine Barrage when properly placed and adequately guarded by patrol boats, support, and sufficient friendly submarines, promises to be one of the cheapest and most effective methods of combating hostile submarines'. However, Washington wanted a Cape Bon–Sicily project to take priority over any of the Adriatic projects and the Bureau of Ordnance did not consider the depth of water involved as a bar to their current form of mines. Sims doubted, however, that the Allies would be enthusiastic for it in preference to the Adriatic or Dardanelles projects. In June the US Planning Section on Sims's staff in London came up with another memorandum (No. 37, 'Estimate of General Situation in the Mediterranean') which included recommendations for a number of mining projects among the many conclusions. The Planning Section wanted to continue present plans for a Sabbioncello barrage; barrages between Otranto–Corfu; an Aegean barrage linking the islands between Euboea and Cape Karapitza on the coast of Asia Minor; surface barrages between Tenedos–Imbros and Imbros–Gallipoli Peninsula; and a Cape Bon–Sicily barrage. The latter, favoured by the Navy Department, was not considered by the Planning Section to be among the most desirable. Sims intended to bring these recommendations before the Allied Naval

Council, but not in a manner to commit the United States unless the project was approved by the Navy Department.[26]

The British differed with the Americans on a few points, for example, the nature and exact location of any additional mine barrages in the Straits of Otranto, and did not favour the Aegean barrage on the grounds there was relatively little submarine activity in the area and the patrols and mines could be used more profitably elsewhere. On the contrary, the British and French (the latter at least initially) favoured a deep minefield between Cape Bon and Sicily and termed it the most urgent requirement after the Dardanelles minefield had been relaid. The French, in contrast to the British, favoured an Aegean barrage and had an additional project of their own in these waters in the form of net barrages in the Euboea channels – that is, between the island of Euboea and the Greek mainland – to shelter a route to Salonika. The Italian desiderata were predictable. Priority should be given to completion of the fixed Otranto barrage, and the recent ill-fated Austrian sortie leading to the loss of the *Szent István* demonstrated that it was hurting the enemy and was essentially correct in concept.[27]

The differing viewpoints inevitably led to an emergency meeting of the Allied Naval Council in London on 23 July, and because of the divergence in views only fairly general conclusions, as set forth in the US Memorandum, were reached. The Council favoured developing a Mediterranean minelaying plan and the first effort should be to complete the Otranto barrage, followed by the establishment of an Aegean barrage and a careful study of the desirability of a Cape Bon–Sicily barrage. The more specific and technical questions would be studied by a special commission due to meet in Malta in August.[28]

The Americans would play a major role in any Mediterranean mining project. They were presently engaged in a large North Sea mining project – which turned out in the long run to be of dubious value – and when it was completed would have a considerable number of ships available. Rear-Admiral Joseph Strauss, in command of the forces laying the North Sea barrage, was due to represent the United States at the Malta Conference which, according to Godfrey, 'has swelled to enormous proportions'. Godfrey and the Mediterranean Staff hoped that they would 'manage to get a clear policy and do not disperse our energies by side shows in every odd channel of the Aegean, as the French would like to do'. He thought one way to avoid this would be 'a preliminary canter' with the Americans before meeting with the French and Italians.[29] Unfortunately, in any situation dealing with many allies one man's 'side show' was another man's 'vital project'.

Sims's ideas were at variance with many of those held by the Allies, but as the Americans would supply much of the material their say as to how it should be used would naturally be great. In these mining projects the Americans probably exerted their greatest influence to date on the course of the war in the Mediterranean. Benson and the Navy Department approved Sims's plans, but with the proviso that mixed command and responsibility for any project should be avoided. The Cape Bon–Sicily project had to be entirely American, the Adriatic to be Italian, supported by the Allies if necessary, and the Aegean and Dardanelles projects to be entirely British. Benson spoke grandly of Allied 'sea frontiers' to safeguard lines of communications. The 'sea frontiers' were Scotland–Orkneys–Norway – the 'Northern barrage'; Britain–France; and Tunisia–Sicily. There were also the operations closing the Adriatic and the Dardanelles, but in the eyes of Washington these Allied projects were only secondary. The Navy Department therefore still favoured the Cape Bon–Sicily project in the Mediterranean, and Sims had to modify his instructions to Rear-Admiral Strauss accordingly. Benson promised that the mine material for the project was practically ready for shipment from the United States, while bad weather in the North Sea after September would prevent the American minelaying force from operating there and, consequently, at least half of it would be available for the Cape Bon–Sicily project in October. Benson also claimed that the United States could supply mine material for the Adriatic and Aegean without detriment to the Cape Bon–Sicily project, subject to developing satisfactory anchors for mines in 600 fathoms, which he expected would take at least two months. These deep anchors would not be necessary for the Cape Bon–Sicily project which could use existing mines, and Benson estimated that the project could probably be completed by 1 December.[30]

The Franco-Italian fixed net barrage itself had been making slow but steady progress and the American naval attaché in Rome reported that, as of mid-July, 10 miles of mine barrage were in place off Otranto, the last buoy was twenty-four miles from Otranto, and the last net nineteen miles. That meant nineteen miles out of an estimated forty-five miles were complete, with an additional five miles of buoys in place. There was material for an additional five miles of completed barrage on hand, but beyond that the supply of steel wire from Britain was the major stumbling block to completion. Commander Train believed that the net, if 25 metres deeper, would be a great success, regretted a 'whole year was lost in hot air between the parties concerned', and thought the British mobile barrage compared to the fixed net a waste of time, energy and fuel. This view, probably heavily influenced by his Italian hosts, was not shared by the Ordnance Section of Sims's staff in London when the Italian naval attaché requested material from the United States for the net barrage. Commander T. A. Thomson of the staff advised the United States government to keep clear of the net barrage whose effectiveness was problematical, and material for a future mine barrage should be given priority over the net barrage. The Americans therefore politely refused.[31] Sims, of course, had a policy of deflecting these private requests for assistance to the Allied Naval Council.

Calthorpe softened his views somewhat on the fixed net barrage and reported to the Admiralty that laying it had met with far less difficulty than he had anticipated. He opened the Malta Conference with a similar statement, congratulating those responsible for laying it, and acknowledging that those officers who had pressed for its trial in the face of his own doubts at the Rome Conference the preceding February had been absolutely right.[32] Calthorpe's remarks had been prompted by the fact that on 3 August UB53 on her way from Pola to the eastern Mediterranean was mined and subsequently sunk – one of the few real victims of the Otranto barrage. The U-boat commander had not realized that the mine-net had been extended and believed he was clear when he struck the mines while surfacing.[33] It might be argued that the loss was due more to surprise than the actual effectiveness of the barrage and had the Germans realized that the net had been extended they would have taken appropriate measures to avoid it. But that was not the way it appeared at the time. Calthorpe always had that lingering preference for the Otranto barrage, mobile rather than fixed, as opposed even to convoy escorts, and in mid-July had reported that sufficient experience had been gained on the mobile barrage to enable him to say he was satisfied that they were beginning to obtain results which fully justified the establishment of those operations, with attacks on enemy submarines passing the barrage increasing in frequency and causing damage, loss, or having an appreciable effect in lowering enemy morale. It is hard to determine the basis for these remarks. UB53 had been the first German submarine lost since June. There had been no German losses in July although the Austrians lost U10 (subsequently salved) to a mine and U20 to the Italian submarine F12. But those losses had been in the northern Adriatic and had nothing to do with the Otranto barrage. Calthorpe also needed more craft to keep the barrage efficient, especially after the French destroyers had been withdrawn for the Aegean. The motor launches and wooden-hull drifters were deteriorating and before the end of the summer he feared that many of them would be unable to keep to the sea. Calthorpe wanted twelve P boats, which had proved so useful in northern waters, more submarines to increase the areas they patrolled, additional American submarine chasers and the maximum number of aircraft and air personnel for the lower Adriatic. The Admiralty were agreeable and intended to replace the wooden-hull drifters with steel-hulled craft, but as usual neither P boats nor destroyers were available.[34]

Both mobile and fixed barrages therefore enjoyed the esteem gained from the almost accidental destruction of UB53 when the Mediterranean mining conference opened at Malta on 6 August. Rear-Admiral Eduardo Salazar, who led the Italian delegation, came fortified with instructions from Revel that, whatever decision was taken regarding minefields in the Straits of Otranto, nothing should be changed in the plans for the mine-net barrage between the eastern end of the Otranto minefield and the island of Fano, and the material to complete this barrage should be supplied before proceeding to other plans. Revel advocated concentrating all efforts on assuring maximum efficiency for one barrage before starting another, and Otranto must necessarily be *the* most important barrage since all submarines operating in the Mediterranean, with the possible exception of the handful at Constantinople, had to pass through these waters.[35] In this determination not to squander their efforts, Revel and Sims were actually of the same mind.

The mining conference lasted four days and, like all Allied conferences, had to deal with a wide range of opinions that were difficult to reconcile. At times the conference broke up into subcommittees to consider certain problems in detail and the discussions were rather more technical than usual. The members of the conference ended by recommending re-establishing the Dardanelles minefield with mines supplied by France and Britain and later laying a minefield against surface ships and submarines between Imbros and Cape Gremea when suitable mines became available. Calthorpe warned, however, that they must not get a false sense of security at the Dardanelles through these minefields since there was nothing which could really insure the destruction of the enemy ships if they came out except a superior fleet capable of engaging them immediately. The conference pleased the Italians by recommending that the Otranto–Fano mine-net barrage should be completed and that the United States should supplement it with deep mines to make it effective up to 85 metres below the surface. The conference also recommended a second Otranto mine barrage to run between Fano and some point on the Italian coast between Santa Maria di Leuca and Otranto. The Italians subsequently agreed to a more northern Cape Cavallo–Saseno line. This second barrage would also be laid by the Americans, subject to their successfully producing a mine suitable for the great depths involved. The conference did not recommend the Cape Bon–Sicily barrage favoured by the US Navy Department because of the difficulties involved in passing the large amount of traffic through the barrage without a very large gate, which would render it ineffective.

For the Aegean the conference recommended the American-proposed Euboea–Andros–Tinos–Mykoni–Nikaria–Furni–Samos–Cape Karapitza barrage. The actual minefields would have been some forty-five miles in length with a single gate in the Doro Channel between Euboea and Andros. The laying and maintenance of the barrage would be an American responsibility but the patrol craft would be British since this was a British zone. The conference concluded by recommending barrages in the northern and southern entrances of the Euboea Channel, a major French concern, and the Allies also recommended that the possibility of a barrage in the Straits of Gibraltar should at least be investigated. The principal objection to the latter was that both ends of the barrier would have to be in neutral Spanish waters. As for the all-important question of priorities, the conference put the Dardanelles first (with the exception of the line Imbros–Cape Gremea), followed by the Adriatic, the Aegean, the entrances to the Euboea Channels and, finally and only after completion of the Aegean barrage, a French-proposed barrage protecting the entrance to the Gulf of Patras.[36]

The Americans emerged from the conference with major responsibilities in the Mediterranean although they failed to obtain what the Navy Department, but not Sims, wanted most: the Cape Bon–Sicily mine barrier. Sims was a bit surprised at British and French objections to it since it had been put on the agenda at French request, but Sims concluded that the latter had evidently changed their mind after discussing the difficulties of getting convoys through the proposed gate. Calthorpe, for his part, concurred with the conference's decisions but would have preferred a deep minefield in the Adventure Bank area south of Malta. British convoys were generally routed over this area and a number of lines of deep mines would constitute a serious risk to submarines seeking to attack the convoys and their escorts.[37]

American intervention had its uncomfortable side and one senses a bit of resentment on the part of Ratyé, for example, when he described how the Americans, while bringing generous and admirable support, also arrived with intangible principles, such as, accepting only homogeneous barrages of either all mines or all nets while, according to Ratyé, good sense would indicate that if you wanted to make barrages effective, it was necessary to combine the two. Nets appeared to be the only instrument suitable at the time for great depths, while mines ought to be used whenever it was possible to employ them.[38] Ratyé admitted that the others had intangible principles, too: the British over the effectiveness of a mobile barrage, and the Italians concerning the necessity for freedom of navigation for their big ships in the Adriatic and opposition to the introduction of foreign warships in their area. But certainly the Americans were a new note in the Mediterranean, another source of conflicting opinions, another ally to be placated, and inevitably yet another complication.

While the Allies planned these grandiose mining barrages directed primarily against submarines, they had not forgotten the threat of the Russian Black Sea Fleet. The problem of insufficient light forces at Mudros formed a considerable part of a long note in August by Vice-Admiral Amet, now commanding the Allied squadrons in the Aegean. The danger existed that the Germans would get their hands on a number of these good Russian destroyers and Amet's forces, despite the reinforcement of the French destroyers from Brindisi, were likely to be insufficient to meet the danger of a raid. Amet had sixteen destroyers on paper (seven French, five British and four Greek), but they were not always available and were also wearing out from hard use. The same was true of his submarines. Amet seems to have had a good imagination and he, or perhaps his staff, developed a number of not-very-pleasant scenarios in which the Allies would be at a serious disadvantage and likely to suffer considerable loss. According to Amet the Allied forces at Mudros ought to include three *escadrilles* of six large fast destroyers each, six fast scouts, ten large American 'hydrophone vedettes' (presumably he meant the submarine chasers), twelve 300–400-ton destroyers and twelve submarines. These figures were somewhat less than those proposed by Darrieus two months before in terms of destroyers and scouts, but now included the American craft. In forwarding and supporting the request, Gauchet provided a list of fourteen submarines of the 1ère Armée navale theoretically available for the Aegean. As of 17 August only seven were actually at Mudros, and of the latter only four were in good condition ready for sea.[39]

The British were equally aware of the danger from the Russian destroyers in the Black Sea, particularly after a report that four Tcerigo-class destroyers (c. 1,325 tons) were completed. There was no Allied destroyer in the Aegean of equivalent gunpower and speed. 'Something ought to be done', commented Commander Dickens, Calthorpe's Deputy Chief of Staff, for it was up to the Allied C.-in-C. to make the necessary dispositions. If anything happened, the British would be responsible at the Dardanelles, and to ensure their destroyer patrol against being wiped out it would have to be much stronger than it was now. The problem was, as Lieutenant-Commander Godfrey pointed out, 'if we panic the only thing that will happen is that we shall be told to send destroyers from the Barrage'. Calthorpe was therefore careful to emphasize that he did not consider the situation could be met by transferring British destroyers from the Adriatic to the Aegean. The Otranto mobile and fixed barrages had to be protected with patrols strong enough not to be overpowered and there had to be sufficient British destroyers in the Adriatic capable of cutting off and sinking raiding enemy destroyers. Calthorpe suggested that if they could not increase the number of destroyers in the Mediterranean, they could at least relieve four British and four French destroyers with eight modern British destroyers, with the older ships available for escort or other work in home waters.[40] Calthorpe's new request set off a considerable debate at the Admiralty where they had already decided to eventually send six M-class destroyers to the Mediterranean when new construction made it possible to relieve them in the Grand Fleet. Nearly everyone agreed that the Mediterranean needed more modern destroyers; the major question was what priority should it be given. Fremantle, now Deputy Chief of Staff, took a negative view and did not think that the mere report that four Russian destroyers of a fairly modern type had been completed justified a further increase of destroyer strength. The French and Italians ought to provide more modern destroyers if they were required, and Fremantle sourly argued that it seemed highly questionable whether the great drain of destroyer forces which protection of the Otranto barrage necessitated was justifiable when they could provide no destroyers at home for offensive anti-submarine operations 'of far greater importance'. In the end, the Mediterranean was allotted the second group of M-class destroyers from the Grand Fleet rather than the fourth as originally intended, and the Admiralty ordered Calthorpe to use in the Aegean the two M- and three S-class destroyers already in the Mediterranean.[41]

The Mediterranean was reinforced in August by additional destroyers from the United States, but only on a limited scale and very slowly. Sims had been extremely disappointed by the long delays in the American destroyer-building programme and had to give priority to the safe arrival of American troops in Atlantic ports. That transport was considerable. In July 357,000 troops (including 15,000 Canadians and Australians) were carried from North American ports to Britain and France and in August 282,449 troops (including 19,750 Canadians) were brought over.[42] The Americans also began routing store ships to French Mediterranean ports via Gibraltar and, on 13 August, Sims reported that since 1 July there had been seventeen of them, mostly large, fast, valuable ships sailing in groups of two with a destroyer as escort rather than included in slow convoys. These store ships were too fast for the American yachts and gunboats stationed at Gibraltar and Sims was forced to assign two new destroyers, the *Dyer* and *Gregory*, to escort them. He proposed to assign all new destroyers to Gibraltar as they arrived until adequate escorts were assured. Sims considered the present escort to be wholly inadequate and anticipated losses when or if submarine activity increased in the western Mediterranean again. As all American destroyers currently in Europe were needed at their present bases to protect troop transports and store ships headed for Atlantic ports, Sims saw no practical method to increase security in the Mediterranean until new destroyers were sent from the United States. Gibraltar also received the repair ship *Buffalo*, 'the best thing that happened to us yet', according to Niblack, for it took the pressure off the dockyard. Nevertheless *Dyer* and *Gregory*, along with those earlier relics from the Philippines, were hard worked and more destroyers were badly needed. Calthorpe visited Gibraltar at the end of August and was very impressed with *Buffalo* ('a model repair ship') and equally so with *Dyer* and *Gregory*, remarking that they were 'beautiful craft. I wish *we* had them for the Dardanelles or Otranto, they are too good for the escort work they are engaged on . . . being very fast.'[43] Calthorpe was buoyed by a decline in shipping losses over the past three months but the remark perhaps also said something about his scale of values, implying there was something demeaning about escort work.

By Autumn 1918 there were about four American store ships arriving in Gibraltar every eight days and discharging about 4,000 tons per day in French Mediterranean ports for the US army. They were sailed via the Spanish coastal route escorted by one destroyer which remained just outside territorial waters and kept her charges inside. The new destroyers *Stribling* and *Luce* were expected to arrive at Gibraltar on 5 and 11 October respectively. The four destroyers on the Gibraltar run would then have been sufficient for American purposes but, of course, very small in the general Mediterranean scheme. However, had the war continued the US army proposed that by mid-July 1919, and possibly before, they would be discharging 15,000 tons per day in Mediterranean ports. This would require more destroyers as escorts, twelve to fifteen, provided they continued to use the Spanish route and the Germans continued to respect it. They would need even more destroyers – about eighteen – if they used direct ocean convoys instead of the coastal route.[44] These figures did not include any destroyers that might have been working with the American minelaying force. It is interesting to observe that the Americans discovered, like their French and Italian allies before them, how useful Spanish neutrality could be. The American naval presence in the Mediterranean anti-submarine campaign was bound to increase, but very slowly and tied strictly to American purposes. Whether or not the Americans would have made any destroyers available for escorting the other Mediterranean convoys once their large building programme began to enter service in substantial numbers is, of course, an open question. They would probably have freed British destroyers from northern waters.

While the Allies had been making their plans for the Mediterranean in the summer of 1918, the tide of the war had definitely turned on land. Ludendorff's massive offensives on the western front failed in the long run to achieve the decisive breakthrough and end the war with German victory. The Germans were stopped, and with their reserves spent and with American forces now pouring into France unimpeded by the U-boats, the Allied commander, Marshal Foch, went over to the offensive. The British victory at Amiens on 8 August – the celebrated 'Black Day of the German Army' – was proof that the tide had turned and that the initiative now lay with the Allies. In Italy the long-awaited Austrian offensive took place along the Piave during 15–24 June and failed. This turn of the tide was not always easy for the distant naval leaders in the Mediterranean to discern since, in the absence of any major encounter in the classic style, they were fighting a war of detail with ceaseless patrol, convoy and escort. The enemy was usually invisible and after a chase or hunt and depth-charge attack there was no certainty that he had been damaged or destroyed. Success was measured by the scale of losses to submarines, or really what did not happen. Submarine sinkings were down compared with what they had been earlier in the year, but the war seemed to go on forever and, as far as the Mediterranean was concerned, Geddes could still write on 12 September 'there is still a great deal to be done before the position ceases to cause us anxiety'.[45] There was another reason why the Mediterranean had not noticed the change in the situation in land warfare. The enemy out here appeared to be on the offensive. The Germans were masters of the Black Sea and if that was far off from the Mediterranean, the Adriatic was not and in the summer of 1918 the Austrians were on the offensive in Albania and seemed to threaten Valona and perhaps even the Allied base on Corfu.

Albania was probably the last offensive undertaken by the Central Powers during the war, ironically not by the Germans but by the XIX Austrian Army Corps. It was really a counteroffensive. At the beginning of July the Italians held the line of the Voyussa River close to Valona, which left the Malakastra heights in Austrian hands, permitting them to keep the entrance and port of Valona under constant observation. General Ferrero, the Italian C.-in-C. in Albania, began an offensive on 7 July to clear the heights. The Italian Supreme Command approved the offensive on the condition that no additional forces would be required. The French in Macedonia co-operated with an attack by the Armée d'orient against the enemy on the right flank of the Italians, while the British provided aerial support and their two monitors in the Adriatic to work on the seaward flank. The Italian attack was successful, cleared the Malakastra heights, and Italian forces eventually advanced to the line of the Semeni River. Commodore Kelly thought at this time that an additional brigade would have ensured the capture of Durazzo, but the Italian Supreme Command refused to reinforce Ferrero whose forces were now depleted by casualties and sickness, particularly malaria. The Austrians were reinforced and began a serious counterattack on 24 August. The Italian Supreme Command, which had refused reinforcements, now ordered a retirement back to the Malakastra heights. Kelly did not consider the present Italian forces to be sufficient to guarantee holding this new position or ensuring the safety of Valona, whose loss would reverse the strategical situation in the lower Adriatic and make the Otranto barrage 'a dream of the past'. Kelly, after consultation with General Ferrero, warned both the Admiralty and Calthorpe of the now-serious situation and requested the earnest and immediate attention of the Supreme War Council. He advised that to re-establish the present situation they needed the immediate dispatch of 4,000 men and 20 light tanks, and added that American Marines would be suitable for these operations. The Admiralty immediately informed the War Office and initiated action through the Allied Naval Council to impress on the Supreme War Council the importance of holding the Malakastra heights and Valona. The War Office, in turn, made strong representations to the Supreme Command through the British military attaché in Italy. Sims took similar steps with General Bliss, the American military representative on the Supreme War Council. The whole Albanian affair seemed to be getting out of hand and the attention aroused was probably most unwelcome to the Italians who had political aspirations in this area. The Supreme Command sent the Puglia Brigade of six battalions to Valona while the British monitors *Earl of Peterborough* and *Sir Thomas Picton* returned to assist with their big guns on the seaward flank. These reinforcements probably assured the safety of Valona but not necessarily the retention of the Malakastra heights. The French, concerned over Corfu, naturally supported the British and American position. Although Revel pointed out that the Austrians had held the Malakastra heights for a few years without serious harm to Valona, and that the Austrians could always observe the base by air, the subject was taken up as an emergency matter by the Allied Naval Council and a suitable recommendation made to the Supreme War Council, tactfully omitting the name of General Ferrero who had connived with Kelly.[46]

Revel had no difficulty in deducing that Ferrero must have put Kelly up to raising the matter with the British government. Ferrero had cabled Revel asking for the British monitors, stating that Kelly concurred in their employment at Valona. That statement certainly gave the game away. Kelly believed that only a timely promise of reinforcements prevented Ferrero from having to retire across the Voyussa to the original Italian lines, for there had been no reserves of any kind available. The British also sent a flight of six Sopwith Camels from No. 66 Wing to Valona. Revel, according to the French naval attaché, blamed the whole Italian retirement on Ferrero advancing too far for his strength. He was confident that the heavy guns of the British monitors would help keep the Italian left flank on the marshy ground between the Malakastra heights and the sea from being turned, but regarded the general situation of the Italian army as a governmental question in which he would not meddle. Orlando was less confident but did not think Valona was threatened and blamed the reverse on Diaz's persistent failure to send reinforcements to Ferrero in time.[47]

Revel was not about to abstain from intervening, however. He asked Diaz's opinion about the Albanian situation, ostensibly to prepare himself for the forthcoming Allied Naval Council, and pointedly mentioned that Kelly was under the direct command of the Italian C.-in-C. in the lower Adriatic who was, in turn, under him, and that Kelly had given his superiors information which did not correspond to the facts and which escaped his competence. He wanted Diaz to request Ferrero not to give information relative to the proceedings of land operations in Albania to British or other Allied naval officers. Revel did point out to Diaz the importance of holding Valona and then went on to affairs that he admitted were beyond his competence, notably that Albania was a delicate and controversial question among the Allies, particularly France. Furthermore, Greece traditionally had aspirations there and the French were likely to favour the latter over Italy. The future of Albania was important for Italy's political and military interests. The Italians should therefore decline any foreign offer of support for their Albanian front because it might have hidden political motives. They should also avoid any situation in which Greek or French reinforcements might arrive before their own. Diaz was, of course, preoccupied with preparations for the long-awaited, final Italian offensive and the Supreme Command replied that the great importance of Valona did not escape it and it would always, when compatible with the higher requirements of the major front, assign men and material commensurate with the necessities of defending the base.[48] In sum, the Supreme Command would devote the minimum resources towards holding Valona and nothing more.

General Badoglio, Diaz's Deputy Chief of Staff, gave similar assurances on behalf of the Supreme Command to the British military attaché, mentioning that the 13th Division was assembling at Brindisi to be ready if required. However, Badoglio thought the Austrians were chiefly concerned with the safety of Durazzo and Elbassan and did not intend to attack Valona. The Supreme Command also did not attach much importance to the Malakastra heights and wondered if there was any special reason for retaining them. General Ferrero had orders not to be drawn into any extensive operations outside the entrenched camp of Valona, and this implied a withdrawal from the heights in the event of a serious attack. The British answer was short and to the point. The Admiralty considered that occupation by the enemy of the Malakastra heights would give him command of the entrance and port of Valona and 'would enable him to see all movements of shipping in Valona Bay which in view of the future Naval Operations in the Lower Adriatic it is of urgent importance should not be allowed'.[49]

The future operation in the lower Adriatic that the British mentioned was, of course, the mine barrage from the mainland to Saseno Island off Valona which everyone anticipated that the Americans would lay. The Americans, however, were about to spring a surprise at the forthcoming meeting of the Allied Naval Council by reverting to their February proposal for a mid-Adriatic barrage. The Navy Department managed to convince Josephus Daniels, Secretary of the Navy, that the situation in the Mediterranean had changed since the past winter and American involvement there would grow perhaps more than any power. The Americans had to push the North Sea barrage in the face of lukewarm support from their Allies, while in the Mediterranean the Allies had not taken kindly to American plans but could not agree on their own. Daniels summarized the new American proposal on 4 September. In the interests of Allied unity and to co-ordinate military and political interests in the eastern Mediterranean, the Navy Department would relinquish its claims to the primacy of the Cape Bon–Sicily barrage and consent to the Dardanelles barrage, assuming its appropriate share of the work, but not violating the territorial waters of Turkey with whom the United States was not at war. In the Adriatic the Americans would assist laying the present Otranto net barrage, but could not augment this barrage with deep mines laid in depths of over 1,200 feet for they had not yet developed a mine which could operate successfully at the extreme depths. This would therefore exclude the mine barrages across the lower Adriatic. The Navy Department proposed as an alternative the Gargano–Curzola barrage. This was a naval operation with a political setting (reported unrest in Austrian provinces) that would, if properly handled, strengthen the entire military situation. The barrage would include an American naval base between Curzola and Sabbioncello with the two places perhaps occupied by American forces. For the naval part of the programme Daniels promised one division of old battleships and the mines necessary for the barrage, together with adequate net protection for the base and also a small air force. Unfortunately, Daniels had to admit that the US War Department did not view the plan with favour because it would detract from the western front. Daniels ordered Sims to take up the matter with the Allied Naval Council.[50]

Sims realized that the recommendations of the Malta Conference on minelaying would have to be considerably modified now that the Navy Department announced that it could not supply mines which could be moored in depths greater than 200–250 fathoms. This was likely to be highly embarrassing for the Americans since they had been so confident in their assertions. Sims also found that the Italians had put in a formal claim to the Allied Naval Council for American resources, submitting a memorandum on the inferiority of anti-submarine measures in the Mediterranean compared with the Atlantic, and asking for an allocation to the Mediterranean of a substantial portion of the craft which the US Navy would have available in the near future. This support was a major Italian priority. Capitano di vascello Sechi, head of the Operations Division of the Stato Maggiore, told the British naval attaché that the Italians wanted to have a squadron of American submarine chasers at Messina, and hoped that Wemyss would not make any trouble with Sims about it. Unfortunately for the Italians, any American assistance was likely to be much less than they had hoped for. Sims anticipated the Allied Naval Council would advise distributing naval forces to further the anti-submarine campaign and protection of vital lines of communication. He admitted that the situation in the Mediterranean 'is undoubtedly serious' but, beyond adding a few American destroyers to the Gibraltar forces to escort US army store ships to Marseilles – and the number was relatively small – he did not think the United States could do more at present.[51]

Sims was obviously embarrassed about the mines. The conclusions of the Malta mining conference had brought the Allies nearer to complete agreement than they had ever been before but such agreement had been reached on the basis of the American statement about their ability to produce satisfactory mines for deep water. For Sims, 'The successful prosecution of the war, the harmonizing of conflicting interests and our national prestige all in my opinion require that our statements as to our ability to produce the mine be fully justified by early performance.'[52]

The fifth meeting of the Allied Naval Council, the first full meeting in over three months, took place in Paris on 13 and 14 September. Wemyss and Sims crossed the Channel to join Revel for the event and mining and barrages in the Mediterranean predictably occupied a good deal of the time. Revel, Wemyss and de Bon were all opposed to the American proposal for a Gargano–Curzola barrage which Sims tried to defend with the argument that it would be exceedingly embarrassing to the enemy even if the Allies could not hold the Sabbioncello Peninsula. Revel's priorities were simple: finish the Otranto–Fano net barrage first and supplement it with mines where the depths were less than 500 metres. De Bon to varying degrees agreed with him, but Sims argued that this would still leave a gap of about thirty miles where submarines could pass under the net and the barrage would be ineffective. De Bon was also anxious, in a related question, to reduce the number of vessels on the mobile barrage once the fixed barrage was completed and reinforced with mines. The light forces released could be used in the Aegean or as convoy escorts. After exhaustive discussion the Allied Naval Council wound up confirming the recommendations made by the Malta Conference concerning the priority of barrages, namely: (1) Dardanelles; (2) Adriatic; (3) Aegean; and (4) Euboea Channel. The Franco-Italian mine-net barrage between Otranto and Fano would be completed and supplemented when possible by successive lines of deep mines moored at different depths below the surface, with the mines to be provided and laid by the United States. The Cape Bon–Sicily and Gibraltar projects were dropped. The Cape Bon–Sicily project was little lamented by the other Allies. Vice-Admiral Salaun, head of the DGGSM, described it 'as more dangerous for Allied navigation than efficacious against the enemy'.[53]

The Council left it up to the Americans to choose the site for a minelaying base in the Mediterranean. De Bon would have liked to see the Americans at Corfu for that would have meant even closer Franco-American collaboration 'and is of a nature to maintain the desirable balance in the influence to be exercised by each of the Allies in the Eastern Mediterranean'. Sims was initially inclined to prefer Corfu, but a study by the US Planning Section recommended Bizerte, partially because Corfu would have been within bombing range of enemy aircraft with, as Sims explained, the potential for disaster if a bomb dropped on a building containing a million pounds of high explosive. The French warmly welcomed the choice and one senses a desire to avoid seeing the Americans co-opted by the British, but little had been done towards realizing the base when the war ended.[54]

The Allies turned down the American proposal for the mid-Adriatic barrage. The Council did not think that the military situation permitted it at the moment and they did not consider it expedient to refer the question to the Supreme War Council. The Italians had actually been warned of the American intentions about Sabbioncello and Curzola just before the meeting by their representatives in Washington. The Italian naval attaché spoke of a landing in Dalmatia and a member of an Italian air mission in the United States spoke of the Americans establishing a base on Curzola to spread anti-Austrian propaganda on the Dalmatian and Croatian coast. Sechi was able to dismiss the last report as 'absurd' and marshalled the familiar staff arguments against any landing on the Dalmatian coast or islands, namely, the ease of an enemy response and the heavy maritime and military commitments involved which were not commensurate with possible gains. In a hastily prepared memorandum for Revel on the eve of his departure for Paris, Sechi argued in favour of cutting off the Austrian advance base at Durazzo by an advance of the Italian army of around sixty kilometres through country not well suited for defence. This would be preferable to an always-risky landing by sea. Sechi and the Stato Maggiore concluded that if the Americans wanted to provide forces for the Adriatic, three brigades could reinforce the Albanian front, while naval forces could go to Valona and Brindisi where they could provide better protection for the Otranto barrage. Any old battleships the Americans had to risk could be used to bombard Durazzo.[55]

Vincenzo Macchi di Cellere, the Italian ambassador in Washington, also learned of the American plans for the Adriatic and reported the growing conviction in American governmental circles that it was desirable to promote the dissolution of Austria-Hungary. He concluded that it would be expedient to have a preliminary exchange of views with the Americans before bringing up the subject of a Dalmatian offensive in the Allied Council to harmonize their views, but if the projected action could have a predominantly Italo-American character the United States would be, to a degree, drawn into their orbit. Revel had already departed for Paris when Sonnino asked his opinion about this new proposal, but the Capo di Stato Maggiore quickly cabled that the negotiations for preparing an exclusively Italo-American operation in Dalmatia had an essentially political character and should be conducted between Rome and Washington and outside the Allied Naval Council. If Sims raised the subject, Revel intended to evade discussion by referring to the Supreme War Council at Versailles for technical examination without binding himself by a formal reply. Revel did just that when the operation was mentioned in the Council, limiting his remarks to saying that the Italian Naval Staff appreciated the high importance of any offensive operations on the eastern shore of the Adriatic provided they were prepared with adequate means for attaining the objective and retaining it in the face of strong enemy counterattacks. Revel added his personal opinion, sending a copy to the king's principal aide-de-camp, that they would obtain American assistance more easily by negotiating directly with the Americans than in the Allied assemblies.[56] This, of course, is exactly what Sims had always tried to avoid by referring questions to the Allied Naval Council.

Before leaving the Sabbioncello–Curzola project it is worth mentioning that the War Office also revived some interest in an Admiralty scheme at the end of September. The Admiralty considered that shallower waters made a Gargano–Curzola barrage more effective than the Otranto barrage provided there was an appropriate base to protect it. They therefore favoured seizing Curzola and the Sabbioncello Peninsula, establishing protected bases in the former, and subsequently taking the islands of Lagosta, Cazza and Pelagosa. The Admiralty estimated that a landing force of 30,000 would be able to take and hold the peninsula and island provided the landing could be protected by the fleet. The troops would, of course, be primarily Italian or, if preferred, the British contingent in Italy.[57] Surprisingly, the Naval Staff made no mention of American troops or of the American plans.

521

The Final Attempt to Appoint a Mediterranean Admiralissimo

The end of the war was a lot closer than some of the Allied naval leaders at the Council meeting in Paris may have realized. In the Mediterranean there was one thing which had consistently eluded them and that was, of course, unity. Unfortunately for the Allies, not everyone was really anxious for it. Less than a week after the first attempt at appointing Jellicoe as Mediterranean admiralissimo collapsed at the Supreme War Council meeting in June, Thaon di Revel presented Orlando with a long memorandum dated 7 June on naval command in the Mediterranean. He elaborated on how the theoretically desirable supreme naval command was less attractive in actual practice, and explained how naval war differed from land war in the absence of uniformity of ships and the speed by which operations developed. Revel also explained how the Adriatic was distinctly different from the North Sea where British admirals had gained most of their experience. The Adriatic was a long rectangle with enemy bases just a few hours' steaming distance away, thereby favouring ambushes and bold action by minuscule ships. The North Sea, on the other hand, was a big square with each side around 400 miles and, except for the minor bases of Ostend and Zeebrugge, the German naval bases were not less than 400 miles from the nearest port on the British coast, and the principal British base, Scapa Flow, was 500 miles from Wilhelmshaven. The surface area was over eight times that of the Adriatic and ambushes and submarines and mines were less to be feared, while minuscule craft were less successful. It was therefore logical that the most competent conduct of naval war in one area could lead to disastrous results in the other, and that the British strategic mentality was not the one most adapted to directing operations in the Adriatic where the Italian navy had acquired, at its expense, precious experience. Revel was obviously depreciating Jellicoe.

Revel also understood political considerations. While the Allies had a common interest in defeating the enemy, they also had other interests which were opposed to each other. The French were traditionally ambitious and reluctant to admit the Italians as equals in acquiring political, economic and commercial influence in the Mediterranean. During the war the French had already given an indication of their policy in regard to Greece and had also displayed designs on the coast of Syria. It was absolutely indispensable that Italy did not appear at the peace negotiations too weakened militarily. While continuing to fulfil its obligations as an ally, once peace was concluded, Italy had to be able to freely exercise the policy conforming to its interests, and those interests and a proper influence in the Mediterranean required an efficient naval force. Ships could not be improvised and it required many years to replace those now running risks in the war, while French ships had been exposed to only minor risks. The Italians not only had to win the naval battle, they had to do so without excessive losses, and they had to make the French expose themselves to the inevitable losses in even a victorious action. Revel wondered what confidence they could have that a supreme allied commander would always keep these factors in mind

The Climax of the War

and act with absolute impartiality in ordering the employment of ships to ensure the foreseeable losses were equally divided. Revel did not even have confidence that a supreme commander would take into account the different characteristics of the ships of each Allied navy. Italian ships were lighter, better armed and faster than corresponding French or British ships, but the inevitable consequence was that their hulls and engines were lighter and less resistant to active service when prolonged beyond certain limits, and if they did not take account of this they ran the risk of having all their light craft immobilized in dockyards after a few months.

Revel proceeded from the general to the particular, criticizing the attempt to take the best part of the Italian fleet and merge it with the French fleet at Corfu, where it would be withdrawn from Revel's authority and placed under Gauchet. The latter was there with the bulk of the French fleet, not for real reasons of a military order but rather to further the political aims of France in the Mediterranean. Revel had some harsh words for Jellicoe as well. Jellicoe had not achieved at Jutland the victory that he might have, and he had not even satisfactorily fulfilled the high post of First Sea Lord that had been given him after that 'half success' since he had left after a short term and had not been employed since. Revel surmised that Jellicoe had influential friends in Parliament and that the British government for reasons of internal politics wanted to find a high position for him. If Jellicoe did not have real command in the different zones of the Mediterranean, the risk would not be great and the situation might be accepted, but it would not be prudent to count on this. Moreover, given the relative importance of each navy's forces in the Mediterranean, the British should be the last to claim command since, according to Revel, the order of power was: (1) France, (2) Italy and (3) Britain. If they considered the burden faced by each Allied navy in the Mediterranean, first place would undoubtedly go to Italy since it was in close contact with the most efficient enemy fleet in the Mediterranean. Revel also feared that an Allied supreme commander might divert light forces from the Adriatic to reinforce the protection of traffic against submarines – a problem which preoccupied the other Allies more than the Austrian fleet. Revel would meet the alleged danger of the Russian Black Sea Fleet by sending to the Aegean a portion of the 'overabundant' French fleet at Corfu.[58]

Revel sent copies of this document to Sonnino, the first aide-de-camp of the king, Del Bono and Grassi in Paris, with orders to the latter to destroy it if he could not keep it in a place of absolute security. Revel's memorandum is a remarkably frank admission of what others had suspected regarding Italian efforts to avoid loss in order to appear in relatively good condition at the Peace Conference. Revel's remarks on Jellicoe are singular and considering their respective experience in handling a fleet in battle or coping with a large government department with world wide responsibilities at a time of crisis they need no comment. There would be little in Revel's handling of the bombardment of Durazzo on 2 October to indicate that he had any special genius for the tactical aspects of naval warfare. Revel did make some good points, such as the overabundance of French capitals ships at Corfu, although he failed to appreciate that the French were there to intercept the Austrian fleet in the unlikely event that it tried to break out of the Adriatic. The Italian fleet at Taranto might well arrive too late and could think only of preventing the return of the Austrians to the Adriatic. Revel also seemed to overlook the necessity for training or joint manœuvres if the French and Italians were really to function effectively together. Nevertheless, given Revel's views on the question of a supreme commander, his tight hold on the Italian navy and his apparent influence with Orlando and Sonnino, was there any use in continuing to try for a unified command? The British knew him as an 'arch obstructionist', but they were going to try.

Orlando was, on the whole, less ferocious than Revel. Before receiving the Capo di Stato Maggiore's memorandum, he discussed the admiralissimo question in a cable to Imperiali which was also intercepted and read by the French. According to Orlando, the consequences of the rupture of negotiations over the naval accord were agreeable to the French and also to the Admiralty but, as for himself, he found it regrettable that there was this reason for mistrust between allies.[59] Geddes, for his part, described the whole unsatisfactory situation in the Aegean, the threat of the Black Sea Fleet and Adriatic complications in a paper for the War Cabinet on 8 June, and concluded with a recommendation for further efforts to get an admiralissimo.[60] Rodd was not sure what had happened at the disastrous Supreme War Council, but after conversations with Sonnino, who claimed to have been surprised at Lloyd George's flare-up over an ostensibly minor point at Versailles, thought that there was a misunderstanding and with a little patience they might have secured the British admiralissimo. The big thing with the Italians, he claimed, was to get the general principle through and trust in time to get over the detail difficulties later. Rodd, of course, knew nothing of Revel's memorandum for the attitude of the Capo di Stato Maggiore was more than a mere 'detail'. Imperiali made the same conciliatory gestures in London during talks with Balfour, and thought that in a strictly private and personal way he had opened the door for future overtures from the British.[61]

Geddes quickly set Rodd straight about the Supreme War Council meeting. Sonnino had not given him the right impression of what had happened at Versailles, for if he thought 'that we split on a matter of minor detail owing to impatience, I can only say that he did not understand the absolute emasculation of the whole scheme involved by the proposals which he voiced and supported on behalf of Admiral di Revel'. Revel, he claimed, knew his proposals 'nullified the whole scheme'. Geddes then described the same attitude of non-cooperation on the part of the Italians concerning repair of warships at the Allied Naval Council which had just ended, and foresaw a widening rift between the British, French and Americans, on the one hand, and the Italians on the other. While the situation remained as it was at the Italian Ministry of Marine, it would be 'perfectly useless' for him to come to Rome to discuss matters. If the Italians were anxious to come to a settlement, they ought to take up the proposals to withdraw Allied light forces from Brindisi and suggest a quiet discussion of the difficulties so that a rift might not appear.[62]

Geddes and the Admiralty did not seem to realize that the French navy was actually almost as opposed to the introduction of the British admiralissimo as Revel and the Italians. De Bon expected the British to resume their efforts despite rebuffs at Versailles and the June meeting of the Allied Naval Council in London, and told the French naval attaché in Rome that they ought to ardently preoccupy themselves with preventing these efforts from materializing. The Italians would help them since they were more determined than ever to maintain that it was useless to send the Italian battleships to Corfu. The French still wanted the Italian dreadnoughts to join Gauchet, something Revel opposed. This was, however, the wrong moment to insist on the replacement of Revel who was stronger than ever by the marvellous stroke of fortune whereby the Italian navy had just sunk the Austrian dreadnought under circumstances which seemed to completely vindicate the views of the Capo di Stato Maggiore. The only reason that Revel might consent to send the battleships to Corfu would be to avoid a British C.-in-C., which de Bon did not think Revel wanted at any price, and de Bon's assurances that any Italian battleships sent to Corfu would be left under an Italian admiral in loose liaison with Gauchet, as well as an assurance that the transfer need not take place immediately, might bring the Italians around. Clemenceau's opinion was that under the present situation the best thing to do would be to drop the question. But de Bon insisted that they had to watch the British, especially their efforts to bring pressure on the Italian government. De Bon concluded that in every respect it seemed the moment was badly chosen to press for greater unity. On one side, Revel's situation was stronger than ever and, on the other side, the success of those efforts for unity would lead to the creation of a British admiralissimo which was contrary to French interests.[63] Revel was in some respects performing a useful service for de Bon. The French might have desired the partial incorporation of those magnificent Italian dreadnoughts into their fleet at Corfu, but not at the price of a British admiralissimo.

Barrère was not anxious to even reopen the question of sending the Italian dreadnoughts to Corfu and wondered if it was actually necessary after the sinking of the *Szent István*. De Bon agreed. Only the loss of the *Szent István* had been confirmed to date – there were erroneous reports of the sinking of a second dreadnought and damage to a third – but, even if the Austrians had lost only one ship, de Bon was convinced that the French squadron at Corfu was perfectly able to dominate the Austrian fleet, and there was no longer any need to occupy themselves with the question of sending Italian dreadnoughts to Corfu. The French had also just obtained what interested them the most – destroyer reinforcements for the Aegean – and they now had an interest in letting recent discussions about a redeployment of Allied naval forces in the Mediterranean fall into complete oblivion.[64]

Geddes assumed wrongly that de Bon was with him and Sims when he circulated a memorandum on the Mediterranean to the War Cabinet on 17 June so that representations could be made through diplomatic channels and 'judicious pressure' brought to bear for more co-operation from the Italian navy. Geddes injected a personal note and charged 'that Admiral di Revel, and he alone, is responsible for the present state of affairs'.[65] In Rome, Rodd was more convinced than ever that there had been a misunderstanding after new conversations with Orlando who denied that the Italians had meant to exclude the Adriatic from any admiralissimo agreement. The British were supported by the American ambassador in Rome who, on instructions from the US State Department, was also complaining about the lack of harmony to Sonnino and apparently receiving the usual reply about special conditions in the Adriatic requiring independence of action.[66]

This American intervention may have been counterproductive, for when Sonnino had a long discussion with Rodd over the subject on 27 June the Italian Foreign Minister reported that the American ambassador had mentioned the antagonism between Revel and the representatives of the other Allies. Sonnino 'began to work himself up into a very bad temper, got very red as he does at these times and tossed the paper about . . . and he murmured some unreasonable insinuation to the effect that the three other Allies came to preliminary agreement and then met Italy with a scheme which they had prepared without her'. Sonnino gradually got calm again and admitted that everyone's nerves were on edge as a result of the long strain of war. Rodd regarded the outburst as 'temperamental' and thought Orlando 'much easier to deal with' but, in fact, much of the interview had been conciliatory, with Rodd and Sonnino carefully examining the Italian transcripts of the meeting at Versailles. The general conclusion was that there did not really seem to be great differences between them and they need only define the nature of operations in the Adriatic that the Italians might undertake on their own initiative. Sonnino was also opposed to the admiralissimo having to refer every case to the Inter-Allied Naval Council and then await their decision, and could not accept any attempt to exclude Revel from the negotiations, although he admitted 'he was of a nervous and excitable temperament'. Sonnino told Rodd that he was prepared to let bygones be bygones and start afresh on this question. He informed Imperiali that he had emphasized to Rodd that it was not prudent for any British minister to come to Rome until they had agreed on the basis of an accord and, above all, they should not raise the matter at Versailles but rather negotiate exclusively by diplomatic means. Sonnino also intended to let the British obtain French consent to an Italo-British formula for agreement. The French again intercepted and read this cable which might have caused some suspicion that their allies were trying to cook something up behind their backs. Geddes was absent at the time and Wemyss ordered no further action was to be taken for the present.[67]

The subject of the admiralissimo was not brought up at the meeting of the Supreme War Council in early July, although with Lloyd George's approval Geddes passed a note to Sonnino at the conference asking him if it would be of any value if they had a private conference. Sonnino indicated, partly by signs across the table, that he considered the matter had been settled at the last meeting and there was no use reopening it. Although Geddes invited him for a private discussion outside and gave him ample opportunity to do so, Sonnino refrained from taking the bait. This was not satisfactory to Geddes who was worried about the lack of light craft at the Dardanelles and was convinced that the Italians were not making the best use of their small craft in the Allied interest. Geddes brought up the matter with Lloyd George on 16 July but the Prime Minister thought that, as a result of recent Italian military success in stopping the Austrian offensive on the Piave, it would be more difficult to do anything than when the question was first raised. Nevertheless, the Italian Minister of the Treasury, Nitti, was due in London shortly and the latter represented in Lloyd George's eyes the 'more liberal minded factor in the situation' as opposed to Sonnino and Revel who represented 'strong military and Jingo interests'. Lloyd George promised to approach Nitti although it is not clear what the results were.[68]

The vigilant Barrère learned from a confidential source, perhaps one of those intercepted telegrams, that Rodd had resumed talks on the admiralissimo, probably on the instructions of his government, and that the Italian government had shown that it was inclined to lend itself 'to this type of clandestine negotiation'. The French ought to put a stop to it since they could not accept it at any price. A supreme command already existed and was held by Gauchet. Leygues wanted Barrère's dispatch called to Clemenceau's attention, but the Premier was not disturbed. He knew that the negotiations were a continuation of those which he considered the Italians had wrecked at Versailles by 'their absurd intransigence' concerning the Adriatic. Clemenceau's interpretation of events was different. Italy had stirred up the idea of the supreme command to elude French command in the hope that the French would not accept British command. The manœuvre did not succeed, for the French accepted British command at sea as just compensation for Foch's supreme command on land. The Italians then made unacceptable reservations which led to the sharp incidents between Lloyd George and Orlando. They had warded off the difficulties of the situation in full accord with the British and, for the moment, Clemenceau was disinterested in any conversations between the British and the Italians although that did not preclude his wanting to know what went on.[69] Clemenceau's attitude was therefore far less jingoistic than Barrère or de Bon. It was a simple deal – Jellicoe for Foch, and nothing to get excited about. Certainly Foch's appointment and position as Supreme Allied Commander on land on the western front disposing of millions of men was far more meaningful than Jellicoe's appointment as Mediterranean admiralissimo to counter the hypothetical threats of the Austrian or Russian Black Sea Fleet would ever be. The strongest argument that Jellicoe's French opponents could raise would have been that the naval appointment might ultimately have its effect on French aspirations in the eastern Mediterranean and Near East. This was certainly a strong motive for a man like the Minister of Marine, Georges Leygues and, ultimately, in the closing days of the war it obviously had its effect on Clemenceau when the jockeying for position began in earnest. But then it was a case of British supremacy at sea prevailing.

The Americans continued to support the British, with Secretary of the Navy Daniels, no doubt influenced by Sims's reports, approaching the State Department for diplomatic assistance in Rome, and the French cryptographers soon learned from Sonnino's report to the Italian ambassador in Paris of the American efforts.[70] The Americans also intervened in another and unofficial manner to revive the flagging efforts towards appointing the admiralissimo. On 3 August, Wemyss wrote to Calthorpe: 'within the last few hours, however, matters have taken one of those extraordinary turns which do sometimes occur and I am writing to tell you that the project has again come into the bounds of practical politics.' The 'extraordinary turn' was the then Assistant Secretary of the Navy and future President of the United States, Franklin Delano Roosevelt, who was in Britain at the time as part of a tour of Allied nations. Geddes and Roosevelt discussed a wide range of subjects but the First Lord apparently brought up the subject of command in the Mediterranean and asked for Roosevelt's assistance in getting Italian co-operation when the Assistant Secretary visited Rome. Rodd was on leave in Britain at the time and the ambassador thought that the Italians would accept Jellicoe as admiralissimo 'if we could have a quiet chat with them'. He recommended that Geddes and Roosevelt should go to Rome together, and that it would be much better if they did not have a French minister with them. Rodd would write privately to Orlando and suggest deferring any visit for three weeks because of the political situation in Italy. Geddes asserted, mistakenly, that the French were 'quite in accord'. They would inform Clemenceau fully, but not at this stage and only after they had heard from Orlando. Geddes claimed that Roosevelt had suggested he accompany him to Rome and the First Lord thought it would be a great mistake to refrain from doing so for, without knowledge of Jellicoe or the naval situation, Roosevelt might come to an unsatisfactory arrangement.[71]

Roosevelt had his own objections, however, and no desire to serve as a front for the British. He therefore elected to go to Rome alone, believing that while the Italians may not have loved the Americans, they at least knew that the Americans had no ulterior motives in the Mediterranean. Geddes, for his part, was faced with a shipping question which necessitated an early meeting of the Supreme War Council in London where the shipping records and information were located and, if the proposal matured, thought they might be able to bring up the admiralissimo question at that meeting thereby eliminating the need for him to go to Rome.[72]

In Rome a very annoyed Thaon di Revel provided Sonnino with Italian conditions for adhering to the admiralissimo proposal, now supported by the United States, which the Italian government had accepted 'for considerations independent of military reasons and beyond my competence', and obviously despite his memorandum of 7 June. Sonnino had these criteria when he met Roosevelt on 9 August and emphasized his adherence in principle to the concept of a supreme commander, but cited the peculiar conditions of the Adriatic which required a certain liberty of action for the Italian C.-in-C. He also asked for the right of the Italian C.-in-C. to appeal to his government against the decision of the admiralissimo, and exclusion of the Allied Naval Council with its seat in London from direction of affairs in the Mediterranean. These were all, by now, familiar Italian claims. Revel repeated them to Roosevelt when the latter visited the Ministry of Marine and had the impression that the Assistant Secretary considered them acceptable as a matter of principle and corresponding to the peculiar strategic characteristics of the naval war in the Mediterranean, especially the

Adriatic. Revel clearly stipulated that a movement of the Italian and Allied fleets away from the Adriatic should take place only if they achieved a significant weakening of the Austrian fleet or an important fraction of the latter took refuge in the Dardanelles. The initiative and direction of all operations in the Adriatic would continue under the leadership and command of the Italian C.-in-C. who would notify his intentions to the Allied C.-in-C. in the Mediterranean and 'take in highest consideration' whatever suggestion the latter would give.[73]

Roosevelt seems to have thought that he had an agreement and cabled Daniels on his way back through France: 'Naval Conference in my opinion result is completion plan for Inter-Allied Commander-in-Chief in Mediterranean Sea, sole reservation being command actual local operations in Adriatic Sea by Italian Admiral.' He had, in fact, muddied the waters thoroughly, having spoken to Orlando about creating a naval general staff in the Mediterranean, Adriatic and Aegean with Jellicoe probably senior member or chairman and a member from each of the Allied navies, which he thought obviated French and Italian objections to a British C.-in-C. and was at least a distinct step towards unity. Rodd's letter to Orlando does not appear to have reached the Italian Prime Minister until after Roosevelt's visit, although Orlando indicated that he would welcome a visit by Geddes and the latter on the basis of a preliminary report from Roosevelt, and Larking thought they were on a 'fair way to settlement'.[74]

Barrère learned of the real purpose of Roosevelt's visit to Rome from a conversation between Charles-Roux, chargé d'affaires at the French embassy, with his American counterpart, Jay, and swung into action, especially after it seemed that Roosevelt had accepted a formula reserving for Italy a certain independence of action in the Adriatic. The conversation between Charles-Roux and Jay convinced Barrère that the British had conducted a sort of flanking movement by way of Washington and Rome to reach an accord *à trois* on naval command in the Mediterranean before raising the question in the Supreme War Council. Barrère claimed that the procedure was symptomatic of present British diplomacy. If the political situation might have led them to accept British command at a given moment, that moment had now disappeared and French political interests did not favour their appearing subordinate to the British in the Mediterranean. In a subsequent cable Barrère added that it appeared strange that without any ostensible motive the French fleet, superior in size to all the Allied forces together in the Mediterranean, was placed under a British admiral. Barrère amplified his telegram with a long dispatch about this agreement among their three principal allies without France on a question of interest to France and in which the British were the prime mover. He termed this an unfortunate proceeding. Barrère claimed that the British had won over the Americans with an analogy about Foch's supreme command on land, but this was a fictitious analogy since a supreme naval commander already existed in the person of Gauchet and there was no military reason to change. Furthermore, France had the preponderant naval force in the Mediterranean. Barrère concluded by stressing France's political interests in the Mediterranean and that the altered situation on the western front made Foch's

529

position unshakable. Consequently Lloyd George no longer had to seek compensation to appease opponents of Foch's command at home, and the French no longer had to pay the expense of that compensation.[75]

It is ironic that both the French and Italians each suspected their ally had gone behind their backs to make a deal with the others. Moreover, Geddes and the British did not have confidence in Roosevelt's judgement. In anticipation of a forthcoming meeting with the Assistant Secretary, Geddes cabled Larking for any information he had on what had happened in Rome, for he feared that Roosevelt's 'lack of intimate knowledge' of the situation had 'misled him into thinking exclusion of Adriatic satisfactory'. The First Lord's fears were confirmed by Larking who 'secretly' obtained copies of the Sonnino–Revel correspondence dealing with Roosevelt's visit. Geddes did not show this information to the Americans when he met with Roosevelt on 28 August.[76] Roosevelt proposed his Inter-Allied naval staff with a representative of each of the navies (British, French, Italian, American and Japanese) and suggested that a British admiral should be 'Chief of Staff'. Operations in the Mediterranean would naturally fall into certain divisions with an Italian C.-in-C. in the Adriatic, a French admiral commanding in the Aegean, a French admiral commanding the main battleship fleet or 'Mediterranean Grand Fleet', and the Naval Staff deciding on a commanding officer for the work of convoy and general anti-submarine operations which were 'becoming more and more one of general participation'. The Naval Staff would suggest command of offensive operations, especially in the Adriatic where the troops employed would probably be American. Roosevelt emphasized that he was putting these proposals down as a personal suggestion 'for a basis of discussion' which ought not to meet with serious opposition from any of the admiralties concerned. Roosevelt, in a covering letter, admitted that 'I have not reached the milk in the coconut' regarding the question of actual authority of the proposed Chief of Staff over the Italian and French fleets, but his visit to Italy made him feel that it would be impossible to get the Italian battleship force placed under Allied command, and the political situation in Italy was such that they should not attempt to force the move. As to the French, their claim to be the most powerful force in the Mediterranean was 'well founded' according to Roosevelt, 'and it can do no harm to call their battleship force the "Grand Fleet of the Mediterranean", a term suggesting at least the same function that the British Grand Fleet is playing in your own North Sea Waters'. Roosevelt's major point was that once the Allied Naval Staff was created, it would become easier later on to get the necessary authority for it.[77]

Ironically, despite French suspicions in fact it must have been the British who were disappointed, for Roosevelt's suggestions were really much ado about nothing, with an innocuous Chief of Staff, French command in the Aegean and at Corfu, and a hint that not even British control of anti-submarine operations was assured since the operations, according to Roosevelt, were 'becoming more and more one of general participation'. What must Geddes and the Admiralty have made out of all this? They probably expressed pleasant generalities and courtesies to smooth their distinguished and important American visitor on his way. Jellicoe was not hopeful, 'although I am told the scheme is not dead I don't myself think it will ever mature'.[78] The French were doing their best to assure that Jellicoe's guess was correct. Clemenceau ordered Jusserand, the French ambassador in Washington, to ask Secretary of State Lansing, not officially but simply for private information, if there was any foundation to the rumour in Italian diplomatic circles that, after agreement with the British, Roosevelt was in Rome negotiating to transfer naval command in the Mediterranean from the French to the British? Lansing was naturally able to deny this, adding that Roosevelt was a facile speaker. Jusserand also called the French Foreign Minister's attention to an earlier report by the French naval attaché in Washington about Roosevelt and his mission to Europe. The French were obviously interested in just who and what this newcomer was, and they must have been intrigued by the naval attaché's report that powerful interests in the US Navy Department, fearing a little his headstrong, active and frank character, had been able for a long time to block Roosevelt's desire to go to Europe. The French naval attaché described him as extremely pro-Allied, and that one could usefully discuss with him all questions of interest to the French navy without forgetting that the assurances he might give on such and such a point would only be personal and might be reviewed and corrected by Washington.[79]

After a few days Lansing was able to give new assurances to Jusserand about the United States attitude on the question of command in the Mediterranean. The American delegate at the Allied Naval Council meeting in London in July had the personal impression that there would be no objection to Jellicoe as commander but the United States would accept whatever the others agreed on. Barrère was also keeping up his barrage from Rome, reporting that Roosevelt had apparently taken from Italy the impression that if the Allies were too exacting the Italians would not be able to continue the war. Barrère charged that certain Italian circles must have exploited Roosevelt's credulity or superficial knowledge to float that rumour, and Washington ought to be warned not to be influenced by Roosevelt's opinion.[80] The French reaction apparently generated enough heat to cause President Wilson to order Secretary of the Navy Daniels to inform him in the future in advance of the names and missions of civilians going abroad because too many men were assuming to speak for the government. The entire affair has been described by a biographer as providing 'a bit of education for Roosevelt'.[81]

The controversy over Roosevelt seems to have been a tempest in a teapot since no one appears to have paid the slightest attention to his proposals for an Inter-Allied Chief of Staff. Geddes and the British returned to negotiating with the Italians on the basis of the criteria given by Sonnino to Rodd earlier in the summer, notably an admiralissimo appointed by the Supreme War Council, each naval commander having the right of appeal against the admiralissimo's decisions, and the Italians undertaking special and ordinary operations in the Adriatic on their own initiative. Geddes and Wemyss agreed that this could serve as the skeleton upon which an organization could be based, but its suitability depended 'largely upon the spirit in which the details are filled in'. The British acknowledged that the admiralissimo would not command forces in action, just as the First Sea Lord of the Admiralty did not command the Grand Fleet after arranging the general distribution and approving large important schemes. But the Admiralty insisted that the admiralissimo should not be in the same position as Foch was in regard to the Supreme War Council for naval warfare was different. Geddes, in an explanatory letter to Lloyd George of 17 September, pointed out that naval warfare was more fluid and less fixed than land warfare and much more technical and detailed in the disposition of forces and consideration of their various qualities in regard to speed, age and armament. Geddes and the Admiralty therefore wanted a close relationship between Jellicoe and the Allied Naval Council, and also stressed the great importance of retaining the full direct responsibility of the chiefs of staff, particularly their own First Sea Lord and the Board of Admiralty. It would therefore be unworkable to cut out the Allied Naval Council and make the admiralissimo directly under the Supreme War Council as Foch was. In fact, according to Geddes, they would be 'better off not to have an Admiralissimo at all'. The Admiralty also, in regard to each commander's right to appeal, insisted that in cases of emergency the admiralissimo should be able to give definite orders to any of the forces under his control.[82]

Geddes left on a mission to the United States at the end of September, but before sailing he was able to obtain a decision from the War Cabinet to proceed on the lines he had proposed. He justified his stand with a copy of another memorandum for the Allied Naval Council on the situation in the Black Sea. The Admiralty estimate of what the situation would be at the end of November included Russian warships in German hands known to be near completion at Nikolaiev (see Table 12.1).

Table 12.1 *Admiralty Estimate of the Potential Naval Balance in the Aegean, September 1918*

	Allied Aegean Squadron	Combined Enemy (Turkish, German and Russian)
Dreadnought battleships	—	1 or 2
Battle cruisers	—	1
Pre-dreadnought battleships	7	4
Cruisers	1	4 (2 Turkish)
Light cruisers	4	1
Destroyers	13	23 (6 Turkish)
Submarines	8	20

Geddes concluded that the position was not satisfactory and, if the enemy made a determined effort, he could sortie from the Dardanelles after the end of November, do great damage in the Aegean and then return to his base. This state of affairs would not have existed had there been a British Mediterranean admiralissimo to use Allied naval forces in the Mediterranean to the best advantage. Geddes's argument was persuasive and he received

Cabinet approval for the Foreign Office to pursue negotiations, since the Admiralty itself could not overcome the obstacles created by the authorities in Rome. He meant, of course, Revel. Geddes considerably overestimated the danger from the Black Sea as we shall shortly see.[83]

By the time the official Cabinet approval was obtained Rodd had actually made significant progress in Rome. He saw Sonnino immediately on his return from leave in Britain, kept the talk on generalities and then arranged to meet privately with Revel on 28 September. The meeting went surprisingly well and a diplomat with considerable experience in Italy apparently got much further than the naval authorities had ever been able to do. A cynic might say that the Macedonian front had broken open, Bulgaria was about to drop out of the war, the Austrians were beginning to retreat in Albania and their status as a belligerent was beginning to look shaky. Consequently, Revel may have considered that the question of an admiralissimo might turn out to be largely an academic one. The talk was on the basis of Sonnino's proposals and the points the British wanted to clear up. Revel did not believe in the Austrian fleet ever leaving the Adriatic due to the difficulties of coaling, and its only possible objective would be refuge in the Dardanelles. Rodd was probably surprised to find Revel agreed with the views of Geddes and Wemyss about the impracticality of putting the admiralissimo under the Supreme War Council, and that there should be no interference in the chain of responsibility between the British Admiralty and the admiralissimo in the Mediterranean. The question of the right of appeal proved more of a problem, but Rodd thought that it could be settled best by naval experts to clear up the ambiguity. Revel actually told Rodd that he thought the appointment in itself was desirable and that he would like to see it carried through as quickly as possible, and he 'had a dig at Admiral de Bon, whom he regarded as responsible for the irritation which had characterised the discussion'. Revel favoured Corfu as the headquarters of the admiralissimo. Rodd also gathered the impression that the choice of Jellicoe was a problem, that he had made some remarks which excited suspicion and that the Italians did not believe he understood conditions in the Adriatic. 'Something which he must have said about the Adriatic has stuck in the memory and produced a sense of misgiving', Rodd explained, and then added, 'The man they all like and believe in here is de Robeck and they look on him as having personal knowledge and experience of all the conditions in these waters.' If the admiralissimo would not command forces in action, a less senior officer might suffice. Rodd was encouraged and considered the time ripe to send a naval expert and, if the latter reached agreement with Revel, the minister would accept it.[84]

Wemyss was not quite as optimistic as Rodd, for Revel seemed inclined to want more independence for the Italian C.-in-C. in the Adriatic than Sonnino had, and the Admiralty had learned by now from hard experience that there was many a slip twixt the cup and the lip as far as agreement over the question was concerned. Wemyss did not think that a British expert should go to Rome before consulting with de Bon in Paris and, in any event, nothing could be done until Geddes returned from America. Geddes agreed and cabled: 'Leave matters until my return.'[85]

Barrère, of course, had been alarmed by the reports from the Stato Maggiore about a possible agreement and asked for permission to bluntly tell Orlando and Sonnino that the French would accept nothing of the kind. Clemenceau told him to abstain, but Barrère insisted that events in the Near East, notably the impending collapse of Turkey, made French naval command in the Mediterranean a primordial necessity.[86] By now the circumstances of the war were overtaking negotiations. Bulgaria asked for an armistice at the end of September and Wemyss wondered if Turkey would soon follow and what the naval situation would then be, or what they would find when they passed through the Straits into the Black Sea. He commented that, had Jellicoe been in the Mediterranean as admiralissimo, it would have been so much easier for them to dispose of their forces.[87] The war ended before negotiations could be resumed. Whether they would have been successful is an open question, and one might also speculate whether de Robeck rather than Jellicoe would have wound up as admiralissimo. It was another 'what-might-have-been' in the Mediterranean.

The Submarine War Winds Down

By the end of June 1918 the advance submarine base of the Germans and Austrians at Cattaro was in an uncomfortable position. The Allied air raids were a steady annoyance and commencing on 6 July there was the additional threat of an Italian advance in Albania, while there were frequent reports from agents of possible Allied landings, the very sort of action the Americans would like to have undertaken with the Marines. Heyssler, now commanding the Austrian Cruiser Flotilla at Cattaro, downplayed the threat as long as the Entente was heavily engaged on the Salonika and Syrian fronts and under the pressure of an Austrian offensive on the Italian front. But once the Austrian offensive in Italy failed, it was not beyond the bounds of possibility that the Entente would try some offensive move, and find support wherever they landed from the unreliable coastal population. The Allied landing would be supported by naval forces too strong for Austrian surface craft or submarines to effectively hinder. The Austro-Hungarian forces in Albania relied on sea transport for supply and Heyssler warned that they could expect the enemy to cut off this communication and thereby prevent rapid reinforcement. Horthy drew AOK's attention to the danger.[88]

Commodore Püllen encountered this feeling of insecurity when he visited Cattaro in early July, aggravated by the fact that the Austrian land commander suspected the loyalty of one of the regiments (composed largely of Ruthenians) which would be available for defence of the base in the event of a civil uprising which might accompany a landing by the Entente. Horthy considered it useless, given the existing ratio of strength, to move his fleet to Cattaro and Püllen had the impression that the weak defences of Cattaro influenced his decision to remain in Pola. They were paying for the neglect of the artillery defences of Cattaro which would have to be strengthened quickly. The threat of Allied landings kept four to six

Austrian submarines tied to the coast near Cattaro or Albania for several weeks to the detriment of the submarine war. Püllen complained that the enemy, merely by spreading reports of planned attacks on Pola, Cattaro and central Dalmatia, gained a considerable morale ascendency and essentially paralysed the Austrian U-boat war.[89]

The German U-boat force in the Mediterranean numbered twenty-seven during the month of July, but two of them had been under repair for close to a year, while the old and now well-worn U33, U34 and U35 were also in dockyard hands for long refits, and the two transports UC20 and UC73 continued their regular run to Tripolitania to the detriment of the submarine war. The small UBIII-class boats now carried the brunt of the war and had proportionately the best success, while the UC minelayers seemed to demonstrate that it was difficult for them to keep contact with convoys and they were best suited for working in restricted areas close to the coast or at the junction of transport routes. The Germans averaged eight boats at sea at the same time and kept their emphasis on the western Mediterranean, but found that the good weather during the summer months made the work of Allied aircraft on anti-submarine patrol especially notable, while the defences in the Straits of Otranto were further improved. German successes were down, but the Mediterranean U-boat command claimed that the standard of success, average tonnage sunk 'per U-boat day' in July (523) stayed at the 1917 average of over 500 tons, while the accomplishments of individual boats were excellent with no U-boat returning to harbour without reporting success.[90]

The month of August saw a further decline in German submarine success. The Mediterranean U-boats were placed under a Befehlshaber (the full title: Befehlshaber der Unterseeboote im Mittelmeer) and, on 27 August, Commodore Grasshoff took over command from Püllen. The Germans, cognizant of the danger of Allied air raids, pushed work on bomb shelters for submarines at Pola and anticipated that by 15 April 1919 – and the return of good flying weather – they would have bomb-proof shelters for five U-boats.[91] The Germans had twenty-eight submarines in the Mediterranean in August, the slight increase was due to the arrival of UB128 under Kapitänleutnant Canaris – the future head of the Abwehr – who had the melancholy distinction of commanding one of the last pair of new U-boats to reinforce the Mediterranean during the war. Canaris passed through the Straits of Gibraltar on the 23rd but did not reach Cattaro until after the beginning of September and achieved no success in the Mediterranean due to stormy weather and excessive consumption of fuel while he was still in the Atlantic. It was symbolic, for counting Canaris the Germans managed to send only eight boats on operations during the month. There were two large new minelayers, U120 and U121, five new UBIII boats and two UCIII minelayers earmarked for the Mediterranean, but they were either unfinished or had not completed their trials by the end of the war. The tonnage sunk per U-boat day in August fell to 417. Grasshoff attributed the decline in results to the lack of U-boats ready for sea, especially the UBIII class, and reported further improvements in the defences at Otranto with the loss of UB53 earlier in the month. This loss may have been due merely to ignorance of the extension of the fixed barrage. Much more ominous for the future was the use of listening devices to detect U-boats trying to break through on the surface at night, combined with a close watch by captive balloons in an area eighty miles long on moonlit nights. The Germans feared during this period that the passage by slow U-boats with small batteries (such as the UCIII boats) would be nearly impossible. The main convoy routes through the Cape Bon–Sicily sector had also been shifted northwards to the shallower waters over the Adventure Bank where the Allies also profited by air cover from the coast of Sicily. This made submarine activity much more difficult. Clearly, the Germans were feeling the Allied countermeasures, but the decline in Allied losses to submarines was still partially related to the number of U-boats the Germans were able to keep at sea. The weekly reports of the BdU Mittelmeer show that in September and October the Germans were able to keep between five and nine boats at sea at the same time, with seven or eight the average at the very end of the war.[92]

In September, Grasshoff experimented with two boats working together, a forerunner of the pack tactics so successfully employed in the Second World War. Kapitänleutnant von Mellenthin of UB49 appears to have originated these tactics in the Mediterranean in January of 1918, operating jointly for a time with UB48 and with different submarines on other cruises. UB49, now under von Mellenthin's successor Oberleutnant zur See Ehrensberger, and UB105 operated for a specified period in late September in the area between the Balearics (Ibiza), Cape Palos and the African coast, and if a convoy was sighted every effort would be made to bring both boats into action against it. The two commanders even had an agreement about an abbreviated wireless code for communicating with one another. Although the boats had individual successes, the experiment did not succeed, partially because no convoys were sighted during the period, there was poor weather and the boats failed to establish wireless contact with each other.[93]

The attempt to repair and refit U-boats suffered from a lack of sufficient labour at Pola where there were approximately 956 German workers and 607 Austro-Hungarian Landstürmer (Home Guard) in September. The Austrians, however, worked very inefficiently according to the Germans, and their capacity for work was expected to decrease still more in the future as a result of the internal situation of the Dual Monarchy.[94] Furthermore, the collapse of Bulgaria at the end of September led Seekriegsleitung – the new naval supreme command established in August with Admiral Reinhard Scheer at its head and Captain Levetzow his Chief of Staff – to order Grasshoff on 27 September to send all available U-boats to attack communications between Gallipoli and the Chalkidiki Peninsula to hinder a landing by the Entente on the northern Aegean coast and help defend the Dardanelles. The Germans still hoped to maintain their supremacy in the Black Sea. They also considered the evacuation of Cattaro, but Grasshoff warned that this would lead to the strangulation of the U-boat war in the Mediterranean within the foreseeable future. They would lose the advantage of the mine-free great depths close to Cattaro and the Austrians would be hard put to keep the shallower waters further north in the Adriatic clear of the mines which the Entente would inevitably lay. Nevertheless, by the end of the month Grasshoff was forced to think the unthinkable, that is, Austria-Hungary would make a separate peace. The Germans quietly began preparations to get as many boats under way as possible if this should materialize, although Grasshoff after a meeting with Horthy on the 29th was still convinced that the Austrians would not make a separate peace.[95]

At the beginning of August and after the frequent reports of possible Entente landings on the Austrian coast, the AOK asked Horthy about the battle-readiness of the fleet and if its spirit and morale had been affected by the February events in Cattaro or the south Slav propaganda being spread through the southern regions of the Dual Monarchy. Horthy immediately replied that the fleet was ready for battle, but morale was obviously a trickier question. He claimed there had been no appearance of ferment since 1 May when, in connection with repercussions of the events of February at Cattaro and strikes on land, a flare up in the fleet was expected and a plot on Tb80 in Pola led by two Slavic ringleaders had been uncovered. Horthy had cracked down quickly with rapid punishment of the ringleaders and he thought this had made a good impression and worked as a deterrent. However, he appears to have been a realist. The opinion in the fleet, which was recruited from all nationalities of the Monarchy, was to a certain extent a mirror of opinion in the Dual Monarchy itself, circumscribed to a degree by discipline. Hostile propaganda could possibly gain ground among certain elements in the fleet. Horthy considered those elements a narrow fraction of the whole, but between this group and the thoroughly reliable elements stood an unsteady and, for the most part, less intelligent mass who, as in February, could be pulled to the revolutionary side. Horthy had dedicated himself to furthering close contact between officers and men and organizing counter-propaganda, and had also tried, without much success because of manpower requirements, to replace older men in the fleet with young sailors. Horthy concluded that the fleet was in hand and in all probability would remain so after and during a hostile action against their coast. He did warn, however, that the torpedo-boat flotilla was being worn out by continuous convoy service and, with no new construction, the flotilla was likely to break down in the foreseeable future.[96] This was a common complaint shared by Horthy's enemies in the Allied navies.

At the beginning of October the Seekriegsleitung ordered that the primary mission of the U-boats for the near future was to attack the Allied supply lines to Salonika and Syria. Grasshoff planned to deploy five of the seven U-boats estimated to be ready between the 5th and 12th to the area west of the line Derna–Sapienza–Ionian Islands. UC52 would lay mines off Corfu and in the Gulf of Patras and work in the northern Ionian, while UC74 would work off Port Said and Alexandria. Grasshoff recognized that disturbing the supply lines to the Macedonian theatre presented special difficulties because a large portion of Allied supplies went by small fast steamers from southern Italian ports to Patras protected by the strong patrols of the Otranto barrage, while the Germans would have to employ a large number of U-boats to effectively disturb the remainder of the traffic flowing into the south-west entrance of the Aegean from Taranto, Messina, Malta and the African coast. Grasshoff himself came down with typhus and had to relinquish his command to Püllen who returned to become BdU on 15 October. He had stopped in Vienna on his way south and realized that by now the future of Austria-Hungary and, consequently, the German bases in the Adriatic was in question. The impending collapse of Austria-Hungary also halted the somewhat leisurely discussions over a naval convention between Austria-Hungary and Germany that had been going on since the preceding April.[97] With the Allied armies now on the offensive in the Balkans and pushing northwards towards the heart of the Dual Monarchy, the Germans were forced to face the problem of saving whatever they could.

The submarine successes in the final months of the war reflect the gradual decline of the Austro-German position, as shown in Table 12.2.[98]

Table 12.2   *Shipping Losses due to Submarines, July–November 1918*

	Sunk by Mediterranean U-Boat Flotillas		Sunk by Constantinople Half Flotilla		Total (All Theatres)	
	Ships	Tonnage	Ships	Tonnage	Ships	Tonnage
July 1918	29	76,629	—	—	113	280,820
Aug. 1918	18	65,377	19	3,904	154	310,180
Sept. 1918	21	35,856	1	1,833	91	171,972
Oct. 1918	11	28,007	19	7,315	73	116,237
Nov. 1918	3	10,233	—	—	3	10,233
Austro-Hungarian submarines sank:						
	Ships	Tonnage				
July 1918	10	235				
Aug. 1918	1	2,209				
Sept. 1918	16	5,502				

Many of the vessels sunk by Austrian submarines at this stage of the war were small Greek and Italian sailing craft, although on 20 September U47 sank the French submarine *Circé* off the Albanian coast. *Circé* had been on anti-submarine patrol and her sole survivor, the second officer, requested that his expectant wife be informed of his survival, a request the Austrians honoured with an uncoded wireless message. On 17 October AOK ordered all Austrian submarines to cease *Handelskrieg* and merely hold themselves ready to defend Dalmatian ports.

In the last part of the war the Germans were still capable of causing losses and in July they had a string of successes which alarmed Geddes and Wemyss. But the old days of easy slaughter so typical of 1916 or 1917 were gone. The Germans also had losses, UB53, as mentioned, in the Otranto barrage on 3 August, and on 4 October UB68 was sunk by gunfire of convoy escorts (the sloop *Snapdragon*, trawler *Cradosin* and steamer *Queensland*) while attacking a convoy south-east of Malta. The submarine had lost trim and broke surface after firing a torpedo. Her commander, Oberleutnant zur

See Karl Dönitz, survived to become leader of the German submarine arm in the Second World War and, for a brief time, successor to Adolf Hitler in 1945. U34, one of the forlorn hope detached to stop the final Allied offensive in the eastern Mediterranean, also disappeared. Her exact fate will probably never be known although the submarine might have been destroyed on 20 or 21 October in the Straits of Otranto by the destroyer *Lizard* and trawler *John Bowler* which dropped depth charges on a suspected submarine after a hydrophone search. The Germans in their final effort nearly achieved a spectacular success when UB48 (Oberleutnant zur See Steinbauer) torpedoed the French battleship *Voltaire* near Cerigotto on the night of 10–11 October. The *Voltaire*, *en route* to Mudros after a refit, did not sink. Capable German submarine commanders demonstrated that right to the end they could sink a ship in convoy – Dönitz had already sunk one ship before he fell victim going after a second – but they could expect retaliation from the escorts. The submarine menace may have been contained, but it was not eliminated. Once this has been said, however, and the point made that the Germans could have a better than average month, such as January 1918, a summary of the tonnage sunk per U-boat day in 1918 shows that the trend was downwards, especially when compared with the first half of 1917 as shown in Table 12.3.[99]

Table 12.3   *Sinkings per U-boat Day, January–August 1918*

	Tonnage sunk per U-boat day
1st Half of 1917	602
January 1918	619
February 1918	546
March 1918	539
April 1918	499
May 1918	518
June 1918	476·3
July 1918	523
August 1918	417

Those statistics compiled by Colonel Beharrell which the Mediterranean Staff found so irksome showed the British that they were on the right track and that convoys were effective. In a review of the eight months prior to 30 June 1918, Beharrell found that there was a tendency for losses in the Mediterranean to decline steadily when a long view was taken. The number of steamers lost in the second quarter of 1918 represented a reduction of 16 per cent on the losses in the first quarter of the year. This was, however, not as large as the reduction in losses in home waters where the percentage reached 21 per cent. The Mediterranean figures were particularly encouraging for there had been a steady increase in traffic in the Mediterranean with the average number of sailings per month during the second quarter of 1918 more than double the corresponding figures for the last quarter of 1917. The situation is shown in Table 12.4.

Table 12.4   *Sailings and Losses in the Mediterranean, November 1917–June 1918*

	Average per Month		
	Nov. and Dec. 1917	1st Quarter 1918	2nd Quarter 1918
Sailings	1,472	2,128	3,164
Losses:			
Total	35	37·6	29·3
Steamers only	32	25·7	21·7
(500 tons and over)			
Tonnage	109,000	108,000	83,000

The ratio of losses to sailings, classified under local convoy, under escort or sailing independently, showed in every case a gradual reduction of risk, although less marked in the case of convoy sailings. The ratios are given in Table 12.5.

Table 12.5   *Ratio of Losses to Sailings in the Mediterranean, November 1917–June 1918*

	Nov. and Dec. 1917	1st Quarter 1918	2nd Quarter 1918
% of loss to convoy sailings	2·2	1·5	1·5
% of loss to escorted sailings	1·9	1·0	0·4
% of loss to unescorted sailings	1·9	1·0	0·2
% of loss to total sailings	2·0	1·2	0·6

The risk for convoyed sailings in the Mediterranean in the second quarter of 1918 was 1·5 per cent which was higher than for United Kingdom convoyed sailings which was 0·6 per cent, but the difference in risk for all sailings was not as great, 0·6 per cent in the Mediterranean compared with 0·5 per cent for United Kingdom traffic.[100]

By August and September 1918 the ratio of loss to sailings had declined still further, as shown in Table 12.6.

Table 12.6   *Ratio of Losses to Sailings in the Mediterranean, August–September 1918*

	August 1918	September 1918
% of loss in convoy	0·51	0·79
% of loss under escort	0·34	0·11
% of loss unaccompanied	0·21	—
% of total sailings	0·35	0·29

The danger areas of the Mediterranean varied as the statistics for average monthly losses, shown in Table 12.7, demonstrated.[101]

Table 12.7   *Danger Areas of the Mediterranean, January–September 1918*

| Area | Average Monthly Losses | | |
	1st Quarter	2nd Quarter	3rd Quarter
Gibraltar–Genoa	4·3	3·7	1·7
Gibraltar–Bizerte	1·0	0·3	0·7
Algeria–France	2·3	5·3	1·0
Italian coasts	3·7	2·3	1·0
Bizerte–Egypt	8·3	6·7	5·7
Aegean–Ionian	3·3	—	1·0
Egypt–Crete	2·7	2·7	3·3

Naturally, the situation was not always so clear to those on the scene. Commodore Baird, Director of Shipping Movements in the Mediterranean, warned in September that with escorts cut down to a minimum for the blockade of the Adriatic, the escort given each convoy was so small it had ceased to be an efficient protection and with the number of surface craft available for the Mediterranean at the maximum 'it will generally be a matter of luck and successful dodging if sinkings remain at their present low level'. Baird discussed a number of reasons for the improved situation, overestimating the percentage of losses to German submarines due to the Otranto barrage and tending to undervalue the convoy system itself. He was not alone. That exceptionally bright young officer and Calthorpe's Assistant Chief of Staff Lieutenant-Commander Godfrey, told Beharrell that personally he had 'no doubt that the very considerable "strafing" that most submarines get when they pass through the barrage eventually finds its reflexion in the reduction of our losses'.[102] But even with the self-inflicted wound which the Otranto barrage represented for the Allies, it was doubtful whether the Germans or Austrians would have reversed the situation when additional submarines came into service at the end of the year or in 1919, provided the number of convoy escorts grew. The trend favoured the Allies because useful craft, such as the British patrol gunboats or Kil class, slow but able to escort the HE–OE convoys from Britain without refuelling, were entering service in increasing numbers while the American destroyer programme, as well as those long-awaited and much delayed Ford boats, would have swelled the ranks of Allied escorts and more and better aircraft added a new dimension of danger to the submarine. This would have been in contrast to the extensive and possibly wasted efforts on new mine barrages. It might be said that the Allies probably would have prevailed in spite of themselves.

The Germans and the Russian Black Sea Fleet

Next to the submarine campaign, Allied naval leaders in the Mediterranean probably spent more energy worrying over the fate of the Russian Black Sea Fleet than any other subject in 1918. Their nightmare was that most of its more modern ships, manned by Germans and Turks, would emerge from the Dardanelles and, with the inability of the Allies to deploy their theoretically superior forces rationally, the Germans and Turks might achieve a local superiority in the Aegean and possibly inflict great damage. But what was the reality behind this threat? It seems to have been far less than the Allies supposed. The conclusion of the Dardanelles campaign at the end of 1916 ended any rational hope that the Allied and Russian navies might have co-operated in the near future and events in the Black Sea tended to fade from view. The naval war in the Black Sea after the Dardanelles campaign – and as reflected in the pages of this book – might almost have been fought in another world. But the Russian navy did not do badly at all. Throughout 1916 they continued the blockades of the Turkish coal district around Zonguldak as well as the Bosphorus, making extensive use of mines to hinder exit and entry. Russian control of the Black Sea was not seriously challenged by the weak German Half Flotilla of submarines at Constantinople. The Russian navy tended to devote more and more of its attention to covering the advance of the Russian army on the Caucasus front and executed a number of successful amphibious operations along the Black Sea coast. The Russians did suffer their worst loss of the war on 20 October when the dreadnought *Imperatriza Maria* blew up and capsized at Sebastopol following a fire in the forward 12-inch gun magazine. The cause was probably accidental rather than sabotage. Russian sea supremacy remained undisturbed, however, throughout most of 1917, although the growing internal crisis, material shortages and lack of activity in yards, reduced active operations to a few of the large destroyers. The Bolshevik triumph in November and subsequent decision to drop out of the war placed the fate of this sizeable and undefeated force in doubt.[103]

The Central Powers concluded an armistice agreement with the Russians at Brest-Litovsk on 15 December 1917 followed by a treaty with the Ukraine on 9 February recognizing the independence of the latter, and on 3 March signed the final treaty of Brest-Litovsk with Russia. The relevant naval clauses called for Russian warships to be gathered in Russian ports and disarmed or detained until conclusion of a general peace. The eastern frontier of the new Ukrainian state was left open, but the republic included Odessa and a Black Sea coastline. The Ukrainians therefore might have claims on some or all of the Black Sea Fleet and this was a source of future confusion. German and Austrian forces marched deep into the Ukraine to secure the wheatfields and on 13 March occupied Odessa, followed by Nikolaiev and its dockyards on the 17th. They continued eastwards and southwards and reached the Crimea and Sebastopol by 1 May. The Moscow government ordered Vice-Admiral N. P. Sablin, C.-in-C. of the Black Sea Fleet, to sail his ships, which included two dreadnoughts, from

Sebastopol to Novorossisk. Sablin's authority was very shaky in a fleet where discipline had to a large extent evaporated. He managed to get fourteen destroyers to leave at midnight on the 13th, but the dreadnoughts *Volya* (ex *Imperator Aleksandr III*) and *Svobodnaya Rossiya* (ex *Imperatriza Ekaterina II*) and four destroyers remained behind. After a month of negotiations the dreadnoughts sailed on the night of 14 May as German patrols entered the city. German artillery fired on them as they departed, the destroyer *Gnyevni* ran aground and the destroyer *Zavyetni* was sabotaged in dockyard hands. The Germans managed to get their hands on the pre-dreadnoughts and a number of smaller ships and submarines after demolition parties failed to carry out their orders. They already controlled those vessels under construction at Nikolaiev, although a shortage of labour and materials made their completion problematical. The two dreadnoughts and a sizeable number of destroyers remained out of their reach at Novorossisk, nominally under Sablin and subject to Moscow's orders. There was, in theory, a Soviet republic at Novorossisk, along with a mutinous Red Army, hoards of refugees, a White volunteer army outside the city, and loose discipline and chaotic diversity of opinion among the crews of the ships, with Sablin's leadership subject to election.[104] Uncertainty and confusion would be the only way to describe the Black Sea Fleet and, of course, the far-distant Allies had only an imperfect idea of what was going on.

Ludendorff definitely had his eye on the Russian warships and, as German troops moved towards the Crimea in April, he suggested that they place some of the Russian warships in service to 'police' the Black Sea. The Turks, who wanted a substitute for the *Breslau*, and Bulgarians also had potentially conflicting claims. This raised some complicated legal and diplomatic problems about ownership of the Russian ships and if they could be considered 'booty' or captured war material after conclusion of the Treaty of Brest-Litovsk. Furthermore, did the Ukrainians have any claim to the ships? The German Foreign Office took the position that Nikolaiev was in Ukrainian territory but the question of ownership of the Russian Black Sea Fleet would have to await a Russian-Ukrainian Peace Treaty.[105] These legal niceties had little meaning for Ludendorff who advised the navy that the acquisition of the Don Basin to provide coal for transporting food and supervision of the political development of the Crimea as a Tartar republic were the ultimate German goals. The Russian warships seized by the Germans might be sold only to the Turks with a clause in the convention that if the latter did not fulfil their obligations the German flag would be raised again. Ludendorff wanted the Admiralstab to bring Vice-Admiral Hopman, the German admiral in the Black Sea, into the picture in order to hinder the Austrians or Bulgarians getting their clutches on the Russian warships.[106]

Vice-Admiral Hopman, the Chief of NATEKO – the Nautisch-Technische Kommission für Schwarze Meere – directed the employment of all naval personnel in the Ukraine and Crimea in agreement with local German army headquarters. The Admiralstab directed the Mittelmeerdivision and other naval units in the Black Sea area to place officers and men at his disposal for manning the Russian ships in Sebastopol, and a detachment of 600 men would also be sent from Germany for the same purpose. After their arrival and the formation of a Marineabteilung Krim, most members of the other Black Sea commands would return to their original units. The primary mission of the Crimean naval detachment was to secure all prizes useful to the navy in Sebastopol and make them ready for sea. The Admiralstab were, however, very circumspect about what would be given to the Turks whose technical and nautical knowledge and capabilities they considered limited. They would have to avoid giving them too many or overly complex ships which would only be a burden for the next few years and which the Turks could not maintain. They therefore opposed making any specific promises to their Turkish allies. Any Russian ships which resisted the entrance of German troops could be disarmed, provisionally commandeered and used for German purposes.[107]

The escape of some of the Russian ships to Novorossisk complicated matters for the Germans. The Supreme Command ordered General Kosch, Oberbefehlshaber in der Krim, to move against the port with the assistance of the *Goeben*. The Admiralstab were opposed to this for there was no security that the Russian warships would remain there and might go to other ports in the Black Sea or Sea of Azov. The Russians would probably scuttle them rather than let them fall into German hands, but one could not really foresee when military operations against those ships would cease. Furthermore, German sea power in the Black Sea was weak, the *Goeben* would face two dreadnoughts and a sizeable number of large modern destroyers which the Turks could not match. The *Goeben*'s damage was not yet fully repaired and the battle cruiser was neither fast enough nor sufficiently battleworthy to face such an undertaking. The *Goeben* did proceed to Sebastopol when the port was captured by the German army in order to make use of the Russian docks. The Turks, for their part, were alarmed that events in the Black Sea might induce the British to attack the Dardanelles, perhaps under cover of smoke as they had recently done in the Zeebrugge raid. They therefore wanted the *Goeben* to return from Sebastopol as soon as possible to be near the Straits, and advised securing the disarmament of the Russian ships at Novorossisk by negotiation with further decisions as to their fate reserved for the future. Ludendorff even suggested towing some of the captured Russian ships to the Dardanelles for use as floating batteries, manned by Turkish crews, with the question of their ownership kept in reserve. The Admiralstab opposed this. The military value of floating batteries in the Straits would be very small and the Germans would gradually have to fully man them and treat them as warships, frustrating the German development programme for the Turkish fleet and the conclusion of a favourable Turco-German naval convention. The Admiralstab opposed giving the Turks anything beyond the *Medjidieh* – a Turkish cruiser mined and sunk off Odessa in 1915 and subsequently salved and put in service by the Russians – and two destroyers. The Turkish navy had trouble finding suitable people for a training detachment in the *Goeben* and if the Turks received more Russian warships they would have to man them with personnel drawn from other naval services useful to the

Germans, such as minesweeping, thereby weakening the Ottoman navy even more. The Admiralstab suggested as an alternative considering the dispatch of land artillery or naval cannon taken from Russian warships for the defences of the Dardanelles.[108] Ludendorff was adamant, however, about treating the Russian ships as 'war booty', and did not agree to a division of the Russian ships among the Black Sea states. The Germans had every interest in strengthening the maritime position of Turkey and he wanted to give the latter ships in addition to a mere substitute for the *Breslau*.[109]

At the beginning of May 1918 the Russian Black Sea Fleet could be said to have been divided into three parts with scattered ships under German control at Ukrainian ports such as Odessa and Nikolaiev, a large portion of the Black Sea Fleet in German hands at Sebastopol, and the ships under Moscow's theoretical control at Novorossisk. The ships in Ukrainian ports included those under construction at Nikolaiev, such as, the dreadnought *Demokratiya* (ex *Imperator Nikolai I*) and 3 light cruisers, as well as 4 turbine-engined destroyers, 2 gunboats and 3 submarines. The bulk of the former Black Sea Fleet at Sebastopol consisted of the pre-dreadnoughts *Ioann Zlatoust* and *Evstafi*, 4 old battleships, 3 cruisers (including ex *Medjidieh*), 1 armed yacht, 3 turbine destroyers, 9 older destroyers, 1 gunboat, 1 yacht-seaplane carrier and 14 submarines (4 very old). Very few of these warships were ready for sea. The uncertain factor was Sablin's force at Novorossisk consisting of the dreadnoughts *Svobodnaya Rossiya* and *Volya*, 10 turbine destroyers and 5 older destroyers. The Germans ruefully acknowledged that it was really more powerful than anything they or the Turks could send against it. The Admiralstab decided that German naval interests required the Russian Black Sea Fleet to be destroyed or disarmed so that for the foreseeable future no Russian fleet threatened Turkey. Germany and its Allies should also acquire worthwhile Russian ships under favourable conditions. Unfortunately, a decision on the actual ownership of the Black Sea Fleet was not expected for some time. Nor were the Germans likely to get any of the ships at Sebastopol in service as quickly as they wanted. Hopman wrote privately to a friend in the Admiralstab that the labour question raised the greatest difficulties with workers not wanting to deviate from the gains of the revolution. Without assistance on the question of labour, it would scarcely be possible for the yards to put more than two to three destroyers back in service within a reasonable space of time. Ironically, Hopman himself was a moderate, basically opposed to the ambitious plans of Ludendorff in the Black Sea and inclined to favour Russia as a potential ally after the war. He also preferred treating the Ukraine as favourably as possible and helping it to create a navy, and he certainly did not advocate claiming Russian ships as 'war booty'.[110]

The fate of those Russian ships produced sharp differences of opinion in Germany with Ludendorff and the General Staff, without any reference to the navy, regarding the ships and naval material as 'war booty' and therefore to be freely disposed of, including promising ships to the Turks. On the other hand, General von Seeckt, Chief of Staff of the Ottoman army, raised the prospect of a 'neutralized Black Sea', a not terribly practical proposal since the Turks could always send warships through the Bosphorus. The popular idea at the Admiralstab was to divide the single powerful naval force in the Black Sea – the former Russian fleet – among the new coastal states carved out of the Russian Empire and buy the useful ships from those uninterested in a navy, and by treaty and influence prevent any one of them from creating a strong fleet. The navy and the Auswärtiges Amt tended to agree but Ludendorff claimed that the army had captured the booty and could do with it as it pleased. The General Staff then negotiated with the Auswärtiges Amt, with the navy scarcely hearing what was going on.[111]

Ludendorff lost patience with the slow progress of negotiations over the ships at Novorossisk and Hindenburg cabled the Kaiser on 10 June that the Germans had already postponed their advance giving the Bolsheviks the opportunity to prepare defences. Ludendorff intended to commence the advance on the 15th if the Germans did not receive assurances that the ships would enter Sebastopol by the 20th. The Russians, however, seemed on the verge of giving in. Captain Tichmenew, interim commander of the Novorossisk naval forces in the absence of Sablin, informed the German harbour commander at Sebastopol that he intended to obey orders from the Russian government and bring his ships to Sebastopol for internment by the 19th at the latest. Hopman, who now received the additional title BMK (Befehlshaber der deutschen Marinekommandos in ehemals russischen Schwarzmeergebiet), reached an agreement with Tichmenew whereby the Germans would pay the Russian officers and men on the interned ships and would be reimbursed later by the Russian government. For the moment, approximately 750 men would remain in the ships, but Hopman intended to reduce this number as soon as possible.[112]

The Germans got much less than they expected. The Bolshevik government had apparently sent secret orders to Novorossisk to scuttle the ships if an order was ever received from Moscow to turn the fleet over to the Germans. But opinion in the fleet at Novorossisk was divided, and there was considerable agitation in those large meetings that were so characteristic of the Russian Revolution. The result of a vote on the issue was approximately 450 for scuttling, 900 for internment in Sebastopol and around 1,000 abstentions. On 18 June, Tichmenew in the *Volya* along with the large destroyers *Bezpokoini*, *Pospyeshni* and *Derski*, the torpedo-boats *Zhivoi* and *Zharki* and an armed merchant cruiser sailed for Sebastopol. The dreadnought *Svobodnaya Rossiya* was torpedoed and sunk by the destroyer *Kertch*, which escaped to Tuapse where she was scuttled the next day. The remaining seven destroyers (including five large modern ones) and torpedo-boats were scuttled in Novorossisk, and German aerial reconnaissance on the 21st reported no more warships afloat in the port.[113] The Germans had therefore lost the use of about half the most modern units they might have anticipated, while the Bolsheviks may have eliminated the potential rival for power which the fleet represented. The Entente, although it was slow to realize it, also had had half the potential danger to its maritime predominance in the Aegean removed.

The German Army High Command was anxious to get some of the ships that had been left behind at Sebastopol ready for police duties in the Black Sea as soon as possible, and under the circumstances full battle readiness was not necessary and could be sacrificed for rapid entry into service. The Admiralstab therefore ordered the destroyers *Schastlivi* (1,110 tons) and *Kapitan Saken* (640 tons), and the torpedo-boat *Zvonki* (350 tons) into service. The destroyers *Buistry* (1,110 tons), *Gnyevni* (1,110 tons) and the torpedo-boats *Zavidni* (350 tons) and *Zhutki* (350 tons) would follow, leaving any repairs which could be deferred to a later date. If necessary, steamers or large motor boats could be armed and used in their place. Approximately 500 men from the German torpedo division would be sent to man the ships, but additional officers were not available and they would have to make use of those already on the scene. The Germans also intended to substitute some of the craft which had just arrived from Novorossisk for some of the ships just mentioned, but the date this could be done was highly uncertain and dependent on difficult political negotiations. The Germans, however, had no interest in Russian salvage operations on the dreadnought *Imperatriza Maria*, which though still capsized had been partially raised.[114]

Ludendorff refused to recognize the ownership of the Russian government over the ships which had returned from Novorossisk to be interned at Sebastopol and wanted to make use of the best of them as quickly as possible. He asked how far they had to alter the agreement with Captain Tichmenew in regard to manning the ships. Captain Tichmenew, 13 officers and approximately 450 men remained aboard those ships as care and maintenance parties and, on 28 June, Hopman reported that the disarmament of the ships was proceeding smoothly with the crews, mostly Ukrainians, working willingly. He also had the problem of approximately 400 men who could not go back to Russia since they had compromised themselves with the Moscow government by bringing the ships to Sebastopol.[115]

The Admiralstab, with the ships actually or nearly in possession, expanded their horizons and decided to put into service under the German flag the dreadnought *Volya*, five destroyers, some submarines and special ships. The Admiralstab also planned to place under the Turkish flag a pre-dreadnought battleship, a cruiser, five destroyers and some submarines and special ships. The big Russian warships naturally required far more in the way of manpower than the handful of destroyers and torpedo-boats that the Germans had previously considered. Obtaining crews was going to be difficult. There were 600 men on their way from Germany and another 500 would follow, plus 80 for the submarines, but the *Volya* alone would require at least 1,000. On 8 July there was a special meeting at the Admiralstab with representatives of the Reichsmarineamt to discuss the problem which became linked with the need to man school ships in home waters, notably the old battleships *Zähringen* and *Schlesien*. The Germans had a surplus crew from the dreadnought *Rheinland* which had suffered severe damage after grounding in the Baltic and was to be converted to a barracks ship. Where should these men be employed? The Admiralstab wanted to put three Buistry-class destroyers in service in the Black Sea and keep two in reserve, but needed more men for the Russian submarines and repair ship *Kronstadt* (renamed *Fleiss*), caretaker parties for the older Russian warships, crews for minesweepers and eight to ten shallow draft craft to counter so-called 'pirates' in the Sea of Azov, and cadres for at least some of the ships the Turks were to receive. The Admiralstab wanted to use the *Volya* for the defence of the Dardanelles and would have to man her heavy artillery on at least a peacetime basis. The Buistry-class destroyers would be used for sorties from the Dardanelles to tie down Allied forces. The conflicting demands for manpower between home waters and the Black Sea had to be reconciled and tended to pit the Reichsmarineamt, anxious for school ships to meet the personnel demands of 1919 and 1920, against the Admiralstab, eager to exploit the momentary advantage in the Black Sea. Vice-Admiral Hebbinghaus of the Reichsmarineamt at one point put the issue bluntly: did they want to continue the U-boat war in 1919 or keep the *Goeben* up to strength? In the end the conference decided that the crew of the *Rheinland* would have to be divided roughly into thirds between *Volya* and the two old battleships to be used as school ships. This meant only approximately 400 additional men for the Black Sea and was inadequate to meet the many new demands.[116] The compromise really satisfied no one and to read the transcript of how these experienced German officers squabbled over specialists, officers and ratings is to realize how limited the options for the Germans in the Black Sea really were.

In early July, von Seeckt, reflecting the position of the Turkish High Command, considered that a better defence of the Dardanelles was desirable and hoped that the Mittelmeerdivision would return to Cospoli and that U-boats would be permanently stationed at the Straits. The diversion of the *Goeben* and the destroyers to the Crimea was clearly unwelcome from his and the Turkish point of view but, by the time his message reached Berlin, *Goeben* had returned to Constantinople and was likely to remain there. Seeckt did not consider an attack imminent, and if undertaken on the scale of 1915 thought it would fail. While a naval attack in great strength and regardless of loss might get through, the Entente would not be able to silence all batteries and, in order to secure supply lines through the Straits, would have to land troops. The preparations for such a landing should be obvious, although the Turks could not station sufficient troops to counter it while such an attack remained unlikely. Seeckt was most emphatic, however, on the necessity of returning the Mittelmeerdivision to Constantinople as soon as the situation in the Black Sea permitted.[117]

Ludendorff was not deterred from his grandiose plans by a lack of personnel. He told the Admiralstab representative at headquarters that he had a strong interest in German seapower in the Black Sea, that is ships with preponderantly German crews, but emphasized somewhat illogically that it was impossible to give the navy recruits. Therefore, and conscious of the disadvantages, he had authorized the German representative at the AOK to ascertain if the Austrians could provide men to man former Russian torpedo-boats under German command, and also if it was possible to send Austrian monitors from the Danube to the Sea of Azov. Ludendorff wanted the *Volya* to be brought far enough along so that making use of Ukrainians (possibly German colonists) or Austrians – but not 'dangerous' Czechs –

and Turkish auxiliary personnel as crew they could show the German flag off Poti, Batum, Trapezund and, most important of all, Constantinople. He opposed giving any of the Russian ships to Bulgaria or the Ukraine and only wanted to provide the Turks with ships useful to the Dardanelles defence.[118]

The Bulgarians did ask if they could purchase 4 modern Russian destroyers, 5 submarines, 3 tugs and 12 mine motor-boats, and Hopman was ready to use Bulgarian crews in some old torpedo-boats and a minesweeping division under German command at Sebastopol. The Admiralstab had no objection to giving them some small units of the former Russian fleet, and such ships would constitute no future danger for Germany or Turkey and would provide schooling for Bulgarian naval personnel which was in the interest of the German navy. The Reichsmarineamt warned, however, that Bulgaria ought not to get anything until a general division of the Russian ships had taken place and Turkish claims were satisfied.[119]

Ludendorff obtained the formality of the Kaiser's approval for putting a dreadnought, five destroyers, some U-boats and special ships into service under the German flag on 12 July. The question of final ownership of the ships would remain open. The OHL did not think that the ships used as floating batteries for the defence of the Dardanelles needed to be fully manned and was also anxious for the Ukraine and Georgia to participate in the 'police' of the Black Sea under German command. The Admiralstab, however, declined the participation of Ukrainian and Georgian craft since training them and the resulting consumption of fuel would be more trouble than the possible advantages. At the most, Ukrainians and Georgians might be employed in German ships for minor duties. The Admiralstab also corrected the army's misconceptions about floating batteries for the Dardanelles defence. Because of enemy aircraft, U-boats and indirect naval gunfire, these batteries had to be completely mobile and would differ from high seas battleships only in the fact that their machinery need not be used for long voyages. They might relinquish their torpedo armament and a small part of their intermediate artillery, and their crews might be reduced to four-fifths normal size. The Admiralstab also intended to move the two best Russian pre-dreadnoughts, *Evstafi* and *Zlatoust*, to the Dardanelles as soon as they could be made ready to sail. They would be manned by Turkish naval personnel, supplemented by Germans. The Turks would be more co-operative in this question if they thought that the ships would remain in their harbours, and the ships would therefore have to fly either the Turkish flag or Turkish and German flags next to one another. Their commissioning might be somewhat hastened by the use of reliable Ukrainian and Georgian qualified seamen.

The Admiralstab advised against detailing Austro-Hungarian officers and men for naval or police duties in the Black Sea because the Germans believed that the Austro-Hungarian navy was scarcely in condition to fulfil German requirements outside the Black Sea, and further diversions would only weaken it still more to the possible detriment of the U-boat war. On the other hand, the Bulgarians with their handful of torpedo-boats or former Russian destroyers might be useful. The Admiralstab made it quite clear to OHL that the desired expansion of German maritime power in the Black Sea and at the Dardanelles was dependent on the fuel question and the Mittelmeerdivision and Turkish fleet had never been allocated enough coal and oil by OHL for proper training or activity. The use of foreign personnel and material would involve intensive training which meant more steaming, and they could therefore expect a considerable increase in consumption of fuel. However, there was no sense in placing more ships in service than they could make battleworthy. Ludendorff was not convinced, however, and still wanted Austrian monitors for the Sea of Azov.[120]

By mid-July 1918 the Germans at Sebastopol had put the repair ship *Kronstadt*, renamed *Fleiss*, into service and intended to send it to Constantinople to serve as an accommodation and repair ship and magazine for the Mittelmeerdivision. The cruiser *Pamyat Merkuriya* was in use as an accommodation ship at Sebastopol. In actual warships the Germans had only the R10 (ex *Zorki*) in service with a mixed German-Turkish crew under the German flag and the submarine US4 (ex *Gagora*) undergoing trials. They also had five shallow draft craft of a variety of sorts for use in the Sea of Azov, where shallow waters prevented use of the torpedo-boats, and the Wedel minesweeping division of four tugs. Hopman expected to have the destroyer R01 (ex *Schastlivi*) in commission within a fortnight, but R02 (ex *Buistry*) was being prepared solely by Russian dockyard personnel and Hopman could not even estimate a completion date. They were refloating R03 (ex *Gnyevni*) but commissioning would depend on the damage sustained when she had grounded trying to escape from Sebastopol over two months before. The destroyer R04 (ex *Kapitan Saken*) needed only a fortnight's overhaul but the work could not be accomplished due to a lack of personnel. The torpedo-boat R11 (ex *Zvonki*) would also be in service soon and the submarine US3 (ex *Utka*) would commence trials as soon as those of US4 were finished.[121] The Germans, in sum, were likely to have had only one large destroyer, two torpedo-boats and one submarine of the former Russian Black Sea Fleet plus the minor craft in service by the end of July. There was, so far, no real reason for the Entente naval leaders to have lost any sleep over them.

The ownership and actual employment of the former Russian ships remained in doubt. On 14 July the Kaiser told Ludendorff that, according to the Auswärtiges Amt, the Ukraine and Russian Republic would have to be in agreement over the ships before they could be used. Ludendorff still did not agree with these legal niceties. The use of the ships was a military necessity for the defence of the Dardanelles and the policing of the Black Sea which could not wait any longer. The Auswärtiges Amt also argued that the Germans were bound by agreement not to use the ships which had returned to Sebastopol from Novorossisk, which meant there were now two categories of former Russian warships, those which had remained at Sebastopol when the German army entered and those which had gone to Novorossisk and subsequently returned. Ludendorff again disagreed: they were not bound by any pledge since the Russians had not fulfilled their part of the agreement in that only part of the ships which fled to Novorossisk returned. Furthermore, the disarmament of ships in harbours not occupied by the Germans was not guaranteed and merchant traffic in the Black Sea and Sea of Azov was in no way secure. Holtzendorff agreed with Ludendorff that they had to get the ships into service as soon as possible for the defence of the Dardanelles, and the navy asked the Auswärtiges Amt to solve their difficulties by reaching prompt agreement with the Ukrainians and Russians. To get around the difficulties, the Reichsmarineamt even prepared estimates of the purchase or charter price of the Russian warships.[122]

There was yet another possible claimant for the Russian ships and an additional complication – Austria-Hungary. Korvettenkapitän Schönthaler, the Austrian naval attaché in Constantinople, had been consistently reporting the growing irritation in Turkey against the Germans over the question of the Russian Black Sea Fleet. Schönthaler thought that it provided opportunities for the Dual Monarchy. Increased Austrian influence in the Ottoman navy would provide opportunities for Austrian officers and men to train after the war when they could assume a reduction in the number of ships that the k.u.k. Kriegsmarine would be able to keep in commission. Schönthaler did not realize what a cruel understatement this would turn out to be. He also recognized the opportunity of getting a foothold in the Black Sea by taking advantage of the German and Turkish shortage of personnel to man at least one or two Russian destroyers with Austrian personnel under the k.u.k. naval ensign. The necessary officers and men might come from disarming old ships or the survivors of the *Szent István*. The Austrian High Command was more interested in the Russian submarines. Arz informed the German General Staff that growing losses and difficulties in the U-boat war required an increase in the numbers of submarines in service and asked for six of the submarines at Sebastopol for use by the Austrian navy in the Mediterranean, asserting that the crews were available. Arz also spoke of the possible purchase of four Buistry destroyers. The Germans replied that there were only two Russian submarines likely to be ready for service in the near future and that these were already manned by German personnel, while the other U-boats at Sebastopol which might be used in the Mediterranean were already occupied by German crews preparing them for commissioning. The Admiralstab observed rather tartly that it was of great interest that the Austrians had personnel available, for they had declined other missions which the Germans had requested of them because of a lack of personnel. Purchase by the Austrians of destroyers was also out of the question until the problem of their ownership was cleared up. A few days later the Admiralstab did agree to the Austrians manning three Russian submarines provided the boats flew the German flag and remained under the command of German officers.[123] The Austrians would work, the Germans would command. The friction and latent rivalry between the two Allies was again apparent.

The Germans solved the question of ownership of the Black Sea Fleet in a supplementary treaty with Russia signed at Berlin on 27 August which included an article on Russian warships and Russian stores seized by

German military forces. The Germans recognized Russia's ownership of the warships seized after ratification of the peace treaty, but the warships 'will remain under German care until the conclusion of the general peace'. The Germans also admitted Russia's claim to be compensated for Russian stores seized outside the Ukraine. A secret letter from the German Foreign Secretary which accompanied the treaty specified that the Germans should be given the use of the Russian warships for 'peaceful aims, in particular for the trawling of mines and coastal harbour and police service'. The agreement included those warships which returned from Novorossisk to Sebastopol, and 'in case of war necessity they might also be used for military aims'. The Germans promised the Russians 'full indemnity for the damages and losses which may be suffered by these ships during this service'. This agreement thereby gave the Germans the use of the Russian warships but, according to the legal experts of the German Foreign Ministry, forestalled any transfer of the ships to another power, and the Germans had to give up the idea of manning some of the ships with their allies. They could, as a way out, place their allies on board 'for training' for up to one-third of the ship's complement after the ship had reached an allied port. The Germans therefore modified their plans and abandoned the proposal to use Bulgarian crews for light craft. In the meantime they collected German crews for the dreadnought *Volya* and four destroyers and some U-boats and, on political grounds, planned for a nucleus crew to bring the *Evstafi* and *Zlatoust* to Constantinople.[124]

The Russian ships themselves were in poor condition and apparently filthy after the Bolshevik period when unruly crews had simply dumped refuse into the bowels of the ship. Hopman warned that they would have to proceed quietly and without warning to avoid damage from sabotage, for Russian opinion even of the officer class, or what remained of it, was turning against Germany, while more ominously Bolshevik propaganda was apparently not without effect on some of the less reliable personnel sent out from Germany. It was really much later than the German leaders thought. The Seekriegsleitung was aware of the danger and issued special orders for secrecy and the simultaneous seizure of all the ships it intended to put into service, even if it could not immediately man them. This now meant *Volya*, six destroyers (five oil- and one coal-burning), all U-boats and the old battleships *Zlatoust* and *Evstafi*. The Turks would not be told until the ships were seized and it would be emphasized to them that the ships remained in the possession of the Russian government and their 'use' by the Germans was the most that the Russian government would allow.[125]

The Germans made their plans with their customary care. Rebeur-Paschwitz was in Berlin for a meeting at the Admiralstab on 4 September and reported that the repairs to the hull of *Goeben* made with caissons were very incomplete, but that it would be very difficult to tow the Russian floating dock from Nikolaiev to Cospoli, which was also under increasing air attack. The best solution would be for *Goeben* to go into dry dock at Sebastopol at the end of October when *Volya* would be in service. The Germans realized that after manning *Volya* there would be no men left for the two older battleships. This was a dilemma, for Kapitän zur See von

Trotha, Chief of Staff to the commander of the High Seas Fleet, admitted that they could not round up any more men for the Black Sea.[126] To avoid possible resistance or sabotage when the time came to seize the ships, the German navy and Foreign Office arranged for a special Russian commissar to be on hand in Sebastopol to assure the Russian crews that the government in Moscow consented to the Germans taking the ships into custody. This plan fell through when the Germans discovered that the commissar would not be able to reach Sebastopol in time, but the Soviet ambassador in Berlin provided Hopman with a written document giving him full powers to take over the ships. The actual takeover went smoothly on 1 October and approximately 200 German naval personnel assumed control of *Volya*, the oil-burning destroyers *Bezpokoini*, *Derski*, *Pospyeshni* and *Puilki*, the coal-burning torpedo-boats *Zhivoi* and *Zharki*, and the auxiliary cruiser *Trajan*. These were all ships which had returned from Novorossisk under the Russian flag in June. The Germans expected to commission *Volya* and the two torpedo-boats within the next few days.[127] *Volya* was not actually put into service until 15 October when her crew came up to full strength. German sailors and Russian workers munitioned the ship and gave her the first thorough cleaning in a long time but, as far as making the dreadnought battle ready, the German personnel not surprisingly had the greatest difficulty with the thoroughly unfamiliar equipment. The three destroyers and a torpedo-boat would not be ready for another month, while another destroyer and four torpedo-boats would require three months.[128] The Germans by this date did not even have a month, but a little over a fortnight before Turkey dropped out of the war, opening the Dardanelles to superior Allied forces.

The commissioning of the *Volya* and the sight of this powerful dreadnought under the German naval ensign was a hollow triumph. By this time Bulgaria had been knocked out of the war and Turkey was wavering, raising the unpleasant question of what would happen to the Mittelmeer-division should the straits be opened to the overwhelmingly superior Allied fleets. The Germans were now embarrassed by the fiction that *Goeben* was a Turkish ship for, in case of a special peace between Turkey and the Entente, the latter might legitimately demand surrender of the ship. The Seekriegs-leitung intended *Goeben* to proceed to Sebastopol to continue the fight and Prince Max of Baden, now Chancellor, agreed that the somewhat specious argument should be given to the Turks that the Germans were preserving the ship for them until after the war and preventing it from falling into the hands of the British.[129]

These plans were, however, far removed from reality if the Turks dropped out of the war and opened the Straits to warships of the Entente, because Sebastopol was ill prepared to resist an assault from the sea. The Germans even had to give up their efforts to put the Russian submarines into service because of the long repair time required and lack of sufficient personnel. The Germans now realized that the Entente would appear in overwhelming strength in the Black Sea and should they capture the Russian ships the Germans as 'custodians' would find it difficult to evade Russian demands for compensation. Ironically, the Germans were now trapped by the very supplementary treaty they had been so anxious to extort from the Russians just two months before. It was a classic example of someone hoisted on their own petard and the Admiralstab recommended getting the ships back to the Russians as quickly as possible.[130]

The Germans faced increasingly unpleasant choices in the Black Sea, for in the armistice negotiations between the British and the Turks at Mudros the British made specific demands about the *Goeben*, notably about disarming the ship and landing the German crew. Rebeur-Paschwitz, with *Goeben* still suffering from open leaks, was indeed ready to hoist his flag on *Volya* and continue resistance at Sebastopol. The Seekriegsleitung was reluctant, however, to relinquish *Goeben* which it considered a German ship and necessary for the continuation of the war in the Black Sea, and proposed that Rebeur-Paschwitz should give up his command of the Turkish fleet, raise the German flag once again in *Goeben* and proceed to Sebastopol.[131] In the end, all this manœuvring was useless once the Turks had concluded an armistice at Mudros on 30 October and Usedom and the Sonderkommando, on Turkish orders and as a part of the terms, had to evacuate the Dardanelles. The Germans finally agreed to turn *Goeben* over to the Turks, largely to safeguard the evacuation of German forces or subjects from the Ottoman Empire. They also prepared to return the former Russian ships.[132] With British forces beginning to sweep the Dardanelles, and with the Allied fleet expected off Constantinople in a day or so, the Germans turned over *Goeben* and the Constantinople U-boats to the Turks on the afternoon of 2 November. For the first time the battle cruiser really was Turkish. With great irony, it was now the turn of the Turkish Minister of Finance to baulk at buying a costly ship which Turkey was likely to neither need nor afford in the immediate future, and the transfer was treated purely as a change of command with the final settlement left open. *Goeben* was treated by the Allies as a Turkish ship and in mid-December under the Turkish and white flag towed from her old anchorage at Stenia to the Gulf of Ismid where she was interned.[133] The old battle cruiser, known as *Yavuz* in Turkish service, was extraordinarily long lived and not broken up until the 1970s.

The Germans now gave up all intention of continuing an offensive naval war in the Black Sea in the interest of securing the evacuation of German subjects from Turkey. Hopman wanted to keep a few Russian ships, such as *Volya*, temporarily in service since the batteries defending Sebastopol were inadequate. He intended to turn the remainder of the Russian ships over to a mixed commission of former Russian officers. The armistice of 11 November concluded on the far off western front also ended these plans, for Article 29 specified that the former Russian ships in the Black Sea were not to be given to either Russia or the Ukraine but rather turned over to the forces of the Entente. The Allied Armistice Commission, however, took cognizance of the Russo-German treaty obligating the Germans to return the ships on conclusion of peace, and the Admiralstab was allowed to order the ships to be turned over to a mixed Russian–Ukrainian commission or any other official body in Sebastopol. In the end the Germans gave the ships to a Ukrainian watch commission (Wachkommando) and turned another five torpedo-boats directly over to the Entente.[134] The Allied fleets finally reached Sebastopol in mid-December.

The odyssey of the Russian Black Sea Fleet was not yet over. There were another two years of civil war and foreign intervention beyond the scope of this book and eventually *Volya* and a remnant of the ships under White Russian control proceeded to Bizerte in 1920, where they were interned and finally broken up by the French. Some of the big guns of *Volya* even wound up being used by the Germans for the defence of Guernsey during the Second World War. The Russian Black Sea Fleet was never the menace that the Allies assumed it would be. The Germans could not put more than one dreadnought and a handful of destroyers and torpedo-boats into service. Even then the dreadnought was to be used primarily for defensive purposes as a floating battery at the Dardanelles, and the *Volya* was not yet worked up when the war ended and was probably far from an efficient unit. This, of course, could have changed if the war lasted long enough. The Germans might have found far more realistic uses for those powerful Russian destroyers, and indeed Rebeur-Paschwitz had thought of using them for a raid to overwhelm the less powerful Allied destroyers on patrol off the Dardanelles. The Allies certainly had more trouble matching destroyers than battleships because of the demands of the anti-submarine war. But even here the Germans succeeded in putting only a few destroyers in service and it would have been a month or two after the Armistice before they would have had enough to consider a raid. The Allies, while aware that the Germans might have had trouble manning the ships, grossly underestimated their difficulties. To paraphrase the famous words of Mahan about the Napoleonic wars, those far distant rusty, dirty and neglected ships at Sebastopol about which the Allies knew little, were all that stood between them and complete peace of mind that they had unchallenged supremacy in surface ships in the Mediterranean.

The Collapse of the Central Powers

The concern over the Russian Black Sea Fleet, German domination of the Black Sea and the limited Austrian counteroffensive in Albania in August 1918 all tended to obscure the fact that the tide of the war had definitely turned against the Central Powers. The Allies on the western front were advancing steadily and in mid-September the collapse of Germany's Allies began. This collapse seemed surprisingly sudden to the naval leaders in the Mediterranean who had been preoccupied with their own affairs, seemingly in isolation, and who traditionally felt neglected by the authorities at home. In Palestine, Allenby had been forced to divert troops to help meet the German offensive on the western front earlier in the year but was able to resume his offensive with the Battle of Megiddo beginning 19 September which led to a Turkish defeat, the capture of Damascus on 1 October and Homs on 16 October, while in Mesopotamia British forces continued their successful advance up the Tigris. The Turks were forced to conclude an armistice at Mudros on 30 October. In the Balkans, the Allied commander, General Franchet d'Esperey, began his attack against the Bulgarians on 14 September and the latter were forced to conclude an armistice on the 29th.

The Bulgarian rout led to action in the Adriatic where Franchet d'Esperey anticipated that the enemy forces in the Balkans would be forced to rely on Durazzo for supplies and asked for some naval action to put the port out of action as an enemy base. Durazzo, however, was in the Italian zone and Gauchet advised Franchet d'Esperey to ask the Minister of War and the Allied Naval Council or Supreme War Council to put pressure on Italy to either undertake the operation herself or let the others do it. Clemenceau reacted immediately, terming the operation urgent and asking the Italians to either do it themselves or let the French act. Gauchet, however, would have had trouble acting alone because of the old problem – his lack of destroyers, sweepers and trawlers. He would have to disorganize the French convoy services and ask the British for light craft drawn from the large number they had on the Otranto barrage. Furthermore, a bombardment would have only a morale effect, and they would have to institute a tight blockade of Durazzo to cut off supplies. This would, in turn, require supporting vessels (possibly the 2nd Division of the 1ère Escadre) as well as armoured cruisers and the use of Valona as a base.[135] All of these actions would involve the French in areas where the Italians were very sensitive.

The Italians also had their eyes on Durazzo but, to date, had done nothing much about the place. They had considered a number of plans since the end of July for a naval attack on Durazzo, or possibly Antivari, but the plans ran into the same old problem which had inhibited Italian action in the Adriatic throughout the war. The probable risks were not justified by the possible gains.[136]

The French request for action against Durazzo put Revel on the spot. Orlando gave him Clemenceau's telegram on the evening of the 26th and passed on the word by telephone that either they had to do it or let the French act, that no other way was possible and he left the final choice to Revel. In case Revel did not believe that they could adopt one or the other solution, they would have to assemble an immediate Council of War (Consiglio di Guerra). Revel decided that he would have to act in spite of the risk and ordered Cusani to prepare plans for a bombardment by the Pisa division of large armoured cruisers. The action was to be rapid and intensive and co-ordinated with air raids conducted with maximum effort. There was no doubt as to what decided Revel: he openly admitted that it would be most onerous if a French naval force entered the Adriatic to carry out the operation.[137]

Revel left Rome to take charge of preparations for the operation the evening of the 28th after telling Orlando that, in addition to a naval bombardment, Durazzo ought to be attacked by land. He told the French that after a preparatory bombardment he intended to sweep a channel to allow destroyers to actually enter Durazzo harbour to destroy magazines, lighters and pontoons at closer range. The Italian navy's desire for a land attack on Durazzo to follow the naval bombardment had political as well as military implications. As Capitano di vascello Sechi, head of the Operations

Division of the Stato Maggiore, explained to a friend, it would be disastrous
with the Balkan front broken open for French or, even worse, Greek troops
to appear as liberators in Albania instead of the Italians.[138]

Commodore Kelly immediately offered to co-operate with all the forces
under his command, including the American submarine chasers. The
Durazzo operation therefore became a true international venture with 5
British light cruisers, 14 British and 2 Australian destroyers, and 11
American submarine chasers under Captain Nelson joining the Italian
forces. This was the closest thing to a fleet action that American naval forces
participated in during the First World War. Revel delayed the operation
until 2 October to enable the dreadnought *Dante Alighieri* to arrive from
Taranto. Revel was in the *Dante* but did not fly his flag. The big
dreadnought flew the flag of Rear-Admiral Mola and escorted by seven
Italian destroyers and flotilla leaders formed one of three groups serving as
advanced covering forces ordered to engage any Austrian vessels coming
out of Cattaro. The other covering forces were a group of three Nibbio
scouts, and the cruisers *Glasgow*, *Gloucester* and *Marsala*, escorted by four
British and Australian destroyers. There were also seven to eight British,
French and Italian submarines on either their normal or extra patrols off the
Austrian bases. Revel ordered the Italian forces at Venice to be ready to
torpedo any large Austrian ships coming out of Pola. The actual force
bombarding Durazzo consisted of the large armoured cruisers *San Giorgio*
(flying the flag of Rear-Admiral Palladini), *San Marco* and *Pisa*, preceded by
four British destroyers fitted as minesweepers, and escorted by four British
destroyers and eight Italian torpedo-boats. This first bombarding group
was followed by a second bombarding group consisting of the British light
cruisers *Lowestoft*, *Dartmouth* and *Weymouth* escorted by four British
destroyers. The American submarine chasers acted as a screen for the
bombarding cruisers and patrolled north and south of the bombarding area.
There were also four to six Mas boats on patrol. British and Italian aircraft
carried out a series of raids throughout the day. This was a formidable force
to employ against a miserable third-rate Albanian harbour which had
rudimentary facilities at best. Unfortunately, Revel reduced the original
scope of the operation by cancelling the plan for destroyers to push into the
port itself to destroy all floating material, while cruisers engaged the
Austrian shore batteries. Revel ordered instead that no unnecessary risks
were to be run 'as any slight loss on the part of the Allies would be claimed
as an enemy victory with corresponding morale effect'. Kelly did not agree
since the principal risks from mines and torpedoes remained the same, and
Calthorpe thought that the operation lost much of its value from the Italian
decision not to press home the attack.[139]

The bombardment of Durazzo on 2 October was the last major action in
the Adriatic during the war and, somewhat ironically, the AOK had
actually ordered its evacuation on 28 September. The Allied action was, in
many ways, using the proverbial hammer to swat a fly for that morning
only the older Austrian destroyers *Dinara*, *Scharfschütze* and the torpedo-
boat Tb87 were in port, along with the steamers *Graz*, *Herzegovina* and
Stambul, and the hospital ship *Baron Call*. The Austrian submarines U29 and

U31 were on patrol in the area. *Baron Call* came out at the beginning of the action and was stopped and inspected by British destroyers but eventually allowed to proceed. Korvettenkapitän Heinrich Pauer, senior Austrian naval officer at Durazzo, kept the three small Austrian warships dodging about in the bay close to land and they escaped with only minor damage, and also evaded torpedo attacks by the Mas boats. The Pisas delivered their long-range bombardment followed by the British cruisers, and during the latter's bombarding run Lieutenant Hermann Rigele in U31 managed to torpedo the *Weymouth*, blowing off the cruiser's stern and killing four men. In Durazzo the *Stambul* was burnt out and sunk; the other pair of steamers escaped with minor damage. There were a number of casualties on shore and several houses were destroyed and considerable lowering of morale followed. U29 attempted to get into position for a torpedo attack but was frustrated by the screening forces and subjected to heavy depth-charge attack. For a long time after the war, the Americans were convinced that the submarine chasers had sunk two submarines that day. They did not. The Austrians, for their part, erroneously thought that the damaged cruiser had sunk.[140]

The Austrians were lucky once again in this final action of the k.u.k. Kriegsmarine, but they realized that stationing light craft at Durazzo would lead to their certain loss in the future. Kelly considered the results of the operation to be 'entirely satisfactory' and thought that grave damage had been done and enormous disorganization caused to an important transport base. Calthorpe did not agree and his Assistant Chief of Staff, Lieutenant-Commander Godfrey, was more scathing:

> A close inshore action, with the consequent possibility of doing material damage to enemy ships and works, would have justified the immobilisation of the *Weymouth* for six months, but to risk mine and submarine merely for the sake of a bombardment at 12,000 yards' range seems extremely futile, especially as we know how ineffectual these long range bombardments are.

As for rewards, aside from acknowledging any individual acts of gallantry, 'the less said about the operation as an operation the better'.[141] Commander Train, relatively sympathetic towards the Italians as usual, had another perspective. The Italians regarded the operation as having been instigated by the French as 'purely a political move to embarrass them', and since the military situation dictated an early evacuation of Durazzo by the Austrians with an inevitable occupation by the Italians, 'to have the port partially destroyed when the Italians arrived, would be, according to the Italians, secret satisfaction to the French'.[142]

The British were aware at the end of September that the situation was about to change in the eastern Mediterranean as well, and finally decided to send a dreadnought to the Aegean. HMS *Superb* was due to leave Britain on 5 October. *Superb* was at first to replace either *Agamemnon* or *Lord Nelson*, but the British decided to leave both in commission for the time being. This would mean there were three British battleships at Mudros, altering the balance *vis-à-vis* the French. The British were also interested in a very different type of warship and on 30 September the British naval attaché in Rome asked Capitano di vascello Sechi of the Stato Maggiore for some Mas boats to be placed under the command of the British admiral at Mudros, possibly led by Lieutenant Gravina, described by Larking as a bold officer well suited to lead a raid on the Bosphorus for the purpose of torpedoing *Goeben*. Revel ordered Sechi to confer directly with Ciano and Gravina, the Mas flotilla leaders, but the subject seems to have dropped from sight, probably being overtaken by events.[143]

Once Bulgaria had concluded an armistice, the inevitable question was: how soon would Turkey follow? Wemyss assumed that there would then be nothing to stop an Allied squadron passing through the Dardanelles, but he wondered what they would meet in the Marmara for they did not know the state of the ships in German hands in the Black Sea. Wemyss could not 'contemplate with equanimity the Allied forces proceeding into those waters under the command of a French Admiral' and Lloyd George agreed with him. The First Sea Lord therefore sent a private telegram to Calthorpe telling him to be ready to leave Malta at short notice for the Aegean where he could hoist his flag in a battleship if he thought it necessary. In order to ensure that the British were properly represented, Wemyss approached Beatty about sending additional dreadnoughts. Calthorpe left Malta on 8 October for Mudros in the light cruiser *Foresight*, but asked for a clarification of his position in regard to Vice-Admiral Amet. Would he take over executive command of the Allied squadron in the Aegean from Amet, or should he deal only with operations connected with landing troops or arising out of a Turkish request for an armistice?[144] Rear-Admiral Hope raised the subject at a conference of naval representatives at Versailles on 10 October and proposed the same arrangements for naval forces as for the military, with the British admiral acting generally under the command of the French C.-in-C. in the Mediterranean. The French objected, the Italians supported the British and the Americans, with no concern in the matter, said nothing. Wemyss put the case to the Cabinet in London. The new operations in the Aegean were likely to include landing troops and stores at subsidiary bases between Salonika and Gallipoli and eventually passage of the fleet through the Dardanelles into the Marmara, occupation of Constantinople and operations in the Black Sea. The British had already commanded the naval portion of the Dardanelles campaign and the arrangements had not conflicted with the French supreme command in the Mediterranean. Thus while the French were concerned with the principal enemy fleet in the Mediterranean, the Austrian, there was no reason why the British should not command in waters remote from the Austrian fleet. The army destined for land operations against Turkey in Europe was mainly British, under a British general who was, in turn, under the supreme authority of a French general officer-commanding-in-chief, and the British naval forces co-operating with these operations would also be mainly British. The dreadnought *Temeraire* had been ordered to follow *Superb* to the Aegean, making two British dreadnoughts and two pre-dreadnoughts at Mudros compared with six French pre-dreadnoughts in the Aegean squadron. Wemyss claimed that now, counting auxiliaries, probably 75 per cent of the naval forces in the Aegean operations would be British. If command at sea in those waters was put into the hands of a non-British admiral, Wemyss claimed that the 'uninstructed public' could say that the Gallipoli operations in 1915 had failed under British command and it was necessary to entrust the duty to another nation. But the war against Turkey had been carried out almost entirely by Britain at the Dardenelles, Egypt, Mesopotamia and Palestine. Wemyss ended with a nationalistic argument:

> Finally, it is in no boastful spirit that I affirm that it may confidently be expected that such operations are far more likely to be brought to a successful issue under the command of a British, rather than of a French Admiral. Throughout the War the British Navy has been increasing in strength, in confidence, and in experience, whilst the French Fleet has been doing exactly the opposite. One cannot contemplate with equanimity the possibility of an Allied Naval Force appearing off Constantinople under the command of any but a British Admiral. Efficiency requires such a step, prestige requires such a step, and the political aspects after the war require such a step.[145]

Wemyss's comments about the French navy were not totally fair regarding smaller craft, particularly those hard-working but now thoroughly worn destroyers. What he presumably meant was, whereas the Grand Fleet had the experience of Jutland and numerous exercises and sweeps at sea, the major French battle fleet had been relatively inactive. Indeed this had also worried Gauchet who was quite conscious of the difficulties of keeping the big ships efficient given the shortage of coal. Wemyss's reasoning carried the day and Lloyd George incorporated many of his arguments in a personal letter to Clemenceau, couching them naturally in more diplomatic language. The Prime Minister wrote:

> I do not see how I could possibly justify to the people of the British Empire that at the moment when the final attack on Turkey was to be delivered, the command of the Naval forces which are overwhelmingly British, in a theatre of war associated with some of the most desperate and heroic fighting by troops from nearly every part of the British Empire, should be handed over to a French Admiral as well.

This question led to what Lloyd George described as 'the only real unpleasantness I ever had with Clemenceau'.[146]

While the British were taking steps to solidify their position in the Aegean, the French were doing the same in regard to Syria and Lebanon. When the capture of Beirut became imminent the French government decided to make as large a naval demonstration as their forces allowed at the moment Allenby's troops entered the city to compensate for the feeble number of French troops with the Allied army and to show the population its interest and naval power. Leygues ordered Gauchet to give the appropriate instructions to Rear-Admiral Varney, commanding the French Syrian Division, and send him the temporary reinforcements necessary for the operation. It was essential that large ships took part in the demonstration. Leygues no doubt had in mind big armoured cruisers with lots of smoke stacks. However, events were moving very rapidly and the first French ships to enter Beirut harbour on 6 October were the small destroyers *Arbalète* and *Coutelas*, while Varney arrived the next day in the yacht *Ariane* to meet a suitably joyous reception. The French quickly began to plan for a landing at Alexandretta, but it was not until after the armistice with Turkey that *Coutelas* landed a small detachment of French and British sailors there on 9 November.[147]

The Italians were also anxious to show the flag in the eastern Mediterranean where their sole representative, the cruiser *Piemonte*, had too small a crew to participate in landing expeditions and Del Bono thought of sending a second-class battleship to the Aegean, preferably flying an admiral's flag.[148] The question was naturally linked to Italian claims in Asia Minor and the French were suspicious that the Italians were seeking to profit from Anglo-French victories in Syria and Macedonia to prepare an independent expedition without the knowledge of their Allies with the objective of securing portions of Turkish territory. The whole issue bristled with potential difficulties which the British were well aware of and wanted to avoid.[149] Revel offered the British the light battleships *Roma* and *Vittorio Emanuele*, but Calthorpe had strong technical objections against their presence in any final operations against Turkey or following an armistice. Mudros was becoming very overcrowded as an anchorage and the Italian battleships had not worked in conjunction with the British and French squadrons and would hardly be a source of strength. There was also the problem of the supply of coal. The British would, if the Italian flag had to be represented, much prefer Mas boats which would indeed be useful either at Constantinople or later in the Black Sea. As Larking's recent request to the Italians about them demonstrated, those familiar with the Mas operations had a genuine respect for them but, of course, the potent little craft did not make the impression a big battleship would and lacked large crews to participate and show the flag in landing operations. According to the British ambassador in Rome, Revel was hurt that apparently he had been purposely left out of the arrangements for the Aegean and, since he had recently been so amenable on the question of the admiralissimo, Rodd urged that Italy should not be entirely forgotten in any naval arrangement. Rodd cabled: 'We have here to do our best to maintain unity and cannot afford to disregard feeling of national pride which seems involved.' In the end and for purely diplomatic reasons, certainly not naval necessity, the Italian battleships joined the Allies in the Aegean.[150]

With the scent of victory in the air the latent competition between the Allies was breaking out into the open. This was notable in the Adriatic where General Ferrero refused to supply a Serbian detachment pursuing the Austrians along with the French in northern Albania, a territory where the Italians claimed special interests. There would be bitter rivalry between the French and the Italians in the Adriatic immediately after the war.[151]

Anglo-French relations were also exacerbated in the Aegean. The friction between the French and Italians had been a constant theme throughout the war, but that between the British and French, at least as far as the navies were concerned, had been muted for both sides in the Mediterranean had tended to work hard to avoid trouble and smooth over or obscure difficulties. This ended in the closing days of the war and there was something close to an open break. The arrival of Calthorpe at Mudros on 11 October signalled the start of the trouble. Calthorpe told Amet that he supposed their respective admiralties had reached agreement on the subject of command but, in the absence of orders from home, he would regard himself as being on a yacht, that is, Amet would direct operations in case of an enemy sortie. Paris sent precise instructions on the 15th. According to the agreement in force Amet would continue to command the Allied squadrons and remained responsible for leading them against enemy naval forces. Calthorpe would directly command British naval forces in the Aegean and would exercise the power of SNO at Mudros and settle all movements of ships other than checking Turkish–German forces. Gauchet, as Allied C.-in-C. retained the higher direction of operations in the eastern Mediterranean and had full liberty to proceed to the Aegean and exercise full prerogatives as commander-in-chief.[152] That assertion may have been a strong hint from the minister to Gauchet to go east.

This was exactly the situation that the British wanted to change with the request from Lloyd George to Clemenceau on 15 October to give Calthorpe full command in the Aegean. Lord Derby caught Clemenceau with the letter at a bad moment just as the Premier was leaving for the front and he 'did not take it very well'. Clemenceau said that it would be difficult to explain to the country that the French command had been done away with in the Mediterranean. Derby replied that it would be easier for Clemenceau to explain this than for Lloyd George to explain that the British fleet 'with its enormous superiority' had been given over to the command of a French admiral. Clemenceau claimed that the French Cabinet would have to consider the matter and Derby expected he would give way in the end, although there would be violent opposition from the Minister of Marine and other members of the government.[153] Derby was correct in his assumption. De Bon, presumably Leygues and diplomats like Barrère had been strongly opposed to Jellicoe as admiralissimo, whereas Clemenceau had not exhibited any strong opposition.

Clemenceau replied to Lloyd George's request on the 21st in what Derby termed 'a disagreeably worded document' ending 'in a blank refusal'. The Premier claimed superiority of numbers had never been the determining factor in the selection of command and the French had received their rights in the Mediterranean by past agreements. He had conceded to British command of the military operations in the Aegean (that is, Milne's advance on Constantinople) and now they wanted command of the naval side, which would eliminate the French from all military action in the Levant. If the British had carried the greater burden in Gallipoli, Mesopotamia and Palestine, the consequence was to weaken the British effort on the western front and leave the major burden in Macedonia to the French. Without belittling Allenby's victories, it was nevertheless Franchet d'Esperey's efforts which had forced Bulgaria to capitulate and had produced the present desperate situation in Turkey. If the British had a privileged position in the regions connecting Egypt and India, the French, as Turkey's principal creditor, had the greater interest at Constantinople. If Clemenceau were to put both military and naval operations against Constantinople under British control his government would be put in an indefensible position with French public opinion. He therefore could not make the sacrifice. The French ambassadors in London and Rome received copies of this exchange and Barrère cheered Clemenceau on: 'Without Foch the Allies would still be in their trenches.'[154]

The situation grew worse when the Turkish government applied for an armistice. Shortly after the Bulgarian collapse the Cabinet of Enver Pasha resigned and was replaced by a government led by Izzet Pasha. On 14 October the Turks asked for an armistice and sent their most important British prisoner, General Townshend, the former defender of Kut, who arrived at Mudros on the 20th with a Turkish delegation to begin talks with Calthorpe. The French insisted, however, that the Allies had already agreed on a draft of peace terms for Turkey at a conference in Paris at the beginning of October and that Franchet d'Esperey or Gauchet ought to be the ones to negotiate. Pichon, according to Derby, was very annoyed and took the line that they had no right to alter the terms of a Turkish Armistice agreed on at Versailles without reference to the French. This, coming on top of the request for a British admiralissimo, made things 'rather awkward'.[155]

Lloyd George answered Clemenceau on the 25th, claiming that the British were not proposing to transfer a command which had hitherto been in the hands of a French admiral to a British admiral, but merely were asking to continue the arrangement whereby a British admiral was in command of the Aegean subject to the control of the Allied C.-in-C. in the Mediterranean – a Frenchman. As for the respective shares of the British and French armies in the defeat of Turkey, Lloyd George admitted that it was difficult to make estimates for the results on all fronts were interrelated, but the British navy had by far the larger share of the defence of Allied communications by sea and even of the Atlantic shore of France. Franchet d'Esperey's successes against Bulgaria had been due to British, Italian, Serbian and Greek, as well as French efforts. The British had no desire to exercise a dominating or preponderant influence at Constantinople, and Lloyd George could not see why Clemenceau wished to deprive them of a naval command that they had exercised ever since 1915 in order that a French admiral might be placed in control of an expedition three-quarters of which was British in matériel and personnel. British public opinion would never tolerate relinquishing naval command in that theatre.[156]

Calthorpe withdrew sixteen destroyers from the Otranto barrage on 18 October in order to be ready for all eventualities in the Aegean, and they were followed by twenty-four trawlers, five divisions of drifters and all the usable motor launches. This, in the words of the American naval attaché in Rome, 'caused the fur to fly down at the Ministry of Marine for several days' for the Italians had not been consulted in advance and there was little left in the Adriatic except the light cruisers and a few destroyers and submarines at Brindisi. The British had then accepted the Italian battleships in the Aegean partially to smooth things over.[157] Train's interpretation was not quite correct. The Italians had anticipated the British move a few days before it took place. Wemyss had hinted at it and the Italian naval attaché in London had tried unsuccessfully to head it off. The Stato Maggiore actually prepared a memorandum on the subject for their attachés in London and Paris and apparently intended to present it at the next session of the Allied Naval Council, but the paper is endorsed as not having been transmitted.[158] Once again the Stato Maggiore's plans were overtaken by events, for the next time the Allied Naval Council met at the end of October it was engaged for the most part in discussing peace terms for Austria-Hungary and Germany.

The British naval forces in the Aegean were to support Milne's advance on land towards Constantinople, including the transport by sea of approximately 5,000 men from Stavros to Dedeagatch. With the arrival of the dreadnoughts *Superb* and *Temeraire*, as well as the sizeable number of destroyers, trawlers and drifters, there could be no doubt who had the preponderant naval force. According to Captain Chetwode, commander of the destroyer flotilla from Brindisi, Mudros was 'chock full of ships and they keep arriving every ten minutes'. He thought 'the whole thing is political . . . the Dardanelles will be open some time and all the different nations want to have more ships there than the other fellow'.[159] No one had demonstrated this more clearly than the British. Seapower was inherently mobile and they had used it when and where they considered it necessary and, in this case, with little regard for their allies. The British had only consented to an alteration of the 1915 arrangement giving them command in the Aegean when a momentary embarrassment led to the French having the preponderant surface force. The British had taken back that preponderance ending what was for them an unnatural situation and they could now safely ignore Amet and the French.

Gauchet finally decided on the 24th to leave for Salonika, for he now considered it indispensible for the C.-in-C. of the Allied naval forces to be in direct contact with the C.-in-C. of the Allied armies in the east, that is, Franchet d'Esperey. Gauchet intended to proceed to Corinth via destroyer and hoist his flag in the armoured cruiser *Jules Michelet* while his flagship *Provence* waited for sufficient escorts to follow him. To the very end the French were plagued by a lack of destroyers. The Aegean was now likely to become even more crowded with ships and admirals.[160] Before Gauchet could depart, the negotiations with the Turks grew serious and Reouf Bey, the new Minister of Marine, and two other negotiators arrived at Mudros and talks began on board the *Agamemnon* the morning of the 27th. On the 26th Paris ordered Amet to concert with Calthorpe over the negotiations – Gauchet thought both were acting as his delegates – and negotiate on the basis of the terms agreed upon by the Allies in Paris. However, Amet was to conclude nothing definite without reference to Paris.[161] Calthorpe had other ideas. He informed Amet that he had been authorized by the British government to arrange the terms of an armistice and the Turkish delegates, as their credentials signed by the Grand Vizier clearly indicated, were accredited to negotiate only with the British. When Amet repeated his desire to share in the negotiations the next day, Calthorpe continued to refuse. He cabled London: 'If he were permitted to do so I am sure it would create difficulty and set back the prospect of an armistice.'[162] There was substantial justice to this, for Amet had been ordered to conclude nothing without approval from Paris.

Leygues fully endorsed the position taken by Amet. There was no agreement between the British, French and Italian governments giving the British admiral the right to negotiate by himself and Calthorpe should wait until the British and French governments were in agreement before concluding an armistice. Neither a barrage of telegrams from Gauchet nor letters from Amet stopped Calthorpe, although Lieutenant-Commander Godfrey described Amet as 'almost battening [sic] on the door of the conference room in the *Agamemnon*'. Calthorpe concluded an armistice with the Turkish delegates on 30 October with hostilities to cease at noon on the 31st. The Allies thrashed out the issue at a conference in Paris to discuss peace terms. The French at first wanted the French and Italian admirals to sign the armistice as well as Calthorpe, but in the end both Sonnino and Clemenceau accepted the *fait accompli*. They had many other things to worry about. Leygues ordered Gauchet to abstain from further measures with Calthorpe. It was just in time. Calthorpe reported receiving 'a somewhat intemperate telegram' from Gauchet about not allowing Amet to be present at the negotiations, but explained that, had he done so, Amet himself had admitted that decisions on every point would have had to be transmitted to Paris for approval. Calthorpe told Gauchet he had taken the course that he considered it was his duty to adopt and regretted that Gauchet considered it to be incorrect. The prompt reply came from the Admiralty: 'You acted quite rightly.'[163]

Clemenceau knew how to accept a *fait accompli*, he had after all been willing to accept Jellicoe as admiralissimo earlier in the year, and Gauchet himself began looking forward to operations in the Black Sea after establishing a base for the French Aegean force at Constantinople, reinforcing it if necessary, opening communications with Constanza and Batum, and preparing to destroy any German ships which might have taken refuge in Russian ports. Leygues authorized Gauchet to proceed to Salonika if he considered it necessary but, in view of the armistice, doubted that this was the case. Moreover, by this time the impending dissolution of Austria-Hungary and imminent armistice in the Adriatic ought to occupy his attention.[164]

The end of the war was now approaching in the Adriatic where, somewhat ironically, the French had informed the British on 16 October that the mine-net barrage at long last had been completed between a point eight miles from Otranto to the island of Fano. The French did not consider that the minefield in the interval between the net barrage and the Italian coast was deep enough and wanted to extend the mine-net barrage close in to the Italian coast. They had the material on hand to do it quickly. The Admiralty agreed on the 29th but by then it was an academic question.[165]

On 24 October, with Austrian forces in Albania in full retreat and with the Germans seeking an armistice on the western front, General Diaz launched his long-awaited offensive on the Italian front leading to the climactic battle of Vittorio Veneto. For a few days the Austrian forces resisted fiercely, but then began to give way on the 29th and by the night of the 30th–31st there was a general collapse. The Austrians concluded an armistice at the Villa Giusti near Padua on the evening of 3 November. By this time the Dual Monarchy itself was in a state of dissolution, a complex subject far beyond the scope of this book.

The Allied leaders considered the draft drawn up by the Allied Naval Council of the naval terms of an armistice with Austria-Hungary at a meeting in Paris on 30 October. They included the surrender of all submarines completed between 1910 and 1918 to the number of 15, all German submarines in Austrian territorial waters after the Armistice, and all the dreadnoughts, the Radetzkys, 4 Spauns, 9 Tátra-class destroyers, 1 minelayer and 6 Danube monitors – all specified by name. Aircraft were to be immobilized. All remaining ships were to be paid off, disarmed and rendered useless in designated naval bases, and the Allies might occupy Pola. On reading this, Clemenceau commented that they had 'left the breeches of the Kaiser and nothing else!' The Allied leaders at the Supreme War Council later reduced the terms to surrender of 3 battleships and 3 light cruisers, but included 12 torpedo-boats in addition to the monitors and destroyers.[166] It was all somewhat academic for the Habsburg Monarchy had ceased to exist.

With the Empire fragmenting, on 16 October Kaiser Karl issued a manifesto offering to turn it into a federal state. Austrian participation in the submarine war outside the Adriatic ceased on the 17th. The Austrian army continued to retreat from Albania, and Durazzo had been evacuated on the 11th and San Giovanni di Medua on the 23rd. By the 23rd Austrian officers were noting the unhealthy effects of the Kaiser's manifesto on discipline in the fleet with a widespread call for a return home and the formation of national committees.[167] The Allied naval leaders had, of course, only a very imperfect knowledge of what was going on across the Adriatic. Nevertheless, while monitoring wireless traffic on 31 October the British listened in fascination when at 08.50 GMT a signal came in the clear from the flagship *Viribus Unitis* at Pola to all ships ordering them to prepare to hoist the 'Croatian flag' at the main top on receipt of the executive signal. The message was signed 'The Central Committee' and when a ship at sea inquired 'Who is the Central Committee?' the cryptic reply was 'We are'. Throughout the day the British heard signals indicating the assumption of control by Yugoslavs and heard the text of Horthy's farewell message to the fleet followed by an enthusiastic and presumably Slavic wireless operator tagging on 'Hurrah, hurrah, hurrah'. The unnamed British intelligence officer had a sense of history and noted: 'Possibly for the last time in history an Austrian Admiral signed himself with the traditional "K.u.K."', and Commodore Kelly's staff, also aware of the momentous events taking place, copied the intelligence summary for the commodore's private papers before it was circulated to the squadron.[168]

On the orders of the Kaiser, Horthy turned over the fleet and naval property to the South Slav National Council in Agram. All men not of South Slav nationality were free to go home, although Horthy urged those who did not take service with the Yugoslav navy to remain at their posts for the period of transfer. Linienschiffskapitän Janko Vuković de Podkapelski was named provisional Yugoslav fleet commander. At approximately 4.45 p.m. on the 31st Horthy turned over the command, and the red-white-red ensign of the k.u.k. Kriegsmarine was lowered for what all realized was the last time. As Horthy stepped ashore with the old ensign under his arm, the new red-white-blue Yugoslav flag was raised in the twilight and greeted with a 21-gun salute. An Austrian officer recalled that none of them could look, while there was general jubilation among the Slavs. That night the ships were fully illuminated for the first time since the war.[169]

The celebrations were premature for during the night, with practically no watch on the harbour entrance being kept, two Italian officers, Tenente medico (Medical Lieutenant) Raffaele Paolucci and Maggiore del Genio navale (Major of Naval Engineers) Raffaele Rossetti, in rubber suits and guiding a torpedo-like, self-propelled mine known as the 'Mignatta' (leech) penetrated the harbour and attached explosive charges to the hull of the *Viribus Unitis*. The charges exploded and *Viribus Unitis* capsized and sank around dawn. Vuković went down with his ship. It has always been a matter of controversy as to how much the Italians really knew of the situation. The Allies also did not recognize the Yugoslav flag and suspected that the change of flag was a ruse to avoid surrendering the ships.[170] In the long run the new Yugoslav state wound up with only a small portion of the former k.u.k. Kriegsmarine.

The Italians also sank the Austrian Lloyd liner *Wien* (7,376 tons) in the attack that night. The steamer had been used as an accommodation ship by the German U-boat crews but the Germans were no longer there. On 10 October the Germans in Pola learned of the departure of an Austrian armistice commission on which Fregattenkapitän Prince von und zu Liechtenstein was the naval member. The Germans finally realized that the game was over and Commodore Püllen reported on the 19th that, despite the undoubted loyalty of the ruling personalities, the Dual Monarchy would be compelled through internal events to conclude peace. This would probably mean the creation of a South Slav state and the end of the use of Adriatic ports as U-boat bases. On the 24th Püllen recommended that all German U-boats ready for sea should leave for home to avoid their surrender becoming a condition of any armistice. The following day Scheer ordered all U-boats ready for sea to sail with the pretext given to the Austrians that they were on a 'special mission'. They were given the same command which had been transmitted to all German U-boats on the 21st, that is, not to conduct commerce war, although they could continue to attack warships but only by day. Püllen, however, was careful to inform Horthy and Commodore Seitz, now commanding the Austrian Cruiser Flotilla at Cattaro, of the real mission of the U-boats which could hardly be kept secret. German personnel began to evacuate Pola on the 28th while Korvettenkapitän Ackermann and staff sailed from Cattaro in the accommodation ship *Cleopatra* on the 30th.[171] All in all, between the 29th and 31st nine U-boats sailed for home from Pola and three from Cattaro. U34 and UC73 which were on operations also received orders by wireless to head for home. The Germans were concerned over the fate of UC74 operating off the coast of Asia Minor and theorized that as the boat lacked fuel for the long voyage home she would have to be interned in Spain. UC74 did eventually reach Barcelona. The Germans blew up or scuttled seven U-boats off Pola (U73, U47, U65, UB48, UC25, UC34 and UC53) one (UB129) at Fiume, one (UC54) at Trieste and one (U72) off Cattaro.[172] The torpedo-boats A82 and A51 were also scuttled.

The Allies would have liked to intercept and destroy those German U-boats heading for home and Captain Nelson reported on 2 November that he had extra chasers ready to reinforce those on the barrage at the first notice of a German exodus, although Sims gave him the impossible order to use every possible means to discriminate between Austrian and German submarines. These orders were, of course, too late. The Germans had already escaped. The Americans also ordered a new group of submarine chasers due to arrive in European waters to proceed to Gibraltar to institute a hunt at the straits, and Rear-Admiral Grant issued special orders for his patrols and made new dispositions in a vain attempt to catch the Germans.[173] This type of 'submarine hunting' had not been successful during the war and it is not surprising that the Allies sank no submarines. The last German loss in the Mediterranean during the war was U34 which was never heard from again after sailing from Pola on 16 October, but the boat was probably lost in the central Mediterranean between the 19th and the 25th. The U-boats remained as deadly as ever, however, and Oberleutnant zur See Heinrich Kukat in UB50 of the II Mediterranean U-Boat Flotilla after passing through the Straits of Gibraltar torpedoed and sank the British battleship *Britannia* off Cape Trafalgar on 9 November – the last British warship to be sunk during the war.[174] Hostilities in the Mediterranean were over, however, and in the next few days Allied warships steamed into the Adriatic to the different ports which had formerly belonged to the Dual Monarchy in order to ensure the execution of the naval clauses of the Armistice. On 12 November, after extensive sweeping, Calthorpe flying his flag in *Superb* led the combined Allied fleet of 4 British, 2 French, and 1 Italian battleships, 1 Greek armoured cruiser, 6 British cruisers and 18 destroyers through the Dardanelles. On the 13th the Allies anchored off Constantinople. The naval war in the Mediterranean was truly over.

Notes: Chapter 12

1 Gauchet to Leygues, 29 May and 1 June 1918, Leygues to Gauchet, 31 May 1918, SHM, Carton A-29; Gauchet to Ratyé, 31 May and 3 June 1918, PRO, Adm 137/2180.
2 Ratyé to Calthorpe, 4 June 1918, Calthorpe to Admiralty, 12 June 1918, Admiralty to Calthorpe, 13 June 1918, British Minister Athens to Calthorpe, 22 June 1918, Calthorpe to British Minister Athens, 23 June 1918, ibid.; Calthorpe to Admiralty, 10 July 1918 and minutes by Coode, 18 July and Hope, 24 July 1918, ibid., Adm 137/1581; Gauchet to Darrieus, 8 June 1918, SHM, Carton A-29.

3 Dumas Diary, 6, 8, 12 and 20 June 1918, Imperial War Museum, London, Dumas MSS, PP/MCR/96, Reel No. 4.

4 Darrieus to Gauchet, 11 June 1918, SHM, Carton Ed-83; Procès Verbal of Meeting of Allied Admirals at Mudros, 18 June 1918, PRO, Adm 137/1581; Darrieus, 'Etude des problemes de guerre concret posé par l'incorporation à la puissance allemande de la flotte russe de la mer noire', 15 June 1918, ibid.

5 Lambert to Geddes, 22 June 1918, PRO, Adm 116/1604; Lambert to Darrieus, 17 June 1918, ibid., Adm 137/1581.

6 Minutes by Coode, 18 July 1918 and Hope, 22 [?] July 1918, draft of letter by Wemyss to French naval attaché, 24 July 1918, ibid.

7 Dumas Diary, 2 and 29 July, 2 and 8 Aug. 1918, loc. cit. at n. 3, Dumas MSS.

8 Sokol, *Österreich-Ungarns Seekrieg*, pp. 553–63; Ufficio Storico, *Marina italiana*, Vol. 7, ch. 24; Edgar Tomicich, 'Die Versenkung des k.u.k. Schlachtschiffes *Szent István* am 10. Juni 1918', *Marine – Gestern, Heute*, vol. 6, nos 1 and 2 (Mar. and June, 1979). Rizzo's Mas15 is preserved as a relic in the Museo del Vittoriano at the base of the Victor Emmanuel II monument in Rome.

9 ANC, Fourth Meetings, 1st and 2nd Sessions, 11 June 1918, and Conclusion LXXVIII, PRO, Adm 137/836, ff. 439, 448–53.

10 ANC, Fourth Meetings, 2nd Session, 11 June 1918, 3rd Session, 12 June 1918, and Conclusion No. LXXXI, ibid., ff. 439–40, 458–60, 464–70.

11 Sims to Benson, 14 June 1918, NARS, RG 45, QC File, Box 464.

12 Sims to Benson, 10 Jan. 1918, ibid., OD File, Box 308. An interesting and full account of the ocean crossing written after the war is in Nelson to Sims, 16 Dec. 1919, ibid., OD File, Box 310. Details of the craft are in Silverstone, *U.S. Warships of World War I*, pp. 182–4.

13 Alexander Moffat, *Maverick Navy* (Middleton, Conn., 1976), p. 90; Sims, *The Victory at Sea*, ch. 6, appropriately titled 'American College Boys and Subchasers'.

14 Benson to Sims, 18 Apr. 1918, NARS, RG 45, OD File, Box 308; Sims to Admiralty, 17 May 1918, PRO, Adm 137/1577.

15 Calthorpe to Geddes, 5 June 1918, Geddes to Sims, 12 June 1918, ibid., Adm 116/1809; notation by Sims on copy of Geddes's letter in NARS, RG 45, OD File, Box 308; Sims to Niblack, 23 May 1918, ibid., TD File, Box 553.

16 Minute by Coode, 29 May 1918, PRO, Adm 137/1577; Sims to Admiralty, 27 May 1918, NARS, RG 45, OD File, Box 308; Sims to Pringle [Queenstown], 11 May 1918, ibid., OR-3 File, Box 335; Sims to Niblack, 13 Apr., 23 May and 2 July 1918, Sims to Pringle, 16 and 18 May 1918, Sims to Benson, 17 May 1918, ibid., TD File, Box 553.

17 Leigh to Sims, 18 June and 2 July 1918, Nelson to Sims, 16 Dec. 1919, ibid., OD File, Box 310; Extracts from Force Commander's Reports, 22 July 1918, p. 5, ibid., TD File, Box 552.

18 Leigh to Sims, 30 July 1918, Sims to Secretary of the Navy (Opns), General Report, 16 Aug. 1918, Extracts from Force Commander's General Reports, 24 Aug. 1918, ibid.; Nelson to Sims, 24 July 1918, ibid., OD File, Box 309; Sims to Benson, 13 Aug. 1918, ibid., OR-1 File, Box 334.

19 Sims to Secretary of the Navy (Operations), General Report, 10 Aug. 1918, ibid., TD File, Box 552.

20 Loftin to Nelson, 9 Sept. 1918, ibid., OD File, Box 310; Sims to Nelson, 3 Oct. 1918, Nelson to Sims, 21 Oct. 1918, ibid., OD File, Box 309.

21 E. C. Spafford to Nelson, 18 Oct. 1918, Nelson to Sims, 25 Oct. 1918, ibid., OD File, Box 310.

22 Sims to Benson, 7 May 1918, ibid., OD File, Box 308; Sims to Benson, 20

Aug. 1918, ibid., OD File, Box 310; Sims to Benson, 2 Aug. 1918, Benson to Sims, 11 Aug. 1918, Sims to Train, 4 Sept. 1918, ibid., OD File, Box 309.

23 Sims, *The Victory at Sea*, pp. 230–1; Heyssler to Keyes, 21 Dec. 1926 in Halpern (ed.), *The Keyes Papers*, Vol. 2, Doc. 161, p. 198; Nelson to Sims, 16 Dec. 1919, pp. 15–16, NARS, RG 45, OD File, Box 310.

24 Sims to Ratyé, 16 Aug. 1918, Sims to Bayly, 24 Aug. 1918, ibid., TD File, Box 553.

25 Stephenson to Kelly, 14 Aug. 1918, PRO, Adm 137/1579.

26 Benson to Sims, 27 May 1918, Sims to Benson, 10 June 1918, NARS, RG 45, QC File, Box 464; Planning Section, Memorandum No. 37 'Estimate of General Situation in the Mediterranean', 17 June 1918, ibid., TX File, Box 568; Sims to Benson, 11 July 1918, ibid., TX File, Box 567.

27 Sims to Hope, 16 July 1918, ibid., OR-1 File, Box 334; differing Allied attitudes are in ANC, Fifth Meetings, Appendix I, Memoranda Nos 163–174 [11–23 July 1918], PRO, Adm 137/836, ff. 561–6.

28 ANC, Emergency Meeting, 23 July 1918, Conclusion LXXXV, ibid., ff. 567–8; Rothiacob to de Bon, 25 July 1918, SHM, Carton Es-19.

29 Godfrey to Ruck Keene, 31 July 1918, Naval Library, Ministry of Defence, London, Godfrey MSS, Mediterranean Papers (I).

30 Benson to Sims, 1 Aug. 1918, NARS, RG 45, TX File, Box 567; Sims to Train [for Strauss], 3 Aug. 1918, ibid., TX File, Box 572.

31 Train, Report No. T-461, Inspection of the Italian Net Barrage, Straits of Otranto, 15 July 1918, ibid., WX-4 File, Box 750; Train to Sims, 16 July 1918, ibid., TD File, Box 553; Cmdr. T. A. Thompson, Memorandum for Chief of Staff, 26 July 1918, ibid., OR-1 File, Box 334; Sims to Italian Naval Attaché, London, 13 Aug., 1918, ibid., TT File, Box 565.

32 Calthorpe to Admiralty, 17 July 1918, PRO, Adm 137/1579; Allied Conference on Mediterranean Mining, Report of Proceedings, 1st Session, 6 Aug. 1918, ibid., Adm 137/836, f. 576.

33 Grant, *U-Boats Destroyed*, p. 133; Spindler, *Handelskrieg*, Vol. 5, p. 201.

34 Calthorpe to Admiralty, 14 July 1918, minutes by Coode, 26 July and 29 Aug., Fisher, 30 July, Director of Air Division, 1 Aug., Hope, 2 Aug., and Duff, 3 Aug. 1918, Admiralty to Calthorpe, 7 Aug. 1918, PRO, Adm 137/1577.

35 Revel, Schema di istruzioni, 31 July 1918, USM, Cartella 1187.

36 Report of the Allied Conference on Mediterranean Minelaying, Recommendations, 15 Aug. 1918, PRO, Adm 137/836, ff. 573–5. On Italian agreement to the Cape Cavallo–Saseno line see: Revel to Triangi, 16 Aug. 1918, USM, Cartella 1187.

37 Sims to Benson, 21 Aug. 1918, NARS, RG 45, TD File, Box 553; Calthorpe to Admiralty, 15 Aug. 1918, PRO, Adm 137/841.

38 Ratyé to de Bon, n.d., SHM, Carton Es-20.

39 Amet, 'Note sur la garde des Dardanelles', 13 Aug. 1918, Gauchet to Leygues, 20 Aug. 1918 (and enclosures), marginal notes by Leygues [?], 8 Sept. 1918, ibid.

40 Minutes by Dickens, 19 Aug., and Godfrey, 19 Aug. 1918, PRO, Adm 137/2180; Calthorpe to Admiralty, 20 Aug. 1918, ibid., Adm 137/1581.

41 Minutes by Coode, 1 Sept., Hope, 3 and 23 Sept., Duff, 4 Sept., Fremantle, 6 Sept. and Wemyss, 24 Sept. 1918, ibid.

42 Capt. Bryon T. Long, Memorandum for Admiral Sims, 24 Aug. 1918, NARS, RG 45, TT File, Box 565.

43 Sims to Benson, 13 Aug. 1918, ibid., CM File, Box 23; Niblack to Sims, 3

Sept. 1918, ibid., TD File, Box 553; Calthorpe to Geddes, 4 Sept. 1918, PRO, Adm 116/1809.

44 Unsigned Memorandum re Gibraltar–Marseilles Convoys, 5 Oct. 1918, NARS, RG 45, CM File, Box 23; Sims to Benson, 10 Oct. 1918, ibid., TP File, Box 560.

45 Geddes to Calthorpe, 12 Sept. 1918, PRO, Adm 116/1809.

46 Kelly to Admiralty, 24 Aug. 1918, minutes by Coode, 31 Aug., Hope, 2 Sept., Wemyss, 3 Sept., and Geddes, 4 Sept. 1918, ANC, Memorandum No. 187, 'Situation in Albania, with Special Reference to Valona', 2 Sept. 1918, Admiralty to War Office, 2 Sept. 1918, ibid., Adm 137/1578; Sims to Benson, 27 Aug. 1918, Sims to Bliss, 27 Aug. 1918, NARS, RG 45, QC File, Box 464; Leygues to Gauchet, 29 Aug. 1918, SHM, Carton A-29. The military operations are covered in detail in Ufficio Storico dello Stato Maggiore dell'Esercito, *Le Truppe Italiane in Albania (Anni 1914–20 e 1939)* (Rome, 1978), ch. 4.

47 Kelly to Admiralty, 30 Aug. 1918, PRO, Adm 137/1578; Saint Pair to Leygues, 30 Aug. 1918, SHM, Carton Ed-95.

48 Revel to Diaz, 28 Aug. 1918, USM, Cartella 1191; Commando Supremo reply cited in: Anon. [possibly Sechi, Chief of Operations Division], 'Appunti pel Commandante Ruspoli', n. d. [Sept. 1918], USM, Cartella 1192. Ruspoli was head of the Allied Naval Council Bureau in Rome.

49 Delmé Radcliffe to War Office, 4 Sept. 1918, Admiralty [Operations Division, Naval Staff] to War Office, 5 Sept. 1918, Kelly to Calthorpe, 16 Sept. 1918, PRO, Adm 137/1578.

50 Unsigned [probably Benson] Memorandum for the Secretary, 4 Sept. 1918, NARS, RG 45, OR-3 File, Box 335; Daniels to Sims, 4 Sept. 1918, ibid., QC File, Box 464.

51 Sims to Benson, 12 Sept. 1918, ibid.; Sechi to Revel, 10 Sept. 1918, USM, Cartella 1191; ANC Memorandum No. 200 Italy, 'Inferiority of Anti-Submarine Protection Measures in the Mediterranean', 27 Aug. 1918, the revised US plans are in ANC Memorandum No. 203, 'Minelaying Operations, Mediterranean', 11 Sept. 1918, PRO, Adm 137/836, ff. 616–17, 627.

52 Sims to Benson, 12 Sept. 1918, NARS, RG 45, TP File, Box 560.

53 ANC, Fifth Meetings, Report of Proceedings, 1st and 2nd Sessions, 13 Sept. 1918, Conclusion No. LXXXV, PRO, Adm 137/836, ff. 527–9; Salaun to de Bon, n.d. [Sept. 1918], SHM, Carton Es-20. Towards the closing days of the war the Americans accepted the Italian proposal for the Brindisi–Saseno location.

54 De Bon to Gauchet, 20 Sept. 1918, SHM, Carton A-136; US Planning Section Memorandum No. 53, 'Mine Base for Operations in Mediterranean', 23 Sept. 1918 (with endorsement by Sims [28 Sept]), NARS, RG 45, TX File, Box 567; Sims to Benson, 2 Oct. 1918, ibid., TD File, Box 553; de Bon to Sims, 5 Oct. 1918, ibid., TD File, Box 552.

55 Sims to Benson, 15 Sept. 1918, ibid., QC File, Box 464; Sechi to Revel, 10 Sept. 1918, USM, Cartella 1192.

56 Macchi di Cellere to Sonnino, 10 Sept. 1918, Sechi to Sonnino, 13 Sept. 1918, Revel to Sonnino, 25 Sept. 1918, ibid.

57 War Office to Fremantle, 30 Sept. 1918, Memorandum by W. Kirke [Assistant Director of Military Operations], 'Operations against Curzola Island and Sabbioncello Peninsula with a view to Forming Anti-Submarine Barrage across the Adriatic', 29 Sept. 1918, Kirke to Fuller, 30 Sept. 1918, PRO, Adm 137/2708.

58 Revel to Orlando, 7 June 1918, USM, Cartella 1192.
59 Orlando to Imperiali, 6 June 1918, copy and translation in SHM, Carton Es-14.
60 No. G.T.-4788, Geddes, 'Command in the Mediterranean', 8 June 1918, PRO, Adm 137/1576.
61 Rodd to Geddes, 9 June 1918, ibid., Adm 116/1649; Imperiali to Orlando, 10 June 1918, The Sonnino Papers [Microfilm], (54 reels, Ann Arbor, Michigan: University Microfilms), Reel 52.
62 Geddes to Rodd, [telegram and letter], 13 June 1918, PRO, Adm 116/1604.
63 De Bon to Saint Pair, 15 June 1918, SHM, Carton Es-19.
64 Saint Pair to Leygues, 15 June 1918, de Bon to Saint Pair, 18 June 1918, SHM, Carton Es-14.
65 Covering note by Geddes to War Cabinet, 17 June 1918, No. G.T.-4876, Geddes, 'Command in the Mediterranean', 13 June 1918, PRO, Adm 116/1810.
66 Rodd to Geddes, 23 June 1918, Rodd to Foreign Office, 24 June 1918, ibid., Adm 116/1604; Train to Sims, 25 June 1918, NARS, RG 45, TD File, Box 553.
67 Rodd to Geddes, 27 June 1918, PRO, Adm 116/1649; Rodd to Foreign Office, 27 June 1918, and notation by Marriott [?] on Admiralty Docket, 30 June 1918, ibid., Adm 137/1576; Sonnino to Imperiali, 27 June 1918, translation and copy in SHM, Carton Es-14.
68 Geddes to Rodd, 16 July 1918, PRO, Adm 116/1649; Steel to Davis, 16 July 1918, Minute by Geddes, 16 July 1918, House of Lords Record Office, London, Lloyd George MSS, F/18/2/2.
69 Barrère to Pichon, 17 July 1918 (and marginal note), SHM, Carton Es-14; Clemenceau to Barrère, 20 July 1918, MAE, Série Y Internationale, Vol. 78.
70 Daniels to Secretary of State, 25 July 1918, Daniels to Sims, 5 [?] Aug. 1918, NARS, RG 45, OR-3 File, Box 335; Sonnino to Bonin, 3 Aug. 1918, copy and translation in SHM, Carton Es-14.
71 Wemyss to Calthorpe, 3 Aug. 1918, microfilm copy, University of California, Irvine, Wemyss MSS; Geddes to Roosevelt, 3 Aug. 1918, Geddes to Balfour, 3 Aug. 1918, Balfour to Geddes, 5 Aug. 1918, PRO, Adm 116/1649. See also Frank Freidel, *Franklin D. Roosevelt: The Apprenticeship* (Boston, Mass., 1952), pp. 350–1.
72 Geddes to Rodd, 8 Aug. 1918, Adm 116/1649; Freidel, *Roosevelt*, p. 351.
73 Revel to Sonnino, 8 Aug. 1918, Sonnino to Revel, 9 Aug. 1918, Revel to Sonnino, 11 Aug. 1918 (with attached Italian criteria in English and French), USM, Cartella 1192. On Roosevelt in Rome see also: Freidel, *Roosevelt*, pp. 362–3; F. Charles-Roux, *Souvenirs diplomatiques: Rome–Quirinal, Février 1916 – Février 1919* (Paris, 1958), pp. 314–16.
74 Roosevelt to Daniels, 14 Aug. 1918, NARS, RG 45, QC File, Box 464; Freidel, *Roosevelt*, p. 363; Rodd to Geddes, 15 Aug. 1918, Geddes to Rodd, 17 Aug. 1918, PRO, Adm 116/1649.
75 Barrère to Pichon, Nos 1739 and 1745, 16 Aug. 1918, idem, Nos 1766 and 388, 17 Aug. 1918, MAE, Série Y Internationale, Vol. 78.
76 Geddes to Larking, 26 Aug. 1918, Larking to Geddes, 27 Aug. 1918 (with minute by Geddes, 28 Aug.), PRO, Adm 116/1649.
77 Roosevelt to Geddes, 28 Aug. 1918 (two letters), ibid.
78 Jellicoe to W. H. Kelly, 29 Aug. 1918, National Maritime Museum, Greenwich, Kelly MSS, KEL/26.
79 Clemenceau to Jusserand, 28 Aug. 1918, Jusserand to Clemenceau, 30 Aug.

and 1 Sept. 1918, Blanpré to Leygues, 16 July 1918, MAE, Série Y Internationale, Vol. 78.

80 Jusserand to Clemenceau, 6 Sept. 1918, Barrère to Pichon, 9 Sept. 1918, ibid.

81 Freidel, *Roosevelt*, p. 364.

82 Erskine to Foreign Office, 13 Sept. 1918, Geddes to Lloyd George, 17 Sept. 1918, Memorandum by the Admiralty on the Proposal of the Italian Government for the Appointment of an Admiralissimo in the Mediterranean, 17 Sept. 1918, loc. cit. at n. 68, Lloyd George MSS, F/18/2/18.

83 Geddes, Admiralty Memorandum for War Cabinet, 25 Sept. 1918, Memorandum by Secretary, Allied Naval Council, 'The Black Sea Fleets', 24 Sept. 1918, PRO, Adm 116/1771; Geddes to Balfour, 27 Sept. 1918, ibid., Adm 116/1649; Foreign Office to Rodd, 1 Oct. 1918, ibid., Adm 137/1576.

84 Rodd to Revel, 25 Sept. 1918, USM, Cartella 1192; Rodd to Geddes, 2 Oct. 1918, Rodd to Wemyss, 29 Sept. 1918, PRO, Adm 116/1649; Rodd to Foreign Office, 2 Oct. 1918, ibid., Adm 137/1576.

85 Wemyss to Rodd, 3 Oct. 1918, Wemyss to Geddes, 7 Oct. 1918, Geddes to Wemyss, 11 Oct. 1918, ibid., Adm 116/1649.

86 Barrère to Pichon, 30 Sept. and 2 Oct. 1918, Pichon to Barrère, 1 Oct. 1918, MAE, Série Y Internationale, Vol. 78.

87 Wemyss to Geddes, 3 Oct. 1918, PRO, Adm 116/1809; Wemyss to Rodd, 3 Oct. 1918, ibid., Adm 116/1649.

88 Heyssler to Horthy, 27 June 1918, OK/MS VIII-1/1 ex 1918, No. 3622; idem, 14 July 1918, OK/MS VIII-1/9 ex 1918, No. 4074.

89 Kriegstagebuch des Führer der Unterseeboote im Mittelmeer, 6, 10–12, 14, 20, 21 July 1918, NARS, T-1022, Roll 74, PG 62066.

90 Grasshoff, Report of July U-boat activities, 3 Sept. 1918, ibid., Roll 928, PG 76421; Minute by Ackermann added to Kriegstagebuch of UC54, 8 Aug. 1918, ibid., Roll 74, PG 61968.

91 Kriegstagebuch des Befehlshabers der Unterseeboote im Mittelmeer, 11, 23 and 27 Aug. 1918, ibid., PG 62066.

92 Püllen to Admiralstab, 12 July 1918, ibid., Roll 1030, PG 76544; BdU, Tätigkeitsmeldung für den 31 August 1918, ibid., Roll 927, PG 76416; Grasshoff, Report of U-boat War in August, 24 Sept. 1918, ibid., Roll 928, PG 76421.

93 Grasshoff to Scheer, 14 Sept. 1918, ibid., Roll 981, PG 76402; Spindler, *Handelskrieg*, Vol. 5, pp. 204–5, 212. On the origin of group tactics, see Bodo Herzog, *60 Jahre Deutsche UBoote, 1906–1966* (Munich, 1968), pp. 169–71, 173, n. 16.

94 BdU Mittelmeer, 'Tätigkeitsberichts – Stützpunktenangelegenheiten, September', 18 Oct. 1918, NARS, T-1022, Roll 927, PG 76416.

95 BdU Mittelmeer, Kriegstagebuch, 27–29 Sept. 1918, ibid., Roll 74, PG 62066.

96 AOK to Horthy, 3 Aug. 1918, Horthy to AOK and Keil, 9 Aug. 1918, OK/MS VIII-1/1 ex 1918, No. 4211.

97 BdU Mittelmeer, Kriegstagebuch, 3, 8 and 15 Oct. 1918, NARS, T-1022, Roll 74, PG 62066; Admiralstab to Seekriegsleitung, 22 Oct. 1918, ibid., Roll 829, PG 75673.

98 Spindler, *Handelskrieg*, Vol. 5, pp. 364–5; Aichelberg, *Unterseeboote Österreich-Ungarns*, Vol. 2, pp. 492–3.

99 ibid., Vol 1, p. 155, Vol. 2, pp. 440–1 and n. 1; Thomazi, *Guerre navale dans l'Adriatique*, pp. 193–4; Grant, *U-Boats Destroyed*, p. 133; idem, *U-Boat Intelligence*, pp. 165–6; Sokol, *Österreich-Ungarns Seekrieg*, pp. 512, 536–40, 567; Spindler, *Handelskrieg*, Vol. 5, pp. 196–7, 202–3; Thomazi, *Guerre navale*

dans la Méditerranée, pp. 68–9. Figures for sinkings per U-boat day culled from Admiralstab, Statistisches über den Ubootskrieg im Mittelmeer, 28 Sept. 1917, NARS, T-1022, Roll 665, PG 75272; and reports of FdU Mittelmeer, ibid., Roll 927, PG 76415, and Roll 928, PG 76421.

100 Director of Statistics, 'Enemy Activity in the Mediterranean', n.d. [25 July 1918], PRO, Adm 116/1604. The anomaly that the percentage of loss in convoy was higher than other forms of traffic is probably explained by the fact that at this late date most ships were convoyed in the more dangerous areas. On this point see Godfrey to Morris, 2 July 1918, loc. cit. at n. 29, Godfrey MSS(I).

101 Director of Statistics, Memorandum, 22 Oct. 1918, PRO, Adm 116/1604. See also tables in Admiralty, *Mediterranean Staff Papers*, pp. 97–8; Corbett and Newbolt, *Naval Operations*, Vol. 5, appendices B and C.

102 Baird to Calthorpe, 28 Sept. 1918, PRO, Adm 137/1576; Godfrey to Beharrell, 16 Sept. 1918, loc. cit. at n. 29, Godfrey MSS(I).

103 For a summary see Greger, *Russische Flotte im Weltkrieg*, pp. 52–64. On the loss of the *Imperatriza Maria* see: J. N. Westwood, 'The end of the *Imperatritsa Mariia*: negligence or sabotage?', *Canadian Slavonic Papers*, vol. 21, no. 1 (Mar. 1979), pp. 66–75.

104 Text of the Treaties reproduced in John W. Wheeler-Bennett, *Brest-Litovsk: The Forgotten Peace* (London, 1938; paperback edn, 1966), appendices II, IV and V. A succinct account of this confusing period is in David Woodward, *The Russians at Sea* (London, 1965), pp. 189–91. German policy is examined in Fischer, *Germany's Aims in the First World War*, ch. 20.

105 Bülow to Admiralstab, 25 Apr. 1918, NARS, T-1022, Roll 708, PG 75674; Capelle to Müller, 24 Apr. 1918, ibid., Roll 572, PG 68320.

106 Telephone Conversation with Captain Retzmann [?] in Gr. H.Q., 29 Apr. 1918, ibid., Roll 708, PG 75679.

107 Admiralstab, 'Richtlinien für Tätigkeit der Kaiserl. Marine in der Ukraine und Krim', 29 Apr. 1918, ibid., PG 75675; Holtzendorff to Oberste Heeresleitung, 24 Apr. 1918, ibid., PG 75674.

108 Holtzendorff to Chef des Generalstabes, 7 May 1918, Holtzendorff to Rebeur-Paschwitz, 7 May 1918, ibid., Roll 670, PG 75348; Bülow to Admiralstab, 27 Apr. 1918, ibid., Roll 664, PG 75248; Bülow to Admiralstab, 12 May 1918, Admiralstab to Bülow, 13 May 1918, Memorandum by Holtzendorff or Admiralstab on Military-Political Situation in the Black Sea, 13 May 1918, ibid., Roll 708, PG 75674.

109 Ludendorff to Admiralstab and Auswärtiges Amt, 14 May 1918, ibid.; Bülow, 'Conversation with Ludendorff', 14 May 1918, ibid., Roll 634, PG 67476.

110 Annex to Report by Naval Member of Ukraine Delegation, 31 May 1918, Admiralstab to Wülfing [naval representative, Kiev], 3 June 1918, ibid., Roll 736, PG 75684; Hopman to Vanselow, 27 May 1918, Hopman to Holtzendorff, 13 June 1918, ibid., Roll 708, PG 75675.

111 Vanselow to Hopman, 23 June 1918, Ludendorff to Admiralstab, 16 Apr. 1918, discussion of Seeckt's proposal in Holtzendorff to Bülow, 3 May 1918, ibid., Roll 708, PG 75674; see also Ritter, *The Sword and the Scepter*, Vol. 4, pp. 283–6.

112 Ludendorff to Auswärtiges Amt, 10 June 1918, NARS, T-1022, Roll 736, PG 75683; Bene to Admiralstab, 17 June 1918, Hopman to Admiralstab, 21 June 1918, ibid., Roll 735, PG 75679.

113 Woodward, *The Russians at Sea*, pp. 191–3; Wheeler-Bennett, *Brest-Litovsk*, pp. 331–2; list of sunken ships in Greger, *Russische Flotte im Weltkrieg*, pp. 70–1; Hopman to Admiralstab, 25 June 1918, Report by Hopman on

remainder of Black Sea Fleet, 19 July 1918, NARS, T-1022, Roll 735, PG 75679.

114 Holtzendorff to Rebeur-Paschwitz and Hopman, 26 June 1918, ibid., Roll 736, PG 75681; on Russian salvage efforts see Admiralstab to Reichsmarineamt, 30 May 1918, Report by Rebuer-Paschwitz, 20 June 1918, ibid., PG 75683.

115 Bülow to Admiralstab, 28 June 1918, Hopman to Admiralstab, 28 June 1918, ibid., Roll 735, PG 75679.

116 Holtzendorff to RMA, 6 July 1918, Minutes of Meeting in Admiralstab, 8 July 1918, ibid., Roll 1030, PG 76543; Memorandum of Meeting on Preparation of Schoolships at Home and Russian warships in the Black Sea, 8 July 1918, ibid., Roll 608, PG 68233.

117 Seeckt to Holtzendorff, 7 July 1918, Koch to Seeckt, 15 July 1918, Seeckt to Hindenburg, 8 July 1918, ibid., Roll 664, PG 75248.

118 Bülow to Admiralstab, 10 July 1918, ibid., Roll 735, PG 75679.

119 Hopman to Admiralstab, 9 July 1918, Admiralstab to Naval Representative at High Command, 16 July 1918, Memorandum by RMA [Hebbinghaus], 15 July 1918, ibid., Roll 736, PG 75682.

120 Bülow to Admiralstab, 12 July 1918, Admiralstab to Holtzendorff, 14 July 1918, ibid., Roll 1030, PG 76543; Ludendorff to Cramon, 16 July 1918, ibid., Roll 735, PG 75679.

121 Admiralstab to Marine Cabinet, 14 July 1918, ibid., Roll 608, PG 68233.

122 Holtzendorff to Admiralstab, 17 and 19 July 1918, Reichsmarineamt to Holtzendorff (and enclosure), 17 July 1918, ibid., Roll 735, PG 75679.

123 Schönthaler to Marinesektion, 28 June 1918, OK/MS VIII-1/8 ex 1918, No. 3396; Zenker to Admiralstab, 2 Aug. 1918, Admiralstab to Zenker, 5 and 8 Aug. 1918, NARS, T-1022, Roll 736, PG 75682.

124 Text of the agreements in Wheeler-Bennett, *Brest-Litovsk*, pp. 433–4, 437; Admiralstab to Seekriegsleitung, 28 Aug. 1918, NARS, T-1022, Roll 736, PG 75681.

125 Hopman to Admiralstab, 19 Aug. 1918, ibid., Roll 708, PG 75675; Scheer to Admiralstab, 5 Sept. 1918, ibid., Roll 736, PG 75681.

126 Minutes of meeting at Admiralstab, 4 Sept. 1918, ibid., Roll 708, PG 75674.

127 Admiralstab to Auswärtiges Amt, 8, 17 and 22 Sept. 1918, Conversation between Geheimrat Nadolny and BII [Admiralstab], 13 Sept. 1918, Auswärtiges Amt to Scheer, 16 and 19 Sept. 1918, Hopman to Admiralstab, 22 Sept. 1918, ibid., Roll 736, PG 75681.

128 Admiralstab to Scheer and Seekriegsleitung, 23 Sept. 1918, Admiralstab to Seekriegsleitung (with translation of note from Joffe [Soviet ambassador]), 24 Sept. 1918, ibid.; Scheer to Müller, 2 Oct. 1918, ibid., Roll 608, PG 68233.

129 Admiralstab to Prince Max of Baden, 10 Oct. 1918, Scheer to Admiralstab, 12 Oct. 1918, ibid., Roll 829, PG 75671.

130 Hopman to Seekriegsleitung, 14 Oct. 1918, ibid., Roll 736, PG 75683; Admiralstab to Kaiser Wilhelm, 21 Oct. 1918, ibid., Roll 608, PG 68233; Admiralstab to Seekriegsleitung, 26 Oct. 1918, ibid., Roll 735, PG 75679.

131 Rebeur-Paschwitz to Admiralstab, 28 Oct. 1918, Seekriegsleitung to Admiralstab, 29 Oct. 1918, Trotha to Seekriegsleitung, 29 Oct. 1918, ibid., Roll 829, PG 75671.

132 Usedom to Seekriegsleitung, 31 Oct. 1918, Scheer to Rebeur-Paschwitz, 1 Nov. 1918, ibid., Roll 1378, PG 60024; Solf [Auswärtiges Amt] to Admiralstab, 30 Oct. 1918, ibid., Roll 829, PG 75671.

133 Rebeur-Paschwitz to Admiralstab, 2 Nov. 1918, ibid. Full account of the Turkish armistice in Grancy to Reichsmarineamt, 6 Feb. 1919, ibid., Roll 538, PG 69133.

134 Hopman to Admiralstab, 8 Nov. 1918, Admiralstab to Hopman, 12 Nov. 1918, Admiralstab to Auswärtiges Amt, 15 Nov. 1918, ibid., Roll 735, PG 75679; Berchen [chargé d'affaires, Kiev] to Auswärtiges Amt, 26 Nov. 1918, ibid., Roll 708, PG 75674.

135 Gauchet to Leygues, 25 and 28 Sept. 1918, Gauchet to Amiral *Bruix* [Du Vignaux], 25 Sept. 1918, Leygues to Gauchet, 27 Sept. 1918, SHM, Carton A-29.

136 Revel to Cusani-Visconti, 28 July, 31 Aug. and 9 Sept. 1918, Mola to Cusani-Visconti, 4 Sept. 1918, Cusani-Visconti to Revel, 4 and 8 Sept. 1918, USM, Cartella 1214/4.

137 Petrozzuli to Revel, 26 Sept. 1918, Revel to Cusani-Visconti, 26 Sept. 1918, Revel, Promemoria, 'Operazioni Navali contro Durazzo', 28 Sept. 1918, USM, Cartella 1231.

138 Gauchet to Amiral *Bruix* [Du Vignaux], 29 Sept. 1918, Leygues to Gauchet, 30 Sept. 1918, SHM, Carton A-29; Sechi to Bisoretta, 28 Sept. 1918, USM, Cartella 1231.

139 Kelly to Admiralty, 4 Oct. 1918, Calthorpe to Admiralty, 25 Oct. 1918, PRO, Adm 137/1578.

140 Printed accounts are: Sokol, *Österreich-Ungarns Seekrieg*, pp. 636–45; Ufficio Storico, *Marina italiana*, Vol. 8, pp. 380–97. The action is not even mentioned in the final volume of Corbett and Newbolt's *Naval Operations*. Pauer's account is in Pauer to Seitz, 3 Oct. 1918, OK/MS VIII-1/1 ex 1918, No. 5375. On lowered morale at Durazzo see AOK to Marinesektion, 6 Oct. 1918, ibid., No. 5270; Seitz to Marinesektion, 3 Oct. 1918, ibid., No. 5157.

141 Kelly to Admiralty, 4 Oct. 1918, Calthorpe to Admiralty, 25 Oct. 1918, PRO, Adm 137/1578; Minute by Godfrey, 14 Oct. 1918, loc. cit. at n. 29, Godfrey MSS, Mediterranean and Black Sea Papers (I).

142 Train, 'Political Side to Italian Bombardment of Durazzo', Report No. R-665, 7 Oct. 1918, NARS, RG 45, WX-4 File, Box 750.

143 Admiralty to Calthorpe, 29 Sept. 1918, Calthorpe to Seymour, 3 Oct. 1918, PRO, Adm 137/2180; Sechi to Revel, 30 Sept. 1918, Revel to Sechi, 1 Oct. 1918, USM, Cartella 137.

144 Wemyss to Geddes, 3 Oct. 1918, PRO, Adm 116/1809; Wemyss to Beatty, 8 Oct. 1918, loc. cit. at n. 71, Wemyss MSS; Calthorpe to Admiralty, 8 Oct. 1918, PRO, Adm 137/2180.

145 Memorandum by Geddes, 'Command of Allied Naval Force in the Aegean', 12 Oct. 1918, ibid., Adm 116/1810.

146 Lloyd George to Clemenceau, 15 Oct. 1918, loc. cit. at n. 68, Lloyd George MSS, F/50/3/37; David Lloyd George, *War Memoirs of David Lloyd George*, 2nd edn, 2 vols (London, n.d. [1936]), Vol. 2, p. 1974.

147 Leygues to Gauchet, 30 Sept. 1918, 1 and 2 Oct. 1918, SHM, Carton A-29; Thomazi, *Guerre navale dans la Méditerranée*, pp. 123–4.

148 Sechi to Revel, 3 Oct. 1918, USM, Cartella 1137; Granville (Athens) to Foreign Office, 8 Oct. 1918, PRO, Adm 137/1581; Train to Sims, 7 Oct. 1918, NARS, RG 45, TD File, Box 553.

149 Pichon to French ambassadors in Rome, London and Washington, 20 and 23 Oct. 1918, MAE, Série Europe 1918–1929, Vol. 77; Pro-Memoria by Italian Embassy, London, 14 Oct. 1918, minutes by DNI, 28 Oct. and Coode, 30 Oct. 1918, Admiralty to Naval Attaché, Athens, 1 Nov. 1918, PRO, Adm 137/1581.

150 Rodd to Foreign Office, 22 Oct. 1918, minutes by Coode, 24 and 26 Oct., and Hope, 27 Oct. 1918, Admiralty to Foreign Office, 27 Oct. 1918, ibid.

151 Gauchet to Leygues, 11 and 16 Oct. 1918, Leygues to Frochot [naval attaché, Rome], 12 Oct. 1918, Frochot to Leygues, 16 Oct. 1918, Franchet d'Esperey to Minister of War, 18 Oct. 1918, Clemenceau to Pichon, 19 Oct. 1918, Clemenceau to Franchet d'Esperey, 20 Oct. 1918, SHM, Carton Es-12; Leygues to Gauchet, 29 Oct. 1918, SHM, Carton A-29.

152 Amet to Gauchet, 11 Oct. 1918, ibid.; Leygues to Gauchet, 15 Oct. 1918, SHM, Carton Es-14.

153 Derby to Lloyd George, 18 Oct. 1918, loc. cit. at n. 68, Lloyd George MSS, F/52/2/40; extract of letter from Derby to Balfour, 18 Oct. 1918, ibid., F/52/2/41.

154 Derby to Lloyd George, 21 Oct. 1918, Clemenceau to Lloyd George (and translation), 21 Oct. 1918, ibid., F/52/2/43; Pichon to Cambon, 23 Oct., Pichon to Barrère, 25 Oct., Barrère to Pichon, 31 Oct. 1918, MAE, Série Y Internationale, Vol. 78.

155 Leygues to Gauchet, 23 Oct. 1918, SHM, Carton A-29; Derby to Balfour, 23 Oct. 1918, loc. cit. at n. 68, Lloyd George MSS, F/52/2/44; draft for an armistice with Turkey is in I.C.-77, Procès-Verbal of Conference, Paris, 6 Oct. 1918, PRO, Cab 28/5.

156 Lloyd George to Clemenceau, 25 Oct. 1918, loc. cit. at n. 68, Lloyd George MSS, F/50/3/39.

157 Train to Sims, 25 Oct. 1918, NARS, RG 45, TD File, Box 553; Leygues to Gauchet, 26 Oct. 1918, SHM, Carton A-134.

158 De Lorenzi to Revel, 11 Oct. 1918, Borghese to Sonnino [?], 11 Oct. 1918, Unsigned draft of letter from Capo di Stato Maggiore to naval attachés in London and Paris with memorandum on Otranto Mobile Barrage, 22 Oct. 1918, USM, Cartella 1191.

159 Chetwode to Kelly, 20 Oct. 1918, loc. cit. at n. 78, Kelly MSS, KEL/24.

160 Gauchet to Leygues, 24 Oct. 1918, Leygues to Gauchet, 26 Oct. 1918, SHM, Carton A-29.

161 Leygues to Gauchet, 26 Oct. 1918, Gauchet to Amet, 27 Oct. 1918, Gauchet to Calthorpe, 27 Oct. 1918, Gauchet to Franchet d'Esperey, 28 Oct. 1918, ibid.

162 Calthorpe to Admiralty, 27 and 28 Oct. 1918, PRO, Adm 137/2180; Amet to Gauchet, 27 and 28 Oct. 1918, SHM, Carton A-29.

163 Leygues to Gauchet, 29 and 31 Oct. 1918, Gauchet to Calthorpe, 30 and 31 Oct. 1918, Amet to Gauchet, 30 and 31 Oct. 1918, ibid.; I.C.-84, Note of a Conversation, Paris, 30 Oct. 1918, PRO, Cab 28/2; Godfrey, *The Naval Memoirs*, Vol. 2, p. 116; Calthorpe to Admiralty, 2 Nov. 1918, Admiralty to Calthorpe, 4 Nov. 1918, PRO, Adm 137/2180.

164 Gauchet to Leygues, 1 and 2 Nov. 1918, Leygues to Gauchet, 1 Nov. 1918, SHM, Carton A-29.

165 Assistant French Naval Attaché to Admiralty, 16 Oct. 1918, Admiralty to Grasset, 29 Oct. 1918, PRO, Adm 137/1579.

166 Paper I.C.-84, Note of a Conversation . . . Paris, 30 Oct. 1918, and Appendix, 'Naval Conditions of an Armistice with Austria-Hungary', PRO, Cab 28/5; ANC, Final Report of the Sixth Meetings, 28 Oct.–4 Nov. 1918, Conference of Naval Representatives, 28 Oct. 1918, and Appendices B and D, ANC, 1st Session, 29 Oct. 1918, and Appendix E, 2nd Session, 31 Oct. 1918 and Appendix F, 3rd Session, 31 Oct. 1918, and Appendix G, ibid., Adm 137/836.

167 A fascinating account is in Khuepach, Tagebuch, October 1918, Kriegsarchiv, Vienna, Nachlass Khuepach, B/200, No. 5/1; see also Sokol, *Österreich-*

Ungarns Seekrieg, ch. 31; Orders to end U-boat war are in Horthy to Marinesektion, 17 Oct. 1918, OK/MS VIII-1/15 ex 1918, No. 5444.

168 Adriatic Intelligence, No. XXVI, 'The Events of the 31st October', 1 Nov. 1918, copy in Kelly MSS, KEL/26, loc. cit. at n. 78.

169 Keil to Militärkanzlei, 30 Oct. 1918, MKSM 69-27/7-3 ex 1918; Horthy to Keil, 31 Oct. 1918, MKSM 69-27/7-6 ex 1918; The record of events on the 31st is by Fregattenkapitän Hugo Volkmann (p. 28) in Nachlass Khuepach, B/200, No. 5/1, loc. cit. at n. 167. Volkmann's record appears to be the basis for Sokol, *Österreich-Ungarns Seekrieg*, pp. 735–7.

170 Ufficio Storico, *Marina italiana*, Vol. 8, pp. 509–19; René Greger, 'Wussten die Italiener davon?', *Marine Rundschau*, vol. 76, no. 7 (July 1979), pp. 445–76; for typical suspicions of a ruse on the change of flag see: Barrère to Pichon, 2 Nov. 1918, SHM, Carton Ed-95.

171 Freyberg to Admiralstab, 10 Oct. 1918, NARS, T-1022, Roll 506, PG 69082; Püllen to Scheer, 19 Oct. 1918, ibid., Roll 829, PG 75668; Püllen to Scheer, 24 Oct. 1918, Scheer to Admiralstab, 25 Oct. 1918, BdU Pola, Kriegstagebuch, 18–30 Oct. 1918 and Nachtrag, 9 Nov. 1918, Report by Kapitänleutnant Wickel, 2 Nov. 1918, ibid., Roll 927, PG 76414.

172 Report of Mediterranean U-boats *en route* home, n.d. [c. 8 Nov. 1918], telephone conversation with German Naval Attaché in Vienna, 2 Nov. 1918, ibid.; Spindler, *Handelskrieg*, Vol. 5, pp. 226–8.

173 Twining to Sims, 1 Nov. 1918, Nelson to Sims, 2 Nov. 1918, NARS, RG 45, OD File, Box 309; Sims to Nelson, 4 Nov. 1918, ibid., OR-1 File, Box 334; Gibraltar Patrol Orders, 29 Oct. 1918, Niblack to Sims, 29 Oct. 1918, ibid., TD File, Box 553.

174 Spindler, *Handelskrieg*, Vol. 5, pp. 195–7, 214–15; Corbett and Newbolt, *Naval Operations*, Vol. 5, pp. 359–60.

Epilogue

The naval war in the Mediterranean had been a frustrating one, and once the defection of Italy from the Triple Alliance ensured that the disparity in strength between the Triple Entente and the Central Powers was huge there would never be a 'Mediterranean Jutland'. The real action came to revolve around submarines, and the British who had significant trade interests represented by the route to the Suez Canal were forced to step in and assume what was virtually direction of the anti-submarine war. They had been only too ready to yield command of surface forces in the Mediterranean to a French admiral at the beginning of the war so that they could concentrate in the north, and a French admiral remained at least nominally commander-in-chief throughout the war. But this was a strange commander-in-chief for, by 1917, Admiral Gauchet seemed more and more preoccupied with his own battle fleet, those seven formidable French dreadnoughts concentrated at Corfu which were certainly the most powerful single squadron in the Mediterranean. However, the prospect that these ships would ever fire their guns in anger became less and less as the war went on, and Gauchet could hardly be an effective commander-in-chief of the whole expanse of the very diverse Mediterranean while confined to the relatively cramped space of his flagship *Provence*, where it was impossible to house the sizeable staff his position really demanded. Corfu, however well placed strategically for checking the Austrian fleet, was geographically out of the way compared with a central location like Malta. Gauchet seemed obsessed with tactical doctrine and arguments such as whether the commander-in-chief himself should control a squadron in action. He would have been a happy man if only the Austrians would have given him a chance with a classic encounter although, due to the heavy demands of the new type of war on flotilla craft, Gauchet would have had difficulty in finding sufficient destroyers at short notice. The French fleet had been destined in prewar days to fight the Triple Alliance, that is, the combined Austrian and Italian forces in the Mediterranean. When this did not occur, it might be said that the capital ships of the French navy never found their real role, especially since the Austrians were not foolish enough to steam out to do battle with overwhelmingly superior forces.

The Italians had a more circumscribed view, for they had their former ally but traditional enemy only a few hours' steaming distance away and, in the relatively confined waters of the Adriatic, they were well aware of the dangers of mines and submarines and determined to shield their precious capital ships until the last moment, exposing them only for a battle against their Austrian counterparts. It was a logical action and we only have to look at the number of British and French battleships sunk going to and from dockyards to defend it. Unfortunately, the officers and men of a complex instrument of war such as a dreadnought or squadron of dreadnoughts grow stale if not properly exercised and by 1918 there were legitimate doubts about the real efficiency of those big ships of the Italian, French and Austrian navies. Moreover, with the exception of the British, they all suffered from a shortage of coal whose consumption had to be carefully monitored.

It was really extraordinary to see how, despite the proven efficiency of the submarine, virtually all the naval leaders remained hypnotized by the big guns of those dreadnoughts. The Austrian fleet never did come out to fight in the Mediterranean but there was always the thought: 'what if they did?' There were undoubtedly some Austrians who wondered whether their country was wise to get into the dreadnought race since they could never hope to match the great maritime powers. On the other hand, it could be argued that they got more than their money's worth out of their handful of modern battleships, for they wound up tying down far more than their own number of French and Italian capital ships. Politics had much to do with this, notably the inability of the French and Italians to combine or co-operate with each other. The k.u.k. Kriegsmarine was a classic example of a fleet-in-being and it must never be forgotten that those big guns of the battle squadron in Pola imposed a certain respect on their opponents and meant that the latter could not operate with impunity in proximity to them without adequate support, and that meant heavy warships which were vulnerable to mines and torpedoes and unwise to risk, particularly in the northern waters of the Adriatic. The big ships watching each other from Taranto, Corfu and Pola tended to checkmate each other, but they were the muscle behind the cruisers and flotilla craft and were part of the complicated equation which, together with minefields and submarine ambushes, limited how far each category of warship could be prudently risked. In the meantime, the submarine campaign against merchant traffic grew in importance and no one ever had enough destroyers or escort craft in the Mediterranean.

The Germans found a fertile field for a portion of their submarine fleet in the Mediterranean, but only a portion for the Mediterranean was a secondary theatre for the two major maritime combatants, Britain and Germany. The great and easy successes of the Germans in the Mediterranean ended by the autumn of 1917 with the introduction of the convoy system. There might be months when losses shot upwards, but the long-term trend was down. The British and their allies were slow to realize the true effectiveness of the convoy and wasted much effort on the Otranto barrage, the results of which were in no way proportionate to the effort expended. The Americans were about to waste even more effort on mine barrages of questionable effectiveness in different areas of the Mediterranean. But the Americans were also on the verge of bringing large numbers of destroyers and escort craft into service in 1919 and this would have been important. The Germans had their own extensive building programme of submarines and the Mediterranean would have received a portion of them – assuming the Germans would have been able to find the crews to man them. The ability of Austria-Hungary, on the other hand, to produce significant numbers of new submarines was very limited. The increased number of German submarines using better tactics, such as working together, might well have kept losses high, but one of the reasons why convoy losses were proportionately higher in the Mediterranean was because the scale of escorts was relatively weak. That would have been changed for the American destroyer programme would have produced a steady stream of American reinforcements at sea in 1919, comparable with American reinforcements on the western front in 1918. Even if the Americans did not go directly to the Mediterranean themselves in large numbers, they would certainly have freed British craft from the north. This, plus the increased number of aircraft employed on anti-submarine patrol, meant that the German and Austrian submarine campaign did not face bright prospects had the war gone on.

The British had never, in their hearts, really accepted French command in the Mediterranean and they steadily chipped away at it. They did so first in the Aegean with the Dardanelles campaign in 1915, and then with a British commander-in-chief at Malta in 1917 to play a leading role in the anti-submarine war. This was not necessarily a conscious series of acts, but represented rather a pragmatic response. The British had a job to do and no one could do it but themselves. The Mediterranean theatre really cried for unity, not just among the different nations but among the far-flung commands of the British and French as well. Calthorpe and Gauchet both experienced difficulty in getting their authority accepted by portions of their own navies. The disunity resulted in a substantial waste of resources which could not always be easily reallocated to where they were most needed. On an international level, the inability of the French and Italians to combine, for perfectly logical reasons in their own eyes, wasted substantial numbers of capital ships. Once again in 1918 the British tried to step into the breech with their proposal that Jellicoe should be Mediterranean admiralissimo, but this was forestalled by the Italian reluctance to include the Adriatic in his command and the more covert opposition by the French navy to what it considered the usurpation of its rights by the British. The very real need for a supreme Allied commander able to allocate resources where they were most needed remained unfulfilled.

The Mediterranean was also an area of 'what might have been's' and where things never happened. The Austrian fleet never went to Constantinople or came out for a replay of Lissa; the French and Italians never tried to capture Cattaro, nor did the Americans ever try to shoot their way into the Bocche; and the US Marines never did manage to add 'Curzola' or 'Sabbioncello' to their battle honours. The Allied nightmare of Germans and Turks manning former Russian warships and breaking out into the Aegean to achieve local supremacy also never happened.

The Mediterranean was also incredibly diverse. By the end of the war, on the Allied side and in addition to British, French and Italian warships, there were Americans, Australians, Russians, Japanese, Greeks and even, on occasion, the odd Portuguese trawler. There were also Brazilian warships

581

and Canadian trawlers working at Gibraltar. It was perhaps inevitable that political and diplomatic rivalries were present. The Central Powers were far less diverse, although in 1918 the Black Sea had the potential to become polyglot with the possibility of Bulgarian, Ukrainian and even Georgian forces working in co-operation with the Germans, Austrians and Turks. The Central Powers also had their own internal rivalries. The Austrians were by no means the complacent stooges of the Germans which some in the Entente readily assumed. Nor for that matter were the Turks.

The question for the Entente is always how well or how poorly did the Allies work together and, in many ways, is like the old problem 'Is the cup half-empty of half-full?' Certainly, there was friction but, on the other hand, the inter-Allied organizations which evolved in the anti-submarine war did fuction, however imperfectly. The British and the Americans worked well together at Gibraltar, and the British and French destroyer forces at Brindisi also seem to have developed a mutual respect for each other. There were many officers who took the idea of an ally seriously and tried to make it work although there was a natural tendency to become disillusioned as time went on. Unfortunately, much of the surface harmony was superficial. Lieutenant-Commander Godfrey described how they had kept the French delegate at Malta, Rear-Admiral Ratyé, 'out of mischief' for months by preparing a 'Guide des Acheminements' or handbook on the routing of shipping and convoys. Godfrey and the Mediterranean Staff cynically realized that it would take so long to be printed that it would be thoroughly out of date when issued and Godfrey advised a friend at the Admiralty to 'keep it simmering' so that it never actually appeared in print until the war was over.[1] Baird, the Director of Shipping Movements, could write after the war: 'I can't understand our Allies. The French and Italian Admirals on the Commission de Malte simply obstructed all the time, and at times it really was hard to keep one's temper. However, we parted the best of friends, and I don't suppose we shall ever meet again.'[2] For the Italian member of the commission, Rear-Admiral Salazar, however, Baird was a 'vero tipo di nordico', a dissembler in an exaggerated fashion, unfair and egoistic. Salazar described a persistent struggle between fixed ideas about absolute control by the British C.-in-C. and the need to get Italian ideas respected when Italian interests were at stake.[3] The French sometimes had similar views about British pretensions but the British doubted French methods and persistence, and both the British and French could be scathing about Italian capabilities while the Italians could imagine their allies did not really understand or appreciate their problems. And so it went on and on.

The Allies were able to keep many of their rivalries muted during the war. But they were always there and with peace they flared up again. Sims wrote perceptively that since the armistice a new war had begun.[4] He was right. French and Italian relations grew poisonous in the Adriatic where the Italians found a new rival in the Yugoslav state, courted by the French. The latent Anglo-French rivalry was to open up in the Near East. Moreover, the Armistice brought little real peace in the eastern Mediterranean world with Allied intervention in south Russia, the Greeks in Asia Minor and the Black Sea area in turmoil. There would be a mutiny in the French fleet in 1919 and

British forces would find themselves on the brink of war with the nationalist Turks in the next few years. The rivalries and lack of harmony among the former Allies which were so evident in the interwar years could be readily discerned in the 1914–18 war. There was also the terrible irony that the first time that Dartige's and Gauchet's old flagship the *Provence* ever fired her guns at a real naval target and received shell fire and serious damage in return would be against the British fleet at Mers-el-Kébir in 1940.

Notes: Epilogue

1 Godfrey to Henderson, 8 Sept. 1918, Naval Library, Ministry of Defence, London, Godfrey MSS, Mediterranean Papers (I).
2 Baird to de Robeck, 5 Jan. 1919, Churchill College, Cambridge, de Robeck MSS, DRBK 5/14.
3 Salazar to Revel, 7 Dec. 1918, USM, Cartella 1191.
4 Sims to Train, 4 Dec. 1918, NARS, RG 45, TD File, Box 553.

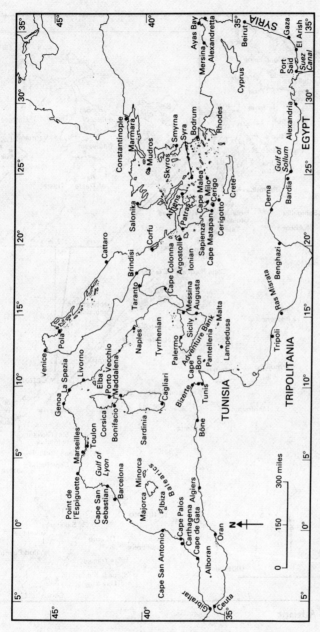

1 The Mediterranean

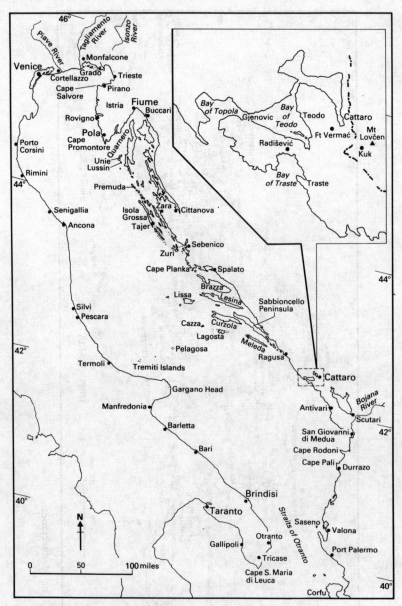

46°

Piave River
Tagliamento River
Isonzo River

Venice
• Monfalcone
Grado
Cortellazzo • Trieste
Cape • Pirano
Salvore
Istria   Fiume
• Buccari
Rovigno •
Pola •   Buccari
Cape
Promontore   Quarnero
Unie
Lussin
Porto
Corsini •
Rimini •
44°
Premuda •
Senigallia •
Ancona •
Isola   Zara
Grossa •   • Cittanova
Tajer •
Zuri   • Sebenico
Cape Planka •   • Spalato
Lissa •   Brazza
Lesina
Silvi •   Cazza   Curzola   Sabbioncello
Pescara •   Lagosta   Peninsula
42°   • Pelagosa   Meleda
Termoli •   Ragusa
Tremiti Islands
Gargano Head
Manfredonia •
Barletta •
Bari •
40°   Brindisi
Taranto
N
Gallipoli   Otranto
0   50   100 miles   Tricase •
Cape S. Maria
di Leuca

Bay of Topola   Bay of Teodo   Teodo   Cattaro
Gjenovic   Ft Vermać   Mt Lovčen ▲
Radišević   Kuk
Bay of Traste   Traste

44°

Cattaro
Antivari •   Bojana River
Scutari
San Giovanni   42°
di Medua •
Cape Rodoni •
Cape Pali •   • Durrazo
Saseno
• Valona
Straits of Otranto   Port Palermo
Corfu   40°

2   The Adriatic

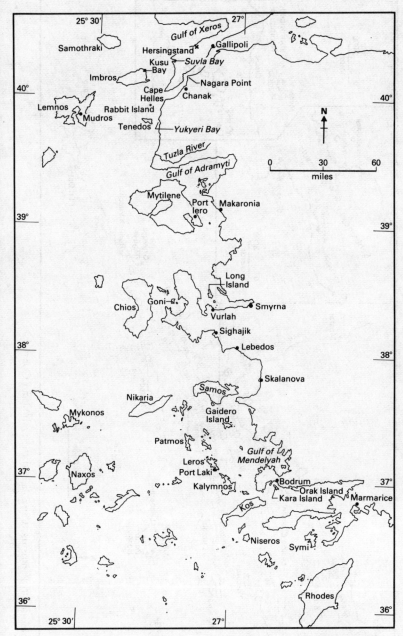

3 Aegean Coast of Asia Minor and approaches to the Dardanelles

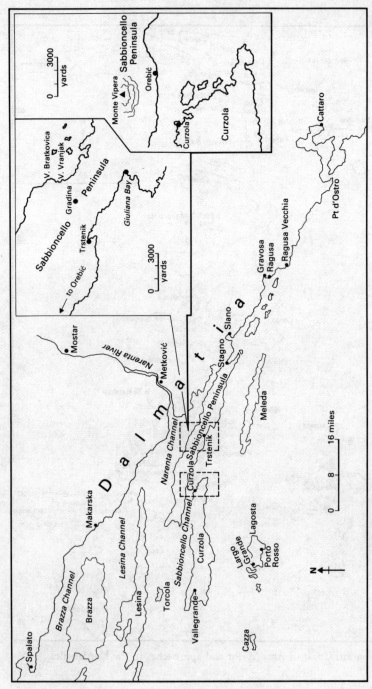

4 Sabbioncello Peninsula, Curzola and the Dalmatian Coast

5 The Aegean

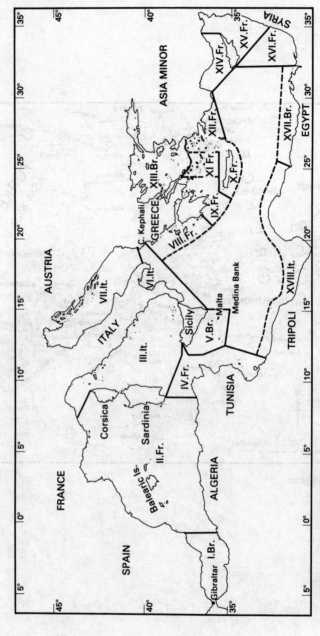

6 Patrol areas established by Paris Conference (December 1915)

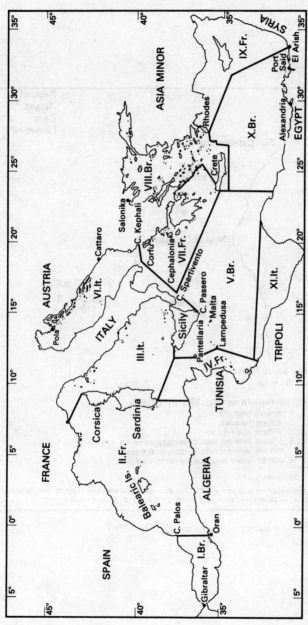

7 Patrol areas established by Malta Conference (March 1916)

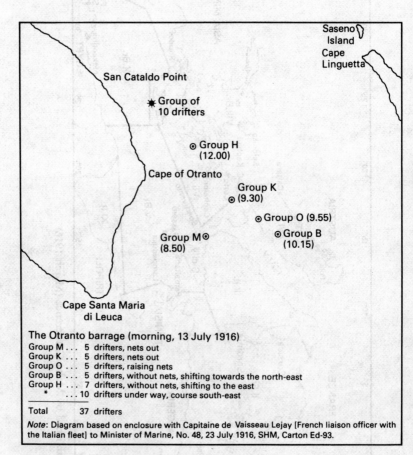

Saseno Island
Cape Linguetta

San Cataldo Point

✳ Group of
10 drifters

⊙ Group H
(12.00)

Cape of Otranto

Group K
⊙ (9.30)

⊙ Group O (9.55)

Group M ⊙
(8.50)

⊙ Group B
(10.15)

Cape Santa Maria
di Leuca

The Otranto barrage (morning, 13 July 1916)

Group M ... 5 drifters, nets out
Group K ... 5 drifters, nets out
Group O ... 5 drifters, raising nets
Group B ... 5 drifters, without nets, shifting towards the north-east
Group H ... 7 drifters, without nets, shifting to the east
        * ... 10 drifters under way, course south-east

Total   37 drifters

Note: Diagram based on enclosure with Capitaine de Vaisseau Lejay [French liaison officer with the Italian fleet] to Minister of Marine, No. 48, 23 July 1916, SHM, Carton Ed-93.

8 The Otranto barrage (morning, 13 July 1916)

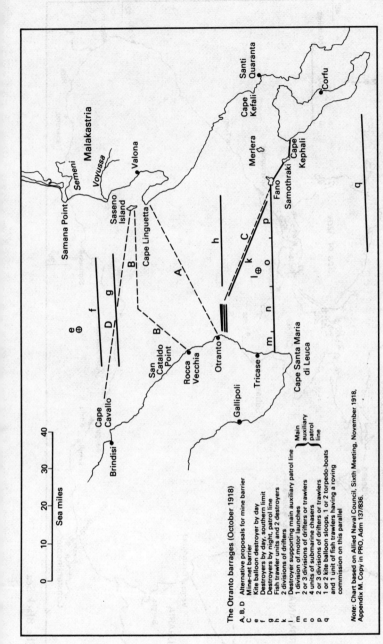

9 The Otranto barrages (October 1918)

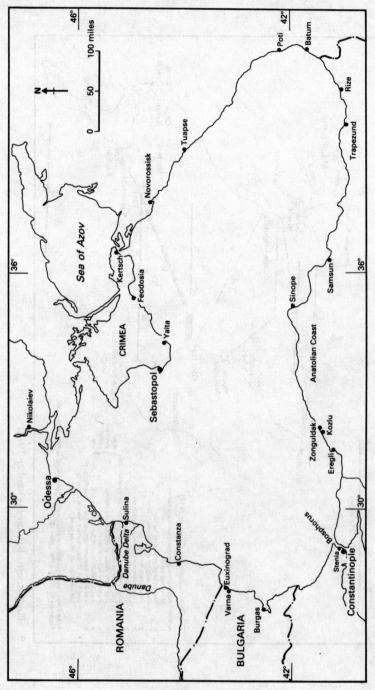

10 The Black Sea

Select Bibliography

Unpublished Materials

The core of this study is based on unpublished material drawn from the archives, but it is not practical to publish a list of the wide range of individual files. These are clearly identified in the notes.

Austria-Hungary

Kriegsarchiv, Vienna. The major repository for surviving records of the k.u.k. Kriegsmarine during the 1914–18 period. The files of the Operationskanzlei/ Marinesektion and the Militärkanzlei des Kaisers und Königs are particularly important. The following Nachlasse are also of great value: Bolfras; Haus; Jedina-Palombini; Kailer; Khuepach; Liechtenstein; Rémy; and Thierry.
Nachlass Erich Heyssler (in private possession).

France

Service Historique de la Marine, Vincennes. Contains a vast amount of material on the French navy during the war as well as useful unpublished studies by French naval officers.
Archives Diplomatiques, Ministère des Affaires Etrangères, Paris. There is some material of value in the series, Guerre, 1914–1918, Y Internationale and Papiers d'Agents, notably Jules Cambon and Camille Barrère.

Germany

National Archives and Records Service, Washington, Microfilm Publication, T-1022, Records of the German Navy, 1850–1945. The so-called 'Tambach Records', an extensive microfilm collection of German naval records captured at Schloss Tambach in 1945, microfilmed in Britain, and subsequently returned to Germany, are of particular value for German naval activities in the Mediterranean. For the purposes of this book, those files which were never microfilmed appear to be the mirror image of those filmed, that is, carbons instead of originals or vice versa.
Bundesarchiv-Militärchiv, Freiburg im Breisgau. In addition to the returned naval materials, the BA-MA have the valuable Nachlasse Firle and Souchon.

Great Britain

Public Record Office, Kew. The major repository of official naval records, found in the Adm series, as well as relevant material in the Cabinet (Cab) and Foreign Office (FO) records. The more useful personal papers include Geddes in the Adm 116 and Grey and Bertie in the FO 800 series.

595

British Library, London: Balfour MSS; Jellicoe MSS; and Keyes MSS.
Churchill College, Cambridge: T. P. H. Beamish MSS; J. R. de Robeck MSS; J. H. Godfrey MSS; R. H. Hall MSS; M. P. A. Hankey MSS; A. A. F. Macliesh MSS; F. Pridham MSS; J. F. Somerville MSS; Tomkinson MSS; and R. Wemyss MSS.
House of Lords Record Office, London: Lloyd George MSS.
Imperial War Museum, London: D. B. Crampton MSS; De Chair MSS; G. Dickens MSS; C. H. Drage MSS; P. W. Dumas MSS; G. M. Eady MSS; H. M. Fitch MSS; L. Gardner MSS; I. W. Gibson MSS; H. Miller MSS; E. Parry MSS; and R. W. Wilkinson MSS.
National Maritime Museum, Greenwich: Clifton Brown MSS; K. Dewar MSS; A. G. Duff MSS; S. R. Fremantle MSS; E. Fullerton MSS; F. T. Hamilton MSS; L. H. Hamilton MSS; J. D. Kelly MSS; W. H. Kelly MSS; D. A. Larking MSS; H. Limpus MSS; B. Milne MSS; H. F. Oliver MSS; J. Porter MSS; and H. Richmond MSS.
Naval Library, Ministry of Defence, London: J. H. Godfrey MSS; and H. B. Jackson MSS. Also contains copies of the detailed studies made by the Naval Staff after the war.
University of California, Irvine: Wemyss MSS (microfilm copy).

ITALY

Ufficio Storico della Marina Militare, Rome. The major repository for a vast amount of Italian naval records for the wartime period as well as the series published by the Stato Maggiore della Marina for internal circulation: 'Chronistoria Documentata della Guerra Marittima Italo-Austriaca, 1915–1918'. The naval archives also hold copies of Italian books dealing with naval subjects which are virtually impossible to obtain outside Italy.
Archivio Centrale dello Stato, Rome. Contains the Carte: Boselli; Brusati; Orlando; and Salandra.
Sonnino Papers, 54 reels, University Microfilms, Ann Arbor, Michigan.

UNITED STATES OF AMERICA

National Archives and Records Service, Washington, DC. The Naval Records of interest for this period are in Record Group 45, especially the TD file (Sims's personal correspondence) and the QC File (Allied Naval Council). Other useful material may be found in Record Group 38, the Office of Naval Intelligence files.

Published Materials

AUSTRIA-HUNGARY

Aichelburg, Wladimir, *Die Unterseeboote Österreich-Ungarns* 2 vols (Graz: Akademische Druck- u. Verlagsanstalt, 1981).
Arz, Artur, *Zur Geschichte des Grossen Krieges, 1914–1918* (Vienna: Amalthea Verlag, 1924; reprint, Graz: Akademische Druck- u. Verlagsanstalt, 1969).
Bayer von Bayersburg, Heinrich, *Unter der k.u.k. Kriegsflagge, 1914–18* (Vienna: Bergland Verlag, 1959).
Bayer von Bayersburg, Heinrich, *Österreichs Admirale und bedeutende Persönlichkeiten der k.u.k. Kriegsmarine, 1867–1918* (Vienna: Bergland Verlag, 1962).

Bayer von Bayersburg, Heinrich, 'Schiff verlassen!', 1914–1918 (Vienna: Bergland Verlag, 1965).

Bayer von Bayersburg, Heinrich, Die Marinewaffen im Einsatz, 1914–1918 (Vienna: Bergland Verlag, 1968).

Bilzer, Franz F., Die Torpedoboote der k.u.k. Kriegsmarine von 1875–1918 (Graz: H. Weishaupt Verlag, 1984).

Conrad, Feldmarschall, Aus Meiner Dienstzeit, 1906–1918, 5 vols (Vienna, Leipzig and Munich: Rikola Verlag, 1921–5).

Cramon, General A. von, Quatre ans au G.Q.G. austro-hongroise (Paris: Payot, 1922).

Czernin, Count Ottokar, In the World War (London: Cassell, 1919).

Glaise-Horstenau, Edmund von, Die Katastrophe: Die Zertrümmerung Österreich-Ungarns und das Werden des Nachfolgestaaten (Vienna, Leipzig and Munich: Amalthea Verlag, 1929).

Glaise-Horstenau, Edmund von, et al., Österreich-Ungarns Letzter Krieg, 1914–1918, 7 vols and 10 supplements (Vienna: Verlag der Militärwissenschaftlichen Mitteilungen, 1930–8.

Greger, René, Austro-Hungarian Warships of World War I (London: Ian Allan, 1976).

Greger, René, 'Wussten die Italiener davon?', Marine Rundschau, vol. 76, no. 7 (July 1979), pp. 445–76.

Horthy, Admiral Nicholas, Memoirs (London: Hutchinson, 1956).

Komjáthy, Miklos (ed.), Protokolle des gemeinsamen Ministerrats der Österreichisch-Ungarischen Monarchie (1914–1918) (Budapest: Akadémiai Kiadó, 1966).

Kunsti, Erich von, Verlorener Strand (Berlin, Vienna and Leipzig: Paul Zsolnay Verlag, 1938).

Marine – Gestern, Heute, Zeitschrift der Arbeitsgemeinschaft für Österreichische Marinegeschichte (Vienna, 1973–).

Martiny, Nikolaus von, Bilddokumente aus Österreich-Ungarns Seekrieg, 1914–1918, 2 vols, 2nd edn (Graz: Akademische Druck- u. Verlagsanstalt, 1973).

May, Arthur J., The Passing of the Hapsburg Monarchy, 1914–1918, 2 vols (Philadelphia, Penn.: University of Pennsylvania Press, 1966).

Oedl, Franz Robert, '50 Jahre Otranto', Österreichische Militärische Zeitschrift (1967), pp. 244–8.

Plaschka, Richard Georg, Cattaro–Prag: Revolte und Revolution (Graz and Cologne: Böhlau, 1963).

Plaschka, Richard Georg, 'Phänomene sozialer und nationaler Krisen in der k.u.k. Marine 1918', Militärgeschichtliches Forschungsamt, Freiburg im Breisgau (ed.), Vorträge zur Militärgeschichte, Vol. 2: Menschenführung in der Marine (Herford and Bonn: E. S. Mittler, 1981), pp. 50–68.

Plaschka, Richard Georg, and Mack, Karlheinz (eds), Die Auflösung des Habsburger-reiches: Zusammenbruch und Neuorientierung im Donauraum (Munich: R. Oldenbourg, 1970).

Polzer-Hoditz, Arthur Count, The Emperor Karl (London and New York; Putnam, 1930).

Regele, Oskar, Feldmarschall Conrad: Auftrag und Erfüllung, 1906–1918 (Vienna and Munich: Verlag Herold, 1955).

Ronge, General Major Max, Kriegs und Industrie Spionage (Zurich, Leipzig and Vienna: Amalthea Verlag, 1930).

Rothenberg, Gunther, The Army of Francis Joseph (West Lafayette, Ind.: Purdue University Press, 1976).

Schmidt-Pauli, Edgar von, Nikolaus von Horthy (Hamburg: Toth Verlag, 1942).

Schupita, Peter, Die k.u.k. Seeflieger: Chronik und Dokumentation der österreichisch-ungarischen Marineluftwaffe (Koblenz: Bernard & Graefe Verlag, 1983).

Sokol, Anthony E., *The Imperial and Royal Austro-Hungarian Navy* (Annapolis, Md.: United States Naval Institute, 1968).

Sokol, Hans Hugo, *Österreich-Ungarns Seekrieg*, 2 vols (Vienna: Amalthea Verlag, 1933; reprint, Graz: Akademische Druck-u. Verlagsanstalt, 1967).

Sokol, Hans Hugo, *Des Kaisers Seemacht: Die k.k. österreichische Kriegsmarine, 1848 bis 1914* (Vienna: Amalthea Verlag, 1980).

Trapp, Georg von, *Bis zum letzten Flaggenschuss: Erinnerungen eines österreichischen U-Boots-Kommandanten* (Salzburg and Leipzig: Verlag Anton Pustet, 1935).

Valiani, Leo, *The End of Austria-Hungary* (London: Secker & Warburg, 1973).

Wagner, Anton, 'Die k.u.k. Kriegsmarine im letzten Jahr des Ersten Weltkrieges', *Österreichische Militärische Zeitschrift* (1968), pp. 409–15.

Wagner, Walter, *Die Obersten Behörden der k.u.k. Kriegsmarine, 1856–1918* (Vienna: Ferdinand Berger, 1961).

Winterhalder, Konter-Admiral Theodor, *Die Österreichisch-Ungarische Kriegsmarine im Weltkrieg* (Munich: J. F. Lehmanns Verlag, 1921).

FRANCE

Andrew, Christopher M., and Kanya-Forstner, A. S., *The Climax of French Imperial Expansion, 1914–1924* (Stanford, Calif.: Stanford University Press, 1981).

Auffray, Bernard, *Pierre de Margerie et la vie diplomatique de son temps* (Paris: Klincksieck, 1976).

Auphan, Amiral, *L'Honneur de servir: mémoires* (Paris: Editions France-Empire, 1978).

Béarn, Hector de, *Souvenirs d'un marin* (Geneva and Paris: La Palatine, 1960).

Bienaimé, Vice-Amiral, *La Guerre navale, 1914–1915: fautes et responsabilités* (Paris: Jules Tallandier, 1920).

Blois, Hubert de, *La Guerre des mines dans la marine française* (Brest and Paris: Editions de la Cité, 1982).

Bonnefous, Georges, *Histoire politique de la troisième république*, Vol. 2: *La Grande Guerre* (Paris: Presses Universitaires de la France, 1957).

Cassar, George H., *The French and the Dardanelles* (London: Allen & Unwin, 1971).

Charles-Roux, F., *Souvenirs diplomatiques: Rome–Quirinal, février 1916–février 1919* (Paris: Arthème Fayard, 1958).

Dartige du Fournet, Vice-Amiral, *Souvenirs de guerre d'un amiral, 1914–1916* (Paris: Plon, 1920).

Debat, Georges, *Marine oblige* (Paris: Flammarion, 1974).

Decoux, Jean, *Adieu marine* (Paris: Plon, 1957).

Docteur, Amiral Jules Théophile, *Carnet de bord, 1914–1919* (Paris: La Nouvelle Société d'Edition, 1932).

Dousset, Francis, *Les Navires de guerre français de 1850 à nos jours* (Brest and Paris: Editions de la Cité, 1975).

Dousset, Francis, *Les Porte-avions français des origines (1911) à nos jours* (Brest and Paris: Editions de la Cité, 1978).

Dumas, Robert, and Guiglini, Jean, *Les Cuirassés français de 23,500 tonnes*, 2 vols (Grenoble: Editions des 4 Seigneurs, 1980).

Ferry, Abel, *Les Carnets secrets (1914–1918)* (Paris: Grasset, 1957).

Forget, Contre-Amiral *et al.*, *En patrouille à la mer* (Paris: Payot, 1929).

France, Assemblée Nationale, Chambre des Députés, *Journal Officiel, les comités-secrets, 1916–1917* (Paris: Imprimerie Nationale, 1919).

France, Ministère de la Guerre, Etat-Major de l'Armée, Service Historique, *Les Armées françaises dans la grande guerre*, Tome VIII, 1ᵉʳ Volume, Annexes (Paris: Imprimerie Nationale, 1924).

Grenoble, Université des Sciences Sociales, Centre de Recherche d'historie de l'Italie et les pays alpins, *La France et l'Italie pendant la première guerre mondiale* (Grenoble: Presses Universitaires de Grenoble, 1976).

Guépratte, Vice-Amiral P.-E., *L'Expédition des Dardanelles, 1914–1915* (Paris: Payot, 1935).

Guerre navale racontée par nos amiraux, La, 4 vols (Paris: Schwarz, n.d.).

Guichard, Louis, *Au large (1914–1918)* (Paris: La Renaissance du Livre, 1919).

Joffre, J. J. C., *Mémoires du Maréchal Joffre*, 2 vols (Paris: Plon, 1932).

Kaspi, André, *La France et le concours américain: février 1917–novembre 1918* (Lille: Service de reproduction des thèses, Université de Lille III, 1975).

King, Jere Clemens, *Generals and Politicians* (Berkeley and Los Angeles, Calif.: University of California Press, 1951).

Labayle-Couhat, Jean, *French Warships of World War I* (London: Ian Allan, 1974).

La Bruyère, René, *Notre marine marchande pendant la guerre* (Paris: Payot, 1920).

Laurens, Adolphe, *Le Commandement naval en Méditerranée, 1914–1918* (Paris: Payot, 1931).

Le Comte, J., 'L'affaire de la *Zenta*', *Revue maritime*, no. 204 (November 1963), pp. 1254–9.

Le Masson, Henri, *Histoire du torpilleur en France* (Paris: Academie de la Marine, n.d. [1966]).

Le Masson, Henri, *Du Nautilus (1800) au Redoutable* (Paris: Presses de la Cité, 1969).

Le Masson, Henri, *Propos maritimes* (Paris: Editions Maritimes et d'Outre-Mer, 1970).

Mitrakos, Alexander S., *France in Greece during World War I: A Study in the Politics of Power* (Boulder, Colo.: East European Quarterly, 1982).

Moreau, Laurent, *A bord du cuirassé "Gaulois": Dardanelles–Salonique, 1915–1916* (Paris: Payot, 1930).

Nouailhat, Yves-Henri, *France et les Etats-Unis, août 1914–avril 1917* (Paris: Publications de la Sorbonne, 1979).

Poincaré, Raymond, *Au service de la France*, 10 vols (Paris: Plon-Nourrit, 1926–33).

Randier, Jean, *La Royale: l'éperon et la cuirasse* (Brest and Paris: Editions de la Cité, 1972).

Ribot, Alexandre, *Lettres à un ami: souvenirs de ma vie politique* (Paris: Editions Bossard, 1924).

Ribot, Dr Al. (Pub.), *Journal d'Alexandre Ribot et correspondence inédites, 1914–1922* (Paris: Plon, 1936).

Roux, Louis, *La Marine marchande* (Paris: Payot, 1923).

Salaun, Vice-Amiral, *La Marine française* (Paris: Les Editions de France, 1934).

Schmidt, Martin E., *Alexandre Ribot: Odyssey of a Liberal* (The Hague: Martinus Nijhoff, 1974).

Suarez, Georges, *Briand: sa vie – son œuvre avec son journal et de nombreux documents inédits*, 6 vols (Paris: Plon, 1938–41).

Taillemite, Etienne, *Dictionnaire des marins français* (Paris: Editions Maritimes et d'Outre-Mer, 1982).

Tanenbaum, Jan Karl, *General Maurice Sarrail, 1856–1929* (Chapel Hill, NC: University of North Carolina Press, 1974).

Tanenbaum, Jan Karl, *France and the Arab Middle East, 1914–1920* (Philadelphia, Penn.: American Philosophical Society, 1978).

Thomazi, A., *La Guerre navale dans l'Adriatique* (Paris: Payot, 1925).

Thomazi, A., *La Guerre navale aux Dardanelles* (Paris: Payot, 1926).

Thomazi, A., *La Guerre navale dans la Méditerranée* (Paris: Payot, 1929).

GERMANY

Bauer, Hermann, *Als Führer der U-Boote im Weltkrieg* (Leipzig: Koehler & Amelang, 1943).

Bauer, Hermann, *Reichsleitung und U-Bootseinsatz 1914 bis 1918* (Lippoldsberg: Klosterhaus Verlag, 1956).

Bergen, Claus (ed.), *U-Boat Stories: Narratives of German U-Boat Sailors* (London: Constable, 1931).

Dönitz, Karl, *Mein wechselvolles Leben* (Göttingen: Musterschmidt Verlag, 1968).

Falkenhayn, Erich von, *General Headquarters and its Critical Decisions* (London: Hutchinson, 1919).

Fischer, Fritz, *Germany's Aims in the First World War*, English edn (New York: W. W. Norton, 1967).

Gayer, U., *Die Deutschen U-Boote in ihrer Kriegführung, 1914–1918* (Berlin: E. S. Mittler, 1930).

Gemzell, Carl-Axel, *Organization, Conflict and Innovation: A Study of German Naval Strategic Planning, 1888–1940* (Lund: Esselte Studium, 1973).

Görlitz, Walter (ed.), *Regierte der Kaiser? Kriegstagebücher, Aufzeichnungen und Briefe des Chefs des Marine-Kabinetts Admiral Georg Alexander von Müller 1914–1918* (Göttingen: Musterschmidt Verlag, n.d. [1959].

Hanssen, Hans Peter, *Diary of a Dying Empire* (Bloomington, Ind.: Indiana University Press, 1955).

Hersing, Otto, *U.21 rettet die Dardanellen* (Zurich, Leipzig and Vienna: Amalthea Verlag, 1932).

Herwig, Holger, *The Politics of Frustration: The United States in German Naval Planning, 1889–1941* (Boston, Mass.: Little, Brown, 1976).

Herwig, Holger, *'Luxury' Fleet: The Imperial German Navy, 1888–1918* (London: Allen & Unwin, 1980).

Herzog, Bodo, *60 Jahre Deutsche UBoote, 1906–1966* (Munich: J. F. Lehmanns Verlag, 1968).

Höhne, Heinz, *Canaris* (London: Secker & Warburg, 1979).

Hopman, Admiral, *Das Kriegstagebuch eines deutschen Seeoffiziers* (Berlin: August Scherl, n.d. [1925]).

Hubatsch, Walther, *Die Ära Tirpitz: Studien zur deutschen Marinepolitik 1890–1918* (Göttingen: Musterschmidt Verlag, 1955).

Hubatsch, Walther, *Der Admiralstab und Die Obersten Marinebehörden in Deutschland 1848–1945* (Frankfurt-on-Main: Bernard & Graefe Verlag, 1958).

Jarausch, Konrad, H., *The Enigmatic Chancellor: Bethmann Hollweg and the Hubris of Imperial Germany* (New Haven, Conn.: Yale University Press, 1973).

Jeschke, Hubert, *U-Boottaktik: Zur deutschen U-Boottaktik, 1900–1945* (Freiburg: Verlag Romach, 1972).

Kopp, Georg, *Two Lone Ships*, English trans. (London: Hutchinson, 1931).

Lorey, Hermann, *Der Krieg in den türkischen Gewässern*, 2 vols (Berlin: E. S. Mittler, Vol. 1: 1928; Vol. 2, 1938).

Mäkelä, Matti E., *Souchon der Goebenadmiral* (Braunschweig: Vieweg, 1936).

Mäkelä, Matti E., *Auf den Spuren der Goeben* (Munich: Bernard & Graefe Verlag, 1979).

Mantey, Vice-Amiral E. von, *Les Marins allemands au combat* (Paris: Payot, 1930).

Michelsen, Andreas, *La Guerre sous-marine (1914–1918)* (Paris: Payot, 1928).

Moraht, Robert, *Werwolf der Meere: U.64 jagt den Feind* (Berlin: Vorhut Verlag Otto Schlegel, 1933).

Mühlmann, Carl, *Das Deutsch-Türkische Waffenbündnis im Weltkriege* (Leipzig: Koehler & Amelang, 1940).

Mühlmann, Carl, *Oberste Heerseleitung und Balkan im Weltkrieg 1914/1918* (Berlin: Wilhelm Lampert Verlag, 1942).

Ritter, Gerhard, *The Sword and the Scepter: The Problem of Militarism in Germany*, 4 vols (Coral Gables, Fla.: University of Miami Press, 1969–73).

Ritter, Paul, *Ubootsgeist: Abenteuer und Fahrten im Mittelmeer* (Leipzig: Verlag K. F. Koehler, 1935).

Rössler, Eberhard, *The U-Boat: The Evolution and Technical History of German Submarines*, Eng. trans. (London and Melbourne: Arms & Armour Press, 1981).

Schulz, Paul, *In U-Boot durch die Weltmeere* (Bielefeld and Leipzig: Velhagen & Klasing, 1931).

Spindler, Arno, *Der Handelskrieg mit U-Booten*, 5 vols (Berlin [Vol. 5, Frankfurt-on-Main]: E. S. Mittler, 1932–66).

Stegemann, Bernd, *Die Deutsche Marinepolitik, 1916–1918* (Berlin: Duncker & Humblot, 1970).

Taylor, John C., *German Warships of World War I* (London: Ian Allan, 1969).

Thomas, Lowell, *Raiders of the Deep* (Garden City, NY: Doubleday, Doran, 1928).

Tirpitz, Admiral [Alfred] von, *My Memoirs*, 2 vols (New York: Dodd Mead, 1919).

Tirpitz, Alfred von, *Deutsche Ohnemachtspolitik im Weltkriege* (Hamburg and Berlin: Hanseatische Verlagsanstalt, 1926).

Trumpener, Ulrich, *Germany and the Ottoman Empire, 1914–1918* (Princeton, NJ: Princeton University Press, 1968).

Trumpener, Ulrich, 'The escape of the *Goeben* and *Breslau*: a reassessment', *Canadian Journal of History*, vol. 6 (1971), pp. 171–87.

Valentiner, Max, *Der Schrecken der Meere: Meine U-Boot Abenteuer* (Zurich, Leipzig and Vienna: Amalthea Verlag, 1931).

GREAT BRITAIN

Allen, Captain G. R. G., 'A Ghost from Gallipoli', *Journal of the Royal United Service Institution*, vol. 108, no. 631 (August 1963), pp. 137–8.

Aspinall-Oglander, Cecil F., *History of the Great War, Military Operations: Gallipoli*, 2 vols in 4 (London: Heinemann, 1929–32).

Beesly, Patrick, *Very Special Admiral: The Life of Admiral J. H. Godfrey, CB* (London: Hamish Hamilton, 1980).

Beesly, Patrick, *Room 40: British Naval Intelligence, 1914–1918* (London: Hamish Hamilton, 1982).

Bell, A. C., *A History of the Blockade of Germany and of the Countries Associated with Her in the Great War, Austria-Hungary, Bulgaria and Turkey* (London: HMSO, 1937 [released to public, 1961]).

Benn, Captain Wedgwood, *In the Side Shows* (London: Hodder & Stoughton, 1919).

Blumberg, General Sir H. E., *Britain's Sea Soldiers: A Record of the Royal Marines during the War, 1914–1918* (Devonport, Devon: Swin, 1927).

Brodie, C. G., *Forlorn Hope 1915: The Submarine Passage of the Dardanelles* (London: W. J. Bryce, 1956).

Buxton, Ian, *Big Gun Monitors* (Tynemouth, Northumb.: World Ship Society & Trident Books, 1978).

Callwell, Major-General Sir C. E., *Field Marshal Sir Henry Wilson: His Life and Diaries*, 2 vols (London: Cassell, 1927).

Cassar, George H., *Kitchener: Architect of Victory* (London: William Kimber, 1977).

Chalmers, Rear-Admiral W. S., *The Life and Letters of David, Earl Beatty* (London: Hodder & Stoughton, 1951).

Chatterton, E. Keble, *Seas of Adventures: The Story of the Naval Operations in the Mediterranean, Adriatic and Aegean* (London: Hurst & Blackett, 1936).

Chatterton, E. Keble, *Beating the U-Boats* (London: Hurst & Blackett, 1943).

Churchill, Winston S., *The World Crisis*, 5 vols in 6 (New York: Scribner's, 1923–31).

Corbett, Julian S. and Henry Newbolt, *Naval Operations*, 5 vols in 9 (London: Longmans, Green, 1920–31).

Cork and Orrery, Admiral of the Fleet, the Earl of, *My Naval Life, 1886–1941* (London: Hutchinson, 1942).

Cunningham of Hyndhope, Viscount, *A Sailor's Odyssey* (London: Hutchinson, 1951).

Dewar, Vice-Admiral K. G. B., *The Navy from Within* (London: Gollancz, 1939).

Dittmar, F. J., and Colledge, J. J., *British Warships, 1914–1919* (London: Ian Allan, 1972).

Elliott, Peter, *The Cross and the Ensign: A Naval History of Malta, 1798–1979* (Cambridge: Patrick Stephens, 1980).

Fayle, C. Ernest, *Seaborne Trade*, 3 vols (London: John Murray, 1920–24).

Fremantle, Admiral Sir Sydney Robert, *My Naval Career, 1880–1928* (London: Hutchinson, 1949).

Gaunt, Admiral Sir Guy, *The Yield of the Years: A Story of Adventure Afloat and Ashore* (London: Hutchinson, 1940).

Gilbert, Martin, *Winston S. Churchill*, Vol. 3: *The Challenge of War, 1914–1916* (Boston, Mass.: Houghton Mifflin, 1971).

Godfrey, J. H., *The Naval Memoirs of Admiral J. H. Godfrey*, 7 vols in 10 (privately printed [Hailsham], 1964–6).

Gooch, John, *The Plans of War: The General Staff and British Military Strategy, 1900–1916* (New York: John Wiley, 1974).

Goodenough, Admiral Sir William E., *A Rough Record* (London: Hutchinson, 1943).

Gordon Lennox, Lady Algernon (ed.), *The Diary of Lord Bertie of Thame, 1914–1918*, 2 vols (London: Hodder & Stoughton, 1924).

Gretton, Vice-Admiral Sir Peter, *Winston Churchill and the Royal Navy* (New York: Coward-McCann, 1969).

Guinn, Paul, *British Strategy and Politics, 1914–1918* (London: Oxford University Press, 1965).

Halpern, Paul G. (ed.), *The Keyes Papers*, Vol. 1: *1914–1918*, Publications of the Navy Records Society, Vol. 117 (London: Navy Records Society, 1975; reprint, Allen & Unwin, 1979).

Halpern, Paul G. (ed.), 'De Robeck and the Dardanelles Campaign', in N. A. M. Rodger (ed.), *The Naval Miscellany, Volume V*, Publications of the Navy Records Society, Vol. 125 (London: Allen & Unwin for the Navy Records Society, 1984), pp. 439–98.

Hampshire, A. Cecil, *The Phantom Fleet* (London: William Kimber, 1960).

Hankey, Lord, *The Supreme Command, 1914–1918*, 2 vols (London: Allen & Unwin, 1961).

Hunt, Barry D., *Sailor-Scholar: Admiral Sir Herbert Richmond* (Waterloo, Ont.: Wilfred Laurier University Press, 1982).

Hurd, Archibald, *The Merchant Navy*, 3 vols (London: John Murray, 1921–9).

James, Admiral Sir William, *The Sky Was Always Blue* (London: Methuen, 1951).

James, Admiral Sir William, *The Eyes of the Navy: A Biographical Study of Admiral Sir Reginald Hall* (London: Methuen, 1955).

James, Admiral Sir William, *A Great Seaman: The Life of Admiral of the Fleet Henry F. Oliver* (London: Witherby, 1956).

Jellicoe, Admiral of the Fleet, Earl, *The Crisis of the Naval War* (London: Cassell, 1920).

Jellicoe, Admiral of the Fleet, Earl, *The Submarine Peril* (London: Cassell, 1934).

Kennedy, Paul M., *The Rise and Fall of British Naval Mastery* (New York: Scribner's, 1976).

Kenworthy, Lieut.-Commander, The Hon. J. M., *Sailors, Statesmen – And Others: An Autobiography* (London: Rich & Cowan, 1933).

Kerr, Admiral Mark, *Land, Sea and Air* (London: Longmans, Green, 1927).

Kerr, Admiral Mark, *The Navy in My Time* (London: Rich & Cowan, 1933).

Keyes, Roger, *The Naval Memoirs*, 2 vols (London: Thornton Butterworth, 1934–5).

Leslie, Shane, *Long Shadows* (London: John Murray, 1966).

Lloyd George, David, *War Memoirs of David Lloyd George*, 2nd end, 2 vols (London: Odhams, n.d. [1936]).

Lumby, E. W. R. (ed.), *Policy and Operations in the Mediterranean, 1912–1914*, Publications of the Navy Records Society, Vol. 115 (London: Navy Records Society, 1970).

Mackenzie, Compton, *Gallipoli Memories* (London: Cassell, 1929).

Mackenzie, Compton, *First Athenian Memories* (London: Cassell, 1936).

Mackenzie, Compton, *Greek Memories* (London: Chatto & Windus, 1939).

Mackenzie, Compton, *Aegean Memories* (London: Chatto & Windus, 1940).

March, Edgar J., *British Destroyers* (London: Seeley Service, 1966).

Marder, Arthur J., *Portrait of an Admiral: The Life and Papers of Sir Herbert Richmond* (London: Cape, 1952).

Marder, Arthur J., *From the Dreadnought to Scapa Flow: The Royal Navy in the Fisher Era, 1904–1919*, 5 vols (London: Oxford University Press, 1961–70).

Marder, Arthur J., *From the Dardanelles to Oran* (London: Oxford University Press, 1974).

Myres, J. N. L., *Commander J. L. Myres, RNVR: The Blackbeard of the Aegean* (London: Leopard's Head Press, 1980).

Parkes, Oscar, *British Battleships*, 2nd edn (London: Seeley Service, 1966).

Parry, Ann (ed.), *The Admirals Fremantle* (London: Chatto & Windus, 1971).

Patterson, A. Temple (ed.), *The Jellicoe Papers*, 2 vols, Publications of the Navy Records Society, Vols 108 and 111 (London: Navy Records Society, 1966–8).

Patterson, A. Temple, *Jellicoe: A Biography* (London: Macmillan, 1969).

Plumridge, John H., *Hospital Ships and Ambulance Trains* (London: Seeley Service, 1975).

Raleigh, Sir Walter, and Jones, H. A., *The War in the Air*, 6 vols (Oxford: Clarendon Press, 1922–37).

Rodger, N. A. M., *The Admiralty* (Lavenham, Suffolk: Terence Dalton, 1979).

Roskill, Stephen W., *The Strategy of Sea Power* (London: Collins, 1962).

Roskill, Stephen W., *Hankey: Man of Secrets*, Vol 1: *1877–1918* (London: Collins, 1970).

Roskill, Stephen W., *Churchill and the Admirals* (London: Collins, 1977).

Roskill, Stephen W., *Earl Beatty: The Last Naval Hero* (London: Collins, 1980).

Salter, J. A., *Allied Shipping Control: An Experiment in International Administration* (Oxford: Clarendon Press, 1921).

Samson, Air Commodore Charles Rumney, *Fights and Flights* (London: Ernest Benn, 1930).

Sueter, Rear-Admiral Murray F., *Airmen or Noahs* (London: Putnam, 1928).

Taffrail [Captain Taprell Dorling], *Endless Story: Being an Account of the Work of the Destroyers, Flotilla Leaders, Torpedo-Boats in the Great War* (London: Hodder & Stoughton, 1931).

Tweedie, Admiral Sir Hugh, *The Story of a Naval Life* (London: Rich & Cowan, 1939).

Usborne, Vice-Admiral C. V., 'The anti-submarine campaign in the Mediterranean subsequent to 1916', *Journal of the Royal United Service Institution*, vol. 69, no. 475 (August 1924), pp. 444–64.

Usborne, Vice-Admiral C. V., *Smoke on the Horizon: Mediterranean Fighting, 1914–1918* (London: Hodder & Stoughton, 1933).

Usborne, Vice-Admiral C.V., *Blast and Counterblast: A Naval Impression of the War* (London: John Murray, 1935).

Weldon, L. B., *'Hard Lying': Eastern Mediterranean, 1914–1919* (London: Herbert Jenkins, 1925).

Wester Wemyss, Admiral of the Fleet, Lord, *The Navy in the Dardanelles Campaign* (London: Hodder & Stoughton, 1924).

Wester Wemyss, Lady, *The Life and Letters of Lord Wester Wemyss* (London: Eyre & Spottiswoode, 1935).

Winton, John, *Convoy: The Defence of Sea Trade, 1890–1990* (London: Michael Joseph, 1983).

'Yamew', 'Mediterranean Convoys, 1918', *Naval Review*, vol. 53, no. 3 (1965), pp. 241–5.

ITALY

Alberti, General Adriano, *Testimonianze straniere sulla guerra italiana, 1915–1918*, 2nd edn (Rome: Ufficio Storico del Commando del Corpo di Stato Maggiore, 1936).

Albertini, Luigi, *Venti anni di vita politica*, Pt 2: *L'Italia nella guerra mondiale*, 3 vols (Bologna: Nicola Zanichelli, 1951–3).

Aldrovandi Marescotti, L., *Guerra diplomatica* (Milan: Mondadori, 1937).

Aldrovandi Marescotti, L., *Nuovi ricordi* (Milan: Mondadori, 1938).

Bagnasco, Erminio, *I Mas e le Motosiluranti italiane, 1906–1966* (Rome: Ufficio Storico della Marina Militare, 1967).

Bargoni, Franco, *Esploratori, fregate, corvette ed avvisi italiani* (Rome: Ufficio Storico della Marina Militare, 1970).

Bernotti, Romeo, *Cinquant'anni nella marina militare* (Milan: Mursia, 1971).

Bravetta, Ettore, *La grande guerra sul mare*, 2 vols (Milan: Mondadori, 1925).

Cadorna, Luigi, *Altre pagine sulla grande guerra* (Milan: Mondadori, 1925).

Cadorna, Luigi, *Luigi Cadorna: Lettere famigliari*, ed. by Raffaele Cadorna (Milan: Mondadori, 1967).

Caraccioli, Mario, *L'Italia e i suoi alleati nella grande guerra* (Milan: Mondadori, 1932).

De Biase, Carlo, *L'Aquila d'Oro: Storia dello Stato Maggiore Italiano (1861–1945)* (Milan: Edizioni del Borghese, 1969).

De Chaurand de Saint Eustache, Felice, *Come L'esercito italiano entro in guerra* (Milan: Mondadori, 1929).

Fioravanzo, Giuseppe, Pollina, C. M., G. Riccardi *et al.*, *I cacciatorpediniere italiani, 1900–1966* (Rome: Ufficio Storico della Marina Militare, 1966).

Fraccaroli, Aldo, *Italian Warships of World War I* (London: Ian Allan, 1970).

Gabriele, Mariano, *Le convenzioni navali della Triplice* (Rome: Ufficio Storico della Marina Militare, 1969).

Gabriele, Mariano, and Friz, Giuliano, *La politica navale italiana dal 1885 al 1915* (Rome: Ufficio Storico della Marina Militare, 1982).

Giamberardino, Oscar di, *L'Ammiraglio Millo* (Livorno: Società Editrice Tirrena, 1950).

Giorgerini, Giorgio and Nani, Augusto, *Le navi di linea italiane (1861–1961)* (Rome: Ufficio Storico della Marina Militare, 1962).

Giorgerini, Giorgio, *Gli incrociatori italiani, 1861–1964* (Rome: Ufficio Storico della Marina Militare, 1964).

Malagodi, Olindo, *Conversazione della guerra, 1914–1919*, 2 vols (Milan and Naples: Riccardo Ricciardi Editore, 1960).

Manfroni, Camillo, *Storia della marina italiana durante la guerra mondiale, 1914–1918*, 2nd edn (Bologna: Nicola Zanichelli, 1925).

Manfroni, Camillo, *Nostri alleati navali: ricordi della guerra Adriatica, 1915–1918* (Milan: Mondadori, 1927).

Martini, Ferdinando, *Lettere (1860–1928)* (Milan: Mondadori, 1934).

Martini, Ferdinando, *Diario, 1914–1918* (Milan: Mondadori, 1966).

Mazzetti, Massimo, *L'esercito italiano nella triplice alleanza: aspetti della politica estera, 1870–1914* (Naples: Edizione Scientifiche Italiane, 1974).

Monticone, Alberto, *Nitti e la grande guerra* (Milan: Dott. A. Guiffrè, 1961).

Monticone, Alberto, *La Germania e la neutralità italiana, 1914–1915* (Bologna: Il Mulino, 1971).

Morabito, Nicola, *La marina italiana in guerra, 1915–1918* (Milan: Omero Maranzoni, 1934).

Pieri, P., *L'Italia nella prima guerra mondiale* (Turin: Einauldi, 1965).

Po, Guido, *Il Grande Ammiraglio Paolo Thaon di Revel* (Turin: S. Lattes, 1936).

Pollina, Paolo M., *I sommergibili italiani, 1895–1962* (Rome: Ufficio Storico della Marina Militare, 1963).

Pollina, Paolo M., *Le torpediniere italiane, 1881–1964* (Rome: Ufficio Storico della Marina Militare, 1964).

Rossi, General Eugenio De, *La vita di un ufficiale italiano sino alla guerra* (Milan: Mondadori, 1927).

Salandra, Antonio, *Italy and the Great War* (London: Arnold, 1932).

Scaroni, Silvio, *Con Vittorio Emanuele III* (Verona: Mondadori, 1954).

Seton-Watson, Christopher, *Italy from Liberalism to Fascism, 1870–1925* (London: Methuen, 1967).

Sonnino, Sydney, *Diario*, ed. by Benjamin F. Brown and Pietro Pastorelli, 3 vols (Bari: Laterza, 1972).

Sonnino, Sydney, *Carteggio, 1914–1916*, ed. by Pietro Pastorelli (Bari: Laterza, 1974).

Ufficio Storico della R. Marina, *La marina italiana nella grande guerra*, 8 vols (Florence: Vallecchi, 1935–42).

Ufficio Storico della Marina [Ammiraglio di Squadra Giuseppe Fioravanzo], *La marina militare nel suo primo secolo di vita (1861–1961)* (Rome: Ufficio Storico della Marina Militare, 1961).

Ufficio Storico della Stato Maggiore dell'Esercito [Generale di Brigata Mario Montanari], *Le Truppe Italiane in Albania (Anni 1914–20 e 1939)* (Rome: Ufficio Storico dello Stato Maggiore dell'Esercito, 1978).

Vigezzi, Brunello, *L'Italia di fronte alla prima guerra mondiale* Vol. 1: *L'Italia neutrale* (Milan and Naples: Riccardo Ricciardi Editore, 1966).

Whittam, John, *The Politics of the Italian Army, 1861–1918* (London: Croom Helm, 1977).

United States of America

Celephane, Lewis P., *History of the Naval Overseas Transportation Service in World War I* (Washington, DC: Naval History Division, 1969).

Cronon, E. David (ed.), *The Cabinet Papers of Josephus Daniels, 1913–1921* (Lincoln, Nebr.: University of Nebraska Press, 1963).

Dorwart, Jeffrey M., *The Office of Naval Intelligence: The Birth of America's First Intelligence Agency, 1865–1918* (Annapolis, Md.: Naval Institute Press, 1979).

Freidel, Frank, *Franklin D. Roosevelt: The Apprenticeship* (Boston, Mass.: Little, Brown, 1952).
Frothingham, Thomas G., *The Naval History of the World War*, 3 vols (Cambridge, Mass.: Military Historical Society of Massachusetts, 1924–1926; reprint, Freeport, NY: Books for Libraries Press, 1971).
Lansing, Robert, *War Memoirs of Robert Lansing* (Indianapolis, Ind.: Bobbs-Merrill, 1935).
Link, Arthur S., *Wilson: Confusions and Crises, 1915–1916* (Princeton, NJ: Princeton University Press, 1964).
Link, Arthur S. (ed.), *The Papers of Woodrow Wilson*, Vol. 35: *October 1, 1915–January 27, 1916* (Princeton, NJ: Princeton University Press, 1980).
May, Ernest R., *The World War and American Isolation, 1914–1917* (Cambridge, Mass.: Harvard University Press, 1959; reprint, Chicago: Quadrangle Books, 1966).
Millholland, Ray, *The Splinter Fleet of the Otranto Barrage* (London: Cresset Press, n.d. [1936]).
Moffat, Alexander, *Maverick Navy* (Middleton, Conn.: Wesleyan University Press, 1976).
Morison, Elting E., *Admiral Sims and the Modern American Navy* (Boston, Mass.: Houghton Mifflin, 1942).
Nutting, William Washburn, *The Cinderellas of the Fleet* (Jersey City, NJ: Standard Motor Construction Co., 1920).
Reilly, John C., and Scheina, Robert L., *American Battleships, 1886–1923* (Annapolis, Md.: Naval Institute Press, 1980).
Silverstone, Paul H., *U.S. Warships of World War I* (London: Ian Allan, 1970).
Sims, Rear-Admiral William Sowden, *The Victory at Sea* (Garden City, NY: Doubleday Page, 1921).
Still, William N., *American Sea Power in the Old World: The United States Navy in European and Near Eastern Waters, 1865–1917* (Westport, Conn.: Greenwood Press, 1980).
Trask, David F., *Captains and Cabinets: Anglo-American Naval Relations, 1917–1918* (Columbia, Mo.: University of Missouri Press, 1972).
United States, Department of State, *Papers Relating to the Foreign Relations of the United States, Supplement: The World War*, 7 vols (Washington, DC: United States Government Printing Office, 1928–32).

GENERAL

Albertini, Luigi, *The Origins of the War of 1914*, 3 vols (London: Oxford University Press, 1952–7).
Balincourt, Commandant de, *Les flottes de combat en 1915* (Paris: Augustin Challamel, 1915).
Basily, Nicolas de, *Memoirs: Diplomat of Imperial Russia, 1903–1917* (Stanford, Calif.: Hoover Institution Press, 1973).
Belot, R. de, and Reussner, André, *La Puissance navale dans l'histoire*, Vol. 3: *De 1914 à 1959* (Paris: Editions Maritimes et d'Outre-Mer, 1960).
Breyer, Siegfried, *Battleships and Battlecruisers, 1905–1970* (Garden City, NY: Doubleday, 1973).
Bush, Captain Eric Wheler, *Gallipoli* (London: Allen & Unwin, 1975).
Castex, Amiral, *Théories stratégiques*, 5 vols (Paris: Société d'Editions Maritimes, Géographiques et Coloniales, 1929–35).
Chack, Paul, and Antier, Jean-Jacques, *Histoire maritime de la première guerre mondiale*, 3 vols (Paris: Editions France-Empire, 1969–74).

Edmonds, Sir James E., *A Short History of World War I* (London: Oxford University Press, 1951).

Einstein, Lewis, *Inside Constantinople: A Diplomatist's Diary during the Dardanelles Expedition, April–September 1915* (New York: E. P. Dutton, 1918).

Esposito, Vincent J. (ed.), *A Concise History of World War I* (New York: Praeger, 1964).

Evans-Pritchard, E. E., *The Sanusi of Cyrenaica* (Oxford: Clarendon Press, 1949).

Falls, Cyril, *The Great War, 1914–1918* (paperback edn, New York: Capricorn Books, 1961).

Falls, Cyril, *Caporetto 1917* (London: Weidenfeld & Nicolson, 1966).

Fayle, C. E., 'Maritime power and continental alliances', *Journal of the Royal United Service Institution*, vol. 70, no. 478 (May 1925), pp. 260–75.

Ferro, Marc, *The Great War, 1914–1918* (London: Routledge & Kegan Paul, 1973).

Gibson, R. H. and Prendergast, Maurice, *The German Submarine War, 1914–1918* (London: Constable, 1931).

Gottlieb, W. W., *Studies in Secret Diplomacy during the First World War* (London: Allen & Unwin, 1957.

Grant, Robert M., *U-Boats Destroyed: The Effect of Anti-Submarine Warfare, 1914–1918* (London: Putnam, 1964).

Grant, Robert M., *U-Boat Intelligence, 1914–1918* (London: Putnam, 1969).

Gray, Edwyn, *The Killing Time: The U-Boat War, 1914–1918* (New York: Scribner's, 1972).

Greger, René, *Die Russische Flotte im Ersten Weltkrieg, 1914–1917* (Munich: J. F. Lehmanns Verlag, 1970).

Guichard, Louis, *Histoire du blocus navale* (Paris: Payot, 1929).

Halpern, Paul G., 'The Anglo-French-Italian Naval Convention of 1915', *Historical Journal*, vol. 13, no. 1 (March 1970), pp. 106–29.

Halpern, Paul G., *The Mediterranean Naval Situation, 1908–1914* (Cambridge, Mass.: Harvard University Press, 1971).

Hezlet, Vice-Admiral Sir Arthur, *The Submarine and Seapower* (New York: Stein & Day, 1967).

Hezlet, Vice-Admiral Sir Arthur, *Electronics and Seapower* (New York: Stein & Day, 1975).

Hough, Richard, *The Great War at Sea, 1914–1918* (London: Oxford University Press, 1983).

Jackh, Ernest, *The Rising Crescent* (New York: Farrar & Rinehart, 1944).

James, Robert Rhodes, *Gallipoli* (New York: Macmillan, 1965).

Jane, Fred T. (ed.), *Jane's Fighting Ships, 1914* (London: Sampson Low, Marston, 1914; reprint, Newton Abbot, Devon: David & Charles, 1968).

Jane's Fighting Ships, 1919, ed. by O. Parkes and Maurice Prendergast (London: Sampson Low, Marston, 1919; reprint, Newton Abbot, Devon: David & Charles, 1969).

Kahn, David, *The Code Breakers: The Story of Secret Writing* (New York: Macmillan, 1967).

Kannengiesser, Hans, *The Campaign in Gallipoli* (London: Hutchinson, 1927).

Larcher, Commandant M., *La Guerre turque dans la guerre mondiale* (Paris: Etienne Chiron and Berger-Levrault, 1926).

Leon, George B., *Greece and the Great Powers, 1914–1917* (Thessaloniki: Institute for Balkan Studies, 1974).

Monasterev, N., *La marina russa nella guerra mondiale, 1914–1917* (Florence: Vallecchi, 1934).

Moorehead, Alan, *Gallipoli* (New York: Harper, 1956).

Mühlmann, Carl, *Der Kampf um die Dardanellen, 1915* (Oldenburg: Stalling, 1927).

Nish, Ian, *Alliance in Decline: A Study in Anglo-Japanese Relations, 1908–1923* (London: Athlone, 1972).

Pomiankowski, Joseph, *Der Zusammenbruch des Ottomanischen Reiches* (Zurich and Vienna: Amalthea Verlag, 1928; reprint, Graz: Akademische Druck-u. Verlagsanstalt, 1969).

Preston, Anthony, *Battleships of World War I* (New York: Galahad Books, 1972).

Silberstein, Gerard E., *The Troubled Alliance: German Austrian Relations, 1914 to 1917* (Lexington, Ky: University Press of Kentucky, 1970).

Theodoulou, Christos, *Greece and the Entente: August 1, 1914–September 25, 1916* (Thessaloniki: Institute for Balkan Studies, 1971).

Weber, Frank G., *Eagles on the Crescent: Germany, Austria and the Diplomacy of the Turkish Alliance, 1914–1918* (Ithaca, NY: Cornell University Press, 1970).

Westwood, John N., 'The end of the *Imperatritsa Mariia:* Negligence or Sabotage?', *Canadian Slavonic Papers*, vol. 21, no. 1 (March 1979), pp. 66–75.

Weyer, B. (ed.), *Taschenbuch der Kriegsflotten 1914* (Munich: J. F. Lehmanns Verlag, 1914; reprinted 1968).

Williamson, Samuel R., *The Politics of Grand Strategy: Britain and France Prepare for War, 1904–1914* (Cambridge, Mass.: Harvard University Press, 1969).

Wolfslast, Wilhelm, *Der Seekrieg, 1914–1918* (Leipzig: Hase & Koehler, 1938).

Woodward, David, *The Russians at Sea* (London: William Kimber, 1965).

Zeman, Z. A. B., *The Gentlemen Negotiators: A Diplomatic History of the First World War* (New York: Macmillan, 1971).

Index

Officers are indexed under the rank held when first mentioned. Warships, including auxiliaries, are listed under 'Warships' and steamers, including hospital ships, are listed under 'Transports'.

609